.

HANDBOOK OF NATURE-INSPIRED AND INNOVATIVE COMPUTING
Integrating Classical Models with Emerging Technologies

HANDBOOK OF NATURE-INSPIRED AND INNOVATIVE COMPUTING
Integrating Classical Models with Emerging Technologies

Edited by

Albert Y. Zomaya
The University of Sydney, Australia

 Springer

Library of Congress Control Number: 2005933256

Handbook of Nature-Inspired and Innovative Computing:
Integrating Classical Models with Emerging Technologies
Edited by Albert Y. Zomaya

ISBN-10: 0-387-40532-1   e-ISBN-10: 0-387-27705-6
ISBN-13: 978-0387-40532-2   e-ISBN-13: 978-0387-27705-9

Printed on acid-free paper.

Printed in the United States of America.

9 8 7 6 5 4 3 2 1   SPIN 10942543

springeronline.com

To my family for their help,
support, and patience.
Albert Zomaya

Table of Contents

CONTRIBUTORS

Editor in Chief
Albert Y. Zomaya
Advanced Networks Research Group
School of Information Technology
The University of Sydney
NSW 2006, Australia

Advisory Board
David Bader
University of New Mexico
Albuquerque, NM 87131, USA

Richard Brent
Oxford University
Oxford OX1 3QD, UK

Jack Dongarra
University of Tennessee
Knoxville, TN 37996
and
Oak Ridge National Laboratory
Oak Ridge, TN 37831, USA

Mary Eshaghian-Wilner
Dept of Electrical Engineering
University of California, Los Angeles
Los Angeles, CA 90095, USA

Gerard Milburn
University of Queensland
St Lucia, QLD 4072, Australia

Franciszek Seredynski
Institute of Computer Science
Polish Academy of Sciences
Ordona 21, 01-237 Warsaw, Poland

Authors/Co-authors of Chapters
Matthew Allen
Computer Science Dept
University of California, Santa
  Barbara
Santa Barbara, CA 93106, USA

Srinivas Aluru
Iowa State University
Ames, IA 50011, USA

Boualem Benatallah
School of Computer Science
  and Engineering
The University of New South
  Wales
Sydney, NSW 2052, Australia

Peter J. Bentley
University College London
London WC1E 6BT, UK

John Brevik
Computer Science Dept
University of California, Santa
  Barbara
Santa Barbara, CA 93106, USA

Rajkumar Buyya
Grid Computing and Distributed
Systems Laboratory and NICTA
  Victoria Laboratory
Dept of Computer Science and
  Software Engineering
The University of Melbourne
Victoria 3010, Australia

Sajal K. Das
Center for Research in Wireless
  Mobility and Networking
  (CReWMaN)
The University of Texas, Arlington
Arlington, TX 76019, USA

Jack Dongarra
University of Tennessee
Knoxville, TN 37996
  and Oak Ridge National Laboratory
Oak Ridge, TN 37831, USA

Peter Eades
National ICT Australia
Australian Technology Park
Eveleigh NSW, Australia

Jens Eisert
Universität Potsdam
Am Neuen Palais 10
14469 Potsdam, Germany
and
Imperial College London
Prince Consort Road
SW7 2BW London, UK

Mary M. Eshaghian-Wilner
Dept of Electrical Engineering
University of California, Los Angeles
Los Angeles, CA 90095, USA

Rasit Eskicioglu
Parallel and Distributed Systems
  Laboratory
Dept of Computer Sciences
The University of Manitoba
Winniepeg, MB R3T 2N2, Canada

Amar H. Flood
Dept of Chemistry
University of California, Los Angeles
Los Angeles, CA 90095, USA

Claude Godart
INRIA-LORIA
F-54506 Vandeuvre-lès-Nancy
Cedex, France

Timothy G. W. Gordon
University College London
London WC1E 6BT, UK

Peter Graham
Parallel and Distributed Systems
  Laboratory
Dept of Computer Sciences
The University of Manitoba
Winniepeg, MB R3T 2N2, Canada

Lili Hai
State University of New York
College at Old Westbury
Old Westbury, NY 11568–0210, USA

Reiner Hartenstein
TU Kaiserslautern
Kaiserslautern, Germany

Seokhee Hong
National ICT Australia
Australian Technology Park
Eveleigh NSW, Australia

Jim Kennedy
Bureau of Labor Statistics
Washington, DC 20212, USA

Alex Khitun
Dept of Electrical Engineering
University of California,
  Los Angeles
Los Angeles, CA 90095, USA

E. V. Krishnamurthy
Computer Sciences Laboratory
Australian National University,
  Canberra
ACT 0200, Australia

Vikram Krishnamurthy
Dept of Electrical and Computer
  Engineering
University of British Columbia
Vancouver, V6T 1Z4, Canada

Mohan Kumar
Center for Research in Wireless
  Mobility and Networking
  (CReWMaN)
The University of Texas,
  Arlington
Arlington, TX 76019, USA

David J. Lilja
Dept of Electrical and Computer
  Engineering
University of Minnesota
200 Union Street SE
Minneapolis, MN 55455, USA

Keith Nesbitt
Charles Sturt University
School of Information Technology
  Panorama Ave
Bathurst 2795, Australia

Daniel Nurmi
Computer Science Dept
University of California, Santa
  Barbara
Santa Barbara, CA 93106, USA

Graziano Obertelli
Computer Science Dept
University of California, Santa
  Barbara
Santa Barbara, CA 93106, USA

Olivier Perrin
INRIA-LORIA
F-54506 Vandeuvre-lès-Nancy
Cedex, France

Hossein Pourreza
Parallel and Distributed Systems
  Laboratory
Dept of Computer Sciences
The University of Manitoba
Winniepeg, MB R3T 2N2, Canada

Fethi A. Rabhi
School of Information Systems,
  Technology and Management
The University of New South Wales
Sydney, NSW 2052, Australia

Arnold L. Rosenberg
Dept of Computer Science
University of Massachusetts Amherst
Amherst, MA 01003, USA

Franciszek Seredynski
Institute of Computer Science
Polish Academy of Sciences
Ordona 21, 01-237 Warsaw, Poland

Leslie Smith
Dept of Computing Science and
  Mathematics
University of Stirling
Stirling FK9 4LA, Scotland

Frank Sommers
Autospaces, LLC
895 S. Norton Avenue
Los Angeles, CA 90005, USA

J. Fraser Stoddart
Dept of Chemistry
University of California,
  Los Angeles
Los Angeles, CA 90095, USA

George G. Szpiro
P.O.Box 6278, Jerusalem, Israel

Javid Taheri
Advanced Networks Research Group
School of Information Technology
The University of Sydney
NSW 2006, Australia

Masahiro Takatsuka
The University of Sydney
School of Information Technology
NSW 2006, Australia

Zahir Tari
Royal Melbourne Institute of
  Technology
School of Computer Science
Melbourne, Victoria 3001, Australia

Kang Wang
Dept of Electrical Engineering
University of California, Los Angeles
Los Angeles, CA 90095, USA

M.M. Wolf
Max-Planck-Institut für Quantenoptik
Hans-Kopfermann-Str. 1
85748 Garching, Germany

Rich Wolski
Computer Science Dept
University of California, Santa
  Barbara
Santa Barbara, CA 93106, USA

Chee Shin Yeo
Grid Computing and Distributed
    Systems Laboratory and NICTA
    Victoria Laboratory
Dept of Computer Science and
    Software Engineering
The University of Melbourne
Victoria 3010, Australia

Joshua J. Yi
Freescale Semiconductor Inc,
7700 West Parmer Lane
Austin, TX 78729, USA

Albert Y. Zomaya
Advanced Networks Research
    Group
School of Information Technology
The University of Sydney
NSW 2006, Australia

PREFACE

The proliferation of computing devices in every aspect of our lives increases the demand for better understanding of emerging computing paradigms. For the last fifty years most, if not all, computers in the world have been built based on the von Neumann model, which in turn was inspired by the theoretical model proposed by Alan Turing early in the twentieth century. A Turing machine is the most famous theoretical model of computation (A. Turing, On Computable Numbers, with an Application to the Entscheidungsproblem, *Proc. London Math. Soc.* (ser. 2), **42**, pp. 230–265, 1936. Corrections appeared in: ibid., **43** (1937), pp. 544–546.) that can be used to study a wide range of algorithms.

The von Neumann model has been used to build computers with great success. It has also been extended to the development of the early supercomputers and we can also see its influence on the design of some of the high performance computers of today. However, the principles espoused by the von Neumann model are not adequate for solving many of the problems that have great theoretical and practical importance. In general, a von Neumann model is required to execute a precise algorithm that can manipulate accurate data. In many problems such conditions cannot be met. For example, in many cases accurate data are not available or a "fixed" or "static" algorithm cannot capture the complexity of the problem under study.

Therefore, The Handbook of Nature-Inspired and Innovative Computing: Integrating Classical Models with Emerging Technologies seeks to provide an opportunity for researchers to explore the new computational paradigms and their impact on computing in the new millennium. The handbook is quite timely since the field of computing as a whole is undergoing many changes. Vast literature exists today on such new paradigms and their implications for a wide range of applications -a number of studies have reported on the success of such techniques in solving difficult problems in all key areas of computing.

The book is intended to be a Virtual Get Together of several researchers that one could invite to attend a conference on `futurism' dealing with the theme of Computing in the 21st Century. Of course, the list of topics that is explored here is by no means exhaustive but most of the conclusions provided can be extended to other research fields that are not covered here. There was a decision to limit the number of chapters while providing more pages for contributed authors to express their ideas, so that the handbook remains manageable within a single volume.

It is also hoped that the topics covered will get readers to think of the implications of such new ideas for developments in their own fields. Further, the enabling technologies and application areas are to be understood very broadly and include, but are not limited to, the areas included in the handbook.

The handbook endeavors to strike a balance between theoretical and practical coverage of a range of innovative computing paradigms and applications. The handbook is organized into three main sections: (I) Models, (II) Enabling Technologies and (III) Application Domains; and the titles of the different chapters are self-explanatory to what is covered. The handbook is intended to be a repository of paradigms, technologies, and applications that target the different facets of the process of computing.

The book brings together a combination of chapters that normally don't appear in the same space in the wide literature, such as bioinformatics, molecular computing, optics, quantum computing, and others. However, these new paradigms are changing the face of computing as we know it and they will be influencing and radically revolutionizing traditional computational paradigms. So, this volume catches the wave at the right time by allowing the contributors to explore with great freedom and elaborate on how their respective fields are contributing to re-shaping the field of computing.

The twenty-two chapters were carefully selected to provide a wide scope with minimal overlap between the chapters so as to reduce duplications. Each contributor was asked to cover review material as well as current developments. In addition, the choice of authors was made so as to select authors who are leaders in the respective disciplines.

ACKNOWLEDGEMENTS

First and foremost we would like to thank and acknowledge the contributors to this volume for their support and patience, and the reviewers for their useful comments and suggestions that helped in improving the earlier outline of the handbook and presentation of the material. Also, I should extend my deepest thanks to Wayne Wheeler and his staff at Springer (USA) for their collaboration, guidance, and most importantly, patience in finalizing this handbook. Finally, I would like to acknowledge the efforts of the team from Springer's production department for their extensive efforts during the many phases of this project and the timely fashion in which the book was produced.

Albert Y. Zomaya

Chapter 1

CHANGING CHALLENGES FOR
COLLABORATIVE ALGORITHMICS

Arnold L. Rosenberg
University of Massachusetts at Amherst

Abstract

Technological advances and economic considerations have led to a wide variety of modalities of *collaborative computing*: the use of multiple computing agents to solve individual computational problems. Each new modality creates new challenges for the algorithm designer. Older "parallel" algorithmic devices no longer work on the newer computing platforms (at least in their original forms) and/or do not address critical problems engendered by the new platforms' characteristics. In this chapter, the field of *collaborative algorithmics* is divided into four epochs, representing (one view of) the major evolutionary eras of collaborative computing platforms. The changing challenges encountered in devising algorithms for each epoch are discussed, and some notable sophisticated responses to the challenges are described.

1   INTRODUCTION

Collaborative computing is a regime of computation in which multiple agents are enlisted in the solution of a single computational problem. Until roughly one decade ago, it was fair to refer to collaborative computing as *parallel computing*. Developments engendered by both economic considerations and technological advances make the older rubric both inaccurate and misleading, as the *multiprocessors* of the past have been joined by *clusters*—independent computers interconnected by a local-area network (LAN)—and by various modalities of *Internet computing*—loose confederations of computing agents of differing levels of commitment to the common computing enterprise. The agents in the newer collaborative computing milieux often do their computing at their own times and in their own locales—definitely not "in parallel."

Every major technological advance in all areas of computing creates significant new scheduling challenges even while enabling new levels of computational efficiency (measured in time and/or space and/or cost). This chapter presents one algorithmicist's view of the paradigm-challenges milestones in the evolution of collaborative computing platforms and of the algorithmic challenges each change in paradigm has engendered. The chapter is organized around a somewhat eccentric view of the evolution of collaborative computing technology through four "epochs," each distinguished by the challenges one faced when devising algorithms for the associated computing platforms.

1. In the epoch of *shared-memory multiprocessors*:
   - One had to cope with partitioning one's computational job into disjoint subjobs that could proceed in parallel on an assemblage of identical processors. One had to try to keep all processors fruitfully busy as much of the time as possible. (The qualifier "fruitfully" indicates that the processors are actually working on the problem to be solved, rather than on, say, bookkeeping that could be avoided with a bit more cleverness.)
   - Communication between processors was effected through shared variables, so one had to coordinate access to these variables. In particular, one had to avoid the potential races when two (or more) processors simultaneously vied for access to a single memory module, especially when some access was for the purpose of writing to the same shared variable.
   - Since all processors were identical, one had, in many situations, to craft protocols that gave processors separate identities—the process of socalled *symmetry breaking* or *leader election*. (This was typically necessary when one processor had to take a coordinating role in an algorithm.)

2. The epoch of *message-passing multiprocessors* added to the technology of the preceding epoch a user-accessible interconnection network—of known structure—across which the identical processors of one's parallel computer communicated. On the one hand, one could now build much larger aggregations of processors than one could before. On the other hand:
   - One now had to worry about coordinating the routing and transmission of messages across the network, in order to select short paths for messages, while avoiding congestion in the network.
   - One had to organize one's computation to tolerate the often-considerable delays caused by the point-to-point latency of the network and the effects of network bandwidth and congestion.
   - Since many of the popular interconnection networks were highly symmetric, the problem of symmetry breaking persisted in this epoch. Since communication was now over a network, new algorithmic avenues were needed to achieve symmetry breaking.
   - Since the structure of the interconnection network underlying one's multiprocessor was known, one could—and was well advised to—allocate substantial attention to network-specific optimizations when designing algorithms that strove for (near) optimality. (Typically, for instance, one would strive to exploit *locality:* the fact that a processor was closer to some processors than to others.) A corollary of this fact

is that one often needed quite disparate algorithmic strategies for different classes of interconnection networks.

3. The epoch of *clusters*—also known as *networks of workstations* (*NOWs*, for short)—introduced two new variables into the mix, even while rendering many sophisticated multiprocessor-based algorithmic tools obsolete. In Section 3, we outline some algorithmic approaches to the following new challenges.

   - The computing agents in a cluster—be they pc's, or multiprocessors, or the eponymous workstations—are now independent computers that communicate with each other over a local-area network (LAN). This means that communication times are larger and that communication protocols are more ponderous, often requiring tasks such as breaking long messages into packets, encoding, computing checksums, and explicitly setting up communications (say, via a hand-shake). Consequently, tasks must now be coarser grained than with multiprocessors, in order to amortize the costs of communication. Moreover, the respective computations of the various computing agents can no longer be tightly coupled, as they could be in a multiprocessor. Further, in general, network latency can no longer be "hidden" via the sophisticated techniques developed for multiprocessors. Finally, one can usually no longer translate knowledge of network topology into network-specific optimizations.

   - The computing agents in the cluster, either by design or chance (such as being purchased at different times), are now often *heterogeneous*, differing in speeds of processors and/or memory systems. This means that a whole range of algorithmic techniques developed for the earlier epochs of collaborative computing no longer work—at least in their original forms [127]. On the positive side, heterogeneity obviates symmetry breaking, as processors are now often distinguishable by their unique combinations of computational resources and speeds.

4. The epoch of *Internet computing*, in its several guises, has taken the algorithmics of collaborative computing precious near to—but never quite reaching—that of distributed computing. While Internet computing is still evolving in often-unpredictable directions, we detail two of its circa-2003 guises in Section 4. Certain characteristics of present-day Internet computing seem certain to persist.

   - One now loses several types of *predictability* that played a significant background role in the algorithmics of prior epochs.
     - Interprocessor communication now takes place over the Internet. In this environment:
       * a message shares the "airwaves" with an unpredictable number and assemblage of other messages; it may be dropped and resent; it may be routed over any of myriad paths. All of these factors make it impossible to predict a message's transit time.
       * a message may be accessible to unknown (and untrusted) sites, increasing the need for security-enhancing measures.
     - The predictability of interactions among collaborating computing agents that anchored algorithm development in all prior epochs no longer obtains, due to the fact that remote agents are typically not

dedicated to the collaborative task. Even the modalities of Internet computing in which remote computing agents promise to complete computational tasks that are assigned to them typically do not guarantee *when*. Moreover, even the guarantee of eventual computation is not present in all modalities of Internet computing: in some modalities remote agents cannot be relied upon *ever* to complete assigned tasks.

- In several modalities of Internet computing, computation is now *unreliable* in two senses:
  - The computing agent assigned a task may, without announcement, "resign from" the aggregation, abandoning the task. (This is the extreme form of temporal unpredictability just alluded to.)
  - Since remote agents are unknown and anonymous in some modalities, the computing agent assigned a task may maliciously return fallacious results. This latter threat introduces the need for computation-related security measures (e.g., result-checking and agent monitoring) for the first time to collaborative computing. This problem is discussed in a news article at ⟨http://www.wired.com/news/technology/0,1282,41838,00.html⟩.

In succeeding sections, we expand on the preceding discussion, defining the collaborative computing platforms more carefully and discussing the resulting challenges in more detail. Due to a number of excellent widely accessible sources that discuss and analyze the epochs of multiprocessors, both shared-memory and message-passing, our discussion of the first two of our epochs, in Section 2, will be rather brief. Our discussion of the epochs of cluster computing (in Section 3) and Internet computing (in Section 4) will be both broader and deeper. In each case, we describe the subject computing platforms in some detail and describe a variety of sophisticated responses to the algorithmic challenges of that epoch. Our goal is to highlight studies that attempt to develop algorithmic strategies that respond in novel ways to the challenges of an epoch. Even with this goal in mind, the reader should be forewarned that

- her guide has an eccentric view of the field, which may differ from the views of many other collaborative algorithmicists;

- some of the still-evolving collaborative computing platforms we describe will soon disappear, or at least morph into possibly unrecognizable forms;

- some of the "sophisticated responses" we discuss will never find application beyond the specific studies they occur in.

This said, I hope that this survey, with all of its limitations, will convince the reader of the wonderful research opportunities that await her "just on the other side" of the systems and applications literature devoted to emerging collaborative computing technologies.

2   THE EPOCHS OF MULTIPROCESSORS

The quick tour of the world of multiprocessors in this section is intended to convey a sense of what stimulated much of the algorithmic work on collaborative computing on this computing platform. The following books and surveys provide an excellent detailed treatment of many subjects that we only touch upon and even more topics that are beyond the scope of this chapter: [5, 45, 50, 80, 93, 97, 134].

2.1   Multiprocessor Platforms

As technology allowed circuits to shrink, starting in the 1970s, it became feasible to design and fabricate computers that had many processors. Indeed, a few theorists had anticipated these advances in the 1960s [79]. The first attempts at designing such *multiprocessors* envisioned them as straightforward extensions of the familiar von Neumann architecture, in which a processor box—now populated with many processors—interacted with a single memory box; processors would coordinate and communicate with each other via shared variables. The resulting *shared-memory multiprocessors* were easy to think about, both for computer architects and computer theorists [61]. Yet using such multiprocessors effectively turned out to present numerous challenges, exemplified by the following:

- Where/how does one identify the parallelism in one's computational problem? This question persists to this day, feasible answers changing with evolving technology. Since there are approaches to this question that often do not appear in the standard references, we shall discuss the problem briefly in Section 2.2.

- How does one keep all available processors fruitfully occupied—the problem of *load balancing*? One finds sophisticated multiprocessor-based approaches to this problem in primary sources such as [58, 111, 123, 138].

- How does one coordinate access to shared data by the several processors of a multiprocessor (especially, a shared-memory multiprocessor)? The difficulty of this problem increases with the number of processors. One significant approach to sharing data requires establishing order among a multiprocessor's indistinguishable processors by selecting "leaders" and "subleaders," etc. How does one efficiently pick a "leader" among indistinguishable processors—the problem of *symmetry breaking*? One finds sophisticated solutions to this problem in primary sources such as [8, 46, 107, 108].

A variety of technological factors suggest that shared memory is likely a better idea as an abstraction than as a physical actuality. This fact led to the development of *distributed shared memory* multiprocessors, in which each processor had its own memory module, and access to remote data was through an interconnection network. Once one had processors communicating over an interconnection network, it was a small step from the distributed shared memory abstraction to explicit *message-passing*, i.e., to having processors communicate with each other directly rather than through shared variables. In one sense, the introduction of interconnection networks to parallel architectures was liberating: one could now (at least in principle) envision multiprocessors with many thousands of processors. On the other hand, the explicit algorithmic use of networks gave rise to a new set of challenges:

- How can one route large numbers of messages within a network without engendering congestion ("hot spots") that renders communication insufferably slow? This is one of the few algorithmic challenges in parallel computing that has an acknowledged champion. The two-phase randomized routing strategy developed in [150, 154] provably works well in a large range of interconnection networks (including the popular butterfly and hypercube networks) and empirically works well in many others.

- Can one exploit the new phenomenon—*locality*—that allows certain pairs of processors to intercommunicate faster than others? The fact that locality can be exploited to algorithmic advantage is illustrated in [1, 101]. The phenomenon of locality in parallel algorithmics is discussed in [124, 156].

- How can one cope with the situation in which the structure of one's computational problem—as exposed by the graph of data dependencies—is incompatible with the structure of the interconnection network underlying the multiprocessor that one has access to? This is another topic not treated fully in the references, so we discuss it briefly in Section 2.2.

- How can one organize one's computation so that one accomplishes valuable work while awaiting responses from messages, either from the memory subsystem (memory accesses) or from other processors? A number of innovative and effective responses to variants of this problem appear in the literature; see, e.g., [10, 36, 66].

In addition to the preceding challenges, one now also faced the largely unanticipated, insuperable problem that one's interconnection network may not "scale." Beginning in 1986, a series of papers demonstrated that the physical realizations of large instances of the most popular interconnection networks could not provide performance consistent with idealized analyses of those networks [31, 155, 156, 157]. A word about this problem is in order, since the phenomenon it represents influences so much of the development of parallel architectures. We live in a three-dimensional world: areas and volumes in space grow polynomially fast when distances are measured in units of length. This physical polynomial growth notwithstanding, for many of the algorithmically attractive interconnection networks—*hypercubes, butterfly networks*, and *de Bruijn networks*, to name just three—the number of nodes (read: "processors") grows *exponentially* when distances are measured in number of interprocessor links. This means, in short, that the interprocessor links of these networks must grow in length as the networks grow in number of processors. *Analyses that predict performance in number of traversed links do not reflect the effect of link-length on actual performance.* Indeed, the analysis in [31] suggests—on the preceding grounds—that only the polynomially growing *meshlike networks* can supply in practice efficiency commensurate with idealized theoretical analyses.[1]

---

[1]Figure 1.1 depicts the four mentioned networks. See [93, 134] for definitions and discussions of these and related networks. Additional sources such as [4, 21, 90] illustrate the algorithmic use of such networks.

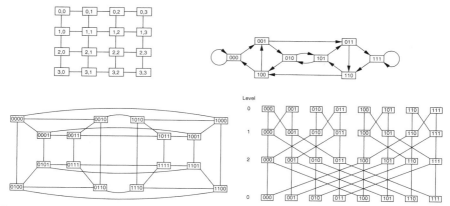

Figure 1.1. *Four interconnection networks. Row 1: the 4 × 4 mesh and the 3-dimensional de Bruijn network; row 2: the 4-dimensional boolean hypercube and the 3-level butterfly network (note the two copies of level 0)*

We now discuss briefly a few of the challenges that confronted algorithmicists during the epochs of multiprocessors. We concentrate on topics that are not treated extensively in books and surveys, as well as on topics that retain their relevance beyond these epochs.

2.2   Algorithmic Challenges and Responses

Finding Parallelism. The seminal study [37] was the first to systematically distinguish between the inherently sequential portion of a computation and the parallelizable portion. The analysis in that source led to *Brent's Scheduling Principle*, which states, in simplest form, that the time for a computation on a p-processor computer need be no greater than $t + n/p$, where t is the time for the inherently sequential portion of the computation and n is the total number of operations that must be performed. While the study illustrates how to achieve the bound of the Principle for a class of arithmetic computations, it leaves open the challenge of discovering the parallelism in general computations. Two major approaches to this challenge appear in the literature and are discussed here.

Parallelizing computations via clustering/partitioning. Two related major approaches have been developed for scheduling computations on parallel computing platforms, when the computation's intertask dependencies are represented by a *computation-dag*—a *directed acyclic graph*, each of whose arcs $(x \rightarrow y)$ betokens the dependence of task y on task x; sources never appear on the right-hand side of an arc; sinks never appear on the left-hand side.

The first such approach is to *cluster* a computation-dag's tasks into "blocks" whose tasks are so tightly coupled that one would want to allocate each block to a single processor to obviate any communication when executing these tasks. A number of efficient heuristics have been developed to effect such clustering for general computation-dags [67, 83, 103, 139]. Such heuristics typically base their clustering on some easily computed characteristic of the dag, such as its *critical path*—the most resource-consuming source-to-sink path, including both computation time and volume of intertask data—or its *dominant sequence*—a source-to-sink path, possibly augmented with dummy arcs, that accounts for the entire makespan of the computation. Several experimental studies compare these heuristics in a variety of settings [54, 68], and systems have been developed to exploit such clustering in devising schedules [43, 140, 162]. Numerous algorithmic studies have demonstrated analytically the *provable* effectiveness of this approach for special scheduling classes of computation-dags [65, 117].

Dual to the preceding clustering heuristics is the process of clustering by *graph separation*. Here one seeks to partition a computation-dag into subdags by "cutting" arcs that interconnect loosely coupled blocks of tasks. When the tasks in each block are mapped to a single processor, the small numbers of arcs interconnecting pairs of blocks lead to relatively small—hence, inexpensive—interprocessor communications. This approach has been studied extensively in the parallel-algorithms literature with regard to myriad applications, ranging from circuit layout to numerical computations to nonserial dynamic programming. A small sampler of the literature on specific applications appears in [28, 55, 64, 99, 106]; heuristics for accomplishing efficient graph partitioning (especially into roughly equal-size subdags) appear in [40, 60, 82]; further sample applications, together with a survey of the literature on algorithms for finding graph separators, appears in [134].

Parallelizing using dataflow techniques. A quite different approach to finding parallelism in computations builds on the *flow of data* in the computation. This approach originated with the VLSI revolution fomented by Mead and Conway [105], which encouraged computer scientists to apply their tools and insights to the problem of designing computers. Notable among the novel ideas emerging from this influx was the notion of *systolic array*—a dataflow-driven special-purpose parallel (co)processor [86, 87]. A major impetus for the development of this area was the discovery, in [109, 120], that for certain classes of computations—including, e.g., those specifiable via nested for-loops—such machines could be designed "automatically." This area soon developed a life of its own as a technique for finding parallelism in computations, as well as for designing special-purpose parallel machines. There is now an extensive literature on the use of systolic design principles for a broad range of specific computations [38, 39, 89, 91, 122], as well as for large general classes of computations that are delimited by the structure of their flow of data [49, 75, 109, 112, 120, 121].

Mismatches between network and job structure. Parallel efficiency in multiprocessors often demands using algorithms that accommodate the structure of one's computation to that of the host multiprocessor's network. This was noticed by systems builders [71] as well as algorithms designers [93, 149]. The reader can appreciate the importance of so tuning one's algorithm by perusing the following studies of the operation of sorting: [30, 52, 52, 74, 77, 92, 125, 141, 148]. The overall groundrules in these studies are constant: one is striving to minimize the worst-case number of comparisons when sorting *n* numbers; only the underlying interconnection network changes. We now briefly describe two broadly applicable approaches to addressing potential mismatches with the host network.

Network emulations. The theory of network emulations focuses on the problem of making one computation-graph—the *host*—"act like" or "look like" another—the *guest*. In both of the scenarios that motivate this endeavor, the host *H* represents an existing interconnection network. In one scenario, the guest *G* is a directed graph that represents the intertask dependencies of a computation. In the other scenario, the guest *G* is an undirected graph that represents an ideal interconnection network that would be a congenial host for one's computation. In both scenarios, computational efficiency would clearly be enhanced if *H's* interconnection structure matched *G's*—or could be made to appear to.

Almost all approaches to network emulation build on the theory of graph embeddings, which was first proposed as a general computational tool in [126]. An *embedding* $\langle \alpha, \rho \rangle$ of the graph $G = (V_G, E_G)$ into the graph $H = (V_H, E_H)$ consists of a one-to-one map $\alpha : V_G \to V_H$, together with a mapping of E_G into *paths* in *H* such that, for each edge $(u, u) \in E_G$, the path $\rho(u, v)$ connects nodes $\alpha(u)$ and $\alpha(v)$ in *H*. The two main measures of the quality of the embedding $\langle \alpha, \rho \rangle$ are the *dilation*, which is the length of the longest path of *H* that is the image, under ρ, of some edge of *G*; and the *congestion*, which is the maximum, over all edges *e* of *H*, of the number of ρ-paths in which edge *e* occurs. In other words, it is the maximum number of edges of *G* that are routed across *e* by the embedding.

It is easy to use an embedding of a network *G* into a network *H* to translate an algorithm designed for *G* into a computationally equivalent algorithm for *H*. Basically: the mapping α identifies which node of *H* is to emulate which node of *G*; the mapping ρ identifies the routes in *H* that are used to simulate internode message-passing in *G*. This sketch suggests why the quantitative side of network-emulations-via-embeddings focuses on dilation and congestion as the main measures of the quality of an embedding. A moment's reflection suggests that, when one uses an embedding $\langle \alpha, \rho \rangle$ of a graph *G* into a graph *H* as the basis for an emulation of *G* by *H*, any algorithm that is designed for *G* is slowed down by a factor $O(\text{congestion} \times \text{dilation})$ when run on *H*. One can *sometimes* easily orchestrate communications to improve this factor to $O(\text{congestion} + \text{dilation})$; cf. [13]. Remarkably, one can *always* improve the slowdown to $O(\text{congestion} + \text{dilation})$: a nonconstructive proof of this fact appears in [94], and, even more remarkably, a constructive proof and efficient algorithm appear in [95].

There are myriad studies of embedding-based emulations with specific guest and host graphs. An extensive literature follows up one of the earliest studies, [6], which embeds rectangular meshes into square ones, a problem having nonobvious algorithmic consequences [18]. The algorithmic attractiveness of the boolean hypercube mentioned in Section 2.1 is attested to not only by countless specific algorithms [93] but also by several studies that show the hypercube to be a congenial host for a wide variety of graph families that are themselves algorithmically attractive. Citing just two examples: (1) One finds in [24, 161] two quite distinct efficient embeddings of complete trees—and hence, of the ramified computations they represent—into hypercubes. Surprisingly, such embeddings exist also for trees that are not complete [98, 158] and/or that grow *dynamically* [27, 96]. (2) One finds in [70] efficient embeddings of butterflylike networks—hence, of the convolutional computations they represent—into hypercubes. A number of related algorithm-motivated embeddings into hypercubes appear in [72]. The mesh-of-trees network, shown in [93] to be an efficient host for many parallel computations, is embedded into hypercubes in [57] and into the de Bruijn network in [142]. The emulations in [11, 12] attempt to exploit the algorithmic attractiveness of the hypercube, despite its earlier-mentioned physical intractability. The study in [13], unusual for its algebraic underpinnings, was motivated by the (then-) unexplained fact—observed, e.g., in [149]—that algorithms designed for the butterfly network run equally fast on the de Bruijn network. An intimate algebraic connection discovered in [13] between these networks—the de Bruijn network is a *quotient* of the butterfly—led to an embedding of the de Bruijn network into the hypercube that had *exponentially* smaller dilation than any competitors known at that time.

The embeddings discussed thus far exploit structural properties that are peculiar to the target guest and host graphs. When such enabling properties are hard to find, a strategy pioneered in [25] can sometimes produce efficient embeddings. This source crafts efficient embeddings based on the ease of recursively decomposing a guest graph G into subgraphs. The insight underlying this embedding-via-decomposition strategy is that recursive bisection—the repeated decomposition of a graph into like-sized subgraphs by "cutting" edges—affords one a representation of G as a binary-tree-like structure.[2] The root of this structure is the graph G; the root's two children are the two subgraphs of G—call them G_0 and G_1—that the first bisection partitions G into. Recursively, the two children of node G_x of the tree-like structure (where x is a binary string) are the two subgraphs of G_x—call them G_{x0} and G_{x1}—that the bisection partitions G_x into. The technique of [25] transforms an (efficient) embedding of this "decomposition tree" into a host graph H into an (efficient) embedding of G into H, whose dilation (and, often, congestion) can be bounded using a standard measure of the ease of recursively bisecting G. A very few studies extend and/or improve the technique of [25]; see, e.g., [78, 114].

When networks G and H are incompatible—i.e., there is no efficient embedding of G into H—graph embeddings cannot lead directly to efficient emulations. A technique developed in [84] can sometimes overcome this shortcoming and produce efficient network emulations. The technique has H emulate G by alternating the following two phases:

Computation phase. Use an embedding-based approach to emulate G piecewise for short periods of time (whose durations are determined via analysis).

Coordination phase. Periodically (frequency is determined via analysis) coordinate the piecewise embedding-based emulations to ensure that all pieces have fresh information about the state of the emulated computation.

This strategy will produce efficient emulations if one makes enough progress during the computation phase to amortize the cost of the coordination phase. Several examples in [84] demonstrate the value of this strategy: each presents a phased emulation of a network G by a network H that incurs only constant-factor slowdown, while any embedding-based emulation of G by H incurs slowdown that depends on the sizes of G and H.

We mention one final, unique use of embedding-based emulations. In [115], a suite of embedding-based algorithms is developed in order to endow a multiprocessor with a capability that would be prohibitively expensive to supply in hard-

---

[2]See [134] for a comprehensive treatment of the theory of graph decomposition, as well as of this embedding technique.

ware. The *gauge* of a multiprocessor is the common width of its CPU and memory bus. A multiprocessor can be *multigauged* if, under program control, it can dynamically change its (apparent) gauge. (Prior studies had determined the algorithmic value of multigauging, as well as its prohibitive expense [53, 143].) Using an embedding-based approach that is detailed in [114], the algorithms of [115] efficiently endow a multiprocessor architecture with a multigauging capability.

The use of parameterized models. A truly revolutionary approach to the problem of matching computation structure to network structure was proposed in [153], the birthplace of the *bulk-synchronous* parallel (*BSP*) programming paradigm. The central thesis in [153] is that, by appropriately reorganizing one's computation, one can obtain almost all of the benefits of message-passing parallel computation while ignoring all aspects of the underlying interconnection network's structure, save its end-to-end latency. The needed reorganization is a form of task-clustering: one organizes one's computation into a sequence of computational "supersteps"—during which processors compute locally, with no intercommunication—punctuated by communication "supersteps"—during which processors synchronize with one another (whence the term *bulk-synchronous*) and perform a stylized intercommunication in which each processor sends *h* messages to *h* others. (The choice of *h* depends on the network's latency.) It is shown that a combination of artful message routing—say, using the congestion-avoiding technique of [154]—and latency-hiding techniques—notably, the method of *parallel slack* that has the host parallel computer emulate a computer with more processors—allows this algorithmic paradigm to achieve results within a constant factor of the parallel speedup available via network-sensitive algorithm design. A number of studies, such as [69, 104], have demonstrated the viability of this approach for a variety of classes of computations.

The focus on network latency and number of processors as the sole architectural parameters that are relevant to efficient parallel computation limits the range of architectural platforms that can enjoy the full benefits of the BSP model. In response, the authors of [51] have crafted a model that carries on the spirit of BSP but that incorporates two further parameters related to interprocessor communication. The resulting *LogP* model accounts for *latency* (the "L" in "LogP"), *overhead* (the "o,")—the cost of setting up a communication, *gap* (the "g,")—the minimum interval between successive communications by a processor, and *processor number* (the "P"). Experiments described in [51] validate the predictive value of the LogP model in multiprocessors, at least for computations involving only short interprocessor messages. The model is extended in [7], to allow long, but equal-length, messages. One finds in [29] an interesting study of the efficiency of parallel algorithms developed under the BSP and LogP models.

3 CLUSTERS/NETWORKS OF WORKSTATIONS

3.1 The Platform

Many sources eloquently argue the technological and economic inevitability of an increasingly common modality of collaborative computing—the use of a *cluster* (or, equally commonly, a *network*) of computers to cooperate in the solution of a computational problem; see [9, 119]. Note that while one typically talks about a network of *workstations* (a *NOW*, for short), the constituent computers in a NOW may well be pc's or multiprocessors; the algorithmic challenges change quantitatively but not qualitatively depending on the architectural sophistication of the "workstations." The computers in a NOW intercommunicate via a LAN—local area network—whose detailed structure is typically neither known to nor accessible by the programmer.

3.2   Some Challenges

Some of the challenges encountered when devising algorithms for NOWs differ only quantitatively from those encountered with multiprocessors. For instance:

- The typically high latencies of LANs (compared to interconnection networks), coupled with the relatively heavyweight protocols needed for robust communication, demand coarse-grained tasks in order to amortize the costs of communication.

Some new challenges arise from the ineffectiveness in NOWs of certain multiprocessor-based algorithmic strategies. For instance:

- The algorithm designer typically cannot exploit the structure of the LAN underlying a NOW.

- The higher costs of communication, coupled with the loose coordination of a NOW's workstations, render the (relatively) simple latency-hiding techniques of multiprocessors ineffective in clusters.

Finally, some algorithmic challenges arise in the world of collaborative computing for the first time in clusters. For instance:

- The constituent workstations of a NOW may differ in processor and/or memory speeds; i.e., the NOW may be *heterogeneous* (be an *HNOW*).

All of the issues raised here make parameterized models such as those discussed at the end of Section 2.2 an indispensable tool to the designers of algorithms for (H)NOWs. The challenge is to craft models that are at once faithful enough to ensure algorithmic efficiency on real NOWs and simple enough to be analytically tractable. The latter goal is particularly elusive in the presence of heterogeneity. Consequently, much of the focus in this section is on models that have been used successfully to study several approaches to computing in (H)NOWs.

3.3   Some Sophisticated Responses

Since the constituent workstations of a NOW are at best loosely coupled, and since interworkstation communication is typically rather costly in a NOW, the major strategies for using NOWs in collaborative computations center around three loosely coordinated scheduling mechanisms—workstealing, cyclestealing, and worksharing—that, respectively, form the foci of the following three subsections.

3.3.1   Cluster computing via workstealing

Workstealing is a modality of cluster computing wherein an idle workstation seeks work from a busy one. This allocation of responsibility for finding work has the benefit that idle workstations, not busy ones, do the unproductive chore of searching for work. The most comprehensive study of workstealing is the series of papers [32]–[35], which schedule computations in a multiprocessor or in a (homogeneous) NOW. These sources develop their approach to workstealing from the level of programming abstraction through algorithm design and analysis through implementation as a working system (called Cilk [32]). As will be detailed imminently, these sources use a strict form of multithreading as a mechanism for subdividing a computation into chunks (specifically, threads of unit-time tasks) that are suitable for sharing among collaborating workstations. The strength and elegance of the results in these sources has led to a number of other noteworthy studies of multithreaded computations, including [1, 14, 59]. A very abstract study of workstealing, which allows one to assess the impact of changes in algorithmic strategy easily, appears in [110], which we describe a bit later.

A. Case study [34]: From an algorithmic perspective, the main paper in the series about Cilk and its algorithmic underpinnings is [34], which presents and analyzes a (randomized) mechanism for scheduling "well-structured" multithreaded computations, achieving both time and space complexity that are within constant factors of optimal.

Within the model of [34], a *thread* is a collection of unit-time tasks, linearly ordered by dependencies; graph-theoretically, a thread is, thus, a linear computation-dag. A *multithreaded computation* is a set of threads that are interconnected in a stylized way. There is a *root thread*. Recursively, any task of any thread T may have $k \geq 0$ *spawn-arcs* to the initial tasks of k threads that are *children* of T. If thread T' is a child of thread T via a spawn-arc from task t of T, then the last task of T' has a continue-arc to some task t' of T that is a successor of task t. Both the spawn-arcs and continue-arcs individually thus give the computation the structure of a tree-dag (see Figure 1.2). All of the arcs of a multithreaded computation represent data dependencies that must be honored when executing the computation. A multithreaded computation is *strict* if all data-dependencies for the tasks of a thread T go to an ancestor of thread T in the thread-tree; the computation is fully strict if all dependencies in fact go to T's parent in the tree. Easily,

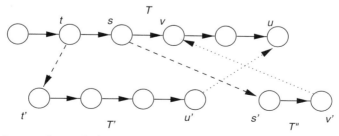

Figure 1.2. *An exemplary multithreaded computation. Thread T' (resp., T'') is a child of thread T, via the spawn-arc from task t to task t' (resp., from task s to task s') and the continue-arc from task u' to task u (resp., from task u' to task u)*

any multithreaded computation can be made fully strict by altering the dependency structure; this restructuring may affect the available parallelism in the computation but will not compromise its correctness. The study in [34] focuses on scheduling fully strict multithreaded computations.

In the computing platform envisioned in [34], a multithreaded computation is stored in shared memory. Each individual thread T has a block of memory (called an *activation frame*), within the local memory of the workstation that "owns" T, that is dedicated to the computation of T's tasks. Space is measured in terms of activation frames.

Time is measured in [34] as a function of the number of workstations that are collaborating in the target computation. T_p is the minimum computation time when there are p collaborating workstations; therefore, T_1 is the total amount of work in the computation. T_∞ is *dag-depth* of the computation, i.e., the length of the longest source-to-sink path in the associated computation-dag; this is the "inherently sequential" part of the computation. Analogously, S_p is the minimum space requirement for the target computation, S_1 being the "activation depth" of the computation.

Within the preceding model, the main contribution of [34] is a provably efficient randomized workstealing algorithm, **Procedure** Worksteal (see Figure 1.3), which executes the fully strict multithreaded computation rooted at thread T. In the Procedure, each workstation maintains a *ready deque* of threads that are eligible for execution; these deques are accessible by all workstations. Each deque has a *bottom* and a *top*; threads can be inserted at the bottom and removed from either end. A workstation uses its ready deque as a procedure *stack*, pushing and popping from the bottom. Threads that are "stolen" by other workstations are removed from the top of the deque. It is shown in [34] that **Procedure Worksteal** is close to optimal in both time and space complexity.

- *For any fully strict multithreaded computation,* **Procedure Worksteal**, *when run on a p-workstation NOW, uses space* $\leq S_1 p$.

Normal execution. A workstation P seeking work removes (pops) the thread at the bottom of its ready deque—call it thread T—and begins executing T's tasks seriatim.

A stalled thread is enabled. If executing one of T's tasks enables a stalled thread T', then the now-ready thread T' is pushed onto the bottom of P's ready deque. (A thread *stalls* when the next task to be executed must await data from a task that belongs to another thread.) /*Because of full strictness: thread T' must be thread T's parent; thread T's deque must be empty when T' is inserted.*/

A new thread is spawned. If the task of thread T that is currently being executed spawns a child thread T', then thread T is pushed onto the bottom of P's ready deque, and P begins to work on thread T'.

A thread completes or stalls. If thread T completes or stalls, then P checks its ready deque.

  Nonempty ready deque. If its deque is not empty, then P pops the bottommost thread and starts working on it.

  Empty ready deque. If its deque is empty, then P initiates workstealing. It chooses a workstation P' uniformly at random, "steals" the topmost thread in P''s ready deque, and starts working on that thread. If P''s ready deque is empty, then P chooses another random "victim."

Figure 1.3. Procedure Worksteal(T) *executes the multithreaded computation rooted at thread* T

- Let **Procedure Worksteal** *execute a multithreaded computation on a p-worksta-tion NOW. If the computation has dag-depth T_∞ and work T_1, then the expected running time, including scheduling overhead, is $O(T_1/p + T_\infty)$. This is clearly within a constant factor of optimal.*

B. Case study [110]: The study in [34] follows the traditional algorithmic paradigm. An algorithm is described in complete detail, down to the design of its underlying data structures. The performance/behavior of the algorithm is then analyzed in a setting appropriate to the genre of the algorithm. For instance, since **Procedure Worksteal** is a randomized algorithm, its performance is analyzed in [34] under the assumption that its input multithreaded computation is selected uniformly at random from the ensemble of such computations. In contrast to the preceding approach, the study in [110] describes an algorithm abstractly, via its state space and state-transition function. The performance/behavior of the algorithm is then analyzed by positing a process for generating the inputs that trigger state changes. We illustrate this change of worldview by describing **Procedure Worksteal** and its analysis in the framework of [110] in some detail. We then briefly summarize some of the other notable results in that source.

In the setting of [110], when a computer (such as a homogeneous NOW) is used as a *worksteating system*, its workstations execute tasks that are generated dynamically via a Poisson process of rate $\lambda < 1$. Tasks require computation time that is distributed exponentially with mean 1; these times are not known to workstations. Tasks are scheduled in a First-Come-First-Served fashion, with tasks awaiting execution residing in a FIFO queue. The *load* of a workstation P at time t is the number of tasks in P's queue at that time. At certain times (characterized by the algorithm being analyzed), a workstation P' can steal a task from another workstation P. When that happens, a task at the output end of P's queue (if there is one) *instantaneously* migrates to the input end of P''s queue. Formally, a work-stealing system is represented by a sequence of variables that yield snapshots of the state of the system as a function of the time t. Say that the NOW being analyzed has n constituent workstations.

- $n_l(t)$ is the number of workstations that have load l.
- $m_l(t) \overset{\text{def}}{=} \sum_{i=0}^{l} n_i(t)$ is the number of workstations that have load $\geq l$.
- $p_l(t) \overset{\text{def}}{=} n_l(t)/n$ is the fraction of workstations of load l.
- $s_l(t) \overset{\text{def}}{=} \sum_{i=l}^{\infty} p_i(t) = m_l(t)/n$ is the fraction of workstations of load $\geq l$.

The *state* of a workstealing system at time t is the infinite-dimensional vector $\vec{s}(t) \overset{\text{def}}{=} \langle s_0(t), s_1(t), s_2(t), \dots \rangle$.

The goal in [110] is to analyze the limiting behavior, as $n \to \infty$, of n-workstation workstealing systems under a variety of randomized workstealing algorithms. The mathematical tools that characterize the study are enabled by two features of the model we have described thus far. (1) Under the assumption of Poisson arrivals and exponential service times, the entire workstealing system is *Markovian:* its next state, $\vec{s}(t+1)$, depends only on its present state, $\vec{s}(t)$, not on any earlier history. (2) The fact that a workstealing system changes state instantaneously allows one to view time as a *continuous* variable, thereby enabling the use of differentials rather than differences when analyzing changes in the variables that characterize a system's state.

We enhance legibility henceforth by omitting the time variable t when it is clear from context. Note that $s_0 \equiv 1$ and that the s_l are nonincreasing, since $s_{l-1} - s_l = p_l$. The systems analyzed in [110] also have $\lim_{l \to \infty} s_l = 0$.

We introduce the general process of characterizing a system's (limiting) performance by focusing momentarily on a system in which no workstealing takes place. Let us represent by dt a small interval of time, in which only one event (a task arrival or departure) takes place at a workstation. The model of task arrivals (via a Poisson process with rate λ) means that the expected change in the variable m_l due to task arrivals is $\lambda(m_{l-1} - m_l) \, dt$. By similar reasoning, the expected change in m_l due to task departures—recall that there is no stealing going on—is just $(m_l - m_{l+1}) dt$. It follows that the expected net behavior of the system over short intervals is

$$\frac{dm_l}{dt} = \lambda \, (m_{l-1} - m_l) - (m_l - m_{l+1}),$$

or, equivalently (by eliminating the ubiquitous factor of n, the size of the NOW),

$$\frac{ds_l}{dt} = \lambda \, (s_{l-1} - s_l) - (s_l - s_{l+1}) \tag{3.1}$$

This last characterization of state changes illustrates the changes' independence from the aggregate number of workstations, depending instead only on the densities of workstations with various loads. The technical implications of this fact are discussed in some detail in [110], with appropriate pointers to the underlying mathematical texts.

In order to analyze the performance of **Procedure Worksteal** within the current model, one must consider how the Procedure's various actions are perceived by the workstations of the subject workstealing system. First, under the Procedure, a workstation P that completes its last task seeks to steal a task from a randomly chosen fellow workstation, P', succeeding with probability s_2 (the probability that P' has at least two tasks). Hence, P now perceives completion of its final task as emptying its queue only with probability $1 - s_2$. Mathematically, we thus have the following modified first equation of system (3.1):

$$\frac{ds_1}{dt} = \lambda \, (s_0 - s_1) - (s_1 - s_2)(1 - s_2) \tag{3.2}$$

For $l > 1$, s_l now decreases whenever a workstation with load l *either* completes a task *or* has a task stolen from it. The rate at which workstations steal tasks is just $s_1 - s_2$, i.e., the rate at which workstations complete their final tasks. We thus complete our modification of system (3.1) as follows:

$$\text{For } l > 1, \quad \frac{ds_l}{dt} = \lambda \, (s_{l-1} - s_l) - (s_l - s_{l+1})(1 + s_1 - s_2) \tag{3.3}$$

The limiting behavior of the workstealing system is characterized by seeking the *fixed point* of system (3.2, 3.3), i.e., the state $\vec{s}$ for which every $ds_l/dt = 0$.

Denoting the sought fixed point by $\pi = \langle \pi_0, \pi_1, \pi_2, \dots \rangle$, we have

- $\pi_0 = 1$, because $s_0 = 1$ for all t;

- $\pi_1 = \lambda$, because

- tasks complete at rate $s_1 n$, the number of busy workstations;
- tasks arrive at rate λn; and
- at the fixed point, tasks arrive and complete at the same rate;

- from (3.2) and the fact that $ds_1/dt = 0$ at the fixed point,

$$\pi_2 = \frac{1 + \lambda - \sqrt{1 + 2\lambda - 3\lambda^2}}{2};$$

- from (3.3) and the fact that $ds/dt = 0$ at the fixed point, by induction,

$$\text{For } l > 2, \pi_l = \left(\frac{\lambda}{1 + \lambda - \pi_2}\right)^{l-2} \pi_2.$$

The message of the preceding analysis becomes clear only when one performs the same exercise with the system (3.1), which characterizes a "workstealing system" in which there is no workstealing. For that system, one finds that $\pi_l = \lambda^l$, indicating that, in the limiting state, tasks are being completed at rate λ. Under the workstealing regimen of **Procedure Worksteal**, we still have the π_l, for $l > 2$, decreasing geometrically, but now the damping ratio is $\frac{\lambda}{1 + \lambda - \pi_2} < \lambda$. In other words, workstealing under the Procedure has the same effect as increasing the service rate of tasks in the workstealing system!

Simulation experiments in [110] help one evaluate the paper's abstract treatment. The experiments indicate that, even with $n = 128$ workstations, the model's predictions are quite accurate, at least for smaller arrival rates. Moreover, the quality of these predictions improve with larger n and smaller arrival rates.

The study in [110] goes on to consider several variations on the basic theme of workstealing, including precluding

(1) stealing work from workstations whose queues are almost empty; and
(2) stealing work when load gets below a (positive) threshold. Additionally, one finds in [110] refined analyses and more complex models for workstealing systems.

3.3.2   Cluster computing via cycle-stealing

Cycle-stealing, the use by one workstation of idle computing cycles of another, views the world through the other end of the computing telescope from workstealing. The basic observation that motivates cycle-stealing is that the workstations in clusters tend to be idle much of the time—due, say, to a user's pausing for deliberation or for a telephone call, etc.—and that the resulting idle cycles can fruitfully be "stolen" by busy workstations [100, 145]. Although cycle-stealing ostensibly puts the burden of finding available computing cycles on the busy workstations (the criticisms leveled against cycle-stealing by advocates of workstealing), the just-cited sources indicate that this burden can often be offloaded onto a central resource, or at least onto a workstation's operating system (rather than its application program).

The literature contains relatively few rigorously analyzed scheduling algorithms for cycle-stealing in (H)NOWs. Among the few such studies, [16] and the series [26, 128, 129, 131] view cycle-stealing as an *adversarial* enterprise, in which the cycle-stealer attempts to accomplish as much work as possible on the "borrowed" workstation before its owner returns—which event results in the cycle-stealer's job being killed!

A. Case study [16]: One finds in [16] a randomized cycle-stealing strategy that, with high probability, succeeds within a logarithmic factor of optimal work production. The underlying formal setting is as follows.

- All of the n workstations that are candidates as cycle donors are equally powerful computationally; i.e., the subject NOW is homogeneous.

- The cycle-stealer has a job that requires d steps of computation on any of these candidate donors.

- At least one of the candidate donors will be idle for a period of $D \geq 3d \log n$ time units (= steps).

Within this setting, the following simple randomized strategy provably steals cycles successfully, with high probability.

Phase 1. At each step, the cycle-stealer checks the availability of all n workstations in turn: first P_1, then P_2, and so on.

Phase 2. If, when checking workstation P_i, the cycle-stealer finds that it was idle at the last time unit, s/he flips a coin and assigns the job to P_i with probability $(1/d)n^{3x/D-2}$, where x is the number of time units for which P_i has been idle. The provable success of this strategy is expressed as follows.

- *With probability $\geq 1 - O((d \log n)/D + 1/n)$, the preceding randomized strategy will allow the cycle-stealer to get his/her job done.*

It is claimed in [16] that same basic strategy will actually allow the cycle-stealer to get $\log n$ d-step jobs done with the same probability.

B. Case study [131]: In [26, 128, 129, 131], cycle-stealing is viewed as a game against a malicious adversary who seeks to interrupt the borrowed workstation in order to kill all work in progress and thereby minimize the amount of work produced during a cycle-stealing opportunity. (In these studies, cycles are stolen from one workstation at a time, so the enterprise is unaffected by the presence or absence of heterogeneity.) Clearly, cycle-stealing within the described adversarial model can accomplish productive work only if the metaphorical "malicious adversary" is somehow restrained from just interrupting every period when the cycle-donor is doing work for the cycle-stealer, thereby killing all work done by the donor. The restraint studied in the *Known-Risk* model of [26, 128, 131] resides in two assumptions: (1) we know the instantaneous probability that the cycle-donor has *not* been reclaimed by its owner; (2) the *life function* P that exposes this probabilistic information—$P(t)$ is the probability that the donor has not been reclaimed by its owner by time t—is "smooth." The formal setting is as follows.

- The cycle-stealer, A, has a large bag of mutually independent tasks of equal *sizes* (which measure the cost of describing each task) and *complexities* (which measure the cost of computing each task).

- Each pair of communications—in which A sends work to the donor, B, and B returns the results of that work to A—incurs a fixed cost c. This cost is kept independent of the marginal per-task cost of communicating between A and B by incorporating the latter cost into the time for computing a task.

- *B* is dedicated to *A*'s work during the cycle-stealing opportunity, so its computation time is known exactly.

- Time is measured in work-units (rather than wall-clock time); one *unit of work* is the time it takes for
  - workstation *A* to transmit a single task to workstation *B* (this is the marginal transmission time for the task: the (fixed) setup time for each communication—during which many tasks will typically be transmitted—is accounted for by the parameter *c*);
  - workstation *B* to execute that task; and
  - workstation *B* to return its results for that task to workstation *A*.

Within this setting, a cycle-stealing opportunity is a sequence of *episodes* during which workstation *A* has access to workstation *B*, punctuated by *interrupts* caused by the return of *B*'s owner. When scheduling an opportunity, the vulnerability of *A* to interrupts, with their attendant loss of work in progress on *B*, is decreased by partitioning each episode into *periods*, each beginning with *A* sending work to *B* and ending either with an interrupt or with *B* returning the results of that work. *A*'s discretionary power thus resides solely in deciding how much work to send in each period, so an *(episode-) schedule* is simply a sequence of positive period-lengths: $S = t_0, t_1, \ldots$. A length-t period in an episode accomplishes $t \ominus c \overset{\text{def}}{=} \max(0, t - c)$ units of work if it is not interrupted and 0 units of work if it is interrupted. Thus, the episode scheduled by S accomplishes $\sum_{i=1}^{k-1}(t_i \ominus c)$ units of work when it is interrupted during period k.

Focus on a cycle-stealing episode whose lifespan ($\overset{\text{def}}{=}$ its maximum possible duration) is L time units. As noted earlier, we are assuming that we know the risk of *B*'s being reclaimed, via a decreasing *life function*,

$$P(t) \overset{\text{def}}{=} Pr(B \text{ has not been interrupted by time } t),$$

which satisfies (1) $P(0) = 1$ (to indicate *B*'s availability at the start of the episode); and (2) $P(L) = 0$ (to indicate that the interrupt will have occurred by time L). The earlier assertion that life functions must be "smooth" is embodied in the formal requirement that P be *differentiable* in the interval $(0, L)$. The goal is to maximize the *expected work production* from an episode governed by the life function P, i.e., to find a schedule S whose expected work production,

$$\text{EXP-WORK}(S; P) \overset{\text{def}}{=} \sum_{i=0}^{L}(t_i \ominus c) P(T_i), \qquad (3.4)$$

is maximum, over all schedules for P. In summation (3.4): each T_i is the partial sum

$$T_i \overset{\text{def}}{=} t_0 + t_2 + \ldots + t_i.$$

The presence of positive subtraction, $\ominus$, in (3.4) makes analyses of life functions difficult technically. Fortunately, one can avoid this difficulty for all but the last term of the summation. Say that a schedule is *productive* if each period—save possibly the last—has length $> c$. The following is proved in [26] and, in the following strict form, in [128].

- One can effectively[3] replace any schedule S for life function P by a productive schedule $\hat{S}$ such that EXP-WORK $(\hat{S}; P) \geq$ EXP-WORK$(S; P)$.

One finds in [131] a proof that the following characterization of optimal schedules allows one to compute such schedules effectively.

- The productive schedule $S = t_0, t_1, \ldots, t_{m-1}$ is optimal for the differentiable life function P if, and only if, for each period-index $k \geq 0$, save the last, period-length t_k is given by[4]

$$P(T_k) = \max(0, P(T_{k-1}) + (t_{k-1} - c) P'(T_{k-1})). \tag{3.5}$$

Since the explicit computation of schedules from system (3.5) can be computationally inefficient, relying on general function optimization techniques, the following simplifying initial conditions are presented in [131] for certain simple life functions.

- When P is convex (resp., concave),[5] the initial period-length t_0 is bounded above and below as follows, with the parameter $\psi = 1$ (resp., $\psi = 1/2$):

$$\sqrt{\frac{c^2}{4} - \frac{cP(t_0)}{P'(t_0)}} + \frac{c}{2} \leq t_0 \leq 2\sqrt{\frac{c^2}{4} - \frac{cP(t_0)}{P'(\psi t_0)}} + c.$$

3.3.3   Cluster computing via worksharing

Whereas workstealing and cycle-stealing involve a transaction between two workstations in an (H)NOW, *worksharing* typically involves many workstations working cooperatively. The qualifier *cooperatively* distinguishes the enterprise of worksharing from the passive cooperation of the work donor in workstealing and the grudging cooperation of the cycle donor in cycle-stealing.

In this section, we describe three studies of worksharing, namely, the study in [2], one of four problems studied in [20], and the most general HNOW model of [17]. (We deal with these sources in the indicated order to emphasize relevant similarities and differences.) These sources differ markedly in their models of the HNOW in which worksharing occurs, the characteristics of the work that is being shared, and the way in which worksharing is orchestrated. Indeed, part of our motivation in highlighting these three studies is to illustrate how apparently minor changes in model—of the computing platform or the workload—can lead to major changes in the algorithmics required to solve the worksharing problem (nearly) optimally. (Since the model of [20] is described at a high level in that paper, we have speculatively interpreted the architectural antecedents of the model's features for the purposes of enabling the comparison in this section.)

All three of these studies focus on some variant of the following scenario. A master workstation P_0 has a large bag of mutually independent tasks of equal sizes and complexities. P_0 has the opportunity to employ the computing power of

---

[3]The qualifier *effectively* means that the proof is constructive.
[4]As usual, f' denotes the first derivative of the univariate function f.
[5]The life function P is *concave* (resp., *convex*) if its derivative P' never vanishes at a point x where $P(x) > 0$, and is everywhere nonincreasing (resp., everywhere nondecreasing).

an HNOW N comprising workstations $P_1, P_2, \ldots, P_n$. P_0 transmits work to each of $N's$ workstations, and each workstation (eventually) sends results back to P_0. Throughout the worksharing process, $N's$ workstations are dedicated to P_0's workload. Some of the major differences among the models of the three sources are highlighted in Table 1.1. The "N/A" ("Not Applicable") entries in the table reflect the fact that only short messages (single tasks) are transmitted in [17]. The goal of all three sources is to allocate and schedule work optimally, within the context of the following problems:

The HNOW-Utilization Problem. *P_0 seeks to reach a "steady-state" in which the average amount of work accomplished per time unit is maximized.*

The HNOW-Exploitation Problem. *P_0 has access to N for a prespecified fixed period of time (the* lifespan*) and seeks to accomplish as much work as possible during this period.*

The HNOW-Rental Problem. *P_0 seeks to complete a prespecified fixed amount of work on N during as short a period as possible.*

The study in [17] concentrates on the HNOW-Utilization Problem. The studies of [2, 20] concentrate on the HNOW-Exploitation Problem, but this concentration is just for expository convenience, since the HNOW-Exploitation and -Rental Problems are computationally equivalent within the models of [2, 20]; i.e., an optimal solution to either can be converted to an optimal solution to the other.

A. Case study [2]: This study employs a rather detailed architectural model for the HNOW N, the HiHCoHP model of [41], which characterizes each workstation P_i of N via the parameters in Table 1.2. A word about message packaging and unpackaging is in order.

- In many actual HNOW architectures, the packaging (π) and unpackaging ($\bar{\pi}$) rates are (roughly) equal. One would lose little accuracy, then, by equating them.

- Since (un) packaging a message requires a fixed, known computation, the (common) ratio ρ/π_i is a measure of the granularity of the tasks in the workload.

- When message encoding/decoding is not needed (e.g., in an HNOW of trusted workstations), message (un)packaging is likely a lightweight operation; when encoding/decoding is needed, the time for message (un)packaging can be significant.

In summary, within the HiHCoHP model, a p-packet message from workstation P_i to workstation P_j takes an aggregate of $(\sigma + \lambda - \tau) + (\pi_i + \bar{\pi}_j \tau)p$ time units.

Table 1.1. *Comparing the models of [2], [20], and [17].*

Model Feature	[2]	[20]	[17]
Does each communication incur a substantial "setup" overhead?	Yes	No	No
Is complex message (un)packaging allowed/accounted for?	Yes	No	N/A
Can a workstation send and receive messages simultaneously?	No	No	Yes
Is the HNOW $N's$ network pipelineable? (A "Yes" allows savings by transmitting several tasks or results at a time, with only one "setup.")	Yes	Yes	N/A
Does P_0 allocate multiple tasks at a time?	Yes	Yes	No
Are $N's$ workstations allowed to redistribute tasks?	No	No	Yes
Are tasks "partitionable?" (A "Yes" allows the allocation of fractional tasks.)	Yes	No	No

Table 1.2. *A summary of the HiHCoHP model.*

Computation-related parameters for $N's$ workstations	
Computation	Each P_i needs ρ_i <u>work units</u> to compute a task. By convention: $\rho_1 \le \rho_2 \le \cdots \le \rho_n \equiv 1$.
Message-(un)packaging	Each P_i needs: $\pi_i \overset{\text{def}}{=} \rho_i \pi_n$ time units per packet to package a message for transmission (e.g., break into packets, compute checksums, encode); $\bar{\pi}_i \overset{\text{def}}{=} \rho_i \bar{\pi}_n$ time units per packet to unpackage a received message.
Communication-related parameters for $N's$ network	
Communication setup	Two workstations require σ time units to set up a communication (say, via a handshake).
Network latency	The first packet of a message traverses $N's$ network in λ time units.
Network transit time	Subsequent packets traverse $N's$ network in τ time units.

The computational protocols considered in [2] for solving the HNOW-Exploitation Problem build on single paired interactions between P_0 and each workstation P_i of N: P_0 sends work to P_i; P_i does the work; P_i sends results to P_0. The total interaction between P_0 and the single workstation P_i is orchestrated as shown in Figure 1.4. This interaction is extrapolated into a full-blown worksharing protocol via a pair of ordinal-indexing schemes for $N's$ workstations in order to supplement the model's power-related indexing described in the "Computation" entry of Table 1.2. The *startup indexing* specifies the order in which P_0 transmits work to $N's$ workstations; for this purpose, we label the workstations $P_{s_1}, P_{s_2}, \ldots, P_{s_n}$ to indicate that P_{s_i} receives work—hence, begins working—before $P_{s_{i+1}}$ does. The *finishing indexing* specifies the order in which $N's$ workstations return their work results to P_0; for this purpose, we label the workstations $P_{f_1}, P_{f_2}, \ldots, P_{f_n}$ to indicate that P_{f_i} ceases working—hence, transmits its results—before $P_{f_{i+1}}$ does. Figure 1.5 depicts a multiworkstation protocol. If we let w_i denote the amount of work allocated to workstation P_i, for $i = 1, 2, \ldots, n$, then the goal is to find a protocol (of the type described) that maximizes the overall work production $W = w_1 + w_2 + \cdots + w_n$.

Importantly, *when one allows work allocations to be fractional*, the work production of a protocol of the form we have been discussing can be specified in

P_0 prepares work for P_i	$P_0 \rightarrow P_i$ setup	P_0 transmits work	P_i unpacks work	P_i does work	P_i prepares results for P_0	$P_i \rightarrow P_0$ setup	P_i transmits results	P_0 unpacks results
$\pi_0 w_i$	σ	λ \; $\tau(w_i - 1)$	$\bar{\pi}_i w_i$	$\rho_i w_i$	$\pi_i \delta w_i$	σ	λ \; $\tau(\delta w_i - 1)$	$\bar{\pi}_0 \delta w_i$
in P_0	in P_0, P_i and network	in network	in P_i			in P_0, P_i and network	in network	in P_0

Figure 1.4. *The timeline for P_0's use of a single "rented" workstation P_i (not to scale)*

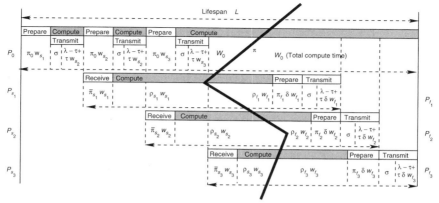

Figure 1.5. *The timeline (*not to scale*) for 3 "rented" workstations, indicating each workstation's lifespan. Note that each P_i's lifespan is partitioned in the figure between its incarnations as some P_{s_a} and some P_{f_b}.*

a computationally tractable, perspicuous way. If we enhance legibility via the abbreviations of Table 1.3, the work production of the protocol $P(\Sigma, \Phi)$ that is specified by the startup indexing $\Sigma = \langle s_1, s_2, \ldots, s_n \rangle$ and finishing indexing $\Phi = \langle f_1, f_2, \ldots, f_n \rangle$ over a lifespan of duration L is given by the following system of linear equations:

$$
\begin{pmatrix}
\mathrm{VC}_1 + \rho_1 & B_{1,2} & \cdots & B_{1,n} \\
B_{2,1} & \mathrm{VC}_2 + \rho_2 & \cdots & B_{2,n} \\
\vdots & \vdots & \cdots & \vdots \\
B_{n-1,1} & B_{n-1,2} & \cdots & B_{n-1,n} \\
B_{n,1} & B_{n,2} & \cdots & \mathrm{VC}_n + \rho_n
\end{pmatrix}
\cdot
\begin{pmatrix}
w_1 \\ w_2 \\ \vdots \\ w_{n-1} \\ w_n
\end{pmatrix}
=
\begin{pmatrix}
L - (c_1 + 2)\,\mathrm{FC} \\
L - (c_2 + 2)\,\mathrm{FC} \\
\vdots \\
L - (c_{n-1} + 2)\,\mathrm{FC} \\
L - (c_n + 2)\,\mathrm{FC}
\end{pmatrix},
\quad (3.6)
$$

where

- SB_i is the set of startup indices of workstations that *start before* P_i;

- FA_i is the set of finishing indices of workstations that *finish after* P_i;

- $c_i \overset{\text{def}}{=} |\mathrm{SB}_i| + |\mathrm{FA}_i|$; and

- $B_{i,j} = \begin{cases} \pi_0 + \tau + \tau\delta & \text{if } j \in \mathrm{SB}_i \text{ and } j \in \mathrm{FA}_i \\ \pi_0 + \tau & \text{if } j \in \mathrm{SB}_i \text{ and } j \notin \mathrm{FA}_i \\ \tau\delta & \text{if } j \notin \mathrm{SB}_i \text{ and } j \in \mathrm{FA}_i \\ 0 & \text{otherwise} \end{cases}$

Table 1.3. Some useful abbreviations

Abbrev.	Quantity	Meaning
$\tilde{\tau}$	$\tau(1 + \delta)$	Two-way transmission rate
$\tilde{\pi}_i$	$\pi_i + \pi_i\delta$	Two-way message-packaging rate for P_i
FC	$(\sigma + \lambda - \tau)$	*Fixed* overhead for an interworkstation communication
VC_i	$\pi_0 + \tilde{\tau} + \tilde{\pi}_i$	*Variable* communication overhead *rate* for P_i

The nonsingularity of the coefficient matrix in (3.6) indicates that the work production of protocol $P(\Sigma, \Phi)$ is, indeed, specified completely by the indexings Σ and Φ.

Of particular significance in [2] are the *FIFO* worksharing protocols, which are defined by the relation $\Sigma = \Phi$. For such protocols, system (3.6) simplifies to

$$\begin{pmatrix} \mathrm{VC}_{s_1} + \rho_{s_1} & \tau\delta & \cdots & \tau\delta \\ \pi_0 + \tau & \mathrm{VC}_{s_2} + \rho_{s_2} & \cdots & \tau\delta \\ \vdots & \vdots & \cdots & \vdots \\ \pi_0 + \tau & \pi_0 + \tau & \cdots & \tau\delta \\ \pi_0 + \tau & \pi_0 + \tau & \cdots & \mathrm{VC}_{s_n} + \rho_{s_n} \end{pmatrix} \cdot \begin{pmatrix} w_{s_1} \\ w_{s_2} \\ \vdots \\ w_{s_{n-1}} \\ w_{s_n} \end{pmatrix} \begin{pmatrix} L - (n+1)\,\mathrm{FC} \\ L - (n+1)\,\mathrm{FC} \\ \vdots \\ L - (n+1)\,\mathrm{FC} \\ L - (n+1)\,\mathrm{FC} \end{pmatrix} \qquad (3.7)$$

It is proved in [2] that, surprisingly,

- *All FIFO protocols produce the same amount of work in L time units, no matter what their startup indexing. This work production is obtained by solving system (3.7).*

FIFO protocols solve the HNOW-Exploitation Problem asymptotically optimally [2]:

- *For all sufficiently long lifespans L, a FIFO protocol produces at least as much work in L time units as any protocol $P(\Sigma, \Phi)$.*

It is worth noting that having to schedule the transmission of results, in addition to inputs, is the source of much of the complication encountered in proving the preceding result.

B. Case study [20]: As noted earlier, the communication model in [20] is specified at a high level of abstraction. In an effort to compare that model with the HiHCoHP model, we have cast the former model within the framework of the latter, in a way that is consistent with the algorithmic setting and results of [20]. One largely cosmetic difference between the two models is that all speeds are measured in absolute (wall-clock) units in [20], in contrast to the relative work units in [2]. More substantively, the communication model of [20] can be obtained from the HiHCoHP model via the following simplifications.

- There is no cost assessed for setting up a communication (the HiHCoHP cost σ). Importantly, the absence of this cost removes any disincentive to replacing a single long message by a sequence of shorter ones.

- Certain costs in the HiHCoHP model are deemed negligible and hence ignorable:
  the per-packet transit rate (τ) in a pipelined network, and
  the per-packet packaging (the π_i) and unpackaging (the $\overline{\pi}_i$) costs.

  These assumptions implicitly assert that the tasks in one's bag are very coarse, especially if message-(un) packaging includes en/decoding.

These simplifications imply that, within the model of [20],

- The heterogeneity of the HNOW N is manifest only in the differing computation rates of N's workstations.

- In a pipelined network, the distribution of work to and the collection of results from each of N's workstation take fixed constant time. Specifically, P_0 sends work at a cost of $t_{\text{com}}^{(\text{work})}$ time units *per transmission* and receives results at a cost of $t_{\text{com}}^{(\text{results})}$ time units *per transmission*.

Within this model, [20] derives efficient optimal or near-optimal schedules for the four variants of the HNOW-Exploitation Problem that correspond to the four paired answers to the questions: "Do tasks produce nontrivial-size results?" "Is N's network pipelined?" For those variants that are NP-Hard, *near*-optimality is the most that one can expect to achieve efficiently—and this is what [20] achieves.

The *Pipelined* HNOW-Exploitation Problem—which is the only version we discuss—is formulated in [20] as an *integer* optimization problem. (Tasks are atomic, in contrast to [2].) One allocates an integral number—call it a_i—of tasks to each workstation P_i via a protocol that has the essential structure depicted in Figure 1.5, altered to accommodate the simplified communication model. One then solves the following optimization problem.

Find: A startup indexing: $\Sigma = \langle s_1, s_2, \ldots, s_n \rangle$
        A finishing indexing: $\Phi = \langle f_1, f_2, \ldots, f_n \rangle$
        An allocation of tasks: Each P_i gets a_i tasks

That maximizes: $\sum_{i=1}^{n} a_i$ (the number of tasks computed)

Subject to the constraint: All work gets done within the lifespan; formally,

$$(\forall 1 \leq i \leq n)[s_i \cdot t_{\text{com}}^{(\text{work})} + a_i \cdot t_i + f_i \cdot t_{\text{com}}^{(\text{results})} \leq L]. \tag{3.8}$$

Not surprisingly, the (decision version of the) preceding optimization problem is NP-Complete and hence, likely computationally intractable. This fact is proved in [20] via reduction from a variant of the Numerical 3-D Matching Problem. Stated formally,

- *Finding an optimal solution to the HNOW-Exploitation Problem within the model of [20] is NP-complete in the strong sense.*[6]

Those familiar with discrete optimization problems would tend to expect a Hardness result here because this formulation of the HNOW-Exploitation Problem requires finding a maximum "paired-matching" in an edge-weighted version of the tripartite graph depicted in Figure 1.6. A "paired-matching" is one that uses both of the permutations Σ and Φ in a coordinated fashion in order to determine the a_i. The matching gives us the startup and finishing orders of N's workstations. Specifically, the edge connecting the left-hand instance of node i with node P_j (resp., the edge connecting the right-hand instance of node k with node P_j) is in the matching when $s_j = i$ (resp., $f_j = k$). In order to ensure that an optimal solution to the HNOW-Exploitation Problem is within our search space, we have to accommodate the possibility that $s_j = i$ and $f_j = k$, for every distinct triple of integers $i, j, k \in \{1, 2, \ldots, n\}$. In order to ensure that a maximum matching in the graph of Figure 1.6 yields this optimal solution, we weight the edges of the graph in accordance with constraint (3.8), which contains both s_i and f_i. If we

---

[6]The strong form of NP-completenes measures the sizes of integers by their magnitudes rather than the lengths of their numerals.

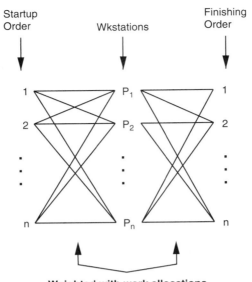

Weighted with work allocations

Figure 1.6. *An abstraction of the HNOW-Exploitation Problem within the model of [20]*

let $\omega(u, v)$ denote the weight on the edge from node u to node v in the graph, then, for each $1 \le i \le n$, the optimal weighting must end up with

$$\omega(s_i, P_i) + \omega(P_i, f_i) = \left\lfloor \frac{L - s_i \cdot t_{\text{com}}^{(\text{work})} - f_i \cdot t_{\text{com}}^{(\text{results})}}{t_i} \right\rfloor.$$

While the desired weighting would lead to an optimal solution, it also leads to NP-Hardness. We avoid this complexity by relinquishing our demand for an *optimal* solution. A simple approach to ensuring reasonable complexity is to decouple the matchings derived for the left-hand and right-hand sides of the graph of Figure 1.6, which is tantamount to ignoring the interactions between Σ and Φ when seeking work allocations. We achieve the desired decoupling via the following edge-weighting:

$$\omega(i, P_j) = \left\lfloor \frac{L/2 - i \cdot t_{\text{com}}^{(\text{work})}}{t_j} \right\rfloor \quad \text{and} \quad \omega(P_j, k) = \left\lfloor \frac{L/2 - k \cdot t_{\text{com}}^{(\text{results})}}{t_j} \right\rfloor.$$

We then find independent left-hand and right-hand maximum matchings, each within time $O(n^{5/2})$. It is shown in [20] that the solution produced by this decoupled matching problem deviates from the true optimal solution by only an additive discrepancy of $\le n$.

- *There is an $O(n^{5/2})$-time work-allocation algorithm whose solution (within the model of [20]) to the HNOW-Exploitation Problem in an n-workstation HNOW is (additively) within n of optimal.*

C. Case study [17]: The framework of this study is quite different from that of [2, 20], since it focuses on the HNOW-Utilization Problem rather than the HNOW-Exploitation Problem. In common with the latter sources, a master workstation enlists the computational resources of an HNOW N in computing a bag of tasks that are equal in both size and complexity. Here, however, the master workstation is a member—call it P_m—of the HNOW N. Moreover, here the bag of tasks is massive, and there is no *a priori* limit to the duration of the worksharing enterprise. Additionally, the form of worksharing considered is different from and, in some ways, more ambitious than in [2, 20]. Now, P_m allocates one task at a time, *and* workstations may redistribute these work allocations (one task at a time) at will, along direct communication links between selected pairs of workstations. Finally, in contrast to the HNOW-Exploitation Problem, one wants here to have the worksharing regimen reach an optimal "steady state," in which the average aggregate number of tasks computed per time-step is maximized. We describe here only the most general of the scheduling results in [17], which places no *a priori* restriction on which pairs of workstations can communicate directly with each other.

As in the HiHCoHP model, each workstation P_i of [17] has a computation rate ρ_i (cf. Table 1.2) which indicates the amount of time P_i takes to compute one task—but the indices here do not reflect relative speeds. Every pair of workstations, P_i and P_j, has an associated cost c_{ij} of transmitting a single task (with all material necessary for its computation) between P_i and P_j, in either direction. To simplify the development, the cost associated with a task is "double-ended," in the sense that it includes the cost of transmitting both that task and (at a later time) the results from that task. If P_i and P_j can communicate directly with one another—for short, are *neighbors*—then c_{ij} is finite; if they cannot, then, by convention, $c_{ij} = \infty$. The communication model in [17] is thus closer to that of [131] than to that of [2], for in the latter, the possible differences between packaging and unpackaging times may render communication costs asymmetric. Several regimens are considered in [17] concerning what processes may occur in parallel. We focus here only on their "base model," in which a workstation can simultaneously receive a task (or a result) from one neighbor, send a task (or a result) to one (possibly different) neighbor, and process some task (that it already has). In summation, if workstation P_i sends a task to workstation P_j at time-step t, then, until time $t + c_{ij}$:

- P_j cannot start executing this task nor initiate another receive operation;

- P_i cannot initiate another send operation.

Within the preceding model, the goal of the study—optimal steady-state performance—is formalized as follows. For each $1 \leq i \leq n$, let $n(i)$ be the set of indices of workstation P_i's neighbors. During a snapshot depicting one unit of activity by the HNOW N:

- k_i is the fraction of time during which P_i is *computing*;

- s_{ij} is the fraction of time during which P_i is *sending* to neighbor P_j;

- r_{ij} is the fraction of time during which P_i is *receiving* from neighbor P_j.

The quantity k_i/ρ_i is the *throughput* of workstation P_i during the isolated time unit. To wit, P_i is capable of computing $1/\rho_i$ tasks in one time unit; in the snapshot, only the fraction k_i of that time unit is spent computing. The goal is to maximize the quantity

$$\text{Throughput-rate} \overset{\text{def}}{=} \sum_{i=1}^{n} \frac{k_i}{\rho_i}, \tag{3.9}$$

subject to the following seven sets of constraints imposed by the model.

1. for all i: $0 \leq k_i \leq 1$
   for all $i, j \in n(i)$: $0 \leq s_{ij} \leq 1$
   for all $i, j \in n(i)$: $0 \leq r_{ij} \leq 1$
   These reflect the fact that k_i, s_{ij}, and r_{ij} are proper fractions.
2. for all $i, j \in n(i)$: $s_{ij} = r_{ji}$
   Each P_j receives whatever each neighbor P_i sends it.
3. for all i: $\Sigma_{j \in n(i)} \, s_{ij} \leq 1$
   for all i: $\Sigma_{j \in n(i)} \, r_{ij} \leq 1$
   These reflect the single-port communication regimen.
4. for all $i, j \in n(i)$: $s_{ij} + r_{ji} \leq 1$
   Even though a link is bidirectional, its bandwidth can never be exceeded. (Multiply the inequality by the bandwidth $1/c_{ij}$ to clarify the constraint.)
5. for all $i \neq m$: $\displaystyle\sum_{j \in n(i)} \frac{r_{ij}}{c_{ij}} = \frac{k_i}{\rho_i} + \sum_{j \in n(i)} \frac{s_{ij}}{c_{ij}}$

   A conservation law: For every P_i except the master P_m—which starts out with "infinitely many" tasks—the number of tasks that P_i receives should equal the number that it computes, plus the number that it relays to other P_j.
6. for all $j \in n(m)$: $r_{mj} = 0$
   Since P_m is saturated with tasks *ab initio*, there can be no advantage to sending it additional tasks.
7. $k_m \equiv 1$
   The model allows P_m to compute without interruption.

The preceding formulation of the goal affords one an efficient alogorithm for optimally solving the HNOW-Utilization Problem on the HNOW N [17].

- *The optimization problem (3.9), augmented with the seven sets of constraints, comprises a linear program whose solution yields the optimal solution for the HNOW-Utilization Problem on the HNOW N.*

- *This linear program finds this schedule in a time polynomial in the size of N, as measured by the number of workstations and the number of direct interworkstation links.*

Significant related studies. One finds in [3] a model that captures the same features as does HiHCoHP but without allowing for workstation heterogeneity. Through use of this model, it is proved that the FIFO Protocol provides optimal solutions for the HNOW-Exploitation Problem in *homogeneous* NOWs.

We remarked earlier that one finds in [20] four variants of the HNOW-Exploitation Problem, not just the one variant we have described. In all four variants, the master workstation sends an allocation of equal-size, equal-complexity tasks to all workstations of the "exploited" HNOW N and receives the results of those tasks; all tasks are assumed to produce the same amount of data as results; all communication is single ported. Two families of worksharing protocols are considered, one of which has work distributed and results collected in the staggered manner depicted in Figure 1.5, and the other of which has work distributed via a scatter operation and results collected via a gather operation.

The HNOW-Rental Problem is studied in [163], under a model in which tasks produce no output and communication can overlap with computation, even on the same workstation. Worksharing proceeds by having the master workstation transmit equal-size chunks of work to the rented HNOW's workstations at a frequency determined by an analysis of the workstations' powers. A near-optimal algorithm is derived within this setting.

One finds in [22, 23, 42] and sources cited therein a model that is simpler than those discussed thus far. These sources employ a very abstract model that suppresses many of the costs accounted for in the other cited studies.

Employing a rather different approach to worksharing, the study in [15] considers how to allocate a single compute-intensive task within an HNOW N. The decision about which workstation(s) will receive the task is made based on an "auction." The master workstation determines which aggregation of N's workstations will—according to the source's cost model—yield the best performance on the auctioned task.

Finally, one finds in [56] a largely experimental study of worksharing in HNOWs whose workstations share resources in a nondedicated manner. As in a Computational Grid (see Section 4.1), the workstations of [56] *timeshare* their cycles with partners' work, rather than dedicating cycles to that work. As in [15], work is allocated among the HNOW's workstations based on anticipated performance on that work; in contrast to [15], "anticipated performance" is explicitly determined empirically; all workstations simultaneously and continuously monitor the anticipated performance of their fellow HNOW members.

4   INTERNET COMPUTING

Advancing technology has rendered the Internet a viable medium for collaborative computing, via mechanisms such as Grid computing (*GC*, for short) and Web-based computing (*WC*, for short). Our interest in these modalities of Internet computing resides in their (not uncommon) use for computing a massive collection of (usually compute-intensive) tasks that reside at a "master" computing site. When so used, the master site views its collaborators as remotely situated "volunteers" who must be supplied with work in a manner that enhances the completion of the massive job.

4.1   The Platform(s)

Computational Grids. A *GC project* presupposes the formation of a *Computational Grid*—a consortium of computing sites that contract to share resources [62, 63]. From time to time, a Grid computing site will send a task to a companion Grid site that has agreed to share its computing cycles. When this companion site returns the result of its current task, it becomes eligible for further worksharing.

Web-based computing. In a *WC project*, a volunteer registers with the master site and receives a task to compute. When a volunteer completes its current task, it revisits the master site to return the results of that task and to receive a new task. Interesting WC projects include [85, 159], which perform astronomical calculations; [137], which performs security-motivated number-theoretic calculations; and [76, 116, 160], which perform medical and biological computations. Such sites benefit from Internet computing either because of the sheer volume of their workloads or because of the computational complexity of their individual tasks.

4.2   Some Challenges

The endeavor of using the Internet for collaborative computing gives rise to two algorithmic challenges that are not encountered in environments in which the computing agents are more tightly coupled. We term these challenges *temporal and factual unpredictability*.

Temporal unpredictability. Remote computing agents in an Internet computing project—be it a WC or GC project—typically tender no guarantee of when the results from an allocated task will be returned to the master site. Indeed, in a WC project, that site typically has no guarantee that a volunteer will *ever* return results. This lack of a time guarantee is an annoyance when the tasks composing the collaborative workload are mutually independent—i.e., form a bag of tasks—but at least one never runs out of tasks that are eligible for allocation. (Of course, if all tasks must eventually be executed—which is *not* the case with several WC projects—then this annoyance must trigger some action, such as reallocation, by the master site.) However, when the tasks in the workload have interdependencies that constrain their order of execution, this temporal unpredictability can lead to a form of gridlock wherein no new tasks can be allocated for an indeterminate period, pending the execution of already allocated tasks. Although safety devices such as deadline-triggered reallocation of tasks address this danger, they do not eliminate it, since the backup remote participant assigned a given task may be as dilatory as the primary one. A major challenge is how to orchestrate the allocation of tasks in a way that minimizes the likelihood of this form of gridlock.

Factual unpredictability. The volunteers who participate in a WC project typically need not authenticate their alleged identities. In many such projects, the sheer number of participants would render the use of costly trusted authentication mechanisms impracticable. This fact renders all interchanges with—and information from—volunteers totally insecure. As noted in Section 1, this situation apparently creates an irresistible temptation for hackers, who plague many WC projects, greatly increasing the overhead for these projects. For this reason, one might suggest using WC only for security-insensitive applications (relating, say, to processing astronomical data [85, 159]) where erroneous or even mischievously or maliciously false results are not likely to have dire consequences. However, many of the most important applications of WC involve very sensitive applications, such as security-related [137] or health-related [76, 116] ones. Indeed, for many applications that generate truly massive numbers of identical tasks, Web-based computing is one of the only imaginable ways to assemble massive computing power at manageable cost. The challenge is to coordinate the volunteers in a WC project in a way that minimizes potential disruptions by hackers, while not excessively slowing down the progress of legitimate participants.

4.3   Some Sophisticated Responses

There have thus far been few rigorously analyzed algorithmic studies of computing on the Internet, via either WC or GC. One significant such study is [17], which studies worksharing in Grids. By rescaling model parameters, this study applies also to worksharing in HNOWs, which is the context in which we discuss it (Section 3.3.3.C). We have opted to reserve this section for studies that address problems unique to Internet computing.

4.3.1   Scheduling to cope with temporal unreliability

A. Case study [133, 136]: These sources craft and study a model that abstracts the process of scheduling computation-dags for either GC or WC. The goal of the model is to allow one to avoid the gridlock encountered when a computation stalls because all tasks that are eligible for execution have been allocated but not yet returned. The model is inspired by the many *pebble games* on dags that have been shown, over several decades, to yield elegant formal analogues of a variety of problems related to scheduling the task-nodes of computation-dags [47, 73, 118]. Such games use tokens called *pebbles* to model the progress of a computation on a dag: the placement or removal of the various available types of pebbles—which is constrained by the dependencies modeled by the dag's arcs—represents the changing (computational) status of the dag's task-nodes. The *Internet-Computing* (*IC*, for short) *Pebble Game* on a computation-dag G involves one player S, the *Server*, and an indeterminate number of players $C_1, C_2, \ldots$, the *Clients*. The Server has access to unlimited supplies of three types of pebbles: ELIGIBLE-BUT-UNALLOCATED (EBU, for short) pebbles, ELIGIBLE-AND-ALLOCATED (EAA, for short) pebbles, and EXECUTED (XEQ, for short) pebbles. The Game's moves reflect the successive stages in the life-cycle of a node in a computation-dag, from eligibility for execution through actual execution. Figure 1.7 presents the rules of the IC Pebble Game. The reader should note how the moves of the Game expose the danger of a play's being stalled indefinitely by dilatory Clients.

There is little that one can do to forestall the chances of gridlock when playing the IC Pebble Game, absent some constraint on the actions of the Clients. Without some constraint, a malicious adversary (read: unfortunate behavior by Clients) could confound any attempt to guarantee the availability of a node containing an EBU pebble—by imposing a pessimal order on the execution of allocated tasks. The constraint imposed by the study in [133, 136] is the assumption that *tasks are executed in the same order as they are allocated.* (Since many GC and WC master sites monitor the state of remote participants, this assumption is not totally fanciful.) With this assumption in place, these studies attempt to optimize the quality of a play of the IC Pebble Game on a dag G by maximizing, at all steps *t, the aggregate number of* EBU *pebbles on G's nodes, as a function of the number of* EAA *and* XEQ *pebbles on G's nodes.*

- At any step of the game, S may place an EBU pebble on any unpebbled source node of G. /* Unexecuted source nodes are always eligible for execution, having no parents whose prior execution they depend on.*/

- Say that Client C_i approaches S requesting a task. If C_i has previously been allocated a task that it has not completed, then C_i's request is ignored; otherwise, the following occurs.

  – If at least one node of G contains an EBU pebble, then S gives C_i the task corresponding to one such node and replaces that node's pebble with an EAA pebble.

  – If no node of G contains an EBU pebble, then C_i is told to withdraw its request, and this move is a no-op.

- When a Client returns (the results from) a task-node, S replaces that task-node's EAA pebble by an XEQ pebble. S then places an EBU pebble on each unpebbled node of G, all of whose parents contain XEQ pebbles.

- S's goal is to allocate nodes in such a way that every node v of G *eventually* contains an XEQ pebble.
  /*This modest goal is necessitated by the possibility that G is infinite.*/

Figure 1.7. *The rules of the IC Pebble Game*

The computation-dags studied in [133, 136] are the four depicted in Figure 1.8: the (infinite) *evolving mesh-dag*, reduction-oriented versions of *mesh-dags* and *tree-dags*, and the *FFT-dag* [48]. It is shown in [133] (for evolving 2-dimensional mesh-dags) and in [136] (for the other dags in Figure 1.8) that a schedule for the dags in Figure 1.8 is optimal if, and only if, it allocates nodes in a *parent-oriented* fashion—i.e., it executes all parents of each node in consecutive steps. This general result translates to the following dag-specific instances.

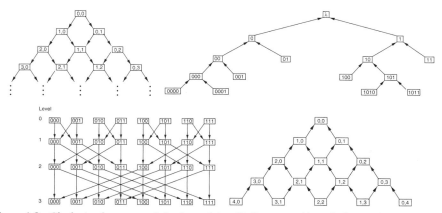

Figure 1.8. *Clockwise from upper left: the evolving (2-dimensional) mesh-dag, a (binary) reduction-tree dag, the 5-level (2-dimensional) reduction-mesh dag, the 4-level FFT-dag*

- *The strategy of executing nodes of evolving mesh-dags along successive levels of the dag—level k comprises all nodes $\langle x, y \rangle$ such that $x + y = k$—is optimal for 2-dimensional mesh-dags. (It is shown in [133] that this strategy is within a constant factor of optimal for mesh-dags of higher (fixed) dimensionalities.)*

The proof for 2-dimensional mesh-dags is immediate from the following observation. No two eligible nodes can reside in the same row or the same column of the mesh-dag at any step of the IC Pebble Game; moreover, all "ancestors" of each EBU node must contain XEQ pebbles. Hence, when there are n EBU nodes on the dag, there must be at least $(\frac{n}{2})$ XEQ nodes "supporting" them. The argument for higher dimensionalities is similar in strategy but significantly more complex.

- *For reduction-oriented mesh-dags, a schedule is optimal if it executes nodes along successive levels of the dag.*

- *For reduction-oriented tree-dags and for the FFT-dag, a schedule is optimal if "sibling" nodes—nodes that share a parent—are always executed in consecutive steps.*

For reduction-mesh dags, the optimality condition follows from the fact that the aggregate number of EBU nodes on the dag at any step of the IC Pebble Game is bounded above by (one plus) the smallest index of a level of the dag that contains a pebble at step t; one therefore wants this index to shrink as slowly as possible. For the other dags, the aggregate number of EBU nodes on the dag at a step of the IC Pebble Game is bounded above by a quantity depending on the structure of the dag and the number of XEQ nodes at that step, *minus the number of nodes that contain* XEQ *pebbles while their siblings don't.*

Significant progress is made in [102] toward developing techniques for crafting optimal schedules for a broad range of computation-dags, by abstracting and generalizing the scheduling principles underlying the case studies in [133, 136].

4.3.2   Scheduling to cope with factual unreliability

There is substantial work going on in the secure-computing community that is aimed at identifying attempts to compromise collaborative computing projects; see, e.g., [144] and sources cited therein. We know, however, of only one study aimed at possibly eliminating hackers from a WC project once they are identified.

A. Case study [132]: This source studies an unusual facet of the security problem in WC. It develops a computationally lightweight scheme for keeping track of which volunteers in a WC project computed which tasks. Much of the scheme employs familiar algorithmic techniques involving search trees for point-and range-queries. The unique aspect of the scheme is a strategy that assigns positive-integer indices to

1. the set of all tasks at the master site,
2. all volunteers (who are allowed to arrive and depart dynamically), and
3. the set of tasks reserved for each volunteer v

and that interrelates the resulting three sets of indices. The interrelation mechanism is a *task-allocation function* (*TAF*, for short), i.e., a *pairing function* φ that maps the set $\mathbf{N} \times \mathbf{N}$ of pairs of positive integers *one-to-one, onto* the set $\mathbf{N}$ of positive integers; symbolically, $\varphi\colon \mathbf{N} \times \mathbf{N} \leftrightarrow \mathbf{N}$. Each copy of the set $\mathbf{N}$ plays the role of one of the indicated sets of indices. The potential practicality of such a scheme demands that the functions φ, φ^{-1}, and $\varphi(u, t+1) - \varphi(u, t)$ all be easily computed; to wit, the "master" site must compute

- $\varphi(v, t)$ to determine the index in the overall workload of the tth task in volunteer v's workload;

- $\varphi^{-1}(t)$ to determine which volunteer, v, was assigned task t, and what index task t has in v's workload; and

- $\varphi(v, t+1) - \varphi(v, t)$ to determine which task to allocate to volunteer v when s/he returns the results of his/her task t.

In a quest for computational ease, the primary focus in [132] is on TAFs that are *additive* (are *ATAFs*, for short). An ATAF assigns each volunteer v a *base task-index* B_v and a *stride* S_v; it then uses the formula

$$\varphi(v, t) = B_v + (t - 1)S_v$$

to determine the workload task-index of the tth task assigned to volunteer v. From a system perspective, ATAFs have the benefit that a volunteer's stride need be computed only when s/he first registers at the website, and can be stored for subsequent appearances.

The main results of [132] determine how to assign base task-indices and strides to volunteers efficiently, both in terms of computing these indices and in terms of having the indices grow as slowly as possible, as functions of the volunteer-index v. The slow growth of B_v and S_v is argued in [132] to facilitate management of the memory in which the tasks are stored. Toward this end, a procedure for

Procedure ATAF-Constructor (φ) (see Figure 1.9) builds on the preceding result to construct ATAFs efficiently.

Step 1. Partition the set of volunteer-task-indices into *groups* whose sizes are powers of 2 (with any desired mix of equal-size and distinct-size groups). Order the groups linearly in some (arbitrary) way.
/*We can now talk unambiguously about group 0 (whose members share *group-index* $g = 0$), group 1 (whose members share group-index $g = 1$), and so on.*/

Step 2. Assign each group a distinct copy of the set $\varnothing$, via a *copy-index* $k(g)$ expressed as a function of the group-index g.
/*We can now talk unambiguously about group g's copy $\varnothing_{k(g)}$ of the odd integers.*/

Step 3. Allocate group g's copy $\varnothing_{k(g)}$ to its members via the ($c = k(g)$) instance of the cited property of the odd integers, using the multiplier 2^g as a *signature* to distinguish group g's copy of the set $\varnothing$ from all other groups' copies.

Figure 1.9. Procedure ATAF-Constructor *(φ), which constructs an ATAF φ*

$$\varphi^{<1>}(x,y) \stackrel{\text{def}}{=} 2^{x-1}[2(y-1)+(2x-1 \bmod 2)]$$

$\langle x,g \rangle$	$\varphi^{<1>}(x,y)$					
$\langle 14,13 \rangle$	8192	24576	40960	57344	73728	$\cdots$
$\langle 15,14 \rangle$	16384	49152	81920	114688	147456	$\cdots$

$$\varphi^{<3>}(x,y) \stackrel{\text{def}}{=} 2^{\lfloor(x-1)/4\rfloor}[8(y-1)+(2x-1 \bmod 8)]$$

$\langle x,g \rangle$	$\varphi^{<3>}(x,y)$					
$\langle 14,13 \rangle$	24	88	152	216	280	$\cdots$
$\langle 15,3 \rangle$	40	104	168	232	296	$\cdots$
$\vdots$	$\vdots$	$\vdots$	$\vdots$	$\vdots$	$\vdots$	$\vdots$
$\langle 28,6 \rangle$	448	960	1472	1984	2496	$\cdots$
$\langle 29,7 \rangle$	128	1152	2176	3200	4224	$\cdots$

$$\varphi^{<\#>}(x,y) \stackrel{\text{def}}{=} 2^{\lfloor\log x\rfloor}\left(2^{1+\lfloor\log x\rfloor}(y-1)+(2x+1 \bmod 2^{1+\lfloor\log x\rfloor})\right)$$

$\langle x,g \rangle$	$\varphi^{<\#>}(x,y)$					
$\langle 28,4 \rangle$	400	912	1424	1936	2448	$\cdots$
$\langle 29,4 \rangle$	432	944	1456	1968	2480	$\cdots$

Figure 1.10.

contructing ATAFs is presented, based on the following well-known property of the set $\emptyset$ of positive odd integers; see [113].

- *For any positive integer c, every odd integer can be written in precisely one of the 2^{c-1} forms: $2^c n + 1, 2^c n + 3, 2^c n + 5, \ldots, 2^c n + (2^c - 1)$, for some nonnegative integer n.*

An explicit expression for the ATAFs of Procedure ATAF-Constructor. If we denote the $2^{k(g)}$ rows of group g as $x_{g,1}, x_{g,2}, \ldots, x_{g,\,2k(g)}$, then for all $i \in \{1, 2, \ldots, k^{(g)}\}$,

$$\varphi(x_{g,i}, y) \stackrel{\text{def}}{=} 2^g[2^{1+k(g)}(y-1)+(2x_{g,i}+1 \bmod 2^{1+k(g)})].$$

Figure 1.10 illustrates the construction via a sampler of argument-result values from three sample ATAFs. The first two exemplified ATAFs, $\varphi^{<1>}$ and $\varphi^{<3>}$, stress ease of computation; the third, $\varphi^{\#}(x,y)$, stresses slowly growing strides.

ACKNOWLEDGMENTS

The research of the author was supported in part by NSF Grant CCR-00-73401. Thanks are due many colleagues who helped in varied ways: by commenting on the text, by pointing out references, and by giving permission to have their work summarized here. I hesitate to enumerate them for fear of inadvertently forgetting some. Let me, therefore, merely assure them of my sincere gratitude.

REFERENCES

[1] U. Acar, G.E. Blelloch, R.D. Blumofe (2002): The data locality of work stealing. *Theory of Computing Systs.* 35, 321–347.

[2] M. Adler, Y. Gong, A.L. Rosenberg (2003): Optimal sharing of bags of tasks in heterogeneous clusters. *15th ACM Symp. on Parallelism in Algorithms and Architectures (SPAA '03)*, 1–10.

[3] J. Agrawal and H.V. Jagadish (1988): Partitioning techniques for large-grained parallelism. *IEEE Trans. Computers 37*, 1627–1634.

[4] W. Aiello, S.N. Bhatt, F.R.K. Chung, A.L. Rosenberg, R.K. Sitaraman (2001): Augmented ring networks. *IEEE Trans. Parallel and Distr. Systs. 12*, 598–609.

[5] S. Akl (1989): *The Design and Analysis of Parallel Algorithms*. Prentice-Hall, Englewood Cliffs, NJ.

[6] R. Aleliunas and A.L. Rosenberg (1982): On embedding rectangular grids in square grids. *IEEE Trans. Comput., C-31*, 907–913.

[7] A. Alexandrov, M.I. Ionescu, K.E. Schauser, C. Scheiman (1997): LogGP: incorporating long messages into the LogP model for parallel computation. *J. Parallel Distr. Comput. 44*, 71–79.

[8] R.J. Anderson and G.L. Miller (1990): A simple randomized parallel algorithm for list-ranking. *Inform. Proc. Lett. 10*.

[9] T.E. Anderson, D.E. Culler, D.A. Patterson, and the HNOW Team (1995): A case for NOW (networks of workstations). *IEEE Micro 15*, 54–64.

[10] M. Andrews, F.T. Leighton, P.T. Metaxas, L. Zhang (1996): Improved methods for hiding latency in high bandwidth networks. *8th ACM Symp. on Parallel Algorithms and Architectures*, pp. 52–61.

[11] F.S. Annexstein (1991): SIMD-emulations of hypercubes and related networks by linear and ring-connected processor arrays. *3rd IEEE Symp. on Parallel and Distributed Processing*, pp. 656–659.

[12] F.S. Annexstein (1994): Embedding hypercubes and related networks into mesh-connected processor arrays. *J. Parallel Distr. Comput. 23*, 72–79.

[13] F.S. Annexstein, M. Baumslag, A.L. Rosenberg (1990): Group action graphs and parallel architectures. *SIAM J. Comput. 19*, 544–569.

[14] N.S. Arora, R.D. Blumofe, C.G. Plaxton (2001): Thread scheduling for multiprogrammed multiprocessors. *Theory of Computing Syst. 34*, 115–144.

[15] M.J. Atallah, C.L. Black, D.C. Marinescu, H.J. Siegel, T.L. Casavant (1992): Models and algorithms for coscheduling compute-intensive tasks on a network of workstations. *J. Parallel Distr. Comput. 16*, 319–327.

[16] B. Awerbuch, Y. Azar, A. Fiat, F.T. Leighton (1996): Making commitments in the face of uncertainty: how to pick a winner almost every time. *28th ACM Symp. on Theory of Computing*, pp. 519–530.

[17] C. Banino, O. Beaumont, L. Carter, J. Ferrante, A. Legrand, Y. Robert (2003): Scheduling strategies for master-slave tasking on heterogeneous processor grids. *IEEE Trans. Parallel and Distr. Syst. 15*, 319–330.

[18] A. Bar-Noy and D. Peleg (1991): Square meshes are not always optimal. *IEEE Trans. Comput. 40*, 196–204.

[19] O. Beaumont, L. Carter, J. Ferrante, A. Legrand, Y. Robert (2002): Bandwidth-centric allocation of independent tasks on heterogeneous platforms. *Int. Parallel Distr. Processing Symp. (IPDPS'02)*.

[20] O. Beaumont, A. Legrand, Y. Robert (2003): The master-slave paradigm with heterogeneous processors. *IEEE Trans. Parallel Distr. Syst. 14*, 897–908.

[21] J.-C. Bermond and C. Peyrat (1989): The de Bruijn and Kautz networks: a competitor for the hypercube? In *Hypercube and Distributed Computers* (F. Andre and J.P. Verjus, eds.), North-Holland, Amsterdam, pp. 279–293.

[22] V. Bharadwaj, D. Ghose, V. Mani (1994): Optimal sequencing and arrangement in distributed single-level tree networks. *IEEE Trans. Parallel Distr. Syst. 5*, 968–976.

[23] V. Bharadwaj, D. Ghose, V. Mani (1995): Multi-installment load distribution in tree networks with delays. *IEEE Trans. Aerospace Electron. Syst. 31*, 555–567.

[24] S.N. Bhatt, F.R.K. Chung, F.T. Leighton, A.L. Rosenberg (1992): Efficient embeddings of trees in hypercubes. *SIAM J. Comput. 21*, 151–162.

[25] S.N. Bhatt, F.R.K. Chung, J.-W. Hong, F.T. Leighton, B. Obrenić, A.L. Rosenberg, E.J. Schwabe (1996): Optimal emulations by butterfly-like networks. *J. ACM 43*, 293–330.

[26] S.N. Bhatt, F.R.K. Chung, F.T. Leighton, A.L. Rosenberg (1997): On optimal strategies for cycle-stealing in networks of workstations. *IEEE Trans. Comput. 46*, 545–557.

[27] S.N. Bhatt, D.S. Greenberg, F.T. Leighton, P. Liu (1999): Tight bounds for on-line tree embeddings. *SIAM J. Comput. 29*, 474–491.

[28] S.N. Bhatt and F.T. Leighton (1984): A framework for solving VLSI graph layout problems. *J. Comput. Syst. Sci. 28*, 300–343.

[29] G. Bilardi, K.T. Herley, A. Pietracaprina, G. Pucci, P. Spirakis (1999): *Algorithmica 24*, 405–422.

[30] G. Bilardi and A. Nicolau (1989): Adaptive bitonic sorting: An optimal algorithm for shared memory machines. *SIAM J. Comput. 18*, 216–228.

[31] G. Bilardi and F.P. Preparata (1995): Horizons of parallel computation. *J. Parallel Distr. Comput. 27*, 172–182.

[32] R.D. Blumofe, C.F. Joerg, B.C. Kuszmaul, C.E. Leiserson, K.H. Randall, Y. Zhou (1995): Cilk: an efficient multithreaded runtime system. *5th ACM SIGPLAN Symp. on Principles and Practices of Parallel Programming (PPoPP'95)*.

[33] R.D. Blumofe and C.E. Leiserson (1998): Space-efficient scheduling of multithreaded computations. *SIAM J. Comput. 27*, 202–229.

[34] R.D. Blumofe and C.E. Leiserson (1999): Scheduling multithreaded computations by work stealing. *J. ACM 46*, 720–748.

[35] R.D. Blumofe and D.S. Park (1994): Scheduling large-scale parallel computations on networks of workstations. *3rd Int. Symp. on High-Performance Distributed Computing*, pp. 96–105.

[36] B. Boothe and A.G. Ranade (1992): Improved multithreading techniques for hiding communication latency in multiprocessors. *19th Int. Symp. on Computer Architecture*.

[37] R.P. Brent (1974): The parallel evaluation of general arithmetic expressions. *J. ACM 21*, 201–206.

[38] R.P. Brent and H.T. Kung (1984): Systolic VLSI arrays for polynomial gcd computation. *IEEE Trans. Comp., C-33*, 731–737.

[39] R.P. Brent, H.T. Kung, F.T. Luk (1983): Some linear-time algorithms for systolic arrays. In *Information Processing 83* (R.E.A. Mason, ed.), North-Holland, Amsterdam, pp. 865–876.

[40] T.N. Bui, S. Chaudhuri, F.T. Leighton, M. Sipser (1987): Graph bisection algorithms with good average case behavior. *Combinatorica 7*, 171–191.

[41] F. Cappello, P. Fraigniaud, B. Mans, A.L. Rosenberg (2005): An algorithmic model for heterogenous clusters: Rationale and experience. *Intl. J. Foundation of Computer Science 16*, 195–216.

[42] Y.C. Cheng and T.G. Robertazzi (1990): Distributed computation for tree networks with communication delays. *IEEE Trans. Aerospace Electron. Syst. 26*, 511–516.

[43] S. Chingchit, M. Kumar, L.N. Bhuyan (1999): A flexible clustering and scheduling scheme for efficient parallel computation. *13th IEEE Int. Parallel Processing Symp.*, pp. 500–505.

[44] W. Cirne and K. Marzullo (1999): The Computational Co-op: gathering clusters into a metacomputer. *13th Int. Parallel Processing Symp.*, pp. 160–166.

[45] M. Cole (1989): *Algorithmic Skeletons: Structured Management of Parallel Computation*. MIT Press, Cambridge, Mass.

[46] R. Cole and U. Vishkin (1986): Deterministic coin tossing with applications to optimal parallel list ranking. *Inform. Contr. 70*, 32–53.

[47] S.A. Cook (1974): An observation on time-storage tradeoff. *J. Comp. Syst. Sci. 9*, 308–316.

[48] T.H. Cormen, C.E. Leiserson, R.L. Rivest, C. Stein (1999): *Introduction to Algorithms* (2nd edition). MIT Press, Cambridge, Mass.

[49] M. Cosnard and M. Tchuente (1988): Designing systolic algorithms by top-down analysis. *3rd Int. Conf. on Supercomputing*.

[50] M. Cosnard and D. Trystram (1995): *Parallel Algorithms and Architectures*. International Thompson Computer Press.

[51] D.E. Culler, R.M. Karp, D. Patterson, A. Sahay, K.E. Schauser, E. Santos, R. Subramonian, T. von Eicken (1996): LogP: towards a realistic model of parallel computation. *C. ACM 39*, 78–85.

[52] R. Cypher and C.G. Plaxton (1993): Deterministic sorting in nearly logarithmic time on the hypercube and related computers. *J. Comput. Syst. Sci. 47*, 501–548.

[53] T.D. deRose, L. Snyder, C. Yang (1987): Near-optimal speedup of graphics algorithms using multigauge parallel computers. *Int. Conf. on Parallel Processing*, 289–294.

[54] M.D. Dikaiakos, K. Steiglitz, A. Rogers (1994): A comparison of techniques for mapping parallel algorithms to message-passing multiprocessors. *6th IEEE Symp. on Parallel and Distributed Processing*, pp. 434–442.

[55] K. Diks, H.N. Djidjev, O. Sykora, I. Vr̆to (1993): Edge separators of planar and outerplanar graphs with applications. *J. Algorithms 14*, 258–279.

[56] X. Du and X. Zhang (1997): Coordinating parallel processes on networks of workstations. *J. Parallel Distr. Comput. 46*, 125–135.

[57] K. Efe (1991): Embedding mesh of trees into the hypercube. *J. Parallel Distr. Comput. 11*, 222–230.

[58] R. Elsässer, B. Monien, R. Preis (2002): Diffusion schemes for load balancing on heterogeneous networks. *Theory of Computing Syst. 35*, 305–320.

[59] P. Fatourou and P. Spirakis (2000): Efficient scheduling of strict multi-threaded computations. *Theory of Computing Syst. 33*, 173–232.

[60] C.M. Fiduccia and R.M. Mattheyses (1982): A linear-time heuristic for improving network partitions. *19th ACM-IEEE Design Automation Conf.*, pp. 175–181.

[61] S. Fortune and J. Wyllie (1978): Parallelism in random access machines. *10th ACM Symp. on Theory of Computing*, pp. 114–118.

[62] I. Foster and C. Kesselman (eds.) (1999): *The Grid: Blueprint for a New Computing Infrastructure*. Morgan-Kaufmann.

[63] I. Foster, C. Kesselman, S. Tuecke (2001): The anatomy of the Grid: enabling scalable virtual organizations. *Intl. J. Supercomput. Appl.*

[64] D. Gannon (1980): A note on pipelining a mesh-connected multiprocessor for finite element problems by nested dissection. *Intl. Conf. on Parallel Processing*, pp. 197–204.

[65] L.-X. Gao, A.L. Rosenberg, R.K. Sitaraman (1999): Optimal clustering of tree-sweep computations for high-latency parallel environments. *IEEE Trans. Parallel Distr. Syst. 10*, 813–824.

[66] V. Garg and D.E. Schimmel (1998): Hiding communication latency in data parallel applications. *12th IEEE Int. Parallel Processing Symp.*, pp. 18–25.

[67] A. Gerasoulis, S. Venugopal, T. Yang (1990): Clustering task graphs for message passing architectures. *ACM Int. Conf. on Supercomputing*, pp. 447–456.

[68] A. Gerasoulis and T. Yang (1992): A comparison of clustering heuristics for scheduling dags on multiprocessors. *J. Parallel Distr. Comput. 16*, 276–291.

[69] M.W. Goudreau, K. Lang, S.B. Rao, T. Suel, T. Tsantilas (1999): Portable and efficient parallel computing using the BSP model. *IEEE Trans. Comput. 48*, 670–689.

[70] D.S. Greenberg, L.S. Heath and A.L. Rosenberg (1990): Optimal embeddings of butterfly-like graphs in the hypercube. *Math. Syst. Theory 23*, 61–77.

[71] V.C. Hamacher and H. Jiang (1994): Comparison of mesh and hierarchical networks for multiprocessors. *Intl. Conf. on Parallel Processing*, I:67–71.

[72] C.-T. Ho and S.L. Johnsson (1986): Graph embeddings for maximum bandwidth utilization in hypercubes. *Intl. Conf. Vector and Parallel Computing*.

[73] J.-W. Hong and H.T. Kung (1981): I/O complexity: the red-blue pebble game. *13th ACM Symp. on Theory of Computing*, pp. 326–333.

[74] Y. Hong and T. Payne (1989): Parallel sorting in a ring network of processors. *IEEE Trans. Comput. 38*, 458–464.

[75] O.H. Ibarra and S.T. Sohn (1990): On mapping systolic algorithms onto the hypercube. *IEEE Trans. Parallel Distr. Syst. 1*, 238–249.

[76] *The Intel Philanthropic Peer-to-Peer program.* ⟨www.intel.com/cure⟩.

[77] C. Kaklamanis and D. Krizanc (1992): Optimal sorting on mesh-connected processor arrays. *4th ACM Symp. on Parallel Algorithms and Architectures*, pp. 50–59.

[78] C. Kaklamanis, D. Krizanc, S.B. Rao (1997): New graph decompositions with applications to emulations. *Theory of Computing Syst. 30*, 39–49.

[79] R.M. Karp and R.E. Miller (1966): Properties of a model for parallel computations: determinacy, termination, queueing. *SIAM J. Appl. Math. 14*, 1390–1411.

[80] R.M. Karp and V. Ramachandran (1990): A survey of parallel algorithms for sharedmemory machines. In *Handbook of Theoretical Computer Science, vol. A* (J. van Leeuwen, ed.). Elsevier Science, Amsterdam, pp. 869–941.

[81] R.M. Karp, A. Sahay, E. Santos, K.E. Schauser (1993): Optimal broadcast and summation in the logP model. *5th ACM Symp. on Parallel Algorithms and Architectures*, pp. 142–153.

[82] B.W. Kernighan and S. Lin (1970): An efficient heuristic procedure for partitioning graphs. *Bell Syst. Technol. J. 49*, 291–307.

[83] S.J. Kim and J.C. Browne (1988): A general approach to mapping of parallel computations upon multiprocessor architectures. *Int. Conf. on Parallel Processing*, III:1–8.

[84] R. Koch, F.T. Leighton, B.M. Maggs, S.B. Rao, A.L. Rosenberg, E.J. Schwabe (1997): Work-preserving emulations of fixed-connection networks. *J. ACM 44*, 104–147.

[85] E. Korpela, D. Werthimer, D. Anderson, J. Cobb, M. Lebofsky (2000): SETI@home: massively distributed computing for SETI. In *Computing in Science and Engineering* (P.F. Dubois, ed.). IEEE Computer Soc. Press, Los Alamitos, CA.

[86] H.T. Kung (1985): Systolic arrays. In *McGraw-Hill 1985 Yearbook of Science and Technology*.

[87] H.T. Kung and C.E. Leiserson (1980): Systolic arrays (for VLSI). In C. Mead and L. Conway, *Introduction to VLSI Systems*, Chapter 8. Addison-Wesley, Reading, MA.

[88] H.T. Kung and W.T. Lin (1983): An algebra for VLSI algorithm design. *Conf. on Elliptic Problem Solvers*, Monterey, CA.

[89] H.T. Kung and R.L. Picard (1984): One-dimensional systolic arrays for multidimensional convolution and resampling. In *VLSI for Pattern Recognition and Image Processing*, Springer-Verlag, Berlin, pp. 9–24.

[90] C. Lam, H. Jiang, V.C. Hamacher (1995): Design and analysis of hierarchical ring networks for shared-memory multiprocessors. *Intl. Conf. on Parallel Processing*, I:46–50.

[91] H.W. Lang, M. Schimmler, H. Schmeck, H. Schroeder (1985): Systolic sorting on a mesh-connected network. *IEEE Trans. Comput., C-34*, 652–658.

[92] F.T. Leighton (1985): Tight bounds on the complexity of parallel sorting. *IEEE Trans. Comput., C-34*, 344–354.

[93] F.T. Leighton (1992): *Introduction to Parallel Algorithms and Architectures: Arrays, Trees, Hypercubes*. Morgan Kaufmann, San Mateo, CA.

[94] F.T. Leighton, B.M. Maggs, S.B. Rao (1994): Packet routing and job-shop scheduling in O(congestion + dilation) steps. *Combinatorica 14*, 167–186.

[95] F.T. Leighton, B.M. Maggs, A.W. Richa (1999): Fast algorithms for finding O(congestion + dilation) packet routing schedules. *Combinatorica 19*, 375–401.

[96] F.T. Leighton, M.J. Newman, A.G. Ranade, E.J. Schwabe (1992): Dynamic tree embeddings in butterflies and hypercubes. *SIAM J. Comput. 21*, 639–654.

[97] G. Lerman and L. Rudolph (1993): *Parallel Evolution of Parallel Processors*. Plenum Press, New York.

[98] K. Li and J. Dorband (1999): Asymptotically optimal probabilistic embedding algorithms for supporting tree structured computations in hypercubes. *7th Symp. on Frontiers of Massively Parallel Computation.*

[99] R.J. Lipton and R.E. Tarjan (1980): Applications of a planar separator theorem. *SIAM J. Comput. 9*, 615–627.

[100] M. Litzkow, M. Livny, M.W. Mutka (1988): Condor – A hunter of idle workstations. *8th Int. Conf. Distr. Computing Syst.*, pp. 104–111.

[101] B.M. Maggs, F. Meyer auf der Heide, B. Vöcking, M. Westermann (1997): Exploiting locality for data management in systems of limited bandwidth. *38th IEEE Symp. on Foundations of Computer Science*, pp. 284–293.

[102] G. Malewicz, A.L. Rosenberg M. Yurkewych (2006): Toward a theory for scheduling dags in Internet-based computing. IEEE Trans. Computers, to appear.

[103] D.W. Matula and L.L. Beck (1983): Smallest-last ordering and clustering and graph coloring algorithms. *J. ACM 30*, 417–427.

[104] W.F. McColl and A. Tiskin (1999): Memory-efficient matrix computations in the BSP model. *Algorithmica 24*, 287–297.

[105] C. Mead and L. Conway (1980): *Introduction to VLSI Systems.* Addison-Wesley, Reading, MA.

[106] G.L. Miller, V. Ramachandran, E. Kaltofen (1988): Efficient parallel evaluation of straightline code and arithmetic circuits. *SIAM J. Comput. 17*, 687–695.

[107] G.L. Miller and J.H. Reif (1989): Parallel tree contraction, Part 1: fundamentals. In *Randomness and Computation*, vol. 5 (S. Micali, ed.), JAI Press, Greenwich, CT, 47–72.

[108] G.L. Miller and J.H. Reif (1991): Parallel tree contraction, Part 2: further applications. *SIAM J. Comput. 20*, 1128–1147.

[109] W.L. Miranker and A. Winkler (1984): Spacetime representations of computational structures. *Computing 32*, 93–114.

[110] M. Mitzenmacher (1998): Analyses of load stealing models based on differential equations. *10th ACM Symp. on Parallel Algorithms and Architectures*, pp. 212–221.

[111] M. Mitzenmacher (1999): On the analysis of randomized load balancing schemes. *Theory of Computing Syst. 32*, 361–386.

[112] J.F. Myoupo (1992): Synthesizing linear systolic arrays for dynamic programming problems. *Parallel Proc. Lett. 2*, 97–110.

[113] I. Niven and H.S. Zuckerman (1980): *An Introduction to the Theory of Numbers* (4th ed.). J. Wiley & Sons, New York.

[114] B. Obrenić (1994): An approach to emulating separable graphs. *Math. Syst. Theory 27*, 41–63.

[115] B. Obrenić, M.C. Herbordt, A.L. Rosenberg, C.C. Weems (1999): Using emulations to enhance the performance of parallel architectures. *IEEE Trans. Parallel Distr. Syst. 10*, 1067–1081.

[116] *The Olson Laboratory Fight AIDS@Home project.* ⟨www.fightaidsathome. org⟩.

[117] C.H. Papadimitriou and M. Yannakakis (1990): Towards an architecture-independent analysis of parallel algorithms. *SIAM J. Comput. 19*, 322–328.

[118] M.S. Paterson, C.E. Hewitt (1970): Comparative schematology. *Project MAC Conf. on Concurrent Systems and Parallel Computation*, ACM Press, pp. 119–127.

[119] G.F. Pfister (1995): *In Search of Clusters*. Prentice-Hall.

[120] P. Quinton (1984): Automatic synthesis of systolic arrays from uniform recurrence equations. *11th IEEE Intl. Symp. on Computer Architecture*, pp. 208–214.

[121] P. Quinton (1988): Mapping recurrences on parallel architectures. *3rd Int. Conf. on Supercomputing*.

[122] P. Quinton, B. Joinnault, P. Gachet (1986): A new matrix multiplication systolic array. *Parallel Algorithms and Architectures* (M. Cosnard et al., eds.) North-Holland, Amsterdam, pp. 259–268.

[123] M.O. Rabin (1989): Efficient dispersal of information for security, load balancing, and fault tolerance. *J. ACM 36*, 335–348.

[124] A.G. Ranade (1993): A framework for analyzing locality and portability issues in parallel computing. In *Parallel Architectures and Their Efficient Use: The 1st Heinz-Nixdorf Symp.*, Paderborn, Germany (F. Meyer auf der Heide, B. Monien, A.L. Rosenberg, eds.) *Lecture Notes in Computer Science 678*, Springer-Verlag, Berlin, pp. 185–194.

[125] J.H. Reif and L.G. Valiant (1987): A logarithmic time sort for linear networks. *J. ACM 34*, 60–76.

[126] A.L. Rosenberg (1981): Issues in the study of graph embeddings. In *Graph-Theoretic Concepts in Computer Science: Proc. Int. Wkshp. WG80* (H. Noltemeier, ed.) *Lecture Notes in Computer Science 100*, Springer-Verlag, Berlin, pp. 150–176.

[127] A.L. Rosenberg (1994): Needed: a theoretical basis for heterogeneous parallel computing. In *Developing a Computer Science Agenda for High-Performance Computing* (U. Vishkin, ed.) ACM Press, New York, pp. 137–142.

[128] A.L. Rosenberg (1999): Guidelines for data-parallel cycle-stealing in networks of workstations, I: on maximizing expected output. *J. Parallel Distr. Comput. 59*, 31–53.

[129] A.L. Rosenberg (2000): Guidelines for data-parallel cycle-stealing in networks of workstations, II: on maximizing guaranteed output. *Int. J. Foundations Comput. Sci. 11*, 183–204.

[130] A.L. Rosenberg (2001): On sharing bags of tasks in heterogeneous networks of workstations: greedier is not better. *3rd IEEE Int. Conf. on Cluster Computing (Cluster'01)*, pp. 124–131.

[131] A.L. Rosenberg (2002): Optimal schedules for cycle-stealing in a network of workstations with a bag-of-tasks workload. *IEEE Trans. Parallel Distr. Syst. 13*, 179–191.

[132] A.L. Rosenberg (2003): Accountable Web-computing. *IEEE Trans. Parallel Distr. Syst. 14*, 97–106.

[133] A.L. Rosenberg (2004): On scheduling mesh-structured computations on the Internet. *IEEE Trans. Comput. 53*, 1176–1186.

[134] A.L. Rosenberg and L.S. Heath (2001): *Graph Separators, with Applications*. Kluwer Academic/Plenum Publishers, New York.

[135] A.L. Rosenberg and I.H. Sudborough (1983): Bandwidth and pebbling. *Computing 31*, 115–139.

[136] A.L. Rosenberg and M. Yurkewych (2005): Guidelines for scheduling some common computation-dags for Internet-based computing. *IEEE Trans. Comput. 54*, 428–438.

[137] *The RSA Factoring by Web Project.* ⟨http://www.npac.syr.edu/factoring⟩ (with Foreword by A. Lenstra). Northeast Parallel Architecture Center.

[138] L. Rudolph, M. Slivkin, E. Upfal (1991): A simple load balancing scheme for task allocation in parallel machines. *3rd ACM Symp. on Parallel Algorithms and Architectures*, pp. 237–244.

[139] V. Sarkar (1989): *Partitioning and Scheduling Parallel Programs for Multiprocessors*. MIT Press, Cambridge, MA.

[140] V. Sarkar and J. Hennessy (1986): Compile-time partitioning and scheduling of parallel programs. *SIGPLAN Notices 21*(7) 17–26.

[141] C.P. Schnorr and A. Shamir (1986): An optimal sorting algorithm for mesh connected computers. *18th ACM Symp. on Theory of Computing*, pp. 255–263.

[142] E.J. Schwabe (1992): Embedding meshes of trees into de Bruijn graphs. *Inform. Proc. Lett. 43*, 237–240.

[143] L. Snyder (1985): An inquiry into the benefits of multigauge parallel computation. *Intl. Conf. on Parallel Processing*, pp. 488–492.

[144] D. Szada, B. Lawson, J. Owen (2003): Hardening functions for large-scale distributed computing. *IEEE Security and Privacy Conf.*

[145] M.M. Theimer and K.A. Lantz (1989): Finding idle machines in a workstation-based distributed environment. *IEEE Trans. Software Eng. 15*, 1444–1458.

[146] C.D. Thompson (1979): Area-time complexity for VLSI. *11th ACM Symp. on Theory of Computing*, pp. 81–88.

[147] C.D. Thompson (1980): *A Complexity Theory for VLSI*. Ph.D. Thesis, CMU.

[148] C.D. Thompson and H.T. Kung (1977): Sorting on a mesh-connected parallel computer. *C. ACM 20*.

[149] J.D. Ullman (1984): *Computational Aspects of VLSI*. Computer Science Press, Rockville, MD.

[150] L.G. Valiant (1983): Optimality of a two-phase strategy for routing in interconnection networks. *IEEE Trans. Comput., C-32*, 861–863.

[151] L.G. Valiant (1989): Bulk-synchronous parallel computers. In *Parallel Processing and Artificial Intelligence* (M. Reeve and S.E. Zenith, eds.) J. Wiley and Sons, New York, pp. 15–22.

[152] L.G. Valiant (1990): General purpose parallel architectures. In *Handbook of Theoretical Computer Science* (J. van Leeuwen, ed.). Elsevier Science, Amsterdam, pp. 943–972.

[153] L.G. Valiant (1990): A bridging model for parallel computation. *C. ACM 33*, 103–111.

[154] L.G. Valiant and G.J. Brebner (1981): Universal schemes for parallel computation. *13th ACM Symp. on Theory of Computing*, pp. 263–277.

[155] P.M.B. Vitanyi (1986): Nonsequential computation and laws of nature. *VLSI Algorithms and Architectures* (Aegean Wkshp. on Computing), *Lecture Notes in Computer Science 227*, Springer-Verlag, Berlin, pp. 108–120.

[156] P.M.B. Vitanyi (1988): Locality, communication and interconnect length in multicomputers. *SIAM J. Comput. 17*, 659–672.

[157] P.M.B. Vitanyi (1988): A modest proposal for communication costs in multicomputers. In *Concurrent Computations: Algorithms, Architecture, and Technology* (S.K. Tewksbury, B.W. Dickinson, S.C. Schwartz, eds.). Plenum Press, New York, pp. 203–216.

[158] A.S. Wagner (1989): Embedding arbitrary binary trees in a hypercube. *J. Parallel Distr. Comput. 7*, 503–520.

[159] C. Weth, U. Kraus, J. Freuer, M. Ruder, R. Dannecker, P. Schneider, M. Konold, H. Ruder (2000): XPulsar@home—schools help scientists. Typescript, University of Tübingen.

[160] S.W. White and D.C. Torney (1993): Use of a workstation cluster for the physical mapping of chromosomes. *SIAM NEWS*, March, 1993, pp. 14–17.

[161] A.Y. Wu (1985): Embedding of tree networks into hypercubes. *J. Parallel Distr. Comput. 2*, 238–249.

[162] T. Yang and A. Gerasoulis (1992): PYRROS: static task scheduling and code generation for message passing multiprocessors. *6th ACM Conf. on Supercomputing*, pp. 428–437.

[163] Y. Yang and H. Casanova (2003): UMR: A multi-round algorithm for scheduling divisible workloads. *17th Int. Parallel and Distributed Processing Symp. (IPDPS'03)*.

Chapter 2

ARM++: A HYBRID ASSOCIATION RULE MINING ALGORITHM

Zahir Tari and Wensheng Wu
Royal Melbourne Institute of Technology

Abstract

Most of the approaches for association rule mining focus on the perform-ance of the discovery of the frequent itemsets. They are based on the algo-rithms that require the transformation of data from one representation to another, and therefore excessively use resources and incur heavy CPU over-head. This chapter proposes a hybrid algorithm that is resource efficient and provides better performance. It characterizes the trade-offs among data rep-resentation, computation, I/O, and heuristics. The proposed algorithm uses an array-based item storage for the candidate and frequent itemsets. In addition, we propose a comparison algorithm (CmpApr) that compares candidate item-sets with a transaction, a filtering algorithm (FilterApr) that reduces the num-ber of comparison operations required to find frequent itemsets. The hybrid algorithm (ARM++) integrates filtering methods within the Partition algo-rithm [7]. Performance analyses from our implementation indicate that ARM++ has better performance and scales linearly.

1   BACKGROUND

We are living in an information age that is overwhelmed by enormous amount of data and information. Data mining within the database community, also known as *knowledge discovery* by the AI community, is the science of automated extraction of useful information or hidden patterns from large databases. Data mining is a new, multidisciplinary field ranging across database technology, sta-tistics, artificial intelligence, machine learning, etc. It normally processes data that have already been collected, such as records of all transactions in a bank, and does not involve the data collection strategy itself.

Data mining is not concerned with a small set of data, as these can be well handled by classical statistical analysis techniques. Data mining focuses on new problems that may arise with large data repositories, such as finding a target within a massive dataset in a short time, finding hidden (i.e. not explicit) relationships amongst a huge volume of information within data repositories (e.g., analysis of emails to detect terrorist threats). Such relationships found through the use of data mining techniques are called *models* or *patterns*. Descriptive models characterize the general properties of the data in the database, while predictive models perform inferences on the current data for predictions. One typical financial application using data mining is the profiling of customer behavior. A bank keeps transaction records of its customers and can use data mining technology to cluster customers into levels of high credit risk, medium credit risk, and trust, which may help them to advertise suitable new products and bank loan approval.

There are many data mining tasks and algorithms. These are often classified into four components [11]:

- Models (pattern structures): these model the underlying structures in a database.

- Score functions: the role is to decide how well the developed model fits with the data.

- Optimization and search methods: these relate to the optimization of the score function and searching over many models and structures.

- Data management strategies: These deal with efficient access and use of data during the search/optimization.

Data mining systems are categorized as follows [12]:

- Classification according to the types of databases to be mined: object-oriented databases, object-relational databases, spatial database, temporal databases and time-series databases, text databases and multimedia databases, heterogeneous databases and legacy databases, and the World Wide Web.

- Classification according to the types of knowledge to be mined: characterization, discrimination, association, classification, clustering, outlier analysis, and evolution analysis.

- Classification according to the types of techniques utilized: machine learning, statistics, pattern recognition, visualization, trees, networks and rules, etc.

- Classification according to the types of applications: finance, telecommunications, DNA, stock markets, etc.

2   MOTIVATION

This chapter focuses on a specific area of data mining, namely, mining of association or relationships between data items. The problem of mining association rules was introduced in [1] and can be defined as follows. Given a set of transactions, where each transaction is a set of items, an association rule is an expression of the form $X \Rightarrow Y$, where X and Y are sets of items. There are two measurements of an association rule; *confidence* and *support*. The *confidence* of a rule represents the percentage of transactions that contain Y out of those that contain X. The *support* of a rule is the percentage of transactions that contain both X and Y. The problem of mining association rules becomes then a two-step process [1–3]. The first step consists of finding all sets of items (called *itemsets*) that have transaction support above minimum support. The *support* for an itemset is the number of transactions that contain the itemset. Itemsets with minimum support are called *frequent* itemsets, and otherwise *small* itemsets. The second step uses the frequent itemsets to generate the desired rules. For a given *frequent* itemset $Y = \{I_1, I_2,....,I_k\}$, $k \geq 2$, it generates all rules that use items from the set $\{I_1,I_2,...,I_k\}$. The antecedent of each of these rules will be a subset X of Y, and the consequent will be the itemset Y-X. If the confidence, i.e., the ratio of the support of Y divided by the support of X, is greater than a confidence factor c, it is an association rule; otherwise, it is not.

Because the number of candidate itemsets and that of transactions are both very large, all the frequent itemsets can be found only in an iterative way, where the itemset with k items is defined as a k-itemset. In this way, iteration means each frequent k-itemset is generated in an increasing order of k. To obtain better performance, different algorithms and data structures have been designed [1-7] to reduce the number of iterations, the number of candidate itemsets, the number of transactions in each iteration, the number of items in each transaction, and the method of comparison between candidate itemsets and transactions to accelerate the identification of a candidate itemset in a transaction. In particular, a lot of work on the efficiency of association rule mining was done in the context of the following approaches: Apriori [2], AprioriTid [2], and Partition [7]. These approaches aim to reduce the execution time by applying heuristics and transforming the data into different representations. However, the transformation of the data from the original form to another will require extra resources and CPU time. On one hand, the required resources are not guaranteed to be available. For example, there might not be enough disk space to hold the transformed data for Partition. This results in the failure of the execution. On the other hand, the time savings from the new data representation might not be able to compensate for the time spent on the transformation. This depends somewhat on the characteristics of the data. To our knowledge, none of the existing algorithms performs as well as others with all the simulation data of different characteristics.

In this chapter, we propose three algorithms, namely, *CmpApr, FilterApr,* and *ARM++*, that aim to improve the performance of association rule mining algorithms at difference stages of the construction of the frequent itemsets. After an evaluation of the performance of the existing algorithms, as shown in Section 5, our findings is that *ARM++* provides a better performance. This gain in performance is mainly related to the fact that ARM++ applies new heuristics in the early stage of association rule mining and changes the data structure when the transformation is beneficial and the resources are available in the late stage. In the early stage, to improve the performance of the existing algorithms, e.g., *Apriori* [2], we come up with two heuristics: (1) a new comparison method, which is implemented in *CmpApr*; and (2) the inherent relations between the data items used to reduce the comparison of unnecessary items, which is implemented in *FilterApr*.

After a detailed analysis of these two heuristics, we realized that the second heuristic reduces the number of comparisons to such an extent that the original beneficial comparison method in *CmpApr* has a negative impact on the execution time in *FilterApr*. Based upon the fact that *FilterApr* is much faster than *CmpApr*, we choose *FilterApr* as the algorithm for the early stage of the algorithm. In the late stage of the algorithm, we use the existing *Partition* [7]. However, we start the conversion of the data only when the estimated transformed data can be held in the memory, thereby minimizing the possible overhead of data I/O operation and extra requirement of disk space.

This chapter is organized as follows. Section 3 reviews some of the major approaches for association rule mining. Section 4 is dedicated to the implementation of the array-based data structure (*ArrayApr*). In Section 5 we describe in detail the three different algorithms, that is, *CmprApr*, *FilterApr*, and *ARM++*. Section 6 provides a detailed analysis of the performance of our algorithms, and finally future extensions of these algorithms are given in Section 7.

3   RELATED WORK

The discovery of frequent itemsets and the construction of association rules are two sub-problems of association rule mining. Our focus here is on the frequent itemset searching of the first sub-problem. The three major data representations used by existing algorithms to store the database are item-lists, candidate-lists, and TID-lists. We describe them and discuss the impact of these data representations on the performance of the algorithms that use them.

3.1   Existing Approaches

AIS [1]
The problem of association rules was first introduced in [1] along with an algorithm that was later called AIS [2]. To find frequent sets, AIS creates candidates "on-the-fly" while it reads the database. Several passes are necessary, and during one pass, the entire database is read, one transaction after the other. Adding items to sets that were found to be frequent in previous passes creates a candidate. Such sets are called *frontier sets*. The candidate that is created by adding an item to a frontier set F is called a *1-extension* of F because one item was added to F. To avoid duplicate candidates, only items that are larger than the largest item in F are considered for 1-extensions. To avoid generating candidates that do not even occur in the database, AIS does not build 1-extensions on blind faith, but only when they are encountered while reading the database.

Associated with every candidate, a counter is maintained to keep track of the frequency of the candidate in the database. When a candidate is first created, this counter is set to 1, and when the candidate is found subsequently in other transactions, this counter is incremented. After a complete pass through all transactions, the counts are examined, and candidates that meet the minimum support requirement become the new frontier sets. This is a simplification because determination of which expansions to include as candidates becomes trickier in the presence of k-extensions and support estimation. For k-extensions, for example, only maximal frequent sets become frontier sets [1].

Unfortunately, the AIS candidate generation strategy creates a large number of candidates, and sophisticated pruning techniques are necessary to decide whether an extension should be included in the candidate set. The methods include a technique called *pruning function optimization* and estimating support for a prospective candidate based on relative frequencies of its subsets. Pruning functions use the fact that a sum of carefully chosen weights per item can rule out certain sets as candidates without actually counting them. An example is the total transaction price. If fewer transactions than the fraction required for minimum support exceed a price threshold, then sets that are more expensive cannot possibly be frequent. These decisions can be fairly costly; moreover, they have to be made repeatedly for many subsets for each transaction. If an unlikely candidate set is rejected, this decision has to be made for every transaction the set appears in.

SETM (Set Oriented Mining)

The SETM algorithm [5] uses only standard database operations to find frequent sets. For this reason, it uses its own data representation to store every itemset supported by a transaction along with the transaction's ID (TID). SETM repeatedly modifies the entire database to perform candidate generation, support counting, and remove infrequent sets.

SETM has a few advantages over AIS because it creates fewer candidates. However, the problem with the SETM algorithm is that candidates are replicated for every transaction in which they occur, which results in huge sizes of intermediate results. Moreover, the itemsets have to be stored explicitly, i.e., by listing their items in ascending order. Using candidate IDs would save space, but then the join could not be carried out as an SQL operation. What is even worse is that these huge relations have to be sorted twice to generate the next larger frequent sets.

Apriori, AprioriTid, and AprioriHybrid Algorithms [2–4,6–8]

The vast number of candidates in AIS caused its authors to design a new candidate generation strategy called *apriori-gen* as part of the algorithms *Apriori* and *AprioriTid* [2]. *Apriori-gen* has been so successful in reducing the number of candidates that it has been used in every algorithm proposed since it was published [3,4, 6–8]. The underlying principle, based on the a priori property, is to generate only those candidates for which all subsets have been previously determined to be frequent. In particular, a $(k+1)$-candidate will be accepted only if all its k-subsets are frequent. Upon reading a transaction T in the counting phase of pass k, *Apriori* has to determine all the k-candidates supported by T and increment the support counters associated with these candidates.

The major problem for *Apriori* is that it always has to read the entire database in every pass, although many items and many transactions are no longer needed in later passes of the algorithm. In particular, the items that are not frequent and the transactions that contain fewer items than the current candidates are not necessary. Removing them would obviate the expensive effort to try to count sets that cannot possibly be candidates.

The shortcoming of *Apriori*, that it could not remove unwanted parts of the database during later passes, has led to the design of *AprioriTid* [2], which uses a different data representation than the item-lists used by *Apriori*. *AprioriTid* can be considered an optimised version of SETM that does not rely on standard database operations and uses *apriori-gen* for faster candidate generation. Therefore, comparing *Apriori* and *AprioriTid* is more interesting because they both generate the same number of candidates and differ mainly in their underlying data representation.

While *Apriori* avoids swapping data to disk, it does not weed out useless items in later passes and hence wastes time on futile attempts to count support of sets involving these items. *AprioriTid*, on the other hand, prunes the data set as described in the previous section and as a result outruns *Apriori* in later passes. Unfortunately, in the second iteration, as a consequence of the candidate-list representation, the data usually do not fit in memory, so swapping is necessary.

Partition [7]

While all the algorithms presented so far are more or less variations of the same scheme, the *Partition* algorithm takes a different approach. *Partition* tries to address two major shortcomings of previous algorithms. The first problem with the previous algorithms is that the number of passes over the database is not known beforehand, regardless of which representation is used. Therefore, the number of I/O operations is not known and is likely to be very large. *AprioriTid* tries to circumvent this problem by buffering the database, but then the database size is limited by the size of main memory. The second problem lies with pruning the database in the later passes, i.e., removing unnecessary parts of the data. AIS and *Apriori* fail to optimize the Item-lists structure. Candidate-lists do permit pruning the database, but they cause problems because of their unpredictably large intermediate results in the early passes.

The approach taken in *Partition* [7] to solve the first problem (unpredictably large I/O-cost) is to divide the database into equally sized horizontal Partitions. An algorithm to determine the frequent sets is run on each subset of transactions independently, producing a set of *local frequent itemsets* for each partition. The partition size is chosen such that an entire partition can reside in memory. Hence, only one read is necessary for this step, and all passes access only the buffered data. To address the second problem (failure to reduce the database size in later passes), *Partition* uses a new "TID-list" data representation both to determine the frequent itemsets for each partition and to count the global supports during the counting phase. TID-lists invert the candidate-list representation by associating with each itemset X a list of all the TIDs for those transactions that support the set. The TID-lists for a k-candidate can be computed easily by intersecting the TID-lists of two of its $(k-1)$-subsets. All TID-lists are sorted so that this intersection can be computed efficiently with a merge-join, which only requires traversing the two lists once.

Like candidate-lists, TID-lists change in every pass and may have to be swapped to disk if there is not enough memory available to store them. Again, the size of intermediate results can be larger than the original data size, and this figure is not known. The reason is the same as that for candidate-lists, with the difference that in *Partition*, TIDs are replicated for every candidate set instead of replicating candidate identifiers for every transaction.

3.2   The ARM++ Approach

If we need to select an algorithm for later iterations of the frequent itemset discovery, which algorithm should we choose? Both *AprioriTid* and *Partition* outperform *Apriori* in the later iterations mainly due to their underlying data structures. All three algorithms generate the same number of candidates and frequent itemsets. For *Partition*, if a k-frequent itemset is in a transaction t, to make this count, it needs only one comparison of the TID-lists of the two $(k-1)$ frequent subsets. In contrast, *AprioriTid* needs two comparisons to detect the existence of two subsets of the k-frequent itemset, in addition to the overhead of the access to the two subsets through the auxiliary data structure. If the data for both algorithms are kept in memory, *Partition* beats *AprioriTid* in terms of performance. With the increasing number of iterations, the gap of the number of comparisons between *Partition* and *Apriori* gets wider.

In this chapter, we propose three new algorithms, varying in the comparison methods, transaction filtering, and transaction transformation. The underlying data structure is described in *ArrayApr*, which stores candidate and frequent itemsets with the proposed array-based data representation rather than the commonly used hash-tree representation [2-4,6–7]. ARM++ is a hybrid algorithm. It is a combination of *FilterApr* and *Partition* [7], where *FilterApr* is used in the early passes (*FilterApr* phase) and *Partition* in the subsequent passes (*Partition* phase). The pivot point is, whenever the estimated TID-list of *Partition* can be held in memory, we switch from *FilterApr* to *Partition*. A brief overview of these algorithms is shown in Table 2.1, and their interdependencies are described in Figure 2.1:

Table 2.1. An Overview of the Proposed Algorithms

Itemset Representation	Data Representation	Comparison Method	Original Algorithm	New Algorithms
Array	Item-list	Itemset vs. Trans	*ArrayApr*	*CmpApr*
Array	Item-list	Sub-trans vs. Itemset	*ArrayApr*	*FilterApr*
Array	Item-list	Sub-trans vs. Itemset	*FilterApr*	*ARM++*
	TID-list	Merge-Join	*Partition*	

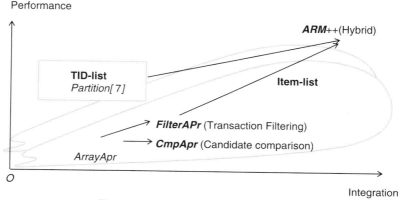

Figure 2.1. Algorithm Evolution Diagram

- *CmpApr* employs a new comparison method, *candidate comparison,* which compares candidate itemsets against a transaction instead of comparing subsets of the transaction with the itemsets. The new array-based data representation of candidate itemsets provides fast access to the items of the itemsets for the new comparison method.

- *FilterApr* harnesses the power of our new transaction filtering, which sharply reduces the number of comparison operations required to find the frequent itemsets among the candidates.

- *ARM++* integrates *FilterApr* with *Partition*. This new hybrid algorithm is the last of our series of optimizations. This new hybrid algorithm aims to make the best use of the available resources, i.e., the memory and secondary storage, to achieve the minimum execution time.

4   ARRAYAPR DATA STRUCTURE

In this section, we first introduce the array-based itemset storage and later show its application in the generation of the candidate and frequent itemsets (Figure 2.2). In contrast to *Apriori*, which uses a tree to store the candidates (that have to be tested against a transaction) in order to reduce the number of comparisons, *ArrayApr* uses the hash function to reach the candidates that are supported by the transaction. Then we explore the functions of the hash-tree during the counting phase and see how they are implemented with the array structure. We have used the data generation technique proposed in [2] to measure the performance of *ArrayApr*. Results of such evaluation are presented in Section 5.

4.1   Arrays: Itemset-counter Table, Hash Table, and Sibling Table

In *ArrayApr*, as in *Apriori*, itemsets are stored separately. However, they are stored in different structures. Our array structure contains three tables: a Hash table, an Itemset-counter table, and a Sibling table. The hash table is part of a hash function, which, given an itemset, can calculate that itemset's mapping address in the Itemset-counter table. After comparing the itemset with its counterpart in the Itemset-counter, we know whether it exists in the itemset-counter table. The sibling table stores the clustering information of itemsets in a bitmap representation. For an itemset in the Itemset-counter table, if the next one in the table is its sibling, its corresponding bit in Sibling Table is "1"; otherwise, it is "0."

For example, {1, 4, 5, 6}, {1, 4, 5, 7}, {1, 4, 5, 9}, and {1, 4, 6, 9} are candidate 4-itemsets. The layout of their storage is shown in Figure 2.2a. After scanning through the database and counting their supports, we assume all are frequent. We copy from the candidate array structure all the frequent itemsets and their clustering information into the frequent Itemset-counter table and the frequent Sibling table, respectively. Then we initialize the hash table based on the itemsets in the Itemset-counter table. After the creation of the frequent itemset

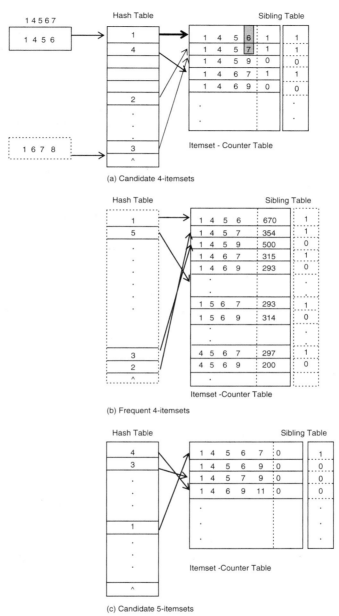

Figure 2.2. Array-based storage of itemsets

array structure, we delete the candidate array structure. The layout of the frequent 4-itemsets is depicted in Figure 2.2b.

The next step is to generate 5-candidates. We scan through the Sibling table of frequent 4-itemsets. If there are siblings, we invoke *apriori-gen* to create the 5-candidates. Instead of generating all the 5-candidates and then detecting their candidacy, immediately after we generate a candidate, we check its candidacy.

In our example, {1, 4, 5, 6}, {1, 4, 5, 7}, and {1, 4, 5, 9} are siblings. First, {1, 4, 5, 6, 7} is created in Phase I of *apriori-gen*. In Phase II, {1, 4, 6, 7}, {1, 5, 6, 7}, and {4, 5, 6, 7} are checked against the frequent Itemset-counter table through the frequent hash table for their existence. We assume all are frequent. The 5-candidate {1, 4, 5, 6, 7} is inserted into the new candidate Itemset-counter table, with its counter and sibling bit initialized to zero. Then we generate another potential 5-candidate {1, 4, 5, 6, 9} in Phase I of *apriori-gen*. In Phase II, {1, 4, 6, 9}, {1, 5, 6, 9}, and {4, 5, 6, 9} are checked against the frequent array structure. We know {1, 4, 6, 9} is there. We assume the other two are both frequent. Hence, {1, 4, 5, 6, 9} is appended to the new candidate Itemset-counter table, with its counter and sibling initialized to zero. Because {1, 4, 5, 6, 9} is an immediate sibling of {1, 4, 5, 6, 7}, the bit corresponding to {1, 4, 5, 6, 7} is set to "1" in the new candidate Sibling table. The last step is the processing of {1, 4, 5, 7, 9}. We assume it is also a candidate. It is appended to the new candidate array structure, with its counter and sibling bit reset. After the creation of the candidate array structure, the frequent Itemset-counter table is reserved for the rule discovery, while the frequent Hash table and frequent Sibling table are deleted. The candidate 5-itemsets are shown in Figure 2.2c.

4.2   Counting

So far, we have discussed the generation of frequent and candidate itemsets with the array structure. Next, we investigate the functions of the hash-tree in the counting phase and see how the array structure can provide the same functionality. We use the example shown in Figure 2.3 to illustrate the functions of the hash tree in the phase of counting. Internal nodes of such a tree are implemented as hash tables to allow fast selection of the next node. To reach the leaf for a set, start with the root and hash on the first item of the set. Reaching the next internal node, hash on the second item and so on until a leaf is found.

Consider now the transaction $T = \{1, 4, 5, 6, 7\}$. *Apriori* needs to identify whether the combinatorial subsets with 4 items of T are candidates. The set of subsets SS of T is $\{s1, s2, s3, s4\}$, where $s1=\{1, 4, 5, 6\}$, $s2=\{1, 4, 5, 7\}$, $s3=\{1, 4, 6, 7\}$, and $s4=\{4, 5, 6, 7\}$. Assume that all are candidates. So there are four candidates, $c1, c2, c3,$ and $c4$, where $c1=s1, c2=s2, c3=s3,$ and $c4=s4$.

Assume further that $c1$ and $c2$ are stored in a leaf node LN_1. Inside LN_1, there is another candidate, {1, 4, 5, 9}, which also has the prefix {1, 4, 5} but is not supported by T. Similarly, $c3$ is stored in a leaf node LN_2 along with another

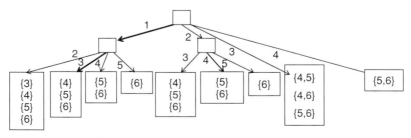

Figure 2.3. Hash tree structure for candidates

candidate {1, 4, 6, 9}. And *c4* is stored in a leaf node *LN₃* with another candidate {4, 5, 6, 9}.

In order to identify the candidacy of the first two subsets, *s1* and *s2, Apriori* reaches *LN₁* from the root by traversing first the edge labeled with item 1, then the one with item 4, and last the one with item 5. The edge selections are implemented as the hash-table loop-ups. *Apriori* tests items 1, 4, and 5 once to reach the leaf. Then it checks all the candidates in the leaf to determine whether they are supported by *T*. The first three items (1, 4, and 5) do not have to be considered any more, but for all the larger items *i* in a candidate set, we have to check whether $i \in T$. Here, the sets of the larger items are stored as item-lists, while the transaction is in the form of a bitmap. In our example, after reaching *LN₁*, we need one comparison to identify a candidate. So after another three comparisons, *s1* and *s2* are found to be candidates, the counters of *c1* and *c2* are increased by 1 separately, while there is no match for {1, 4, 5, 9}. For *s3*, after reaching *LN₂*, we need another two comparisons. Also, we need another six comparisons for *s4* after reaching *LN₃*. In Figure 2.4, the paths to locate sets {1, 4, 5, 6}, {1, 4, 5, 7}, {1, 4, 6, 7}, and {4, 5, 6, 7} are marked with bold arrows. The associated items are in bold.

The above example demonstrates three functions of the hash tree in *Apriori*:

- Store the candidate/frequent itemsets: *c1, c2, c3,* and *c4* are stored in the hash tree.

- Identify the status of a set of items, i.e., whether it is a candidate/frequent itemset: *s1, s2, s3,* and *s4* are candidates.

- Further, if an itemset is a candidate, locate the position of the candidate and its counter. The counters of *c1, c2, c3,* and *c4* are found and incremented.

In contrast to *Apriori*, we employ the Itemset-counter array to store the itemsets, along with the auxiliary Hash table and Sibling table to achieve the same functionality provided by the hash-tree:

- All the frequent itemsets and candidate itemsets are stored in the Array structure.

- For any given set of items, if it is a candidate/frequent itemset, the hash function maps it to a bucket within its hash table that points to an itemset in the

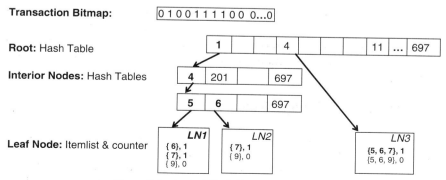

Figure 2.4. *Apriori* Hash Tree storage for itemsets

Itemset-counter table. The given itemset and the one in the table are the same, e.g., {1, 4, 5, 6} in Figure 2.2a. Otherwise, the hash function maps it to an empty bucket within its hash Table, e.g., {1, 6, 7, 8} in Figure 2.2a.

- Because both the itemset and its counter are stored together in the Itemset-counter table, once the itemset is located, the counter can be incremented quickly.

Let us use the same example as that for *Apriori*, $T = \{1, 4, 5, 6, 7\}$ to illustrate how the Array structure works. When comparing the transaction against the candidate itemset, instead of initializing a bitmap for each transaction, we generate clusters of possible candidate itemsets. For $SS = \{s1, s2, s3, s4 \mid s1=\{1, 4, 5, 6\}$, $s2=\{1, 4, 5, 7\}$, $s3=\{1, 4, 6, 7\}$, $s4=\{4, 5, 6, 7\}\}$, there are three clusters: *cluster1* = {1, 4, 5, 6, [7]}, *cluster2* = {1, 4, 6, 7}, and *cluster3* = {4, 5, 6, 7}. Because in a cluster, all the itemsets are the same except for their last items, we need only store item 7 instead of {1, 4, 5, 7} in *cluster1*. Then we compare each cluster with the candidate itemsets. For *cluster1*, the hash function leads *s1* to its corresponding position in the Itemset-counter table with four comparisons. The counter of the itemset increases by 1. Next, for *s2*=[7], there are two ways to check its candidacy. If the sibling chain is short, say, less than 4, we compare item 7 with the last item of the next itemset along the sibling chain until these items match, or until 7 is less than the last item of the next itemset along the chain. If the chain is long, for all the itemsets in the cluster, the hash function generates their addresses in the Itemset-counter table all at once, so we can check directly their existence in the Itemset-counter table. Because both the candidate itemsets and the itemsets in the clusters are stored in ascending order, the two methods generate the same results.

In our example, the sibling chain is three itemsets long, less than 4. Hence, on the fifth comparison, we compare 7 with the last item of {1, 4, 5, 7}. They match, so the counter of the next itemset increases by 1. Because there is nothing left in *cluster1*, we move on to *cluster2*. The hash function maps subset {1, 4, 6, 7} to its corresponding entry in the Itemset-counter table. With four comparisons, we match the subset with the itemset and increase the counter by 1. In the same manner, with four comparisons, we locate and increase the counter of {4, 5, 6, 7}.

5   ARM++: A HYBRID ALGORITHM FOR ASSOCIATION RULES

This section presents three new algorithms, which vary in their comparison methods, transaction filtering, and transaction transformation. As in *ArrayApr*, the candidate and frequent itemsets in all the new algorithms are stored with the new array-based data representation rather than the common hash-tree representation [2,3,4,6,7].

5.1   Methods of Comparison: *CmpApr*

For a transaction and a set of candidate itemsets, there are two ways to compare them. Existing *Apriori*-based algorithms [2,6] only compare the transaction against the candidate itemset by hashing the items in the transaction against the hash-tree. Up to now, all our discussions have been based upon this method, namely, *subset comparison*. For example, in *ArrayApr*, in the kth iteration, given a transaction, for all subsets that are k-candidates, k comparisons are needed to determine the candidacy of each subset. However, for the subsets that are not candidates, the comparison stops after the first mismatch between the candidate and the subset, so the number of comparisons might be less than k for each subset. In this example, we assume that six comparisons are needed to determine the candidacy of a subset in the sixth iteration, no matter whether it turns out to be a candidate or not. With a transaction of 20 items, for the subset comparison method, ignoring the overhead of hashing, the number of item comparisons is

$$\binom{20}{6} * 6 = 232,560.$$

However, there is another comparison method, namely, *candidate comparison*. It compares the candidate itemsets against the transaction. The transaction is initialized in a bitmap. We assume that the number of comparisons between a k-candidate and the transaction is k, though it might be less if the candidate is not supported by the transaction. We continue with the previous example. If there are 8,192 candidates in the 6th iteration, the number of item comparisons is 8,192 * 6 = 49,152. In this case, it is obvious that candidate comparison performs better than its counterpart. Also, the candidate comparison method does not have the hashing overhead. The description of *candidate_compare()* routine is given in Function 1 (see below).

Nevertheless, candidate comparison does not guarantee a smaller number of comparisons. For the same transaction, in the third iteration with 28,000 candidates, the subset comparison generates $\binom{20}{3} * 3 = 3,420$ comparisons, while candidate comparison requires 28,000 *3 = 84,000 comparisons.

Candidate_compare
1) $m=1$
2)   **while** $m <= |C_k|$ % $|C_k|$ is the number of candidates in C_k %
3)   **if** all items i in $c_m \in T$ % c_m is the mth candidate in C_k %
4) c_m.count ++
5) m++
6)   **while** c_m is sibling of c_{m-1} % skip the first k-1 items of the
                                                sibling candidates %
7)   **if** k^{th} item in $c_m \in T$
8) c_m.count++
9)   **end-if**
10) m++
11)   **end-while**
12)   **else**   % skip all the sibling candidates %
13) m++   % because none is supported by T %
14)   **while** c_m is sibling of c_{m-1}
15) m++
16)   **end-while**
17)   **end-if**
18)   **end-while**
   end.

Function 1: Candidate_compare

In our candidate comparison method, the comparison of sibling candidates within a cluster can be accelerated in the same fashion as described in subsection 2.2. After we find that a sibling candidate is supported by a transaction, its siblings only need to check whether or not their last items are in the transaction bitmap. This process is implemented in steps 6–11 of Function 1. Similarly, in steps 14–16, once we find that a candidate is not supported, all the comparisons of its siblings with the transaction are skipped. The candidate comparison benefits from our array structure, since, when we compare the items in a candidate with a transaction, all the items are stored adjacently.

Our new algorithm, *CmpApr*, is described in Algorithm 1 (see below). It is based upon both the subset comparison (step 8–11) and the candidate comparison (step 6). From the above example, we can see that in the early iterations, when we have a large number of candidates and a comparatively small number of subsets in a transaction, the subset comparison method is better. In the later iterations, when we have a small number of candidates and comparatively large number of subsets in a transaction, the candidate comparison method is preferable. Fortunately, when we start to process a transaction, we know the number of items in the transaction, the length of candidates, and the number of candidates. For a transaction with $|T|$ items in the kth iteration, we can precalculate the number of subsets, $\binom{|T|}{k}$. If it is smaller than the number of candidates, we select the traditional subset comparison method; otherwise, we use our candidate comparison method. Preference is given to the latter when the number of subsets equals the number of candidates, because the overhead of the hashing function is larger than that of the initialization of the transaction into a bitmap. The condition statement of step 5 incorporates the above selection criteria.

CmpApr
1) $L_0 = \emptyset$, $k = 1$
2) $C_1 = \{ \{i\} \mid i \in I \}$
3) **while** ($C_k \neq \emptyset$) **do**
   % count support %
4)   **forall** transactions $T \in D$
5)   **if** $(estCmp(|T|, k) > = |C_k|)$ % In *CmpApr*, $estCmp(|T|, k) = \binom{|T|}{k}$%
6) $candidate\_compare(C_k, T)$
7)   **else**
             % *ArrayApr* body: subset comparison %
8) $C_t = subset(C_k, T)$
9)   **forall** $c \in C_t$
10) $c.count ++$
11)   **end-forall**
12)   **end-if**
13)   **end-forall**
14) $L_k = \{c \in C_k \mid c.count \geq n * s_{min}\}$
15) $C_{k+1} = generate\_candidates(L_k)$
16) $k++$
17) **end-while**
18) **return** $L = \bigcup_k L_k$
end.

Algorithm 1 *CmpApr*

5.2   Online Transformation: *FilterApr*

This subsection describes the *FilterApr* algorithm, which is used for the subset comparison. This algorithm introduces two layers of filtering. The first is called *transaction transformation*, which occurs while the transactions are being read; the other is called *subset transformation*, which happens during the subset generation from transactions.

Within an iteration, if an item in a transaction is not part of the frequent itemsets supported by the transaction, it is *useless* since it contributes nothing to the generation of frequent itemsets; otherwise, it is *useful*. Processing the data without the useless items is vitally important. As mentioned earlier, *AprioriTid* and *Partition* outperform *Apriori* in the later iterations in that their underlying data structures, itemset-list and TID-list, store only the useful data. During the counting phase, both algorithms save the overhead of computation associated with items of no interest, whilst *Apriori* cannot efficiently trim the item-list structure and has to process the subsets containing useless items. Because *FilterApr* reads and then drops the useless items before checking the candidacy of the subsets of the transactions, the number of the comparisons in *FilterApr* is much less than that in *ArrayApr*, though the filtering in *FilterApr* is not as efficient as the built-in pruning of the useless items in itemset-list and TID-list.

5.2.1   Transaction Transformation

The essence of transaction transformation is to screen out useless items before the real processing. We achieve this by building a set of transaction filers derived from the candidate itemsets.

The items in a transaction that do not appear in any of the supporting frequent itemsets in the kth iteration can be dropped in the kth iteration. However, we have a problem in applying this property to practice. Before we finish the kth iteration, we don't know which candidate is frequent. A workable and less stringent property is that the items in a transaction that do not appear in any of the candidate itemsets in the kth iteration can be removed. Before the start of the kth iteration, we can build an *item filter* with only those items that appear in the k-candidates. The filter is implemented as a bitmap. In the kth iteration, all items that do not belong to the filter will be discarded; only items that exist in it will be processed.

For example, suppose we have only four candidate itemsets $\{1, 4, 5, 6\}$, $\{1, 4, 5, 7\}$, $\{1, 4, 5, 9\}$, and $\{1, 4, 6, 9\}$ in the fourth iteration. A transaction $T = \{2, 3, 4, 5, 6, 7, 9, 10\}$, with *item filter*, will be trimmed down to $\{4, 5, 6, 7, 9\}$. However, if we investigate the above example more carefully, we find there is no item 1 in the transaction, whereas item 1 is the very first item of all the candidate itemsets. This means that none of the itemsets is supported by the transaction. Therefore, without item 1, all the items in T are useless. Our example shows that the set of possible candidate items at a particular position of all candidate itemsets can determine the potential usefulness of an item in a transaction.

We call all the possible items at a position j of the candidate k-itemsets the *necessary candidate items* of position j, denoted by I_j, where,

$$I_j = \{i_j \mid i_j \text{ is the } j^{th} \text{ item of } c \cap c \in C_k\}.$$

In our example, the necessary candidate items of position 1, I_1, is $\{1\}$, I_2 is $\{4\}$, I_3 is $\{5, 6\}$, and I_4 is $\{6, 7, 9\}$.

In order to use the necessary candidate items to filter the transactions, let us consider the procedure of the generation of the subsets of a transaction. In the kth iteration, from the start of a transaction T, the first item t_1 in T can only be the first item of a subset. For t_1 to be useful, the subset or one of the subsets, in which t_1 is the first item, must be a candidate. Hence, the first useful item t_1 must belong to I_1, i.e., $t_1 \in I_1$. The second transaction item t_2 can be either the first or the second item of a subset. For t_2 to be useful, the subset or one of the subsets, in which t_2 is the either the first item or the second item, must be a candidate. Hence, the second useful item t_2 must belong to either I_1 or I_2, i.e., $t_2 \in I_1 \cup I_2$. Hence, for the useful m^{th} item in transaction T, t_m, we have

$$t_m \in \bigcup_1^m I_j, \text{ where } m < k.$$

The useful k^{th} item and the useful items after it in a transaction have to appear in our item filter. Hence, we have

$$t_n \in \bigcup_1^k I_j, \text{ where } n \geq k \cap n \leq |\mathrm{T}|.$$

If we look from the other side of the same transaction T^R, that is, from the end going backwards, the last useful item of a transaction, t^R_1, can only be the last item of some of the candidate itemsets, i.e., $t^R_1 \in I_k$. The second-to-last useful item of a transaction, t^R_2, can be either the last or the second-to-last of some of the candidate itemsets, i.e., $t^R_2 \in I_k \cup I_{k-1}$. Hence, for the mth-to-last useful item in the transaction, t^R_m, we have

$$t^R_m \in \bigcup_k^{k-m+1} I_j, \text{ where } m < k.$$

The kth-to-last useful item and the useful items before it in a transaction have to appear in our item filter. Hence, we have

$$t^R_n \in \bigcup_k^1 I_j, \text{ where } n \geq k \cap n \leq |\mathrm{T}^R|.$$

Based upon our analysis of the subset generation from the transaction, we can derive the *possible transaction items* at position j of a transaction from the necessary candidate items. The formal definition is in Figure 2.5. A graphical representation is shown in Figure 2.6.

We define *transaction_transform( )* in Function 2, as shown below. Forward possible transaction items are used in steps 1–9, the item filter is used in steps 11–19, and backward possible transaction items are used in steps 20–28. Before

Forward possible transaction items: $T_m = \bigcup_1^m Ij, (m = 1, 2, ..., k-1)$

Item filter: $T_k = \bigcup_1^k Ij,$

Backward possible transaction items: $T^R_m = \bigcup_k^{k-m+1} Ij, (m = 1, 2, ..., k-1)$

Figure 2.5. Transaction Transformation Filters

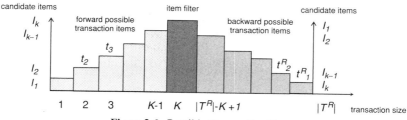

Figure 2.6. Possible Transaction Items

the start of the kth iteration, we can generate the possible transaction item filters from the candidate itemsets in the form of a bitmap. When we read a transaction, we apply the possible transaction item filters by invoking *transaction_transform( )* to remove the useless items from the transaction. After the invocation, if the length of the transformed transaction is not less than k, we continue to count its support; otherwise, the transaction is discarded, since it will not support any k-candidates. This process is implemented in step 30.

Transaction_transform

1) $m=1, j=1$ % Phase I: Forward possible transaction items %
2) **while** ($m<k \cap j< |T|$)   % transaction T %
3)   **if** ($t_j \in T_m$)   % useful item %
4) $m{+}{+}, j{+}{+}$
5)   **else**   % useless, discarded %
6)   mark t_j to be discarded
7) $j{+}{+}$
8)   **end-if**
9) **end-while**

10) **if** (m is $k \cap j < |T|$)   % k potentially useful items, items not transformed %
11)   **while** ($j \le |T|$)   % Phase II: Item filter %
12)   **if** ($t_j \in T_k$)
13) $m{+}{+}, j{+}{+}$
14)   **else**
15)   mark t_j to be discarded
16) $j{+}{+}$
17)   **end-if**
18)   **end-while**
19)   adjust T to remove discarded item

20) $m=1, j=|T|$ % Phase III: Backward possible transaction items %
21)   **while** ($m<k \cap j \ge 0$)
22)   **if** ($t_j \in T^R_m$)   % useful item %
23) $m{+}{+}, j{-}{-}$
24)   **else**   % useless, discarded %
25)   mark t_j to be discarded

26)   *j*—
27)   **end-if**
28)   **end-while**
29) **end-if**
30) adjust *T* to remove discarded item
31) **return** *T*
end.

Function 2: *Transaction_transform*

Transaction transformation works on the transactions based upon the possible transaction items, which are generated from necessary candidate items according to the relationship between the items at a particular position in the transaction and the items at a particular position in the candidate itemsets.

5.2.2   Subset Transformation

Transaction transformation finishes before the generation of the subset. The next layer of filtering, *subset transformation*, works on the subsets generated from the transactions to reduce the combinatorial subset space for the support counting. We discover the inter-item relationships between the adjacent items of the candidate itemsets and use these heuristics to avoid the generation of useless subsets, which turn out to be small itemsets.

In the previous example, with only four candidates at the fourth iteration, namely, $\{1, 4, 5, 6\}$, $\{1, 4, 5, 7\}$, $\{1, 4, 5, 9\}$, and $\{1, 4, 6, 9\}$, and a transaction $T = \{1, 4, 5, 6, 7, 9\}$, the transaction transformation cannot trim T any more. The subsets generated from T with four items are

$$s_1 = \{1, 4, 5, 6\}, s_2 = \{1, 4, 5, 7\}, s_3 = \{1, 4, 5, 9\}, s_4 = \{1, 4, 6, 7\},$$
$$s_5 = \{1, 4, 6, 9\}, s_6 = \{1, 5, 6, 7\}, s_7 = \{1, 5, 6, 9\}, s_8 = \{1, 6, 7, 9\}.$$

From the candidate itemsets, we know that after the first item, 1, the only possible second item is 4. So only those subsets with the second item as 4 are generated. We have s_1, s_2, s_3, s_4, and s_5 left. After the second item 4, the possible third items are 5 or 6. The remaining five subsets have no problems. After the third item 5, the possible fourth items are 6, 7, or 9. s_1, s_2, and s_3 survive the test. After another third item, 6, the only possible fourth item is 9. s_4 is discarded and s_5 is generated. In the example, after our *possible subset item* test, subset s_4, s_6, s_7, and s_8 are discarded "on-the-fly" instead of being passed on to the hashing function to check their candidacy.

The heuristics behind the usage of inter-item relationships are these: when we generate a subset from the first item to the last, the set of $(j+1)^{th}$ possible subset items can be limited based upon the known j^{th} item. In the example shown above, without the knowledge of the third item, we can only use the set of necessary candidate items at position 4, i.e., $I_4 = \{6, 7, 9\}$. We cannot filter any item. Once we know that the third item is 6, the fourth possible subset item is 9, so we can filter out s_4.

In order to save the inter-item relationship, we apply the module-2^n $(n \geq 0)$ operation on the item at the $(j-1)^{th}$ $(j > 1)$ position of a candidate itemset. If the result is i, we add the jth item of the candidate to the ith set of possible subset items. Actually, we split I_j, the sets of the necessary candidate items at the jth position, into 2^n sets of *possible subset items* (*PSI*). We denote the ith set of possible subset items at position j by PSI_{ji}. There is an exception for I_j: it will not be divided, since there are no items before the first. The number, 2^n, into which the possible subset items split the necessary candidate items is called the *splitting factor*. For fast detection, we select the splitting factor as a number to the power of 2.

In the kth iteration, similar to the k *possible transaction item* filters created for the transaction transformation, we build $k*2^n$ *possible subset item* filters, which are also in the form of a bitmap. The possible subset item filters of our previous example, with the splitting factor of 2, are shown in Figure 2.7. The dashed lines mark the module operations on the items.

The splitting factor is a measurement of how thoroughly *PSI*s represent the inter-item relationships among the candidate itemsets. With a splitting factor of 1, *PSI*s reduce to the possible candidate itemsets. The larger the splitting factor, the more fully *PSI*s represent the inter-item relationship, and the better they screen out useless subsets. However, the memory requirement of *PSI*s increases linearly with the splitting factor. The trade-off of the space-and-time problem of the splitting factor is further investigated with experimental results in subsection 6.2. Subset transformation is based upon the set of PSIs and is described below as Function 3. For each subset, *subset_transform* marks its usefulness.

Subset_Transform
1) set c useful
2) $m=2$ % start from the second item %
3) **while** ($m \leq k$)
4)   previous $= c_{m-1}$ MOD 2^n % calculate which set of PSI %
5)   **if** c_m in $PSI_{m, previous}$ % subset item in the Possible Subset Items %
6) m++   % check next subset item %
7)   **else**
8)   set c useless
9)   break   % skip to next subset %
10)   **end-if**
11) **end-while**
end.

Function 3: Subset_Transform

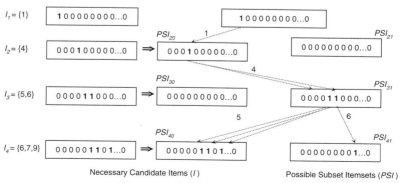

Figure 2.7. Possible Subset Items

To integrate transaction transformation and subset transformation, we come up with a new routine, *filterCount( )*. It applies the transaction transformation in step 3 and the subset transformation in step 8, as defined in Function 4. Firstly, the transaction transformation reduces the number of items in the transactions to be processed in the counting phase. Secondly, the subset transformation reduces the number of subsets to be detected for candidacy.

filterCount( )
```
 1) forall transactions T ∈ D
 2)    % Transaction transformation %
 3)    T = transaction_transform(T)
 4)    if |T| ≥ k
 5)       C_t = subset(C_k, T)
 6)       forall c ∈ C_t
 7)          % Subset Transformation %
 8)          subset_transform(c)
 9)          if c is useful
10)             c.count ++
11)          end-if
12)       end-forall
13)    end-if
14) end-forall
end.
```
Function 4: *filterCount()*

To end this section, we propose a new algorithm, *FilterApr*, as shown in Algorithm 2 below. It uses *filterCount( )* in step 4 to find all the frequent itemsets.

FilterApr
```
 1) L_0 = ∅, k = 1
 2) C_1 = { {i} | i ∈ I }                          % all 1-itemsets %
 3) while ( C_k ≠ ∅ ) do
 4)    filterCount()
 5)    L_k = {c ∈ C_k | c.count ≥ n * s_min}
 6)    C_{k+1} = apriori_gen(L_k)
 7)    k++
 8) end-while
 9) return L = ⋃_k L_k
end.
```
Algorithm 2: FilterApr

5.3   *ARM++*: A Fast Algorithm

In this section, we combine *FilterApr* with *Partition* [7] to propose a new algorithm, *ARM++*, as defined in Algorithm 3. It is a hybrid of *FilterApr* in the early passes (*FilterApr* phase) and *Partition* in the subsequent passes (*Partition* phase).

The pivot point is that whenever the estimated TID-list of *Partition* can be held in memory, we switch from *FilterApr* to *Partition*.

5.3.1 Implementation of *ARM++*: Partition Phase

Being similar to *Partition*, in steps 24–31 of the partition phase, *ARM++* works with the TID-list representation. The count for a candidate is determined immediately after it has been generated from two frequent sets. To compute the count, the TID-lists of the two frequent sets are joined using a merge-join.

One minor difference between *ARM++* of the partition phase and *Partition* is that *ARM++* uses the same Array structure to store frequent sets and the same candidate generation technique as those in *ArrayApr*. Use of the same data structure and the candidate generation code further simplifies the comparison between TID-lists and item-lists, because our results are not obscured by different storage and candidate generation procedures.

5.3.2 No Partitioning of data

The very reason *Partition* divides the data into several parts is that it cannot keep all the TID-lists in memory, especially in the early iterations. With the iteration number increasing, the number of candidates decreases sharply. Also, with the length of the candidate itemsets increasing, they are less likely to be supported by transactions. Hence, in the later iterations, it is possible to cache all the TID-lists in memory if it is not possible in the early iterations.

When the size of the TID-lists exceeds the amount of free memory, the data that cannot be held in memory will be swapped onto the disk by the virtual memory system. This process is not only time-consuming but also not always possible. Given a large database that occupies nearly all the disk space, there might not be enough space for the swapping area. For example, with our 79.6 MB simulation data containing only 1,000,000 transactions, for support as low as 0.25%, with an average transaction size as long as 20 and an average itemset length of 6, in the third iteration, there are 12,933 frequent itemsets. The minimum length of the TID-lists is 2,500, and each TID takes 4 bytes. Hence, we need a minimum of 123 MB to store the TID-lists before the start of the third iteration. With physical memory of 64 MB, and free disk space of 64 MB, my computer cannot run *Partition*, since there is not enough space to store the data in the format of a TID-list. After eight or more iterations, the memory requirement to store the TID-lists of the candidate itemsets drops to no more than 25 MB, so one partition is enough. In this case, my computer can run *Partition* from the eighth iteration.

Based upon the above analysis, with large databases on the disk, it is likely that we do not have enough free space to store the intermediate TID-lists. So we implement *ARM++* as a hybrid of *FilterApr* and *Partition*. In the early iterations, before the TID-lists can be held in memory in step 6, we adopt *FilterApr*. Once we can start *Partition* without splitting the data, we transform the data from item-list format into TID-list in steps 9–22 and switch to *Partition*. In the partition phase, *ARM++* has only one partition, so the whole TID-list is held in memory; there is no extra disk space needed to store the intermediate TID-list, as in the case of multiple partitioning. Another advantage is that we can test the performance of the TID-list data structure against that of the item-list in the later iterations without the impact of partitioning.

ARM++
1) $L_0 = \emptyset$, $k = 1$
2) $C_1 = \{ \{i\} \mid i \in I \}$
3) transformed-to-TID = false
4) **while** ($C_k \neq \emptyset$) **do**
5)   **if**($\sum_{|C_{k+1}|} \min_k |C_k|$ > available mem) % the estimated size TID-lists vs. avail. mem.%
6)   *filterCount*()
7)   **else**
            % transfer from item-list to TID-list %
8)   **if** NOT transformed-to-TID
9)   **forall** transactions $T \in D$
10) $T = transaction\_transform(T)$
11)   **if** $|T| \geq k$
12) $C_t = subset(C_k, T)$
13)   **forall** $c \in C_t$
14) $subset\_transform(c)$
15)   **if** c is useful
16) $c.count ++$
17) $T(c) += T.id$ % add transaction id to tid-list %
18)   **end-if**
19)   **end-forall**
20)   **end-if**
21)   **end-forall**
22)   transformed-to-TID = true
23)   **else**
                % Partition Phase%
24)   **forall** candidates c of size k
25) $T(c) = generate\_TID\_list(c)$
26)   **if** ($|T(c)| \geq n * S_{min}$)
27) $L_k = L_k \cup \{c\}$
28)   **else**
29) $drop\_candidate(c)$
30)   **end-if**
31)   **end-forall**
32)   **end-if**
33) $L_k = \{c \in C_k \mid c.count \geq n * s_{min}\}$
34) $C_{k+1} = apriori\_gen(L_k)$
35) $k++$
36) **end-while**
37) **return** $L = \bigcup_k L_k$
end.

Algorithm 3: *ARM++*

5.3.3 Estimation of the size of intermediate TID-list data

When we implement the above strategy, we need to determine the size of the TID-lists of all $(k+1)$-candidates before the start of the $(k+1)^{th}$ iteration. We can calculate the potential maximum size of the data when we use *apriori-gen* to generate the $k+1$ candidates.

After the kth scan, we already know the support of each k-frequent itemset. Based upon the first property of *a priori*, the support of any $k+1$ frequent itemset is equal to or less than that of its child k-frequent itemset with the smallest support. In *Partition,* the support for a candidate is generated at the same time the candidate is generated. If the count is no less than the minimum support, the candidate becomes a frequent itemset; otherwise, it is discarded. The length of the TID-list of a frequent/candidate itemset c_{k+1} is actually its support. Hence, the maximum possible length of the TID-list of the candidate, $|c_{k+1}|_{max}$, is the minimum of all the supports of the k^- containing frequent itemsets of the candidate, i.e., $|c_{k+1}|_{max} = \min_k |C_k|$, where $c_k \subset c_{k+1}$. For example, given four 3-frequent itemsets {3 169 377}, {3 169 555}, {3 337 555}, and {169 337 555} with their supports, i.e., 326, 327, 333, and 310, respectively, the support of {3 169 377 555} cannot exceed 310.

Before the start of the $(k+1)^{th}$ iteration, we have gathered all the supports for k-frequent itemsets. In step 34, when we derive $k+1$ candidates from k-frequents, for each generated candidate, we can calculate the maximum possible length of its TID-list, $|c_{k+1}|_{max} = \min_k |C_k|$. The sum of such lengths associated with all candidates, $\sum_{|C_{k+1}|} \min_k |C_k|$, is the estimation of the size of the TID-list data of the $(k+1)^{th}$ iteration. In step 5, if the sum is equal to or less than the size of the free memory, we know if we start to transform the data from itemlist to TID-list in the $k+1$ iteration, we do not need to swap the resulting data. In this case, while we count the supports of the candidates in the $k+1$ iteration using modified *FilterApr* in steps 9–22, if a transaction includes some candidates, we save the ID of the transaction into the TID-list buffers associated with the candidates. After the $k+1$ iteration, we enter the partition phase of *ARM++*.

5.3.4 Combining 1-itemsets and 2-itemsets counting

Let us consider the performance of the TID-list and item-list. It is in the later iterations that the savings on the computation of irrelevant items give *Partition* an edge over *FilterApr*. However, in the second iteration, *FilterApr* outperforms *Partition*. Consider a database of $m = 1,000$ items, all of which we assume to be frequent, when the support is very low. This means that all 2-combinations of those items, $m*(m-1)/2$, at the level of 500,000 candidates have to be evaluated by *Partition* in pass 2. Assume further that there are 10,000,000 transactions with an average of 20 items. The average length of a TID-list for a *1*-itemset is therefore $10,000,000*20/1,000 = 200,000$ TIDs. One merge-join to count a candidate requires as many comparisons as there are items in the longer list; thus, $500,000 * 200,000 = 10^{11}$ comparisons are necessary during pass 2. This figure is usually even larger because the lists that are longer than average cause more comparisons than assumed here. We can estimate the number of hash operations performed by *FilterApr*. In iteration 2, with so large a number of candidate itemsets, *FilterApr* would use subset comparison based upon the Array structure. Again, we assume that all items are frequent. The approximation of the comparison is $\binom{20}{2}$* 10,000,000 = 3.8* 10^9.

As shown in the above example, in the second iteration, both the *Apriori* and *Partition* require a large number of comparisons to locate the candidate itemsets. We can optimize the counting in the second iteration by counting the support for 2-candidates directly, saving all the comparison overheads. Further, the direct counting can be done in the first scan of the database. We can combine the *1*-itemset and *2*-itemset counting in the first iteration, saving the I/O cost of one scan of the data. The performance results of all the above algorithms, *ArrayApr, CmpApr, FilterApr,* and *ARM++*, in Section 5 are generated with this optimization.

6   PERFORMANCE ANALYSIS

This section illustrates the performance of the proposed algorithms. In particular, we demonstrate the effects of online transformation of transactions, which significantly reduce the CPU overhead in the early iterations. Also, we present the efficiency of TID-lists in the later iterations whenever the resources needed for execution are available. We evaluate the algorithms with two different methods. The first is based upon the execution time of different algorithms listed in Figures 2.8, 2.9, and 2.10. It gives preference to the actual execution time of the different parts of the algorithms. However, the implementation tools and underlying execution environment also have direct impact on the execution time. This makes the comparison result of algorithms tested on different platforms obscured by factors other than the algorithms themselves. The second method is based upon the number of integer comparisons involved in the algorithm of the frequent itemset discovery, as specified in Table 2.2. Because it is independent of the implementation tools and testing platform, this method genuinely reflects the efficiency of the algorithm.

All our algorithms use the *a priori* [2] optimization to reduce the number of candidate itemsets. In addition, *CmpApr* adopts different comparison methods to reduce the number of comparisons. *FilterApr* reduces the combinatorial search space by cutting the number of items in the transactions as well as the number of subsets of the transactions. In the early iterations, *FilterApr* outperforms

Table 2.2. Number of comparisons to determine the candidacy of itemsets

Algorithm	No. Subset Comparisons	No. Candidate Comparisons	No. TID Comparisons	Total	Time (Sec.)
ArrayApr	3,735,752,027	0	0	3,735,752,027	20,952.00
CmpApr	518,788,343	1,924,005,176	0	2,442,793,519	1,856.92
FilterApr	191,467,720	0	0	191,467,720	174.66
ARM++	85,722,627	0	17,432,961	103,155,588	108.42
Item-list ideal	137,343,148	0	0	137,343,148	N/A

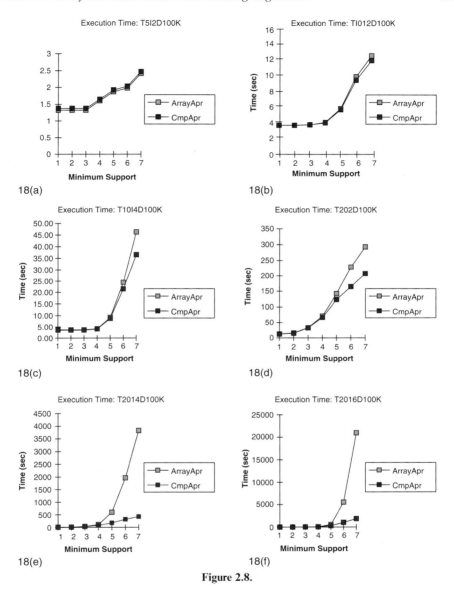

Figure 2.8.

Partition, which might require too much space to hold the intermediate result, thereby making it impossible to execute. However, *Partition* [7] needs only one comparison to determine the existence of a candidate itemset in a transaction, while *FilterApr* needs n comparisons in the nth iteration. That is the reason why *Partition* outperforms *FilterApr* in later iterations. As a compromise of *FilterApr* and *Partition,* *ARM++* also considers the availability of resources. It executes *FilterApr* in the early iterations when resources are not enough for *Partition.* Then it shifts to *Partition* whenever the resources are available for execution.

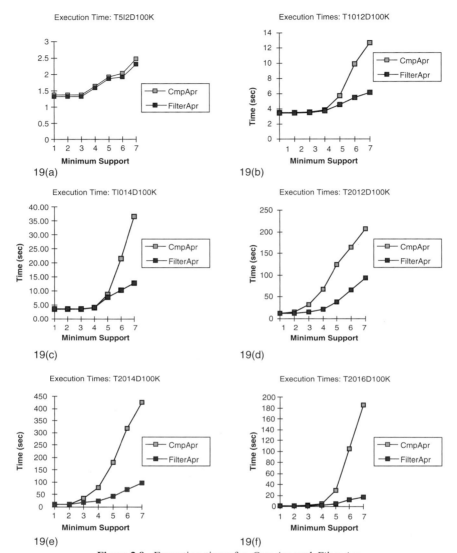

Figure 2.9. Execution times for *CmpApr* and *FilterApr*

6.1   Compare Candidate Comparison
and Subset Comparison

In this section, we compare the performance of *ArrayApr* and that of
CmpApr. *ArrayApr* is our implementation of the *a priori* optimization on the candidate itemsets stored in the array structure. Its performance shows the effect
of *a priori* without any other heuristics. In addition to the subset comparison
used in *ArrayApr*, *CmpApr* selectively uses candidate comparison to reduce the
number of comparisons and thus reduces the overall computation time.

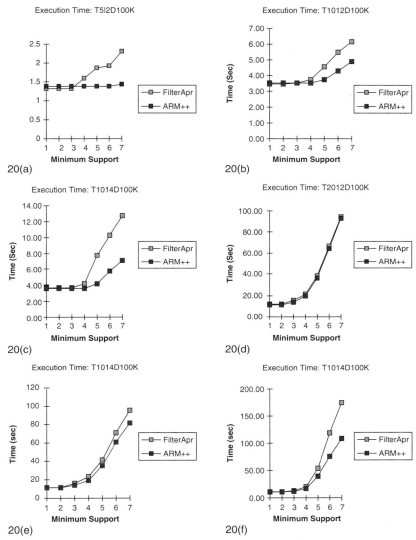

Figure 2.10. Execution times for *FilterApr* and *ARM++*

Execution time. Figure 2.8 shows the execution time for the six synthetic datasets of 100,000 transactions given in Table 2.3 for decreasing values of minimum support. In the figure, as well as in Figures 2.9 and 2.10, the values of 1, 2, 3, 4, 5, 6, and 7 on the *X*-axis represent the minimum support threshold of 2%, 1.5%, 1%, 0.75%, 0.5%, 0.33%, and 0.25%, respectively. As value on the *X*-axis increases from 1 to 7, the minimum support drops from 2% to 0.25%, and the execution times of the algorithms increase. This is because with the decrease of the minimum support, the total numbers of candidate itemsets and of frequent itemsets increase, both of which take more time to generate. Moreover, if we compare Figure 2.8(a) through Figure 2.8(f), we find that as the average length of transactions increases, the execution time increases. Further, for the same average length

Table 2.3. Synthetic Data Sets

Name	|T|	|I|	|D|	Data Size(corr=0.5, c=0.5)
T5.I2.100K	5	2	100,000	2.33 MB
T10.I2.100K	10	2	100,000	4.19 MB
T10.I4.100K	10	4	100,000	4.23 MB
T20.I2.100K	20	2	100,000	7.99 MB
T20.I4.100K	20	4	100,000	7.97 MB
T20.I6.100K	20	6	100,000	7.97 MB
T5.I2.500K	5	2	500,000	11.6 MB
T10.I2.500K	10	2	500,000	20.9 MB
T10.I4.500K	10	4	500,000	21.1 MB
T20.I2.500K	20	2	500,000	39.9 MB
T20.I4.500K	20	4	500,000	39.8 MB
T20.I6.500K	20	6	500,000	39.8 MB
T5.I2.1M	5	2	1,000,000	23.3 MB
T10.I2.1M	10	2	1,000,000	41.9 MB
T10.I4.1M	10	4	1,000,000	42.3 MB
T20.I2.1M	20	2	1,000,000	79.9 MB
T20.I4.1M	20	4	1,000,000	79.7 MB
T20.I6.1M	20	6	1,000,000	79.6 MB
T10.I4.2M	10	4	2,000,000	84.6 MB
T10.I4.5M	10	4	5,000,000	211 MB
T10.I4.10M	10	4	10,000,000	423 MB

of transactions, with the increase of the average length of itemsets, the execution time also increases. Both these outcomes result from the increase of the numbers of frequent itemsets and of candidate itemsets.

With a small average length of transactions, small average length of itemsets, and high minimum support rate, the numbers of candidate itemsets and of frequent itemsets are much less than those with large average length of transaction, large average length of itemsets, and low minimum support rate. We can see that the "easiest" dataset is T5I2D100K at the highest support setting of 2%, while the "hardest" is T20I6D100K at the lowest support setting (0.25%).

It is with the hard dataset that the effect of reduction of the algorithm search space can show up. With the easy dataset, the gain in the reduction of the number of candidate and frequent itemsets is so small that it might not offset the extra complexity introduced. As to the performance comparison of *ArrayApr* and *CmpApr*, for example, the execution times of *CmpApr* on T5I2D100K are slightly longer than those of *ArrayApr* with all settings of minimum support. With T10I2D100K, the speed gain of *CmpApr* over *ArrayApr* is marginal. It is with the hardest dataset that the true efficiency of *CmpApr* is fully represented. Therefore, in the following discussion, we will focus on the performance of the algorithms on the hardest dataset, both in terms of the time and the number of comparisons that occurred.

As shown in Figure 2.8(f), the improvement in execution times for the hardest dataset is quite significant. The execution time improves from 20,952 seconds to 1,856.92 seconds. Since both *ArrayApr* and *CmpApr* use the same candidate itemset generation technique and process the same transactions, the latter mainly benefits from the candidate comparison method. Subset comparisons are much more expensive than candidate comparison because of the overhead of hashing functions. Before each subset comparison, the position of the subset has to be calculated based upon the content of the subset. The longer the subset, the higher the overhead of hashing. Though special optimization has been implemented on the hashing calculation, it is still very expensive, considering the fact that it is required for each subset. In contrast, for candidate comparison, the candidates are stored in the array structure sequentially. The comparisons are conducted in the order of the candidate itemset, so there is no extra cost in determining the positions of candidate itemsets.

6.2   Transform Transactions and Subsets

This subsection compares the performance of *CmpApr* and that of *FilterApr*. *CmpApr* uses a different comparison method to reduce the number of item comparisons as well as the cost of each comparison, while *FilterApr* reduces both the number of items in the transactions and the subsets of transactions.

Execution time. Figure 2.9 shows the execution times of both *CmpApr* and *FilterApr*. With all the data sets, *FilterApr* outperforms *CmpApr*. Especially for the hardest data set, the execution time drops significantly from 1,856.92 seconds to 174.66 seconds. Since *FilterApr* only uses the comparatively slower subset comparison, the improvement is mainly due to the significant reduction in the number of subsets of transactions. There is overhead associated with the transaction transformation, which processes data at the speed of 1 MB/second. We derive this number by subtracting the sequential input throughput with transformation of about 4 MB/second from the measured raw sequential of about 5 MB/second. Compared with the time saved, this optimization is very effective. One good feature about subset filtering is that the longer the subset, the more information about the interrelationship between the adjacent items, the more powerful the transaction transformation, and the more significant the reduction on the execution time.

Number of comparisons. In subset comparison, for each subset of a transaction, we need to determine whether it is a candidate or not. The subsets of a transaction are generated combinatorially from the items of the transaction. Transaction transformation reduces the number of subsets by filtering out the useless items and the unnecessary subsets generated from the retained items. In Table 2.2, the total number of item comparisons of *FilterApr* is 7.84% of that of *CmpApr*, and execution time of *FilterApr* is 9.4% of that of *CmpApr*. We can see that the filters increase the hit-ratio by removing over 92% of futile item comparisons.

6.3   Integrate FilterApr and Partition

Here we compare the performance of *FilterApr* and that of *ARM++*. Because *FilterApr* and *ARM++* share the same algorithm in the early iterations, actually we compare the performance of *FilterApr* and the *Partition* phase of *ARM++* in the later iterations. Although *FilterApr* has employed several new optimizations to improve its performance, in the later iteration, the TID-list underlying *ARM++*

beats the item-structure behind *FilterApr*. In the kth iteration, to compute a count for a candidate itemset, *ARM++* needs only one comparison of the TIDs of its two sub-itemsets, while *FilterApr* needs o(k) comparisons, i.e., the comparisons of the k items of the subset with the items in one or multiple hash buckets. Recall *itemset-list* also needs o(k) comparisons. Inherently, the TID-list is the best among the three possible structures in later iterations. However, the size of the TID-list is in proportion to the number of the transactions in the database. For data with the same support for the same number of frequent itemsets, the length of TID-lists of the database with 10,000,000 transactions would be 100 times those of the database with 100,000 transactions. In contrast, *FilterApr* needs no extra memory to hold the database. It works on the original database, and the processing can be accelerated with the help of filters.

Execution time. Figure 2.11 shows the execution times of both *FilterApr* and *ARM++*. For the hardest data set, the execution time drops from 174.66 seconds down to 108.42 seconds. As discussed above, the improvement is due to the adoption of *Partition* in the later iterations of execution. Similar to the subset comparison, there is hashing overhead associated with the TID comparison. Therefore, TID comparison is much quicker than the candidate comparison. However, in *ARM++*, there is an overhead to transform the data from the item-structure to the TID-structure when switching from *FilterApr* to *Partition*. As to the memory requirement, the filters in *FilterApr* requires less than 104 KB memory. When *ARM++* switching to the *Partition* phase, we use all the available 64 MB of memory to store the intermediate TID-lists.

Number of comparisons. In Table 2.2, for *ARM++*, there is a new column, *No. TID Comparisons*, to summarize the number of item comparisons based upon the TID-lists. The total number of item comparisons of *ARM++* is 53.88% of that of *FilterApr*, and the execution time of *ARM++* is 62.07% of that of *FilterApr*. We can see that the adoption of the TID-list increases the hit-ratio by removing over 46% of the unnecessary item comparisons.

In the first column, we list an *Item-list Ideal* algorithm, which represents the perfect algorithm based upon item-structure where none of the item comparisons is related to any small itemsets. Actually, the total number of item comparisons of *ARM++* is only 75% of that of the *Item-list Ideal* algorithm. This demonstrates that the underlying TID-list data structure can provide a more efficient comparison method than the item-structure in the later iterations.

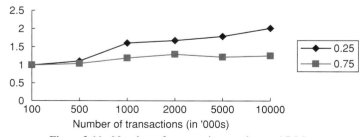

Figure 2.11. Number of transactions scale-up: ARM++

Scalability. Figure 2.11 shows the scalability of the *ARM++* when the number of transactions scales up. The number of transactions ranges from 100 K, 500 K, 1 M, 2 M, 5 M, up to 10 M. The minimum supports of the experiments are set to 0.25% and 0.75%. *ARM++* scales linearly with the increasing number of transactions.

6   CONCLUSIONS

Based upon our study of association rule mining, we have proposed a sequential algorithm, *ARM++*, which achieves better performance with the available resources and displays near-linear scale-up behavior. We believe that *ARM++* is the first attempt to integrate different algorithms based upon the available resources. In the early iterations, it requires fewer resources than *Partition*, and in the late iterations, it performs faster than *FilterApr*. In our analysis of different algorithms, we compare both their execution times and the number of comparisons involved. The execution of different algorithms at different stages is performance oriented and resource based. The flexibility of the approach enables us to integrate the latest research result in the association rule mining and related field.

Unfortunately, the utilization of computer power was limited to a single machine due to the sequential nature of our algorithm, so our future work will consist of extending the proposed algorithms in a context of heterogeneous environments. Several algorithms have been proposed [3,4,6] that aim to reduce execution time by running on multiple machines and minimizing costly intercommunication. However, all these algorithms are designed for parallel machines or homogeneous network environments, where the performance of each node or machine is the same or similar and the connection is reliable and fast. In a heterogeneous network environment, the power of each machines varies, and the throughput of network connection between different machine varies. Because usually there are multiple jobs running at the same time, the local resources, i.e., CPU, memory, disk, and communication resources, change over time. The challenge is to maximize performance while using minimum resources.

ACKNOWLEDGMENT

This project is supported by the ARC (Australian Research Council) Linkage-project LP0347217 (titled "Designing a Scalable and Robust Infrastructure for Highly Dynamic Web Services") and SUN Microsystems.

REFERENCES

[1] R. Agrawal, T. Imielinski, and A. Swami (1993): Mining Association Rules between Sets of Items in Large Databases. *Proc. SIGMOD International Conference on Management of Data*, Washington, DC, pp. 207–216.

[2] R. Agrawal and R. Srikant (1994): Fast Algorithms for Mining Association Rules. *Proc. Very Large Database International Conference*, Santiago, pp. 487–498.

[3] R. Agrawal and J.C. Shafer (1996): *Parallel Mining of Association Rules: Design, Implementation and Experience*. Research Report RJ10004, IBM Almaden Research Center, San Jose.

[4] D. W. Cheung, V. T. Ng, A. W. Fu, and Y. Fu (1996): Efficient Mining of Association Rules in Distributed Databases. *IEEE Trans. Knowledge Data Eng. 8*(6), 911–921.

[5] M. Houtsma, and Arun Swami (1995): Set-Oriented Mining for Association Rules in Relational Databases. *IEEE Int. Conf. on Data Engineering* pp. 25–33.

[6] J.S. Park, M-S Chen, and P. S. Yu (1995): An Effective Hash-Based Algorithm for Mining Association Rules. *Proc. SIGMOD Int. Conf. Management of Data*, pp. 175–186.

[7] A. Savasere, E. Omiecinski, and S. Navathe (1995): An Efficient Algorithm for Mining Association Rules in Large Databases. *Proc. Very Large Database Int. Conf.*, Zurich, pp. 432–444.

[8] R. Srikant and R. Agrawal (1996): Mining Quantitative Association Rules in Large Relational Tables. *Proc. SIGMOD Int. Con. on Management of Data*, Montreal, pp. 1–12.

[9] http://www. almaden.ibm.com/cs/quest/syndata.html

[10] R. Srikant and R. Agrawal: Mining Quantitative Association Rules in Large Relational Tables. *SIGMOD 96*, Montreal, pp. 1–12.

[11] D. Hand, H. Mannila, and P. Smyth (2001): *Principles of Data Mining*. MIT Press, Cambridge, MA.

[12] J. Han and M. Kamber (2001): *Data Mining—Concepts and Techniques*. Academic Press, New York.

Chapter 3

MULTISET RULE-BASED PROGRAMMING PARADIGM FOR SOFT-COMPUTING IN COMPLEX SYSTEMS

E. V. Krishnamurthy
Australian National University
and
Vikram Krishnamurthy*
University of British Columbia

Abstract

This chapter describes a rule-based multiset distributed programming paradigm as a unifying theme for conventional as well as soft and innovative computing, e.g., Markov Chain Monte Carlo (MCMC)-based Bayesian inference; biological, chemical, DNA, dynamical, genetic, immuno-, and membrane computation; and nature-inspired, self-organized criticality and active walker (swarm and ant intelligence) models. The computations are interpreted as the outcome arising out of deterministic, nondeterministic, or stochastic interaction among elements in a multiset object space that includes the environment. These interactions are like chemical reactions, and the evolution of the multiset can mimic biological evolution. Since the reaction rules are inherently parallel, any number of actions can be performed cooperatively or competitively among the subsets of elements so that the elements evolve toward an equilibrium or an emergent state. Practical realization of this paradigm is achieved through a coordination programming language using Multiset and transactions. This paradigm permits carrying out parts or all of the computations independently in a distributed manner on distinct processors and is eminently suitable for cluster and grid computing. Some important applications of this paradigm are described.

* Research was supported by the National Sciences and Engineering Research Council (NSERC) Canada.

1   INTRODUCTION

Most systems we observe in nature are complex dynamical systems that consist of a large number of degrees of freedom. Further, they may contain several inhomogeneous subsystems that are spatially and temporally structured on different scales and characterized by their own dynamics and interacting with each other in a complex manner. Such complex systems often exhibit collective ("Emergence") behavior that is difficult to model deterministically, based entirely on the properties of the individual subsystems. Probabilistic models such as stochastic dynamical systems provide an efficient methodology for modeling such complex systems by capturing the average behavior of the system at different spatial and temporal scales. Despite the relative simplicity of a probabilistic model (in terms of the number of degrees of freedom) compared with a deterministic model, the dynamics of the resulting stochastic system are often highly nonlinear, implying that it is not possible to obtain analytical expressions for the distributions or statistics such as mean and variance. Thus we need to resort to Monte Carlo simulation-based methods to compute estimates of the distribution and statistics. These Monte Carlo estimators are based on the strong law of large numbers, which under suitable regularity conditions (e.g., geometric ergodicity of the dynamical system) states that the arithmetic mean of the simulated random samples converges strongly (with probability one) to the true statistic. This simulation-based approach for computing estimates of the distribution and statistics of a stochastic dynamical system can be viewed as "*soft computation*," since unlike conventional computation, where exactness is our goal, we allow here for the possibility of error and randomness. Soft computation needs to be supported by a suitable choice of a datastructure and an associated programming paradigm. It is the object of this chapter to describe a unifying programming paradigm for carrying out soft computation in complex systems.

A programming paradigm is a class of programs that solve different problems while having the same control structure [6, 7, 70]. This permits us to write a generic program—called a *program shell*—that implements the common control structure. The program includes a few unspecified data types and procedures that vary from one application to another. We can then devise a parallel application program by substituting the types and procedures needed for a specific application.

In this chapter we describe a unified multiset programming paradigm (UMPP) that constitutes a unifying theme for several widely used computational schemes. These include all conventional algorithms, Markov chain Monte Carlo (MCMC) [26], Particle filters [27], *evolutionary algorithms*, such as classifier systems, probabilistic bucket brigade learning [19], *genetic algorithms* [8, 12, 29, 30, 32, 61, 62], *genetic programming* [42], *membrane computing* [74], *immunocomputing* [33], *Self-organized criticality* [10], and *active walker models* (ants with scent or multiwalker-paradigm, where each walker can influence the other through a shared landscape), also called *Stigmergy* [9, 11, 18, 23, 24, 38, 39, 60, 56, 40] *stochastic marked point processes* [78, 81], *random graph models* [15, 25], *biomimicry* [72], and *DNA computing* [2, 58]. Also it is applicable to nonequilibrium systems interacting with surroundings [63, 76] using feedback mechanisms involving catalytic reactions—as, for example, the production of ATP (adenosine triphosphate) from ATP. These lead to the necessity for the *open-world hypothesis* (rather than the closed-world assumption used in logic) to discover newer unknown possibilities, e.g., self-organization and active walks (swarm intelligence: see [11, 23, 39, 56]).

1.1 Structure of Unified Multiset Programming Paradigm (UMPP)

The UMPP proposed in this chapter consists of the following features [65, 37, 41, 80] that mimic evolutionary behavior in a biological system and innovative aspects of other nonclassical computational schemes [85]:

1. One or more object spaces that contain elements whose information is structured in an appropriate way to suit the problem at hand (e.g., the genomic library).
2. A set of interaction rules that prescribes the context for the applicability of the rules to the elements of an object space. Each rule consists of a left-hand side (a pattern or property or attribute) of named objects and the conditions under which they interact, and a right-hand side that describes the actions to be performed on the elements of the object space, if the rule becomes applicable, based on some deterministic or probabilistic criteria. For example, techniques in the *lock-key paradigm* [20, 21] abstracted from shape matching in molecular biology form the basis for molecular computing. The lock-key paradigm arises from the notions of complementarity and the union of opposites that pervade the entire science and natural philosophy. It is based on the recognition of an object (molecule) through complementary shape matching.
3. A control strategy that specifies the manner in which the elements of the object space will be chosen and interaction rules will be applied, the kinetics of the rule-interference (inhibition, activation, diffusion, chemotaxis), and a way of resolving conflicts that may arise when several rules match at once. This is analogous to the selection strategy (possibly stochastic) in a biological system.
4. A mechanism to evaluate the elements of the object space in order to determine the effectiveness of rule application (e.g., evaluating fitness for survival in a biological system).

Thus, UMPP provides a stochastic framework of *generate and test* for a wide range of problems [92, 62]. Also, the system structure of UMPP, consisting of components and their interaction, is supported by contemporary software architecture design [5].

1.2 Computational Features of UMPP

The UMPP has the following computational features:

1. Interaction-based: The computations are interpreted as the outcome of interacting elements of the object space that produce new elements (or the same elements with modified attributes) according to specific rules. Hence, the intrinsic (genotype) and acquired properties due to interaction (phenotype) can both be incorporated in the object space. Since the interaction rules are inherently parallel, any number of actions can be performed *cooperatively or competitively* among the subsets of elements so that the new elements evolve toward an equilibrium or unstable or chaotic state. Such an evolution may retain certain invariant properties of the attributes of the elements.

2. Content-based activation of rules: The next set of rules to be invoked is determined solely by the contents of the object space, as in the context of chemical reactions. This feature is very powerful, since it provides for automating the discovery of solutions, as in genetic programming [42].

3. Pattern matching: Search takes place to bind the variables in such a way as to satisfy the left-hand side of the rule. It is this characteristic of pattern (or attribute) matching that gives the rule-based paradigm its distinctive capabilities for innovative computing [36, 85, 91].

4. Simplicity of implementation: The implementation involves three basic tasks:
   a. Searching for elements of the object space satisfying the interaction condition
   b. Carrying out the action to these elements, ensuring that certain invariants hold before and after the actions
   c. Evaluation of the new elements in the object space for the required termination or equilibrium or self-organized criticality or emergent states

5. Suitable for deterministic, nondeterministic, and probabilistic evolutionary modes: The object space mentioned above is analogous to phase space in dynamical systems. It permits the introduction of a probabilistic formulation in rule applications. As each element of the ensemble changes over time, its phase point is carried into a new phase point. The evolution of the resulting probability cloud (e.g., probability mass function associated with the discrete phase points) in phase space corresponds to a distributed probabilistic computation. Thus this paradigm is suitable for deterministic exact computation when the initial conditions are exactly specified and the evolution is governed by a deterministic system. It is also suitable for approximate probabilistic computation when the initial conditions and interactions are not complete and not well specified. The probabilistic computation mode is useful when one wants to derive macroscopic or bulk properties of matter from the rules governing a large number of objects, as in a statistical mechanical system interacting with an environment.

6. Choice of objects and actions: We can use strings, arrays, sets, trees and graphs, multisets, tuples, molecules, particles, and even points as the basic elements of computation and perform suitable actions on them by defining a suitable topology, geometry, or metric space. Accordingly, this approach is widely applicable to several innovative computing approaches.

The rest of this chapter is organized as follows. In Sections 2 and 3, general properties and those of rule-based paradigms are developed. In Section 4, we use these properties to give a complete description of the UMPP. In Section 5, examples are given that are completely modeled by UMPP. These are, respectively, Markov Chain Monte Carlo methods, Classifier/Bucket Brigade systems, Genetic Algorithms, Genetic Programming, Oscillatory Chemical Reactions, Swarm and Ant-Colony techniques, and Conrad's Lock-Key Paradigm, membrane and immunocomputing, and quantum field theory. In Section 6, UMPP is interpreted in terms of relational databases. Section 7 explains the molecular DNA computation using multiset datastructure. Section 8 presents some simulation examples of adaptive learning algorithm for Nernst potential, and adaptive spreading code optimization in wireless CDMA systems. Section 9 contains some concluding remarks.

2   DEFINITIONS AND FORMALIZATION

We define the following terms:

System. A system is a set of objects together with relationships between objects and their attributes.

Environment. For a given system, the environment is the set of all objects, a change in whose attributes affects the system, and also those objects whose attributes are changed by the behavior of the system.

Specification. We also define a specification of a *deterministic computation* as a description that, when executed, would transform the given input object space into a desired output object space satisfying the prescribed attributes.

The main feature of the general rule-based paradigm is the specification of the program:

$G(R, A)(M)$ = If there exists elements a, b, c, . . . in an object space M such that an interaction rule R $(a, b, c, . . .)$ involving elements a, b, c is applicable, then $G(R, A)((M\text{-}\{a, b, c,. . \}) + A(a, b, c,. . .))$; else M.

Here M denotes the initial object space. This is a multiset or a bag in which a member can have multiple occurrences [14]. The sign "−" denotes the removal (annihilation) of the interacted elements; it is the multiset difference. The sign "+" denotes the insertion (or creation) of new elements after the action A; this is multiset union. Note that R is a condition text (or an interaction condition that is a boolean) that determines when some of the elements of the object space M can interact. The function A is the action text that describes the result of this interaction.

The function R can be interpreted as the query evaluation function in a database M, and the function A can be interpreted as the updating function for a set of database instances. Hence, if one or several interaction conditions hold for several nondisjoint subsets at the same time, the choice made among them can be nondeterministic. This leads to competitive parallelism. However, if the interaction condition holds for several disjoint subsets of elements in the database at the same time, the actions can take place independently and simultaneously. This leads to cooperative parallelism.

Deterministic Iterative Computation. This paradigm is a deterministic iterative dynamic computation consisting of applications of rules that consume the interacting elements of the object space and produce new or modified elements in the multiset. This is essentially *Dijkstra's Guarded Command Program* [45]. It is well known that the Guarded Command approach serves as a universal distributed programming paradigm for all conventional algorithms with deterministic or nondeterministic components [70]. So we will not elaborate on this aspect any further.

Termination. To achieve termination of rule application, the interaction conditions R have to be designed so that the elements in the object space can interact only if they are in opposition to the required termination condition. When all the elements meet the termination condition, the rules are not applicable and the computation halts, leaving the object space in an equilibrium state (or a fixed point of the iterative dynamics).

Nontermination, instability and irreversibility. These cases arise when the rules continue to fire indefinitely. Then the object space can be in a nonequilibrium state. It is also possible that the evolution of the system is chaotic.

As an example, consider the rule-based iterative deterministic dynamical system:

For $X(0)$ in the range $[-1,1]$,
if $X(i) \geq 0$ then $G(X(i+1)) = -2X(i) +1$;
else $G(x(i+1)) = 2X(i)+1$

The two rules for $X(i) \geq 0$ and $X(i) < 0$ are mutually exclusive and do not compete. This generates a chaotic dynamical system that is unstable and has a dense orbit in the interval $[-1,1]$ [17, 56].

3   TYPES OF RULE-BASED SYSTEMS

Several types of rule-based systems are used in computer science [31, 41, 65, 80]:
1. Monotonic. Here the application of one rule does not prevent or interfere with the application of another rule that could have also been applied at the time when the first rule was selected.
2. Nonmonotonic. Here the application of one rule interferes with the application of another rule.
3. Partially commutative. If the application of a particular sequence of rules transforms the system from state 1 to state 2, then any interleaved set of rules in the sequence would equally well create the same transformation from state 1 to state 2.
4. Commutative. A system that is both monotonic and partially commutative is called *commutative*.

Commutative systems are useful for problems in which changes occur but can be reversed and the order in which operations occur is not critical. Non-partially commutative production systems are useful when irreversible changes occur; here the order is important.

The implementation of a production system operates in three-phase cycles: matching, selecting, and execution. The cycle halts when the elements of the database satisfy a termination condition. The task of match phase is similar to query matching—that is, unification of the rules with the database. This phase returns a conflict set that satisfies the conditions of different rules. In the select phase, we select those compatible rules after conflict resolution. In the execution phase, all selected rules are fired and actions are implemented.

Parallelism can be achieved in the matching and execution phases as follows:
In the matching phase, we can
1. Match in parallel several partitions of the rule set
2. Match several partitions of the object space
   In the execution phase, we can
1. Execute several rule actions on the object space elements if these are independent (interrule actions)
2. Execute several instantiations of the same rule simultaneously (intrarule actions)

3.1   Kinetics of the Multiset Rule-based Systems

In order to speed up the use of UMPP, we need to consider how to permit multiple rule execution concurrently. This offers the possibility of carrying out parts or all of computations in parallel on distinct processors or performing multiple simulations simultaneously in a grid or cluster computing environment. Such possibilities would require the analysis of how the rules interfere with each other. There are three ways in which the rules can interfere [35, 37, 41, 55, 43, 45]. We call these interference rules *Turing's kinetic rules*, as they are similar to those enunciated by Turing [88] to describe the development of shape, form, and pattern in organisms (chemical morphogenesis rules: see [69]).

1. **Enabling dependence (ED)**. Rule i and rule j are called *enable dependent* if the application (or firing) of rule i updates (writes, or W) the elements of the object space, and creates the required precondition that is read (R) by rule j and causes it to fire. As a special case, the update can be either insertion ($W+$) or deletion ($W-$) of elements, and the precondition of rule j to fire is respectively the presence ($R+$) or absence (R) of those identical elements. (In parallel programming, these WR, $W+R+$, $W-R-$ types of dependencies are called *dataflow dependence*).

2. **Inhibit dependence (ID)**. Rule i and rule j are called *inhibit dependent* if the application (or firing) of rule i updates (W) the elements of the object space, and disables the required precondition that is read (R) by rule j and prevents it from firing. As a particular case, the updates can be either insertion ($W+$) or deletion ($W-$) of elements, and the precondition of rule j to fire can be respectively the absence ($R-$) or presence ($R+$) of those elements. The WR, $W+R-$, or $W- R+$ types of dependencies are called *inhibit dependencies*.

3. **Opposition dependence (OD)**. Rule i and rule j are said to be *opposition dependent* if the following situation holds. Rule i updates (W) or deletes ($W-$) or adds ($W+$) elements, while rule j respectively overwrites (W) or simply adds ($W+$) or deletes (W) the same elements. (In parallel programming, this WW type of dependence is called *data-output dependence*).

The rules are called *compatible* if they are not inhibit dependent (ID) and not opposition dependent (OD). The communication among the objects takes place through ED and ID. Note that a rule can enable (be autocatalytic) or inhibit itself.

We can relate the parallelism in production rules with vector, pipeline, and data parallelism thus:

1. Vector parallelism. If all the rules are compatible, then we can apply all the rules simultaneously, e.g., a vector addition.

2. Pipeline parallelism. Here multiple rules are fired in parallel and passing data in a pipeline fashion, e.g., multienzyme reactions, where at each membrane an "imprisoned" enzyme performs a given operation and then sends it on to the next stage [76].

3. Data parallelism. Multiple instantiations of the same rule are fired in parallel based on distinct data, e.g., forming matrix products.

The rule-based paradigm can be supported by a database transaction processing system if we identify the condition text with a database query evaluation function (to find those elements or subsets of elements of the database satisfying particular conditions) and the action text with the updating operation in the database. Such identification relates the rule-based programming style and the database transactional programming style [59]. When one or more reaction conditions hold for several disjoint subsets at the same time, the query or Read (R) operation and the update (W) operation can take place concurrently. This parallelism corresponds to *cooperative parallelism*.

If, however, one or more conditions hold for nondisjoint subsets of the database, then a transaction is chosen among the alternatives either nondeterministically or probabilistically, as dictated by a random number generator. The actions on the chosen subset are executed atomically and committed. In other words, the chosen subset undergoes an *asynchronous atomic update*. This ensures that the process of matching and the follow-up actions satisfy the four important properties called *ACID properties* [49]: Atomicity (indivisibility and either all or no actions carried out), Consistency (before and after the execution of a transaction), Isolation (no interference among the actions), and Durability (no failure). Once all the actions are carried out and committed, the next set of conditions is considered. As a result of the actions followed by commitment, we derive a new database; this may satisfy new conditions of the text, and the actions are repeated by initiating a new set of transactions. This set of transformations halts when there are no more transactions executable or the database does not undergo a change for two consecutive steps, indicating a new consistent state of the database. Such a scheme would correspond to *competitive parallelism*.

The implementation of a rule based-system for mathematical problems requires that the application of the rules eventually terminates. Termination for a rule set is guaranteed if rule processing always reaches a stable state in which none of the rules will be enabled to react. However, note that rule processing does not terminate if rules provide new conditions to fire indefinitely—that is, if actions of Ri create the right conditions for Rj to fire. This would correspond to cyclic computations and could lead to circularity or a deadlock situation.

3.2   Closed-World Assumption and Closed Systems

In conventional computer programming, we usually choose a commutative production system that is sure to lead us to termination of the program corresponding to a fixed point. This is achieved by choosing the positive world of facts in which any fact that is not present (or cannot be derived from other assertions) is assumed to be false. This assumption is called the *Closed World Assumption* (*CWA*; [31]). It is an important assumption used in database design that is based on first-order logic. The Gamma paradigm described by Banatre and Me'tayer [6] is based on the closed-world assumption and corresponds to a commutative production system; here we do not check for facts that are not present or derivable. If CWA does not hold, we have a nonmonotonic system. CWA is valid only in first-order logic or for Horn clauses in second-order logic [31].

First-order logic has the three important properties:
1. Completeness. It is complete with respect to the domain of interest. That is, all facts needed to solve a problem are present in the system or can be derived from the given rules.
2. Consistency. All axioms are contradiction free.
3. Monotonicity. The only way it can change is that new facts can be added as they become available.

If these new facts are consistent with all other facts that have been asserted, then nothing ever will be retracted from the set of facts that are known to be true.

Formal reasoning requires the CWA to specify what can be produced from the rules. This means that a formal system, no matter how well constructed, will not be able to model the changes in a nonstationary world. Therefore, if any of the above properties are not satisfied, conventional first-order logic cannot be applied and we need to use nonmonotonic logic.

Classical dynamics (also called *rational mechanics*) uses the laws of reasoning based on CWA and a monotonic production rule system. Given a well-defined initial state, we can precisely compute the evolutionary trajectory in the phase space and a well-defined final state of the system. This is because such a system is characterized by a deterministic set of equations (or rules) of motion, we have complete knowledge about the system, and no other unknown fact exists. Hence it is a closed system that is reversible or invariant under the transformation of a positive to negative time coordinate. Such a closed system does not usually interact with the environment and there is no energy or mass exchange outside the system [76].

CWA assumes that anything that is not necessarily true should be assumed to be false. It has two limitations:

1. It only operates on individual predicates and not on interactions among them.
2. It assumes that all the predicates have their instances listed. This is true perhaps in the database context but not otherwise. But, in general, we cannot completely describe all predicates, and the assumption that the world is closed is not valid—we must assume that the world is open.

Nonmonotonic systems [1] can contain empirical statements and plausible set of rules that make the system open.

3.3   Open Systems

An open system, unlike a closed system, is characterized by a system interacting with an environment. Its evolution is *not governed* by a deterministic set of equations of motion, and we are usually concerned about the average behavior of the system as it evolves. For the open system, we need to introduce probabilities due to the following reasons:

1. Ignorance of the relevant variables and functions involved in the rules to represent a given problem domain.
2. Inadequacy of the rules to model a given system and its environment, since we do not know whether an object belongs to a system or whether it belongs to an environment or how to subdivide the objects to establish a dichotomy of sets of related objects into a system and an associated environment.
3. The introduction of a probabilistic approach permits us to take into account all possible sequences of events into the future, from the most to the least probable.

Open systems interact with the environment accompanied by an exchange of energy, entropy, and matter. These systems are characterized by a nonmonotonic production system in which we need to discover new rules that may violate old rules. Examples of such systems are thermodynamical and nonequilibrium systems, including chaotic and self-organized critical systems; and non-Markovian active-walker models, where the system and the environment interact with each other. Such systems need probabilistic modes of computation to account for ignorance of some relevant variables or functions and inadequacy of the rule sets due to interaction with the environment. This computation is imprecise, reflecting the average behavior of the system [66].

As described in [71] and [47], closed systems with no dissipation of energy have zero metric entropy, while open systems are dissipative and have a positive metric entropy. Thus we have two major classes of systems or machines, ordinary (O) and dissipative (P), which are based on metric entropy as described below:

Ordinary or Zero Metric Entropy Machines (O)

These are completely structured, deterministic, exact behavior (or algorithmic) machines.

This class contains the machines in Chomskiian hierarchy [43]:

1. *Finite State machines: obey regular grammar or type 3 grammar;*
2. *Push down-stack machines: obey context-free grammar or type 2 grammar;*
3. *Linear bounded automata: obey context-sensitive or type 1 grammars;*
4. *Turing Machines that halt: obey an unrestricted or type 0 grammar, and*
5. *Exactly integrable Hamiltonian flow machines.*

Such machines are, in principle, information lossless; their outputs contain all the required information as dictated by the programs. Further, the fixed point of a terminating Turing computation is an analogue of an attractor or equilibrium point in an integrable Hamiltonian system.

Positive Metric Entropy Machines (P)

The Lyapunov exponent of a dynamical system is a measure of the sensitivity of the state of the system to its initial conditions. A nonlinear dynamical system with an attractor that has a positive Lyapunov exponent exhibits chaotic behavior—the attractor is exponentially sensitive to the initial condition of the system. Such systems are analogues of a problem that stands at the border of computability and noncomputability, where we do not know whether the computation halts or reaches a fixed point. To be at the edge of computability is analogous to entering a route to chaos in dynamics. Thus chaos in dynamical systems and noncomputability can be considered as parallels in their respective domains. Undecidable (nonterminating) partially recursive schemes also exhibit chaoslike behavior, such as lack of predictability and decidability! In fact, it is suspected that deterministic chaos corresponds to Godel's undecidability.

Nonintegrable positive entropy machines exhibit various degrees of irregular dynamics:

1. *Ergodicity.* Here the set of points in phase space behave in such a way that the time-average along a trajectory equals the ensemble average over the phase space. Although the trajectories wander around the whole phase space, two neighboring initial points can remain fully correlated over the entire time of evolution. Ergodicity in a dynamical system is a result of nonintegrable perturbation in an integrable system [57]. The term *ergodicity* in dynamical systems means *statistical homogeneity*. This means the trajectory starting from any initial state can access all other states in the phase space.

2. *Mixing.* The initial points in the phase space can spread out to cover the space in time but at a rate weaker than the exponential (e.g., inverse power of time).

3. *Bernoullicity, K-flow, or chaos.* The trajectories cover the phase space in such a way that the initially neighboring points separate exponentially and the correlation between two initially neighboring points decays with time exponentially. It is with this class of irregular motion that we define classical chaos. These trajectories lie on the border and beyond the Turing computable region; that is, they belong to partial recursive schemes leading to undecidability.

4. *Nonequilibrium systems.* These systems exhibit emergent behavior, such as chemical and biological machines and living systems.

Each of the above properties implies all the properties above, e.g., within a chaotic region the trajectories are ergodic on the attractor and wander around the desired periodic orbit. Classical motion is chaotic if the flow of the trajectories in a given region of phase space has positive Lyapunov exponents that measure the rate of exponential separation between two neighboring points in the phase space. Chaos indicates hypersensitivity on the initial conditions. Also, the system becomes inseparable (metric transitivity), and the periodic points are dense. That is, the whole dynamical system is not simply a sum of parts; it functions as a whole, leading to what is known as *emergence*. Also, strange attractors with fractal dimensions govern such dynamic systems!

Thus, to simulate open systems, we need to combine zero and positive entropy machines to carry out computation and also provide environmental interaction. This can be achieved by the introduction of entropy through random choices.

The introduction of positive entropy through the injection of either chaoticity (deterministic randomness) or stochasticity (statistical randomness) has several advantages [44, 46, 50, 67]:

1. It provides ergodicity of search orbits. This has the property that every point in the set of accessible states is approached arbitrarily closely during the iteration. This property ensures that searching is done through all possible states of the solution space, since there is a finite probability that an individual can reach any point in problem space with one jump.

2. It provides solution discovery capabilities (as in genetic programming) due to embedded randomness [82]. This property arises due to the fact that chaotic orbits are dense and have a positive Lyapunov exponent, two initially close orbits can separate exponentially from each other.

3. It cuts down the average running time of an otherwise worst–case running time-algorithm. We pay for this gain by producing an output that has an error with a small probability. Accordingly, we cannot claim that the solutions would always exist, and even if they exist, they are exact.

4. It can solve problems of high complexity by facilitating cross-fertilization across discipline; e.g., genetics (genetic algorithms), thermodynamics (simulated annealing), statistical mechanics (particle transport), and complex systems (active-walker, self-organization, and percolation models).

5. Also, stochastic mechanisms plays a vital role in many physical processes involving motion of particles: e.g., mechanisms such as diffusion, aimless drift of particles, convection, annihilation of particles from the population, and creation of particles. These mechanisms change the local density of the population. Numerous physical and social systems behave in this manner.

Remarks

1. It is possible that quasi-ergodic behavior arises, resulting in the entrapment of the orbit in isolated regions. This behavior can be avoided by using perturbations to the chaotic orbit that are highly sensitive to initial conditions or by using more than one Markov chain, with the initial states reasonably apart.
2. Prigogine [76] suggests the use of nonunitary transformations, called *star-Hermitean operators*, to extend the capabilities of computational systems to reflect average behavior. That is, the tools of both equilibrium and nonequilibrium quantum statistical mechanics are needed to create open systems.

3.4   Simulating Open Systems

A way to simulate a mixture of the zero and positive entropy machines is by choosing the mode of application and the action set of a rule-based program to be either deterministic, nondeterministic, probabilistic, or fuzzy. Rule application policy in a production system can be modified by

1. Assigning probabilities/fuzziness for applying the rule
2. Assigning strength to each rule by using a measure of its past success
3. Introducing a support for each rule by using a measure of its likely relevance to the current situation.

The above three factors provide for competition and cooperation among the different rules. In particular, the probabilistic rule system can lead to emergence and self-organized criticality. Thus, the capabilities of class O machines can be enlarged by simulating special features of class P machines—using nondeterminism, randomness, approximation, probabilities, equilibrium statistical mechanical (e.g., simulated annealing), and nonequilibrium statistical mechanical (e.g., genetic algorithms and the Ant algorithm) approaches.

We will describe in Section 4 how the probabilistic rule-based paradigm can simulate the open system.

4   THE STOCHASTIC RULE-BASED PARADIGM

In every closed logical, physical, chemical, or biosystem, certain properties (or attributes) do not change (are conserved) or remain invariant when the system evolves over time, moving from one state to another. Such attributes are called *invariants* and play an important role in the specification of the system. A deterministic rule-based paradigm in a closed system ensures that when an interaction triggers an action, certain specified invariants always hold before and after the actions. However, in open systems—such as complex systems, which consist of a large number of simple elements interacting with each other and the environment—new properties such as self–organized criticality and the active walk system can emerge [56]. Such systems are dissipative, do not necessarily satisfy predetermined invariant conditions (such as conservation of certain specific properties), and need to use probabilistic rule selection and modification. Here, the probabilistic rule paradigm plays an important role [83].

In Section 3 we discussed the necessity for the introduction of probabilistic variant of the production rule paradigm for nonmonotonic or open systems. This paradigm is obtained by introducing probabilities for selection when one or more reaction conditions hold for several nondisjoint subsets at the same time. In this case, the choice made among these subsets is determined by a random number generator that selects the ith possible subset with a probability $p(i)$ to perform the required actions, thus providing for probabilistic competition among the different choices. This results in the Unified rule-based Multiset Programming Paradigm (UMPP) and is defined by the function

$PG(R(p(i), A)(M) =$ if there exists elements $a, b, c, \ldots$ belonging to an object space M (a multiset) such that $R(a, b, c, \ldots)$, then $G(R,A)((M-\{a, b, c, \ldots\}) + A(a, b, c, \ldots))$, else M,

where each of the possible number of subsets i that satisfy the conditions R is chosen with a probability $p(i)$ and the corresponding text of action A is implemented. Note that the sum of $p(i)$ equals 1. Also, when $p(i)$ is not specified, the choice can be deterministic or nondeterministic. Thus UMPP can contain within itself the deterministic, nondeterministic, and probabilistic components.

The UMPP is useful in many ways:

1. It can be used to realize evolutionary algorithms such as classifier systems, probabilistic, bucket brigade learning, the genetic algorithms [8, 12, 29, 30, 32, 61], self-organized criticality, and active walker models—ants with scent or multiwalker-paradigm, where each walker can influence the other through a shared landscape based on nondeterministic or probabilistic action [11, 23, 56].
2. The multiset datastructure used in UMPP is suitable to describe physical events. It can represent pointlike variables in physics (time, space, velocity, or other quantity) or discreteness of events intrinsic to the physical processes (intrinsic point processes) or arising out of observations (observational point processes) [64, 78, 81]. Also it can represent iterative dynamical systems, including cellular automata [36, 91] and evolving networks [25].
3. It can support the design of a wide variety of programs to seek answers to questions such as:
   a. Which is the most likely state that a system will reach if supplied with a given input sequence?
   b. What is the average survival time of a population that is subject to reproduction and death of its members?
   c. How long does it to take to learn a particular concept?
   d. Can a system reach self-organized criticality?
   e. Can a system become chaotic?

4.1   Properties of UMPP

The nondeterministic as well as probabilistic computations are organized in two phases [44]:

Phase 1: Guessing or tossing (random choice)
Phase 2: Evaluation and verification of the validity of the result

These two phases work interactively. Thus nondeterministic and probabilistic computations are no more than guess-check and toss-check actions. In the guessing or tossing phase, we apply certain reaction rules probabilistically to individual elements satisfying the required conditions and perform the required actions. In the verification phase, we evaluate either the individual elements of the database or a selected subset or the whole database using some acceptance criteria.

As mentioned in Section 2, the deterministic and nondeterministic UMPP programs are based on two-valued logic, and they terminate when the interaction conditions (guards) are false [45]. But to determine the speed of convergence and termination of the probabilistic UMPP paradigm, we need to use probabilistic arguments. In practice, to detect a fixed point (or equilibrium), we need to use some acceptance criteria, and at the end of each trial evaluate an individual element or a selected subset or the whole object space, to decide whether to repeat the trial or to halt. That is, the evaluation of the object space can take place at different levels of granularity depending upon the problem domain. Also, the acceptance criteria may be chosen dependent on or independent of the number of previous trials, and the choice of probabilities can remain static or can vary dynamically with each trial. Thus, depending upon the evaluation granularity, acceptance criteria, and the manner in which the probability assignments are made, we can devise various strategies. We will give examples of these in Section 5.

4.2   Iterative Dynamics of UMPP

In Section 2 we described the deterministic iterative scheme that can either lead to a fixed point for closed systems or exhibit aperiodic and chaotic behavior or self-organization when applied to open systems. In the stochastic approach, we need to deal with stochastic difference or differential equations. For search and optimization problems, one could use either chaoticity or stochasticity in iterative schemes to create ergodicity. While it is still not known whether chaoticity or stochasticity is superior in computational performance, the stochastic method seems to be more easily amenable for proof techniques and seems to be more robust under dynamic noise. This is a major research area currently [17]. Since UMPP can deal with deterministic, nondeterministic (deterministic random and chaoticity), and stochasticity, it permits simulating a variety of schemes, namely, piecewise deterministic, piecewise stochastic, and nondeterministic systems encountered in time-varying systems, and point processes that have a variety of applications [78, 64, 81].

UMPP provides a suitable model for understanding a large class of evolutionary events. Such a model is applicable to very wide areas in biological and social systems that are characterized by different kinds of attractors belonging to four classes, called *Wolfram classes* [91]:

1. Evolution to a fixed homogeneous state in living systems (limit points in dynamical systems) corresponding to fixed points in programming
2. Evolution to simple separated periodic structures in living systems (or limit cycles in dynamical systems) corresponding to competitive cycles of deadlock or livelock in concurrent computation
3. Evolution to chaotic behavior, yielding aperiodic patterns in living systems (strange attractors in dynamical systems) that have no correspondence in computer science

4. Evolution to complex patterns of localized structures in living systems, which have no analog in dynamical systems or in computer science.

In addition, phase transitions can arise between the various classes. For example, between periodic and chaotic behavior there is a phase transition. While the periodic and chaotic regions are governed by rules, the transition region is not governed by any rules. Thus one proceeds through a complexity hierarchy from simple to complex upto the transition region and beyond that complex to simple dynamics. The phase transition therefore separates the space of computation into an ordered and a disordered regime, which can be thought to correspond with halting and nonhalting computations. The transients grow very rapidly in the vicinity of a transition between ordered and disordered dynamics. Dynamics in the vicinity of the phase transition gives rise to a critical slowing down, and the various complexity classes (constant, linear, polynomial, exponential) are encountered. Critical slowing down of a system appears like the exponential slowdown in computing the solution of an intractable or nonpolynomial time-solution problem.

Phase transition-like phenomenon arises in a wide variety of algorithms and heuristics used for search problems in the NP class or beyond [96] and in random graph models [15]. Although simulation is a poor substitute, there seems to be no other way to guess the threshold of certain properties like phase transition in complex systems. However, no satisfactory conclusions have been arrived at so far to distinguish NP-complete problems or many other similar properties from the phase transition point of view.

5 REALIZATION OF UMPP AND EXAMPLES

Practical realization of the UMPP can be achieved through a coordination programming language using Multiset and transactions; the design details will be published elsewhere.

5.1 Markov Chain Monte-Carlo and Randomized Grid Bayesian Inference

The Markov Chain Monte Carlo (MCMC) methods [79], which include simulated annealing, data augmentation, and Metropolis Hastings-type algorithms, are used to construct the *a posteriori* probability density function of a random dynamical system. The UMPP proposed in Section 4 can realize such MCMC methods as follows: the first condition text (say, R /pi) prescribes the nature of random variable (i.e., probability distribution function) to be used for the selection of the elements of the database and also a set of *deterministic criteria* for the acceptance or rejection of the elements. The corresponding action text (A) implements these conditions and accepts or rejects the elements as and when they are randomly generated (on the fly). Following the rejection of elements, the second condition text (say, R* /p*i) prescribes a *probabilistic criterion* to accept (or reject) some of the earlier rejected elements; the corresponding action text A* implements these conditions. The condition text R* /p*i is then varied as a function of the current number of trials and a parameter called *temperature* [61]. The effect of this variation is such that the probability of accepting a new solution that is worse than the current solution decreases with the degree of the deterioration of the solution, and more significantly with the run time of the method.

More recently, a recursive (real-time) MCMC algorithm called a *particle filter* [27], has been developed. This algorithm iteratively updates the currently available set of particles into a new set of particles so that the empirical probability distribution of the particles closely follow the true distribution. That is, the simulated evolution of the particles mimics the real system. This algorithm is based on randomized grids for propagating the conditional density of the state of a dynamical system given noisy observations. Then sequential importance sampling, together with the Bayes rule, is used to update the weights of the grid points from a priori distribution to a posteriori distribution. In order to avoid degeneracy problems, a random resampling method is used to eliminate low-probability points in the grid. This step mimics evolution in the sense that it eliminates most poorly adapted species (selective extinction or death). It is clear that these steps can be completely captured by the UMPP. In MCMC methods, the granularity of the evaluation takes place at the elemental level, and hence these methods permit on-the-fly acceptance of elements, thereby providing high concurrency in the implementation.

The use of Multiset facilitates the realization of the Multiple Particle Filter approach recently described by Yuen and MacDonald [94]. It can be computationally advantageous by splitting a multidimensional problem into multiple low-dimensional ones if there is sufficient degree of independence among the components in the estimation problem.

5.2   Classifier / bucket-Brigade systems

The classifier system [8, 12, 29, 30, 32, 61] is a parallel rule-based production system based on two-valued logic. Each classifier can be regarded as a separate instruction that takes messages as input and produces messages as output. As in a production system, there is a match cycle, where each rule is matched against the state of the short-term memory containing a message list M. If its preconditions are satisfied by at least one message, then the classifier is activated, and an execute cycle carries out the required actions and posts an external message. All external communications are via the message list. Thus all internal control and external communication reside in the same data structure. The classifier system can therefore be realized by the rule-based model, if the messages are represented by a database of appropriate type. When the classifier system is used deterministically, it iterates for a fixed number of times or until the message list does not change for two successive atomic steps. It has been shown in Forrest [29] that

1. any finite function can be computed by some classifier system in a single match-and-execute step, with an arbitrary amount of parallelism, by distributing the representation of the function over enough number of processors, and
2. a classifier system can be made to behave completely sequentially.

These two properties permit the classifier system to behave with maximal parallelism or completely sequentially. Thus a classifier system offers a flexible formalism that permits optimization of the three parameters, namely, the number of processors (classifiers), the length of computation, and the amount of inter-processor communication.

In the Bucket-Brigade system (BBS) [8, 12, 29, 30, 32, 34], the classifier system is generalized by introducing two factors, called the *strength* and the *activation* of each rule based on its relevance and support from other rules.

1. *Strength of the individual rule.* The strength of each rule is based on its success.
2. *Support and relevance of the rule.* Each rule is evaluated by its likely relevance to the current situation and support from other rules.

Here, the first rule reflects the success of the individual rule, while the second rule reflects the performance of the collection of the different rules acting as a whole, by evaluating the relevance of each individual and providing support for its activity.

These two factors, namely, the strength and the support, provide for competition and cooperation among the different rules. When a posted message matches a rule, each classifier makes a bid proportional to its strength; hence, highly fit rules are given preference. The bid made by an activated classifier is then proportionately divided and sent as a reward to other classifiers earlier responsible for activating it. Thus if a rule is instrumental in permitting other rules to fire *favorably*, it receives payoff and hence its strength will be increased; otherwise, its strength is decreased due to bidding. In the steady state, the strength remains invariant. BBS is useful to construct a database whose attributes are not known in advance but are adaptive or evolving probabilistically. The UMPP can realize the BBS, if the probabilities p_i are replaced by strengths and at the end of each atomic update, the actions are evaluated and the strengths are reassigned depending upon downstream and upstream payoff.

The ant algorithm and swarm intelligence use an approach similar to BBS (see subsection 5.7 below).

5.3   Genetic Algorithm

The genetic algorithm goes a step further than the BBS: after selecting the most successful rules, these rules are combined by selecting pairs and performing crossover and mutation. The crossover may be thought of as a combination of independent rules, while the mutation may be thought of as an error in input or an approximation.

The genetic algorithm [8, 12, 29, 30, 32, 68, 13, 62, 84, 83, 90] chooses an initial population of objects called *chromosomes*, represented by a multiset M of binary strings with a length of m bits. Then it performs on M three different probabilistic operations that mimic the operations found in nature, namely, selective reproduction, crossover, and mutation. These operations can therefore be represented in the UMPP using four transactions:

Transaction 1 evaluates the given generation for assigning the selection probabilities q to initiate the actions for the creation of a new generation.

Transaction 2 performs reproduction; its condition text enables us to select probabilistically those strings that are fit, and its action text replaces the original multiset with the fittest strings.

Transaction 3 performs crossover; its condition text picks up any two elements and the crossover site; the corresponding action text performs crossover and returns the two offspring back to the multiset.

Transaction 4 performs mutation; its condition text gives the probabilistic conditions to select a string as well as the site for mutation; the action text performs mutation and returns the string back to the multiset. This sequence of transactions is then repeated until the multiset is stable or does not undergo a change.

If the reproduction, crossover, and mutation are performed sequentially, one after another, then the UMPP is given by the composition of the four transactions applied to M. We can introduce concurrency among the three transactions 2, 3, and 4, subject to the constraint that they act on different strings. Such a genetic algorithm is called an *elitist model*, where the parents and offspring together can undergo selective reproduction, crossover, and mutation [32, 61, 84].

Note that the evaluation transaction cannot be interleaved with others. In implementing the paradigm, therefore, we must decide how to interleave tasks of different types and size (granularity). This problem is called *multilevel atomicity*. It is possible to interleave the simulated annealing algorithm with the genetic algorithm; the accepted elements in the annealing algorithm can undergo selection, mutation, and crossover or other new operations listed in Michalewicz [61].

The correspondence between the genetic algorithm and UMPP is summarized below:

Genetic Algorithm	UMPP
Generation	Iteration of the multiset
String	Elements
Crossover, Mutation	Interaction
Selection	Deterministic, Probabilistic Choice
Evaluation	Pattern matching, Evaluation
Fitness	Test
Population Fitness	Global test of the multiset
Family fitness	Local test of sets of varying granularity
History	Computational history

5.4 Genetic Programming

Koza's [42] genetic programming can be ably supported and implemented with the very general multiset data structure by a proper choice of the features described in the Introduction, namely, the choice initial object spaces, set of reaction rules and their probabilities, the self-activation of the rules, the control strategy, and the termination condition for evaluating the fitness of elements.

5.5. Evolutionary Optimization

In nature, highly specialized complex structures emerge when their most inefficient elements are selectively driven to extinction. Evolution progresses by selecting against the few most poorly adapted species, rather than by expressly breeding those species best adapted to the environment. The experimental approach by Boettcher and Percus [10] uses the extremal optimization (EO) processes in which the least fit variables are progressively eliminated [35]. The EO process uses a different strategy in comparison to simulated annealing. In simulated annealing, the system is forced to equilibrium dynamics by accepting or rejecting local changes. EO, however, takes the system to a far-from-equilibrium position, and persistent selection against the worst fitness (i.e., selective extinction or death) leads to a near-optimal solution. Also, EO differs from the genetic algorithm (GA); whereas GA keeps track of entire gene pools of states from which to select and breed an improved generation of solutions, EO operates only with local updates on a single copy of the system, with improvements achieved instead by elimination of the bad. EO also differs from the greedy strategy, which aims at improving the solution at each step and as a result falls into a local optimum. EO, however, can fluctuate between good and bad solutions and can enable us to cross barriers and approach new regions in configuration space. Note that EO can be simulated using UMPP.

5.6 Oscillatory Chemical Reactions

We mentioned in Section 3 that the rule processing does not terminate if and only if rules provide new conditions to fire indefinitely—that is, actions of a rule Ri create the right conditions for another rule Rj to fire. This leads to circularity in definition or a deadlock. Usually in computer science we do not want this situation to happen, as it leads to a wasteful consumption of resources and instability. However, such a cyclic system occurs commonly in biology and seems to form the basis of all living systems. For example, the energy-rich molecule adenosine triphosphate (ATP) is produced through a succession of reactions in the glycolytic (sugar-splitting) cycle that involves ATP at the start. To produce ATP, we need ATP. These reactions correspond to catalytic reactions that arise in nonequilibrium systems, where a set of reactants produce a set of products that react with some of the reactants and continue reacting indefinitely as an oscillatory reaction. These reactions, for example, can be of the form in which one of the initial reactants A and another reactant X produce Y, and Y produces Z, and Z produces X. Such reactions have rates that are determined by the concentration of the reactants and the products. Such oscillatory systems are called *nonequilibrium systems* or the Brusselator model [76, 86, 87] and can be realized using UMPP.

The Brusselator model consists of the four production rules:

$$(1) \ A \rightarrow X; \ (2) \ BX \rightarrow YD; \ (3) \ XXY \rightarrow XXX; \ (4) \ X \rightarrow E$$

Thus this model is a multiset $M = \{A, B, X, Y, E\}$ and a set of reaction rules R defined above among the elements. Note that an element can undergo self-mutation on its own (autolysis) or due to interaction with the environment, e.g., in the rules for

$$A \rightarrow X \text{ or } X \rightarrow E.$$

We can also incorporate the rate of reaction within each rule, which can be either deterministic or probabilistic. By varying the reaction rates or rates of application of rules to the system, the number of elements X and Y can diverge, become unstable, oscillate, or converge.

For example, a simple simulation shows that the relative frequencies of application of rule (1) and rule (2) can produce varying kinds of effects in the population (numbers) of X and Y.

5.7   Swarm and Ant Colony Paradigm

A swarm (consisting of birds, ants, cellular automata) is a population of interacting elements that is able to optimize some global objective through cooperative search of space. Interactions that are relatively local are often emphasized [39, 11, 24, 60, 56]. There is a general stochastic tendency in a swarm for individuals to move toward a center of mass in the population on critical dimensions, resulting in convergence to an optimum. In real number space, the parameters of a function space can be conceptualized as a point. Here, individual elements in the multiset are points in space, and change over time is represented as movement of points, representing particles with velocities, and the system dynamics is formulated in UMPP using the following rules:
1. *Stepping rule*. The state of each individual element is updated in many dimensions, in parallel, so that the new state reflects each element's previous best success, e.g., the position and momentum (velocity) of each particle.
2. *Landscaping rule*. Each element is assigned a new best value of its state that depends on its past best value and a suitable function of the best values of its interacting neighbors, with a suitably defined neighborhood topology and geometry.

Remark: The above two rules are similar to the strength and support of rules used in BBS in subsection 5.2 above. The first rule reflects the betterment of the individual, while the second rule reflects the betterment of the collection of the individuals in the neighborhood as a whole by evaluating the relevance of each individual and providing support for its activity.

All elements in the multiset or selected chunks are updated using rules (1) and (2). These two rules permit us to model Markovian random walks, which are independent of the past history of the walk and non-Markovian random walks, which are dependent upon past history—such as self-avoiding, self-repelling, and active random-walker models. This can result in a swarm (a self-organizing system) whose global nonlinear dynamics emerges from local rules due to stochasticity or chaoticity introduced by the parameter variation. In nonlinear dynamics, the beautiful property of superposition (namely, the linear combinations of solutions are also solutions and such solutions form a linear vector space) is lost. As a result, there is no general solution. Also, analytic solutions are rare and nonexistent; solutions may exhibit singularities not present in the equations of motion, and these may be sensitive to initial conditions. Further, interesting new properties may show up: low-dimensional attractors, bifurcations, and chaos. Accordingly, various kinds of attractors (as described in Section 4.2) can arise that result in fractal dimensions, presenting a swarmlike, flocklike appearances depending upon the Jacobian of the mapping [57]. Thus, in nonlinear dynamics, integration (solving differential equations) and finding attractors are the key issues.

5.8   Conrad's Lock–Key Paradigm

Conrad and Zauner [20, 21, 22, 95] suggest the lock–key paradigm as the basis for molecular computing. This paradigm arises from the notions of complementarity and the union of opposites that pervade the entire science and natural philosophy. The lock–key paradigm is based on the recognition of an object (molecule) through complementary shape matching. This assumes the existence of a suitably defined "complement" among pairs of objects. Such a complement can be defined for molecular structures at three levels [16]:

1. Primary level. Here we refer to purely syntactic attributes, as in the Watson–Crick complement of a sequence (got by interchanging purines and pyrimidines: A (Adenine) for T (Thymine) and conversely, and G (Guanine) for C (Cytosine) and conversely; or
2. Secondary level. Here we refer to the structure that describes local internal arrangements (alpha helices and beta sheets); or
3. Tertiary level. Here we deal with the 3-D configuration of the structure, namely, the geometric and topological features that are complementary.

To simulate the lock–key paradigm at the above three levels, we need to have a database of elements with complementary attributes, much as in a relational database. However (unlike in a database), here the query and retrieval take place through molecular reaction when a pair matches (at the primary, secondary, or tertiary level according to a specified rule), followed by the required actions (e.g., chemoreceptors for gustation and olfaction). The rule system can be explicit as in a production system or can be implicit as in a dynamical system, where energy minimization brings the required elements into physical contact to self-assemble and generate the required actions. Thus the complementarity paradigm is applicable to both the computational and dynamical systems. It is also useful in synthetic biology [89, 48].

5.9   Membrane and Immunocomputing

The basic datastructure used in membrane [74] and biomolecular immunocomputing [33] are multisets with a priority relation among rules, and the rules are applied in a conditional manner. UMPP provides all these features.

5.10   Quantum Field Theoretical Computations

In the "occupation number formalism" used in Quantum Field theoretical computation [75], states are characterized by a specification of how many particles there are in each of a complete set of single-particle states [51]. The occupation number notation is a multiset datastructure or a bag that has repetitive elements in a set [70]. The repeated elements correspond to indistinguishable objects in the same state. For example, the shell notation for atoms:

$(1s)^2$, $(2s)^2$ $(2p)^1$ meaning that two electrons are in state 1s, two are in state 2s, and one is in the state 2p. This can be written in the multiset notation as $\{1s.2, 2s.2, 2p.1\}$.

Thus, the occupation number formalism in quantum physical computations can be implemented in UMPP. Also, UMPP can simulate the evolution of states of quantum systems with arbitrarily many particles described by vectors in the Fock space by appropriate choice of rules and actions that satisfy the desired invariant properties.

Quasi-particles are entities in quantum field theory. These consist of a main particle surrounded by a cloud of associated particles that are in certain definite relationship to the main particle. Thus a quasi-particle provides for a collective operation, and hence it simplifies the analysis of the evolution of a system through its propagation. This is the main reason for the use of quasi-particles in physics, as well as in the mutiset parallel computational paradigm. Thus quasi particles behave like user-defined objects that encapsulate data and procedures that can be mobile, e.g., agents in distributed systems.

6 RELATIONAL DATABASE MODEL AND LOCK–KEY PARADIGM

The lock–key paradigm is closely related to rule-based programming and the relational database model. The relational database model consists of one or more relations, each expressed as a set of tuples, often expressed as a table. Each row of this table represents one of the tuples, and each column represents one of the component positions of all the tuples. The tuples are also called *attributes*.

The following properties [41] of relational database programming make it suitable for biosystems:
1. Entire relations are accepted as inputs, and conceptually complete relations are delivered as results.
2. The contents of relations change as a function of time.
3. The relations are always finite, unlike in ordinary computing, where we deal with infinite relations.
4. Individual elements in tuples are always simple ground constants with no variables or complex structures.

Among the many operators of relational algebra, the most important one, which we need for computation with molecular biosystems, is a variant of the join operation. The join operation accepts two relations and joins them along the columns if the attribute names and domains are common to both. Thus it builds up relationships among the relations. However, we still have ground constants as elements of tuples, limiting the expressive power of the relational algebra to that of the first-order logic. When the join condition involves only comparing equality, it is called *equijoin*. Thus when equijoin is performed, we will have one or more pairs of attributes with identical values. In order to remove the superfluous elements, a new operation called *natural join* is used in relational databases. It is basically an equijoin operation followed by the removal of superfluous elements.

In the lock–key or complementarity paradigm, we indeed need a modification of natural join in which the attributes are not equal but are complementary: after the operation the result is a single tuple. We call this new operation *conjoin* to indicate that two objects are united into one, after the natural join of their complementary attributes. The conjoin of two relations R and S, denoted by $R<>S$, is formed by taking each tuple r from R and each tuple s from S and comparing them. If the component of r for A_i equals the complement of the component of

s for B_j, then we form one tuple from r and s; otherwise, no tuple is formed. This requires a lock–key matching of attribute values that are mutually complementary. While forming the tuple from r and s, we take the components of r followed by the components of s, but indicating the match. Note that the conjoin operation is no more expensive than the natural join, since we look for complementary features in each defined attribute. Using conjoin, we can realize the three types of complementary paradigms—primary, secondary or tertiary—with well-defined attributes. Note that the conjoin operation need not necessarily result in a unique tuple, since matching may not be unique.

6.1   Algorithm Conjoin

Consider conjoining relations R with attributes $\{A,B\}$ and relation S with attributes $\{B^*,C\}$, where B^* is a suitably defined complement of B. The algorithm for conjoin, based on a nested "for" loop, is as follows:

for each tuple r in R **do**
   for each tuple s in S **do**
   if r and s are complements on their B and B^* attributes
      then
   conjoin the tuple matching r and s on attributes A, B, B^*, and C

The above algorithm would take $O(rs)$ time, since we need to pair all the tuples.

6.2   Conjoin and Self-Assembly

In nature, the conjoin is a fundamental operation carried out by RNA polymerase, the enzyme that synthesizes a complementary RNA copy of one or more genes of a DNA molecule. The RNA serves to direct the synthesis of the proteins encoded by those genes. The polymerase essentially carries out a "for" loop; in each cycle, it takes a small molecule (one of the four nucleotide pyrophosphates, ATP, GTP, CTP, or TTP, whose base is complementary to the base about to be copied on the DNA strand) from the surrounding solution, forms a covalent bond between the nucleotide part of the small molecule and the existing uncompleted RNA strand, and releases the pyrophosphate part into the surrounding solution as a free pyrophosphate molecule (PP). The enzyme then shifts forward one notch along the DNA in order to copy the next nucleotide and repeats. The proofreading of DNA replication and repairing damage requires a similar "for" loop. Conrad [20] proposes a jigsaw puzzle model for self-assembly based on the lock–key paradigm and the energy minimization criteria. In this model, energy plays an important role in directing the computation, unlike the models (such as Turing machine) used in computer science.

7   MOLECULAR DNA COMPUTATION

The DNA molecular computation scheme introduced by Adelman [2] [16, 58, 77, 54, 28] models the actual instance of a problem rather than providing a universal approach to computation. It provides for a fine-grained parallelism based on the free-energy minimization (annealing) associated with the self-assembly properties of DNA sequences. That is, the physical structure of the machine is specific so as to cater to the need for solving a single problem instance [96].

The actual computation proceeds in three phases:

Phase 1. Encoding phase: Here the input is encoded into a multiset whose elements are DNA sequences and their Watson–Crick complements (WCC) so that the required conditions R for the chemical reactions A driven by chemical free-energy minimisation are feasible.

Phase 2. Action (chemical reaction) phase: The encoded molecules chemically react with each other autonomously to form supermolecular complexes (new elements of the multiset) through the association of WCC sequences. Each of the complexes denotes a partial solution to the problem.

Phase 3. Solution selection and termination: The complexes are selected and tested for the existence of the solution or as to whether they satisfy the termination condition of the solution expected.

The above three phases are the basic steps in UMPP. Note that the updating action A (Phase 2) in the conditional in $G(R,A)(M)$, namely: if there exists elements $a,b,c,\ldots,\ldots$ belonging to a multiset M such that $R(a,b,c,\ldots)$, then

$$G(R,A)((M-\{a,b,c,\ldots\}) + A(a,b,c,\ldots)), \text{ else } M$$

is implemented autonomously by the free-energy minimization. However, Phase 3 requires a test for the solution through external physicochemical means, such as polymerase reaction, gel electrophoresis, and hybridization probing.

7.1 Molecular multiset data structure

Adelman's approach uses the biological–chemical reaction in DNA molecules to solve the Hamilton Path Problem (HPP)–[2, 73]: Given a graph G, is there a path through the graph that visits every node in the graph exactly once? This is a proverbially hard problem for which no polynomial time solutions are as yet known.

The data structure chosen is a chemical graph whose vertices are uniquely labeled by a short even-member sequence of DNA consisting of nucleotides A, G, C, or T. This sequence is called *oligonuleotide* and is a single-stranded DNA molecule. Each edge is an ordered pair of nodes (i,j). Such an edge is denoted by the oligonuleotide that combines the righthalf of the DNA sequence $(R(i))$ representing the vertex i and the left -half of the sequence $(L(j))$ representing the vertex j.

To join any two edges (i,j) and (j,k), a chemical reaction known as *ligation* is used. This consists in tying two edges together by using a WCC oligonuleotide of j (in which A is replaced by T and conversely, and C is replaced by G and conversely). Thus the fusing of two edges denoted by the ordered triplet (i,j,k) is represented by the fused double-stranded DNA sequence $R(i),L(j),R(j), L(k)$, in which the middle part $L(j) R(j)$ is ligated to WCC $(j) = L(j^*) R(j^*)$. This double-stranded sequence is denoted by

$\{R(i), (L(j) \& L(j^*)), (R(j) \& R(j^*)), L(k)\}$, where "&" denotes an elementwise nucleotide fusing operation that can be looked upon as conjoin operation earlier described in a relational database context .

Adeleman's algorithm consists of three basic tasks:
1. Using molecules to represent elements of multiset
2. Self-assembly of elements of the multiset satisfying the reaction condition
3. Checking for termination conditions

The above tasks are implemented by Adelman to find the Hamilton path using the following four steps:
1. Synthesize a random path in the graph
2. Retain only those paths that satisfy the condition specified for the beginning and ending vertices of the path.
3. Keep only those paths that contain exactly n different vertices
4. Check for termination by looking for only those paths that go through all the vertices at least once.

7.2 Molecular Chemical Transactions

Adelman uses different types of chemical and physico–chemical operations (these may be called *genetic engineering* operations): copy, paste, amplification, extraction, identification zero-test, sum, for which we use the computer science term *transaction* meaning that these need to have four important properties called ACID properties [49, 95]: Atomicity (indivisibility and either all or no actions carried out), Consistency (before and after the execution of a transaction), Isolation (no interference among the actions), and Durability (no failure).

1. *Copy/ replicate.* This synthesizes a large number of copies of any single-stranded DNA. That is, it creates a large number of copies of the elements of a multiset M.
2. *Paste or create double strands.* This produces a combination of elements of multisets, resulting in a multiset containing new elements that can be ordered sequences containing WCC fused subsequences. Such a fusion creates double strands. This set of elements can be represented by a parallel elementwise operation on subsequences, denoted by "&". This operation is chemically achieved through self-assembly by free-energy minimization.
3. *Selective amplify.* This operation is different from "copy" in that it is a higher-level or macro-copy operation that replicates any selected element (single- or double-stranded DNA) whose attributes are specified. This operation is externally achieved either through cloning or through the more efficient polymerase reaction (PCR). This is analogous to the selective reproduction strategy widely used in the genetic algorithms.
4. *Extraction.* This operation extracts sequences of specified lengths. It is carried out using the physicochemical operation known as *gel electrophoresis*. This operation is similar to the message pattern matching used in classifier and production systems. Also, it is similar to the selection or projection operation used in the theory of recursive functions to select the k elements among n ordered elements.
5. *Identification.* This operation selects those sequences of specified lengths that contain specified subsequences. Using hybridization probes of subsequences that are complementary to the selected subsequence, individual vertices are identified.

6. *Zero test.* this operation determines whether or not there is a DNA strand. This is a fundamental operation required in the recursive functions.

7. *Sum or merge.* Given two multisets M and N, the sum denoted by $M+N$ is the multiset where each element has a multiplicity that is a sum of its multiplicity in M and N.

In DNA computing, knowledge is represented by omission of negative facts. Propositions that are not given are assumed to be false; that is, we use the *Closed world assumption (CWA)*, in which only positive facts are stated. As mentioned earlier, CWA is valid only for Horn clauses; that is, if there are non-Horn clauses, we cannot make the closed-world assumption [31]. For nonequilibrium systems interacting with their surroundings through an entropy flow, this assumption is invalid [76]. Most such systems use feedback mechanisms involving catalytic reactions, as, for example, production of ATP (adenosine triphosphate) from ATP. Such reactions arise from far-from-equilibrium conditions. These lead to the necessity for the *Open-world hypothesis*, which leads to newer phenomena such as self-organization and active walks (swarm intelligence) [11, 23, 39, 56].

Finally, we observe that we can combine neural and molecular computing. The genetic code may be looked upon as a string of spin variables undergoing dynamical development in the course of reproduction. Analogous to Hopfield's spin-glass approach for neural nets, Anderson and others have formulated a model for the evolution of organisms using a fitness landscape. Kuhn's model uses the concept of RNA replication and autocatalysis driven by temperature cycling [38]. A population of organisms (strings of + or − spins $S(i)$) is encouraged to conjugate randomly in pairs during a cooling cycle, and if two shorter strings (RNA polymers) are conjugated end to end on a third longer one, they are allowed to bond to each other, giving a long single RNA polymer. The strings are then subjected to a heating cycle, where they separate and also encounter a fitness function that can be identified by a spin-glass Hamiltonian and that serves as a criterion for survival into the next conjugation. The fitness landscape is a spin-glass function. The use of autocatalysis seems to extend the power of first-order logic to overcome the limitations of the closed-world assumption.

8   DISCRETE ADAPTIVE STOCHASTIC OPTIMIZATION

Searching and exploration form the basis for many types of data analysis, adaptive learning, and pattern classification problems. Adaptive systems need to use some form of search operation to explore a feature space that describes all possible configurations of the system. Usually we are interested in "optimal" or "near optimal" configurations defined with respect to a specific problem domain. Such problem domains are usually high dimensional with no single optimal solution and are multimodal, i.e., they can have many local and global optimal solutions.

In general, finding the global maximum and minimum of multimodal problems with high dimensions and conflicting constraints turnsout to be exponential in complexity, and usually the problems are NP-complete or even NP-hard [46].

Therefore, conventional search techniques are inefficient. We need to use a probabilistic approach that is adaptable to the particular problem domain so that the search space can be sampled to yield near-optimal solutions with a high probability. Any such adaptive (learning) search methods are characterized by taking the following aspects into account:

1. How are solutions (parameters, hypotheses) represented? What data structures are used?
2. What search operators are used in moving from one configuration to the next? How is the adaptive step defined?
3. What type of search is conducted by applying the search operators iteratively? How is the search space explored and exploited?
4. Is the adaptive system supervised (interactive) or unsupervised (noninteractive)?
5. How can problem-specific knowledge be incorporated into the adaptive learning algorithm?

8.1   Example

Consider the following discrete stochastic optimization problem. Let $\Theta = \{1, 2, \ldots, S\}$ denote a finite set and consider the following problem: Compute

$$\theta^* = \min_{\theta \in \Theta} E\{X_n(\theta)\},$$

where E denotes mathematical expectation and, for any fixed $\theta \in \Theta$, $\{X_n(\theta)\}$ denotes a sequence of independent and identically distributed (iid) random variables that can be generated for any choice of $\theta \in \Theta$. If the density function of $X_n(\theta)$ is not known, then it is not possible to analytically evaluate the above expectation, and hence θ^*. In such a case, one needs to resort to simulation-based stochastic approximation to compute the optimal solution θ^*.

A brute-force approach of computing the optimal solution to the problem involves exhaustive enumeration over all Θ and proceeds as follows: For each $\theta \in \Theta$, generate a large number N of random samples $X_1(\theta)$, $X_2(\theta), \ldots X_N(\theta)$. Then compute an estimate of $E\{X_n(\theta)\}$ using the sample average (arithmetic mean)

$$G_N(\theta) = (X_1(\theta) + X_2(\theta) + \ldots + X_N(\theta)/N.$$

By Kolmogorov's strong law of large numbers (which is one of the most fundamental consequences of the ergodic theorem for iid processes), $G_N(\theta) \to E\{X_n(\theta)\}$ with probability one as $N \to \infty$. This and the finiteness of Θ imply that

$$\arg \max_{\theta \in \Theta} G_N(\theta) \to \arg \max_{\theta \in \Theta} E\{X_n(\theta)\} \text{ as } N \to \infty.$$

However, the above brute-force procedure is extremely inefficient—evaluating $G_N(\theta)$ at values $\theta \in \Theta$ with $\theta \neq \theta^*$ is wasted effort, since it contributes nothing towards evaluating $G_N(\theta^*)$. What is required is an intelligent dynamic scheduling (search) scheme that decides at each time instant which value of θ to evaluate next, given the current estimates, in order to converge to the maximum θ^* with minimum effort.

There are several different classes of methods that can be used to solve the above discrete stochastic optimization problem [3, 52]. When the feasible set Θ is small (usually 2 to 20 elements), statistical ranking and selection methods and multiple comparison methods can be used to locate the optimal solution. However, for large Θ, the computational complexity of these methods becomes prohibitive. The above problem can also be viewed as a multiarmed bandit problem, which is a special kind of infinite-horizon Markov decision process with an "indexable" optimal policy. However, as mentioned in Andradottir [4], multiarmed bandit solutions and learning automata procedures often tend to be conservative because they are designed to spend as much time as possible at the optimum solution.

8.2   Stochastic Approximation Algorithm

In recent years a number of discrete stochastic approximation algorithms have been proposed. Several of these algorithms [3], including simulated annealing-type procedures and stochastic ruler, fall into the category of random search. Here we present a globally convergent discrete stochastic approximation algorithm based on the random search procedures in Andradottir [3]. The basic idea is to generate a homogeneous Markov chain, taking values in Θ that spend more time at the global optimum than at any other element of Θ. This generation consists of the following UMPP steps:

Step 0: Initialization. At time $n=0$, select starting point $\theta_0 \in \Theta$ randomly with uniform probability. Set $D_0 = e_\theta 0$, where e_i denotes the S-dimensional unit vector with 1 in the ith position and zeros elsewhere. Set the initial solution estimate $\hat{\theta}_0 = x_0$.

Step 1: Sampling. At time n, sample $u_n \in \Theta - \{\theta_n\}$ with uniform distribution.

Step 2: Evaluation and acceptance.
Evaluate the random sample costs $X_n(\theta_n)$ and $X_n(u_n)$.
If $X_n(\theta_n) > X_n(u_n)$, then set $\theta_{n+1} = \theta_n$; else set $\theta_{n+1} = u_n$.

Step 3: Update duration time vector at time $n+1$ as $D_{n+1} = D_n + e_{\theta_n}$

Step 4: Update estimate of maximum at time n as $\hat{\theta}_n = \arg \max_{i \in \{1,2,\ldots,S\}} D_{n+1}(i)$
Set $n \to n+1$ and go to Step 1.
Then, as proved in Andradottir [3], under suitable conditions (e.g., if the density function with respect to which the expected value is defined above is symmetric), the estimate $\hat{\theta}_n$ generated by the above random search stochastic approximation algorithm converges with probability one to the global optimum θ^*. It is also shown in Andradottir [3] that the algorithm is attracted to the global optimum, i.e., the algorithm spends more time at the global optimum than at any other candidate value. That is, for sufficiently large n, the duration time vector D_n has its maximum element at θ^*.

8.3   Applications

The above discrete stochastic approximation algorithm has several applications. For example, in Krishnamurthy and Chung (2003), it is used to learn the behavior of an ion channel (large protein molecule) in a nerve cell membrane to estimate the Nernst potential efficiently. In Krishnamurthy, Wang and Yin [53], a recursive version of the algorithm is used to optimize the spreading code of a CDMA spread spectrum transmitter over a fading wireless channel. More recently, in Yin, Krishnamurthy and Ion [93], an adaptive version of the above algorithm is presented that can track a slowly time-varying global optimum. For a weak convergence analysis and complexity aspects of this adaptive algorithm, [93, 52].

9   CONCLUSION

This chapter presents a unified rule-based multiset programming paradigm (UMPP) as a general model and unifying theme for conventional and soft-computing. The introduction of probabilistic choices in a multiset chemical reaction model provides a soft-computational model to study evolutionary biological, chemical, and physical systems based on intermittent feedback from the environment. Unlike conventional computation, where exactness is our goal, in soft computation, we allow the possibility of error and randomness to model features that are inherent in problems arising in nature. The paradigm described here provides a new programming environment based on a distributed architecture for classifier, bucket brigade, genetic, and molecular algorithms as well as ant-algorithms, swarm intelligence, membrane and bio-immunology computing, multiple-particle filtering, adaptive stochastic optimization and self-organized criticality. This paradigm is well suited for cluster and grid computing.

REFERENCES

[1] A.N. Abdallah (1995): *The Logic of Partial Information*, Springer Verlag, New York.

[2] L.M. Adelman (1994): Molecular computation of solutions to combinatorial problems, *Science, 266*, 1021–1024.

[3] S. Andradottir (1996): A global search method for discrete stochastic optimization, *SIAM Journal of Optimization, 6*, 2(1), 513–530.

[4] S. Andradottir (1999): Accelerating the convergence of random search methods for discrete stochastic optimization, *ACM Transactions on Modelling and Computer Simulation, 9*, 4(1), 349–380.

[5] R. Backhouse and J. Gibbons (2003): Generic Programming, *Lecture Notes in Computer Science*, Vol. 2793, Springer Verlag, New York.

[6] J.-P. Banatre, D.L. Me'tayer (1990): The Gamma model and its discipline of programming, *Science of Computer Programming, 15*, 55–77.

[7] J.-P, Banatre, D.L. Me'tayer (1993): Programming by Multiset transformation, *Comm. ACM, 36*, 98–111.

[8] R.K. Belew, S. Forrest (1988): Learning and programming in classifier systems, *Machine Learning 3*, 193–223.

[9] T. Blackwell and J. Branke (2004): Multi-swarm optimization in dynamic environments, *Lecture Notes in Computer Science*, Vol. 3005, pp. 489–500, Springer Verlag, New York.

[10] S. Boettcher, and A. Percus (2000): Nature's way of optimizing, *Artificial Intelligence*, 119, 275–286.

[11] E. Bonabeau, M. Dorigo and G. Theraulaz (1999): *Swarm Intelligence: From Natural to Artificial Systems*, Oxford University Press, U.K.

[12] L.K. Booker, D.E. Goldberg, J.H. Holland (1986): Classifier systems and Genetic Algorithms, *Artificial Intelligence*, 40, 235–282.

[13] J. Branke, H.C. Andersen and H. Schmeck (1996). Global selection methods for massively parallel computers, in *Evolutionary Computing*, T.C. Fogarty, ed., *Lecture Notes in Computer Science*, *1143*, 175–188, Springer Verlag, New York.

[14] C.S. Calude, et al., (2001): Multiset processing, *Lecture Notes in Computer Science*, Vol. 2235, Springer Verlag, New York.

[15] C. Cannings and D.D. Penman (2003): Models of Random graphs and their applications, *Handbook of Statistics*, C.R. Rao, ed., *21*, 51-91, North Holland, Amsterdam.

[16] N. Campbell (1996): *Biology*, Benjamin/Cummings, New York.

[17] K.S. Chan, and H. Tong (2002): *Chaos: A Statistical Perspective*, Springer, New York.

[18] S. Chu, et al., (2003): Parallel ant colony systems, *Lecture Notes In Artificial Intelligence*, *2871*, 279–284, Springer Verlag, New York.

[19] C.A.C. Coello, D.A. Van Veldhuizen, G.B. Lemont (2002): *Evolutionary Algorithm for Solving Multi-objective Problem*, Kluwer, New York.

[20] M. Conrad (1992): Molecular computing paradigms, *Computer*, 25, 6–68.

[21] M. Conrad, K.-P. Zauner (1997): Molecular computing: From conformational pattern recognition to complex processing networks, in *Bioinformatics, Lecture Notes in Computer Science 1278*, 1–10, Springer Verlag, New York.

[22] M. Conrad, K-P Zauner (1998): DNA as a vehicle for the self-assembly model of computing, *Biosystems*, *45*, 59–66.

[23] M. Dorigo, G.D. Caro and M. Sampels (2002): Ant algorithms, *Lecture Notes in Computer Science*, Vol. 2463, Springer Verlag, New York.

[24] M. Dorigo, and T. Stutzle (2004): *Ant Colony Optimization*, M.I.T. Press, Cambridge, Mass.

[25] S.N. Dorogovtsev, and J.F.F. Mendes, (2003): *Evolution of Networks*, Oxford University Press, Oxford.

[26] A. Doucet et al., (2000): *Sequential Monte-Carlo Methods in Practice*, Springer, New York.

[27] A. Doucet, N. Gordon, V. Krishnamurthy, (2001): Particle filters for state estimation of jump Markov linear systems, *IEEE Trans. Signal Processing*, *49*, 613–624.

[28] J.L. Fernandez-Villacanas, J.M. Fatah, S. Amin (1998): Computing with evolving proteins, *Parallel and Distributed Processing*, J. Rolim, ed. *Lecture Notes in Computer Science*, Vol. 1388, Springer Verlag, New York, pp. 207–215.

[29] S. Forrest (1991a): *Parallelism and Programming in Classifier Systems*, Morgan Kauffman, San Mateo, California.

[30] S. Forrest (1991b): *Emergent Computation*, M.I.T Press, Cambridge, Mass.

[31] M.H. Genesereth, N. Nilsson, (1987): *Logical Foundations of Artificial Intelligence*, Morgan Kaufmann, Los Altos, California.

[32] D.E. Goldberg, (1989): *Genetic Algorithms in Search, Optimisation and Machine Learning*, Addison Wesley, Reading, Mass.

[33] L. Goncharova, et al., (2003): Biomolecular immunocomputing, *Lecture Notes in Computer Science*, *2787*, 102-110, Springer Verlag, New York.

[34] J.J. Grefenstett, (1988): Credit assignment in rule discovery systems based on genetic algorithms, *Machine Learning*, *3*, 225–245.

[35] J.H. Holland, et al., (1987): *Induction*, M.I.T. Press, Cambridge, Mass.

[36] A. Ilachinski, (2002): *Cellular Automata*, World Scientific, Singapore.

[37] T. Ishida (1991): Parallel, distributed and multiagent production systems, *Lecture Notes in Computer Science*, 890, Springer Verlag, New York.

[38] S.A. Kauffman (1993): *The Origins of Order*, Oxford University Press, Oxford.

[39] J. Kennedy and R.C. Eberhart, (2001). *Swarm Intelligence*, Morgan Kauffman, London.

[40] P. Kevin MacKeown (1997): *Stochastic Simulation in Physics*, Springer, New York.

[41] P.M Kogge, (1991): *The Architecture of Symbolic Computers*, McGraw Hill, New York.

[42] J.R. Koza, (1994): *Genetic Programming II*, M.I.T. Press, Cambridge, Mass.

[43] E.V. Krishnamurthy, (1985): *Introductory Theory of Computer Science*, Springer Verlag, New York.

[44] E.V. Krishnamurthy (1986): Solving problems by random trials, Science and computers, (A volume dedicated to Nicholas Metropolis), G.C. Rota, ed., *Advances in Mathematics*, *10*, 61-81, Academic Press, New York.

[45] E.V. Krishnamurthy, (1989): *Parallel Processing*, Addison Wesley, Reading, Mass.

[46] E.V. Krishnamurthy (1996): Complexity issues in parallel and distributed computing, in *Handbook of Parallel and Distributed Computing*, Chapter 4, A. Zomaya, ed., McGraw Hill, New York.

[47] E.V. Krishnamurthy, (2003): Algorithmic entropy, phase transitions, and smart systems, *Lecture Notes in Computer Science*, *2659*, 333–342, Springer Verlag, New York.

[48] E.V. Krishnamurthy, (2004): Rule-based Multiset Programming Paradigm, Applications to Synthetic Biology, Third Workshop on Non-Silicon Computation, (NSC-3), Munich, in *31st International Symposium on Computer Architecture*, Munich, June 2004.

[49] E.V. Krishnamurthy, V.K. Murthy, (1992): *Transaction Processing Systems*, Prentice Hall, Sydney.

[50] V. Krishnamurthy, and E.V. Krishnamurthy, (1999): Rule-based Programming Paradigm: A formal basis for biological, chemical and physical computation, *Biosystems*, *49*, 205–228.

[51] E.V. Krishnamurthy, and V. Krishnamurthy (2001): Quantum field theory and computational paradigms, *International Journal of Modern Physics*, *12*C, 1179–1201.

[52] V. Krishnamurthy, and S.H. Chung (2003): Adaptive learning algorithms for Nernst potential and I-V curves in nerve cell membrane ion channels modelled as hidden Markov models, *IEEE Transactions NanoBioScience*, *2*(4), 266–278.

[53] V. Krishnamurthy, X. Wang, G. Yin (2004): Adaptive Spreading Code Optimization and Adaptation in CDMA via Discrete Stochastic Approximation, *IEEE Transactions Information Theory*, 50(9), 1927–1949.

[54] I. M. Kulic (1998): Evaluating polynomials on the molecular level—a novel approach to molecular computers, *Biosystems*, 45, 45–57.

[55] S. Kuo, D. Moldovan, (1992): The state of the art in parallel production systems, *J. Parallel and Distributed Computing*, 15, 1–26.

[56] L. Lam (1998): *Nonlinear Physics for Beginners*, World Scientific, Singapore.

[57] A.J. Lichtenberg and M.A. Liberman, (1983): *Regular and Stochastic Motion*, Springer Verlag, New York.

[58] R.J. Lipton (1995): DNA solution to hard computational problems, *Science*, 268, 542-545.

[59] W. Ma,, E.V. Krishnamurthy and V.K. Murthy (1995): Multran—A coordination programming language using multiset and transactions, *Proc. Neural, Parallel and Scientific Computing*, 1, 301-304, Dynamic Publishers, Inc., U.S.A.

[60] N. Meuleau and M. Dorigo, (2002): Ant colony optimization and stochastic gradient descent, *Artificial Life*, 8, 103–121.

[61] Z. Michalewicz (1992): *Genetic Algorithms + Data Structures = Evolution Programs*, Springer Verlag, New York.

[62] Z. Michalewicz and D.B. Fogel (2000): *How to Solve It: Modern Heuristics*, Springer Verlag, New York. (1992,

[63] D. Midgley (2003): *Systems Thinking*, Vols. 1–4, Sage Publications, London.

[64] R.K. Milne (2001): Point processes and some related processes, *Handbook of Statistics*, 19, 599–641, C.R.Rao, ed., North Holland, Amsterdam.

[65] D.P. Miranker (1991), *TREAT: A New Efficient Match Algorithm for AI Production Systems*, Pitman, London.

[66] B. Misra, I. Prigogine and M. Courbage (1979), From deterministic dynamics to probabilistic descriptions, *Physica*, 98A, 1–26.

[67] R. Motwane and P. Raghavan (1995), *Randomized Algorithms*, Cambridge University Press, Cambridge.

[68] H. Muehlenbein (1991), Evolution in time and space-the parallel genetic algorithm, in *Foundations of Genetic algorithms*, Rawlins, G., ed., Morgan Kaufmann, San Mateo, California, 316–337.

[69] J.D. Murray (2003): *Mathematical Biology*, Springer, New York.

[70] V.K. Murthy and E.V. Krishnamurthy (1995): Probabilistic Parallel Programming based on multiset transformation, *Future Generation Computer Systems*, 11, 283–295.

[71] V.K. Murthy and E.V. Krishnamurthy, (2003): Entropy and Smart systems, *International Journal of Smart Engineering Systems*, 5, 481-499.

[72] K.M. Pacino (2002): Biomimicry of bacterial foraging for distributed optimization and control, *IEEE Control magazine*, 22(3), 52-68.

[73] C.H. Papadimitriou (1985): *Computational Complexity*, Addison Wesley, Reading, Mass.

[74] G. Paun (2003): Membrane computing, *Lecture Notes in Computer Science*, FCT 2003, 2751, 284–295, Springer Verlag, New York.

[75] D. Petrina, Ya., (1995): *Mathematical Foundations of Quantum Statistical Mechanics*, Kluwer Academic Publishers, London.

[76] I. Prigogine (1980): *From Being to Becoming*, W.H. Freeman, San Fransisco.

[77] N.G. Rambidi (1997): Biomolecular computer: roots and promises, *Biosystems*, *44*, 1–15.

[78] R.D. Reiss (1993): *A Course on Point processes*, Springer Verlag, New York.

[79] C.P. Robert and G. Casella (1999) *Monte Carlo Statistical Methods*, Springer Verlag.

[80] E. Rich, K. Knight (1991): *Artificial Intelligence*, McGraw Hill, New York.

[81] J.D. Scargle and G.J. Babu (2003), Point processes in astronomy, *Handbook of Statistics*, C.R. Rao, ed., 21, 795–825, North Holland, Amsterdam.

[82] R.J. Solomonoff (1995): The discovery of algorithmic probability: A guide for the programming of true creativity, *Lecture Notes in Computer Science*, *904*, 1–22.

[83] J.C. Spall (2003): *Introduction to Stochastic Search and Optimization*, Wiley-Interscience, New York.

[84] W.M. Spears, and K.A. De Jong (1993): An overview of evolutionary computation, *Machine Learning ECLML-93, Lecture Notes in Computer Science*, *667*, 442-459, Springer Verlag, New York.

[85] S. Stepney, J.A. Clark et al., (2003): Artificial Immune System and the grand challenges for non-classical computation, *Lecture Notes in Computer Science*, *2787*, 204–216, Springer Verlag, New York.

[86] D. Straub (1997): *Alternative Mathematical Theory of Nonequilibrium Phenomena*, Academic Press, New York.

[87] Y. Suzuki, et al., (2001): Artificial Life applications of a class of P systems: Abstract rewriting systems on Multisets, *Lecture Notes in Computer Science*, *2235*, 299–346, Springer Verlag, New York.

[88] A.M. Turing (1952): The chemical basis for morphogenesis, *Phil. Trans. Roy. Soc. London*, *237*, 37–79.

[89] W. Wayt Gibbs (2004): Synthetic life, *Scientific American*, *290*(5), 48–55.

[90] D. Whitley T. Starkweather (1990): Genitor: a distributed Genetic algorithm, *J. Experimental and Theoretical Artificial Intelligence*, *2*, 184–214.

[91] S. Wolfram (2002): *A New Kind of Science*, Wolfram Media Inc., Champaign, Ill.

[92] X. Yao, (2003): The evolution of evolutionary computation, *Lecture Notes in Artificial Intelligence*, *2773*, 19–20, Springer Verlag, New York.

[93] G. Yin, V. Krishnamurthy and C. Ion (2004): Regime Switching Stochastic Approximation Algorithms with application to adaptive discrete stochastic optimization, *SIAM Journal of Optimization*, *14*(4), 1187–1215.

[94] D.C.K. Yuen and B.A. MacDonald (2004): Theoretical considerations of multiple particle filters for simultaneous localization and map-building, *Lecture Notes in Computer Science*, *3213*, 203–209.

[95] K.-P. Zauner, M. Conrad (1996): Parallel computing with DNA: toward the Anti-Universal Machine, *Proc. PPSN-IV, Lecture Notes in Computer Science*, 1141, Springer Verlag, New York.

[96] W. Zhang and R. Korf (1996): A study of complexity transitions on the asymmetric travelling salesman problem, *Artificial Intelligence*, *81*, 223–239.

Chapter 4

EVOLUTIONARY PARADIGMS

Franciszek Seredynski
Polish-Japanese Institute of Information Technology and Polish
Academy of Sciences

Abstract

In recent years, evolutionary computation (EC) techniques have became one of the most popular heuristic search methods successively applied to solve complex research and real-life problems. This chapter presents an overview of the field of EC. Main concepts of biological evolution and some biological paradigms are shown, their influence on EC is discussed, and a general computational scheme currently used in EC is presented. The best recognized classes of EC algorithms are described, such as *Evolution Strategies, Genetic Algorithms, Genetic Programming, Evolutionary Programming*, and *Learning Classifier Systems*. However, the main emphasise is on the class of Genetic Algorithms (GAs). Mechanisms of controlling evolutionary process in GAs are discussed, the most known variants of GAs are presented, and current issues of development of GAs are considered.

1 EVOLUTION, LEARNING, AND EVOLUTIONARY COMPUTATION

1.1 Lamarckian Evolution

In the nineteenth century, several theories of biological evolution were proposed and three of them are used today to different degrees in evolutionary computing (EC). These are (e.g., [31,85,102]) *Lamarckian evolution, Darwinian evolution* (Darwin, 1859), and the theory proposed by Baldwin known as the *Baldwin effect* (Baldwin, 1896). Some other concepts introduced later, such as *species, niches*, or *coevolution* of species, are also used in EC.

One of the first concepts of evolution was the one proposed by J. B. Lamarck. He suggested that the experience of organisms during their lifetime—their ability of adaptation—may directly influence evolution over many generations. This meant that traits such as the development of some organs (or the degeneration of others) across individuals' lifetimes to make activity more efficient, or learned behaviors such as how to avoid preditors, could be passed on to offspring by inheritance alone, and the offspring would not need to learn these traits. He believed that after some number of generations, this process could lead to the emergence of new species.

Using the notion of the *phenotype* as the observed characteristics of an organism and the notion of the *genotype* as the actual genetic structure of the organism, one can see Lamarckian evolution as a mapping from the phenotype to the genotype, where environment and individual experience directly change the individual genetical makeup. While today Lamarckian evolution is not an accepted model of biological evolution, some research in the field of EC used this model and shown that the search process may converge to a local optimum [131] or that it can sometimes improve (e.g. [1,54]) the effectiveness of an evolutionary algorithm.

1.2   Darwinian Evolution

Today the best known evolutionary algorithms (EAs) are loosely based on simulated Darwinian evolution. Darwin's theory pointed out two main factors of an evolutionary process: *natural selection* and *genetic variation*. Natural selection, which is today briefly described as the principle of survival of the fittest, states that the individuals whose variations are better adapted to the environment have a greater probability of surviving and reproducing, and selection is the mechanism that reduces the number of less-adapted individuals. Shortly after the publication of Darwin's theory, Gregor Mendel discovered the genetic basis of inheritance, and later some scientists like Hugo de Vries developed the concept of genetic mutations. Research from *genetics* shows that genes determine individual characteristics and only genes are transmitted thorough generations. The genetic material of the organisms is the result only of a continual variation of individuals, with possible influences from environmental conditions.

In contrast to Lamarckian evolution, the driving force of Darwinian evolution is a mapping from the genotype to the phenotype. This means that the environment and genetic information determine characteristics of individuals. Today the EC community interprets Darwinian evolution as a life-cycle of some organisms, as presented in Figure 4.1.

It is assumed that a population $P(t) = \{x_1^t, \ldots, x_n^t\}$ consisting of n individuals of the same species begins its life-cycle in generation t, called also an iteration t. The individuals live in some environment where they get food, struggle with illnesses, and avoid predators. At the end of their lifetime, the fitness of each individual in the population is evaluated, and this fitness is the basis to apply in some way the principle of natural selection, which gives a higher chance of survival to more fit individuals. Next, for those members of the population that survived, genetic mechanisms are applied to reproduce them by creating new individuals (offspring, children) that inherit features of their parents. As a last step of the life-cycle of the current population, it is assumed that new members of the population replace partially or fully the old members, and they are considered as members of a new population that begins a new life-cycle, termed generation $t + 1$.

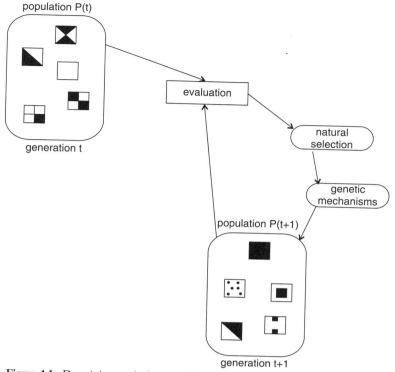

Figure 4.1. Darwinian evolution as a life-cycle of a population of individuals

1.3 Baldwin Effect

Baldwin suggested the idea that individual learning can change the course of evolution. The individual learning does not affect directly the genetic code of the individual, but individuals with increased learning capabilities may have higher probabilities to survive, which may result in an increasing number of their off-spring. If, e.g., a new predator appears [85] in the environment of some species, individuals capable of learning to avoid the predator will be favored. As the pro-portion of such individuals in the population grows, the population will be able to support a more diverse gene pool, allowing the evolutionary process to adapt more rapidly. This may in turn enable the standard evolutionary process to more quickly evolve a genetic trait to avoid the predator. This mechanism is called the *Baldwin effect*. Some results of applying the Baldwin effect in EC show [131] that the search process converges to the global optimum, while the search process without learning converges to local optimum. Also, positive effects of the application of the Baldwin effect were observed in experiments with evolving neural networks [57] and in modeling immune systems [96].

1.4 Species and Niches

The concepts of *species* and *niches* existing in biology and ecology, respec-tively, has been recently recognized by EC community (see section 3.3) to create new EAs. While the process of emerging species is not fully understood, there is some agreement concerning the main principles of the development of species [31]. Biological species are recognized more by their phenotypic differences than by genetic criteria. It is assumed that interbreeding may happen only between individuals of the same species. New traits in the population may be a result only of such processes as reproduction, mutation, gene flow, and genetic drift, which are realized on genes pool of the same species. It is believed that traits favored by the mechanism of natural selection may lead to the appearance of new species.

Members of the same species occupy an ecological region called a *niche*. The ecological niche is associated with a survival strategy of the species, the environment in which the species' relations to food and enemies are established.

1.5   Coevolution

The prevailing number of EAs is based on simulations of the life-cycle of a population of a single species. The open new area of EC are EAs based on a paradigm of *coevolution* of different species (see section 3.5). Coevolution can be defined [31] as a change in the genetic composition of one or more species in response to a genetic change in another, which happens during the evolutionary process as the result of interactions between different species. Different species can occupy different niches or share the same niches. They may compete for one or more resources. In the outcomes of coevolution, different forms of coexistence between species can be observed.

When coexistence has the form of *competition* between different species, the presence of each species is associated with reducing the growth of another species. Some kind of equilibrium between species can appear. When the relation between two species is based on *exploitation*, then the presence of one species stimulates the growth of the second species, while this second species inhibits the grow of the first. This form of coexistence is based on interaction between species having a character of either a *predator–prey* interaction, resulting in the extinction of one species, or a *host–parasite* interaction, leading to two coevolving species where extinction does not take place. Most of the predator–prey forms of interaction are based on the original model of Lotka and Voltera [75,127].

If the last form of coexistence, *cooperation*, takes place between species, then the presence of each species stimulates the growth of the other species.

1.6   Evolutionary Algorithms

Evolutionary Algorithms (EAs) are search, optimization, and learning techniques based on the Darwinian concept of natural evolution and biology. Today there are several well-established streams of EAs: Evolutionary Strategies (ESs), Genetic Algorithms (GAs), Genetic Programming (GP), Evolutionary Programming (EP) and Learning Classifier Systems (LCSs) [11,35,55,71,82,90,139,137,90]. A common accepted term referring to this type of computation is *evolutionary computation* (EC). Despite the differences between these streams, which will be shown later, they all use the basic notions and mechanisms of evolution and biology, such as (1) a population of individuals, (2) the fitness of an individual, (3) the

birth/death cycle of individuals, (4) inheritance, and (5) reproduction, variation, and selection/competition.

Figure 4.2 shows a general computational scheme for EAs. The scheme can
also be presented with the use of the following pseudocode:

0. Construct a representation (an individual of a population) of a solution for a
   given problem;

   $t \leftarrow 0$

1. Randomly create an initial population $P(t)$ of individuals
2. Evaluate fitness of all individuals in $P(t)$
3. If a **termination condition** is satisfied then go to Step 5 else go to Step 4
4. Apply selection and genetic operators in $P(t)$;

   4'. *Optionally*: apply competition mechanisms;

   4''. *Optionally*: apply local search algorithms;

   $t \leftarrow t + 1$; go to Step 2;

5. *Optionally*: If **restart** then go to Step 6, else go to Step 7
6. $t \leftarrow 0$;

   Generate modified initial population $P(t)$; go to Step 2

7. Consider the best individual from $P(t)$ as a solution of the problem.

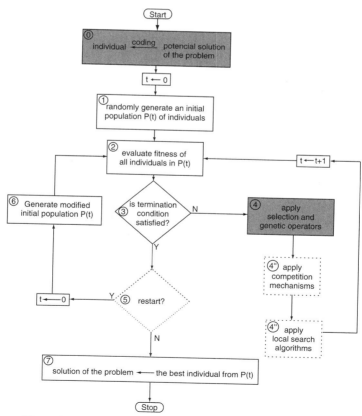

Figure 4.2. Computational scheme of an evolutionary algorithm

Steps 4', 4'', 5, and 6 are not used in classical versions of EAs. As a *termination condition*, a predefined number of generations of simulated evolutionary process is usually used, or some more complex stopping criteria can be applied, like, e.g., "stop if the fitness of the best individual in the population has not increased during the predefined number of generations."

The main differences between the streams of EAs lie in Steps 0 and 4 of the computational scheme of EAs. Let us consider the issue of a *representation* [107] of a solution of a problem to be solved (Step 0 in the computational scheme of ES). For this purpose, it is useful to consider two separate spaces (e.g., [9]): a solution space and a search space (see Figure 4.3). If we want, e.g., to design a car with specific features, then we can imagine a space of solutions of the problem (see Figure 4.3, left) as a set of potential solutions. A single actual solution is a collection of parameters of a desired construction and is called a *phenotype*. Some EAs search for a solution directly in a solution space, i.e., in the space of phenotypes. However, some other EAs search a solution indirectly in a search space, which is constructed by mapping to it objects from the solution space. A *genotype* is an object of the search space and represents a coded version of parameters of a corresponding phenotype from the solution space. Figure 4.3 (right) shows an example of a search space of genotypes used in GAs. A binary string is a representation of a genotype. Values of a single gene called *alleles* code parameters of searched solutions. A collection of genes is called a *chromosome*. Evolving individuals from the search space requires mapping genotypes into space of phenotypes to read correctly an actual quality of a solution.

ESs differs also in Step 4, where selection and genetic operators are applied. The differences are in the type of operator, the means of their construction, and the order of their application.

2   EVOLUTION STRATEGIES

Evolution Strategies (ESs) were independently developed by Rechenberg and Schwefel in the early 1960s in Germany as a method to solve practical optimiza-

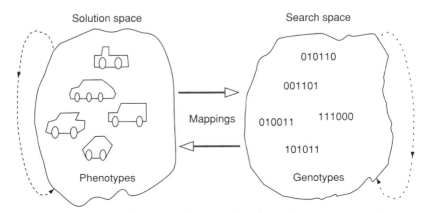

Figure 4.3. Solution space (phenotypes) and search space (genotypes)

tion problems in engineering. For continuous optimization problems, ES directly processes a real-valued n-dimensional vector $\mathbf{x}$ that is associated with the extremum of a function $F(\mathbf{x}) : R^n \rightarrow R$. It means that there is no process of coding (see Figure 4.2) of potential solutions (phenotypes in a solution space) to a problem into individuals of a population (genotypes in a search space) and that ES directly operates on phenotypes (see Figure 4.3).

A number of ESs have been developed (see, e.g., [61,104,113,90,10]). All of them are described using a specific notation, and in particular the following notation of parameters is used: μ—the size of parent population, λ—the size of offspring population, ρ—the size of family (parents) $(1 \leq \rho \leq \mu)$. An individual $\mathbf{v}$ is a pair of float-valued vectors $\mathbf{v} = (\mathbf{x}, \boldsymbol{\sigma})$, where $\mathbf{x} = (x_1, x_2, \ldots, x_n)$ is a point in a solution space, and $\boldsymbol{\sigma} = (\sigma_1, \sigma_2, \ldots, \sigma_n)$ is a vector of standard deviations. The earliest ES was based on a population consisting of one individual only, and was referred to as $(1 + 1)$ -*ES*.

2.1   The $(1 + 1)$ -*ES*

The $(1 + 1)$ -*ES* algorithm, also called *two-member* ES, is based on a simple mutation-selection scheme. An initial population at generation $t = 0$ consists of one parent $\mathbf{v}^t$. One offspring is created by an operator of *mutation*, which adds to components of the vector $\mathbf{x}^t$ normally distributed random numbers, i.e.,

$$x^{t+1} = x^t + N(0, \sigma), \tag{1}$$

where $N(0, \boldsymbol{\sigma})$ is a vector of normally distributed (isotropic Gaussian), independent random numbers with a mean of 0 and standard deviations $\boldsymbol{\sigma}$. An explanation for this operator is the biological observation that offspring are similar to their parents and that small changes are more likely than larger ones. It is possible to use other distributions [11] such as nonisotropic Gaussian or other continuous distributions, two-point distribution in binary search spaces, or "move operators" for combinatorial optimization problems.

When the population temporarily contains two individuals, the operator of *deterministic selection* is applied. The selection operator selects the better of the two individuals, which then moves to the next generation. The algorithm is continued until a termination condition is satisfied. One can notice that the evolution process is based mainly on the mutation operator.

While it can be proved that the algorithm converges to a global optimum when $\sigma_i = const$, the algorithm may get stuck after a certain number of generations. Rechenberg observed [104] that progress in evolution exists only for a small bandwidth (evolution window) of mutation strength. He proposed a statistical inference method called *1/5-rule* to control σ during the evolutionary process. The rule says that ϕ—a quotient of a number of successful mutations (which improved the fitness of individuals) to the total number of mutations—should be equal to 0.2: if a current value of ϕ is greater than 0.2, then the standard deviation σ associated with the operator of mutation should be increased, and when ϕ is less than 0.2, the σ should be decreased. Recently some other techniques using adaptation or self-adaptation and based on statistical inference or an evolutionary approach were proposed (see, e.g., [10,11]) to control σ.

2.2   The $(\mu + 1)$ -*ES*

The algorithm assumes an existing population consisting of μ individuals, where $\mu > 1$. Two individuals are selected randomly from the population to create one offspring by using an operator of *discrete recombination*. The offspring $(\mathbf{x}, \sigma)$ has components x_i and σ_i, which are randomly copied from parents. Next, as in $(1 + 1)$-ES, the operator of mutation is performed on the offspring. Finally, the operator of deterministic selection is applied, which removes from the population of the size $\mu + 1$ the least fit individual.

2.3   The $(\mu + \lambda)$ -*ES*

The $(\mu + \lambda)$-ES algorithm is a natural extension of the previous one. In the algorithm, μ parents (usually $\mu \leq \lambda$) produce λ offspring. Offspring are mutated, but the mutation operator is modified by introducing an additional level, where σ is controlled by the mutation operator, instead of the internal strategy handling σ (e.g., *1/5-rule*). If $(\mathbf{x}, \sigma)$ is an offspring obtained in the result of the recombination operator, then the two-level mutation operator converts it into an individual ($\mathbf{x}'$, σ') in the following way: first, the σ component of the individual is modified into σ': $\sigma' = \sigma e^{N(0, \Delta\sigma)}$, and next the component $\mathbf{x}$ of the individual is modified: $\mathbf{x}' = \mathbf{x} + N(0,\sigma')$, where $\Delta\sigma$ is a step-size meta-control parameter.

The temporary population of size $\mu + \lambda$ is next reduced by deterministic selection to μ best individuals. This kind of selection is called (+) selection. The algorithm can be recommended for the solution of combinatorial and discrete problems. In such cases, e.g., for the Traveling Salesman Problem (TSP), an individual is a permutation list containing a sequence of cities to be visited in predefined order, and permutation operators of mutation similar to those used in GAs are applied. Note that in all cases considered so far, ES algorithm parents survive until they are replaced by fittest offspring, and well-adapted individuals may survive forever. This feature may give rise to some disadvantages of the $(\mu + \lambda)$-ES, such as, e.g., getting stuck on a problem with an optimum that moves over time.

2.4   The (μ, λ) -*ES*

To avoid disadvantages associated with $(\mu + \lambda)$-ES, a modification of this algorithm known as (μ, λ) -*ES* was proposed. As in the previous algorithm, a μ-member population of parents produces λ offspring by means of recombination and mutation. However, the selection operator is applied only to the population of offspring, reducing it to μ parents of the next generation, and this kind of selection is called (,) selection. While the general computational scheme of ES is as shown in Figure 4.2, Step 4 of ES is presented in Figure 4.4 and contains a sequence of operators executed in the following order: recombination, mutation, and selection.

2.5   ES with Self-adaptation: $(1, \lambda) - \sigma\text{SA} - \text{ES}$

Observation and comparison of behavior of $(\mu + \lambda)$ and $(\mu, \lambda) - ES$ models show (e.g., [10,11]) that (1) if mutation strength is for some reason constant, then

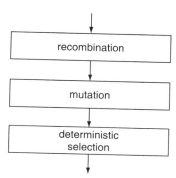

Figure 4.4. Order of selection and genetic operators applied in ESs

(,) strategies lead to a saturation behavior, and (2) if the mutation strength cannot be scaled down, the (+) strategy is always beneficent. Also, for both models, the existence of an evolution window was observed, with a value of mutation that provided evolutionary progress. This leads to the necessity of developing more general algorithms such as $(\mu \dot{+} \lambda) - ES$, where both strategies can be used, or $(\mu/\mu, \lambda) - ES$ with recombination.

In [114], *contemporary* ESs were proposed. These are referred as $(\mu, \kappa, \lambda, \rho) - ES$ and allow a gradual transition from either $(\mu, \lambda) - ES$ or $(\mu, \lambda) - ES$ by introducing a lifespan parameter κ—the upper limit for life span ($\kappa \geq 1$), $\lambda \geq \mu$ if $\kappa = 1$; and ρ—the number of ancestors for each descendant ($1 \leq \rho \leq \mu$). The (,) and (+) strategies can be used depending on the value of κ.

The more general solution for controlling mutation rate and its scalability are ESs with self-adaptation, such as, e.g., $(1, \lambda) - \sigma SA - ES$ [10,11]. Each individual in the algorithm includes object parameters and evolvable (*endogenous*) strategy parameters. Endogenous strategy parameters control the variation of the individual's object parameters by mutation. These are inherited together with the object parameters.

2.6 Advanced ES Techniques

A number of advanced ES techniques are currently under study [10,11]. The general $(\mu/\rho \dot{+} \lambda) - ES$ algorithm uses the μ/ρ recombination and both (,) and (+) strategies. The recombination is applied to ρ ($\rho \leq \mu$) parents. The ρ parents (also called a ρ-*family*) produce one offspring. If $\rho < \mu$, then the members of the ρ-family are chosen randomly from the set of μ parents, and if $\rho = \mu$, then all μ parents are involved in the process of creating a child. The recombination is applied to the object parameters and can be applied also to endogenous strategy parameters.

The Meta-ES (or hierarchically organized ES) $[\mu'/\rho' \dot{+} \lambda' (\mu_i/\rho_i \dot{+} \lambda_i)^\gamma] - ES$, $i = 1, 2, \ldots, \lambda'$, gives a possibility of mixed structural and parameter optimization. There are λ' populations in the algorithm, and γ (the exogenous strategy parameter) sets an isolation period time between them. The outer $[] - ES$ (structure evolution) improves parameters of the inner $() - ES$ (parameter evolution) populations.

Another approach to construct adaptive ES search techniques to control the variation operators (mutation, recombination) is based on use of statistical information. While the 1/5-rule (see, section 2.1) is the simplest example of such a technique, currently more advanced algorithms are used, such as the *Cumulative Step-size Adaptation* (CSA) algorithm or the *Covariance Matrix Adaptation* (CMA) algorithm.

3   GENETIC ALGORITHMS

Genetic Algorithms (GAs)[34, 46, 81] were originally developed in the late 1960s at the University of Michigan by John Holland and his team, who conducted their research on robust, adaptive systems. Later, GAs were refined by De Yong, Goldberg, Michalewicz, and many others. While the computational scheme of GAs is as shown in Figure 4.2, GAs distinctively differ in Steps 0 and 4 from the other EAs, in particular from ESs, in the following ways: (1) a search space of genotypes is used, and a binary string is a representation of a genotype, as shown in Figure 4.3 (Step 0 in Figure 4.2), and (2) the sequence of selection and genetic operators is usually, as shown in Figure 4.5, performed in the following order: *stochastic selection*, *crossover* (corresponding to operator *recombination* in ESs), and *mutation* (Step 4 in Figure 4.2).

Overviews concerning current issues on GAs can be found in [133, 55, 35].

3.1   Simple Genetic Algorithm

Selection and genetic operators of a Simple Genetic Algorithm (SGA) [46] have the following properties: (1) *proportional selection* is used, alternatively called a selection with a *roulette wheel*, (2) a *single-point crossover* is performed on each chromosome, with a probability p_c, and (3) a *single-bit mutation* is performed with a probability p_m. These selection and genetic operators are shown in Figure 4.6.

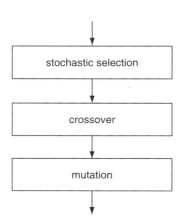

Figure 4.5. Order of selection and genetic operators applied in GAs

The proportional selection operator provides a method of stochastic selection that selects an individual i (to survive and have a chance for mating) with a probability

$$p_i = \frac{f_i}{\sum_{j=1}^{n} f_j} \qquad (2)$$

proportional to its fitness f_i, where n is the size of the population. Assuming that there are five individuals in a population with fitness 27, 45, 11, 5, and 32, respectively, one can construct the roulette wheel with five areas (see Figure 4.6a), each corresponding to a single individual, that are proportional to their probability of selection. A single spin of the wheel results in a selection of one individual corresponding to the area of the roulette pointed to by a pointer when the wheel stops spinning. The selection is completed after spinning the wheel five times.

Each individual that passes selection is chosen next, with a probability p_c for mating. A single-point crossover is performed on two parent individuals (see Figure 4.6b). A random position is chosen in both chromosomes, and two children individuals are produced after the exchange of genetic material. The choice of which parent contributes the bit for a given position of children can be also determined by an additional string called the *crossover mask*. For the crossover shown in Figure 4.6b, the crossover mask is 111100. The 1s and 0s of the crossover mask define the contribution of bits of parent $P1$ and parent $P2$, respectively, to the child $Ch1$. The second child uses the same mask but switches the roles of the two parents.

After crossover, a genetic mutation operator is performed. Each locus of each chromosome of the population is selected for mutation, with a probability p_m.

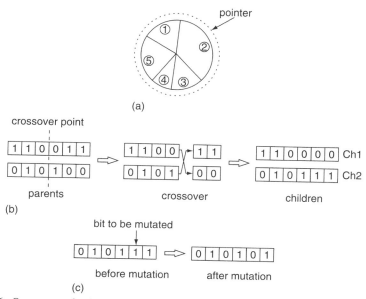

Figure 4.6. Operators of selection, crossover, and mutation used in SGA: (a) roulette wheel (proportional selection), (b) single-point crossover, (c) single-bit mutation

If mutation takes place, a corresponding bit switches its value either from $0 \rightarrow 1$ (see Figure 4.6c) or from $1 \rightarrow 0$.

SGA has good theoretical foundations [128], but most applications do not use it. The main problems with SGA are the following: (1) premature convergence to a local optimum, because of sensitivity of such parameters as population size or crossover/mutation rate, (2) strong convergence to the wrong solution for the problems known as *deceptive problems* [46], and (c) possible poor representation and poor operators for some problems. For these reasons, a number of extensions of SGA have been proposed, and for practical applications, customized/hybrid GAs with domain-dependent representations and operators are frequently designed.

3.2   Mechanisms to Control Evolutionary Process in GAs

Representations and Encoding

Representation is one of the key issues influencing the performance of EAs used as optimizers. As mentioned earlier, when the problem of optimization with EA use is considered, it is useful to consider two spaces: the phenotype space representing the original definition of the problem and the genotype space representing encoded solutions. The purpose of representation is to assign genotypes to corresponding phenotypes [102, 107], which is often called *genotype–phenotype mapping*. This mapping can be done in different ways. It influences the suitability of applied genetic operators and the performance of the evolutionary process.

The most common representation applied in GAs is a *binary* string used, e.g., in SGA. In some problems binary encoding is natural, e.g., for the 0-1 *knapsack* problem that is very well known in operational research. In such cases there is no distinction between genotype and phenotype spaces. The same result takes place when *continuous* encoding (similar to that used in ESs) with real-valued vectors is used for function optimization problems. For some discrete nonbinary problems, e.g., the *rotor stacking problem* [102], a discrete alphabet of higher cardinality might be appropriate.

One of the problems that may arise when the standard binary code is used is that adjacent genotypes may not have adjacent phenotypes. In such cases, the use of *Gray code* may be preferable and more effective. Some recent research [132, 133] shows that Gray encoding reduces the number of local optima, which is important for local search algorithms, and beats binary encoding in many test problems.

For some, problems (e.g., TSP, flowshop problem, multiprocessor scheduling), natural encoding is a *permutation* representation. For these problems, special crossover operators must be designed because the standard crossover operators usually fail to preserve the permutation. For other problems, e.g., *tree optimization problems*, a graph can be represented by its characteristic vector.

Incorporating problem-specific knowledge in the representation can increase [107] the GA performance. This can be done in particular by (1) considering specific properties of the optimal solutions, e.g., trees and stars, and (2) delivering to the population solutions that are similar to the optimal solution.

Currently, analytical models do not exist that describe the influence of representation on the performance of EAs, but there are some general recommendations [107]. Goldberg's recommendations [46] are based on (1) the principle of meaningful building blocks and (2) the principle of minimal alphabets, and are oriented on effective processing schemata in GAs. Radcliff [101] suggests that representation and operators cannot be considered separately from each other and makes some recommendations [116] on how to design representation-independent EAs. According to Palmer [92], (1) encoding should represent all possible phenotypes, and all possible individuals should be equally represented in the set of all possible genotypic individuals, (2) encoding should encode no infeasible solutions, should possesses locality and be adjusted to a set of genetic operators, and should minimize nonlinearities in fitness functions, and (3) decoding of the phenotype from the genotype should be easy.

One of the open issues in current research on representation in GAs concerns the use of redundant representation (see, e.g., [106]), where the number of genotypes is larger than the number of phenotypes.

Population Manipulation

Population size and the individual replacement strategy are very sensitive parameters [102, 55] of GAs. An analysis performed by Goldberg and his colleagues [48] suggested a linear dependence of population size on string length. However, some empirical results (see, e.g., [112]) show that population sizes as small as 30 are adequate in many cases, e.g., for binary-encoded problems, but for higher-cardinality alphabets, much larger populations are needed. For a minimum population size, a principle was suggested in [100] that every point in the search space should be reachable in the initial population by crossover operation only. Some reports also show (e.g., [2]) that including in the initial population some good-quality solution obtained from another metaheuristic can improve the performance of GAs but may also lead to premature convergence to a poor solution.

The most traditional individual replacement strategy used in GAs is a *generational* reproduction: a current population is completely replaced by offspring generated by selection and genetic operators. Such a replacement strategy is used in SGA and most GAs. De Yong proposed [34] a simple strategy called *elitism*, which ensures the survival of the best individual in the population, and the concept of *population overlaps*, which assumes replacing only a fraction G (*generation gap*) of the population in each generation. He also introduced a *crowding* operator, which specifies the number of individuals initially selected as candidates to be replaced by a newly generated offspring. A new offspring replaces the most similar individual, where the similarity measure can be, e.g., the *Hamming distance* between individuals.

The opposite strategy is assumed by *steady-state* reproduction. In each generation, only one or two individuals are created, which replace the worst individuals. This strategy can be modified [102] in such a way that candidates for replacement are chosen from those worse than the median. Another modification of this strategy, useful for optimization in dynamic environments [15], suggests replacing [125] the *oldest* instead of the worst individual but not replacing it [122] when it is currently the best in the population.

Selection

The selection operators used in GAs operate on the fitness of individuals. The mechanism of the *roulette wheel* used in SGA to implement *proportional selection* can be changed by introducing an *n*-armed spinner (*n* is the size of the population) [102] providing *stochastic universal selection,* an effective method of implementating proportional selection. The *scaling* problem associated with roulette-wheel selection—i.e., when values of individual fitness in subsequent generations become less distinguished and *selection pressure* becomes weaker—can be solved by a number of algorithms proposed in [46].

Ranking selection does not need scaling and is more efficient. It sorts individuals in each generation according to their decreasing/increasing fitness and assigns new values of selection probability. Selection probabilities assigned to ranked individuals can increase linearly or nonlinearly, creating in this way a *linear ranking* selection or a *nonlinear ranking* selection, respectively. A number of algorithms exist [4, 81] for assigning linear or nonlinear probabilities to ranked individuals. The algorithms provide a possibility for control of the selection pressure.

Another effective and simple selection operator is *tournament selection*. It requires choosing k individuals from a population (often $k = 2$), comparing their fitness, and selecting the most fit as the winner of the tournament. A variant of tournament selection is called *strict* tournament, and it has similar properties to ranking selection. To provide higher selection pressure, yet another version of tournament selection is used, which is called *soft* tournament. In this case, the winner of the selection is accepted with some predefined probability.

In *truncation selection*, some percentage of the best individuals of a population is selected, and parents from this selected subset only are chosen randomly for mating. A comparison and theoretical analysis of selection schemes can be found in [13].

Search Operators

Crossover

Two sources of bias exist [102] that can be exploited in GAs by crossover operators: *positional bias* and *distributional bias*. From this point of view, much empirical evidence supports the opinion that one-point crossover is not the best crossover construction. *Two-point crossover* and generally *multipoint crossover* are logical extensions of the one-point crossover. In the two-point crossover, offspring are created by substituting intermediate segments of one parent into the middle of the second parent string. The intermediate segment is represented in the crossover mask by a contiguous block of 1s with the borders of the segments created randomly. For the crossover mask 001110, two-point crossover will create offspring 110101 and 010010.

The crossover operator that removes any bias is *uniform crossover*. It combines bits sampled uniformly from two parents. For the crossover mask with random string of bits 101100, two identical offspring are created: 110000. When the mask is created using a Bernoulli distribution, this uniform crossover is referred as UX.

As presented above, crossover operators are suitable for problems with binary representation. However, for problems with permutation representation, they can produce infeasible solutions and therefore cannot be applied. For permutation problems such as TSP, sequencing, or scheduling, a number of nonlinear crossover operators have been constructed. Among these, the best known are (1) PMX (Partially Mapped Crossover), which exchanges a partial segment between parents, (2) CX (Cycle Crossover), which finds all mapping cycles between parents and next copies elements of the two parents to the offspring in corresponding positions, (3) OX (Order Crossover), which randomly selects several of the same elements in both parents and next makes exchanges between parents in those selected positions, (4) HUX crossover, a variant of uniform crossover in which exactly half the bits are exchanged, (5) the *edge recombination* crossover, and others [81]. Recently, the *edge assembly* crossover [89] was proposed and applied successfully for solving TSP problem for more than 3000 cities.

Mutation.

Mutation in GAs is usually considered as a secondary genetic operator. The purpose of mutation is to introduce some randomness into the search and to prevent the optimization process from getting stacked into local optima. Most variants of GAs apply mutation with a constant low rate, e.g., 0.005. Some research used higher mutation rates ranging from 0.001 up to 0.01, but it was found that higher mutation rates may transform the optimization process performed by the GA into a random search process. The appropriate value of the mutation rate of the GA for a given optimization problem is an open research issue.

The formula for the near optimal value of the probability of mutation p_m for a set of test functions was found experimentally [112] to be

$$p_m = \frac{1.7}{n\sqrt{l}}, \tag{3}$$

where n is the population size and l is the length of a chromosome. However, theoretical analysis conducted in [87] using the ONEMAX function shows that the optimal mutation rate for any unimodal binary function is approximated by the formula

$$p_m = \frac{1}{n}. \tag{4}$$

Results of research presented in [7] suggest that the mutation rate should change dynamically during the evolutionary searching process in the following way:

$$p_m(t) = (2 + \frac{l-2}{T-1}t)^{-1}, \tag{5}$$

where t is the current generation and T is the total number of generations. These results show that the mutation rate probability should change from an initial value of 1/2 to 1/*l*. In [91] it was shown that the value of optimal mutation rates in GAs differs according to whether recombination is used or not. A new mutation operator proposed in [22] and named *minimum-allele-reserve-keeper* ensures a minimum amount of each allele in each locus with the least possible amount of gene inversion. In [33], a nature-based mutation operator called the *frame-shift* is proposed.

A number of novel GAs with new mutation operators have been proposed recently. In [58], a *parental mutation GA* is proposed in which mutation occurs not only in offspring but also at the parental level. In [124], a novel genetic algorithm named the *Split Search GA* was proposed to fully utilize the mutation operator. Experimental results using this algorithm show that increasing the role of mutation in the evolutionary search may be beneficial.

Competition Mechanisms

A typical competition mechanism that can be applied (see Figure 4.2) is *elitism* (see section 3.2). It assumes always keeping the best individual in the current population to replace the worst individual in the next generation, if the individual in the next generation is worse that the best one in the previous population. Another competition mechanism is applying *truncation* selection (see section 3.2) to the population of parents and children.

Local Search Algorithms

Local search algorithms are based on the idea of iterative improvement of a current solutions and are often used in GAs. A number of local search algorithms have been developed. The best known of these are the following:

- *next ascent bit-climbing*: a *flip-list* describing the order of flipping of a selected chromosome is created, and (1) the bit of the chromosome corresponding to the actual position on the flip-list is flipped, (2) the flip is accepted if the new string has a higher fitness than before flipping, and (3) after flipping all bits according to the flip-list, the string with the highest fitness is considered to be a solution

- *steepest ascent bit-climbing*: as in the next-ascent algorithm, bits of a chromosome are flipped in a predefined sequence; however, after flipping a current bit according to the flip-list, (1) the remaining sequence of bits is sequentially flipped; for each new string, fitness is evaluated, and after that the flip is removed, (2) the bit (from the sequence of flipped bits) that obtained the highest fitness of the chromosome is accepted, and (c) the procedure is continued for the next bit from the flip-list

- *random bit-climbing (RBC)* [28]: similar to the next-ascent algorithm, but the flip-list is defined as a permutation of bits' positions in the chromosome; permutations are generated until no improving flips are found

- Lamarckian evolution [131] (see section 1.1)

- Baldwin effect [131] (see section 1.3)

- *(1+1)-ES* [37] (see section 2.1)

- *random mutation hill-climbing* or random local search [83, 129], which works like a simple standard evolutionary algorithm (EA), which is mutation based and works with population size 1 (referred to as *(1+1)-EA*) but with a different mutation operator

- *Random Walk with Uniform (or Normal) Distribution* [37]

Recently some other local search algorithms have been proposed. These are (1) the *quad search* algorithm [130], a specialized form of steepest ascent that operates on a reduced neighborhood and uses a Gray encoding, (2) *consecutive exchange* [23], a modification of the *2-Opt* heuristic combined with *tabu search*, and (3) a local search strategy based on the idea of iterative improvement of a solution via a series of neighbor moves until no improvement can be made [62].

Restart
One method to prevent GAs from prematurely converging to local optima before discovering a global solution is periodically restarting GA (see Figure 4.2) according to some restart strategy that can be either *static* or *dynamic* [42]. The restart can be performed with the use of a new seed. When GAs are applied in dynamic environments [15], the important issue is the content of the initial population of GA after restarting. The new initial randomly created population usually contains some percent of the population from the previous run.

3.3   Variants of GAs

SGA with *elitism*.
This is one of the simplest extensions of SGA (see Figure 4.2).

Hybrid GAs
This variant includes a wide range of GAs currently used or proposed that apply local search algorithms (see section, 3.2 and Figure 4.2).

Genitor [134]: A Steady-State GA
This algorithm uses rank-based selection and a *steady-state* strategy for reproduction. In each generation, only one (or two) individuals are created. Two-point crossover with reduced surrogates is used to produce a pair of children, and then one of them is selected randomly for mutation. The offspring displace the worst individual in the population.

CHC [36]
A fixed population of size 50 is used. Members of the population are paired randomly, and only parents sufficiently different are mated. As crossover, a reduced surrogate HUX is used, and no mutation is applied to offspring. Truncation selection is used and restart is applied, in which a new population is created by using the best solutions from the previous population with 30% mutation.

GENOCOP [81]
This variant is a GA-based hybridized evolutionary system used in several versions for solving constrained optimization problems. Real-numbers representation and a number of crossover and mutation operators are employed.

Breeder GA [88]
Breeder GA is an SGA-style algorithm developed to solve continuous problems directly, without the need for a discrete genotype. The parameters of the algorithm that control the evolutionary process are (1) population size, (2) mutation rate, and (3) selection intensity. Mutation is performed at a rate of $1/l$ (l is string length), which is claimed to be optimal. A form of truncation selection used in breeding is applied, namely, the best individual takes place in all matings.

GAVaPS [81]

Population size in the algorithm can vary during the evolutionary process, and it depends on the *age* of an individual, which is its parameter. An individual that exceeds its *lifetime* is eliminated from the population. The value of lifetime is determined at each generation, and it depends on some population statistics.

Niching Algorithms

In many applications such as multimodal or multiobjective optimization, dynamic function optimization, or machine learning, the important issues are (1) the maintenance of diversity of a population and converging to different solutions, and (2) preventing premature convergence when only one solution is required. These issues are addressed by *niching algorithms*. One of the first mechanisms introduced to support diversity is *crowding* [34], which assures that new individuals replace similar individuals in a population. The mechanism of *fitness sharing* [46] forces similar individuals to share their fitness. The *mating restriction mechanism* [32] prevent recombination between individuals in different niches. *Deterministic crowding* [76] modifies crowding by a mechanism of minimizing the sum of parent-to-offspring distance. Recently the mechanism of *probabilistic crowding* [80] was proposed and a concept of *niching pressure* was introduced [115] and used in the context of agent-based EC systems.

Multiobjective Evolutionary Algorithms

Multiobjective Evolutionary Algorithms (MOEAs) are one of the current trends in developing EAs. An excellent overview of current issues, algorithms, and existing systems in this area is presented in [24,25].

Evolutionary Optimization in Dynamic Environments

EAs for time-varying environments are the subject of current study within the area of EC. Different aspects of dynamic optimization problem are discussed in [15], along with evolutionary concepts to solve these problems.

Parallel GAs

See section 3.4.

Coevolutionary GAs

See section 3.5.

Competent GAs

See section 3.6.

3.4   Parallel GAs

Single-population Master-Slaves Model

The *single-population master-slaves model* [18,51,61] offers the easiest and simplest way of parallelizing single-population GAs and is presented in Figure 4.7a. A master-processor runs the GA performing selection and genetic operators.

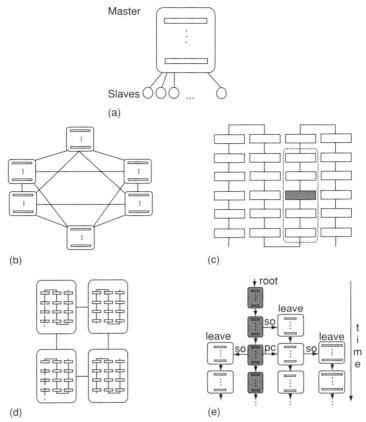

Figure 4.7. Types of parallel GAs: (a) single-population master-slaves model, (b) island model, (c) diffusion model (cellular GAs, fine-grained parallel GAs), (d) hierarchical parallel GAs, (e) hierarchical genetic strategy

The operation of fitness evaluation is parallelized. Due to this parallelization, the fitness of individuals in the population can be calculated *in parallel* by slave-processors, if a corresponding number of processors is available.

Island Model

In the *island model*, also called the *migration* or *multiple population model* [18,19,119,77,61], a population of GA is divided (see Figure 4.7b) into some number of subpopulations, called *islands* or *demes*, which are located on different, usually MIMD-class processors. Each subpopulation is a complete GA and evolves *in parallel*, exchanging periodically with other subpopulations the best individuals. A population structure composed of subpopulations is defined by the topology of a communication graph, which specifies a neighborhood for each subpopulation and serves to exchange individuals between neighbor subpopulations. Both the number of subpopulations and the topology of the communication graph are user-defined parameters.

Each subpopulation runs during some predefined number of generations called an *epoch*, in the same way as it is done in the one-population GA. After each *epoch*, neighbor subpopulations communicate by exchanging some number of their best individuals, which migrate and then are assimilated into subpopulations in such a way as to maintain a constant size of the subpopulation. The *island model* outperforms the one-population GA, providing a nearly linear speed-up when parameters of the algorithm are well tuned. Current modifications of the model introduce a variable subpopulation size of each island, different lengths of chromosomes in subpopulations, and asynchronous interactions between islands.

Diffusion Model

In the *diffusion model*, also called the *neighborhood, fine-grained,* or *cellular model* [18,119,97,61], each individual from a GA population is placed into a single processor, typically of the SIMD class. A neighborhood relation is set between all individuals by considering each individual as a node of a user-defined communication graph, which can be linear (see Figure 4.7c) or planar. Additionally, a local neighborhood of each individual is specified (see dotted area for the shadowed individual in Figure 4.7c). All selection and genetic operators are defined locally on such (possibly overlapping) neighborhoods. Different local mating strategies [50] and different neighborhood sizes and shapes [109] can be used.

Hierarchical Parallel GAs

Hierarchical parallel GAs are the result of an attempt to integrate the advantages of the master-slaves, island, and diffusion models [18]. In [73], the island model was combined with the diffusion model to solve the scheduling problem efficiently, and the idea of such a hierarchical model is presented in Figure 4.7d. A hierarchical model combining both the island and master-slaves models can be found in [46].

Hierarchical Genetic Strategy

Recently, in [110], a parallel GA referred as *hierarchical genetic strategy* has been proposed. It is a variable-length chromosome multipopulations GA model with a number of subpopulations changing dynamically in time (see Figure 4.7e). The algorithm starts from a single population (root) of chromosomes of the same length. During the evolutionary process, new subpopulations (leaves) can be created by using two operators: a *prefix comparison* operator and a *sprouting* operator. The root population can create a new subpopulation by using the sprouting operator when a promising individual appears, and this will be detected by the comparison operator. The new subpopulation always contains chromosomes with increased length and runs in parallel with the root subpopulations. The process of creating new subpopulations can be continued by both root and leaves subpopulations. The stop criterion of a running subpopulation is a stagnation of evolutionary process in a subpopulation.

3.5   Coevolutionary GAs

The idea of *coevolutionary algorithms* comes from the biological observation that coevolving some number of *species*, defined as collections of phenotypically similar individuals, is more realistic than simply evolving a population containing representatives of one species. So, instead of evolving a population (global or distributed) of similar individuals representing a global solution, it is more appropriate to coevolve subpopulations of individuals representing specific parts of the global solution. Four coevolutionary algorithms, presented below, depict specific lines of the research currently conducted in this area.

Coevolutionary Genetic Algorithms

The *Coevolutionary GA* [93,94], described in the context of the constraint satisfaction problem and the neural network optimization problem, is based on a *predator–prey* paradigm [56]. The algorithm operates on two subpopulations: the main subpopulation $P^1()$, containing individuals $\bar{x}$, and an additional subpopulation $P^2()$, containing individuals $\bar{y}$ coding some constraints, conditions, or simply test points concerning a solution $\bar{x}$. Both or only one subpopulation evolves to optimize a global function $f(\bar{x}, \bar{y})$.

A single act of coevolution is based on the independent selection of individuals $\bar{x}$ and $\bar{y}$ from subpopulations in order to encounter them and evaluate their $f(\bar{x}, \bar{y})$. The manner of assigning fitness to the individuals stems from the predator–prey relation: success of one individual should mean failure of the second one. During one generation, individuals are confronted a predefined number times. At the end of the evolution process, the best individual from $P^1()$ is considered to be a solution of a problem.

Cooperative Coevolutionary Genetic Algorithms

The *Cooperative Coevolutionary GA* (CCGA) has been proposed [98] in the context of a function optimization problem and is one of the best-known coevolutionary algorithms. Each of N variables x_i of the optimization problem is considered as a species with its own chromosome structure, and subpopulations for each variable are created. A global function $f(\bar{x})$ is an optimization criterion. To evaluate the fitness of an individual from a given subpopulation, it is necessary to communicate with selected individuals from all subpopulations.

In the initial generation ($t = 0$), individuals from a given subpopulation are matched with randomly chosen individuals from all other subpopulations. The fitness of each individual is evaluated, and the best individual in each subpopulation is found. The process of *cooperative coevolution* starts from the next generation ($t = 1$). For this purpose, in each generation a cycle of operations is repeated in a round-robin fashion. Only one current subpopulation is active in a cycle, while the other subpopulations are frozen. All individuals from the active subpopulation are matched with the best values of the frozen subpopulations. When the evolutionary process is completed, a composition of the best individuals from each subpopulation represents a solution of a problem. The algorithm has been successfully used in different applications (e.g., [65]).

Loosely Coupled Genetic Algorithms

The *Loosely Coupled GA* (LCGA) [117,119] is a coevolutionary algorithm exploring a paradigm of *competitive coevolution* and motivated by noncooperative models of game theory.

For an optimization problem described by some function (a global criterion) of N variables, local chromosome structures are defined for each variable, and local subpopulations are created for each of them. With each subpopulation, a locally defined function is associated, if possible, that describes relations between the variable associated with the population and other variables and subpopulations. This relation is described by a communication graph called a *graph of interaction*. While the purpose of each subpopulation is to optimize own local function under constraints defined by the influence of other local variables, an optimization of a global criterion is expected as the result of achieving by subpopulations some equilibrium, equivalent to a Nash equilibrium point in noncooperative models of game theory. If local functions are not known, the subpopulations directly optimize the global criterion.

The LCGA works in such a way that after initialization of subpopulations, each subpopulation performs in parallel the same set of operations in each generation. Each individual in a subpopulation is matched with randomly chosen individuals from subpopulations according to the interaction graph, and its fitness is calculated according to a local (or global) function assigned to a subpopulation. This matching is repeated for each individual a predefined number of times. Next, standard GA operators are applied locally in subpopulations. The evolutionary process is continued for a predefined number of generations until the system achieves the state of equilibrium equivalent to a Nash equilibrium point.

LCGAs have been applied to solve the *multiprocessor mapping and scheduling* problem [118] and the function optimization problem [120].

Coevolutionary Distributed Genetic Algorithm

The *Coevolutionary Distributed Genetic Algorithm* (CDGA), described [63,79] in the context of integrated manufacturing planning and scheduling, combines features of diffusion models with coevolutionary concepts. N coevolving species with their own genotypes represent partial solutions to a problem, e.g., plans for a particular component to be manufactured in a machine shop. The quality of each partial solution can be evaluated by a local function. The challenge is designing an optimal schedule to minimize the total cost of executing, in parallel, a set of plans represented in a given subpopulation. A global measure of the performance of a given plan, executed in parallel together with all plans from a population, is a global function taking into account a possible conflict in the use of common resources in the machine shop, and resolved by a local arbitrator.

A population of the CDGA is composed of subpopulations occupying a predefined number of cells arranged in some user-defined topological structure, e.g., a toroidal grid. In each cell, there are single representatives (individuals) of each species and also an individual representing an arbitrator. Only individuals of the same species from neighborhood subpopulations take part in the breeding.

Coevolution, i.e., an influence of another species on a given species, is taken into account by calculating a value of a global function. An offspring that is a result of breeding in a given local neighborhood replaces an individual in this neighborhood.

3.6   Competent GAs

A theoretical explanation of the work of SGA and a number of its extensions is based on the Holland's concept of *building blocks* (BBs) [46]. According to this concept, to find a global optimum of a problem GA requires identifying and grouping together partial solutions-schemata (BBs) with above-average value of fitness. For many hard optimization problems such as permutation problems, GAs and especially SGA have a problem doing that. These problems are frequently modeled by designing hard multimodal optimization problems called *deceptive problems* (see, e.g., [46,69])—combinations of *deceptive subfunctions* that mislead GAs to converge to a global optimum. Related to the deceptive problems is the *linkage problem*, which states that no fixed operators of recombination are able to provide mixing individuals with arbitrary codes to obtain proper BBs.

One possible solution to deceptive-like problems is to apply problem-specific coding and operators. A more general approach is to design more flexible and powerful GAs, which are referred to as *competent GAs* [47,69]. A number of competent GAs have been developed, and all of them fall into one of two classes [69]: (1) algorithms (the *fast messy GA* [49], the *gene expression messy GA* [5], and the *linkage learning GA* [52]) based on evolving the representation of solutions or adapting recombination operators, and (b) algorithms (the *extended compact GA* [53] and the *Bayesian optimization algorithm* (BOA) [95]) based on extracting information from a set of promising solutions.

Fast Messy GAs and OmeGA

In messy GAs [47,69], the genes (messy genes) of a chromosome (messy chromosome) are represented by a pair of number (*gene locus, gene value*). For example, the chromosome ((2 0)(4 1)(1 1)(3 0)(5 1)) represents the binary string 10011. Messy chromosomes may have different lengths, and they may be *underspecified* or *overspecified*. As in SGA, selection and genetic operators are used. However, the traditional crossover is replaced by *cut and split operators*.

In the fast messy GA (*fmGA*), two loops—outer and inner—are performed. In each cycle of the outer loop, three phases of the inner loop are performed. In the first, *initialization phase*, a population of individuals containing all possible genic and allelic combinations is created. In the second phase, called the *building-block filtering phase*, the population is filtered in such a way as to contain a high proportion of gene combinations belonging to BBs. In the *juxtapositional phase*, tournament selection and genetic operators are applied to form a high-quality solution.

To apply *fmGA* for solving permutation problems, the definition of messy gene is modified: a *random key* (real random number) instead of a binary digit (for gene value) is used, and such a extension of the algorithm is called *ordering messy GA* (*OmeGA*) [69]. For the TSP with five towns, a possible genotype may look like ((1, 0.26)(2, 0.22)(3, 0.72)(4, 0.19)(5, 0.20)). After sorting keys, the following phenotype is decoded: ((4, 0.19)(5, 0.20)(2, 0.22) (1, 0.26) (3, 0.72)), which corresponds to the permutation (4 5 2 1 3). One can easily check that the traditional single-point crossover operator will always generate feasible offspring when random key vectors are used.

Gene Expression Messy GA

The overall organization of the *gene expression messy GA* (*gemGA*) [5,47] is similar to that in *fmGA*, but the representation and the basic mechanism of the algorithm are different. The *gemGA* has no variable-length chromosomes and no under- or overspecification, and genes are stored in regular arrays. As was the case of *fmGA*, the main purpose of the *gemGA* is to determine the linkage groups, and the most important innovation of the algorithm to do that is the idea of *transcription* or *antimutation*. During the one-bit perturbation of each string, the perturbations that improve the structure are ignored and perturbations that degrade the structure are selected as possible linkage group candidates for subsequent processing.

3.6.3   Linkage Learning GA

In the *linkage learning GA* (*LLGA*) [52,47], the main concepts of the organization and the messy representation of chromosomes are similar to those in *fmGA* except that chromosomes have a circular structure. The main innovation of this messy algorithm is the mechanism called *probabilistic expression*, which reorders chromosomes in such a way as to detect important BBs in the encoding. The *extended compact GA* [53] is a more efficient version of the *LLGA*.

3.6.4   Bayesian Optimization Algorithm

The *Bayesian optimization algorithm* (*BOA*) [95,47] is a messy GA that identifies linkage-like data in a population through the construction of Bayesian networks. Traditional selection operators (truncation and tournament) are applied to choose a subset of solutions in the population that is used to construct a good Bayesian network modeling that subset. The probabilistic model corresponding to the structure of the Bayesian network is used next to generate a new population.

4   GENETIC PROGRAMMING

Genetic Programming (GP) is an evolutionary optimization technique proposed by Koza [70]. The general computational scheme of EA presented in Figure 4.2 is still valid for GP, but the main differences from other evolutionary techniques concern (1) a representation of a solution (Step 0), and (2) the order of selection and genetic operators (Step 4). Solutions are represented by trees (see Figure 4.8), which provide a flexible way of describing computer programs in

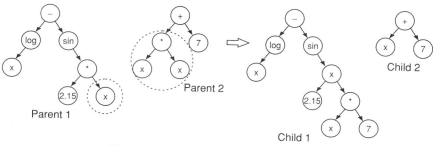

Figure 4.8. Individuals and crossover in GP

LISP language, functions, or variable length structures. To represent a tree in GP, a potential solution of a problem and a set of *functions* and *terminals* corresponding to a given problem domain must be provided by a user. For the individuals represented in Figure 4.8, the set of functions is $F = \{ +, *, log, sin\}$ and the set of terminals is $T = \{2.15, 7, x\}$. Two individuals, *parent1* and *parent2*, represent the expressions $log (x) - sin(2.15 * x)$ and $x^2 + 7$, respectively. After calculation of fitness of each individual, selection and genetic operators are applied. Figure 4.9 shows the order of application of the operators. Members of a new generation are created either by a selection operator with a probability p_s or by a crossover operator with a probability p_c or by a mutation operator with a probability p_m ($p_s + p_c + p_m = 1$). A crossover operator creates offspring by exchanging subtrees in parents, as shown in Figure 4.8.

Advanced GP issues concern developing *automatically defined functions* and specialized operators such as *permutation, editing*, or *encapsulation* [71,72]. One

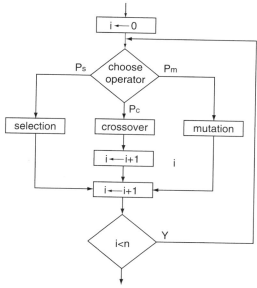

Figure 4.9. Order of selection and genetic operators used in GP

of the research issues concerns developing methodologies to reduce the search space and increase search efficiency. *Context-Free Grammar-based GP*, or *Constrained GP* [66], belongs to some proposed methodologies for automatic processing of additional constraints. Recently [67], a methodology using automatically adapting GP representation has been proposed. GP techniques have been recently used to solve problems of classification and pattern recognition, data mining, forecasting, programming parallel computers and cellular automata, synthesis of analog circuits, and many others.

5   EVOLUTIONARY PROGRAMMING

Evolutionary Programming (EP) is another evolutionary technique developed by Fogel and co-workers [38]. It uses finite state machines (FSMs) as a representation of solutions (see Step 0 in Figure 4.2) in a population of individuals. Surprisingly, it does not use a crossover operator but only mutation and stochastic selection, as shown in Figure 4.10. In its standard version, μ parents create by Gaussian mutation μ offspring, and tournament selection is usually applied. The basic cycle of EP is similar to $(\mu + \mu) - ES$. EP has been used as an approach to artificial intelligence [40] and to combinatorial optimization problems [39]. Recently [140], in the context of multimodal function optimization, *fast EP* has been proposed by introducing a new mutation operator based on Cauchy random numbers. Currently [41], a *meta EP* type of EP is used with multiple mutation operators and is built in to individual parameters to allow self-adaptation.

6   LEARNING CLASSIFIER SYSTEMS

Learning Classifier Systems (LCSs) are a class of rule-based learning machines in which rules are generated and modified by GA [14,46]. Two approaches to LCSs are known: the Pittsburgh approach (see, e.g., [3]) and, much more popular, the Michigan approach. An LCS maintains a population of production rules called *classifiers*. Each rule consists of two parts: a condition part and an action part. The condition part is built using the ternary alphabet {0, 1, #}, where the # symbol matches both 0 and 1. If the condition part of a classifier matches the input sent from the environment (defined by an application), the action part is executed. If more rules match an input from the environment a

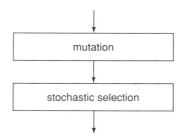

Figure 4.10. Order of selection and genetic operators used in EP

conflict resolution algorithm should be performed. Classifiers interacting with the environment receive *rewards* and their fitness is updated, usually by use of the *bucket brigade* algorithm in classical LCSs. Periodically, GA is applied to produce new rules, but only a small amount of the population is changed during one generation.

Classical LCSs [14,46] appeared from the simplification of Holland's initial work [59] and have been successfully applied in many areas, in particular for data mining (e.g., [60]) and complex control problems (e.g., [122]). In their implementation, a direct reward allocation scheme was used, which was problematic when applied to complex delayed reward tasks [8]. First strength-based ZCSs [135] and sometime later an extended classifier system (XCS) [136] were proposed as a solution to problems encountered in classical strength-based LCSs, and most current research and development is focused on this class of LCSs (e.g., [17,30,137]).

Figure 4.11 shows a simplified version of XCS. It consists of a number of classifiers sets: the *population set* [P] of all classifiers (initially empty); the *match set* [M]—the set of classifiers whose conditions match the current environmental input; and the *action set* [A]—the set of classifiers whose actions will be send to the environment. For a classifier, in addition to the condition and action parts and fitness, some other parameters are specified, such as *prediction p, error ε,* and fitness *F*. All these parameters are modified by the system predictions with the use of learning techniques. The action of a classifier is chosen based on the predicted payoffs of the matching rules. GA is applied not to the whole population of rules

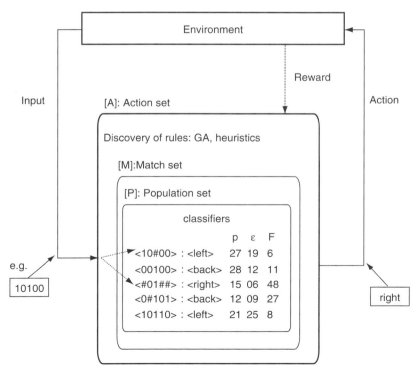

Figure 4.11. Concept of XCS learning classifier system

but only to rules from the *action set*. The wheel roulette or tournament selection and genetic operators of crossover and mutation are applied. A pair of offspring is added to the population [P] and replaces two other classifiers from this population.

Recently (e.g., [16,45,123]), Anticipatory Learning Classifier Systems (ALCSs) have emerged in which model-based reinforcement learning is used and, instead of GAs, heuristics are used for improvement of rules.

7   CONCLUSIONS

In this chapter, an overview of the field of EC has been presented. The main emphasis has been on genetic algorithms, the most popular class of EC. However, other important classes of EC were also presented, such as evolution strategies, genetic programming, evolutionary programming, and learning classifier systems. The purpose of the overview has been to present the current state of the field of EC and to discuss the most promising directions of developments in the field.

The EC is a relatively young research area in which the main stream of research is oriented toward experimentation. Despite this emerging state of the field, EC has already proved its potential in solving many theoretical and practical problems. Techniques of EC have been successfully applied to solve, in particular, such commercial problems as [29] cellular telephone tower placement, optical fiber network design, a securities trading system, or process scheduling.

While the theory of EC is still under development, some advances in building such a theory can be noted [102,128]. The *no free lunch theorem* [138] shows that the performance of all search metaheuristics and algorithms averaged over all possible functions is the same if they satisfy certain conditions. The cumulative effects of selection, crossover and mutation operators on evolutionary processes can be studied by designing *Markov chain* models. Properties of GAs can be rigorously proven by the *exact dynamical system model*, covering in particular the original *schema theorem*, and GA dynamics can be approximated by the *statistical mechanics* approach. The concept of *landscape* and some methodologies (e.g., Walsh representation) can be used to predict the performance of GA for solving some problems.

The well-established field of EC serves also as a platform for development of new population-based search algorithms. *Differential evolution* (e.g., [99]), *memetic algorithms* (e.g., [86]), *cultural algorithms* [105], or *probabilistic incremental program evolution* [108] are examples of such search algorithms that are tightly coupled with EC. *Artificial immune systems* (e.g., [31, 64]) and *particle swarm optimization* (e.g., [12,68]) represent search algorithms that are based on new paradigms, but their intersection with evolutionary concepts is visible.

REFERENCES

[1] D. Ackley, M. Litman (1994): A case for Lamarckian evolution. In: *Langton C (ed) Artificial Life III*, Reading, MA, Addison Wesley.

[2] R. K. Ahuja, J. B. Orlin (1997): Developing fitter GAs. *Inform J. Computing*, 9: 251–253.

[3] J. Bacardit, J. M. Garrel (2003): Evolving multiple discretizations with adaptive intervals for a Pittsburgh rule-based learning classifier system. In: [21]: 1818–1831.

[4] T. Bäck, D. B. Fogel, Z. Michalewicz (eds) (1997): *Handbook of Evolutionary Computation*, IOP Publishing Ltd. and Oxford University Press.

[5] S. Bandyopadhyay, H. Kargupta, G. Wang (1998): Revisiting the GEMGA: scalable evolutionary optimization through linkage learning. *Proc. of the Fourth Int. Conf. on Evolutionary Computation*: pp. 603–608.

[6] W. Banzhaf, et al. (eds) *Proc. of the Genetic and Evolutionary Computation Conference GECCO'99*, Morgan Kaufmann Publishers.

[7] T. Bäck, M. Schütz (1996): Intelligent mutation rate control in canonical genetic algorithms. In: Ras Z W, Michalewicz M (eds) *Foundations of Intelligent Systems*, Springer, *LNAI 1079*: 158-167.

[8] A. Barry (2003): Limits in long path learning with XCS. In: [21]: 1832–1843.

[9] P. J. Bentley, D. W. Corne (eds.)(2002): *Creative Evolutionary Systems*, Morgan Kaufmann.

[10] H. Beyer -G (2001): The theory of evolution strategies, *Natural Computing Series*, Springer, Heidelberg.

[11] H. Beyer -G (2003): Introduction to evolution strategies. In: [44]: 384–426.

[12] T. M. Blackwell (2003): Swarms in dynamic environments. In [20]: 1–12.

[13] T. Blickle, L. Thiele (1996): A comparison of selection schemes used in evolutionary algorithms. *Evolutionary Computation*, 4: 361–394.

[14] L. B. Booker, D. E. Goldberg, J. H. Holland (1989): Classifier systems and genetic algorithms. *Artificial Intelligence 40*: 235–282.

[15] J. Branke (2002): *Evolutionary Optimization in Dynamic Environments*, Kluwer Academic Publishers.

[16] M. V. Butz (2002): Biasing exploration in an anticipatory learning classifier system. In: Lanzi et al. (eds) *Advances in Learning Classifier Systems*, LNAI 2321, Springer: 3–22.

[17] M. V. Butz, K. Sastry, D. E. Goldberg (2003): Tournament selection: stable fitness pressure in XCS. In: [21]: 1857–1869.

[18] E. Cantu-Paz (2003): Parallel genetic algorithms. In: [44]: 241–257.

[19] E. Cantu-Paz (1999): Topologies, migration rates, and multi-population parallel genetic algorithms. In: [6]: 91–98.

[20] E. Cantu-Paz et al. (eds) (2003): Genetic and Evolutionary Computation-GECCO 2003, Part I, LNCS 2723, Springer.

[21] E. Cantu-Paz et al. (eds) (2003): Genetic and Evolutionary Computation-GECCO 2003, Part II, LNCS 2724, Springer.

[22] Z. S. H. Chan, H. W. Ngan, A. B. Rad (1999): Minimum-allele-reserve-keeper (MARK): a fast and effective mutation scheme for genetic algorithm. In: [6], *1*: 106–113.

[23] H. Choe, S-S. Choi, B-R. Moon (2003): A hybrid genetic algorithm for hexagonal tortoise problem. In: [20]: 850–861.

[24] C. A. Coello Coello (1999): A comprehensive survey of evolutionary-based multiobjective optimization techniques. *Knowledge and Information Systems 1*(3):269–308.

[25] C. A. Coello Coello, D. A. Van Veldhuizen, G. B. Lamont (2002): Evolutionary Algorithms for Solving Multi-objective Problems. Kluwer Academic.

[26] D. Corn, M. Dorigo, F. Glover (eds) (1999): New Ideas in Optimization. McGraw-Hill, London, 1999.

[27] Y. Davidor, H-P. Schwefel, R. Manner (eds) (1994): Parallel Problem Solving from Nature—PPSN III, LNCS 866, Springer.

[28] L. Davis (1991): Bit-climbing, representational bias, and test suite design. In: L. Booker, R. Belew (eds) *Proc. of the 4th Int. Conf. on GAs*, Morgan Kaufmann: 18–23.

[29] L. D. Davis (1999): Commercial applications of evolutionary computation: some case studies. In: [43]: 38–51.

[30] D. Dawson (2003): Improving performance in size-constrained extended classifier systems. In: [21]: 1870–1881.

[31] L. N. De Castro, J. Timmis (2002): Artificial Immune Systems: A New Computational Intelligence Approach, Springer.

[32] K. Deb, D. E. Goldberg (1989): An investigation on niche and species formation in genetic function optimization. In: Schaffer J D et al. (eds) *Proc. of the Third Int. Conf. on Genetic Algorithms*. Morgan Kaufmann Publishers: pp. 42–50.

[33] I. De Falco, A. Iazzetta, E. Tarantino (1999): Towards a simulation of natural mutation. In: [6], *1*: 156–163.

[34] K. De Jong (1975): An Analysis of the Behavior of a Class of Genetic Adaptive Systems. Doctoral dissertation, University of Michigan, Ann Arbor, Michigan.

[35] K. De Jong (2003): Evolutionary computation: a unified approach. In: [44]: 644–652.

[36] L. J. Eshelman (1991): The CHC adaptive search algorithm: how to have safe search when engaging in nontraditional genetic recombination. In: G. J. E. Rawlins (ed) Foundations of Genetic Algorithms, Morgan Kaufmann, San Mateo, CA: 265–283.

[37] F. P. Espinoza, B. S. Minsker, D. E. Goldberg (2003): Performance evaluation and population reduction for a self adaptive hybrid genetic algorithm (SAHGA). In: [20]: 922–933.

[38] L. J. Fogel, A. J. Owens, M. J. Walsh (1966): Artificial Intelligence Through Simulated Evolution. John Wiley, Chichister, UK.

[39] D. B. Fogel (1993): Applying evolutionary programming to selected traveling salesman problems. *Cybern. Syst.*, *24*: 27–36.

[40] D. B. Fogel (1995): Evolutionary Computation. Towards a New Philosophy of Machine Intelligence, IEEE Press.

[41] G. B. Fogel, K. Chellapilla (1999): Simulated sequencing by hybridization using evolutionary programming. In: *Proc. of the 1999 Congress on Evolutionary Computation*, *1*: 463–469.

[42] A. S. Fukunaga (1998): Restart scheduling for genetic algorithms. In: A. E. Eiben et al.(eds) Parallel Problem Solving from Nature—PPSN V, Springer, LNCS *1498*: 357–366.

[43] GECCO-1999: 1999 Genetic and Evolutionary Computation Conference. Tutorial Program. Orlando, Florida, July 14, 1999.

[44] GECCO-2003: 2003 Genetic and Evolutionary Computation Conference. Tutorial Program. Chicago, Illinois, July 13, 2003.

[45] P. Gerard, O. Sigaud (2003): Designing efficient exploration with MACS: modules and function approximation. In: [21]: 1882–1893.

[46] D. E. Goldberg (1989): Genetic Algorithms in Search, Optimization, and Machine Learning, Addison-Wesley, Reading, Massachusets.

[47] D. E. Goldberg (2002): The Design of Innovation. Lessons from and for Competent Genetic Algorithms. Kluwer Academic Publishers, Boston/ Dordrecht/London.

[48] D. E. Goldberg, K. Deb, J. H. Clark (1992): Genetic algorithms, noise and the sizing of population. *Complex Systems*, 6: 333–362.

[49] D. E. Goldberg, K. Deb, H. Kargupta, G. Harik (1993): Rapid, accurate optimization of difficult problems using fast messy genetic algorithms. *Proc. of the Fifth Int. Conf. on Genetic Algorithms*: 56–64.

[50] M. Gorges-Schleuter (1992): Comparison of local mating strategies in massively parallel genetic algorithms. In: [78]: 553–562.

[51] J. Grefenstette (1997): Efficient implementation of algorithms. In: [4]: E2.1:1–E2.1:6.

[52] G. R. Harik (1997): Learning gene linkage to efficiently solve problems of bounded difficulty using genetic algorithms. Unpublished doctoral dissertation, University of Michigan, Ann Arbor, also IlliGAL Report No. 97005.

[53] G. R. Harik (1999): Linkage Learning via Probabilistic Modeling in the ECGA. IlliGAL Report No. 99010, Urbana, IL, University of Illinois at Urbana-Champaign.

[54] W. Hart , R. Belew (1995): Optimization with genetic algorithm hybrids that use local search. In: R. Below and M. Mitchell (eds.) Adaptive Individuals in Evolving Populations: Models and Algorithms, Reading, MA, Addison Wesley.

[55] R. Heckendorn (2003): An introduction to genetic algorithms: theory and practice. In: [44]: 225–240.

[56] W. D. Hillis (1992): Co-evolving parasites improve simulated evolution as an optimization procedure. In: C. G. Langton et al. (eds) Artificial Life II. Addison-Wesley.

[57] G. E. Hinton, S. J. Nowlan (1987): How learning can guide evolution. *Complex Systems*, *1*: 495–502.

[58] T. P. Hoehn, C. C. Pettey (1999): Parental and cyclic-rate mutation in genetic algorithms: an initial investigation. In: [6], *1*: 297–304.

[59] J. H. Holland (1985): Properties of the bucket brigade algorithm. In: J. J. Grefenstette (ed) *Proc. of the 1st Int. Conf. on Genetic Algorithms and Their Applications*: 1–7.

[60] J. H. Holmes (1996): A genetics-based machine learning approach to knowledge discovery in clinical data. J. American Medical Informatics Association Supplement.

[61] F. Hoffmeister, T. Bäck (1992): Genetic Algorithms and Evolution Strategies: Similarities and Differences. Technical Report No SYS-1/92, University of Dortmund.

[62] G. Huang , A. Lim (2003): Designing a hybrid genetic algorithm for the linear ordering problem. In: [20]: 1053–1064.

[63] P. Husbands (1994): Distributed coevolutionary genetic algorithms for multi-criteria and multi-constraint optimization. In: T. C. Fogarty (ed) Evolutionary Computing, LNCS 865, Springer: 150–165.

[64] IEEE Trans. on Evolutionary Computation (2002). Special issue on artificial immune systems, *6*, 3(1).

[65] A. Iorio, X. Li (2002): Parameter control within a co-operative co-evolutionary genetic algorithm. In: M. Guervos et al. (eds) *Proc. of the Seventh Conf. on Parallel Problem Solving from Nature (PPSN VII)*, Springer: pp. 247–256.

[66] C. Z. Janikow (1996): A methodology for processing problem constraints in genetic programming. *Computers and Mathematics with Applications*, vol. 32, No 8: 97–113.

[67] C. Z. Janikow, R. A. Deshpande (2003): Adaptation of representation in GP. In: C. H. Dagli et al. (eds) *Smart Engineering System Design*, *13*: 45–50.

[68] J. Kennedy, R. C. Eberhart (1999): The particle swarm: social adaptation in information-processing systems. In: [26]: 379–387.

[69] D. Knjazew (2002): OmeGA. A Competent Genetic Algorithm for Solving Permutation and Scheduling Problems. Kluwer Academic Publishers, Boston/Dordrecht/London.

[70] J. R. Koza (1992): Genetic programming: on the programming of computers by natural selection. MIT Press, Cambridge, MA.

[71] J. R .Koza (2003): Introduction to genetic programming. In: [44]: 1–34.

[72] W. B. Langdon , R. Poli (2003): Foundations of genetic programming. In: [44]: 53–105.

[73] S. -C. Lin, E. D. Goodman, W. F. Punch, III (1997): Investigating parallel genetic algorithms on job shop scheduling problems. In: Evolutionary Programming VI, LNCS 1213, Springer: 383–393.

[74] J. Lis, A. E. Eiben (1996): A multi-sexual genetic algorithm for multiobjective optimization. In: T. Fukuda, T. Furuhashi (eds) *Proc. of the 1996 Int. Conf. on Evolutionary Computation*. IEEE: 59–64.

[75] A. J. Lotka (1925), Elements of Physical Biology, Williams and Wilkins, Baltimore.

[76] S. W. Mahfoud (1992): Crowding and preselection revisited. In: [78]: 27–36.

[77] W. N. Martin, J. Lienig, J. P. Cohoon (1997): Island (migration) models: evolutionary algorithms based on punctuated equlibria. In: [4]: C6.3:1–C6.3:16.

[78] R. Männer, B. Manderick (eds) (1992): Parallel Problem Solving from Nature, 2. North-Holland.

[79] M. McIlhagga , P. Husbands, R. Ives (1996): A comparison of optimization techniques for integrating manufacturing, planning and scheduling. In: [126]: 604–613.

[80] O. J. Mengshoel, D. E. Goldberg (1999): Probabilistic crowding: deterministic crowding with probabilistic replacement. In: [6]: 409–416.

[81] Z. Michalewicz (1996): Genetic Algorithms + Data Structures = Evolution Programs, Springer-Verlag, Berlin.

[82] Z. Michalewicz (1995): Evolutionary computation: an overview. In: J. Komorowski (eds) *Proc. of the 8th Scandinavian Conf. on Artificial Intelligence*. IOS Press, *28*: 322–337.

[83] M. Mitchell, J. H. Holland, S. Forrest (1994): When will a genetic algorithm outperform hill climbing. In: J. D. Cowan et al. (eds) Advances in Neural Information Processing Systems, vol. 6, Morgan Kaufmann: 51–58.

[84] M. Mitchel (1996): An Introduction to Genetic Algorithms. The MIT Press, Cambridge Massachusetts.

[85] T. M. Mitchell (1997): Machine Learning. McGraw-Hill.

[86] P. Moscato (1999): Memetic algorithms: a short introduction. In: [26]: 219–244.

[87] H. Mühlenbein (1992): How genetic algorithms really work I. Mutation and hillclimbing. In: [78]: 15–25.

[88] H. Mühlenbein, D. Schlierkamp-Voosen (1994): The science of breeding and its application to the breeder genetic algorithm. *Evolutionary Computation*, *1*: 335–360.

[89] Y. Nagata, S. Kobayashi (1997): Edge assembly crossover: a high-power genetic algorithm for the traveling salesman problem. In: T. Bäck (ed) Proc. of 7th Int. Conf. on Genetic Algorithms, Morgan Kaufmann, San Francisco, CA: 450–457.

[90] V. Nissen, J. Biethahn (1995): An introduction to evolutionary algorithms. In: J. Biethahn and V. Nissen (eds) Evolutionary Algorithms in Management Applications, Springer: 3–97.

[91] G. Ochoa, I. Harvey, H. Buxton (1999): On recombination and optimal mutation rates. In: [6], *1*: 488–496.

[92] C. C. Palmer (1994): An Approach to a Problem in Network Design using Genetic Algorithms. Unpublished Ph.D. thesis, Polytechnic University, Troy, NY.

[93] J. Paredis (1994): Co-evolutionary constraint satisfaction. In: [27]: 46–55.

[94] J. Paredis (1996): Coevolutionary life-time learning. In: [126]: 72–80.

[95] M. Pelikan, D. E. Goldberg, E. Cantu-Paz (1999): BOA: The Bayesian optimization algorithm. In: [6]: 525–532.

[96] A. S. Perelson, R. Hightower, S. Forrest (1996): Evolution and somatic learning in V-Region genes. *Research in Immunology*, *147*: 202–208.

[97] C. C. Pettey (1997): Diffusion (cellular) models. In: [4]: C6.4:1–C6.4:6.

[98] M. A. Potter, K. A. De Yong (1994): A cooperative coevolutionary approach to function optimization. In: [27]: 249–257.

[99] K. V. Price (1999) An introduction to differential evolution. In: [26]: 79–108.

[100] C. R. Reeves (ed) (1993): Modern Heuristics Techniques for Combinatorial Problems. Blackwell Scientific, Oxford, UK.

[101] N. Radcliffe (1992), Non-linear genetic representations. In: [78]: 259–268.

[102] C. R. Reeves, J. E. Rowe (2003): Genetic Algorithms: Principle and Perspectives: A Guide to GA Theory. Kluwer Academic Publishers.

[103] S. Ronald (1997): Robust encoding in genetic algorithms: a survey of encoding issues. In: *Proc. of the Forth Int. Conf. on Evolutionary Computation*, Piscataway, NJ, IEEE: 43–48.

[104] I. Rechenberg (1994): Evolutionsstrategie. Frommann-Holzboog Verlag, Stuttgart.

[105] R. G. Reynolds (1999): Cultural algorithms: theory and applications. In: [26]: 367–377.

[106] F. Rothlauf (2003): Population sizing for the redundant trivial voting mapping. In: [21]: 1307–1319.

[107] F. Rothlauf (2003): Representations for genetic and evolutionary algorithms. In: [44]: 203–224.

[108] R. Salustowicz, J. Schmidhuber (1999): From probabilities to programs with probabilistic incremental program evolution. In: [26]: 433–450.

[109] J. Sarma, K. A. De Jong (1996): An analysis of the effects of neighborhood size and shape on local selection algorithms. In: [126]: 236–244.

[110] R. Schaefer, J. Kolodziej (2003): Genetic search reinforced by the population hierarchy. In: K. A. De Jong, R. Poli, J. E. Rove (eds) Foundations of Genetic Algorithms 7, Morgan Kaufmann: 383–399.

[111] J. D. Schaffer (ed)(1989): *Proc. of 3rd Int. Conf. on Genetic Algorithms*, Morgan-Kaufmann, San Mateo, CA.

[112] J. D. Schaffer, R. A. Caruana, L. J. Eshelman, R. Das (1989): A study of control parameters affecting online performance of genetic algorithms for function optimization. In: [111]: 51–60.

[113] H -P. Schwefel (1995): Evolution and Optimum Seeking, Wiley, New York.

[114] H -P. Schwefel, C. Rudolph (1995): Contemporary evolution strategies. In: Third Int. Conf. on Artificial Life, LNCS 929, Springer Verlag: 893–907.

[115] R. E. Smith, C. Bonacina (2003): Mating restriction and niching pressure: results from agents and implications for general EC. In: [21]: 1382–1393.

[116] D. Surry, N. Radcliffe (1996): Formal Algorithms + Formal Representations = Search Strategies. In: [126].

[117] F. Seredynski (1994): Loosely coupled distributed genetic algorithms. In: [27]: 514–523.

[118] F. Seredynski (1997): Competitive coevolutionary multi-agent systems: the application to mapping and scheduling problems. *Journal of Parallel and Distributed Computing, 47*: 39–57.

[119] F. Seredynski (1998): New trends in parallel and distributed evolutionary computing. Fundamenta Informaticae 35, IOS Press: 211–230.

[120] F. Seredynski, A. Y. Zomaya, P. Bouvry (2003): Function Optimization with Coevolutionary Algorithms. In: M. A. Klopotek et al. (eds) Intelligent Information Processing and Web Mining, Advances in Soft Computing, Springer: 13–22.

[121] R. E. Smith, B. A. Dike, R. K. Mehra, B. Ravichandran, A. El-Fallah (1999): Classifier systems in combat: two-sided learning of maneuvers for advanced fighter aircraft. In: Computer Methods in Applied Mechanics and Engineering, Elsevier.

[122] J. E. Smiths, F. Vavak (1999): Replacement strategies in steady state genetic algorithms: dynamic environments. *Journal of Computing and Information Technology, 7*(1): 49–59.

[123] W. Stolzmann (2003): Anticipatory classifier systems. In: [44]: 493–517.

[124] R. Tsang, P. Lajbcygier (2002): Optimizing technical trading strategies with split search genetic algorithms. In: S.-H. Chen (ed) Evolutionary Computation in Economic and Finance. Physica-Verlag, Heildeiberg, New York: 333–358.

[125] F. Vavak, T. C. Fogarty, K. Jukes (1996): A genetic algorithm with variable range of local search for tracking changing environments. In: [126].

[126] H -M. Voight et al. (eds) (1996): Parallel Problem Solving from Nature-PPSN IV, Springer, LNCS 1411.

[127] V. Volterra (1926): Variazoni e Fluttuazioni Del Numero D'individui in Specie Animali Conviventi. *Memorie della R. Accaddemia Nazionale dei Lincei, 2*: 31–113.

[128] M. D. Vose (1999): The Simple Genetic Algorithm. MIT Press.

[129] I. Wegener, W. Carsten (2003): On the optimization of monotone polynomials by the (1 + 1) EA and randomized local search. In: [20]: 622–633.

[130] D. Whitley, D. Garrett, J -P. Watson (2003): Quad search and hybrid genetic algorithms. In: [21]: 1469–1480.

[131] D. Whitley, V. S. Gordon, K. Mathias (1994): Lamarckian evolution, the Baldwin effect and function optimization. In: [27]: 6–15.

[132] D. Whitley (1999): A free lunch proof for Grey versus binary encoding. In: [6]: 726–733.

[133] D. Whitley (2003): Evaluating search algorithms. In: [44]: 132–147.

[134] D. Whitley (1989): The GENITOR algorithm and selection pressure: why rank-based allocation of reproductive trials is best. In: [111]: 116–121.

[135] S. W. Wilson (1994): ZCS: A zeroth level classifier system. *Evolutionary Computation 2*(1): 1–18.

[136] S. W. Wilson (1995): Classifier fitness based on accuracy. *Evolutionary Computation 3*: 149–175.

[137] S. W. Wilson (2003): Structure and Function of the XCS classifier system. In: [44]: 547–555.

[138] D. H. Wolpert, W. G. Macready (1997): No free lunch theorems for optimization. *IEEE Trans. on Evolutionary Computation*, 1: 67–82.

[139] X. Yao (1996): An overview of evolutionary computation. *Chinese Journal of Advanced Software Research, 3*, 1:(1) 12–29.

[140] X. Yao (1999): Evolutionary programming made faster. *IEEE Trans. on Evolutionary Computation, 3*, 2(1): 82–102.

Chapter 5

ARTIFICIAL NEURAL NETWORKS
Javid Taheri and Albert Y. Zomaya
The University of Sydney

Artificial Neural Networks have been one of the most active areas of research in computer science during the last fifty years, with periods of intense activity interrupted by episodes of hiatus [1]. The premise for the evolution of the theory of artificial neural networks stems from the basic neurological structure of living organisms. Cells are the most important constituent of these life forms. These cells are connected by *synapses*, which are the links that carry messages between cells. In fact, by using synapses to carry the pulses, cells can activate each other with different threshold values to form a decision or memorize an event.

Inspired by this simplistic vision of how messages are transferred between cells, scientists invented a new computational approach, which became popularly known as Artificial Neural Networks (or Neural Networks for short), and used it extensively to target a wide range of problems in many application areas. Although the shape or configurations of different neural networks may look different at the first glance, the networks themselves are almost similar in structure.

A neural network consists of *cells* and *links*. Cells are the computational part of the network that perform reasoning and generate activation signals for other cells, while links connect the different cells and enable messages to flow among cells. Each link is usually a one-directional connection with a weight that affects the carried message in a certain way. This means that a link receives a value (message) from an input cell, multiplies it by a given weight, and then passes it to the output cell.

In its simplest form, a cell can have three states (of activation), namely, +1 (TRUE), 0, and −1 (FALSE), to represent three states: activation, unknown, and deactivation. Figure 5.1 shows a simple network with two inputs and one output. Table 5.1 gives the output for all possible inputs in such a network. As can be seen, this network simply separates the sample space into two completely individual subspaces.

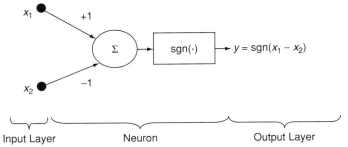

Figure 5.1. *A neural network with two inputs and one output*

Table 5.1 Truth table of the network in Figure 5.1

x	-1	0	$+1$
y			
-1	0	-1	-1
0	1	0	-1
$+1$	1	1	0

1   A GENERIC NEURAL NETWORK

Figure 5.1 shows a simple instant of a neural network. Cells (or neurons) can have more sophisticated structure that can handle complex problems. These neurons can be linear or nonlinear functions with or without biases. Figure 5.2 shows two simple neurons that can have biased and unbiased states.

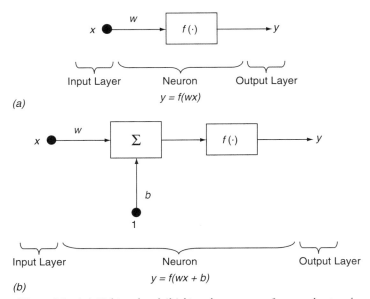

Figure 5.2. *(a) Unbiased and (b) biased structures of a neural network*

1.1 Single-Layer Perceptron

The single-layer perceptron is one of the simplest classes of neural networks [1]. The general overview of this network is shown in Figure 5.3, where the network has n inputs and generates only one output. The input of the function $f(\cdot)$ is actually a linear combination of the network's inputs. In this case, W is a vector of neuron weights, X is the input vector, and y is the only output of the network. These inputs are defined as follows:

$$y = f(W \cdot X + b)$$
$$W = (w_1 \quad w_2 \quad \ldots \quad w_n)$$
$$X = (x_1 \quad x_2 \quad \ldots \quad x_n)^T$$

The above-mentioned basic structure can be extended to produce networks with more than one output. In this case, each output has its own weights and is completely uncorrelated to the other outputs. Figure 5.4 shows such a network, with the following formulas:

$$Y = F(W \cdot X + B)$$

$$W = \begin{bmatrix} w_{1,1} & w_{1,2} & \ldots & w_{1,n} \\ w_{2,1} & & & \\ \ldots & & & \\ w_{m,1} & & \ldots & w_{m,n} \end{bmatrix}$$

$$X = (x_1 \quad x_2 \quad \ldots \quad x_n)^T$$
$$Y = (y_1 \quad y_2 \quad \ldots \quad y_m)^T$$
$$B = (b_1 \quad b_2 \quad \ldots \quad b_m)^T$$
$$F(\cdot) = (f_1(\cdot) \quad f_2(\cdot) \quad \ldots \quad f_m(\cdot))^T$$

where
n: number of inputs
m: number of outputs
W: weighing matrix
X: input vector
Y: output vector
$F(\cdot)$: array of output functions

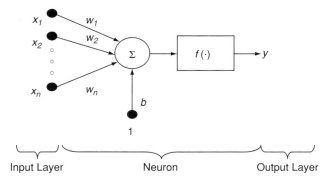

Figure 5.3. *A single-output (single-layer) perceptron*

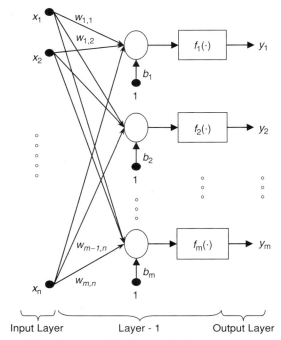

Figure 5.4. *A multioutput single-layer perceptron*

2 MULTILAYER PERCEPTRON

A multilayer perceptron can be simply constructed by concatenating several single-layer perceptron networks. Figure 5.5 shows the basic structure of such a network, which has the following parameters [1]:

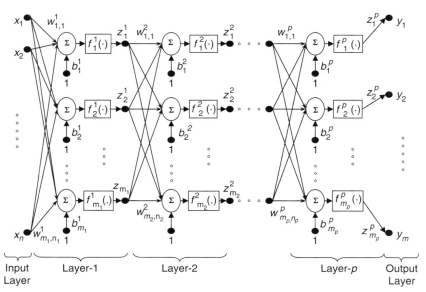

Figure 5.5. *The basic structure of a multilayer neural network*

X: input vector
Y: output vector
n: number of inputs
m: number of outputs
p: total number of layers in the network

while
m_i: number of outputs for the *i*th layer
n_i: number of inputs for the *i*th layer

Note that in this network, every internal layer of the network can have its own number of inputs and outputs only by considering the concatenation rule, i.e. $n_i = m_{i-1}$. The output of the first layer is calculated as follows:

$$Z^1 = F^1(W^1 \cdot X + B^1)$$

$$W^1 = \begin{bmatrix} w^1_{1,1} & w^1_{1,2} & \cdots & w^1_{1,n} \\ w^1_{2,1} & & & \\ \cdots & & & \\ w^1_{m_1,1} & & \cdots & w^1_{m_1,n} \end{bmatrix}$$

$$X = (x_1 \quad x_2 \quad \cdots \quad x_n)^T$$
$$B^1 = (b^1_1 \quad b^1_2 \quad \cdots \quad b^1_{m_1})^T$$
$$Z^1 = (z^1_1 \quad z^1_2 \quad \cdots \quad z^1_{m_1})^T$$
$$F^1(\cdot) = (f^1_1(\cdot) \quad f^1_2(\cdot) \quad \cdots \quad f^1_{m_1}(\cdot))^T$$

As a result, the output of the second layer would be

$$Z^2 = F^2(W^2 \cdot Z^1 + B^2)$$

$$W^2 = \begin{bmatrix} w^2_{1,1} & w^2_{1,2} & \cdots & w^2_{1,n} \\ w^2_{2,1} & & & \\ \cdots & & & \\ w^2_{m_2,1} & & \cdots & w^2_{m_2,m_1} \end{bmatrix}$$

$$B^2 = (b^2_1 \quad b^2_2 \quad \cdots \quad b^2_{m_2})^T$$
$$Z^2 = (z^2_1 \quad z^2_2 \quad \cdots \quad z^2_{m_2})^T$$
$$F^2(\cdot) = \left(f^2_1(\cdot) \quad f^2_2(\cdot) \quad \cdots \quad f^2_{m_2}(\cdot)\right)^T$$

Finally, the last-layer formulation can be given as

$$Y = Z^p = F^p(W^p \cdot Z^{p-1} + B^p)$$

$$W^p = \begin{bmatrix} w^p_{1,1} & w^p_{1,2} & \cdots & w^p_{1,n} \\ w^p_{2,1} & & & \\ \cdots & & & \\ w^p_{m_1,1} & & \cdots & w^p_{m_p,m_{p-1}} \end{bmatrix}$$

$$B^p = (b^p_1 \quad b^p_2 \quad \cdots \quad b^p_{m_p})^T$$

$$Z^p = (z_1^p \quad z_2^p \quad \cdots \quad z_{m_p}^p)^T$$
$$F^p(\cdot) = \left(f_1^p(\cdot) \quad f_2^p(\cdot) \quad \cdots \quad f_{m_p}^p(\cdot) \right)^T$$

Note that, in such networks, the complexity of the network rises quickly based on the number of layers. Practically experienced, each multilayer perceptron can be evaluated by a single-layer perceptron with a comparatively huge number of nodes.

2.1   Function Representation

Two of the most popular uses of neural networks is to represent (or approximate) functions and model systems. Basically, a neural network would be used to imitate the behavior of a function by generating relatively similar outputs in comparison with the real system (or function) over the same range of inputs.

2.1.1   Boolean Functions

Neural networks were first used to model simple Boolean functions. For example, Figure 5.6 shows how a neural network can be used to model an AND operator, while Figure 5.7 gives the truth table. Note that "1" stands for "TRUE" while "−1" represents a "FALSE" value. The network in Figure 5.6 actually simulates a linear (function) separator, which simply divides the decision space into two parts.

2.1.2   Real-Value Functions

In real-value functions, the network weights must be set so that the network can generate continues outputs of a real system. The generated network is also intended to act as an extrapolator that can generate output data for inputs that are different from the training set.

To clarify this, assume that the data set given in Table 5.2 is produced by a real-world phenomenon (or system). The idea here is for a neural network (Figure 5.8) to regenerate the same data and also be able to produce other values for sets of unforeseen inputs (i.e., extrapolate). Figure 5.9 shows graphically the output of both the system and the neural model.

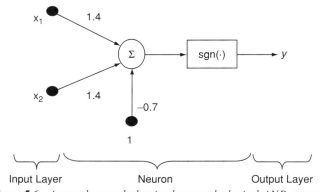

Figure 5.6. *A neural network that implements the logical AND operator*

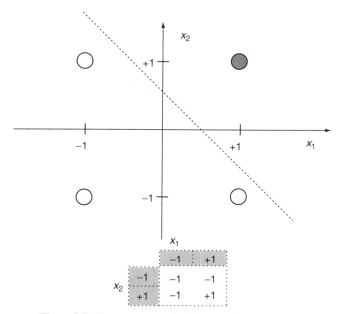

Figure 5.7. *Representation for the network in Figure 5.6*

Table 5.2. Truth table for an instance of a real value function

X_1 / X_2	−3	0	3
−3	0.97	0.43	−3.49
0	1.85	0.28	−1.18
3	4.26	1.0	−1.36

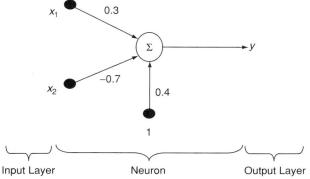

Figure 5.8. *A neural network that implements a simple real function*

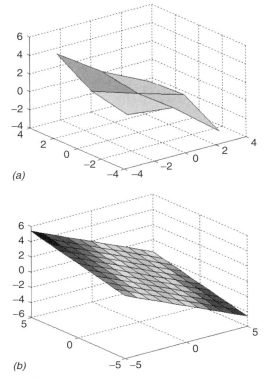

Figure 5.9. *The real values (a) and its corresponding neural model (b)*

3   LEARNING SINGLE-LAYER MODELS

The main, and most important, application of all neural networks is their ability to model a process or learn a behavior of a system. Toward this end, several algorithms have been proposed to train the adjustable parameters of a network (i.e., W). Basically, training a neural network to adjust the Ws is categorized into two different classes: supervised and unsupervised [2–6].

3.1   Supervised Learning

The main purpose of supervised learning is to "teach" a network to copy the behavior of a system or a function. In this case, there is always a need to have a "training" data set. The network topology and the algorithm with which the network is trained are highly interrelated. In general, a topology of the network is chosen first and then an appropriate training algorithm is used to tune the weights (W) [7, 8].

3.1.1.   Perceptron Learning

As mentioned earlier, the perceptron is the most basic form of neural networks. Essentially, this network tries to classify input data by mapping it onto a plane (Figures 5.3 and 5.4). In this approach, to simplify the algorithm, suppose that the network's input is restricted to $\{+1, 0, -1\}$, while the output can be $\{+1, -1\}$. The aim of the algorithm is to find an appropriate set of weights, W, by sampling a training set, T, that will capture the mapping that associates each input to an output, i.e.,

$$W = (w_0\ w_1\ \ldots\ w_n)$$
$$T = \{(R^1, S^1), (R^2, S^2), \ldots, (R^L, S^L)\}$$

where n is the number of inputs, R^i is the ith input datum, S^i represents the appropriate output for the ith pattern, and L is the size of the training data set. Note that, for the above vector W, w_n is used to adjust the bias in the values of the weights. Perceptron Learning can be summarized as follows:

Step 1: Set all elements of the weighting vector to zero, i.e., $W = (0\ 0\ \ldots\ 0)$.
Step 2: Select the training pattern randomly, the kth datum.
Step 3: IF the current W hasn't been classified correctly, i.e., $W.R^k \neq S^k$, THEN modify the weighing vector as follows: $W \leftarrow W + R^k\ S^k$.
Step 4: Repeat steps 1–3 until all data are classified correctly.

The following example is used to demonstrate how this network functions. Assume a network with two inputs and one output used to classify the data of Table 5.3. The different iterations that the network will undergo are as follows:

Iteration	Current W	Choice	OK ?	Action
1	<0 0 0>	T5	NO	W=W–T5
2	<–2 3 –1>	T6	YES	
3	<–2 3 –1>	T4	YES	
4	<–2 3 –1>	T2	YES	
5	<–2 3 –1>	T1	NO	W=W+T1
6	<0 3 0>	T2	YES	
7	<0 3 0>	T1	NO	W=W+T1
	<2 3 1>	Works for all training data; algorithm terminates.		

In this case, the final answer would be $W = [2\ 3\ 1]$. Figure 5.10 shows the network after it converges to the previous answer, while Figure 5.11 graphically shows the output of the network.

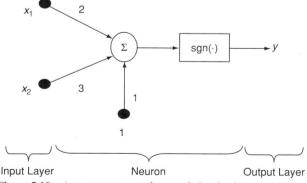

Figure 5.10. *A perceptron neural network for the data in Table 5.3*

Table 5.3. A sample training set for a perceptron

Name	Input		Output
	X_1	X_2	Y
T_1	2	0	1
T_2	1	2	1
T_3	3	4	1
T_4	-3	-2	-1
T_5	2	-3	-1
T_6	-1	-1	-1

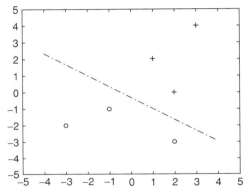

Figure 5.11. *The output of the network of Figure 5.10*

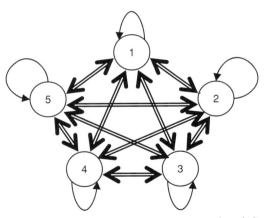

Figure 5.12. *A sample linear auto-associative network with five nodes*

3.2 Linear Auto-Associative Learning

An auto-associative network is another type of network that has some type of memory. In this network, the input and output nodes are basically the same. Hence, when a datum enters the network, it passes through the nodes and converges to the closest memorized datum, which was previously stored in the network during the training process [1]. Figure 5.12 shows an instance of such network with five nodes.

It is worth noting that the weighing matrix of such network is not symmetrical. That is, $w_{i,j}$, which relate node i to node j, may have different values than $w_{j,i}$. The main key of designing such a network is in the training data set. In this case, the assumption is to have orthogonal or approximately orthogonal training data, i.e.,

$$\langle T_i, T_j \rangle \approx \begin{cases} 0 & i \neq j \\ 1 & i = j \end{cases}$$

where T_i is the ith training data and $\langle \cdot \rangle$ is the inner product of two vectors. Based on the above, the weight matrix for this network is calculated as follows, where $\otimes$ stands for outer product of two vectors:

$$W = \sum_{i=1}^{N} T_i \otimes T_i$$

As can be seen, the main advantage of this network is in its one-shot learning process, accomplished by considering orthogonal data. Note that, even if the input data are not orthogonal in the first place, they can be transferred to a new space by a simple transfer function.

To demonstrate the use of this network, assume the three-node network of Figure 5.13. In this network, the inputs and outputs of the network are basically same. Also, assume that the data in Table 5.4 need to be stored in the network.

In this case, the training data set is approximately orthogonal, i.e.,

$\langle T_1, T_1 \rangle = 0.9902$
$\langle T_2, T_2 \rangle = 1.0025$
$\langle T_1, T_2 \rangle = -0.0066$

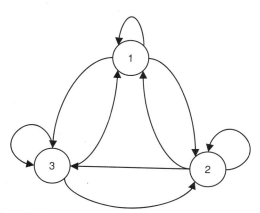

Figure 5.13. *An auto-associative network with three nodes*

Table 5.4. Training data for a sample auto associate network

T_1	<−0.29 0.90 0.31>
T_2	<0.94 0.33 −0.1>

Therefore, the weight matrix would be calculated as follows:

$$W = T_1 \otimes T_1 + T_2 \otimes T_2 =$$

$$\begin{bmatrix} 0.0841 & -0.2610 & -0.0899 \\ -0.2610 & 0.8100 & 0.2790 \\ -0.0899 & 0.2790 & 0.0961 \end{bmatrix} + \begin{bmatrix} 0.8836 & 0.3102 & -0.0940 \\ 0.3102 & 0.1089 & -0.0330 \\ -0.0940 & -0.0330 & 0.0100 \end{bmatrix}$$

$$= \begin{bmatrix} 0.9677 & 0.0492 & -0.1839 \\ 0.0492 & 0.9189 & 0.2460 \\ -0.1839 & 0.2460 & 0.1061 \end{bmatrix}$$

To show how the above network functions, assume that the following data, which are not part of the training data set, are fed into the network: $T = < 0.8$ 0.5 $0.33 >$. Figure 5.14 shows how this network converges to an output. Figures 5.14a and 5.14b show the $\| T - T_1 \|$ and $\| T - T_2 \|$ cases, respectively.

3.2.1 Iterative Learning

Iterative learning is another approach that can be used to train a network. In this case, the network's weights are modified smoothly, in contrast to the one-shot learning algorithms. In general, network weights are set to some arbitrary values first, and then training data are fed to the network. In this case, in each training cycle, network weights are modified smoothly. Then the training process proceeds until it achieves an acceptable level of acceptance for the network. However, the training data could be selected sequentially or randomly in each training cycle [9–11].

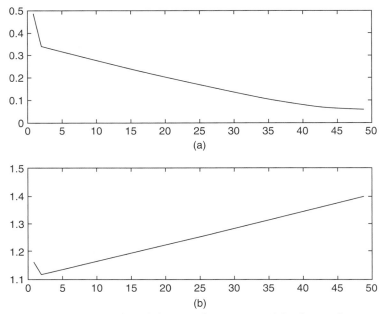

Figure 5.14. *Convergence of the network in Figure 5.13 for the new data set*

3.2.2   Hopfield's Model

A Hopfield neural network is another example of an auto-associative network [1, 12–14]. There are two main differences between this network and the previously described auto-associative network. In this network, self-connection is not allowed, i.e., $w_{i,i} = 0$ for all nodes. Also, inputs and outputs are either 0 or 1. This means that the node activation is recomputed after each cycle of convergence as follows:

$$S_i = \sum_{j=1}^{N} w_{i,j} \cdot u_j(t) \tag{1}$$

$$u'_j = \begin{cases} 1 & if \ S_i \geq 0 \\ 0 & if \ S_i < 0 \end{cases} \tag{2}$$

After feeding a datum into the network, in each convergence cycle, the nodes are selected by a uniform random function, the inputs are used to calculate (1), and then (2) follows to generate the output. This procedure is continued until the network converges.

The proof of convergence for this network uses the notion of *energy*. This means that an energy value is assigned to each state of the network, and through the different iterations of the algorithm, the overall energy is decreased until it reaches a steady state. To show the workings of this network, one can train this network to learn the data set given in Table 5.5. In this case, the weights matrix would be as follows:

$$W = \sum_{i=1}^{N} T_i \otimes T_i = \begin{bmatrix} 1 & 1 & 1 & 1 \\ 1 & 1 & 1 & 1 \\ 1 & 1 & 1 & 1 \\ 1 & 1 & 1 & 1 \end{bmatrix} + \begin{bmatrix} 1 & 1 & -1 & -1 \\ 1 & 1 & -1 & -1 \\ -1 & -1 & 1 & 1 \\ -1 & -1 & 1 & 1 \end{bmatrix}$$

$$+ \begin{bmatrix} 1 & -1 & -1 & -1 \\ -1 & 1 & 1 & 1 \\ -1 & 1 & 1 & 1 \\ -1 & 1 & 1 & 1 \end{bmatrix} = \begin{bmatrix} 3 & 1 & -1 & -1 \\ 1 & 3 & 1 & 1 \\ -1 & 1 & 3 & 3 \\ -1 & 1 & 3 & 3 \end{bmatrix} \rightarrow \begin{bmatrix} 0 & 1 & -1 & -1 \\ 1 & 0 & 1 & 1 \\ -1 & 1 & 0 & 3 \\ -1 & 1 & 3 & 0 \end{bmatrix}$$

Now, suppose that the following input is applied to the network:

$$T = \begin{bmatrix} -1 \\ 1 \\ -1 \\ -1 \end{bmatrix}$$

Table 5.5. Training data for a Hopfield neural network

T_1	<1 1 1 1>
T_2	<−1 −1 1 1>
T_3	<1 −1 −1 −1>

In this case, the network output would be

$$W \cdot T = \begin{bmatrix} 3 \\ -3 \\ -1 \\ -1 \end{bmatrix} \rightarrow \begin{bmatrix} 1 \\ -1 \\ -1 \\ -1 \end{bmatrix} \equiv T_3$$

Note that, in this case, the network convergence occurs in only one cycle, although it may need more iteration for other inputs.

3.2.3   Mean Square Error (MSE) Algorithms

MSE algorithms emerged as an answer to the deficiencies experienced by using perceptrons and other simple networks [1, 15]. One of the most important reasons is the inseparability of training data. If the data used to train the network are naturally inseparable, the training algorithm never terminates (Figure 5.15).

The other reason for using this technique is to converge to a better solution. In perceptron learning, the training process terminates right after finding the first answer, regardless of its quality (i.e., sensitivity of the answer). Figure 5.16 shows an example of such a case. Note that, although the answer found by the perceptron algorithm is correct (Figure 5.16a), the answer in (Figure 5.16b) is more robust. Finally, another reason for using MSE algorithms, which is crucial for most neural network algorithms, is speed of convergence.

The MSE algorithm attempts to modify the network weights based on the overall error of all data. In this case, assume that network input and output data are represented by T_i, R_i for $i = 1...N$, respectively. Now the MSE error is defined as follows:

$$E = \frac{1}{N} \sum_{i=1}^{N} (W \cdot T_i - R_i)^2$$

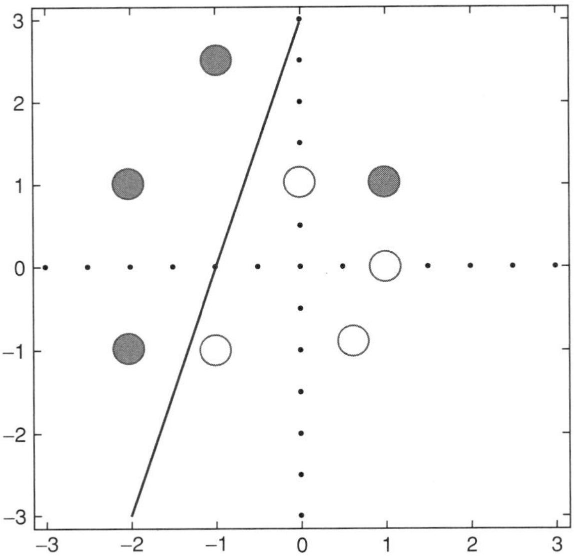

Figure 5.15. *An example of an inseparable training data set*

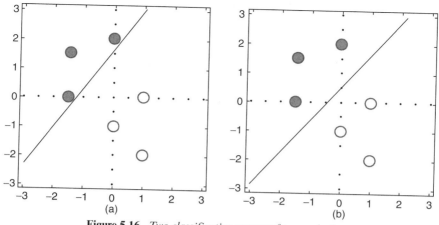

Figure 5.16. *Two classification answers for sample data*

Note that the stated error is the summation of all individual errors for all the training data. In spite of all the advantages of this training technique, there are several disadvantages. For example, the network might not be able to correctly classify the data if they are widely spread apart (Figure 5.17). The other disadvantage is that speed of convergence may completely vary from one set of data to another.

3.2.4 The Widow-Hoff Rule or LMS Algorithm

In the widow-Hoff algorithm, the network weights are modified after each iteration [1, 16]. A training datum is selected randomly, and then the network weights

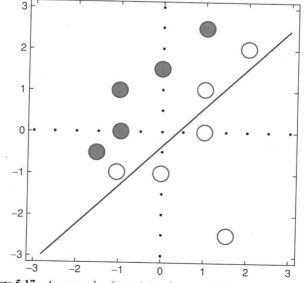

Figure 5.17. *An example of a training data set with spread-out members*

are modified based on the corresponding error. This procedure continues until it converges to the answer. For a randomly selected k^{th} entry in the training data, the error is calculated as follows:

$$\varepsilon = (W \cdot T_k - R_k)^2$$

Now the gradient vector of this error would be

$$\nabla \epsilon = \langle \frac{\partial \epsilon}{\partial W_0} \frac{\partial \epsilon}{\partial W_1} \cdots \frac{\partial \epsilon}{\partial W_N} \rangle$$

Hence,

$$\frac{\partial \epsilon}{\partial W_j} = 2 (W \cdot T_k - R_k) \cdot T_k$$

Based on the Widow-Hoff algorithm, the weights should be modified opposite to the direction of the gradient. As a result, the final update formula for the weighting matrix W would be

$$W' = W - \rho \cdot (W \cdot T_k - R_k) \cdot T_k$$

Note that ρ is known as the learning rate and absorbs the multiplier of value 2.

3.4   Unsupervised Learning

Unsupervised learning networks attempt to cluster input data without the need for the traditional "learn by example" technique that is commonly used for neural networks. Note that clustering applications tend to be the most popular type of applications for which these networks are normally used. The most popular networks in this class are K-means, Kohonen, ART1, and ART2 [17-21].

3.4.1   K-Means Clustering

K-means clustering is the simplest technique used for classifying data. In this technique, a network with a predefined number of clusters is considered, and then each datum is assigned to one of these clusters. This process continues until all data are checked and classified properly. The following algorithm shows how this algorithm is implemented.

Step 1: Consider a network with K clusters.

Step 2: Assign all data to one of the above clusters, with respect to the distance from the center of the cluster and each datum.

Step 3: Modify the center of the assigned cluster.

Step 4: Check all data in the network to ensure proper classification.

Step 5: If a datum has to be moved from one cluster to another one, then update the center of both clusters.

Step 6: Repeat steps 4 and 5 until no datum is wrongly classified.

Figure 5.18 shows an example of such a network when applied for data classification with correct and incorrect numbers of clusters. As can be seen, if the number of clusters is properly guessed, then this algorithm can be very effective.

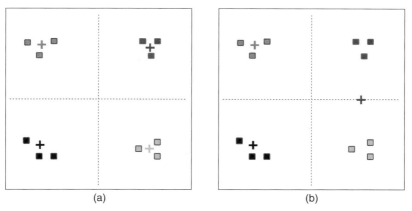

Figure 5.18. *Results of applying a k-means clusterer with (a) appropriate and (b) inappropriate numbers of clusters*

3.4.2   Kohonen Clustering

The Kohoner classification method clusters input data based on a topological representation of the data. The outputs of the network are arranged so that each output has some neighbors. Thus, during the learning process, not only one output but a group of close outputs are modified to classify the data. To clarify the situation, assume that a network is supposed to learn how a set of data is to be distributed in a two-dimensional representation (Figure 5.19).

In this case, each point is a potential output with a predefined neighborhood margin. For example, the cell marked X and eight of its neighbors are given. Therefore, whenever this cell gets selected for an update, all its neighbors are included in the process too. The main principle behind this approach for classifying input data is analogous to principles of biology. In a mammalian brain, all vision, auditory, and tactile sensors are mapped into a number of cell sheets. Therefore, if one of the cells is activated, all cells close to it will be affected, but with different intensity levels.

Now assume that a training data set, T_i for $i = 1...N$, is available and that the network must classify it based on a similarity measure. The main idea here is for

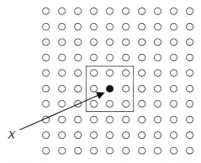

Figure 5.19. *Output topology of a sample Kohonen network*

the network to assign at least one of its output weights to fire for a particular training datum. To achieve this, for each training datum, the closest output is found, and then the corresponding weights are modified in order to get the minimum possible Euclidean distance, i.e. to minimize $\| T_k - W_{m,n} \|$. Another consideration during this training process is the learning rate of the algorithm. In general, at the outset, the network is trained with a fast learning rate, while in the final stages of the training process, the training data hardly change the network weights. The following procedure explains the details of this classifier:

Step 1: Define the algorithm step size $\rho(t) = \left(1 - \frac{t-1}{L}\right)$, where L is the predefined number of iterations.
Step 2: Generate a grid network with the dimension of the input data.
Step 3: Assign all network weights to random data.
Step 4: Select a random training data, T_k.
Step 5: Find the closest output of the network to T_k, and let this be $O_{m,n}$.
Step 6: Modify $O_{m,n}$ and its neighboring weights, with a predefined margin, as follows: $W_{x,y} = W_{x,y} + \rho(t) \cdot (T_k - W_{x,y})$.
Step 7: Set $t \leftarrow t + 1$ and repeat steps 4–7 until $t = L$.

Figure 5.20 shows the random data that need to be classified, while Figure 5.21 shows the end result for a number of iterations.

3.4.3   ART1

This neural classifier, known as *Adaptive Resonance Theory* or *ART*, deals with digital inputs ($T_i \in \{0,1\}$). In this network, each "1" in the input vector represents information, while a "0" entry is considered noise or unwanted information. In ART, there is no predefined number of classes before the start of classification; in fact, the classes are generated during the classification process.

Moreover, each class prototype may include the characteristics of more than a training datum. The basic principle of such a network relies on the similarity factor for data classification. In summary, every time a datum is assigned to a cluster, firstly, the nearest class with this datum is found, and then, if the similar-

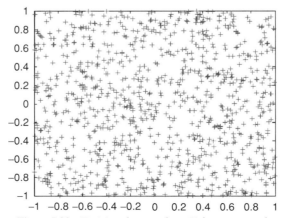

Figure 5.20. *Training data set for a Kohonen network*

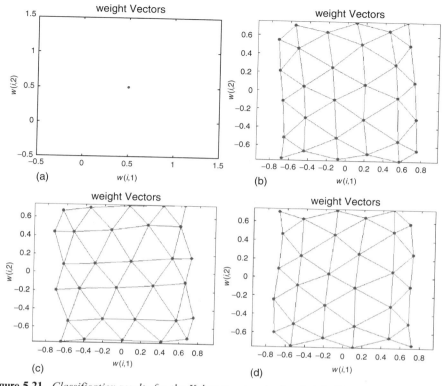

Figure 5.21. *Classification results for the Kohonen network after (a) 0, (b) 10, (c) 20, and (d) 30 iterations*

ity of this datum to the class prototype is more than a predefined value, known as a *vigilance factor*, the datum is assigned to this class and the class prototype is modified to have more similarity with the new data entry [1, 22, 23].

The procedure below shows how this algorithm is implemented. However, the following points need to be noted First.

1. $\|X\|$ is the number of 1s in the vector $\mathbf{X}$.
2. $X \cdot Y$ is the number of common 1s between the vectors $\mathbf{X}$ and $\mathbf{Y}$.
3. $X \cap Y$ is the bitwise AND operator applied on vectors $\mathbf{X}$ and $\mathbf{Y}$.

Step 1: Let β be a small number, n be the dimension of the input data, and ρ be the vigilance factor ($0 \le \rho < 1$).

Step 2: Start with no class prototype.

Step 3: Select a training datum by random, T_k.

Step 4: Find the nearest unchecked class prototype, C_i, to this datum by minimizing $\dfrac{C_i \cdot T_k}{\beta + \|C_i\|}$.

Step 5: Test whether C_i is sufficiently close to T_k by verifying $\dfrac{C_i \cdot T_k}{\beta + \|C_i\|} > \dfrac{T_k}{\beta + \rho}$.

Step 6: If C_i is not similar enough, then assign a new class prototype and go to step 3.

Step 7: If it is sufficiently similar, check the vigilance factor:

$$\frac{C_i \cdot T_k}{\|T_k\|} \geq \rho$$

Step 8: If the vigilance factor is exceeded, then modify the class prototype by $C_i = C_i \cap T_k$ and go to step 3.

Step 9: If the vigilance factor is not exceeded, then find another unchecked class prototype (step 4).

Step 10: Repeat steps 3–9 until none of the training data causes any change in class prototypes.

3.4.4 ART2

ART2 is a variation of ART1, with the following differences:
1. Data are considered continuous and not binary.
2. The input data are processed before passing them to the network. Actually, the input data are normalized, and then all elements of the result vector that are below a predefined value are set to zero and the vector is normalized again. The process is used for noise cancellation.
3. When a class prototype is found for a datum, the class prototype vector is moved fractionally toward the selected datum. As a result, contrary to the operation of ART1, the weights are moved smoothly toward a new datum. The main reason for such a modification is to "memorize" previously learnt rules.

The following algorithm demonstrates the working of ART2:

Step 1: Let; n be the dimension of the input data; α be a positive small number given by $\alpha \leq 1/\sqrt{n}$; λ be the normalized factor such that $0 < \lambda < 1/\sqrt{n}$; and ρ be the vigilance factor ($0 \leq \rho < 1$).

Step 2: Process all the training data for $k = 1 \cdot N$ as follows:
Normalize T_k.
Set all elements of T_k to 0 if they all are less or equal to λ.
Normalize T_k again.

Step 3: Start with no class prototype.

Step 4: Select a training datum randomly, T_k.

Step 5: Find the nearest unchecked class prototype, C_i, to this datum by minimizing $C_i \cdot T_k$.

Step 6: Test whether C_i is sufficiently close to T_k by verifying $C_i \cdot T_k \geq \alpha \cdot \sum_j T_j^k$.

Step 7: If C_i is not similar enough, then assign a new class prototype and go to step 4.

Step 8: If it is sufficiently similar, check the vigilance factor: $C_i \cdot T_k \geq \rho$.

Step 9: If the vigilance factor is exceeded, then modify the class prototype by

$$C_i = \frac{(1-\beta) \cdot C + \beta \cdot T_k}{\|(1-\beta) \cdot C + \beta \cdot T_k\|} \text{ and go to step 4.}$$

Step 10: If the vigilance factor is not exceeded, then try to find another unchecked class prototype (step 5).

Step 11: Repeat steps 3–9 until none of the training data causes any change in class prototypes.

3.5   Learning in Multiple-Layer Models

As mentioned earlier, multilayer neural networks consist of several con-catenated single-layer networks [1, 24–26]. The inner layers, known as hidden layers, may have different number of inputs and outputs. Because of this added complexity, the training process becomes more involved. This section presents two of the most popular multilayer neural networks.

3.6   Back-Propagation Algorithm

The back-propagation algorithm is one of the most powerful and reliable techniques that can be used to adjust network weights. The main principle of this approach is to use the gradient information of a cost function to modify the net-work's weights.

However, the use of such an approach to train multilayer networks is a little different from applying it to single-layer networks. In general, multilayer net-works are much harder to train than single-layer ones. In fact, convergence of such networks is much slower and very error sensitive.

In this approach, an input is presented to the network and allowed to "for-ward" propagate through the network. The output is calculated, and then the output is compared with a "desired" output (from the training set) and an error is calculated. This error is then propagated "backward" into the network, and the different weights are updated accordingly. To simplify the description of this algorithm, consider a network with a single hidden layer (and two layers of weights), as shown in Figure 5.22. In relation to this network, the following def-initions apply. Of course, the same definitions can be easily extended to larger networks.

T_i, R_i for $i = 1...L$: The training set of input and outputs, respectively.
N, S, M: The size of the input, hidden, and output layers, respectively.
W^1: Network weights from the input layer to the hidden layer.
W^2: Network weights from the hidden layer to the output layer.
X, Z, Y: Input and output of the hidden layer and the network output, respec-tively.
$F^1(\cdot)$: Array of network functions for the hidden layer.
$F^2(\cdot)$: Array of network functions for the output layer.
These definitions lead to the following formulas:

$$Z = F^1(W^1 \cdot X)$$

$$W^1 = \begin{bmatrix} w_{1,1}^1 & w_{1,2}^1 & \cdots & w_{1,n}^1 \\ w_{2,1}^1 & & & \\ \cdots & & & \\ w_{s,1}^1 & & \cdots & w_{s,n}^1 \end{bmatrix}$$

$$X = (x_1 \quad x_2 \quad \cdots \quad x_n)^T$$
$$Z = (z_1 \quad z_2 \quad \cdots \quad z_s)^T$$
$$F^1(\cdot) = (f_1^1(\cdot) \quad f_2^1(\cdot) \quad \cdots \quad f_s^1(\cdot))^T$$

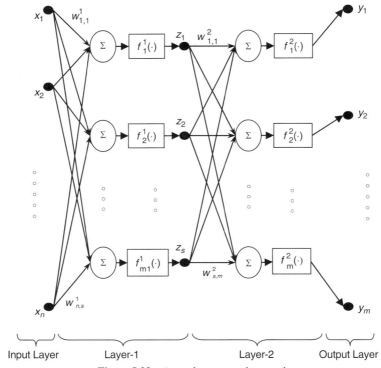

Figure 5.22. *A two-layer neural network*

$$Y = F^2 \left(W^2 \cdot Z \right)$$

$$W^2 = \begin{bmatrix} w_{1,1}^2 & w_{1,2}^2 & \cdots & w_{1,s}^2 \\ w_{2,1}^2 & & & \\ \cdots & & & \\ w_{m,1}^2 & & \cdots & w_{m,s}^2 \end{bmatrix}$$

$$F^2(\cdot) = \left(f_1^2(\cdot) \quad f_2^2(\cdot) \quad \cdots \quad f_m^2(\cdot) \right)^T$$

Now assume that the cost function for this optimization process is defined as

$$E = \frac{1}{2L} \sum_{k=1}^{L} \sum_{j=1}^{M} \left(R_j^{(k)} - Y_j^{(k)} \right)^2$$

where $Y_j^{(k)}$ and $R_j^{(k)}$ are the actual and desired outputs of the network, respectively. In this case, k represents the kth training datum and j is the jth output.

In this case, the following formulas represent the details:

$$Y_j^{(k)} = f_j^2 \left(\sum_{s=1}^{S} w_{j,s}^2 \cdot Z_s^{(k)} \right) \equiv f_j^2 \left(net2_j^{(k)} \right)$$

$$Z_s^{(k)} = f_s^1 \left(\sum_{i=1}^{N} w_{s,i}^1 \cdot x_i^{(k)} \right) \equiv f_s^1 \left(net1_s^{(k)} \right)$$

Now, the main cost function can be rewritten as follows:

$$E = \frac{1}{2L}\sum_{k=1}^{L}\sum_{j=1}^{M}\left(R_j^{(k)} - f_j^2\left(\sum_{s=1}^{S}w_{j,s}^2 \cdot f_s^1\left(\sum_{i=1}^{N}w_{s,i}^1 \cdot x_i^{(k)}\right)\right)\right)^2$$

Based on the gradient algorithm, with the assumption that all functions in the network are derivable, the following would apply for the output layer:

$$\frac{\partial E}{\partial w_{f,g}^2} = -\frac{1}{L}\sum_{k=1}^{L}\left(R_f^{(k)} - Y_f^{(k)}\right)\frac{\partial Y_f^{(k)}}{\partial w_{f,g}^2}$$

$$= -\frac{1}{L}\sum_{k=1}^{L}\left(R_f^{(k)} - Y_f^{(k)}\right)\frac{\partial f_f^2\left(net2_f^{(k)}\right)}{\partial net2_f^{(k)}}\frac{\partial net_f^{(k)}}{\partial w_{f,g}^2}$$

$$= -\frac{1}{L}\sum_{k=1}^{L}\lambda_{2_f}^{(k)} \cdot Z_g^{(k)}$$

where

$$\lambda_{2_f}^{(k)} = (R_f^{(k)} - Y_f^{(k)})f_f^2(net_f^{(k)})$$

The gradient formulas for the hidden layer would be as follows:

$$\frac{\partial E}{\partial w_{f,g}^1} = \frac{1}{L}\sum_{k=1}^{L}\frac{\partial E}{\partial Z_f^{(k)}}\frac{\partial Z_f^{(k)}}{\partial w_{f,g}^1}$$

$$= -\frac{1}{L}\sum_{k=1}^{L}\sum_{j=1}^{M}\left(R_j^{(k)} - Y_j^{(k)}\right)\frac{\partial f^2\left(net_j^{(k)}\right)}{\partial net_j^{(k)}}w_{j,f}^2\frac{\partial Z_j^{(k)}}{\partial w_{f,g}^1}$$

$$= -\frac{1}{L}\sum_{k=1}^{L}\sum_{j=1}^{M}\lambda_{2_j}^{(k)} \cdot w_{j,f}^2\frac{\partial f^1\left(net_f^{(k)}\right)}{\partial net_f^{(k)}} \cdot X_g^{(k)}$$

$$= -\frac{1}{L}\sum_{k=1}^{L}\lambda_{1_f}^{(k)} \cdot X_g^{(k)}$$

where

$$\lambda_{1_f}^{(k)} = \dot{f}_f^1\left(net_f^{(k)}\right)\sum_{j=1}^{M}w_{j,f}^2 \cdot \lambda_{2_j}^{(k)}$$

To summarize the above technique, the back-propagation algorithm for a two-layer network can be derived as follows:

Step 1: Create a network with a predefined number of nodes in the hidden layer, and random weights for all links.

Step 2: Select a kth entry consisting of an input and desired output.

Step 3: Compute $net1_i^{(k)}$ and $Z_i^{(k)}$ for $i = 1... S$:

$$net1_i^{(k)} = \sum_{r=1}^{N} = w_{r,i}^1 \cdot X_r^{(k)}, Z_i^{(k)} = f_i^1(net1_i^{(k)})$$

followed by $net2_j^{(k)}$ and $Y_j^{(k)}$ for $j = 1...M$:

$$net2_i^{(k)} = \sum_{i=1} = w_{i,j}^2 \cdot Z_i^{(k)}, Y_j^{(k)} = f_j^2(net2_j^{(k)})$$

Step 4: Computer $\lambda_1 i^{(k)}$ and $\lambda_2 j^{(k)}$ for $i = 1 ... S$ and $j = 1...M$:

$$\lambda_{2_j}^{(k)} = \left(R_j^{(k)} - Y_j^{(k)} \right) f_j'\!\left(net2_j^{(k)} \right)$$

$$\lambda_{1_i}^{(k)} = f_i'\!\left(net1_i^{(k)} \right) \sum_{j=1}^{M} w_{i,j}^2 \cdot \lambda_{2_j}^{(k)}$$

Step 5: Calculate the gradient over the input batch:

$$\frac{\partial E}{\partial w_{i,j}^2} = \frac{\partial E}{\partial w_{i,j}^2} + \lambda_{2_j}^{(k)} \cdot Z_i^{(k)}$$

$$\frac{\partial E}{\partial w_{i,j}^1} = \frac{\partial E}{\partial w_{i,j}^1} + \lambda_{1_j}^{(k)} \cdot X_i^{(k)}$$

Step 6: Repeat steps 2–5 for all training data.
Step 7: Update the network weights as follows:

$$w_{i,j}^1(new) \leftarrow w_{i,j}^1(old) - \frac{\mu}{L}\frac{\partial E}{\partial w_{i,j}^1}$$

$$w_{i,j}^2(new) \leftarrow w_{i,j}^2(old) - \frac{\mu}{L}\frac{\partial E}{\partial w_{i,j}^2}$$

Step 8: Repeat steps 2–7 until a predefined accuracy measure is reached for the network.

3.7   Radial Basis Functions

The Radial Basis Function (RBF) neural network is another popular multi-layer neural network [27–31]. The RBF network consists of two layers, one hidden layer and one output layer. In this network, the hidden layer is implemented by radial activation functions while the output layer is simply a weighted sum of the hidden-layer outputs.

The RBF neural network is able to model complex mappings, which perceptron neural networks can only accomplish by means of multiple hidden layers. The outstanding characteristics of such a network makes it applicable for a variety of applications, such as function interpolation [32, 33], chaotic time series modeling [34, 35], system identification [36–38], control systems [39, 40], channel equalization [41–43], speech recognition [44, 45], image restoration [46, 47], motion estimation [48], pattern classification [49], and data fusion [50].

3.7.1   Network Topology

The main topology of this network is as shown in Figure 5.23. Many functions were introduced for possible use in the hidden layer; however, radial functions (Gaussian) remain the most effective to use for data or pattern classification. The Gaussian functions are defined as follows:

$$\Phi_j(X) = \exp\left[-(X - \mu_j)^T \Gamma_j^{-1}(X - \mu_j) \right]$$

where $j = 1, 2, \ldots, L$, L represents the number of nodes in the hidden layer, X is the input vector, μ_j and Γ_j are the mean vector and covariance matrix of the jth Gaussian function, respectively. In some approaches, a polynomial term is

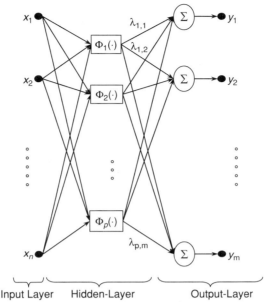

Figure 5.23. *The basic structure of an RBF network*

appended to the above expression, while in others the functions are normalized to the sum of all Gaussian components as in the Gaussian mixture estimation. Geometrically, a radial basis function in this network represents a bump in the N-dimensional space where N is the number of entries (input vector size). In this case, the μ_j represents the location of this bump in the space and Γ_j models its shape. The output layer of this network is a linear combination of the hidden layer outputs, as follows:

$$Y_k(X) = \sum_{i=1}^{L} \lambda_{i,k} \cdot \Phi_i(X)$$

where L is the number of outputs of the hidden layer, Y_k is the kth output, and $\lambda_{i,k}$ is a linear factor (connection weight) from the ith hidden layer output to the kth network output. In the classification application, the actual output of the network is usually limited by a sigmoid function to be between 0 and 1:

$$Z_k = \frac{1}{1 + \exp\left[-Y_k(X)\right]}$$

3.7.2 Training Algorithms

Because of the nonlinear behavior of this network, the training procedure of the RBF network (as in multilayer networks) is approached in a completely different manner from that of single-layer networks. In this network, the aim is to find the center and variance factor of all hidden-layer Gaussian functions as well as the optimal weights for the linear output layer. In this case, the following cost function is usually considered to be the main network objective:

$$Min\left(\sum_{i=0}^{N} \left(\left[Y(T_i) - R_i \right]^T \cdot \left[Y(T_i) - R_i \right] \right) \right)$$

where N is the number of inputs in the training data set, $Y(X)$ is the output of the network for input X, and $\langle T_k, R_k \rangle$ is the kth training data pair. So the actual output of the network is a combination of a nonlinear computation followed by a linear operation. Therefore, finding an optimal set of weights for hidden layers and output layer parameters is hardly achievable.

In this case, several approaches were used to find the optimal set of weights; however, none of these can provide any guarantees that optimality can be achieved. For example, many approaches suggest that the hidden-layer parameters are set randomly and that the training procedure is just carried on for the output linear components. In contrast, in some other cases, the radial basis functions are homogenously distributed over the sample space before the output linear weights are found. However, the back-propagation algorithm seems to be the most suitable approach for training such a network.

Note that, in this approach, numerous iterations might be needed to converge to a suitable answer, so the probability of getting stuck in local minima during training process is unavoidable. To solve this problem, several algorithms were suggested that use another classification technique, such as K-means [51], to guess the initial location of the radial functions in the space. However, the following approach is mentioned as one of the simplest but most powerful approaches to tune these sensitive weights. The main idea of this technique is similar to that of Kohonen's training routine. In this method, the parameters of the radial basis functions are set randomly, and for each training datum, the closest radial basis function in the hidden layer is selected and modified. The following algorithm shows the details:

Step 1: Generate an RBF neural network with a predefined number of Gaussian functions in the hidden layer, namely, L functions.

Step 2: Set the center of these Gaussian functions randomly, and, set their variance using a predefined fixed value.

Step 3: Select a random datum from the training data, T_k.

Step 4: Find the closest center of these Gaussian function with reference to the following criterion: $\underset{1 < j < P}{Min} \left(\| T_k - \mu_j \| \right)$, where μ_j is the center of the jth Gaussian function, μ^*.

Step 5: Modify the center of the closest function as $\mu^* = \mu^* + \gamma(T_k - \mu^*)$, where γ is an arbitrary small positive value as the learning rate.

Step 6: Repeat Steps 3–5 until all radial functions are almost fixed in space.

Step 7: Calculate the output-layer linear weights by Least Mean Squares or any other optimization routine.

Note that, during step 3–5, when the centers of the radial functions are calculated, some radial functions might get close to each other during the process, while others will never be affected. Therefore, an RBF neural network with an excessive number of radial functions is usually generated first; then, after the result generated by steps 3–5 is examined, the optimal number of radial functions is guessed and the training algorithm is restarted. Figure 5.24 shows an RBF network with two radial functions in the hidden layer that managed to learn the behavior of a given data set.

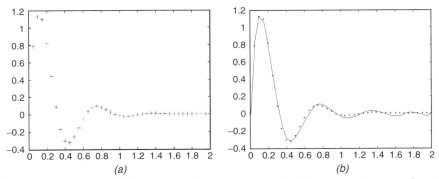

Figure 5.24. *(a) A typical data set for an RBF neural network (b) corresponding network output after training*

4   LEARNING VECTOR QUANTIZATION

The Learning Vector Quantization (LVQ) network is another popular classification technique that can be used for data clustering [52–54]. In this technique, a two-layer network topology is used to classify the data, which can be used in either supervised or unsupervised training.

In the supervised mode, a training data set is used to adjust the network parameters (Figure 5.25). The first layer of this network follows the "winner-takes-all" routine, while the second layer is linear. Basically, in the winner-takes-all topology, the input vector is fed to the layer, and based on the layer outputs, only one of the outputs is set to "1" and the rest to "0." The basic topology of this layer is usually the distance between network weights and the input datum. This process is followed by a comparator to evaluate the outputs of different nodes and to emphasize the largest element by setting it to "1" and the others to "0."

4.1   Learning Algorithm

Because of the nonlinear nature of the first layer, the training of such a network requires certain considerations. The back-propagation and other learning methods that try to adjust network parameters by using gradient information of the cost function cannot be readily applied here. However, a similar formulation is used here with some modifications.

The main idea of the LVQ algorithm is based on a simple rule. A number of hidden nodes with random weights are set as the first layer to build subclasses, and then some of these subclasses are merged together to make up the final network output. In this case, the final classes are assumed to have approximately equal number of subclasses (Figure 5.26).

The other key element of this technique is the use of fixed subclass assignments during the whole process of training. In fact, the second-layer weight matrix is set only once, and the training process modifies the parameters of the

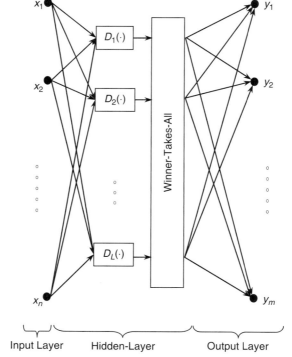

Figure 5.25. *Basic structure of a LVQ network*

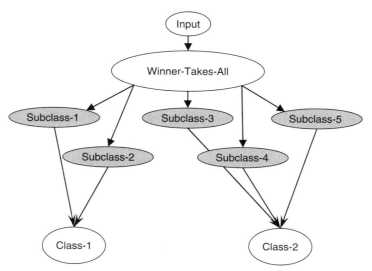

Figure 5.26. *Subclass association of an LVQ network*

first layer only. Based on this classification technique, the weight matrix of the output layer has only a "1" entry in each column, to distinguish the final class, and several 1s in each row to assign several subclasses to a class. Now each training data entry is fed into the network, and its corresponding output is calculated, based on the current network parameters. In this case, the parameters of the nodes in the first layer that won (or lost) the competition are slightly moved toward (or away from) this datum if the network correctly (incorrectly) classifies this entry.

The following algorithm describes the overall procedure and the $\langle T_k, R_k \rangle$ represents the kth training entry (input, output).

Step 1: Set random weights for all L nodes in the first layer.

Step 2: Assign different subclasses to the same class randomly and homogenously, because these weight won't be changed during the training process.

Step 3: Select a random training datum, T_k.

Step 4: Find the neuron in the first layer that is closest to this input, i^*.

Step 5: Calculate the final output answer for the input vector.

Step 6: If the network output is the same as the desired value, R_k, then adjust the weights of the i^* nodes of the first layer as follows: $w_{i^*} \leftarrow w_{i^*} + \lambda(T_k - w_{i^*})$.

Step 7: If the network output is not the same as the desired value, R_k, then adjust the weights of the i^* nodes of the first layer as follows: $w_{i^*} \leftarrow w_{i^*} - \lambda(T_k - w_{i^*})$.

Step 8: Repeat steps 3–7 until all data are correctly classified.

Note that λ is the learning rate, which can be set to a constant or modified during the training process.

To clarify this procedure, assume that the training data set is as follows:

$$\langle T, R \rangle = \left\{ \left\langle \begin{bmatrix} 0 \\ 0 \end{bmatrix} \begin{bmatrix} 1 \\ 0 \end{bmatrix} \right\rangle, \left\langle \begin{bmatrix} 0 \\ 1 \end{bmatrix} \begin{bmatrix} 1 \\ 1 \end{bmatrix} \right\rangle, \left\langle \begin{bmatrix} 1 \\ 0 \end{bmatrix} \begin{bmatrix} 0 \\ 0 \end{bmatrix} \right\rangle, \left\langle \begin{bmatrix} 1 \\ 1 \end{bmatrix} \begin{bmatrix} 0 \\ 1 \end{bmatrix} \right\rangle \right\}$$

Also, assume that the weights matrix of the first and second layer is set as follows:

$$W^1 = \begin{bmatrix} 0.1 & 0.2 \\ 0.2 & 0.3 \\ 0.3 & 0.1 \\ 0.2 & 0.2 \end{bmatrix} \text{ and } W^2 = \begin{bmatrix} 1 & 1 & 0 & 0 \\ 0 & 0 & 1 & 1 \end{bmatrix}$$

Now, suppose the second training datum is selected to train the network. Therefore, the output of the first layer would be

$$A(1) = \begin{bmatrix} \|[0.1 \ \ 0.2] - [0 \ \ 1]\| \\ \|[0.2 \ \ 0.3] - [0 \ \ 1]\| \\ \|[0.3 \ \ 0.1] - [0 \ \ 1]\| \\ \|[0.2 \ \ 0.2] - [0 \ \ 1]\| \end{bmatrix} = \begin{bmatrix} 0.8062 \\ 0.7280 \\ 0.9487 \\ 0.8246 \end{bmatrix} \xrightarrow{compete} \begin{bmatrix} 0 \\ 0 \\ 1 \\ 0 \end{bmatrix}$$

and the output of the network would be

$$A(2) = W^2 \cdot A(1) = \begin{bmatrix} 1 & 1 & 0 & 0 \\ 0 & 0 & 1 & 1 \end{bmatrix} \cdot \begin{bmatrix} 0 \\ 0 \\ 1 \\ 0 \end{bmatrix} = \begin{bmatrix} 0 \\ 1 \end{bmatrix} \neq \begin{bmatrix} 1 \\ 1 \end{bmatrix} = R_2$$

Note that the network output is different from the desired output. Therefore, the weighing vector of the second node of the first layer is modified as follows:

$$w_3 = \begin{bmatrix} 0.3 \\ 0.1 \end{bmatrix} - 0.2 \cdot \left(\begin{bmatrix} 1 \\ 1 \end{bmatrix} - \begin{bmatrix} 0.3 \\ 0.1 \end{bmatrix} \right) = \begin{bmatrix} 0.16 \\ -0.08 \end{bmatrix}$$

The final weight matrix for the first layer would be

$$W^1 \leftarrow \begin{bmatrix} 0.1 & 0.2 \\ 0.16 & -0.08 \\ 0.3 & 0.1 \\ 0.2 & 0.2 \end{bmatrix}$$

This procedure should be continued until all the data have been correctly classified.

5   NEURAL NETWORK APPLICATIONS

This section briefly reviews a number of application areas in which neural networks have been used effectively. This is by no means an exhaustive list of applications.

5.1   EXPERT SYSTEMS

One popular application is the use of neural networks as expert systems. Several definitions have been presented to clearly distinguish this kind of systems from other approaches [55–57]. Generally, an expert system is defined as a system than can imitate the action of a human being for a given process. This definition does not restrict the design of such systems by traditional Artificial Intelligence approaches. Therefore, a variety of such systems can be built by using Fuzzy Logic, Neural Networks, and Neuro-Fuzzy techniques. In most of these systems, there is always a knowledge-based component that holds information about the behavior of the system as simple rules followed by operators (usually in Fuzzy Systems) or a large database collected from the system performance that a neural network can be trained to emulate (Figure 5.27).

5.2   NEURAL CONTROLLERS

Neural controllers are a specific class of expert systems that deal with the process of regulating a liner or nonlinear system (Figure 5.28). There are two methods to train such system, namely, supervised and unsupervised. In the super-

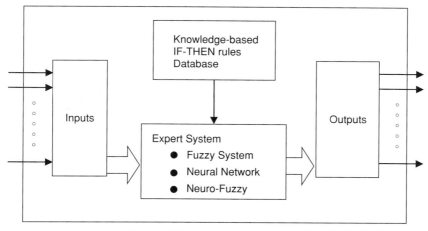

Figure 5.27. *A generic expert system*

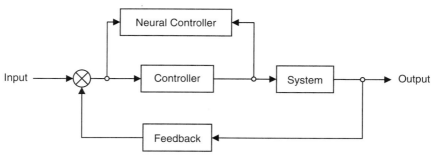

Figure 5.28. *A neural network controller*

vised approach, another controller usually exists, and the neural controller is trained to imitate its behavior. In this case, the neural controller is connect in parallel to the other controller, and during the process, by sampling inputs and outputs, the network is trained to generate similar outputs for similar inputs of the real controller. This process is known as *online training*. In contrast, in the case of offline training, a database of the real-controller inputs and outputs can be employed to train the network [58-60].

6   DECISION MAKERS

In the specific class of decision makers, which can also be viewed as an expert system, a neural network is used to make critical decisions in unexpected situations. One such application is popular in financial markets such as stock market applications. One of the main characteristics of such systems that distinguish them from simple expert systems is their stability. In fact, these systems must be able to produce acceptable output for untrained situations. Therefore, a sufficiently rich data set must be used for the training process [61–63] (see Figure 5.29).

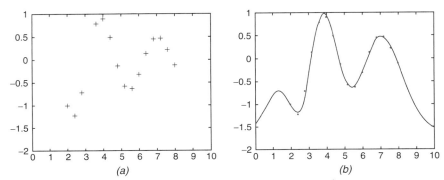

Figure 5.29. *(a) Sample data and (b) network output after training*

7   ROBOT PATH PLANNING

Another complex scenario in which neural networks have been used with some promise is that of robot path planning. In this case, the robot tries to navigate its way to reach a target location. The situation can be made more complicated by adding obstacles in the environment or even other mobile robots. Normally, this situation is modeled as an optimization problem in which some cost function is minimized (e.g., minimize the distance that the robot needs to travel) while satisfying certain constraints (e.g., no collisions) [64–66] (see Figures 5.30 and 5.31).

8   ADAPTIVE NOISE CANCELLATION

Neural networks have been used very effectively to filter noise. In this case, the target signal (in the training set) is the nonnoisy signal that the input should be

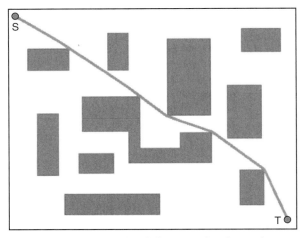

Figure 5.30. *An optimal path for a sample robot work space*

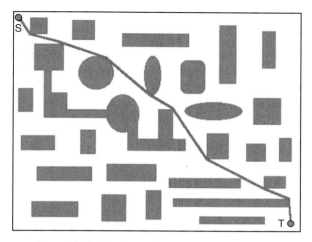

Figure 5.31. *A robot work space with deep U-traps*

generating. The network must learn how to imitate the noise and in the process manage to neutralize it. Many approaches have been introduced in the literature over the years, and some of these have been deployed in real environments [67–69]. An example is provided in Figures 5.32 and 5.33.

9   CONCLUSION

In this chapter, a general overview of artificial neural networks has been presented. These networks vary in their sophistication from the very simple to the more complex. As a result, their training techniques vary as well as their capabilities and suitability for certain applications. Neural networks have

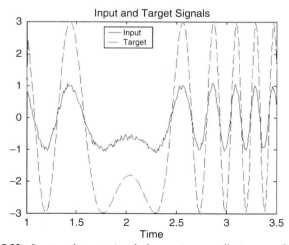

Figure 5.32. *Input and target signals for a noise-cancellation neural network*

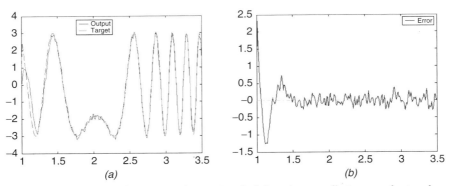

Figure 5.33. *Final performance and error signal of the noise-cancellation neural network*

attracted a lot of interest over the last few decades, and it is expected they will be an active area of research for years to come. Undoubtedly, more robust neural techniques will be introduced in the future that could benefit a wide range of complex applications.

REFERENCES

[1] S. I. Gallant (1993): *Neural Network Learning and Expert Systems*, MIT Press.
[2] N.B. Karayiannis and A.N. Venetsanopoulos, (1993) Efficient learning algorithms for neural networks (ELEANNE), *IEEE Transactions on Systems, Man and Cybernetics*, *23*(5), 1372–1383.
[3] M.H. Hassoun and D.W. Clark (1988): An adaptive attentive learning algorithm for single-layer neural networks, in *Proceedings of the IEEE International Conference on Neural Networks*, *1*, 431–440.
[4] M.E. Ulug (1994): A single layer fast learning fuzzy controller/filter: Neural Networks, in *Proceedings of the IEEE World Congress on Computational Intelligence*, *3*, 1662–1667.
[5] N.B. Karayiannis and A.N. Venetsanopoulos (1992): Fast learning algorithms for neural networks, *IEEE Transactions on Circuits and Systems II: Analog and Digital Signal Processing*, *39*(7), 453–474.
[6] T. Hrycej (1991): Back to single-layer learning principles, in *Proceedings of the International Joint Conference on Neural Networks*, Seattle, *2*, 945.
[7] M.J. Healy (1991): A logical architecture for supervised learning: Neural Networks, in *Proceedings of the IEEE International Joint Conference on Neural Networks*, *1*, 190–195.
[8] R.D. Brandt and L. Feng (1996): Supervised learning in neural networks without feedback network, in *Proceedings of the IEEE International Symposium on Intelligent Control*, pp. 86–90.

[9] Y. Gong and P. Yan (1995): Neural network based iterative learning controller for robot manipulators, in *Proceedings of the IEEE International Conference on Robotics and Automation*, *1*, 569–574.

[10] S. Park and T. Han (2000): Iterative inversion of fuzzified neural networks, *IEEE Transactions on Fuzzy Systems*, 8(3), 266–280.

[11] X. Zhan, K. Zhao, S. Wu, M. Wang, and H. Hu (1997): Iterative learning control for nonlinear systems based on neural networks, in *Proceedings of the IEEE International Conference on Intelligent Processing Systems*, *1*, 517–520.

[12] C.J. Chen, A.L. Haque, and J.Y. Cheung (1992): An efficient simulation model of the Hopfield neural networks, in *Proceedings of the International Joint Conference on Neural Networks*, *1*, 471–475.

[13] G. Galan-Marin and J. Munoz-Perez (2001): Design and analysis of maximum Hopfield networks, *IEEE Transactions on Neural Networks*, *12* (2), 329–339.

[14] N.M. Nasrabadi and W. Li (1991): Object recognition by a Hopfield neural network, *IEEE Transactions on Systems, Man and Cybernetics*, *21* (6), 1523–1535.

[15] J. Xu, X. Zhang, and Y. Li (2001): Kernel MSE algorithm: a unified framework for KFD, LS-SVM and KRR, in *Proceedings of the International Joint Conference on Neural Networks*, *2*, 1486–1491.

[16] T. Hayasaka, N. Toda, S. Usui, and K. Hagiwara (1996): On the least square error and prediction square error of function representation with discrete variable basis, in *Proceedings of the Workshop on Neural Networks for Signal Processing*, *6*, 72–81. IEEE Signal Processing Society.

[17] D.-C. Park (2000): Centroid neural network for unsupervised competitive learning, *IEEE Transactions on Neural Networks*, *11*(2), 520–528.

[18] W. Pedrycz and J. Waletzky (1997): Neural-network front ends in unsupervised learning, *IEEE Transactions on Neural Networks*, 8(2), 390–401.

[19] D.-C. Park (1997): Development of a neural network algorithm for unsupervised competitive learning, in *Proceedings of the International Conference on Neural Networks*, *3*, 1989–1993.

[20] K.-R. Hsieh and W.-T. Chen (1993): A neural network model which combines unsupervised and supervised learning, *IEEE Transactions on Neural Networks*, *4* (2), 357–360.

[21] A.L. Dajani, M. Kamel, and M.I. Elmastry (1990): Single layer potential function neural network for unsupervised learning, in *Proceedings of the International Joint Conference on Neural Networks*, *2*, 273–278.

[22] M. Georgiopoulos, G.L. Heileman, and J. Huang (1991): Properties of learning in ART1, in *Proceedings of the IEEE International Joint Conference on Neural Networks*, *3*, 2671–2676.

[23] G.L. Heileman, M. Georgiopoulos, and J. Hwang (1994): A survey of learning results for ART1 networks, in the *Proceedings of the IEEE International Conference on Neural Networks*, IEEE World Congress on Computational Intelligence, *2*, 1222–1225.

[24] J. Song and M.H. Hassoun (1990): Learning with hidden targets, in the *Proceedings of the International Joint Conference on Neural Networks*, *3*, 93–98.

[25] H.K. Kwan (1991): Multilayer feedbackward neural networks, in *Proceedings of the International Conference on Acoustics, Speech, and Signal Processing, 2*, 1145–1148.

[26] J.F. Shepanski (1988): Fast learning in artificial neural systems: multilayer perceptron training using optimal estimation, in *Proceedings of the IEEE International Conference on Neural Networks, 1*, 465–472.

[27] N.B. Karayiannis and M.M. Randolph-Gips (2003): On the construction and training of reformulated radial basis function neural networks, *IEEE Transactions on Neural Networks, 14* (4), 835–846.

[28] J.A. Leonard and M.A. Kramer (1991): Radial basis function networks for classifying process faults, *IEEE Control Systems Magazine, 11*(3), 31–38.

[29] R. Li, G. Lebby, and S. Baghavan (2002): Performance evaluation of Gaussian radial basis function network classifiers, *SoutheastCon, 2002, Proceedings IEEE*, pp. 355–358.

[30] F. Heimes and B. van Heuveln (1998): The normalized radial basis function neural network, in *Proceedings of the IEEE International Conference on Systems, Man, and Cybernetics, 2*, 1609–1614.

[31] R.J. Craddock and K. Warwick (1996): Multi-layer radial basis function networks. An extension to the radial basis function, in the *Proceedings of the IEEE International Conference on Neural Networks, 2*, 700–705.

[32] J.C. Carr, W.R. Fright and R.K. Beatson (1997): Surface interpolation with radial basis functions for medical imaging, *IEEE Transactions on Medical Imaging, 16*(1), 96–107.

[33] M.A. Romyaldy Jr. (2000): Observations and guidelines on interpolation with radial basis function network for one dimensional approximation problem, in the *Proceedings of the 26th Annual Conference of the IEEE Industrial Electronics Society, 3*, 2129–2134.

[34] H. Leung, T. Lo, and S. Wang, (2001): Prediction of noisy chaotic time series using an optimal radial basis function neural network, *IEEE Transactions on Neural Networks, 12*(5), 1163–1172.

[35] R. Katayama, Y. Kajitani, K. Kuwata, and Y. Nishida (1993): Self generating radial basis function as neuro-fuzzy model and its application to nonlinear prediction of chaotic time series, in a *Proceedings of the Second IEEE International Conference on Fuzzy Systems*, pp. 407–414.

[36] K. Warwick and R. Craddock (1996): An introduction to radial basis functions for system identification. A comparison with other neural network methods, in the *Proceedings of the 35th IEEE Decision and Control Conference, 1*, 464–469.

[37] Y. Lu, N. Sundararajan and P. Saratchandran (1996): Adaptive nonlinear system identification using minimal radial basis function neural networks, in *Proceedings of the IEEE International Conference on Acoustics, Speech, and Signal Processing, 6*, 3521–3524.

[38] S. Tan, J. Hao, and J. Vandewalle (1995): A new learning algorithm for RBF neural networks with applications to nonlinear system identification, in *Proceedings of the IEEE International Symposium on Circuits and Systems, 3*, 1708–1711.

[39] T. Ibayashi, T. Hoya, and Y. Ishida (2002): A model-following adaptive controller using radial basis function networks, in *Proceedings of the International Conference on Control Applications, 2,* 820–824.

[40] P.K. Dash, S. Mishra and G. Panda (2000): A radial basis function neural network controller for UPFC, *IEEE Transactions on Power Systems, 15*(4), 1293–1299.

[41] J. Deng, S. Narasimhan, and P. Saratchandran (2002): Communication channel equalization using complex-valued minimal radial basis function neural networks, *IEEE Transactions on Neural Networks, 13*(3), 687–696.

[42] J. Lee, C.D. Beach, and N. Tepedelenlioglu (1996): Channel equalization using radial basis function network, in *Proceedings of the IEEE International Conference on Neural Networks, 4,* 1924–1928.

[43] J. Lee, C.D. Beach, and N. Tepedelenlioglu (1996): Channel equalization using radial basis function network, in *Proceedings of the IEEE International Conference on Acoustics, Speech, and Signal Processing, 3,* 1719–1722.

[44] R. Sankar and N.S. Sethi (1997): Robust speech recognition techniques using a radial basis function neural network for mobile applications, in *Proceedings of IEEE Southeastcon,* pp. 87–91.

[45] H. Ney (1991): Speech recognition in a neural network framework: discriminative training of Gaussian models and mixture densities as radial basis functions, in *Proceedings of the IEEE International Conference on Acoustics, Speech, and Signal Processing, 1,* 573–576.

[46] I. Cha and S.A. Kassam (1994): Nonlinear image restoration by radial basis function networks, in *Proceedings of the IEEE International Conference on Image Processing, 2,* 580–584.

[47] I. Cha and S.A. Kassam (1996): Nonlinear color image restoration using extended radial basis function networks, in *Proceedings of the IEEE International Conference on Acoustics, Speech, and Signal Processing, 6,* 3402–3405.

[48] A.G. Bors and I. Pitas (1998): Optical flow estimation and moving object segmentation based on median radial basis function network, *IEEE Transactions on Image Processing, 7* (5), 693–702.

[49] D. Gao and G. Yang (2002): Adaptive RBF neural networks for pattern classifications, in *Proceedings of the International Joint Conference on Neural Networks, 1,* 846–851.

[50] C. Fan, Z. Jin, J. Zhang, and W. Tian (2002): Application of multisensor data fusion based on RBF neural networks for fault diagnosis of SAMS, in *Proceedings of the 7th International Conference on Control, Automation, Robotics and Vision, 3,* 1557–1562.

[51] J.T. Tou and R.C. Gonzalez (1974), *Pattern Recognition,* Reading, MA, Addison-Wesley.

[52] Z.-P. Lo, Y. Yu, and B. Bavarian (1992): Derivation of learning vector quantization algorithms, in *Proceedings of the International Joint Conference on Neural Networks, 3,* 561–566.

[53] P. Burrascano (1991): Learning vector quantization for the probabilistic neural network, *IEEE Transactions on Neural Networks, 2*(4), 458–461.

[54] N.B. Karayiannis and M.M. Randolph-Gips (2003): Soft learning vector quantization and clustering algorithms based on non-Euclidean norms: multinorm algorithms, *IEEE Transactions on Neural Networks*, *14*(1), 89–102.

[55] L. Medsker (1994): Design and development of hybrid neural network and expert systems, in *Proceedings of the IEEE International Conference on Neural Networks*, IEEE World Congress on Computational Intelligence, *3*, 1470–1474.

[56] M.S. Kurzyn (1993): Expert systems and neural networks: a comparison, Artificial Neural Networks and Expert Systems, in *Proceedings of the First International Two-Stream Conference on Neural Networks*, New Zealand, pp. 222–223.

[57] A.V. Hudli, M.J. Palakal and M.J. Zoran (1991): A neural network based expert system model, in *Proceedings of the Third International Conference on Tools for Artificial Intelligence*, pp. 145–149.

[58] W.-Y. Wang, C.-Y. Cheng and Y.-G. Leu (2004): An online GA-based output-feedback direct adaptive fuzzy-neural controller for uncertain nonlinear systems, in *IEEE Transactions on Systems, Man and Cybernetics, Part B*, *34*(1), 334–345.

[59] Y. Zhang, P.-Y. Peng and Z.-P. Jiang (2000): Stable neural controller design for unknown nonlinear systems using backstepping, *IEEE Transactions on Neural Networks*, *11*(6), 1347–1360.

[60] A.L. Nelson, E. Grant and G. Lee (2003): Developing evolutionary neural controllers for teams of mobile robots playing a complex game, in *Proceedings of the IEEE International Conference on Information Reuse and Integration*, pp. 212–218.

[61] L. Rothrock (1992): Modeling human perceptual decision-making using an artificial neural network, in *Proceedings of the International Joint Conference on Neural Networks*, *2*, 448–452.

[62] S. Mukhopadhyay and H. Wang (1999): Distributed decomposition architectures for neural decision-makers, in *Proceedings of the 38th IEEE Conference on Decision and Control*, *3*, 2635–2640.

[63] G. Rogova, P. Scott, and C. Lolett (2002): Distributed reinforcement learning for sequential decision making, in *Proceedings of the Fifth International Conference on Information Fusion*, *2*, 1263–1268.

[64] J. Taheri and N. Sadati, (2003): Fully modular online controller for robot navigation in static and dynamic environments, in *Proceedings of the 2003 IEEE International Symposium on Computational Intelligence in Robotics and Automation*, *1*, 163–168.

[65] N. Sadati and J. Taheri (2002): Genetic algorithm in robot path planning problem in crisp and fuzzified environments, in *Proceedings of the IEEE International Conference on Industrial Technology*, *1*, 175–180.

[66] N. Sadati and J. Taheri (2002): Solving robot motion planning problem using Hopfield neural network in a fuzzified environment, in *Proceedings of IEEE International Conference on Fuzzy Systems*, *2*, 1144–1149.

[67] R. Bambang (2002): Active noise cancellation using recurrent radial basis function neural networks, in *Proceedings of the Asia-Pacific Conference on Circuits and Systems*, *2*, 231–236.

[68] C.K. Chen and T.-D. Chiueh (1996): Multilayer perceptron neural networks for active noise cancellation, in *Proceedings of the IEEE International Symposium on Circuits and Systems*, 3, 523–526.

[69] L. Tao and H.K. Kwan (1999): A neural network method for adaptive noise cancellation, circuits and systems, in *Proceedings of the IEEE International Symposium on Circuits and Systems*, 5, 567–570.

Chapter 6

SWARM INTELLIGENCE
James Kennedy
Bureau of Labor Statistics

Swarm intelligence refers to a kind of problem-solving ability that emerges in the interactions of simple information-processing units. The concept of a swarm suggests multiplicity, stochasticity, randomness, and messiness, and the concept of intelligence suggests that the problem-solving method is somehow successful. The information-processing units that compose a swarm can be animate, mechanical, computational, or mathematical; they can be insects, birds, or human beings; they can be array elements, robots, or standalone workstations; they can be real or imaginary. Their coupling can have a wide range of characteristics, but there must be interaction among the units. Given the diversity of paradigms that call themselves swarm intelligence, this chapter will focus on the particular approach known as *particle swarm optimization*.

1   PARTICLE SWARMS

The particle swarm algorithm is based on a certain insight regarding human behavior and cognition. The insight is simple, as is the algorithm that follows from it. Simply put: *people learn to make sense of the world by talking with other people about it*. This not-very-technical observation enables us to design a family of computer algorithms that encode some population of individuals who propose solutions to a problem, and then are able to refine those solutions by interacting with their "peers," picking up suggestions from their neighbors, and adjusting their own patterns of variables.

Over time, in one of these programs, individuals begin to find good problem solutions, even when the problem is very difficult—for instance, when it is multimodal, nonlinear, noisy, or nondifferentiable. This technique has been used for binary problems, multiobjective problems, dynamic problems that keep changing, and many other tough kinds of problems. It has been used for a variety of engineering problems, from the maintenance of electrical grids to the classification of physiological variables in early diagnosis of disease.

As will be seen, there have been, over the past decade, many variations in the particle swarm algorithm. Some versions are almost unrecognizable, and some variations are extremely minor tweaks that enhance performance significantly. The following sections will introduce the canonical form of the algorithm and some common variations, and then discuss some ongoing research on different problem domains and different lines of alteration of the algorithm.

1.1   General Characteristics

Every known version of the particle swarm algorithm has certain characteristics. First, every version employs a *population* of particles. The number of these is typically far less than in the usual evolutionary algorithm; most researchers use twenty to fifty particles in a population.

Second, every particle swarm has some sort of *topology* describing the interconnections among the particles. The "traditional" topologies, which are becoming somewhat antiquated in light of current research but are still widely used, are call *gbest* and *lbest*. The *gbest* topology (or *sociometry*, since it is often considered to be like a kind of social network) can be thought as a fully interconnected population; that is, every member of the population can be influenced by every other one. In the standard particle swarm, this means that particles are affected by the individual that has found the best problem solution so far—the very best one in the population. Thus, though *gbest* contains the greatest possible number of connections between pairs of population members, in practice it really only means keeping track of the best solution found. The *lbest* sociometry is a ring lattice, where every particle is connected to the particles on either side of it in the population array. As will be seen, the advantage of this structure is that subpopulations can converge independently on diverse optima in the problem space. Thus the *lbest* topology, while typically slower to converge on an optimum, is also less susceptible to the allure of local optima; its search is slower and more thorough than *gbest*'s. Thousands of other topologies have been tested, as will be described below.

A third characteristic of every particle swarm is some choice of a *change rule*. The particle moves through the search space, selecting a point at time t that is dependent on its position at $t-1$, its previous successes, and the previous successes of its neighbors. There is a "standard" formula for determining the next step, but this has evolved over time, and some researchers even have tried replacing the formula with a kind of random number generator. It may seem that the particle swarm is typified by the trajectories of the particles through the search space, but this view is only correct if the concept of "trajectory" is stretched to include random search around a center.

Evolutionary search is often described in terms of two phases, called *exploration* and *exploitation* [28]. The search algorithm first searches the environment for good regions, and then, having found a good region of the search space, looks for the best point in that region. In the particle swarm, however, step-size—the range of investigation of a particle in the search space—is scaled to consensus in the neighborhood; if a particle and its neighbors have had success in a particular area, then that area will be searched, but if some neighbors are still investigating other regions of the problem space, the particle will still tend to explore widely. Concepts such as exploration versus exploitation seem to assume certain characteristics of the search space—for instance, that it contains subdivisions that are locally monotonic. The particle swarm's assumptions are more flexible; a well-designed particle swarm can search multiple regions of the space simultaneously, and particles can switch flexibly from one locally optimal region to another.

A fourth characteristic of all known particle swarms is what may loosely be termed the *interaction rule*. A particle considers its successes and some other particles' successes in determining the next point to test in the search space. How this point is chosen, though, may follow any of a number of possible rules, and the list of rules is growing as researchers push the limits of what is known in this young field.

1.1.1 The Canonical Algorithm

This section will present the most common form of particle swarm algorithm as it currently exists, and discuss some of its features.

1.1.2 Constants and Initialization

There is no law that says that particles must be initialized randomly through the problem space, but that is the general practice, given that there is no special knowledge about a better way to do it. Three variables need to be initialized, most importantly the positions of the particles, represented algebraically as $\vec{x}_i$, and their velocities $\vec{v}_i$. If the researcher chooses to initialize $\vec{v}_i$ to a vector of zeroes, then $\vec{p}_i$ should be different from $\vec{x}_i$ in order to make the particles move; but more frequently, $\vec{p}_i = \vec{x}_i$ for the first iteration, and nonzero velocity values propel the particle through the search space in some randomly chosen direction.

Xmax is simply a constant that defines the range of the search space. It may vary on each dimension, but is simplified here as a single constant, as many test functions treat variables identically. The constant Vmax has a history that will be described below. It may be used to constrain search during the iterative phase of the algorithm, but it is a heuristic device only; in the canonical version, Vmax simply serves to initialize particle velocities in-bounds.

The "acceleration constants" phi1 and phi2 and the "constriction coefficient" chi (φ_1, φ_2, and χ) are the result of analysis by Maurice Clerc, described below. The value of chi is derived from the sum of the two phi constants by a formula, and phi1 and phi2 are set to sum to 4.1, just because it works.

1.1.3 Neighborhood Best

In the canonical particle swarm, each particle is influenced by its best neighbor. The set of particles to which a particle i is topologically connected is called i's *neighborhood*. The neighborhood may be the entire population or some subset of it. Normally the algorithm loops through the neighborhood, comparing the best function results found so far (*pbest*[k]), and assigns the index of the best particle to the variable g. Note that not all versions of the particle swarm use the best neighbor; some use an average of all neighbors' previous successes, but these versions are relatively new and not standard.

Table 6.1. Pseudocode representation of the canonical particle swarm algorithm.

Xmax ← range of search space
Vmax ← proportional to range of search space
phi = 4.1
chi = 0.792

Initialize
    for i = 1 to number of particles
        for j = 1 to number of problem dimensions
            $x[i][d]$ = uniform rand() in Xmax // position of particle i on dimension d
            $v[i][d]$ = uniform rand() in ± Vmax
            $p[i][d]$ = $x[i][d]$ // for start
        $pbest[i]$ = eval($p[i]$) // arbitrary for initialization
        if $pbest[i] < pbest[gbest]$ then $gbest = i$

Iterate
    for i = 1 to number of particles
        g = index of neighbor with best $pbest[i]$

    //Select point to test
    for j=1 to dimension
        $v[i][d]$ = chi × ($v[i][j]$ + rand()× phi1 × ($p[i][d] - x[i][d]$) + rand()× phi2 × ($p[g][d] - x[i][d]$))
    for j = 1 to dimension
        $x[i][d]$ = $x[i][d]$ + $v[i][d]$

    // Evaluate new point
    eval = eval($x[i]$)

    // If it's better than best so far
    if eval < $pbest[i]$ then do
        $pbest[i]$ = eval
        for j = 1 to dimension
            $p[i][j]$ = $x[i][j]$
        if $pbest[i] < pbest[gbest]$ then $gbest = i$
Until termination criterion is met

1.1.4   Selecting a Point to Test

The particles oscillate around a point defined as a stochastic average between the individual particle's previous best and the best neighbor's previous best. This oscillation is the result of a formula that adjusts the particle's velocity at each time-step. As the particle gets farther from the mean, the velocity becomes smaller until it reverses direction and the particle goes the other way.

As the two terms added to $v[i][d]$ are weighted by uniformly distributed random numbers, the pattern is not cyclic; it gets its characteristic amplitude and wavelength from the value of phi, but does not strictly adhere to a periodic pattern. But this source of irregularity is not the most important source of variation in the particle's trajectory. More importantly, the particle may find a new point in the search space that is better than its previous best. Further, some member of its neighborhood might find a better point. In this case, it may be that the "best neighbor" at time t is different from that at $t-1$, or it may simply be that the same neighbor has found a better point, so that $p[g][d]$ has changed, even though g has not. These improvements, of course, guide the progress of the algorithm and are central to its ability to optimize complex functions. The result, though, is an aperiodicity of the particles' trajectories that is very hard to comprehend: this messy, complicated, ever-evolving, highly interactive process is what we call *swarm intelligence*.

The amplitude of the oscillation turns out to be a very important feature of the particle swarm search strategy. It can be seen to have two components. First, as seen above, the formula, even in its deterministic form, produces a wave that searches back and forth. But more importantly, and more difficult to grasp, the difference between the individual's previous best $p[i][d]$ and the neighborhood best $p[g][d]$ wanders constantly as a result of the random coefficients applied to each variable. The random coefficients vary between 0.0 and 1.0, meaning that, if a coefficient equals zero, that variable ($p[i][d]$ or $p[g][d]$) will have no effect. If both coefficients are near zero, the velocity will retain its previous value, and if both are near 1.0, the velocity may be greatly modified. The particle may move into a region on the next step that is bounded by a sort of hyperrectangle, bounded by the current position plus the $t-1$ velocity in the corner where all the random numbers equal zero, and the current position plus the $t-1$ velocity plus the differences between the current position and both previous bests, multiplied by their acceleration constants φ_1 and φ_2, when the random numbers equal 1.0.

The size of this hyperrectangle is defined by the difference, on each dimension, between $p[i][d]$ and $p[g][d]$. The meaningful implication of this is that the range of the search is modulated by the difference between particles' previous best points – what we call *consensus*. When a particle and its neighbor have found success in the same region of the search space, they "agree" on where to look for even better points. The degree of consensus scales the extent of the search.

In sum, the particle selects points in the search space based on a kind of oscillatory trajectory that carries it back and forth around the region defined by where it has had success before, and where its neighbors have found good solutions.

1.1.5   The Evaluation

The particle swarm searches for the minimum or maximum of a function, and evaluates the entire function all at once. In a sense this resembles the measurement of *fitness* in evolutionary computation methods. Importantly, this approach is distinguished from the variable-by-variable type of evaluation seen in cognitivistic – i.e., traditional artificial intelligence – approaches to problem solving in computer programs. It is not possible to assign credit to variables in terms of their contribution to the evaluation of an entire pattern, nor does it turn out to be necessary.

1.2   The Sociocognitive Metaphor

Traditional AI grew up together with cognitive psychology, as a reaction to the behaviorism that prevailed in psychology in the middle of the twentieth century. The behaviorists had essentially blocked any study of mental phenomena in the universities, so the "cognitive revolution" began with a commonsense approach, looking at the thinking processes of the individual as an isolated unit. That point of view is consistent with the *experience* of thinking; that is, our thoughts seem like a private monologue or story, occurring in our own phenomenological worlds.

Social psychologists, though, were forming another perspective on cognition. Many studies showed that individuals' beliefs, memories, attitudes, and thought processes were heavily influenced by those around them. As early as 1936, Sherif [67] was showing how reported perceptions were shaped by norms; Asch's [5] famous conformity experiments showed how behavior could be shaped by the influence of others; Crutchfield [19] and Deutsch and Gerard [21] further focused in on factors affecting the social influence of groups on individuals. At the same time, persuasion researchers from Hovland [36] to Cialdini (e.g., [13]) were noting that the choices people make are directly and irrefutably affected by their social atmosphere.

An important study by Nisbett and Wilson [55] showed that people are often unaware of their own cognitive processes, and are unable to report verbally how their own minds arrived at a conclusion – many self-reported cognitive processes are better described as "rationalizations" than "descriptions" of cognitive processes. Note that early AI was largely based on self-reported processes [54]; as such, it is clear that there will be room for improvement over the heuristic algorithms employed in traditional artificial intelligence paradigms.

Fundamental to the particle swarm algorithm is a view of cognition as a social process. The internal monologue of thought is easily seen as an imagined conversation between the thinker and some other – the other may be another person, another instance of the self, or, it seems possible, the self may perceive itself as the listener as another imagined individual produces the monologue. In any case, Levine, Resnick, and Higgins [50] noted that, "Outside the laboratory and the school, cognition is almost always collaborative" (p. 599). According to them, intersubjectivity, a shared understanding of the task and context, is required for coordinated cognitive activity, and they proposed research in a new field they call *sociocognition*, which comprises the integration of social interaction and cognition. Their statement was adamant: "Although some might claim that the brain as the physical site of mental processing requires that we treat cognition as a fundamentally individual and even private activity, we are prepared to argue that all mental activity – from perceptual recognition to memory to problem solving – involves either representations of other people or the use of artifacts and cultural forms that have a social history" (p. 604).

Consider, for example, the topic of false memory, for instance as researched by Elizabeth Loftus [51]. Loftus has shown repeatedly that memories created by suggestion are indistinguishable from "real" memories, that is, memories generated by the individual's first-hand perception of a situation. This research supports the view of memory as a social construction. Decades of work by Albert Bandura [8] has consistently shown the numerous and important ways that human cognition is a function of social learning; Bandura focuses on observational learning, mostly, where the individual sees how someone else has solved a problem, and imitates that. Likewise, Latané's social impact theory research [56] shows an individual's attitudes and beliefs to be a simple function of the strength, immediacy, and number of others who hold that attitude or belief. Very recent research by Wegner [72] shows that even "conscious will" is largely illusory.

The starting-point then for understanding the metaphor underlying this problem-solving technique is to understand that human intelligence itself operates through interaction among individuals. Our conscious experience of thinking is not a good scientific description of cognition. It appears that a better description would focus less on internal, private processes, and more on interpersonal dynamics.

Cognitive dissonance theory [30; 31] portrays the mind as a set of cognitive elements related to one another in complex logical and affective ways. The individual is motivated to find and maintain consistency among the elements; for instance, it is uncomfortable to hold two beliefs that logically contradict one another, or to find oneself in agreement with someone one doesn't like. In the current view, "dissonance" is the result of a cognitive evaluation function, where a vector of cognitive elements and their interrelationships is input, and a single measure of goodness is produced. Thinking, then, is seen to be a process of optimization, of constant searching for ways to arrange and rearrange beliefs and attitudes so as to produce the most consistent – least dissonant – pattern. One important aspect of this process is that people simply talk to one another, and observe one another, and learn from one another how to make sense of a confusing world.

Particle swarms are most typically used by engineers and others who apply mathematics to difficult tasks. These innovators need a method that works, something that can solve hard problems with a minimum of tweaking. The two perspectives on the algorithm, the sociocognitive perspective and the engineering perspective, constantly interact symbiotically to produce new developments in the field—new ways to make the algorithm work better, faster, and more efficiently. The metaphor of interacting human minds is a rich one for improving the paradigm. For instance, we may ask:

- Is human social interaction best conceived as averaging between two points of view?

- Are individuals influenced equally by everyone they know? And, if not, how are the differences best summarized in a computer algorithm?

- Is influence reciprocal between individuals?

- Are individuals affected by other individuals, or by statistical norms of their group?

. . . and so on. Thinking about these kinds of questions sometimes results in new variations of the algorithm, oftentimes with improved optimization results. The social–psychological and applied-mathematical facets of the algorithm benefit mutually from one another.

1.3   Origins of the Present-Day Canonical Particle Swarm

This section describes some steps in the development of the algorithm since its initial discovery in 1994. A subsequent section will describe some current research frontiers, and finally, some speculation about future directions will be offered.

1.3.1   Social Psychology and Genetic Algorithms

The seeds of the particle swarm were planted when the present author worked with Bibb Latané and his colleagues at the University of North Carolina, creating computer simulations of social systems using the Warsaw Simulation System [56]. These simulations, which were supported by decades of human-subjects research by Latané on social impact theory, were based on cellular automata [74]; a population was coded as a grid of individuals who interacted with one another according to rules programmed by the researcher. The outstanding finding of that research was that simple local interaction rules, similar to what Latané had derived from his experimentation and observational research with human subjects, could result in consistent and meaningful large-scale patterns of belief, attitude, and behavior in the society.

In 1992, the present author began meeting with a computational intelligence brown-bag lunchtime group, comprising mostly engineers and computer scientists (including Russ Eberhart), at a research institute that shall remain nameless. In those lively discussions it became apparent that the social dynamics simulated in the Psychology Department at Chapel Hill had much in common with the dynamics simulated in evolutionary computation. Populations of individuals interacted, the population changed over time, and global order emerged from local behavior.

The most important difference had to do with the presence of something called "a problem." The evolutionary algorithms were being used to find the optima of complicated mathematical functions, whereas the social simulations simply iterated to an equilibrium state. But it seemed obvious that social systems do solve problems; the state of human knowledge, for instance, does improve over time. What would happen if the states of the individuals in the social simulations were evaluated on the basis of some measure of goodness, similar to cognitive dissonance?

There are important differences between evolutionary and social–psychological processes. One of the biggest philosophical differences has to do with selection. Evolutionary methods find increasingly better problem solutions by killing off worse-performing members of the population and letting better ones reproduce; each iteration represents a "generation" in the history of the population. Societies, though, retain individuals over iterations; an iteration is simply a unit of time. Individuals are seen as changing over time, rather than being replaced.

The fundamental principle of evolution is competition for survival. Individuals who are allowed to survive may reproduce. Mutation, crossover, and/or other operators may affect the offspring, and as the fittest of each generation is allowed to survive and reproduce, the quality of the population, typically, improves over time.

The fundamental principle of the particle swarm is cooperation and sharing of knowledge. Every individual participates in the population's improvement as both teacher and learner. Over time, due to a kind of ratchet effect [69], the patterns of variables improve. Individuals that communicate with one another tend to gravitate into the same regions of the problem space, as better-performing individuals influence lesser ones. Depending on the population topology and other factors, the individuals may cluster around diverse local optima, or they may all end up in the same region. When local optima have been well searched, it is quite probable that the particles are clustered around the global optimum, or at least an excellent local one.

1.3.2   Flocking and Schooling

The first particle swarm program was written by modifying a bird-flocking simulation. Two disparate groups of researchers in the 1980s [64; 33] had derived very similar models of the dynamics of bird flocks. Reynolds, working from a computer-graphics perspective (e.g., he wanted to be able to portray realistic bird-flock animations on a computer screen), concluded that bird flocking could be simulated using three rules:

- Separation: steer to avoid colliding with local flockmates
- Alignment: try to move in the same average direction as local flockmates
- Cohesion: steer to move toward the perceived center of the local flock

Heppner, a biologist, made three-dimensional movies of bird flocks, and carefully studied the dynamics of their choreography. His model, though it was developed independently of Reynolds', contained essentially the same three rules, plus a fourth: attraction to a roost. His flocks eventually settled down.

The present author had been experimenting with these flocking models, and added one more feature, with surprising results [45]. Inspired by Heppner's "attraction to a roost," "cornfield vector" was added, which in the first program was simply a two-dimensional point on the plane of the computer monitor. This point was considered to simulate some food on the ground; birds flying past might see the food, or some sign of the presence of food, and most importantly, birds flying past could see that other birds seemed to be zeroing in on some target. Thus, members of the flock were attracted toward positions that other members of the flock had found to be relatively near to food.

The first experiments were shocking. The flock immediately converged on the point on the screen, as if sucked in by a vacuum cleaner.

That first algorithm worked as follows: each bird

- evaluated its distance from the cornfield
- identified some "neighbors" who were nearby on the display plane
- identified which of its neighbors had come closest to the target point, and where that had happened (note that the location of the point was not known, but only the distance from it)
- if its position was to the right of (above) its own previous best point, then it moved some random amount to the left (down), else it moved a random amount to the right (upward)
- if its position was to the right of (above) the best neighbor's best point, it moved a random amount to the left (down), otherwise right (upward)

The success of the food-searching program prompted the second set of experiments, conducted the same day. The evaluation of distance from an arbitrary point on the screen was replaced by an XOR feedforward neural network. A network was defined with two input nodes, three hidden nodes, and one output, requiring nine connection weights and four biases. Thus optimizing the weights (including biases) meant searching through a thirteen-dimensional space. Weights were initialized with random values, and the program ran iteratively. For testing purposes, two of the weights were graphed on the screen, meaning that the entire flock could be watched as a display of swarming particles (at this time, the algorithm was yet unnamed). The code for evaluating the network was cut from some public-domain source code and pasted into the program where the evaluation of distances to the cornfield vector had been.

Again, the flock had no difficulty finding an optimal matrix of weights. The plotted points zoomed immediately, it seemed, with no hesitation, toward a configuration that resulted in squared error in the network very near zero.

At this point, I sent some code to Russ Eberhart, who compiled it and agreed that this new algorithm did seem to successfully optimize the weights in the network. He and I have worked together on the paradigm ever since.

1.3.3   The Evolution of the Paradigm

We made several changes to the paradigm almost immediately. First, since the task of identifying neighbors in the search space (a vestige of the flocking simulation) was very expensive computationally, we experimented with topological neighbors, both *gbest* and *lbest*, and found that these worked just as well. The advantage here was that neighborhoods were constant, and did not have to be recalculated on every iteration depending on the positions of all the particles in the search space.

Another important change in the first weeks of experimentation involved replacing the inequality rule. The very first versions simply said that if a particle's current position was greater than the stochastic average of its and its neighbor's *pbests*, it would change by a negative amount, and if it was less than the target it would change by a positive amount. The new version used the distance, on each dimension, between the particle's present position and the stochastic average of the previous bests:

```
v[i][j] = v[i][j] +
    rand() × (phi1) × (p[i][d] − x[i][d]) +
    rand() × (phi2) × (p[g][d] − x[i][d]);
        if v[i][d] > Vmax then v[i][d] = Vmax;
        else if v[i][d] < -Vmax then v[i][d] = -Vmax;
x[i][d] = x[i][d] + v[i][d];
```

There was some initial experimentation with the two constants, called above phi1 and phi2; some experiments found that it was better to have the first one bigger than the second, and some found it was better to make the second constant bigger. These two constants, randomly weighted, assign weight to the two "differences," where the first is an "individual" (sometimes "cognitive") term, and the second is an "other" (or "social") term. Because it did not appear that one weighting scheme or the other was superior across a range of situations, and in the interest of parsimony, we decided to make the two constants equal, and let the random number generator make the decision about which should be larger.

Now that the two phi constants were established to be equal to one another, the system still needed to have values defined for them and for Vmax. Numerous studies were conducted, both published and unpublished, and by convention most researchers felt that a value of 2.0 worked well for each phi. Values that were too low tended to allow the particle to wander too far from promising regions of the search space, and values too high tended to jerk the particle back and forth unproductively.

Vmax was a different kind of problem. Vmax set a limit for the velocity, which otherwise was defined by the size of the previous iteration's velocity and the two differences. Without Vmax the system simply exploded, for reasons that were initially not understood. If the velocity was not limited, it would become larger and larger with each iteration until it exceeded the data type range. With Vmax the particle's trajectory became pseudocyclic, oscillating (or maybe "twitching" is a better word for it) around the average of the previous bests.

When the difference between the individual's and other's pbests were large, Vmax had the effect of slowing the exploratory search by limiting the particle's trajectory to "smallish" steps between the two pbests and slightly beyond them. When the difference between them was small, though, especially when it was small relative to Vmax, the amplitude of the trajectory was modulated by Vmax, and the particle was not able to converge in the later stages of search.

What was the right size for this constant? Research with neural networks and standard testbed problems typically concluded that a value of approximately 4.0 was appropriate. But several papers were published during this time that noted the inability of the swarm to converge on optima – it is usually desirable for an optimizer to search in smaller steps as it approaches the peak of an optimal region. It was clear that something needed to be done about this unsatisfying situation.

1.3.4   Controlling Explosion and Convergence

The present author presented a paper at the 1998 Evolutionary Programming conference (Kennedy, [40]), which plotted the trajectories of some one-dimensional deterministic particles, where the previous bests were combined and did not change with time. In other words, these simplified particles followed the rule:

$$v = v + (\text{phi}) \times (p - x)$$
$$x = x + v$$

These graphs showed, first of all, that particles without random coefficients did not explode; their trajectories were very orderly and well-behaved. Second of all, the trajectories for each value of phi were unique, often presenting the appearance that the particle in discrete time was skipping across underlying waveforms, which varied with the value of phi. The graphs were presented to the conference as a kind of puzzle. Why does the system explode when randomness is added? What is the nature of the underlying wave patterns?

These questions resulted in several avenues of research. In an informal talk to a workshop at the Congress of Computational Intelligence in Anchorage later that same year, Doug Hoskins noted that simply varying phi between two values would cause the velocity to increase out of control. He compared this effect to pumping a swing, where the change in the coefficient added energy to the system.

Ozcan and Mohan [57, 58] analyzed the simplified particle system and determined that the particle was "surfing the waves" of underlying sinusoidal patterns. They proposed that particles might be equipped with "sensors" that determined what kind of search was being conducted; if a particle stayed in a region too long, for instance, a coefficient could be adapted to enlarge the scope of search.

At about this time, Shi and Eberhart [24, 23] introduced a convention they called the "inertia weight," which depreciated the contribution of the *t*-1 velocity. By using an inertia weight less than 1.0, it was possible to control the explosion of the algorithm. The inertia weight algorithm was implemented as

```
v[i][j] = W × v[i][j] +
    rand()× (phi1) × (p[i][d] − x[i][d]) +
    rand()× (phi2) × (p[g][d] − x[i][d]);
x[i][d] = x[i][d] + v[i][d];
```

where W was the new coefficient in the algorithm. Several values were experimented with; those researchers settled on a method of reducing the value of the inertia weight, typically from about 0.9 to about 0.4, over the course of the iterations. Though Vmax was no longer necessary for controlling the explosion of the particles, Eberhart and Shi continued to use it, often setting Vmax = Xmax, in order to keep the system within the relevant part of the search space.

In France, Maurice Clerc was developing a mathematical analysis of the system in order to understand the explosion and convergence properties of the particle swarm. He reduced the simplified, deterministic, one-dimensional, single-particle system to an algebraic matrix, by the following steps.

The simplified, deterministic algorithm can be depicted algebraically as

$$v_{t+1} = v_t + \varphi_1 \otimes (p_i - x_i) + \varphi_2 \otimes (p_g - x_i)$$
$$x_{t+1} = x_t + v_{t+1}$$

And then, by substitution,

$$p = \frac{\varphi_1 p_i + \varphi_2 p_g}{\varphi}, \text{ where } \varphi = \varphi_1 + \varphi_2$$
$$y = p - x_t$$

Given these transformations, the system can be written as

$$v_{t+1} = v_t + \varphi y_t$$
$$x_{t+1} = -v_t + (1 - \varphi) y_t$$

which can be represented in matrix form:

$$P_t = \begin{pmatrix} v_t \\ y_t \end{pmatrix}$$

$$M = \begin{pmatrix} 1 & \varphi \\ -1 & 1 - \varphi \end{pmatrix}$$

The velocity and position of the system are then calculated:

$$P_{t+1} = M \cdot P_t$$

or, to generalize:

$$P_t = M^t \cdot P_0$$

To control explosion, Clerc reasoned, one must ensure that M^t approaches a limit of zero as time approaches infinity. This is done by ensuring that the eigenvalues of M are less than 1 in module. Clerc accomplished this by application of a system of "constriction coefficients."

The simplest and most widely used version is Clerc's Type 1" constriction:

$$v_t + 1 = \chi (v_t + \varphi_1 \otimes (p_i - x_i) + \varphi_2 \otimes (p_g - x_i))$$
$$x_{t+1} = x^t + v^t + 1$$

where the constriction coefficient χ is defined as

$$\chi = \frac{2k}{\left| 2 - \varphi - \sqrt{\varphi^2 - 4\varphi} \right|}, \text{ where } \kappa \in [0,1] \text{ and } \varphi > 4.0 \text{ (usually } \kappa = 1.0 \text{ and } \varphi = 4.1.$$

Adding randomness, multidimensionality, and population size brings us back to the pseudocode example given in Table 6.1, the canonical particle swarm of the present time. It should be noted that the Type 1" constriction scheme is mathematically equivalent to the inertia-weight model, with appropriate values of coefficients.

1.4 Current Directions in Particle Swarm Research

Research on the particle swarm has fanned out in many different directions. For this chapter we will touch briefly on some developments and refer the reader to primary sources. This section will cover several specific problem domains to which the algorithm has been applied, and a later section will discuss variations in the algorithm itself.

1.4.1 Multiobjective optimization

It sometimes happens that a problem is defined in terms that require solving multiple problems simultaneously. Often the solutions to the various problems conflict with one another, and the best solution is a kind of compromise. The boundary between the two problems' solution regions tends to comprise multiple points; that is, there can be a set of solutions that equally well satisfies the conflicting demands. The set of solutions is called a *Pareto set*.

Optimization discussed to this point has searched for a single best solution to a problem. In using the particle swarm for multiobjective optimization, however, most researchers try to find a method where each particle represents a single point on the Pareto front and the overall solution is distributed across the entire population. To this writer, at least, the real problem of multiobjective optimization with particle swarms is the coordination of individuals. Human societies are full of reciprocity, roles, and specialization; the ordinary particle swarm has none. The work of a society may be seen as multiobjective optimization – you need to heat your house as well as feed the family, as well as maintain transportation, etc. There are many objectives that must all be met to ensure survival and comfort. And this multiplicity of objectives is met through role specialization. Similarly, researchers are currently experimenting with ways for particles to "specialize" within the context of a multiobjective problem.

Mexican researcher Coello Coello [17, 18] has developed a particle swarm variation he calls MOPSO, for *m*ultiobjective *p*article *s*warm *o*ptimization. MOPSO imposes a kind of grid on the search space, and maintains a global repository of nondominated vectors (e.g., vectors that best meet the optimization criteria) in each section of the grid. Each hypercube section of the grid is assigned a fitness that is inversely proportional to the number of points in it; this gives advantage to sections with fewer particles and helps in finding distributed solutions. Rather than having particles influence one another, solutions stored in the repository are substituted for the best neighbor; the repository member to influence a particle is chosen through roulette-wheel selection. Coello Coello reports that MOPSO performed "competitively" with other algorithms, in terms of the goodness of solutions found, and was computationally faster than other methods.

Parsopoulos and Vrahatis [59] adapted some techniques from genetic algorithms in order to develop a "multi-swarm" that could optimize multiple objectives simultaneously. The vector-evaluated genetic algorithm (Shaffer, [66]) subdivides the population into sections assigned to each of the objectives. Parsopoulos and Vrahatis's vector-evaluated particle swarm optimization (VEPSO) approach divided the population into two swarms for testing on two-objective problems. Each swarm was evaluated on one of the criteria, but social influence came from the best-performing particle in the other swarm.

Hu and Eberhart [37] modified the particle swarm in a different way to get it to optimize two simultaneous objectives. A different neighborhood was created on each iteration, using the K neighbors that were nearest in the fitness value space of the first objective function, where K was the neighborhood size. The neighbor to influence was then chosen as the one that had done the best so far on the second objective function. The particle's previous best, *pbest*, was only updated when a multiobjective solution was found that dominated the previous *pbest*.

Hu and Eberhart [37] note that there is no well-established measure for performance on multiobjective problems. Nevertheless, they report good results with their particle swarm on a set of standard problems from the literature.

In sum, several groups of researchers are approaching the multiobjective optimization case from different angles, slowly converging on a set of procedures for solving these knotty problems with particle swarms. These approaches necessitate some thinking about how the particles can interact with one another in order to blanket the solution space; each particle must find its appropriate role in the solution set.

The metaphor of human sociocognition should supply researchers with plenty of ideas for this interesting challenge. How do people coordinate their activities? Human social influence is something more than imitation – what are the factors that influence people to behave differently from one another, yet in concert? Consideration of these questions might result in simple yet effective advances in particle swarm theory.

1.4.2 Dynamic Problems

An obvious weakness with the particle swarm approach is its dependence on past successes as indicators of the locations of possible future successes. When the problem holds still, this can be sufficient, but many problems, especially in the real world, are constantly changing. Thus a particular type of difficult situation exists when the optima move around the parameter space.

In one of the earliest studies of this problem, Carlisle and Dozier [10] periodically replaced the previous best vector $\vec{p}_i$ with the current position $\vec{x}_i$, essentially "forgetting" past successes. They tested this modification using a dynamic version of the sphere function $f(\vec{x}) = \sqrt{\sum (g_j - x_j)^2}$, which is a simple measure of the distance from a particle's current position to the optimum $\vec{g}$, which was moved around the parameter space. Carlisle and Dozier tested two conditions, one in which the previous best was reset at regular intervals, and one where the previous best was reset when the particle detected that the optimum had moved some specified distance from its previous position. They also manipulated the speed with which the optimum moved.

In the no-reset control condition, the "full model" particle swarm was able to optimize well when the target moved slowly, but suffered when it moved fast. (A "social-only" version, using

$$v[i][j] = W \times v[i][j] + \text{rand}() \times (\text{phi2}) \times (p[g][d] - x[i][d])$$

also performed quite well in all tests.) Resetting more frequently resulted in the population performing better when the target was moving fast, but worse when it moved slowly; resetting less frequently had the opposite result. Resetting when a criterion had been breached also resulted in improvement, but nothing better than what was found using the simpler technique. In a later paper [11], these researchers took the approach of posting a "sentry" particle, which evaluated changes in the objective function in order to tell the swarm when to make adjustments.

Eberhart and Shi [25, 26] had similar ideas. After every 100 iterations, they reset the population using a technique similar to Carlisle and Dozier's, setting the "previous best" to the evaluation of the current position. They compared their results to previous work with evolutionary algorithms by Angeline [2] and Bäck [6] and found that error in tracking the optimum with the particle swarm was "several orders of magnitude less than that obtained by either Angeline or Bäck." Besides the three-dimensional sphere functions that the other authors had tested, Eberhart and Shi looked at higher dimensions and found that resetting the previous bests was sufficient to track optima in all cases.

Hu and Eberhart [38] reevaluated the best particle to detect changes in the position of the optimum. The *gbest* particle was evaluated using two different techniques. *Changed-gbest-value* meant that the *gbest* position was evaluated at every iteration, and change in its evaluation meant that the evaluation function had changed. In the *fixed-gbest-value method*, the *gbest*, and sometimes the second-best, particle was monitored; if it did not change for a certain number of iterations, e.g., if improvement ceased, then it was assumed that the function had changed, and a response was needed.

The response was to reinitialize part of the population. These researchers experimented with various proportions, as well as various numbers of iterations set to wait in the fixed-*gbest*-value condition before responding. Their results show that the populations were able to track dynamic optima quite well, especially when a small percent (10%) of the particles were rerandomized in response to change.

In sum, results so far are showing the particle swarm to be competitive with evolutionary computation methods for optimizing dynamically changing functions. Several tricks have been proposed for overcoming the particle swarm's reliance on memory for previous successes, which are not relevant if a problem has changed significantly.

1.5   Binary Particle Swarms

Much of the literature on genetic algorithms is focused on the binary implementation, probably because that was the focus of Holland's [35] pioneering work. At any rate, binary implementations can be useful for encoding discrete spaces as well as numeric ones—for instance, through noting the presence or absence of a feature. Thus it would seem useful to be able to run the particle swarm on binary spaces.

Kennedy and Eberhart [44] proposed a very simple adjustment to the canonical algorithm of the day (this was before the inertia weight and constriction coefficients had been discovered). The method involves a change in the way velocity is conceptualized. Whereas in real numbers velocity is a change in position, when optimizing variables in a discrete space velocity might better be thought of as a probability threshold.

Thus, where the real-numbered algorithm was given as

v[i][d] = khi × (v[i][j] +
    rand()× phi1 × (p[i][d] − x[i][d]) +
    rand()× phi2 × (p[g][d] − x[i][d]))
x[i][d] = x[i][d] + v[i][d]

the probability-threshold technique "squashes" $v[i][d]$ into the (0,1) interval, then generates a random number from a uniform distribution and compares it to the threshold. If the random number is less than the threshold, the variable $x[i][d]$ will be assigned the value of 1, and otherwise 0. A common sigmoid function is used for squashing:

$$S(x) = \frac{1}{1 + \exp(-x)}$$

Thus the binary algorithm can be written as

v[i][d] = khi × (v[i][j] +
    rand()× phi1 × (p[i][d] − x[i][d]) +
    rand()× phi2 × (p[g][d] − x[i][d]))
if rand() < S(v[i][d]) then x[i][d] = 1
else x[i][d]=0

Kennedy and Spears [48] compared this algorithm with several varieties of genetic algorithms (GAs), using Spears' multimodal random problem generator;

the binary particle swarm was the only algorithm of four that were tested (GA with mutation and no crossover, GA with crossover and no mutation, GA with both crossover and mutation, and particle swarm) to find the global optimum on every single trial. And it found the optimum fastest, except for the simplest condition, with low dimensionality and a small number of local optima, where it was slightly outperformed by the mutation-only GA (which was the worst in other conditions).

Agrafiotis and Cedeño [1, 12] used particle swarms to select a set of features that optimized some chemical criterion. When they wanted K features to be selected, they modified a particle swarm so that the locations of particles were treated as probabilities in a roulette wheel. The probabilities were calculated as

$$p_{ij} = \frac{x_{ij}^{\alpha}}{\sum x_{ij}^{\alpha}}$$

where α is a scaling factor they call *selection pressure*. Values of α greater than 1.0 lead to a tendency to favor the selection of highly fit features, while values below 1.0 give more approximately the same probability of selection to all features. These authors used $\alpha=2$ in their experiments. The x_{ij} variables are constrained to the interval [0,1]. The roulette-wheel selection is performed K times to select K features.

Agrafiotis and Cedeño found that their particle swarm method performed better than simulated annealing in two ways. First, the fitness of the best models found by particle swarms were better than the best found by simulated annealing; as the authors comment, "although annealing does converge with greater precision [less variance in results], it converges to sub-optimal models that are perhaps more easily accessible in the fitness landscape." Second, particle swarms produced a more diverse set of good solutions; the authors explain this outcome by saying that the particle swarm "casts a wider net over the state space and [,] capitalizing on the parallel nature of the search," is able to find disparate solutions.

Other versions of the binary particle swarm have been suggested. Mohan and Al-kazemi (2001), for instance, have proposed an array of approaches. They call their binary algorithms DiPSO, for *di*screte *p*article *s*warm *o*ptimization. Their multiphase discrete particle swarm optimization model, called M-DiPSO, assigned coefficients to the three terms on the right-hand side of the velocity adjustment, and used a hill-climbing technique to select the next position. In their reported experiments, they used coefficients of (1, 1, −1) sometimes and (1, −1, 1) other times, depending in part on the *phase* of the algorithm. The phase is switched if some number of iterations (they used five) has gone by without improvement. In effect, the phase-switching means that sometimes particles are attracted to one of the two bests, and sometimes are repelled. Thus, by alternating phases, the system explores more thoroughly.

1.6 Topology and Influence

In the very first particle swarms, every individual was influenced by the very best performer in the population. Since only the best member of a particle's neighborhood actually influences it, this was equivalent to a social network where every individual was connected to every other one. Early experimentation, however, found advantages with a topology where each individual was connected to its adjacent neighbors in the population. These two approaches were called *gbest* (for "global best") and *lbest* ("local best").

It was noted that the *gbest* topology had a tendency to converge very quickly on good problem solutions but had a (negative) tendency to fail to find the best region of the search space. *Lbest*, on the other hand, was slower but explored more fully, and typically ended up at a better optimum. The simple explanation is that the local-influence topology buffers and slows the flow of information so that individuals can search collaboratively with their neighbors in one region of the search space while other particles search in other regions.

Kennedy [41] experimented with some alternative social-network structures and found that varying the topology had a big effect on results. A paper by Watts and Strogatz [71] had shown that changing a small number of random links in a social network could drastically shorten the mean distance between nodes without affecting the degree of clustering, defined as the proportion of nodes' neighbors that were neighbors of one another.

Kennedy's 1999 paper arranged the particle swarm population of twenty particles into various configurations and then modified the configurations, or "sociometries," by randomly varying one connection. The sociometries used were classical ones [9], including

- the wheel, where one population member was connected to all the others, with no other connections in the population

- the ring, equivalent to *lbest* or a ring lattice, where all individuals were connected with their immediate neighbors

- the star, equivalent to *gbest*, with all individuals connected to all others, and

- random edges, with every individual randomly connected to two others

The small-world manipulations were not especially effective in that study, as the populations were really too small for that phenomenon to show itself. The differences between the various topologies, however, were quite noticeable, and further research explored that aspect of the algorithm more thoroughly.

It is useful to think for a minute about how information spreads in a particle swarm population. When a particle *i* finds a relatively good problem solution, it still may not be the best thing found in *j*'s neighborhood (*i* and *j* being linked), and so *j* will not be affected by *i*'s discovery. Eventually, though, if *i* has actually found a good region of the search space, its performance will improve as it explores that area, until it does become the best in *j*'s neighborhood. Then *j* will be attracted to search the region between (and beyond) them, and may eventually find that *i* has indeed found a higher peak in the fitness landscape. In this case, *j*'s performance will improve, its "previous best" will be in *i*'s region, and *j*'s other neighbors will be attracted to that region. It is perhaps overly facile to simply say that information has "spread" from *i* to *j*'s neighbors.

Kennedy and Mendes [46] tested several thousand random graphs, sociometries that were optimized to meet some criteria, including average degree or number of links per individual, variance of degree (high or low), clustering, and variance in clustering. They used two distinct measures of a particle swarm's problem-solving ability. The first, "performance," is the best function result obtained after some number of iterations. In order to compare across functions, these results were standardized, that is, they were transformed to give a mean of 0.0 and standard deviation of 1.0; results could then be averaged across problems. The second measure, called "proportion," was the proportion of trials in which a particular version of the algorithm met criteria from the literature that indicate that the global optimum has been found. For instance, in a multimodal problem there may be many local optima, the peaks of which will be relatively good results, but there is, in the test suite used in this research, only one globally best solution.

Kennedy and Mendes found that different topologies were successful depending on which measure was used. For instance, when looking at performance – best function result at 1,000 iterations – the best swarms comprised sociometries with high degree; that is, each individual had many connections to others. But the best swarms by proportion – the ability to find the global optimum – were mostly of moderate degree. The best by this measure had a degree of five (mean degrees of 3, 5, and 10 were tested in that study).

Kennedy and Mendes [47] included another modification of the particle swarm, which they called the *fully informed particle swarm (FIPS)*. Recall that Clerc analyzed a particle swarm of one particle, where the two terms added to the velocity were collapsed into one. He concluded that the coefficient φ should equal 4.1, with a χ constriction factor of approximately 0.7298, calculated from the formula given above. Since two terms are added to the velocity in a real particle swarm, i.e., the term representing the particle's own previous best and that representing the neighborhood best, the φ coefficient was divided by two, with half being assigned to each term.

Kennedy and Mendes noted that there was no reason the coefficient should not be subdivided even further. Thus they modified the particle swarm by adjusting the velocity using information drawn from all the neighbors, not just the best one. So where the canonical particle swarm can be depicted algebraically as

$$\vec{v}_i \leftarrow \chi\left(\vec{v}_i + U(0,\varphi_1) \otimes (\vec{p}_i - \vec{x}_i) + U(0,\varphi_2) \otimes (\vec{p}_g - \vec{x}_i)\right)$$
$$\vec{x}_i \leftarrow \vec{x}_i + \vec{v}_i$$

the FIPS algorithm is given as

$$\vec{v}_i \leftarrow \chi\left(\vec{v}_i + \sum_{n=1}^{N_i} \frac{U(0,\varphi) \otimes (\vec{p}_{nbr(n)} - \vec{x}_i)}{N_i}\right)$$
$$\vec{x}_i \leftarrow \vec{x}_i + \vec{v}_i$$

where $nbr(n)$ is the particle's nth neighbor.

The FIPS algorithm does not perform very well at all with the *gbest* topology, or in fact with any with high degree in the population topology. With *lbest*, however, or with topologies where particles have very few (e.g., three) neighbors, FIPS performs better than the canonical particle swarm as measured by both performance and proportion in a suite of standard test functions.

Sociometry, then, was found to be a more important factor in a FIPS swarm than in one where information was taken only from the best neighbor. It seems intuitively obvious that information from many neighbors may include conflicts, since these neighbors may have found success in different regions of the search space; thus the averaged information is likely to be unhelpful. In versions using the best neighbor only, though, a bigger neighborhood is more likely to contain better information, as a bigger net is likely to catch a bigger fish. All in all, the FIPS particle swarm with appropriate sociometry outperformed the canonical version on all the testbed problems.

It is interesting to go back to the sociocognitive metaphor here for understanding and for new ideas. Ideas sweep through a population, one person to another, with "better" ideas – ones that explain the most with the least inconsistency – prevailing. But the variables that affect social influence are very complex. Theorists such as Latané focus on high-level factors, while others look "inside the head" at cognitive factors; one traditional social-psychological view looks at qualities of the message source, the message itself, and the recipient of the message [61].

In designing a particle swarm, then, it is not immediately obvious how one should code the interactions of individual particles. It is certainly reasonable to assume that people tend to accept information from experts and authorities, that is, people who seem to have achieved some success, but it is also reasonable to say that people accept information from people they know well, and that people accept information that fits well with their previous views. The interpersonal flow of information still does not have a well-fitted, comprehensive theory specific enough to be implemented in a computer program. Still, it seems that the particle swarm algorithm can and will be improved by integrating more of what is known about human social behavior. It is expected that the nature of the interactions of the particles will undergo important changes in years to come.

1.7   Gaussian Particle Swarms

The velocity-adjustment formula is arbitrary. It is entirely possible that a different formula could be used to move the particles back and forth around the average of their own successes and good points found by their neighbors. A few researchers have tampered with the formula, but not very much.

Kennedy [43] conducted an experiment to discover the distribution of the points that are searched by the canonical particle swarm. The individual and neighborhood bests were defined as constants, -10 and $+10$ in that study, and the formula was iterated a million times to produce a histogram. The histogram revealed that the algorithm searches a bell-shaped region centered halfway between the two best points, and extending significantly beyond them. (This last effect is often referred to as "overflying" the best points.) The distribution appeared to be a typical gaussian bell curve.

This result should not be surprising when one considers that the points are chosen by averaging pairs of random numbers. The central limit theorem would predict that the means would be normally distributed. This point was also noted by Secrest and Lamont [65] as well as Higashi and Iba [34].

Kennedy modified the algorithm by substituting a gaussian random number generator for the velocity change formula, using the midpoint between $p[i][d]$ and p[g][d] on each dimension as the mean of the distribution, and their difference as the standard deviation. Thus the resulting algorithm can be algebraically described as

$$\vec{x}_i \leftarrow G\left(\frac{\vec{p}_i + \vec{p}_g}{2}, \left|\vec{p}_i - \vec{p}_g\right|\right)$$

where $G(mean,\ s.d.)$ is a gaussian random number generator.

Other versions were tested, for instance by using the mean of all neighbors, à la FIPS, for $\vec{p}_g$ in the gaussian formula just given. Some versions selected random neighbors from the population, some used the population best, and some used an "interaction probability" (IP) threshold of 0.50; this meant that a vector element was only changed if a probability test was passed. Half the time, then, $x[i][d]=p[i][d]$.

The best performing version in that study was the random-neighbor, IP=0.50 version, though other versions were quite competitive. There did not seem to be any significant performance difference between the gaussian versions and the canonical algorithm with velocity.

It would seem, then, that the door is open for experimentation with new formulas for moving the particle. What is the best strategy for exploring a wide variety of problem spaces? The adjustment of velocity by traditional terms based on the differences may not be the best approach.

1.8   Particle Swarms and Evolutionary Computation

A reader familiar with evolutionary computation will have noted that the gaussian perturbation suggested here is similar to that employed in evolutionary programming and especially evolution strategies. Evolutionary programming does not employ crossover or recombination, but only mutation, which is usually gaussian or Cauchy distributed. Evolution strategies (ESs), however, do typically feature interaction between population members, which is called *recombination* and is considered metaphorically to resemble the mixing of phenotypes in sexual reproduction.

In fact, intermediate recombination in ES is very similar to the interactions of individuals in gaussian particle swarms. Parents are selected, similar to the individual particle and its best neighbor, and averages are calculated for each vector element. These means are then perturbed through gaussian mutation with a standard deviation that is evolved, in ES, as a vector of "strategy parameters" along with the object parameters that are being optimized [7].

This adaptation of strategy parameters in ES means that optimization of an n-dimensional problem requires at least a $2n$-dimensional vector to be adapted iteratively, as there is a standard-deviation variable for every function parameter. Why isn't this necessary in the particle swarm? The answer is that the standard deviation of the "mutation" in the particle swarm is determined by the distance between the individual and its source of social influence. This is true whether the velocity formula is used, or gaussian randomness: the adaptation is inherent.

One other evolutionary computation paradigm uses consensus to determine step-size, and that is *differential evolution (DE)* [62]. In DE, a vector drawn from a population is modified by some values that are derived from the differences between two other vectors that are randomly drawn from the population. Thus, as in the particle swarm, the variance of change, or step-size, is determined by the size of differences among population members.

In both ES and DE, problem solutions that will interact with one another are chosen at random. The particle swarm, however, has a topological structure such that each problem solution has a subset of the population with which it will share information. (This is arguable in the *gbest* versions.) Some ES researchers have experimented with fixed topologies [73], but what can this possibly mean in a simulation of evolution? It would seem to mean that two parents have two children, who then mate with one another and have two children, who then mate with one another and so on. If the neighborhood size exceeds two, then the incest is somewhat less intense, as siblings will only mate occasionally. But it is certainly not like anything in nature.

Thus we discover a chasm between the evolutionary methods and the ones we are calling *social*, which has to do with the persistence of the individual over time. Darwinisan evolution, at least as it is implemented in computer programs, functions through *selection*, differential reproduction probabilities depending on fitness. The social models (here we can include the ant swarms, cultural algorithm [63], and some of the fixed-topology ES versions just mentioned), on the other hand, feature the survival of individuals from one "generation" (the word is not appropriate here, and is used to make that point) to the next.

Evolution introduces a bias toward better problem solutions by allowing only the fitter population members to reproduce. The parents are, at least potentially, replaced at each turn, leaving offspring that are altered copies of themselves. The particle swarm implements a positive bias by a process that may be properly called *learning*; that is, the states of individuals are changed by their experiences, which include interactions with one another.

It can be argued that particle swarms instantiate a kind of selection, if one considers the previous bests, e.g., $\vec{p}_i$, as the parent individual, and the current location $\vec{x}_i$ as something like an offspring [4, 43]. Each iteration then presents an occasion for competition between the parent and the child, and if the child is better it kills the parent and takes its place. This view calls to mind (1+1)-ES, where a candidate solution is mutated, and if the descendant is better than the parent, then the descendent becomes the ancestor for the next generation.

But first – is this evolution at all? Selection cannot be taken to have occurred in every situation where a better exemplar is chosen over a lesser one, for instance (1+1)-ES.

Philosophically central to this issue is the question of what makes up an individual. We can imagine, for instance, a kind of biological kingdom where an orgasm gave its own life to its offspring and perished at the moment the torch was passed. In this case, observers would almost certainly develop a vocabulary that allowed them to track the vital "spirit" as it passed from generation to generation. In other words, if A transferred its life-force to B, and at the moment B accepted it A lost it, then B would probably be named A-Junior, or A-the-ninetieth, or something to indicate that the spirit of A was in this particular organism. The life-force passed through the generations would be considered "the individual," and the organism inhabited by it at the moment would be some other kind of transient thing. The lack of such a concept seems to be what is missing in attempts to explain the particle swarm, and certain kinds of ES, as evolutionary processes. It is the concept that in describing an individual's sense of continuity from moment to moment, from day to day, is called *self* or *ego*.

The various EC paradigms have a tendency to blend together, being separated as much by sociological boundaries as technical differences. One method uses tournament selection, another uses roulette-wheel selection, by tradition as much as by necessity. Yet though there is much overlap, and much that can be learned by one paradigm from another, there are also some hard differences. I am arguing here that the use of selection distinguishes an evolutionary group of algorithms from another group in which individuals survive over iterations. I am also suggesting, gently, that some processes that have been labeled "evolutionary" are not. For instance, it seems very inelegant to try to explain how selection is at work when one parent gives birth to one offspring at a time and eventually perishes when it is replaced by its own child.

It seems more appropriate, in these cases, to view population members as persistent individuals that change over time – that learn. These are two different kinds of methods for biasing a population's performance toward improvement: reproduction allowing only for the fittest members of the population, versus change or learning in individuals over time. These two methods can be combined in an application, as Angeline showed in 1998, where he added selection to a particle swarm and found that performance was improved. But they are not variations on the same thing.

The "social" family of algorithms relies on the interactions between individuals, which in EC is called *crossover* or *recombination*. For instance, several researchers have written "cognition-only" particle swarm programs, where the last, social, term of the velocity adjustment was simply omitted. These versions are uniformly terrible at finding any optimum unless they are initialized near it and there is a clear monotonic gradient. It is the influence of neighbors that forces a particle to explore the space more widely when there is diversity in the population, and more narrowly when there is agreement. It is social influence that tells the particle where to look, and tells it how big its steps should be through the space. And the sociometric structure of the population helps determine how quickly it will converge on an optimum, as opposed to maintaining searches of diverse regions. In sum, the interactions among individuals are crucial to the "social" family of algorithms.

Why isn't crossover, for instance, a qualifying characteristic for membership in the "social" group? That is because social creatures don't die as soon as they socialize. Oh, we could find some kind of black-widow analogy, but we would be stretching it. The behaviors of truly social organisms are changed through their interactions with their conspecites; this behavior change is called *learning*, and when behaviors are learned from others, it is called *social learning* [8].

1.9   Memes

It would appear that, in discussing the evolution of cognitive patterns in a population, we must be talking about the same thing that people who talk about memes are talking about. Memes [28] are patterns, perhaps ideas, snatches of music, behavioral patterns, that seem to spread through a population, as if taking on a life of their own.

The evolutionary nature of memes seems self-evident, which should of course be a sign that something is wrong.

I imagine that a meme is like a schema in Holland's analysis of the behavior of genetic algorithms. On a ten-dimensional binary genetic representation, say, 1001010011, it may be that one subset of bits, say the 101 starting at the fourth site, confers some important fitness value and comprises some kind of logically interrelated genetic pattern.

In this case, then, the entire bitstring 1001010011 must be considered to be the cognitive state of some individual. As the meme spreads through the population, more and more individuals will find their fourth, fifth, and sixth mental slots filled with the meme-pattern 101. This appears to be the only way that a meme could be represented.

This view is fine for a static snapshot of the population. We see that some individuals contain or embody the meme, and others don't. Theoretically, what we expect to see in our simulation is some dynamic representation of the adoption of the meme by new population members (and eventually its replacement by some other meme).

But let us imagine that this population is modeled by a genetic algorithm (GA) of some sort. We have an immediate problem, which is that population members have to die. Whether we implement crossover or mutation, or both, we are expected to kill off the less fit members of the population and replace them with a new generation. Because the GA works by selection, it is necessary that only a subset produce offspring, and that the offspring replace the ancestors. It is simply not going to be possible to model the spread of memes in a population using a genetic algorithm.

Richard Dawkins [28] invented the concept of memes, or at least introduced the term to our vocabulary. So it is noteworthy that his innovative EC program, "Biomorphs," represents a kind of asexual evolution that utterly fails to mimic the supposed behavior of memes. A single Biomorph on the screen is selected, and clicked, and then a new generation of Biomorphs appears, all of which are descended from the one that was clicked on in the previous generation. They are all slightly mutated forms of the original, and the rest of the previous generation has disappeared, died, gone forever.

It does not seem reasonable to believe that memes are "evolutionary" at all, in any Darwinian sense. The evolution of ideas belongs to the second class of paradigms, the social methods. It is not hard at all to model memetic evolution, for instance, in a particle swarm, where individuals are manifest as vectors of variables, which can even be binary variables; in this case, the meme can be portrayed as a pattern in the vector, say 101 starting in the fourth site on a ten-dimensional bitstring. The spread of the meme is seen in changes in the states of population members, with the particular meme 101 moving through the social network from individual to individual as it is adopted by new population members.

This modeling is possible because individuals maintain their identities over time, and learn by changing. While a meme may be a distinct and easily identifiable pattern of behavior, it does not have a life of its own; it does not leap from person to person like a virus (which memes are frequently compared to), infecting one mind after the other. No, the active agent is the individual, the teenage kid who adopts the behavior. Just as a language has no existence independent of its speakers – even writing is only a pattern of marks to someone can't read it – so the phenomena known as memes only have their existence in the states of those who participate in them, own them, use them, adopt them, provide habitation for them.

2   EXTERIORIZING THE PARTICLE SWARM

The particle swarm algorithm is only a recipe for solving problems, and does not need to be run in a computer program. At least two implementations demonstrate that some parts of the program can be run in the real world.

A major pharmaceutical company needed a medium for growing bacteria [16]; this involved finding an optimal mixture of ingredients for the particular organism. In order to solve this problem, Cockshott and Hartman mixed up some batches with random amounts of each ingredient, introduced the organism to it, and waited for it to grow. After some period of time, they measured the amount of the organism that had grown in each mixture, and, using that measure as an "evaluation function," calculated proportions of the ingredients, from the particle swarm formulas, to try in the next round of trials. In their research, time-steps were weeks long, and measurement occurred outside the computer, but the particle swarm recipe was followed literally.

Cockshott and Hartman report that the optimized ingredient mix they eventually derived was over twice as good as a mix found using traditional methods. Also, interestingly, the mix discovered through the particle swarm process was very different from other mixes that had been found; it lay outside what had been considered the "feasible" regions of the search space.

Kennedy [42] wrote a program that extended the particle population to include a human being. A user interface displayed a "problem," which was to find the desired pattern of squares on a grid similar to a checkerboard. Underlying the problem was an NK landscape function, which could be adjusted to make the problems more or less hard; the landscape could be monotonic, which would allow a simple greedy strategy of flipping colors one at a time, or local optima could be introduced. The user in the "exteriorized particle swarm" was also shown his own previous best pattern, as well as the best pattern so far found by a population of particles.

While no carefully designed experiment was conducted, informal testing indicated that the presence of the humans, who were allowed to use any cognitive strategy they wished, did not improve the performance of the swarm. Further, the global optimum was found at least as often by a computational particle as by a human one.

These instances show the particle swarm to be more than a type of computer program; it is a way of doing things. The algorithm is derived from observations of human behaviors, and can be turned around and used as a process for guiding human behavior, for instance for getting "out of the box," finding solutions to problems that have proven intractable.

2.1   The Future of the Particle Swarm

There is something satisfying in thinking about the particle swarm paradigm itself as a big particle swarm. The method originated in the integration of bird-flocking, neural networks, social psychology, evolutionary computation, and other diverse subjects, and continues to evolve through the blending of existing particle swarm theory with new topics and situations. In the particle swarm tradition, much of the work has been reported and discussed at conferences and symposia, and much of the research has been collaborative, as researchers explore their own ideas and adopt the ideas of their colleagues. This section will speculate on the future of particle swarms in terms of applications, tweaks, and theory.

2.1.1   Applications

The particle swarm is most often used as a tool for engineers, and its applications cover an extremely wide domain. As it is a method for optimizing vectors of variables, and many engineering problems require exactly that; as it is a fast and efficient method for problem-solving, with a minimum of parameters to adjust; and as it is very easy to code and maintain, and is unpatented and otherwise free of burden, the paradigm is used in many applications.

The most common use of particle swarms is in optimizing the weights in feed-forward neural networks. These networks are often used for the analysis of complex, e.g., nonlinear, data. Since the problem space of the neural net typically contains many local optima, gradient descent approaches such as backpropagation of error are sometimes inadequate; the solution is highly dependent on the starting point.

Eberhart and Shi [24] extended the use of the particle swarm beyond the weight matrix, letting it optimize the structure of the network as well. Since each node in the standard feedforward network has a sigmoid transfer function, by using the function

$$output_i = \frac{1}{(1 + e^{-k \cdot input})}$$

Eberhart and Shi optimized the exponent coefficient k, which is the slope of the function, along with the network weights. This parameter was allowed to take on negative as well as positive values. If k became very small, the node could be eliminated. Thus, it is possible, using this method, to generate a network structure along with the weights.

Particle swarms have been used on problems in domains as diverse as reactive power and voltage control by a Japanese electric utility [76], diagnosis of human tremor [22], and multiple-beam antenna arrays [32]. Ujjin and Bentley [70] used particle swarm optimization in a worldwide web "recommender system," which helps users navigate through Internet entertainment and shopping sites. Xiao et al. [75] used the algorithm for clustering genes.

It is not possible to imagine the range of future applications of the particle swarm. Any problem that has multiple variables is a candidate for analysis with this approach.

2.1.2 Tweaks

The particle swarm algorithm has been modified in many ways, some of them fundamental and some trivial. For instance, the Vmax constant, which was necessary in versions without inertia or constriction factors, is now optional; some researchers still set a value for Vmax just to keep the particles from going "outside the solar system" [27]. Eberhart and his colleagues, for instance, commonly set Vmax equal to the range of the problem space. The inertia weight has undergone numerous adjustments: sometimes it decreases over time, and sometimes it is given a random value within a range. The constants that weight the two terms adjusting the velocity are usually equal, but not always, and sometimes larger or smaller values are used for them. Sometimes the velocity is modified by one term instead of two, sometimes by more than two.

Clerc's analysis seems to have shown the best values for some of the system constants, and contemporary particle swarm researchers usually adhere to his recommendations [15]. But, as has been seen, even these analytically derived values are sometimes tweaked.

Individuals in the particle swarm imitate successes: is this a realistic depiction of human behavior? It is obvious that much more interesting particle trajectories could be discovered by modeling processes from nature. Sometimes humans rebel against their groups, especially when these become too restrictive or when individuals are not attaining satisfaction. Human specialization has already been mentioned; this topic is especially relevant when discussing multiobjective optimization, where each particle represents a point in the Pareto set, and the pattern across the population comprises the entire problem solution. Even when a problem has only one objective, it is important to maintain diversity in the population in order to prevent stagnation and premature convergence.

The topology of the particle swarm has been modified quite a lot, as well. Several researchers have experimented with adaptive topologies [14], where some rules are programmed for pruning connections and adding others. If we think of all that is known about the complexities of human social networks, groups, and relationships, we see that there is a vast gold mine of things to try, ways to organize the population so that knowledge spreads realistically from person to person. Should links between particles be symmetrical? Should they be weighted probabilistically or made fuzzy? What are the best topological structures in general, and are there problem features that correlate with topology features? There are very many questions here, to be answered by some future researchers.

The particle swarm has been hybridized with various evolutionary computation and other methodologies. Angeline's incorporation of selection has been mentioned. Something similar was used by Naka et al. [53]. Zhang and Xie [77] hybridized the particle swarm with differential evolution, and reported good results. Parsopoulos and Vrahatis [60] used the nonlinear simplex method to initialize the particle swarm parameters. Clearly, tricks from other disciplines can be borrowed and integrated with the basic particle swarm framework. It is expected that future research in this area will open up new and powerful approaches to optimization and problem solving.

2.1.3.   Theory

The particle swarm is not very well defined. For instance, Zhang and Xie [77] remark that the gaussian particle swarm is "a variety of evolution strategies." Of course, the present viewpoint is that some varieties of evolution strategies are particle swarms, but, point of view aside, it is clear that evolutionary methods overlap, and that the theory of particle swarm optimization is still in its infancy.

Clerc's remarkable analysis of the single particle's trajectory moved the field ahead significantly, and allowed the development of universal parameters that fit every problem and did not need to be adjusted. The next step is a comparable analysis at a higher level, looking at the whole population's trajectory through the search space. Perhaps one of the readers of this chapter will have an insight that makes such a global analysis possible. The analysis needs to explain not only the interactions of individual particles but also the global dynamics of the entire population, and needs to explain how graph-theory aspects of the population topology interact with convergence properties of the particles.

A theme of the current chapter is the richness of the metaphor of human behavior for informing developments in the digital implementations of the algorithm. The point of this is really that human beings are the most intelligent thing we know. We tend to define intelligence in terms of human behavior, whether intentionally or not. The human mind classifies, remembers, communicates, reasons, and empathizes better than any computer product known. And so the question is, what are the qualities of human behavior that make it so intelligent? The particle swarm approach ventures to guess that interpersonal interaction is an important part of it, and draws on the science of social psychology for inspiration. Programs that solve problems through interactions of computational entities are a kind of validation of social-psychological theorizing, and so the metaphor and the engineering tool inform one another.

What is really needed is a general theory of populations that includes evolutionary algorithms as well as social ones. It appears that a rather small toolbox can construct a great variety of problem-solving methods. For instance, gaussian perturbation can be seen in evolutionary programming, evolution strategies, and particle swarms, and the interactions of individuals in particle swarms greatly resemble crossover or recombination in evolutionary algorithms. But selection is different from learning. Topological linkage can be seen in particle swarms and some ES versions, and the type of interaction can be similar in those paradigms, e.g., gaussian mutation around a midpoint between neighbors or parents.

And what is essential for a particle swarm? It appears that the velocity formula is arbitrary, and it has been shown that it is not necessary to interact with the best neighbor. What is left? It appears that the essence of the particle swarm is a population of individuals that persist over time and learn from one another. Hopefully the future will provide a comprehensive theory that explains the variations in methods for such implementations.

REFERENCES

[1] D. K. Agrafiotis and W. Cedeño (2002): Feature selection for structure-activity correlation using binary particle swarms. *Journal of Medicinal Chemistry*, *45*, 1098–1107.

[2] P. J. Angeline (1997): Tracking Extrema in Dynamic Environments. *Evolutionary Programming*, pp. 335–345.

[3] P. Angeline (1998a): Evolutionary optimization versus particle swarm optimization: Philosophy and performance differences. In V. W. Porto, N. Saravanan, D. Waagen, and A. E. Eiben, (eds.), *Evolutionary Programming VII*, 601, 610. Berlin: Springer.

[4] P. J. Angeline (1998b): Using selection to improve particle swarm optimization. *IEEE International Conference on Evolutionary Computation*, Anchorage, AK, USA.

[5] S. Asch (1956): Studies of independence and conformity: I. A minority of one against a unanimous majority. *Psychological Monographs*, 70 (9).

[6] T. Bäck (1998): On the behavior of evolutionary algorithms in dynamic environments. In D. B. Fogel, H.-P. Schwefel, Th. Bäck, and X. Yao (eds.), *Proc. Fifth IEEE Conference on Evolutionary Computation (ICEC'98)*, Anchorage AK, pp. 446–451, IEEE Press, Piscataway, NJ.

[7] T. Bäck, F. Hoffmeister, and H. Schwefel (1991): A survey of evolution strategies. In Lashon B. Belew and Richard K. Booker (eds.), *Proc. 4th International Conference on Genetic Algorithms*, pp. 2–9, San Diego, CA, Morgan Kaufmann.

[8] A. Bandura (1986): Social Foundations of Thought and Action: A Social Cognitive Theory. Englewood Cliffs, NJ: Prentice-Hall.

[9] A. Bavelas (1950): Communication patterns in task-oriented groups. *Journal of the Acoustical Society of America*, *22*, 727–730.

[10] A. Carlisle and G. Dozier (2000): Adapting particle swarm optimization to dynamic environments. *Proc. Int. Conf. Artificial Intelligence*, 2000, 429–434, Las Vegas, NV, USA.

[11] A. Carlisle and G. Dozier (2002): Tracking Changing Extrema with Adaptive Particle Swarm Optimizer. *ISSCI, 2002 World Automation Congress*, Orlando, FL, USA, June, 2002.

[12] W. Cedeño and D. K. Agrafiotis (2003): Using particle swarms for the development of QSAR models based on k-nearest neighbor and kernel regression. *Journal of Computer-Aided Molecular Design*, *17*, 255–263.

[13] R. B. Cialdini (1984): Influence: The Psychology of Persuasion. Quill Publishing.

[14] M. Clerc (1999): The swarm and the queen: Towards a deterministic and adaptive particle swarm optimization. *Congress on Evolutionary Computation*, Washington, D. C., pp. 1951–1957.

[15] M. Clerc and J. Kennedy (2002): The particle swarm: explosion, stability, and convergence in a multi-dimensional complex space. *IEEE Transactions on Evolutionary Computation*, *6*, 58–73.

[16] A. B. Cockshott and B. E. Hartman (2001): Improving the fermentation medium for Echinocandin B production. Part II: Particle swarm optimization. Process Biochemistry, *36*, 661–669.

[17] C. A. Coello Coello and S. Lechuga (2001): MOPSO: A Proposal for Multiple Objective Particle Swarm Optimization. Technical Report EVOCINV-01-2001, Evolutionary Computation Group at CINVESTAV, Sección de Computación, Departamento de Ingeniería Eléctrica, CINVESTAV-IPN, México.

[18] C. A. Coello Coello and M. S. Lechuga (2002): MOPSO: A proposal for multiple objective particle swarm optimization. *IEEE Congress on Evolutionary Computation,* 2002, Honolulu, HI, USA.

[19] R. S. Crutchfield (1955): Conformity and character. *American Psychologist, 10,* 191–198.

[20] R. Dawkins (1989): The Selfish Gene, 2nd ed. Oxford: Oxford University Press.

[21] M. Deutsch and H. B. Gerard (1955): A study of normative and informational social influences upon individual judgment. *Journal of Abnormal and Social Psychology, 51,* 629–636.

[22] R. C. Eberhart and X. Hu (1999): Human tremor analysis using particle swarm optimization. *Proc. Congress on Evolutionary Computation 1999,* Washington, D. C. 1927–1930. Piscataway, NJ: IEEE Service Center.

[23] R. C. Eberhart and Y. Shi (2000): Comparing inertia weights and constriction factors in particle swarm optimization. *Proc. CEC 2000,* San Diego, CA, pp. 84–88.

[24] R. C. Eberhart and Y. Shi (1998): Evolving artificial neural networks. *Proc. 1998 Int. Conf. Neural Networks and Brain,* Beijing, P. R. C., PL5–PL13.

[25] R. C. Eberhart and Y. Shi (2001a): Tracking and optimizing dynamic systems with particle swarms. *Proc. Congress on Evolutionary Computation 2001,* Seoul, Korea. Piscataway, NJ: IEEE Service Center.

[26] R. C. Eberhart and Y. Shi (2001b): Particle swarm optimization: developments, applications and resources. *Proc. Congress on Evolutionary Computation 2001,* Seoul, Korea. Piscataway, NJ: IEEE Service Center.

[27] R. C. Eberhart (2003): Introduction to particle swarm optimization (tutorial). *IEEE Swarm Intelligence Symposium,* Indianapolis, IN, USA.

[28] A. E. Eiben and C. A. Schippers (1998): On evolutionary exploration and exploitation. Fundamenta Informaticae. IOS Press.

[29] J. E. Fieldsend and S. Singh (2002): A multi-objective algorithm based upon particle swarm optimisation, an efficient data structure and turbulence. *Proc. 2002 U.K. Workshop on Computational Intelligence* (Birmingham, UK, 2–4 Sept. 2002), pp. 37–44.

[30] L. Festinger (1957): A Theory of Cognitive Dissonance. Evanston IL: Row, Peterson.

[31] L. Festinger (1954/1999): Social communication and cognition: A very preliminary and highly tentative draft. In E. Harmon-Jones and J. Mills (eds.), Cognitive Dissonance: Progress on a Pivotal Theory in Social Psychology. Washington D. C.: AP Publishing.

[32] D. Gies and Y. Rahmat-Samii (2003): Reconfigurable array design using parallel particle swarm optimization. *Proceedings of 2003 IEEE Antennas and Propagation Symposium* (in press).

[33] F. Heppner and U. Grenander (1990): A stochastic nonlinear model for coordinated bird flocks. In S. Krasner (ed.), The Ubiquity of Chaos. Washington, D. C.: AAAS Publications.

[34] N. Higashi and H. Iba (2003): Particle swarm optimization with gaussian mutation. *Proc. IEEE Swarm Intelligence Symposium 2003 (SIS 2003)*, Indianapolis, IN, USA, pp. 72–79.

[35] J. H. Holland (1975): Adaptation in Natural and Artificial Systems. Ann Arbor: The University of Michigan Press.

[36] C. Hovland (1982): Communication and Persuasion. New York: Greenwood.

[37] X. Hu and R. C. Eberhart (2002a): Multiobjective optimization using dynamic neighborhood particle swarm optimization. *Proceedings of the IEEE Congress on Evolutionary Computation (CEC 2002)*, Honolulu, HI, USA, pp. 1677–1681.

[38] X. Hu and R. C. Eberhart (2002b): Adaptive particle swarm optimization: detection and response to dynamic systems. *IEEE Congress on Evolutionary Computation*, Honolulu, HI, USA.

[39] X. Hu (2002): Multiobjective optimization using dynamic neighborhood particle swarm optimization. *IEEE Congress on Evolutionary Computation*, Honolulu, HI, USA.

[40] J. Kennedy (1998): The behavior of particles. Evolutionary Programming VII: *Proc. Seventh Annual Conference on Evolutionary Programming*, San Diego, CA, pp. 581–589.

[41] J. Kennedy (1999): Small worlds and mega-minds: effects of neighborhood topology on particle swarm performance. *Proc. Congress on Evolutionary Computation 1999*, pp. 1931–1938. Piscataway, NJ: IEEE Service Center.

[42] J. Kennedy (2000): Human and Computer Learning Together in the Exteriorized Particle Swarm. Socially Intelligent Agents: The Human in the Loop, pp. 83–89. Technical Report FS-00-04, AAAI Press.

[43] J. Kennedy (2003): Bare bones particle swarms. *Proc. IEEE Swarm Intelligence Symposium 2003 (SIS 2003)*, Indianapolis, IN, USA, 80–87.

[44] J. Kennedy and R. C. Eberhart (1997): A discrete binary version of the particle swarm algorithm. *Proc. 1997 Conf. on Systems, Man, and Cybernetics*, 4104–4109. Piscataway, NJ: IEEE Service Center.

[45] J. Kennedy and R. C. Eberhart (1995): Particle swarm optimization. *Proc. IEEE Int. Conf. on Neural Networks*, 4, 1942–1948. Piscataway, NJ: IEEE Service Center.

[46] J. Kennedy and R. Mendes (2002): Population structure and particle swarm performance. *IEEE Congress on Evolutionary Computation*, Honolulu, HI, USA.

[47] J. Kennedy and R. Mendes (2003): Neighborhood topologies in fully-informed and best-of-neighborhood particle swarms. *In Proc. 2003 IEEE SMC Workshop on Soft Computing in Industrial Applications (SMCia03)*, Binghamton, NY.

[48] J. Kennedy and W. M. Spears (1998): Matching algorithms to problems: an experimental test of the particle swarm and some genetic algorithms on the multimodal problem generator. *Proc. Int. Conf. on Evolutionary Computation*, pp. 78–83. Piscataway, NJ: IEEE Service Center.

[49] B. Latané (1981): The psychology of social impact. American Psychologist, *36*, 343–356.

[50] J. M. Levine, L. B. Resnick, and E. T. Higgins (1993): Social foundations of cognition. *Annual Review of Psychology, 44*, 585–612.

[51] E. F. Loftus and K. Ketcham (1994): The Myth of Repressed Memory: False Memories and Allegations of Sexual Abuse. New York: St. Martin's Press.

[52] C. K. Mohan and B. Al-kazemi (2001): Discrete particle swarm optimization. *Proc. Workshop on Particle Swarm Optimization*. Indianapolis, IN: Purdue School of Engineering and Technology, IUPUI (in press).

[53] S. Naka, T. Genji, K. Miyazato, and Y. Fukuyama (2002): Hybrid particle swarm optimization based distribution state estimation using constriction factor approach. *Proc. Joint 1st International Conference on Soft Computing and Intelligent Systems and 3rd International Symposium on Advanced Intelligent Systems (SCIS & ISIS)*.

[54] A. Newell and H. Simon (1963): GPS: A program that simulates human thought. In Feigenbaum and Feldman. (ed.), Computers and Thought. McGraw-Hill, New York.

[55] R. E. Nisbett and D. W. Wilson (1977): Telling more than we can know: Verbal reports on mental processes. *Psychological Review, 84,* 231–259.

[56] A. Nowak, J. Szamrej, and B. Latané (1990): From private attitude to public opinion: A dynamic theory of social impact. *Psychological Review, 97,* 362–376.

[57] E. Ozcan and C. Mohan (1999): Particle swarm optimization: surfing the waves. *Proc. 1999 Congress on Evolutionary Computation*, 1939–1944. Piscataway, NJ: IEEE Service Center.

[58] E. Ozcan and C. K. Mohan (1998): Analysis of a simple particle swarm optimization system. *Intelligent Engineering Systems Through Artificial Neural Networks, 8,* 253–258.

[59] K. E. Parsopoulos and M. N. Vrahatis (2002a): Particle swarm optimization method in multiobjective problems, *Proceedings of the 2002 ACM Symposium on Applied Computing (SAC 2002)*, pp. 603–607.

[60] K. E. Parsopoulos and M. N. Vrahatis (2002b): Initializing the particle swarm optimizer using the nonlinear simplex method. In A. Grmela and N. E. Mastorakis (eds), Advances in Intelligent Systems, Fuzzy Systems, Evolutionary Computation, pp. 216–221. WSEAS Press.

[61] R. E. Petty and J. T. Cacioppo (1981): Attitudes and persuasion: Classic and contemporary approaches. Dubuque, IA: Wm. C. Brown.

[62] K. V. Price (1999): An introduction to differential evolution. In D. W. Corne, M. Dorigo, F. Glover (eds), New Ideas in Optimization. McGraw Hill.

[63] R. G. Reynolds (1994): An introduction to cultural algorithms. *Proc. Third Annual Conference on Evolutionary Programming*, pp. 131–139.

[64] C. W. Reynolds (1987): Flocks, herds, and schools: A distributed behavioral model. *Computer Graphics, 21,* 25–34.

[65] B. R. Secrest and G. B. Lamont (2003): Visualizing particle swarm optimization—gaussian particle swarm optimization. *Proc. IEEE Swarm Intelligence Symposium 2003 (SIS 2003)*, Indianapolis, IN, USA, pp. 198–204.

[66] J. D. Schaffer (1985): Multiple objective optimization with vector evaluated genetic algorithms. In *Genetic Algorithms and their Applications: Proceedings of the First International Conference on Genetic Algorithms*, pp. 93–100.

[67] M. Sherif (1936): The Psychology Of Social Norms. New York: Harper Brothers.

[68] Y. Shi and R. C. Eberhart (1998): Parameter selection in particle swarm optimization. *Proc. Seventh Annual Conference on Evolutionary Programming*, pp. 591–601.

[69] M. Tomasello (1999): The Cultural Origins of Human Cognition. Cambridge, MA: Harvard University Press.

[70] S. Ujjin and P. J. Bentley (2003): Particle swarm optimization recommender system. I*n Proc. IEEE Swarm Intelligence Symposium 2003*, Indianapolis, IN, USA.

[71] D. Watts and S. Strogatz (1998): Collective dynamics of small-world networks. *Nature, 363*:202–204.

[72] D. M. Wegner (2002): The Illusion of Conscious Will. Cambridge, MA: The MIT Press.

[73] K. Weinert, J. Mehnen, and G. Rudolph (2001): Dynamic Neighborhood Structures in Parallel Evolution Strategies (Technical Report). Reihe CI 112/01, SFB 531, University of Dortmund.

[74] S. Wolfram (1994): Cellular Automata and Complexity: Collected Papers. Reading, MA: Addison-Wesley.

[75] X. Xiao, R. Dow, R. C. Eberhart, B. Miled, and R. J. Oppelt (2003): Gene clustering using self-organizing maps and particle swarm optimization. *Second IEEE International Workshop on High Performance Computational Biology*, Nice, France.

[76] H. Yoshida, Y. Fukuyama, S. Takayama, and Y. Nakanishi (1999): A particle swarm optimization for reactive power and voltage control in electric power systems considering voltage security assessment. *1999 IEEE International Conference on Systems, Man, and Cybernetics, 6,* 502.

[77] W. J. Zhang and X. F. Xie (2003): DEPSO: hybrid particle swarm with differential evolution operator. *IEEE Int. Conf. on Systems, Man & Cybernetics (SMCC)*, Washington, D. C. USA.

Chapter 7

FUZZY LOGIC
Javid Taheri and Albert Y. Zomaya
The University of Sydney

The principles of Fuzzy Logic were introduced several decades ago by Lotfi Zadeh [1]. The thrust of Zadeh's work was in the realization that decision making in the real world is not crisp. Most of the time, decisions are not "binary" in nature, such as yes/no, black/white, up/down, etc. Events and decisions tend to be "fuzzy," and a good example is the case of a glass of water that can be described as full or empty. Now, if one is to take a sip of water, then the glass is neither empty nor full, but in between. If the process continues until the glass is empty, then one can say that the glass has undergone different states from the time it was full to the time it became empty. It is obvious that the above phenomenon cannot be described by using binary logic and different rules need to be adopted to account for the different levels of "fuzziness" that any a decision process can take.

1 FUZZY PRINCIPLES

1.1 Multivalue Algebra

The most important difference between fuzzy and binary representations is the way a variable is quantized. The binary world uses two values (0 or 1) to represent each phenomenon, while in the fuzzy world variables are quantized by a function that takes a smooth shape ranging from 0 to 1 [1, 2].

1.2 Simplicity versus Accuracy

Fuzzy logic attempts to formulate an environment not accurately but in a simple manner. In modern sciences, especially mathematics and physics, there is an accurate formulation for every event. On the other hand, if an event cannot be explained accurately, a decision can be made with a given probability. Fuzzy logic tends to simplify the process of making a decision, especially in cases where an exact formula is very difficult to derive or does not exist.

1.3   Probability versus Possibility

To explain the interplay between probability and possibility, let's return to our earlier example, the glass of water. If one is to say that this is "a glass containing water with the probability of 0.5," it means that the whole glass might contain water or some other liquid like gasoline. On the other hand, if one uses the expression that this is "a glass containing water with the possibility of 0.5," it means that the liquid is definitely a mixture of water and another unknown liquid. Another distinguishing factor between these two expressions is the sample spaces they represent. In probability, the sum of all events that could happen should add up to 1.0, while in the case of possibility, the sum can be smaller or larger than 1.0.

1.4   Fuzzy Sets

A fuzzy set is a fundamental component of a fuzzy system [2]. Traditionally, a *set* is a collection of elements or objects that can be of finite or infinite size. In this case, a given element, x, can be a member of set A, or otherwise. So the answer to the question "Does x belong to set A?" is either true or false. In contrast, each fuzzy set is a set of ordered pairs and is usually defined as follows:

$$\tilde{A} = \left\{ \left(x, \mu_{\tilde{A}}(x) \right) \right\}$$

where $\mu_{\tilde{A}}(x)$ is the *membership function* and represents the degree of truth or compatibility of variable x with the set. Figure 7.1 shows a simple fuzzy set with following definition:

$$\tilde{A} = \left\{ \left(\left(x, \mu_{\tilde{A}}(x) \right), \mu_{\tilde{A}}(x) = \left(1 + (x - 5)^2 \right)^{-2} \right) \right\}$$

1.5   Fuzzy Numbers

A fuzzy number $\tilde{M}$ is called positive (negative) if its membership function is such that [2]

$$\mu_{\tilde{M}}(x) = 0, \forall\, x < 0\ (x > 0)$$

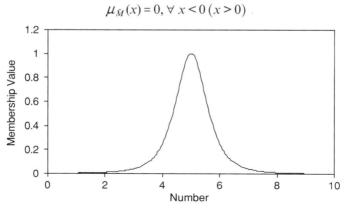

Figure 7.1. Representation of the fuzzy numeral "approximately 5"

1.6   Basic Set-Theoretic Operations

Different logic operations are defined for fuzzy sets and numbers. The basic logic operations of union, intersection, and complement are usually defined as follows [2].

1.6.1   Union

The union of two fuzzy sets $\tilde{A}$ and $\tilde{B}$ is

$$\tilde{C} = \tilde{A} \cup \tilde{B} = \left\{ \left(x, \mu_{\tilde{C}}(x) \right), \mu_{\tilde{C}}(x) = \max\left(\mu_{\tilde{A}}(x), \mu_{\tilde{B}}(x) \right) \right\}$$

1.6.2   Intersection

The intersection of two fuzzy sets $\tilde{A}$ and $\tilde{B}$ is

$$\tilde{D} = \tilde{A} \cap \tilde{B} = \left\{ \left(x, \mu_{\tilde{D}}(x) \right), \mu_{\tilde{D}}(x) = \min\left(\mu_{\tilde{A}}(x), \mu_{\tilde{B}}(x) \right) \right\}$$

1.6.3   Complement

The complement of a fuzzy set $\tilde{A}$ is

$$\overline{\tilde{A}} = \left\{ \left(x, \mu_{\overline{\tilde{A}}}(x) \right), \mu_{\overline{\tilde{A}}}(x) = 1 - \mu_{\tilde{A}}(x) \right\}$$

Figure 7.2 shows the results of the above operations on fuzzy sets $\tilde{A}$ and $\tilde{B}$. These definition are simple and don't obey advance set-theoretic operations such as monotonicity, commutativity, and associativity. To overcome this problem, several complex definitions have been proposed in the literature [2].

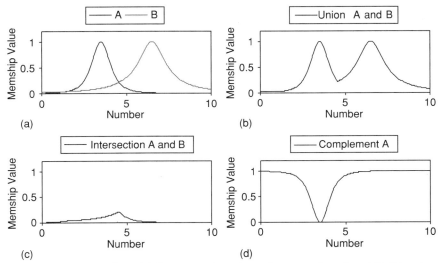

Figure 7.2. Fuzzy operations. (a) Representation of two fuzzy numbers A and B; (b) union of A and B; (c) intersection of A and B; (d) complement of A

2   FUZZY SYSTEMS

Figure 7.3 shows a generic fuzzy system. In all fuzzy systems, there are three main components: Rule Database, Fuzzification, and Defuzzification.

2.1   Fuzzy rules

Fuzzy systems are based on the preliminary information given to the system as fuzzy rules. These rules, which are written as linguistic commands, are usually not so precise. In fact, they are written to enable decision to be made in cases where there is imprecise or no preliminary information about the system under considerations. The following rules represent instances of generic fuzzy rules:

- IF "Salary is High" then "Tax is High"

- IF "Speed is Low" then "Accident Probability is Low"

- IF "Left Obstacle is Near" and "Front Obstacle is Near" then "Turn Right Quickly" and "Reduce Speed"

The above rules may have single or multiple antecedents and/or consequences.

2.2   Fuzzification

One of the most important components of every fuzzy system is the fuzzification phase, during which the crisp values from a real-world system are managed so that they can be processed by the fuzzy system [2]. Fuzzy rules, as seen earlier, are linguistic expressions that need to be further clarified, as in the case of the following rule:

IF "Salary is High" then "Tax is High"

So what does "High" mean? How high does the salary need to be so that it is considered "High"? Also, what is "High" in the context of how much tax needs to be paid? The process of defining this kind of information for a fuzzy system is known as *fuzzification*. To achieve this, knowledge-based information is

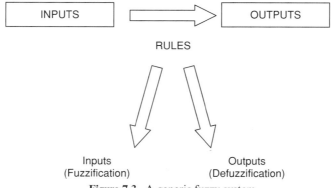

Figure 7.3. A generic fuzzy system

categorized into several parts as membership functions or fuzzy sets. Then a label is assigned to each part. For example, "Salary" could be categorized as shown in Figure 7.4. Note that membership functions designed to separate the different classes of salary earnings are overlapped smoothly to reduce the sensitivity of the fuzzy system.

2.3   Defuzzification

This process attempts to generate a crisp value for each fuzzy output generated by the fuzzy system. The following methods are the most popular for the *defuzzification* process.

2.3.1   Center of Area (COA)

In this case, the crisp value is calculated as the integral of the output fuzzy number weighted by the value of the membership function, which can be defined as follows:

$$u^{COA} = \frac{\int_U u.\mu^C(u)\,du}{\int_U \mu^C(u)\,du}$$

where $\mu^C(u)$ is the membership function of the fuzzy value.

2.3.2   Center of Sum (COS)

This defuzzification method is a simplified version of COA and is defined as follows:

$$u^{COA} = \frac{\int_U u.\mu^C(u)\,du}{\int_U \mu^C(u)\,du}$$

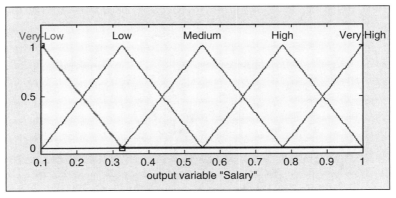

Figure 7.4. Fuzzification of the variable "Salary"

2.3.3   Mean of Maximum (MOM)

The maximum of the fuzzy number is computed, and then the average of both the maximum and the actual number is the defuzzified version.

2.3.4   Smallest of Maximum (SOM)

The maximum of the fuzzy number is computed, and then the smallest value is considered as the defuzzified number [2].

2.3.5   Largest of Maximum (LOM)

The maximum of the fuzzy number is computed, and then the largest value is considered as the defuzzified number [2]. To clarify the above definitions, Figure 7.5 shows how a fuzzy variable can be defuzzified.

2.4   Mamdani Fuzzy Systems

The Mamdani system is one of the two most famous fuzzy systems and is usually used for making fuzzy decisions [2–5]. In this system, the input and output variables are all fuzzified with several membership functions. For example, assume that a fuzzy system is designed to define the salary of an employee. Also suppose that the salary of an employee is related to his/her work experience and education level.

Figure 7.6 provides an overview of the above system. Although the output of this system is the level of salary, the first step is to fuzzify the input variables with membership functions. Towards this end, work experience (WrkExp) is fuzzified by three triangular membership function (Figure 7.7) as Beginner, Intermediate, or Expert, and the Education level (Edu) is fuzzified by three membership functions (Figure 7.8) as High School Diploma, Bachelor Degree, or Post Graduate Degree. The output of the system, Salary, is fuzzified by five labels (Figure 7.9) as Very-Low, Low, Medium, High, and Very-High. Note that, to generalize the controller, all variables are normalized to 1.0.

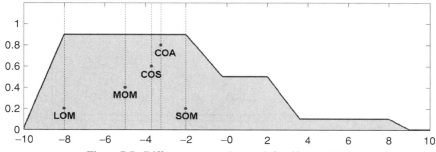

Figure 7.5. Different approaches to defuzzify a variable

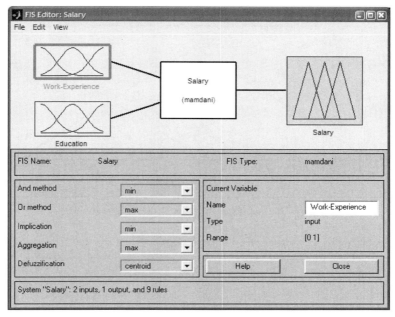

Figure 7.6. The general overview of Mamdani's salary system

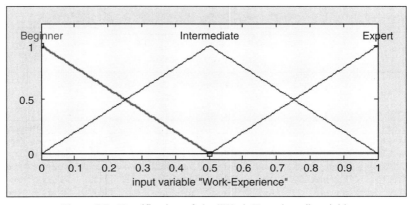

Figure 7.7. Fuzzification of the "Work-Experience" variable

Table 7.1 lists the rules of this system. To clarify how this fuzzy system computes the salary of an employee, the general data flow of this system is shown in Figure 7.10, while the general surface view of this system is shown in Figure 7.11.

Note that there are two other logic operations that need to be performed to compute the final fuzzy answer: *implication* and *aggregation*. These two operators are usually defined as AND and OR operators [2]. In this example, the COA is chosen as the defuzzification method. The Work Experience and Education Level variables are set to 0.1 and 0.3, respectively. Therefore, the Salary output for these inputs is 0.365. The general Surface View of this controller is presented in Figure 7.11.

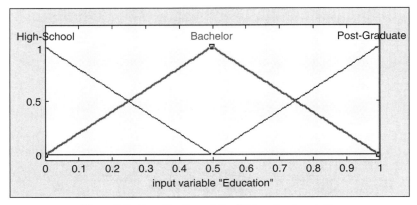

Figure 7.8. Fuzzification of the "Education" variable

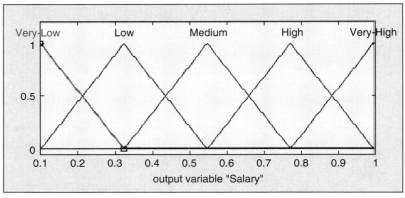

Figure 7.9. Fuzzification of the "Salary" variable

Table 7.1: Fuzzy rules for the system of Figure 7.6

Antecedent				→	Consequence
IF	WrkExp is Beginner	And	Edu is High School	Then	Salary is Very-Low
IF	WrkExp is Beginner	And	Edu is Bachelor	Then	Salary is Low
IF	WrkExp is Beginner	And	Edu is Post Graduate	Then	Salary is Medium
IF	WrkExp is Intermediate	And	Edu is High School	Then	Salary is Low
IF	WrkExp is Intermediate	And	Edu is Bachelor	Then	Salary is Medium
IF	WrkExp is Intermediate	And	Edu is Post Graduate	Then	Salary is High
IF	WrkExp is Expert	And	Edu is High School	Then	Salary is Medium
IF	WrkExp is Expert	And	Edu is Bachelor	Then	Salary is High
IF	WrkExp is Expert	And	Edu is Post Graduate	Then	Salary is Very High

2.5   Sugeno Fuzzy Systems

The Sugeno fuzzy system is another class of fuzzy systems that is usually used for control system applications [2, 6]. The output of each rule in this system is a linear, or in some cases a nonlinear, combination of its inputs. The output of the different rules is augmented to calculate the final output, which is actually the weighted sum of the rules.

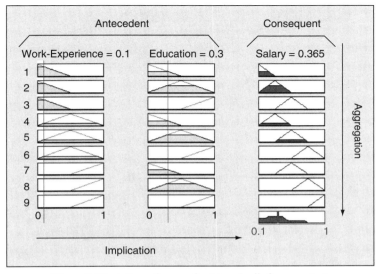

Figure 7.10. A flow diagram for Mamdani's fuzzy system

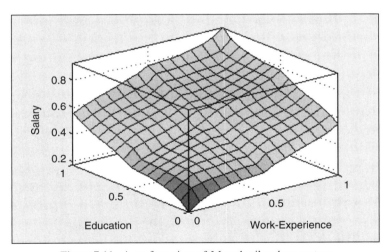

Figure 7.11. A surface view of Mamdani's salary system

To clarify the above, a Sugeno fuzzy system is designed to solve the salary problem given previously. Figure 7.12 shows the general overview of the system. The way the input variables are fuzzified is exactly the same as in Mamdani's version of this controller. The only difference is in defining the output for each fuzzy rule. In this case, five different formulas are defined to determine the salary category. To simplify the problem, these formulas are selected as constant numbers (although they can be any linear or nonlinear combination of the inputs) labeled as Very-Low, Low, Medium, High, and Very-High, with the following definitions:

Very-Low   =   0.1

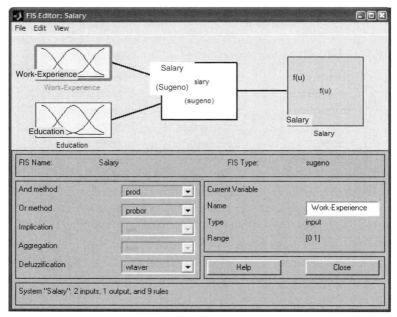

Figure 7.12. A general overview of Sugeno's salary system

Low   =   0.25
Medium   =   0.5
High   =   0.75
Very-High   =   1.0

The rules of Table 7.1 are applicable here, with the only difference being how the output is defined. Figure 7.13 shows a general overview of the rules firing scheme when the input variables are 0.1 and 0.3 for Work Experience and Education Level, respectively. In this case, the salary output is 0.232. The general Surface View of this system is given in Figure 7.14.

2.6   Fuzzy Decision Makers

Fuzzy decision makers are another class of fuzzy systems used for real-world applications [7-9]. In these systems, a predefined number of simple rules are embedded into the system, and then the system is allowed to make its own decisions, even in the case of unknown events for which the system was never trained.

To demonstrate the general idea of such systems, assume that one knows how the system must behave in extreme conditions, as shown in Figure 7.15, which is drawn for the examples provided in the last two sections to set the amount of salary for an employee. Then the aim of the whole system is to decide for all conditions inside the plate shown in Figure 7.15, while the rules are actually written for the known conditions that are marked with spheres (the system is trained for these points as its rules).

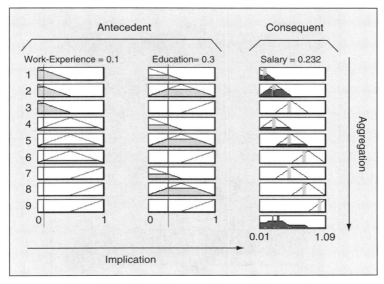

Figure 7.13. A flow diagram of Sugeno's fuzzy system

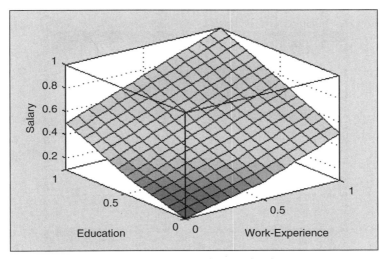

Figure 7.14. A surface view of Sugeno's salary system

2.7 Fuzzy Controller

Fuzzy Controllers are the other type of system employed for systems control [10–13]. The most famous example of this kind of system is reverse car parking. This example is one of the Demos of the Matlab® Releases, Version 13, Fuzzy Toolbox [14]. Figure 7.16 shows the initial conditions of a car to be parked, while Figure 7.17 shows the trajectory of the car position when the fuzzy controller is parking the car.

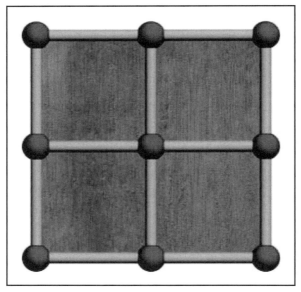

Figure 7.15. The rules are composed for the marked areas, although the system is able to make its decision for all the points

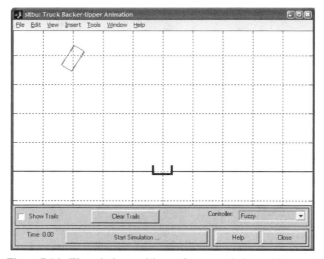

Figure 7.16. The relative positions of a car and the parking spot

2.8   Fuzzy Classifiers

Fuzzy classifiers are other classes of systems with different functionalities. [16, 17]. The aim here is to cluster objects, for example, in cases of system identification, time-series prediction, and noise cancellation. For further information, please refer to the Fuzzy Toolbox of the Matlab®, released version 13 [14].

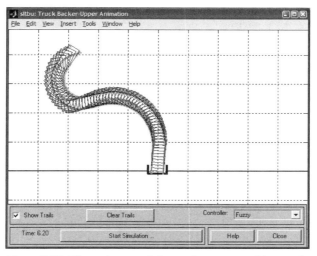

Figure 7.17. The trajectory of the car in reverse parking mode

3   DATA CLUSTERING ALGORITHMS

Clustering algorithms are used extensively not only to organize and categorize data but also to compress them in order to construct a model [17–24]. Through use of clustering techniques, data are partitioned into several groups such that the similarity within a group is larger than the similarities with other groups. These techniques are usually used in conjunction with radial basis functions or fuzzy modeling to determine the initial locations of the radial basis functions or fuzzy *IF – THEN* rules. In this case, a similarity function is usually defined to take two variables and generate a small output for similar inputs and large numbers for nonsimilar ones. It is important to note that clustering techniques used for structure identification in neural or fuzzy models are highly heuristic, and it is possible to find a data set in which none of the clustering techniques is applicable.

3.1   K-Means Clustering

The K-means algorithm partitions a group of n vectors x_j: $j = 1,...,n$ into c groups G_i: $i = 1,...,c$, and finds a cluster center in each group such that a cost function of dissimilarity measure is minimized [19,20]. To achieve this outcome, let's assume that

$$ J = \sum_{i=1}^{c} J_i = \sum_{i=1}^{c} \left(\sum_{k,\, x_k \in G_i} \left\| x_k - c_i \right\|^2 \right) $$

where $J_i = \sum_{k,\, x_k \in G_i} \left\| x_k - c_i \right\|^2$ is a cost function within group i.

The partitioned groups are typically defined by a $c \times n$ binary membership matrix U, where the elements u_{ij} are 1 if the jth data point x_j belongs to group i and 0 otherwise.

$$u_{ij} = \begin{cases} 1 & \left\| x_j - c_i \right\|^2 \leq \left\| x_j - c_k \right\|^2 \\ & k \neq i \\ 0 & \text{otherwise} \end{cases}$$

The membership matrix U has the following properties:

1. $\displaystyle\sum_{i=1}^{c} u_{ij} = 1 \qquad \forall j = 1,...,n$

2. $\displaystyle\sum_{i=1}^{c}\sum_{j=1}^{n} u_{ij} = n$

Finally, after every iteration, c_i should be updated as follows:

$$c_i = \frac{1}{|G_i|}\sum_{k,\, x_k \in G_i} x_k \text{ where } \qquad |G_i| = \sum_{j=1}^{n} u_{ij}$$

Note that the algorithm is inherently iterative, and no guarantee can be made that it will converge to an optimum solution. The performance of the K-means algorithm depends on the initial position of the cluster centers.

3.2   Fuzzy C-Means Clustering

Fuzzy C-means clustering (FCM), also known as fuzzy ISODATA, is a data clustering algorithm in which each data point belongs to a cluster to a degree specified by a membership grade [20,21].

FCM partitions a collection of n vectors $x_j: j = 1,...,n$ into c fuzzy groups $G_i: i = 1,...,c$, and finds a cluster center in each group such that a cost function of dissimilarity measure is minimized. To accommodate the introduction of fuzzy partitioning, the membership matrix U is allowed to have elements with values ranging between 0.0 and 1.0 such that

$$\sum_{i=1}^{c} u_{ij} = 1 \qquad \forall j = 1,...,n$$

The cost function for FCM is then a generalization of

$$J(U, c_1, c_2,..., c_c) = \sum_{i=1}^{c} J_i = \sum_{i=1}^{c}\sum_{j=1}^{n} u_{ij}^m \times d_{ij}^2$$

where u_{ij} is between 0 and 1; c_i is the cluster center of fuzzy group i; $d_{ij} = \left\| c_i - x_j \right\|$; and $m \in [1,\infty)$ is a weighting exponent.

The necessary conditions for the above equation to reach a minimum can be determined by

$$\overline{J}(U, c_1, c_2,..., c_c, \lambda_1, \lambda_2,..., \lambda_n) = \sum_{i=1}^{c}\sum_{j=1}^{n} u_{ij}^m \times d_{ij}^2 + \sum_{j=1}^{n} \lambda_j \left(\sum_{i=} u_{ij} - 1\right)$$

where $\lambda_j; j = 1,...,n$ are the Lagrange multipliers for the n constraints. A solution of the above problem should lead to the following formulas:

$$c_i = \frac{\displaystyle\sum_{j=1}^{n} u_{ij}^m \times x_j}{\displaystyle\sum_{j=1}^{n} u_{ij}^m}$$

and

$$u_{ij} = \cfrac{1}{\displaystyle\sum_{k=1}^{c} \left(\cfrac{d_{ij}}{d_{kj}}\right)^{\frac{2}{m-1}}}$$

As in the previous case, no guarantee ensures that FCM will converge to an optimum solution. The performance depends on the initial cluster centers.

3.3 Mountain Clustering Method

The mountain clustering method is a relatively simple and effective approach to approximate estimation of cluster centers on the basis of a density measure called the *mountain function* [22, 23]. This method can be used to obtain initial cluster centers that are required by more sophisticated cluster algorithms such as fuzzy C-mean. This clustering method involves three major steps. The first step forms a grid over the data space. The second step entails constructing a mountain function representing a data density measure:

$$m(v) = \sum_{i=1}^{N} \exp\left(-\frac{\|v - x_i\|^2}{2\sigma^2}\right)$$

where x_i is the ith data point and σ is an application specific constant. The mountain function can be viewed as a measure of *data density*, since it tends to be higher if more data points are located nearby and lower if fewer data points are around. The third step involves selecting the cluster centers by sequentially destructing the mountain function. First, the point in the candidate centers $v \in V$ that has the greatest value for the mountain function is found. This point will be considered as the first cluster center c_1.

Now let

$$m_{new}(v) = m(v) - m(c_1) \exp\left(-\frac{\|v - c_1\|}{2\beta^2}\right)$$

After the subtraction operation, the second cluster center is selected as the point $v \in V$ that has the greatest value for the new mountain function. This process of revising the mountain function and finding the next cluster center continues until a sufficient number of cluster centers are reached.

Mountain clustering can also be applied to identify the structure of a fuzzy model. To do this, firstly, a training data set is used to find cluster centers (x_i, y_i), and then a zero-order Sugeno fuzzy model is formed in which the ith rule is expressed as

IF X is close to x_i THEN Y is close to y_i

Then other tuning methods can be used to tune the rules further.

3.4 Subtracting Clustering

A new approach in fuzzy clustering is *subtractive clustering*, in which data points (not grid points) are considered as candidates for cluster centers [24]. With this method, the computation is simply proportional to the number of data points and independent of the dimensional of the problem under consideration, since each data point is potentially a candidate for a cluster center. Then, a *density measure* at data point x_i is defined as

$$D_i = \sum_{j=1}^{n} \exp\left(-\frac{\|x_i - x_j\|^2}{\left(\frac{r_a}{2}\right)^2}\right)$$

where r_a is a positive constant. The radius r_a defines a neighborhood; data points outside this radius contribute only slightly to the density measure.

When the density measurement for each data point has been calculated, the data point with the highest density measure is selected as the first cluster center. Let x_{c_1} be the point selected, with D_{c_1} as its density measure. Now the density measure for each data point x_i is revised by the formula

$$D_i = D_i - D_{c_1} \exp\left(-\frac{\|x_i - x_{c_1}\|^2}{\left(\frac{r_b}{2}\right)^2}\right)$$

where another r_b is a positive constant. Note that the constant r_b is normally larger than r_a to prevent closely spaced cluster centers. In general, $r_b = 1.5 \, r_a$.

After the density measure for each data point is revised, the next cluster center x_{c_2} is selected and all the density measures for data points are revised again. This process is repeated until sufficient cluster centers have been generated.

Like the mountain clustering algorithm, the subtractive clustering algorithm can be launched to determine fuzzy rules. For instance, assume that the center for the ith cluster is c_i in an M-dimensional and that the consequent parts are assumed to have RBFN membership. In this case, the membership function μ can be assigned as

$$\mu_i = \exp\left(-\frac{\|x_i - p_i\|^2}{(r_b/2)^2}\right)$$

3.5   Fuzzy Rules Generation

As explained earlier, each fuzzy system consists of three main components: input variables that must be fuzzified, output variables that must be defuzzified, and the most important part, namely, the rules database. The rules of a fuzzy system are the part of the system that actually relates the outputs to the inputs. It is obvious that without appropriate rules, the system may function inefficiently. Although rule generation is the most important part of a fuzzy system, it has rarely been considered because of its complexity.

Several approaches have been presented to help designers of fuzzy systems develop their rules in an efficient and concise way. However, most of these approaches have limited applicability. This section attempts to introduce some effective approaches to generate fuzzy rules [25–31]. Further, appropriate fuzzification and defuzzification methods are also important because they are correlated with the rules of the system.

3.6 Fuzzy Rules from Fuzzy Knowledge

The first approach employed for generating fuzzy rules is based on the experience of actual system operators, who usually intuitively know how to control the system. In this case, the fuzzy designer codes the ideas of an expert user into linguistic expressions, as seen earlier. The only thing the designer must consider is the consistency of the coding process so as to achieve maximum robustness of the system.

To clarify this situation, suppose a controller must be designed to control the temperature and flow of a shower using Hot and Cold values as inputs. In this case, the simplest controller can be that of Figures 7.18 and 7.19. Note that this system is a simple feedback controller that tries to reduce the difference between the actual temperature and flow rates and the desired ones (Feedback Errors).

To achieve this result, temperature and flow errors are both fuzzified by three triangular membership functions, as shown in Figures 7.20 and 7.21, while the outputs of the system are represented with three trapezoidal membership functions, as shown in Figure 7.22. Figures 7.23 and 7.24 show the temperature and flow rate of the system when their desired values are changes with square waveforms. Table 7.2 lists the rules for this system. This example is one of the Matlab® Fuzzy Logic Toolbox Demos [14].

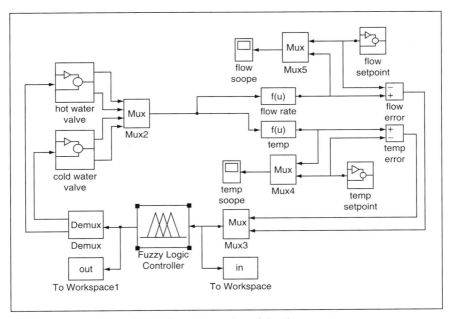

Figure 7.18. General overview of the shower system

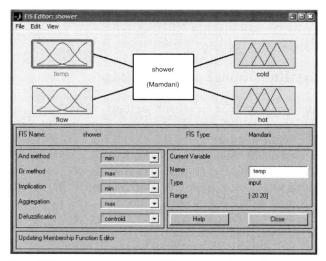

Figure 7.19. General overview of Mamdani's shower fuzzy system

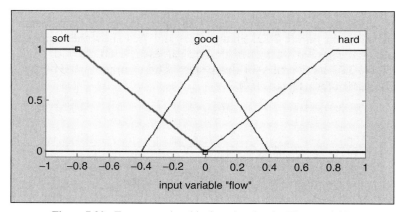

Figure 7.20. Fuzzy membership function for the Flow variable

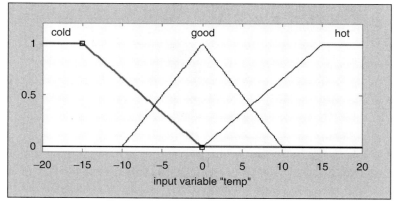

Figure 7.21. Fuzzy membership function for the Temp variable

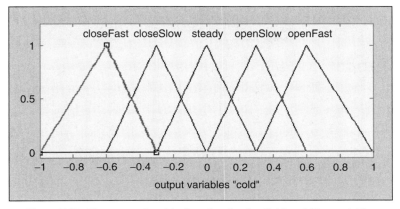

Figure 7.22. Fuzzy membership function for the Cold and Hot variables

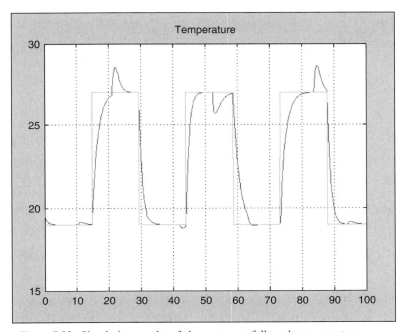

Figure 7.23. Simulation results of the system to follow the temperature curve

3.7   Fuzzy Rules from Fuzzy Patches

Fuzzy patches are actually fuzzy clusters that are generated by a given fuzzy clustering technique. Then a rule is written for each patch to imitate the behavior of the system in that condition. These patches can also be used to design a controller. In fact, the controller is designed so that it compensates the behavior of the system for each one of the patches. Then some other fuzzy rules are added to the system just to achieve overall stability for the system.

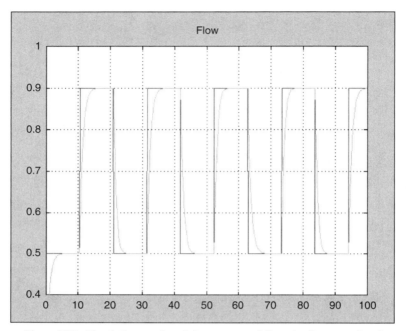

Figure 7.24. Simulation results of the system to follow the flow rate signal

3.8 Tuning Fuzzy Rules

Once the general structure of a fuzzy system has been determined, the system must be tuned to have the best performance. This process is usually performed by some optimal control routines that tune the parameters of the membership functions. In some cases, these routines even change the whole structure of the fuzzification and defuzzification processes [29].

3.9 Tuning Fuzzy Systems Using Gradient Descent Training

In this section, it is assumed that the structure of the fuzzy system is known and that the aim is to tune the parameters. In this case, a fuzzy system with a Gaussian membership function and COA defuzzification method is considered:

$$
f(x) = \frac{\displaystyle\sum_{l=1}^{M} \overline{y}^{l} \left[\prod_{i=1}^{n} \exp\left(-\left(\frac{x_i - \overline{x}_i^{l}}{\sigma_i^{l}} \right)^2 \right) \right]}{\displaystyle\sum_{l=1}^{M} \left[\prod_{i=1}^{n} \exp\left(-\left(\frac{x_i - \overline{x}_i^{l}}{\sigma_i^{l}} \right)^2 \right) \right]}
$$

where M is the number of rules and $\overline{y}^{l}, \overline{x}_i^{l}, \sigma_i^{l}$ are free parameters to be adjusted. Note that, although the structure of the system is chosen, the whole system has not been designed yet because of the $\overline{y}^{l}, \overline{x}_i^{l}, \sigma_i^{l}$ parameters. To determine these

Table 7.2. Fuzzy rules for the system shown in Figure 7.18

	Antecedent			→		Consequent	
IF	Temp is Cold	And	Flow is Soft	Then	CldVlv is OpenSlow	And	HotVlv is OpenFast
IF	Temp is Cold	And	Flow is Good	Then	CldVlv is CloseSlow	And	HotVlv is OpenSlow
IF	Temp is Cold	And	Flow is Hard	Then	CldVlv is CloseFast	And	HotVlv is CloseSlow
IF	Temp is Good	And	Flow is Soft	Then	CldVlv is OpenSlow	And	HotVlv is OpenSlow
IF	Temp is Good	And	Flow is Good	Then	CldVlv is Steady	And	HotVlv is Steady
IF	Temp is Good	And	Flow is Hard	Then	CldVlv is CloseSlow	And	HotVlv is CloseSlow
IF	Temp is Hot	And	Flow is Soft	Then	CldVlv is OpenFast	And	HotVlv is OpenSlow
IF	Temp is Hot	And	Flow is Good	Then	CldVlv is OpenSlow	And	HotVlv is CloseSlow
IF	Temp is Hot	And	Flow is Hard	Then	CldVlv is CloseSlow	And	HotVlv is CloseFast

parameters, it is helpful to represent the fuzzy system $f(x)$ as a feedforward network—specifically, the mapping from the input $x \in U \subset \Re^n$ to the output, $f(x) \in V \subset \Re$.

Now in order to design the parameters by the Gradient Descent Method, the matching error of the system is assigned as follows:

$$e^p = \frac{1}{2}(f(x_0^p) - y_0^p)^2$$

Considering a minimization problem, the $\bar{y}^l, \bar{x}_i^l, \sigma_i^l$ parameters should be adjusted such that e^p is minimized. In this case, using the gradient descent algorithm, the following formulas are used to tune these parameters. $\bar{y}^l$ would be adjusted as follows:

$$\bar{y}^l(q+1) = \bar{y}^l(q) - \alpha \left.\frac{\partial e}{\partial \bar{y}^l}\right|_q$$

$$\frac{\partial e}{\partial \bar{y}^l} = (f - y)\frac{\partial f}{\partial a}\frac{\partial a}{\partial \bar{y}^l} = (f - y)\frac{1}{b}z^l$$

$$\bar{y}^l(q+1) = \bar{y}^l(q) - \alpha \frac{f - y}{b}z^l$$

$\bar{x}_i^l$ as follows:

$$\bar{x}_i^l(q+1) = \bar{x}_i^l(q) - \alpha \left.\frac{\partial e}{\partial \bar{x}_i^l}\right|_q$$

$$\frac{\partial e}{\partial \bar{x}_i^l} = (f - y)\frac{\partial f}{\partial z^l}\frac{\partial z^l}{\partial \bar{x}_i^l}$$

$$\bar{x}_i^l(q+1) = \bar{x}_i^l(q) - \alpha \frac{f - y}{b}(\bar{y}_i^l(q) - f)z^l \frac{2(x_{0i}^p - \bar{x}_i^l(q))}{\sigma_i^{l^2}(q)}$$

and finally σ_i^l as follows:

$$\sigma_i^l(q+1) = \sigma_i^l(q) - \alpha \left.\frac{\partial e}{\partial \sigma_i^l}\right|_q$$

$$\frac{\partial e}{\partial \sigma_i^l} = (f - y)\frac{\partial f}{\partial z^l}\frac{\partial z^l}{\partial \sigma_i^l}$$

$$\sigma_i^l(q+1) = \sigma_i^l(q) - \alpha \frac{f - y}{b}(\bar{y}^l(q) - f)z^l \frac{2(x_{0i}^p - \bar{x}_i^l(q))^2}{\sigma_i^{l^3}(q)}$$

This algorithm is also called the *error back-propagation training algorithm*. The following algorithm is the final procedure that can be used to adjust the parameters of a fuzzy system using the gradient descent technique.

Step 1: Structure determination and initial parameter setting

Choose the fuzzy system in the above form and determine the M. Have in mind that larger values for M need more computation as well, but better accuracy. The initial parameters $\bar{y}^l(0)$, $\bar{x}_i^l(0)$, $\sigma_i^l(0)$ must be chosen carefully, too. These initial parameters may be determined according to the linguistic rules from experts or any other clustering technique.

Step 2: Present input and calculate the output of the fuzzy system

For a given input–output pair (x_0^p, y_0^p), $p = 1,2,...$, the following auxiliary parameters are calculated, where q is the iteration cycle:

$$z^l = \prod_{i=1}^{n} \exp\left(-\left(\frac{x_{0i}^p - \bar{x}_i^l(q)}{\sigma_i^l(q)}\right)^2\right)$$

$$b = \sum_{l=1}^{M} z^l$$

$$a = \sum_{l=1}^{M} \bar{y}^l(q)z^l$$

$$f = \frac{a}{b}$$

Step 3: Update the parameters

Modify the parameters $\bar{y}^l(q+1)$, $\bar{x}_i^l(q+1)$, σ_i^l (q + 1) based on the results of Step 2, where $y = y_0^p$.

Step 4: Repeat Steps 2 and 3 with $q = q + 1$ for a predefined number of iterations, or until the output error of the system $|f - y_0^p|$ becomes less than another predefined value ε.

Step 5: Repeat Steps 2 through 4 with $p = p + 1$, that is, update parameters using the next input–output pair (x_0^{p+1}, y_0^{p+1}).

Step 6: Repeat the whole training procedure if applicable.

If desirable and feasible, set $p = 1$ and repeat Steps 2–5 until the designed fuzzy system is satisfactory. For online control and dynamic system identification, this step is not feasible because the input–output pairs are provided one-by-one in a real-time fashion. However, for pattern recognition problems where the input–output pairs are provided offline, this step is desirable.

Note that, because of the nature of the above training algorithms, choosing the initial parameters is crucial to the success of the algorithm. If the initial parameters are chosen close to the optimal ones, the algorithm has a good chance of converging to the optimal solution; otherwise, the algorithm may converge to a nonoptimal solution or even diverge.

Setting the Initial Parameters

The choice of initial parameters is detrimental to the overall quality of the final solution. In some cases, these parameters can be selected by experts, but in other occasions this is not possible. So, to solve the above identification problem, the following method is proposed for setting the initial parameters [29].

An online initial parameter choosing method:

Step 1: Collect the input–output pairs

$$(x_0^{k+1}, y_0^{k+1})$$

where

$$x_0^{k+1} = (y(k),...,y(k - n + 1),u(k),...,u(k - m + 1))$$

for the first

$$y_0^{k+1} = y(k + 1)$$

M points ($k = 1, ..., M - 1$).
Note that the training algorithm is actually started when $k = M - 1$.
Step 2: Choose the initial parameters
     These parameters are chosen as $\bar{y}^l(0) = y_0^l$ and $\bar{x}^l(0) = x_{0i}^l$, while $\sigma_i^l(0)$
   can be
set according to one of the following criteria:
1. Set $\sigma_i^l(0)$ to a small number

2. Set $\sigma_i^l(0) = \dfrac{\max\limits_{l=1,...,M}(x_{0i}^l) - \min\limits_{l=1,...,M}(x_{0i}^l)}{M}, i = 1, ..., n + m$

3. Set $\sigma_i^l(0)$ so that it makes the membership functions uniformly cover the
   range of x_{0i}^l from $l = 1$ to $l = M$.
The following lemma is a stability proof of the presented technique.

Lemma: For any arbitrary $\varepsilon > 0$, there exist $\sigma^* > 0$ such that the fuzzy system
$\hat{f}(x)$, with the preceding initial parameters $\bar{y}^l$, $\bar{x}_i^l$, and $\sigma_i^l = \sigma^*$, has the property that

$$\left| \hat{f}(x_0^{k+1}) - y_0^{k+1} \right| < \epsilon \qquad k = 0, 1, ..., M - 1.$$

Note that, by using this method, the first M input–output pairs will be properly matched. Thus, if these first M input–output pairs contain important features of the unknown system $f(x)$, it is very likely that, after training, the fuzzy identifier will converge rapidly and determine the unknown parameters of the system.

3.10   Design of Fuzzy Systems Using Recursive Least Squares

The gradient descent algorithm in the previous section tries to minimize the
criterion $e^p (e^p = \frac{1}{2}(f(x_0^p) - y_0^p)^2)$, which actually accounts for the matching error

of only one input–output pair (x_0^p, y_0^p). In other words, the training algorithm updates the parameters to match one input–output pair at a time. In this new approach, a training algorithm that minimize the summation of the matching errors for all the input–output pairs up to p is used to adjust the training parameters; that is, the objective here is to design a fuzzy system $f(x)$ to minimize the following cost function:

$$J_p = \sum_{j=1}^{p} \left(f(x_0^j) - y_0^j \right)^2$$

Moreover, the fuzzy system is designed iteration by iteration in a recursive manner; that is, if f_p is the fuzzy system designed to minimize J_p, then f_p should be represented as a function of f_{p-1}. To accomplish this, the recursive least squares algorithm is used as follows:

Step 1: Suppose that $U = [\alpha_1, \beta_1] \times ... \times [\alpha_n, \beta_n] \subset \mathfrak{R}^n$. Then, for each $[\alpha_i, \beta_i]$,
   $i = 1, 2, ..., n$, define N_i fuzzy sets as $A_i^{l_i}$, $l_i = 1, 2, ..., N_i$, which cover $[\alpha_i, \beta_i]$
   homogenously.
Step 2: Construct the fuzzy system from the following $\prod_{i=1}^{n} N_i$ fuzzy *IF – THEN*
   rules as follows:

$$IF \ x_1 \ is \ A_1^{l_1} \ and \ ... \ and \ x_n \ is \ A_n^{l_n} \ THEN \ y \ is \ B^{l_1,...,l_n}$$

where $l_i = 1, 2,..., N_i$, $i = 1, 2,..., n$, and $B^{l_1,...,l_n}$ is any fuzzy set with center at $\bar{y}^{l_1...l_n}$ (which is free to change). In particular, when the fuzzy system with product inference engine, singleton fuzzifier, and COA defuzzifier is chosen with the following formula:

$$f(x) = \frac{\sum_{l_1=1}^{N_1} \cdots \sum_{l_n=1}^{N_n} \bar{y}^{l_1, ..., l_n} \left[\prod_{i=1}^{n} \mu_{A_i^{l_i}}(x_i) \right]}{\sum_{l_1=1}^{N_1} \cdots \sum_{l_n=1}^{N_n} \left[\prod_{i=1}^{n} \mu_{A_i^{l_i}}(x_i) \right]}$$

where $\bar{y}^{l_1, ..., l_n}$ are free parameters (that need to be properly chosen).

Step 3: Collect the free parameters $\bar{y}^{l_1, ..., l_n}$ into the $\prod_{i=1}^{n} N_i$ -dimensional vector as follows:

$$\theta = (\bar{y}^{1...1}, ..., \bar{y}^{N_1 1...1}, \bar{y}^{121...1}, ..., \bar{y}^{N_1 21...1}, \bar{y}^{1N_2...N_n}, ..., \bar{y}^{N_1 N_2...N_n})^T$$

to form $f(x) = b^T(x) \cdot \theta$, where

$$b(x) = (b^{1...1}, ..., b^{N_1 1...1}, b^{121...1}, ..., b^{N_1 21...1}, b^{1N_2...N_n}, ..., b^{N_1 N_2...N_n})^T$$

and

$$b^{l_1, ..., l_n}(x) = \frac{\prod_{i=1}^{n} \mu_{A_i^{l_i}}(x_i)}{\sum_{l_1=1}^{N_1} \cdots \sum_{l_n=1}^{N_n} \left[\prod_{i=1}^{n} \mu_{A_i^{l_i}}(x_i) \right]}$$

Step 4: Choose the initial parameters $\theta(0)$ as follows:

If there are linguistic rules from experts whose *IF* parts agree with the *IF* parts of one of the existing rules, then choose $\bar{y}^{l_1, ..., l_n}(0)$ to be the centers of the *THEN* part fuzzy sets in these linguistic rules; otherwise, choose $\theta(0)$ arbitrary in the output space $V \subset \Re$; or from a clustering algorithm.

Step 4: For $p = 1, 2,...$, compute the parameter θ using the following recursive least squares algorithm:

$\theta(p) = \theta(p-1) + K(p) \cdot [y_0^p - b^T(x_0^p) \check{\ } \theta(p-1)]$
$K(p) = P(p-1) \cdot b(x_0^p) \cdot [b^T(x_0^p) \cdot P(p-1) \cdot b(x_0^p) + 1]^{-1}$
$P(p) = P(p-1) - P(p-1) \cdot b(x_0^p).$
$\quad [b^T(x_0^p) \cdot P(p-1) \cdot b(x_0^p) + 1]^{-1} b^T(x_0^p) \cdot P(p-1)$

where $\theta(0)$ is chosen from Step 4, and $P(0) = \sigma I$, where σ is a large constant. In this fuzzy system, the parameters $\bar{y}^{l_1, ..., l_n}$ are equal to the corresponding elements in $\theta(p)$.

4 DESIGN OF FUZZY SYSTEMS USING CLUSTERING

In this section, the input–output pairs are used to design the rules for the fuzzy system. Basically, the input–output pairs are grouped into clusters and one rule is formulated for each cluster [32–37].

4.1   An Adaptive Fuzzy System

Suppose that N input–output pairs (x_0^l, y_0^l), $l = 1, 2,..., N$, are given and the task is to construct a fuzzy system $f(x)$ that can match all the N pairs with a given accuracy. That is, for any given $\varepsilon > 0$, it is required to satisfy $|f(x_0^l) - y_0^l| < \varepsilon$ for all $l = 1, 2,..., N$. In this case, the optimal fuzzy system is considered as

$$f(x) = \frac{\sum_{l=1}^{N} y_0^l \exp\left(-\frac{|x - x_0^l|^2}{\sigma^2}\right)}{\sum_{l=1}^{N} \exp\left(-\frac{|x - x_0^l|^2}{\sigma^2}\right)}$$

while the membership functions are

$$\mu_{A_i^l}(x_i) = \exp\left(-\frac{|x - x_0^l|^2}{\sigma^2}\right)$$

In this case, the designed optimal fuzzy system will have one rule for one input–output pair. Therefore, the larger the number of input–output pairs, the larger the number of rules in the system. To solve this problem, various clustering techniques can be used to categorize the input–output pairs and, consequently, reduce the number redundant rules.

4.2   Design of Fuzzy System Using Nearest-Neighbor Clustering

Use of the nearest-neighbor technique is one of the most effective ways to design fuzzy systems [34, 35]. This technique can be summarized as follows:

Step 1: Starting with the first input–output pair (x_0^l, y_0^l), establish a cluster center x_c^1 at x_0^l, and set $A^1(1) = y_0^1$, $B^1(1) = 1$. Select a radius r.

Step 2: Suppose that the algorithm is going to assign the kth input–output pair (x_0^k, y_0^k), $k = 2, 3,...$, to a cluster when there are M clusters with centers at $x_c^1, x_c^2,..., x_c^M$.

Step 3: Compute the distance of x_0^k to those M cluster centers, and then find the nearest cluster to x_0^k, namely, $x_c^{l_k}$. Then:

- If $|x_0^k - x_c^{l_k}| > r$, establish x_0^k as a new cluster center $x_c^{M+1} = x_0^k$, set
  $A^{M+1}(k) = y_0^k$, $B^{M+1}(k) = 1$

  and keep

  $A^l(k) = A^l(k-1)$
  $B^l(k) = B^l(k-1)$ for all $l = 1, 2,...,M$.

- If $|x_0^k - x_c^{l_k}| \leq r$, do the following:

$$A^{l_k}(k) = A^{l_k}(k-1) + y_0^k$$

$$B^{l_k}(k) = B^{l_k}(k-1) + 1$$

and set

$$A^l(k) = A^l(k-1)$$

$$B^l(k) = B^l(k-1)$$

for all $l = 1, 2, ..., M$.

Step 3: If x_0^k does not establish a new cluster, then the designed fuzzy system based on the k input–output pairs (x_0^j, y_0^j), $j = 1, 2, ..., k$ is

$$f_k(x) = \frac{\sum_{l=1}^{M} A^l(k) \exp\left(-\frac{\left|x - x_c^l\right|^2}{\sigma^2}\right)}{\sum_{l=1}^{M} B^l(k) \exp\left(-\frac{\left|x - x_c^l\right|^2}{\sigma^2}\right)}$$

Step 4: If x_0^k establishes a new cluster, then the designed fuzzy system is

$$f_k(x) = \frac{\sum_{l=1}^{M+1} A^l(k) \exp\left(\frac{-\left|x - x_c^l\right|^2}{\sigma^2}\right)}{\sum_{l=1}^{M+1} B^l(k) \exp\left(\frac{-\left|x - x_c^l\right|^2}{\sigma^2}\right)}$$

Step 5: Repeat by returning to Step 2 with $k = k+1$ until the process converges to a satisfactory solution.

5   FUZZY APPLICATIONS

This section presents two popular applications that demonstrate the potential of fuzzy logic in solving complex problems [36–38].

6   APPLICATION TO NONLINEAR DYNAMIC SYSTEM IDENTIFICATION

System identification is a process of determining an appropriate model for a system based on measurement form sensors [36, 37]. This process is important because many applications in science and engineering depend on the accurate modeling of a real-world system. In this section, a fuzzy system is used to approximate the unknown nonlinear components of a dynamic system. Now, consider a discrete-time nonlinear dynamic system as follows:

$$y(k+1) = f(y(k), ..., y(k-n+1), u(k), ..., u(k-m+1))$$

where f is an unknown function that needs to be "identified", u and y are the inputs and outputs of the system, respectively, and n and m are positive integers. Now let $\hat{f}(x)$ be the fuzzy system that is supposed to be an approximate of the real system f.

$$y(k+1) = \hat{f}(y(k),...,y(k-n+1),u(k),...,u(k-m+1))$$

Based on the identification scheme given in Figure 7.25, the aim is to adjust the parameters of $\hat{f}(x)$ such that the output of the identification model $\hat{y}(k+1)$ converges to the output of the real system $y(k+1)$ as $k \to \infty$.

To achieve this outcome, any of the previously presented tuning algorithms can be used with the following formulation. The input–output pairs in this problem are (x_0^{k+1}, y_0^{k+1}), where

$$x_0^{k+1} = (y(k),..., y(k-n+1), u(k),..., u(k-m+1))$$
$$y_0^{k+1} = y(k+1) \qquad\qquad k = 0, 1, 2,...$$

Now the system parameters are modified iteration by iteration to follow the real output.

6.1   Fuzzy robot navigator

Robot control is another area that benefited from advances in fuzzy logic [38]. A fuzzy navigator is designed to control a robot that moves around a room containing several static obstacles (chairs, tables, etc) and dynamic obstacles (humans). Now the idea is that a fuzzy navigator will aid the robot to get to any arbitrary point in the room from any other arbitrary point without colliding with any static or dynamic obstacle [39].

In summary, the robot is equipped with ultrasonic sensors to detect its surrounding obstacles. These sensors are mounted on the front, left, and right side of the robot. Three completely individual controllers were designed to seek the goal, avoid obstacles, and follow edges in the room. Figure 7.26 shows the general overview of the controller, while Figures 7.27 and 7.28 are two examples of launching the proposed algorithm in the presence of dynamic and static obstacles. In these figures, the robot starts from the "S" point to get the target point "T".

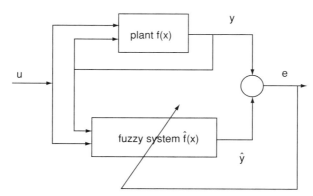

Figure 7.25. A fuzzy identification system

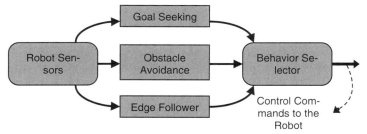

Figure 7.26. A fuzzy robot navigator

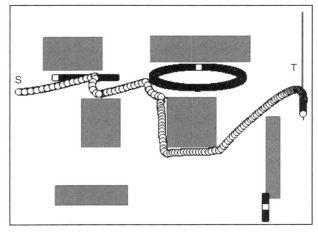

Figure 7.27. A path generated in the presence of static and dynamic obstacles with a moving target

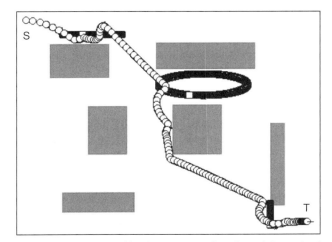

Figure 7.28. A path generated in the presence of static and dynamic obstacles

Static obstacles are shown in gray, are dynamic (moving) obstacles are shown in black. The robot itself is shown as a circle with a tick to show its head angle. Note that, in Figure 7.27, the target is also a moving point, such as a carriage.

7   CONCLUSION

In this chapter, a general overview of the fuzzy logic has been presented. The premise of fuzzy logic relies on the fact that decisions in the real world may not be clear-cut, especially in complex scenarios. Fuzzy logic is a powerful tool that can be applied to a wide range of applications ranging from fuzzy control to fuzzy decision makers and fuzzy classifiers.

REFERENCES

[1]   B. Kosko (1994): Fuzzy Thinking: The New Science of Fuzzy Logic. *Hyperion*, Reprint edition.

[2]   H.-J. Zimmermann (2001): Fuzzy Set Theory and its Applications, 4th ed. Kluwer Academic Publishers.

[3]   H. Ying, Y. Ding, S. Li, and S. Shao (1999): Comparison of necessary conditions for typical Takagi-Sugeno and Mamdani fuzzy systems as universal approximators, *IEEE Transactions on Systems, Man and Cybernetics (Part A)*, *29*(5), 508–514.

[4]   Y. Ding, H. Ying, and S. Shao (2000): Necessary conditions on minimal system configuration for general MISO Mamdani fuzzy systems as universal approximators, *IEEE Transactions on Systems, Man and Cybernetics (Part B)*, *30*(6), 857–864.

[5]   P. Liu (2002): Mamdani fuzzy system: universal approximator to a class of random processes, *IEEE Transactions on Fuzzy Systems*, *10* (6), 756–766.

[6]   K. Tanaka, T. Taniguchi, and H. O. Wang (2000): Generalized Takagi-Sugeno fuzzy systems: rule reduction and robust control, in *Proc. Ninth IEEE International Conference on Fuzzy Systems*, *2*, 688–693.

[7]   V. Catania, G. Ficili, S. Palazzo, and D. Panno (1995): A fuzzy decision maker for source traffic control in high speed networks, in *Proc. International Conference on Network Protocols*, pp. 136–143.

[8]   Q. M. Wu and C. W. de Silva (1993): Automatic adjustment of the cutting position of a vision-based fish processing machine, in *Proc. IEEE Pacific Rim Conference on Communications*, Computers and Signal Processing, *2*, 702–705.

[9]   H. R. Beom and H. S. Cho (2000): Sonar-based navigation experiments on a mobile robot in indoor environments, in *Proc. IEEE International Symposium on Intelligent Control*, pp. 395–401.

[10] H.M. Tai and S. Shenoi (1994): Robust fuzzy controllers, in *Proc. IEEE International Conference on Systems, Man, and Cybernetics*, *1*, 85–90.

[11] S. Galichet and L. Foulloy (1995): Fuzzy controllers: synthesis and equivalences, *IEEE Transactions on Fuzzy Systems*, *3*(2), 140–148.

[12] W. Barra, Jr. (1998): A practical and useful self-learning fuzzy controller, in *Proc. Int. Conf. Control (Control '98)*, Sept. 1-4, 1998, *1*, 290–295.

[13] C. W. Tao and J. Taur (1999): Design of fuzzy controllers with adaptive rule insertion, *IEEE Transactions on Systems, Man and Cybernetics (Part B)*, *29*(3), 389–397.

[14] Fuzzy Toolbox, Matlab Released Version 13.

[15] S. Abe (1998): Dynamic cluster generation for a fuzzy classifier with ellipsoidal regions, *IEEE Transactions on Systems, Man and Cybernetics (Part B)*, *28*(6), 869–876.

[16] J. G. Marin-Blazquez and Q. Shen (2002): From approximative to descriptive fuzzy classifiers, *IEEE Transactions on Fuzzy Systems*, *10*(4), 484–497.

[17] O. Takata, S. Miyamoto, and K. Umayahara (2001): Fuzzy clustering of data with uncertainties using minimum and maximum distances based on L1 metric, in *Proc. Joint 9th IFSA World Congress and 20th NAFIPS International Conference*, *5*, 2511–2516.

[18] L.-J. Kau (2003): Adaptive predictor with dynamic fuzzy K-means clustering for lossless image coding, in *Proc. 12th IEEE International Conference on Fuzzy Systems*, *2*, 944–949.

[19] N. Watanabe and T. Imaizumi (2001): Fuzzy k-means clustering with crisp regions, in *Proc. 10th IEEE International Conference on Fuzzy Systems*, *1*, 199–202.

[20] Y. Bo, G. J. Klir, and J. F. Swan-Stone (1995): Evolutionary fuzzy C-means clustering algorithm, in *Proc. Joint Fourth IEEE International Conference on Fuzzy Systems and the Second International Fuzzy Engineering Symposium*, *4*, 2221–2226.

[21] M.-C. Hung and D.-L. Yang (2001): An efficient Fuzzy C-Means clustering algorithm, in *Proc. IEEE International Conference on Data Mining*, pp. 225–232.

[22] J. W. Lee, S. H. Son, and S. H. Kwon (2001): Advanced mountain clustering method, in *Proc. Joint 9th IFSA World Congress and 20th NAFIPS, July 1*, 275–280.

[23] P. J. Costa Branco, N. Lori, and J. A. Dente (1995): An autonomous approach to the mountain-clustering method, in *Proc. Third International Symposium on Uncertainty Modeling and Analysis and Annual Conference of the North American Fuzzy Information Processing Society*, pp. 649–654.

[24] W.-Y. Liu, C.-J. Xiao, B.-W. Wang, Y. Shi, and S.-F. Fang (2003): Study on combining subtractive clustering with fuzzy C-means clustering, in *Proc. Int. Conf. Machine Learning and Cybernetics*, *5*, 2659–2662.

[25] S. Mitra and Y. Hayashi (2000): Neuro-fuzzy rule generation: survey in soft computing framework, *IEEE Transactions on Neural Networks*, *11*(3), 748–768.

[26] C.-S. Fahn, K.-T. Lan, and Z.-B. Chern (1999): Fuzzy rules generation using new evolutionary algorithms combined with multilayer perceptrons, *IEEE Transactions on Industrial Electronics*, *46*(6), 1103–1113.

[27] T.M. McKinney and N. Kehtarnavaz (1997): Fuzzy rule generation via multi-scale clustering, in *Proc. IEEE International Conference on Systems, Man, and Cybernetics*, *4*, 3182–3187.

[28] J. Wang, L. Shen, and J.-F. Chao (1997): An efficient method of fuzzy rules generation, in *Proc. IEEE International Conference on Intelligent Processing Systems*, *1*, 295–299.

[29] Y. Shi, M. Mizumoto, N. Yubazaki and M. Otani (1996): A learning algorithm for tuning fuzzy rules based on the gradient descent method, in *Proc. IEEE International Conference on Fuzzy Systems*, *1*, 55–61.

[30] X. Chang, W. Li, and J. Farrell (2000): A C-means clustering based fuzzy modeling method, in *Proc. Ninth IEEE International Conference on Fuzzy Systems*, *2*, 937–940.

[31] M.-S. Chen and R.-J. Liou (1999): An efficient learning method of fuzzy inference system, in *Proc. IEEE International Fuzzy Systems*, *2*, 634–638.

[32] T.-W. Hung, S.-C. Fang, and H. L. W. Nuttle (1999): An easily implemented approach to fuzzy system identification, in *Proc. 18th International Conference of the North American Fuzzy Information Processing Society*, pp. 492–496.

[33] Y. Wang and G. Rong (1997): A self-organizing neural-network-based fuzzy system, in *Proc. Fifth International Conference on Artificial Neural Networks*, pp. 106–110.

[34] I. Burham Turksen, B. A. Sproule, and C. A. Naranjo (2001): A k-nearest neighborhood based fuzzy reasoning schema, in *Proc. 10th IEEE International Conference on Fuzzy Systems*, *1*, 236–239.

[35] L.-X. Wang (1993): Training of fuzzy logic systems using nearest neighborhood clustering, in *Proc. Second IEEE International Conference on Fuzzy Systems*, *1*, 13–17.

[36] F. Wan, L.-X. Wang, H.-Y. Zhu, and Y.-X. Sun (2001): Generating persistently exciting inputs for nonlinear dynamic system identification using fuzzy models, in *Proc. IEEE International Conference on Fuzzy Systems*, *1*, 505–508.

[37] A. Lo Schiavo and A. M. Luciano (2001): Powerful and flexible fuzzy algorithm for nonlinear dynamic system identification, *IEEE Transactions on Fuzzy Systems*, *9*(6), 828–835.

[38] J. Taheri and N. Sadati (2003): A fully modular online controller for robot navigation in static and dynamic environments, in *Proc. IEEE International Symposium on Computational Intelligence in Robotics and Automation*, *1*, 163–168.

Chapter 8

QUANTUM COMPUTING
J. Eisert[1,2] and M. M. Wolf[3]
[1]Imperial College London,
[2]Universität Potsdam
[3]Max-Planck-Institut für Quantenoptik

Quantum mechanics is one of the cornerstones of modern physics. It governs the behavior and the properties of matter in a fundamental way, in particular on the microscopic scale of atoms and molecules. Hence, what we may call a classical computer, i.e., those machines on or under the desktops in our offices together with all their potential descendants, are themselves following the rules of quantum mechanics. However, they are no quantum computers in the sense that all the inside information processing can perfectly be described within classical information theory. In fact, we do not need quantum mechanics in order to explain how the zeros and ones – the bits – inside a classical computer evolve. The reason for this is that the architecture of classical computers does not make use of one of the most fundamental features of quantum mechanics, namely, the possibility of superpositions. Throughout the entire processing of any program on a classical computer, each of the involved bits takes on either the value zero or one. Quantum mechanics, however, would in addition allow superpositions of zeros on ones, that is, bits – now called *qubits* (quantum-bits) – that are somehow in the state zero and one at the same time. Computing devices that exploit this possibility, and with it all the essential features of quantum mechanics, are called *quantum computers* [1]. Since they have an additional capability, they are at least as powerful as classical computers: every problem that can be solved on a classical computer can be handled by a quantum computer just as well. The converse, however, is also true, since the dynamics of quantum systems is governed by linear differential equations, which can in turn be solved (at least approximately) on a classical computer. Hence, classical and quantum computers could in principle emulate each other, and quantum computers are thus no hypercomputers.[1]

---

[1]A *hypercomputer* would be capable of solving problems that cannot be handled by a *universal Turing machine* (the paradigm of a classical digital computer). The most famous example of

So why quantum computing? And if there is any reason, why not just simulate these devices (which do not exist yet anyhow) on a classical computer?

1   WHY QUANTUM COMPUTING?

1.1   Quantum computers reduce the complexity of certain computational tasks

One reason for quantum computers is that they will solve certain types of problems faster than any (present or future) classical computer – it seems that the border between *easy* and *hard* problems is different for quantum computers than it is for their classical counterparts. Here *easy* means that the time for solving the problem grows polynomially with the length of the input data (as with the problem of multiplying two numbers), whereas hard problems are those for which the required time grows exponentially. Prominent examples for hard problems are the traveling salesman problem, the graph isomorphism problem, and the problem of factoring a number into primes.[2] To the surprise of all, Peter Shor showed in 1994 that the latter problem could efficiently be solved by a quantum computer in polynomial time [2]. Hence, a problem that is hard for any classical computer becomes easy for quantum computers.[3] Shor's result gets even more brisance from the fact that the security of public key encryption, i.e., the security of home banking and any other information transfer via the Internet, is heavily based on the fact that factoring is a hard problem.

One might think that the cost for the exponential speedup gained with quantum computers would be an exponential increase in the required accuracy for all the involved operations. This situation would then be reminiscent of the drawback of analogue computers. Fortunately, this is not the case, and a constant accuracy is sufficient. However, achieving this "constant" is without doubt experimentally highly challenging.

1.2   Quantum systems can efficiently simulate other quantum systems

Nature provides many fascinating collective quantum phenomena such as superconductivity, magnetism, and Bose–Einstein condensation. Although all

---

such a problem is the *halting problem*, which is in modern terminology the task of a universal crash debugger, which is supposed to spot all bugs leading to crashes or infinite loops for any program running on a universal Turing machine. As shown by Turing, such a debugger cannot exist.

[2] These problems are strongly believed to be hard (the same is, by the way, true for a special instance of the computer game "Minesweeper"). However, in all cases, there is no proof that a polynomial-time algorithm cannot exist. The question whether there exists such an algorithm (for the traveling salesman or the minesweeper problem) is in fact the notorious $P \stackrel{?}{=} NP$ question, for whose solution there is even a prize of 1 million.

[3] In fact, Shor's algorithm strikes the *strong Church-Turing thesis*, which states that every reasonable physical computing device can be simulated on a probabilistic Turing machine with at most a polynomial overhead.

properties of matter are described and can in principle be determined from the laws of quantum mechanics, physicists have very often serious difficulties in understanding them in detail and in predicting them by starting from fundamental rules and first principles. One reason for these difficulties is that the number of parameters needed to describe a many-particle quantum system grows exponentially with the number of particles. Hence, comparing a theoretical model for the behavior of more than, say, thirty particles with experimental reality is not possible by simulating the theoretical model numerically on a classical computer without making serious simplifications.

When thinking about this problem of simulating quantum systems on classical computers, Richard Feynman came to the conclusion in the early 1980s that such a classical simulation typically suffers from an exponential slowdown, whereas another quantum system could in principle do the simulation efficiently with bearable overhead [3].

In this way a quantum computer, operated as a *quantum simulator*, could be used as a link between theoretical models formulated on a fundamental level and experimental observations. Similar to Shor's algorithm, a quantum simulator would yield an exponential speedup compared with a classical computer. An important difference between these two applications is, however, that a useful Shor-algorithm quantum computer would require thousands of qubits, whereas a few tens of qubits could already be useful for the simulation of quantum systems. We will resume the idea of a quantum simulator in Sections 6 and 7.

1.3   Moore's law has physical limits

Apart from the computational power of a quantum computer there is a much more banal argument for incorporating quantum mechanics into computer science: *Moore's law*. In 1965 Intel cofounder Gordon Moore observed an exponential growth in the number of transistors per square inch on integrated circuits and he predicted that this trend would continue [4]. In fact, since then this density has doubled approximately every 18 months.[4] If this trend continues, then around the year 2020 the components of computers will be at the atomic scale, where quantum effects are dominant. We thus will inevitably have to cope with these effects, and we can either try to circumvent and eliminate them as long as possible and keep on doing classical computing or try at some point to make use of them and start doing quantum computing.

1.4   Even small quantum circuits may be useful

Besides the quantum computer with its above-mentioned applications, quantum information science yields a couple of other useful applications that might be easier to realize. The best example is quantum cryptography, which enables one to transmit information with "the security of nature's laws" [5]. However, small

---

[4]Actually, not every prediction of the pioneers in computer business was that Farsighted: For instance, in 1943 Thomas Watson, chairman of IBM, predicted a world market for five computers, and in 1977 Digital Equipment Corp. founder Ken Olson stated that "there is no reason anyone would want a computer in their home."

building blocks of a quantum computer, i.e., small quantum circuits, may be useful as well. One potential application, for instance, is in precision measurements, as in atomic clocks [6, 7], which are important in global positioning systems as well as in synchronizing networks and distant telescopes. By generating quantum correlations between the N relevant atoms in the atomic clock, a quantum circuit could in principle reduce the uncertainty of the clock by a factor of $\sqrt{N}$.

Another application of small quantum circuits is *entanglement distillation*: in order to distribute entangled states over large distances, we have to send them through inevitably noisy channels, thereby losing some of the entanglement. Fortunately, however, we can in many cases *distill* a few highly entangled states out of many weakly entangled ones [8, 9].

2   FROM CLASSICAL TO QUANTUM COMPUTING

Let us now have a closer look at the way a quantum computer works. We will do so by comparing the concepts of classical computing with the basics of quantum computing. In fact, many classical concepts have very similar quantum counterparts, like bits become qubits, and the logic is still often best explained within a circuit model [10, 1]. However, there are also crucial differences, which we will describe below.

2.1   Qubits and quantum parallelism

The elementary information carriers in a quantum computer are the *qubits* – quantum bits [11]. In contrast to classical bits, which take on a value of either zero or one, qubits can be in every *superposition* of the state vectors $|0\rangle$ and $|1\rangle$. This means that the vector $|\Psi\rangle$ describing the (pure) state of the qubit can be any linear combination

$$|\Psi\rangle = \alpha |0\rangle + \beta |1\rangle \tag{1}$$

of the vectors $|0\rangle$ and $|1\rangle$ with complex coefficients α and β.[5] In the same way, a system of many qubits can be in a superposition of *all* classically possible states

$$|0, 0,...,0\rangle + |1, 0,..., 0\rangle + ... + |1, 1,...,1\rangle. \tag{2}$$

The basis $\{|0, 0,...,0\rangle, |0, 1,...,0\rangle,...,|1, 1,...,1\rangle\}$ that corresponds to the binary words of length n in a quantum system of n qubits is called the *computational basis*.[6] Using the superposition of Eq. (2) as an input for an algorithm means somehow running the computation on all classically possible input states at the same time. This possibility is called *quantum parallelism*, and it is certainly one of the reasons for the computational power of a quantum computer. The mathematical structure behind the composition of quantum systems is the *tensor product*.

---

[5] The "Dirac notation" $|\cdot\rangle$ is frequently used in quantum mechanics. Eq. (1) could as well be written in the standard vector notation, i.e., $\Psi = (\alpha, \beta)$ such that $|0\rangle$ and $|1\rangle$ correspond to the basis vectors $(1, 0)$ and $(0, 1)$, respectively.

[6] In finite-dimensional quantum systems such as those we encounter here, the computational basis spans the *Hilbert space* associated with the physical system.

Hence, vectors like $|0, 0, ..., 0\rangle$ should be understood as $|0\rangle \otimes ... \otimes |0\rangle = |0\rangle^{\otimes n}$. This implies that the dimension of space characterizing the system grows exponentially with the number of qubits.

Physically, qubits correspond to effective two-level systems like the ground state and excited state of an atom, the polarization degree of freedom of light, or the up- and down-orientation of a spin-1/2 particle (see Section 9). Such a physical system can be in any *pure state* that can be represented by a normalized vector of the above form.[7] A pure state of a composite quantum system that is not a product with respect to all constituents is called an *entangled* pure state.

2.2 Read-out and probabilistic nature of quantum computers

An important difference between classical and quantum computers is in the read-out process. In the classical case, there is not much to say: the output is a bit-string obtained in a deterministic manner, i.e., repeating the computation will lead to the same output again.[8] However, due to the probabilistic nature of quantum mechanics, the situation is different for a quantum computer. If the output of the computation is, for instance, the state vector $|\Psi\rangle$ in Eq. (1), α and β cannot be determined by a single measurement on a single specimen. In fact, $|\alpha|^2$ and $|\beta|^2$ are the probabilities for the system to be found in $|0\rangle$ and $|1\rangle$, respectively. Hence, the absolute values of these coefficients can be determined by repeating the computation, measuring in the basis $|0\rangle$, $|1\rangle$, and then counting the relative frequencies. The actual outcome of every single measurement is thereby completely indeterminate. In the same manner, the state of a quantum system consisting of n qubits can be measured in the computational basis, which means that the outcome corresponding to some binary word occurs with the probability given by the square of the absolute value of the respective coefficient. So, in effect, the probabilistic nature of the read-out process on the one hand and the possibility of exploiting quantum parallelism on the other hand are competing aspects when it comes to comparing the computational power of quantum and classical computers.

2.3 The circuit model

A classical digital computer operates on a string of input bits and returns a string of output bits. The function in between can be described as a logical circuit

---

[7]States in quantum mechanics, however, can also be *mixed*, in contrast to pure states, which can be represented as state vectors. A general and hence mixed quantum state can be represented by a *density operator* ρ. A density operator ρ is a positive operator, $\rho \geq 0$, which is normalized, tr$[\rho]$ = 1. For qubits, the state space, i.e., the set of all possible density matrices representing possible physical states, can be represented as a unit ball, called the *Bloch ball*. The extreme points of this set are the pure states that correspond to state vectors. In the Bloch picture, the pure states are located on the boundary of the set: the set of all pure states is hence represented by a unit sphere. The concept of mixed quantum states is required in quantum mechanics to incorporate classical ignorance about the preparation procedure, or when states of parts of a composite quantum system are considered.

[8]Within the circuit model described above, this observation is trivial, since all the elementary gates are deterministic operations. Note that even *probabilistic* classical algorithms run essentially on deterministic grounds.

built up out of many elementary logic operations. That is, the whole computation can be decomposed into an array of smaller operations – gates – acting only on one or two bits, like the AND, OR, and NOT operation. In fact, these three gates together with the COPY (or FANOUT) operation form a *universal* set of gates into which every well-defined input–output function can be decomposed. The complexity of an algorithm is then essentially the number of required elementary gates, resp. its asymptotic growth with the size of the input.

The circuit model for the quantum computer [10, 1] is actually very reminiscent of the classical circuit model: of course, we have to replace the input–output function by a quantum operation mapping quantum states onto quantum states. It is sufficient to consider only those operations that have the property of being unitary, which means that the computation is taken to be logically reversible. In turn, any unitary operation can be decomposed into elementary gates acting only on one or two qubits. A set of elementary gates that allows for a realization of any unitary to arbitrary approximation is again referred to as being *universal* [12, 10]. An important example of a set of universal gates is, in this case, any randomly chosen one-qubit rotation together with the *CNOT (Controlled NOT)* operation, which acts as

$$|x, y\rangle \mapsto |x, y \oplus x\rangle, \tag{3}$$

where $\oplus$ means addition modulo 2 [13]. As in the classical case, there are infinitely many sets of universal gates. Notably also, any generic (i.e., randomly chosen) two-qubit gate (together with the possibility of switching the leads in order to swap qubits) is itself a universal set, very much like the NAND gate is for classical computing [12].[9] Notably, any quantum circuit that makes use of a certain universal set of quantum gates can be simulated by a different quantum circuit based on another universal set of gates with only polylogarithmic overhead [16, 17, 1]. A particularly useful single-qubit gate is the *Hadamard gate*, acting as

$$|0\rangle \mapsto H|0\rangle = (|0\rangle + |1\rangle)/\sqrt{2}, \quad |1\rangle \mapsto H|1\rangle = (|0\rangle - |1\rangle)/\sqrt{2}. \tag{4}$$

A *phase gate* does nothing but multiply one of the basis vectors with a phase,

$$|0\rangle \mapsto |0\rangle, |1\rangle \mapsto i|1\rangle, \tag{5}$$

and a *Pauli gate* corresponds to one of the three unitary Pauli matrices (see Figure 8.1). The CNOT, the Hadamard, the phase gate, and the Pauli gate are quantum gates of utmost importance. Given their key status in many quantum algorithms, one might be tempted to think that with these ingredients alone (together with measurements of Pauli operators: see below), powerful quantum algorithms may be constructed that outperform the best-known classical algorithm to a problem. This intuition is yet not correct: it is the content of the *Gottesman-Knill theorem* that any quantum circuit consisting of only these ingredients can be simulated effi-

---

[9]Any such generic quantum gate has so-called *entangling power* [14], in that it may transform a product state vector into one that can no longer be written as a tensor product. Such quantum mechanical pure states are called *entangled*. In the intermediate steps of a quantum algorithm, the physical state of the system is, in general, highly multiparticle entangled. In turn, the implementation of quantum gates in distributed quantum computation requires entanglement as a resource [15].

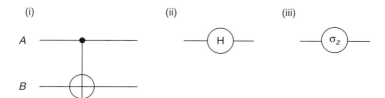

Figure 8.1. Representation of (i) a quantum CNOT gate, (ii) a Hadamard gate, and (iii) a Pauli σ_z gate. In the CNOT gate, the first qubit, here denoted as A, is typically referred to as control, the second qubit B as target. The CNOT gate is a quantum version of the XOR gate, made reversible by retaining the control.

ciently on a classical computer [1, 18]. The proof of the Gottesman-Knill theorem is deeply rooted in the stabilizer formalism that we will encounter later in the context of quantum error correction.

One of the crucial differences between classical and quantum circuits is that, in the quantum case, the COPY operation is not possible. In fact, the linearity of quantum mechanics forbids a device that copies an unknown quantum state – this is known as the *no-cloning theorem*.[10] The latter has far-reaching consequences, of which the most prominent is the possibility of quantum cryptography coining this "no-go theorem" into an application [5].

2.4   How to program a quantum computer?

The good thing about the classical computer on which this chapter has been written is that it is programmable. It is a single device capable of performing different operations depending on the program it is given: word processing, algebraic transformations, displaying movies, etc. In more abstract terms, a classical computer is a *universal gate array*: we can program *every* possible function with n input and n output bits by specifying a program of length $n2^n$. That is, a fixed circuit with $n(1 + 2^n)$ input bits can be used in order to compute any function on the first n bits in the register. Is the same true for quantum computers? Or will these devices typically be made-to-measure with respect to a single task?

Nielsen and Chuang showed that quantum computers cannot be universal gate arrays [20]. Even if the program is itself given in form of a quantum state, it would require a program register of infinite length in order to perform an arbitrary (unitary) operation on a finite number of qubits – universality was shown to be only possible in a probabilistic manner. In this sense, quantum computers will not be the kind of all-purpose devices that classical computers are. In practice, however, any finite set of quantum programs can run on a quantum computer with a finite program register. This issue applies, however, to the programming of a quantum computer with a fixed hardware, which is, needless to say, still in the remote future as a physical device.

---

[10]If one knows that the state vector is either $|0\rangle$ or $|1\rangle$, then a cloning machine is perfectly consistent with rules of quantum mechanics. However, producing perfect *clones* of an arbitrary quantum state as given by Eq. (1) is prohibited, as has been shown by Wootters, Zurek, and Dieks [19].

2.5   Quantum error correction

When it comes to experimental realizations of quantum computers, we will have to deal with errors in the operations, and we will have to find a way to protect the computation against these errors: we have to find a way of doing *error correction*. Roughly speaking, error correction in classical computers is essentially based on two facts:

1. Computing with classical bits itself provides a simple means of error correction in the form of a *lock-in-place mechanism*. If, for instance, two bits are realized by two different voltages (as is the case in our computers, as well as in our brains), then the difference can simply be chosen large enough such that typical fluctuations are small compared with the threshold separating the two bits.
2. The information can be copied and then stored or processed in a redundant way. If, for instance, an error occurs in one of three copies of a bit, we can recover the original information by applying a majority vote. Of course, there are much more refined versions of this method.

Unfortunately, in quantum computers we cannot use either of these ideas in a straightforward manner because

1. there is no lock-in-place mechanism, and
2. The no-cloning theorem forbids copying the state of the qubits.

To naively measure the state of the system to find out what error has actually happened before correcting it does not help, since any such attempt would necessarily disturb the state in an irreversible manner. So at the very beginning of quantum information science, it was not clear whether or not, under physically reasonable assumptions, fault-tolerant quantum computing would be possible. It was obvious from the beginning on, in turn, the goal of suitable quantum error correction would need to be achieved in some way. Without appropriate error correction techniques, the promise of the Shor-class quantum computer as a computational device potentially outperforming modern classical computers could quite certainly not be met.

Fortunately, Steane, Shor, and many other researchers showed that error correction is nevertheless possible and that the above problems can indeed be overcome [21–24]. The basic idea is that a logical qubit can be protected by encoding it in a nonlocal manner into several physical qubits. This amounts to a lossless encoding in longer code words to make the states robust against the effects of noise, without the need to actually copy the quantum state under consideration and introduce redundancy in the literal sense.

3   ELEMENTARY QUANTUM ALGORITHMS

In the same scientific paper in which David Deutsch introduced the notion of the universal quantum computer, he also presented the first quantum algorithm [25].[11] The problem that this algorithm addresses, later referred to as Deutsch's problem, is a very simple one. Yet the *Deutsch algorithm* already exemplifies the

---

[11]Quantum Turing machines were first considered by Benioff [26] and developed by Deutsch [25].

advantages of a quantum computer through skillfully exploiting quantum parallelism. Like the Deutsch algorithm, all other elementary quantum algorithms in this section amount to deciding which *black box*, out of finitely many alternatives, one has at hand. Such a black box is often also referred to as an *oracle*. An input may be given to the oracle, one may read out or use the outcome in later steps of the quantum algorithm, and the objective is to identify the functioning of the black box. It is assumed that this oracle operation can be implemented with some sequence of quantum logic gates. The complexity of the quantum algorithm is then quantified in terms of the number of queries to the oracle.

3.1   Deutsch algorithm

With the help of this algorithm, it is possible to decide whether a function has a certain property with a single call of the function, instead of the two calls that are necessary classically. Let

$$f : \{0, 1\} \rightarrow \{0, 1\} \tag{6}$$

be a function that has both a one-bit domain and range. This function can be either *constant* or *balanced*, which means that either $f(0) \oplus f(1) = 0$ or $f(0) \oplus f(1) = 1$ holds. The problem is to find out with the minimal number of function calls whether this function f is constant or balanced. In colloquial terms, the problem under consideration may be described as a procedure to test whether a coin is fake (has two heads or two tails) or genuine.

Classically, it is obvious that two function calls are required to decide which of the two allowed cases is realized, or, equivalently, what the value of $f(0) \oplus f(1)$ is. One way to compute the function f on a quantum computer is to transform the state vector of two qubits according to

$$|x, y\rangle \mapsto U_f |x, y\rangle = |x, f(x) \oplus y\rangle. \tag{7}$$

In this manner, the evaluation can be realized unitarily. The above map is what is called a standard quantum oracle (as opposed to a minimal quantum oracle [27], which would be of the form $|x\rangle \mapsto |f(x)\rangle$). The claim now is that by using such an oracle, a single function call is sufficient for the evaluation of $f(0) \oplus f(1)$. In order to show this, let us assume that we have prepared two qubits in the state with state vector

$$|\Psi\rangle = (H \otimes H)|0, 1\rangle, \tag{8}$$

where H denotes the Hadamard gate of Section 2. We now apply the unitary U_f once to this state, and finally apply another Hadamard gate to the first qubit. The resulting state vector hence reads as (see Figure 8.2)

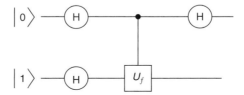

Figure 8.2. The circuit of the Deutsch algorithm.

$$|\Psi'\rangle = (H \otimes 1) \, U_f (H \otimes H) \, |0, 1\rangle. \tag{9}$$

A short calculation shows that $|\Psi'\rangle$ can be evaluated to

$$|\Psi'\rangle = \pm |f(0) \oplus f(1)\rangle \, H |1\rangle. \tag{10}$$

The second qubit is in the state corresponding to the vector $H|1\rangle$, which is of no relevance to our problem. The state of the first qubit, however, is quite remarkable: encoded is $|f(0) \oplus f(1)\rangle$, and both alternatives are decidable with unit probability in a measurement in the computational basis, since the two state vectors are orthogonal.[12] That is, with a single measurement of the state, and notably, with a single call of the function f of the first qubit, we can decide whether f is constant or balanced.

3.2   Deutsch–Jozsa algorithm

The Deutsch algorithm does not yet imply superiority of a quantum computer as compared with a classical computer, as far as query complexity is concerned. After all, it merely requires one function call instead of two. The situation is different in the case of the extension of the Deutsch algorithm known as *Deutsch–Jozsa algorithm* [29]. Here, the task is again to find out whether a function is constant or balanced, but f is now a function

$$f : \{0, 1\}^N \to \{0, 1\}, \tag{11}$$

where N is some natural number. The function is guaranteed to be either constant, which now means that either $f(i) = 0$ for all $i = 0,..., 2^N - 1$ or $f(i) = 1$ for all i, or balanced. The function is said to be balanced if the image under f takes the value 1 as many times as it takes the value 0. The property of being balanced or constant can be said to be a global property of several function values. It is a promised property of the function, which is why the Deutsch–Jozsa algorithm is being classified as a *promise algorithm*. There are only two possible black boxes available, and the tasks is to find out which one is realized.

It is clear how many times one needs to call the function on a classical computer: the worst-case scenario is that after $2^N/2$ function calls, the answer has been always 0 or always 1. Hence, $2^N/2 + 1$ function calls are required to know with certainty whether the function is balanced or constant (a result that can be significantly improved if probabilistic algorithms are allowed for). Quantum mechanically, again, a single function call is sufficient. Similarly to the above situation, one may prepare $N + 1$ qubits in the state with state vector

$$|\Psi\rangle = H^{\otimes(N + 1)} |0, ..., 0, 1\rangle, \tag{12}$$

and apply to it the unitary U_f as in Eq. (7), acting as an oracle, and apply $H^{\otimes N} \otimes 1$ to the resulting state, to obtain (see Figure 8.3)

$$|\Psi'\rangle = (H^{\otimes N} \otimes 1) \, U_f H^{\otimes(N + 1)} |0, ..., 0, 1\rangle. \tag{13}$$

---

[12]Note that the algorithm presented here is not quite the same as in the original paper by Deutsch, which allowed for an inconclusive outcome in the measurement. This deterministic version of the Deutsch algorithm is due to Cleve, Ekert, Macchiavello, and Mosca [28].

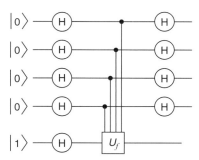

Figure 8.3 The circuit of the Deutsch–Jozsa algorithm.

In the last step, one performs a measurement on the first N qubits in the computational basis. In effect, one observes that if the function f is constant, one obtains the measurement outcome corresponding to $| 0, ..., 0\rangle$ with certainty. For any other output, the function is balanced. So again, the test for the promised property can be performed with a single query, instead of $2^N/2 + 1$ classically.[13]

In the end, the performance of the Deutsch–Jozsa algorithm is quite impressive. If there is any drawback to it, it is that, unfortunately, the algorithm is to some extent artificial in nature and lacks an actual practical application emerging in a natural context. The astonishing difference in the number of queries in the quantum and classical case also disappears if classically probabilistic algorithms are allowed for: in fact, if we use a probabilistic algorithm, a polynomial number of queries achieves an exponentially good success probability.

3.3 Simon's algorithm

Simon's problem is an instance of an oracle problem that is hard classically, even for probabilistic algorithms, but tractable for quantum computers [32]. The task is to find the period p of a certain function $f : \{0, 1\}^N \to \{0, 1\}^N$, which is promised to be 2-to-1 with $f(x) = f(y)$ if and only if $y = x \oplus p$. Here, x and y denote

---

[13]A number of related problems show very similar features. In the *Bernstein–Vazirani algorithm* [30], once again a function $f : \{0, 1\}^N \to \{0, 1\}$ is given, promised to be of the form

$$f(x) = ax \tag{14}$$

for $a, x \in \{0, 1\}^N$ for some natural number N. ax denotes the standard scalar product $ax = a_0x_0 + ... + a_{2}N{-}1\, x_{2}N{-}1$. How many measurements are required to find the vector a of zeros and ones? Classically, one has to perform measurements for all possible arguments, and in the end solve a system of linear equations. With the standard oracle $|x, y\rangle \mapsto |x, f(x) \oplus y\rangle$ at hand, in its quantum version in the Bernstein–Vazirani algorithm, only a single call of the oracle is required. Although it has been convincingly argued that one does not have to evoke the metaphor of quantum parallelism to interpret the functioning of the quantum computer in the Bernstein–Vazirani problem – the difference from quantum to classical lies rather in the ability to reverse the action of a CNOT gate by means of local operations on the control and target qubits – the surprisingly superior performance of the quantum algorithm to its classical counterpart is self-evident.

binary words of length N, where $\oplus$ now means bitwise addition modulo 2. The problem can be stated as a decision problem as well, and the goal would then be to decide whether or not there is a period, i.e., whether f is 2-to-1 or 1-to-1.

Classically the problem is hard, since the probability of having found two identical elements x and y after $2^{N/4}$ queries is still less than $2^{-N/2}$. Simon's quantum solution is the following: start with a state vector $(H|0\rangle)^{\otimes N}|0\rangle^{\otimes N}$ and run the oracle once, yielding the state vector $2^{-N/2} \sum_x |x\rangle|f(x)\rangle$. Then measure the second register.[14] If the measurement outcome is $f(x_0)$, then the state vector of the first register will be

$$\frac{1}{\sqrt{2}}\left(|x_0\rangle + |x_0 \oplus p\rangle\right). \tag{15}$$

Application of a Hadamard gate to each of the N remaining qubits leads to

$$\frac{1}{2^{(N+1)/2}} \sum_y \left((-1)^{x_0 \cdot y} + (-1)^{(x_0 \oplus p) \cdot y}\right)|y\rangle \tag{16}$$

$$= \frac{1}{2^{(N-1)/2}} \sum_{p \cdot y = 0} (-1)^{x_0 \cdot y}|y\rangle. \tag{17}$$

If we finally measure the first register in computational basis, we obtain a value y such that $y \cdot p = 0$ modulo 2. Repeating this procedure in order to get $N-1$ linearly independent vectors $y_1, ..., y_{N-1}$, we can determine p from the set of equations $\{y_i \cdot p = 0\}$. To this end we have to query the oracle $\boldsymbol{O}(N)$ times.[15] Hence, we get an exponential speedup compared with any classical algorithm. And in contrast to the Deutsch–Jozsa algorithm, this exponential gap remains if we allow for probabilistic classical algorithms.[16] Simon's algorithm has much in common with Shor's algorithm: they both try to find the period of a function,[17] both yield an exponential speedup, and both make use of classical algorithms in a post-processing step. Actually, Shor's work was inspired by Simon's result.

4   GROVER'S DATABASE SEARCH ALGORITHM

The speedup due to the quantum algorithms presented for the Deutsch-Jozsa and Simon problems is enormous. However, the oracle functions are constrained to comply with certain promises, and the tasks considered hardly appear in practical applications. In contrast, Grover's algorithm deals with a frequently appearing problem [33]: *database search*.

Assume we have an unsorted list and want to know the largest element, the mean, whether there is an element with certain properties, or the number of such elements. All these are common problems or necessary subroutines for more com-

---

[14]Note that this step is not even necessary – it is merely pedagogical.

[15]This symbol is the "big-O" Landau symbol for the asymptotic upper bound. In the rest of this chapter, this notation will be used even if the asymptotic behavior could be specified more precisely.

[16]Simon's problem is an instance of an oracle problem relative to which BPP≠BQP. That is, classical and quantum polynomial-time complexity classes for bounded error probabilistic algorithms differ relative to Simon's problem.

[17]Whereas Simon's problem is to find a period in $(Z_2)^N$, Shor's algorithm searches for one in Z_{2^N}.

plex programs. Due to Grover's algorithm, all these problems in principle admit a typically quadratic speedup compared with classical solutions. Such an improvement in performance might not seen very spectacular; however, the problems to which it is applicable are quite numerous,[18] and the progress from ordinary Fourier transform to the FFT has already demonstrated how a quadratic speedup in an elementary routine can boost many applications.

Consider the problem of searching a marked element $x_0 \in \{1, ..., N\}$ within an unsorted database of length $N = 2^n$. Whereas classically we have to query our database $\mathbf{O}(N)$ times in order to identify the sought element, Grover's algorithm will require only $\mathbf{O}(\sqrt{N})$ trials. Let the database be represented by a unitary[19]

$$U_x 0 = \mathbf{1} - 2 \, |x_0\rangle \langle x_0|, \tag{18}$$

which flips the sign of $|x_0\rangle$ but preserves all vectors orthogonal to $|x_0\rangle$. The first step of the algorithm is to prepare an equally weighted superposition of all basis states $|\Psi\rangle = \frac{1}{\sqrt{N}}\sum_x |x\rangle$. As we have seen previously, this step can be achieved by applying N Hadamard gates to the state vector $|0\rangle$. Next, we apply the *Grover operator*

$$G = U_\Psi \, U_x 0, \quad U_\Psi = 2 \, |\Psi\rangle \langle \Psi| - \mathbf{1} \tag{19}$$

to the state vector $|\Psi\rangle$. Geometrically, the action of G is to rotate $|\Psi\rangle$ towards $|x_0\rangle$ by an angle $2\,\varphi$, where $\sin\varphi = |\langle \Psi|x_0\rangle| = 1/\sqrt{N}$. The idea now is to iterate this rotation k times until the initial state is close to $|x_0\rangle$, i.e.,

$$G^k|\Psi\rangle \approx |x_0\rangle \tag{20}$$

Measuring the system (in computational basis) will then reveal the value of x_0 with high probability.

So, how many iterations do we need? Each step is a $2\,\varphi$-rotation, and the initial angle between $|\Psi\rangle$ and $|x_0\rangle$ is $\pi/2 - \varphi$.[20] Using that for large N $\sin\varphi \approx \varphi$, *we see that $k \approx \pi\sqrt{N}/4$ rotations will do the job*, and the probability of obtaining a measurement outcome different from x_0 will decrease as $\mathbf{O}(1/N)$. Since every step in the Grover iteration queries the database once, we need only $\mathbf{O}(\sqrt{N})$ trials compared with $\mathbf{O}(N)$ in classical algorithms. To exploit this speedup, we need of course an efficient implementation not only of the database-oracle U_{x_0} but also of the unitary U_Ψ. Fortunately, the latter can be constructed out of $\mathbf{O}(\log N)$ elementary gates.

What if there are more than one, say M, marked elements? Using the equally weighted superposition of all the respective states instead of $|x_0\rangle$, we can essentially repeat the above argument and obtain that $\mathbf{O}(\sqrt{N/M})$ queries are required in order to find one out of the M elements with high probability. However, performing further Grover iterations would be overshooting the mark: we would rotate the initial state beyond the sought target, and the probability for finding a

---

[18]For instance, the standard solution to all NP-complete problems is doing an exhaustive search. Hence, Grover's algorithm would speed up finding a solution to the traveling salesman, the Hamiltonian cycle, and certain coloring problems.

[19]$|x_0\rangle \langle x_0|$ means the projector onto the vector $|x_0\rangle$. That is $U_x 0 \, |x\rangle = (-1)^{\delta x, x_0} |x\rangle$.

[20]This clarifies why we start with the state vector $|\Psi\rangle$: the overlap $|\langle \Psi|x_0\rangle|$ does not depend on x_0.

marked element would rapidly decrease again. If we initially do not know the number M of marked elements, this problem is, not serious, however. As long as $M \ll N$, we can still gain a quadratic speed-up by simply choosing the number of iterations randomly between 0 and $\pi \sqrt{N}//4$. The probability of finding a marked element will then be close to $1/2$ for every M. Notably, Grover's algorithm is optimal in the sense that any quantum algorithm for this problem will necessarily require $O(\sqrt{N/M})$ queries [34].

5   EXPONENTIAL SPEED-UP IN SHOR'S FACTORING ALGORITHM

Shor's algorithm [2] is without doubt not only one of the cornerstones of quantum information theory but also one of the most surprising advances in the theory of computation itself: a problem that is widely believed to be *hard* becomes *tractable* by refering to (quantum) physics – an approach completely atypical for the theory of computation, which usually abstracts away from any physical realization.

The problem Shor's algorithm deals with is *factorization*, a typical NP problem. Consider for instance the task of finding the prime factors of 421301. With pencil and paper, we might well take more than an hour to find them. The inverse problem, the multiplication 601×701, can, however, be solved in a few seconds, even without having pencil and paper at hand.[21] The crucial difference between the two tasks of multiplication and factoring is, however, how the degree of difficulty increases with the length of the numbers. Whereas multiplication belongs to the class of "tractable" problems for which the required number of elementary computing steps increases polynomially with the size of the input, every known classical factoring algorithm requires an exponentially increasing number of steps. This is what is meant when we say that factoring is an "intractable" or "hard" problem. In fact, it is this discrepancy between the complexity of the factoring problem and its inverse that is exploited in the most popular public key encryption scheme based on RSA -its security heavily relies on the assumed difficulty of factoring. In a nutshell, the idea of Shor's factoring algorithm is the following:

1. *Classical part:* Using some elementary number theory, one can show that the problem of finding a factor of a given integer is essentially equivalent to determining the period of a certain function.

2. *QFT for period-finding:* Implement the function from step (1) in a quantum circuit and apply it to a superposition of all classical input states. Then perform a discrete quantum Fourier transform (QFT) and measure the output. The measurement outcomes will be probabilistically distributed according to the inverse of the sought period. The latter can thus be determined (with certain probability) by repeating the procedure.

---

[21] Actually, it takes eleven seconds for a randomly chosen Munich schoolboy at the age of 12 (the sample size was one).

3. *Efficient implementation:* The crucial point of the algorithm is that the QFT as well as the function from step (1) can be efficiently implemented, i.e., the number of required elementary operations grows only polynomially with the size of the input. Moreover, the probability of success of the algorithm can be made arbitrarily close to 1 without exponentially increasing the effort.

Clearly, the heart of the algorithm is an efficient implementation of the QFT. Since Fourier transforms enter into many mathematical and physical problems, one might naively expect an exponential speedup for all these problems as well. However, the outcome of the QFT is not explicitly available but "hidden" in the amplitudes of the output state, which cannot be measured efficiently. Only global properties of the function, like its period, can in some cases be determined efficiently.

Nevertheless, a couple of other applications are known for which the QFT leads again to an exponential speedup compared with the known classical algorithms. The abstract problem, which encompasses all these applications, is known as the *hidden subgroup problem* [1]. Another rather prominent representative of this type is the discrete logarithm problem. Let us now have a more detailed look at the ingredients for Shor's algorithm.

5.1 Classical part

Let N be an odd number we would like to factor and $a < N$ be an integer that has no nontrivial factor in common with N, i.e., $gcd(N, a) = 1$. The latter can efficiently be checked by Euclid's algorithm.[22] A facot of N can then be found indirectly by determining the period p of the function $f : \mathbb{Z} \longrightarrow \mathbb{Z}_N$, defined as

$$f(x) = a^x \bmod N. \tag{21}$$

Hence, we are looking for a solution of the equation $a^p - 1 = 0 \bmod N$. Assuming p to be even, we can decompose

$$a^p - 1 = (a^{\frac{p}{2}} + 1)(a^{\frac{p}{2}} - 1) = 0 \bmod N, \tag{22}$$

and therefore either one or both terms $(a^{\frac{p}{2}} \pm 1)$ must have a factor in common with N. Any nontrivial common divisor of N with $(a^{\frac{p}{2}} \pm 1)$, again calculated by Euclid's algorithm, yields thus a nontrivial factor of N.

Obviously, the described procedure is only successful if p is even and the final factor is a nontrivial one. Fortunately, if we choose a at random,[23] this case occurs with probability larger than one half unless N is a power of a prime. The latter case can, however, be checked again efficiently by a known classical algorithm, which returns the value of the prime. Altogether, a polynomial time algorithm for determining the period of the function in Eq. (21) leads to a probabilistic polynomial time algorithm that either returns a factor of N or tells us that N is prime.

---

[22]In $\boldsymbol{O}((\log N)^3)$ time.
[23]For each randomly chosen a, we must again check whether $gcd(N, a) = 1$. The probability for this can be shown to be larger than $1/\log N$. The total probability of success is thus at least $1/(2 \log N)$.

5.2   Quantum Fourier Transform

The step from the ordinary discrete Fourier transform (based on matrix multiplication) to the Fast Fourier Transform (FFT) has been of significant importance for signal and image processing as well as for many other applications in scientific and engineering computing.[24] Whereas the naive way of calculating the discrete Fourier transform

$$\hat{c}_y = \frac{1}{\sqrt{n}} \sum_{x=0}^{n-1} c_x e^{\frac{2\pi i}{n} xy} \qquad (23)$$

by matrix multiplication takes $\boldsymbol{O}(n^2)$ steps, the FFT requires $\boldsymbol{O}(n \log n)$. The *quantum Fourier transform* (QFT) [2, 35–37] is in fact a straightforward quantum generalization of the FFT, which can, however, be implemented using only $\boldsymbol{O}((\log n)^2)$ elementary operations – an exponential speedup!

Let now the computational basis states of q qubits be characterized by the binary representation of numbers $x = \sum_{i=1}^q x_i 2^{i-1}$ via

$$|x\rangle = |x_1,...,x_q\rangle. \qquad (24)$$

That is, in this subsection, x denotes from now on a natural number or zero and not a binary word. Then for $n = 2^q$, the QFT acts on a general state vector of q qubits as $\sum_x c_x |x\rangle \mapsto \sum_y \hat{c}_y |y\rangle$. This transformation can be implemented using only two types of gates: the Hadamard gate and conditional phase gates P_d, acting as

$$|a,b\rangle \mapsto |a,b\rangle e^{\delta_{a+b,2}\pi i/2^d}, \qquad (25)$$

which rotate the relative phase conditionally by an angle $\pi 2^{-d}$, where d is the "distance" between the two involved qubits.

Figure 8.4 shows the quantum circuit, which implements the QFT on $q = 3$ qubits. The extension of the circuit to more than three qubits is rather obvious and since $q(q + 1)/2$ gates are required, its complexity is $\boldsymbol{O}(q^2) = \boldsymbol{O}((\log n)^2)$. Being only interested in an approximate QFT, we could reduce the number of gates even further to $\boldsymbol{O}(\log n)$ by dropping all phase gates P_d with $d \geq m$. Naturally, the accuracy will then depend on m.[25]

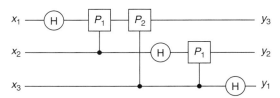

Figure 8.4 The circuit of a discrete quantum Fourier transform on three qubits. The gate P_d adds a conditional relative phase $\pi/2^d$, where d is the distance between the two involved qubits in the circuit.

---

[24]Although FFT is often attributed to Cooley and Tukey in 1965, it is now known that by 1805 Gauss had already used the algorithm to interpolate the trajectories of asteroids [38].
[25]An ε-approximation of the QFT (in the 2-norm) would require $\boldsymbol{O}(q \log(q/\varepsilon))$ operations, i.e., m is of the order $\log(q/\varepsilon)$ (cf. [35]).

5.3   Joining the pieces together

Let us now sketch how the QFT can be used to compute the period p of the function in Eq. (21) efficiently. Consider two registers of q qubits each, where $2^q = n \geq N^2$ and all the qubits are in the state vector $|0\rangle$ initially. Applying a Hadamard gate to each qubit in the first register yields $\frac{1}{\sqrt{n}}\sum_x |x,0\rangle$. Now suppose we have implemented the function in Eq. (21) in a quantum circuit that acts as $|x,0\rangle \mapsto |x, f(x)\rangle$, where x is taken from $\mathbb{Z}_n$. Applying this to the state vector and then performing a QFT on the first register, we obtain

$$\frac{1}{n}\sum_{x,\,y=0}^{n-1} e^{\frac{2\pi i}{n}xy}\, |y, f(x)\rangle. \tag{26}$$

what will the distribution of measurement outcomes look like if we now measure the first register in computational basis? Roughly speaking, the sum over x will lead to constructive interference whenever y/n is close to a multiple of the inverse of the period p of f, and will yield destructive interference otherwise. Hence, the probability distribution for measuring y is sharply peaked around multiples of n/p, and p itself can be determined by repeating the whole procedure $\mathbf{O}(\log N)$ times.[26] At the same time, the probability of success can be made arbitrary close to 1. In the end, we can easily verify whether the result, the obtained factor of N, is valid or not.

What remains to be shown is that the map

$$|x,0\rangle \mapsto |x, f(x)\rangle, \qquad f(x) = a^x \bmod N \tag{27}$$

can be implemented efficiently. This can be done by repeatedly squaring in order to get $a^{2^j} \bmod N$ and then multiplying a subset of these numbers according to the binary expansion of x. This requires $\mathbf{O}(\log N)$ squarings and multiplications of $\log N$-bit numbers. For each multiplication, the "elementary-school algorithm" requires $\mathbf{O}((\log N)^2)$ steps. Hence, by implementing this simple classical algorithm on our quantum computer, we can compute $f(x)$ with $\mathbf{O}((\log N)^3)$ elementary operations. In fact, this part of performing a standard classical multiplication algorithm on a quantum computer is the bottleneck in the quantum part of Shor's algorithm. If there could be a more refined *quantum modular exponentiation* algorithm, we could improve the asymptotic performance of the algorithm.[27]

Altogether, the quantum part of Shor's factoring algorithm requires on the order $(\log N)^3$ elementary steps, i.e., the size of the circuit is cubic in the length of the input. As described above, additional classical preprocessing and postprocessing is necessary in order to obtain a factor of N. The time required for the

---

[26]For the cost of more classical postprocessing, it is even possible to reduce the expected number of required trials to a constant (cf. [2]).

[27]In fact, modular exponentiation can be done in $\mathbf{O}((\log N)^2 \log\log N \log\log\log N)$ time by utilizing the Schönhagen–Strassen algorithm for multiplication [39]. However, this is again a classical algorithm, first made reversible and then run on a quantum computer. If there exists a faster quantum algorithm, it would even be possible that breaking RSA codes on a quantum computer is asymptotically faster than the encryption on a classical computer.

classical part of the algorithm is, however, polynomial in $\log N$ as well, such that the entire algorithm does the job in polynomial time. In contrast, the running time of the number field sieve, which is currently the best classical factoring algorithm, is $\exp[\mathbf{O}((\log N)^{\frac{1}{3}}(\log \log N)^{\frac{2}{3}})]$. Moreover, it is widely believed that factoring is a classically hard problem, in the sense that no classical polynomial time algorithm exists. However, it is also believed that proving the latter conjecture (if it is true) is extremely hard, since it would solve the notorious $P \overset{?}{=} NP$ problem.

6   ADIABATIC QUANTUM COMPUTING

Shor's factoring algorithm falls into a certain class of quantum algorithms, together with many other important algorithms, such as the algorithm for computing orders of solvable groups [40] and the efficient quantum algorithm for finding solutions of Pell's equation [41]: it is an instance of a hidden subgroup problem. In fact, it has turned out in recent years that it appears difficult to leave the framework of hidden subgroup problems and to find novel quantum algorithms for practically relevant problems. This motivates the quest for entirely new approaches to finding such new algorithms. The algorithm of [42] based on *quantum random walks* [43] is an important example of such a new approach, although the problem it solves does not appear in a particularly practical context. Another approach is the framework of adiabatic quantum algorithms:

In 2000, Farhi, Goldstone, Gutmann, and Sipser introduced a new concept to the study of quantum algorithms, based on the adiabatic theorem of quantum mechanics [44]. The idea is the following: let $f : \{0, 1\}^N \longrightarrow \mathbb{R}$ be a cost function for which we would like to find the global minimum, assumed to be in $x \in \{0, 1\}^N$. In fact, any local combinatorial search problem can be formulated in this way. For simplicity, suppose that this global minimum is unique. Introducing the *problem Hamiltonian*

$$H_T = \sum_{z \in \{0,1\}^N} f(z) |z\rangle \langle z|, \tag{28}$$

the problem of finding the $x \in \{0, 1\}^N$ where f attains its minimum amounts to identifying the eigenstate $|x\rangle$ of H_T corresponding to the smallest eigenvalue $f(x)$, i.e., the *ground state energy* associated with H_T. But how does one find the ground state in the first place? The key idea is to consider another Hamiltonian, H_0, with the property that the system can easily be prepared in its ground state, which is again assumed to be unique. One then interpolates between the two Hamiltonians, for example linearly:

$$H(t) = \frac{t}{T} H_T + (1 - \frac{t}{T}) H_0, \tag{29}$$

with $t \in [0, T]$, where T is the *run time* of the adiabatic quantum algorithm. This Hamiltonian governs the time evolution of the quantum state of the system from time $t = 0$ until $t = T$. According to the Schrödinger equation, the state vector evolves as $i\partial_t |\Psi(t)\rangle = H(t)|\Psi(t)\rangle$. In a last step, one performs a measurement in the computational basis. If one obtains the outcome associated with $|x\rangle$, then the measurement result is just x, the minimal value of the function f. In this case the probabilistic algorithm is successful,—an outcome that happens with *success probability* $p = |\langle x|\Psi(T)\rangle|^2$.

What are the requirements for such an algorithm to work, i.e., to result in x with a large success probability? The answer to this question is provided by the *quantum adiabatic theorem*: If the Hamiltonian $H(t)$ exhibits a nonzero spectral gap between the smallest and the second-to-smallest eigenvalue for all $t \in [0, T]$, then the final state vector $|\Psi(T)\rangle$ will be close to the state vector $|x\rangle$ corresponding to the ground state of H_T, if the interpolation happens sufficiently slowly, meaning that T is sufficiently large. The initial state is then said to be adiabatically transferred with arbitrary accuracy into the desired ground state of the problem Hamiltonian, which encodes the solution to the problem. The typical problem of encountering local minima that are distinct from the global minimum can in principle not even occur. This kind of quantum algorithm is referred to as an *adiabatic algorithm*.

Needless to say, the question is how large a time T has to be chosen. Let us denote with

$$\Delta = \min_{t \in [0, T]} (E_t^{(0)} - E_t^{(1)}) \tag{30}$$

the minimal spectral gap over the time interval $[0, T]$ between the smallest $E_t^{(0)}$ and the second-to-smallest eigenvalue $E_t^{(1)}$ of $H(t)$, associated with eigenvectors $|\Psi_t^{(0)}\rangle$ and $|\Psi_t^{(1)}\rangle$, respectively, and with

$$\Theta = \max_{t \in [0, T]} \left| \left\langle \Psi_t^{(1)} \middle| \partial_t H(t) \middle| \Psi_t^{(0)} \right\rangle \right|. \tag{31}$$

Then, according to the quantum adiabatic theorem, the success probability satisfies

$$p = |\langle \Psi_T^{(0)}|\Psi(T)\rangle|^2 \geq 1 - \varepsilon^2 \tag{32}$$

if

$$\epsilon \geq \frac{\Theta}{\Delta^2}. \tag{33}$$

The quantity Θ is typically polynomially bounded in N for the problems one is interested in, so the crucial issue is the behavior of the minimal gap Δ. Time complexity is now quantified in terms of the run time T of the adiabatic algorithm. If one knew the spectrum of $H(t)$ at all times, then one could immediately see how fast the algorithm could be performed. Roughly speaking, the larger the gap, the faster the algorithm can be implemented. The problem is that the spectrum of $H(t)$, which can be represented as a $2^N \times 2^N$ matrix, is in general unknown. Even to find lower bounds for the minimal spectral gap is extraordinarily difficult, unless a certain symmetry highly simplifies the problem of finding the spectrum. After all, in order for the Hamiltonian to be "reasonable," it is required to be *local*, i.e., it is a sum of operators that act only on a bounded number of qubits in N. This restriction is very natural, since it means that the physical interactions involve always only a finite number of quantum systems [45]. Note that, as an indication whether the chosen run time T for an adiabatic algorithm is appropriate, one may start with the initial Hamiltonian and prepare the system in its ground state, interpolate to the problem Hamiltonian and – using the same interpolation – back to the original Hamiltonian [46]. A necessary condition for the algorithm to have been successful is that, finally, the system is to a good approximation in the ground state of the initial Hamiltonian. This is a method that should be accessible to an experimental implementation.

Adiabatic algorithms are known to reproduce the quadratic speedup in the Grover algorithm for unstructured search problems [47]. But adiabatic algorithms can also be applied to other instances of search problems: In [48], adiabatic algorithms have been compared with simulated annealing algorithms, finding settings in which the quantum adiabatic algorithm succeeded in polynomial time but simulated annealing required exponential time. There is, after all, some numerical evidence that for structured NP hard problems like MAX CLIQUE and 3-SAT, adiabatic algorithms may well offer an exponential speedup over the best classical algorithm, again assuming that $P \neq NP$ [44]. In fact, it can be shown that adiabatic algorithms can be efficiently simulated on a quantum computer based on the quantum circuit model, provided that the Hamiltonian is local in the above sense (see also the subsequent section). Hence, whenever an efficient adiabatic algorithm can be found for a specific problem, this implies an efficient quantum algorithm [45]. The concept of adiabatic algorithms may be a key tool to establish new algorithms beyond the hidden subgroup problem framework.

7   SIMULATING QUANTUM SYSTEMS

A typical application of computers is that of being workhorses for physicists and engineers who want to simulate physical processes and compute practically relevant properties of certain objects from the elementary rules of physics. If many particles are involved, the simulation might become cumbersome or even impossible without exploiting serious approximations. This is true classically as well as quantum mechanically[28]: simulating turbulences is not necessarily easier than dealing with high temperature superconductors. There is, however, a crucial difference between classical and quantum systems regarding how many are "many particles." Whereas the dimension of the classical phase space grows linearly with the number of particles, the size of the quantum mechanical Hilbert space increases exponentially. This fact implies that the exact simulation of an arbitrary quantum system of more than 25 qubits is already no longer feasible on today's computers. Consider, for instance, a closed system of N (say 25) qubits whose time evolution is determined by a Hamiltonian H via Schrödinger dynamics,

$$|\Psi(t)\rangle = e^{-iHt}|\Psi(0)\rangle. \tag{34}$$

Since H is a Hermitian $2^N \times 2^N$ matrix, it is, although often sparse, extremely hard to exponentiate – for $N = 25$, it has about 10^{15} entries!

Once we have the building blocks for a *universal* quantum computer of N qubits, i.e., a universal set of gates, we can in principle simulate the dynamics of any closed N-qubit system. That is, we can let our quantum computer mimic the time evolution corresponding to any Hamiltonian we were given by some theorist

---

[28]Even the types of differential equations we have to solve can be very similar. The classical diffusion equation is, for instance, essentially a real version of the quantum mechanical Schrödinger equation.

and then perform some measurements and check whether the results, and with them the given Hamiltonian, really fit the physical system in the laboratory. Despite the naivete of this description, one crucial point here is whether or not the simulation can be implemented efficiently on our quantum computer. In fact, it can, as long as the Hamiltonian

$$H = \sum_{l}^{L} H_l \qquad (35)$$

is again a sum of *local* Hamiltonians H_l acting only on a few particles.[29] The basic idea leading to this result is the following [49]:

The evolution according to each H_l can be easily simulated, i.e., with an overhead that does not grow with N. Since the different H_l in general do not commute, we have $\Pi_l e^{-iH_l t} \neq e^{-iHt}$. However, we can exploit Trotter's formula

$$\lim_{k \to \infty} \left(\prod_{l=1}^{L} e^{-iH_l \frac{t}{k}} \right)^k = e^{-iHt} \qquad (36)$$

in order to move in the direction in Hilbert space corresponding to H by concatenating many infinitesimal moves along H_1, H_2, ... To use Lloyd's metaphor, this is like parallel parking with a car that can only be driven forward and backward. In fact, this process is part of everyday life not only for car drivers but also for people, say, working in nuclear magnetic resonance, where sophisticated pulse sequences are used in order to drive a set of spins to a desired state. The important point, however, is that in such a way e^{-iHt} can be efficiently approximated with only a polynomial number of operations. Moreover, the number of required operations scales as $\boldsymbol{O}(\text{poly}(1/\varepsilon))$, with the maximal tolerated error ε.

The evolution of closed discrete systems is not the only thing that can be simulated efficiently. If, for instance, the terms H_l in Eq. (35) are tensor products and L is a polynomial in N, this simulation also works [1]. Moreover, the evolution of open systems; approximations of systems involving continuous variables [50, 51]; systems of indistinguishable particles, in particular fermionic systems [52], and equilibration processes [53] have been studied as well.

Since the simulation of quantum systems has already become an interesting application for a few tens of qubits, we will see it in the laboratories long before a "Shor class" quantum computer will be built that strikes classical factoring algorithms (and thus requires thousands of qubits) [54]. In fact, we do not even need a full quantum computer setup, i.e., the ability to implement a universal set of gates, in order to simulate interesting multipartite quantum systems [55].

8   QUANTUM ERROR CORRECTION

Quantum error correction aims at protecting the coherence of quantum states in a quantum computation against noise. This noise is due to some physical interaction between the quantum systems forming the quantum computer and their environment—an interaction that can never be entirely avoided. It turns out that reliable quantum computation is indeed possible in the presence of noise,

---

[29]That is, every H_l involves at most a number of particles independent of N.

a finding that was one of the genuinely remarkable insights in this research field. The general idea of quantum error correction is to encode logical qubits into a number of physical qubits. The whole quantum computation is hence performed in a subspace of a larger dimensional Hilbert space, called the *error correcting code subspace*. Any deviation from this subspace leads to an orthogonal *error subspace*, and can hence be detected and corrected without losing the coherence of the actual encoded states [56]. Quantum error correcting codes have the ability to correct a certain finite-dimensional subspace of error syndromes. These error syndromes could, for example, correspond to a *bit-flip error* on a single qubit. Such bit-flip errors are, however, by no means the only type of error that can occur to a single qubit. In a *phase flip error*, the relative phase of $|0\rangle$ and $|1\rangle$ is interchanged. Quantum error-correcting codes can be constructed that correct for such bit-flip and phase errors or both. In a quantum computing context, this error correction capability is still not sufficient. It is the beauty of the theory of quantum error correcting codes that indeed, codes can be constructed that have the ability to correct for a *general error* on a single qubit (and for even more general syndromes). What this means we shall see after our first example.

8.1   An introductory example

The simplest possible encoding that protects at least against a very restricted set of errors is the following: Given a pure state of a single qubit with state vector $|\Psi\rangle = \alpha|0\rangle + \beta|1\rangle$, this state can be protected against bit-flip errors of single qubits by means of the *repetition encoding* $|0\rangle \mapsto |0,0,0\rangle$ and $|1\rangle \mapsto |1,1,1\rangle$, such that $|\Psi\rangle$ is encoded as

$$|\Psi\rangle = \alpha|0\rangle + \beta|1\rangle \mapsto \alpha|0,0,0\rangle + \beta|1,1,1\rangle. \tag{37}$$

This encoding, the idea of which dates back to work by Peres as early as 1985 [57], can be achieved by means of two sequential CNOT gates to qubit systems initially prepared in $|0\rangle$. Note that this encoding does not amount to a copying of the input state, which would be impossible anyway. If an error occurs that manifests itself in a *single* bitflip operation to any of the three qubits, one can easily verify that one out of four mutually orthogonal states is obtained: these states correspond to no error at all, and a single bit flip error to any of the three qubits. This encoding, while not yet being a quantum error-correcting code in the actual sense, already exemplifies an aspect of the theory: With a subsequent measurement that indicates the kind of error that has occurred, no information can be inferred about the values of the coefficients α and β. A measurement may hence enquire about the error without learning about the data.

While already incorporating a key idea, this encoding is nevertheless not a particularly good one to protect against errors: If a different error than a bit-flip occurs, then the measurement followed by an error correction cannot recover the state. Moreover, and maybe more seriously, the state cannot be disentangled from the environment, if the error is due to some physical interaction entangling the state with its environment. Let us consider the map involving the qubit undergoing the error and the environment, modeled as a system starting with state vector $|\Psi_0\rangle$, according to

$$|0, \Psi_0\rangle \mapsto |1, \Psi_0\rangle, \text{ and } |1, \Psi_0\rangle \mapsto |0, \Psi_1\rangle, \tag{38}$$

such that the environment becomes correlated with the qubit undergoing the error. This process is typically referred to as *decoherence*. The above encoding cannot correct for such an error and recover the original state. Such an entangling error, however, corresponds instead to the generic situation happening with realistic errors. In Preskill's words, the manifesto of quantum error correction is to fight entanglement with entanglement [56]. What he means is that the unwanted but unavoidable entanglement of the system with its environment should be avoided by means of skillfully entangling the systems in a quantum error-correcting code, followed by appropriate correction.

8.2   Shor code

There are, notably, error correcting codes that can correct for any error inflicted on a single qubit of the code block. That such quantum error correcting codes exist was first noted by Steane and Shor in independent seminal work in 1995 and 1996 [21, 23]. *Shor's 9 qubit code* is related to the above repetition code by encoding again each of the qubits of the codewords into three other qubits, according to $|0\rangle \mapsto (|0,0,0\rangle + |1,1,1\rangle)/\sqrt{2}$ and $|1\rangle \mapsto (|0,0,0\rangle - |1,1,1\rangle)/\sqrt{2}$. If effect, in the total encoding, each logical qubit is encoded in the state of nine physical qubits, the codewords being given by

$$|0\rangle \mapsto (|0,0,0\rangle + |1,1,1\rangle)(|0,0,0\rangle + |1,1,1\rangle)(|0,0,0\rangle + |1,1,1\rangle)/\sqrt{8}, \tag{39}$$

$$|1\rangle \mapsto (|0,0,0\rangle - |1,1,1\rangle)(|0,0,0\rangle - |1,1,1\rangle)(|0,0,0\rangle - |1,1,1\rangle)/\sqrt{8}, \tag{40}$$

In a sense, the additional encoding of the repetition code mends the weaknesses of the repetition code itself. Such an encoding of the encoding is called a *concatenation of codes*, which plays an important role in quantum error correction. What errors can it now correct? If the environment is initially again in a pure state associated with state vector $|\Psi_0\rangle$, then the most general error model leads to the joint state vector

$$(\alpha|0\rangle + \beta|1\rangle)|\Psi_0\rangle = (\alpha|0\rangle + \beta|1\rangle)|\Psi_0\rangle + (\alpha|1\rangle + \beta|0\rangle)|\Psi_1\rangle$$
$$+ (\alpha|0\rangle - \beta|1\rangle)|\Psi_2\rangle + (\alpha|1\rangle - \beta|0\rangle)|\Psi_3\rangle, \tag{41}$$

where no assumption is made concerning the state vectors $|\Psi_0\rangle$, $|\Psi_1\rangle$, and $|\Psi_2\rangle$, and $|\Psi_3\rangle$. One particular instance of this map is the one where

$$|\Psi_0\rangle = |\Psi_2\rangle = |0\rangle, |\Psi_1\rangle = |1\rangle, |\Psi_3\rangle = -|1\rangle. \tag{42}$$

One can convince oneself that when disregarding the state of the environment (reflected by the partial trace), this error is a quite radical one: in effect, it is as if the qubit is discarded right away and replaced by a new one, prepared in $|0\rangle$. The key point now is that the Shor code has the ability to correct for any such error if applied to only one qubit of the codeword, and to completely disentangle the state again from the environment. This includes the complete loss of a qubit, as in the previous example. In a sense, one might say that the continuum of possible errors is discretized, leading to orthogonal error syndromes that can be reliably distinguished with measurements, and then reliably corrected. But then, one might say, typical errors affect not only one qubit in such a strong manner but rather all qubits of the codeword. Even then, if the error is small and of the order $O(\varepsilon)$ in ε, characterizing the fidelity of the affected state versus the input, after error correction it can be shown to be of the order $O(\varepsilon^2)$.

8.3   Steane code

Steane's 7-qubit quantum error-correcting code is a good example of how the techniques and the intuition from classical error correction can serve as a guideline to construct good quantum error-correcting codes [21, 22]. Steane's code is closely related to a well-known classical code, the [7, 4, 3]-*Hamming code*. The starting point is the *parity check matrix* of the [7, 4, 3]-Hamming code, given by

$$h = \begin{pmatrix} 0 & 0 & 0 & 1 & 1 & 1 & 1 \\ 0 & 1 & 1 & 0 & 0 & 1 & 1 \\ 1 & 0 & 1 & 0 & 1 & 0 & 1 \end{pmatrix}. \tag{43}$$

The codewords of the classical Hamming code are all binary words v of length 7 that satisfy $hv^T = 0$, which is meant as addition in $\mathbb{Z}_2$. It is a straightforward exercise to verify that there are in total 16 legitimate codewords (the kernel of h is four-dimensional). In the classical setting, if at most a single unknown bit-flip error occurs to a word v, leading to the word v', it can be easily detected: if the error happens on the ith bit, then, from the very construction of h, hv'^T is nothing but a binary representation of i, indicating the position of the error. If $hv'^T = 0$, one can conclude that $v' = v$, and no error has occurred.

The 7-*qubit Steane code* draws from this observation. It is now defined as follows: For the logical $|0\rangle$, the quantum codeword is the superposition of the eight codewords of the classical Hamming code with an odd number of 0s, represented in terms of state vectors. The latter term means that the binary word $x_1,...,x_7$ is represented as $|x_1,...,x_7\rangle$. The logical $|1\rangle$ is encoded in a similar state vector corresponding to an even number of 0s. That is,

$$|0\rangle \mapsto (|0,0,0,0,0,0,0\rangle + |0,0,0,1,1,1,1\rangle + |0,1,1,0,0,1,1\rangle$$
$$+ |0,1,1,1,1,0,0\rangle + |1,0,1,0,1,0,1\rangle + |1,0,1,1,0,1,0\rangle \tag{44}$$
$$+ |1,1,0,0,1,1,0\rangle + |1,1,0,1,0,0,1\rangle)/\sqrt{8}$$

$$|1\rangle \mapsto (|0,0,1,0,1,1,0\rangle + |0,0,1,1,0,0,1\rangle + |0,1,0,0,1,0,1\rangle$$
$$+ |0,1,0,1,0,1,0\rangle + |1,0,0,0,0,1,1\rangle + |1,0,0,1,1,0,0\rangle \tag{45}$$
$$+ |1,1,1,0,0,0,0\rangle + |1,1,1,1,1,1,1\rangle)/\sqrt{8}.$$

The central idea now is that, in the quantum situation, one can make use of the idea of how the syndrome is computed in the classical case. When appending a system consisting of three qubits, the transformation $|v'\rangle|0,0,0\rangle \mapsto |v'\rangle|hv'\rangle$ can be realized in a unitary manner, and the measurement of the state of the additional qubits reveals the syndrome. But this procedure, one might be tempted to think, is merely sufficient to correct for bit-flip errors from the construction of the [7, 4, 3]-Hamming code. This is not so, however: a rotation of each qubit of the quantum codewords with a Hadamard gate H, as described in Section 2 with $|0\rangle \mapsto (|0\rangle + |1\rangle)/\sqrt{2}$ and $|1\rangle \mapsto (|0\rangle - |1\rangle)/\sqrt{2}$, will yield again a superposition of binary words. In fact, it is again a superposition of Hamming codewords, and bit-flip errors in this rotated basis correspond to phase flips in the original basis. So applying the same method again will in fact detect all errors. The encodings of the Shor and the Steane code are shown in Figure 5.

8.4   CSS and stabilizer codes

The formalism of *Calderbank–Shor–Steane* (CSS) *codes* [58, 22] takes the idea seriously that the theory of linear codes can almost be translated into a theory of quantum error-correcting codes. Let us remind ourselves what $[n, k, d]$ in the above notation specifying the classical Hamming code stands for: n is the length of the code, k the dimension, and d the distance—the minimum Hamming distance between any two codewords. At most $\boldsymbol{O}(d-1)/2$ errors can be corrected by such a code. Any such linear code is specified by its *generator matrix G*, which maps the input into its encoded correspondent. The parity check matrix h can be easily evaluated from this generator matrix. Associated with any linear code is its *dual code* with generator matrix h^T. The construction of *CSS codes* is based not on one but on two classical codes: on both an $[n_1, k_1, d_1]$ code C_1 and an $[n_2, k_2, d_2]$ code C_2 with $C_2 \subset C_1$, such that both the former code and the dual of the latter code can correct for m errors. The quantum error-correcting code is then constructed for each codeword x_1 of C_1 as a superposition over codewords of C_2, again represented as pure states of qubits.

With this construction, much of the power of the formalism of classical linear error correcting codes can be applied. It turns out that with such CSS codes, based on the classical theory, up to m errors can be detected and corrected, indicating that good quantum error-correcting codes exist that can correct for more than general errors on single qubits. The above Steane code is already an example of a CSS code, but one that corrects for only a single error. Is Steane's 7-qubit quantum code the shortest quantum code that can correct for a general error to a single qubit? The answer is no, and it can be shown that five qubits are sufficient, as was first pointed out by Laflamme, Miquel, Paz, and Zurek on the one hand [24] and by Bennett et al. [59] on the other. What can also be shown, in turn, is that no even shorter quantum code can exist with this capability. This insight is important when considering the hardware resources necessary to design a quantum computer incorporating error correction.

This 5-qubit code is a particular instance of a so-called *stabilizer code* [18]. The stabilizer formalism is a very powerful means to grasp a large class of unitary quantum operations on states, as well as state changes under measurements in the computational basis. Essentially, instead of referring to the states themselves, the idea is to specify the operators that "stabilize the state," i.e., those operators the state vector is an eigenvector of with eigenvalue 1. It turns out that it is often far easier and more transparent to specify these operators than to specify the state vectors. The power of the stabilizer formalism becomes manifest when considering the *Pauli group*, i.e., the group of all products of the Pauli matrices and the identity with appropriate phases. Based on this stabilizer formalism, an important class of stabilizer codes can be constructed that are a genuine generalization of the CSS codes and also embody the 9-qubit Shor code. But the significance of the stabilizer formalism goes much beyond the construction of good quantum error-correcting codes. The *Gottesman-Knill theorem* that has been mentioned previously in Section 2 can, for example, be proved using this formalism.

There is a notable link between stabilizer codes and quantum error-correcting codes based on graphs. A large class of quantum error-correcting codes can be constructed based on a graph, where edges, roughly speaking, reflect an interaction pattern between the quantum systems of the quantum codewords [18, 60]. It turns out that these *graph codes* present an intuitive way of constructing error-correcting codes, and they exactly correspond to the stabilizer codes. It is an interesting aspect that the *graph states* [60, 61] associated with graph codes can also serve a very different purpose: they themselves form a universal resource for measurement-based *one-way quantum computation* [62]. In this scheme, a particular instance of a graph state is initially prepared as a resource for the quantum computation. Implementing a quantum algorithm amounts to performing measurements on single qubits only (but not necessarily in the computational basis), thereby realizing an effective unitary transformation on the output qubits.

8.5   Fault-tolerant quantum computation

Very nice, one might say at this point, it is impressive that errors affecting quantum systems can be corrected. But is there not a crucial assumption hidden here? Clearly, when one is merely storing quantum states, errors are potentially harmful, and this danger can be very much attenuated by means of appropriate quantum error correction. But so far, we have assumed that the encoding and decoding of the quantum states can be done in a perfectly reliable manner, without errors at all. Given the degree of complexity of the circuits necessary to do such an encoding (see, e.g., Figure 8.5), amounting essentially to a quantum computation, it does not seem very natural to assume that this computation can be done without any errors. After all, one has to keep in mind that the whole procedure of encoding and decoding complicates the actual computation and adds to the hardware requirements.

It was one of the very significant insights in the field that this assumption is, unrealistic as it is, unnecessary. In the recovery process, errors may be allowed for, leading to *fault-tolerant recovery*, as has been shown in seminal work by Shor [63], with similar ideas having been independently developed by Kitaev [64]. Fault-tolerant recovery is possible as long as the error rate in this process is sufficiently low. But then, it might not be optimal to first encode, then later (when appropriate) decode, perform a quantum gate, and then encode the state again. Instead, it would be desirable to find ways of implementing a universal set of gates in the space of the encoded qubits itself. This leads to the theory of *fault-tolerant quantum computation*. That this is possible has again been shown by Shor [63], who devised fault-tolerant circuits for two-qubit CNOT gates, rotations, and three-qubit *Toffoli gates* acting as $|x, y, z\rangle \mapsto |x, y, z \oplus xy\rangle$[30]. This might still not be

---

[30]Note that, quite surprisingly, Toffoli and Hadamard gates alone are already universal for quantum computation, thereby eliminating the need for general single-qubit rotations [65, 16].

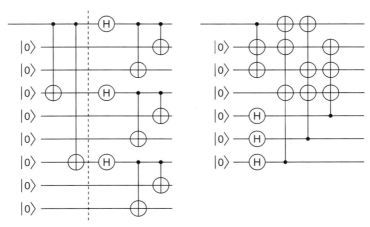

Figure 8.5. The encoding circuits of the Shor (left) and Steane (right) quantum codes. To the left of the dotted line, the depicted circuit corresponds to the repetition code. The first line corresponds to the input qubit.

enough: from quantum error correction above, alone, as described it is not clear how to store quantum information for an arbitrarily long time with high fidelity. Knill and Laflamme demonstrated that this is possible with *concatenated encoding*, meaning that the encoded words are encoded again to some degree of hierarchy, and appropriate error detection and correction are performed [66, 67]. Uniting these ingredients, it became evident that a threshold for the required accuracy of general fault-tolerant quantum computation can be identified, allowing in principle for arbitrarily long quantum computation with high fidelity. Several nonequivalent *threshold theorems*, asking essentially for only a constant error rate, have been developed that hold under a number of different assumptions [56, 68, 64, 18, 67]. Such schemes for achieving reliable quantum computation at a constant error rate can be achieved with a polylogarithmic overhead in both the time and space of the computation to be performed. Hence, the additional cost in depth and size of the quantum circuit is such that the superiority of quantum algorithms like Grover's and Shor's algorithms over their classical counterparts is essentially preserved.

So, in a nutshell, quantum error correction, together with techniques from fault-tolerant quantum computation, significantly lessens the threat posed by the unavoidable decoherence processes from which any quantum computer will suffer. To preserve the coherence of the involved quantum over the whole quantum computation remains the central challenge of realization. The theory of quantum error correction, however, shows that the pessimism expressed in the mid 1990s, culminating in the statement that these daunting problems cannot be overcome as a matter of principle, was not quite appropriate.

9   HOW TO BUILD A QUANTUM COMPUTER

We have seen so far what purposes a quantum computer may serve and what tasks it may perform well (better than any classical computer), and we have sketched what the underlying computational model is like. Also, ways have been described to fight the decoherence due to coupling with the environment, and eventually to the same devices that are designed to perform the readout. The crucial question remains: how can a quantum computer be built? What are the physical requirements to appropriately isolate a quantum computer from its environment? What is the physical hardware that can maintain the promise of the quantum computer as a supercomputing device?

Needless to say, there are no satisfactory answers to these questions so far. On the one hand, progress has been made in recent years in the experimental controlled manipulation of very small quantum systems that cannot be called other than spectacular, in a way that was not imaginable not long ago. Quantum gates have been implemented in the quantum optical context, and with nuclear magnetic resonance (NMR) techniques, even small quantum algorithms have been realized. On the other hand, however, it seems fair to say that a universal quantum computer as a physical device that deserves this name is still in the remote future. The only thing that seems safe to say is that none of the current experimental efforts probably deals with exactly the physical system that will be used in an eventual realization of a Shor-class quantum computer. Supposedly, completely new ways of controlling individual quantum systems will have to be devised, potentially combining previous ideas from quantum optics and solid state physics. Any such implementation will eventually have to live up to some requirements that have perhaps been most distinctly formulated by DiVincenzo as generic requirements in practical quantum computation [69], (see Figure 8.6). It is beyond the scope of this chapter to give an introduction to the very rich literature on physical implementations of quantum computers. After all, this is the core question that physicists seek to address in this field. Instead, we will sketch a few key methods that have been proposed as potentially promising or that have already been demonstrated in experiments.

9.1   Quantum optical methods

Among the most promising methods to date are quantum optical methods where the physical qubits correspond to *cold ions in a linear trap*, interacting with laser beams. A plethora of such proposals have been made, dating back to seminal work by Cirac and Zoller [70]. In the latter proposal, qubits are identified with internal degrees of freedom of the ions, which are assumed to be two-level systems for practical purposes. Single qubit operations can be accomplished by means of a controlled interaction with laser light, shone onto the ions by different laser beams that can individually address the ion. The ions repel each other

---

> (i) Scalable physical system with well-characterized qubits
> (ii) Ability to initialize the state of the qubits to a simple fiducial state
> (iii) Long decoherence times, much longer than the gate operation time
> (iv) Universal set of quantum gates
> (v) Qubit specific measurement capability

Figure 8.6. The DiVincenzo criteria of what requirements must be met in any physical implementation of a quantum computer.

by Coulomb interaction, forming a string of ions, with adjacent ions being a couple of optical wavelengths apart from each other. More challenging, of course, is to find ways to let two arbitrary qubits interact to realize a two-qubit quantum gate. This outcome can be achieved by means of exciting the collective motion of the canonical degrees of freedom of the ions with lasers, i.e., by using the lowest-level collective *vibrational modes*. Several refinements of this original proposal aim at realizing the gates faster, and in a way that does not require extremely low temperatures or is less prone to decoherence [71]. Such quantum gates have already been realized in experiments, notably the implementation of two-qubit quantum gates due to work by Monroe and coworkers [72] with a single ion and by Blatt and coworkers [73] with a two-ion quantum processor.

Alternatively to using degrees of freedom of motion to let quantum systems interact, this goal can be achieved by means of the tools of *cavity quantum electrodynamics* (cavity QED) [74, 75]. The key idea is to store neutral atoms inside an optical cavity formed, for example, by two optical supermirrors. The interactions required to perform two-qubit gates are moderated by means of the interaction of the atoms with a single quantized mode of a high-Q optical cavity. In [74] it is assumed that adjacent atoms are separated by a few wavelengths of the cavity mode, interacting with laser beams in an individual manner (standing qubits); but atomic beams passing through the cavity have also been considered, both theoretically and experimentally (flying qubits). Two regimes can in general be distinguished: the strong coupling limit, where coherent atom–cavity dynamics dominates cavity losses and spontaneous emission, and the bad cavity limit, where cavity loss rate is much larger than the atom–cavity coupling.

Still using a quantum optical setting, but without a quantum data bus in the closer sense, are proposals that make use of *controlled collisions* of cold atoms. This outcome can be realized, for example, with neutral atoms in *optical lattices*, where direct control over single quantum systems can be achieved [76].

Not to be confused with the classical optical computer, in the *optical quantum computer* the qubits are encoded in the state of field modes of light [77]. The state is manipulated by means of optical elements such as beam splitters, mirrors, phase shifts, and squeezers. The advantage – that photons are not very prone to decoherence – is at the same time the disadvantage, since letting them interact is difficult, as is realizing strong Kerr nonlinearities without significant losses. Yet in order to circumvent the latter problem, instead of requiring that a given task is accomplished with unit probability, one may effectively realize the required nonlinear interactions by means of measurements of the photon number. This is possible at the cost of the scheme becoming probabilistic. Notably, Knill, Laflamme, and Milburn have proposed a scheme for universal quantum computation employing optical circuits that merely consist of passive linear optical elements (hence excluding squeezers), together with photon counters that have the ability to distinguish 0, 1, and 2 photons [78].

Finally, the vibrational modes of molecules can be employed to serve as qubits in *molecular quantum computers* [79]. Both single qubit and two-qubit gates can be implemented in principle by suitably shaped femtosecond laser pulses, the form of which can be computed by applying techniques from control theory. Drawbacks are problems related to the scalability of the setup.

9.2   Solid-state approaches

Solid-state approaches serve as an alternative to quantum optical settings. Several different systems have been considered so far, including proposals for *quantum dot* quantum computers with dipole–dipole coupling. Ideas from solid-state physics and cavity QED can be combined by considering solid-state quantum computers, where gates can be realized by controlled interactions between two distant quantum dot spins mediated by the field of a high-Q microcavity [80, 81]. The Kane proposal is concerned with a *silicon-based nuclear spin quantum computer*, where the nuclear spins of donor atoms in doped silicon devices correspond to the physical qubits [82]. The appeal of the proposal due to Ladd is that it sketches a silicon quantum computer that could potentially be manufactured using current fabrication techniques with semi-conductor technology and current measurement techniques [83]. Finally, SQUIDs, *superconducting quantum interference devices*, with the quantized flux serving as the qubit, could be candidates for a physical realization of a quantum computer.

9.3   NMR quantum computing

Probably the most progressed technology so far in a sense is bulk ensemble quantum computation based on *nuclear magnetic resonance* (NMR) techniques [84, 85]. This idea is different from those previously described in that no attempt is made to control the state of individual quantum systems, trapped or confined in an appropriate way. Instead, the state of nuclear spins of 10^{20}–10^{23} identical molecules is manipulated using well-developed tools from NMR technology. Bulk techniques are used not only because the standard machinery of NMR is available but also because the nuclear spin state of a single molecule can hardly be properly prepared. This setup literally allows for quantum computation with a cup of coffee. Single qubit gates can be realized fairly easily. With appropriate hand-tailored molecule synthesis and a sophisticated magnetic field pulse sequence, a 7-qubit NMR quantum computer has been realized that implements a shortened and simplified version of Shor's algorithm [85]. However, quantum computation with bulk NMR techniques comes with a caveat. Although the most progress has so far been made in this area, it has been convincingly argued that the scalability of these kinds of proposals is limited by serious problems: notably, the signal is exponentially reduced in the number of qubits by effective pure-state preparation schemes in an exponential manner in the number of qubits [31].

10   PRESENT STATUS AND FUTURE PERSPECTIVES

In the information age, where DVDs, wireless LAN, RSA encryption, and UMTS are the antiquated technologies of tomorrow, quantum information theory aims to understand the old rules of quantum mechanics from the new perspective of information theory and computer science. In contrast to some earlier approaches to a better *understanding* of quantum mechanics, this approach is very pragmatic, leaving aside all metaphysical issues of interpretation and transforming former apparent paradoxes into future applications. The most challenging and outstanding of these is the universal quantum computer. Its potential is not yet fully understood. At the moment there are essentially two classes of very promising quantum algorithms: search algorithms based on Grover's database search and applications of the quantum Fourier transform like Shor's factoring and discrete logarithm algorithms.[31] In particular, the latter yield an exponential speedup compared with the best-known classical algorithms. For which other problems can we expect such a speedup? The killer application would of course be a polynomial-time algorithm for NP-complete problems. Being optimistic, one could consider results in adiabatic computing as supporting evidence for this desire. However, the optimality of the quadratic speedup in search algorithms might be evidence to the contrary. Moderating our optimism a bit, we could try to find efficient quantum algorithms for problems that are believed to be hard classically but not NP-complete. The hottest candidate among such problems is probably the graph isomorphism problem, for which, despite considerable effort, no efficient quantum algorithm has been found so far.

What role does entanglement play in quantum computers? This question is in general not entirely answered yet. However, if we consider a quantum computer unitarily acting on a pure input state, then an exponential speedup compared with classical computers can only be achieved if the entanglement present in intermediate states of the computation increases with size of the input [87, 88].[32] It appears that computations based on such (rather typical) quantum evolutions can in general not be simulated efficiently on classical computers.

Let us finally speculate on how a quantum computer will eventually look. What will be its hardware? In the past, the most successful realization was NMR, where even small quantum circuits have been implemented. Unfortunately, it has been convincingly argued that this implementation is not scalable to larger circuits. For the near future, ion traps and, in particular regarding the simulation of quantum systems, optical lattices seem to be quite promising, whereas in the remote future solid-state realizations would be desirable. However, progress is never smooth:

> *Where a calculator on the ENIAC is equipped with 18,000*
> *vacuum tubes and weighs 30 tons, computers in the future may*
> *have only 1,000 tubes and perhaps only weigh 1 1/2 tons.*
> *(Popular Mechanics, March 1949)*

---

[31]More recent progress in this direction includes polynomial-time quantum algorithms for estimating Gauss sums [86] and solving Pell's equation [41].

[32]As shown by Vidal [88], the evolution of a pure state of N qubits can be simulated on a classical computer by using resources that grow linearly in N and exponentially in the entanglement. Similarly, the evolution of mixed states, on which the amount of correlation is restricted, can be efficiently simulated. Note that subexponential speedups as in Grover's search algorithm could also be achieved without entanglment, or with a restricted amount of it [89].

REFERENCES

[1] M. Nielsen, I. L. Chuang (2000): Quantum Computation and Information. Springer: Berlin Heidelberg New York.

[2] P. W. Shor (1994): Proc 35th Annual Symposium on Foundations of Computer Science, IEEE Press; Shor PW (1997): *SIAM J Comp 26*:1484.

[3] R. P. Feynman (1996): Feynman lectures on computation. Addison-Wesley, Reading; Feynman RP (1982): *Int J Theor Phys 21*:467.

[4] G. E. Moore (1965): Electronics *38*:8.

[5] N. Gisin, G. Ribordy, W. Tittel, H. Zbinden (2002): *Rev Mod Phys 74*:145.

[6] D. J. Wineland, J. J. Bollinger, W. M. Itano, F. L. Moore (1992): *Phys Rev A* 46:R6797; Wineland DJ, Bollinger JJ, Itano WM (1994): *Phys Rev A 50*:67.

[7] S. F. Huelga, C. Macchiavello, T. Pellizzari, A. K. Ekert, M. B. Plenio, J. I. Cirac (1997): *Phys Rev Lett 79*:3865.

[8] C. H. Bennett, G. Brassard, B. Popescu, J. A. Smolin, W. K. Wootters (1996): *Phys Rev Lett 76*:722.

[9] P. Horodecki, R. Horodecki (2001): *Quant Inf Comp 1*(1):45.

[10] D. Deutsch (1989): *Proc R Soc London A 525*:73.

[11] B. Schumacher (1995): *Phys Rev A 51*:2738.

[12] A. Barenco, D. Deutsch, A. Ekert, R. Jozsa (1995): *Phys Rev Lett 74*:4083; Barenco A, Bennett CH, Cleve R, DiVincenzo DP, Margolus N, Shor PW, Sleator T, Smolin J, Weinfurter H (1995): *Phys Rev A 52*:3457.

[13] J. Preskill (1998): Lecture Notes for Physics 229: Quantum Information and Computation. CalTech: Pasadena.

[14] D. Collins, N. Linden, S. Popescu (2001): *Phys Rev A 64*:032302.

[15] J. Eisert, K. Jacobs, P. Papadopoulos, M. B. Plenio (2000): *Phys Rev A* 62:052317; Gottesman D (1998): quant-ph/9807006; J. I. Cirac, W. Dür, B. Kraus, M. Lewenstein (2001): *Phys Rev Lett 86*:544.

[16] A. Y. Kitaev (1997): *Russian Mathematical Surveys 52*:1191.

[17] R. Solovay (1995): Unpublished.

[18] D. Gottesman (1997): Stabilizer Codes and Quantum Error Correction. PhD thesis, CalTech, Pasadena.

[19] W. K. Wootters, W. H. Zurek (1982): *Nature 299*:802; Dieks D (1982): *Phys Lett A 92*:271.

[20] M. A. Nielsen, I. L. Chuang (1997): *Phys Rev Lett 79*:321.

[21] A. Steane (1996): *Phys Rev Lett 77*:793.

[22] A. Steane (1996): *Proc R Soc London 452*:2551.

[23] P. W. Shor (1995): *Phys Rev A 52*:2493.

[24] R. Laflamme, C. Miquel, J. P. Paz, W. H. Zurek (1996): *Phys Rev Lett* 77:198; E. Knill, R. Laflamme, A. Ashikhmin, H. Barnum, L. Viola, W. H. Zurek (2002): quant-ph/0207170.

[25] D. Deutsch (1985): *Proc R Soc London A 400*:97.

[26] P. Benioff (1980): *J Stat Phys 22*:563.

[27] V. Vedral, A. Barenco, A. Ekert (1996): *Phys Rev A 54*:147.

[28] R. Cleve, A. Ekert, C. Macchiavello, M. Mosca (1998): *Proc R Soc London A* 454:339.

[29] D. Deutsch, R. Jozsa (1992): *Proc R Soc London* A *439*:553.

[30] E. Bernstein, U. V. Vazirani (1997): *SIAM J Comput 26*:1411.

[31] N. D. Mermin (2004): *IBM Journal of Research and Development* 48, 53.

[32] D. R. Simon (1994): *Proc 35th Annual Symposium on Foundations of Computer Science*:166.

[33] L. K. Grover (1996): Proceedings STOC:212.

[34] C. H. Bennett, E. Bernstein, Brassard, U. Vazirani (1997): *SIAM J Comput* 26:1510.

[35] Coppersmith (1994): *IBM Research Report RC* 19642.

[36] A. Y. Kitaev (1995): quant-ph/9511026.

[37] M. Pueschel, M. Roetteler, T. Beth (1998): quant-ph/9807064.

[38] M. T. Heideman, D. H. Johnson, C. S. Burrus (1984): Gauss and the history of the fast Fourier transform, *IEEE ASSP Magazine* 1(4):14.

[39] D. Knuth (1973): The Art of Computer Programming II. Addison-Wesley: Reading, MA.

[40] J. Watrous (2000): quant-ph/0011023.

[41] S. Hallgren (2002): *Symposium on the Theory of Computation* (STOC).

[42] A. M. Childs, R. Cleve, E. Deotto, E. Farhi, S. Gutmann, D. A. Spielmann (2002): *Proc ACM Symposium on Theory of Computing* (STOC 2003).

[43] D. Aharonov, A. Ambainis, J. Kempe, U. Vazirani (2001): *Proc ACM Symposium on Theory of Computing* (STOC 2001).

[44] E. Farhi, J. Goldstone, S. Gutmann, M. Sipser (2000): quant-ph/0001106; E. Farhi, J. Goldstone, S. Gutmann, J. Lapan, A. Lundgren (2001): Science 292:472.

[45] D. Aharonov, A. Ta-Shma (2003): quant-ph/0301023.

[46] V. Murg, J. I. Cirac (2004): *Phys Rev A* 69: 042320.

[47] J. Roland, N. J. Cerf (2003): *Phys Rev A* 65:042308.

[48] E. Farhi, J. Goldstone, S. Gutmann (2002): quant-ph/0201031.

[49] S. Lloyd (1996): Science 273:1073.

[50] B. M. Boghosian, W. Taylor (1998): D. Physica 120:30.

[51] C. Zalka (1998): *Proc R Soc London A* 454:313.

[52] D. S. Abrams, S. Lloyd (1997): *Phys Rev Lett* 79:2586; Ortiz G, Gubernatis JE, Knill E, Laflamme R (2001): *Phys Rev A* 64:022319.

[53] B. M. Terhal, D. P. DiVincenzo (2000): *Phys Rev A* 61:22301.

[54] E. Jané, G. Vidal, W. Dür, P. Zoller, J. I. Cirac (2003): *Quant Inf Comp* 3(1):15.

[55] M. Greiner, I. Bloch, O. Mandel, T. W. Hänsch, T. Esslinger (2001): *Phys Rev Lett* 87:160405; M. Greiner, O. Mandel, T. Esslinger, T. W. Hänsch, I. Bloch (2002): *Nature 415*:39.

[56] J. Preskill (1998): *Proc R Soc London* A, 454:385.

[57] A. Peres (1985): *Phys Rev A 32*:3266.

[58] A. R. Calderbank, P. W. Shor (1996): *Phys Rev A 54*:1098.

[59] C. H. Bennett, D. DiVincenzo, J. Smolin, W. Wootters (1996): *Phys Rev A 54*:3824.

[60] D. Schlingemann (2002): *Quant Inf Comp 2*:307.

[61] M. Hein, J. Eisert, H. J. Briegel (2004): *Phys Rev A 69: 062311*.

[62] R. Raussendorf, H. J. Briegel (2000): *Phys Rev Lett 86*:5188; Raussendorf R, Browne DE, Briegel HJ (2003): *Phys Rev A 68*:022312.

[63] P. W. Shor (1996): *Proc 37th Annual Symposium on Fundamentals of Computer Science, IEEE*:56.

[64] A. Y. Kitaev (1997): *Russian Mathematical Surveys 52*:1191.

[65] D. Aharonov (2003): quant-ph/0301040.

[66] E. Knill, R. Laflamme (1996): quant-ph/9608012.

[67] E. Knill, R. Laflamme, W. H. Zurek (1998): Science *279*:342.

[68] D. Aharonov, M. Ben-Or (1999): quant-ph/9906129.

[69] D. DiVincenzo (2000): *Fort Phys 48*:771.

[70] J. I. Cirac, P. Zoller (1995): *Phys Rev Lett 74*:4091.

[71] S. Scheider, D. F. V. James, G. J. Milburn (1999): *J Mod Opt 7*:499; Sørensen A. Mølmer K. (1999): *82*:1971; Jonathan D, Plenio MB, Knight PL (2000): *Phys Rev A 62*:42307.

[72] C. Monroe, D. M. Meekhof, B. E. King, W. M. Itano, D. J. Wineland (1995): *Phys Rev Lett 75*:4714.

[73] F. Schmidt-Kaler, H. Häffner, M. Riebe, S. Gulde, Q. P. T. Lancaster, T. Deuschle, C. Becher, C. F. Roos, J. Eschner, R. Blatt (2003): *Nature 422*:408.

[74] T. Pellizzari, S. A. Gardiner, J. I. Cirac, P. Zoller (1995): *Phys Rev Lett 75*:3788.

[75] Q. A. Turchette, C. J. Hood, W. Lange, H. Mabuchi, H. J. Kimble (1995): *Phys Rev Lett 75*:4714; Domokos P, Raimond JM, Brune M, Haroche S (1995): *Phys Rev Lett 52*:3554.

[76] D. Jaksch, H. J. Briegel, J. I. Cirac, C. W. Gardiner, P. Zoller (1999): *Phys Rev Lett 82*:1975.

[77] G. J. Milburn (1989): *Phys Rev Lett 62*:2124.

[78] E. Knill, R. Laflamme, G. J. Milburn (2001): *Nature 409*:46; Ralph TC, White AG, Munro WJ, Milburn GJ (2001): *Phys Rev A 65*:012314; Lapaire GG, Kok P, Dowling JP, Sipe JE (2004): *Phys Rev A 68*:042314; Scheel S, Nemoto K, Munro WJ, Knight PL (2003): *Phys Rev A 68*:032310.

[79] C. M. Tesch, R. de Vivie-Riedle (2002): *Phys Rev Lett 89*:157901; Vala J, Amitay Z, Zhang B, Leone SR, Kosloff R (2002): *Phys Rev A 66*:062316.

[80] M. S. Sherwin, A. Imamoglu, T. Montroy (1999): *Phys Rev A 60*:3508.

[81] A. Imamoglu, D. D. Awschalom, G. Burkard, D. P. DiVincenzo, D. Loss, M. Sherwin, A. Small (1999): *Phys Rev Lett 83*:4204.

[82] B. E. Kane (1998): *Nature 393*:133.

[83] T. D. Ladd, J. R. Goldman, F. Yamaguchi, Y. Yamamoto, E. Abe, K. M. Itoh (2002): *Phys Rev Lett 89*:017901.

[84] N. A. Gershenfeld, I. L. Chuang, S. Lloyd (1996): Phys Comp 96, *Proc of the 4th Workshop on Physics and Computation*:134; Gershenfeld NA, Chuang IL (1997): Science 275:350; Cory DG, Fahmy AF, Havel TF (1997): *Proc Natl Acad Sci USA 94*:307.

[85] L. M. Vandersypen, M. Steffen, G. Breyta, C. S. Yannoni, M. H. Sherwood, I. L. Chuang (2001): *Nature 414*:883.

[86] W. van Dam, G. Seroussi (2003): *Proc RSoc London A 459*:2011.

[87] R. Jozsa, N. Linden (2002): quant-ph/0201143.

[88] G. Vidal (2003): *Phys Rev Lett 91*:147902.

[89] S. Lloyd (2000): *Phys Rev A 61*:010301.

Chapter 9

COMPUTER ARCHITECTURE

Joshua J. Yi[1] and David J. Lilja[2]

[1]Freesale Semiconductor Inc.
[2]University of Minnesota

1   INTRODUCTION

Originally proposed in 1945 by John von Neumann, the von Neumann architecture has become the foundation for virtually all commercial processors. von Neumann machines have three distinguishing characteristics: 1) the stored-program concept, 2) the partitioning of the processor into different functional components, 3) and the fetch-execute cycle.

The key idea behind the stored-program concept is that the series of instructions that form the program are stored in processor-accessible memory. By contrast, for processors that do not utilize the stored-program concept, the instructions of the program need to be fed into the processor as the program is running or the program needs to be hard coded into the processor. Storing the program in memory where the processor can easily access it is obviously more efficient than feeding in each instruction while the program is running. Also, reprogramming a stored-program concept processor is as simple as loading the next program into memory, which is more flexible than physically reprogramming the processor.

The second key characteristic of von Neumann architectures is that the processor is partitioned into components for input, output, computation, and control. Figure 9.1 shows how these components are connected together. The input and output components allow the processor to communicate to the user through other parts of the computer. For example, the processor receives information from the user through the keyboard and mouse while displaying information to the user through the monitor. The arithmetic-logic unit (ALU) is the component in the processor that actually does the computations. Computations can be divided into two categories: arithmetic and logical. Examples of the former include addition, subtraction, multiplication, division, etc. for integer and floating-point (real) numbers; examples of the latter include AND, OR, XOR, NOT, etc. In current-generation processors, the ALU is not a single monolithic

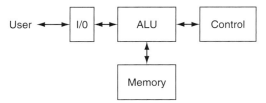

Figure 9.1. Basic components of a von Neumann architecture

component. Rather, multiple, distributed functional units perform its tasks; this partitioning decreases the overall execution time of each type of operation. Finally, the purpose of the control logic is to coordinate the flow of instructions and data between the different components of the processor by producing a sequence of signals that synchronizes the operation of each of the processor's components with respect to the other components. The control unit is necessary to ensure correct execution of the fetch-execute cycle, which is the third and final characteristic of a von Neumann architecture.

As its name implies, the fetch-execute cycle consists of two steps: instruction fetch and instruction execution. Since the program is stored in the computer's memory, to fetch an instruction, the processor must first retrieve each instruction from the computer's memory before the instruction can be executed. To retrieve the proper instruction, the processor sends the value of the program counter (PC), which holds the memory address of the next instruction, to memory, which returns the instruction stored at that memory location. After receiving that instruction, the processor calculates the address of the subsequent instruction and stores it into the PC. Usually, the address of the next instruction is simply the address of the instruction immediately following the current instruction. However, due to branch and jump instructions (which are the result of the function and subroutine calls, IF statements, etc.), the next instruction may not be the next sequential instruction, but will instead be located somewhere else in memory. Storing the address of the next instruction into the PC completes the instruction fetch part of the fetch-execute cycle.

The other half of the fetch-execute cycle, instruction execution, consists of several smaller substeps. The first substep is instruction decode, which occurs immediately after the instruction is fetched. In this substep, the decode logic analyzes the instruction to determine what kind of instruction it is (add, multiply, AND, branch, load, store, etc.), how many input operands there are, and where the input operands come from. After the processor decodes the instruction, it first gathers the values of the input operands, as specified by the instruction. For example, before the processor can compute the result of "1+2," it first needs to retrieve the values of the two input operands (1 and 2) from the specified registers or memory locations. In the next substep, the processor executes the instruction. In the case of arithmetic and logical instructions, the processor computes a new output value. In the case of load and store instructions, the processor accesses memory to either retrieve a value from memory (load) or write a value to memory (store). And in the case of branch instructions, the processor determines whether the branch condition is true or false and then calculates the memory address of the next instruction. Table 9.1 summarizes the action of these three types of instructions. Finally, in the last substep, the result of the instruction is stored into a register or a memory location so that is it available for the next instruction. After finishing execution, the processor fetches the next instruction and restarts the fetch-execute cycle all over again.

To summarize, instruction fetch retrieves the next instruction that the processor will execute, and in instruction execution, the processor performs the work that is specified by that instruction. By repeatedly fetching and executing instructions, the processor executes a program.

Although proposed over 50 years ago, the three fundamental characteristics of a von Neumann architecture, the stored-program concept, partitioned processor components, and the fetch-execute cycle, still remain the foundation of modern-day processors.

2   RISC VERSUS CISC

It is important to realize that the characteristics of a von Neumann architecture specify only how the processor is organized and how it operates from a functional point of view. As a result, two processors could have very different implementations, but both could still be von Neumann architectures. Given this freedom of implementation, computer architects have proposed two implementations that represent very different design philosophies. The first approach is known as the reduced instruction set computer, or more commonly by its acronym RISC. The second implementation is the complex instruction set computer, or CISC.

At heart of the difference between these two design philosophies is the processor's instruction set architecture (ISA). The instruction set is the set of assembly-level instructions that the processor is capable of executing and the set of registers that are visible (directly accessible) to an assembly-language programmer.

2.1   RISC: Reduced Instruction Set Computers

The basic design philosophy for RISC processors is to minimize the number and complexity of the instructions in the instruction set, in addition to defining uniform-length instructions. Adding more complex or nonuniform instructions into the processor's instruction set makes it more difficult for the processor to execute efficiently, since each of those instructions may have its own individual idiosyncrasies that may require specialized hardware in order to execute those cases. A processor can execute instructions much more efficiently when they are simple and uniform in length, since less complex "one-size-fits-all" hardware can be used for all instructions.

In addition to reducing the complexity of the hardware, minimizing the number of instructions in the processor's instruction set has the effect of reducing the

Table 9.1. Actions of the three main instruction types

Instruction Type	Action
Arithmetic and Logical	Computes new results
Load and Store	Reads from and writes to memory
Branch	Checks condition, determines next instruction

bus widths between internal processor components. Since each instruction has its own unique identifier, known as the *opcode*, adding additional instructions to the processor's instruction set may result in needing to add additional bits to the opcode. Adding more bits to the opcode may increase the number of bits needed for each instruction, which in turn increases the width of each internal bus.

Using simple and uniform-length instructions has two consequences. First, only load and store instructions are allowed to access memory; this simplifies the specification and execution latency of the instruction set's arithmetic and logical instructions. Instead of allowing an add instruction to directly add the values in two memory locations, two load instructions are used to first load those values into the processor's registers before the add instruction can execute. After computing the result, the add instruction has to use a store instruction to write its result to memory. This type of architecture is known as a "register-to-register" architecture, since all instructions with the exception of loads and stores can only read their input operands from and write their output values to the register file. Obviously, as compared with allowing each arithmetic or logical instruction to directly access memory, using load instructions to first load the values for input operands and then using a store instruction to store the output value requires three additional instructions (two loads and one store). While this increases the total instruction count when a program executes, it does not change the amount of "work" (steps necessary to execute the program) that the processor needs to do. Since this approach reduces the complexity of the hardware, this approach may still allow the processor to execute the program in less time than a CISC processor. In other words, it is easier to design hardware that executes a few types of instructions over and over again instead of designing hardware to execute many different types of instructions just a few times.

The other consequence of executing simple and uniform-length instructions is that there are fewer ways for load and store instructions to generate the address that is used to access memory. Since these ways of accessing memory are relatively simple, the compiler may need to insert additional instructions to help generate the correct address. For example, when traversing a linked-list in C, if more complex addressing modes were allowed, each load instruction could potentially retrieve the base address for the next link in the list. In a RISC processor, two loads are needed to retrieve the base address of the following link in the list.

In summary, since each RISC instruction is relatively simple and is uniform in length, programs compiled for a RISC processor contain additional instructions to move data between the processor and memory, to support more complex addressing modes, or to execute pieces of more complex tasks than a CISC processor. These additional instructions obviously increase the number of dynamic instructions that the processor executes, in addition to increasing the size of the compiled program. On the other hand, since all the instructions are simple and of uniform length, the hardware for the RISC processor is relatively simple and therefore more efficient, i.e., has a higher clock rate than the equivalent CISC processor. Simply stated, RISC processors trade off the execution of a larger number of instructions for a faster clock frequency.

2.2   CISC: Complex Instruction Set Computers

The basic design philosophy behind a CISC processor is nearly opposite to that of the RISC processor. First, instead of using several simple instructions to accomplish a single task, a CISC processor may use only one or two more complex instructions. Second, instead of having a set of relatively simple, uniform-length instructions, the instruction set for CISC processors consists of many complex instructions that are nonuniform in length and have multiple addressing modes. Third, instead of allowing only load and store instructions to access memory, in a CISC processor, arithmetic and logical instructions can access memory directly. As a result of these differences, a CISC processor typically executes fewer instructions to run the same program than the RISC processor does. Also, the size of the compiled program for the CISC processor, in terms of bytes, is also smaller than the size of the RISC program.

Obviously, these three differences have a very significant effect on the actual implementation of the hardware. Since each CISC instruction is much more complex than its RISC counterpart, the hardware needed to execute each CISC instruction is correspondingly more complex. In general, increasing the complexity of hardware decreases the speed at which the hardware executes instructions. As a result, the clock frequency of CISC processors is typically lower than the clock frequencies of RISC processors. Since each CISC instruction does more work than does a RISC instruction, each CISC instruction takes more time, as measured in clock cycles, to execute. Therefore, not only is the clock rate of CISC processors slower than that of RISC processors but also it typically takes more clock cycles to execute a CISC instruction than for a RISC instruction. However, the trade-off is that one CISC instruction does the same amount of work as several RISC instructions.

In summary, the design philosophy of CISC processors is to support very complex instructions that can be nonuniform in length. The upsides of this design philosophy are that each instruction does a significant amount of work and that the total size of the program is smaller. The downsides are that it takes more clock cycles to execute each instruction and that the hardware is very complex and consequently slower than the equivalent RISC processor.

2.3   Performance Analysis of RISC versus CISC

Although the previous two sub-sections compared RISC and CISC processors somewhat indirectly, this section uses the formula below to directly compare the performance of these two processors. The time required to execute a program is summarized below (see Eq. 1).

$$T_e = n * \text{CPI} * T_c \qquad (1)$$

T_e is the total execution time of the program. n is the total number of dynamic (executed) instructions in the program, CPI is the average number of clock cycles needed to execute each instruction, and T_c is the time per clock cycle.

As this formula shows, the total execution time of the program depends on the number of instructions that the processor has to execute, the average number of clock cycles that each instruction takes, and the amount of time in a clock cycle (i.e., the reciprocal of the clock frequency). Therefore, to reduce a program's execution time, a computer architect can 1) reduce the number of instructions that the processor executes, 2) reduce the average number of clock cycles that it takes to execute each instruction, and/or 3) decrease the time per clock cycle (increase the clock frequency).

Since RISC processors execute more instructions than CISC processors do, the value of n is higher for RISC processors. However, the corresponding trade-off is that each RISC instruction takes fewer clock cycles when executing the same program, which means that the CPI for RISC processors is lower. Finally, since the hardware for RISC processors is less complex, the clock period for RISC processors also is typically lower for a given technology.

Ultimately, the key question is, which design philosophy is the better approach? The answer is usually RISC, and the reason is called pipelining, which is explained in more depth in the following section. Due to its design philosophy of simple and uniform-length instructions, RISC processors benefit more from pipelining than the typical CISC processor does. Since pipelining is more difficult to implement on a CISC processor, and since it yields lower performance benefits for a CISC processor, RISC processors have evolved into the principal design philosophy used in the design of most current processors.

3   EXPLOITING PARALLELISM: PIPELINING AND MULTIPLE INSTRUCTION ISSUE AND EXECUTION

3.1   Pipelining

To reduce a program's execution time, computer architects need to either decrease the number of instructions that the processor executes, reduce the CPI of each instruction, or reduce the clock period. However, since the number of instructions in the program cannot be reduced at run-time by the hardware and since the clock period is limited by the minimum transistor width, the only viable option for computer architects to reduce the program's execution time is to reduce the CPI. Since it is very difficult to directly decrease the CPI of any individual instruction, the principal method to decrease the processor's CPI is to increase the number of instructions that are executing concurrently, i.e., executing instructions in parallel.

For example, assume that it takes a processor 5 clock cycles to fetch and execute an add instruction. This corresponds to a CPI of 5 cycles for that instruction. Then also assume that the multiply instruction that immediately follows the add instruction takes another 5 cycles. When these two instructions execute sequentially, i.e., one after another, the add instruction finishes after 5 cycles. In the next cycle, cycle 6, the multiply starts and then finishes 4 cycles later, in cycle 10. Therefore, in the case of sequential execution, the average CPI for these two instructions is 5 cycles.

On the other hand, assume that the multiply instruction starts executing one cycle after the add and that there are sufficient hardware resources to execute both instructions in parallel. The add instruction starts executing in cycle 1, while the multiply instruction starts executing one cycle later in cycle 2. In cycle 5, the add instruction finishes, while the multiply instruction does not finish until cycle 6. In this case, the average CPI for these two instructions is 3 cycles. In this example, executing two sequential instructions in parallel reduces the average CPI from 5 cycles to 3 cycles, or by 40%.

In the previous example, the execution of the add and multiply instructions was pipelined. The basic idea behind pipelining is that hardware resources should be as busy as possible. In a pipelined processor, the processor's hardware resources are organized into "stages." Each major task of instruction execution maps to one or more pipeline stages. Then, to execute an instruction, the instruction enters the pipeline and goes through each stage of the pipeline until its result is written to the register file or to memory and it exits the pipeline.

Within the fetch-execute cycle, the processor performs several tasks to execute an instruction. Generally, these are fetch, decode, issue and obtain input operand values, execute, and writeback (store the newly computed results back to the register file or to memory). Assuming that each of these tasks is organized into its own pipeline stage, and assuming that output buffers are placed after each pipeline stage to store the results of that pipeline stage, the result is a classical 5-stage pipeline. In this case, the first stage of the pipeline is the fetch stage, the second stage is the decode stage, and so on.

Each pipeline stage performs its task on only one instruction at a time, or in other words, there is only one instruction in each stage. Unless there are data and/or control dependences between instructions, each instruction spends only one cycle in each pipeline stage. (A more detailed explanation of data and control dependences is given in the following section, but for now, it is only necessary to understand that data and control dependences force delays between instructions, which increases the average CPI.) Since each instruction spends only a single cycle in each pipeline stage and since there is only one instruction in each pipeline stage, the number of cycles that it takes to execute a program with n instructions, without any data or control dependences, is (see Eq. 2):

$$\text{Total Cycles} = m + (n-1) \qquad (2)$$

m is the number of pipeline stages. Assuming that the program is running on a processor with 5 pipeline stages, the first instruction in the program enters the pipeline at cycle 1 and then exits the pipeline after cycle 5. Therefore, the execution time of the first instruction is 5, or m, cycles. Then, since each following instruction starts one cycle after the instruction before it and finishes one cycle after it, once the first instruction finishes, since one instruction finishes executing every cycle, the remaining $n-1$ instructions require only an additional $n-1$ cycles. Consequently, an n-instruction program takes only $m + (n-1)$ cycles in order to execute the program completely.

By contrast, for an unpipelined processor, since each instruction takes m cycles to finish executing and since the following instruction cannot start executing until the previous one finishes, the total execution time is $n * m$ cycles. The speedup of a pipelined processor – as compared with an unpipelined one – for a very large program (n→ ∞), is (see Eq. 3):

$$\text{Speedup}_{n \to \infty} = \frac{\text{Unpipelined}}{\text{Pipelined}} = \frac{n*m}{m+(n-1)}$$

$$= \frac{1}{\frac{1}{n} + \frac{1}{m} - \frac{1}{n*m}} = \frac{1}{0 + \frac{1}{5} - 0} = \frac{1}{0.2} = 5 \qquad (3)$$

Therefore, for a 5-stage pipeline, when there are a very large number of instructions and when there are no data or control dependences, the execution time of a program that runs on a 5-stage pipelined processor is 5 times faster than the execution time of the same program on an unpipelined one.

In summary, the use of pipelining reduces the execution time of a program by overlapping the execution of different instructions. Pipelined processors exploit the parallelism inherent in programs to decrease the program's execution time. In the ideal case, when there are not any data or control dependences, a pipelined processor with m stages is m times faster than an unpipelined one. However, in typical programs, data and control dependences do exist and can severely degrade the processor's performance from its theoretical peak performance.

3.2   Data and Control Dependences

Data and control dependences are the by-products of relationships between instructions. There are three kinds of data dependences: output, anti, and flow. In a pipeline, these three dependences cause write-after-write, write-after-read, and read-after-write hazards, respectively, if the dependences occur between instructions that are in the pipeline simultaneously.

Output and antidependences are known as *name dependences*, since they are the result of two instructions sharing a register or memory location (name), but not with a producer and consumer relationship. In the case of an output dependence, both instructions write their output values to the same storage location, typically a register. This dependence is only a problem when both instructions are allowed to execute in parallel and where the second instruction may finish before the first. To ensure correct program execution, the first instruction needs to write its output value to the register before the second instruction writes its output value.

In an antidependence, the second instruction writes to the register that the first instruction needs to read from. To ensure correct program operation, the first instruction needs to read the value from the shared register before the second instruction overwrites the current value. Since output and antidependences are name dependences, assigning the second instruction to write to a different register will remove this dependence while maintaining correct program execution.

Flow dependences are the result of a producer and consumer relationship between two instructions. A flow dependence exists between the two only if the first instruction writes to a register from which second one reads. Therefore, to ensure that the second instruction executes correctly (computes its output value using the correct input values), the second instruction must delay its read of the shared register until after the first instruction writes to it. Since flow dependences have to be honored, they are known as "true dependences". Unfortunately, since the value of the producer flows directly to the consumer, the processor cannot execute both instructions in parallel. Instead, the second instruction has to wait for the first to produce its result. Proposing architectural techniques to mitigate the effect of these dependences and/or to completely break them are very common topics in computer architecture research and are discussed in Section 3.3 to Section 4.

The following segment of assembly code gives examples of output, anti, and flow dependences. In particular, an output dependence exists between instructions 1 and 3 (through register r1), an antidependence exists between instructions 1 and 2 (through register r2), and a flow dependence exists between instructions 2 and 3 (through register r2).

```
1. add r1, r2, r3      // r1 = r2 + r3
2. sub r2, r4, r5      // r2 = r4 − r5
3. mult r1, r2, r6     // r1 = r2 * r6
```

The problem with forcing two instructions to execute in a specific order is that it forces the first instruction to finish executing before the second can start or, at the very least, decreases the amount of overlap in the execution of the two instructions, either of which increases the CPI. From a pipeline point of view, dependences prevent two instructions from executing in adjacent stages. Instead, when a dependence exists between two instructions, pipeline "bubbles" (NOP or "no-operation") must be placed between the two instructions. The pipeline has "stalled" when it executes NOPs instead of instructions. Alternatively, instructions without any dependences can be placed between the two instructions.

Finally, it is important to state that data dependences also exist when two instructions are not back-to-back. That is, an output, anti, or flow dependence can exist between two instructions that are separated by several other instructions.

While data dependences are due to the fact that two instructions read from or write to the same register or memory location, control dependences stem from the fact that the target (i.e., the next instruction) of the control (i.e., branch) instruction is unknown until the branch instruction finishes executing. Consequently, the processor cannot fetch and start executing the next instruction in parallel with the branch until after it completes execution. This forces the processor to either fill the pipeline with other instructions or with NOPs.

When a pair of dependent instructions are in the pipeline together, the dependence between the two instructions can cause a hazard. In other words, the dependence between instructions evolves from being a potential problem to an actual one, i.e., incorrect program execution.

3.3. Multiple Instruction Issue and Execution: SuperScalar and VLIW Processors

Although pipelining can dramatically improve the processor's performance, a hazard between any pair of instructions can dramatically degrade a processor's performance, since the processor has to stall the pipeline until the first instruction either reads its input value from, or writes its output value to, the shared register or memory location. Although this ensures correct program execution, not only does this increase the average CPI, it also has the effect of preventing instructions that are not dependent on the first instruction from being fetched and/or executed. Therefore, to avoid this problem, higher performance processors have the capability of fetching and executing multiple instructions in the same cycle to avoid being stalled by a single data dependence. This allows the processor to extract parallelism in another "dimension" to further improve upon the base processor's performance. Since these types of processors can issue and subsequently execute multiple instructions in the same cycle, these processors are typically called *n*-way issue processors (e.g., 4-way issue, 8-way issue, etc.).

To clarify, pipelining reduces a program's execution time by allowing one instruction to start executing in every cycle. A multiple issue processor, on the other hand, further reduces the program's execution time by allowing multiple instructions to start executing in every cycle. In other words, a multiple issue processor duplicates the pipeline such that multiple pipelines operate in parallel.

To support the simultaneous issue and execution of multiple instructions, several changes and additions need to be made. First, hardware structures like the register file need to be multiported so that multiple instructions can read from and write to them. Second, the buses between hardware components need to be widened to accommodate the flow of additional instructions. Third, additional hardware needs to be added to ensure that the processor can operate at peak efficiency or will operate correctly. An example of the former is the register renaming hardware. Since output and antidependences can be removed by simply renaming the shared register, the processor temporarily retargets the second instruction to write to another temporary register. In this way, the first instruction is able to read from or write to the shared register without the possibility of a premature write from the second instruction.

The reorder buffer (ROB) is an example of a component that is added to the processor to ensure that the processor executes the program correctly. Since multiple instructions begin executing every cycle and since a multiple-issue processor is pipelined, in any given cycle, there are several instructions that are currently executing. Since some instructions may finish executing before a preceding instruction, the processor needs to ensure that those instructions do not write their values to the register file or to memory, since they could be overwritten by what should be a preceding instruction. To store output values that are not yet ready to be written to the register file or memory, the processor uses a ROB. This hardware structure holds the results of instructions until each instruction is ready to write its value to the register file or memory in the correct order.

Computer architects classify current-generation processors into one of two groups: superscalar processors and very-long instruction word (VLIW) processors. Both of these processors use pipelining and multiple instruction issue and execution to increase the amount of parallelism. The difference between the two is in how the instructions are scheduled, that is, the order in which the instructions are to be executed. In a VLIW processor, the compiler schedules the order in which instructions will execute based on several factors, including any data and control dependences between instructions, the number and type of available functional units, and the expected execution latency of each instruction. After determining a set of instructions that meets the compiler's scheduling criteria, the compiler groups these instructions together to form a superinstruction, the very-long instruction word. Since the compiler has already determined that each group of instructions is free of any dependences within the group, each bundle of instructions can be fetched, executed, and retired (finished) together.

Use of the compiler to perform the instruction scheduling reduces the complexity of the hardware, since there is no need for complex scheduling logic, which could decrease the hardware's speed. Furthermore, since the compiler determines the instruction execution schedule at compile time, the potential exists for the compiler to construct a better schedule than would be possible by using only hardware. The compiler has the advantage of having more time than the hardware does when trying to determine an optimal schedule, and the compiler can examine more instructions at a time. However, the big problem with static (i.e., compiler-determined) instruction scheduling is that run-time information, such as the program's inputs, is not available. Not having the actual inputs of the program available to the compiler can significantly limit the compiler's ability to statically schedule a program.

By contrast, a superscalar processor dynamically, i.e., at run-time, determines the order of execution for the program's instructions. More specifically, after the instructions are decoded, the processor examines the decoded instructions to determine which ones are ready for execution. (An instruction is ready to be executed after it has received its input operands. An instruction that is not ready for execution must wait for its producer instruction(s) to compute the corresponding input value(s).) Depending on the issue policy, the issue logic in the processor then selects a subset of the ready instructions and issues (sends) them to the functional units for execution. If the processor has an *in-order* issue policy, the processor issues only ready instructions from the oldest unissued instruction up to the first nonready instruction. If the oldest unissued instruction is not ready, then no instructions are issued in that cycle. By contrast, if the processor has an *out-of-order* issue policy, it issues as many ready instructions as possible, up to the issue width limit. Therefore, in the event that there are several ready instructions after the first nonready one, an out-of-order processor is able to issue those instructions out of program order, bypassing the nonready instruction to issue as many ready instructions as possible. Since ready instructions do not need to wait for older, unready instructions, out-of-order issue can yield significant performance improvements as compared with in-order issue.

On the other hand, the advantage that in-order processors have over out-of-order ones is simpler hardware design. Since the processor only checks the oldest few instructions, instead of all unissued instructions, less complex hardware is needed to issue the instructions. The trade-off is that ready instructions younger than the first nonready one cannot be issued that cycle. Consequently, a single nonready instruction blocks further instruction issue, which slows down the instruction execution rate. Although the out-of-order processor is able to issue any instructions that are ready, the issue logic hardware is much more complex, since the processor needs to examine all unissued instructions to find the maximum number of ready instructions that can be issued that cycle. This requirement obviously increases the complexity of the issue logic.

In summary, the fundamental difference between VLIW and superscalar processors is when the actual order in which the instructions are executed is determined – either statically at compile-time or dynamically at run-time.

3.4   The Memory Gap and MultiLevel Caches

One of biggest problems facing computer architects, now and in the future, is the "memory gap." The origin of this problem is that the speed of processors is increasing faster than the speed of memory is increasing. Therefore, as processor clock frequencies increase, the number of *cycles* required to access memory also increases. Since it may take a few hundred cycles to retrieve the data for a load instruction, the processor will eventually stop issuing any more instructions, since it cannot find more ready ones. Shortly after the processor stops issuing instructions, the processor finishes executing the last few issued instructions, and further instruction execution stops completely. Therefore, until memory returns the value of the load instruction, the processor is completely idle. For multiway issue processors, this phenomenon is especially problematic, since the processor cannot execute any more instructions for several hundred cycles while it is waiting for the results of a load instruction. Instead of executing *n* instructions per cycle, where *n* is the maximum issue width, for a few hundred cycles, the processor stalls, i.e., "instruction slots" are wasted. Obviously, if the processor has to stall frequently to wait for memory accesses, the execution time of the program will be much higher than if the processor did not have to wait for memory accesses. To further exacerbate this problem, in addition to the increasing memory gap, the issue width of processors is also increasing. This means that even more instruction slots will be wasted in the future as the gap between processor and memory speeds increases.

To combat this problem, computer architects add small, fast memory structures called *caches* between the processor and memory (RAM). Caches exploit *spatial and temporal locality* to improve the performance of the memory hierarchy. Due to spatial locality, the next memory reference is likely to access an address that is close, physically, to the last one. Due to temporal locality, the next memory reference is likely to access an address that was recently accessed. The memory references of typical applications exhibit both kinds of locality due to the use of loops and the linearly increasing value of the PC. Thus, to improve the performance of the memory hierarchy, caches store data around the most recently accessed addresses.

When the program begins execution, the cache is said to be "cold," or completely empty. As the processor requests data from different addresses, the cache stores the values at those addresses and nearby addresses. When the cache becomes full, selected entries in the cache are overwritten based on the organization of the cache and its replacement policy. When the processor requests the value for a memory address that is already in the cache, the cache can send the value to the processor, instead of forcing the processor to retrieve the value from main memory. This situation is referred to as a *cache hit*. The opposite situation is referred to as a *cache miss*. Since the latency of a cache hit is much lower than the latency for a memory access, the number of cycles needed to retrieve the value for that address will be much lower. Then, if a significant percentage of the memory accesses are cache hits, the average number of cycles needed for memory accesses – and, subsequently, the total program execution time – will be much lower. Generally, as the cache hit rate increases, the number of cycles required for a memory access decreases.

To balance the cost and performance benefits of cache memories, computer architects use multiple levels of cache. The level-1 (L1) cache, the level of cache closest to the processor, is the smallest but also the fastest. Since a cache exploits spatial and temporal locality, a small cache can still have a high cache hit rate but a low hit latency. A cache with a low hit latency but a high hit rate minimizes the memory access time. Due to the stored program concept, instructions are stored and fetched from memory. However, since the memory access patterns of instructions and data are very different, the L1 cache is usually split into two L1 caches, one for instructions and one for data, to further improve the cache hit rate. Each level of cache, L2, L3, etc., between the L1 cache and main memory is larger and can hold more data, but is slower. Each level of cache services the memory accesses that were missed in the caches between that cache and the processor, albeit with a higher access time.

To illustrate how multilevel caches can decrease the average latency of memory access, first assume that the memory hierarchy consists of an L1 data cache, a combined L2 cache, and main memory, which have hit latencies of 2, 10, and 150 cycles, respectively. Also assume that the hit rate for L1 is 80% and for L2 is 90%, while the hit rate for main memory is 100%. Then, for 1000 load instructions, 800 (1000 * 0.80) are L1 hits, 180 (200 * 0.90) are L2 hits, and the remaining 20 are memory hits. The average latency for these load instructions is (see Eq. 4):

$$\text{Average Latency} = [(800 * 2) + (180 * 10) + (20 * 150)]/1000$$
$$= 6400 / 1000 = 6.4 \text{ cycles} \qquad (4)$$

By comparison, without the L1 and L2 caches, the average memory latency of these 1000 load instruction is 150 cycles (the access time of main memory), which will substantially increase the CPI. Therefore, as this example shows, by adding some small, fast caches to exploit spatial and temporal locality, computer architects are able to dramatically improve the performance of the memory subsystem.

3.5   Policies and Additions for High-Performance Memory

To further improve the performance of the memory hierarchy, computer architects have implemented two policies into the memory hierarchy and its interface with the processor core. The first policy, *load bypassing*, allows load instructions to bypass preceding store instructions in the order in which load and store instructions are issued to the memory hierarchy [11]. Since load instructions retrieve values from memory that are needed by the processor for further computations, decreasing the latency of load instructions has a larger effect on the program's execution time than does decreasing the latency of the store instructions. One way to decrease the effective latency of a load instruction is to issue it sooner than otherwise would normally occur. The one caveat to this policy is that the addresses for all store instructions preceding this load must be known, i.e., calculated, before the load is allowed to access the memory hierarchy. The reason for this is that a preceding store instruction may write to the same memory location as the load. If the load is allowed to skip ahead of a store that writes to the same memory location from which the load reads, then the load will retrieve the wrong value from memory since the store did not first write its value. If the address of the load differs from the address(es) of all of the preceding stores, then load is allowed to skip ahead of those stores.

A more aggressive version of this policy allows the load to access memory even when the addresses for all preceding store instructions are not known. This version defers the address check until after the load retrieves its value from memory. If none of the addresses of the preceding stores matches the address of the load, then the load forwards its value to the processor core. If the address of a preceding store matches the address of the load, the load discards its value. In the former case, the load instruction retrieves its value from memory a few cycles earlier than it could have if it waited for the address calculation of the preceding store instructions.

In the following example, instruction 3 can execute can before instructions 1 and 2, since the memory address of instruction 3 (A) differs from the addresses for instructions 1 and 2 (B and C). However, instruction 4 can bypass only instruction 2, since its address (B) matches the memory address of instruction 1.

1. st B, r1   // B = R1
2. st C, r2   // C = r2
3. ld A, r3   // r3 = A
4. ld B, r4   // r4 = B

When the address of the load matches the address of a preceding store – as is the case for instructions 1 and 4 – and if both addresses have been computed, then *load forwarding* can be used to improve the processor's performance [9]. With load forwarding, the value of the store is directly sent to the load. In the event that two preceding stores write the same address, the load instruction receives its value from the second store. Sending the results of the store to the load directly has three benefits. First, it allows to the load to execute before the store, even though the store precedes the load and accesses the same address. Second, since the load obtains its value directly from the store instruction, it does not have to wait until the store instruction has first written its value to memory before accessing the memory hierarchy to retrieve that value. Finally, since the load instruction does not need to access memory, the amount of traffic within the memory hierarchy is reduced.

In addition to the cache size, the other factor that affects the cache hit rate is its associativity. The associativity can be defined as the number of cache entries where a specific memory address can be stored. In a direct-mapped cache, each memory address can only be stored in one cache entry. On the other hand, in a fully associative cache, any memory address can go in any of the cache entries. Since many addresses map to the same cache entries, increasing the associativity increases the number of locations in which the data for a memory address can be stored, which decreases the likelihood that that memory address will be overwritten when the cache is full. Two issues limit the degree of associativity. First, increasing the cache's associativity requires additional hardware for comparators and multiplexors, although the capacity of the cache, as measured in bytes, does not increase. Second, due to this additional hardware, the access time of highly associative caches is higher than caches with the same capacity but a lower degree of associativity.

One very simple, yet highly effective, way of effectively increasing the cache's associativity is to use a *victim cache* [3]. A victim cache is a small, fully associative cache that stores cache blocks that are evicted from the L1 data cache. A cache block is a group of consecutive memory addresses that are moved in and out of the cache together. Cache blocks are evicted from the cache whenever empty entries in which an incoming block can be stored in cannot be found. Whenever a cache evicts a block, the next access to that block will require a higher access latency, since that cache block is present only in a level of cache that is further away from the processor. By contrast, when using a victim cache, evicted cache blocks remain in a level of cache closer to the processor. Although the victim cache is fully associative, its access time is similar to or lower than the access time of the L1 data cache, since it is so small. Use of a victim cache in parallel with the L1 data cache effectively increases the associativity of the L1 data cache since cache blocks can now be stored in the victim cache. Use of a victim cache in combination with the L1 data cache increases the hit rate of caches closest to the processor, which increases the processor's performance.

3.6   Branch Prediction: Speculative Bypass of Control Dependences

As described in Section 3.2, a control dependence stems from the fact that the instruction that should execute after a branch instruction is not known until after the branch has executed. However, waiting to the fetch the next instruction until after the branch has finished executing decreases the instruction throughput through the processor, which in turn increases the execution time of the program. Although the next instruction to follow the branch cannot be known with absolute certainty before the branch has started to execute, while the processor is waiting for the branch instruction to execute, the processor can predict the address of the branch target, i.e., the next instruction to execute, speculatively execute that instruction and the ones that follow it, and then verify whether the prediction was correct after branch finishes executing.

The processor component that makes predictions on the branch direction and target is the *branch predictor*. When the prediction is correct, the processor has successfully guessed which instructions will execute next and, consequently, the instructions that the processor had previously executed are correct. However, if the processor guesses wrong on which direction the branch will take next, then all the instructions that the processor speculatively executed are also wrong and need to be discarded. To return the processor to the correct state, the instructions that were speculatively executed need to be discarded and removed from the pipeline, and the processor needs to fetch and start executing instructions on the other path. The number of cycles that the processor needs to restore the processor state is known as the *branch misprediction penalty*. During this time, the processor is idle and not executing any instructions, which decreases the processor's performance. To maximize the performance of the processor, computer architects attempt to minimize the branch prediction penalty.

Two other key issues affect the processor's performance when using branch prediction. First, the number of stages in the pipeline affects how many cycles elapse before the branch predictor can verify the accuracy of the prediction. To verify the accuracy of the branch prediction, the branch predictor compares the result of the branch with the prediction. However, the longer the pipeline, the more cycles it takes for the processor to compute the result of the branch for verification—and the more cycles it takes for the processor to verify the prediction, the more cycles the processor spends executing instructions that will never be used. Since the number of stages in the pipeline directly affects the number of cycles that are needed to execute the branch, the number of stages consequently affects the processor's performance as it relates to branch prediction.

Second, the other issue is the branch prediction accuracy. The branch prediction accuracy is defined as the number of correct predictions divided by the total number of predictions. Since the length of the processor's pipeline and the branch misprediction penalty apply only when the branch predictor makes a misprediction, maximizing the number of correct predictions limits the performance degradation due to these two factors. Therefore, computer architects attempt to maximize the branch prediction accuracy.

Branch predictors consist of three main components: the branch history table (BHT), the branch target buffer (BTB), and some logic. The BHT is an on-chip table that stores the last n-directions for a few thousand branches. In the fetch stage, when a branch instruction is fetched from memory, the processor uses the branch's PC as an index into the BHT. The branch logic uses its algorithm and the branch's recent history to make a prediction as to whether the branch is taken or not. If the branch predictor predicts that the branch is not taken, then the next instruction that the processor will execute is the instruction that immediately follows the branch. If the branch predictor predicts that the branch is taken, then the branch logic uses the PC to access the BTB to quickly determine the address of the next instruction that is to be executed so that instruction can be fetched from memory. The BTB is a table that stores the addresses of recently-taken branch targets. Use of a BTB allows the processor to immediately start fetching the instruction at the predicted branch target instead of waiting for that address to be computed. After the branch executes, the processor updates the BHT with the direction of the branch and the BTB, if the branch is taken.

It is important to note that since the BHT is much smaller than the maximum number of entries that a PC could index, only a few bits from the least significant end of the PC are used to index the BHT; the remaining more significant bits are ignored. Consequently, since the entire PC is not needed to access the BHT, multiple branch instructions that have the same bit pattern for the BHT index will map to the same BHT entry. This situation is known as *aliasing*, and it can affect the branch predictor's accuracy since the branch history for another branch could be used to make predictions for the current branch instruction instead of its own history.

One simple branch predictor makes its predictions based on the last direction that is stored in the BHT for that branch, or another branch in the event of aliasing. If the last direction that the branch took was taken, then the branch predictor predicts that the branch will be taken again. The opposite prediction occurs when the branch was most recently not taken. After the branch executes, the BHT stores the direction that the branch actually took. Since only one bit is needed to store whether this branch was taken or not, this predictor is known as a one-bit predictor. While this branch predictor has the advantage of minimal BHT size and fair branch prediction accuracy, the major problem with it is that it tends to make mispredictions when entering and when leaving a loop.

For example, assume that the processor executes a loop with five iterations. For the first four iterations, the branch is taken; only the last iteration is not taken. Since the one-bit predictor immediately writes the most recent direction into the BHT, when entering the loop, the last direction that is stored in the BHT is not taken. Therefore, the branch predictor will predict "not-taken" for the first iteration when the direction is actually taken. After the first iteration, the BHT stores "taken" as the last direction for that branch and is subsequently able to make three correct predictions in a row for the next three iterations. However, for the fifth iteration, the branch predictor predicts "taken" when the branch is actually not taken. This results in another misprediction, and the branch predictor stores "not-taken" into the BHT, which will cause yet another misprediction when the branch executes the next time. This results in a 60% prediction accuracy due to mispredictions for the first and fifth iterations.

To solve this problem, a two-bit branch predictor can be used. The difference between the one-bit and the two-bit branch predictors is that the one-bit predictor changes its prediction in response to a single misprediction while the two-bit predictor requires two mispredictions to change its prediction. In the above example, the two-bit predictor would accurately predict the branch's direction for the first four iterations, making a misprediction only for the last iteration. Therefore, in this example, although the two-bit predictor requires twice the number of history bits in the BHT, it results in an 80% prediction accuracy, which is a very significant difference.

Other than one- and two-bit predictors, computer architects have proposed several other branch predictors to achieve higher branch prediction accuracies. One- and two-bit branch predictors are fairly accurate for floating-point programs where the branch behavior is relatively well behaved. But for integer programs, where the branch behavior is less well behaved, one- and two-bit branch predictors do not account for the effect that other branch instructions may have on the direction that the current branch will take and consequently have poor branch prediction accuracy.

In contrast, correlating and two-level predictors use the history of the most recently executed branch instructions to make a prediction. While there are several flavors and varieties of each, the basic operation for these two predictors is relatively similar. These branch predictors use a bit pattern that represents the taken/not-taken behavior of several recent branches as an index into a table of one- or two-bit prediction counters [10]. To store the direction of each of the m most recently executed branch instructions, these branch predictors use an m-bit shift register known as the *branch history register* (BHR). After a branch instruction finishes executing, BHR shifts the bits such that the oldest branch is overwritten and the youngest is stored on the other end of the shift register. The m-bits of the BHR are then used to index the *pattern history table* (PHT) that has 2^m entries. Each entry of the PHT is a one- or two-bit predictor that ultimately makes the branch prediction. It is important to note that basic versions of these predictors do not use the PC of the branch instruction, which may lead to aliasing in the PHT. To reduce the chance of deconstructive aliasing, variants of these predictors use at least part of the PC to index the PHT.

In summary, the basic assumption for these predictors is that whenever a series of branch instructions has the same history as another series, then the direction of the current branch can be predicted based on past behavior of the branch that followed each series of branch instructions.

After a processor jumps to and finishes executing a subroutine, it needs to return to the point in the program that called the subroutine. To accomplish this, the processor could use the PC of the branch instruction, which corresponds to the subroutine return, to access the BTB to determine what the next instruction is. The problem with this solution is that the subroutine could be called from several places in the program and that the calls may be interleaved. Therefore, the target (return) address could constantly change, depending on which place in the program called the subroutine. To avoid interrupting the instruction fetch process, computer architects have designed the *return address stack* (RAS) to store the address of the target instruction [4]. When a subroutine is called, the processor pushes the return address onto the RAS. If that subroutine calls another subroutine, or itself, another return address is pushed onto the stack. Then, when each subroutine has finished executing, the processor simply pops each return address off the RAS and resumes fetching instructions starting at the return address.

3.7   Branch Predication: Non-Speculative Bypass of Control Dependences

Although recently proposed and implemented branch predictors have become very complex – and accordingly require a large amount of chip area and dissipate a large amount of power – the control-flow of some branch instructions is so complex that they are hard to predict very accurately. To achieve higher branch prediction accuracy, which subsequently results in significantly higher processor performance, it is very important to accurately predict the direction of these difficult-to-predict branches. For reasons described above, difficult-to-predict branches severely degrade performance, since they interrupt the instruction fetch stream and since misprediction recovery requires several clock cycles.

One solution to this problem, called *branch predication*, is to simply fetch and execute instructions down both directions of the branch [7]. After the branch executes, the correct direction is known and instructions down the correct path are saved while instructions down the wrong path are ignored and discarded. To accomplish this, the branch instruction is converted to a compare instruction where the result of the compare is written to a *predicate register*. A predicate register is added as an input operand to each instruction down one path; instructions down the other path are assigned another predicate register. The value of the predicate register indicates whether the branch instruction was taken or not and subsequently whether the output values of that instruction should be saved or not. When the predicate register is set to zero, all instructions that have that predicate register as an input operand are discarded; meanwhile, the value of the predicate register for the instructions on the other path is 1. When the predicate register is set to 1, the instructions that use that predicate register are saved and eventually write their output values to the register file.

Since the processor executes instructions on both branch paths, the processor effectively predicts the direction of the branch with 100% accuracy. Therefore, why should branch predication not be applied to all branch instructions to achieve a 100% prediction accuracy? First, the cost of branch predication is that the processor must devote resources to executing some instructions that will be discarded. Therefore, the processor's execution rate is lower when the branch direction is unknown than after the branch direction has been resolved. Second, applying branch predication to all branch instructions means that even highly predictable branch instructions will be converted. This means that instead of making a high-accuracy prediction and then maximizing the rate of execution along that path, the processor sacrifices that high rate of execution for a much lower one to achieve a slight improvement in the branch prediction accuracy. Therefore, to maximize performance, branch predication should be applied only to difficult-to-predict branches.

In 2000, Intel began to ship the production version of the Itanium processor. One of the most notable features of this processor was its implementation of branch predication. Although initial academic studies suggested performance improvements of 30% or more, the performance improvement due to branch predication was a modest 2% [2]. Two key reasons were given to account for this discrepancy. First, there were several differences in the production and academic versions of the compiler and the hardware. One key difference was in the level of detail between the academic and production versions. For instance, the academic studies did not account for the effect of the operating system and factors such as the effects of cache contention and pipeline flushes. These relatively small differences tend to reduce the performance of the real machine. Second, the benchmarks that were used to generate each set of performance results differed. In the benchmark suite that was used on the production hardware, branch execution latency and the misprediction penalty accounted for a smaller percentage of the program's execution time than in the benchmark suite for the academic studies. Despite these differences and the difference in the performance results, the authors of [2] state that as the Itanium processor and its compiler mature, the performance impact of branch predication will increase.

3.8   High Performance Instruction Fetch: The Trace Cache

From a conceptual point of view, the instruction fetch and execute components of the processor exist in a producer-and-consumer relationship. The instruction fetch components, which includes the branch predictor and instruction cache, "produce" instructions by retrieving them from memory and placing them into a buffer known as the instruction fetch queue. The instruction execute components, which include the issue logic and the processor's functional units, "consume" the instructions by executing them and writing their results to the register file and memory. As the issue width increases, the rate at which the processor consumes instructions increases, which increases the processor's performance. However, to maintain the processor's performance as the issue width increases, the instruction fetch components need to produce the instructions at a similarly high rate or the processor's performance will suffer.

The problem with conventional instruction fetch mechanisms is that they can only fetch a single cache block from memory per cycle if the cache block contains a branch instruction that is predicted to be taken. When a cache block does not contain any branch instructions or when it contains a branch instruction that is predicted to be not taken, the next cache block is fetched next from memory. However, if the cache block has a branch instruction that is predicted to be taken, then the processor cannot fetch any more cache blocks until after the next block is brought into the processor. This severely limits the rate at which instructions can be fetched.

One solution to this problem is the *trace cache* [8]. The trace cache stores a trace of instructions that were previously executed together consecutively. Accordingly, the trace cache implicitly contains the record of which direction each branch instruction in the trace took. The trace cache is accessed in parallel with the L1 instruction cache, using the PC for the next instruction. When the processor finds a matching trace – one that has a matching set of predicted branch directions – in the trace cache, instructions are retrieved from the trace cache instead of from the L1 instruction cache. Otherwise, the processor fetches instructions from the instruction cache.

The advantage of using a trace cache is that by organizing the instructions into a trace, the instructions from multiple taken branches can be fetched from memory together in a single cycle. This gives the instruction fetch components the potential to meet the execution core's consumption rate. The disadvantage is that the processor designers must devote a substantial amount of chip area to the trace cache.

3.9   Value Prediction: Speculative Bypass of Data Dependences

As described in Section 3.2, in addition to control dependences, data dependences – register or memory dependences between instructions – also can severely degrade the processor's performance. The counterpart to branch prediction (speculative bypass of control dependences) is *value prediction*, which exploits *value locality* to improve the processor's performance.

Value locality is the "likelihood of the recurrence of a previously seen value within a storage location" in a processor [6]. In other words, value locality is the probability that an instruction produces the same output value.

Value prediction is a microarchitectural technique that exploits value locality. Based on the past values for an instruction, the value prediction hardware predicts what the output value could be. After predicting the output value, the processor forwards that predicted value to any dependent instructions – instructions that need that value as an input operand – and then speculatively executes those dependent instructions based on the predicted value. To verify the prediction, the processor executes the predicted instruction normally. If the prediction is correct, the processor resumes normal execution and can write the values of the speculatively executed instructions to the register file and memory. If the prediction is incorrect, then all the dependent instructions need to be reexecuted with the correct value.

It is important to realize that without value locality, value prediction would not be able to improve the processor's performance, since it would be virtually impossible to accurately choose the correct value for an instruction from 2^m different values, where m is the number of bits in each number (typically 32 or 64).

Last-value prediction is the simplest version of value prediction. Last-value prediction stores the last output value of each instruction into the value prediction table. Upon encountering the next instance of that instruction, the processor uses the last output value as the predicted value. For example, if a particular add instruction computed the output value of 2 last time, then when that add instruction next executes, the last value predictor predicts that the add will again produce an output value of 2.

While last-value prediction can yield reasonably high prediction accuracies for some instructions, its accuracy is very poor when it tries to predict the values of computations such as incrementing the loop index variable. Therefore, to improve the prediction accuracy of last-value prediction for these and similar computations, computer architects have proposed the stride-value value predictor. For this predictor, the predicted value is simply the sum of the last output value for that instruction and the stride, which is the difference of the last two output values. For instance, when the output value history for an instruction is 1, 2, 3, 4, 5, etc., the stride value predictor will predict that the next output values will be 6, 7, 8, etc. Note that when the stride value equals zero, the stride value predictor functions as a last-value predictor.

Although stride-value prediction has a higher prediction accuracy than last-value prediction, the two predictors are fundamentally the same. Consequently, for more complex output value patterns such as 1, 4, 7, 9, 1, 4, 7, 9, ... 1, 4, 7, 9, etc., both value predictors have very poor performance. One value predictor that can accurately predict this irregular pattern is the finite-context method predictor. This predictor stores the last n output values for an instruction and then uses some additional logic to determine which of those n values should be used as the predicted value.

In summary, value prediction improves the processor's performance by allowing it to execute instructions earlier than would otherwise be possible, if the prediction is correct. This potential performance gain comes at the cost of prediction verification and a potentially very large value prediction table.

3.10 Value Reuse: Nonspeculative Bypass of Data Dependences

During the course of a program's execution, a processor executes many redundant computations. A redundant computation is one that the processor had performed earlier in the program. Any and all computations can be redundant. It is important to note that an optimizing compiler may not be able to remove these redundant computations during the compilation process, since the actual input operand values may be unknown at compile time – possibly because they depend on the inputs to the program.

Redundant computations affect the program's execution time in two ways. First of all, executing the instructions for redundant computations increases the program's dynamic instruction count. Secondly, these redundant computations affect the average CPI, since they produce the values for other instructions in the program (a flow dependence exists between these instructions and others). Unfortunately, while redundant, these computations need to be executed to ensure correct program operation. Consequently, the hardware cannot simply disregard these computations.

Value reuse is a microarchitectural technique that improves the processor's performance by dynamically removing redundant computations from the processor's pipeline [12]. During the program's execution, the value reuse hardware compares the opcode and input operand values of the current instruction against the opcodes and input operand values of all recently executed instructions, which are stored in the value reuse table (VRT). If there is a match between the opcodes and input operand values, then the current instruction is a redundant computation and, instead of continuing its execution, the current instruction gets its output value from the result stored in the VRT. On the other hand, if the current instruction's opcode and input operand values do not match those found in the VRT, then the instruction is not a recent redundant computation and it executes as it normally would. After finishing the execution for each instruction, the value reuse hardware stores the opcode, input operand values, and output value for that instruction into the VRT. Value reuse can be applied at the level of individual instructions or to larger units, such as basic blocks [5].

The key difference between value prediction and value reuse is that value prediction is speculative whereas value reuse is nonspeculative. Consequently, the predictions of the value predictor must be verified with the actual result of the predicted instruction, and recovery must be initiated if the prediction is wrong. By contrast, since the computation and inputs are known, the results for value reuse are nonspeculative and do not need to be verified, since they cannot be wrong.

While value reuse is able, through table lookups, to generate the output value of an instruction sooner than would otherwise be possible, two key problems limit its performance. First, to ensure that multiple instructions can access and retrieve their output values from the VRT within one or two cycles, the number of entries in the VRT has to be relatively low. Therefore, the VRT can only hold a small number of redundant computations. The second problem is that since VRT is finite in size and since it constantly stores the inputs and outputs of the most recently executed instructions, the VRT may eventually become filled with computations that are not very redundant. Therefore, instead of storing the redundant computations that are very frequently executed, which account for a large fraction of the program's execution time, the VRT may store redundant computations that are relatively infrequently executed and that have very little impact on the program's execution time.

3.11   Prefetching

As described in Section 3.4, the performance of the memory hierarchy is the result of two factors: the hit latency of the caches (or memory) and the hit rate of the caches. Since the hit latency is determined by how the cache is implemented, its size, associativity, and location (on-chip or off-chip), computer architects can only improve the hit rate to decrease the memory access time of load instructions. One such approach is a mechanism called *prefetching* [15].

What prefetching attempts to do is to retrieve a cache block of instructions or data from memory and put that block into the cache before the processor requests those instructions or data from memory, i.e., needs to use them. For prefetching to significantly improve the performance of the memory hierarchy, a prefetching algorithm needs to do two things. First, it needs to predict those address(es) for which the processor will access memory. Due to very complex memory access patterns that are prevalent in nonscientific applications, accurate prediction of which address(es) will be needed in the near future is very difficult. Second, for prefetching to be most effective, the prefetching algorithm needs to place the block of memory into the cache before the processor requests those instructions or data. However, due to wide-issue processors and very long memory latencies that are only getting longer, the prefetch algorithm must determine which block of memory to retrieve several hundred cycles or more before the processor actually makes that request. On the other hand, bringing the desired memory block into the cache far before it is needed may result in that memory block being replaced by another, higher-priority memory block. Therefore, the timeliness aspect of prefetching really means that the prefetched block needs to be brought into the cache as close as possible to when the processor will consume those values. Bringing that block into the cache too early or too late may not significantly improve the processor's performance.

Prefetch algorithms can be initiated either solely by hardware or with some assistance from the compiler. In the former case, the prefetching algorithm is completely implemented in the hardware. As a result, the hardware determines which addresses to prefetch and at what time. In the latter case, the compiler inserts prefetch instructions into the assembly code. Those instructions tell the hardware prefetch mechanism when to prefetch and for what to address to prefetch. For software prefetching, the compiler analyzes the assembly code to determine which load instructions will seriously degrade the processor's performance. For those instructions, the compiler then inserts the necessary prefetch instructions into the code at a point that it determines is sufficiently far away from the point in time when the processor will actually use that value.

One very well-known prefetching technique is *next-line prefetching*. When using next-line prefetching, after a cache miss, in addition to fetching the cache block that contains the address that caused the cache miss, the processor also fetches the next sequential cache block and places that block in a prefetch buffer, which is a small, fully associative cache. By fetching the next cache block, this prefetching algorithm is counting on the program to exhibit spatial locality and on addresses in the next cache block to be requested soon. Storing the prefetched cache block in a prefetch buffer reduces the amount of cache pollution, which is caused by bringing in blocks that will not be used before they are evicted or evicting blocks that will be used in the near future.

Finally, due to the increasing memory gap, designing and implementing more effective prefetching algorithms remains a very active area of research in computer architecture.

4 MULTITHREADED ARCHITECTURES: NEXT-GENERATION MULTIPROCESSOR MACHINES

4.1 Speculative Multithreaded Processors

Scientists and engineers, in an effort to decrease the execution time of their programs, commonly run their programs on multiprocessor systems. Ideally, after parallelizing the code, each processor can execute its portion of the program without having to wait for other processors to catch up or to produce values for it. A deeply nested loop, where each loop iteration does not depend on the value of a previous loop iteration, is ideal for parallelization, since it does not contain any cross-iteration dependences. While this situation is common for scientific floating-point applications, the loops in integer (nonscientific) programs typically have cross-iteration data dependences that make them very difficult to run on a multiprocessor system. These data dependences force the other processors in the system to stall until the processor running that previous loop iteration generates the needed value.

To address this issue, computer architects have proposed *speculative multi-threaded processors* as a potential solution to allow integer programs to efficiently run on multiprocessor systems. A representative example of a speculative multi-threaded processor is the Superthreaded Architecture (STA) [13]. In the STA, the compiler analyzes the program to determine which loops can be efficiently parallelized to decrease the overall program execution time. Since, at compile time, the compiler may not be able to determine whether a potential cross-iteration dependence will actually be one at run-time, the compiler flags that address. To ensure that those addresses that the compiler has flagged are handled properly at run-time, the STA uses an on-chip buffer called the *memory buffer*.

Other than the memory buffer, the only other additions to the base processor, which can either be an "off-the-shelf" superscalar or VLIW processor, are a little additional logic for interprocessor communication and for processor execution synchronization. Each processor is connected to two other processors via a uni-directional ring. As with typical multiprocessor systems, each processor has its own private L1 data cache but shares the L2 cache with the other processors. The memory buffer is a private cache.

When a program begins executing on the STA, only one processor is active; the remaining processors are idle, waiting for the program to reach a loop (parallel region). The start of the parallel region is denoted by a special instruction. After the active processor executes that special instruction, it forks off the next processor in the unidirectional ring and begins execution of its iteration in the parallel region. Meanwhile, the next processor copies the set of values that are needed for parallel execution and then forks off its own processor. This process repeats itself until all processors are executing an iteration of the loop.

When each processor in the system begins parallel execution, the processor allocates space in the memory buffer for each potential cross-iteration dependence that the compiler flagged. When a load instruction accesses the memory hierarchy, the memory buffer and L1 data cache are accessed in parallel, although the data can be present only in one structure. When the address for the load instruction is found in the L1 data cache, the processor continues execution as normal. However, when address is found in the memory buffer, the processor needs to wait until either another processor generates that value or another processor updates it, if the value is not already there. On the other hand, when a processor generates a value for an address that is found in the memory buffer, the processor forwards that value across the unidirectional ring to the other processors. Therefore, by using the compiler to flag potential cross-iteration dependences, the memory buffer to track and update the status of those dependences, and the unidirectional ring to pass values from processor to processor, the

STA architecture is able to parallelize and efficiently run programs that have cross-iterations dependences.

When a processor finishes its iteration, it checks to see if all processors that are executing a previous iteration are finished. If not, the processor stalls until they are finished. If so, then the processor writes its values back to memory. After a processor writes its values to memory, the state of memory is the same as if this iteration just finished executing on a uni-processor.

Finally, since there are an indeterminate number of iterations for some loops, it is not known until run-time which processor will be the one to execute the last iteration. To maintain high performance given this uncertainty, each processor keeps forking off another processor as if no uncertainty exists. When the processor that executes the last iteration detects that it is the last iteration, it kills all successor iterations running on the "downstream" processors. That processor then starts executing another sequential region of code while all other processors are idle. This cycle of sequential and parallel execution continues until the program is finished.

In conclusion, speculative multithreaded processors, such as the Superthreaded Architecture, allow multiprocessor systems to efficiently execute programs with many cross-iteration data dependences. To accomplish this, hardware like the memory buffer is added to the base processor to ensure that potential cross-iteration dependences are handled correctly.

4.2   Simultaneous Multithreading

When multiple programs are running on the same uniprocessor system, the operating system allows each program to execute for a certain amount of time before swapping that program out for another one. Before the next program can start running, the processor state of the current program must be saved to memory. Then after the processor state of the next program is loaded into the processor, the next program can begin executing. Obviously, repeated storage and loading of the processor state of each program adds extra overhead to the time it takes to execute both programs. On the other hand, running more than one program at a time may allow the processor the hide the latency of cache misses by running another program while the memory hierarchy services the cache miss.

Some operating systems and processors switch programs only when there are caches misses. This allows one program to efficiently execute the low latency parts of the code and then allows another program to run while high latency parts of the code are being serviced. Although this setup allows the execution of two programs to overlap, it still incurs the cost of saving and loading the processor state.

A hardware improvement on this approach is *simultaneous multithreading* [14]. A simultaneous multithreading (SMT) processor allows two or more programs, or threads, to simultaneously execute on the same processor. Therefore, instead of fetching only the instructions for a single program, an SMT processor fetches the instructions for multiple programs at the same time. Instead of decoding and issuing instructions from a single program, an SMT processor decodes, issues, and executes the instructions for multiple programs. Finally, instead of writing the results for a single program to the register file, an SMT processor writes the result of each program to its own register file to maintain proper program execution semantics. An SMT processor also replicates other base processor resources to support multiple hardware-based program threads.

Suppose that eight programs are running on a SMT processor. Of those eight programs, only two are active at any given time. To execute both programs, the SMT processor first needs to fetch instructions for both programs at the same time. After fetching instructions from both programs, the instructions execute on the processor as would the instructions for a single program, with the obvious exception that instructions for one program do not use the results from the other. Whenever a load instruction experiences a cache miss, the SMT processor stops fetching instructions for that program and starts fetching and executing the instructions for another program. Use of a round-robin fetch policy ensures that progress is made in executing each program.

It is important to note that the start-to-finish time of any one program running on an SMT processor will be longer than the start-to-finish time of the same program running on a conventional uniprocessor of similar resources, since the other programs compete for the processor's resources. However, the SMT processor is able to decrease the overall execution time of all n programs by executing them in parallel at a fine-grain level as opposed to executing them serially on the conventional uniprocessor machine.

SMT processors are able to decrease the execution time of multiple programs for three reasons. First, by allowing instructions from multiple instructions to execute simultaneously, the SMT processor can find more instructions that are ready to issue, since dependences, both control and data, do not exist between the instructions of two different programs. As a result, the SMT processor can reduce the average CPI across all programs. Second, by supporting multiple program execution at a very fine-grain level, the SMT processor is able to avoid the cost of storing and loading the processor state. Third, by swapping out each program after it incurs a cache miss, the SMT processor is able to hide the memory latency of a load instruction in one program by executing instructions in another program.

Finally, although their names are similar, simultaneous multithreading and speculative multithreading have several major differences. First, an SMT processor is a single, very wide-issue processor, while a speculative multithreaded processor is a multiprocessor system. Second, SMT processors decrease the overall execution time of multiple programs, while speculative multithreaded processors decrease the execution time of a single program. Given these differences, these two approaches could be combined together to form a multiprocessor system that can quickly execute a single program or multiple programs.

5   CONCLUSION: FUTURE TRENDS AND ISSUES

Over the past few decades, computer architects have improved the performance of processors in one of three ways: increasing the processor's clock frequency, executing multiple instructions simultaneously via pipelining, and executing multiple instructions in parallel via wide-issue processors. Although these approaches have significantly improved the processor's performance, at least two factors limit further performance gains purely by using these techniques.

First, as described in Section 3.4, the disparity in the rates of increase in the processor speed and the memory speed has led to a memory gap that will only widen in the future. To ensure that the processor is able to fetch an adequate number of instructions to feed the execution core and to ensure that data dependences between load instructions and other types of instructions do not become the bottleneck, computer architects need to find additional methods of decreasing the average memory latency. Compounding this problem is that memory bandwidth will increasingly become a limiting factor on any solutions [1]. As a result, instead of trading off memory bandwidth for memory latency, computer architects will need to find other solutions that decrease the average memory latency without dramatically increasing the memory bandwidth requirements. Solutions to this problem may include novel methods of prefetching data and instructions, different cache and memory hierarchy designs, and new technologies that reduce the memory latency.

Another problem that has already become a major one is the power dissipation of modern processors. Microarchitectural techniques such as branch prediction, prefetching, and value prediction are all speculative techniques that rely on predicting in what direction the branch will go, what instructions or data are needed next, and what values a particular instruction will produce, respectively, to improve the processor's performance. Although these techniques are very effective in improving the processor's performance, they also consume a lot of additional energy to do so. The extra energy that these and other speculative techniques consume increases the power consumption, which lowers the battery life of laptop computers or raises the temperature of the processor to dangerous levels. Consequently, for any performance enhancements, computer architects must balance increased performance with increased power consumption.

In conclusion, to maintain the phenomenal rate of improvement in microprocessor performance, computer architects need to implement the techniques that have been discussed in this chapter. Also, architects need to develop other techniques of improving the performance without exceeding power consumption goals.

REFERENCES

[1] D. Burger, J. Goodman, and A. Kägi (1996): Memory Bandwidth Limitations of Future Microprocessors, *International Symposium on Computer Architecture*.

[2] Y. Choi, A. Knies, L. Gerke, and T. Ngai (2001): The Impact of If-Conversion on Branch Prediction and Program Execution on the Intel Itanium Processor, *International Symposium on Microarchitecture*.

[3] N. Jouppi (1990): Improving Direct-Mapped Cache Performance by the Addition of a Small Fully-associative Cache and Prefetch Buffers, *International Symposium on Computer Architecture*.

[4] J. Hennessy and D. Patterson (1996): Computer Architecture: A Quantitative Approach, Morgan-Kaufman.

[5] J. Huang and D. J. Lilja (2003): Balancing Reuse Opportunities and Performance Gains with Sub-Block Value Reuse, *IEEE Transactions on Computers, 52*, 1032–1050.

[6] M. Lipasti, C. Wilkerson, and J. Shen (1996): Value Locality and Load Value Prediction, *International Conference on Architectural Support for Programming Languages and Operating Systems.*

[7] S. Mahlke, R. Hank, R. Bringmann, J. Gyllenhaal, D. Gallagher, and W. Hwu (1994): Characterizing the Impact of Predicated Execution on Branch Prediction, *International Symposium on Microarchitecture.*

[8] E. Rotenberg, S. Bennett, and J. Smith (1996): Trace Cache: A Low Latency Approach to High Bandwidth Instruction Fetching, *International Symposium on Microarchitecture.*

[9] J. Shen and M. Lipasti (2003): Modern Processor Design, Fundamentals of Superscalar Processors, McGraw-Hill.

[10] J. Silc, B. Robic, and T. Ungerer (1999): Processor Architecture: From Dataflow to Superscalar and Beyond, Springer-Verlag.

[11] D. Sima, T. Fountain, and P. Kacsuk (1997): Advanced Computer Architectures, A Design Space Approach, Addison Wesley Longman.

[12] A. Sodani and G. Sohi (1997): Dynamic Instruction Reuse, *International Symposium on Computer Architecture.*

[13] J. Tsai, J. Huang, C. Amlo, D. Lilja, and P. Yew (1999): The Superthreaded Processor Architecture, *IEEE Transactions on Computers*, 48(9).

[14] D. Tullsen, S. Eggers, and H. Levy (1995): Simultaneous Multithreading: Maximizing On-Chip Parallelism, *International Symposium on Computer Architecture.*

[15] S. VanderWiel and D. Lilja (2000): Data Prefetch Mechanisms, *ACM Computing Surveys*, 32(2), 174–199.

Chapter 10

A GLANCE AT VLSI OPTICAL INTERCONNECTS: FROM THE ABSTRACT MODELINGS OF THE 1980S TO TODAY'S MEMS IMPLEMENTATIONS (A SURVEY REPORT)

Mary M. Eshaghian-Wilner
University of California Los Angeles
Lili Hai
State University of New York College
at Old Westbury

Abstract

This chapter presents a brief overview of some of the major research contributions in the area of VLSI computing with optical *interconnects* from the early modelings of the 1980s to today's MEMS implementations. Both free-space and fiber-guided interconnects are covered. Various models and architectures with optical interconnects are shown, and aspects of their algorithmic design are also reviewed. The chapter concludes with a brief discussion of some of the current advancements in MEMS and nanotechnology that could pave the way towards the actual implementation of some of the theoretical models that were proposed in the 1980s, and eventually towards designing of all optical systems. The materials presented in this chapter are compiled from some of the references that are listed chronologically at the end of the chapter.

1   INTRODUCTION

Optical Computing was a very active area of research in the 1980s. But the work tapered off because of the materials limitations that seemed to prevent manufacturing of efficient and cost-effective VLSI optical computing chips. Now, optical computing is back. New types of conducting polymers can be used to make transistor-like switches smaller and 1,000 times faster than silicon transistors. Also, researchers have now shown that photons can be trapped long enough to store data. Even with all these advances, we may not see these technologies on our computers for another 15 years or so. In the near term, however, optical computers will most likely be hybrid electro-optical systems. The early 1980s introduced the design of such architectures in which computations are done electronically and communications are done optically. This chapter presents an overview of such electro-optical architectures, with an emphasis on the design of optical interconnection mediums for those architectures.

Today, computers perform logic operations in just a few nanoseconds. Tomorrow's optical computers are expected to be 1,000 to 100,000 times faster. All current computer device technologies are limited by the speed of electron motion. The speed of electrons in copper wires is literally half the speed of light in vacuum, while the speed of light in photonic circuits is the speed of light in vacuum – the highest attainable speed, as stated by Einstein's principle that signals cannot propagate faster than the speed of light. Furthermore, unlike a copper cable, which sends electricity one pulse at a time, optical fibers can transmit several pieces of data as waves of different colors of light, which can travel down an optical fiber simultaneously. With free-space optics, beams can cross each other without distorting the information that they carry. All these advances support such promising statements as the one made by Dr. Abduldayem of NASA, who said, "Optically, we can solve a problem in one hour which would take an electronic computer 11 years to solve – and they would be more immune to noisy data."

While optical circuits do not dissipate as much heat as silicon chips do, today's materials that are required to support photonic circuits require too much power to work in consumer products. Coming up with the right materials may take five years or more, and it may be a decade after that before optical computing products appear. Therefore, at least in the near term, optical computers will most likely be hybrid electro-optical systems where computations are done electronically and communications optically. The rest of this chapter surveys some of the advancements made to date towards design of optical interconnects on a chip, and the chapter is organized as follows.

In Section 2 we present an overview of abstract models for computing on a chip with optical interconnects. In Section 3 we review architectures with free-space optical interconnects, and in Section 4 we review architectures using fiber-guided interconnects. The Optical Reconfigurable Mesh, a selected hybrid electro-optical architecture, is presented in Section 5. Section 6 discusses the nanoscale and MEMS implementation of architectures with optical interconnects.

2   ABSTRACT MODELS

This section of the chapter presents the theoretical aspects of computing with optical interconnects on VLSI chips. In this section, we first present an overview of the optical model of computation (OMC), which represents a VLSI chip enhanced with free-space optical interconnects. We then present a review of other models, some of which were based on OMC. We will also discuss some simulation and application algorithms for OMC type of models.

2.1 The Optical Model of Computation and Related Models

In this section, we introduce the Optical Model of Computation (OMC), which is an abstraction of computing chips with optical interconnects. Similar to the VLSI model of computation, which was proposed by Thompson in the late 1970s, this generic model can be used to understand the limits of computational efficiency in using optical technology.

Unique qualities of the optical medium are its abilities to be directed for propagation in free space and to have two optical channels cross in space without interaction. These properties allow optical interconnects to utilize all three dimensions of space.

One of the first attempts to use free-space optics as a means of data communications was in [4]. In these authors hybrid GaAs/Si approach to data communication, a GaAs chip with optical sources was connected in a hybrid fashion (with conventional wire bond techniques) to an Si chip such that light was generated only along the edges of the Si chip. The sources were of the edge-emitting or surface-emitting types. The optical signals were routed to the appropriate locations on the Si chip using conventional and/or holographic optical elements. The Si chip contained detectors to receive the optical data streams generated by the sources. Since the detector–amplifier combinations were fabricated in Si, every computational component on the Si chip was capable of receiving data.

Based on the properties of free-space optics and VLSI technology, an optical model of computation is defined as follows [23, 37]:

An optical model of computation represents a network of N processors, each associated with a memory module, and a deflecting unit capable of establishing direct optical connection to another processor. The interprocessor communication is performed satisfying the following rules:

- *At any time a processor can send at most one message. Its destination is another processor or a set of processors (broadcasting).*

- *The message will succeed in reaching the processor if and only if it is the only message with that processor as its destination at that time step.*

- *All messages succeed or fail (and thus are discarded) in unit time.*

To ensure that every processor knows when its message succeeds, we assume that the OMC is run in two phases. In the first phase, read/write messages are sent, and in the second, values are returned to successful readers and acknowledgments are returned to successful writers. We assume that the operation mode is synchronous and that all processors are connected to a central control unit. The above definition is supplemented with the following set of assumptions for accurate analysis.

- Processors are embedded in an Euclidean plane referred as the *processing layer*.

- Each of the processing/memory elements occupies unit area.

- Deflectors are embedded in an Euclidean plane referred as the *deflecting layer*.

- Each deflecting unit occupies at least one unit area.

- The deflecting layer is collinear to the processing layer.

- I/O is performed at I/O pads. Each I/O pad occupies at least one unit area or, one unit area.

- The total volume is the sum of the space occupied by the processing layer, the deflecting layer, and the space for optical beams.

- The intercommunication is done through free-space optical beams.

- Time is measured in terms of number of units of clock cycles.

- An optical beam carries a constant amount of information in one unit of time, independent of the distance to be covered.

- A deflector is capable of redirecting an incident beam in one unit of time.

- A processor can perform a simple arithmetic/logic operation in one unit of time.

- The time, T, for computation is the time between the arrival of the first input and the departure of the last output.

To be able to compare our results with those that use Thomson's VLSI model of computation, without loss of generality, assume that there are N processors placed on an $N^{1/2} \times N^{1/2}$ grid called the processing layer. Similarly, there are N deflecting modules on a layer above the processing layer, called the deflection layer. The interconnection beams are established in the free-space between these two layers, as shown in the Figure 10.1 below. Hence, the amount of data that can be exchanged in a cycle between two sets of processors (two-way information transfer rate) is N. The time T required to solve a problem is the number of cycles

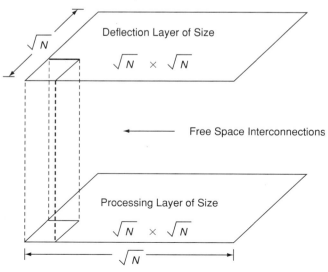

Figure 10.1. The OMC model

required to exchange the minimum required information (I). This leads to $A\,T = \Omega\,(I)$, where A is the area occupied by the processing layer.

A related model is VLSIO [20], which is a three-dimensional generalization of the wire model of the two-dimensional VLSI model with optical beams replacing the wires as communication channels. Compared with the three-dimensional VLSI model of computation, our model is more resource efficient. The simulation of many parallel organizations using the OMC requires a considerably smaller amount of volume than their layout in the three-dimensional VLSI model. For example, the layout volume of an N processor hypercube can be reduced from $O(N^{3/2})$ to $O(N\,logN)$ with OMC.

The Optical communication parallel Computer model (OCPC), presented in a USC technical report by Anderson and Miller [24], is a well-studied theoretical model, which was inspired by and based on the OMC model that was also developed at USC but as part of Eshaghian's Ph.D. thesis [23]. In the next section, the algorithmic design issues of OMC and OCPC models have been elaborated.

Lastly, note that although fiber optics provide superb bandwidth as compared with electrical wires, from a computational point of view, networks with fiber optical connections lead to VLSI space-time trade-offs similar to the traditional electrical interconnects. For this reason, the OMC model was designed to capture just the computational power of free-space optical interconnects, which are drastically different from electrical interconnects. An abstract model called the "Hypernetwork Model" was introduced by Zheng to represent architectures using fiber optics [68]. A hypernetwork M is essentially a graphical representation of the underlying topology of a given network of processors interconnected with fiber optics. More specifically, it is a network whose underlying structure is a hypergraph, in which each vertex corresponds to a unique processor of the hypernetwork, and each hyperedge corresponds to a multiconnect component that connects the processors. Zheng states, "The class of optical multiconnect components excludes those that provide fixed parallel connections in the form of image relay using lenses and mirrors." Optical multiconnect components can be multi-access fiber buses- or star couplers, as described in Section 4.

2.2 Simulation and Application Algorithms

The OCPC and OMC models have been appealing to the theoretical community [50, 53, 66, 67] because they present a technology through which it is possible to efficiently simulate PRAM algorithms. The main underlying assumption in the basic shared and distributed-memory PRAM models is that the intercommunication delay in every step of computation is constant. In other words, using electrical interconnections, one would need to have a fully interconnected network to realize such a unit-delay intercommunication requirement. Implementation of a fully connected network with electrical interconnections, where there is bounded fan-in fan-out to processors, leads to a lower bound of $\Omega(log\ N)$ delay. Therefore, every step of a PRAM algorithm will require $\Omega(log\ N)$ time when implemented in electrical circuits with bounded degree nodes. With optical interconnects as shown in OMC, and therefore on OCPC too, because any processor can communicate with any other processor directly through its dynamically reconfigurable deflecting unit, the unit-delay interconnectivity assumed in PRAM can be realized in real time (constant delay) with bounded fan-in fan-out processors.

Goldberg, Matias and Rao [50] presented a randomized simulation of an N $log\ log\ N$ EREW PRAM on the N processor OCPC in which, with high probability, each step of the PRAM takes $O(log\ logN)$ steps to simulate on OCPC. Prior to these results, the simulation of EREW PRAM was described by Valiant on an OCPC [33]. Valiant had given a constant delay simulation of Bulk Synchronous Parallel (BSP) computer on the OCPC, and also had given an $O(log\ N)$ randomized simulation of an $N\ log\ N$ processor EREW PRAM on an N processor BSP computer. Another simulation with delay $O(log\ N\ log\ log\ N)$ was given by Gereb-Graus and Tsantilas [40]. A fundamental problem that deals with contention resolution on the OCPC is that of realizing an h-relation. In this problem, each processor has at most h messages to send and at most h messages to receive. Following Anderson and Miller [24], Valiant [33], and Gereb-Graus and Tsantilas [40], Goldberg, Jerrum, Leighton, and Rao [45] solved the problem in time $O(h + log\ log\ N)$ for an N processor OCPC. A lower bound of $\Omega(log\ log\ N)^{1/2}$ expected time was obtained by Goldberg, Jerrum, and MacKenzie [67].

More recently, MacKenzie and Ramachandran [66] showed that the ERCW PRAM (using the "Tolerant" protocol for resolving write conflicts) with n global memory cells and unlimited local memory, is computationally equivalent to the OCPC. This finding is in contrast to the statements given in [66] that the OCPC model is equivalent to an EREW PRAM, a restriction that was not made in OMC. In [23, 37], both exclusive and concurrent write features of OMC were analyzed and applied in solving problems. In the following, a set of application algorithms as opposed to PRAM simulation algorithms for OMC are shown. The first is a set of optimal EREW algorithms for some geometric problems, and the second is a set of ERCW solutions [37]. Please note that, due to space limitations, the details of the algorithms are not presented. Furthermore, just a few of the algorithms are explained.

Optimal EREW algorithms

In this section, we present $O(log\ N)$ algorithms for problems such as finding connected components and locating the nearest neighboring figure to each figure in an $N^{1/2} \times N^{1/2}$ digitized image. We are concerned with black and white (binary) images, where the black pixels are 1-valued and white pixels are 0-valued.

An early step in intermediate-level image processing is identifying figures in the image. In a *0/1* picture, the connected 1s are said to form a figure. Thus, associated with each PE is a label, which is the unique ID of the figure to which the PE belongs. An $N^{1/2} \times N^{1/2}$ digitized picture may contain more than one connected region of black pixels. The problem is to identify to which figure (label) each I belongs.

Given an $N^{1/2} \times N^{1/2}$ 0/1 image, all figures can be labeled, and the nearest figure to all figures can be found, in $O(log\ N)$ time using an $(N^{1/2} / log^{1/2} N) \times (N^{1/2} / log^{1/2} N)$-OMC.

The first part of the algorithm requires sequential processing of *log N* elements by each PE. Then, once the size of the processors and the pixels match, the following is done for labeling the figures. For details on how the nearest neighboring figures are found, refer to the original manuscript [33].

The basic idea of the labeling algorithm is to identify the outer and inner boundaries of each figure, and then uniquely label all the connected ones surrounded by each of these boundaries. To assure circular boundaries, the input image is magnified by a factor of two along each dimension. Each pixel then locally determines whether it is a boundary pixel or not by checking if at least one of its four adjacent pixels along the x- and y-axis hold a 0. The pixels along each boundary are linked to form a circular list. The direction of pointers is determined as shown in Figure 10.2. The details for two selected segments are shown. Others can be formulated similarly.

Now only the outer-boundary PEs take part in the computation to identify the least-numbered PE in their list. Each PE, during iteration $i + 1$, sets its pointer to the pointer of the PE to which it was pointing at the end of iteration i. Since this has the effect of doubling the distance "jumped" during each iteration, in $O(\log N)$ time all the PEs in each list know the least-numbered PE in their list. The final step is the propagation of the unique IDs of each of the outer boundaries to its inner region. Broadcasting of IDs is done in parallel along each row of the image. It is easy to see that, since the figures do not cross, there is always a unique ID broadcasted to each of the inner PEs.

Constant-Time ERCW algorithms

One of the most attractive properties of optics is superposition. This property suggests that the resultant disturbance at any point in a medium is the algebraic sum of the separate constituent waves. Hence, it enables many optical signals to pass through the same point in space at the same time without causing mutual interference or crosstalk. Using this property, Giles and Jenkins [21] showed how a single memory element could be read by many processors at the same time. In

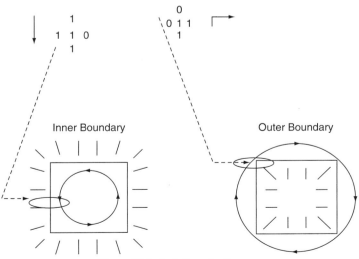

Figure 10.2. Labeling the figures

this section, we employ this characteristic to allow concurrent writes if all the requesting processors want to write a 1. This leads to a constant running time of the following geometric algorithms, under the assumption that broadcasting can be done in unit time:

Given an $N^{1/4} \times N^{1/4}$ image, using a $N^{1/2} \times N^{1/2}$ OMC, in $O(1)$ time,

- *For a single figure, its convex hull and a smallest enclosing box can be found.*

- *For each figure, the nearest neighboring* figure *can be identified.*

3   FREE-SPACE OPTICAL INTERCONNECTS

In this section, we present an overview of various architectures with free-space optical interconnects. We categorize these into two groups: static crossbars and dynamic reconfigurable architectures. Architectures with static crossbar free-space interconnectivity are those in which the connectivity is achieved for N input ports to N output ports with free-space beams deflected by N^2 fixed passive optical elements. On the other hand, in architectures with dynamic free-space interconnectivity, the interconnectivities among any combination of N elements can be achieved through the reconfiguration of N deflecting units.

3.1   Crossbar Architectures

Two types of crossbar architectures are presented in this section. The first is of the type referred to in the literature as a *matrix crossbar*, and the second is an electro-optical crossbar. The switching speed of these designs is discussed and compared with classical electrical interconnects.

3.1.1   Matrix Crossbars

The paper by Sawchuck et al. [8] presents an overview of various types of matrix crossbars. The basic idea behind these architectures is that, there are N input ports, which could represent processors, and there are N output ports, representing destination processors or memory modules. To interconnect these N points to each other, each of the N processors sends a free-space beam directed to N deflecting units. Therefore, for an array of N input ports, there will be a deflecting matrix of size N^2. Depending on which deflecting units are set beforehand, the input is routed to the desired output processors. This type of architecture allows both one-to-one connectivity as well as connectivity through broadcasting. The deflecting units essentially mask the inputs to the outputs. The masks on the holograms can be reprogrammed but this process is rather slow. But once the holograms are programmed, they will act as passive components to directly pass through the incident beams to desired locations. Another technique used for reconfiguring the connections is to use acousto-optical devices. In this regime, an acoustic wave generated in the acousto-optical device interacts with the incident beam and causes it to be redirected to the desired location. The reconfiguration time here is limited by the speed of acoustic waves, which will be on the order of microseconds, as compared to the switching speed in electrical crossbars, which is on the order of nanoseconds. Combining optical and electrical crossbar concepts, in the next section we will show an electro-optical crossbar that has a nanoseconds switching speed.

3.1.2   The Electro-Optical Crossbar

Electro-optical crossbar design uses a hybrid reconfiguration technique for interconnecting processors. There are N processors, each located in a distinct row and column of the $N\times N$ processing layer. For each processor, there is a hologram module having N units, such that the ith unit has a grating plate with a frequency leading to a deflection angle corresponding to the processor located at the grid point (i,i). In addition, each unit has a simple controller and a laser beam. To establish or reconfigure to a new connection pattern, each processor broadcasts the address of the desired destination processor to the controller of each of N units of its hologram module using an electrical bus (see Figure 10.3). The controller activates a laser (for conversion of the electrical input to an optical signal) if its ID matches the broadcast address of the destination processor. The connection is made when the laser beams are passed through the predefined gratings. Therefore, since the grating angles are predefined, the reconfiguration time of this design is bounded by the laser switching time, which is in the order of nanoseconds using gallium arsenide (GaAs) technology.

This architecture is faster than the previous designs and compares well with the clock cycle of current supercomputers. One of the advantages of this simple design is in its implementability in VLSI, using GaAs technology. Unlike the previous designs, this can be fabricated with very low cost and is highly suitable for applications where full connectivity is required. In such applications, the processor layer area can be fully utilized by placing N optical-beam receivers in each of the vacant areas to simultaneously interconnect with all the other processors.

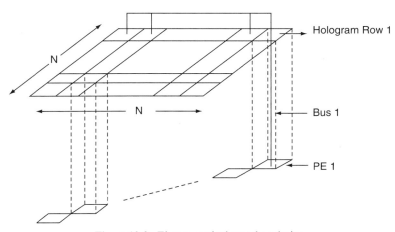

Figure 10.3. Electro-optical crossbar design

3.2   Dynamically Reconfigurable Architectures

In this section, we present a class of optical interconnection networks as a realization of the OMC presented in the previous section. The architectures presented here are reconfigurable and can interconnect any permutation of processors to one another. Unlike the crossbar architectures in the last section, here there are just N deflecting units for interconnecting N inputs to N outputs. Each of the proposed designs uses a different optical device technology for redirection of the optical beams to establish a new topology, and represents an upper bound on the volume requirement of OMC.

3.2.1   Optical Mesh Using Mirrors

In optical mesh design using mirrors, there are N processors on the processing layer of area N. Similarly, the deflecting layer has area N and holds N mirrors. These layers are aligned so that each of the mirrors is located directly above its associated processor (see Figure 10.4). Each processor has two lasers. One of these is directed up towards the arithmetic unit of the mirror, and the other is directed towards the mirror's surface. A connection phase would consist of two cycles. In the first cycle, each processor sends the address of its desired destination processor to the arithmetic unit of its associated mirror using its dedicated laser. The arithmetic unit of the mirror computes a rotation degree such that both the origin and destination processors have equal angle with the line perpendicular to the surface of the mirror in the plane formed by the mirror, the source processor, and the destination processor. Once the angle is computed, the mirror is rotated to point towards the desired destination. In the second cycle, connection is established by the laser beam carrying the data from the source to the mirror and, from the mirror, being reflected towards the destination. Since the connection is made through a mechanical movement of the mirror, using the current MEMS technology described later in this chapter, this leads to an order of

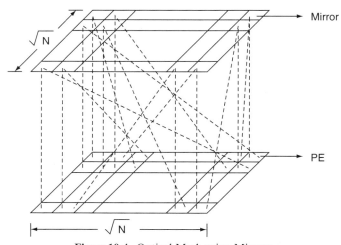

Figure 10.4. Optical Mesh using Mirrors

microsecond reconfiguration time. The space requirement of this architecture is $O(N)$ under the following assumption: each mirror is attached to a simple electromechanical device, which takes one unit of space and can rotate to any position in one unit of time.

3.2.2   Reconfiguration Using Acousto-Optical Devices

In reconfiguration using acousto-optical devices, N processors are arranged to form a one-dimensional processing layer, and the corresponding acousto-optical devices are similarly located on a one-dimensional deflecting layer (see Figure 10.5). The size of each of the acousto-optical devices is proportional to the size of the processing array, leading to an $O(N^2)$ area deflection layer. Similar to the design using mirrors, every processor has two lasers, and each connection phase is made up of two cycles. In the first cycle, each processor sends the address of its desired destination processor to the arithmetic unit of its associated acousto-optical device using its dedicated laser. Each arithmetic unit computes the frequency of the wave to be applied to the crystal for the redirection of the incoming optical beam to the destination processor. Using the other laser in the second cycle, each processor sends its data directly to the mirror located above it. This mirror is fixed such that its reflected beam passes through its corresponding acousto-optical device and then gets redirected towards the desired processor. One of the advantages of this architecture over the previous design is that it has a reconfiguration time of the order of microseconds due to the speed of sound waves. The other advantage is its broadcasting capability, which is due to the possibility of generating multiple waves through a crystal at a given time. Furthermore, the above can be extended to interconnect a two-dimensional grid of processors as follows:

Using an $N^{1/2} \times N^{1/2}$ processing layer, and an $N^{1/2} \times N^{1/2}$ array of acousto-optical devices as the deflecting layer of size $O(N^2)$, one step of OMC can be realized in $O(\log^2 N)$ time.

The area is obtained with similar arguments as in the one-dimensional case. The time complexity is due to the movement of data using the standard divide-and-conquer techniques. At the ith step, a block size 2^i is divided into two blocks of half the size. Each subblock contains only the data locations. To route up $O(i)$ elements residing in the queue of each of the processors, the ith step is simulated by $O(i)$ iterations.

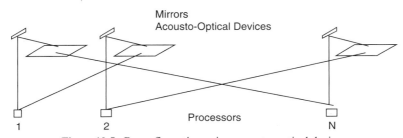

Figure 10.5. Reconfiguration using acousto-optical devices.

4   FIBER-GUIDED OPTICAL INTERCONNECTS

In this section, we first present a brief description of different types of modulations used with fiber optics, including time division multiplexing (TDM) and wavelength division multiplexing (WDM). Next we present two classes of architectures: first are those that use star couplers, and second are those that use shared fiber buses. Architectures in both these categories should be representable by the hypernetwork model described previously [68]. For a more detailed review of fiber-guided optical interconnects, see the survey paper by Sahni [74].

TDM is a technique of sending multiple signals on a carrier in the form of one complex signal, and then recovering the original signals separately at the receiving end. The network bandwidth is divided into fixed bandwidth segments. Each segment is assigned to a data source. One data source (using one channel) is given its own time slot to use the network. Usually, a time slot has a length for one bit or one byte transmission. The data from each channel is transmitted in turn in a regular sequence, cycling back from the last channel to the first one. TDM is a scheme allowing several low-speed channels multiplexed into a single high-speed channel for the transmission and then decomplexed back to the low-speed channels at the destinations of transmissions. Currently, TDM transmission speed in backbone terrestrial optical transmission systems are 2.4 Gbit/s and 10 Gbit/s with some deploying equipment. Recent advances reported by Cisco Systems have resulted in speeds of 40 Gbit/s.

WDM is another optical transmission technique where a single optical fiber transmits multiple optical signals by using different wavelength for each signal stream. In other words, WDM allows multiple signal travel in parallel at different speed in one optical fiber. The wavelengths used for WDM are chosen in a certain range of frequencies. Three ranges so far applied are, 850 nm, 1310 nm and 1550 nm. The wavelength of 1550 nm is found to be the best having the minimum loss in a fiber. In today's WDM systems, each channel or wavelength can operate at up to 2.5 to 40 Gbit/s.

In the 1990s, Dense Wavelength Division Multiplexing (DWDM) was developed to meet the rapidly growing *demands* of network bandwidth (300% growth per year). In a recent report by Cisco Systems, the following statement was made about DWDM: "Without having to lay new fiber, the effective capacity of existing fiber plant can routinely be increased by a factor of 16 or 32. Systems with 128 and 160 wavelengths are in operation today, with higher density on the horizon. The specific limits of this technology are not yet known." This approach essentially enables a single fiber to carry more than one terabit/s of information.

4.1   Multistage Fiber Interconnection Networks

Traditional multistage interconnection networks such as the Omega network can be implemented using optical interconnects, where electrical wires are replaced by fiber optics and the intermediate switches are replaced by passive optical couplers. A passive optical coupler of size K connects one of the K inputs to up to K outputs. Therefore, the K inputs coming into a coupler will be processed sequentially in K steps.

The Partitioned Optical Passive Stars (POPS) topology [61] is an "all-optical" interconnection architecture. In the POPS network, source nodes send data to the destination nodes through passive optical couplers. All links for sending and receiving data in source and destination nodes are optical devices. A set of two parameters, *n* and *d*, uniquely determines the implementation of a POPS network. The *n* is the size, the number of nodes, of the system. The *d* is the degree, the number of links to source/destination nodes, of a coupler. The number of groups partitioned is represented by $g = n/d$.

A POPS of g groups has g^2 couplers because each coupler group contains g couplers to connect with the nodes in g-1 other source node groups and the source nodes in its own partition. If the g coupler groups are denoted by G_i, $0 \leq i < g$, the g couplers in each G_i will be denoted by C_{ij}, $0 \leq j < g$.

Each source node has g transmitters. We denote g transmitters of a node to be T_0, T_1, ..., T_{g-1}. Any source node in group G_i, $0 \leq i < g$, connects to one coupler of g groups as follows: T_0 to $C_{0,i}$, T_1 to $C_{1,i}$, ..., T_{g-1} to $C_{g-1,i}$. Similarly, each destination node has g receivers. But those g receivers connect to g couplers in the same coupler group as that destination node. So if a destination node is in group G_i and the g receivers of the node are denoted as R_0, R_1, ... R_{g-1}, they will connect to the couplers as R_0 to $C_{i,0}$, R_1 to $C_{i,1}$, ..., R_{g-1} to $C_{i,g-1}$.

Thus, for any source node N_i, $0 \leq i < n$, sending a message to a destination node N_j, $0 \leq j < n$, the data transmission path is as follows. Assume N_i is in group G_p, $0 \leq p < g$, and N_j is in group G_q, $0 \leq q < g$. N_i sends a message to g couplers $C_{0,p}$, $C_{1,p}$, ..., $C_{g-1,p}$ of which coupler C_{qp} is in coupler group G_q. When the message is received by C_{qp} and is broadcast to all destination nodes connected to G_q, the node N_j receives the message.

By this interconnection, the POPS network presents the advantage that the network diameter is 1. However, the passive optical coupler in POPS can only receive one signal at a time from its source nodes, even though it can broadcast a signal to all destination nodes connected to it. Proper partitioning can alleviate the bandwidth problem caused by this limitation, as POPS does. But for any POPS architecture with $d > 1$, the multisignals from multisource nodes still have to be received sequentially by a coupler. Only one source link is activated at a given time for a coupler to prevent collisions. The TDM technique is a good choice for the optical source links in POPS for static network traffic. For the dynamic message traffic, an arbitration protocol on a per coupler basis has to be specified, and WDM protocols can be adapted. More details can be found in [61].

4.2 ARRAYS WITH MULTIPLEXED FIBER OPTICAL BUSES

The architectures presented here are either one- or two-dimensional arrays of processors that are interconnected through shared buses, where the buses are fiber-optical buses. Similar to the traditional bus-based architectures using electrical interconnects, switches can be set to reconfigure the buses. The main difference here is due to the fact that the optical versions of these bus-based architectures benefit from the high bandwidth offered through fiber optics. Also, time and wavelength multiplexing can be performed on the fiber-optical buses. Here is an overview of some of the architectures proposed using these concepts.

APPB: *Array Processors with (Optical) Pipelined Buses* (APPB) [35] are linear arrays with n processors connected to a folded optical bus (also could be two directional buses). The upper bus segment, named the *transmitting bus*, is for processors to send messages out, and the lower bus segment, named the *receiving bus*, is for processors to read messages. Some conditions have to be met to guarantee that different messages do not overlap when traveling in the same waveguide. A complete bus cycle is necessary to transmit data from all processors. Several message routing approaches can be used in the linear pipelined optical bus. Two major mechanisms are used. The first uses the TDM scheme [42] with a waiting time function, and the second is the coincident pulse technique [16]. Both methods are for one-to-one mapping routing and broadcasting. A single node can receive no more than one message at a time.

AROB: The *array with reconfigurable optical buses*, (AROB) [54], was designed with two major objectives: (1) to be able to simulate efficiently the reconfiguration mechanism of a traditional reconfigurable network, and (2) to add to the reconfigurable network the optical communication capabilities of the APPB-like structure. A (two-dimensional) (2D) AROB uses optical waveguides for the links of interconnection and optical switches for reconfiguration. Each link between ports of two adjacent nodes is composed of transmitting and receiving segments, and each includes three waveguides exactly similar to the optical bus of APPB. The reconfiguration or the switch setting consists of two operations: (1) setting of the segment termination nodes so that there are no connections between any internal ports; and (2) setting of the intermediate nodes so that one port connects to another port internally. After each switch setting, a set of disjoint linear optical bus segments appears in the system. Each segment is unidirectional. A pair of pulses is sent by the leading node to the reference, and then they select waveguides synchronously on the transmitting segment. Those pulses will reach the receiving bus segment at the same time. When all nodes on the segment receive those coincident signals, they can determine the configuration of the receiving bus. A 2D AROB can simulate an $n \times n$ reconfigurable mesh with a constant factor slowdown. However, note that the column/row *permutation* can be implemented in one bus cycle.

LARPBS: The *linear array with a reconfigurable pipelined bus system*, (LARPBS) [62], is a one-dimensional parallel computing model. On its APPB-like optical bus segment, two sets of optical switches, RSR (i) and RST(i), $0 \le i < n$ (where n is the number of nodes in the system), are inserted for each node i. Each set of RSR(i) includes three switches on three receiving bus sections between node i and node $i + 1$. The three switches in RST(i) are for three transmitting bus sections in coincident pulse technique. Those switches are used for bus reconfigurations and are called *reconfigurable switches*. The control of setting RSR(i) and RST(i) is in the node i. There are two states of a switch set, namely, straight and cross. If the RSR(i) and RST(i) are set to straight, the node i is an intermediate node in a bus segment (do not count the two end nodes in the whole bus).

For example, if all reconfigurable switches on the bus are set to straight, the system will be a regular pipelined bus system. If RSR*(i)* and RST*(i)* are set to cross, the bus is split into two segments: one contains node 0 to node *i* and another contains node *i+1* to node *n-1*. Another important feature in LARPBS is the conditional delay for the writing. Between a pair of neighbored nodes, *i* and *i+1*, $0 \leq i < n-2$, a conditional delay unit is inserted on the transmitting segments and controlled by the node *i+1*. Note that node 0 has no conditional delay unit. This feature is very useful for algorithms such as finding a binary prefix sum. By setting the delay unit straight or cross to represent the value of 0 or 1 in a node, each node *i* can count the delay time to determine the sum of node 0 to node *i* in the coincident pulse scheme.

5 A SELECTED HYBRID ARCHITECTURE

Over the years, many architectures with electro-optical interconnects have been proposed. The OTIS architecture presented in [43] and the Optical Reconfigurable Mesh (ORM) architecture presented in [72] are examples of such systems. Here we explain the ORM system, which is one of the more recent architectures that can be implemented with MEMS, and can be used in nanoscale structures as discussed later in the chapter.

5.1 The Optical Reconfigurable Mesh

A 4×4 optical reconfigurable mesh (ORM) is shown in figure 10.6a and 10.6b. There are two layers in the ORM: the deflection layer and the processing layer. The deflection layer consists of N^2 deflecting units, while the processing layer consists of N^2 processing units. The processors on the processing layer are interconnected as a reconfigurable mesh and can also intercommunicate optically using the deflection layer. The reconfigurable mesh model used here is standard. The reconfigurable mesh of size N^2 consists of an $N \times N$ array of processors connected to a grid-shaped reconfigurable broadcast bus, where each processor has a locally controllable bus switch. The switches allow the broadcast bus to be divided into subbuses, providing smaller reconfigurable meshes or reconfigurable bus segments. The detailed structure of a processing unit in the processing layer and the detailed structure of a deflecting unit in the deflection layer are also shown in Figure 10.6. In the following subsections, we describe each of those components.

5.1.1 The Processing Unit

There are $N \times N$ processing units on the processing layer and three optical transmitters and one receiver residing in each processing unit. One of the transmitters, TR(1), is directed towards the control unit of the deflection unit. The second one, TR(2), is directed towards the reconfigurable mirror (RM) of the deflection unit, and the third one, TR(3), is directed towards the fixed mirror (FM) of the deflection unit. Each processing unit has a constant number of *log N* bit memory cells and simple computation capabilities. It is connected to other processing units in the mesh by the electrical reconfigurable buses. Each processing unit

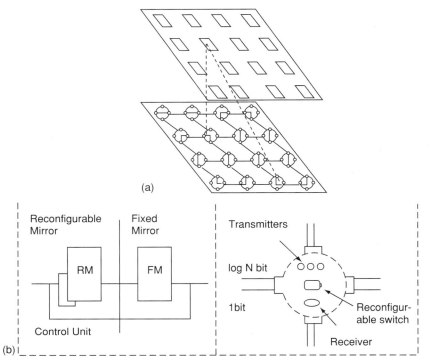

Figure 10.6. A 4×4 Optical Reconfigurable Mesh (ORM). (a). optical routing from Processor p (2, 2) to processor p (2, 4); (b) The structure of the processing unit

controls the internal reconfigurable switches and is responsible for sending and receiving data to and from the other processing units. We index the processing unit in the ith row and the jth column of the mesh on the processing layer as $P(i,j)$ in which $1 \le i, j \le N$ (see Figure 10.6b).

5.1.2   The Deflection Unit

The deflecting layer contains $N \times N$ deflecting units. Each deflecting unit consists of two mirrors and an arithmetic control unit. One of the mirrors is a fixed mirror (FM), which transfers data from the processor under it to a fixed address whenever it is used. Another mirror is a reconfigurable mirror (RM). The control unit receives an address from the processor under it, translates the address and controls the direction of the RM (see Figure 10.6b). Since the angle of the FM is fixed, the processor can send data directly from one dedicated transmitter to its destination without going through the control unit. We define each deflecting unit (a mirror and the related control unit) located directly above $P(i,j)$ as $M(i,j)$.

5.2   Data Movement in ORM

The data can be routed in three different ways in this architecture. In the first, *electrical routing*, the routing is done only through electrical buses. The second one, *optical routing*, uses free-space optics. The third type, *electro-optical routing*, uses both electrical and optical free-space connections to allow a complete connection among N processors. Each of the movements is described below. For application of these data movement techniques for solving some communication-intensive tasks, see the Ph.D. thesis of Lili Hai, where the first O(log N) time algorithm for finding the convex hulls of all figures in an N × N 0/1 image has been presented.

5.2.1 Electrical Routing

The electrical routing in ORM is similar to those for reconfigurable meshes. The electrical routing in ORM is any routing from one node to another or a broadcast, which uses electrical buses in the reconfigurable mesh only. This type of communication is suitable for providing arbitrary connections in the processing layer.

5.2.2 Optical Routing

The optical routing in ORM is the routing through optical free-space interconnections only. The data transfer does not use any electrical bus in the system. All N^2 processors can communicate in unit time delay as long as there is only one read or write from or to each location. How such an optical connection is established between two processors through the RM is described below.

A connection phase consists of two cycles. In the first cycle, each processor sends the address of its desired destination processor to the arithmetic control unit of its associated mirror using its dedicated laser TR(1). The arithmetic control unit of the mirror computes a rotation degree such that both the origin and destination processors have an equal angle with the line perpendicular to the surface of the mirror in the plane formed by the mirror, the source processor, and the destination processor. Once the angle is computed, the mirror is rotated to point to the desired destination. In the second cycle, the connection is established by the laser beam, TR(2), carrying the data from the source to the mirror and then from the reflected mirror towards the destination. An example of an optical routing from processor P(2,2) to processor P(4,3) is shown in Figure 10.6a.

The read operation has two phases. In the first phase, the read requirement and the reader's address are sent to the processor, which stores the desired data. In the second phase, the data are sent back to the reader, depending on the reader's address. Both phases use the two-cycle write routing method.

5.2.3 Electro-Optical Routing

Electro-optical routing establishes an efficient full connectivity among only the N processors situated diagonally in the processing layer of the N^2 processors in the ORM (i.e., for processors $P(j, j)$ where $1 \leq j \leq N$). This routing technique uses electrical buses on the processing layer and fixed mirrors on the deflection layer.

This connection for electro-optical routing is implemented as follows. Each processor $P(j, j)$ is associated with the jth row of the deflection unit, where the row contains N fixed mirrors. The ith fixed mirror in that row for $1 \leq i \leq N$ is directed to the processing unit $P(i,i)$. There are two possible types of routing:

Exclusive Read Exclusive Write (EREW) and Concurrent Read Concurrent Write (CRCW). We explain both methodologies below. (The other two techniques described earlier, electrical and optical routings, are EREW.)

The variety of techniques available in this architecture makes ORM a very powerful computing model. For example, using combinations of the electrical, the optical, and the electro-optical routing techniques, it was shown in Hai's Ph.D. thesis [60] that the convex hull of *multiple* figures in a digitized image of size $N \times N$ could be found in $O(logN)$ time using an $N \times N$ ORM. To the best of our knowledge, this is the fastest known solution to this problem using any known parallel model or structure with N^2 processors. All previous solutions had a running time of $O(log^2N)$. *The proof of this theorem is rather lengthy and, due to space limitations, is not presented here. Interested readers should refer to the thesis.*

EREW Electro-optical Routing
In this routing, any PE $P(i,i)$ sends data to $P(k,k)$ in the following way:
1. $P(i,i)$ sends the data to $P(i,k)$ through the electrical row bus;
2. $P(i,k)$ sends data to $P(k,k)$ through transmitter TR(3) and its deflector $M(i,k)$.

CRCW Electro-optical Routing
Definition: The CRCW access model for N diagonal processors on the ORM is defined as follows:

- *In one write step, each $P(i,i)$ can send one write request to $P(k,k)$, $k \neq i$. If there is more than one write request to $P(i,i)$, $P(i,i)$ will receive only one of them.*

- *In one read step, each $P(i,i)$ can send one read request to $P(k,k)$, $k \neq i$. The reader (multiple readers are allowed) can get the requested data back in the same step.*

Now we prove the following:
The concurrent write and the concurrent read of N PEs can be done on the ORM in $O(1)$ time.

We show this by giving the following constant time algorithm. We assume that the read or write operation signal (operation command) is known by all PEs. The following steps are executed in constant time.

Write Operation

There are three steps in this operation. In step 1, the destination address for a write request is broadcast to the row i by each $P(i,i)$. The processor (in row i, for each i) with a j index matching the destination address is an active processor in this step. This processor is responsible for sending the data to the destination, and therefore its optical light beam is activated. In step 2, a single write request is chosen among multiple write requests directed to a processor. In this step, the losers become inactive. In step 3, the chosen write request is sent to each destination. The implementation details of each step are as follows:
1. Initially, the ORM performs the row bus connection. Each $P(i,i)$ sends a write request destination address j to the row i. The address can be received by all

PEs through the row buses of the mesh. Each PE compares the address with its own column index. The $P(i,j)$ will mark itself as an active PE if the address j is matched to its column index. The others in row i do nothing.

2. All PEs of the ORM perform the column bus connection except that each active PE disconnects its north port from its south port. Each active PE sends a signal to the south port and checks the north port. If an active PE does not receive any signal from its north, it means that it is a northmost active PE in the column, so it activates the light beam. All the other active PEs become inactive. The piece of data in $P(i,i)$ for which the $P(i,j)$ is active is the chosen one for writing data to $P(j,j)$.

3. Each $P(i,i)$ sends the writing data to the row again. The data are received by active $P(i,j)$ and sent to $P(j,j)$ through the activated laser beam. Since there is only one sender left in each column after step 2, each $P(j,j)$ will receive at most one piece of data from the free space in the step.

Read Operation

The concurrent read operation contains two phases. In the first phase, the readers send read requests to the destination $P(j,j)$. During this step, the electrical and optical routes for $P(j,j)$ to send the data back to multiple readers are established.

In the second phase, the data are sent to the readers by $P(j,j)$. Two variables, R and C, are used in each PE to implement the operation. The implementation is as follows (see Figure 10.7):

1. The ORM does the row bus connection. Each $P(i,i)$ sends the address of the destination processor, j, and the read request (requested memory cell address) to row i. When j is matched to the column index of a PE, $P(i,j)$ saves the read request and sets the variable $R = 1$.

2. The ORM does the column buses connection. Each $P(i,i)$ sends the address of the destination processor, j, to column i. Each PE compares j with its row index. If they match, the PE sets the variable $C = 1$.

3. The ORM keeps the column buses connection. The PE whose $R = 1$ is an active PE in this step. Find the northmost active PE in each column. This PE activates the light beam and sends the read request to $P(j,j)$ using transmitter TR(3).

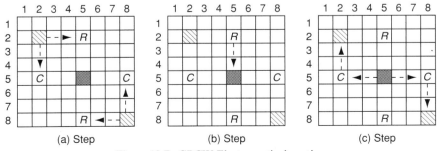

Figure 10.7. CRCW Electro optical routing

This action can be done because the read request has been saved in this PE in step 1 and the active $P(i,j)$ uses its $M(i,j)$ to connect the optical path to $P(j,j)$.

4. The ORM does the row bus connection. Each PE with $C = 1$ is an active PE now, that activates its light beam using transmitter TR(3). The requested data are retrieved by each $P(j,j)$ and broadcast to row j. Then the data are sent to the requester $P(i,i)$ through the bus and the light beam of $P(j,i)$ using transmitter TR(3) as shown in Figure 10.7c.

6   CURRENT TECHNOLOGIES AND BEYOND

This section addresses some of the recent advances in MEMS and nanoscale technology. Using these technologies, we first show that it would now be possible to implement MEMS architectures on an integrated chip with dynamic free-space interconnectivity and, second, how such concepts can be carried onto designs of nanoscale architectures that are subject to quantum effects.

6.1   MEMS

The idea of fabricating tiny movable devices on chips was first conceived in the late 1960s, and strong research and development activity in this field started around 1980 [79]. Since then, many results have appeared that show theoretical modelings, new materials, fabrication processes, actuation mechanisms, and sensing methods. The impact that the micro-electro-mechanical systems (MEMS) already have had in various applications, such as in sensing applications, has been very noteworthy. The art of integration via MEMS technology has led to the development of a huge array of integrated microsystems with rich and versatile functionality. A host of new applications, particularly in biology and medicine, appears to be imminent.

Optical MEMS is a relatively new and highly productive discipline within MEMS. The Optical MEMS conference started in 1996 and in just a few years has grown significantly. Several journals have been dedicated to Optical MEMS. An interesting issue of *Journal of Lightwave Technology* is dedicated to "Optical MEMS and Its Future Trends" and was edited by Lin, Wu, Sawada, and Mohr [79]. One interesting aspect of this issue, especially as applied to this chapter, is that it contains papers that discuss the integration of movable micromirrors in a chip.

The paper by Ji and Kim [75] is an example of this discussion. In that paper, the authors show that they have designed and fabricated an addressable 4×4 array of micromirrors capable of providing up to 90 degrees of angular deflection. Each micromirror is composed of a single crystalline silicon mirror plate supported by aluminum springs, which provides an extremely flat reflective surface, and a compliant spring material that enables the integration of the device into a limited area without mitigating its performance. A mirror rotation angle of more than 80 degrees can be obtained by applying an external magnetic field. Furthermore, the authors state that this angle can be increased by the use of an electrostatic force. Each mirror plate and its associated springs occupy an area of 500×500 µm^2. A 10 µm thick layer of single-crystal silicon is used as the mirror plate for obtaining a flat surface. The authors' design allows for selective actuation of some of the micromirrors while the others remain clamped by electrostatic force.

Note that the industry seems to be significantly ahead of academia in designing micromirror arrays. The digital micromirror device, (DMD), is built by DLP, which is a division of Texas Instruments. DMD is a micromirror system with approximately a million individually switchable micromirrors. Each mirror has a length of 13 µm and can be switched in 15 microseconds for maximum precision. The array of Micro-opto-electro-mechanical System (MOEMS) mirrors built by Lucent Technologies is an array of 100 million switchable micromirrors. This essentially can operate as a peta-bit switch that works for 1,296 ports, each containing 40 separate signals, and each of the signals can carry 40 giga-bits per second.

These kinds of advancements clearly indicate that we are now able to implement the OMC-based models with reconfigurable mirrors, such as the Optical Mesh or the ORM architecture. The nano-electro-mechanical systems (NEMS) implementation of these types of architectures will open yet another gate of possibilities towards the efficient implementation of VLSI architectures with reconfigurable mirrors. In the next section, we talk about some of the ideas currently under development for integrating the MEMS implementations of ORM with quantum-level nanoscale computing structures in a multiscale system.

6.2   Nanoscale

Here we discuss a three-dimensional nanoscale electro-optical architecture called *H3D-QCA* [80]. In this architecture, just as in the OMC model, there are two layers: the processing layer below and the deflecting layer on top. The processors can intercommunicate using a standard reconfigurable mesh through the local switchable connections and also using the reconfigurable MEMS mirrors with free-space optical interconnects. Each of the processors contains some local memory and is attached to a quantum cellular automata (QCA) cube. In each cube there are quantum cells (see Figure 10.8).

The implementation of QCA using quantum dots is quite well known through the work of researchers at Notre Dame University, but has the limitation that it operates under low temperatures. A solution to this is to implement the cells using molecules. Using molecular magnetic switches, we can simulate a QCA that operates at room temperature.

The computations within the QCA cubes are done in a fashion similar to a standard QCA except that the two-dimensional QCA logic circuits are laid out in three dimensions. In other words, the QCA blocks can be used to compute millions of logic operations locally by techniques already developed for QCA. The computations are done as the neighboring cells interact with each other through quantum tunneling effects. Once the local computations within each cube are completed, the results are forwarded to their corresponding processing units. The processors can then store the data in their local memory and/or intercommunicate with other processing units using the electronically reconfigured mesh and/or the micro-electro-mechanical mirrors.

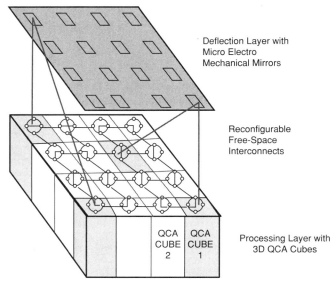

Figure 10.8. *H3D-QCA* architecture

7   CONCLUSION AND FUTURE RESEARCH

Research began in the early 1980s in optical computing, with the goal of replacing electronics with a technology that could enable the building of significantly faster computers. The limitations in the materials that were needed to fabricate all optical computing systems caused work in this area to taper off. Architectures and models were designed that were hybrid, combining optical interconnects with electronic circuits. This chapter has presented an overview of some of the work that has been done since the 1980s in designing electro-optical computing architectures with optical interconnects. The treatment here is far from exhaustive, but rather focuses on architectures representing very distinct connectivity styles. The chapter concluded with a brief discussion of what is now possible with MEMS and nanoscale technology. In our opinion, optical computing is back again as a research area that needs to be revisited with respect to the advancements made during the past twenty years. What lies ahead in the next few decades could be the study of the synergy of optical computing and quantum computing.

REFERENCES

The listed references, not all of which are cited in this chapter as a whole highlight some of the major contributions to the field of optical inter-connections. Please note that each reference item is tagged with a letter A, B, D, J, S, or T following the year of publication. These tags respectively identify the corresponding Optics article as: (A) Architecture/Algorithm paper, (B) Book, (D) Dissertation, (J) Journal/special issue, (S) Survey paper, or (T) Theoretical paper. Although not all the reference items are cited in this chapter, they all have had a significant role in shaping the field of optical interconnections since the 1980s. This list is far from exhaustive, but rather focuses on a class of architectures representing very distinct connectivity styles.

[1] [1980-S1] H. M. Gibbs, S. L. McCall, T. N. C. Venkatesan (1980): Optical Bistable Devices: The Basic Components of All-Optical Systems? *Op. Engg.*

[2] [1982-S1] P.W. Smith (1988): On the Physical Limits of Digital Optical Switching and Logic Elements. *Bell Sys. Tech. J.*

[3] [1983-S1] H. J. Caulfield, J. A. Neff, and W. T. Rhodes (1983) Optical computing: The Coming Revolution in Optical Signal Processing. *Laser Focus, 19*(11), 100–109.

[4] [1984-S1]J. W. Goodman, F. Leonberger (1984): S. Y. Kung, and R. A. Athale, Optical Interconnections for VLSI Systems. *Proceedings of the IEEE. 72*(7), 850–866.

[5] [1984-S2] A. A. Sawchuck (1984): T. C. Strand, Digital Optical Computing. *Proceedings of IEEE, 72*, 758–779.

[6] [1985-S1] B. Clymer and S. A. Collins (1985): Jr., Optical Computer Switching Net-work. *Op. Engg. 24*, 74–81.

[7] [1986-A1] K Brenner, A. Huang, and N. Streibel (1986): Digital Optical Computing with Symbolic Substitution. *App. Op. 25*, 3054–3064.

[8] [1986-A2] A. A. Sawchuk, B. K. Jenkins (1986): Dynamic Optical Interconnections for Parallel Processors. *Op. Comp.*

[9] [1986-S1] P.R. Haugen, S. Rychnovsky, A. Husain and L.D., Hutcheson (1986): Optical interconnects for high speed computing. *Op. Eng. 25*, 1076–1085

[10] [1986-S2] B.S. Wherrett (1986): Architectural Aspects of Optical Computing. *Photonic Logic and Information Processing.*

[11] [1986-S3] B. K. Jenkins, C. L. Giles (1986): Parallel Processing Pardigms and Optical Computing. *Optical Computing.*

[12] [1986-S4] T. E. Bell (1986): Optical Computing: A Field in Flux. *IEEE Spectrum 23*(8), 34–5,7

[13] [1986-S5] A. W. Lohmann (1986): What Classical Optics can do for the Digital Optical Computer. *App. Op. 25*, 1543–549

[14] [1986-S6] D.H. Hartman (1986): Digital High Speed Interconnects: A Study of the Optical Alternative. *Optical Engineering. 25*, 1086–1102

[15] [1987-A1] I. M. I. Habbab, M. Kavehrad, and C. E. W. Sundberg (1987): Protocals for Very High-Speed Optical Fiber Local Area Networks using a Passive Star Topology. *J. Lightwave Tech.* LT05:1782–1793

[16] [1987-A2] D. M. Chiarulli, R. G. Melhem, and S. P. Levitan (1987): Using Coincident Optical Pulses for Parallel Memory Addressing. *Comp.*

[17] [1987-S1] A. A. Sawchuk, B. K. Jenkins, and C.S. Raghavendra, and A. Varma (1987): Optical Crossbar Networks. *IEEE Comp. 20*(6), 50–60

[18] [1987-S2] M. J. Murdocca (1987): Digital Optical Computing with One-Rule Cellular Automata. *Applied Optics.*

[19] [1987-S3] L. D. Hucheson, P. Haugen, A. Husain (1987): Optical Interconnects replace hardwire. *IEEE Spectrum.*

[20] [1987-T1] R. Barakat and J. Reif (1987): Lowerbounds on the Computational Efficiency of Optical Computing Systems. *Applied Optics. 26*(6), 1015–1018

[21] [1988-A1] B. K. Jenkins and C. L. Giles (1988): Superposition in Optical Computing. *Proceedings of International Conference on Optical computing.* Toulon, France.

[22] [1988-B1] D. G. Feitelson (1988): *Optical Computing: A Survey for Computer Scientists.* The MIT Press, Cambridge, MA.

[23] [1988-D1] M. M. Eshaghian (1988): Parallel Computing with Optical Interconnects. Ph.D. Thesis, University of Southern California.

[24] [1988-T1] R. J. Anderson and G. L. Miller (1988): Optical Communication for Pointer Based Algorithms. Technical Report CRI 88-14, University of Southern California.

[25] [1988-T2] M. R. Feldman, S. C. Esener, C. C. Guest, and S. H. Lee (1988) Comparison between Optical and Electrical Interconnects based on Power and Speed Considerations. *Applied Optics. 27,* 1742–1751.

[26] [1989-A1] A. Hartman, and S. Redfield (1989): Design Sketches for Optical Crossbar Switches intended for Large-Scale Parallel Processing Applications. *Optical Engg. 28*(4), 315–327.

[27] [1989-A2] F. Kiamiley, S. Eseneer, R. Paturi, Y. Feinman, P. Mercier, C.C. Guest, and S. H. Lee (1989): Programmable Optoelectronic Multiprocessors and their Comparison with Symbolic Substitution for Digital Optical Computing. *Op. Eng.* 28 April 1989.

[28] [1989-J1] S. H. Lee, and R. A. Athale (1989): Optical Computing. *Opt. Eng.* (special issue) *April.*

[29] [1989-S1] S. Toborg, and K. Hwang (1989): Exploring Neural Network and Optical computing Technologies. In *Parallel Processing for Supercomputers and Artificial Intelligence.* K. Hwang and D. Degroot, (eds) McGraw Hill.

[30] [1989-S2] P.B. Berra, A. Ghafoor, M. Guiznani, S. J. Marcinkowski, and P. A. Mitkas (1989): Optics and Supercomputing. *Proceedings of the IEEE,* 77(12), 1797–1815.

[31] [1989-T1] M. R. Feldman, C. C. Guest, T. J. Drabik, and S. C. Esener (1989): Comparison between Electrical and Free Space Optical Interconnects for Fine Grain Processor Arrays based on Interconnect Density Capabilities. *Appl. Optics. 28,* 3820–3829.

[32] [1990-S1] F. B. McCormick and M. E. Prise (1990): Optical Circuitry for Free-space Interconnections. *Appl. Optics. 29,* 2013–2018.

[33] [1990-T1] L. G. Valiant (1990): General Purpose Parallel Architectures, Chapter 18 of the *Handbook of Theoretical Computer Science.* J. Van Leeuwen Elsevie, (ed).

[34] [1991-A1] A. Benner, H. Jordan, and V. Heuring (1991): Digital Optical Computing With Optically Switched Directional Couplers. *Optical Eng., 30,* 1936–1941.

[35] [1991-A2] Z. Guo, R.G. Melhem, R. Hall, D. Chiarulli, and S. Levitan (1991): Pipe-lined Communications in Optically Interconnected Arrays. *J. Parallel and Distributed Comp. 12*(3), 269–282.

[36] [1991-B1] A. D. McAulay (1991): *Optical Computer Architectures: The Application of Optical Concepts to Next Generation Comp.* Wiley, New York, NY.

[37] [1991-T1] M. M. Eshaghian (1991): Parallel Algorithms for Image Processing on OMC. *IEEE Transactions on Comp. 40*(7), 827–833.

[38] [1992-A1] V. P. Heuring, H. F. Jordan and J. P. Pratt (1992): Bit-serial Architecture for Opt. Comp. *Applied Optics, 31*, 3213–3224.

[39] [1992-T1] A. Louri and A. Post (1992): Complexity Analysis of Optical-Computing paradigms. *App. Optics. 31*, 5568–5583.

[40] [1992-T2] M. Gereb-Graus and T. Tsantilas (1992): Efficient Optical Communication in Parallel Computers. *Proceedings of the ACM Symposium on Parallel Algorithms and Architectures. 4*, 41–48.

[41] [1993-A1] S. Wei, E. Schenfeld (1993): Hierarchical Interconnection Cache Networks. In the *Proceedings of the International Parallel Processing Symposium*, pp. 135–141.

[42] [1993-A2] C. Qiao and R. Melhem (1993): Time-division Optical Communications in Multiprocessor Arrays, *IEEE Transactions on Comp. 42*(5), 577–590.

[43] [1993-A3] G. C. Marsden, Ph. J. Marchand, P. Havery, and S. Esener (1993): Optical Transpose Interconnection System Architectures. *Opt. Lett. 18*(13), 1083–1085.

[44] [1993-J1] Melhem, R., and D. Chiarulli (1993): Special Issue of Optical Computing and Interconnection Systems. *In the J. of Parallel and Distributed Comp. 17*(3).

[45] [1993-T1] L A. Goldberg, M. Jerrum, T. Leighton, and S. Rao (1993): A Doubly Logarithmic Communication Algorithm for the Completely Connected Optical Communication Parallel Computer. In *Proceedings of ACM Symposium on Parallel Algorithms and Architectures*, pp. 300–309.

[46] [1994-A2] M. M. Eshaghian, S. H. Lee, and M. E. Shaaban (1994): Optical Techniques for Parallel Image Computing. *Journal of Parallel and Distributed Comp. 3*(2), 190–201.

[47] [1994-A3] D. M. Chiarulli, S. P. Levitan, R. G. Melhem, M. Bidnurkar, R. Ditmore, G. Gravenstreter, Z. Guo, C. Qiao, M. F. Sakr, and J. P. Teza (1994): Optoelectronic Buses for High-Performance Comp. *Proceedings of the IEEE, 82*(11), 1701–1710.

[48] [1994-B1] J. Jahns and S.H. Lee (1994): *Optical Computing Hardware, Academic Press, Boston.*

[49] [1994-S1] H. S. Hinton et al. (1994): Free-Space Digital Optical Systems. *Proceedings of IEEE, Special Issue on Opt. Comp. Sys.* Nov. 1994. *82*(11), 1632–1649.

[50] [1994-T1] L. A. Goldberg, Y. Matias, and S. Rao (1994): An Optical Simulation of Shared Memory. *ACM Symposium on Parallel Algorithms and Architectures.*

[51] [1995-R1] P. Berthome, Th. Duboux, T. Hagerup, I. Newman, A. Schuster (1995): Self-simulation for the Passive Optical Star Model. *European Symposium on Algorithms, Lecture Notes in Comp. Sci., 979*, 369–380.

[52] [1995-S1] D. Feitelson, L. Rudolph (1995): The Promise of Optical Free-space Inter-connections for Concurrent Memory Access. *Technical Report 95-6*, Institute of Computer Science, Hebrew University, Jerusalem.

[53] [1995-T1] S. Rao, T. Suel, T. Tsantilas, (1995): Efficient Communication using Total-Exchange, *International parallel Processing Symposium.*

[54] [1996-A1] S. D. Pavel and S. G. Akl (1996): Matrix operations using arrays with Reconfigurable optical buses. *J. Parallel Algorithms and App. 8*, 223–242.

[55] [1996-D1] I. G. Yayla (1996): Speed and Energy Comparison between Electrical and Electro-optical Interconnects and Application to Opto-electronic Comp. Ph.D. Thesis, University of California, San Diego.

[56] [1996-R1] A. Aggarwal, A. Bar-Noy, D. Coppersmith, R. Ramaswami, B. Schieber, M. Sudan (1996): Efficient Routing in Optical Networks. *J. ACM.* *43*(6), 973–1001.

[57] [1996-S1] T. Yatagai (1996): Optical Computing and Interconnect. *Proceedings of IEEE*, *84*(6), June 1996, 828–852.

[58] [1997-A1] E. Harder, S. K. Lee, H. A. Choi (1997): On Wavelength Assignment in WDM Optical Networks. *Proceedings MPPOI '97*, Montreal, Canada.

[59] [1997-J1] M. M. Eshaghian and E. Schenfeld (1997): Special issue on Parallel Computing with Optical Interconnects. In the *J. Parallel and Distributed Comp. 41*(1).

[60] [1997-T1] L. Hai (1997): Efficient Parallel Computing with Optical Interconnects. Ph.D. Thesis, New Jersey Institute of Tech.

[61] [1998-A1] R. Melhem, G. Gravensteter, D. Chiarulli, and S. Levitan (1998): The Communication Capabilities of Partitioned Optical Passive Stars Networks. In *Parallel Computing using Optical Interconnection.* (K. Li, Y. Pan and S. Zheng (eds)) Kluwer Academic Publishers.

[62] [1998-A2] Y. Pan, M. Hamdi, and K. Li (1998): Efficient and Scalable Quicksort on a Linear Array with a Reconfigurable Pipelined Bus System. *Future Generation Computer Systems, 13*(6), 501–513.

[63] [1998-A3] T.H. Szymanski, A. Au, M. Lafrenire-Roula, V. Tyan, B. Supmonchai, J. Wong, B. Zerrouk, and S.T. Obenaus (1998): Terabit Optical Local Area Networks for Multiprocessing Systems. *Applied Optics, Special Issue on Massively Parallel Optical Interconnects for Multiprocessor Systems, 37*(2), 264–275.

[64] [1998-A4] D. C. Hoffmeister, J. Chu, J. A. Perreault, and P. Dowd (1998): Lightning Network and Systems Architecture. In K. Li, Y. Pan, and S. Zheng (eds). *on Parallel Computing using Optical Interconnections.* Kluwer Academic Publishers.

[65] [1998-B1] K. Li, Y. Pan, and S. Zheng (1998): Parallel Computing using Optical Interconnections. Kluwer Academic Publishers.

[66] [1998-T1] P. D. MackKenzie and V. Ramachandran (1998): ERCW PRAMs and Optical Communication. *Theoretical Comp. Sci. 196*, 153–180.

[67] [1998-T2] L.A. Goldberg, M. Jerrum, P. Mckenzie (1998): An Ω (loglogn)$^{\frac{1}{2}}$ Lower-bound for Routing in Optical Networks. *SIAM J. Comp.*

[68] [1998-T3] S. Q. Zheng (1998): An abstract Model for Optical Interconnection Networks. In K. Li, Y. Pan and S. Zheng (eds) *on Parallel Computing using Optical Interconnections*, Kluwer Academic Publishers.

[69] [1999-A1] P. Lalanne, J. Hazart, P. Chavel, E. Cambril, and H. Launois (1999): Transmission Polarizing Beam Splitter Grating. *J. Optics, A: Pure App. Opt. 1*, 215–219.

[70] [1999-A2] M. Raksapatcharawong, T. M. Pinkston, and Y. Choi (1999): Evaluation of Design Issues for Optoelectronic Cores: A Case Study of the WARPII router. *J. Optics, A: Pure Applied Optics, 1*, 249–254.

[71] [1999-A3] S. J. Fancey, M. R. Taghizadeh, G. S. Buller, M. P. Y. Desmulliez, and A. C. Walker (1999): Optical components of the smart-pixel optoelectronic connection (SPOEC) project. *J. Optics, A: Pure Applied Optics. 1*, 304–306.

[72] [2000-A1] B. Webb, and A. Louri (2000): A Class of Highly Scalable Optical Cross-bar-Connected Interconnection Networks (SOCNs) for Parallel Computing Systems. In *IEEE Transactions on Parallel and Distributed Sys. 11*(5).

[73] [2001-A1] L. Hai (2001): An Optically Interconnected Reconfigurable Mesh, *J. Parallel and Distributed Comp. 61*, 737–747.

[74] [2001-S1] Sartaj Sahni (2001): Models and Algorithms for Optical and Optoelectronic Parallel Computers. *Int. J. on Foundations of Comp. Sci. 12(3)*.

[75] [2003-A1] C.-H. Ji, and Y.-K. kim (2003): Electromagnetic Micromirror Array with Single-Crystal Silicon Mirror Plate and Aluminum Spring. *In J. Lightwave Tech. 21*(3).

[76] [2003-J1] L. Lin, M. Wu, R. Sawada, and J. Mohr (2003): edited special issue on Optical MEMS and Its Future Trends. In *J. Lightwave Tech. 21*(3).

[77] [2003-R1] S. yao, B. Mukherjee, S.J. Ben Yoo, and S. Dixit (2003): A Unified Study of Contenstion-Resolution Schemes in Optical packet-Switched Networks. *J. Lightwave Tech. 21*(3).

[78] [2003-R2] M. M. Eshaghian (2003): Nanoscale Computing Structures. *Proceedings of the 7th World Multi-conference on Systemics, Cybernetics, and Informatics, SCI2003*, Florida.

[79] [2003-S1] M. Mehta (2003): ISRC Future Technology topic Brief. Bauer College of Business Administration, University of Houston, Texas.

[80] [2006-S1] M. M. Eshaghian, Amar H. Flood, Alexander Khitun, Vwani Roychowdhury, J. Fraser Stoddart and Kang Wang (2006): Molecular and Nanoscale Computing and Technology. In A. Zomaya (ed), entitled *Handbook of Nature-Inspired and Innovative Computing*, Springer USA.

Chapter 11

MORPHWARE AND CONFIGWARE
Reiner Hartenstein
TU Kaiserslautern

Abstract

This chapter introduces morphware as the basis of a second machine paradigm, which mainly has been introduced by the discipline of embedded system design, targeting the system on chip (SoC). But more recently SoC design is adopting more and more computer science (CS) mentality and also needs the services of computer science (CS) professionals. CS is going to include the morphware paradigm in its intellectual infrastructure. The time has come to bridge the traditional hardware–software chasm. A dichotomy of two machine paradigms is the road map to upgrade CS curricula by evolution, rather than by revolution. This chapter mainly introduces morphware platforms as well as their models and architectures.

1   INTRODUCTION

Morphware [1] [2] is the new computing paradigm, the alternative RAM-based general-purpose computing platform model. The traditional hardware–software chasm distinguishes software running on programmable computing engines (microprocessors) *driven by instruction streams* scanned from RAM, as well as application-specific fixed hardware like accelerators that are not programmable after fabrication. The operations of such accelerators are primarily *driven by data streams*. Such accelerators are needed because of the microprocessor's performance limits caused by the sequential nature of its operation—by the *von Neumann bottleneck*.

John von Neumann's key achievement has been the simple common model called the *von Neumann machine paradigm* ([3, 4], von Neumann has not invented the computer). His model provides excellent guidance in CS education and also narrows the almost infinite design space. However, the contemporary common model of computing systems is the cooperation of the (micro)processor and its accelerator(s), including an interface between both (Figure 11.1). This model

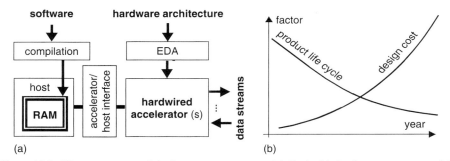

Figure 11.1. The common model of computer systems. (a) Embedded microprocessor model; (b) impact of the second design crisis.

holds not only for embedded systems but also for the PC needing accelerators not only for running its own display. Accelerators are a kind of slaves. The operating system and other software are running on the microprocessor, which is the host and master of the accelerators. The host may send parameters (for example, mode select, start, stop, reset, etc.) and receive interrupts and some result data.

The host operation is *instruction–stream driven*. The instruction stream is managed by the program counter inside the host processor. The accelerator usually has no program counter; its operations are *data–stream driven* (see *data stream* interface in Figure 11.1). Not only in terms of efficiency, this model especially makes sense for data-intensive applications, where *multiple data streams* are interfaced to the accelerator Figure 11.1. Only a few very sophisticated architectures are difficult to map onto this model. In the case of computation–intensive applications with very low data traffic to/from the accelerator, a single data stream generated by the host may be sufficient. This model (for details, see the next section and Section 3.1 ff. is as simple as the host's von Neumann (vN) model, which is also important for educational purposes (for details, see also Section 3.1).

By the way, *data–stream–driven computing (or flowware–based computing*: this term will be defined later) had already been used implicitly by the first programmers. In a von–Neumann–based, instruction–stream–driven environment, the less efficient *detour* over the application control-structures has been the only viable solution. However, by avoiding the (vN) bottleneck, a data–stream–driven environment permits much more direct and efficient solutions. For more detailed explanations, see Section 11.3.

vN processor programming is supported by compilers, whereas traditional accelerator development has been and is done with electronic design automation (*EDA*), tools [5]—for acronyms, see Figure 11.2.

More recently, however, such accelerator design has been affected by the second *design crisis* (Figure 11.1b). Compared with microprocessor design, the SoC design productivity in terms of gates per day is slower by a factor of about 10^{-4} [6]. Another symptom of increasing design implementation problems and the *silicon technology crisis* has been the drastically decreasing number of wafer starts for newer technology fabrication (Figure 11.3a) and the still decreasing low number of *application-specific IC* design starts (Figure 11.3c). Another major cost fac-

AM	anti-machine (DS machine)	ISP	instruction stream processor
AMP	data stream (AM) processor	LSI	Large Scale ICs
ASIC	application-specific IC	LUT	Look-Up Table
asMB	autosequencing Memory Bank	MCGA	Mask-Configurable Gate Array
BIST	Built-In Self-Test	MPGA	(see MCGA)
CFB	Configurable Function Block	MSI	Medium Scale ICs
CLB	Configurable Logic Block	MW	Morphware
COTS	commodity off the shelf	PC	Personal Computer
CPU	"central" processing unit: DPU	PS	Personal Supercomputer
	(with instruction sequencer)	pSoC	programmable SoC
cSoC	configurable SoC	rDPU	reconfigurable DPU
CW	Configware	rDPA	reconfigurable DPA
DAC	Design Automation Conference	RA	reconfigurable array
DPA	data path array (DPU array)	RAM	random access memory
DS	data stream	rAMP	reconfigurable AMP
DPU	data path unit (without sequencer)	RC	reconfigurable computing
ecDPU	emulation-capable DPU	rGA	reconfigurable gate array
EM	evolutionary methods	RL	reconfigurable logic
EDA	electronic design automation	RTR	run-time reconfiguration
EH	evolvable morphware ("evolvable	SoC	(an entire) System on a Chip
	hardware")	SSI	Small Scale ICs
FPGA	field-programmable gate array	SW	Software
FRGA	field-reconfigurable gate array	System	C C dialect f.Hw/Sw co–design
FW	Flowware	UML	Unified Modeling Language
GNU	GNU's Not Unix (consortium)	Verilog	a popular C-like HDL
HDL	Hardware Description Language	VHDL	VHSIC Design Language
			an HDL)
HPC	High-Performance Computing		
HW	Hardware	VHSIC	Very High Speed ICs
IC	integrated circuit	VLSI	Very Large Scale ICs
IP	intellectual property	vN	von Neumann

Figure 11.2. Acronyms

tor of the application-specific silicon, needed for accelerators, is increasing mask cost (Figure 11.3b), driven by growing wafer size and the growing number of masks needed. ASIC stands for mask–configurable gate arrays and similar methodologies [7] that need fewer masks than *full custom ICs* requiring the full mask set of the fabrication process [8].

1.1 Morphware

Illustrated by Makimoto's wave model [9, 10], the advent of morphware is the most important revolution in silicon application since the introduction of the microprocessor [11]. Emerging in the 1980s and now having moved from a niche market to mainstream, this third class of platforms now fills the gap between vN–type procedural compute engines and application–specific hardware. It is *morphware*, the fastest growing segment of the semiconductor market. (for terminology, see also Figure 11.5). The most important benefit of morphware is the opportunity to replace hardwired accelerators by RAM–based reconfigurable accelerators so that application–specific silicon can be mostly avoided, as is well-known from running software on the vN–type microprocessor. This will be

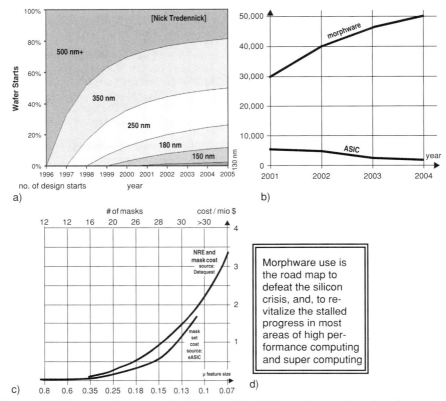

Figure 11.3. The second design crisis (silicon crisis). a) Decreasing number of wafer starts, b) growing number of morphware-based design starts [13] vs. declining number of ASIC design starts [13]; demonstrating that morphware already has reached mainstream status; c) increasing mask set cost and total NRE cost; d) providing the road map on the way out of the silicon crisis.

explained in the following paragraphs. The very high and still increasing number of morphware–based design starts (Figure 11.3c) demonstrates the benefit of using replacement morphware platforms instead of ASICs, where the backlog of design starts over morphware has exceeded a factor of more than 10 and is growing further.

> von Neumann's key achievement is the simple common model called the *von Neumann machine paradigm.*

Morphware is structurally programmable hardware, where the interconnect between logic blocks and/or functional blocks, as well as the active functions of such blocks, can be altered individually by *downloading configware*, down to the *configuration memory (configuration RAM)* of a morphware chip (also compare Figure 11.6e). So we need two kinds of input sources: Traditional *software* for programming instruction streams, and *configware* for structural reconfiguration of morphware.

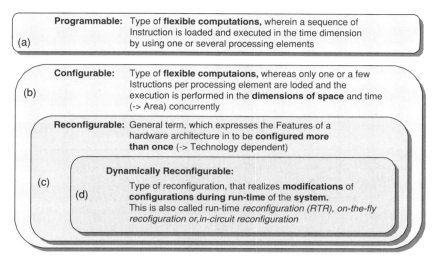

Figure 11.4. Contributions to terminology [12]: Programmable vs. (re)configurable.

	Platform	Program source	Machine paradigm
	Hardware	(not program-mable)	(None)
Mor-phware	Fine grain morphware	*Configware*	
	Coarse grain morphware (data-stream-based)	*Configware & flowware*	Anti-machine*
Hard-wired proces-sor	Data-stream-based computing	*Flowware*	
	Instruction-stream-based computing	Software	Von Neu-mann

* see Section 19.3.6 and Figure 11.23.

Figure 11.5. Terminology.

Before going into more detail, we should take a first step in clarifying the *termi-nology* around reconfigurability [12]. To highlight the key issues in distinguishing the classical vN paradigm from morphware, we should define the term *reconfig-urable*, because *reconfiguration* in general has many different meanings. In com-puting sciences, the terms *programmable* refer to the *time domain*, where *programming* means *instruction scheduling* (Figure 11.4a). The term *configurable* introduces the *space domain*, where *configuration* means *the setup of structures* and preadjustment of logic blocks or function blocks (Figure 11.4b). *Reconfiguration* means, that a platform can be configured several times for different structures (Figure 11.4c), whereas Mask–Configurable Gate Arrays (see Section 2) can be con-figured only once. Configuration or reconfiguration usually is *impossible during run time*. But *dynamically reconfigurable* (Figure 11.4d) means that partial reconfigura-tion may happen at run time. A warning to educators: Dynamically reconfigurable

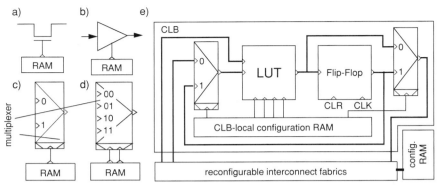

Figure 11.6. Programmable switches and blocks used in FRGAs. a) Pass transistor; b) Tristate buffer; c) two–way multiplexer; d) four–way multiplexer, e) simplified example of a configurable Logic Block (CLB).

or *self–reconfigurable* systems are more bug prone than others and are more difficult to explain and to understand.

By introducing morphware, we obtain a new general model of embedded computers (Figure 11.7a): *The accelerator has become reconfigurable*. It has been changed from hardware (Figure 11.1a) to morphware. As mentioned previously, accelerator operation is usually data–stream–based. Because of its *non–von Neumann machine principles*, an accelerator has *no von Neumann bottleneck* and may be interfaced to a larger number of data streams (Figure 11.23c, d). With a

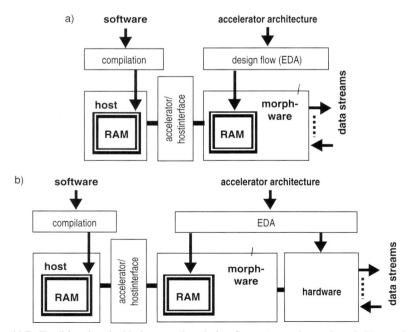

Figure 11.7. Traditional embedded computing design flow. a) morphware based; b) morphware/hardware–based.

morphware accelerator (Figure 11.7a), the host may also use the host/accelerator interface to organize the reconfiguration process (this will be explained later). Also, mixed–type accelerators are possible (Figure 11.7b): Hardware and morphware. However, a few architectures include morphware directly inside the vN microprocessor. Here the morphware is used for *flexible instruction set extensions* [14, 15], a modern version of the vN model only, where morphware is connected to the *processor bus* (Figure 11.8a). Also most *network processors* use instruction set extensions [16]. This situation is different from the common model shown in Figure 11.7, where morphware is just connected to the host's *memory bus* (Figure 11.8b).

1.2   Two RAM-based machine paradigms

We now have two different RAM–based input source paradigms: One for scheduling (programming) the instruction streams, to be scanned *from RAM program memory <u>during</u> run time* by sequences of instruction fetches, and the other for configuring structures by downloading configware code *to the configuration RAM <u>before</u> run time*. Downloading configware code is a kind of pseudo–instruction fetch (but here <u>not</u> at run time) where, however, such "instructions" or expressions may be much more powerful than microprocessor instructions. The configuration RAM is often called *hidden RAM*, because it is not nicely concentrated into a matrix, as in typical RAM components sold by IC vendors. Physically, the individual memory cells in a morphware device are located close to the switch point or connect point they are controlling (see the flip–flops *FF* in Figure 11.10c and d). Also, the addressing method used by morphware for downloading reconfiguration code is often different from that of classical RAM.

> Data–stream–driven computing had already been used implicitly by the first programmers.

It was recognized rather early that morphware had introduced a fundamentally new machine paradigm. Field–reconfigurable Custom Computing Machines (FCCM) [17], the name of an annual conference series, is an indication. A major

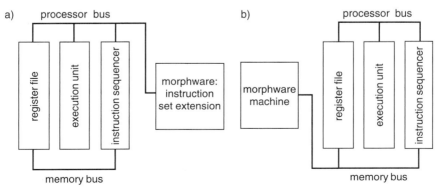

Figure 11.8. Alternative morphware applications. a) von Neumann processor with morphware–based instruction set extension; b) von Neumann host with morphware–based coprocessor.

number of experimental computing machines of this kind have been implemented, mostly from academia (for a survey covering the years 1995 and earlier, see [18]).

As mentioned earlier, the use of commodity off–the–shelf (COTS) morphware for acceleration can avoid the very costly need for application–specific silicon. Both kinds of platforms support *rapid downloading of patches, upgrades, or even new applications* down to the RAM program memory, even via the Internet. The consequence is a change of the business model for accelerators. *Personalization before fabrication*, typical of hardwired accelerators, can be replaced by the business model of the microprocessor, using *personalization after fabrication*—at the customer's site.

It is very important to distinguish, that the personalization source for vN microprocessors is *software*, and for morphware it is *configware*. Because of the growing importance of configware we currently observe a growing *configware industry*—a kind of emerging competitor to the *software industry*. Morphware has become an essential and indispensable ingredient in SoC (System on a Chip) design and beyond. Morphware meanwhile is used practically everywhere, so this chapter has no room for a survey to mention all uses. A good reading source is the volumes of proceedings (published by Springer in its LNCS series [19]) of Field–Programmable Logic [20], the annual international conference on Field–Programmable Logic and its applications, and the largest conference in this area.

2   FINE-GRAIN MORPHWARE

Since their introduction in 1984, *Field–Reconfigurable Gate Arrays* (*FRGAs*, often also called FPGAs), or *reconfigurable Gate Arrays* (*rGAs*) have become the most popular implementation media for digital circuits. For a reading source on the role of rGAs (providing 148 references), see [21]. The very high and increasing number of design starts on FRGAs demonstrates that the mask–configurable ASICs were already the losers years ago (Figure 11.3c). The technology-driven progress of FRGAs (for key issues, see [22]) is much faster than that of microprocessors. FRGAs with 50 mio system gates are coming soon [23]. It is well known that the growth rate of the integration density of microprocessors is much slower than Moore's law. However, because of the high degree of layout regularity, the integration density of FRGAs is moving at the same speed as Moore's law [9]. But because of the high percentage of wiring area, the transistor density of FRGAs is memory behind by two orders of magnitude [9]. However, the number of transistors per chip on FRGAs had surpassed that of microprocessors already by the early 1990s and is now higher by two orders of magnitude [9].

2.1   The Role of rGAs

We may distinguish two classes of morphware: *Fine-grain* reconfigurable morphware, and *coarse–grain* reconfigurable morphware. Reconfigurability of fine granularity means that the functional blocks have a datapath width of about one bit. This means that programming, at a low abstraction level, is logic design. Practically all products on the market are *FPGAs* (field–programmable gate arrays, better called *FRGAs* or *rGAs*: (*(field–)reconfigurable gate arrays*), although some vendors prefer different terms as kinds of brand names, like, for instance, Programmable Logic Device (PLD), or reconfigurable logic device LD. Morphware platforms and their applications have undergone a long sequence of transitions. First, FPGAs appeared as cheap replacements for *MPGAs* (or *MCGAs*: Mask-Configurable Gate Arrays). Even today, FRGAs are the reason for the shrinking ASIC markets (Figure 11.3c), since for FPGAs no application-specific silicon is needed—a dominating cost factor in low production volume products. (ASIC fabrication cost is much lower—only a few specific masks are needed than that of other integrated circuits.) Later, the area proceeded into a new model of computing possible with FRGAs. The next step was making use of the possibility for debugging or modifications during the last day or week, which also led to its adoption by the *rapid prototyping* community which also has led to the introduction of *ASIC emulators* faster than simulators. The next step is direct *incircuit execution* for debugging and patching at the last minute.

> Meanwhile, morphware is used practically everywhere.

From a terminology point of view, the historic acronyms *FPGA* and *FPL* are a bad choice, because programming, i.e., scheduling, is a *procedural* issue in the *time domain*. The term *PLD* is also a bad choice and should be replaced by *rLD*. A program determines a *time sequence* of executions. In fact, the FP in FPGA and in FPL (the acronym for *field–programmable*), actually means *field reconfigurable*, which is a structural issue *in the space domain: configuration in space*. For a clearly consistent terminology, it would be better to use *FRGA (field–reconfigurable gate array)* or *rGA* instead of FPGA. Throughout this chapter the term *rGA* or *FRGA* will be used instead of *FPGA*. For terminology, see Figure 11.2, Figure 11.5, and Sections 2.5 and 4.1.

The most important architectural classes of rGAs are (see [24]) island architecture (Xilinx), hierarchical architecture (Altera), and row–based architecture (Actel). A more historic architecture is *mesh–connected*, sometimes also called *sea of gates* (introduced by Algotronix) [25]. A simple example of Configurable Logic Block block diagram is shown in Figure 11.6. Its functional principles by multiplexer implementation are shown in Figure 11.9a and b, where in CMOS technology, only 12 transistors are needed for the fully decoded multiplexer (Figure 11.9c). The island architecture is illustrated in Figure 11.10a. Figure 11.10b show details of *switch boxes* and *connect boxes*. Figure 11.10c shows the circuit diagram of a *cross point* in a switch box, and, Figure 11.10d shows the same from within a connect box. The thick wire in Figure 11.10b illustrates how these interconnect resources are configured to connect a pin of one CLB with a pin of another CLB. The total configuration of all wires of an application is organized by a *placement and routing* software. Sometimes more interconnect resources are needed than are available, so for some CLB not all pins can be reached. Due to such *routing congestion*, it may happen that a percentage of CLBs cannot be used.

2.2 Commercially available FRGAs

A wide variety of fine-grain morphware products is available from a number of vendors, such as the market leader Xilinx [26], the second largest vendor Altera

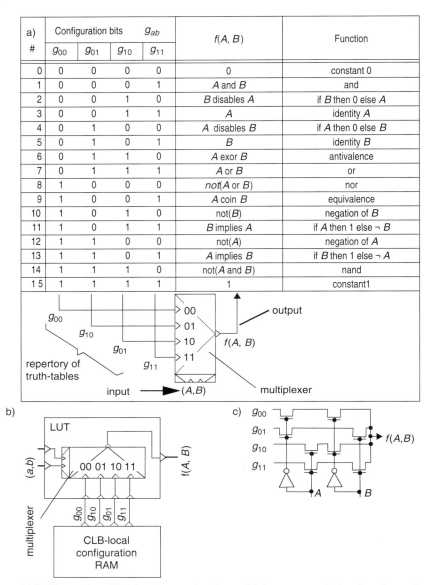

Figure 11.9. Illustrating LUT implementation by multiplexer: example for functions of two variables. a) illustration of the function generator; b) multiplexer circuit; c) illustration of LUT (look-up table) block use within CLB (compare Figure 11.6e).

[27], and many others. A variety of evaluation boards and prototyping boards is also offered. COTS (commodity off the shelf) boards for FRGA–based developments are available from Alpha Data, Anapolis, Celoxica, Hunt, Nallatech, and others, to support a broad range of in–house developments. As process geometries have shrunk into the deep–submicron region, the logic capacity of FRGAs has greatly increased, making FRGAs a viable implementation alternative for larger and larger designs. FRGAs are available in many different sizes and prices

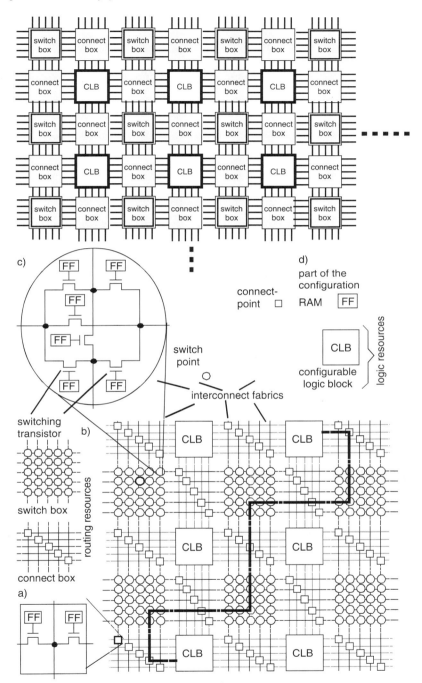

Figure 11.10. Illustrating FRGA island architecture fine-grain morphware resources. a) Global view of interconnect fabrics; b) detailed view (only one configured "wire" shown); c) connect point circuit of a switch box; d) connect point circuit of a connect box.

per piece, ranging from 10 US–dollars to FRGAs with many more than a million usable gates for more than 1000 US–dollars. Xilinx has preannounced FRGAs with 50 *mio* system gates around 2005 [23]. Modern FRGAs support mapping entire systems onto the chip by offering on board all components needed, such as several memory banks for user data; one or several microprocessors like ARM, PowerPC, MIPS, or others; a major number of communication interfaces (WAN, LAN, BoardAN, ChipAN etc.) supporting contemporary standards; up to several GHz bandwidth; JTAG boundary scan circuitry to support testing; sometimes even multipliers

Also, FRGAs featuring low power dissipation [28] or better radiation tolerance (for aerospace applications) are offered. Several major automotive corporations have contracts with FRGA vendors to develop morphware optimized for this branch of industry. Some commercially available FRGAs also support partial columnwise reconfiguration so that different talks may reside in the array and may be swapped individually. This setup may also support *dynamic reconfiguration* (*RTR*: run–time reconfiguration), where some tasks may be in the execution state, while at the same time other tasks are being reloaded. Dynamic reconfiguration, however, tends to be tricky and difficult to understand and to debug. But static reconfiguration is straightforward and easier to understand. Because reconfiguration is slow multi–context morphware has also been discussed, but is not yet available commercially. Multicontext morphware features several alternative internal reconfiguration memory banks, for example two or four banks, so that reconfiguration can be replaced by an ultrafast context switch to another memory bank.

2.3   Applications

Morphware is used practically everywhere, so this section can mention only a few examples. Most early FRGA applications have been rapid prototyping [25, 29, 30], rather than directly implementing products on morphware platforms. *Rapid prototyping* and *ASIC emulation* are still important for the development of hardwired integrated circuits. Since, in IC design, flow simulation may take days or even weeks, a remedy has been *ASIC emulation*, using huge emulation machines called *ASIC emulators*.

Earlier such machines included racks full of boards equipped with masses of FRGAs of the low density available at that time. Through acquisitions the three major EDA vendors now offer ASIC emulators, along with compilers: Cadence has acquired Quickturn, Synopsys has acquired IKOS, and Mentor Graphics has bought Celaro, also offering such service over the Internet. Another R&D scene and market segment calls itself *Rapid Prototyping*, where for smaller designs less complex emulation boards are used, such as Logic emulation PWB (based on the Xilinx Virtex FRGA series, which can emulate up to 3 million gates), and the DN3000k10 ASIC Emulator from the Dini Group.

The terminology is reconfigurable vs. programmable. The semantics is structural vs. procedural.

Another morphware application area is scientific high–performance computing (HPC) where often the desired performance is hard to attain through "traditional" high–performance computing. For instance, the gravitating n-body problem is one of the grand challenges of theoretical physics and astrophysics [31, 32]. Hydrodynamic problems fall into the same category, where often numerical modeling can be used only on the fastest available specialized hardware.

Analytical solutions exist for only a limited number of highly simplified cases. For example interpretation of dense centers of galactic nuclei, observed with the Hubble Space Telescope, by uniting the hydrodynamic and the gravitational approach within one numerical scheme. The maximum particle number was limited until recently to about 10^5 even on the largest supercomputers. For astrophysics, the situation improved thanks to the GRAPE special purpose computer [33]. To improve flexibility, a hybrid solution has been introduced with AHA-GRAPE, which includes auxiliary morphware [31]. Other morphware–based machines such as, WINE II, MDGRAPE [34], and MDM (Modular Dynamics Machine) [35–37] are also used for modeling and simulation in molecular dynamics [31, 33, 38].

Because of the availability of high–density FRGAs, the scenario has drastically changed. The trend is to deliver the FRGA–based solution directly to the customer, at least for lower production volumes. Not only microcontrollers or simple logic circuits are easy to transfer onto a FRGA platform; practically everything can migrate onto morphware. A single FRGA type may replace a variety of IC types. Design and debugging turn–around times can be reduced from several months to weeks or days. Patches or upgrades may take only days, hours, or even minutes, and may even be carried out at the customer's site or remotely over the Internet or wireless communication, which means a change of the business model—an important benefit for innovative efforts in remote diagnosis and other customer services.

A future application of emulation may serve to solve the long–term microchip spare-part problem in areas such as industrial equipment, military, aerospace, automotive, etc., with product lifetimes up to several decades [39]. The increasing spare-part demand stems from the increasing number of embedded systems, the limited lifetime of microchip fabrication lines (mostly less than 7–10 years), and the decreasing lifetime of unused microchips. When a modern car with several dozen embedded microchips needs electronic spare–parts 10 or 15 years later, the microchip fab line no longer exists, and a major percentage (or all) of the parts kept in spare–parts storehouses have faded away. The hope of keeping an old fab line alive that could deliver long–lasting robust products at low NRE cost seems to be an illusion. *Retro emulation* might be the only viable solution, where reverse engineered products are emulated on FRGAs, since application–specific silicon will not be affordable due to low microchip production volumes in these areas and rapidly increasing mask cost.

Fortunately now, with FRGAs, a new kind of IC platform is available so that we can switch from hardware to morphware, which can be "rewired" at run time. Because of their general–purpose properties, FRGAs are a suitable platform for reverse engineering of required but unavailable spare parts. Morphware is the fastest growing segment of the IC market [Dataquest]. Also for industries such as the automotive, aerospace, military, or industrial electronics such a common morphware platform would be a promising route to avoid very high mask costs,

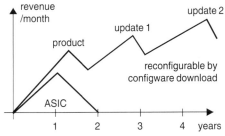

Figure 11.11. accelerator longevity [40].

to reduce the number of IC types needed, to accelerate IC time to market, and to solve long–term spare–part supply problems by retro emulation.

> In morphware application, the lack of algorithmic cleverness is an urgent educational problem.

The new business model of morphware brings a new dimension to digital system development and has a strong impact on SoC design (System–on–Chip). Performance by parallelism is only one part of the story. The time has come to fully exploit morphware flexibility to support very short turn–around time for real–time, in–system debugging, profiling, verification, tuning, field maintenance, and field upgrades. One of the consequences of the new business model is the adoption of a computer science mentality for developing all kinds of electronics products, where patches and upgrades are carried out at the customer's site (Figure 11.11), or even via the internet using Run–Time Reconfiguration (RTR). This approach is also an important remedy to the current embedded system design crisis, caused by skyrocketing design cost coinciding with decreasing product lifetime, by providing product longevity (Figure 11.1b).

2.4   Application Development support

Morphware is the fastest growing segment of the integrated circuit (IC) market, currently relying on a growing large user base of HDL–savvy designers. A number of books are available that give an introduction to application development using FRGAs [29, 41–45]. Not only is the configware industry rapidly growing, offering IP cores [46] and libraries for morphware platforms but also a rapidly growing branch of the EDA industry offers tools and design environments to support configware development. Complete design flows from HDL sources such as VHDL [47] are offered by Mentor Graphics [48], Synplicity [49], Celoxica [50], and others. A key issue is the integration of IP cores into the design flow. At DAC [51], a task force has been set up to solve standards problems.

> Sloppy terminology is a severe problem which torpedoes diffusion and education.

There are also design flows [52, 53] from Matlab sources [54], and a tool to generate HDL description from Unified Modeling Language has been reported [55]. An emerging trend is going to input sources of higher abstraction levels like the languages Handel–C by Celoxia, Precision–C from Mentor Graphics, SystemC [56, 57], a C dialect [58] by Synopsys [59] targeting HW/CW/SW co-design. Matlab indicates a tendency to go to even higher abstraction level of mathematical formulas. The emerging use of *term rewriting systems (TRS)* for design is another indication of this trend [60–63].

Also, a wide variety of vendors are offering tools not covering the entire design flow, such as those for debugging, timing estimation [64], simulation, verification, placement and routing, and other tasks, as well as soft IP cores. Examples include the CoreConnectBus (Xilinx), Parameterizes Processor (Xilinx), IPbus interface (Xilinx), embedded software development tools (Wind River, GNU, and others), Integrated Bus Analyzer (Xilinx), board support package for interface software (Xilinx), and over 40 processor IP models (Xilinx), [23]. Still a research area is morphware operating systems, to load and coordinate multiple tasks to be resident in a single FRGA. PACT has this sort of an OS for its XPP coarse–grain reconfigurable array (see Section 3), which can be *partly recon-figured* rapidly in parallel while neighboring reconfigurable data path units (rDPUs) are still processing data. Reconfiguration is triggered externally or even by special event signals originating within the array, *enabling self–reconfiguring designs* [65]. In general, there is still room for new tools and design flows offering improved quality and designer productivity. Key issues for the performance of FRGAs implemented in deep–submicron processes are the following three factors: the quality of the CAD tools used to map circuits into the FRGA, the quality of the FRGA architecture, and the electrical (i.e., transistor–level) design of the FRGA. In order to investigate the quality of different FRGA architectures, we need EDA tools capable of automatically implementing circuits in each FRGA architecture of interest.

19.2.5   Education

Education is an important area of application development support because it prevents a shortage of qualified professionals. In morphware application, the lack of algorithmic cleverness is one of the urgent educational problems. For instance, how can we implement a high–performance application for low-power dissipation on 100 datapath units running at 200 MHz, rather than on one processor running at 20 GHz? An example is the migration of an application from a very fast digital signal processor to a low power implementation on FRGA, yielding speedup factors between 5 and 22 [66]. The transformation of the algorithm from the software domain to fine–grain morphware required an enormous effort by the student-in-charge of this project, because such algorithmic cleverness is not yet taught within typical curricula.

The data stream paradigm has been around for almost three decades. Software uses it indirectly through inefficient instruction–stream implementations. Due to poor synthesis methodology, its direct use by systolic arrays remained a niche until the mid–1990s.

CS education is becoming more and more important for embedded system development, because SoC design has rapidly adopted CS mentality [67]. The amount of program code implemented for embedded systems doubles every 10 months and will reach 90% of all codes being written by the year 2010 [68]. Currently, a typical CS graduate with von–Neumann–only mentality does not have the skills needed for HW/CW/SW partitioning decisions nor the algorithmic cleverness needed to migrate an application from software onto an FRGA. The failure to teach the important skills, needed to map applications onto morphware in our CS curricula will cause a major disaster. Our current graduates are not qualified for the IT labor market of the near future [72].

Terminology is a key issue. It is very important to maintain a clear and consistent terminology. Sloppy terminology is a severe problem that torpedoes diffusion, education, and efforts to bridge communication gaps between disciplines. Too many experts using their own nonconsensus terminology are creating massive confusion: their colleagues often do not know what they are really talking about.

I have had my own frustrating experiences with contradictory terminology when teaching VHDL and Verilog in the same course [73]. Students have been confused by most of the terminology because, for almost each important term in this area, there have been usually three different definitions: 1) what the student associates with the term when hearing it for the first time, 2) how the term is used by VHDL experts, and 3) how it is used by Verilog experts.

Terminology should be tightly linked with common models. In both hardware and software, the *design space* has almost infinite size. Not only students get lost in this space without any guidance by models that narrow the design space. A machine paradigm is needed. The *von Neumann paradigm* has been highly successful for 50 years; but now because of the *dominance of morphware* we need a new, second, machine paradigm that can be used as a general model for guidance due to: (1) Its well–defined terminology, and (2) its simplicity: the *anti–machine paradigm* (see Section 3.6). The term *reconfigurable* has too many different meanings in too many different areas, including everyday life. For this reason the term *morphware* is often much better. Because terminology is so domain specific, you can guess a person's field by his or her use of terminology. When somebody associates *blacksmith* with *hardware*, you know this person is an IT professional. When somebody associates downloading drivers or other software into the RAM of a von Neumann machine with *reconfiguration*, you know that this person is not familiar with morphware and its environment.

2.6   Innovative Applications

Terms like *evolvable hardware* (EH) or in fact, *evolvable morphware (EM)*, *Darwinistic Methods* for system design, or *biologically inspired system design* point to a newer research area stimulated by the availability of fine-grain morphware. Also, retro emulation is an innovative application. It is an efficient way of re–engineering unavailable electronics parts for replacement to solve the long-term microchip spare-part problem in areas such as industrial equipment, military, aerospace, automotive, etc., with product lifetimes up to several decades. But in the future, reverse engineering can be avoided, it the implementation of all IC architectures are FRGA based from the beginning.

The antimachine has no von Neumann bottleneck. No caches are needed.

FRGAs may be good platforms to achieve *fault tolerance* by self–healing mechanisms [74, 75]. Partial rerouting can circumvent wires or CLBs found to be faulty. A NASA single–chip spacecraft has been discussed (breaking many paradigms in spacecraft design [76]), which is based on a high–density FRGA, does not need an operating system, and uses fault tolerance to reduce the need for radiation hardening. Currently available commercial FRGA architectures insufficiently support such rearrangements at run time. More research is required to obtain better architectural support [74, 77].

Another interesting area deals with *soft CPUs*, also called *FRGA CPUs*, i.e., microprocessors implemented by mapping their logic circuits onto an FRGA. Examples are the *MicroBlaze*, a 32–bit Harvard architecture from Xilinx [78], Altera's *Nios* processor [27], the ESA *SPARC LEON* open source core [79, 80], the *LEON2* processor [81], which is a synthesizable VHDL model of a 32-bit processor compliant with the SPARC V8 architecture, and the *Dragonfly* 8-bit core [78]. Of course, soft processors run about a factor of 3 to 5 times slower than their hardwired versions. By the way, designing soft CPUs is a popular subject of lab courses offered by a large number of universities.

2.7 Scalability and Relocatability

Relocation, even dynamically at run time, of configware macros is subject of the new area of configware operating systems [69–71]. Some FRGAs are so large that more than 100 soft CPUs can be mapped onto such a single chip. Will future giga–FRGAs permit the mapping of practically everything, including large rDPAs, onto a single morphware chip? This leads to the question of FRGA scalability. For instruction set processors, the von Neumann bottleneck guarantees full relocatability of code. Within very large FRGAs, however, relocatability might be limited by routing congestion (Figure 11.12a). But *Structured Configware Design* (a design philosophy derived from structured VLSI design [82]) is a promising approach to solve the relocatability problem (Figure 11.12b), so that FRGAs may be universal as microprocessors.

3 COARSE-GRAIN MORPHWARE

In contrast to fine-grain morphware using CLBs of smallest datapath width (~1 bit), coarse-grain morphware uses rDPUs (reconfigurable Data Path Units) with wide data paths, e.g., 32 bits wide. Instead of FRGAs, we have rDPAs (reconfigurable DPU Arrays). As an example, Figure 11.13 shows the result of mapping an image-processing application (SNN filter) onto a primarily mesh-based KressArray [83] with 160 rDPUs of 32-bit path width. This array is interfaced to 10 data streams: nine input streams and one output stream. Figure 11.14 shows some details of the XPU (xtreme processing unit), a commercially available rDPA from PACT AG [84–87]. Figure 11.15 illustrates the differences in the execution mechanisms. At vN execution (Figure 11.15a), exactly one operation is

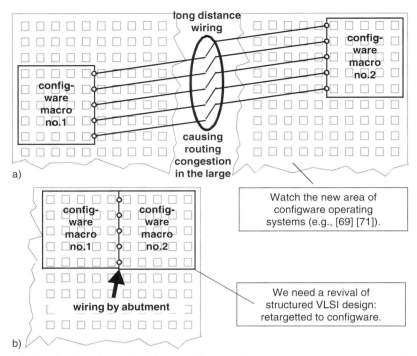

Figure 11.12. Solving a) the FRGA scalability problem b) automated structured configware design.

carried out per clock cycle. Intermediate results are stored in registers. For migration of such an algorithm from vN to an rDPA like PACT XPP (Figure 11.15b), a subsequence is mapped from time to space and executed in parallel on the array.

As soon as this operation is completed, the next chunk of parallelized code is executed. Intermediate results may be communicated by a buffer (see Figure 11.15b).

Usually an rDPA is a pipe network, not a multiprocessor or multicomputer network, since DPUs do not show a program counter (for details, see later sections of this chapter). Coarse–grain morphware has been a research area for more than a decade (for a survey, see [88, 89]). Since it plays an important role in wireless communication [90, 91], *software–defined radio* [92], and multimedia processing, not only performance but also MIPS / mW are key issues. Figure 11.16 shows that FRGAs just fill the efficiency gap and the flexibility gap between hardwired platforms and instruction set processors. Coarse-grain arrays, however, almost attain the efficiency of hardwired platforms (Figure 11.16), when mesh-based architectures using wiring by abutment are used so that no separate routing areas are needed [9]. Also, configuration memory being an order of magnitude smaller than that of FRGAs, contributes to this area/power efficiency [9].

Breaking away from the current mindset requires more than traditional technology development and infusion. It requires managerial commitment to a long-term plan to explore new thinking [96].

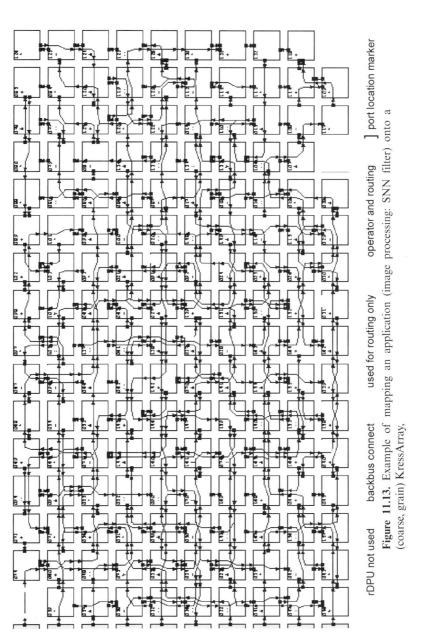

rDPU not used   backbus connect   used for routing only   operator and routing   ] port location marker

Figure 11.13. Example of mapping an application (image processing: SNN filter) onto a (coarse, grain) KressArray,

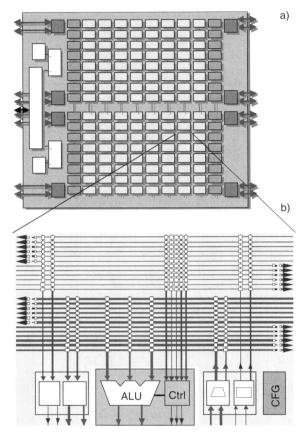

Figure 11.14. Configurable XPU (xtreme processing unit from PACT. a) Array structure; b) rDPU.

3.1   Pipe Networks and Flowware

We have to distinguish between two different domains of programming in time: *Instruction scheduling* and *data scheduling*. The programming code for von Neumann–like devices is an *instruction schedule*, compiled from *software* (Figure 11.17b). The programming code for resources like systolic arrays and other DPA (arrays of DPUs) is a *data schedule*, which can be compiled from *flowware* defining, which data item has to appear at which port at which time. Such data schedules manage the flow of *data streams*. This is illustrated in Figure 11.7a, showing a typical *data stream* notation introduced with *systolic arrays more than 20 years ago*.

The first *flowware–based* paradigm, the systolic array, got stuck in a niche for a long time (throughout the 1980s and beyond) because of the wrong synthesis method—until the *supersystolic array* made it viable for morphware. This

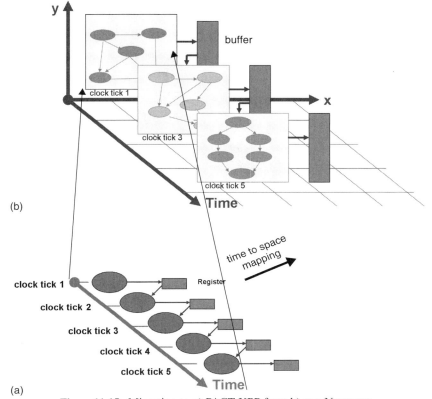

Figure 11.15. Migration to a) PACT XPP from b) von Neumann.

will be explained later. A systolic array [93–95] is a pipe network. The term *systolic* reminds us of the multiple data streams clocked into and out of such a pipe network and of its similarity to the heart and the bloodstreams entering and leaving it. Its DPUs never have instruction sequencers. The mode of DPU operation is transport triggered by data items. If synchronization is done by handshake instead of clocking, a systolic array may be also called a *wavefront array*.

The traditional systolic array could be used only for applications with strictly regular data dependencies, because array synthesis methods used linear projections or algebraic methods resembling linear projections. Such synthesis methods yield only strictly uniform arrays with linear pipes. The Data Path Synthesis System (DPSS) [83], however, uses simulated annealing (the mapper in Figure 11.17c), which removes the traditional application limitations, enabling the synthesis of *supersystolic arrays* featuring and also any kind of nonuniform arrays with any freeform pipes, such as zigzag, spiral, completely irregular, and many others. Due to this drastically improved flexibility, reconfigurable arrays (rDPAs) also make sense. The KressArray Xplorer, including a mapper, has been implemented as a design space explorer to optimize rDPU and rDPA architectures [97–99]. For more details on Xplorer, see Section Figure 3.4.

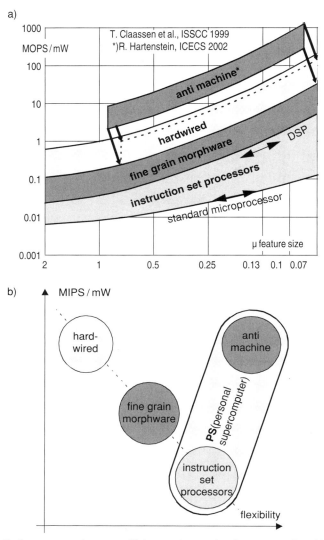

Figure 11.16. Performance and energy efficiency: a) vs. technology generation; b) vs. flexibility.

3.2   Data streams and flowware languages

More recently, data–stream–based computing has been popularized by a number of academic projects, such as SCCC [100], SCORE [101, 102], ASPRC [103], BEE [104, 105], KressArray [97, 98], and more [106]). The specifications of data streams can be expressed by *flowware language*. Data streams are created by executing flowware code on *auto–sequencing memory modules* (asM). Figure 11.19 a shows a distributed memory array of such asM modules driving data streams from/to the rDPA surrounded by the asMs. All enabling architectural resources for flowware execution are available [107, 108, 110, 111]. The new R&D discipline of application–specific distributed memory architectures [107] has arrived just in time

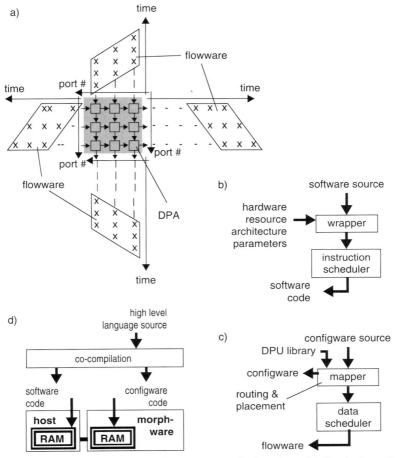

Figure 11.17. Compilation. a) a systolic array example (matrix multiplication) to illustrate flowware and its role; b) compilation for von Neumann platforms; c) configware / flowware compilation for morphware platforms; d) software / configware co/compilation.

to provide a methodology of architectural resources for processing flowware. Two alternative memory implementation methodologies are available [107, 112, 113], either specialized memory architectures using synthesized address generators (e.g., APT by IMEC [107]) or flexible memory architectures using programmable general–purpose address generators [109, 114]. Performance and power efficiency are supported especially by sequencers, which do not need memory cycles even for complex address computations [107], having been used also for the smart memory interface of an early antimachine architecture [114, 115].

Flowware may also be described by higher–level flowware languages [116], which are similar to high level software languages like C (Figure 11.21). Both languages have jumps, loops, and nested loops. The main differences between software and flowware is that, flowware semantics is based on one or several data counters, whereas software refers to only a single program counter. Because of

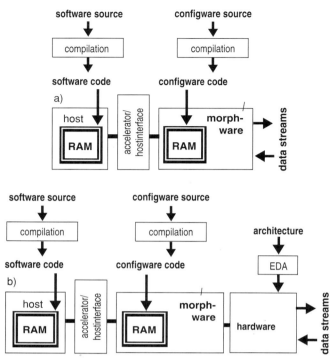

Figure 11.18. Modern embedded computing design flow. a) Software / configware codesign; b) software / configware / hardware codesign.

multiple data counters, flowware also features parallel loops, which are not supported by software languages. Flowware is much simpler because it does not need to express data manipulation.

Because of the wrong synthesis method, the systolic array, the first flowware–based paradigm, got stuck in a niche for a long time—until the super–systolic array made it viable for morphware.

For good morphware application development support, an integrated synthesis system is useful that efficiently supports configware / flowware codesign, such as, for instance, DPSS [83] (Figure 11.19b), so that the user does not need to care about the configware / flowware interaction. A well–designed dual–paradigm language covering both [116] the flowware paradigm and the configware paradigm, and supporting the communication between both segments, would be useful for designer productivity. Examples for multiple–scope languages are already existing hardware languages like VHDL [47] or Verilog [43], which support the co–description of hardware and software constructs and also alleviate the handling of hardware / software communication. The strong trend within EDA toward higher abstraction levels, heralded by new languages like System–C [56–58] and others, opens a path toward integrated codesign frameworks coordinating all three paradigms covering hardware, morphware, software, configware, and flowware.

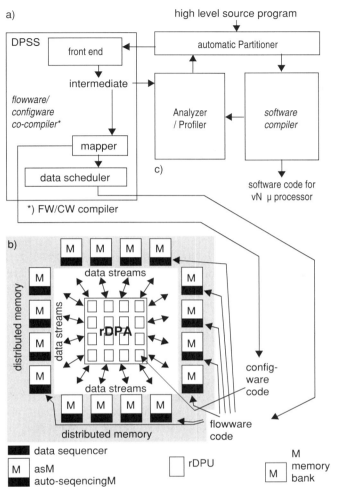

Figure 11.19. Flowware/configware/software cocompilation. a) Becker's partitioning cocompiler; b) antimachine target example.

The flowware–based common model of data–stream–based computing may be used for both hardware and morphware. There is, in principle, no difference, whether DPAs are hardwired or reconfigurable (rDPAs). The only important difference is the binding time of placement and routing before fabrication (hardware) or after fabrication (morphware: Compare Figure 11.27).

3.3   Coarse-Grain Arrays

Because the number of CFBs is by orders of magnitude smaller than that of CLBs in FRGAs, mapping takes only minutes or less instead of hours. Since computational data paths have regular structure potential, full custom designs of *reconfigurable datapath units* (rDPUs) are drastically more area–efficient, Coarse–grained architectures provide operator–level CFBs and very area–efficient datapath routing switches. A major benefit is massive reduction of configuration memory and configuration time, and drastic complexity reduction of the P&R (placement and routing) problem. Several architectures will be briefly outlined (for details, see [88]).

Primarily mesh–based architectures arrange their PEs mainly as a rectangular 2-D array with horizontal and vertical connections that support rich communication resources for efficient parallelism and encourage nearest neighbor links between adjacent PEs. Typically, longer lines are also added with different lengths for connections over distances larger than one. The *KressArray* [83] is primarily a mesh of rDPUs physically connected through wiring by abutment. *MATRIX* [117] is a multigranular array of 8–bit CFBs (basic with vN microprocessor core) *Reconfigurable Architecture Workstation (RAW)* [118] provides a 4–by–4 array RISC multiprocessor architecture of NN–connected 32–bit modified MIPS R2000 microprocessors. The *(Dynamically Reconfigurable Architecture for Mobile Systems (DReAM)* Array [119]) is for next–generation wireless communication.

Some RAs are based on one or several linear arrays, like *(Reconfigurable Pipelined Datapath) (RaPiD)* [120] and *PipeRench* [121]. Architectures using crossbars include *(Programmable Arithmetic Device for DSP) PADDI*, which uses a central reduced crossbar (difficult to rout) and a two level hierarchy of segmentable buses; *PADDI–1* [122, 123], and *PADDI–2* [124]. The *Pleiades* Architecture [66] is a kind of generalized low–power *PADDI–3*.

3.4   Compilation Techniques

The first step in introducing morphware–oriented compilation techniques in application development for embedded systems is the replacement of EDA (Figure 11.7a and b) by compilation also for the morphware part (Figure 11.18a and b). This step of evolution should be accompanied by a clean model that has been introduced in the course of history. Partly in synchrony with Tsugio Makimoto's Wave model [9, 10], Nick Tredennick summarizes the history of silicon application [125] in three phases (Figure 11.22a–c): Hardwired components like SSI, MSI, and LSI circuits which *cannot be programmed*; have fixed resources; and fixed algorithms (Figure 11.22a). The introduction of the microprocessor changes this set up to fixed resources but variable algorithms (Figure 11.22b). We need *only one programming source: Software* (Figure 22e). The advent of morphware has made both resources and algorithms variable (Figure 11.22c). We need *two programming sources: Configware* to program the resources, *and flowware* to program the data streams running through the resources (Figure 11.22f). An early implementation is the DPSS (Figure 11.17c, see also Section 3.1).

3.5   Cocompilation

Separate compilation of software and configware (Figure 11.18a and b) gives only limited support to reach the goal of good designer productivity. Especially to introduce *software / configware / flowware codesign* to CS professionals and CS curricula, we need *cocompilation techniques* to support application development at high abstraction levels. Figure 11.17c shows the typical structure of a *software / configware partitioning / cocompiler* (Figure 11.17c), where the configware part (DPSS in Figure 11.19b) includes both a *configware code generator* and a *flowware code generator. CoDe–X* was an early implementation of a compiler of this kind, which was a *partitioning cocompiler* (Figure 11.19b and c), accepting C language input (pointers are not supported), which partitions source input to run on a symbiosis of a host and a rDPA [126–128]. This partitioner (Figure 11.19c) was based on the identification of usability of *loop transformations* [129–134]. This partitioner was implemented via *simulated annealing*. An additional *analyzer / profiler* (Figure 11.19c) was used for further optimization. Figure 11.19b shows the flowware / configware compiler (a version of the DPSS) as explained above, which was used as a subsystem inside the CoDe–X co–compiler. Figure 11.20a gives some DPSS details. *ALE–X* is an intermediate form derived from the C language.

Language category	Software languages	Flowware languages
Sequencing managed by	Read next instruction, goto (instruction address), jump (to instruction address), instruction loop, nesting, **_no_** *parallel loops*, escapes, instruction stream branching	Read next data item, goto (data address), jump (to data address), data loop, nesting, *parallel loops*, escapes, data stream branching
Data manipulation	Yes	Not needed
State register	Program counter	Single or multiple data counter(s)
Instruction fetch	Memory cycle overhead	No overhead
Address computation	Massive memory cycle overhead	Drastically reduced overhead

It is time to bridge the hardware / software chasm. We need a Mead-&-Conway–like edu rush [135].

A newer version of DPSS includes *KressArray Xplorer* (Figure 11.20a), a design space explorer to optimize KressArray DPU and rDPA architectures [98, 99]. As shown in Figure 11.20a mapping based on architecture description one yields a different array configuration than that based on architecture description two. Figure 11.20b illustrates the high flexibility of the KressArray family concept accepted by Xplorer. Path width and mode of each nearest neighbor connection can be individually selected. Also, a wide variety of second–level of *back bus interconnect* resources are available (not shown in the figure) featuring highly parallel buses or bus segments. Other design space explorers include *DSEs (Design Space Explorers*, survey: [88]), which use automatic guidance systems or design assistants to give advice during the hardware (and morphware) design flow, e.g., by DPE (Design Planning Environment) [136]; *Clio* [137] (both for VLSI); and DIA (for ASICs) [138]. *Platform Space Explorers (PSEs)* are used to find an optimum vN processor array, as with DSE [139], *Intelligent Concurrent Object-oriented Synthesis (ICOS)* [140], and *DSE for Multimedia Processors (DSEMMP)* [141].

3.6   A Dichotomy of Two Machine Paradigms

Traditionally hardware experts have been needed for morphware application development (Figure 11.7a, compare Section 2.4). Because of the rapid growth of

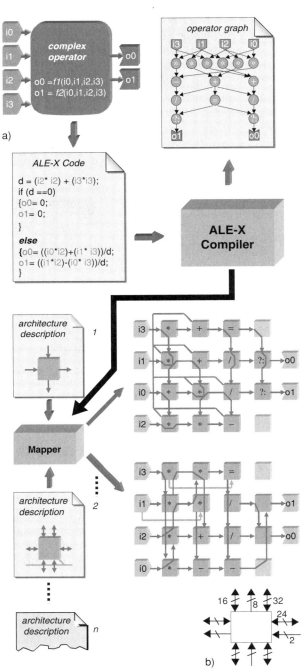

Figure 11.20. KressArray Xplorer (design space explorer [97]). a) Simplified example to illustrate platform space exploration by finding an optimized array depending on rDPU architecture (1 or 2); b) KressArray family rDPU example architecture illustrating flexibility.

Language category	Software Languages	Flowware Languages
Sequencing managed by	Read next instruction, goto (instruction address), jump (to instruction address), instruction loop, nesting, **_no parallel loops_**, escapes, instruction stream branching	Read next data item, goto (data address), jump (to data address), data loop, nesting, *parallel loops*, escapes, data stream branching
Data manipu-lation	Yes	Not needed
State register	Program counter	Single or multiple data counter(s)
Instruction fetch	Memory cycle overhead	No overhead
Address com-putation	Massive memory cycle overhead	Drastically reduced overhead

Figure 11.21. Software languages versus flowware languages.

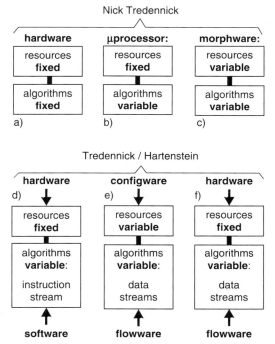

Figure 11.22. Nick Tredennick's digital system classification scheme. a) Hardwired; b) programmable in time; c) reconfigurable; d) von Neumann–like machine paradigm; e) reconfigurable antimachine paradigm, f) Broderson's hardwired antimachine.

the amount of code to be implemented for embedded systems [68], CS graduates are now also needed to handle the amount of work to be done. This expansion is hardly possible without moving to higher abstraction levels. Because it focuses on the design space, as the *von Neumann paradigm* does for software a second machine paradigm is needed as a simple guideline to implement flowware (and configware). This *antimachine paradigm* is summarized in Figure 11.23b–d. In contrast to the von Neumann paradigm (Figure 11.23a), the sequencer (data counter) has moved to the memory (as part of asM, an auto–sequencing memory bank), while the DPU of the antimachine has no sequencer (Figure 11.23b). The anti machine paradigm [141] also supports multiple data streams by multiple asMs providing multiple data counters (Figure 11.23c, d). That's why the antimachine has no von Neumann bottleneck. It does not need caches because of multiple data streams. Caches do not help because new data mostly have new values.

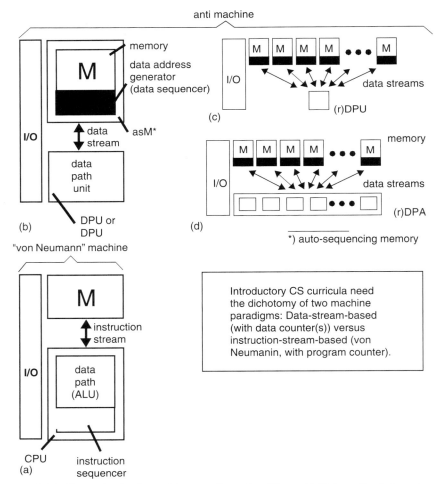

Figure 11.23. Illustrating basic machine paradigms (see Figure 11.19 legend). a) data–stream–based antimachine with simple DPU; b) with rDPU and distributed memory architecture; c) with DPU array (DPA or rDPA); d) von Neumann.

The enabling technologies for the antimachine architecture implementations are available [107, 108, 110–114, 142–144]. Figure 11.26a shows details of an antimachine mapped onto a KressArray, and Figure 11.26b shows the details mapped onto a PACT XPP array. The antimachine paradigm is useful for both morphware-based machines and hardwired machines ([145], etc.). The antimachine should not replace von Neumann: We need both machine paradigms. We need morphware to strengthen the declining vN paradigm.

The antimachine is not a *dataflow machine* [146] because it had been established by an old (now obsolete) research area that focused on an arbitration–driven machine, which checks, for each operator, whether all operands are available. In case of a reject, this operator can be resubmitted later. Such a machine operation is indeterministic, and for an algorithm, the total order of execution cannot be predicted. The execution of the vN machine and of the antimachine, however, is deterministic. However, the dataflow languages that have come along with this indeterministic paradigm [147] could also be useful sources for the antimachine.

4 THE IMPACT OF MORPHWARE ON COMPUTING SCIENCES

As labeled in Figure 11.24(3) the growth rate of algorithmic complexity [148] is higher than that of Moore's law (1), while the growth rate of microprocessor integration density (2) is far behind Moore's law. The improvement of computational efficiency in terms of mA needed per MIPS (5) has slowed down and is moving towards saturation. The performance requirements for wireless communication

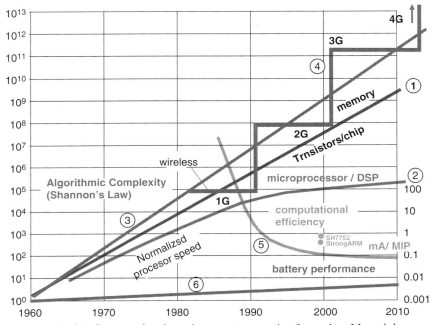

Figure 11.24. Computational requirements are growing faster than Moore's law.

(4) are rising by huge steps from device generation to device generation. Also, a number of other application areas such as multimedia or scientific computing (Section 2.3) suffer from a similar growth of requirements. Traditional HPC needs too much power: about 100W per gigaFLOPS [55]. Forth coming microprocessor generations promise only marginal performance improvements (Figure 11.25). A highly promising alternative is the microprocessor interfaced to a suitable coarse-grain array (Figure 11.17d), maybe for converting a PC into a PS (personal supercomputer). But such a PS will be accepted by the market only when it is accompanied by a good cocompiler (Figure 11.19b and c), the feasibility of which has been demonstrated [126–128].

The future of the microprocessor is no longer very promising: only marginal improvements can be expected for performance area efficiency (Figure 11.25). Power dissipation is becoming worse, generation by generation. The intel Itanium 2 on 130 nm technology with 410 million transistors dissipates 130 Watts at 1.3 Volts operating voltage [91] compared with 130 Watts at 1.6 Volts for the first Itanium. Traditional HPC (High Performance Computing) using such or similar microprocessors needs about 100W per gigaFLOPS [55]. Pipelined execution units within vN machines yield only marginal benefit for the price of sophisticated speculative scheduling strategies. Multithreading needs substantial overhead for any kind of multiplexing [149]. All these bad signs get added to the old limitations like the vN bottleneck [9, 147, 150–154]. Because of the increasing weakness of the microprocessor, we need a new computing paradigm as an auxiliary resource to cooperate with the microprocessor (Figure 11.16b). Morphware has arrived just in time. The future acceptance of the stand-alone operation of morphware is not very likely. Adding an rDPA and a good cocompiler to a microprocessor (Figure 11.17d) enables the PC to become a PS (personal supercomputer).

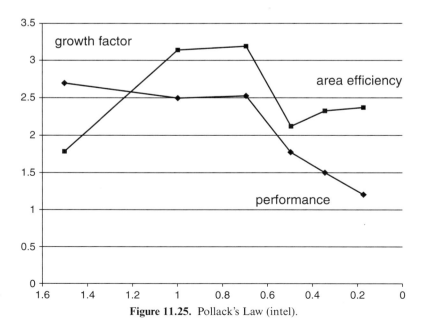

Figure 11.25. Pollack's Law (intel).

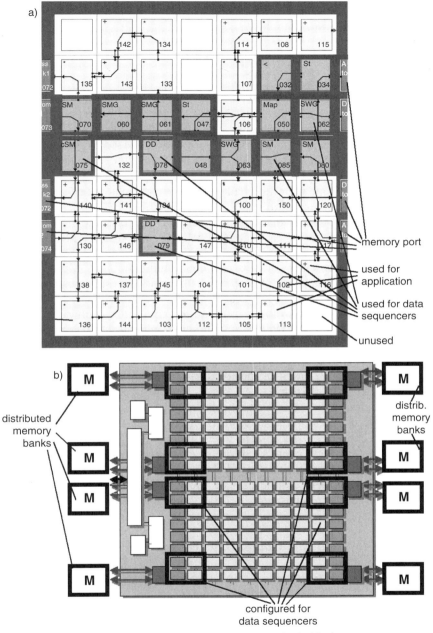

Figure 11.26. Antimachine mapped a) onto KressArray: synthesizable data sequencers mapped by KressArray Xplorer together with an application (linear filter) onto a KressArray; b) onto PACT XPP (another application example, distributed memory shown).

> Static reconfiguration is straightforward and easy to understand. But dynamic reconfiguration tends to be tricky and difficult to understand and to debug.

SoC design rapidly adopts a CS mentality [67]. The amount of program code implemented for embedded systems doubles every 10 months and will reach 90% of all codes being written by the year 2010 [68]. Currently, a typical CS graduate with von–Neumann–only mentality does not have the skills needed for HW / CW / SW partitioning decisions, nor the algorithmic cleverness needed to transfer an application from software onto an FRGA. There is a trend to convey the codesign of embedded computing systems from the domain of hardware expertise over to CS methodologies. To cope with this challenge to CS curricula, the new antimachine paradigm and new compilation methods are needed.

The hardware/software chasm in professional practice and in education is causing damage amounting to billions of EURO each year worldwide. It is the main reason for the productivity gap in embedded system design. Meanwhile, it is widely accepted that morphware is a new computing paradigm. Morphware provides the enabling fundamentals to cope with this crisis. It is time to bridge the hardware/software chasm. We need a Mead–&–Conway–like rush [135]. We are already on the way. Scientific computing is using more and more Morphware. The international HPC conference IPDPS is coming along with the rapidly growing Reconfigurable Architectures Workshop (RAW [155, 156]). The number of attendees from HPC coming to conferences like FPL [20] and RAW is rapidly increasing. Special interest groups of professional organizations are changing their scope, e.g., PARS [32, 157–159].

There is sufficient evidence that morphware is breaking through as a new computing paradigm. Breaking away from the current mindset requires more than traditional technology development and infusion. It requires managerial commitment to a long-term plan to explore new thinking [96]. Morphware has just achieved its breakthrough as a second class of RAM–based programmable data processing platforms—a counterpart of the RAM–based von Neumann paradigm. Morphware combines very high flexibility and programmability with the performance and efficiency of hardwired accelerators.

4.1   Reconfigurable Computing versus Parallel Processing

A comprehensive treatment of important issues in parallel computing is provided by *The Sourcebook for Parallel Computing* [150], a key reference giving a thorough introduction to parallel applications, software technologies, enabling technologies, and algorithms. Classical parallelism by concurrent computing has a number of disadvantages over parallelism by antimachines having no von Neumann bottleneck, as is discussed elsewhere [105, 114, 151, 152]. In parallel computing, unfortunately, the scaling of application performance often cannot match the peak speed the resource platforms seem to provide, and the programming burden for these machines remains heavy. The applications must be programmed to exploit parallelism in the most efficient way possible. Today, the responsibility for achieving the vision of scalable parallelism remains in the hands of the application. Amdahl's Law explains just one of several reasons for inefficient resource utilization [153]. vN–type processor chips are almost all memory, because the architecture is wrong [105]. Here the metric for what is a good solution has been wrong all along [105].

Reconfigurable versus parallel computing is also a very important issue for terminology—to avoid confusion. At the circuit level, all transistors look the same. So the question is how to distinguish switching within a reconfiguration fabric from other switching activities in an IC. The antimachine model introduced in section 3.6 is a good guideline for definition of the term *reconfigurable*. Switching during run time of instruction–stream–based operations, such as, addressing the register file is no reconfiguration. Switching inside a memory address decoder is also not reconfiguration. What about microprogramming? Is it reconfiguration? A microprogrammable instruction-set processor can be modeled by the nested machine model, showing that a microinstruction stream is also an instruction stream [149]. This means that running microcode *is not reconfiguration—it is execution* of a micro instruction stream. The following definitions will help us to avoid confusion. An important difference between reconfigurable computing and concurrent computing is determined by the binding time (Figure 11.27). Another important criterion is whether the code semantics is *structural* or *procedural*.

- The routing of data, addresses, and instructions during run time ***is not*** reconfiguration.

- Loading an instruction–stream–driven device to the program memory ***is not*** *reconfiguration*. It is procedural–style *programming* (instruction scheduling).

- Changing before their run time the effective *structure* of data paths and other resources: ***is definitely*** reconfiguration.

- Depending on the method used, dynamic reconfiguration (RTR) may be a hybrid, where parts of the system are running to manage the reconfiguration of other parts. (This chapter has already mentioned that RTR is quite a difficult subject.)

Within reconfigurable computing systems, the "instruction fetch" (i.e., setup of all computational resources and of all related communication paths) happens

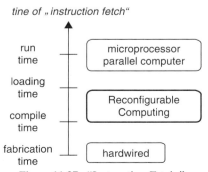

Figure 11.27. "Instruction Fetch."

before run time (Figure 11.27). We call this *reconfiguration* because it changes the effective structure of data paths and similar resources. Within concurrent computing systems, however, the instruction fetch and setup of all related communication paths happens *during* run time (Figure 11.27), which we *do not call reconfiguration*. The main difference with respect to performance is the amount of switching activity at run time, which is low for reconfigurable systems and high for instruction–stream–driven parallel computing. Depending on the application and the architecture, massively parallel concurrent systems may suffer heavily from communication congestion at run time. Because run time is more precious than compilation time, this migration of switching activities over to compile time or leading time is a welcome performance property of the morphware paradigm. Unfortunately, the distinction between parallel and reconfigurable computing is blurred by some projects labeled "reconfigurable" but that, in fact, deal with classical parallel computing on a single chip.

4.2   New Taxonomy Needed

We now live in a time exhibiting a shortage of analysts writing good and comprehensive surveys. What is currently missing and should soon be the subject of research is an all–embracing taxonomy of architectures and algorithms covering both areas, classical parallel computing and supercomputing, as well as reconfigurable computing. We need a taxonomy of architectures providing guidance in designing modern high–performance computing systems using resources from both areas, or to decide which area's resources provide the more promising alternatives. We also need all–embracing taxonomy algorithms to support the migration of applications or parts of applications from one area to another, for instance, from a vN platform to fine-grain morphware, or to coarse–grain morphware, or to mixed platforms. Such a taxonomy of algorithms should also survey the amount of interconnect resources needed by vN to morphware migration. Depending on the algorithm class, the interconnect requirements may show extremely wide variety. Some kinds of algorithms may be very easy to convert into pipelines, whereas others, for instance the parallelized Viterbi algorithm, may require enormously complex interconnect structures. A new taxonomy should be developed rapidly that supports the algorithmic cleverness needed for a good morphware–based designer productivity and for retrieving high–quality design solutions.

We need a new taxonomy of architectures and algorithms.

We should not hesitate to reform CS and CSE curricula in order to prevent disqualification in the job market in the near future. Introductory undergraduate programming lab courses should not support the development of a procedural-only mindset. Such courses should rather be a guide to the world of embedded systems, requiring algorithmic cleverness for partitioning an application problem into cooperating software, flowware, and configware blocks. The exercises of such courses should feature varieties of tasks, including several subtasks of different nature, such as, (1) software implementation of the problem, (2) flowware implementation of the problem, and (3) partitioning the problem into (3a) a software part, (3b) a flowware part, and (3c) development of the interface needed for its dual-paradigm coimplementation.

5   CONCLUSIONS

Morphware has become an essential and indispensable ingredient in SoC (System on a Chip) design and beyond. Already HDLs like VHDL (which is an Ada dialect), Verilog (a C dialect), and others are languages of higher abstraction levels and should be taught also to CS students.

The hardware/software chasm in professional practice and in education causes damage amounting to billions of EURO each year worldwide. It is the main reason for the productivity gap in embedded system design. Meanwhile, it is widely accepted that morphware is a new computing paradigm. Morphware provides the enabling fundamentals to cope with this crisis.

But most current work on reconfigurable systems is specialized and is not motivated by long-term aspects—wearing blinders that limit the view to particular applications, architectures, or tools. The long–term view, however, shows a heavy impact of reconfigurable computing upon the intellectual infrastructures of CS and CSE. This chapter has drafted a road map for upgrading CS and CSE curricula and for bridging the gap between a procedural and a structural mentality. The impact of morphware on CS will help to achieve this by evolution, rather than by revolution. You all should be evangelists for the diffusion of the visions needed to take this road and move out of the current crisis.

REFERENCES

[1] http://www.darpa.mil/ipto/programs/pca/vision.htm
[2] http://morphware.net/
[3] A. Burks, H. Goldstein, J. von Neumann (1946): Preliminary discussion of the logical design of an electronic computing instrument. US Army Ordnance Department Report.
[4] H. Goldstein, J. von Neumann, and A. Burks (1947): Report on the mathematical and logical aspects of an electronic computing instrument. *Princeton Institute of Advanced Study*.
[5] D. Jansen et al. (2003): The electronic design automation handbook, Kluwer.
[6] P. Gillick (2003): State of the art FPGA development tools. *Reconfigurable Computing Workshop*, Orsay, France.
[7] M. J. Smith (1997): Application specific integrated circuits, Addison Wesley.
[8] D. Chinnery and K. Keutzer (2002): Closing the gap between ASIC & custom, Kluwer.
[9] R. Hartenstein (invited paper) (1987): The Microprocessor is no more general purpose *Proc. IEEE International Symposium on Innovative Systems (ISIS)*, Austin, Texas.

[10] T. Makimoto (keynote) (2000): The rising wave of field–programmability, *Proc. FPL 2000*, Villach, Austria, August 27–30, Springer-Verlag, Heidelberg/New York.

[11] F. Faggin, M. Hoff, S. Mazor, and M. Shima (1996): The history of 4004. *IEEE Micro*. Dec. 1996.

[12] J. Becker (invited tutorial) (2003): Reconfigurable computing systems. *Proceedings Escola de Microelectrônica da SBC–Sul (EMICRO 2003)*. Rio Grande, Brasil, September.

[13] B. Lewis (2002): Gartner Dataquest, October 28.

[14] P. Athanas (1992): An adaptive Machine Architecture and Compiler for Dynamic Processor Reconfiguration Ph.D thesis, Brown University, Providence, Rhode Island.

[15] S. Vassiliadis, S. Wong, and S. Cotofana (2001): The MOLEN rm–coded processor. *Proc. FPL*.

[16] M. Iliopoulos, T. Antonakopoulos (2000): Reconfigurable network processors based on field-programmable system level integrates circuits. *Proc. FPL*.

[17] http://www.fccm.org

[18] R. Hartenstein (1995): Custom computing machines. *DMM'95*, Smolenice, Slovakia.

[19] http://www.springer.de/comp/lncs/

[20] http://fpl.org

[21] S. Hauck (1998): The role of FPGAs in reprogrammable systems. *Proc. IEEE*.

[22] V. Betz, J. Rose, and A. Marquardt (eds.) (1999): Architecture and CAD for deep-submicron FPGas. Kluwer.

[23] S. Hoffmann (2003): Modern FPGAs, reconfigurable platforms and their design tools. *Proc. REASON summer school*. Ljubljana, Slovenia, August 11–13.

[24] D. Soudris et al. (2002): Survey of existing fine grain reconfigurable hardware platforms. *Deliverable D9 AMDREL consortium (Architectures and Methodologies for Dynamically Reconfigurable Logic)*.

[25] J. Oldfield and R. Dorf (1995): Field–programmable gate arrays: Reconfigurable logic for rapid prototyping and implementation of digital systems. Wiley-Interscience.

[26] http://www.xilinx.com

[27] http://www.altera.com

[28] V. George and J. Rabaey (2001): Low–energy FPGAs: Architecture and design. Kluwer.

[29] Z. Salcic and A. Smailagic (1997): Digital systems design and prototyping using field programmable logic. Kluwer.

[30] J. Hamblen and M. Furman (2001): Rapid prototyping of digital systems. Kluwer.

[31] R. Männer and R. Spurzem et al. (1999): AHA-GRAPE: Adaptive hydrodynamic architecture–GRAvity PipE. *Proc. FPL*.

[32] G. Lienhart (2003): Beschleunigung hydrodynamischer N–Körper–simulationen mit rekonfigurierbaren rechensystemen. *Joint 33rd Speedup and 19th PARS Workshop*. Basel, Switzerland, March 19–21.

[33] N. Ebisuzaki et al. (1997): *Astrophysical Journal, 480*, 432.

[34] T. Narumi, R. Susukita, H. Furusawa, and T. Ebisuzaki (2000): 46 Tflops Special– purpose computer for molecular dynamics simulations WINE-2. *Proc. 5th Int'l Conf. on Signal Processing.* Beijing 575–582.

[35] T. Narumi, R. Susukita, T. Koishi, K. Yasuoka, H. Furusawa, A. Kawai, and T. Ebisuzaki (2000): 1.34 Tflops molecular dynamics simulation for NaCl with a special–purpose computer: MDM. SC2000, Dallas.

[36] T. Narumi, A. Kawai, and T. Koishi (2001): An 8.61 Tflop/s molecular dynamics simulation for NaCl with a special–purpose computer: MDM. SC2001, Denver.

[37] T. Narumi, R. Susukita, T. Ebisuzaki, G. McNiven, and B. Elmegreen (1999): Molecular dynamics machine: Special–purpose computer for molecular dynamics simulations. *Molecular Simulation, 21*, 401–415.

[38] T. Narumi (1998): *Special–Purpose Computer for Molecular Dynamics Simulations Ph D dissertation*, University of Tokyo.

[39] T. Thurner (2003): Trends in der automobile–elektronik; *GI/ITG FG AH - Zielplan–Workshop at FDL 2003.* Frankfurt /Main, Germany.

[40] T. Kean (invited keynote) (2000): It's FPL, Jim–but not as we know it! Market opportunities for the New commercial architectures. *Proc. FPL.*

[41] R. Zeidman (2002): Designing with FPGAs and CPLDs. *CMP Books.*

[42] U. Meyer-Baese (2001): Digital signal processing with field programmable gate arrays (With CD-ROM). Springer-Verlag.

[43] K. Coffman (1999): Real World FPGA design with verilog. Prentice Hall.

[44] R. Seals and G. Whapshott (1997): Programmable logic: PLDs and FPGAs. McGraw-Hill.

[45] G. Martin and H. Chang (ed.) (2003): Winning the SoC revolution: Experiences in real design. Kluwer.

[46] G. Ou and M. Potkonjak (2003): Intellectual property protection in VLSI design. Kluwer.

[47] P. J. Ashenden (2001): The designer's guide to VHDL (2nd Ed.), Morgan Kaufmann.

[48] http://www.mentor.com/fpga/

[49] http://www.synplicity.com/

[50] http://www.celoxica.com/

[51] http://www.dac.com

[52] http://www.mathworks.com/products/connections/product_main. shtml?prod_id=304

[53] http://www.celoxica.com/methodology/matlab.asp

[54] http://www.mathworks.com/

[55] I. Jones (2003): DARPA funded Directions in embedded computing. *Reconfigurable Computing Workshop.* Orsay, France, Sept.

[56] T. Grötker et al. (2002): System design with system-C. Kluwer.

[57] http://www.synopsys.com/products/concentric_systemC/cocentric_ systemC_ds.html

[58] http://www.systemc.org/

[59] http://www.synopsys.com/

[60] J. Hoe, Arvind: Hardware synthesis from term rewriting systems. *Proc. VLSI'99.* Lisbon, Portugal.

[61] M. Ayala-Rincón et al. (2003): Efficient computation of algebraic operations over dynamically reconfigurable systems specified by rewriting–logic environments. *Proc. 23rd SCCC. IEEE* CS press.

[62] M. Ayala-Rincón et al. (2003): Architectural specification, exploration and simulation through rewriting-logic. *Colombian J. Comput. 3*(2), 20–34.

[63] M. Ayala-Rincón et al. (2003): Using rewriting–logic notation for functional verification in data–stream–based reconfigurable computing. *Proc. FDL 2003 (Forum on Specification and Design Languages)*. Frankfurt /Main, Germany, September 23–26.

[64] P. Bjureus et al. (2002): FPGA Resource and timing estimation from matlab execution traces *10th Int'l Workshop on Hardware/Software Codesign*. Estes Park, Colorado, May 6–8.

[65] V. Baumgarten, G. Ehlers, F. May, A. Nückel, M. Vorbach, and M. Weinhardt (2003): PACT XPP -A self–reconfigurable data processing architecture. *The J. Supercomputing. 26*(2), Sept. 2003, 167–184.

[66] J. Rabaey (1997): Reconfigurable processing: The solution to low-power programmable DSP. *Proc. ICASSP*.

[67] http://public.itrs. net/Files/2002Update/2002Update.htm

[68] N. N., Department of Trade and Industry (DTI), London, UK, 2001

[69] H. Simmler et al. (2000): Multitasking on FPGA coprocessors. *Proc. FPL*

[70] H. Walder and M. Platzner (2003): Reconfigurable hardware operating systems: From design concepts to realizations. *Proc. ERSA 2003*.

[71] H. Walder and M. Platzner (2004): A runtime environment for reconfigurable hardware operating systems. *Proc. FPL 2004*.

[72] R. Hartenstein (invited paper) (2002): Reconfigurable computing: Urging a revision of basic CS curricula. *Proc. 15th Int'l Conf. on Systems Engineering (ICSENG02)*. Las Vegas, USA, 6–8 Aug. 2002.

[73] course ID=27 in: http://vlsil.engr.utk.edu/~bouldin/C OURSES/HTML/courselist.html

[74] C. Stroud et al. (2002): BIST-based diagnosis of FPGA interconnect. *Proc. IEEE Int'l. Test Conf.*

[75] P. Zipf (2002): *A Fault Tolerance Technique for Field–Programmable Logic Arrays Dissertation*. Univ. Siegen, Germany.

[76] http.//directreadout.gsfc.nasa.gov

[77] M. Abramovici and C, Stroud (2000): Improved BIST–based diagnosis of FPGA logic blocks. *Proc. IEEE Int'l Test Conf.*

[78] http://www.xilinx.com/events/docs/e sc_sf2001_microblaze.pdf

[79] http://www.leox.org/

[80] J. Becker and M. Vorbach (2003): An industrial/academic configurable system– on–chip project (CSoC): Coarse.grain XPP/Leon–based architecture integration. DATE.

[81] http://www.gaisler. com/leonmain.html

[82] C. Mead and L. Conway (1980): Introduction to VLSI systems design. Addison-Wesley.

[83] R. Kress et al.: A datapath synthesis system (DPSS) for the reconfigurable datapath architecture. *Proc. ASP-DAC'95*

[84] http://pactcorp.com

[85] V. Baumgarten et al. (2001): PACT XPP – A self–reconfigurable data processing architecture. ERSA.

[86] J. Becker, A. Thomas, M. Vorbach, and G. Ehlers (2002): Dynamically reconfigurable systems–on–chip: A core-based industrial/academic SoC synthesis project. *IEEE Workshop Heterogeneous Reconfigurable SoC.* Hamburg, Germany, April 2002.

[87] J. Cardoso and M. Weinhardt (2003): From C programs to the configure–execute model. DATE.

[88] R. Hartenstein (2001): A decade of research on reconfigurable architectures. DATE.

[89] W. Mangione-Smith et al. (1997): Current issues in configurable computing research. *IEEE Computer*, Dec 1997.

[90] J. Becker, T. Pionteck, and M. Glesner (2000): An application–tailored dynamically reconfigurable hardware architecture for digital baseband processing. SBCCI.

[91] M. Sauer (2003): Issues in concept development for embedded wireless SoCs. *GI/ITG FG AH -Zielplan-Workshop.* Frankfurt/Main, Germany.

[92] A. Wiesler, F. Jondral (2002): A software radio for second and third generation mobile systems. *IEEE Trans. on Vehicular Technology. 51*, (4), July.

[93] N. Petkov (1992): Systolic parallel processing. North-Holland.

[94] M. Foster, H. Kung (1980): Design of special-purpose VLSI chips: Example and opinions. *ISCA.*

[95] H. T. Kung (1982): Why systolic architectures? *IEEE Computer 15*(1), 37–46

[96] http://directreadout.gsfc.nasa.gov

[97] U. Nageldinger et al. (2000): Generation of design suggestions for coarse-grain reconfigurable architectures *FPL 2000.*

[98] U. Nageldinger (2001): *Coarse–grained Reconfigurable Architectures Design Space exploration Dissertation*, – downloadable from [99]

[99] http://xputers.informatik.uni-kl.de/papers/publications/Nageldinger Diss.html

[100] J. Frigo et al. (2001): Evaluation of the streams–C C–to–FPGA compiler: An applications perspective. *FPGA.*

[101] T.J. Callahan: Instruction–level parallelism for reconfigurable computing. *FPL'98*

[102] E. Caspi et al. (2000): Extended version of: Stream computations organized for reconfigurable execution (SCORE). *FPL '2000.*

[103] T. Callahan (2000): Adapting software pipelining for reconfigurable computing. CASES

[104] H. Kwok-Hay So, BEE (2000): *A Reconfigurable Emulation Engine for Digital Signal Processing Hardware M.S. thesis*, UC Berkeley.

[105] C. Chang, K. Kuusilinna, R. Broderson (2002): The biggascale emulation engine. *FPGA.*

[106] B. Mei et al. (2003): Exploiting loop–level parallelism on coarse–grained reconfigurable architectures using modulo scheduling. DATE 2003.

[107] M. Herz et al. (invited paper) (2002): Memory organization for data–stream–based reconfigurable computing *ICECS.*

[108] M. Herz et al. (1997): A novel sequencer hardware for application specific computing. *Proc. ASAP.*

[109] H. Reinig et al. (1995): Novel sequencer hardware for high–speed signal processing. *Proc. Design Methodologies for Microelectronics*, Smolenice, Slovakia.

[110] M. Herz (2001): *High Performance Memory Communication Architectures for Coarse-grained Reconfigurable Computing Systems Ph.D. thesis*, Kaiserslautern – downloadable from: [111]

[111] http://xputers.informatik.uni-kl.de/papers/publications/HerzDiss.html

[112] F. Catthoor et al. (2002): Data access and storage management for embedded programmable processors. Kluwer.

[113] F. Catthoor et al. (1998): Custom memory management methodology exploration of memory organization for embedded multimedia systems design. Kluwer.

[114] M. Weber et al. (1988): MOM–map oriented machine. In (E. Chiricozzi, A. D'Amico (ed.) *Parallel Processing and Applications*. North-Holland.

[115] A. Hirschbiel et al. (1987): A flexible architecture for image processing. *Microprocessing and Microprogramming. 21*, 65–72.

[116] A. Ast et al. (1994): Data–procedural languages for FPL–based machines. *FPL'94.*

[117] E. Mirsky and A. DeHon (1996): MATRIX: A reconfigurable computing architecture with configurable instruction distribution and deployable resources. *Proc. IEEE FCCM'96.* April 17–19 Napa, CA, USA.

[118] E. Waingold et al. (1997): Baring it all to software: RAW machines. *IEEE Computer.* 86–93.

[119] J. Becker et al. (2000): Architecture and application of a dynamically reconfigurable hardware array for future mobile communication systems. *Proc. FCCM'00.* April 17–19, Napa, CA, USA.

[120] C. Ebeling et al. (1996): RaPiD: Reconfigurable pipelined datapath. *Proc. FPL'96.*

[121] S. C. Goldstein et al. (1999): PipeRench: A coprocessor for streaming multimedia acceleration. *Proc. ISCA'99*, May 2–4 Atlanta.

[122] D. Chen and J. Rabaey (1990): PADDI: Programmable arithmetic devices for digital signal processing. *VLSI Signal Processing IV*, IEEE Press.

[123] D. C. Chen and J. M. Rabaey (1992): A reconfigurable multiprocessor IC for rapid prototyping of algorithmic-specific high–speed DSP data paths. *IEEE J. Solid–State Circuits. 27(12).*

[124] A. K. W. Yeung and J. M. Rabaey (1993): A reconfigurable data–driven multiprocessor architecture for rapid prototyping of high throughput DSP algorithms. *Proc. HICSS-26.* Jan. Kauai, Hawaii.

[125] N. Tredennick (1995): Technology and business: Forces driving microprocessor evolution. Dec. *Proc. IEEE.*

[126] J. Becker et al. (1998): Parallelization in co–compilation for configurable accelerators. *Proc. ASP-DAC'98.*

[127] J. Becker (1997): *A partitioning compiler for computers with Xputer–based Accelerators Ph.D. Dissertation*, University of Kaiserslautern. downloadable from [128].

[128] http://xputers.informatik.uni-kl.de/papers/publications/BeckerDiss.pdf

[129] L. Lamport (1974): The parallel execution of Do-loops. *C. ACM 17, 2*, Feb.

[130] D. Loveman (1977): Program improvement by source–to–source transformation. *J. ACM 24*, 1.

[131] W. Abu-Sufah, D. Kuck, and D. Lawrie (1981): On the performance enhancement of paging systems through program analysis and transformations. *IEEE-Trans. C-30*(5).

[132] U. Banerjee (1979): *Speed–up of ordinary programs; Ph.D. Thesis*, University of Illinois at Urbana-Champaign, Oct. DCS Report No. UIUCDCS-R-79-989.

[133] J. Allen, K. Kennedy (1984): Automatic loop interchange. *Proc. ACM SIG–PLAN'84, Symp. on Compiler Construction*, Montreal, Canada, SIGPLAN Notices June 19, 6.

[134] J. Becker and K. Schmid (1998): Automatic parallelism exploitation for FPL–based accelerators. *Hawaii Int'l. Conf. on System Sciences (HICSS'98)*, Big Island, Hawaii.

[135] http://xputers.informatik.uni-kl.de/staff/hartenstein/eishistory_en.html

[136] D. Knapp et al. (1991): The ADAM design planning engine. *IEEE Trans CAD*.

[137] J. Lopez et al. (1992): Design assistance for CAD frameworks. *Proc. EURODAC'92*. Hamburg, Sept. 7–10, Germany.

[138] L. Guerra et al. (1998): A methodology for guided behavioral level optimization. *Proc. DAC'98*, June 15–19, San Francisco.

[139] C. A. Moritz et al. (1999): Hot Pages: software caching for RAW microprocessors. MIT. LCS-TM-599, Aug. Cambridge, MA.

[140] P.-A. Hsiung et al. (1999): PSM: An object–oriented synthesis approach to multiprocessor design. *IEEE Trans VLSI Systems 4/1*. March.

[141] J. Kin et al. (1999): Power efficient media processor design space exploration. *Proc. DAC'99*. June 21–25, New Orleans, http://anti-machine.org.

[142] K. Schmidt et al. (1990): A novel ASIC design approach based on a new machine paradigm. *J. SSC* -invited reprint from *Proc. ESSCIRC*.

[143] W. Nebel et al. (1984): PISA, a CAD package and special hardware for pixel-oriented layout analysis. *ICCAD*.

[144] R. Hartenstein et al. (1990): A novel paradigm of parallel computation and its use to implement simple high performance hardware. *Future Generation Computer Systems 791/92*, -invited reprint fr. Proc. InfoJapan'90 (Int'l Conf. Commemorating the 30th Anniversary Computer Society of Japan), Tokyo, Japan.

[145] C. Chang et al. (2001): The biggascale emulation engine (Bee). summer retreat UC Berkeley.

[146] D. Gajski et al. (1982): A second opinion on dataflow machines. *Computer*, Feb.

[147] J. Backus (1978): Can programming be liberated from the von Neumann style? A functional style and its algebra of programs. *Communications of the ACM*, August, *20*(8), 613–641.

[148] J. Rabaey (keynote) (2000): Silicon Platforms for the Next Generation Wireless Systems. *Proc. FPL*.

[149] G. Koch et al. (1975): The universal bus considered harmful. *Proc. 1st EUROMICRO Symposium on the microarchitecture of computing systems.* Nice, France, North Holland.

[150] J. Dongarra, I. Foster, G. Fox, W. Gropp, K. Kennedy, L. Torczon, and A. White (ed.) (2002): The sourcebook of parallel computing. Morgan Kaufmann.

[151] Arvind et al. (1983): A Critique of Multiprocessing the von Neumann Style. *Proc. ISCA.*

[152] G. Bell (keynote) (2000): All the chips outside. The architecture challenge. *Proc. ISCA.*

[153] G. Amdahl (1967): Validity of the single processor approach to achieving large-scale computing capabilities. *AFIPS Conference Proceedings.* (30).

[154] J. Hennessy (1999): ISCA25: Looking backward, looking forward. *Proc. ISCA.*

[155] http://www.ece.lsu.edu/vaidy/raw04/

[156] http://xputers.informatik.uni-kl.de/raw/index_raw.html

[157] http://www.iti.uni-luebeck.de/PARS/

[158] http://www.speedup.ch/

[159] http://www.hoise.com/primeur/03/articles/monthly/AE-PR-04-03-61.html

Chapter 12

EVOLVING HARDWARE
Timothy G. W. Gordon and Peter J. Bentley
University College London

1   INTRODUCTION

In the hundred years since John Ambrose Fleming invented the diode at University College London and gave birth to the field, electronics has become a well-understood engineering discipline. This solid grounding of knowledge has allowed the commercial semiconductor industry to grow at a remarkable rate in the intervening years, both in volume and in the complexity of hardware. As a result, the now-famous Moore's Law has held true for almost forty years [85]. But problems are beginning to emerge. For the industry to flourish, the growth in hardware complexity must continue, but it is becoming clear that current design methodologies applied to silicon-based technologies can no longer support the present rate of scaling.

In the medium term, the requirement for new and innovative designs is set to grow as it becomes necessary to squeeze more and more out of the technologies we already have. The long-term solution is likely to lie in the development of new circuit medium technologies. But even when new circuit media do eventually become commercially feasible, they are likely at best to require features in our designs that our current circuit methodologies are not aimed at providing, such as fault tolerance, and at worst require a complete rewriting of the design rules. So it is clear that there is a significant requirement for innovative circuit designs and design methodologies, and the cost of developing these in man-hours of research and design is likely to be considerable.

Over the past decade, a new field applying evolutionary techniques to hardware design and synthesis has emerged. These techniques may be able to give us a new option. We can use evolution to design automatically, or at least aid in the design and realization of innovative circuits. This field has been coined *evolutionary electronics*, *hardware evolution*, and *evolvable hardware*, amongst others. Here it will be referred to as *evolvable hardware*.

The field of evolvable hardware draws inspiration from a range of other fields, as shown in Figure 12.1. For many years computer scientists have modeled their learning algorithms on self-organizing processes observed in nature. Perhaps the most well-known example is the artificial neural network (ANN) [93]. Others include the collective decision-making of ant colonies [12], the adaptive ability of immune systems [98], the growth of self-similar structures in plants [64], and of course Darwinian evolution [19]. Collectively, work on such algorithms is known as *bio-inspired software*, which is shown at the intersection of Computer Science and Biology in Figure 12.1.

Ideas from nature have also been used in electronic engineering for many years; for instance, simulated annealing algorithms are used in many circuit partitioning algorithms. (Simulated annealing algorithms are based on the physical phenomenon of annealing in cooling metals.) Interest in using ideas from nature has grown in recent years to the extent that the field of bio-inspired hardware is now firmly established in its own right. This field uses many of the ideas adopted from nature by software developers, and some new ones, to allow fault tolerance, reconfigurability, and even automatic circuit design in modern hardware. The field of evolvable hardware is shown at the intersection of Computer Science, Biology, and Electronic Engineering in Figure 12.1. The focus of this chapter is in this central area.

The interrelationships between areas of hardware design and synthesis, and evolutionary computation are shown in Figure 12.2. Digital hardware synthesis is traditionally a combination of two processes. First, a human-designed circuit specification is mapped to a logical representation through the process of logic synthesis. This is represented as the lower right-hand set in Figure 12.2. This netlist then undergoes further combinatorially complex optimization processes in order to place and route the circuit to the target technology. This area is represented as the lower left-hand set in Figure 12.2. Many modern electronic design automation (EDA)[1] tools use intelligent techniques in these optimization algorithms, and research into the use of evolution for these purposes abounds [18, 74]. Hence we see the set representing evolutionary design intersect with that of

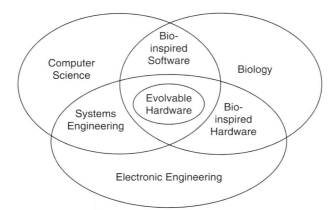

Figure 12.1. The field of evolvable hardware originates from the intersection of three sciences

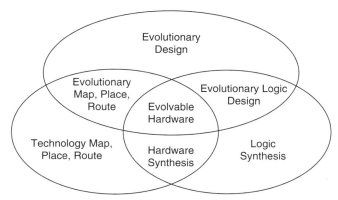

Figure 12.2. Evolvable hardware can include aspects of hardware design and optimization techniques

technology mapping, placement, and routing in Figure 12.2 to yield evolutionary mapping, placement, and routing. However, circuit design, along with some optimization decisions during the synthesis process, is still in the domain of the human designer. It has only been recently that significant interest has developed in implementing evolutionary techniques higher up the VLSI design flow at circuit design, a move that can allow evolution to generate creative designs that can rival or improve on human ones. The most widespread examples of this have been to use evolution for the design of logic, as represented by the intersection of the areas of evolutionary design and logic synthesis in Figure 12.2. Some of the work in this intersection falls into the field of evolvable hardware. However, much work at the logical level is carried out in the spirit of evolving programs or other forms of logic, and so is beyond the scope of this chapter.

The rest of the chapter is organized as follows. Section 2 begins with a brief discussion of how evolvable hardware can be realized, and surveys its areas of application. The field is still young, and there are several problems that must be tackled before large-scale commercial use of the techniques will become viable. Section 3 discusses key past and current research into evolvable hardware by focusing on the two largest and most actively researched of these problems, namely, generalization and evolvability, along with the most important benefit of evolvable hardware in our eyes: innovation. We use "level of abstraction," "learning bias," and "evolving platform" as the main features to map out this research.

A distinction commonly made is the difference between *extrinsic evolution*, where candidate circuit designs are evaluated in simulation, and *intrinsic evolution*, where candidate circuit designs are synthesized and evaluated directly on programmable logic devices (PLDs). In the case of circuits evolved intrinsically, the choice of platform used can have a profound effect on evolution's performance. Criteria for choosing a suitable platform are discussed at the end of Section 3, along with an appraisal of platforms that have been used for evolvable hardware to date. Section 4 presents some of our recent work into a new branch of evolvable hardware, developmental hardware evolution, which has the potential to solve many of the evolvability issues in the field. Finally, a summary will be given in Section 5.

2   EVOLVABLE HARDWARE IN PRACTICE

Evolutionary Computation is the field of solving problems using search algorithms inspired by biological evolution. These algorithms are collectively known as *evolutionary algorithms*. They model the principles of selection, variation, and inheritance that are the basis of the theory of Darwinian evolution, and have been applied to a huge spectrum of problems, from classic optimization [52] to the creation of original music [5]. Typically they work on a population of prospective solutions in parallel. Each member of the population is evaluated according to a problem-specific *fitness function* that tests how well each solution performs a required task and then assigns that solution a fitness score. A *selection* operator then probabilistically chooses solutions with higher fitness from the population to form the basis of a new generation of solutions. These solutions are then varied, commonly by randomly altering each solution to model *mutation* and/or by recombining two solutions in some way to model sexual reproduction—a procedure commonly called *crossover*. The process is then iterated for a number of generations until a stopping condition is met, for instance, the discovery of a solution with a given fitness or the completion of a predefined number of generations.

This chapter concerns the application of evolutionary algorithms to the automatic design of electronic circuits. In order to familiarize the reader with how circuits might be evolved, an example is now presented.

2.1   An Example of Evolvable Hardware

The class of evolutionary algorithms most commonly used in evolvable hardware is the *genetic algorithm*. Most commonly, these operate on a fixed-size population of fixed-length binary strings called *chromosomes*. Each chromosome encodes a common set of parameters that describe a collection of electronic components and their interconnections. Thus, each set of parameter values represents an electronic circuit. The set of all possible combinations of parameter values defines the *search space* of the algorithm, and the circuits that they represent define the *solution space* of the algorithm. Traditionally, every parameter set in the search space encodes a unique circuit description in the solution space. For every chromosome/circuit pair, the chromosome is called the *genotype* and the circuit is called the *phenotype*.

An example of evolvable hardware is shown in Figure 12.3. The algorithm begins by initializing the bits of each chromosome with random values. The chromosomes are then evaluated in turn by creating a circuit based on the parameter values, either as a simulated model of the circuit or as a concrete circuit embodied in reconfigurable hardware (an example of which is shown in Section 5). The circuit's fitness for performing the target task is then measured by passing to it a set of test values and evaluating the veracity of the circuit's output. The selection operator then probabilistically populates the next generation of chromosomes such that chromosomes with high fitness are more likely to be selected. There are many methods to achieve this, a common approach being *two-member tournament selection* [19]: the operator selects two individuals at random and compares their fitness. Only the individual with the highest fitness is inserted into the next

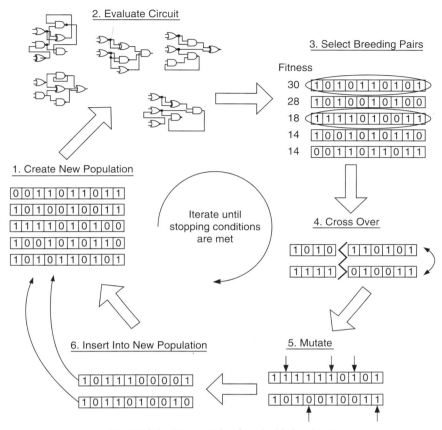

Figure 12.3. An example of evolvable hardware

generation. If the two have equal fitness, the individual to be inserted is chosen at random. Once the new population has been selected, it is varied. Common variation operators are *one-point crossover* and *point mutation* [19]. One-point crossover recombines two chromosomes by choosing a position at random along the chromosome and swapping every bit beyond this point between the strings. It is stochastically applied according to a fixed probability. Point mutation independently inverts each bit in the chromosome according to a fixed probability. These operators are applied to all members of the new population. Often, in addition to these operators, the best member of the original population is copied into the new population unchanged, a strategy called *elitism* [19]. The new population is now complete, and the algorithm then iterates the steps of evaluation, selection, and variation until a circuit that functions adequately is found or a prespecified number of generations is completed.

Using evolution to design circuits in this way brings a number of important benefits to electronics, allowing design automation and innovation for an increasing range of applications. Some of the more important areas where evolvable hardware can be applied include the following:

- Automatic design of low-cost hardware

- Coping with poorly specified problems

- Creation of adaptive systems

- Creation of fault-tolerant systems

- Innovation in poorly understood design spaces

The remainder of this section will explore research in these areas in a little more detail.

2.2   Automatic Design of Low-Cost Hardware

Automation has been used in circuit synthesis for many years. Traditional digital design involves the mapping of an abstract human-designed circuit to a specific technology through the application of simple minimization, placement, and routing rules. As our capability for synthesizing more complex circuits has grown, so has the need for more resourceful processes to handle the combinatorially complex mapping procedures. Intelligent techniques such as simulated annealing [97] and ANNs [133] have been routinely used to search these exploding spaces of mappings and minimizations for some time. More recently, so has evolution [18, 74].

Evolvable hardware allows us to take the automation of circuit production a step further, automating how to generate the actual circuit design from a behavioral specification and simultaneously automating the circuit synthesis process. The behavioral specification presented to the evolvable system may be as simple as a series of circuit input signals that the system must match to a corresponding predefined set of output signals, although other representations of circuit behavior may be used, often including environmental conditions or simulated error test cases or depending on the requirements of the circuit. How the representation and contents of the circuit specification affect the functionality of circuits is currently the center of much interest and is discussed in more detail under the heading of *generalization* in Section 3.

In applications where a suitable behavioral specification has been found, evolvable hardware can remove the necessity for a designer, or at least reduce the design time that is required, thus reducing production costs. This advantage is particularly useful when design costs are a significant proportion of total cost, for instance for hardware that is produced in low volumes. Evolvable hardware even allows us to evolve designs to suit an individual. Many medical applications have not been suitable for hardware solutions owing to the expense of personalization. Evolvable hardware allows cheap, fast solutions to such applications. For example, a system has been developed to control a prosthetic hand by recognition of patterns of myoelectric signals in a user's arm [45]. The implementation is an entirely hardware-based solution with reconfigurable logic, a hardware genetic algorithm unit, a CPU core for evaluation, a chromosome memory, and a random number generator implemented on the same integrated chip.

Evolution can also be used to reduce production costs on larger scales by optimizing circuits that fail to meet their required specifications due to variations during fabrication. For instance, [88] corrected variations in the frequency of intermediate frequency filters by using evolution to control the output of a series of transconductance amplifiers. This is a useful tool in the case of analogue circuit designs, where individual component behaviors can vary quite markedly, and in particular for designs where power and size are important, since tuning the components in this way allows smaller, low-power components to be used. In light of this, intermediate frequency filters tuned using this technique are already in use in commercial mobile communications products [87]. The idea of using evolution to counteract fabrication variations has also been explored for digital circuits. For instance, Takahashi, Kasai, et al. incorporated programmable delay elements in the registers of a memory test pattern generator [112], thus allowing the evolved circuits to compensate for not only clock skew but also any variations in data delays throughout the circuit. Simulation results demonstrated that an almost 50% improvement in production yield was possible using this method. Such improvements in yield can reduce production costs considerably.

2.3   Poorly Specified Problems

For some problems, it is difficult to specify functionality succinctly but easy to specify a behavioral description. Computer scientists have used evolution to handle problems with such poor specifications for many years. ANNs have been applied to problems such as noisy pattern recognition [93]. Evolvable hardware techniques have similarities with and advantages over ANNs, as noted by Yao and Higuchi [132]. Both can be feed-forward networks, and both can learn non-linear functions successfully. But, in addition, hardware is by nature a fast medium, and in many cases, such as when restricted to feed-forward networks, evolved hardware designs are more easily understood than ANNs. Therefore this approach is often suited to problems usually tackled with ANNs but that require fast operation and good solution tractability. Evolvable hardware suitable for such purposes has already been developed for industrial use [88].

One problem where evolved hardware can rival ANNs is pattern recognition. For example, Sekanina has successfully evolved image noise filters that rival the best traditionally designed circuits [100]. One of the advantages of evolutionary systems is the ease with which learning biases can be incorporated. For instance, Higuchi et al. have evolved high-speed robust classifiers [34, 42] Good generalization characteristics were incorporated into the solutions by specification of a bias based on machine learning theory. More recently, do Amaral et al. evolved fuzzy functions that can be used as building blocks in the construction of fuzzy logic controllers [11].

2.4   Adaptive systems

With sufficient automation (i.e., real-time synthesis provided by PLDs), evolvable hardware has the potential to adapt autonomously to changes in its environment. This ability can be very useful in situations where real-time manual control over systems is not possible, such as on deep space missions. It could be particularly useful when unexpected conditions are encountered.

Stoica et al. have noted that current lack of validation for online evolutionary systems means that critical spacecraft control systems, and other mission-critical systems, cannot currently be placed under evolutionary control [104]. Greenwood and Song have proposed using evolutionary techniques in conjunction with formal verification techniques to circumvent this problem [22]; however, to date only noncritical systems such as sensor processing systems have been explored, for example, adaptive data compression systems [15]. Other systems that could benefit from the ability to autonomously evolve are power management systems and controller deployment mechanisms for booms, antennae, etc. [91]

Several other adaptive hardware compression systems have also been developed. Two systems have been developed at the Electrotechnical Lab. (ETL), both using predictive coding. The first predicts each pixel, using a standard prediction function, from a subset of surrounding pixels selected by a genetic algorithm. It has proved successful in compressing bi-level images for high precision electrophotographic printers, outperforming JBIG, the ISO standard for bi-level image compression, by an average of around 50%. Since then the method has been proposed as a new ISO standard [94]. The second approach breaks images into smaller sections and uses evolution to model a function for each section [95]. They also suggested that a similar system could be used for real-time adaptive compression of video signals. A similar technique was used by Sekanina to evolve adaptive circuits that filter image noise in changing environments [99].

Many other adaptive filters have been evolved, including digital finite impulse response (FIR) filters, commonly used in audio applications such as noise and echo cancellation [125, 131] and their more complex but less reliable counterparts, infinite impulse response (IIR) filters [100]. Analogue adaptive filters have also been evolved. For example, Zebulum et al. presented signal extraction filters capable of adaptively amplifying the strongest component of the input signal while attenuating others, thus improving a hypothetical signal/noise ratio [135]. Through evolution, these circuits could be adapted to new input profiles.

Online scheduling hardware has also been developed, most notably adaptive cell scheduling systems for ATM networks, that responds to changes in traffic flow [59, 65]. In a related field, Damiani et al. have developed an online adaptive hashing system that could be used to map cache blocks to cache tags dependent on the access patterns of the data over time [9].

2.5   Fault-Tolerant Systems

Ongoing advances in component miniaturization have not been complemented by improvements in fabrication reliability. This means that many modern VLSI circuit designs must be tolerant to fabrication faults. It is expected that this issue will become even more important in future circuit technologies. Miniaturization also exposes components to a greater risk of operational faults—for instance, due to the effects of power fluctuations or ionizing radiation. Reliability is of paramount importance for many systems, such as medical equipment and transport control systems. Military and spacecraft systems are particularly susceptible to reliability problems, as they are regularly subjected to harsh conditions. Current techniques for fault tolerance rely on the presence of additional redundant components and thorough testing, either at the point of manufacture or online, and add considerable cost and design complexity. Fortunately, evolvable hardware provides a number of mechanisms to introduce fault tolerance into circuits.

A class of adaptive system that was not mentioned in Section 2.4 comprises circuits that can adapt to faults in their own hardware, thus providing a mechanism of fault recovery. An early demonstration of this ability was that of Higuchi et al. [34], where an adaptive hardware system learned the behavior of an expert robot controller by example using a genetic algorithm. More recently, Vigander demonstrated that a simple evolutionary system could restore most but not all functionality to a 4-bit × 4-bit multiplier that had been subjected to random faults [130]. Complete functionality could be restored by applying a voting system to select between several alternative circuits that had been repaired by evolution. Sinohara et al. used a multiobjective evolutionary algorithm that allowed essential functionality to be restored at the expense of secondary behavior that was not deemed to be important by the designer, such as power dissipation [102]. This algorithm was demonstrated in the repair of NOR gates and inverters. Hounsell and Arlsan have explored the repair of an evolved FIR filter after the injection of multiple faults [38]. They examined two different recovery methods. The first was to recall the final population of the evolutionary run that created the original filter design, and the second was to seed a new random population with a copy of the original design. Both mechanisms recovered functionality faster than rerunning evolution with a completely random population, with population seeding outperforming population recall by a small margin. Zebulum et al. demonstrated evolutionary recovery with a 4-bit DAC that had initially been evolved using traditionally designed operational amplifiers and smaller DACs evolved in earlier experiments as building blocks. Faults were introduced into one of the operational amplifiers. The recovered circuit outperformed the circuit that had initially been evolved. It was suggested that operational amplifiers were not useful building blocks for evolution. Gwaltney and Ferguson investigated fault recovery in an evolved analogue motor controller [26], again by re-evolving the population that gave rise to the best nonfaulty controller after introducing faults. They discovered that evolution could recover from faults in some components better than others, although at least some functionality was restored in all cases.

Louis [70] combined an evolutionary approach with a case-based memory, where partial solutions to similar, previously attempted problems were inserted into the evolutionary population. This process demonstrated that better quality solutions to parity problems could be evolved in less time than when using evolution alone and suggested that this method might prove useful for fault recovery.

Most evolutionary fault recovery systems that have been demonstrated to date have only explored recovery from errors introduced into the logic of the circuit. However, Lohn et al. have demonstrated an evolutionary fault recovery system that can repair routing in addition to logic [66], which they suggest is important for modern routing-rich programmable devices. Another type of fault is the failure of a component at extreme temperatures. Stoica et al. have observed that multipliers, Gaussian curve generators, and logic gates that have evolved under standard conditions degrade or fail at extreme temperatures. However, when re-evolved at those temperatures, the circuits regained functionality in all cases.

Fault detection is traditionally dealt with by incorporating additional hardware into a design to perform a built-in self test (BIST). Garvie and Thompson have demonstrated that evolution can be used to design small adders and multipliers that incorporate BIST at very low additional cost by sharing components between BIST and the circuit function [17]. Innovative circuit designs such as this will be discussed in Section 2.6.

A number of other bio-inspired online autonomous hardware, fault-tolerance mechanisms have been developed for both fault detection [7] and recovery [72, 126]. Although these have been proposed as a platform for evolutionary experiments, they do not use evolution as an adaptive repair mechanism, and so will not be considered further here.

Fault *tolerance* refers to systems that are inherently tolerant to faults, rather than systems that can detect and/or recover from faults. Evolution has proved an ideal candidate for the exploration of fault-tolerant systems and is discussed under the heading of *generalization* in Section 3.3.

2.6   Design Innovation in Poorly Understood Design Spaces

Traditional circuit designers tend to work on a problem from the top down, decomposing the problem into smaller subproblems that have limited interactions and then repeating the process until only a number of small problems remain that are well understood in the field of circuit design and have known solutions. Each decomposition carefully directs the process towards these solutions by using formal design rules. Evolution works differently. It works from the bottom up, adding components together to make partial solutions to the design problem, which are in turn combined and tinkered with, until the solution meets the design criteria. This idea is discussed more fully in Section 3. For now, we shall discuss when this approach might be useful.

The clearest cases for application are design spaces for which we have very limited knowledge of how components will interact, and so design rules have not yet been developed. Advances in electronic engineering are beginning to generate new kinds of circuit technologies for which the design spaces are often very poorly understood. In these cases, evolution can prove a useful technique in searching for innovative designs, since it can be guided purely by the behavior of the evolving circuit rather than by relying on domain knowledge. An example of this is the field of nanoelectronics, where Thompson and Wasshuber have successfully evolved innovative (but at this stage not particularly useful) single-electron NOR gates [122].

There is also a set of current technologies for which traditional logic synthesis techniques have not yet been designed but that are becoming increasingly important for circuit designers. Many programmable logic technologies provide XOR gates and multiplexers, but digital design rules are best suited to generating sum-of-products solutions that do not map well to these elements. In these cases, an evolutionary approach can work directly with a design abstraction suitable for the technology and potentially search areas of space that a traditional designer would miss if using the techniques above, and this approach may discover more parsimonious solutions, as has been demonstrated by Miller et al. [76].

Beyond these technologies, there are design spaces where the interactions are so complex that it has not been possible to develop formal methods to partition and decompose the design space. For instance, when compared to the design space of digital logic, analogue design is much less well understood. Hence circuit design in this domain requires more expert knowledge. Evolutionary algorithms have proved very successful in discovering human-competitive (and better) analogue circuit designs [1, 51].

Perhaps the most successful application of evolution to complex design spaces is the automatic design of antennas. Traditional antenna designs are based on a handful of known, regular topologies. Beyond these, the interactions between elements become too complex to abstract. Linden has demonstrated that evolution is capable of discovering an array of highly unconventional, irregular antenna designs [63] and has shown that evolved antennas can be evolved and operate effectively in real-world settings using transmission of real data [61] and transmission where the signal path is obstructed [61]. Such is evolution's performance when applied to antenna design that an evolved antenna is undergoing flight qualification testing for NASA's upcoming Space Technology 5 mission [69], and if successful will be the first evolved hardware in space.

A more subtle and perhaps surprising point is that evolution searches an inherently different area of search space than traditional designers do. Because of this difference, it is possible for evolution to discover innovative solutions even for well-understood design spaces, since some useful circuits lie beyond the areas of solution space we would normally explore if we were to tackle the problem. This outcome, of course, demands that evolution is allowed to work without the design constraints that we would normally place on circuit designs, as was first demonstrated by Thompson. Currently, this approach has not yet yielded any significant real-world applications, but the concept has prompted a great deal of research, as discussed in Section 3.

Current evolutionary techniques only works well for small problems, since the search spaces can become vast for large circuits. A great deal of research is currently directed at scalability, which is discussed later in this chapter. That said, we can still make use of evolution by finding small yet innovative designs that are evolved to produce limited interactions and so can be used by traditional designers as building blocks for larger circuits. Such building blocks have been found for both analogue and digital designs [1, 78]. This approach has also been advocated for use at higher abstractions [101], where it was suggested that evolved or evolvable IP cores could now be provided for commercial use in programmable logic devices. It has also been suggested that previously evolved building blocks may help evolution discover larger circuits [135].

Finally, evolution has proved to be very successful at the generation of circuits that incorporate several functions within one set of shared components, a task for which there is little domain knowledge. We have described an example of this in Section 2.5, where adders and multipliers were evolved to incorporate a BIST function. A related idea is that of polymorphic electronics [108], where a circuit is evolved to perform multiple functions using a shared set of components, with each function becoming apparent under different environmental conditions. For example, a circuit might perform as an AND gate at one temperature and an OR gate at another. Such circuits might prove very useful for military and intelligence purposes.

Design innovation is, in our eyes, the most significant benefit of evolvable hardware; hence, research in this area is discussed in more detail in Section 3.

3   RESEARCH IN EVOLVABLE HARDWARE

Having discussed the benefits of evolvable hardware, and some of the applications that these benefits allow, this section reviews the main thrusts of research in this field. The research is decomposed into three areas: innovation, generalization and evolvability.

3.1   Innovation

Traditional circuit designers decompose a problem from the top down, iteratively splitting the task into smaller and smaller subproblems by applying constraints on their interactions. This partitioning is *actively directed* to reach a set of subproblems contained within the reservoir of electronics and materials knowledge, and is known as *abstraction*. These subproblems can then be individually modeled as an encapsulated physical device, without the need to understand its complex internal interactions. An example is a digital memory device, which can be mapped to an array of analogue circuits that use different techniques to achieve similar input/output characteristics. When the subproblems are reassembled, care must be taken to ensure that the constraints made during the partitioning process are adhered to. For example the digital memory device mentioned above is often constructed of high-gain analogue components, so we must ensure that its output is allowed to saturate before it is passed to another part of the circuit.

Evolution uses a different approach. It works from the bottom up, attempting to find correlations between sets of components that consistently improve the behavior of a circuit with respect to the problem at hand. Unlike traditional design, the direction of its search does not have to be directed by previous knowledge. If evolution is set up in such a way that it can *exploit* correlations between the components it manipulates and the observed external behavior of a circuit, then circuit designs can be discovered using this behavior alone as a guide, regardless of the complexities of the interactions within the circuit.

In Section 2 we discussed four areas of application for innovative evolutionary design: familiar design technologies with relaxed abstractions, programmable logic abstractions, complex design technologies, and new design technologies. These are now discussed in turn.

3.1.1   Relaxing Abstractions

Seminal work on the relaxation of design abstractions was carried out by Thompson. He first set out to show that evolution could successfully manipulate the dynamics and structure of circuits when the dynamical and structural constraints that traditional designers depend on heavily had been relaxed. He demonstrated this [120] by evolving a complex recurrent network of high-speed gates at a netlist level abstraction to behave as a low-frequency oscillator. Fitness was measured as an average error based on the sum of the differences between desired and measured transition periods. Circuits were evaluated in simulation using an asynchronous digital abstraction. Hence a search space containing only circuits that used behavior modeled by the simulator was searched, with the space strictly partitioned into units of logic gates. However, as the simulator allowed the gates to interact asynchronously, the selection operator could explore the asynchronous dynamics of the model, being free to make use of any such behavior or ignore it as it saw fit.

The required behavior of the circuit was successfully evolved, showing that it is possible for evolution to search without the constraints (in this case, synchronous constraints) usually needed by traditional designers. Further, a graph-partitioning algorithm showed that the structure of the circuit contained no significant structural modules, as would be seen through the successive abstraction approach of a traditional top-down approach. Thompson also showed that the circuit behavior relied on methods that would not have been used by traditional designers. So not only had evolution found a solution by searching the space beyond conventional circuit design space but also it had found a solution that that actually *lay within* this space.

Thompson went on to show that evolution with relaxed restrictions on circuit dynamics was possible in physical hardware, rather than simulation [120]. The hardware was a finite-state machine for a robot controller. However, whether the states were controlled synchronously by a given clock or not was under genetic control, an architecture Thompson termed a *dynamic state machine (DSM)*. The evolved robot controller used a mixture of synchronous and asynchronous behavior and interacted with the environment in a complex dynamical manner to produce behavior that would not have been possible using the finite-state machine abstraction with such limited resources. Importantly, he suggested that the ability of such a parsimonious controller to interact in such a complex manner with its environment was not attributable to the DSM architecture. Rather, it arose from the ability of evolution to *exploit* it. Again, evolution had found a circuit that traditional design techniques could not generate by avoiding a traditional design constraint, which in this case was the synchrony imposed on the finite-state machine abstraction. But in addition, evolution had found a circuit that used the rich dynamics that can arise by relaxing design constraints to perform a real task, demonstrating that such dynamics can give rise to *useful behavior* in the real world.

Thompson also carried out the first intrinsic evolution of a circuit evaluated on an FPGA. A 10×10 area of a Xilinx XC6126 bitstream was evolved. Almost all bits in the bitstream corresponding to this area were evolved directly as the bits of the chromosome of a genetic algorithm [116]. Thereby Thompson set about evolving a circuit at the lowest level of abstraction possible with the device he had—that of the *physical behavior* of the target technology. The task was to evolve a circuit to discriminate between 1 kHz and 10 kHz signals. Fitness was calculated by subjecting each circuit to five 500 ms bursts of each signal in a random order, and awarding high fitness to circuits with a large difference between the average voltage of the output during these bursts. The average voltages were measured with an analogue integrator. The only input to the circuit was the 1 kHz/10 kHz signal—no clock was given, and hence the task required that a continuous-time arrangement of components be found that discriminated between signals many orders of magnitude longer than the delay afforded by each individual component. The resulting circuit used a fraction of the resources that a traditional designer would need to achieve the same task. Following months of analysis, Thompson and Layzell described the functionality of the circuit as "bizarre," and to date, the nature of some of the mechanisms it uses are still not completely understood, although the authors postulated that the circuit made use of the *underlying physics of the substrate* in a way that traditional design would consider too complex to consider.

Later, Thompson and Layzell carried out a similar experiment, this time providing the circuit with a 6 MHz oscillator signal that could be used or ignored as evolution required [121]. The prime motivation for the experiment was to investigate robustness, and so evaluation was carried out under a range of conditions specified by an operational envelope. Hence the constraints to the system were the same as before, except that a soft bias towards robust behavior had been added through the fitness function. However, an additional dynamical resource had been provided. The resulting circuit made use of the clock, and the design was simulated by using the PSpice digital simulator. The simulated design behaved exactly like that of the real circuit, showing that evolution had found a solution within the digital design abstraction of the simulator, even through the constraints did not explicitly require that. However, analysis of the simulation waveforms showed a large number of transient signals. This finding allows us to conclude that potentially useful circuits lie within the digital abstraction that are *undiscoverable* using traditional digital design methodologies owing to their greedy, top-down nature, and that at least some of these circuits *can* be discovered using evolution.

3.1.2   Programmable Logic Abstractions

In Section 2 we noted that most digital circuit design methodologies are geared towards producing logic in the canonical sum-of-products form. However, many programmable logic devices support additional components that are not easily utilized by such an abstraction, such as XOR gates, multiplexers, and lookup tables (LUTs). Miller et al. have conducted research into the discovery of innovative circuits, one of their main motivations being the derivation of new design principles that could be applied to logic abstractions such as those found in programmable logic devices. They note [78] that Boolean or other algebraic rules can map from a truth table of required circuit behavior to an expression in terms of that algebra. They then suggest that a bottom-up evolutionary approach could search not only the class of expressions that the algebraic rules map to but also a larger space of logical representations beyond commonly used algebras.

In an attempt to demonstrate this idea, they successfully evolved one- and two-bit adders based on the ripple adder principle using a feed-forward netlist representation of AND, OR, NOT, XOR and MUX gates. This space lies beyond the commonly used Boolean and Reed–Muller algebra spaces but is of interest since the multiplexer is available as a basic unit in many technologies. This argument is very similar to Thompson's in principle—that the discovery of innovative circuits can be facilitated through the modification of design abstractions implemented through representational biases.

Many of the circuits reported in this and other work [83, 76] were unusual but interesting because of their efficiency in terms of gate count. They lay in the space of circuits making use of multiplexers and XOR gates, outside the space of traditional atomic Boolean logic units. The authors argued that these circuits were unlikely to be found using traditional algebraic methods, and so evolutionary "assemble-and-test" was a useful way that such a space can be explored. The work continued with the evolution of two-bit and three-bit multipliers. All work was carried out using gate-level logic simulation. Similar work has been carried out with multiple valued algebras [46].

Another aspect of this group's work is the contention that *design principles* useful to traditional designers could be discovered by searching for patterns in evolved circuits. In particular, they hypothesis that by evolving a series of modules of increasing size, design principles that the modules have in common may be extracted from them. The authors [78], [83] evolved many one and two bit adders, and by inspection deduced the principle of the ripple adder. Although knowledge of this principle already exists in the domain, they went on to argue that evolution discovered and made use of it with no prior knowledge or explicit bias. Since the design principle could be extracted a comparison of one- and two-bit adders that had evolved to use the principle, they asserted that evolution could be used as a method of design principle discovery.

More recent work in this area has concentrated on developing an automatic method of principle detection [76, 77]. Having successfully evolved two- and three-bit multipliers that are much more compact than those of traditional design, the authors have integrated a data mining procedure to search for design principles [43]. The learning algorithm used for the data mining process is an instance-based learning technique called Case Based Reasoning [84], (Chapter 8). We shall argue in our discussion on scalability in Section 3.4 that by modeling biological development we might be able to allow evolution to automatically encapsulate such design principles without the need to resort to other learning techniques and to use evolution itself to select for design principles that are inherently evolvable.

3.1.3   Complex Design Technologies

In Section 2, we noted that there are complex design spaces for which it has not been possible to develop formal methods to partition and decompose the design space, and that evolutionary algorithms offer an alternative approach to the use of a human expert. An example of this kind of design space is that of analogue circuit design.

One traditional technique of simplifying an analogue design space is to fix the topology of the circuit to a design with well-known characteristics and to modify only parameters relating to the components within the design. A good deal of work using evolutionary algorithms in analogue circuit design takes this approach, and can be considered to have more in common with evolutionary optimization than evolutionary circuit design [3]; [88]. However, as the field of evolvable hardware has developed, researchers have begun to allow evolution to explore analogue circuit topologies. For instance, Grimbleby developed a hybrid genetic algorithm/numerical search method that used the genetic algorithm to search topologies and a numerical design optimization method to select parameter values for the evolved topologies [23]. Additionally, Koza et al. and Lohn and

Columbano have both developed evolutionary circuit design methods that explore both topology and component parameters [67]; [50]. These two methods are of particular interest to us since they do not use a fixed mapping of genotype to phenotype. The benefits of using such an approach, and details of these two examples in particular, are discussed at length in Section 3.4.

With the advantages of evolutionary design in mind, Gallagher has recently advocated a return to the development of analogue computers [16], which today have been almost completely replaced by their digital counterparts. He distinguished two classes of analogue computers. The first is *direct* computers, which are designed to reproduce the behavior of a physical system directly. The example he gave was of a serial RLC circuit. This can be considered as directly modeling a damped harmonic oscillator, where inductance is equivalent to mass, capacitance is equivalent to the inverse of spring elasticity, and resistance is equivalent to frictional damping. Indirect analogue computers simply implement complex mathematical functions using building blocks that embody simple mathematical functions, such as adders and integrators. Gallagher suggests that the demise of the analogue computer is mostly due to a combination of the difficulty in discovering direct implementations of required computations and the difficulty in constructing accurate indirect models due to compound errors in component precision. He went on to point out that intrinsic evolution actually discovers direct implementations, since the circuit is designed purely to replicate a specified behavior rather than to perform a mathematical function, and that for applications where size and power are vital, evolving direct analogue models should be considered as a serious alternative to digital models of analogue computations.

An impressive example of evolution's ability to manipulate interactions that are too complex for human designers to fathom is that of antenna design. We have already mentioned in Section 2 that evolution is capable of discovering an array of highly unconventional, irregular antenna designs. Early work in this field used simulation; however, Linden [60] went a step further. He intrinsically evolved an array of wires connected with reed switches, which are mechanical switches that are closed by an induced magnetic field, controllable from a computer. The antennas that he evolved made use of the complex electromechanical coupling between wire segments that resulted from the fields of the reed switches. Human designers would be unable to exploit such complex nonlinear physical interactions in a controlled manner.

3.1.4   New technologies

In Section 2, we briefly discussed that evolutionary design is likely to be a useful tool for new circuit design technologies for which no domain knowledge exists. Thompson [119] suggested that until a model of a new technology is derived, only a blind search technique such as evolution can be of use to design circuits in it. He first noted that as we move towards nanoscale circuitry, we cannot continue to suppress quantum effects so that our macroscopic models fit; rather, we must make use of them. He then described a system of this third class. The system consisted of an array of quantum dots between which electrons could only pass by quantum mechanical tunnelling. The task was to evolve a NOR gate by modifying effectively only the size, shape, and position of the dots. Thus, evolved circuits would rely on tunnelling effects to perform a logical function. (The task was carried out in simulation, but the concept is unaffected.) The evolved circuit used a property called *stochastic resonance* in which the thermal energy of the electrons allows stochastic transmission of a signal. This is an innovative property never before considered for the design of electronic circuits, be they single-electron or not. That evolution discovered this property demonstrates its ability to blindly design in the absence of any useful design rules.

There are also hopes to exploit quantum effects in another way: through quantum computing. Quantum computers do not process bits. Instead, they process qbits, which exist in a superposition of states. This allows n coupled qubits to represent a superposition of 2^n states, and operators acting upon the qubits operate on the superposition of states in parallel. This means that, as the number of superposed bits the operators operate upon increases, the processing power of the device increases exponentially with respect to traditional computing devices. Once quantum circuits are developed that can operate on superpositions of even tens of bits, they are likely to have enormous computing power. Theory has pointed to a number of rudimentary quantum gates that could be used to develop quantum circuits, although practice suggests that the number of interconnected gates is likely to become a limiting factor in their design. This realization has led a number of researchers to begin searching for innovative parsimonious sets of quantum gates using evolutionary algorithms [71]; [111].

Several researchers have also suggested that the field should be designing new technologies to suit evolutionary algorithms rather than the reverse. Miller and Downing have noted that all of today's electronic components have been designed specifically for top-down design methodologies and that researchers in hardware evolution have been "abusing" these components [75]. They argue that biological evolution is clearly capable of evolving extremely complex structure by *exploiting the physics* of the surrounding environment, and so we should be looking for substrates that exhibit rich, complex internal interactions and must be reconfigurable, ideally by small applied voltages. They suggest that substances that exist in a state on the edge of disorder would be good candidates, as they would exhibit the rich interactions necessary while being able to quickly relax to a homogeneous quiescent state. The Candidates they have suggested include liquid crystals, electroactive polymers, and voltage-controlled colloids.

Amorphous computers have also recently been suggested as a substrate amenable to evolution. Amorphous computers are essentially large collection of simple, wireless units that perform computations. These units are unreliable, not geometrically aligned, and can only communicate locally, but they are likely to be relatively easy to synthesize in extremely large arrays, as compared with other future technologies. However, no computational paradigm exists that can take advantage of their massively distributed function. Future nanoscale devices are also likely to have an amorphous structure, as Miller and Downing have pointed out [75]; hence, this could be a major issue for upcoming computational devices. Haddow and van Remortel have suggested that, by combining the principles of biological development and evolvable hardware, it may be possible to realize designs for amorphous computers [28].

3.2   Generalization

In the section above, we have discussed what we believe to be the primary motivation for work on evolvable hardware, namely, its ability to create innovative hardware. In this and the next section, we discuss the two greatest hurdles to evolvable hardware's viability for general real-world applications. The first of these is the difficulty of generalization.

Inductive learners such as evolutionary algorithms infer hypotheses from observed training examples of some kind. In the case of evolvable hardware, we test prospective circuits by exposing them to different conditions, most commonly a range of input signals, and observing the circuit outputs in order to evaluate fitness. If it is infeasible for all possible training examples to be observed by the learner, then the learner generalizes beyond the cases it has observed. Modern real-world circuits can process hundreds of input signals, and to observe each possible combination of these just once, even at millions of training cases a second, would take longer than the age of the universe. For sequential circuits, the number of training cases is infinite. And as we shall see later in this section, unseen signal inputs are but one (admittedly important) example of unseen operating conditions that we might hope a circuit to generalize across. Clearly, the ability to generalize is vital to the long-term future of evolvable hardware.

Two approaches to applying bias towards generalization can be found in the literature:
1. Introduce domain knowledge about the *structure* of circuits that exhibit the required generalization characteristics, perhaps in the form of a heuristic.
2. Introduce knowledge about the *behavior* of circuits that exhibit the required generalization characteristics, and rely on evolution to learn about the structure of circuits that exhibit the required behavior in addition to the primary task.

We now explore work on generalization, first by considering the special case of generalization across unseen input signal cases.

3.2.1   Generalization Across Input Vectors

Several researchers have explored input generalization under the framework of pattern recognition, a familiar problem in the area of generalization and therefore well suited to the study of this problem. As we mentioned in Section 2, many systems have been developed that demonstrate that evolvable hardware can generalize to unseen test cases for real-world pattern recognition data, such as image and signal classification [34]; [90] and image and signal noise filtering [100]; [131]. Yao and Higuchi have implied that the success of evolvable hardware in problems like these relies in some way on the use of a hard bias towards feed-forward networks of nonlinear processing units, likening their function to ANNs [132]. This bias is an example of case 1 above. Iwata et al. successfully managed to improve upon the generalization abilities of this kind of system by applying additional knowledge, again in the style of case 1 above [42]. They introduced a heuristic commonly used in the machine learning literature to improve generalization. The heuristic emerges from the application of the Minimum Description Length (MDL) principle to the discovery of maximum a posteriori hypotheses in Bayesian settings, and biases the search towards small circuits. For details of this interpretation of MDL, see Mitchell, [84] Chapter 6).

Miller and Thomson investigated the generalization abilities of a system evolving two- and three-bit multipliers with respect to the size of the input training sets [80, 81] and were far less successful. The task was to evolve a functional circuit from a subset of the truth table. They found that if evolution was presented with a subset of training cases throughout the entire evolutionary run, it was not able to produce general solutions. This finding suggests that in the setting of this problem and algorithm there was no implicit bias towards generality, even though they again enforced a hard representational bias towards feed-forward networks. They also reported that even when evolution was provided with a new set of training cases randomly drawn from the truth table every generation, general solutions were still not found, suggesting that evolution had little memory in the context of this problem.

Miller and Thomson also investigated the evolution of square root functions [80, 81]. In these cases, they discovered that some acceptable solutions were generated when evolution was limited to an incomplete training set. These cases occurred when the missing training cases tested low-order bits, which contributed less to the fitness. This outcome seems to answer the puzzle as to why their earlier experiments failed to generalize, as we shall now explain with reference to another experiment.

Imamura, Foster, and Krings also considered generalization in Miller's multiplier problems [40] and concurred that evolving fully correct circuits to many problems was extremely difficult without access to a full training set. They pointed out that the problem was exacerbated in functions where each test vector contained equal amounts of information relevant to the problem, such as the case of the three-bit multiplier studied by Miller and Thomson. However they suggested that in cases where the data contained a large amount of "don't care" values, evolvable hardware could be successful using a smaller test vector. Real-world pattern classification data contain redundant information, which explains why they succeeded where the multiplier problem failed. Indeed, since many input sets exhibit this property, it seems reasonable to assume that for any real-world problem some level of redundancy is likely to exist, although the problem of how to select test vectors remains. Immamura, Foster, and Krings suggested an adaptive approach of allowing the evolving system to search for useful subsets of test vectors.

3.2.2 Generalizing Across Operating Environments Though Representation

Just as it is unrealistic for the algorithm to train from every conceivable circuit input, in most cases it is unrealistic to train under every conceivable operating environment. Operating environments might include a range of technologies or platforms on which the designed circuit should operate, as well as a range of conditions to which the embodied circuit may be subjected.

Traditional designers usually manage such generalization by imposing hard biases on the nature of the circuit. These biases are again representational abstractions that encode domain knowledge known to produce behavior common across all necessary operating environments. The abstractions are then mirrored on the physical hardware through some constraint on the hardware's behaviour. A circuit that behaves correctly in all necessary conditions should then follow. For example, a gate-level digital design abstraction requires that the physical gates of the target technology behave as perfect logic operators. In most technologies, these gates are represented by transistors—physical devices that behave like high-gain amplifiers. Timing constraints and operating environment constraints specified by the manufacturer of the physical device are imposed on the real hardware. This ensures that, when an abstract computation takes place, the voltages of the transistors within each logic gate have reached saturation, and any transient behavior generated before saturation has dissipated. From this point forward, the outputs can be treated as logical values. In synchronous systems, these constraints are usually imposed with respect to a clock. The manufacturer will then guarantee that for a range of operating conditions, the device will behave as it appeared to within the design abstraction. The design is then portable across a range of devices and operating conditions.

Evolutionary circuit design often takes a similar approach to the traditional design process by applying design abstractions used by traditional designers. Many circuits have been evolved at levels of abstractions that would limit the search to circuits with good generalization characteristics. However, the only case we are familiar with where representational design abstractions have been imposed *specifically* to ensure good generalization is that of Stoica and colleagues [109], where a very high level of generalization was required. The experiment involved evolving transistor level circuits, and a representational bias was imposed that prevented input signals from connecting to transistor gates rather than to source or drain inputs, thus improving the loading characteristics of the evolved circuits. (The experiment is discussed in more detail in Section 3.3.3.)

3.2.3   Generalization Across Operating Environments by Inference from Examples

In cases where no knowledge is available about the structure of solutions that generalize across all operating environments, the only solution is for evolution to infer this information from examples.

Early work with intrinsically evolved circuits by Thompson focused on design innovation through relaxation of constraints [115, 116, 117]. Thompson successfully evolved a circuit to distinguish between two frequencies, using a Xilinx XC6200 FPGA. However, he then went on to note the lack of robustness to environmental conditions such as temperature, electronic surroundings, and power supply that may occur. He also noted that the design was not portable when moved not only to a different FPGA, but also to a different area of the same FPGA. Similar results have been reported by Masner et al. [73]. Thompson went on to explore how solutions that generalized well across a range of operating environments could be evolved [18]. He took a previously evolved FPGA circuit that discriminated between two tones. He then specified a number of parameters for an operational envelope which, when varied, affected the performance of this circuit: temperature, power supply, fabrication variations, packaging, electronic surroundings, output load, and circuit position on the FPGA. The final population from the previous experiment was then allowed to evolve further, this time on five different FPGAs maintained at the limits of environmental conditions specified by the operational envelope parameters. Although there was no guarantee that the circuit would generalize to behave robustly under all environmental conditions within the envelope, Thompson found a level of robustness evolved in four out of five cases. Hence, it appears that the biases he had introduced into the evolutionary algorithm were sufficient to promote good operating-condition generalization characteristics for the evolution of the 6200 architecture.

In a similar vein, Stoica et al. [106] explored the operation of circuits in extreme temperatures. Their initial experiment involved testing both traditionally designed circuits and circuits evolved under standard conditions (multipliers, Gaussian curve generators, and logic gates) to see whether they degrade or fail at extreme temperatures. This was primarily an experiment in evolutionary fault recovery, and they demonstrated that all circuits could regain functionality when evolved under extreme conditions. However, it is interesting to note that a population of 50 circuits re-evolved for 200 generations in this manner often exhibited degraded performance under standard conditions, whereas before they had functioned perfectly. This finding suggests that generalization qualities are easily lost if a consistent bias towards them is not asserted during evolution.

A problem closely related to Thompson's exploration of portability is the portability of extrinsically evolved analogue circuits to physical devices. Analogue circuit simulators tend to simulate circuit behavior very closely, and so it might be expected that extrinsically evolved circuits would generalize well to the real circuit. However, this does not happen in practice. One issue is that some behaviors that simulate according to the physics programmed into the simulator may not be feasible in the chosen implementation technology. A common example is that simulators fail to prevent the simulation of extremely high currents, and so evolution is free to take advantage of them in its design. Koza et al. have evolved many circuits extrinsically at an analogue abstraction using the Berkeley SPICE simulator [50], but have found that these circuits are practically infeasible because they rely on extremely high currents. Additionally, analogue simulators use very precise operating conditions. The circuits of Koza et al. are evolved to operate at 27°C, and so there is no explicit bias towards generalization across a range of temperatures.

When evolving networks of transistors intrinsically, Stoica et al. have come across the reverse problem: circuits evolved intrinsically may operate as expected under the conditions prevailing when they were evolved, but may not operate acceptably in software [105]. Their solution to the problem was to evaluate some circuits of each generation intrinsically, and some extrinsically. This they termed *mixtrinsic evolution* [107]. They also suggested that another use of mixtrinsic evolution would be to reward solutions that operate differently in simulation than when instantiated in a physical circuit. This would encourage innovative behavior not captured by simulation. They later developed a method [25] to include several different software models, based on various different processes, analysis tests, and timing resolutions.

The issues of portability discussed above have only dealt with portability between simulation and PLDs. An issue of extreme importance for evolutionary circuit design is whether designs evolved either extrinsically on PLDs or intrinsically are portable to custom application-specific integrated circuits (ASICs), which cannot be used during mixtrinsic evolution. Until recently, this question had been left unanswered, but Stoica et. al [109] evolved transistor-level gates using a combination of comprehensive fitness testing on each individual and mixtrinsic testing across the population. Comprehensive tests included transient analyses at different frequencies, testing a number of loads. Mixtrinsic tests were SPICE analysis on several process models and a range of voltages and temperatures. Additionally, a representational bias was imposed to improve loading characteristics, as mentioned in Section 3.3.2. Tests that were carried out mixtrinsically during evolution were carried out in full on the final evolved solutions, and revealed that some but not all of the circuits performed robustly across all tests. All circuits exposed to the full range of validation were successfully validated in silicon, showing that with careful validation procedures, portability of evolved designs to ASIC technologies is possible.

The concept of the ability of circuits to function under various environmental conditions can be extended to include the capacity of circuits to operate in the presence of faults. This was first investigated by Thompson [115, 116, 117]. He evolved a DSM-based robot controller problem (discussed in Section 3.2.1) in the presence of single-stuck-at (SSA) faults in the RAM used to hold a lookup table of state transitions for the state machine. Rather than testing each candidate solution exhaustively across all sets of possible faults, he aimed to test only the fault that caused the most degradation in each controller. He recognized that the population was likely to be made up of individuals of various designs, and hence the highest degradation of performance was unlikely to be caused by the same fault in the RAM. To circumvent this problem, at each generation he averaged the RAM bits across the DSMs of the entire population to give what he termed a *consensus individual*. Faults were only introduced once a good solution was found, and then the population was tracked to see how it performed. He found that solutions that were tolerant to most SSA faults existing in the initial population of evolved solutions, for reasons discussed in Section 3.3.4, but as evolution proceeded in the presence of faults, tolerance was lost as the algorithm concentrated on tolerating the single worst fault until eventually solutions tolerant to any single fault were discovered.

Canham and Tyrell extended this work to more complex faults that commonly develop in FPGA architectures [8]. They emulated a Xilinx 6200 series architecture on a Xilinx Virtex FPGA and introduced simulated SSA faults in the logic of the configurable logic blocks (CLBs), and short circuit faults between the inputs and outputs of the CLBs during evolution. The resultant circuits were compared against a set of control circuits that were evolved in the absence of faults and found a large increase in fault tolerance that could not be explained purely by "junk" faults occurring in unused areas of the FPGA.

Hartmann et al. have evolved fault-tolerant circuits using nonperfect digital gates called messy gates [30]. Various levels of noise were injected into digital gate models simulated using SPICE, and digital circuits were evolved. The circuits are manipulated by evolution at the gate level, but the evaluation of circuits was carried out using SPICE. The authors discovered that adders and multipliers could be evolved under high levels of noise. They postulated that the noise smoothed the fitness landscape as highly fit circuits that depended on each gate to perform function were no longer present in the search space.

3.2.4 Inherent Generalization

Another fascinating model for fault tolerance is that the biases of the evolutionary algorithm have an inherent tendency to generate solutions that generalize across certain conditions. Thereby, evolved circuits would exhibit robustness to changes in those particular conditions "for free."

Thompson has also postulated that evolved circuits may be inherently robust to some types of fault. He observed that an evolutionary algorithm will by nature be drawn to optima surrounded by areas of high fitness, and suggested that as a result, a single bit mutation from such an optimum will also tend to also have a high fitness. He then conducted experiments on an artificial NK landscape to demonstrate this. For details of this type of landscape, see work by Kauffman and Levin [47]. He then proposed that such an effect could have beneficial engineering consequences if a mutation were to cause a change in the circuit that is similar to a fault—namely, that the evolved system is likely to be inherently robust to such faults. He went on to highlight this by using the evolution of the DSM robot controller described in Section 3.3.3 as an example. Each bit of the RAM that encoded the controller's state machine was directly encoded in the chromosome, and so mutation of one of these bits had a effect similar to a "single stuck at" (SSA) fault. Examination of the effect of SSA faults on a previously evolved state machine revealed that it was quite robust to faults. However, since state machines for this problem with similar fitness could not be easily generated by any means other than evolution, statistical tests of the evolved machine's resilience to faults could not be carried out.

Following this experiment, Masner et al. [73] carried out studies of the effect of representational bias on the robustness of evolved sorting networks to a range of faults. The aim of the work was to explore the relationship between size and robustness of sorting networks using two representations—tree and linear. They noted that robustness first increases and then decreases with size, and is therefore not due purely to the existence of redundant nonfunctional gates in the sorting networks. They also noted that the linear representation tended to decrease in robustness with respect to size faster than the tree representation.

Layzell has suggested that robustness of solutions can also be generated at the level of populations [55]. In particular, he was interested in the ability of another member of the population to be robust with respect to a fault that causes the original best solution to fail. This outcome he called *populational fault tolerance (PFT)*. He went on to demonstrate that PFT is inherent in certain classes of evolved circuit and to test various hypotheses that could explain its nature. As with Masner et al., he noted that fault tolerance did not seem to be a result of redundant units based on the current design. Instead, he showed that descendants of a previously best and inherently different design were still present in redundant genes in the members of the population. It was these individuals that provided PFT. He demonstrated that this situation did not result from the presence of a diverse range of distinct solutions in the final population when he repeated the experiment using a single hillclimber to evolve solutions and then generated 50 single-bit mutants of this single individual. These individuals presented a similar tolerance to fault, confirming that the fault tolerance was inherent to the *incremental* nature of evolutionary processes in general: the entire population contained remnants of inherently different solutions that had been explored earlier.

This fact suggests that PFT is somewhat of a misnomer, since one might expect it to refer to tolerance owing to the nature of a population-based search. Tyrrell et al. have explored what might be called "true" populational fault tolerance [127]. Unlike Layzell's work, population diversity was encouraged by evolving oscillators using a population of 16 hillclimbers that did not interact with each other. This setup ensured that the evolved solutions did not share a common evolutionary history, so any fault tolerance observed could not be a result of the effect proposed by Layzell above. When faults were introduced to the oscillators that caused the best member of the population to fail, another member of the population often retained relatively high fitness. This demonstrates that population diversity can also play a role in evolved fault tolerance.

3.3   Performance and Evolvability

A good deal of research in the field of evolvable hardware is devoted to the following:

- improving the quality of solutions that evolution discovers for a given problem

- improving the scalability of evolution to larger and/or more complex problems

- improving the speed with which evolution finds acceptable solutions

These ideas are highly interrelated since they all aim to improve the performance of the evolutionary search in order to achieve slightly different goals.

3.3.1   Representations

Selection of a good representation is crucial to the performance of an evolutionary algorithm. As discussed in Section 2, the representation of an evolutionary algorithm defines how solution space is mapped onto search space. This process affects the performance of the algorithm as it delimits the solutions present in the search space, thereby fixing the density of acceptable solutions in the search space. Many researchers, particularly in the early days of evolvable hardware, believed that performance could be improved by reducing the size of the search space and increasing the density of good solutions lying within it. This approach will be discussed in due course. However, representation has a second effect. In Section 2 we discussed how it partly specifies the order of traversal of search space, since it sets the distance between any given points in space. Hence, it changes the *nature* of the search space. It is becoming increasingly recognized that having a small-sized space is not as important as having a space that allows evolution to discover incremental improvements in fitness that will lead it to a solution [10, 2, 115]. We define a search space that allows this process to occur an *evolvable* search space.

Miller and Thomson have explored how changes in circuit geometry affect the evolvability of a two-bit multiplier [79, 80, 81] and how the functionality-to-routing ratio affects the evolvability of netlist representations of the SBOX problem space [79, 80, 81]. It appears that evolvability is affected profoundly but erratically by both factors, making it difficult to draw many direct conclusions. Miller and Thomson did note, however, that evolvability was improved by allowing cells dedicated to routing signals between functional cells. However, because these studies may be dependent on the problem, the biases imposed by the specific operators used within the algorithm, and the level of abstraction at which the experiments were conducted, again it is dangerous to read too much into this work.

3.3.2 Function Level Evolution

The function-level approach to improving evolvability was proposed by Murakawa et al. [89] and has since been adopted by many others [124, 99, 123]. Murakawa et al. pointed out that the size of the search space for a binary genetic algorithm increases at a rate of 2^n for every addition n genes, and suggested that as evolution tackles larger problems, the explosion in search-space size prevents the algorithm from searching effectively. One solution they proposed was function-level evolution. Here they suggested that instead of using gate-level representations, domain knowledge could be used to select high-level computational units, such as adders, subtractors, and sine generators, that could be represented directly in the chromosome. thereby reducing the size of the chromosome necessary to represent an acceptable solution. Although this approach has proved to be successful for limited problems, there are several issues that indicate it is not a long-term solution. First is the problem of domain knowledge, which requires an experienced designer to select suitable function-level units for the problem at hand. Furthermore, if little or no domain knowledge exists for the problem, it may not be suitable for a function-level approach. Second, the approach is not scalable to problems of increasingly greater complexity without introducing more domain knowledge through the selection of more powerful functions. Third, once an abstraction has been made through the selection of function-level units, evolution will be limited to search the space of this abstraction, and any innovative solutions at a lower abstraction will be unattainable. Finally, and perhaps most importantly, the functional units are selected using domain knowledge from traditional design processes. As we have discussed throughout this chapter, evolution performs a bottom-up search rather than a top-down design. In Section 3.4.1, we pointed out that there is very little domain knowledge about the *evolvability* of circuit design spaces, and so even functions selected by experienced designers may not be of value when attempting to solve a problem using an evolutionary algorithm.

Indeed, Thompson argued that coarse-grained representations such as those employed by function-level evolution may reduce the evolvability of a hardware design space [115, 116, 117], since the addition to or removal from a circuit design of a complex function is likely to have a more dramatic effect on the overall function of the circuit than simple function. Thompson makes a strong argument that traditional evolution has the capability to search larger spaces than those advocated by Murakawa et al. [89]. In particular, he suggests that there may be features of many hardware design landscapes that allow us to search large spaces beyond the point where the evolving population has converged in fitness. Such a feature, he suggested, was the neutral network.

3.3.3   Neutral Networks

Neutral networks can be conceived as collections of genotypes with phenotypes of identical fitness that are arranged in search space so as to make pathways or networks that can be navigated by evolution through the application of its genetic operators. It has been suggested that *genetic drift* along such networks can allow evolution to escape local optima that they would otherwise be anchored to [39]. The idea of neutral mutations has been recognized in the field of evolutionary biology for some time but has only in recent years been used as a paradigm for search in evolutionary computation. Harvey suggested that taking full advantage of neutral networks would require a redesign of evolutionary algorithms, and in light of this he proposed the Species Adaptation Genetic Algorithm (SAGA) [31], which advocates incremental changes in genotype length and a much greater emphasis on mutation than is common for genetic algorithms. Thompson, however, managed to prove his point using only a fixed-length genetic algorithm with a SAGA-style mutation rate to search an incredibly large circuit design space (2^{1800}) for good solutions. This he succeeded in doing, and when the algorithm was stopped owing to time constraints, fitness was still increasing even though the population had converged long before [32]. Analysis of the evolutionary process did indeed reveal that a converged population had drifted along neutral networks to more fruitful areas of the search space. He attributed much of this behavior to the increased mutation rate, a change to the static procedural mapping of the algorithm. He went on to speculate that neutral networks might be a feature of a great deal of design spaces, including many hardware design spaces.

Vassiliev and Miller have explored neutrality in the three-bit multiplier logic netlist space. Their work [128, 129] suggests that neutral changes at the start of an evolutionary run occur because of high redundancy in the genotype. As the run continues and fitness becomes higher, redundancy is reduced. However, the number of neutral changes does not drop as quickly, suggesting that selection *promotes* neutral changes in order to search the design space. They then went on to show that when neutral mutations were forbidden, the evolvability of the landscape was reduced. They have also proposed that the search for innovation may be assisted by using current designs as a starting point for evolution, and proposed that a neutral bridge could be used to lead from conventional design space to areas beyond [128, 129].

Much of the work on neutrality uses evolutionary strategies as opposed to the more traditional genetic algorithm. Evolutionary strategies do not use the crossover operator, and because of this, their use in studies of neutral mutations, the driving force of evolution in the neutral network paradigm, simplifies analysis.

3.3.4   Incremental Learning

Following the function-level approach, Torresen proposed another idea based on evolving more complex components to improve scalability. Inspired by results from the use of automatically defined functions in genetic programming, and recognizing that an incremental, bottom-up process might improve scalability, he suggested that evolution could be handed the task of evolving higher-level functions. He also suggested that the process could be repeated incrementally so as to produce a complex solution based on a series of modules that had been iteratively encapsulated into larger ones. Thus he dubbed the approach *increased complexity evolution*. However, he still needed a mechanism to modularize the problem into less complex subtasks that would each present a more evolvable landscape than that of the entire task.

He suggested that the complexity of the problem could be subdivided by a traditional functional decomposition, and demonstrated the process with a pattern recognition task where a number of character images were to be classified according to character. Each output of the circuit corresponded to an individual character and was to be set high only if the pattern under test corresponded to that character. He manually decomposed the problem into a set of circuits where each would be evolved to detect only a single character. His results showed that there was a significant increase in evolutionary performance when decomposing the problem in this way. Unfortunately, his demonstration implicitly included domain knowledge by applying the idea of top-down decomposition to a problem that is amenable to such an approach. Additionally, he also stopped short of demonstrating the benefits such an approach could bring to scalability, since he did not present a demonstration of evolution at a higher level of abstraction using the evolved circuits as primitives. Finally, the opportunity for an incrementally evolved system to innovate is curtailed by this approach, in this case by the imposition of a traditional top-down design that was implicitly imposed. Although this method does not fundamentally solve the problem of scalability it may be useful when knowledge is available as to how a problem might be decomposed. For example, Hounsell and Arslan [37] decomposed a three-bit multiplier problem by output pins in this manner. In this case, they automatically integrated the individual circuits, which were evolved extrinsically, using standard logic minimization techniques, thereby automating the technique and addressing to some extent the issue of parsimony that Torresen had not touched upon. Kazadi et al. [48] have extended the idea further by removing the requirement of combining evolved circuits using traditional minimization techniques, thereby increasing the opportunities for innovative circuit design. They achieved this by first evolving the correct behavior for a single output and then selecting a single parsimonious solution and encapsulating it as a module. The module was then used as a primitive for another stage of evolution in which correct behavior for an additional output was required. The process was iterated until correct behavior for all outputs was observed. Although this method can automate the generation of a complete circuit, it is still relies on decomposition by output producing evolvable subproblems.

Lohn et al. have compared a number of incremental-type systems. They compared three dynamic fitness functions against a static one [68]. The dynamic fitness functions increased in difficulty during an evolutionary run. One had a fixed increase in difficulty, based on domain knowledge; one had a simple adaptive increase based on the best fitness within the population; and one put the level of difficulty under genetic control by coevolving the problem and the solution. The results showed that the coevolutionary system performed best on an amplifier design problem, but the static system performed best of all. When discussing potential reasons as to why the incremental systems showed poorer performance, Lohn et al. recognized that the discontinuity in the fitness landscapes resulting from the adaptive nature of the fitness functions might have reduced the evolvability of the systems.

3.3.5   Dynamic Representations

Another proposal from ETL to improve the speed of evolution was to use a variable length representation, with the aim of reducing the size of the search space necessary for a problem. Applied to a pattern recognition problem, performance was improved over an algorithm that did not use variable-length representations, in terms of both solution parsimony and efficacy [44].

A similar approach was taken by Zebulum in an experiment to evolve Boolean functions using a chromosome of product terms that were summed by the fitness function [139]. However, the search order of representation space differed from the ETL experiments. Inspired by the observation that complex organisms have evolved from simpler ones, the population was seeded with short chromosomes. This approach assumes a correlation between complex behavior and complex structure. As we discussed earlier, Thompson has demonstrated that this is not necessarily true, since complexity in behavior can arise from interactions of a simple system with a complex environment [120]. However, the simplicity of the simulation used to evaluate circuit designs in this example may mean that in this case the assumption holds. A new operator was introduced to increase chromosome length, under the control of a fixed parameter. Hence a simple pressure to move from short representations to long ones was set. It was found that a low rate of increase allowed fully functional but more parsimonious solutions to be found over a larger rate.

In both these examples, each gene in the representation was mapped directly to a Boolean function, and the representation space was searched by adding and removing genes guided by evolution in the first case, and by adding genes guided by a simple heuristic in the second case. In both cases, only the size of the space searched was changeable, rather than any arrangement of the order; hence, the *evolvability* of the space remained unaltered.

3.3.6   Development

The use of evolution itself to explore representation space as a meta-search in addition to the search of design space is an attractive idea. This leaves the question of how to do so such that the search of representations achieves the following:

- it allows evolution to explore innovative design spaces;

- it allows evolution to explore design spaces of varying evolvability, not just size.

We have already explained that evolution searches design space from the bottom up, and that this is unlike approaches imposed by traditional top-down design, allowing evolution to explore innovative areas of design space. We have also already mentioned how we have little understanding of how to make such searches more evolvable.

One approach we can take is to turn to nature to gain some insight into evolvability. The proof that bottom-up evolutionary design can be highly evolvable is all around us in the form of extremely complex biological organisms. However, Dawkins has noted that that the organisms that evolved early in evolutionary history have since then evolved the least [10], since most simple organisms present today are virtually unchanged since their appearance in the fossil record, whereas organisms that have evolved in more modern times have continued to evolve increasingly complex structure. This led Dawkins to suggest that biological evolution has over time discovered evolvable mechanisms that it has used to generate increasingly complex organisms: there has been an evolution of evolvability. This has led us to believe that we should look to differences between the mechanisms that simple and higher organisms employ to map from genotype to phenotype for sources of evolvability. A striking feature of higher organisms is their modularity. The period of evolutionary history in which organisms first made use of complex modular structures, the Cambrian period, heralded the appearance of Metazoan organisms and was marked by an explosion of evolution [49]. This would suggest that the idea of decomposing a problem into modules to improve evolvability is a good one. The mechanisms of problem decomposition previously used to evolve hardware designs relied on top-down human design abstractions. The mechanism by which all Metazoan organisms map genotype to phenotype is quite different. It is the process of development. Development provides a mechanism for evolutionary control over a *bottom-up* modularization process. It allows evolution to make use of any innovative design features it discovers at lower abstractions and to encapsulate them for reuse at a higher level of abstraction.

Development maps genotype to phenotype in an *indirect* process. It provides a series of instructions describing how to construct an organism [4]. It is also a *generative* process. It uses abstraction and iteration to manage the flow of control within the series of instructions [36]. In this sense, it can be likened to a traditional declarative computer program. Developmental systems that employ these ideas in an abstract sense have been explored for a number of years in the context of ANN design. They directly evolve programs that explicitly describe how a system should develop. The language in which the programs are described employ fixed, explicit mechanisms for abstraction and reuse. Such systems have been labeled as *explicit* developmental systems by Bentley and Kumar [4]. One such system is cellular encoding [24]. More recently, the same method has been used by Koza et al. to evolve analogue circuits [50]. The basic technique is to evolve trees of developmental steps using genetic programming (GP). Each developmental step, encoded as a GP node, explicitly codes for a phenotype modification. A fixed "embryonic" phenotype is "grown" by applying a tree of rules to it. Koza used automatically defined functions (ADFs) to explicitly provide modularity, and automatically defined copies (ADCs) to provide iteration. Lohn and Columbano have used a similar approach, but with a linear mapping representation that is applied to an embryonic circuit in an unfolding manner, rather than a circuit-modifying one [67]. The representational power is limited, although some but not all of these limitations have more recently been removed by introducing new operators [6]. Although both systems have managed to evolve innovative designs, only Koza has demonstrated examples of modularization and reuse in his solutions, and these have been limited to a few examples that do not produce modularization and reuse on the order of that seen in biological organisms. This result might suggest that there are other features of biological development important to evolvability that are not captured by implementing such abstract ideas of modularization, reuse, and growth alone. To benefit from using a developmental genotype–phenotype mapping, the process by which biological development achieves these features should be modeled more closely.

Biological development describes the transformation of a single-celled embryo into a complex adult organism. The entire process is by no means completely understood. It encapsulates a huge array of interactions between genes, their products, and the environment, from microscopic to macroscopic, some of seemingly minor importance, some ubiquitous to all stages of development. One mechanism that has a hand in all stages of development is DNA transcription. Transcription regulates the rate of gene expression through the presence of proteins called transcription factors, which either increase (activators) or decrease (inhibitors) the transcription rate of a particular gene. All transcription factors are proteins that are generated by the expression of other genes. Thus a dynamic, autocatalytic network of gene products specifies which genes are expressed. These networks are called *gene regulatory networks (GRNs)* [103]. Such networks may be arranged as modules, controlled by a master control gene [58]. When activated, the master control gene causes a cascade of activity throughout a GRN module and generates a complex feature in a phenotype.

Evolution is able to manage the flow of control for the developmental program over time by manipulating gene products involved in GRNs. However, another mechanism is required to communicate flow of control over space. To achieve this, biology makes use of two processes: growth and induction. Growth occurs through cellular division; thus, regulatory substances within an ancestor cell can be distributed to all the cell's descendents as they spread through space. Development can control this process, for instance, by constraining the location of a regulatory substance within a cell such that, after cell cleavage, it is present only in one daughter cell. Such regulatory substances are known as *cytoplasmic determinants*. Induction is quite different. Here a cell encodes regulatory information as a chemical signal, which is transmitted to nearby cells. A variety of inductive signal types have been identified [103] that pass information over various localities and at various rates.

Evolutionary design systems that model these processes are termed *implicit* by Bentley and Kumar [4]. Flow of control in implicit systems is commonly modeled by successively rewriting a symbolic description of a simple object according to a set of rewriting rules. The map between genotype and phenotype is specified by a fixed start symbol for the rule rewriting process, and the grammar is evolved. One type of system that models both transcription and growth are L-Systems. These have been explored in the context of circuit design by Haddow and Tufte [27]. The L-System they used was context free; hence, the rules were rewritten such that there was no communication between adjacent structures. Hence, no concept of induction was modeled. Miller has explored a similar growth-based system that incorporated a limited amount of context [82]. The phenotype consists of a single embryonic cell. The chromosome encodes a set of functions to determine the inputs and function of the cell and whether it should divide to produce two daughter cells. At each developmental timestep, the functions are executed in all current cells, and the process iterates. The arguments of shared functions are the positions of the inputs, current function, and location of that cell. Functions were used to determine the connections and function in the next step of development. Hence a form of communication is captured by the model through the labels of each cell's current neighbours affecting the current cell's next state. However, the communication between cells (and hence the model of induction) is present in a highly abstract and limited sense, and the role of induction in the development of the circuit cannot be separated from the role of growth.

3.3.7   An Example of Developmental Evolutionary Circuit Design

The recent work of Gordon [20] provides an alternative approach. With the eventual goal of evolving complex, functioning circuits, an exploratory system based on the three principles of being generative, implicit, and context-driven was designed. It was decided that a rule-based system could satisfy all three criteria. Like biological organisms, the phenotype is composed of "cells", but unlike biological organisms, the cells in our model are laid out on a two-dimensional grid, mirroring the medium of electronic circuits. This layout has the advantage of being easily mapped to a circuit design for a programmable logic device such as a Field Programmable Gate Array (FPGA), and so was in keeping with our aim of developing a system with as little computational overhead as possible. To update the entire individual for a single developmental timestep, the set of rules that make up the chromosome is tested against the "chemical environment" that is modeled in each of these cells. For each cell, only the rules that match that cell's environment are activated. If the environment differs between cells, it is possible for different rules to be activated in each cell, which leads to their environments being altered in different ways. In this way, different chemical environments can be maintained between cells. By modeling a cell's context with only transcription factors (proteins that activate genes) and ignoring all other chemistry present in biological cells, we were able to keep our model as simple as possible yet encapsulate the key features that provide a generative, implicit, context-driven process.

Transcription factor proteins were modeled as binary state variables. Each gene was modeled as a rule. The precondition of the rule specified which proteins must be present (activators) and which must be absent (inhibitors) in order for that particular gene to activate. The postcondition of the rule defines the protein that is generated if the rule is activated. An example rule is shown in Figure 12.4.

For a rule like this to be activated, the proteins in the environment must match the pattern of proteins specified in the rule precondition. There are five bits in the rule precondition for each protein in the model. The final three bits define the protein concentration that the operator will act upon. Hence a rule can specify concentration values to range from 0 to 7. The first two bits of the protein condition specify the operator—not equal to (00), less than or equal to (01), greater than or equal to (10), or equal to (11). The specific protein to be tested is determined by the locus of these bits. A set of these rules makes up the chromosome

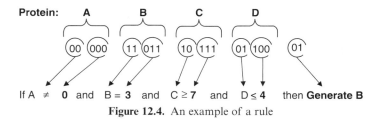

Figure 12.4. An example of a rule

and defines how the proteins interact over time. At each timestep in the developmental process, the environment is inspected to determine which proteins are present, and then each rule is inspected to determine whether the environment matches the rule. If it does, the rule is activated; the protein defined in the rule's postcondition is generated and goes on to make up part of the protein environment of the following timestep.

Context is a key feature of our model—cells must be able to affect their neighbor's environment. In our model, this is achieved through the interaction of proteins. Each cell inspects its neighbors to determine what proteins they are generating. The protein concentration detected by a cell is determined thus: for each protein, the cell sums the total number of neighbors that are generating that protein. If the cell itself is also generating that protein, it adds an additional 3 concentration points to the total. Thus the maximum concentration can be 7 points, since as 4 are contributed by the neighbors and 3 by the cell itself. To simulate this process, the cell model for our exploratory system contains a protein detector and a protein generator in order to record the proteins that are present in the cell and the proteins that are detected by the cell, respectively. To summarize, a complete developmental timestep for a cell proceeded thus:

1. For each protein in the model, the cell's protein detector sends a query to each of its von Neumann neighbors (i.e., the four neighbors to the north, south, east, and west on a 2D grid) to determine if they are generating that protein. It also queries its own generator, and sums the results from the neighbors and itself (with an additional bias towards itself) to give a detected concentration for that protein.

2. The rule set is tested against the pattern of proteins detected by the detector in step 1. As each rule with a precondition matching the cell's current pattern of *detected* proteins is activated, the cell's protein *generator* is updated to represent the protein specified in the rule postcondition.

These two steps are then repeated for a number of cycles, as shown in Figure 12.5, allowing the pattern of proteins formed across the global array of cells to change until a stable state or cycle of states is reached, or until development is halted after a predetermined number of timesteps. Gordon provides Full details [20].

The system described above so far models the process of forming patterns of gene products. What remains is for a mechanism to be introduced by which the patterns of gene products generate a circuit design. Each cell in our cellular array is mapped directly to a configurable logic block (CLB) on a Xilinx Virtex FPGA, and the activity of the genes in each cell are linked to alterations in the functional components in the CLB. This means that in addition to proteins, the models of

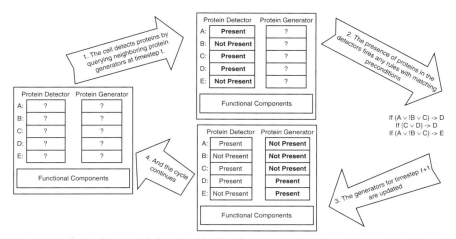

Figure 12.5. A developmental timestep highlighting the protein interaction model with a cell

our cells also contain functional components that map directly to functional components in a CLB. In order to keep the initial model simple, we added as few components as possible to our cell model. Each cell has four input wires that could be driven by its local neighbors, two 4-input lookup tables (LUTs), and an output wire from each LUT. The LUTs map directly to two of the four LUTs in a Virtex CLB, and the input and output wires map directly to manually selected single lines between the CLBs. For details of the Virtex architecture and how this mapping was made, see the work of Gordon and Bertley [21].

To allow these functional components to be altered by gene activity, we introduced new postconditions to the rules. These coded for an alteration to the logic in a CLB. Over the course of development, the activities of these circuit-altering postconditions were recorded by activity counters – one counter in each cell for each circuit-altering postcondition—and once development was complete, the activity counters were inspected in order to determine what alterations should be made to a predefined template circuit on the Virtex. Gordon and Bertley give details of this process [21].

Numerous experiments have been carried out on this model and variations of it [19]. The results showed the importance of good intercellular communication to improve development's ability to generate and maintain a range of patterns. The work has shown that the computational power of this developmental model is sufficient to allow the learning of patterns that map to fully functional adder circuits [20]. This is an important step towards tackling real-world problems with development.

3.4   Platform Research

We have now reviewed most current research into evolvable hardware. We have seen that many researchers believe that working at low levels of abstraction can have advantages. We have also seen that mechanisms to explore evolvability and generalization are being actively investigated. What we have not considered is the availability of platforms for low-abstraction hardware evolution.

In this section, we cover the platforms that have been reported in the evolvable hardware literature. Some are commercially available, and some have been developed by researchers. Commercial devices have not been developed with evolvable hardware as a primary goal, and so most struggle to compete with dedicated evolvable hardware on performance, versatility, and ease of use for our purposes. However, they do have advantages of availability and cost (although some that were used for early research are now no longer available), and so many researchers have explored their use for evolvable hardware.

3.4.1   Criteria for successful evolutionary platforms

Thompson [115] has listed a number of criteria for intrinsic circuit evolution platforms. These are discussed below:

Reconfigurable an unlimited number of times. Many field programmable devices are designed to be programmed only once. Others are designed to be programmed a small number of times, but repeated configuration can eventually cause damage. Evolutionary experiments can require millions of evaluations, and so devices for intrinsic experiments should be able to be reconfigured infinitely.

Fast and / or partial reconfiguration. If millions of evaluations are needed, the evaluation process should be fast. Modern programmable devices have millions of configurable transistors and consequently have large configuration bitstreams. This can mean that downloading the configuration becomes the bottleneck of the evolutionary process. The brute force solution to this problem is to use devices with high bandwidth configuration ports. Another solution is to evaluate many individuals at once, as proposed by Higuchi, Iba, and Manderick, among others [33]. Batch evaluation limits the type of evolutionary algorithm to those with large populations, ruling out the use of steady-state genetic algorithms or low-population evolutionary strategies. A more elegant solution is that of partial reconfiguration, where only the changes from the current configuration need to be uploaded. This yields similar bandwidth use with no constraints on the learning algorithm.

Indestructibility or validity checking. In conventional CMOS technologies, a wire driven from two sources can result a short circuit if one drives the wire to a different voltage level than another. The high currents generated from such an event are extremely undesirable, as they can damage the device, and so should be prevented by hard constraints, rather than the softer ones advocated so far. Some hardware platforms are designed around an architecture with which contention is impossible. For those that are not, there are two options—either an abstract architecture can be imposed on top of the real hardware, or circuits can be tested for contention before they are synthesized, and evaluated by an alternative means if such a condition is detected.

Fine-grain reconfigurability. In order to allow evolution the ability to innovate, evolution must be able to manipulate candidate circuits at a low level of abstraction. Hence a good platform needs fine-grain control over the evolving platform.

Thompson also points out the distinction between fine-grain architectures and fine-grain reconfigurability—namely, that although a device's architecture may be based on repeated large units, if these can be reconfigured at a finer level, then this criterion will be met.

Flexible I/O. The method of supplying input and retrieving output from an evolved circuit can affect the feasibility of successful evolution, so a platform that allows experimentation with this is useful.

Low cost. This is of particular importance when the motive behind using evolution is to lower costs through design automation.

Observability. In order to analyze how evolved circuits work, their internal signals need to be probed. However, when working with low-design abstractions, it may be impossible to avert the potential of signal probes to change the behavior of the circuit, and the probed signal architectures should be chosen with this as a consideration.

3.4.2   Platforms

Bearing these criteria in mind, the platforms that have been used or proposed for use for evolvable hardware experiments are now considered briefly. These can be classified into three groups: commercial digital, commercial analogue, and research platforms. They are tabulated below.

Commercial Analogue Platforms
Zetex TRAC [14]: Based around 2 pipelines of 10 op-amps + programmable capacitors, resistors. Linear and nonlinear functions successfully evolved. Large-grained reconfigurability and limited topology limit worth for evolution.
Anadigm FPAA(Inc. 2003): Up to 4 reconfigurable blocks with programmable interconnect. CABs contain 2 op-amps, capacitor banks, serial approximation register. Large-grained reconfigurability limits worth for evolution. No reports on use for evolvable hardware.
Lattice ispPAC [92]: Designed for filtering applications. Based on programmable amplifiers. Limited reconfigurability (~10,000x) limits suitability for evolvable hardware.
Motorola MPAA020 [136]: 20 cells containing an op. amp, comparator, transistors, capacitors, and SRAM. A range of circuits has been evolved. Much of the bitstream is proprietary. Geared towards circuits based around the op. amp. No longer available.

Commercial Digital Platforms
Xilinx 6200 [115, 116, 117, 50, 121]: Developed for dynamic reconfig. apps. Fast and infinite reconfig., fully or partially. Homogenous fine-grained architecture of MUXes. All configurations valid. Good I/O. Expensive, no longer available.
Xilinx XC4000 [57]: Low cost, infinite but slow reconfig. SRAM LUT based architecture. Damaged by invalid configurations. Parts of bitstream proprietary and undisclosed. Reconfigurable at resource level using Xilinx JBits software. No longer available.

Xilinx Virtex/II/II Pro [35, 56]: Medium cost. SRAM LUT based architecture. Can be reconfigured infinitely and quickly, fully and partially. Can be damaged by random configurations. Some of the bitstream is proprietary and undisclosed, but most hardware resources can be reconfigured using Xilinx JBits software. Virtex II provides embedded multipliers, Virtex II Pro provides embedded CPU core. Widely available.

Research Platforms
FPTA [105, 53, 13]: Reconfigurable at transistor level, additionally supporting capacitors and multiple I/O points. Programmable voltages control resistances of connecting switches for use as additional transistors. Some versions allow variable channel height and width. FPTA2 provides 8×8 array of FPTA cells Fits criteria for evolvable hardware well.
Embryonic Arrays [113, 126]: Bio-inspired fault tolerant FPGA architecture. Programmable cells usually based on MUXtrees. New POEtic tissue designed to support hierachical logical genotype, developmental and phenotype layers. Interesting architecture for developmental hardware evolution.
Palmo [29]: PWM-based signaling rather than true analogue. Based around array of integrators. All configurations valid.
Evolvable Motherboard [54]: Array of analogue switches, connected to six interchangeable evolvable units. Evolution of gates, amplifiers, and oscillators demonstrated using bipolar transistors as evolvable unit. Good I/O. Board-based architecture is not suitable for real-world problems due to size, cost, and number of evolvable units.
FIPSOC [86]: Complete evolutionary system aimed at mixed signal environments. Analogue and digital units. CPU and memory to encode evolutionary algorithm. Analogue units based around amplifiers. Digital units based on LUTs and flip-flops. Context-based dynamic reconfiguration suitable for real-time adaptive systems.
PAMA [96]: Fixed analogue MUX array allowing interconnection of interchangeable evolvable units. Current version implements a 32 16:1 bidirectional low on-resistance MUX/deMUX allowing for random configurations.

4   SUMMARY

The problems of electronic circuit design are increasing as demand for improvements increases. In this review, we have introduced a promising new type of solution to these difficulties: evolvable hardware. This emerging field exists at the intersection of electronic engineering, computer science, and biology.

The benefits brought about by evolvable hardware are particularly suited to a number of applications, including the design of low-cost hardware, poorly specified problems, creation of adaptive systems, fault-tolerant systems, and innovation.

The chapter has also reviewed and analyzed current research trends in evolvable hardware in depth. In particular, the research focusing on innovation, evolvability, and platforms have been described, and a recent example of a developmental evolutionary electronics system designed by the authors has been provided.

Evolvable hardware is still a young field. It does not have all the answers to the problems of circuit design, and there are still many difficulties to overcome. Nevertheless, these new ideas may be one of the brightest and best hopes for the future of electronics.

ACKNOWLEDGMENTS

The authors would like to thank Dr. Peter Rounce for his insights and advice.

REFERENCES

[1] V. Aggarwal (2003): *Evolving sinusoidal oscillators using genetic algorithms.* 2003 NASA/DoD Conference on Evolvable Hardware, Chicago, IL, USA, IEEE Comput. Soc., Los Alamitos, CA, USA.

[2] L. Altenberg, (1995): The Schema Theorem and Price's Theorem. *Foundations of Genetic Algorithms 3*. D. Whitley and M. D. Vose. San Mateo, CA, U.S.A., Morgan Kaufmann: 23–49.

[3] T. Arslan and D. H. Horrocks (1995): The Design of Analogue and Digital Filters Using Genetic Algorithms. *15th SARAGA Colloquium on Digital and Analogue Filters and Filtering Systems*, London, U.K.

[4] P. J. Bentley and S. Kumar (1999): Three Ways to Grow Designs: A Comparison of Embryogenies for an Evolutionary Design Problem. *Proceeding of the Genetic and Evolutionary Computation Conference*, Orlando, FL, U.S.A.

[5] J. A. Biles (1994): GenJam: A Genetic Algorithm for Generating Jazz Solos. *Proceedings of the 1994 International Computer Music Conference*, San Francisco, CA, U.S.A., International Computer Music Association.

[6] J. P. B., Botelho, L. B. Sa, et al. (2003): An experiment on nonlinear synthesis using evolutionary techniques based only on CMOS transistors. *2003 NASA/DoD Conference on Evolvable Hardware*, Chicago, IL, USA, IEEE Comput. Soc., Los Alamitos, CA, USA.

[7] D. W. Bradley and A. M. Tyrrell (2001): The architecture for a hardware immune system. *Proceedings Third NASA/DoD Workshop on Evolvable Hardware*. EH 2001. 12–14 July 2001, Long Beach, CA, USA, IEEE Comput. Soc., Los Alamitos, CA, USA.

[8] R. O. Canham and A. M. Tyrrell (2002): Evolved Fault Tolerance in Evolvable Hardware. *2002 World Congress on Computational Intelligence*, Honolulu, HI, U.S.A., IEEE, Piscataway, NJ, USA.

[9] E., Damiani and V. Liberali, et al. (2000): Dynamic Optimisation of Nonlinear Feed-Forward Circuits. *3rd International Conference on Evolvable Systems*, Edinburgh, U.K.

[10] R. Dawkins, (1989): The evolution of evolvability. *Proceedings of Artificial Life: The Quest for a New Creation*, Santa Fe, U.S.A., Addison-Wesley.

[11] J. F. M., do Amaral, J. L. M. do Amaral, et al. (2002): Towards Evolvable Analog Fuzzy Logic Controllers. *2002 NASA/DoD Conference on Evolvable Hardware*, Alexandria, VA, U.S.A., IEEE Press.

[12] M. Dorigo, and G. Di Caro (1999): The Ant Colony Optimization Metaheuristic. *New Ideas in Optimization*. D. Corne, M. Dorigo and F. Glover. London, UK, McGraw-Hill: 11–32.

[13] I., Ferguson, A. Stoica, et al. (2002): An Evolvable Hardware Platform based on DSP and FPTA. *2002 Genetic and Evolutionary Computation Conference*, Memlo Park, CA, U.S.A., AAAI Press.

[14] S. J. Flockton and K. Sheehan (1999): A system for intrinsic evolution of linear and non-linear filters. *Proceedings of the First NASA/DoD Workshop on Evolvable Hardware.* 19–21 July 1999, Pasadena, CA, USA, IEEE Comput. Soc., Los Alamitos, CA, USA.

[15] A. Fukunaga and A. Stechert (1998): Evolving Nonlinear Predictive Models for Lossless Image Compression with Genetic Programming. *Third Annual Genetic Programming Conference*, Madison, WI, U.S.A.

[16] J. C. Gallagher, (2003): The once and future analog alternative: evolvable hardware and analog computation. *2003 NASA/DoD Conference on Evolvable Hardware*, Chicago, IL, USA, IEEE Comput. Soc., Los Alamitos, CA, USA.

[17] M. Garvie and A. Thompson (2003): Evolution of Self-diagnosing Hardware. *5th International Conference on Evolvable Systems*, Trondheim, Norway, Springer-Verlag.

[18] N., Göckel, R. Drechsler, et al. (1997): A Multi-Layer Detailed Routing Approach based on Evolutionary Algorithms. *Proceedings of the IEEE International Conference on Evolutionary Computation*, Indianapolis, IN, U.S.A.

[19] D. E. Goldberg (1989): Genetic algorithms in search, optimization, and machine learning. Reading, Mass.; Harlow, Addison-Wesley.

[20] T. G. W. Gordon (2003): Exploring Models of Development for Evolutionary Circuit Design. *2003 Congress on Evolutionary Computation*, Canberra, Australia.

[21] T. G. W. Gordon and P. J. Bentley (2002): Towards Development in Evolvable Hardware. *2002 NASA/DoD Conference on Evolvable Hardware*, Washington D.C., U..S.A.

[22] G. W. Greenwood and X. Song (2002): How to Evolve Safe Control Strategies. *2002 NASA/DoD Conference on Evolvable Hardware*, Alexandria, VA, U.S.A., IEEE Press.

[23] J. B. Grimbleby (2000): Automatic Analogue Circuit Synthesis Using Genetic Algorithms. *IEE Proceedings on Circuits Devices and Systems 147*(6): 319–323.

[24] F. Gruau (1994): Neural Network Synthesis Using Cellular Encoding and the Genetic Algorithm. *Laboratoire de l'Informatique du Parallilisme.* Lyon, Ecole Normale Supirieure de Lyon: 151.

[25] X., Guo, A. Stoica, et al. (2003): Development of consistent equivalent models by mixed-mode search. *IASTED International Conference on Modeling and Simulation*, Palm Springs, California, U.S.A.

[26] D. A. Gwaltney and M. I. Ferguson (2003): Intrinsic hardware evolution for the design and reconfiguration of analog speed controllers for a DC Motor. *2003 NASA/DoD Conference on Evolvable Hardware*, Chicago, IL, USA, IEEE Comput. Soc., Los Alamitos, CA, USA.

[27] P. C., Haddow, G. Tufte, et al. (2001): Shrinking the Genotype: L-systems for EHW? *The 4th International Conference on Evolvable Systems*: From Biology to Hardware, Tokyo, Japan.

[28] P. C. Haddow and P. van-Remortel (2001): From here to there: future robust EHW technologies for large digital designs. *Proceedings Third*

NASA/DoD Workshop on Evolvable Hardware, Long Beach, CA, USA, IEEE Comput. Soc., Los Alamitos, CA, USA.

[29] A., Hamilton, K. Papathanasiou, et al. (1998): Palmo: Field Programmable Analogue and Mixed-signal VLSI for Evolvable Hardware. *2nd International Conference on Evolvable Systems*, Lausanne, Switzerland, Springer-Verlag, Berlin, Germany.

[30] M., Hartmann, P. Haddow, et al. (2002): Evolving robust digital designs. *2002 NASA/DoD Conference on Evolvable Hardware*. 15–18 July 2002, Alexandria, VA, USA, IEEE Comput. Soc., Los Alamitos, CA, USA.

[31] I. Harvey, (1991): Species Adaptation Genetic Algorithms: The basis for a continuing SAGA. *1st European Conference on Artificial Life*, Paris, France.

[32] I. Harvey and A. Thompson (1997): Through the labyrinth, evolution finds a way: A silicon ridge. *1st International Conference on Evolvable Systems*, Tsukuba, Japan, Springer-Verlag, Berlin, Germany.

[33] T., Higuchi, H. Iba, et al. (1994): Evolvable Hardware. *Massively Parallel Artifical Intelligence*. Cambridge, MA, U.S.A., MIT Press: 398-421.

[34] T., Higuchi, M. Iwata, et al. (1996): Evolvable hardware and its application to pattern recognition and fault-tolerant systems. *Proceedings of Towards Evolvable Hardware*: An International Workshop. 2–3 Oct. 1995, Lausanne, Switzerland, Springer-Verlag, Berlin, Germany.

[35] G., Hollingworth, S. Smith, et al. (2000): The Intrinsic Evolution of Virtex Devices Through Internet Reconfigurable Logic. *Proceedings of the Third International Conference on Evolvable Systems*, Edinburgh, U.K.

[36] G. Hornby (2003): Generative Representations for Evolutionary Design Automation. Department of Computer Science. Waltham, MA, U.S.A., Brandeis University.

[37] B. I. Hounsell and T. Arslan (2000): A novel genetic algorithm for the automated design of performance driven digital circuits. *2000 Congress on Evolutionary Computation*, La Jolla, CA, USA, IEEE, Piscataway, NJ, USA.

[38] B. L. Hounsell and T. Arslan (2001): Evolutionary design and adaptation of digital filters within an embedded fault tolerant hardware platform. *Proceedings Third NASA/DoD Workshop on Evolvable Hardware*. EH 2001. 12–14 July 2001, Long Beach, CA, USA, IEEE Comput. Soc., Los Alamitos, CA, USA.

[39] M. A., Huynen, P. F. Stadler, et al. (1996): Smoothness within ruggedness: The role of neutrality in adaptation. *Proceedings of the National Academy of Science* 93.

[40] K., Imamura, J. A. Foster, et al. (2000): The test vector problem and limitations to evolving digital circuits. *2nd NASA/DoD Workshop on Evolvable Hardware*, Palo Alto, CA, U.S.A., IEEE Comput. Soc., Los Alamitos, CA, USA.

[41] A. Inc. (2003): AN120E04 FPAA Data Sheet, http://www.anadigm.com. 2004.

[42] M., Iwata, I. Kajitani, et al. (1996): A pattern recognition system using evolvable hardware. *4th International Conference on Parallel Problem Solving from Nature PPSN IV*, Berlin, Germany, Springer-Verlag, Berlin, Germany.

[43] D., Job, V. Shankararaman, et al. (1999): Hybrid AI Techniques for Software Design. *Proceedings of the 11th International Conference on Software Engineering and Knowledge Engineering*, Kaiserslautern, Germany.

[44] I., Kajitani, T. Hoshino, et al. (1996): Variable length chromosome GA for evolvable hardware. *3rd IEEE International Conference on Evolutionary Computation*, Nagoya, Japan, IEEE, New York, NY, USA.

[45] I., Kajitani, T. Hoshino, et al. (1999): An Evolvable Hardware Chip and Its Application as a Multi-Function Prosthetic Hand Controller. *16th National Conference on Artificial Intelligence*, Orlando, FL, U.S.A., AAAI Press.

[46] T., Kalganova, J. F. Miller, et al. (1998): Some aspects of an evolvable hardware approach for multiple-valued combinational circuit design. *2nd International Conference on Evolvable Systems, Lausanne*, Switzerland, Springer-Verlag, Berlin, Germany.

[47] S. Kauffman and S. Levin (1987): Towards a General Theory of Adaptive Walks on Rugged Landscapes. *Journal of Theoretical Biology. 128*: 11-45.

[48] S., Kazadi, Y. Qi, et al. (2001): Insufficiency of piecewise evolution. *3rd NASA/DoD Workshop on Evolvable Hardware*, Long Beach, CA, USA, IEEE Comput. Soc., Los Alamitos, CA, USA.

[49] M. Kirschner and J. Gerhart (1998): Evolvability. *Proceedings of the National Acadamy of Science 95*(8): 420–8427.

[50] J., Koza, F. H. I. Bennett, et al. (1999): *Genetic Programming III*. San Francisco, California, U.S.A., Morgan-Kauffmann.

[51] J. R., Koza, M. A. Keane, et al. (2000): Automatic creation of human-competitive programs and controllers by means of genetic programming. *Genetic Programming and Evolvable Machines 1*(1-2): 121–64.

[52] W. B. Langdon, (1997): Scheduling Maintenance of Electrical Power Transmission. *Artificial Intelligence Techniques in Power Systems*. K. Warwick and A. O. Ekwue. London, IEE Press: 220-237.

[53] J., Langeheine, J. Becker, et al. (2001): A CMOS FPTA chip for intrinsic hardware evolution of analog electronic circuits. *Proceedings Third NASA/DoD Workshop on Evolvable Hardware. EH 2001*. 12–14 July 2001, Long Beach, CA, USA, IEEE Comput. Soc., Los Alamitos, CA, USA.

[54] P. Layzell (1998): A new research tool for intrinsic hardware evolution. *2nd International Conference on Evolvable Systems*, Lausanne, Switzerland, Springer-Verlag, Berlin, Germany.

[55] P. Layzell and A. Thompson (2000): Understanding Inherent Qualities of Evolvaed Circuits: Evolutionary History as a Predictor of Fault Tolerance. *3rd International Conference on Evolvable Systems*, Edinburgh, U.K., Springer-Verlag.

[56] D. Levi (2000): HereBoy: a fast evolutionary algorithm. *The Second NASA/DoD Workshop on Evolvable Hardware.*, Palo Alto, CA, USA, IEEE Comput. Soc., Los Alamitos, CA, USA.

[57] D. Levi and S. A. Guccione (1999): GeneticFPGA: evolving stable circuits on mainstream FPGA devices. *1st NASA/DoD Workshop on Evolvable Hardware*, Pasadena, CA, U.S.A., IEEE Comput. Soc., Los Alamitos, CA, USA.

[58] E. B. Lewis (1992): Clusters of master control genes regulate the development of higher organisms. *Journal of the American Medical Association 267*: 1524–1531.

[59] J. H. Li and M. H. Lim (2003): Evolvable Fuzzy System for ATM Cell Scheduing. *5th International Conference on Evolvable Systems*, Trondheim, Norway, Springer-Verlag.

[60] D. S. Linden (2001): A system for evolving antennas in-situ. *Proceedings Third NASA/DoD Workshop on Evolvable Hardware. EH 2001.* 12–14 July 2001, Long Beach, CA, USA, IEEE Comput. Soc., Los Alamitos, CA, USA.

[61] D. S. Linden (2002): An evolvable antenna system for optimizing signal strength in-situ. *IEEE Antennas and Propagation Society International Symposium*, vol.1, 16–21 June 2002, San Antonio, TX, USA, IEEE, Piscataway, NJ, USA.

[62] D. S. Linden (2002): Optimizing signal strength in-situ using an evolvable antenna system. *2002 NASA/DoD Conference on Evolvable Hardware.* 15–18 July 2002, Alexandria, VA, USA, IEEE Comput. Soc., Los Alamitos, CA, USA.

[63] D. S. Linden and E. E. Altshuler (1999): Evolving wire antennas using genetic algorithms: a review. *Proceedings of the First NASA/DoD Workshop on Evolvable Hardware.* 19–21 July 1999, Pasadena, CA, USA, IEEE Comput. Soc., Los Alamitos, CA, USA.

[64] A. Lindenmayer (1968): Mathematical models for cellular interactions in development I Filaments with one-sided inputs. *Journal of Theoretical Biology 18*: 280–289.

[65] W., Liu, M. Murakawa, et al. (1997): ATM cell scheduling by function level evolvable hardware. *1st International Conference on Evolvable Systems*, Tsukuba, Japan, Springer-Verlag, Berlin, Germany.

[66] J., Lohn, G. Larchev, et al. (2003): A Genetic Representation for Evolutionary Fault Recovery in Virtex FPGAs. *5th International Conference on Evolvable Systems, Trondheim*, Norway, Springer-Verlag.

[67] J. D. Lohn and S. P. Colombano (1998): Automated analog circuit synthesis using a linear representation. *2nd International Conference on Evolvable Systems*, Lausanne, Switzerland, Springer-Verlag, Berlin, Germany.

[68] J. D., Lohn, G. L. Haith, et al. (1999): A comparison of dynamic fitness schedules for evolutionary design of amplifiers. *1st NASA/DoD Workshop on Evolvable Hardware*, Pasadena, CA, USA, IEEE Comput. Soc., Los Alamitos, CA, USA.

[69] J. D., Lohn, D. S. Linden, et al. (2003): Evolutionary Design of an X-Band Antenna for NASA's Space Technology 5 Mission. *2003 NASA/DoD Conference on Evolvable Hardware*, Chicago, IL.

[70] S. J. Louis (2003): Learning for evolutionary design. *2003 NASA/DoD Conference on Evolvable Hardware*, Chicago, IL, USA, IEEE Comput. Soc., Los Alamitos, CA, USA.

[71] M., Lukac, M. A. Perkowski, et al. (2003): Evolutionary Approach to Quantum and Reversible Circuits Synthesis. *Artificial Intelligence Review 20*(3-4): 361–417.

[72] N. J. Macias and L. J. K. Durbeck (2002): Self-assembling circuits with autonomous fault handling. *2002 NASA/DoD Conference on Evolvable Hardware*. 15–18 July 2002, Alexandria, VA, USA, IEEE Comput. Soc., Los Alamitos, CA, USA.

[73] J., Masner, J. Cavalieri, et al. (1999): Representation and robustness for evolved sorting networks. *1st NASA/DoD Workshop on Evolvable Hardware*, Pasadena, CA, U.S.A., IEEE Comput. Soc., Los Alamitos, CA, USA.

[74] P. Mazumder and E. M. Rudnick (1999): *Genetic Algorithms for VLSI Design, Layout and Test Automation.* Upper Saddle River, NJ, U.S.A., Prentice-Hall.

[75] J. F. Miller and K. Downing (2002): Evolution in materio: looking beyond the silicon box. *2002 NASA/DoD Conference on Evolvable Hardware*. 15–18 July 2002, Alexandria, VA, USA, IEEE Comput. Soc., Los Alamitos, CA, USA.

[76] J. F., Miller, D. Job, et al. (2000): Principles in the Evolutionary Design of Digital Circuits -Part I. *Genetic Programming and Evolvable Machines* 1(1/2): 7–35.

[77] J. F., Miller, D. Job, et al. (2000): Principles in the Evolutionary Design of Digital Circuits -Part II. *Genetic Programming and Evolvable Machines* 1(3): 259–288.

[78] J. F., Miller, T. Kalganova, et al. (1999): The Genetic Algorithm as a Discovery Engine: Strange Circuits and New Principles. *Proceedings of the AISB Symposium on Creative Evolutionary Systems*, Edinburgh, U.K.

[79] J. F. Miller and P. Thomson (1998): Aspects of Digital Evolution: Evolvability and Architecture. *5th International Conference on Parallel Problem Solving from Nature*, Amsterdam, The Netherlands, Springer-Verlag.

[80] J. F. Miller and P. Thomson (1998): Aspects of digital evolution: geometry and learning. *Proceedings of Second International Conference on Evolvable Systems*: From Biology to Hardware. (ICES 98). 23–25 Sept. 1998, Lausanne, Switzerland, Springer-Verlag, Berlin, Germany.

[81] J. F. Miller and P. Thomson (1998): Evolving Digital Electronic Circuits for Real-Valued Function Generation using a Genetic Algorithm. *3rd Annual Conference on Genetic Programming*, San Francisco, CA, U.S.A,.

[82] J. F. Miller and P. Thomson (2003): A Developmental Method for Growing Graphs and Circuits. *5th International Conference on Evolvable Systems*, Trondheim, Norway, Springer-Verlag.

[83] J. F., Miller, P. Thomson, et al. (1997): Designing electronic circuits using evolutionary algorithms. Arithmetic circuits: a case study. Applications of Computer Systems. *Proceedings of the Fourth International Conference*. 13–14 Nov. 1997, Szczecin, Poland, Wydwnictwo i Drukarnia Inst. Inf. Polytech. Szczecinskiej, Szezecin, Poland.

[84] T. M. Mitchell (1997): *Machine Learning.* London, McGraw-Hill.

[85] G. E. Moore (1965): Cramming More Components Onto Integrated Circuits. *Electronics* 38(8): 114–117.

[86] J. M., Moreno, J. Madrenas, et al. (1998): Feasible, evolutionary and self-repairing hardware by means of the dynamic reconfiguration capabilities of

the FIPSOC devices. *2nd International Conference on Evolvable Systems*, Lausanne, Switzerland, Springer-Verlag, Berlin, Germany.

[87] M., Murakawa, T. Adachi, et al. (2002): An AI-calibrated IF filter: a yield enhancement method with area and power dissipation reductions. *2002 IEEE Custom Integrated Circuits Conference*, Singapore.

[88] M. Murakawa, S. Yoshizawa, et al. (1998): Analogue EHW chip for inter-mediate frequency filters. *Proceedings of Second International Conference on Evolvable Systems: From Biology to Hardware*. (ICES 98). 23–25 Sept. 1998, Lausanne, Switzerland, Springer-Verlag, Berlin, Germany.

[89] M. Murakawa, S. Yoshizawa, et al. (1996): Hardware evolution at function level. *5th Conference on Parallel Problem Solving from Nature*, Berlin, Germany, Springer-Verlag, Berlin, Germany.

[90] M. Murakawa, S. Yoshizawa, et al. (1999): The GRD chip: Genetic recon-figuration of DSPs for neural network processing. *IEEE Transactions on Computers* 48(6): 628–639.

[91] J. Plante, H. Shaw, et al. (2003): Overview of Field Programmable Analog Arrays as Enabling Technology for Evolvable Hardware for High Reliability Systems. *2003 NASA/DoD Conference on Evolvable Hardware*, Chicago, IL, U.S.A., IEEE Press.

[92] E. Ramsden (2001): The ispPAC family of reconfigurable analog circuits. *3rd NASA/DoD Workshop on Evolvable Hardware*, Long Beach, CA, USA, IEEE Comput. Soc., Los Alamitos, CA, USA.

[93] D. E. Rumelhart, B. Widrow, et al. (1994): The Basic Ideas in Neural Networks. *Communications of the ACM 37*(3): 87–92.

[94] H. Sakanashi, M. Iwata, et al. (2001): A Lossless Compression Method for Halftone Images using Evolvable Hardware. *4th International Conference on Evolvable Systems*, Tokyo, Japan, Springer-Verlag.

[95] M. Salami, M. Murakawa, et al. (1996): Data compression based on evolv-able hardware. *1st International Conference on Evolvable Systems from Biology to Hardware*, Tsukuba, Japan, Springer-Verlag, Berlin, Germany.

[96] C. C. Santini, R. Zebulum, et al. (2001): PAMA-programmable analog mul-tiplexer array. *3rd NASA/DoD Workshop on Evolvable Hardware*, Long Beach, CA, USA, IEEE Comput. Soc., Los Alamitos, CA, USA.

[97] Sechen (1988): *VLSI Placement and Global Routing Using Simulated Annealing*. Boston, MA, U.S.A, Kluwer Academic Publishers.

[98] L. A. Segel and I. Cohen, Eds. (2001): Design Principles for the Immune System and Other Distributed Autonomous Systems. *Santa Fe Institute Studies in the Sciences of Complexity*. New York, Oxford University Press.

[99] L. Sekanina (2002): Evolution of digital circuits operating as image filters in dynamically changing environment. *8th International Conference on Soft Computing*, Brno, CZ.

[100] L. Sekanina (2003): Easily Testable Image Operators: The Class of Circuits Where Evolution Beats Engineers. *2003 NASA/DoD Conference on Evolvable Hardware*, Chicago, IL, U.S.A., IEEE Press.

[101] L. Sekanina (2003): Towards Evolvable IP Cores for FPGAs. *2003 NASA/Dod Conference on Evolvable Systems*, Chicago, IL, U.S.A., IEEE Press.

[102] H. T. Sinohara, M. A. C. Pacheco, et al. (2001): Repair of analog circuits: extrinsic and intrinsic evolutionary techniques. *Proceedings Third NASA/DoD Workshop on Evolvable Hardware*. EH 2001. 12–14 July 2001, Long Beach, CA, USA, IEEE Comput. Soc., Los Alamitos, CA, USA.

[103] J. M. W. Slack (1991): *From Egg to Embryo*. Cambridge, Cambridge University Press.

[104] A. Stoica, A. Fukunaga, et al. (1998): Evolvable hardware for space applications. *Second International Conference on Evolvable Systems: From Biology to Hardware*. (ICES 98). 23–25 Sept. 1998, Lausanne, Switzerland, Springer-Verlag, Berlin, Germany.

[105] A. Stoica, D. Keymeulen, et al. (1999): Evolutionary experiments with a fine-grained reconfigurable architecture for analog and digital CMOS circuits. *Proceedings of the First NASA/DoD Workshop on Evolvable Hardware*. 19–21 July 1999, Pasadena, CA, USA, IEEE Comput. Soc., Los Alamitos, CA, USA.

[106] A. Stoica, D. Keymeulen, et al. (2001): Evolvable hardware solutions for extreme temperature electronics. *3rd NASA/DoD Workshop on Evolvable Hardware.*, Long Beach, CA, USA, IEEE Comput. Soc., Los Alamitos, CA, USA.

[107] A. Stoica, R. Zebulum, et al. (2000): Mixtrinsic Evolution. *3rd International Conference on Evolvable Systems*, Edinburgh, U.K.

[108] A. Stoica, R. Zebulum, et al. (2002): On polymorphic circuits and their design using evolutionary algorithms. *20th IASTED International Multiconference on Applied Informatics*, Innsbruck, Austria, ACTA Press, Anaheim, CA, USA.

[109] A. Stoica, R. S. Zebulum, et al. (2003): Silicon validation of evolution-designed circuits. *2003 NASA/DoD Conference on Evolvable Hardware*, Chicago, IL, USA, IEEE Comput. Soc., Los Alamitos, CA, USA.

[110] S. Sundaralingam and K. C. Sharman (1998): Evolving Complex Adaptive IIR Structures. *9th European Signal Processing Conference*, Rhodes, Greece.

[111] A. J. Surkan and A. Khuskivadze (2002): Evolution of quantum computer algorithms from reversible operators. *2002 NASA/DoD Conference on Evolvable Hardware*. Alexandria, VA, U.S.A., IEEE Comput. Soc., Los Alamitos, CA, USA.

[112] E. Takahashi, Y. Kasai, et al. (2003): A Post-Silicon Clock Timing Adjustment Using Genetic Algorithms. *2003 Symposium on VLSI circuits*, IEEE Press.

[113] G. Tempesti, D. Mange, et al. (2002): The BioWall: an electronic tissue for prototyping bio-inspired systems. *2002 NASA/DoD Conference on Evolvable Hardware*, Alexandria, VA, U.S.A., IEEE Comput. Soc., Los Alamitos, CA, USA.

[114] A. Thompson (1995): Evolving electronic robot controllers that exploit hardware resources. Advances in Artificial Life. *Third European Conference on Artificial Life. Proceedings. 4–6 June 1995*, Granada, Spain, Springer-Verlag, Berlin, Germany.

[115] A. Thompson (1996): An Evolved Circuit, Intrinsic in Silicon, Entwined with Physics. *1st International Conference on Evolvable Systems*, Springer-Verlag.

[116] A. Thompson (1996): Hardware Evolution. Brighton, U.K., University of Sussex.

[117] A. Thompson (1996): Silicon Evolution. *Proceedings of the 1st Annual Conference on Genetic Programming*, Stanford, CA, U.S.A.

[118] A. Thompson (1998): On the automatic design of robust electronics through artificial evolution. *Proceedings of Second International Conference on Evolvable Systems*: From Biology to Hardware. (ICES 98). 23–25 Sept. 1998, Lausanne, Switzerland, Springer-Verlag, Berlin, Germany.

[119] A. Thompson (2002): Notes on design through artificial evolution: Opportunities and algorithms. *Adaptive computing in design and manufacture 5*(1): 17–26.

[120] A. Thompson, I. Harvey, et al. (1996): Unconstrained Evolution and Hard Consequences. *Towards Evolvable Hardware: The Evolutionary Engineering Approach*. E. Sanchez and M. Tomassini. Berlin, Germany, Springer-Verlag. *1062*: 136–165.

[121] A. Thompson and P. Layzell (2000): Evolution of Robustness in an Electronics Design. *Proceedings of the 3rd International Conference on Evolvable Systems*: *From Biology to Hardware*, Edinburgh, U.K.

[122] A. Thompson and C. Wasshuber (2000): Evolutionary design of single electron systems. *Proceedings. The Second NASA/DoD Workshop on Evolvable Hardware*. 13–15 July 2000, Palo Alto, CA, USA, IEEE Comput. Soc., Los Alamitos, CA, USA.

[123] R. Thomson and T. Arslan (2003): The evolutionary design and synthesis of non-linear digital VLSI systems. *2003 NASA/DoD Conference on Evolvable Hardware*, Chicago, IL, USA, IEEE Comput. Soc., Los Alamitos, CA, USA.

[124] J. Torresen (2000): Possibilities and limitations of applying evolvable hardware to real-world applications. *Proceedings of FPL 2000. 10th International Conference on Field Programmable Logic and Applications*. 27–30 Aug. 2000, Villach, Austria, Springer-Verlag, Berlin, Germany.

[125] G. Tufte and P. C. Haddow (2000): Evolving an adaptive digital filter. *Proceedings. The Second NASA/DoD Workshop on Evolvable Hardware*. 13–15 July 2000, Palo Alto, CA, USA, IEEE Comput. Soc., Los Alamitos, CA, USA.

[126] A. Tyrrell, E. Sanchez, et al. (2003): POEtic Tissue: An Integrated Architecture for Bio-inspired Hardware. *5th International Conference on Evolvable Systems*, Trondheim, Norway.

[127] A. M. Tyrrell, G. Hollingworth, et al. (2001): Evolutionary strategies and intrinsic fault tolerance. *3rd NASA/DoD Workshop on Evolvable Hardware*. EH 2001, Long Beach, CA, USA, IEEE Comput. Soc., Los Alamitos, CA, USA.

[128] V. Vassilev and J. F. Miller (2000): The Advantages of Landscape Neutrality in Digital Circuit Evolution. *Proceedings of the 3rd International Conference on Evolvable Systems*: *From Biology to Hardware*, Edinburgh, U.K.

[129] V. Vassilev and J. F. Miller (2000): Embedding Landscape Neutrality To Build a Bridge from the Conventional to a More Efficient Three-bit

Multiplier Circuit. *Genetic and Evolutionary Computation Conference*, Las Vegas, NV, U.S.A.

[130] S. Vigander (2001): Evolutionary Fault Repair of Electronics in Space Applications. Trondheim, Norway, Norwegian University Sci. Tech.

[131] K. A. Vinger and J. Torresen (2003): Implementing evolution of FIR-filters efficiently in an FPGA. *2003 NASA/DoD Conference on Evolvable Hardware*, Chicago, IL, USA, IEEE Comput. Soc., Los Alamitos, CA, USA.

[132] X. Yao and T. Higuchi (1997): Promises and challenges of evolvable hardware. *1st International Conference on Evolvable Systems: From Biology to Hardware*, Tsukuba, Japan, Springer-Verlag, Berlin, Germany.

[133] J. S. Yih and P. Mazumder (1990): A Neural Network Design for Circuit Partitioning. *IEEE Transactions on Computer Aided Design 9*(10): 1265–1271.

[134] R. S. Zebulum, M. Aurélio Pacheo, et al. (1997): Increasing Length Genotypes in Evolutionary Electronics. *7th International Conference on Genetic Algorithms*, East Lansing, MI, U.S.A.

[135] R. S. Zebulum, D. Keymeulen, et al. (2003): Experimental results in evolutionary fault-recovery for field programmable analog devices. *2003 NASA/DoD Conference on Evolvable Hardware*, Chicago, IL, USA, IEEE Comput. Soc., Los Alamitos, CA, USA.

[136] R. S. Zebulum, M. A. Pacheco, et al. (1998): Analog circuits evolution in extrinsic and intrinsic modes. *2nd International Conference on Evolvable Systems*, Lausanne, Switzerland, Springer-Verlag, Berlin, Germany.

Chapter 13

IMPLEMENTING NEURAL MODELS IN SILICON
Leslie S. Smith
University of Stirling

Abstract

Neural models are used in both computational neuroscience and in pattern recognition. The aim of the first is understanding of real neural systems, and of the second is gaining better, possibly brainlike performance for systems being built. In both cases, the highly parallel nature of the neural system contrasts with the sequential nature of computer systems, resulting in slow and complex simulation software. More direct implementation in hardware (whether digital or analogue) holds out the promise of faster emulation both because hardware implementation is inherently faster than software and the operation is much more parallel. There are costs to this: modifying the system (for example, to test out variants of the system) is much harder when a full application-specific integrated circuit has been built. Fast emulation can permit direct incorporation of a neural model into a system, permitting real-time input and output. Appropriate selection of implementation technology can help to make simplify interfacing the system to external devices. We review the technologies involved and discuss some example systems.

1   WHY IMPLEMENT NEURAL MODELS IN SILICON?

There are two primary reasons for implementing neural models: one is to attempt to gain better and possibly brainlike performance for some system, and the other is to study how some particular neural model performs. Current computer systems do not approach brainlike system performance in many areas (sensing, motor control, and pattern recognition, for example, to say nothing of the higher level capabilities of mammalian brains). There has been considerable research into how the neural system attains its capabilities. Implementing neural systems in silicon can permit direct applications of this research by permitting neural models to run rapidly enough to be applied directly to data. It is true that increases in workstation performance have allowed some software implementations of neural models to run in real time, but the highly parallel nature of neural systems, coupled with increasing interest in the application of more sophisticated (and computationally more expensive) neural models, has caused interest in more direct implementation to be maintained. Interest in applying neural models to sensory and sensory-motor systems has made attaining real-time performance a critical factor. Real sensory systems are highly parallel, with multiple parallel channels of information, so even though each channel might be implementable in real-time in software, implementing multiple channels implies hardware implementation.

The study of how particular models of neural systems perform is one aspect of computational neuroscience. Such studies are usually carried out in software, since this allows easy alteration of and experimentation with systems. However, models of the highly parallel architecture of neural systems run slowly on standard computers. This has led to interest in the use of parallel computer systems for such models [1, 2] and to interest in silicon implementations. Some researchers in computational neuroscience would like to apply their models directly to real data (implying real-time operation). Even if parallel computers can provide the speed required, it is easier and cheaper to interface silicon implementations to external hardware.

Recently, another motivation for silicon implementation has arisen as well. The continuing applicability of Moore's Law (which states that the number of transistors on a chip doubles every 18 to 24 months) suggests that we shall soon have chips with more than 10^8 transistors but that we may also have chips whose transistors may be relatively noisy. Such large numbers of transistors seem to entail highly parallel algorithms if these transistors are not to sit unused almost all of the time [3]. Further, biological systems seem to produce relatively robust solutions with relatively noisy components, something that standard computer systems cannot achieve. This has led to increased interest in the study and implementation of neural models directly in silicon.

1.1   What this review covers—and what it omits

This review covers the implementation of a number of different types of model neuron, ranging from the very simple McCulloch–Pitts neuron to highly complex multicompartment models. It includes implementations of integrate-and-fire neurons and other models of intermediate complexity. It does not cover those silicon chips that are primarily concerned with using these neural models to solve a particular problem. We do describe some of the implementation techniques used for the back-propagated delta rule and the Boltzmann machine, but we do not review all these chips, concentrating instead on specific issues such as synapse implementation or noise. A more detailed review of such chips may be found in [4].

1.2   Organization of this review

We start by outlining the organization and structure of a real neuron. This overview will allow us to see the different aspects of neuron behavior that are being modelled. We review the different types of models for neural systems that have been proposed, differentiating between those that deal with simple vector input (in which time is either irrelevant or occurs only in terms of the order in which the input vectors are presented), and those in which the precise timing of the inputs matters. We then discuss the different technologies for implementation and describe how different types of model neurons have been implemented. We discuss some applications, and consider what has been and can be expected to be achieved by using these different implementation technologies.

2   AN OUTLINE OF A REAL NEURON

Real neurons, like all real cells, are very complex. The aim of this subsection is to describe a neuron at a level of detail and in a language that is informative to a wide range of scientists and that can also be used to illustrate what is actually being modeled in particular implementations. A detailed neurophysiological description of real neuron operation may be found in [5], part II, and in [6].

There are many different types of neurons, and these very enormously in morphology (shape) and extent, as well as in the details of their biophysics. Neurons are found in a very wide range of animal species: invertebrate, insect, and vertebrate. What they all share is operation using electric charge. The operation of the neuron relies on the neuron's excitable membrane. The membrane of any cell is its outermost layer: its boundary. In neurons, this membrane is a bilipid membrane that contains ionic channels (see Figure 13.2). What makes the membrane excitable is the way in which its characteristics alter depending on the (localized) voltage across the membrane. The purely bilipid part of the membrane is essentially a very thin insulator, separating the relatively conducting electrolytes inside and outside the cell. The ionic channels (and there are many different types of ionic channel) embedded in this membrane allow selected (charged) ions to cross the membrane. Unbalanced movement of ions into and out of the neuron alters the potential difference between the inside and the outside of the neuron (see Figure 13.3). The ions of particular significance here are potassium (K^+), sodium (Na^+), and calcium (Ca^{++}). There is some disagreement as to whether ion channels are static or can move around inside the membrane [7].

In the absence of any input to the neuron, the excitable membrane will maintain the inside of the neuron at a particular potential relative to the outside of the neuron. This resting membrane potential is usually on the order of -65 mV (millivolts) (though this does vary across different populations of neurons). This resting potential results from the movement of ions, primarily due to the different ionic concentrations inside and outside of the neurons, and this is maintained by the Na^+–K^+ pump which keeps the Na^+ concentration inside the cell low and the K^+ concentration inside the cell high (see Figure 13.3). External inputs to the neuron result in the increase of this potential (known as *depolarization* in the neurophysiology community) or decrease of this potential (*hyperpolarization*).

Before discussing the details of how this potential changes, we consider the overall structure of a neuron: see Figure 13.1. The neuron has a cell body (the soma), and in most neurons, this has projections. These projections are of two types: the dendrites and the axon. The dendrites have a treelike structure (hence

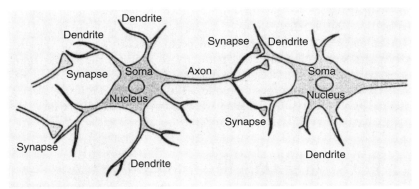

Figure 13.1. Overall structure of a neuron (actually, a local interneuron). Figure modified from [5] (Figure 2.8), with permission.

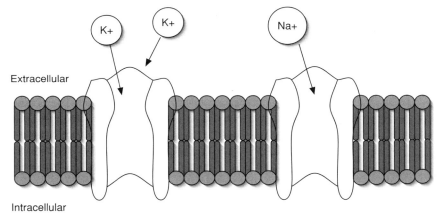

Figure 13.2. Patch of cell neuron membrane. Ion channels are embedded in the bilipid membrane. The membrane is made up of molecules each with a hydrophilic end (circle) and a hydrophobic end (lines), and is impermeable to ions. There are many types of ion channels, each consisting of a protein embedded in the membrane: different proteins have different permeabilities to ions because of the conformation of the protein. Additionally, the protein confirmation itself may be dependent on the voltage across the membrane, so the ion channel's behavior may be dependent on the voltage across the membrane as well.

their name, which comes from the Greek δενδρον [dendron], a tree) and are located where inputs to the neuron arrive. The axon, which also has a branching structure, transfers the output of the neuron to other neurons. These two projections can be difficult to tell apart in electron micrographs, but they have different populations of ion channels in their membranes, and they function in different ways.

Connections between neurons take place at synapses. Mostly, each synapse is between the axon of one neuron (the presynaptic neuron) and the dendrite of

---

[1]There are also axo-axonic and dendro-dendritic synapses, as well as axonic synapses that contact the cell body.

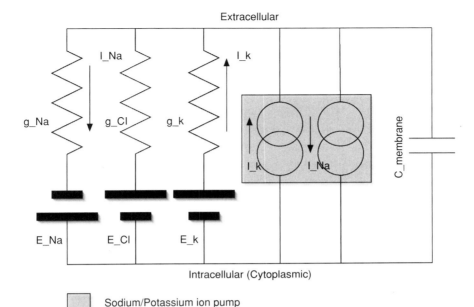

Figure 13.3. Equivalent circuit of a patch of membrane. The arrows show the direction of the ion movement (which is the same direction as current transfer). The sodium–potassium pump maintains the inside of the cell at a negative potential (more Na⁺ ions are transferred out than K⁺ ions are transferred in). The capacitance is provided by the (insulating) bilipid membrane.

another neuron (the postsynaptic neuron).[1] It is through the synapse that the potential at that point in the presynaptic axon alters the potential at that point in the postsynaptic neuron's dendrite. Brains contain a large number of highly interconnected neurons, and each interconnection consists of a synapse. Some neurons (e.g., cortical pyramidal neurons) may have as many as 10,000 synapses on their dendrites. There are therefore a very large number of synapses in animal brains. According to Koch [6], in primates there are about 100,000 cells, and about 6×10^8 synapses per cubic mm in the cortex.

In an animal brain, synapses are of many different types. Actual synaptic operation is complex. Many synapses operate by releasing small bubbles (called *vesicles*) of a chemical (called a *neurotransmitter*) from the presynaptic axon into the space (called the *cleft*) between the presynaptic axon and the postsynaptic dendrite (see Figure 13.4). In one type of synapse (ionotropic), this process directly affects the ionic channels on the dendrite, causing some of them to open and to allow influx or efflux of ions, altering the potential at that point in the postsynaptic dendrite. In another type of synapse (metabotropic), the effect is less direct, altering the ion transport of neighboring proteins. Clearly, both types of synapse require some time for the effect of the presynaptic pulse to be felt postsynaptically, and this effect (called *postsynaptic potentiation* or *PSP*) takes some time to decay as well. There are many types of both ionotropic and metabotropic synapses (often classified by the neurotransmitters used). Ionotropic synapses are faster in operation than metabotropic synapses.

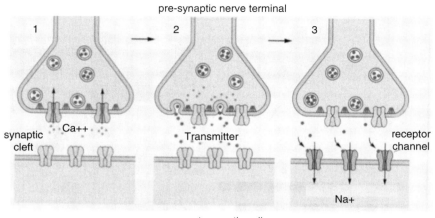

pre-synaptic nerve terminal

post-synaptic cell

Figure 13.4. Diagram showing the operation of an ionotropic synapse. Modified with permission from [5] (Figure 10.7).

When the potential alteration is depolarizing, the synapse is said to be *excitatory*, and when the potential alteration is hyperpolarizing, the synapse is said to be *inhibitory*. These small alterations in potential are summed on the dendrites. On many neurons, this summation appears to be essentially linear within a certain range of potentials: outside of this range, ion channels alter their configuration, and the dendrite ceases to be linear. This nonlinearity may occur at some small portion of the dendrite, due, for example, to many nearby synapses being simultaneously stimulated. On some neurons, synapses are located on spines on the dendrite (spiny neurons, as opposed to smooth neurons), leading, it is believed, to greater ionic and electrical isolation of each synapse. Some researchers believe that the dendrites perform a considerable amount of processing (the neurophysiology is discussed in Section 19.3.2 of [6], and modeling in [8]), and that there are essentially nonlinear processes operating on the neuron that provide neurons with considerable information processing power.

In many neurons, it is the potential at a particular part of the neuron, the *axon hillock* (located on the soma of the neuron, at the root of the axon projection) that is of particular importance. At this trigger zone on the neuron, there is a large concentration of particular types of sodium channels. The result is that when the voltage at this location increases beyond a certain threshold value (usually about −48 mv), a particular set of voltage-sensitive ion channels opens and allows the influx of Na$^+$ ions, rapidly increasing the depolarization. This results in even more of these channels opening, causing a very fast and large rise in the membrane potential. As a result of this increased depolarization, two things occur: firstly, the sodium ion channels close, and secondly, another set of ionic channels opens, allowing the efflux of a different set of ions (K$^+$), causing the potential to drop nearly as rapidly as it rose (see Figure 13.5). This potential increase and decrease is regenerated along the axon, resulting in a spikelike signal passing along the axon, arriving at the synapses that this axon makes. Because the spike is regenerated, its shape is characteristic of the mechanism of its production and does not carry information. It is worth noting that (1) the sodium ion

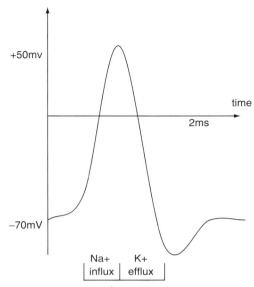

Figure 13.5. Graph of depolarization on an axon during an action potential (spike).

channels are not able to reopen immediately, so there is an inbuilt maximal rate at which these spikes can be produced by the neuron, and (2) the potassium efflux normally overshoots, causing a brief after-spike hyperpolarization. The delay in the reusability of the sodium channels results in the neuron's absolute and relative refractory period: that is, the period during which the neuron cannot fire again, and the period during which it is more difficult for the neuron to fire again.

The actual propagation speed of the spike is relatively slow due to both the nature of the conductance and the distributed resistance and capacitance of the axon. It can be speeded up by a process known as myelinization. In myelinization, glial cells form a myelin insulation a round the axon, reducing its capacitance, and allowing the spike to jump (by electrical conductivity, rather than by regeneration) from point to point (actually, to breaks in the myelin, known as Nodes of Ranvier) along the axon. Actual propagation speeds vary from 1 mm/sec to 100 mm/s inside brains (and faster along peripheral nerves).

Not all neurons actually produce spikes: some output graded potentials. Indeed, not all neurons have actual dendrites: some receive synapses only on the soma itself. In many synapses, the alteration in potential produced depends also on the potential at the synapse. In particular, some synapses (shunting synapses) tend to drive the potential back towards the resting potential (and thus are either excitatory or inhibitory, depending on the local potential). In addition, synapses do not always have exactly the same effect postsynaptically as a result of a presynaptic spike. Many synapses are depressing synapses: the effect of the first few spikes (after a period of presynaptic inactivity) is much larger than that caused by later spikes. Other synapses are facilitating: after a period of presynaptic inactivity, the effect of a train of spikes gradually increases. These effects appear to be due partly to depletion of presynaptic neurotransmitter, and partly to changes at the membrane on the postsynaptic dendrite (see [9], chapter 10).

One important aspect of real neural systems is that they alter in response to their inputs. They adapt, so identical inputs at different times can have different effects. This adaptation takes place over many time scales: it may occur rapidly, as a result of a single event, or very slowly over the lifetime of the animal. Early in the animal's life, the neural system grows. There is a great deal of evidence that the stimulation it receives is critical in adjusting the processing that takes place to the actual input arriving (e.g., in vision: see chapter 56 of [5]). In mammals many synapses are formed but do not last. Changes inside the system take many forms: in addition to growth and decay of synapses, there are structural and biochemical alterations at synapses, alterations in neuron morphology, and subtler changes due to hormones and diffusable neurotransmitters such as nitrous oxide (NO) and peptides. Neural models have tended to focus almost exclusively on changes at synapses. In addition to the short-term synaptic alteration above (called *dynamic synapse behavior*), synapses can also become stronger over a longer period (*long-term potentiation, LTP*), or become weaker over a longer period (*long-term depression, LTD*). Somehow, out of all these forms of adaptation, the system appears to learn: we see systemwide changes that provide appropriate changes in behavior.

There are many views on how much of the detail of the behavior of neurons is important for understanding their information-processing capabilities. These views range from the view that only the firing of the neuron matters to views that voltage-based processing on the dendrite is crucial in information processing, to views that it is the detail of the quantum effects upon the movement of ions and the conformation of proteins that matter. Some believe that the firing of neurons is essentially for information transfer, and that what happens on the dendrites is critical to information processing (see [6] chapter 20, and [10]). These differences in beliefs are at the root of the many models that we will now describe.

3   SIMPLE (TIME-FREE) NEURON MODELS

The simplest neural models do not include time: that is, each neuron's input is considered as a vector, and the output is computed from this input without regard for what the neuron's previous input (or output) had been. There is no internal state inside the neuron that would allow previous inputs to affect current operation. Networks of such neurons can be made sensitive to previous inputs if the network contains loops (because the state information is contained in these new inputs), but even then, these networks are sensitive only to the order of the inputs and not to their actual timing. This type of neuron model is the basis for most of the current work in neural networks for pattern recognition. Such models have been implemented on analogue computers, digital computers, and in various types of hardware.

3.1   The McCulloch–Pitts model

The earliest model was the McCulloch-Pitts neuron [11]. This model forms the weighted sum of its (vector) input and produces a binary output, which is 1 if the weighted sum exceeds some threshold, and 0 otherwise. This can be written

$$A = \sum_{i=1}^{n} w_i X_i \tag{1}$$

followed by $Y = 1$ if $A > \theta$, and $Y = 0$ otherwise. Here w_i is the weight characterizing the synapse from input i, X_i is the ith input, A is the activity of the neuron, θ is the threshold, and Y is the neuron's output.

The model has been formed by (1) considering each spiking neuron as a two-state device, in which the neuron is either firing (output = 1) or not (output = 0), and (2) considering each synapse as characterized by a single number (w_i). An excitatory synapse has $w_i > 0$, and an inhibitory synapse has $w_i < 0$. The effect of the presynaptic neuron on the postsynaptic neuron is found by simple multiplication. The overall effect of all the presynaptic neurons—the activity, A—is a simple linear sum: the dendrite is reduced to a single point. The nonlinearity is introduced only at the end, where the activity is thresholded to produce the output.

What makes this very simple model interesting is that it can be used to do computation. It is straightforward to design simple NOT, AND, and OR gates, and these can be assembled to provide any logical predicate. The addition of a clock allows one to build a digital computer from such devices.

3.2   Learning systems

Many extensions to this simple model have been proposed. In terms of basic operation, these extensions have often been relatively minor, such as graduating the output. The knowledge that real neural systems are not preprogrammed (at least in vertebrates) but adapt or learn has been very influential, partly because useful adaptation has proven very difficult to achieve in traditional computer systems, and partly because there are many problems for which a purely algorithmic solution is virtually impossible to find, whereas examples of correct behavior are quite simple to produce. A system based on learning might be able to solve such problems.

The earliest form of neural learning was suggested by Hebb [12]. In this form of learning, synapses that connect neurons that fire together are strengthened. This type of learning can be applied to make simple learning systems. These have been investigated in the context of both time-free models and models that include time: in the time-free case, they can provide a basis for certain self-organizing systems [13]. We will discuss the case including time in more detail in Section 5.4.3. We first discuss learning systems that have a teacher: that is, learning systems in which there is a known correct output for many of the possible inputs. We return to systems without a teacher in Section 3.3.

3.2.1   Perceptrons

One of the earliest learning systems was the perceptron [14], in which some of the geometry of the dendrite was reintroduced. What the perceptron is best known for is the perceptron learning rule [14]. This rule (described in many Neural Networks textbooks, (e.g., [15,16])) was the first one discussed that allowed the neural model to adapt itself so as to produce the desired input:output mapping. It was limited to a single layer of simple perceptrons (i.e., perceptrons which had the dendrite geometry removed) with binary outputs (which are the same as McCulloch–Pitts neurons), but was shown to be able to generate any logical predicate that this architecture could permit. This was the first truly adaptive system, and it was hugely influential. It led to various forms of implementation (see Section 5).

3.2.2   The Delta rule

The Delta rule is another learning algorithm for the same architecture [17, 18]. This rule minimizes the Euclidean (least squares) distance between the actual output and the desired output by adjusting the weights (and is sometimes known as the *least mean squares rule*). It is applicable to units whose output is a continuously increasing function of the weighted sum of the inputs. The unit output function may be linear (i.e., the output is simply a constant times the activity A from Equation 1), or may be a squashing function such as a logistic:

$$Y = 1/(1 + \exp(-k_1 A + k_2)) \tag{2}$$

where Y is the output, and k_1 and k_2 are constants that determine the magnitude and location of the maximum slope. The logistic function has a value that is always between 0 and 1. Other squashing functions (e.g., tanh) have also been utilized. Again, it has been shown that the Delta rule can produce any output that the particular single-layer architecture could produce, and given small enough weight changes, will converge to a solution (see, e.g., Section 5.4 of [15]). The way in which the network is used is that a set of (input, output) pairs is produced, and these are then applied to the network as the input and the desired output for this input. The weights are then adjusted to reduce the error: that is, the square of the sum of the differences between the desired and actual outputs.

However, the limited computational ability of the single-layer architecture was proven in [19]. The architecture can only produce linearly separable mappings. Minsky and Papert's doubt as to whether it could be extended either to more complex perceptron networks or to a larger class of functions led to a decrease in the effort extended in neural computing (see [15], Section 1.2) in the 1970s and early 1980s.

3.2.3   The Hopfield network and the Boltzmann machine

Two new adaptation algorithms were introduced for similar types of neurons in the early 1980s, one for binary neurons (the Hopfield model, and its extension, the Boltzmann machine), and the other an extension of the Delta rule (the back-propagated Delta rule). Both of these networks were hugely influential, and both were implemented in various forms in hardware.

Hopfield's network [20] is symmetrical: that is, $w_{ij} = w_{ji}$, where w_{ij} is the weight from presynaptic neuron j to postsynaptic neuron i. This network is not a simple layer of neurons, but has cycles. Updating the network was done neuron by neuron, asynchronously, and the Hopfield proved that the network eventually settles into a stable state. It was therefore the first network to have a dynamical behavior, although this was not normally used in its operation. The network is considered to have an overall energy

$$E = -\frac{1}{2} \sum_{i,j=1}^{N} w_{ij} X_i X_j \qquad (3)$$

where the neuron's output, X_i, is either +1 or 1, rather than +1 or 0, and updating each neuron's state minimizes this total energy, E. The network could be trained to be an associative memory by applying the vectors to be stored and then adjusting the weights so as to minimize E. Hopfield and others (as is clearly explained in [15]) showed that such a network could remember a maximum of $0.138N$ vectors. These could be recalled by providing the network with an incomplete vector, thus providing content-addressable memory.

An important extension to this network was the Boltzmann machine [21]. In this network, the original Hopfield network is extended by adding new nodes that are not connected to the outside world. These so-called hidden nodes can learn to form internal representations that can allow the network to learn additional vectors and can be used to allow the network to classify its inputs by examining the hidden unit state. However, the learning technique also has to change (since the Hopfield learning recipe cannot train weights to and from hidden nodes). The learning algorithm used is statistical in nature: essentially, it uses concepts from statistical physics and Boltzmann distributions (hence the algorithm's name) to set these weights. A comprehensible description may be found in [15], chapter 7 or in [16], chapter 11. Using such techniques in software is exceedingly slow. However, the idea that this type of network could learn some form of internal representation helped rekindle interest in the whole area, and the slowness of the algorithm in software helped motivate implementations of this type of network in silicon.

3.2.4   The back-propagated Delta rule

The best known of the simple neural network learning rules is the back-propagated Delta rule. Discovered independently at least five times [22–26], it permits a Delta rule like network to be extended from a simple single layer to a feed-forward network (see Figure 13.6). The basic idea is that errors at the output layer are funneled back to the units of each hidden layer: for details see any book on neural networks, e.g., [15] chapter 6, or [16], chapter 4. Once the error at a unit is known, it can be used to adjust the weights to that unit, essentially using the original Delta rule.

There are two problems with the back-propagated Delta rule: firstly, it is no longer the case that continued application of the learning rule will necessarily allow the network to learn the input:output mapping, even although it may be possible for the architecture to do so; and secondly, learning tends to be slow. The result of the first problem is that one cannot be sure that the network produced is the best network possible given the (input:output) pairs that have been provided. So-called local error minima can result in the network stopping learning before it has done as well as it can. Further, if the (input:output) pairs contain some noise (perhaps the result of measurement errors), it is quite possible for the network to attempt to learn this noise. A great deal has been written about the best ways in which to use this type of network. Certainly, like the Boltzmann machine, it is capable of extracting information about the (input:output) pairs provided and coding this into its weights. Learning is slow because the mapping

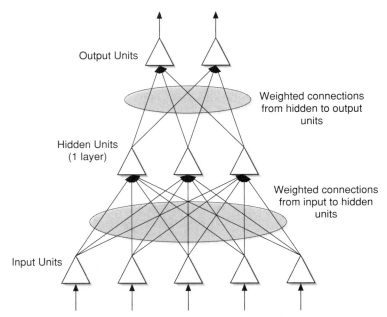

Figure 13.6. Feed-forward neural network. The input layer simply transfers its inputs through (adjustable) weighted synapses to the hidden layer. There may be a number of hidden layers, with different numbers of units. The radial basis function network [16] has a similar structure, with one hidden layer, whose units have a peak response at one point in the input space.

between the weights and the error (the so-called error surface) can be very complex: gradient descent methods applied to high-dimensional complex surfaces must move slowly because they otherwise risk missing the desired minima of the surface. The error surface may also contain local minima: if the weights are trapped in one of these, the performance will be suboptimal.

Because of the wide possible applicability of this network, and because it is slow to train, many attempts have been made to implement it directly into hardware. These are reviewed in Section 5.3.

Many extensions to this rule have been described and many have been concerned with improving the form of the gradient descent, attempting to make it closer to steepest descent (some are described in [16], chapter 4). Others have attempted to replicate the hidden layer's effects by recoding the input. The idea here is that what the back-propagated Delta rule does in its hidden layers is to recode the input so that the mapping from the recoded input to the output becomes separable, thus permitting the Delta rule to be used. This is essentially the basis for the Radial Basis Function network [27], (see also [16] chapter 5), which performs recoding and uses the simple Delta rule between the recoded input and the desired output.

Bishop [28] has shown that these types of network essentially implement a form of statistical algorithm. This does not reduce the utility of these systems, and indeed helps to explain why they are so useful. However, it does show that the limitations of this type of algorithm are essentially the same as the limitations of the statistical techniques.

3.2.5 Learning sequences

All the above rules can be turned into systems that learn sequences of inputs, either classifying the sequence or attempting sequence completion. In such sequences it is the order of the elements, not their precise times, that matters. Learning can be achieved in a number of ways: a window through the sequence can be used as the input to the network (i.e., the last n elements of the input are used as input, and the output target might be the next element in the sequence), or a network with loops may be used, in which case information about the previous sequence element is held internally inside the network (see, e.g., [29]). What networks of these types cannot achieve is learning anything that requires information about the precise timing (as opposed to order) of the input vectors.

3.3   Self-organizing systems

Self-organizing systems are systems that adjust their behavior in response to their input. No correct output is provided: instead, the system adjusts its internal parameters so as to detect some regularity in the input. Such situations commonly occur in sensory perception: the input is of very high dimensionality (for example, there is one value per light sensor in a camera system, or one value per bandpass filter in a sound sensor), yet although this suggests a very high number of possible inputs, real inputs are confined to some relatively small subspace. In other words, the probability distribution functions of each of the (scalar) inputs are not independent. It is usually the case that the aim of self-organizing systems is to adjust the weights in the system so as to produce outputs (usually of lower dimensionality than the input) that catch the important aspects of the variation in the input.

The idea of neural processing as data reduction goes back to [30]. Simple Hebbian learning systems have some utility in this area: consider a number of inputs that converge on a single output. Assume that the synapses are excitatory, and that a number of coincident inputs are required to make the output neuron fire. Inputs which co-occur in large enough numbers to make the output unit fire will tend to increase their weights, making the output neuron more sensitive to these inputs. However, simple Hebbian learning alone fails to work effectively because the weights increase without limit. Below, we discuss two algorithms that add something to Hebbian learning and that have been candidates for silicon implementation. A useful introduction to this field may be found in [16], chapter 8.

3.3.1 Learning vector quantisation

Learning vector quantization (LVQ) is used to map a number of inputs (each with a scalar value) into one of a number of outputs. LVQ is one of a class of algorithms known as competitive learning algorithms (see [15], chapter 9). This class of algorithms clearly produces outputs of lower dimensionality: the mapping is from some subset of R^N to $\{1..M\}$ where N is the number of inputs and

M the number of output units. Normally, all the input units have synapses to all the output units, initially with random weights. The learning algorithm has a Hebbian aspect, in that weights between input units and output units that fire are increased. However, usually only one output unit is allowed to be active at a time, and the weights to that unit are adjusted in such a way that the total weight (or the total squared weight) remains the same. Some variants also reduce the weights on some of the synapses on inactive output units.

LVQ algorithms are of particular interest in compressive coding: by replacing the input vector with the code for the output unit that best represents it, a very considerable reduction in data volume can be achieved. Further, the LVQ network adjusts itself to the statistics of the data. Because such coding is frequently required in real time (for example, for transmitting coded images), there is considerable interest in the hardware implementations of LVQ systems.

3.3.2   The Kohonen mapping network

The Kohonen mapping network is a variant of LVQ in which not only the weights of the winning unit are adjusted but also weights to nearby units are adjusted (see [16], chapter 9, or [31]). This description presupposes a definition of "nearby", forcing the designer to place some form of topology on the output units. For example, the output units might be organized in one dimension (as points on a line or a circle) or in two dimensions (as points on a grid or on the surface of a sphere or cylinder or torus). The network is trained by being exposed to many input vectors, and the weights to the output units are adjusted. Usually, the number of units whose weights are adjusted for each winning pattern is gradually reduced.

After training, novel inputs will normally result in some localized area of the output units being activated. In this way, high-dimensional data are mapped into some area on a surface. Such data compression can be very useful for sensory information, for example, in robotics or surveillance. Often the requirement is that training can be relatively slow, but operational results are required quickly for real-time applications. This situation has led to interest in silicon implementations of this technique.

4   MODELS THAT INCLUDE TIME

Model neurons that include time are those in which the actual timing of the input (as opposed to the order of the input) matters. Models of this form can be sensitive to the actual timing of their inputs, as opposed to their order: the neurons contain internal time-varying state. The simplest form of neural model that includes time is the integrate-and-fire model. Such neurons can process general time-varying signals, but their outputs are normally spike trains. In common with spike trains of real neurons, the actual shape of the spike is irrelevant. All that matters is the timing of the spike. Thus, the output can be characterized by

$$S = \{t_i : i = 1 \ldots n\}, t_i < t_{i+1}$$

where t_i is the time of the ith spike train in a train of n spikes. More complex models model the neuron in more detail, sometimes including the membrane itself and sometimes including the actual production of the spike.

4.1   The leaky integrate-and-fire model

The leaky integrate-and-fire neuron has a very long history: the concept can be traced back to 1907 [32]. In this neuron model, the dendrites are modeled as single points at which the synaptic inputs are summed, while current leaks away linearly: a detailed description can be found in [6], chapter 14. Below threshold, the voltagelike state variable at that point, A, is described by the equation

$$\frac{dA}{dt} = -\frac{A}{\tau} + I(t) \qquad (4)$$

where τ is the time constant of the point neuron (i.e., a [reciprocal] measure of its leakiness), and $I(t)$ is the total external input to the neuron (see Figure 13.7). In the presence of positive input, the activity A can rise to the threshold θ. When this threshold is crossed from below, the neuron emits a spike, and A is reset to some initial value. The mechanism of spike generation is generally ignored in the model, and the output is characterized entirely by the sequence of spike times. This type of neuron is sometimes known as a *point neuron*, because all the geometry of the dendrite has been shrunk to a single point. If R is infinite, then the neuron is not leaky, and it simply integrates its input until it reaches the threshold. If τ is small, then more recent inputs have a larger effect on A. If $I(t)$ is made up of a number of excitatory synaptic inputs, each of which is not large enough to cause A to exceed θ, then the neuron will act as a coincidence detector, firing when a number of its excitatory inputs occur at about the same time, allowing A to reach θ in spite of the leakage.

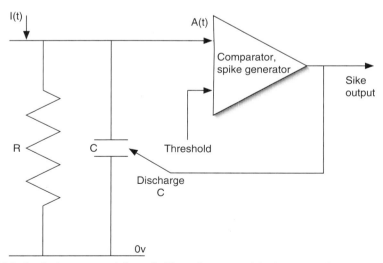

Figure 13.7. Leaky integrate-and-fire unit. The resistor R models the overall (fixed) leakage of the membrane (if omitted, there is no leakage), and the capacitor C models the overall capacitance of the membrane. The time constant $\tau = RC$. When a spike occurs, the capacitor is discharged.

4.1.1   Other point neuron models

The leaky integrate-and-fire model is the best known (and most frequently implemented) of the models that represent the dendrite as a single point. Another important model is Gerstner's spike response model [33,34], in which the threshold is dynamic and the shape of the postsynaptic potential is modeled. The dynamic threshold permits the neuron's refractory period and relative refractory period to be included in this relatively simple model.

In Equation 4, the leakage is linear. Feng and Brown [35] suggest a nonlinear leakage coefficient (equivalent to making $\tau = \tau(A)$), with the result that under certain conditions, inhibitory input can increase the firing rate [36]. Izhikevich [37] reviews a number of point neuron type models, both from the point of view of neural plausibility and computational efficiency. Not surprisingly, the more biologically plausible models take much more computing time. Izhikevich has proposed a new model [38] based on bifurcation analysis, which can generate realistic neural output from a simple simulation.

4.2   More detailed neuron models

Compartmental neuron models divide up the neuron into a number of sections (or compartments), each of which is modeled individually, with electrical current feeding into neighboring sections. The advantage is that the whole neuron (soma, dendrites, and axon) may be modeled with a degree of accuracy that can be determined by the modeller. The morphology may be simulated (at least as far as branching and neurite diameter is concerned), and each section may be given different properties. The usual techniques are based on the Hodgkin–Huxley equations (see [6], chapter 6, and [5] chapter 7), and these allow different populations of ion channels in each compartment to be modeled. Essentially, a nonlinear leakage current is associated with each ion type. There are some standard simulation tools developed for this type of simulation, most notably Neuron [39].

There are also simplified models, often based on the Hodgkin–Huxley equations—for example, the FitzHugh–Nagumo equations and the Morris–Lecar equations (both reviewed in [6], chapter 7, and discussed in terms of computational efficiency in [37]). Indeed, Feng and Brown's model [35] is a version of the FitzHugh–Nagumo model. These models can aid the speed of computation (in software) and possibly the complexity of a hardware implementation.

4.3   Learning in models that include time

Neural models that include time generally have a spike-based output. This spike output may be thought of either as coding a value in terms of its instantaneous spiking rate (rate coding) or by the precise timing of the spikes. In rate coding (and also in the case where the output is not a sequence of spikes, but a continuously varying value), it is possible to apply, for example, Hebbian-type learning rules as discussed in section 3.2. There are no equivalents of the Delta rule or the perceptron learning rule that make specific use of these types of code. These learning rules are based on the idea of a single vector input producing a single vector output. One can still use this formulation of a network that uses rate-coded spiking neurons, but no advantage is being taken of the neurons including time.

Although rate-coded and graded-output neurons clearly can have more sophisticated learning rules, there has been more interest in learning rules for spike timing-coded neurons. This case is of particular interest to computational neuroscientists, since it may inform brain science. There has been particular interest in temporal versions of Hebbian learning rules (reviewed in [40] and also in chapter 10 of [34]). To apply Hebbian learning to spiking neurons, we need to reconsider what "firing together" means: the usual view is that, for excitatory synapses, those whose postsynaptic currents assist in making the postsynaptic neuron fire are strengthened, while those whose postsynaptic currents do not help are weakened. Generally, these new rules do not alter synaptic strength unless the postsynaptic neuron fires: thus their effect is to strengthen synapses that were active just before the postsynaptic neuron fired and to weaken those that were active just after the postsynaptic neuron fired. Although such learning rules have not yet been demonstrated to be effective in applied neural networks, there is considerable interest in silicon implementations of this type of rule (see Section 5.4.3).

5   TECHNIQUES FOR HARDWARE IMPLEMENTATION

Hardware implementation of neural models and networks of neural models can allow these systems to operate in real time and to use the massive parallelism inherent in these types of design. Sequential computers cannot provide true parallelism, and parallel computers are expensive: further, there is often a mismatch between the very intense intercommunication required for neural computers and the relatively low bandwidth parallelism provided by the cheaper forms of parallel computer, such as networks of transputers or Beowulf clusters [41].

In fact, direct hardware implementation of neural systems and networks has a relatively long history. Prior to the advent of the workstation, neural modelers were forced either to use mainframe computers or to develop their own hardware. Models of excitable membranes using discrete components were developed [42–45], as well as full neurons [46]. More computationally oriented models of perceptron-based machines were built [47,48]. This chapter is not the place for a full review of this historically interesting material: however, the history does show that dedicated hardware for neural systems is not a new idea. Modern neural hardware developers are primarily interested in chip-based implementation. This focus has certainly made the resulting hardware smaller (the neural model of the avian retina developed by Runge et al. [49] ran to 50 circuit boards!), though more difficult to test and modify.

There are many possible ways of organizing a review of implementations of neural models. In a much earlier article [50], these were organized by chip type. In [4], they are organized by actual chip, and in [51], a table of chips and their characteristics is provided. Here, we review some of the issues, then discuss the analogue versus digital issue, and then look at the question of whether the implementations use static (time-free) or dynamic (including time) approaches.

5.1   VLSI implementation of neural models

Chip-based implementations are very attractive to the neural system implementor. Not only are they small (and easily incorporated into complete systems)
but also most design systems proffer at least some facilities for testing the design
prior to actual chip manufacture. Further, if the implementation is successful, the
designer will normally receive a number of chips, allowing more than one
researcher to work with the implementation. In addition, reusing designs or sections of designs is relatively straightforward. However, implementors of neural
systems in silicon do not have the luxury of developing a new silicon technology,
and so must use technologies that were developed for other purposes, such as for
high-speed digital processors.

The basic implementation techniques are summarized in Table 13.1. There are
many different possibilities within each of these classes of implementation technique. Analogue implementations are normally custom integrated circuits. These
may use the linear range of the field-effect transistors (above threshold) or the
very-low-power exponential part of their range (subthreshold). Digital implementation techniques range from software (i.e., implementation on a normal
computer) to field-programmable gate array (FPGA: a technology in which an
array of electrically programmable gates can be interconnected in an electrically programmable way) to application-specific digital integrated circuits (digital
ASIC). Of course, these technologies may be mixed, even on the same chip. We
note in passing that field-programmable analogue arrays (FPAAs) are in development (see, for example, [52]), although they are not yet nearly large enough to
replace complex analogue ASICs. The downside of hardware implementation is
the length of the timescale from design (or modification) to implementation. For
all the hardware implementation techniques (except FPGA), change of design
means refabrication, and this process generally takes months. On occasion, focused
ion beam (FIB) machines (see, e.g., http://www.feico.com/support/fiblab.htm) can
be used to modify devices, but this option is often not available, or else is inappropriate for the modification required. FPGAs can be reprogrammed quickly: they
are a technology with aspects of both hardware and software.

In Table 13.1, the "Degree of Implementation" [53] column relates to the
extent to which all the elements of all neurons exist as separate hardware components. Fully implemented systems have identifiable (and different) circuit elements for each entity being modeled. Real neural systems are fully implemented.
Most analogue implementations are also fully implemented. However, full imple-

Table 13.1. Summary of characteristics of different implementation techniques for
implementing neural systems.

Implementation Technology	Degree of Implementation	Real-time Speed	Power System	Consumption
Subthreshold a VLSI	High	High	Yes	Very low
Above threshold a VLSI	High	Very high	Yes	Medium
dVLSI	Low	High	Possible	Medium to high
FPGA	Low-medium	Medium	Possible	Medium to high
Workstation software	Minimally low	Low	Not usually	High
DSP based software	Low	Medium-high	Possible	High

mentation is not usually possible for digital VLSI implementations since replicating, e.g., digital multipliers at each synapse would make the circuit impossibly large: instead, the same functional unit may be reused frequently. For example, one digital multiplier may well be used as part of the implementation of many synapses. Such a virtual design (again using the terminology of [53]) trades off the speed of the functional unit against its area and the switching involved in multiplexing signals to the functional unit. By careful design, real-time performance may still be possible, but even with fast digital electronics, it is not guaranteed. FPGA- and DSP-based implementation are not normally fully implemented. Depending on the design chosen, component re-use will occur to a greater or lesser extent. Pure software implementations use the CPU(s) of the workstation for all computational tasks and have the lowest degree of implementation. Even implementations on parallel sets of workstations (e.g., Beowulf) simply tend to distribute the different parts of larger simulations across a number of workstations. DSP chips are also software driven and are normally controlled from a workstation. The degree of implementation depends on the details of the design (for example, on the number of chips used). The systems are easily reconfigurable, but because they are special purpose, they require specific software packages and can be difficult to program.

5.2   Analogue or digital VLSI

The first choice facing a designer intent on implementing a neural model in VLSI is whether to use an analogue or a digital design. If an ASIC is being produced, it is very likely that the technology being used for chip manufacture might have been developed for digital designs. When the implementor is attempting to build an analogue ASIC, or, indeed, any target except a digital ASIC (for example, a mixed (or hybrid) design: part digital and part analogue), problems arise. The quoted feature size for a particular technology (λ) is intended for use in the production of digital gates. For such gates, all that matters is that the realized circuit conforms with the designed circuit and that the switching voltage between an FET being on and off is within a particular range. For above-threshold analogue VLSI, the implementor is attempting to use the linear part of the transistor's characteristic, and so is reliant on the actual placing and shape of the transistor's I_{ds}/V_{gs} characteristic. This reliance can lead to matching problems, though it does appear to be the case that these problems are not major. However, for subthreshold aVLSI, the designer is reliant on the characteristic of the transistors before they turn on (i.e., I_{ds}/V_{gs} below threshold). This is not a characteristic that digital chip designers generally care about since it does not impact on their designs.

Why then would anyone consider analogue implementation? We discuss below some of the differences in implementation characteristics implied by these two different approaches.

5.2.1   Signal coding

The primary difference between digital and analogue systems is in how signals are coded. Digital signals are discrete values, valid at specific instants, and analogue signals are continuous values in continuous time. In a digital system, the two primary parameters of a signal are sampling rate and sample length. In an analogue system, the parameters are bandwidth, slew rate (maximal rate at which a signal can change), noise level, and drift. (Drift causes the analogue signal to change slowly [perhaps due to temperature variation], again reducing overall accuracy.) There is a third form of coding, namely, spike encoding, that provides spikes at specific instants, which we discuss further in Section 5.4.

In a digital system, the sampling rate determines the signal bandwidth: the maximal bandwidth is half the sampling rate. The bandwidth determines the maximal rate at which values (such as postsynaptic potentials) can change, For fully implemented systems, both analogue and digital systems normally have plenty of bandwidth in hand compared with real neural systems. However, digital systems are not normally fully implemented, so they need to have a higher bandwidth. If a particular piece of circuitry is used in P different ways (for example, a digital multiplier might be used in P different synapses), then its processing bandwidth (or speed) must be at least P times the actual required bandwidth. The sampling rate also determines the accuracy with which the time of an event can be determined: this can be important for spiking neurons (see also Section 5.4).

In a digital system, sample length determines the accuracy with which a value can be held: theoretically, an analogue system holds a value precisely, but the effect of noise is that the value is no longer precise, and drift causes further difficulties. Maximizing sample length leads to space problems: for most circuitry, the number of gates required is at best proportional to sample length.

5.2.2   Memory technologies

Memory is required in neural systems to hold constant values (such as thresholds, delays, or characteristics for ion channels) as well as variable values such as those characterizing synapses or any other aspect of the model that can alter. Digital memory techniques are well known: memory consists of a string of bits, each held either as a static RAM (sRAM) or a dynamic RAM (dRAM) cell. dRAM requires frequent refreshing, and both sRAM and dRAM are volatile and thus require reinitializing on power cycling. Another possibility is to use electrically erasable programmable read-only memory (EEPROM or flash memory) techniques to provide nonvolatile but rewritable memories.

Analogue memory elements are more problematic. In discrete systems, fixed values may be held by selecting discrete components (usually resistors and/or capacitors) with particular values. This approach is not practical on analogue VLSI chips: resistors can be fabricated, but their accuracy is low, and capacitors of any reasonable size take up too much space. One method of keeping values in analogue systems is to use a digital storage solution combined with a digital-analogue convertor (DAC). Such a system can provide accurate storage, with storage for each value taking up little space. If many values are required (as might be the case for synapse weight storage), this usually means using a smaller number of DACs and sharing them, with a consequent need for additional routing of signals.

True analogue VLSI storage generally uses either the charge on a capacitor or floating gate technology [54]. The simplest technique relies on simply storing some charge on a capacitor, which is essentially isolated. However, this charge tends to leak away, and so a refresh system is often introduced. A variant on this technique for increasing the quality of this form of representation is to use the ratio of the charge stored on two neighboring capacitors, relying on them both leaking at the same rate [55]. Such memories are essentially volatile. Restoration of these values often makes use of external digitally held values and an on-chip DAC. Floating-gate technology proffers the possibility of longer-term nonvolatile analogue storage: it is based on the same techniques that are used for EEPROM, but attempts to retain an analogue value [54, 56, 57]. Extended analogue storage is not a requirement of standard digital technology, and so is not supported in design systems. This can make chip development more difficult because the devices are often not supported in simulation environments.

The above techniques are for storing constant values. However, an important aspect of neural simulations (and particularly of neural networks) is adaptivity: we need to be able to adjust values, and to adjust them gradually. This process consists of first determining what the parameter alteration should be (discussed in Sections 5.3.1 and 5.4.3), and second, implementing some mechanism for on-chip parameter alteration. For digital storage, there is no difficulty in adjusting a binary string: what is required is either an adder or a step-up/step-down counter, or each value may be rewritten, having been recalculated elsewhere. For analogue systems, the problem requires novel solutions. This is not a new problem: specialized devices for weight storage and updating in the analogue domain have a long history (see Section 8.2 of [53]). The original Perceptron Mark 1 used motor-driven potentiometers. Later, Widrow introduced the memistor, a copper/electrolyte variable-resistance electrochemical cell. Some systems expect weight adjustments to be determined and effected from outside of the chip: weights are recalculated and then updated using a digital computer interface (e.g., [55, 58]). If the neural simulation is to be be trained without an external computer, then it should incorporate internal adaptation. For capacitative storage, there must be some mechanism for gradually increasing or gradually decreasing the charge stored on the capacitor. For floating-gate techniques, there needs to be a mechanism for charging and discharging the floating gate. Meador [56] suggested using pairs of floating-gate transistors and transferring charge between them. Diorio [57] uses hot-current injection to add electrons to its floating gate and Fowler–Nordheim tunneling to remove them. External checking of the actual weight may be required because of variations in chip processing. This is still an area of active research: Hsu et al. [59] have developed Diorio's ideas in a competitive learning chip, and Morie et al. [60] are developing a multinanodot floating-gate technique for postsynaptic pulse generation.

5.2.3   Simple arithmetic operations

Whether one is using a simple neuron like that in Equation 1 or a more complex neuron with an explicit dendrite, one needs to use arithmetic operations both for calculating neuron output and for any internal parameter alteration. For example, to calculate the postsynaptic activation one requires at least a multiply; to compute the total activation, one requires addition. In a digital implementation, these process imply the use of adders and multipliers, and in an analogue implementation the use of circuitry that can sum voltages (or currents) and perform multiplication on whatever circuit value is being used to represent the output, activation, or synaptic data.

Such arithmetic operators occur very frequently in neural models. In real neurons, these operations are accomplished using (for synapses) the effects of altering release probabilities for presynaptic neurotransmitter vesicles and changing the probabilities of opening postsynaptic ion channels, and (for the activation summation) by charge summation inside the dendrite. Both these operations take up very little space indeed. In digital systems, very fast adders and multipliers can easily be built. Adders tend to be relatively small, but multipliers tend to be larger. Depending on the multiplier implementation, one has a choice between having the latency and the size of the multiplier increase linearly with operand length (or having the latency increase as the log of the operand length) and having the size of the multiplier increase as the square of operand length [61]. In either case, it is not practical to use a separate multiplier per synapse for neural network implementation, although it can be practical to use one adder per neuron for activation summation.

In analogue implementation, simple multiplication of positive values (single-quadrant multiplication) is relatively straightforward. Thus, if a neuron's output can be guaranteed to be positive, and the weight is known to be excitatory (inhibitory), the product can be added to (subtracted from) the postsynaptic activity. However, the most popular time-free neural model (back-propagation) has neurons whose weights can be either excitatory or inhibitory, and can change between these during training. In addition, some versions of back-propagation use a $\tanh(A)$ output function, rather than a logistic $(1/(1 + \exp(-A)))$ function, resulting in outputs being either negative or positive. Thus, either two-quadrant or even four-quadrant multiplication is required. This can be problematic, since it is very easy for the product to be outside the linear range of the multiplier (see [62], chapter 6).

In analogue implementations, it is possible to use the transfer characteristics of MOSFETs (or of circuits of MOSFETs) directly, even when these are nonlinear. This option was one of the driving forces behind the Mead's original proposal to use subthreshold a VLSI for neural modeling (and for neuromorphic systems) [62]. In this way, exponential functions, differentiators, and integrators can be built directly (see also [63]). This approach is clearly much more space efficient than developing digital circuits for the same function, and this is the reason why subthreshold a VLSI systems have a very high degree of implementation. However, design is more difficult (or perhaps more skilled), and one is reliant on the silicon implementation behaving in exactly the same way as the designer's model, which, as discussed earlier, may be difficult to achieve.

5.3   Implementing simple time-free neuron model networks

An implementation of a simple time-free neuron model consists of an implementation of the synapses, of the dendrites, and of the generation of the output of the model neuron. In addition, it is necessary to implement the interconnection between the neurons. Further, for adaptive systems, one must also implement both parts of the mechanism for adaptation. The primary difficulties arise at synapses. The problems are computation of postsynaptic potential and computation (and implementation) of synaptic parameter alterations. If there are many neurons, there may also be problems associated with neuron interconnection.

The dendrites accumulate the activity passed to them by the synapses. This is a simple additive process (see Eq. 1). In a digital implementation, this is simple addition, with the number of bits used determining both the precision of the result and when overflow or underflow might occur. In an analogue implementation, either currents or voltages may be summed. Accuracy is then a function of noise, drift, and the linearity of the system. Analogue equivalents to overflow and underflow occur when the current or voltage reaches its limit.

The output of the neuron may be binary (for McCulloch–Pitts neurons or perceptrons, for example), or it may be graded (for a linear threshold unit, for example). In digital implementations, the former is achieved by numerical comparison with a fixed (binary-coded) threshold, and therefore requires an adder. In analogue implementations, this adder is replaced by a comparator, and the threshold is required to be stable. Where the output is graded (as is the case for Delta rule [plain and and back-propagated] and for the Radial Basis Function networks), some function must be applied to the activity. This may be simple multiplication (for linear units) or a logistic function (Eq. 2) or some other function. Accurate implementation may be quite complex in a digital implementation. Sometimes look-up tables are used to speed up this operation. Generally, the output function is shared between a number of neurons on the same chip (partial implementation). In analogue implementations, it may be virtually impossible to achieve exactly the output function required. However, in both the Delta and back-propagated Delta rule, it is not the exact function that matters but rather that the function is a squashing function, which is smooth and always has a positive derivative. Given suitable limits to the activity of the neuron, this outcome can often be achieved relatively easily and compactly in an analogue implementation. One can claim some biological plausibility for this approach as well, since the activation at the axon hillock (where spiking is initiated) will necessarily limit as it tends towards both positive and negative values due to the opening of additional ion channels. Both this form of limitation and the limitation on maximal spiking rates are likely to have similar forms of characteristics, but are unlikely to follow some analytical mathematical function.

Lastly, model neuron outputs must be connected to the appropriate synapses. Each neuron output may be connected to many different synapses, though each synapse is normally connected to only one neuron output. In a digital implementation, this outcome is best achieved by the use of some form of bus, particularly if the synapses are not fully implemented. The bus allows values to be directed to whichever element of circuitry is implementing that synapse at that time: it is straightforward to calculate whether the bus speed is sufficiently high, and to replicate it if required. In an analogue system, it is more common to use a rectangular array of synapses, as discussed in the next section.

5.3.1   Synapses for time-free neurons

The emulation of synapses is critical in silicon implementations of model neurons. As with real neurons, synapses are by far the most frequently occurring element of model neural networks. Because a single model neuron may have so many synapses, the system designer is faced with a choice between replicating a small amount of circuitry and hence a simple synapse (full implementation) or sharing the circuitry between a number of synapses (partial implementation). Replicating large amounts of circuitry is generally not practical.

The basic function of a synapse in a network of time-free neurons is to allow a presynaptic input to affect the postsynaptic neuron. Simple implementations of synapses are generally multiplicative: the change in postsynaptic activity is proportional to the presynaptic input, and the constant of proportionality is known as the weight, as in Eq. (1). For simple binary neurons, this set up can be implemented by adding or substracting a constant (weight-dependent) amount from the activity. For graded output neurons, multiplication of the output of the presynaptic neuron and the weight is required. Digital multipliers are standard circuit components but contain a considerable amount of circuitry. Full implementation of such multipliers results in the synapse numbers becoming the limiting factor in what can be placed on a single chip, while partial implementation implies precise switching of the presynaptic input and the appropriate weight, and of the resulting product.

Mechanisms for weight storage were discussed in Section 5.2.2. Chips normally have the weights on-chip, although some may require the weights to be downloaded at start-up. Analogue synapses are often stored in a rectangular array, as illustrated in Figure 13.8. For example, the Intel 80170NX chip [55] has a 160 by 64 array of synapses. Each set of synapses belonging to a single neuron is in a vertical column. The presynaptic inputs from a single neuron are in a hor-

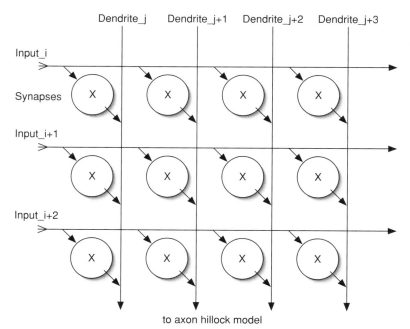

Figure 13.8. Synapses (each a simple multiplier) are arranged in a rectangular formation. Dendrites accumulate current from all synapses to that neuron.

izontal line. Where the two meet, there is a synapse (though some may have no effect). The vertical lines accumulate this input (whether as a current I_{syn} or a voltage V_{syn}) and apply this to the simulated axon hillock. Weight storage precision can affect the system in terms of both the system displaying the correct behavior once trained and the system being able to work correctly during training. (This is a general problem in digital signal processing: see [64].) In general, attaining correct behavior once trained is less demanding than attaining appropriate behaviour during training: 4 to 8 bits is enough for almost any application [65,66].

For specific fixed applications, weights may be set externally and fixed. Generally, synaptic adaptivity is attained by weight alteration, which requires that the weights be updatable. We discussed mechanisms for updating the weight in Section 5.2.2: here we are interested in determining what this weight update should be. This calculation may take place on-chip or off-chip. Different neural network algorithms make different changes: with the exception of the perceptron rule and the Hopfield network, however, these changes are often small. Further when using the back-propagated Delta rule, small changes often occur a long way from the best solution due to nearly flat areas in the error/weight space. If the weight update calculation is off-chip, this situation may not present a problem since high-precision arithmetic will be available off-chip. However, if the changes are calculated on-chip, there can be difficulties with digital weight storage update calculation when the weight change becomes less than one bit. (Indeed, these problems apply equally at weight update, even if the changes are calculated at high precision.) This critical point results in a sudden performance breakdown [67] in training, although such precision is not required in recall. Digitally stored analogue weights suffer from exactly the same problem. There has been considerable software exploration of this problem [68]. In a purely analogue system, weights can often be adjusted by very small amounts (exactly how small depends on the details of the implementation), limited by the noise and drift in the system. Failure from this source tends to be less sudden. Changing purely analogue weights can be an imprecise affair, and some systems allow a "chip in the loop" form of updating (e.g., the Intel 80170 [69]), where the effect of the weight update is tested immediately and the update is possibly repeated.

5.3.2 Developed hardware for time-free neurons

Hardware time-free neuron implementations have been around for some time (see [4,51]): a number of chips have been produced commercially and by University Departments (see [70] for a list). A number of the major semiconductor manufacturers have also produced chips: Intel produced the 80170NX (or Electronically Trainable Artificial Neural Network, ETANN) [69], an essentially analogue device directly implementing a number of neurons. Synapses were implemented using the difference between voltages on two neighboring floating gates. The values were externally determined and nonvolatile, with analogue multipliers at each synapse. IBM produced the ZISC036 (ZISC, for zero instruction set computer) [71], a digital chip implementing a radial basis function with on-chip learning. This chip could load and evaluate a vector in about 4 microseconds. Motorola collaborated with Adaptive Solutions to develop CNAPS [72], which is essentially a specialized DSP device that can be programmed to implement neural network applications in a highly efficient fashion. Phillips produced Lneuro [73] and Lneuro 2.3 [74], both digital implementations. Both were intended as special-purpose processors used in conjunction with a computer. Lneuro2.3 was intended also for other signal and image-processing applications. Siemens produced the SYNAPSE-3 neurocomputer, based on their MA16 chip [75,76], a digital chip that can be programmed to perform many different neural network algorithms at high speed. Many other smaller companies (and many university departments) also developed neural network chips in the early 1990s.

Very few of these chips appear to be currently in production, even though the technology of neural networks is quite widely applied. There are two reasons why neural network chips have not taken off. The first is that workstation prices have tumbled while at the same time their performance has rocketed. The result is that (1) training up neural networks does not take an unreasonably long time, even when large amounts of data are involved, and (2) using neural network software after training is very fast: real-time performance is often possible without special hardware. Since most users do not really care, how long training takes, so long as recall is fast, there is no commercial advantage in building systems a round neural network chips. The second reason is that neural networks themselves (and therefore neural network chips) are components in larger systems. These systems are required in order to massage the data into a form where it can be used directly with a time-free neural network: generally these systems already require a PC, so adding on some neural network software to complete the system is a much more attractive proposition than adding on neural network hardware. Neural network chips tend to be in use either in specialized defense applications (e.g., Irvine Sensors 3DANN devices, see http://www.irvine-sensors.com) or in visual sensors (e.g. NeuriCam, see www.NeuriCam.com). There is still interest in developing neural network chips for algorithms: the Boltzmann machine's capability for generating representations (and for using noise in the algorithm itself) has led to continuing interest in that algorithm ([77,78]). In addition, there has been interest in hardware for the more recent products of expert algorithms [79], resulting in a mixed-signal (hybrid) implementation [80].

Perhaps a third reason can be added as well: as is clear from the paragraph above, there has been no agreement among chip designers as to the best way to implement this type of device. Technologies have varied from specialized analogue systems to specialized digital systems to systems that were essentially adapted digital signal processors. All these approaches work, but none had a specific competitive edge.

5.4   Implementing spiking neurons

The earliest implementations of spike-based neurons used existing pulse-based technologies. Interest in this approach appears to have decreased in favor of more biologically plausible systems based on integrate-and-fire neurons.

5.4.1   Pulse-based neuron implementations

Pulse-based techniques have been used in signal processing for many years. Signals take the form of a train of pulses, usually with the signal in an inactive (zero) state most of the time. Such signals have advantages over level coded signals: they are low power (assuming that power consumption is minimal during the zero period), reasonably noise immune, and easily regenerated if the pulse edge is flattened. There are essentially three basic techniques for coding (modulating) values onto pulses: pulse height modulation, pulse width modulation, and pulse frequency modulation. These techniques are, up to a point, independent of each other. One can argue that these pulse-based techniques do have a degree of neural plausibility: pulse frequency modulation is the same as biological spike-rate coding. One can argue that pulse height modulation is what is happening at synapses, although the postsynaptic smearing of the precise spike timing could also be interpreted as pulse width modulation.

A number of groups have developed pulse-based neural systems. Murray's group [81–83] used pulse frequency modulation for neuron-to-neuron communication, and pulse width modulation inside the neuron for neuron state (or activity). Their chips were used in robot controllers. Richert's group [84] also used pulse height modulation. Hamilton [83] uses pulse height modulation for postsynaptic currents. The systems produced are relatively compact and low power, and can process and produce time-varying signals (for example, by modulating the pulse frequency). One problem is that it takes time to decode such pulse outputs: one needs to sample pulses for some time in order to estimate the value represented by a pulse frequency coded signal. Lehmann describes circuits for implementing classical conditioning [85] and for biologically inspired learning [86] in pulsed neural networks.

5.4.2 Point neurons

Point neurons such as leaky integrate-and-fire (LIF) neurons are more accurate models than time-free models because, even although they reduce the dendrite to a single point, they do model behavior in time. The mathematical model for this neuron is described in Eq. (4). Implementing such a neuron can be achieved very directly in discrete analogue electronics, as was shown in Figure 13.7. The capacitor C models the membrane capacitance, and the resistor R models the (constant) membrane leakage (in Eq.(4), $\tau = RC$). The threshold θ is modeled using a comparator. Circuitry to generate the spike is required, as is circuitry to discharge the capacitor when a spike is generated. Additional aspects of LIF neurons, such as an absolute refractory periods (the period after spiking during which the neuron cannot fire), relative refractory periods (the period following the absolute refractory period during which it is more difficult to make the neuron fire), postsynaptic current pulse shaping, and spike output shaping can, if required, also be implemented directly in analogue circuitry. The problem with such analogue models in size and complexity: researchers are usually interested in experimenting with networks of LIF neurons, and in adaptation in such networks. It is impractical (or perhaps just unfashionable) to produce discrete analogue implementations of such networks. Such direct implementations are larger, and one has to build each one individually. However, considering the difficulties involved in VLSI implementation, and the fact that many hardware implementations are used for experimenting with relatively small networks (taking advantage of speed, rather than size), there may still be a place for such discrete component-based systems.

Researchers are often more interested in software and hardware implementations of such networks. Software for such neurons is straightforward to develop. There are two basic techniques used. The direct approach involves modeling the development of the voltage on each neuron using discreticized time (where the timestep is chosen to be small enough to capture the behavior being studied). This approach is useful for small numbers of neurons and can permit the modeling of postsynaptic current pulse shaping. Where large numbers of neurons are to be simulated, this approach can be slow. The alternative is the next spike time approach. In this case, the effect of each spike's arrival is modeled. Membrane voltages are updated only when a spike arrives, relying on the fact that for a neuron with fixed threshold and no noise, spiking is always the direct effect of the most recent excitatory presynaptic pulse. The effect is that the simulation time becomes dependent on the level of spiking and on the degree of interconnection. This technique has been used by [2, 87–89] for simulating large numbers of neurons. In addition, Grassman and Cyprian [89] have developed special-purpose hardware to support this.

Neither of these software techniques will work in real time unless the network being simulated is small. Hardware implementations offer this possibility. Both digital [90, 91] and analogue [58, 92–95] implementations have been built. Digital implementations using the direct approach are attractive, since we can update the representation of the membrane voltage with each timestep. Turning Equation 4 into voltage and discreticizing gives

$$V(t + \Delta t) = V(t) - \frac{\Delta t}{\tau} V(t) + \frac{I(t)\Delta t}{C} \tag{5}$$

where $V(t)$ is the voltage on the membrane, Δt is the timestep, and $I(t)$ is the postsynaptic current injected. If we use floating-point arithmetic throughout, this presents few problems. However, using fixed-point (which takes up much less chip space), we run into problems when $\frac{\Delta t}{\tau} V(t)$ or $\frac{I(t)\Delta t}{C}$ disappears because they are less than the smallest number representable. This occurs when either number is less than $\frac{\theta}{2^n}$ for an n-bit representation. This problem is serious, particularly for attempts at fully implemented chips [91]. The problem can result in the failure of continuous small inputs to push the V over the threshold. Further, attempting to gain better accuracy for spike times by decreasing Δt makes the problem worse. Only increasing the length of the representation really helps.

Including a refractory period (relative or absolute) presents few problems: the absolute refractory period uses a timer, and the neuron simply may not fire during this time. The relative refractory period requires adjusting the value of θ: though not implemented in the examples above, it could be implemented either by setting θ to a high value and then decrementing it towards its rest value, or using a number of θ values and setting the values with the aid of another timer.

Analogue implementations suffer from different problems. The most crucial problem is that the timing expected from LIF neurons does not match well with the values of R and C (and hence τ) that can be produced with standard analogue technologies. (Meador's design [56] appears to integrate signals in less than 1 μs.)

We would like values for τ of around 20 ms. This would imply that $RC = 0.02$. Capacitors are produced using areas of metal (often deposited aluminium) separated by a thin layer of silicon dioxide. The capacitance is directly proportional to the area, making it impossible to fabricate a number of large capacitors on a single chip. The maximal value realistically achievable is of the order of 1 pF, or 10^{-12} F. This value implies a value for R of $2*10^{10}$, or 20 GΩ. Resistors are produced either as tracks of polysilicon or by using transistors with fixed V_{gs} as resistors. The former produces only resistors with low values: the latter can produce much higher values of resistance by utilizing the part of the transistor characteristic just below the transistor's conduction threshold. However, in this region, the drain-source resistance is an exponential function of V_{gs}, so precision (and stability) of this resistance requires both precision (stability) in V_{gs}. Unless one is willing to manually trim V_{gs} for each neuron, this also requires reproducibility of below-threshold currents across the chip. Chicca et al. [95] used careful layout, with an additional metal layer, but report about 16% variation in leakage current over one chip.

Switched capacitor techniques [96] have been used to increase the value of R achievable, and hence to reduce the value of C that needs to be implemented. Switched capacitor techniques introduce a digital switching signal to partially discharge the capacitor. This results in problems associated with hybrid systems, particularly adding noise to circuitry that is attempting to use precise analogue values. This situation can be problematic, requiring very careful circuit and system design. Additionally, the use of switched circuit designs also can make the precise timing of spike generation (resulting from the activation exceeding the threshold) become phase entrained to the switching signal [97].

Liu and Minch [94] have achieved a degree of adjustment in firing rate in response to perturbations in the neuron's overall input by adapting the integrate-and-fire neuron's threshold upwards in response to each generated spike, and gradually downwards otherwise. The decrease uses a tunneling mechanism with a time constant of seconds or minutes. Indiveri [98] achieves spike frequency adaptation by charging a capacitor. In addition, this low power chip has a refractory period. A different variety of point neuron has been implemented by Patel and DeWeerth [99]. Their approach implements a more complex (but more biologically realistic) model neuron: the Morris–Lecar model [100]. Their aVLSI implementation is particularly relevant to the design of neural oscillators, since it can produce outputs with frequencies in the range of 0.1 Hz to 1 Khz, depending on circuit parameters.

5.4.3   Synapses for spiking neurons

Spiking neuron synapses receive a train of pulses, rather than values. These spike trains are digital in the sense that a spike is an all-or-nothing event, yet analogue in the sense that in an unclocked implementation, the spike time is unconstrained. Although real neuron spikes are of the order of 1ms in duration, implemented spikes are often much shorter (about 100 ns in [93]), or they may be coded simply as event times, with no duration assumed at all. Implementing these synapses means translating these pulse trains (or event lists) into activity changes. One way of achieving this outcome is to inject a small amount of current for each spike. The exact amount and the direction of current injection depend on the synaptic weight and on whether the weight is inhibitory or excitatory. Such current pulses may be fixed length and height modulated (as in [83, 93]), or could use other pulse modulation techniques. The use of pure pulse-based techniques does tend to result in relatively small synapses [81, 83].

Simple modulated current injection for each spike assumes that the shape of the postsynaptic current is rectangular. One result of this is that if the activity is near threshold, and a spike arrives at an excitatory synapse, then the threshold is instantly reached, and the postsynaptic neuron fires at once. Though there are occasions when this outcome can be useful, resulting in instant synchronization of firing neurons, it is certainly not biologically realistic, and can cause problems if neurons are reciprocally connected without a refractory period. In simulations, the effect of the synapse is often approximated by an alpha function, $\alpha t \exp(-\alpha t)$: in hardware implementations, the noninstantaneous effect of the synapse can be implemented using capacitances (only really practical in subthreshold aVLSI where minute currents are used), or by using a table lookup (in a digital system).

Weight storage and manipulation can be the same as for time-free neurons. The time parameter means that there are additional options in terms of synaptic weight changes. In addition to the long-lasting changes discussed earlier, synapses may have shorter-term changes—for example they may be depressing or facilitating (see Section 2). A simple depressing synapse has been implemented by Rasche and Hahnloser [101]. The weight on this synapse is set by the charge on a capacitor, which each incoming spike discharges. This capacitor is slowly being charged up to its maximal level (which corresponds to the synapse's original weight). The result is that a sequence of closely spaced presynaptic spikes have a gradually decreasing effect: if, however, there is then a gap, the synapse recovers to its initial weight. Liu and Minch [94] have also implemented a depressing synapse, but with a longer time constant: their work is aimed at maintaining neural processing in the face of rising input spike frequencies.

A number of different mechanisms for altering weights in spiking neuron networks have been suggested. Some of these are extensions of techniques used in time-free networks. Maass has suggested how spiking neuron firing times might be interpreted in order to implement a spiking neuron equivalent of the backpropagation learning algorithm [102]. However, such rules do not take advantage of the capabilities of spiking networks to use patterns over time, and have low biological plausibility. Designers of spiking neural networks have generally been interested in more biologically plausible rules, perhaps because there has not been a spiking equivalent of a perceptron network or a Delta rule. Instead, such designers have been interested in variations on the original Hebbian learning rules, particularly temporally asymmetric Hebbian learning [40].

There has been considerable interest in the implementation of such rules. Bofill et al. [103] have produced one possible circuit. This form of a VLSI implementation has been used to detect synchrony by taking advantage of the tendency of this implementation of the rule towards making weights go to one of their endpoints [104]. Chicca et al. [95] have implemented a bistable excitatory Hebbian synapse. Paired presynaptic spiking input and postsynaptic neural activity result in the synapse being strengthened towards its higher level, but otherwise the synapse decays towards its lower level. There is also a stochastic element in the synaptic strength variation. In [105] these, authors report that each synapse uses 14 transistors.

One specific synapse that has received a great deal of attention is the synapse between the inner hair cell of the the organ of Corti (in the cochlea, in the inner ear) and the neurons of the spiral ganglion whose axons form the auditory nerve. The reason for interest in this synapse is that this synapse is part of the transduction of the movement of the membranes in the cochlea into a neural signal, and maintaining precise timing is known to be important for finding the direction of sound. Software models have been built (reviewed in the similar manner as in [106]), as have hardware implementations. These often include depression (since the biological synapses appear to be depressing). Hardware implementations are popular, as they permit real-time implementations of biologically inspired auditory models. The first silicon implementation is discussed in [107], and the field is reviewed in [108]. The most sophisticated version is in [109].

5.4.4 Interconnecting spiking neuron systems

Single chips may contain a number of spiking neuron implementations, and for small networks, it is sometimes possible to produce the whole network on a single chip. In general, however, one will want to connect up neurons on different chips. In addition, it is often the case that the inputs to the network and the outputs from the network will be required off-chip. On chips that contain a small number of neurons, one can connect neurons and the appropriate synapse using point-to-point wiring. For larger numbers of neurons, this approach is impractical.

The address/event representation (AER) was introduced for this purpose (see [110] for a tutorial introduction). This is a time-division multiplexing system that uses a digital bus to transfer spikes from neurons to the appropriate synapses. It allows for interconnection to be described in biologically natural ways, and also for reprogrammable configuration. "Virtual" wiring is possible as well. There is ongoing work on chip-based support at the Institute for Neuroinformatics in Zurich, Switzerland.

5.5 Implementing more complex neuron models

Many researchers are not satisfied with time-free or point neuron models. It is well known that real neurons are far more complex than either of these models. The computational properties of time-free neural models have been well investigated over many years. Networks of point neurons and learning mechanisms for point neurons are still under research. Point neurons make the implicit assumption that there is no interaction between the different inputs that arrive on the dendrite. Even although relatively complex postsynaptic functions may be used, what arrives at the thresholding element is simply the (linear) sum of these inputs.

Yet there is a school of thought (discussed in [111]), which holds that the spikes from neurons are simply the mechanism whereby neurons communicate their results, and that complex processing can take place on the neuron itself, possibly even without any spiking occurring at the axon hillock. Such a view seems attractive when one considers both the complex morphology of many neurons and the nonuniform placing of ion channels on these neurons. Even the briefest inspection of neural images shows that the dendrites have very considerable complexity: indeed, many types of neuron are differentiated by their dendrite shapes.

The limiting factors in the accuracy of neuron simulation are time and space. One could model neurons right down to the molecular or atomic level. Before a researcher produces a model, the researcher normally has some particular idea that they want to investigate. More complex models of full neurons have normally been either compartmental models or models of dendrites: others have gone further and have modeled patches of membrane (though such models are rarely modeling full neurons).

5.5.1   Multicompartment neurons

Software implementations of compartmental models model the dendrites, cell body, and axon as an interconnected set of cylinders and branches. Each modeled element has its inputs and outputs to and from adjacent elements, as well as its various cross-membrane leakage currents modeled. In addition, postsynaptic currents from model synapses can be included in the modeled elements. The most prevalent package for this is Neuron [39]. This form of model is generally slow, though this depends on the number of compartments being modeled. However, even although hardware implementation would clearly be faster, it is rarely attempted, primarily because such simulations are carried out with a view to understanding detailed neuron operation (for example, the effects of synapses on distal and proximal dendrites, and the effects of branching both in dendrites and axons) rather than actual information processing.

There has been more interest in hardware implementation of dendrites. Extending the dendrite beyond a single point means that the activity of the neuron is no longer a single value but is a function of location as well as time. Further, the precise time ordering of presynaptic signals will have an effect on this activity. Mel [8] has provided a major review of information processing on the dendrite, concluding that dendrites from single neurons could perform logical operations or discriminate between images. Elias [112] and Northmore and Elias [113] have developed an analogue VLSI dendrite implementation which can process spike trains. In [114], they have used switched capacitor techniques to achieve the range of membrane resistances required. Simple dendritic processing has been used to design an aVLSI chip that is sensitive to the direction of motion [115]. In [116], learning in dendritic systems is emulated. There is current interest in combining model dendrites with temporal Hebbian learning: recent research suggests that the precise timing of presynaptic and postsynaptic signals [40], and the location of the synapse on the dendrite [117], can affect the way in which weights characterizing synapses alter. Dendritic models are usually combined with spike-generating entities, and sometimes with models of delay in the axon, due to axon diameter (wide axons conduct faster) and even myelinization[2] to produce models of whole neurons in which precise spike timing can be modeled.

---

[2]Myelin is a protein produced by glial brain cells. It is often wrapped around axons, reducing both their leakage and their capacitance, and allowing much faster transfer of action potentials (see [5], chapter 4).

5.5.2   Implementing models of excitable membranes

The lowest level of neural modeling currently attempted is modeling of excitable membranes. The impetus for producing such models is clear: as discussed in Section 2, ion channels embedded in the membrane are the primary mechanism whereby the potential of the neuron is modified or altered. The aim of this work has generally been "explanatory neuroscience" [118], rather than biologically inspired computing. It is not possible to emulate multiple different yet interacting ion species directly in electronics. Electronic systems have only one charge carrier, the electron. Similarly, one cannot model multiple varieties of voltage-sensitive (and ion-type-sensitive) ion channels. These can be modeled in software, but such models are slow and complex.

The idea of using subthreshold FETs to emulate the exponential conductance properties of ion channels is discussed at length in Mead's book [62], where he calls it *eclectronics*. A highly influential implementation of the spiking characteristics of the soma and axons was produced by Mahowald and Douglas [119]. This aVLSI implementation implements bulked ion channels (rather than individual ones) and is essentially a silicon compartment model. It was the first to achieve this goal in hardware and thus to operate in real time. A more detailed discussion of the elements of this chip can be found in [120]. A number of other authors have followed this early start: Rasche, Douglas, and Mahowald [121] added extra conductances, and Rasche and Douglas [122] have developed this concept and have produced a more robust chip. Both [119] and [122] implement these ion channels as a circuit, rather than as a single transistor, as implied by Mead. Implementing ion channels as single transistors was attempted in [123]: however, it proved difficult to get the range of behaviors one would want from a range of different types of ion channels. Shin and Koch [124] provide an aVLSI implementation of an adaptive algorithm that permits an electronic neuron to enable it to adapt its current threshold to the mean of the input current. Rasche [125] has produced aVLSI adaptive dendrite that can operate in widely varying levels of overall neural activity. This form of adaptation allows the dendrite to signal changes from the short-term mean of their input. Rasche and Douglas [126] have developed the silicon axon so that it can support both forward and backward propagation of spikes. Minch et al. [127] have produced a silicon axon that recreates a pulse along its length.

Real synapses, of course, are not simple mulipliers. One form of synapse (a chemical synapse: see [5] chapter 10) consists in essence of a set of ion channels on the postsynaptic membrane that are opened when neurotransmitter is released presynaptically. This occurs in response to presynaptic action potentials. Such a synapse has been implemented in aVLSI by Rasche and Douglas [128], where they provide equivalent circuits for (bulk) AMPA and NMDA conductances.

5.5.3   Applications of hardware spiking neurons

What evidence is there that more sophisticated neural hardware, such as that of point neurons, might have application, when those for time-free neurons (discussed in Section 5.3.2) have proven largely a graveyard for silicon implementations? Firstly, these chips can process time-varying signals directly. They do not require the signal to be sampled initially. Thus a minimum of extra hardware is required (bringing the signal into the desired voltage/current range, or pulse coding it, for example), greatly simplifying the direct interfacing of the neural network system with the devices providing input and accepting output from the network. If interfacing the chip does not entail using a PC, then there is more advantage to be gained from direct hardware implementation.

Although such silicon neural systems have not yet found industrial applications, there have been applications for this type of technology in the neuromorphic field. These applications vary from line following in a robot [129] to sound direction finding [130, 131], including sonar [132], to real-time image analysis [133, 134] to motor control [135]. They have been applied particularly in autonomous systems, where the simplicity of interfacing the implemented neuron to the rest of the system has been important. Even where digital computers are part of the overall system, there are still advantages in using hardware-implemented neural systems, particularly at the sensor-processing end of the system. Their explicit parallelism can permit effective real-time exploitation of the signals being interpreted, distributing the processing in an effective way.

The other application area for hardware neural implementations is in modeling and interfacing to real neural systems. One interesting example of modeling neural systems is Tobi Delbruck's "Physiologist's Friend" chip [136], a model of a visual cortical neuron with retinal sensors that can model the receptive field of a visual cortical neuron well enough to be used instead of a live animal for training psychology or physiology students. In addition, spiking silicon neurons are one of the underlying technologies that may permit effective sensory implants [137], both auditory [138] and visual [139]. These prosthetic applications may prove to be an important growth area for this type of technology, where small size and ultra-low power consumption are critical.

There is also rather less disagreement about the most appropriate technologies to use for implementing these systems. Most implementations are either analogue or hybrid, using aVLSI (often largely subthreshold, partly because of its low power consumption and partly to take advantage of its nonlinear circuit elements) and sometimes combining this with pulse techniques. One recent paper [140] uses a mixture of excitatory and inhibitory neurons, implemented in subthreshold aVLSI, with separate dendrites for different types of input. The analogue circuitry produces an essentially digital output, using strong positive feedback to provide a robust selection output—robust against the actual level of the input. This mixture of analogue and digital, inspired by biology yet not constrained to follow it exactly, is conceptually reasonably simple (and thus efficiently implementable) and able to implement an algorithm. This approach may represent a direction that could lead to a greater range of applications.

6   CONCLUSION

Modeling neurons at a number of different levels has uncovered a number of what appear to be computational principles of the brain. These have then been used in electronic systems or in software and where appropriate in hardware as well. Neural network technology is now well established. Whether the novel computational paradigms from more sophisticated model neurons will prove useful remains to be seen. Initial applications seem to suggest that the first areas of application will be in what is currently the niche area of autonomous systems. Other research areas (with titles like "the disappearing computer" or "the ubiquitous computer") suggest that greater autonomy for computer-based systems will be required, so this niche area may well come to be more important.

It is, however, still the case that brains can do many things that are not possible in current electronic systems. Neuromorphic systems have been proposed as one set of techniques for capturing some of these capabilities. They have indeed helped to explain some of the brain's sensory capabilities, particularly in vision and in motor control. Yet the deeper, less peripheral capabilities of brains remain essentially untouched. It is an open question as to which, if any, of the other aspects of neural systems apart from those already modeled might provide a clue as to the nature of these capabilities. Currently, spiking systems are being investigated by many laboratories. These certainly show promise for parallel processing of time-varying signals. However, so far, investigation of spiking systems has thrown no light on awareness, self-consciousness, or indeed, consciousness. Even planning is still entirely in the domain of old-fashioned software.

There are a number of candidate "biotechnologies" for possible further investigation. These range from the interactions between the different ion types gated by the zoo of ion channels found in neurons to interactions between elements of neurons at the quantum level (as suggested by Hammeroff and Penrose). Modeling these systems in software or hardware presents one way of investigating these possibilities. There are other possibilities as well, such as producing hybrid machines, part electronic and part neural [141].

There are difficulties in producing simulations of interacting ions or of systems at the quantum level on normal computers. Such computers are inherently deterministic, and this makes the modeling of stochastic or quantum systems slow and cumbrous. It is possible that Moore's Law will come to the rescue: as feature sizes decrease, gates and transistors become more noisy do to various noise effects, making the emulation of stochastic systems in hardware much simpler (even if it does make building deterministic systems that much harder). It may yet be that there are general principles of another sort of computation grounded in this stochasticity, and that understanding these using modeling will provide some other general principles, perhaps even shedding light on some of the brain's deeper capabilities.

ACKNOWLEDGMENTS

The support of the UK EPSRC (grant number GR/R64654) is acknowledged.

REFERENCES

[1] P. Hammarlund and O. Ekeberg (1998): Large neural network simulations on multiple hardware platforms. *Journal of Computational Neuroscience 5*, 443–459.

[2] E. Claverol, A. Brown, and J. Chad (2001): Scalable cortical simulations on Beowulf architectures. *Neurocomput. 43*, 307–315.

[3] D. Hammerstrom (2001): Biologically inspired computing. [Online]. Available: http://www.ogi.ece.edu/strom

[4] Neural network hardware. [Online]. (1998): Available: http://neuralnets.web.cern.ch/NeuralNets/nnwlnHepHard.html

[5] E. Kandel, J. Schwartz, and T. Jessell (2000): *Principles of Neural Sci.* (4th Ed.) McGraw Hill.

[6] C. Koch (1999): *Biophysics of Computation.* Oxford.

[7] T. Bell (1991): A channel space theory of dendritic self-organisation. AI Laboratory, Free University of Brussels, Tech. Rep. 91–4.

[8] B. Mel (1994): Information processing in dendritic trees. *Neural Comput. 6*, 1031–1085.

[9] D. Aidley (1999): *The Physiology of Excitable Cells.* (4th Ed.) Cambridge University Press.

[10] S. Hammeroff (1999): The neuron doctrine is an insult to neurons. *Behavioural and Brain Sciences, 22*, 838–839.

[11] W. McCulloch and W. Pitts (1943): A logical calculus of ideas immanent in nervous activity. *Bulletin of Mathematical Biophysics, 5*, reprinted in [142].

[12] D. Hebb (1949): *The Organization of Behavior.* Wiley, New York. partially reprinted in [142].

[13] J. Anderson (1995): *An Introduction to Neural Networks.* Cambridge, MA: MIT Press.

[14] F. Rosenblatt (1962): *Principles of Neurodynamics.* Spartan, New York.

[15] J. Hertz, A. Krogh, and R. Palmer (1991): *Introduction to the Theory of Neural Computation.* Addison Wesley.

[16] S. Haykin (1999): *Neural Networks: A Comprehensive Foundation.* (2nd Ed.) Macmillan.

[17] B. Widrow and M. Hoff (1960): Adaptive switching circuits, In *1960 IRE WESCON Convention Record.* New York: IRE, *4*, 96–104.

[18] R. Rescorla and A. Wagner (1972): A theory of pavlovian conditioning: The effectiveness of reinforcement and nonreinforcement. In *Classical Conditioning II: Current Research and Theory* (A. Black and W. Prokasy, eds) Appleton-Century-Crofts, New York: 64–69.

[19] M. Minsky and S. Papert (1969): *Perceptrons.* MIT Press, Cambridge partially reprinted in [142].

[20] J. Hopfield (1982): Neural networks and physical systems with emergent collective computational abilities. *Proceedings of the National Academy of Sciences. USA, 79*, 1982, reprinted in [142].

[21] D. Ackley, G. Hinton, and T. Sejnowski (1985): A learning algorithm for boltzmann machines. *Cognitive Science, 9*, reprinted in [142].

[22] A. Bryson and Y.-C. Ho (1969): *Applied Optimal Control.* Blaisdell, New York.

[23] P. Werbos (1974): Beyond regression: New tools for prediction and analysis in the behavioral sciences. Ph.D. dissertation, Harvard University.

[24] D. Parker (1985): Learning logic. Center for Computational Research in Economics and Management Science, Massachusetts Institute of Technology, Cambridge, MA, Tech. Rep. TR–47.

[25] Y. Le Cun (1985): Une procédure d'apprentissage pour réseau à seuil assymétrique. In *Cognitiva 85: A la Frontière de l'Intelligence Artificielle des Sciences de la Connaissance des Neurosciences*, (Paris 1985). CESTA, Paris: 599–604.

[26] D. Rumelhart, G. Hinton, and R. Williams (1986): Learning representations by back-propagating errors. *Nature, 323*, 533–536, reprinted in [142].

[27] J. Moody and C. Darken (1988): Learning with localized receptive fields. In *Proceedings of the 1988 Connectionist Models Summer School*, (D. Touretzky, G. Hinton, and T. Sejnowski, eds) (Pittsburg). Morgan Kaufmann, San Mateo 133–143.

[28] C. Bishop (1995): *Neural networks for Pattern Recognition*. Clarendon Press, Oxford.

[29] J. Elman (1990): Finding structure in time. *Cognitive Science. 14*, 179–211.

[30] H. Barlow (1959): Sensory mechanisms, the reduction of redundancy and intelligence. *The Mechanisation of Thought Processes: NPL Symposium, 10.*

[31] T. Kohonen, T. Huang, and M. Schroeder (2000): *Self-organizing Maps.* (3rd ed.) Springer-Verlag.

[32] L. Lapique (1907): Sur l'excitation electrique des nerfs. *J. Physiology. Paris*, 620–635.

[33] W. Gerstner (1995): Time structure of the activity in neural network models. *Physical Reviews E. 51*, 738–758.

[34] W. Gerstner and W. Kistler (2002): *Spiking Neural Models*. Cambridge.

[35] J. Feng and D. Brown (2000): Integrate-and-fire models with nonlinear leakage. *Bulletin of Mathematical Biology. 62*, 467–481.

[36] J. Feng and G. Wei (2001): Increasing inhibitory input increases neuronal firing rate: when and why? Diffusion process cases. *J. Phys. A. 34*, 7493–7509.

[37] E. Izhikevich. Which model to use for cortical spiking neurons? submitted to *IEEE Transactions of Neural Networks.*

[38] ——— , Simple model of spiking neurons, accepted for publication in *IEEE Transactions of Neural Networks.*

[39] M. Hines and N. Carnevale (1997): The NEURON simulation environment. *Neural Computation. 9*, 1179–1209.

[40] G. Bi and M. Poo (2001): Synaptic modification by correlated activity: Hebb's postulate revisited. *Annual Review of Neuroscience. 24*, 139–166.

[41] L. Smith (2002): Using Beowulf clusters to speed up neural simulations. *Trends in the Cognitive Science. 6*, 231–232.

[42] R. Fitzhugh (1966): An electronic model of the nerve membrane for demonstration purposes. *J. Appl. Physiology. 21*, 305–308.

[43] R. Johnson and G. Hanna (1969): Membrane model: a single transistor analog of excitable membrane. *J. Theoretical Biology. 22*, 401–411.

[44] E. R. Lewis (1968): An electronic model of the neuroelectric point process. *Kybernetik. 5*, 30–46.

[45] G. Roy (1972): A simple electronic analog of the squid axonmembrane: the neuro FET. *IEEE Transactions on Biomedical Engineering. BME-18*, 60–63.

[46] W. Brockman (1979): A simple electronic neuron model incorporating both active and passive responses. *IEEE Transactions on Biomedical Engineering.* BME-26, 635–639.

[47] F. Rosenblatt (1958): The perceptron: a probabilistic mode for information storage and processing in the brain. *Psychological Rev. 65*, 386–408.

[48] B. Widrow (1962): Generalization and information storage in networks of ADALINE neurons. In *Self-Organizing Systems* (G. Yovitts, ed) Spartan Books.

[49] R. Runge, M. Uemura, and S. Viglione (1968): Electronic synthesis of the avian retina. *IEEE Transactions on Biomedical Eng.*, BME-15, 138–151.

[50] L. Smith (1989): Implementing neural networks. In *New Developments in Neural Computing* (J. Taylor and C. Mannion, eds) Adam Hilger, 53–70.

[51] I. Aybay, S. Cetinkaya, and U. Halici (1996): Classification of neural network hardware. *Neural Network World. 6*(1), 11–29.

[52] "AN220E04 datasheet: Dynamically reconfigurable FPAA," Anadigm, 2003.

[53] R. Hecht-Nielsen, *Neurocomputing.* Addison-Wesley, 1990.

[54] E. Vittoz, H. Oguey, M. Maher, O. Nys, E. Dijkstra, and M. Cehvroulet (1991): Analog storage of adjustable synaptic weights. In *VLSI Design of Neural Networks.* (U. Ramacher and E. Rueckert, eds) Kluwer Academic.

[55] "80170nx electrically trainable analog neural network," Intel Corporation, 1991.

[56] J. Meador, A. Wu, C. Cole, N. Nintunze, and P. Chintrakulchai (1991): Programmable impulse neural circuits. *IEEE Transactions on Neural Networks. 2*(1), 101–109.

[57] C. Diorio, P. Hasler, B. Minch, and C. Mead (1996): A single-transistor silicon synapse. *IEEE Transactions on Electron Devices. 43*(11), 1982–1980.

[58] L. Smith, B. Eriksson, A. Hamilton, and M. Glover (1999): SPIKEII: an integrate-and-fire aVLSI chip. *Int. J. Neural Syst. 9*(5), 479–484.

[59] D. Hsu, M. Figueroa, and C. Diorio (2002): Competitive learning with floating-gate circuits. *IEEE Transactions on Neural Networks. 13*, 732–744.

[60] T. Morie, T. Matsuura, M. Nagata, and A. Iwata (2003) A multinanodot floating-gate mosfet circuit for spiking neuron models. *IEEE Transactions on Nanotechnology. 2*, 158–164.

[61] D. Green (1999) *Digital Electronics* (5th ed.) Prentice Hall.

[62] C. Mead (1989): *Analog VLSI and Neural Systems.* Addison-Wesley.

[63] S.-C. Liu, J. Kramer, G. Indiveri, T. Delbruck, and R. Douglas (2002): *Analog VLSI: Circuits and Principles.* MIT Press.

[64] E. Ifeachor and B. Jervis (2002): *Digital Signal Processing: A Practical Approach* (2nd ed.) Prentice Hall.

[65] M. Hohfield and S. Fahlman (1997): Probabilistic rounding in neural network learning with limited precision. *Neurocomputing. 4*, 291–299.

[66] E. Sackinger (1997): Measurement of finite precision effects in handwriting and speech recognition algorithms. In *ICANN 97: LNCS 1327* (W. Gerstner, A. Germond, M. Hasler, and J.-D. Nicoud, eds), Springer Verlag, 1223–1228.

[67] P. Moerland and E. Fiesler (1997): Neural network adaptations to hardware implementations. In *Handbook of Neural Computation* (E. Fiesler and R. Beale, eds) IOP Publishing.

[68] S. Draghici (2002): On the capabilities of neural networks using limited precision weights. *Neural Networks. 15*, 395–414.

[69] I. Corporation (1990): 80170NN electrically trainable analog neural network. *Datasheet.*

[70] C. S. Lindsey, B. Denby, and T. Lindblad. Neural network hardware. [Online]. Available: http://www.avaye.com/ai/nn/hardware/index.html

[71] A. Eide (1994): An implementation of the zero instruction set computer (zisc036) on a pc/isa-bus card, [Online]. Available: citeseer.nj.nec.com/ eide94implementation.html

[72] H. McCartor (1991): Back propagation implementation on the adaptive solutions cnaps neurocomputer chip. In *Advances in Neural Information Processing Systems 3*, (R. Lippmann, J. Moody, and D. Touretzky, eds), Morgan Kaufmann pp. 1028–1031.

[73] N. Mauduit, M. Duranton, and J. Gobert (1992): Lneuro 1.0: A piece of hardware LEGO for building neural network systems. *IEEE Transactions on Neural Networks. 3*(3).

[74] Y. Deville (1995) Digital VLSI neural networks: from versatile neural processors to application-specific chips. *Proc. of the International Conference on Artificial Neural Networks ICANN'95*, Paris, France, Industrial Conference, Session 9, VLSI and Dedicated Hardware.

[75] U. Ramacher, J. Beichter, W. Raab, J. Anlauf, N. Bruels, U. Hachmann, and M. Weseling (1991): Design of a 1st generation neurocomputer. In *VLSI Design of Neural Networks*, (U. Ramacher and E. Rueckert, eds), Kluwer Academic.

[76] U. Ramacher, W. Raab, J. Anlauf, U. Hachmann, J. Beichter, N. Bruls, R. Manner, J. Glas, and A. Wurz (1993): Multiprocessor and memory architecture of the neurocomputer SYNAPSE-1. *Proc. International Conference on Microelectronics for Neural Networks*. Edinburgh, pp. 227–232.

[77] H. Chen and A. Murray (2002): A continuous restricted Boltzmann machine with a hardware amenable training algorithm. In *Proceedings of ICANN 2002*, pp. 426–431.

[78] — , A continuous restricted Boltzmann machine with an implementable training algorithm. In *IEEE Proceedings on Vision Image and Signal Processing*.

[79] G. Hinton, B. Sallans, and Z. Ghahramani (1999): A hierarchical community of experts. In *Learning in Graphical Models* (M. Jordan, ed) MIT Press pp. 479–494.

[80] P. Fleury and A. Murray (2003): Mixed-signal VLSI implementation of the products of experts' contrastive divergence learning scheme. In *Proceedings of ISCAS 2003. 5*, pp. 653–656.

[81] A. Murray, L. Tarassenko, H. Reekie, A. Hamilton, M. Brownlow, D. Baxter, and S. Churcher (1991): Pulsed silicon neural nets—following the biological leader. In *Introduction to VLSI Design of Neural Networks* (U. Ramacher, ed), Kluwer pp. 103–123.

[82] A. Murray, S. Churcher, A. Hamilton, A. Holmes, G. Jackson, R. Woodburn, and H. Reekie (1994) Pulse-stream VLSI neural networks. *IEEE MICRO*, pp. 29–39.

[83] A. Hamilton, S. Churcher, P. Edwards, G. B. Jackson, A. Murray, and H. Reekie (1994): Pulse-stream VLSI circuits and systems: the EPSILON neural network chipset. *Int. J. Neural Sys.* 4(4), 395–405.

[84] P. Richert, L. Spaanenburg, M. Kespert, J. Nijhuis, M. Schwarz, and A. Siggelkow (1991): ASICs for proto-typing pulse-density modulated neural networks. In *Introduction to VLSI Design of Neural Networks* (U. Ramacher, ed), Kluwer pp. 125–151.

[85] T. Lehmann (1997): Classical conditioning with pulsed integrated neural networks: Circuits and system. pt. II, *IEEE Transactions on Circuits and Systems, 45(6)*, 720–728.

[86] T. Lehmann and R. Woodburn (1999): Biologically-inspired learning in pulsed neural networks. In *Learning on Silicon: Adaptive VLSI Neural Systems* (G. Cauwenberghs and M. Bayoumi, eds) Kluwer, pp. 105–130.

[87] L. Watts (1993): Event driven simulation of networks of spiking neurons. In *Advances in Neural Information Processing Systems 6* (J. Alspector, J. Cowan, and G. Tesauro, eds), pp. 927–934.

[88] A. Nishwitz and H. Glünder (1995): Local lateral inhibition—a key to spike synchronization. *Biological Cybernetics.* 73(5), 389–400.

[89] L. Smith, B. Eriksson, A. Hamilton, and M. Glover (1999): Fast digital simulation of spiking neural networks and neuromorphic integration with SPIKELAB. *Int. J. Neural Sys.* 9(5), 473–478.

[90] S. Lim, A. Temple, S. Jones, and R. Meddis (1998): Digital hardware implementation of a neuromorphic pitch extraction system. In *Neuromorphic Systems: Engineering Silicon from Neurobiology* (L. Smith and A. Hamilton, eds), World Scientific.

[91] N. Mtetwa, L. Smith, and A. Hussain (2000): Stochastic resonance and finite resolution in a network of leaky integrate-and-fire neurons. In *Artificial neural networks—ICANN 2002*. Springer, Madrid, Spain pp. 117–122.

[92] S. Wolpert and E. Micheli-Tzanakou (1996): A neuromime in VLSI. *IEEE Transactions on Neural Networks, 7*(2), 300–306.

[93] M. Glover, A. Hamilton, and L. Smith (1998): Analogue VLSI integrate and fire neural network for clustering onset and offset signals in a sound segmentation system. In *Neuromorphic Systems: Engineering Silicon from Neurobiology* (L. Smith and A. Hamilton, eds), pp. 238–250.

[94] S.-C. Liu and B. A. Minch (2001): Homeostasis in a silicon integrate and fire neuron. In *Advances in Neural Information Processing Systems 13, Papers from Neural Information Processing Systems (NIPS) 2000, Denver, CO, USA* (T. K. Leen, T. G. Dietterich, and V. Tresp, eds), MIT Press, pp. 727–733.

[95] E. Chicca, D. Badoni, V. Dante, M. D'Andreagiovanni, G. Salina, L. Carota, S. Fusi, and P.D. Giudice (2003): A vlsi recurrent network of integrate-and-fire neurons connected by plastic synapses with long term memory. *IEEE Transactions on Neural Network.* 14(5), 1409–1416.

[96] J. Mavor, M. Jack, and P. Denyer (1983): *Introduction to MOS LSI Design.* Addison Wesley.

[97] B. Eriksson (2002): A critical study of a hardware integrate-and-fire neural network. Master's thesis, University of Stirling, Department of Computing Science and Mathematics.

[98] G. Indiveri (2003): A low-power adaptive integrate-and-fire neuron circuit. In *Proc. IEEE International Symposium on Circuits and Systems.* May 2003.

[99] G. Patel and S. P. DeWeerth (1997): Analog VLSI Morris-Lecar neuron. *Electronics Letters, 33,* 997–998.

[100] C. Morris and H. Lecar (1981): Voltage oscillations in the barnacle giant muscle fiber. *Biophysics J. 35,* 193–213.

[101] C. Rasche and R. Hahnloser (2001): Silicon synaptic depression. *Biological Cybernetics. 84,* 57–62.

[102] W. Maass (1997): Networks of spiking neurons: The third generation of neural network models. *Neural Networks. 10* (9), 1659–1671.

[103] A. Bofill, R. Woodburn, and A. Murray (2001): Circuits for VLSI implementation of temporally-asymmetric Hebbian learning. In *Neural Information Processing Systems.* Vancouver.

[104] A. Bofill-i-Petit and A. Murray (2003): Synchrony detection by analogue VLSI neurons with bimodal STDP synapses. accepted for NIPS 2003.

[105] E. Chicca, G. Indiveri, and R. Douglas (2003): An adaptive silicon synapse. In *Proc. IEEE International Symposium on Circuits and Systems.* May.

[106] M. Hewitt and R. Meddis (1991): An evaluation of eight computer models of mammalian inner hair-cell function. *J. Acoustical Soc. Am. 90*(2), 904–917.

[107] J. Lazzaro and C. Mead (1989): Circuit models of sensory transduction in the cochlea. In *Analog VLSI Implementations of Neural Networks.* Kluwer pp. 85–101.

[108] I. Grech, J. Micallef, and T. Vladimirova (1999): Silicon cochlea and its adaptation to spatial localisation. *IEE Proceedings—Circuits Devices and Systems. 146*(2), 70–76.

[109] A. van Schaik and A. McEwan (2003): An analog VLSI implementation of the meddis inner hair cell model. *EURASIP J. Applied Signal Processing.*

[110] K. Boahen, Point-to-point connectivity between neuromorphic chips using address-events. *IEEE Transactions on Circuits and Systems II. 47*(5), 416–434.

[111] I. Segev, M. Rapp, Y. Manor, and Y. Yarom (1992): Analog and digital processing in single nerve cells: dendritic integration and exonal propagation. In *Single Neuron Computation* (T. McKenna, J. Davis, and S. Zornetzer, eds) pp. 173–198.

[112] J. Elias (1993): Artificial dendritic trees. *Neural Comput. 5*(4), 648–664.

[113] D. Northmore and J. Elias (1996): Spike train processing by a silicon neuromorph: The role of sublinear summation in dendrites. *Neural Comput. 8*(6), 1245–1265.

[114] J. Elias and D. Northmore (1995): Switched-capacitor neuromorphs with wide-range variable dynamics. *IEEE Transactions on Neural Networks. 6*(6), 1542–1548.

[115] M. Ohtani, H. Yamada, K. Nishio, H. Yonezu, and Y. Furukawa (2002) Analog LSI implementation of biological direction-sensitive neurons. part 1 *Japanese Journal of Applied Physics, 41,* 1409–1416.

[116] W. Westerman, D. P. Northmore, and J. G. Elias (1998): A hybrid (hardware/software) approach towards implementing hebbian learning in silicon neurons with passive dendrites. In *Neuromorphic Systems: Engineering Silicon from Neurobiology.* (L. Smith and A. Hamilton, eds), World Scientific.

[117] A. Saurdagiene, B. Porr, and F. Woergoetter (2004): How the shape of pre- and post-synaptic signals can influence STDP: A biophysical model, accepted for *Neural Comput.*

[118] R. Douglas, M. Mahowald, and K. Martin (1996): Neuroinformatics as explanatory neuroscience. *Neuroimage.* S25–S27.

[119] M. Mahowald and R. Douglas (1991): A silicon neuron. *Nature, 354* (6354), 515–518.

[120] R. Douglas and M. Mahowald (1995): A construction set for silicon neurons. In *An Introduction to Neural and Electronic Networks* (S. Zornetzer, J. L. Davis, C. Lau, and T. McKenna, eds) Academic Press pp. 277–296.

[121] C. Rasche, R. Douglas, and M. Mahowald (1998): Characterization of a silicon pyramidal neuron. In *Neuromorphic Systems: Engineering Silicon from Neurobiology* (L. Smith and A. Hamilton, eds) World Scientific.

[122] C. Rasche and R. Douglas (2001): An improved silicon neuron. *Analog Integrated Circuits and Signal Processing.* 23(3), 227–236.

[123] C. Breslin and L. Smith (1999): Silicon cellular morphology. *International Journal of Neural Systems.* 9(5), 491–495.

[124] J. Shin and C. Koch (1999): Adaptive neural coding dependent con the time-varying statistics of the somatic input current. *Neural Computation.* 11(8), 1893–1913.

[125] C. Rasche (1999): An aVLSI basis for dendritic adaptation. *IEEE Transactions on Circuits and Systems II.* 48(6), 600–605.

[126] C. Rasche and R. Douglas (2001): Forward- and backpropagation in a silicon dendrite. *IEEE Transactions on Neural Networks.* 12(2).

[127] B. A. Minch, P. Hasler, C. Diorio, and C. Mead (1995): A silicon axon. In *Advances in Neural Information Processing Systems* (G. Tesauro, D. Touretzky, and T. Leen, eds) 7. The MIT Press, pp. 739–746.

[128] C. Rasche and R. Douglas (1999): Silicon synaptic conductances. *J. Comput. Neuroscience.* 7(1), 33–39.

[129] R. Mudra and G. Indiveri (1999): A modular neuromorphic navigation system applied to line following and obstacle avoidance tasks. In *Experiments with the Mini-Robot Khepera: Proceedings of the 1st International Khepera Workshop* (A. A. Loeffler, F. Mondada, and U. Rueckert, eds), pp. 99–108.

[130] C. Schauer, T. Zahn, P. Paschke, and H. Gross (2000): Binaural sound localization in an artificial neural network. In *IEEE International Conference on Acoustics, Speech, and Signal Processing*, pp. 865–868.

[131] A. van Schaik and S. Shamma (2003): A neuromorphic sound localizer for a smart mems system. In *IEEE International Symposium on Circuits and Systems.* pp. 864–867.

[132] G. Cauwenberghs, R. Edwards, Y. Deng, R. Genov, and D. Lemonds (2002): Neuromorphic processor for real-time biosonar object detection. In *IEEE International Conference on Acoustics, Speech, and Signal Processing (ICASSP).* pp. 3984–3987.

[133] G. Crebbin and M. Fajria (2000): Integrate-and-fire models for image segmentation. In *Visual Communications and Image Processing 2000*, pp. 867–874.

[134] T. Netter and N. Franceschini (2002): A robotic aircraft that follows terrain using a neuromorphic eye. In *IEEE/RSJ International Conference on Intelligent Robots and Systems (IROS 2002)*, pp. 129–134.

[135] M. Lewis, M. Hartmann, R. Etienne-Cummings, and A. Cohen (2001): Control of a robot leg with an adaptive aVLSI CPG chip. *Neurocomputing. 38*, 1409–1421.

[136] T. Delbrck, S.-C. Liu, E. Chicca, G. M. Ricci, and S. Bovet. (2001): The physiologist's friend chip. [Online]. Available: http://www.ini.unizh.ch/tobi/friend/chip/index.html

[137] T. Berger, M. Baudry, R. Brinton, J. Liaw, V. Marmarelis, A. Park, B. Sheu, and A. Tanguay (2001): Brain-implantable biomimetic electronics as the next era in neural prosthetics. *Proceedings of the IEEE. 89*(7), 993–1012.

[138] T. Lande, J. Marienborg, and Y. Berg (2000): Neuromorphic cochlea implants. In *IEEE International Symposium on Circuits and Sys. (ISCAS 2000)*, pp. 401–404.

[139] E. Maynard (2001): Visual prostheses. *Annual Review of Biomedical Engineering. 3*, 145–168.

[140] R. Hahnloser, R. Sarpeshkar, M. Mahowald, R. Douglas, and H. Seung (2000): Digital selection and analogue amplification coexist in a cortex-inspired silicon circuit. *Nature. 405*, 947–951.

[141] T. DeMarse, D. Wagenaar, A. Blau, and S. Potter (2001): The neurally controlled animat: Biological brains acting with simulated bodies. *Autonomous Robots. 11*, 305–310.

[142] J. Anderson and E. Rosenfeld (eds) (1988): *Neurocomputing: Foundations of Research*. MIT Press, Cambridge.

Chapter 14

MOLECULAR AND NANOSCALE COMPUTING AND TECHNOLOGY

*Mary M. Eshaghian-Wilner, Amar H. Flood, Alex Khitun,
J. Fraser Stoddart, and Kang Wang*
University of California, Los Angeles

Due to the continued scaling of CMOS chips, it is expected that the feature size of devices will reach the atomic and molecular scales in the next decades. However, there is concern that this scaling effort may come to an end. Nanoscale CMOS and other novel nano-devices promise improved performance for information processing. But there are many issues and challenges associated with the design of such nano-systems. This chapter attempts to present a very brief overview of nanoscale and molecular computing technology. Several nanoscale and molecular computing elements and architectures proposed by the authors are described, and their performance and limitations are discussed. The chapter includes a brief tutorial on various existing nanoscale and molecular devices. These include molecular switches, resonant tunnel diodes, tunnel diodes, single electron transistors, carbon nanotube field-effect transistors, quantum dots, and spin systems. Nanoscale computing modules such as quantum- and spin-based cellular logic arrays and molecular-based cellular automata, all made from the switches presented here, are discussed. These modules are an integral part of a hierarchical 3-D multiscale architecture presented. A set of nano quantum and molecular self-assembled structures, including molecular crossbars are also shown. The materials presented here are compiled from the reference articles listed at the end of the chapter.

1   INTRODUCTION

Nanotechnology may offer a potentially viable manufacturing technology that allows precise control of the structure of matter by working with atoms and molecules [68]. It entails the ability to build molecular systems with atom-by-atom precision, yielding a variety of systems and nanomachines. It will allow many things to be manufactured at low cost. It will lead to the production of systems including nanoelectronic circuits and nanomachines. The development of nanotechnology in the broadest sense has immediate implications, since we can design a whole new range of machines from nanoscale objects. These nano objects may be made of bits of crystal of inorganic, organic, and even biological materials. The development and use of molecular nanotechnology – the building up from atoms – will be slower because it will take time to find the exact point where changing only a few atoms in a structure will make a difference. The single electron device (e.g., memory) may be a case where molecular technology research will be commercialized more easily.

A consequence of Moore's Law is that the individual feature sizes of electronic components decrease every year despite the continued difficulty in fabricating smaller and smaller electronic components. Following on from Moore's Law, ITRS (*The International Technology Roadmap for Semiconductors*, 2003 edition) anticipates that by the year 2009 the feature sizes of devices will become less than 45 nm, where the electronic properties of the materials will change from obeying classical physics to the wave nature of quantum physics. Transistors may eventually reach a limit of one electron per bit. Current CMOS technology has reached the 90-nm feature size in manufacture.

The scaling effort is intended to increase device density, functionality, and performance along with cost benefits. Therefore, shrinking of the device feature size will continue in the future until the limits and cost benefits are reached. In research, devices with a gate feature size of about 10 nm have been demonstrated, as is schematically shown in Figure 14.1 (from INTEL Components Research). The ultimate feature size of CMOS may reach 5–7 nm, for which the tunneling between source and drain may be the limiting factor. As devices are scaled down, there are many technical challenges and fundamental limits. The challenging issues range from lithography, power dissipation (power supply), short-channel effect, and gate oxide to interconnect delays.

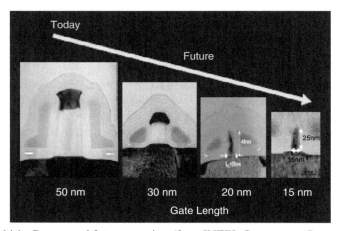

Figure 14.1. Current and future gate sizes (from INTEL Components Research 2002).

In the nanoscale regime, electrons in a solid no longer flow like particles; rather, they can better be described as quantum mechanical—as a wave. This wave behavior makes it possible for electrons to do remarkable things, such as instantly tunneling through an insulating layer that normally would be impermeable. To understand how and when quantum effects come into play, we must consider what happens to a semiconductor device as it becomes smaller. As we reduce the size, the net electron transit time through the devices is shorter, and hence there is an incentive for making electronic devices smaller and smaller. However, there are more fundamental effects, such as the fact that for individual atoms and molecules the electronic states are discrete and quantized. Quantum effects become observable when the separation between these energy levels becomes larger than the thermal energy that allows rapid transitions at operating temperature. As the physical dimensions of the devices are reduced, the separation between the discrete energy levels increases and quantum effects persist to higher temperatures. A school of thought believes that these effects might be used to our advantage— if we knew how to control them. Nanoelectronics is the emerging field of building electronic devices at the atomic level to harness these small-scale "quantum" properties of nature. The field unites physicists, chemists and biologists in order to understand how nature works at the atomic scale and how we can control it. For more details, see [14, 39, 41, 75, 83, 87].

Another new and exciting interdisciplinary field is the area of molecular electronics, which is concerned with the exploitation of organic compounds in electronic and optoelectronic devices. It is possible to build electronic devices based on molecular switches of different designs [47, 48, 62, 76, 84]. The key issue in designing a molecular-based switch, as compared with a scaled switch such as a transistor, is being able to control the flow of electrons. Use of a molecule that switches by the relative mechanical movements of its component parts, as in bistable [2] rotaxanes and [2] catenanes, is one method, from which it has been possible to fabricate a 64-bit RAM device [82]. Another way to do this in a molecule is to control the overlap of electronic orbitals. For example, with the right overlap it may be possible for electrons to flow, but if the overlap can be controllably perturbed, it may be possible to block the flow.

The task of fabricating and testing such tiny molecular devices is possible by utilizing one of two simple methods, based on (1) the use of a scanning tunneling microscope (STM), and (2) the fabrication of electrode-molecule-electrode (EME) devices. STMs use a sharpened conducting tip with a bias voltage applied between the tip and the substrate. When the tip is brought within < 1 nm of a molecular layer that is on the surface of a substrate, electrons from the molecular sample begin to tunnel across the 1 nm gap into the tip or vice versa, depending upon the sign of the bias voltage. The tunneling process is quantum mechanical, and therefore, it takes advantage of wave properties to move an electron through an energy barrier at lower energies than if the electron was a particle. EME devices can be prepared by utilizing closely packed molecular monolayers deposited onto a bottom electrode, using the Langmuir-Blodgett (LB) technique [7], such that a Ti [62] or Au [97] electrode can be vapor deposited on top without damaging, or penetrating through, the molecules. The electronic properties of the EME device can be interrogated using simple I-V measurements.

Over the past 40 years, scientists have investigated and tried to understand unusual quantum phenomena, but an important question is whether or not it is possible that a new kind of computer can be designed based entirely on quantum principles. The extraordinary power of the quantum computer is a result of a phenomenon called *quantum parallelism*, a mechanism that enables multiple calculations to be performed simultaneously. This is in contrast to a classical computer that can only perform operations one at a time, albeit very quickly [80]. The field of quantum computation had remained a largely academic one until the 1990s, when it was shown that, for certain key problems, quantum computers could, in principle, outperform their classical counterparts. Since then, research groups around the world have been racing to pioneer a practical system. However, trying to construct a quantum computer at the atomic scale is far from easy, since it requires the ability to manipulate and control single atoms. "Wiring" quantum bits together via coherent wave interactions is a challenging task. In addition, it requires the manipulation of electrons and protons within individual atoms without disturbing the coherence of the particle's spins. These systems may need to be constructed with molecular mimics or even using biological materials.

The objective of the present chapter is to present a very brief overview of nanoscale computing elements, structures, and architectures. Nanoscale elements include nano CMOS, SET, molecular devices, and others. We will study the design and fabrication of nanoscale chips for computing using Nano and Molecular elements. While the architectures presented may employ quantum and tunneling effects because of the device feature size being below 10 nm, the style of the computation used is classical rather than quantum.

The rest of the chapter is organized as follows. In the next section, we present a brief tutorial on various existing nanoscale and molecular devices. These include molecular switches, resonant tunnel diodes, tunnel diodes, single electron transistors, carbon nanotube field-effect transistors, quantum dots, and spin systems. Next, in Section 3, we review a set of nanoscale computing modules, such as quantum and spin-based cellular logic arrays, and molecular-based cellular automata, all made from the switches presented here. These modules will be an integral part of a hierarchical 3-D multi-scale architecture. In Section 5, we discuss self-assembled structures including molecular and quantum-based self-assemblies. A discussion of design issues and challenges for nanoscale and molecular computing is presented in Section 6. Concluding remarks and future research are presented in Section 7.

2   SWITCHING ELEMENTS

In this section, we present a very brief description of various basic elements, devices, and units used in designing molecular and nanoscale computing structures and architectures. The basic devices presented here are used in the architectures and structures presented in the later Sections of this chapter. For a more detailed overview of some of these devices, refer to an earlier publication by Goldbaher-Gordon et al. [24].

2.1 Molecular Switches

Solid-state electronic devices based on molecular switches have been proposed as the active units in both nonvolatile random access memory circuits and as the reconfigurable bits for a custom configurable logic-based computing machine [82]. The central element of such devices is based on the simple EME configuration, which forms a molecular switch tunnel junction that can be electrically switched between high and low conductance states. The mounting evidence, both experimental and theoretical, is consistent with the molecule's role in the devices' switching mechanism [82, 90, 96, 98]. Consequently, it may be possible for device characteristics, such as volatility, on/off current ratios, and absolute conductance, to be tuned by altering the internal structure of the molecules. Furthermore, the molecules are designed to operate individually, which is anticipated to allow these devices to be scaled, ultimately to a very small number of molecules, if not a single one.

An integrated systems-oriented approach has guided the team of Heath and Stoddart [82] to develop and demonstrate molecular-switch tunnel junctions (MSTJs) capable of 64-bit RAM with multiple write, read and erase cycles. The MSTJ devices have been scaled from microns down to nanometer-sized devices and, further, to a situation where [91] a single semiconducting carbon nanotube is utilized as one of the electrodes. These devices are essentially fabricated the same way at each length scale. A silicon nanowire or single semiconducting carbon nanotube is prepared, and wired for electrical connectivity, on an SiO_2 substrate. An LB monolayer of closely packed molecular switches is transferred to the substrate, and a Ti top electrode is vapor-deposited on top of the monolayer through a mask at an angle orthogonal to the bottom electrode. An Al electrode is deposited on top of the Ti one for electrical connectivity. The remaining part of the monolayer, which is not covered by the crossbar, is finally washed away. The mechanism of switching and electrical transport in these devices relies on molecular properties and hence represents a significant development in the design and integration of organic compounds within an electronics paradigm.

The Stoddart group at UCLA has been developing voltage-driven molecular switches from the classes of compounds known as bistable [2] catenanes, [2] rotaxanes, and [2] pseudorotaxanes for their use as the active components in solid-state molecular switch devices.

These molecules, shown in Figure 14.2 can be rationally designed to provide many advantages. First, voltage-addressable bistability can be designed into these molecules, and this bistability can be thoroughly characterized in the solution phase using various optical and NMR spectroscopies. Second, the bistable [2]catenanes, [2]rotaxanes and [2]pseudorotaxanes display slightly different overall structures, yet they contain the same voltage-activated subunits that allow their switching mechanisms to behave in a similar way within the devices. Third, these compounds are prepared using a modular synthetic approach that allows them to be optimized and customized. For example, to facilitate the formation of Langmuir monolayers, amphiphilicity can be incorporated into their molecular structures. This property allows for the preparation of closely packed monolayers that can easily be deposited on Si electrodes. The quality of the films is paramount

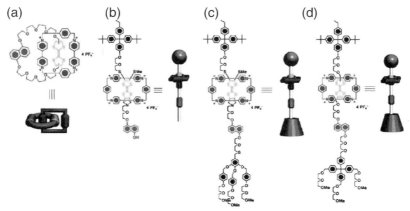

Figure 14.2. From left to right, molecular structures and graphical representations of the switchable molecules. (a) A bistable [2]catenane. (b) An amphiphilic, bistable [2]pseudorotaxane. (c, d) Two versions of amphiphilic, bistable [2]rotaxanes. In all these molecular switches, the solution-phase switching mechanism is based on voltage-driven oxidation of the tetrathiafulvalene (TTF) unit, followed by Coulombic repulsion-driven motion of the tetracationic cyclophane component so that it encircles the dioxynaphthalene (DNP) ring system.

for obtaining a working device and is assured using in-situ techniques prior to deposition of the top electrode.

The MSTJs based on bistable [2] catenanes, [2] rotaxanes and [2] pseuodrotaxanes are as dependent on the electrode material as they are on the molecule [93]. While MSTJs based on the three different molecular structures have demonstrated switching characteristics in devices, it is noteworthy that the same result has not been obtained when wholly metallic materials have been employed as both of the electrodes. In all cases, operational devices were only obtained when the bottom electrode was either polycrystalline silicon, with its native oxide layer, or a single semiconducting carbon nanotube. The switching voltages were all about +2 V (switch on) or −2 V (switch off), the on/off current ratios were about 10, the device's switching was observed to be thermally activated and displayed volatility, and only switchable molecules defined a binary character in the device, in contrast to nonswitchable control compounds. However, when Pt was used as the bottom electrode, in place of Si or C, the results were different [88, 89]. Although switching of the device between on and off states was observed, it was a phenomenon that was not isolated to switchable molecules. The switching mechanism from devices built on Pt electrodes was ultimately determined to be due to electromigratory nanofilament growth [100]. Moreover, in single-molecule break junction measurements [101] conducted at low temperature, the differential conductance between two platinum wires, across a switchable rotaxane, indicate that the electron transport properties of the single-molecule EME are dominated by the electrode-molecule interface. It is conceivable that a Schottky-like barrier is present at this novel type of heterojunction. One useful rule of thumb that is suggested from these observations is that, in order to resolve the contribution of the molecule to the device's electrical transport properties, it may be important to utilize electrodes that are made of materials with a similar work function to those of the carbon that constitute organic compounds.

The design of switchable molecules and MSTJ structures alike has resulted from an interplay between synthetic chemists and device builders. This approach has allowed for both elements to evolve in order to fit the boundary conditions determined by the other one. In this way, a new technology – switchable molecules – has been integrated successfully into memory devices. Moreover, the potential to perform logic also invites investigation. The challenge faced when utilizing crossbars, or 2-D networks at the nanoscale, is one of circuit design [88] and one that has not been outside the team's consideration. Specifically, Williams' research group at HP – the third team member with Heath and Stoddart – has developed a demultiplexer and multiplexer system, thus providing the necessary proof of principle demonstration of how to electrically address nanoscale wires and junctions. Such an integrated systems-oriented approach supports the efforts of a team of many research groups geared towards the development of molecular electronic devices.

2.2 Devices with Negative Differential Resistance

The first tunneling diode was proposed by Esaki and Tsu in 1970 [2], and the first negative-differential resistance was observed in 1973 [3]. In 1974, resonant tunneling through a double-barrier resonant-tunneling diode (RTD) was reported [4]. Among the many nanoelectronic devices proposed, the RTD has been very extensively explored for nanoelectronic circuit applications because of its compact size, high speed, device design flexibility, and negative differential resistance. RTD has been realized with nanofabrication techniques such as molecular beam epitaxy (MBE), atomic layer deposition (ALD), and metal-organic chemical vapor deposition (MOCVD). Figure 14.3 shows a typical band diagram with quantized energy levels of the RTD and I-V characteristics.

Initially, with low voltage across the RTD (point A in Figure 14.3), the electrons are below the resonance level, so the probability for the electrons to tunnel is extremely small. As the voltage through the RTD increases, the emitter region is wrapped upwards, and the collector region is warped downwards. Eventually, the band of electrons in the emitter is lined up with the resonant level, allowing tunneling to the collector (peak point B). With higher voltage, the electrons are pushed past the resonant energy level, which decreases the tunneling probability (point C). If the voltage increases further, some electrons become able to flow over the top of the quantum barriers, and the current will rise.

For RTD devices, two material characteristics are important for achieving high current density and high peak-to-valley ratio. These are (1) large enough energy band discontinuities and (2) material compatibility (lattice mismatch). The best performance of RTDs has been achieved with a III-V semiconductor [45]. An oscillator of InAs/AlGaAs RTD demonstrated works at over 700 GHz [21]. Also, a few logic circuits using RTDs have been proposed [37]. Among these are logic gates consisting of RTDs and HBT, Boolean function circuits, cellular neural networks, etc. The first tunnel diode SRAM cell was proposed by Goto et al., and it consisted of only one FET and two tunnel diodes [2]. Since then, tunneling devices [6, 41, 42] have attracted a great deal of interest, particularly in SRAM applications [33]. In a tunneling-based SRAM cell [60], tunneling current flows continuously to maintain one of several stable states. Figure 14.14 shows forward

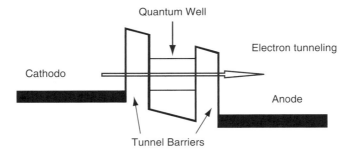

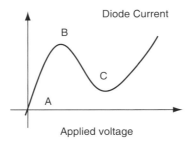

Figure 14.3. Energy levels of the RTD and IV characteristics.

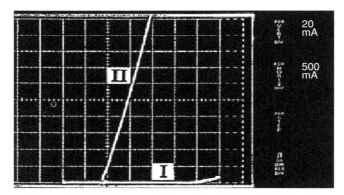

Figure 14.4. I-V characteristics of the Si-Based SRAM cell.

I-V characteristics of the Si-Based SRAM cell [16]. The lower branch of the curve, which is marked as state I, occurs as the diode is brought from zero bias. As the forward bias is increased above a transition voltage (3.5V in the figure), the diode switches to the low-resistance branch, which is marked as state II. It has recently been shown that for tunneling-based SRAM, the standby power/bit can approach the limit of technology-dependent leakage by reducing the NDR tunneling current [44]. (Large-scale integration (LSI) transistor/RTD technology has been demonstrated in compound semiconductor material systems [31].) Tunneling-based static and dynamic RAMs are expected to reduce the standby power/bit (less than 1 pW for gigabit applications) [10, 17].

In contrast, the silicon-based Si/SiGe RTD demonstrated to date has a relative power current density and a smaller peak-to-valley ratio than those of III-IV materials [77]. The small peak-to-valley ratio is due to the fact that the band offsets are too small and the effective mass is too large. Even though silicon-based RTDs have not been integrated with CMOS, silicon tunnel RTD devices have recently been reported [22, 28, 29], and they can be readily integrated with current Si technologies [7].

Negative differential resistance is the key property of RTDs to be used in computational devices. It can be exploited to design compact bistable–multistable circuits [15], Cellular Neural Networks (CNN) [70], Neuromorphic Architecture [23], and Cellular Automata [94].

2.3   Carbon Nano-Tube Field Effect Transistors

Nanotubes (NTs) form another class of nanostructures. The first experimental realization of individual Y-junction carbon NT diodes was recently accomplished [59]. The I-V measurements on these diodes show rectifying behavior at room temperature, suggesting potential device applications. Other earlier studies on carbon p-n junction diodes can be seen in the references [49, 50, 52]. These simple devices demonstrate the general concept of rectifying operation. Besides the rectifying behavior, Leonard and Tersoff [63] recently recognized that in NT two-terminal devices, tunneling through a potential barrier can lead to negative differential resistance (NDR). They treated theoretically both a nanotube p-n junction and an undoped metal-nanotube-metal junction by calculating quantum transport, using a self-consistent potential in tight-binding approximation. The predicted peak-to-valley current ratio, even at room temperature, exceeds by orders of magnitude those seen in existing devices.

Molecular field-effect transistors (FETs), three-terminal switching devices with single-wall and multiwall carbon NTs, were fabricated and demonstrated [38, 43]. With the application of a voltage to a gate electrode, the nanotube can be switched from a conducting to an insulating gate. At room temperature, some devices show a transistor action similar to that of p-channel field-effect transistors [54], whereas others behave like gate-voltage independent wires. At room temperatures, transport is usually dominated by Coulomb blockade. At higher temperature, power law behaviors are observed in the bias and temperature dependences of conductance. With the use of the gate electrode, the conductance of a single-wall NT-FET could be modulated by more than five orders of magnitude. However, large-diameter multiwall NTs typically show no gate effect; on the other hand, structural deformation can modify their electronic structure sufficiently to yield the FET behavior.

It should be noted that the above NT-FETs were fabricated on top of high-work-function metal electrodes such as platinum or gold. These devices have generally high-contact resistance and were unipolar with hole-transport characteristics. To investigate the origin of the p-type characteristics of semiconducting NTs, Martel et al. [73] fabricated carbon NT FETs with titanium carbide contacts and passivated with a uniform SiO_2 layer (see Figure 14.5). In contrast to the above-mentioned devices, the titanium-carbide-contacted FET showed that an apparent barrier height for carrier injection could be modulated by the gate

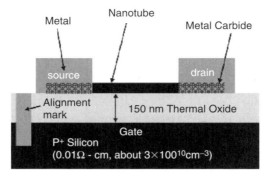

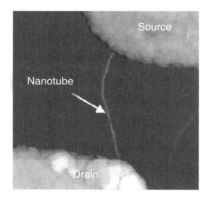

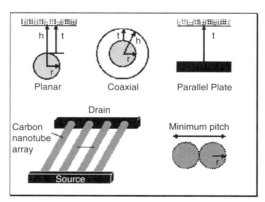

Figure 14.5. Carbon nanotube FET (CNFETs); see Martel et. al. [67]. Two gate electrode configurations (planar and coaxial) CNFETs.

field, allowing the FETs to be ambipolar with a low contact resistance for both n- and p-type conduction. This finding suggests that the usual p-type characteristic of NT FETs is not an intrinsic property of a nanotube, but rather appears to be a property of the nanotube–metal junction contacts. Moreover, the ambipolar properties of NT FETs may therefore be exploited for implementation of complementary logics.

Significant progress in CNT fabrication has been made possible by utilizing electric-field-directed deposition. Single-walled carbon nanotubes were synthesized by chemical vapor deposition of methane at controlled locations on a substrate using patterned catalytic island [58]. Combined synthesis and microfabrication techniques allows a large number of ohmically contacted nanotube devices with controllable length to be placed on a single substrate.

2.4 Single Electron Transistors

As the feature size goes to the nanometer scale, the number of electrons that the gate controls will continue to decrease and eventually reach a single electron. Device functions may be realized by controlling a single electron, referred to as a *single-electron transistor (SET)*. The SET emits an electron to a small silicon island coupled to two external reservoirs (source and drain) through a tunneling barrier, and the potential barrier of the island can be controlled by a gate or multiple gates, as shown in Figure 14.6. Because the size of the island is on the order of nanometers, the capacitance may be on the order of aF, and the charging energy ($e^2/2C$) becomes more than tens of meV. In this case, the Coulomb blockade is even visible at room temperature. The drain current controlled by the gate voltage exhibits periodic oscillations with a period of (e/C_g), called *Coulomb oscillations*.

Due to the unique features described above, single-electron transistors offer the following advantages for some circuit applications: (1) good scalability, in which the principle of the Coulomb blockade permits single-electron devices to operate at very small physical dimensions, down to the atomic scale, making ultra-large-scale integration possible; (2) ultra-low-power dissipation, simply

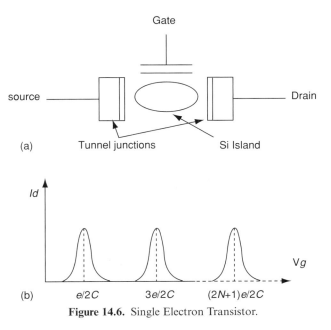

Figure 14.6. Single Electron Transistor.

because these transistors use a very small number of electrons and there is little or no standby power dissipation; and (3) faster operation, with a small capacitance, even though the current is low [61]. The single-electron transistor has another interesting feature in that a large-threshold voltage shift can be achieved by adding only one electron to charge the gate [32]. As the size of the floating is shrunk to tens of nanometers, the storage of a single electron results in a threshold voltage shift much greater than the charging energy.

Based on the Coulomb blockade effect, several circuit applications in logic and memory have been proposed and simulated [11, 13, 55, 64, 72]. Single-electron flash memory is the first single-electron device demonstrated to operate at room temperature, in which one electron stored in the floating gate represents one bit of information [25]. Single-electron transistor with multiple gates was proposed to implement complicated logic functions, with a small number of devices with respect to the conventional CMOS, by making full use of a unique feature of SETs of an oscillatory conductance as a function of the gate voltage. Takahashi et al. [67] confirmed that a two-gate SET functioned as an XOR gate operating at 40 K. Figure 14.7 shows (a) a SET inverter realized with capacitively coupled SET transistors (the offset charges q are specified to insure proper inverter operation) and (b) a SET inverter realized with resistively coupled SET transistors.

Note that, although many logic schemes have been proposed, no logic family has been thoroughly characterized experimentally. One of the problems is that it has been difficult to fabricate complex circuits with the very small feature sizes necessary (< 100 nm) for single electronics circuits. In order for SET circuits to function, the energy that is necessary to add an electron to a device must be larger than the characteristic thermal energy k_BT. According to the published data [72], the speed of SET logic circuits is very slow, and the gate delay is more than tens of milliseconds. Actually, this large delay is not a fundamental characteristic of SET itself but results from the interconnect.

The main challenge in integration of SET devices in VLSI circuits is the charge offset problem. This problem manifests itself as a random offset due to the presence of spurious charge in the island or the region near to it. Since the source-drain current versus the gate voltage is periodic (see Figure 14.6), the random

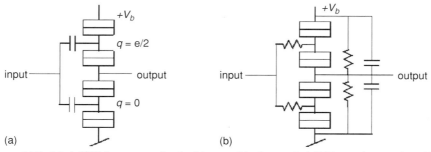

Figure 14.7. (a) A SET inverter realized with capacitively coupled SET transistors. The offset charges q are specified to insure proper inverter operation. (b) A SET inverter realized with resistively coupled SET transistors.

offset makes the threshold voltage of each island different, and thus it is impossible to predict the "high" or "low" state. An anticipated solution to this problem may come from the use of fault-tolerant architecture [23] compensating for the deviation in a single device performance.

2.5 Quantum Dots

Quantum dots (QDs) are nano-sized deposits of one semiconductor embedded in another semiconductor. Since the dot material has an energy band gap that is smaller than that of the surrounding material, it can trap charge carriers. While quantum dots are particles made up of hundreds to thousands of atoms, in many of their characteristics they behave like a single gigantic atom. The optical and transport properties of quantum dots – particularly the ease of customizing those properties by adjusting the size or composition of the dots – make them very suitable for molecular electronics. In the category of QDs, there are individual dots (a.k.a. *artificial atoms*), as well as coupled dots (*quantum-dot molecules*), and a composite device of four or five QDs called a *QD cell*. The integration of these into various architectures is shown later in this chapter. The following is a brief discussion on how quantum dots compare with RTD and SETs as explained in [24].

The essential structural feature that all three of these devices (RTD, SET, and QD) have in common is a small "island" composed of semiconductor or metal in which electrons may be confined. The island's role is analogous to that of the channel in an FET. The extent of confinement of the electrons in the island is different in these three devices. In QD, the island confines electrons with *zero* classical degrees of freedom remaining. In RTDs, because of the size, the island confines electrons with *one or two* classical degrees of freedom. And in SETs, the island confines electrons with *three* classical degrees of freedom. The composition, shape, and size of the island give the different types of solid-state nanoelectronic devices their distinct properties. It should be noted that as the feature size of RTD and equivalent devices get smaller, they eventually behave as SET.

2.6 Spins

As explained in the overview article by Awschalom et al. [78], devices that rely on an electron's spin to perform their functions form the foundation of spintronics or magnetoelectronics. Electrons have a property called spin that can be oriented in one direction or the other – called *spin-up* or *spin-down*. When electron spins are aligned, they create a large-scale net magnetic moment. Magnetism is an intrinsic physical property associated with the spins of electrons in a material.

In an ordinary electric current, spins are oriented at random and hence play no role in determining the resistance of a wire or the amplification of a transistor circuit. Spintronic devices, in contrast, rely on differences in the transport of spin-up and spin-down electrons. In a ferromagnet, such as iron or cobalt, the spins of certain electrons on neighboring atoms tend to line up. In a strongly magnetized piece of iron, this alignment extends throughout much of the metal. When a current passes through the ferromagnet, electrons of one spin direction tend to be obstructed. The result is a spin-polarized current in which all the electron spins point in the other direction.

In 1990, Supriyo Datta and Biswajit A. Das, then at Purdue University, proposed a design for a spin-polarized field-effect transistor, or spin FET. The Datta–Das spin FET has a ferromagnetic source and drain so that the current flowing into the channel is spin-polarized. When a voltage is applied to the gate, the spins rotate as they pass through the channel and the drain rejects these antialigned electrons. Macroscopic spin transport was first demonstrated in n-doped gallium arsenide. Recent experiments have successfully driven coherent spins across complex interfaces between semiconductor crystals of different composition. For more information, refer to the cited overview article [78].

3   COMPUTING MODULES

Having presented the basic nano and molecular switching elements, we now proceed with an overview of a set of computing modules that can be built using those switches. These modules will be integrated to form the high-level architectures presented in the next section. The computing modules presented here are Quantum-based, Spin-based, and Molecular-based.

3.1   Quantum-Based Computing Modules

The Quantum Cellular Automata (QCA) has been extensively studied by a group of researchers at the University of Notre Dame for several years [12, 57]. The basic idea behind QCA is that when the level of integration is very small, then cells interact with each other through quantum effects and tunneling. By utilizing quantum dots, the size of an elementary cell can be shrunk down to hundreds or tens of nanometers, and the intercell interaction can be realized via quantum tunneling without wires. Moreover, the product of energy of switching, E, and of switching time, τ, may approach the fundamental limit $E \cdot \tau \leq \hbar$. Through use of this concept, simple cells have been developed mainly using five quantum dots called a *quantum dot molecule*. The five dots are close enough to enable electrons to tunnel between the dots. The barriers between cells are assumed to be sufficient to completely suppress intercellular tunneling. Two electrons occupy each cell. The occupancy can be stabilized because of the large energy splitting between different charge states of the cell. The Coulomb interaction between electrons in a cell acts to produce two distinct cell states with different charge configurations. If the barriers to tunneling are sufficiently high, the two-electron ground-state wave function in the cell will localize the two electrons on antipodal sites. This localization is due to Coulomb exclusion, a phenomenon closely related to the well-known Coulomb blockade of current, and results in nearly exact quantization of charge in each dot.

There are two possible configurations with the electrons on opposite corners of the dots, as shown in Figure 14.8. The polarization of the states is defined as +1 and −1. Binary information can be encoded using cell polarization. A cell polarization of +1 corresponds to a bit value of 1; a cell polarization of −1 corresponds to a bit value of 0. The Coulomb interaction between cells causes the

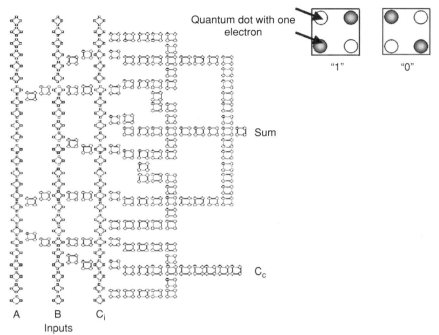

Figure 14.8. An implementation of a binary Full Adder using QCA (adapted from the QCA website)

state of one cell to affect the state of a neighboring cell. Even a slight polarization in a neighboring cell induces essentially complete polarization in the target cell. This means that at every stage the signal level is restored. This restoration will enable a line of QCA cells to act as a robust binary wire. Similarly, a series of logic gates can be built using a specific arrangement of such cells. Therefore, it is possible to implement logic circuits in QCA. A schematic for a full adder is shown in Figure 14.8.

The details of how to lay out the QCA circuit arrays in 3-D is shown in the next section. However, at the moment, there are a number of difficulties in making QCA work efficiently. One of the main difficulties at this time is that its operation is limited to low temperatures. One solution here may be to implement the QCA molecularly.

3.2   Spin-Based Computing Modules

Eventually, an atomic-level Cellular Automota (CA) may be built on individual nuclear or electron spins. The original idea to use nuclear spins for quantum computing was proposed by Kane [36] (see Figure 14.9).

Initially, the aim of associating nuclear spins via hyperfine interaction was to perform a quantum superposition (entangled state) of all spins in an array.

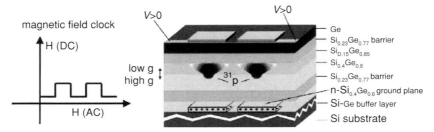

Figure 14.9. Magnetic field-driven spin CA. A single electron spin device may be used as an elementary cell. The nearest neighboring spins are coupled by exchange interaction. The strength of coupling is controlled by the local electric and global magnetic fields.

However, as we explained before, our focus is just on classical computations subject to quantum effects and not "quantum computing." The problem is significantly simplified if we eliminate the very stringent demand of quantum coherency and consider nuclear spins as semiclassical two-state systems. When using spins, the maximum cell density is defined not by the cell size itself but by the intercell distance, which in turn is restricted by the interatom distance.

Similar to the QCA presented in the last section, logical functions and circuits can be implemented using spins, where the spin's direction can act as a binary switch. A binary signal is communicated from one electron to the next by spin coupling. There are no physical wires; the quantum-mechanical interaction plays the role of wires. Figure 14.10 shows how spins implement various logic functions. For a more detailed description, refer to the paper on Granular Nanoelectronics [20].

3.3   Molecular-Based Computing Modules

Cellular Automata (CA) is a distributed data-processing system that consists of many identical processing elements (cells) regularly arrayed on a plane. The data that the CA manipulates are a pattern of the cell states. Each cell changes its state in each discrete time through interactions with its nearest neighbors. The cellular automation receives an input pattern and converts the pattern into different patterns in next time steps using a set of rules. Finally, it renders the result as the output. We discuss here a molecular-based CA. Molecular electronics has recently attracted attention, since there is great potential in implementing new molecules (mainly organic) for a variety of electronics and optoelectronic functionalities [25]. A significant feature offered by molecular electronics is the possibility of building an intelligent molecule, that can be self-assembled by chemical syntheses and whose state can be linked to its nearest connecting neighboring molecules. The intelligent molecules may function as an ALU. It has only recently become possible to obtain some kinds of intelligent polymer molecules attached to solid surfaces [35]. Powerful chemical methods are now available for creating polymeric modules that can be assembled in a variety of ways to perform useful, intelligent molecule functions. An example of an optically driven NAND logic gate based on intelligent molecules is described in an article by Crandall and Lewis [9].

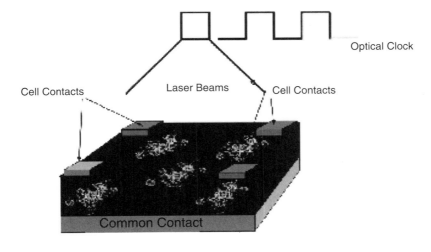

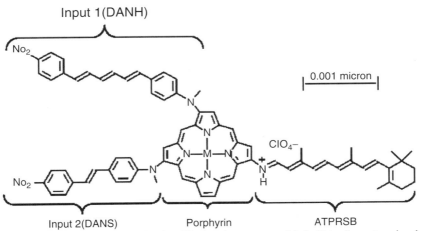

Figure 14.10. Optically driven molecular CA. An elementary cell is built by "smart molecules." Interactions among the nearest molecules may be initiated by optical pulses.

In Figure 14.10, we have schematically shown such a "smart molecular"-based CA. An elementary cell consists of one smart molecule with a driving electrode. The electrode serves to initiate the molecule to the initial state and also to provide the reading of the final resultant state. Association among the neighboring molecules is done though chemical bonds. Time-step synchronization may be done by optical pulses. Potentially, a number of different logic functions can be realized by one smart molecule, for example, activated by optical pulses at different wavelengths.

There are several significant drawbacks intrinsic to molecular schemes. The most important one is thermal instability. Indeed, most polymers become unstable and decomposed at several hundred degrees, implying thermal budget restrictions in fabrication. Thermal instability can also cause reliability problems due to breakdown of chemical bonds. The minimum size of the molecular CA is limited by the size of the intelligent molecule, which usually exceeds a few nanometers.

4   HIGH-LEVEL ARCHITECTURES

The computing modules presented in the previous sections can be assembled together to form various computing architectures. Here we present two high-level architectures. The first one is a hierarchical multiscale architecture whose basic computing modules can be any of the three modules presented in the previous section. The second architecture is neuromorphic, which presents a different style of computing paradigm. This high-level architecture also can be implemented with quantum dots, RTDs, and/or spins.

4.1   Multiscale Architecture Design

Here we discuss the integration of the nanoscale computing modules, described in the last section, into a three-dimensional hierarchical multiscale computer architecture, as shown in Figure 14.11. In this architecture, there are two layers: the processing layer below, and the deflecting layer on top. The processors can intercommunicate by using a standard reconfigurable mesh through the local switchable connections and also by using the reconfigurable microelectromechanical (MEMS) mirrors with free-space optical interconnects. Each of the processors contains some local memory and is attached to a nanoscale computing cube. In each cube there are nanoscale cells laid out in a three-dimensional format as shown. Each cube essentially can be the 3-D implementation of either the QCA, spin-based circuitry, or the molecular cellular automata.

The implementation of the architecture shown in Figure 14.11, using the quantum dot cellular automata logic circuitry that is quite well known from the work of researchers at Notre Dame University, has a low-temperature operation limitation. A solution to this problem could be to implement the cells using molecules, as described in the previous section. By using molecular magnetic switches, we can simulate the QCA that operates at room temperature. For more details, refer to [92].

In the QCA implementation, the computations within each QCA cube are done in a similar fashion as a standard QCA, except that the two-dimensional QCA logic circuits are laid out in three dimensions, as shown at the bottom right of Figure 14.11. In other words, the QCA blocks can be used to compute millions of logic operations locally by techniques already developed for QCA. The computations are done as the neighboring cells interact with each other through quantum tunneling effects. Once the local computations within each cube are completed, the results are forwarded to their corresponding processing units. The processors can then store the data in their local memory and/or intercommunicate with other processing units using the electronically reconfigured mesh and/or the micro-electromechanical mirrors.

It is possible to replace the QCA cubes with spin-based computational cubes. The overall operation at the architectural level is still the same. Computations are done within the cubes using quantum effects but based on spins instead of based on the polarities of the quantum cells. Once the cubes complete the computations, they send their results to their cube-designated processor, which will intercommunicate with other cubes using electro-optical interconnectivity. The cubes can also be replaced by molecular cellular automata units, where the computations within the cubes are governed by a set of rules as described in the previous section. Once the results of each cube are obtained, the operation among the MEMS-level processors proceeds via the electro-optical connectivity available.

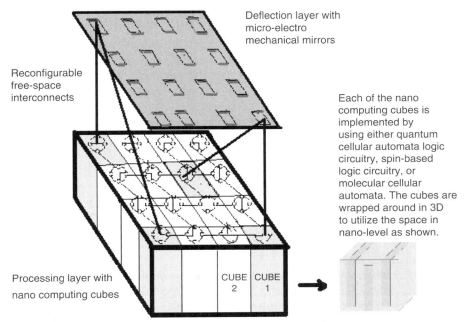

Figure 14.11. A hierarchical multiscale architecture.

Whether the cells are implemented using quantum dots, spins, and/or molecules, it is easy to see that the space-time trade-offs of this multiscale model are similar to those for three-dimensional VLSI, which is $VT^{3/2} = \Omega(I)^{3/2}$. The difference here is that the VLSI three-dimensional model was not implementable due to fabrication limitations on the number of layers, but now we have a technology that could eventually allow a 3-D construction at the nanoscale level.

4.2   Neuromorphic Architecture Design

Neuromorphic architectures, shown below, are a class of nanoelectronic circuits that exploit the charging behavior in resistively/capacitively linked arrays of nanometer-sized metallic islands (quantum dots), self-assembled on a resonant tunneling diode, to perform neuromorphic computation. These circuits produce associated memory effects and realize the additive short-term memory or content-addressable memory models of neural networks without requiring either large-area/high-power operational amplifiers or massive interconnectivity between devices. These two requirements had seriously hindered the application of neural networks in the past. Additionally, the circuits can solve NP-complete optimization problems (such as the traveling salesman problem) using single electron charge dynamics, exhibit rudimentary image-processing capability, and operate at room temperature, unlike most quantum devices. Two-dimensional (2-D) processors, with a 100×100 pixel capacity, can be fabricated in a nanoscale area. For more details, see the publication by Roychowdhury et. al. [23].

5   SELF-ASSEMBLED STRUCTURES

As anticipated, the device feature size will be reduced to the nanometer regime. Self-assembly appears to be one of the most promising techniques to reach such scales economically. However, several barriers exist. The most critical are the control of the placement, the size, the uniformity, and the placement of self-assembled nanostructures. In what follows, we talk about two different types of self-assembly. One is regular arrays of quantum dots and the other is a molecular approach.

5.1   Regular Arrays of Quantum Dots

The control of the placement of nano-islands is of high practical importance for a number of potential applications, such as quantum dot-based lasers, single-electron transistors, and quantum computers. On most occasions, the self-assembled quantum dots are randomly distributed on substrate surfaces due to the spontaneous nucleation process.

Only recently, an ordered arrangement of self-assembled nano-island has been reported [27,51]. First, Kamins et al. [27] reported that Ge dots were well aligned along the two edges of the pre-grown Si stripe mesas on patterned Si (001) substrates. Then, G. Jin et al. [51] observed a cooperative arrangement of self-assembled dots on one-dimensional (1-D) ridges of Si stripe mesas formed by selective epitaxial growth. The cooperative arrangement of Ge dots was obtained with a degree of periodicity to place the dots at the desired location – an essential requirement for information processing. Moreover, the aligned Ge dots on the ridges had a *mono*-modal distribution, in contrast with a *bi*-(even *multi*-) modal distribution of self-assembled Ge dots normally observed on planar Si (001) substrates. Figures 14.12 and 14.13 show ordered arrangement of self-assembled Ge quantum dots on selectively grown Si mesas on pattern substrates prepared with a conventional photolithography [51]. This approach enables us to realize regimented arrays of high-density nano-structures at low cost and free of defects and damages.

This approach of using substrate patterns to achieve the regimented placement also provides self-assembly of the nearest neighbor interconnects. Moreover, using tilted substrates, we are able to form regular surface steps via appropriate surface treatments, such as annealing. These regular atomic steps have been used as a template for the formation of ordered dot arrays. It is also possible to control the surface reconstruction via a surface modification to accomplish the ordering structures in an atomic scale. What has been demonstrated is just the beginning, and there are abundant opportunities to explore new principles and methods not yet discovered to achieve regimented structures for scales down to the atomic level.

5.2   Molecular Self-Assembly

An interesting alternative for circuit fabrication, when devices are scaled to a few tens of nanometers in size and smaller, is the bottom-up, self-assembly-based manufacturing approach being developed in molecular electronics research programs.

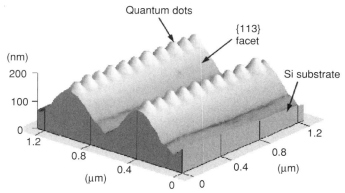

Figure 14.12. Three-dimensional AFM image of the cooperative arrangement of self-assembled Ge dots on <110>-oriented Si stripe mesas with a window width of 0.6 μm. Self-aligned and well-spaced 1D arrays of Ge dots are formed on the ridges of the Si mesas after the deposition of 10 ML Ge. The growth temperature is 630°C. The sidewall facets of the Si stripe mesas are confirmed to be {113} facets. The dimensions of the Ge islands are about 80 nm wide and about 20 nm high, and the period of the Ge islands is about 110 nm.

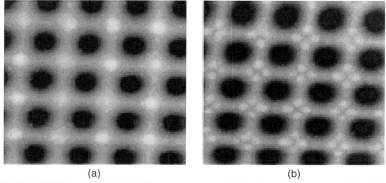

Figure 14.13. AFM images of the 2-D arrangement of Ge dots on Si mesas with different Ge amounts. (a) 0.4 nm – one dot; (b) 1.3 nm – four dots. The growth temperature is 600° C. The scale of the images is 4×4 μm^2.

However, at this time there are many challenges in developing circuitry by this approach. For example, self-assembly leads most readily to periodic structures, and, while the starting material for such approaches may be highly purified, the assembly steps themselves are unlikely to be perfect. Furthermore, various structural parameters of a circuit that are obtained through lithographic patterning, such as the length, diameter, orientation, and separation of the wires, can be substantially more difficult to control by using chemical assembly. Also, nanowires with the most desirable electrical characteristics, such as single-walled carbon nanotubes, do not necessarily have the chemical properties required for controlled self-assembly.

Single Crossbars: The relevance of the crossbar circuit for molecular electronics was first reported by Heath et al. [34]. Later a room-temperature, minimal-lithography technique for chemically assembling small deterministic crossbars of single-walled carbon nanotubes (SWNT) was presented [79]. Results indicate that it is possible to fabricate deterministic wiring networks from SWNTs by using chemical self-assembly. While this process is currently limited to the fabrication of relatively small crossbars (4 × 4 and less), preliminary results indicate that the optimization of several experimental handles may lead to the assembly of large-scale structures without requiring the use of lithographic techniques. Thus, relatively inexpensive routes toward fabricating designed circuits with characteristic dimensions on the order of a few nanometers may be possible. Three SWNT crossbars of varying structural characteristics are shown in Figure 14.14. A key result of this work is that the pitch of the crossbar was controllable and correlated with the length of the SWNT ropes. Although progress is being made, it has been difficult, up until recently, to exercise the level of control required in order to attain the

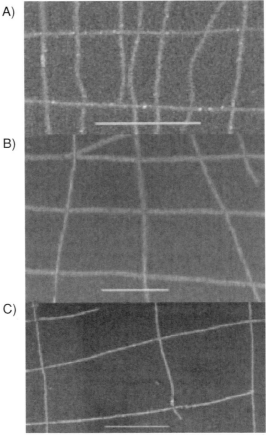

Figure 14.14. Scanning electron micrographs of SWNT crossbars with varying pitch. Scale bars are 500 nm for A) and B), and 1 μm for C). The diameter of the ropes is not well measured with this technique, but can be measured with force microscopy. The shortest (500 nm) wires are characterized by diameters of 1–2 nm, while the longest (20μm) wires possess diameters ranging from 10 to 15 nm. SWNT rope lengths [μm]: A) 3.7 ± 0.3 & 1.2 ± 0.33; B) 2.8 ± 0.53; C) 3.8 ± 1.2.

required density and complexity by utilizing processes that are amenable to large-scale manufacture. Lieber's group has demonstrated the large-scale alignment and multilevel fabrication of ultra-high-density Si nanowire elements for electronic applications [99]. The precise alignment of the nanowires was provided by the self-organizational principle inherent in large-aspect ratio wires orienting at the air–water interface, like the timber in a log run. These arrays of nanowires, deposited as LB films and patterned using lithographic techniques, form the basis for one class of circuitry based on crossbars.

The crossbar junction represents one of the simplest elements that can be considered as an active device when the two wires are separated by an insulating dielectric or a molecular switch. Bistable nanotube mechanical junctions [66], as well as various EME junction devices–diodes [98], molecular switch tunnel junctions [62], and junctions exhibiting negative differential resistance [65], have all been demonstrated at the device level.

The opportunity to build functional electronic components from semiconducting nanowires offers ultra-high-density circuitry, which has been facilitated by recent advances in nanowire fabrication. Lieber has developed a method for growing nanowires that provide the ability to modulate the doping along a Si nanowire between high and low levels [95]. In addition, nanowires can be grown with core shell structures [81] from two different materials, wherein the sheath can be removed, exposing the inner core. While these new classes of nanowires provide a similar level of nanometer-scaled control over the electronic structure, which is displayed in molecular electronic components, they do not display the facility to undergo a molecule's geometry rearrangements. When these highly structured nanomaterials are coupled with the new handling techniques for laying down nanowires in a controlled way using the LB method, the door to a new class of nanoelectronic devices founded on custom-designed nanowires may be opening.

Crossbar Networks: During the development of nanometer scale switches, traditional circuit designs may not be able to take maximum advantage of the unique properties and scale conferred. Consequently, the crossbar junction appears to be the basis from which to consider (see Figure 14.15) higher levels of complexity for the formation of crossbar networks. It is possible to conceive of different schemes to design 1-D [48, 69, 71] or 2-D networks for memory or logic purposes.

The state-of-the-art crossbar networks are tiled in 2-D, in which each crossbar is a two-terminal switching device. This higher level of complexity in circuit design sets one fundamental limitation: each crossbar has to be independently addressable. In cases where the 2-D networks have been fabricated in the past, as in ferroelectric [18] and magnetoresistive [56] crosspoint memories, the key issue has been that of half-select. In a crossbar network, each wire crosses many others at their crosspoints and this can lead to a situation where switches are incorrectly selected. However, when a rotaxane-based molecular switch is used at the crossbar, half select is no longer a problem. The bistable molecular switches are voltage gated, which means that only those crosspoints that are defined by a potential difference, which exceeds a certain threshold voltage, will lead to an addressed crosspoint. All the other wires crossing the two that are used to address the crosspoint of interest are below the switching threshold and are therefore not mistakenly switched. Through use of bistable [2] rotaxane-based molecular switches, it has been possible to generate a memory array and to perform simple logic such as an AND or XOR gate [82].

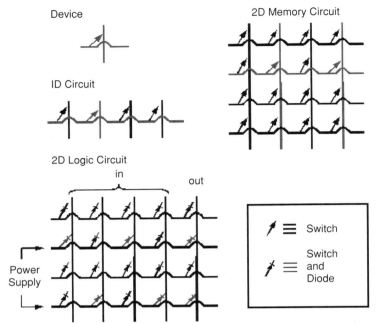

Figure 14.15. It is possible to utilize a crossbar in increasing levels of complexity to attain memory and perform logic. The crossbar networks can be composed of switches or diodes, in which molecules may provide the key active component in order to realize such devices. (Adapted from [82].)

6   DESIGN ISSUES AND CHALLENGES

In this section, we talk about the design issues and challenges in nanoscale and molecular computing architectures.

6.1   Unidirectionality Issues

A major drawback of the proposals for logic implementations based on bistable devices without directionality such as the QCA lies in their failure to ensure propagation of the logic signal from the input to the output. That is, if two bistable devices are connected together in series, then there must be some isolation between the input and output so that the input drives the output and not the reverse. Coulomb interactions between two identical charge polarizations are reciprocal, so it is impossible to distinguish the input polarization from the output polarization. In other words, the output influences the input just as much as the input influences the output. Consequently, logic signals cannot propagate unidirectionally from the input to the output, from one stage to the next, leading to an operational failure. This occurs because the input cannot uniquely and predictably determine the output. This problem is pathological in many proposed schemes of nano-electronic architecture: one needs to ensure that the signals propagate from the input to the outputs and that the whole system does not get stuck in metastable states. For more details, see the article by Anantrand and Roychowdhury [46].

On the other hand, the cellular automata-based architectures with local connectivity also have shortcomings: they offer no mechanism for loading the initial program into the cellular array of quantum devices. As a result, they are also of questionable efficacy.

In neuromorphic schemes, unidirectional signal propagation from the input to the output is effected through a *clocking mechanism*. For example, when the OR gates in the first layer are operational, the AND gate in the succeeding stage is disabled. Once the OR gates have reached stable states, then a clock pulse is applied to initialize the AND gate. This scheme avoids the potential problem of the AND gate acting as an input to the OR gates, and instead allows the OR gates to drive the AND gate. The same strategy can be extended to the case of multi-level circuits. Such a scheme of multiphase clocking ("push-clock" and "drop-clock") is also used in conventional charge-coupled devices (CCDs). Moreover, this multiphase clocking scheme will enable *pipelining*. That is, every other level in a multilevel circuit can operate simultaneously, and a new set of inputs can be fed to the circuit every other clock cycle. This setup allows the implementation of a high throughput logic block.

6.2 Fault-Tolerant Designs

In order to replace conventional CMOS circuits with nanoscale devices, we first have to demonstrate nano-devices with combined memory and logic functions. Recent investigations suggest that "smart molecules" could be a possible first step toward constructing molecular nanoscale computing modules. To date, the unprecedented accuracy required for positioning single molecules into an array of growing, perfectly ordered quantum dots to form a controlled array is a road block for practical realization of the proposed schemes. In general, any attempt to construct a large number of identically operating devices integrated on a large scale usually suffers from inevitable material imperfections. Potentially, this problem may be resolved by progress in advanced fabrication techniques (for example, a high level of self-assembly). Another possible solution is the use of fault tolerance or self-correction mechanisms to allow for faults in logic functionalities, rather than simply working toward perfecting fabrication processes [19, 23, 30]. Clearly, progress in both areas will be helpful.

Any computational architecture at the nanoscale level should display inherent fault-tolerant properties. Nanostructure devices will probably have more variability in their characteristics than their earlier-generation microstructure counterparts. Any scheme that ignores this fact and relies on every quantum dot being perfect will almost inevitably be impractical. In order to ensure fault tolerance, one can allow a cluster of islands to represent a gate, rather than a single dot or just a few dots. Note that the size of the arrays for each gate can be varied depending on the state of the technology. By providing larger arrays, one can increase fault tolerance.

6.3   Challenges of Molecular Computing

There are a number of issues facing the emerging field of molecular electronics that need to be addressed. At a fundamental level, bistable [2] rotaxane-based switches are believed to permit electron transport primarily by tunneling through quantized energy levels. Consequently, by tuning the molecular subunits that constitute the rotaxanes, it may be possible to enhance the on/off current ratio and therefore widen the areas of applicability of molecular computing. One other key area relates to how exactly molecular electronic components can be fully harnessed by employing unique computer circuits. This is a salient thesis in this chapter, and therefore an integrated systems-oriented approach forms a central feature and returns the problem to one of interdisciplinary description–what are molecular properties, and how do they impact on the architecture? The driving force to face this challenge may be provided less by fundamental discovery than by market forces. This situation is not unfamiliar in the area of electronics, where it is Moore's Law that has guided scientists and engineers alike into the molecular and quantum domains.

7   CONCLUSION

In this chapter, we have presented an overview of various nanoscale and molecular computing architectures. We have given a brief tutorial on various existing nanoscale and molecular devices. These include molecular switches, resonant tunnel diodes, tunnel diodes, single electron transistors, carbon nanotube field-effect transistors, quantum dots, and spin systems. We have next discussed a set of nanoscale computing modules, such as quantum and spin-based cellular logic arrays, and molecular-based cellular automata, all made from the switches presented here. These modules are an integral part of the hierarchical 3-D multi-scale architecture presented. We have also showed a set of quantum and molecular self-assembled structures including molecular crossbars. The fabrication of these architectures currently faces a number of challenges, as discussed in this chapter. Nanoscale and molecular computing is a promising alternative to today's CMOS technology but is in an infancy stage, with many interesting design issues yet to be studied and resolved.

ACKNOWLEGMENTS

We acknowledge with great thanks Dr. Vwani Roychowdhry for his contributions as a consultant to this project.

REFERENCES

[1] [1960-01] E. Goto, K. Mutara, K. Nakazawa, T. Moto-Oka, Y. Matsuoka, Y. Ishibashi, T. Soma, and E. Wada. (1960): Esaki diode high speed logical circuits, *IRE Transactions on Electronics and Computing 9*, 25.

[2] [1970-01] L. Esaki and R. Tsu (1970): Superlattice and negative differential conductivity in semiconductors, IBM *Journal of Research and Development 14*, 61.

[3] [1973-01] L.L. Chang, L. Esaki, W.E. Hpoward, and R. Ludeke (1973): Structures grown by molecular beam epitaxy (GaAs and GaAs-Ga/sub 1-x/Al/sub x/As), *Journal of Vac. Science and Technology 10*, 11, 9.

[4] [1974-01] L.L. Chang, L. Esaki, and R. Tsu (1974): Resonant tunneling in semiconductor double barriers, *Applied Physics Letters 24*, 593.

[5] [1976-01] J. Holland (1976): Studies of the spontaneous emergence of self-replicating systems using cellular automata and formal grammars, *in Automata Languages Development,* North-Holland Publishing Co., Amsterdam, The Netherlands, pp. 385.

[6] [1987-01] V.J. Goldman, D.C. Tsui, and J.E. Cunningham (1987): Observation of intrinsic bistability in resonant-tunneling structures, *Physical Review Letters 58*, 1256.

[7] [1990-01] A. Miura, T. Yakihara, S. Uchida, S. Oka, S. Kobayashi, H. Kamada, and M. Dobashi (1990): Monolithic sampling head IC, *IEEE Trans. Microwave Theory and Technology 38*, 1980.

[8] [1991-01] A. Ulman (1991): An Introduction to Ultrathin Organic Films from Langmuir-Blodgett to Self-assembly, Academic Press, San Diego.

[9] [1992-01] B.C. Crandall and J. Lewis (1992): Nanotechnology Research and Perspectives, The MIT Press Cambridge, pp. 149–170.

[10] [1992-02] Y.-C. Kao, A.C. Seabaugh, and H.-T. Yuan (1992): Vertical integration of structured resonant tunneling diodes on InP for multi-valued memory applications, *Int. Conference on Indium Phosphide and Related Materials 489.*

[11] [1992-03] J.R. Tucker (1992): Complementary digital logic based on the `Coulomb blockade,' *Journal of Applied Physics*, 72, 4399.

[12] [1993-01] C.S. Lent, P.D. Togaw, and W. Porod (1993): Bistable saturation in coupled quantum dots for quantum cellular automata, *Applied Physics Letters 62*, 714.

[13] [1993-02] K. Yano, T. Ishii, T. Hashimoto, T. Kobayashi, F. Murai, and K. Seki (1993): A room-temperature single-electron memory device using fine-grain polycrystalline silicon, *IEDM Technical Digest 541.*

[14] [1994-01] P. Balasingam and V.P. Roychowdhury (1994): Nanoelectronic functional devices, Purdue University Technical Report: TR-EE 94-24.

[15] [1994-02] K. Maezawa, T. Akeyoshi and T. Mizutani (1994): Functions and applications of monostable-bistable transition logic elements (MOBILE's) having multiple-input terminals, *IEEE Transactions On Electron Devices 41*, 148.

[16] [1995-01] T.K. Carns, X. Zheng, and K.L. Wang (1995): A novel high speed, three element Si-based static random memory (SRAM) cell, *IEEE Electron Device Letters 16*, 256.

[17] [1995-02] K. Itoh, K. Sasaki, and Y. Nakagome (1995): Trends in low-power RAM circuit technologies, *Proceedings of IEEE 83*, 524.

[18] [1995-03] R.E. Jones, Jr., P.D. Maniar, R. Moazzami, P. Zurcher, J.Z. Witowski, Y.T. Lii, P. Chu, and S.J. Gillispie (1995): Ferroelectric non-volatile memories for low-voltage, low-power applications, *Thin Solid Films 270*, 584.

[19] [1996-01] S. Bandyopadhyay and V.P. Roychowdhury (1996): Computational paradigms in nanoelectronics: quantum coupled single electron logic and neuromorphic networks, *Japan. J. Appl. Phys. 35*, 3350.

[20] [1996-02] S. Bandyopodhyay and V.P. Roychowdhury (1996): Granular nanoelectronics: The logical gateway to the 21st Century, *IEEE Potentials*.

[21] [1996-03] E.R. Brown and C.D. Parker (1996): Resonant tunnel diodes as submillimetre-wave sources, *Philos. Trans. R. Soc. London, Ser. A 354*, 2365.

[22] [1996-04] J.Koga and A. Toriumi (1996): Room temperature negative differential conductance in three-terminal silicon surface tunneling device, *IEDM Technical Digest 265*.

[23] [1996-05] V.P. Roychowdhury, D.B. Janes, S. Bandyopadhyay, and X. Wang (1996): Collective computational activity in self-assembled arrays of quantum dots: a novel neuromorphic architecture for nanoelectronics, *IEEE Transactions on Electron Devices 43*, 1688.

[24] [1997-01] D. Goldhaber-Gordon, M.S. Montermerlo, J.C. Love, G.J. Opiteck, and J.C. Ellenbogen (1997): Overview of nanoelectronic devices, *Proceedings of IEEE*.

[25] [1997-02] J. Jortner and M. Ratner (1997): Molecular Electronics, Oxford, U.K.

[26] [1997-03] T.I. Kamins, E.C. Carr, R.S. Williams, and S.J. Rosner (1997): Deposition of three-dimensional Ge islands on Si(001) by chemical vapor deposition at atmospheric and reduced pressures, *Journal of Applied Physics 81*, 211.

[27] [1997-04] T.I. Kamins and R.S. Williams (1997): Lithographic positioning of self-assembled Ge islands on Si(001), *Physical Letters 71*, 1201.

[28] [1997-05] S.J. Koester, K. Ismail, K.Y. Lee, and J.O. Chua (1997): Operation of a novel negative differential conductance transistor fabricated in a strained Si quantum well, *IEEE Electron Device Letters 118*, 432.

[29] [1997-06] K. Morita, K. Morimoto, H. Sorada, K. Araki, K. Yuki, M. Niwa, T. Uenoyama, and K. Ohnaka (1997): Si interband tunnelling diode through a thin oxide with a degenerate poly-Si electrode, *in Extended Abstracts from the 3rd International Workshop Quantum Functional Devices 175*.

[30] [1997-07] V.P. Roychowdry, D.B. Janes and S. Bandyopadhyay (1997): Nanoelectronic architecture for Boolean logic, *Proc. IEEE 85*, 574.

[31] [1997-08] A. Seabaugh, B. Brar, T. Broekaert, G. Frazier, P. van der Wagt, and E. Beam (1997): Resonant tunneling circuit technology: has it arrived?, *GaAs IC Symposium and Technology Digest 119*.

[32] [1997-09] J.J. Welser, S. Tiwari, S. Rishton, K.Y. Lee, and Y. Lee (1997): Room temperature operation of a quantum-dot flash memory, *IEEE Electron Devices Letters 18*, 278.

[33] [1997-10] X. Zhu, X. Zheng, M. Pak, M.O. Tanner, and K.L. Wang (1997): Si bistable diode utilizing interband tunneling junctions, *Applied Phyics Letters 71*, 2190.

[34] [1998-01] J.R. Heath, P.J. Kuekes, G.S. Snider, R.S. Williams (1998): A defect tolerant computer architecture: Opportunities for nanotechnology, *Science 280*, 1716.

[35] [1998-02] K.M. Horn, B.S. Swartzentruber, G.C. Osbourn, A. Bouchard, and J.W. Bartholomew (1998): Electronic structure classifications using scanning tunneling microscopy conductance imaging, *Journal of Applied Physics 84*, 2487.

[36] [1998-03] B.E. Kane (1998): A silicon-based nuclear spin quantum computer, *Nature 393*, 133.

[37] [1998-04] C.H. Lin, K. Yang, M. Bhattacharya, X. Wang, X. Zhang, J.R. East, P. Mazumder, and G.I. Haddad (1998): Monolithically integrated InP-based minority logic gate using an RTD/HBT heterostructure, *International Conference on Indium Phosphide and Related Materials 419*.

[38] [1998-05] R. Martel, T. Schmidt, H.R. Sea, T. Hertel, and P. Avouris (1998): Single- and multi-wall carbon nanotube field-effect transistors, *Applied Physics Letters 73*, 2447.

[39] [1998-06] J.H. Reif (1998): Alternative computational models: A comparison of biomolecular and quantum computation, *Proceeding of the 18th International Conference on Foundations of Software Technology and Theoretical Computer Science*.

[40] [1998-07] M. Rodder, S. Hattangady, N. Yu, W. Shiau, P. Nicolllian, T. Laaksonen, C.P. Chao, M. Mehrota, C. Lee, S. Murtaza, and S. Aur (1998): IEDM Tech. Dig. 623.

[41] [1998-08] A.C. Seabaugh and R. Lake (1998): Beyond-the-roadmap technology: Silicon heterojunctions, optoelectronics, and quantum devices, *Encyclopedia of Physics 22*, 335.

[42] [1998-09] J.P. Sun, G.I. Haddad, P. Mazumder, and J.N. Shulman (1998): Resonant tunneling diodes: models and properties, *Proceedings of IEEE 86*, 641.

[43] [1998-10] S.J. Tans, R.M. Verschueren, and C Dekker (1998): Room temperature transistor based on a single carbon nanotube, *Nature 393*, 49.

[44] [1998-11] J.P.A. van der Wagt, A.C. Seabaugh, and E.A. Beam (1998): RTD/HFET low standby power SRAM gain cell, *IEEE Electron Device Letters 19*, 7.

[45] [1998-12] T. Waho, T. Itoh, and M. Yamamoto (1998): Ultrahigh-speed resonant tunneling circuits, *in Second International Workshop on Physics and Modeling of Devices based on Low-Dimensional Structures,* p.73.

[46] [1999-01] M.P. Anantram and V.P. Roychowdhury (1999): Metastable states and information propagation in a one-dimensional array of locally coupled bistable cells, *Journal of Applied Physics 85*.

[47] [1999-02] J. Chen, M.A. Reed, A.M. Rawlett, and J.M. Tour (1999): Large on-off ratios and negative differential resistance in a molecular electronic device, *Science 286*, 1550.

[48] [1999-03] C.P. Collier, E.W. Wong, M. Belohradsky, F.M. Raymo, J. F. Stoddart, P.J. Kuekes, R.S. Williams, and J. R. Heath (1999): Electronically configurable molecular-based logic gates, *Science 285*, 391.

[49] [1999-04] K. Esfarjani, A.A. Farajian, Y. Hashi, and Y. Kawazoe (1999): Electronic and transport properties of N-P doped nanotubes, *Applied Physics Letters 74*, 79.

[50] [1999-05] A.A. Farajian, K. Esfarjani, and Y. Kawazoe (1999): Nonlinear coherent transport through doped nanotube junctions, *Physical Review Letters 82*, 5084.

[51] [1999-06] G. Jin, J. L. Liu, S. G. Thomas, Y. H. Luo, K. L. Wang, and B. Y. Nguyen (1999): Controlled arrangement of self-organized Ge islands on patterned Si (001) substrates, *Applied Phyiscs Letters 75*, 2752.

[52] [1999-07] F. Leonard and J. Tersoff (1999): Novel length scales in nanotube devices, *Physical Review Letters 83*, 5174.

[53] [1999-08] K. Likharev (1999): Single-electron devices and their applications, *Proceedings of IEEE*, 87.

[54] [1999-09] J. Nygard, D.H. Cobden, M. Bockrath, P.L. McEuen, and P.E. Lindelof (1999): Electrical transport measurements on single-walled carbon nanotubes, *Applied. Physics A 69*, 297.

[55] [1999-10] Y. Ono, Y. Takahashi, K. Yamazaki, H. Namatsu, K. Kurihara, and K. Murase (1999): Si complementary single-electron inverter, *IEDM Technical Digest 367*.

[56] [1999-11] S.S.P. Parkin, K.P. Roche, M.G. Samant, P.M. Rice, R.B. Beyers, R.E. Scheuerlein, E.J. O'Sullivan, S.L. Brown, J. Bucchigano, D.W. Abraham, Y. Lu, M. Rooks, P.L. Trouilloud, R.A. Wanner, and W.J. Gallagher (1999): Exchange-biased magnetic tunnel junctions and application to nonvolatile magnetic random access memory, *J. Appl. Phys. 85*, 5828.

[57] [1999-12] G. Snider, A. Orlov, I. Amlani, X. Zuo, G. B. Stein, C. Lent, J. Mez, and W. Porod (1999): Quantum-dot cellular automata, *Journal of Applied Physics*.

[58] [1999-13] H.T. Soh, C.F. Quate, A.F. Morpurgo, C.M. Marcus, J. Kong, and H. Dai (1999): Integrated nanotube circuits: Controlled growth and ohmic contacting of single-walled carbon nanotubes, *Appl. Phys. Lett. 75*, 627.

[59] [1999-14] A.S. Vedeneev, J. Li, C. Papadopoulos, A. Rakitin, A.J. Bennett, H.W. Chik, and J.M. Xu (1999): Molecular-scale rectifying diodes based on Y-junction carbon nanotubes, *Proceedings of IEDM 231*.

[60] [1999-15] J.P.A. van der Wagt (1999): Tunneling-based SRAM, *Proceedings of IEEE, 87*, 571.

[61] [1999-16] K. Yano, T. Ishii, T. Sano, T. Mine, F. Muri, T. Hashimoto, T. Kobayashi, T. Kure, and K Seki (1999): Single-electron memory for giga-to-tera bit storage, *Proceedings of IEEE 87*, 633.

[62] [2000-01] C.P. Collier, G. Mattersteig, E.W. Wong, Y. Luo, K. Beverly, J. Sampaio, F.M. Raymo, J.F. Stoddart, and J.R. Heath (2000): A [2]catenane-based solid state electronically reconfigurable switch, *Science 289*, 1172.

[63] [2000-02] F. Leonard and J. Tersoff (2000): Negative differential resistance in nanotube devices, *Physical Review Letters 85*, 4767.

[64] [2000-03] Y. Ono and Y. Takahashi (2000): Single-electron pass-transistor logic: operation of its elemental circuit, *IEDM Technical Digest 297*.

[65] [2000-04] M.A. Reed and J.M. Tour (2000): Computing with molecules, *Sci. Am. 282*, 86.

[66] [2000-05] T. Rueckes, K. Kim, E. Joselevich, G.Y. Tseng, C.-L. Cheung, and C.M. Lieber (2000): Carbon nanotube-based nonvolatile random access memory for molecular computing, *Science 289*, 94.

[67] [2000-06] Y. Takahashi, A. Fujiwara, K. Yamazaki, H. Namtsu, K. Kurihara, and K.Murase (2000): Multigate single-electron transistors and their application to an exclusive-OR gate, *Applied Physics Letters 76*, 637.

[68] [2000-07] M. Wilson, K. Kannangara, G. Smith, M. Simmons, B. Raguse (2000): Nanotechnology, Basic Science and Emerging Technologies, Chapman & Hall/CRC.

[69] [2001-01] A. Bachtold, P. Hadley, T. Nakanaishi, and C. Dekker (2001): Logic circuits with carbon nanotube transistors, *Science 294*, 1317.

[70] [2001-02] M. Hanggi and L.O. Chua (2001): Cellular neural networks based on resonant tunneling diodes, *Int. Journal of Circuit Theory and Applications 29*, 487.

[71] [2001-03] Y. Huang, X. Duan, Y. Cui, L. J. Lauhon, K.-H. Kim, and C.M. Lieber (2001): Logic gates and computation from assembled nanowire building blocks, *Science 294*, 1313.

[72] [2001-04] D.H. Kim, S.-K. Sung, J.S. Sim, K.R. Kim, J.D. Lee, B.-G. Park, B.H. Choi, S.W. Hwang, and D. Ahn (2001): Single-electron transistor based on a silicon-on-insulator quantum wire fabricated by a side-wall patterning method, *Appl. Phys. Lett. 79*, 3812.

[73] [2001-05] R. Martel, V. Derycke, C. Lavoie, J. Appenzeller, K.K. Chan, J. Tersoff, and P. Avouris (2001): Ambipolar electrical transport in semiconducting single-wall carbon nanotubes, *Physics Review Letters 87*, 256805.

[74] [2001-06] R. Martel, H.-S.P. Wong, K. Chan, and P. Avouris (2001): Carbon nanotube field effect transistors for logic applications, *International Electron Devices Meeting. Technical Digest* (Cat. No.01CH37224) IEEE 751.

[75] [2001-07] M.T. Niemier and Peter Kogge (2001): Exploring and exploiting wire-level pipelining in emerging technologies, *28th Annual Symposium on Computer Architecture*.

[76] [2001-08] M.A. Reed, J. Chen, A.M. Rawlett, D.W. Price, and J.M. Tour (2001): Molecular random access memory cell, *Appl. Phys. Lett. 78*, 3735.

[77] [2001-09] P. See, D.J. Paul, B. Hollander, S. Mantl, I.V. Zozoulenko, and K.-F. Berggren (2001): High performance Si/Si/sub 1-x/Ge/sub x/ resonant tunneling diodes, *IEEE Electron Device Letters 22*, 182.

[78] [2002-01] D.D. Awschalom, M.E. Flatté, and N. Samarth (2002): Spintronics, *Scientific American,* May.

[79] [2002-02] M.R. Diehl, S.N. Yaliraki, R.A. Beckman, M. Barohona, and J.R. Heath (2002): Self-assembled, deterministic carbon nanotube wiring networks, *Angew. Chem. Int. Ed. 41*.

[80] [2002-03] A.Y. Kitaev, A.H. Shen, and M.N. Vyalyi (2002): Classical and quantum computation, *American Mathematical Society*.

[81] [2002-04] L.J. Lauhon, M.S. Gudiksen, C.L. Wang, and C.M. Lieber (2002): Epitaxial core-shell and core-multishell nanowire heterostructures, *Nature 420*, 57.

[82] [2002-05] Y. Luo, C.P. Collier, J.O. Jeppesen, K.A. Nielsen, E. DeIonno, G. Ho, J. Perkins, H.-R. Tseng, T. Yamamoto, J.F. Stoddart, and J.R. Heath

(2002): Two-dimensional molecular electronics circuits, *ChemPhysChem 3*, 519.

[83] [2002-06] S.E. Lyshevski (2002): MEMS and NEMS, Systems, Devices, and Structures, CRC Press.

[84] [2002-07] J.K. Mbdindyo, T.E. Mallouk, J.B. Mattzela, I. Kratochvilova, B. Razavi, T.N. Jackson, and T.S. Mayer (2002): Template synthesis of metal nanowires containing monolayer molecular junctions, *J. Am. Chem. Soc. 124*, 4020.

[85] [2002-08] M.J. Krawczyk, K. Kulakowski, and A.Z. Maksymowicz (2002): New cellular automaton designed to simulate geometration in gel electrophoresis, Elsevier, *Computer Physics Communications 147*, 1-2(1), 354–7, Netherlands.

[86] [2002-09] T. Yang, R.A. Kiehl, and L.O. Chua (2002): Chaos in circuits and systems, *World Scientific*, pp. 577-91.

[87] [2003-01] G. Bourianoff (2003): The future of nanocomputing, *IEEE Computer, August.*

[88] [2003-02] Y. Chen, G.-Y Jung, D.A.A. Ohlberg, X. Li, D.R. Stewart, J.O. Jeppesen, K.A. Nielsen, J.F. Stoddart, and R.S. Williams (2003): Nanoscale molecular-switch crossbar circuits, *Nanotechnology 14*, 462.

[89] [2003-03] Y. Chen, D.A.A. Ohlberg, X. Li, D.R. Stewart, R.S. Williams, J.O. Jeppesen, K.A. Neilsen, J.F. Stoddart, D.L. Olynick, and E. Anderson (2003): Nanoscale molecular-switch devices fabricated by imprint lithography, *Appl. Phys. Lett. 82*, 1610.

[90] [2003-04] W. Deng and W. A. Goddard, Ab initio simulation of the Heath-Stoddart electronic devices *J. Am. Chem. Soc., submitted.*

[91] [2003-05] M.R. Diehl, D.W. Steuerman, H.-R. Tseng, S.A. Vignon, A. Star, P.C. Celestre, J.F. Stoddart, and J.R. Heath (2003): Single-walled carbon nanotube-based molecular switch tunnel junctions, *ChemPhysChem 4*, 1335.

[92] [2003-06] M.M. Esahghian (2003): Nanoscale Ccomputing structures, *Proceedings of the 7th World Multi-conference on Systemics, Cybernetics, and Informatics, SCI2003*, Florida, July.

[93] [2003-07] J.R. Heath and M.A. Ratner (2003): Molecular electronics, *Physics Today*, May, 43.

[94] [2003-08] A. Khitun, S. Hong, and K.L. Wang (2003): Semiconductor tunneling structure with self-assembled quantum dots for multi-logic cellular automata module, *SPIE-International Society Optical Engineering, Proceedings of SPIE 5023*, pp.445-8.

[95] [2003-09] C.M. Lieber (2003): Presentation at the DARPA PI Review Meeting for the Moletronics Program, Virginia.

[96] [2003-10] Y. Luo, H.-R. Tseng, D.W. Steuerman, J. F. Stoddart, and J. R. Heath, Conservation of molecular mechanisms in solution, half devices and full devices, *Angew. Chemie Int. Ed.*, manuscript in preparation.

[97] [2003-11] R.M. Metzger (2003): Unimolecular electrical electrical rectifiers, *Chem. Rev. 103*, 3803.

[98] [2003-12] H.-R. Tseng, D. Wu, N. Fang, X. Zhang, and J.F. Stoddart (2003): Nanoelectromechanical switching in a self-assembled monolayer of [2]rotaxanes on gold, *ChemPhysChem*, in press.

[99] [2003-13] D. Whang, S. Jin, Y. Wu, and C.M. Lieber (2003): Large-scale hierarchical organization of nanowire arrays for integrated nanosystems, *Nano Lett. 3*, 1255.

[100] [2003-14] R.S. Williams (2003): Presentation at the DARPA PI Review Meeting for the Moletronics Program, VA.

[101] [2003-15] H. Yu, Y. Luo, K Beverly, J.F. Stoddart, H.-R. Tseng, and J.R. Heath (2003): The molecule-electrode interface in single-molecule transistors, *Angew. Chemie Int. Ed. 42*, 5706.

Chapter 15

TRENDS IN HIGH-PERFORMANCE COMPUTING

Jack Dongarra

University of Tennessee and Oak Ridge
National Laboratory

1   HISTORICAL PERSPECTIVE

In last 50 years, the field of scientific computing has undergone rapid change—
we have experienced a remarkable turnover of technologies, architectures, vendors,
and the usage of systems. Despite all these changes, the long-term evolution of performance seems to be steady and continuous, following Moore's Law rather closely.
In 1965 Gordon Moore, one of the founders of Intel, conjectured that the number
of transistors per square inch on integrated circuits would roughly double every year.
It turns out that the frequency of doubling is not 12 months, but roughly 18 months
[8]. Moore predicted that this trend would continue for the foreseeable future. In
Figure 15.1, we plot the peak performance over the last five decades of computers
that have been called *supercomputers*. A broad definition for a supercomputer is that
it is one of the fastest computers currently available. These are systems that provide
significantly greater sustained performance than that available from mainstream
computer systems. The value of supercomputers derives from the value of the problems they solve, not from the innovative technology they showcase. By performance
we mean the rate of execution for floating-point operations. Here we chart KFlop/s
(Kiloflop/s, thousands of floating-point operations per second), MFlop/s
(Megaflop/s, millions of floating-point operations per second), GFlop/s (Gigaflop/s,
billions of floating–point operations per second), TFlop/s (Teraflop/s, trillions
of floating-point operations per second), and PFlop/s (Petaflop/s, 1,000 trillions of
floating-point operations per second). This chart shows clearly how well Moore's
Law has held up over almost the complete lifespan of modern computing—we see
an increase in performance averaging two orders of magnitude every decade.

In the second half of the 1970s, the introduction of vector computer systems
marked the beginning of modern supercomputing. A vector computer or vector
processor is a machine designed to efficiently handle arithmetic operations on
elements of arrays, called *vectors*. These systems offered a performance advantage

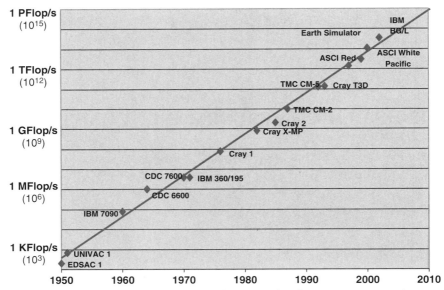

Figure 15.1. Moore's Law and peak performance of various computers over time.

of at least one order of magnitude over conventional systems of that time. Raw performance was the main, if not the only, selling point for supercomputers of this variety. However, in the first half of the 1980s, the integration of vector systems into conventional computing environments became more important. Only those manufacturers that provided standard programming environments, operating systems, and key applications were successful in getting the industrial customers that became essential for survival in the marketplace. Performance was increased primarily by improved chip technologies and by producing shared-memory multiprocessor systems, sometimes referred to as *symmetric multiprocessors* or *SMPs*. An SMP is a computer system that has two or more processors connected in the same cabinet, managed by one operating system, sharing the same memory, and having equal access to input/output devices. Application programs may run on any or all processors in the system; assignment of tasks is decided by the operating system. One advantage of SMP systems is scalability; additional processors can be added as needed up to some limiting factor determined by the rate at which data can be sent to and from memory.

Fostered by several government programs, scalable parallel computing using distributed memory became the focus of interest at the end of the 1980s. A distributed memory computer system is one in which several interconnected computers share the computing tasks assigned to the system. Overcoming the hardware scalability limitations of shared memory was the main goal of these new systems. The increase of performance of standard microprocessors after the Reduced Instruction Set Computer (RISC) revolution, together with the cost advantage of large-scale parallelism, formed the basis for the "Attack of the Killer Micros." The transition from Emitted Coupled Logic (ECL) to Complementary Metal-Oxide Semiconductor (CMOS) chip technology and the usage of "off the shelf" commodity microprocessors instead of custom processors for Massively Parallel Processors or MPPs was the consequence. The strict definition of an MPP is a machine with many interconnected processors, where "many" is dependent on the state of the art. Currently, the majority of high-end machines have fewer than 256 processors, with the highest number on the order of 10,000 processors. A more practical definition of an MPP is a machine whose architecture is capable of having many processors—that is, it is scalable. In particular, machines with a distributed memory design (in comparison with shared memory designs) are usually synonymous with MPPs, since they are not limited to a certain number of processors. In this sense, "many" is a number larger than the current largest number of processors in a shared-memory machine.

2   STATE OF SYSTEMS TODAY

The acceptance of MPP systems not only for engineering applications but also for new commercial applications, especially for database applications, emphasized different criteria for market success, such as stability of the system, continuity of the manufacturer, and price/performance. Success in commercial environments is now a new, important requirement for a successful supercomputer business. Due to these factors and the consolidation in the number of vendors in the market, hierarchical systems built with components designed for the broader commercial market are currently replacing homogeneous systems at the very high end of performance. Clusters built with off-the-shelf components are also gaining more and more attention. A cluster is a commonly found computing environment consisting of many PCs or workstations connected together by a local area network. The PCs and workstations, which have become increasingly powerful over the years, can together be viewed as a significant computing resource. This resource is commonly known as a cluster of PCs or workstations and can be generalized to a heterogeneous collection of machines with arbitrary architecture.

At the beginning of the 1990s, while the multiprocessor vector systems reached their widest distribution, a new generation of MPP systems came on the market, claiming to equal or even surpass the performance of vector multiprocessors. To provide a more reliable basis for statistics on high-performance computers, the Top500 [4] list was begun. This report lists the sites that have the 500 most powerful installed computer systems. The best LINPACK benchmark performance [9] achieved is used as a performance measure to rank the computers. The Top500 list has been updated twice a year since June 1993. In the first Top500 list in June 1993, there were already 156 MPP and SIMD systems present (31% of the total 500 systems).

The year 1995 saw remarkable changes in the distribution of the systems in the Top500 according to customer types (academic sites, research labs, industrial/commercial users, vendor installations, and confidential sites). Until June 1995, the trend in the Top500 data was a steady decrease of industrial customers, matched by an increase in the number of government-funded research sites. This trend reflects the influence of governmental High Performance Computing (HPC) programs that made it possible for research sites to buy parallel systems, especially systems with distributed memory. Industry was understandably reluctant to follow this path, since systems with distributed memory have often been far from mature or stable. Hence, industrial customers stayed with their older vector systems, which gradually dropped off the Top500 list because of low performance (see Figure 15.2).

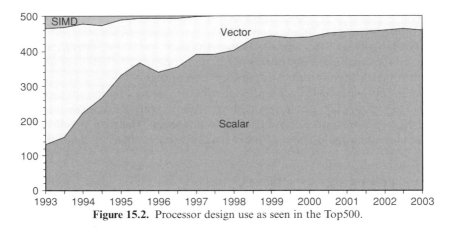

Figure 15.2. Processor design use as seen in the Top500.

Beginning in 1994, however, companies such as SGI, Digital, and Sun began selling symmetric multiprocessor (SMP) models in their workstation families. From the very beginning, these systems were popular with industrial customers because of the maturity of the architecture and their superior price/performance ratio. At the same time, IBM SP systems began to appear at a reasonable number of industrial sites. While the IBM SP was initially intended for numerically intensive applications, in the second half of 1995 the system began selling successfully to a larger commercial market, with dedicated database systems representing a particularly important component of sales.

It is instructive to compare the growth rates of the performance of machines at fixed positions in the Top500 list with those predicted by Moore's Law. To make this comparison, we separate the influence of increasing processor performance and that of the increasing number of processors per system on the total accumulated performance. (To get meaningful numbers, we exclude the SIMD systems for this analysis, since these tend to have extremely high processor numbers and extremely low processor performance.) In Figure 15.3 we plot the relative growth of the total number of processors and of the average processor performance, defined as the ratio of total accumulated performance to the number of processors. We find that these two factors contribute almost equally to the annual total performance growth—a factor of 1.82. On average, the number of processors has grown by a factor of 1.30 each year and the processor performance by a factor 1.40 per year, compared to the factor of 1.58 predicted by Moore's Law.

3   PROGRAMMING MODELS

The standard parallel architectures support a variety of decomposition strategies, such as decomposition by task (task parallelism) and decomposition by data (data parallelism). Data parallelism is the most common strategy for scientific programs on parallel machines. In data parallelism, the application is decomposed by subdividing the data space over which it operates and assigning different processors to the work associated with different data subspaces. Typically, this strategy involves some data sharing at the boundaries, and the programmer is

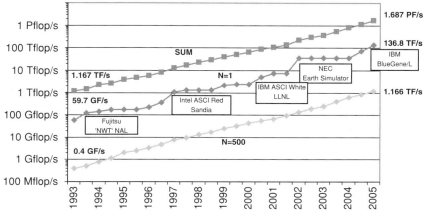

Figure 15.3. Performance growth at fixed Top500 rankings.

responsible for ensuring that this data sharing is handled correctly—that is, that data computed by one processor and used by another is correctly synchronized.

Once a specific decomposition strategy is chosen, it must be implemented. Here the programmer must choose the programming model to use. The two most common models are

- the shared-memory model, in which it is assumed that all data structures are allocated a common space that is accessible from every processor; and

- the message-passing model, in which each processor (or process) is assumed to have its own private data space, and data must be explicitly moved between spaces as needed.

In the message-passing model, data are distributed across the processor memories; if a processor needs to use data that are not stored locally, the processor that owns those data must explicitly "send" the data to the processor that needs them. The latter must execute an explicit "receive" operation, which is synchronized with the "send," before it can use the communicated data.

To achieve high performance on parallel machines, the programmer must be concerned with scalability and load balance. Generally, an application is thought to be scalable if larger parallel configurations can solve proportionally larger problems in the same running time as smaller problems on smaller configurations. Load balance typically means that the processors have roughly the same amount of work, so that no one processor holds up the entire solution. To balance the computational load on a machine with processors of equal power, the programmer must divide the work and communications evenly. This division can be challenging in applications applied to problems that are unknown in size until run time.

4   FUTURE TRENDS

Based on the current Top500 data (which cover the last 13 years) and the assumption that the current rate of performance improvement will continue for some time to come, we can extrapolate the observed performance and compare these values with the goals of government programs such as the Department of Energy's Accelerated Strategic Computing Initiative (ASCI), High Performance Computing and Communications, and the PetaOps initiative. In Figure 15.4, we extrapolate the observed performance using linear regression on a logarithmic scale. This means that we fit exponential growth to all levels of performance in the Top500. This simple curve fit of the data shows surprisingly consistent results. Based on the extrapolation from these fits, we can expect to see the first 100 TFlop/s system by 2005. By 2005, no system smaller than 1 TFlop/s should be able to make the Top500 ranking.

Looking even farther into the future, we speculate that based on the current doubling of performance every twelve to fourteen months, the first PetaFlop/s system should be available around 2009. Due to the rapid changes in the technologies used in HPC systems, there is currently no reasonable projection possible for the architecture of the PetaFlops systems at the end of the decade. Even as the HPC market has changed substantially since the introduction of the Cray 1 three decades ago, there is no end in sight for these rapid cycles of architectural redefinition.

There are two general conclusions we can draw from these figures. First, parallel computing is here to stay. It is the primary mechanism by which computer performance can keep up with the predictions of Moore's law in the face of the increasing influence of performance bottlenecks in conventional processors. Second, the architecture of high-performance computing will continue to evolve at a rapid rate. Thus, it will be increasingly important to find ways to support scalable parallel programming without sacrificing portability. This challenge must be met by the development of software systems and algorithms that promote portability while easing the burden of program design and implementation.

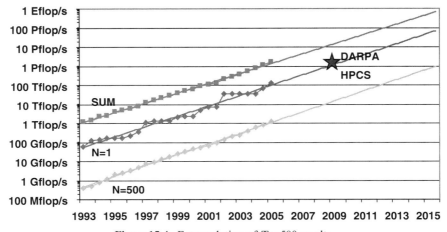

Figure 15.4. Extrapolation of Top500 results.

4.1   Grid Computing

Grid computing provides for a virtualization of distributed computing and data resources such as processing, network bandwidth, and storage capacity to create a single system image, providing users and applications seamless access to the collective resources. Just as an Internet user views a unified instance of content via the Web, a grid user essentially sees a single, large virtual computer.

Grid technologies promise to change the way organizations tackle complex computational problems. However, the vision of large-scale resource sharing is not yet a reality in many areas—Grid computing is an evolving area of computing, where standards and technology are still being developed to enable this new paradigm.

The early efforts in Grid computing started as projects to link US supercomputing sites, but now that initiative has grown far beyond its original intent. In fact, there are many applications that can benefit from the Grid infrastructure, including collaborative engineering, data exploration, high-throughput computing, and of course distributed supercomputing.

Ian Foster [12] defines a Grid as a system that

- coordinates resources that are not subject to centralized control . . . (A Grid integrates and coordinates resources and users that live within different control domains—for example, the user's desktop vs. central computing, different administrative units of the same company, or different companies—and addresses the issues of security, policy, payment, membership, and so forth that arise in these settings. Otherwise, we are dealing with a local management system.)

- . . . using standard, open, general-purpose protocols and interfaces . . . (A Grid is built from multipurpose protocols and interfaces that address such fundamental issues as authentication, authorization, resource discovery, and resource access. As discussed further below, it is important that these protocols and interfaces be standard and open. Otherwise, we are dealing with an application-specific system.)

- . . . to deliver nontrivial qualities of service. (A Grid allows its constituent resources to be used in a coordinated fashion to deliver various qualities of service, relating for example to response time, throughput, availability, and security, and/or co-allocation of multiple resource types to meet complex user demands so that the utility of the combined system is significantly greater than that of the sum of its parts.)

At its core, grid computing is based on an open set of standards and protocols — e.g., Open Grid Services Architecture (OGSA) — that enable communication across heterogeneous, geographically dispersed environments. With grid computing, organizations can optimize computing and data resources, pool them for large capacity workloads, share them across networks, and enable collaboration.

A number of challenges remain to be understood and overcome in order for Grid computing to achieve widespread adoption. The major obstacle is the need for seamless integration over heterogeneous resources to accommodate the wide variety of different applications requiring such resources.

5   TRANSFORMING EFFECT ON SCIENCE AND ENGINEERING

Supercomputers have transformed a number of science and engineering disciplines, including cosmology, environmental modeling, condensed matter physics, protein folding, quantum chromodynamics, device and semiconductor simulation, seismology, and turbulence. As an example, consider cosmology—the study of the universe, its evolution and structure—where one of the most striking paradigm shifts has occurred. A number of new, tremendously detailed observations, deep into the universe, are available from such instruments as the Hubble Space Telescope and the Digital Sky Survey [2]. However, until recently, it has been difficult, except in relatively simple circumstances, to tease from mathematical theories of the early universe enough information to allow comparison with observations.

However, supercomputers have changed all that. Now cosmologists can simulate the principal physical processes at work in the early universe over space–time volumes sufficiently large to determine the large-scale structures predicted by the models. With such tools, some theories can be discarded as being incompatible with the observations. Supercomputing has allowed comparison of theory with observation and thus has transformed the practice of cosmology.

Another example is the DOE's Accelerated Strategic Computing Initiative (ASCI), which applies advanced capabilities in scientific and engineering computing to one of the most complex challenges in the nuclear era—maintaining the performance, safety, and reliability of the nation's nuclear weapons without physical testing. As a critical component of the agency's Stockpile Stewardship Program (SSP), ASCI research develops computational and simulation technologies to help scientists understand aging weapons, predict when components will have to be replaced, and evaluate the implications of changes in materials and fabrication processes for the design life of aging weapons systems. The ASCI program was established in 1996 in response to the Administration's commitment to pursue a comprehensive ban on nuclear weapons testing. ASCI researchers are developing high-end computing capabilities far above the current level of performance, as well as advanced simulation applications that can reduce the current reliance on empirical judgments by achieving higher resolution, higher fidelity, 3-D physics, and full-system modeling capabilities for assessing the state of nuclear weapons.

Parallelism is a primary method for accelerating the total power of a supercomputer. That is, in addition to continuing to develop the performance of a technology, multiple copies are deployed that provide some of the advantages of an improvement in raw performance, but not all.

Employing parallelism to solve large-scale problems is not without its price. The complexity of building parallel supercomputers with thousands of processors to solve real-world problems requires a hierarchical approach—associating memory closely with Central Processing Units (CPUs). Consequently, the central problem faced by parallel applications is managing a complex memory hierarchy, ranging from local registers to far-distant processor memories. It is the communication of data and the coordination of processes within this hierarchy that represent the principal hurdles to effective, correct, and widespread acceptance of parallel computing. Thus, today's parallel computing environment has architectural complexity layered upon a multiplicity of processors. Scalability, the ability for hardware and software to maintain reasonable efficiency as the number of processors is increased, is the key metric.

The future will be more complex yet. Distinct computer systems will be networked together into the most powerful systems on the planet. The pieces of this composite whole will be distinct in hardware (e.g., CPUs), software (e.g., operating system), and operational policy (e.g., security). This future is most apparent when we consider geographically distributed computing on the Computational Grid [10]. There is great emerging interest in using the global information infrastructure as a computing platform. By drawing on the power of high-performance computing resources that are geographically distributed, it will be possible to solve problems that cannot currently be attacked by any single computing system, parallel or otherwise.

Computational physics applications have been the primary drivers in the development of parallel computing over the last twenty years. This set of problems has a number of features in common, despite the substantial specific differences in problem domain:

1. Applications were often defined by a set of partial differential equations (PDEs) on some domain in space and time.
2. Multiphysics often took the form of distinct physical domains with different processes dominant in each.
3. The life cycle of many applications was essentially contained within the computer room, building, or campus.

These characteristics focused attention on discretizations of PDEs, the corresponding notion of resolution being equivalent to accuracy, and solution of the linear and nonlinear equations generated by these discretizations. Data parallelism and domain decomposition provided an effective programming model and a ready source of parallelism. Multiphysics, for the most part, was also amenable to domain decomposition and could be accomplished by understanding and trading information about the fluxes between the physical domains. Finally, attention was focused on the parallel computer, its speed and accuracy, and relatively little attention was paid to I/O beyond the confines of the computer room.

The Holy Grail for software is *portable performance*. That is, software should be reusable across different platforms and should provide significant performance, say, relative to peak speed, for the end user. Often, these two goals seem to be in opposition to each other. Languages (e.g., Fortran, C) and libraries (e.g., Message Passing Interface (MPI) [7] and Linear Algebra Libraries, i.e., LAPACK [3]) allow the programmer to access or expose parallelism in a variety of standard ways. By employing standards-based, optimized libraries, the programmer can sometimes achieve both portability and high performance. Tools (e.g., svPablo [11] and Performance Application Programmers Interface (PAPI) [6]) allow programmers to determine the correctness and performance of their codes and, if falling short in some ways, to suggest various remedies.

ACKNOWLEDGMENTS

This research was supported in part by the Applied Mathematical Sciences Research Program of the Office of Mathematical, Information, and Computational Sciences, U.S. Department of Energy, under contract DE-AC05-00OR22725 with UT-Battelle, LLC.

REFERENCES

[1] E. Brooks (1989): The Attack of the Killer Micros. Teraflop Computing Panel, Supercomputing '89, Reno, Nevada.

[2] Donald G. York et al. September (2000): The American Astronomical Society. The Sloan Digital Sky Survey: Technical Summary, *The Astronomical Journal*, *120*:1579–1587.

[3] E. Anderson, Z. Bai, C. Bischof, S. Blackford, J. Demmel, J. Dongarra, J. Du Croz, A. Greenbaum, S. Hammaring, A. McKenney, and D. Sorensen (1999): *LAPACK Users' Guide – Third Edition*. SIAM Publication, Philadelphia.

[4] Top500 Report. http://www.top500.org/

[5] J. Dongarra, K. London, S. Moore, P. Mucci, and D. Terpstra (2001): Using PAPI for Hardware Performance Monitoring on Linux Systems. Terpstra. In *Proceedings of the Conference on Linux Clusters: The HPC Revolution*.

[6] S. Browne, J. Dongarra, N. Garner, G. Ho, and P. Mucci (2000): A Portable Programming Interface for Performance Evaluation on Modern Processors. *International Journal of High Performance Computing Applications*, *14*(3), 189–204.

[7] M. Snir, S. Otto, S. Huss-Lederman, D. Walker, and J. Dongarra (1996): MPI: The Complete Reference. MIT Press, Boston.

[8] G.E. Moore (1965): Cramming More Components onto Integrated Circuits. *Electronics 38*(8), 114–117.

[9] J.J. Dongarra (2003): Performance of Various Computers Using Standard Linear Equations Software (Linpack Benchmark Report). University of Tennessee Computer Science Technical Report, CS-89-85. http://www.netlib.org/benchmark/performance.pdf

[10] I. Foster and C. Kesselman (eds) (1998): *Computational Grids: Blueprint for a New Computing Infrastructure*. Morgan Kaufman.

[11] L. DeRose and D. A. Reed (1999): SvPablo: A Multi-Language Architecture-Independent Performance Analysis System. *Proceedings of the International Conference on Parallel Processing (ICPP'99)*, Fukushima, Japan.

[12] I. Foster, What is the Grid? A Three Point Checklist. *GRIDToday,* July 20, 2002.

Chapter 16

CLUSTER COMPUTING: HIGH-PERFORMANCE, HIGH-AVAILABILITY, AND HIGH-THROUGHPUT PROCESSING ON A NETWORK OF COMPUTERS

Chee Shin Yeo[1], Rajkumar Buyya[1], Hossein Pourreza[2], Rasit Eskicioglu[2], Peter Graham[2], Frank Sommers[3]
[1]The University of Melbourne, Australia
[2]The University of Manitoba, Canada
[3]Autospaces, LLC

1   INTRODUCTION

The first inspiration for cluster computing was developed in the 1960s by IBM as an alternative to linking large mainframes in order to provide a more cost-effective form of commercial parallelism [1]. At that time, IBM's Houston Automatic Spooling Priority (HASP) system and its successor, Job Entry System (JES), allowed the distribution of work to a user-constructed mainframe cluster. IBM still supports clustering of mainframes through its Parallel Sysplex system, which allows the hardware, operating system, middleware, and system management software to provide dramatic performance and cost improvements while permitting large mainframe users to continue to run their existing applications.

However, cluster computing did not gain momentum until the convergence of three important trends in the 1980s: high-performance microprocessors, high-speed networks, and standard tools for high-performance distributed computing. A possible fourth trend is the increasing need of computing power for computational science and commercial applications, coupled with the high cost and low accessibility of traditional supercomputers. These four building blocks are also known as *killer-microprocessors, killer-networks, killer-tools,* and *killer-applications,* respectively. The recent advances in these technologies and their availability as cheap and commodity components are making clusters or networks of computers such as Personal Computers (PCs), workstations, and Symmetric Multiple-Processors (SMPs) an appealing solution for cost-effective parallel computing. Clusters, built using commodity-off-the-shelf (COTS) hardware components as well as free, or commonly used, software, are playing a major role in redefining the concept of supercomputing. And consequently, they have emerged as mainstream parallel and distributed platforms for high-performance, high-throughput, and high-availability computing.

The trend in parallel computing is to move away from traditional specialized supercomputing platforms, such as the Cray/SGI T3E, to cheaper and general-purpose systems consisting of loosely coupled components built up from single or multiprocessor PCs or workstations. This approach has a number of advantages, including being able to build a platform for a given budget that is suitable for a large class of applications and workloads.

The emergence of cluster platforms was driven by a number of academic projects, such as Beowulf [2], Berkeley NOW [3], and HPVM [4], that prove the advantage of clusters over other traditional platforms. These advantages include low-entry costs to access supercomputing-level performance, the ability to track technologies, incrementally upgradeable system, open-source development platforms, and vendor independence. Today, clusters are widely used for research and development in science, engineering, commerce, and industry applications that demand high-performance computations. In addition, clusters encompass strengths such as high availability and scalability that motivate wide usage in non-supercomputing applications as well, such as clusters working as web and database servers.

A cluster is a type of parallel or distributed computer system that consists of a collection of inter-connected stand-alone computers working together as a single integrated computing resource [1, 5]. The typical architecture of a cluster is shown in Figure 16.1. The key components of a cluster include multiple standalone computers (PCs, workstations, or SMPs), operating systems, high-performance interconnects, middleware, parallel programming environments, and applications.

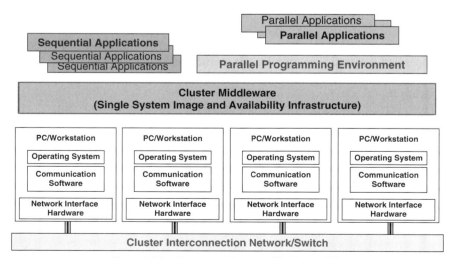

Figure 16.1. Cluster architecture (R. Buyya [1]).

The remaining part of this chapter focuses on cluster-specific components and their functionality, along with representative examples. It assumes that the reader is familiar with the standard commodity hardware and software components such as stand-alone computers, operating systems such as Linux and Windows, and standard communication software such as TCP/IP.

2 INTERCONNECTION TECHNOLOGIES AND COMMUNICATION SOFTWARE

Clusters need to incorporate fast interconnection technologies in order to support high-bandwidth and low-latency interprocessor communication between cluster nodes. Slow interconnection technologies had always been a critical performance bottleneck for cluster computing. Today, improved network technologies help realize the construction of more efficient clusters.

Selecting a cluster interconnection network technology depends on several factors, such as compatibility with the cluster hardware and operating system, price, and performance. There are two metrics to measure performance for interconnects: bandwidth and latency. Bandwidth is the amount of data that can be transmitted over the interconnect hardware in a fixed period of time, while latency is the time needed to prepare and transmit data from a source node to a destination node.

Table 16.1 gives a summary of some interconnection technologies, which are then compared as shown in Table 16.2. The comparisons examine factors that include bandwidth, latency, hardware availability, support for Linux, maximum number of cluster nodes supported, how the protocol is implemented, support for Virtual Interface Architecture (VIA), and support for Message Passing Interface (MPI). VIA [9] is a standard for the low-latency communication software interface that was developed by a consortium of hardware producers and academic institutions and that has been adopted for use by most cluster vendors. MPI [10] provides message passing through a set of libraries that users can use to develop parallel and distributed applications. This means that MPI provides the communication layer for user applications and thus ensures portability of application code across all distributed and parallel platforms.

With the current popularity of cluster computing, it is increasingly important to understand the capabilities and potential performance of various network interconnects for clusters. Furthermore, due to the low cost of clusters and their growing acceptance within the scientific community, many recent cluster builders are not computer scientists or engineers and thus have limited technical computing skills. This new group of cluster builders is less interested in features such as Network Interface Card (NIC) programmability and special messaging libraries. Instead, they are concerned with two primary factors: cost and performance. While cost is easily determined and compared, performance is more difficult to assess, particularly for users who may be new to cluster computing.

Several performance assessments of cluster systems, and of specific interconnects, have been performed [15–19]. Unfortunately, much of the work done has, in some sense, been "comparing apples to oranges." This is because most existing performance analyses have been forced to compare results for interconnects being

Table 16.1. Examples of some interconnection technologies.

Interconnection Technology	Description
Gigabit Ethernet	• Provides a reasonably high bandwidth given its low price, but suffers from relatively high latency, thus restricting Gigabit Ethernet as a good choice. However, the low price of Gigabit Ethernet is appealing to building clusters. • http://www.10gea.org
Giganet cLAN	• Giganet cLAN was developed with the goal of supporting VIA in hardware, and it supports a low latency. But it provides only a low bandwidth of less than 125 MBytes/s, thus making it not a viable choice for implementing fast cluster networks. • http://www.giganet.com
Infiniband [6]	• The latest industry standard based on VIA concepts and released in 2002, Infiniband supports connecting various system components within a system such as interprocessor networks, I/O subsystems, or multiprotocol network switches. This makes Infiniband independent of any particular technology. • http://www.infinibandta.org
Myrinet [7]	• The current most widely used technology for fast cluster networks. The key advantage of Myrinet is that it operates in user space, thus bypassing operating system interferences and delays. • http://www.myrinet.com
QsNet II	• The next generation version of QsNet, based on a high-performance PCI-X interface as compared with QsNet's PCI interface. QsNet II is able to achieve 1064 MBytes/s, support 4096 nodes, and provide 64-bit virtual address architecture. • http://www.quadrics.com
Scalable Coherent Interface (SCI) [8]	• The first interconnection technology standard specified for cluster computing. SCI defines a directory-based cache scheme that can keep the caches of connected processors coherent, and is thus able to implement virtual shared memory. • http://www.scizzl.com

used on different cluster systems (since any given cluster seldom has more than one or two interconnects available). To be as useful as possible, interconnect performance assessments should

- be based on timing runs done on real hardware using real programs, thereby eliminating any issues related to either limitations of simulation or overtuning of synthetic benchmarks;

- use identical cluster node hardware for all runs with all network interconnects so that the results do not have to be carefully "interpreted" to account for possible performance variations due to differences in system components other than the network interconnect;

- concurrently consider as many different network interconnects as possible to avoid possible discrepancies between independent experiments done at different times; and

- include a number of real-world applications in addition to the key benchmark suites commonly used to assess cluster performance in order to provide greater confidence that the results observed are not simply those that

Table 16.2. Comparison of some interconnection technologies (updated version from [11]).

Comparison Criteria	Gigabit Ethernet	Giganet cLAN	Infiniband	Myrinet	QsNet II	Scalable Coherent Interface (SCI)
Bandwidth (MBytes/s)	< 100	< 125	850	230	1064	< 320
Latency (μs)	< 100	7-10	< 7	10	< 3	1–2
Hardware Availability	Now	Now	Now	Now	Now	Now
Linux Support	Now	Now	Now	Now	Now	Now
Max. No. of Nodes	1000s	1000s	> 1000s	1000s	4096	1000s
Protocol Implementation	Hardware	Firmware on adaptor	Hardware	Firmware on adaptor	Firmware on adaptor	Firmware on adaptor
Virtual Interface Architecture (VIA) Support	NT/Linux	NT/Linux	Software	Linux	None	Software
Message Passing Interface (MPI) Support	MVICH [12] over M-VIA [13], TCP	3rd Party	MPI/Pro [14]	3rd Party	Quadrics	3rd Party

can be expected of, in particular, well-tuned benchmark code (results for real applications are likely to be more indicative of what new cluster users can expect from their applications than are results from well-established benchmarks).

A subset of the authors (Pourreza, Eskicioglu, and Graham) have conducted performance assessments of a number of interconnects identified in Table 16.2 by taking timings when running identical applications on identical cluster nodes. Repeated isolated runs were made of a number of standard cluster computing benchmarks (including the NAS parallel benchmarks [20] and the Pallas benchmarks [21]), as well as some real world parallel applications[1] on first- and second-generation Myrinet [7], SCI [8], and Fast (100 Mbps) and Gigabit (1000 Mbps) Ethernet, and the key results are summarized below. For those readers who are interested, additional details are available in [23].

For small-scale compute clusters, most first-time cluster builders tend to choose between a very low-cost commodity interconnect (most commonly, Fast or Gigabit Ethernet) and a more expensive but higher performance interconnect (such as Myrinet or SCI). In many cases, this choice is made prior to any serious investigation of the interconnection needs of the application(s) to be run on the cluster and is often determined by simply asking the question, "Can our budget afford a fast interconnect?" This approach is undesirable and may lead to frustration with the resulting cluster performance, due to two possible reasons: one is that the selected network interconnect is inadequate for the work to be done, and the other is that the money spent on an underutilized interconnect could have been better spent on other useful components, such as faster processors and larger memory. Cluster builders could easily avoid these problems by following some simple guidelines and considering the performance characteristics of the various interconnects as determined by independent analysis.

In general, the cost of commodity interconnects is currently approximately an order of magnitude lower than the cost of high-performance interconnects. The wide price differential means that, whenever possible, it is highly desirable to use a commodity interconnect. The primary difference between commodity and high-performance interconnects is the latency of sending messages and, to a somewhat lesser extent, the bandwidth available for messaging. This naturally means that high-performance interconnects are most desirable when the applications to be run over them communicate frequently (particularly if they exchange many small messages). Applications that communicate only infrequently and that exchange larger messages often perform quite well using commodity interconnects. These general observations are confirmed by the example graphs shown below.

The cost of Fast (100 Mbps) Ethernet is now so low that a common strategy among many first-time cluster builders is to start by using Fast Ethernet for their interconnect and then upgrade when necessary (or when they have a better idea of their application characteristics and hence requirements). Given the extremely low cost of Fast Ethernet, there is little concern if the equipment is used only for

---

[1]Among these applications were PSTSWM (http://www.csm.ornl.gov/chammp/pstswm), a shallow-water model commonly used as part of larger Global Climate Models (GCMs), and Gromacs [22] (http://www.gromacs.org), a molecular dynamics package.

a short period of time. Furthermore, many cluster builders will keep their Fast Ethernet network to carry maintenance traffic (such as NIS, NFS, and remote logins) even after adding a high-performance interconnect to their cluster. Thus, they avoid "polluting" the high-speed interconnect with unnecessary traffic that might interfere with the actual executing programs. In addition, if the Fast Ethernet equipment is no longer required, it can be easily redeployed for usage elsewhere in the organization. Gigabit Ethernet is also increasingly being treated in a similar fashion, even though it is more expensive. But the advantages of Gigabit Ethernet are a longer lifespan as an active interconnect and the ability to support a much wider range of applications.

All the timings reported are done on an eight-node Linux cluster (with RedHat 9.0, kernel 2.4.18 smp and gcc 3.2.2). Each node has a dual Pentium III, 550-MHz processor with 512 MB of shared SDRAM memory and local IDE disks (all I/O activity in the experiments occurs on local disks to eliminate the effects of NFS access). Each node also has first- and second-generation Myrinet, GigaNet, Fast Ethernet, Gigabit Ethernet, and point-to-point SCI (Dolphin WulfKit) Network Interface Cards (NICs). All NICs except the SCI NICs are connected to dedicated switches. The SCI NICs are interconnected in a 4x2 mesh configuration. The Fast Ethernet network is also used for "maintenance" traffic, but steps were taken to ensure that traffic "maintenance" would be minimal during the experiments. Although each node has a dual processor, only a single processor is used for running most of the applications, since most small-scale cluster nodes are still uniprocessor. The results from the best performing version of MPI that is available for each interconnect are reported. The public-domain GNU compilers (gcc and g77 version 3.2.2) are used to compile all applications because GNU compilers are the most commonly used by most cluster builders. All timings are taken in isolation from other work and logins (in other words, no other applications are running while the timings are being taken, no other users are allowed to log in, and the operating systems on all nodes are only running cluster-essential software daemons). This setup represents the characteristics of a "production" cluster environment. Results for the GigaNet interconnect are not reported due to lack of a suitable MPI implementation. Also, results using the second-generation Myrinet NICs are omitted, since the cluster nodes do not support 64-bit transfers, which is one of the key benefits of second-generation Myrinet. Through experimentation, we discovered that without such wide transfers, there is little difference between the two generations of Myrinet.

The base performance of the various interconnects (in terms of bandwidth and latency) are shown in Figures 16.2 and 16.3, respectively. The relative figures for the four networks are as expected, with Fast Ethernet clearly being inferior to all the other interconnects and Gigabit Ethernet being noticeably below SCI and Myrinet despite advertising a similar raw bandwidth. Even from these results, it is clear that fast Ethernet would likely only be suitable for the most compute-bound applications.

The NPB suite consists of a number of parallel programs implemented using MPI that have a variety of communication patterns and frequencies (some of the programs are compute bound, while others are communication bound). All programs are derived from real-world program codes. The sample results shown below are for the FT and LU benchmarks. The FT-A benchmark (shown in

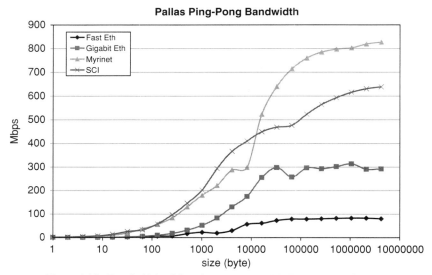

Figure 16.2. Bandwidth of four interconnects (H. Pourreza et al. [23]).

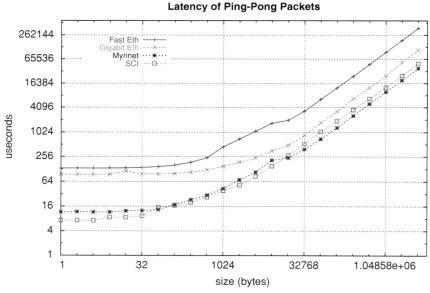

Figure 16.3. Latency of four interconnects (H. Pourreza et al. [23]).

Figure 16.4) implements a Fourier Transform (on relatively small data – the "-A" suffix) and is quite communication bound, while the LU-A benchmark (shown in Figure 16.5) implements LU decomposition (also on small data) and is relatively compute bound. The trends seen for FT are consistent with those described earlier and expected. The fact that LU is more compute bound is reflected by the improved relative performance of the commodity interconnects in Figure 16.5.

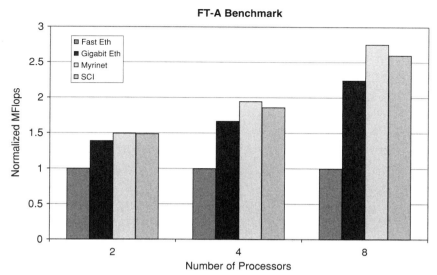

Figure 16.4. The NPB FT-A benchmark (H. Pourreza et al. [23]).

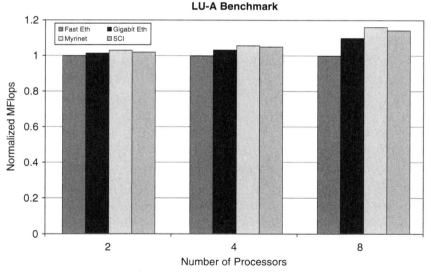

Figure 16.5. The NPB LU-A benchmark (H. Pourreza et al. [23]).

Figures 16.6 and 16.7 show speedup values for FT-A and LU-A on the four interconnects, in this case using all 16 processors in the cluster. Again, the impact of LU's being compute bound is clearly evident, reinforcing the idea that strongly compute-bound code can make good use of cheap, commodity interconnects.

It is useful to note that the overall results obtained for the large, real-world MPI applications are highly consistent with the results for the NPB suite. Both sample applications (PSTSWM and GROMACS) are moderately compute bound

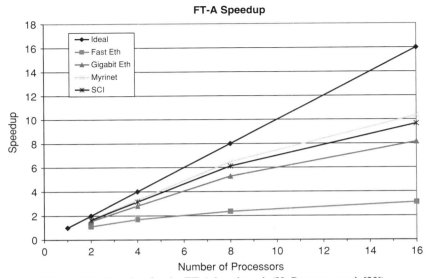

Figure 16.6. Speedup for the FT-A benchmark (H. Pourreza et al. [23]).

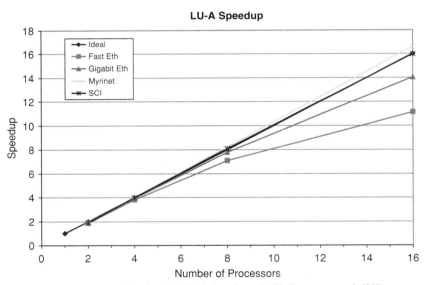

Figure 16.7. Speedup for the LU-A benchmark (H. Pourreza et al. [23]).

(PSTSWM more so than GROMACS). As a result, Fast Ethernet is an undesirable interconnect to use when running them. It is interesting to note that the effect of the point-to-point interconnects in SCI also begin to have a negative impact in GROMACS (presumably since some of the nodes must forward messages on behalf of other nodes).

From the graphs shown (as well as other related work) and considering the cost of the networking equipment, it is clear that fast Ethernet is no longer a desirable choice for a cluster interconnect unless cost is an overriding consideration (in which case, poor cluster performance for all but the most compute-bound applications must be expected). Despite its extremely low raw latency, SCI can experience problems when used in a point-to-point configuration due to the overhead of forwarding "third-party" messages. To take full advantage of SCI's capabilities, the cluster programmer must be prepared to expend significant effort to ensure that the application is structured to minimize nondirect communication. This task is often onerous and should not be taken lightly. Of all interconnects, Myrinet offers the best and most consistent performance but is also (not surprisingly) the highest-cost interconnect. Gigabit Ethernet, a commodity interconnect, offers surprisingly good performance for a fair range of applications (excluding those that are heavily communication bound) and is likely a good interconnect for many cluster builders if they expect their applications to be at least partially compute bound. Gigabit Ethernet is now significantly cheaper than Myrinet and other similar interconnect technologies (e.g., GigaNet and Infiniband). Further, with the appropriate switches, better performance can be obtained with Gigabit Ethernet using "Jumbo" frames. But, of course, the best way to select an interconnect is by benchmarking the application(s) to be run. If this is not possible, the use of the guidelines described and tests based on the NPB suite appear to be reasonable alternatives.

3   SINGLE SYSTEM IMAGE (SSI)

The Single System Image (SSI) [24] represents the view of a distributed system as a single unified computing resource. SSI provides better usability for the users, since it hides from them the complexities of the underlying distributed and heterogeneous nature of clusters. SSI can be established through one or several mechanisms implemented at various levels of abstraction in the cluster architecture: hardware, operating system, middleware, and applications.

The design goals for SSI cluster-based systems focus on complete transparency of resource management, scalable performance, and system availability in supporting user applications. Key SSI attributes that are generally considered desirable include point of entry, user interface, process space, memory space, I/O space, file hierarchy, virtual networking, job management system, and control point and management. Table 16.3 summarizes how SSI can be achieved at different levels of abstraction, with examples. The next section explains the cluster resource management systems.

3.1.1   SSI at the Operating System Level

The operating system in each of the cluster nodes provides the fundamental system support for the combined operation of the cluster. The operating system provides services such as protection boundaries, process/thread coordination, interprocess communication, and device handling, thus creating a high-level software interface for user applications.

Table 16.3. Achieving Single System Image (SSI) at different levels of abstraction.

Level of Abstraction	Description and Examples
Hardware	Implementing SSI at the Hardware layer (lowest level of abstraction) allows the user to view a cluster as a shared-memory system. Some examples are • Memory Channel [25] • Distributed Shared Memory (DSM) [26, 27]
Operating System	Modifying the existing operating system kernel to support SSI. Some examples are • MOSIX [28] • Solaris MC [29] • UnixWare [30, 31] Constructing a new operating system layer that integrates operating systems on each node. Some examples are • GLUnix [32]
Middleware	Implementing SSI at the Middleware layer is most common for clusters. Using a programming environment for development and execution of applications. Some examples are • Parallel Virtual Machine (PVM) [33] Installing resource management systems (RMSs) that manage resources and applications in the cluster. Some examples are • Condor [34] • Loadleveler [35] • Load Share Facility (LSF) [36] • Open Portable Batch System (OpenPBS) [37] • Sun Grid Engine (SGE) [38] • Libra [39]
Application	Implementing SSI at the Application layer (highest level of abstraction) provides an application-specific user interface. Some examples are • PARMON [40] • Linux Virtual Server [41] • Problem Solving Environments [42]

A cluster operating system is desired to have the following features:

- *Manageability*: Ability to manage and administrate local and remote resources.

- *Stability*: Support for robustness against system failures with system recovery.

- *Performance*: All types of operations should be optimized and efficient.

- *Extensibility*: Provide easy integration of cluster-specific extensions.

- *Scalability*: Able to scale without impact on performance.

- *Support*: User and system administrator support is essential.

- *Heterogeneity*: Portability over multiple architectures to support a cluster consisting of heterogeneous hardware components. May be achieved through the use of middleware.

There are two main types of cluster operating systems: free and commercial. Examples of free releases are Linux and MOSIX. Linux [43] is the most widely used cluster operating system, since it is free, open-source, and has a wide user and developer community. MOSIX [28] is a set of extensions built on top of the Linux kernel that enables process migration in a cluster environment to support automatic load balancing.

Commercial releases of cluster operating systems are proprietary and shipped with commercial clusters. Examples include IBM's AIX [44], SGI's IRIX [45], Sun's Solaris MC [29], HP/Compaq's Tru64 [46], SCO's Unixware [30], and Microsoft's Windows NT/2000 [47] and Windows Server family.

4   RESOURCE MANAGEMENT SYSTEM (RMS) MIDDLEWARE

A cluster resource management system (RMS) acts as a cluster middleware that implements the SSI [24] for a cluster of machines. It enables users to execute jobs on the cluster without needing to understand the complexities of the underlying cluster architecture. An RMS manages the cluster through four major branches, namely, *resource management*, *job queuing*, *job scheduling*, and *job management*.

Figure 16.8 shows a generic architecture of a cluster RMS. An RMS manages the collection of resources such as processors and disk storage in the cluster. It maintains status information on resources so as to know what resources are available, and it can thus assign jobs to available machines. The RMS uses job queues that hold submitted jobs until there are available resources to execute the jobs. When resources are available, the RMS invokes a job scheduler to select from the queues what jobs to execute. The RMS then manages the job execution processes and returns the results to the users upon job completion.

The advent of Grid computing [48] further enhances the significance of the RMS in clusters. Grid brokers can discover Grid resources such as clusters and submit the jobs via an RMS. The RMS then manages and executes the jobs before returning the results back to the Grid brokers. To enable effective resource management on clusters, numerous cluster management systems and schedulers have been designed. Table 16.4 gives a summary of some examples of RMSs.

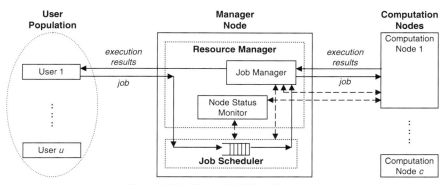

Figure 16.8. Cluster RMS architecture.

Table 16.4. Examples of Resource Management Systems (RMSs) middleware.

RMS	Organization	Brief Description and Website
Condor	University of Wisconsin–Madison	• Able to detect and execute jobs on idle nondedicated machines. • http://www.cs.wisc.edu/condor
Loadleveler	IBM	• Manages resources and jobs for IBM clusters. • http://www.ibm.com/servers/eserver/clusters/software
Load Share Facility (LSF)	Platform Computing	• Adopts a layered architecture that supports many extension utilities. • http://www.platform.com/products/LSF
Open Portable Batch System (OpenPBS)	Altair Grid Technologies	• Supports multiple scheduling policies based on extensible scheduler architecture. • http://www.openpbs.org
Sun Grid Engine (SGE)	Sun Microsystems	• The Enterprise edition supports scheduling of jobs over multiple clusters within an organization. • http://gridengine.sunsource.net
Libra	University of Melbourne	• Supports resource allocation based on computational economy principles and users' quality of service requirements. • http://www.gridbus.org/libra

Condor [34], developed by the University of Wisconsin–Madison, not only is able to manage a cluster of dedicated machines but also allows execution of jobs on nondedicated machines that are otherwise left idle. Condor can automatically detect these idle machines and use them via checkpointing and migration of job processes. Idle machines are placed into a Condor pool so that they are allocated for job execution, and are taken out of the pool when they become busy. Condor also provides extensions for using multiple Condor pools. A technique in Condor called *flocking* allows jobs submitted within a Condor pool to execute on another separate pool of machines. A version of Condor called *Condor-G* also supports the utilization of Globus [49] software that provides the infrastructure for authentication, authorization, and remote job submission of Grid resources.

LoadLeveler [35] is a resource management system developed by IBM to manage resources for IBM cluster products. LoadLeveler schedules jobs and provides functions for building, submitting, and processing jobs. When a user submits a job, LoadLeveler examines the job command file to determine what resources the job requires. Based on the jobs' requirements, it determines which machines are best suited to provide these resources and the best time for the job to be dispatched to the machines, and then dispatches the job at that time. To aid this process, LoadLeveler uses job queues to store the list of jobs that are waiting to be processed. LoadLeveler also uses a classification mechanism called *job classes* to schedule jobs to run on machines. For example, a job class called "short" contains short running jobs, while a job class called "weekend" contains jobs that are only allowed to run on the weekends. Job classes can be defined by the administrator to restrict which users can use a specific job class and what jobs can run on a particular machine.

LSF [36] is a loosely coupled cluster solution for heterogeneous systems, allowing LSF extension modules to be installed to provide advanced services.

This setup is possible due to LSF's design, which is based on a layered architecture. The base layer consisting of *Base System* and *Server Daemon* layers and provides low-level cluster services such as dynamic load balancing and transparent access to the resources available on all participating machines in the cluster. Other LSF utilities are then supported on top of the base layer at the *Utilities* layer. Examples of LSF utilities include *LSF Batch*, which provides a centralized resource management system for the cluster; *LSF MultiCluster*, which enables users to access resources on multiple LSF clusters in different geographic locations; and *LSF Analyzer*, which generates reports about the cluster by processing historical workload data.

OpenPBS [37] is the open-source version of the Portable Batch System (PBS). PBS was developed for NASA to control job execution and to manage resources for Numerical Aerodynamic Simulation (NAS) applications. It aims to be a flexible and extensible batch-processing system that supports multiple scheduling policies and job migration to meet the unique demands of heterogeneous computing networks. Currently, a new commercial version of PBS called PBSPro is available with more advanced features, such as supporting preemption, a backfilling algorithm, and advanced reservations for scheduling. OpenPBS adopts an independent scheduler architecture that enables the administrator to modify the existing default scheduling policies more easily to suit different requirements of the cluster. The administrator can create his own new customized scheduler that defines what types of resources and how much of each resource can be used by each job.

SGE [38] is currently an open-source project by Sun Microsystems which aims to establish community-driven standards that facilitate execution of computationally intensive applications. The user is able to submit batch, interactive, and parallel jobs to SGE. SGE also provides transparent workload distribution within the cluster and supports check pointing that enables jobs to migrate automatically between machines without user intervention based on load demands. The Enterprise Edition of SGE supports resource management and scheduling over multiple clusters within an organization. This setup enables the negotiation of resource and job policies to facilitate cooperation across multiple clusters.

Libra [39] is a computational economy-driven scheduling system that aims to improve the value of utility delivered to the user and the quality of services, as opposed to existing cluster RMSs that focus on a system-centric approach to resource management. Developed as part of the Gridbus Project at the University of Melbourne, Libra is designed to support allocation of resources based on the users' quality of service (QoS) requirements. It is intended to work as an add-on to the existing queuing and resource management system. The first version has been implemented as a plug-in scheduler to PBS. The scheduler offers market-based, economy-driven service for managing batch jobs on clusters by scheduling CPU time according to user-perceived value (utility), determined by the user's budget and deadline rather than by system performance considerations. Libra shows that the deadline and budget-based proportional resource allocation strategy improves both the utility of the system and user satisfaction as compared to system-centric scheduling strategies. We believe that this feature of Libra helps enforce resource allocation based on service level agreements when cluster services are offered as a utility on the Grid.

5   CLUSTER PROGRAMMING MODELS

All of a cluster's subsystems, from I/O to job scheduling to the choice of node operating system, must support the applications the cluster is designed to run. While small clusters are often constructed to support a single class of applications, such as serving Web pages or database applications, larger clusters are often called on to dedicate parts of their resources to different kinds of applications simultaneously [50, 51]. These applications often differ not only in their workload characteristics but also in the programming models they employ. The programming models employed by an application, in turn, determine the key performance characteristics of a cluster application. This section details the most important programming models used to construct cluster-aware applications; the next section provides examples of cluster applications constructed with one or more of these models.

Cluster computing programming models have traditionally been divided into categories based on the relationship of programs to the data the programs operate on [52]. The Single-Instruction, Single-Data (SISD) model defines the traditional von Neumann computer. Multiple-Instruction, Multiple-Data (MIMD) machines include most of today's clusters as well as parallel computers. In the Single-Instruction, Multiple-Data (SIMD) model, each processor executes the same program. Finally, the Multiple-instruction, Single-Data model (MISD) defines systems where multiple programs operate on the same data. MIMD has emerged as the most prevalent programming model on clusters.

In addition to dividing cluster programming models based on how programs relate to data, programming models can also be categorized on how they exploit a cluster's inherent parallelism. On that basis, cluster computing programming models can roughly be divided into two categories. The first category of models allows a serial (nonparallel) application to take advantage of a cluster's parallelism. The second category of models aids in the explicit parallelization of a program. Since cluster users are much more familiar with creating a serial program than with developing explicitly parallel applications, the first category of programming models have become dominant in cluster computing applications.

Pfister [5] coined the term *SPPS (serial program, parallel subsystem)* to describe a common technique of running a serial program on a cluster. In SPPS, many instances of a serial program are distributed on a cluster. A parallel subsystem provides input to each serial program instance and captures output from those programs, delivering that output to users. Because there are multiple programs on the clusters, operating on multiple data, SPPS is a form of MIMD. This section describes the two most common categories of SPPS programming models: distributed shared virtual memory-based systems, and message passing as illustrated by the Message Passing Interface (MPI) standard. Finally, programming models based on virtual machines are explained.

The SPPS model facilitates a division of labor in developing a cluster application: it allows a domain expert to write serial programs and delegates the task of creating an often complex parallel subsystem to highly skilled parallel programming specialists. The parallel subsystem in an SPPS-style cluster application is increasingly provided in the form of off-the-shelf middleware.

For example, Database Management Systems (DBMS) and Transaction Processing Monitors (TPM) routinely apply the SPPS technique to hide the complexity of parallel operations from users. A database query is typically submitted from a serial program to a cluster-aware DBMS subsystem responsible for query processing. That subsystem may process the query in a parallel fashion, possibly involving many cluster nodes. The query results are then returned to the serial program [53]. SPPS is used in scientific applications as well, allowing a scientist to focus on writing a serial program and submit that serial program for parallel execution on a cluster. An example is found in FermiLab's Cooperative Processes Software (CPS) [54].

When many instances of a serial program operate in parallel, those instances must coordinate work through a shared cluster resource, such as distributed shared memory or a message-passing infrastructure. The primitive operations that coordinate the work of concurrently executing serial programs on a cluster define a *coordination language* [55]. A coordination language is often described in terms of an Application Programming Interface (API) to a parallel subsystem. Such an API offers bindings to one or more programming languages. Another way to describe a coordination language is to use declarative scripting, which differs from API since it describes the required conditions and relationships and lets the computer system determine how to satisfy them. A coordination language, together with a programming language, defines the programming model of a cluster parallel application. Table 16.5 shows some examples of cluster programming models.

The *Linda tuplespace* system [56] exploits distributed shared memory [57] to facilitate the parallel execution of a serial program on a cluster. Linda defines primitive operations on a shared memory resource, allowing data items – *tuples* – to be written to that memory, read from shared memory, and deleted from shared

Table 16.5. Examples of cluster programming models.

Programming Environment	Coordination Language	Supported Programming Language	Website
Linda	API	C, Fortran	• http://www.cs.yale.edu/cswwworig/Linda/linda.html
JavaSpaces	API	Java	• http://www.sun.com/jini • http://www.jini.org
Message Queues	API	C, C++, Java	• http://www.microsoft. com/windows2000/technologies/communications/msmq/default.asp • http://www-306.ibm.com/software/integration/mqfamily • http://www.sun.com/software/products/message_queue
Message-Passing Interface (MPI)	API	C, C++, Fortran	• http://www.mpi-forum.org
JavaGroups	API	Java	• http://www.jgroups.org/javagroupsnew/docs
Parallel Virtual Machine (PVM)	API	C, C++, Fortran	• http://www.csm.ornl.gov/pvm/pvm_home.html
Parameter Sweep	Script-based constructs	Declarative programming	• http://www.csse.monash.edu.au/~davida/nimrod

memory. A tuple is similar to a database relation. A serial process with access to the shared memory writes data items to memory, marking each item with an attribute indicating that that item requires processing. Another process awaiting newly arriving tuples removes such an item from the shared memory, performs computations on that data item, and deposits the results into the shared memory. The original submitter of the job then collects all the results from the tuplespace. Each process operating on a tuplespace is typically a serial program, and the Linda system facilitates the concurrent execution of many such programs.

JavaSpaces [58] is an object-oriented Linda system that takes advantage of Java's platform-independent code execution and mobile code facility. Mobile code allows not just data but also code to move from one cluster node to another at run-time. A master node runs a JavaSpace process, providing a shared memory resource to other cluster nodes that act as workers. When a worker removes a job request from the shared JavaSpace, the operating codes for that job dynamically download to that worker. The worker executes that downloaded code and places the output of that execution into the JavaSpace. JavaSpaces, therefore, facilitates the automatic run-time distribution of code to cluster nodes. JavaSpaces also provides optional transactional access to the shared memory resource, which is especially helpful in the case of very large clusters with frequent node failures.

While *message queues* first became popular with SMPs as a load-distribution technique [5], distributed message queues have become increasingly popular with clusters as well. Distributed queues are a form of distributed shared memory with the added property of ordered message delivery. Most message queues in commercial use also provide transactional access to the queue.

While distributed shared memory facilitates communication via a shared cluster resource, the message-passing model coordinates work by sending and receiving messages between processes. The *Message-Passing Interface (MPI)* [10] standard defines a programming model for message passing, along with a series of functions to support that programming model. Language bindings to MPI functions exist for a variety of languages, such as C, C++, and Fortran. In addition, a Java-based version of MPI specifies how this programming model can be used from Java programs [59].

In the MPI model, a set of processes are started at program startup. There is one process per processor, but each processor may execute a different process. Thus, MPI is a message-passing programming model for MIMD systems. During program execution, the number of processes in an MPI program remains fixed.

MPI processes are named, and processes send and receive messages in a point-to-point fashion based on process name. Processes can be grouped, and collective communication functions can be used to perform global operations on a group, such as broadcast and synchronization. Message exchanges in MPI can convey the communication context in which a message exchange occurs. MPI even offers a process the ability to probe its environment and to probe for messages, allowing MPI programs to use both synchronous and asynchronous message exchange.

In addition to defining message exchange semantics, the MPI programming model provides explicit support for the construction of parallel programming libraries suitable for execution on a cluster [60]. Libraries written for the MPI standard are portable and can be reused by higher-level application software. The chief MPI tools for library construction are communication contexts, process groups, virtual topologies, and cached attributes. An MPI construct called a *communicator* encapsulates all these functions in a reusable fashion.

An MPI process group is an ordered collection of processes that defines the scope for process names and for collective communication. Because the system can differentiate between processes sharing a context, communication context allows partitioning of information during message exchange. Separate contexts by MPI libraries insulate communication internal to the library execution from external communication.

An MPI *communicator* can be thought of as a group identifier associated with a context. *Intra*-communicators operate on a single group, whereas *inter*-communicators are used for point-to-point communication between two groups of processes. While intra-communicators let a library developer encapsulate communication internal to a library, inter-communicators bind two groups together, with communication contexts shared by both groups.

The MPI standard limits itself to defining message passing semantics and functions and to defining the primitives required for reusable libraries. MPI does not provide an infrastructure for program construction and task management. Those responsibilities are left to MPI implementations. The most popular implementation of the MPI standard is MPICH [61]. Available as an open-source package, MPICH supports the latest MPI 2 standard [10]. MPI has recently been extended for Grid communication with the MPICH-G library [62].

While MPI provides a comprehensive message-passing library of over 150 functions, several of the key MPI concepts have influenced the design of smaller, special-purpose message-passing libraries. *JavaGroups* [63] is an open-source Java toolkit for reliable multicast communication on a cluster, or even on a wide-area network. Similar to MPI, JavaGroups facilitates the creation of processes groups and also allows the processes to dynamically join or leave groups. An automatic membership-detection infrastructure in JavaGroups handles the removal of non-responsive group members. Communication in JavaGroups can be point-to-point from one group member to another, or group communication (from one group member to an entire group). Several cluster-aware Java applications rely on JavaGroups for group message passing, such as the JBoss application server [64].

In addition to message passing and virtual shared memory, programming models based on virtual machines also facilitate the parallel execution of serial programs on a cluster (SPPS). The *Parallel Virtual Machine (PVM)* [33] consists of daemon processes, to be executed on all cluster nodes, and an application programming library. PVM presents heterogeneous cluster resources as a homogenous environment to a program. The PVM daemon process can run on machines with widely differing computational capabilities, from notebooks to supercomputers. PVM offers language bindings to C and C++ as a set of API functions, and a binding to Fortran as a series of subroutines.

Using PVM is straightforward. First, the user starts up the PVM daemons on the set of cluster nodes he or she wishes to incorporate into the shared cluster resource. Next, the user writes a set of serial programs, includes calls to the PVM routines, and links those programs with the PVM libraries. Finally, the user executes a "master" program on one machine. That program, through the PVM API calls, will spawn other programs, "slaves," on other cluster nodes as needed. Those programs communicate with each other through a simple message-passing mechanism. The run concludes with the termination of the initial serial master program. Code for each slave program must be made available to the PVM daemon on each node prior to executing the master.

Each serial program running on the nodes that make up a PVM instance typically runs as a task on a host's operating system. Therefore, the unit of parallelism in PVM is a *task*. A group of such tasks make up a PVM program. PVM tasks are identified by a task ID, typically an integer. Task IDs are assigned by PVM, and intertask communication takes place in PVM based on task IDs. Currently, PVM does not use MPI for intertask message-passing communication. However, an effort is under way to incorporate the benefits of MPI into PVM [65].

A PVM task can belong to one or more task groups during its execution. Task groups in PVM are dynamic: a task can join or leave a task group during its execution without having to notify other tasks in a given group. PVM also supports group communication primitives: a task can broadcast a message not only to other members of the group to which it currently belongs but also to tasks belonging to other task groups.

Parameter Sweep supports parallelism by executing the same program with different parameters in parallel as individual processes. An example of a tool that supports parameter sweep is Nimrod [66], which performs parameter sweep over a cluster of computers. Nimrod provides a script-based declarative programming language for defining parameter-sweep specification. It allows users to define varying values for key parameters to be studied in a simple script. Using the script, it automatically generates the required data files for each program, depending on the set of parameters. Nimrod then selects a computer for each program, transfers the generated data files and other required files for each program to the selected workstation for execution, and transfers back the execution results.

6   CLUSTER APPLICATIONS

One category of applications where cluster computing is rapidly becoming the architecture of choice is Grand Challenge Applications (GCA). Grand Challenge Applications (GCAs) [67] are defined as fundamental problems in science and engineering with broad economic and scientific impact whose solution can be advanced by applying High Performance Computing and Communications (HPCC) technologies.

The high scale of complexity in GCAs demands an enormous amount of resource needs, such as processing time, memory space, and communication bandwidth. A common characteristic of GCAs is that they involve simulations that are computationally intensive. Examples of GCAs are applied fluid dynamics, environmental modeling, ecosystem simulation, biomedical imaging, biomechanics, molecular biology, molecular design, cognition, and computational sciences.

Other than GCAs, cluster computing is also being applied in other applications that demand high availability, scalability, and performance. Clusters are being used as replicated storage and backup servers that provide the essential fault tolerance and reliability for critical applications. For example, the Internet search engine Google [68] uses cluster computing to provide reliable and efficient Internet search services. There are also many commercial cluster products designed for distributed databases and web servers. In the following subsections, we will discuss some of these applications and examine how cluster computing is used to enable them.

6.1.1 Google Search Engine

Internet search engines enable Internet users to search for information on the Internet by entering specific keywords. A widely used search engine, Google [68] uses cluster computing to meet the huge quantity of worldwide search requests that comprise a peak of thousands of queries per second. A single Google query needs to use at least tens of billions of processing cycles and access a few hundred megabytes of data in order to return satisfactory search results.

Google uses cluster computing as its solution to the high demand of system resources, since clusters have better price–performance ratios than alternative high-performance computing platforms, and also use less electrical power. Google focuses on two important design factors: reliability and request throughput.

Google is able to achieve reliability at the software level so that a reliable computing infrastructure can be constructed on clusters of 15,000 commodity PCs distributed worldwide. The services for Google are also replicated across multiple machines in the clusters to provide the necessary availability. Google maximizes overall request throughput by performing parallel execution of individual search requests. This means that more search requests can be completed within a specific time interval.

A typical Google search consists of the following operations:
1. An Internet user enters a query at the Google webpage.
2. The web browser searches for the Internet Protocol (IP) address via the www.google.com Domain Name Server (DNS).
3. Google uses a DNS-based load-balancing system that maps the query to a cluster that is geographically nearest to the user so as to minimize network communication delay time. The IP address of the selected cluster is returned.
4. The web browser then sends the search request in Hypertext Transport Protocol (HTTP) format to the selected cluster at the specified IP address.
5. The selected cluster then processes the query locally.
6. A hardware-based load balancer in the cluster monitors the available set of Google Web Servers (GWSs) in the cluster and distributes the requests evenly within the cluster.
7. A GWS machine receives the request, coordinates the query execution, and sends the search result back to the user's browser.

Figure 16.9 shows how a GWS operates within a local cluster. The first phase of query execution involves index servers consulting an inverted index that matches each query keyword to a matching list of documents. Relevance scores are also computed for matching documents so that the search result returned to the user is ordered by score. In the second phase, document servers fetch each document from disk to extract the title and the keyword-in-context portion of the document. In addition to the two phases, the GWS also activates the spell checker

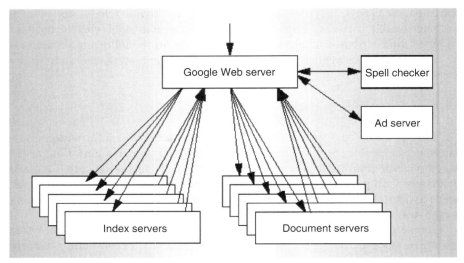

Figure 16.9. Google query-serving architecture (L. A. Barroso et al. [68]).

and the ad server. The spell checker verifies that the spelling of the query key-words is correct, while the ad server generate advertisements that relate to the query and may therefore interest the user.

6.1.2   Petroleum Reservoir Simulation

Petroleum reservoir simulation facilitates a better understanding of petroleum reservoirs, which is crucial to better reservoir management and more efficient oil and gas production. Petroleum reservoir simulation is an example of GCA, since it demands intensive computations in order to simulate geological and physical models. For example, the Center for Petroleum and Geosystems Engineering of the University of Texas at Austin is constructing a new parallel petroleum reservoir simulator called General Purpose Adaptive Simulator (GPAS) [69] using a cluster of 64 dual-processor servers with a total of 128 processors.

A typical petroleum reservoir simulator consists of a coupled set of nonlinear partial differential equations and constitutive relations that describe the physical processes occurring in a petroleum reservoir. There are two most widely used sim-ulators. The first is the black oil simulator, which uses water, oil, and gas phases for modeling fluid flow in a reservoir. The second is the compositional simulator, which uses phases with different chemical species for modeling physical processes occurring in a reservoir. Previously, compositional simulators were used less often, since they are more complicated and thus require more intensive memory and processing requirements. With the advent of cluster computing, more researchers are using compositional simulators that use more data to characterize reservoirs.

The GPAS [69] is a compositional petroleum reservoir simulator that can per-form more accurate, efficient and high-resolution simulation of fluid flow in permeable media. It uses a finite-difference method that divides a continuous domain into smaller cells to solve the governing partial differential equations. The higher number of cells produces more accurate results but requires more computation time. A fully implicit solution results in a structure of nonlinear equations that are then resolved using Newton's method. However, large sparse linear systems of equations are needed to obtain a numerical solution of these nonlinear equations. Therefore, the Portable Extensible Toolkit for Scientific Computation (PETSc) [70], a set of tools for solving partial differential equations, is used to solve these linear systems.

To handle the parallel processing requirements, an Integrated Parallel Accurate Reservoir Simulator (IPARS) framework has been developed to separate the physical model development from parallel processing. IPARS provides input and output, memory management, domain decomposition, and message passing among processors to update overlapping regions. Communications between the simulator framework and a physical model are carried out through FORTRAN subroutine calls provided within the IPARS, thus hiding the complexities from the physical model developers, who only need to call the FORTRAN subroutines to perform corresponding tasks.

6.1.3 Protein Explorer

The Bioinformatics Group at RIKEN Genomic Sciences Center in Japan is currently building the world's first petaflops supercomputer. The *Protein Explorer (PE)* system [71] will be a specialized system for molecular dynamics simulations—specifically, protein simulations—and is expected to be ready in early 2006. The PE system will be a PC cluster equipped with special-purpose engines to calculate nonbonded interactions between molecular atoms. These calculations constitute the most time-consuming portion of the simulations. The PE project is motivated by the national Protein 3000 project in Japan that was initiated in 2002 with the goal of solving the structures of 3,000 proteins by the year 2007.

Figure 16.10 shows the components of the PE system. It will be a cluster of 256 dual-processor nodes giving a total of 512 processors, connected via Gigabit Ethernet. Each cluster node has two special-purpose engine boards (with 12 MDGRAPE-3 chips on each board) connected to it, giving it a total of 6,144 chips.

The cluster nodes will transmit the coordinates and the other data of particles for the molecular dynamics simulation to the special-purpose engines, which then calculate the nonbonded forces such as Coulomb force and van der Walls force between particles before returning the results to the hosts. In other words, the special-purpose engines only focus on computing the most complex portion of the simulation, that is, calculating the nonbonded forces. All the coordination and other calculations are handled by the cluster nodes themselves.

6.1.4 Earthquake Simulation

Earthquake simulation is classified as a GCA, given its high modeling and computational complexities [72]. First, multiple spatial scales characterize the earthquake source and basin response, ranging from tens of kilometers for the basin dimensions to hundreds of kilometers for earthquake sources. Second,

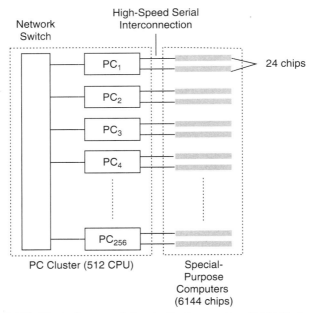

Figure 16.10. Block diagram of Protein Explorer system (M. Taiji et al. [71]).

temporal scales differ—from hundredths of a second for depicting the highest frequencies of the earthquake source to several minutes of shaking within the basin. Third, many basins have highly irregular geometry. Fourth, the soils in the basins comprise heterogeneous material properties. And fifth, there remains great uncertainty into the modeling process due to the indirect observation of geology and source parameters.

An ongoing research project in the United States [72] focuses on developing the capability for generating realistic inversion-based models of complex basin geology and earthquake sources. This capability could then be used to model and forecast strong ground motion during earthquakes in large basins such as Los Angeles (LA). Ground motion modeling and forecasting is essential to studying which structures will become vulnerable during the occurrence of an earthquake. This modeling can be used to design future earthquake-resistant structures and to retrofit existing structures so as to mitigate the effects of an earthquake. The Los Angeles region was chosen for the case study because it is the most highly populated seismic region in the USA, has well-characterized geological structures (including a varied fault system), and has extensive records of past earthquakes.

The earthquake simulation is conducted using a terra-scale HP AlphaServer cluster that has 750 quadruple-processor nodes at the Pittsburgh Supercomputing Center (PSC). It simulates the 1994 Northridge earthquake in the Greater LA Basin at 1 Hz maximum frequency resolution and 100 m/s minimum shear wave velocity. The resulting unstructured mesh contains over 100 million grid points and 80 million hexahedral finite elements, ranking it as one of the largest unstructured mesh simulations ever conducted. It is also the most highly resolved simulation of the Northridge earthquake ever done. It sustains nearly a teraflops over 12 hours in solving the 300 million wave propagations.

The simulations are based on multiresolution mesh algorithms that can model the wide range of length and time scales depicting earthquake response. Figure 16.11 shows the process of generating a mesh using the etree method. That method is used for earthquake simulations in heterogeneous basins, where the shear wave velocity and maximum resolved frequency determine the local element size. At the initial "construct" step, an octree is constructed and stored on disk. The decompositions of the octants are dependent on the geometry or physics being modeled, thus resulting in an unbalanced octree. Then the balance step recursively decomposes all the large octants that violate the 2-to-1 constraint until there are no more illegal conditions, thus creating a balanced octree. Finally, in the transform step, mesh-specific information such as the element–node relationship and the node coordinates are derived from the balanced octree and separately stored in two databases: one for the mesh elements, another for the mesh nodes.

For the balancing step, the whole domain is first partitioned into equal-size blocks. Then, internal balancing enforces the 2-to-1 constraint within each block. Finally, boundary balancing is used to resolve interactions between adjacent blocks. This local balancing step is very effective, since it can achieve a speedup ranging from 8 to 28, depending on the size of the meshes being balanced.

Figure 16.12 shows snapshots at different times of the simulation of the wave propagation throughout the basin based on the 1994 Northridge earthquake. These snapshots reflect the directivity of the ground motion along the strike from the epicenter and the concentration of motion near the fault corners.

6.1.5 Image Rendering

The Scientific Computing and Imaging (SCI) Institute at University of Utah has explored cluster-based scientific visualization [73] using a 32-node visualization cluster composed of commodity hardware components connected with a high-speed network. The OpenGL [74] scientific visualization tool, Simian, has been modified to create a cluster-aware version of Simian that supports parallelization by making explicit use of remote cluster nodes through a message-passing interface (MPI). Simian is able to generate 3D images for fire-spread simulations that model scenarios such as when a missile located within a pool of jet fuel catches fire and explodes. The use of image rendering for fire-spread simulations enables researchers to a better visualize the destructive effects.

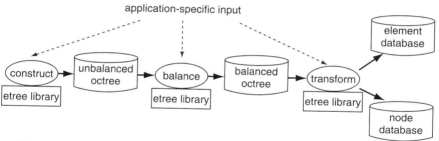

Figure 16.11. The etree method of generating octree meshes (V. Akcelik et al. [72]).

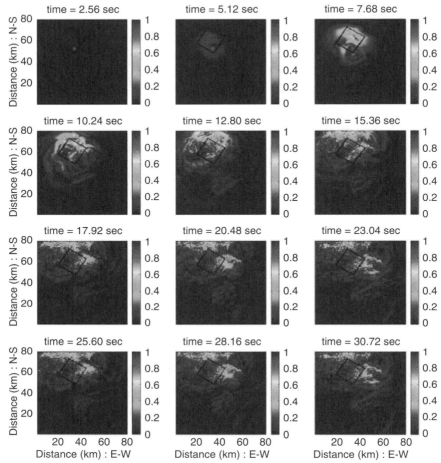

Figure 16.12. Snapshots of propagating waves from simulation of 1994 Northridge earthquake (V. Akcelik et al. [72]).

Normally, Simian uses a swapping mechanism to manage datasets that are too large to load into the available texture memory, resulting in low performance and interactivity. For the cluster-aware Simian, large datasets are divided into subvolumes that can be distributed across multiple cluster nodes, thus achieving the interactive performance. This "divide-and-conquer" technique first decomposes the dataset into subvolumes before distributing the subvolumes to multiple remote cluster nodes. Each node is then responsible for rendering its subvolume by using the locally available graphics hardware. The individual results are finally combined using a binary-swap compositing algorithm to generate the final image. This enables the cluster-aware Simian to visualize large-scale datasets and maintain interactive rates without the need for texture swapping.

Figure 16.13. Visualization of fire-spread datasets (C. Gribble et al. [73]).

Figure 16.13 shows the visualization of two fire-spread datasets simulating a heptane pool fire, generated by the cluster-aware version of Simian using eight cluster nodes. The top row of Figure 16.13 shows two views (side and top views) of the h300_0075 dataset, while the bottom row shows the h300_0130 dataset.

SUMMARY

We have discussed the motivation for cluster computing as well as the technologies available for building cluster systems. The emphasis placed on the use of commodity-based hardware and software components to achieve high performance, availability, and scalability means that cluster computing is a more cost-effective platform compared with traditional high-performance platforms.

We have examined the various cluster-specific components such as interconnection technology, operating system, middleware, and programming model. We have discussed the performance of a number of common cluster interconnects. We have also presented various parallel programming models and concepts of single system image and its realization at the cluster resource management level. The rapid research and development of cluster hardware and software components has enhanced the usage of cluster computing for a wide variety of applications, both in scientific and commercial domains. We have studied some of these applications and how clusters are used to implement them.

For recent developments and innovations in cluster computing technologies and their applications, we recommend readers to refer to the Proceedings of the IEEE Task Force on Cluster Computing (TFCC) [75] events such as the ClusterXY [76] and CCGridXY [77] conference series.

REFERENCES

[1] R. Buyya (ed) (1999): *High Performance Cluster Computing: Architectures and Systems, 1*, Prentice Hall.

[2] The Beowulf Cluster site, http://www.beowulf.org

[3] T. E. Anderson, D. Culler, and D. A. Patterson (1995): A Case for NOW (Network of Workstations), *IEEE Micro, 15*(1), 54–64.

[4] A. Chien, S. Pakin, M. Lauria, M. Buchanan, K. Hane, L. Giannini, and J. Prusakova (1997): High Performance Virtual Machines (HPVM): Clusters with Supercomputing APIs and Performance, *Proc. 8th SIAM Conference on Parallel Processing for Scientific Computing (PP97)*, Minneapolis, USA.

[5] G. F. Pfister (1998): *In Search of Clusters, 2nd Edition*, Prentice Hall.

[6] T. Shanley (2002): *Infiniband Network Architecture*, Addison-Wesley.

[7] N. J. Boden, D. Cohen, R. E. Felderman, A.E. Kulawik, C.L. Seitz, J.N. Seizovic, and Wen-King Su (1995): Myrinet: A Gigabit-per-second Local Area Network, *IEEE Micro, 15*, (1), 29–36.

[8] K. Alnaes, E. H. Kristiansen, D. B. Gustavson, and D. V. James (1990): Scalable Coherent Interface, *Proc. 1990 IEEE International Conference on Computer Systems and Software Engineering (CompEuro '90)*, Tel-Aviv, Israel, pp. 446–453.

[9] D. Cameron and G. Regnier (2002): *Virtual Interface Architecture*, Intel Press.

[10] Message Passing Interface (MPI) Forum, http://www.mpi-forum.org

[11] M. Baker, A. Apon, R. Buyya, and H. Jin (2002): Cluster Computing and Applications, *Encyclopedia of Computer Science and Technology, 45* (Supplement 30), A. Kent and J. Williams (eds), Marcel Dekker, pp. 87–125.

[12] MVICH: MPI for VIA, http://old-www.nersc.gov/research/FTG/mvich

[13] M-VIA: VIA for Linux, http://old-www.nersc.gov/research/FTG/via

[14] MPI/PRO, http://www.mpi-softtech.com

[15] M. Banikazemi, J. Liu, D. K. Panda, and P. Sadayappan (2001): Implementing TreadMarks over Virtual Interface Architecture on Myrinet and Gigabit Ethernet: Challenges, Design Experience, and Performance Evaluation, *Proc. 2001 International Conference on Parallel Processing (ICPP '01)*, Valencia, Spain, pp. 167–174.

[16] Z. Lan and P. Deshikachar (2003): Performance Analysis of a Large-Scale Cosmology Application on Three Cluster Systems, *Proc. 2003 IEEE International Conference on Cluster Computing (Cluster 2003)*, Hong Kong, China, pp. 56–63.

[17] A. J. van der Steen (2003): An Evaluation of Some Beowulf Clusters, *Cluster Computing, 6*(4), 287–297.

[18] H. Chen, P. Wyckoff, and K. Moor (2000): Cost/Performance Evaluation of Gigabit Ethernet and Myrinet as Cluster Interconnects, *Proc. 2000 Conference on Network and Application Performance (OPNETWORK 2000)*, Washington, USA.

[19] J. Hsieh, T. Leng, V. Mashayekhi, and R. Rooholamini (2000): Architectural and Performance Evaluation of GigaNet and Myrinet Interconnects on Clusters of Small-Scale SMP Servers, *Proc. 2000 ACM/IEEE Conference on Supercomputing (SC2000)*, Dallas, USA.

[20] D. H. Bailey, E. Barszcz, J. T. Barton, D. S. Browning, R. L. Carter, L. Dagum, R. A. Fatoohi, P. O. Frederickson, T. A. Lasinski, R. S. Schreiber, H. D. Simon, V. Venkatakrishnan, and W. K. Weeratunga (1991): The NAS Parallel Benchmarks, *International Journal of Supercomputing Applications*, 5(3), 63–73.

[21] Pallas MPI Benchmarks, http://www.pallas.com/e/products/pmb/index.htm

[22] E. Lindahl, B. Hess, and D. van der Spoel (2001): GROMACS 3.0: a package for molecular simulation and trajectory analysis, *Journal of Molecular Modeling*, 7(8), 306–317.

[23] H. Pourreza, R. Eskicioglu, and P. C. J. Graham (2004): Preliminary Performance Assessment of Four Cluster Interconnects on Identical Hardware, *Proc. 18th International Symposium on High Performance Computing Systems and Applications (HPCS2004)*, Winnipeg, Canada.

[24] R. Buyya, T. Cortes, and H. Jin (2001): Single System Image (SSI), *International Journal of High Performance Computing Applications*, 15(2), 124–135.

[25] Hewlett-Packard, Memory Channel, http://www.hp.com/techservers/systems/symc.html

[26] A Comprehensive Bibliography of Distributed Shared Memory, http://dsm-biblio.cs.umanitoba.ca/WEB

[27] Distributed Shared Memory (DSM), http://www.cs.umd.edu/~keleher/dsm.html

[28] A. Barak and O. La'adan (1998): The MOSIX multicomputer operating system for high performance cluster computing, *Future Generation Computer Systems*, 13(4–5), 361–372.

[29] Y. A. Khalidi, J. M. Bernabeu, V. Matena, K. Shirriff, and M. Thadani (1995): Solaris MC: A Multi-Computer OS, *Sun Microsystems Technical Report TR-95-48*.

[30] SCO Unixware, http://www.thescogroup.com/products/unixware713

[31] B. Walker and D. Steel (1999): Implementing a Full Single System Image UnixWare Cluster: Middleware vs. Underware, *Proc. International Conference on Parallel and Distributed Processing Techniques and Applications (PDPTA99)*, Las Vegas, USA, pp. 2767–2773.

[32] D. P. Ghormley, D. Petrou, S. H. Rodrigues, A. M. Vahdat, and T. E. Anderson (1998): GLUnix: A Global Layer Unix for a Network of Workstations, *Software: Practice and Experience*, 28(9), 929–961.

[33] V. S. Sunderam (1990): PVM: A framework for parallel distributed computing, *Concurrency: Practice and Experience*, 2(4), 315–339.

[34] University of Wisconsin-Madison, *Condor Version 6.6.2 Manual*, 2004.

[35] IBM, *LoadLeveler for AIX 5L V3.2 Using and Administering, SA22-7881-01*, 2003.

[36] Platform Computing, *LSF V4.1 Administrator's Guide*, 2001.

[37] Altair Grid Technologies: *OpenPBS Release 2.3 Administrator Guide*, 2000.

[38] Sun Microsystems, *Sun ONE Grid Engine, Administration and User's Guide*, Oct. 2002.

[39] J. Sherwani, N. Ali, N. Lotia, Z. Hayat, and R. Buyya (2004): Libra: A Computational Economy based Job Scheduling System for Clusters, *Software: Practice and Experience*, 34(6), 573–590.

[40] R. Buyya (2000): PARMON: a portable and scalable monitoring system for clusters, *Software: Practice and Experience*, *30*(7), 723–739.

[41] W. Zhang (2000): Linux Virtual Server for Scalable Network Services, *Linux Symposium*, Ottawa, Canada.

[42] E. Gallopoulos, E. Houstis, and J. R. Rice (1994): Computer as thinker/doer: problem-solving environments for computational science, *IEEE Computational Science and Engineering*, *1*(2), 11–23.

[43] Linux Online, http://www.linux.org

[44] IBM AIX: UNIX Operating System, http://www.ibm.com/servers/aix

[45] SGI IRIX, http://www.sgi.com

[46] HP/Compaq Tru64, http://www.tru64unix.compaq.com

[47] Microsoft Windows 2000: http://www.microsoft.com/windows2000

[48] I. Foster and C. Kesselman (eds), (1999): *The Grid: Blueprint for a New Computing Infrastructure*, Morgan Kauffman Publishers.

[49] I. Foster and C. Kesselman (1997): Globus: A Metacomputing Infrastructure Toolkit, *International Journal Supercomputer Applications*, *11*(2), 115–128.

[50] R. Evard, N. Desai, J. Navarro, and D. Nurmi (2002): Clusters as large-scale development facilities, *Proc. 2002 IEEE International Conference on Cluster Computing (Cluster 2002)*, Chicago, USA.

[51] N. Pundit (2002): CPlant: The Largest Linux Cluster, *Newsletter of IEEE Task Force on Cluster Computing*, *4*(1), Fall.

[52] M. Flynn (1972): Some computer organizations and their effectiveness, *IEEE Transactions on Computers*, *21*(9), 948–960.

[53] S. Ghandeharizadeh and F. Sommers (2001): Parallel Databases and Decision Support Systems, *Handbook of Data Mining and Knowledge Discovery*, W. Klosgen and J. Zytkow (eds), Oxford University Press.

[54] T. Nash (1992): Cluster Computing at FermiLab, presentation to IEEE SSS.

[55] G. Papadopoulos and F. Arbab (1998): Coordination models and languages, *Centrum voor Wiskunde en Informatica Technical Report SEN-R9834*.

[56] N. Carriero and D. Gelernter (1990): *How to Write Parallel Programs: A First Course*, MIT Press.

[57] K. Li and P. Hudak (1986): Memory Coherence in Shared Virtual Memory Systems, *Proc. 5th Annual ACM Symposium on Principles of Distributed Computing*, Calgary, Canada, pp. 229–239.

[58] J. Waldo et al. (2001): *The Jini Specifications, 2nd Edition*, Addison-Wesley.

[59] B. Carpenter, V. Getov, G. Judd, T. Skjellum, and G. Fox (1998): MPI For Java: Position Document and Draft API Specification, *Java Grande Forum Technical Report JGF-TR-03*.

[60] A. Skjellum, N. E. Doss, and P. V. Bangalore (1993): Writing Libraries in MPI, *Proc. Scalable Parallel Libraries Conference,* Mississippi State, USA, pp. 166–173.

[61] W. Gropp, E. Lusk, N. Doss, and A. Skjellum (1996): A High-Performance, Portable Implementation of the MPI Message Passing Interface Standard, *Parallel Computing*, *22*(6), 789–828.

[62] I. Foster, and N. Karonis (1998): A Grid-Enabled MPI: Message Passing in Heterogeneous Distributed Computing Systems, *Proc. 1998 IEEE/ACM Supercomputing Conference (SC98)*, Orlando, USA.

[63] JavaGroups, http://www.jgroups.org/javagroupsnew/docs

[64] JBoss, http://www.jboss.org

[65] G. Fagg and J. Dongarra (1996): PVMPI: An Integration of the PVM and MPI Systems, *Calculateurs Parallèles*, 8(2), 151–166.

[66] D. Abramson, R. Sosic, J. Giddy, and B. Hall (1995): Nimrod: A Tool for Performing Parametised Simulations Using Distributed Workstations, *Proc. 4th IEEE Symposium on High Performance Distributed Computing (HPDC95)*, Pentagon City, USA, pp. 112–121.

[67] National Coordination Office for Informational Technology Research and Development, Grand Challenge Applications, *High Performance Computing and Communications: Foundation for America's Information Future*, http://www.nitrd.gov/pubs/blue96/section.2.6.0.html

[68] L. A. Barroso, J. Dean, and U. Holzle (2003): Web search for a planet: The Google cluster architecture, *IEEE Micro*, 23(2), 22–28.

[69] T. Uetani, B. Guler, and K. Sepehrnoori (2002): Parallel Reservoir Simulation on High Performance Clusters, *Proc. 6th World Multi-Conf. on Systemics, Cybernetics and Informatics (SCI2002)*, V.

[70] Portable Extensible Toolkit for Scientific Computation (PETSc), http://www-unix.mcs.anl.gov/petsc

[71] M. Taiji, T. Narumi, Y. Ohno, N. Futatsugi, A. Suenaga, N. Takada, and A. Konagaya (2003): Protein Explorer: A Petaflops Special-Purpose Computer System for Molecular Dynamics Simulations, *Proc. 2003 ACM/IEEE Supercomputing Conference (SC2003)*, Phoenix, USA.

[72] V. Akcelik, J. Bielak, G. Biros, I. Epanomeritakis, A. Fernandez, O. Ghattas, E. J. Kim, J. Lopez, D. O'Hallaron, T. Tu, and J. Urbanic (2003): High Resolution Forward and Inverse Earthquake Modeling on Terascale Computers, *Proc. 2003 ACM/IEEE Supercomputing Conference (SC2003)*, Phoenix, USA.

[73] C. Gribble, X. Cavin, M. Hartner, and C. Hansen (2003): Cluster-based Interactive Volume Rendering with Simian, *University of Utah School of Computing Technical Report UUCS-03-017*.

[74] OpenGL, http://www.opengl.org

[75] IEEE Task Force on Cluster Computing, http://www.ieeetfcc.org

[76] ClusterXY - IEEE Intl. Conference on Cluster Computing, http://www.cluster comp.org

[77] CCGridXY - IEEE Intl. Symposium on Cluster Computing and the Grid, http://www.ccgrid.org

Chapter 17

WEB SERVICE COMPUTING: OVERVIEW AND DIRECTIONS

Boualem Benatallah[1], Olivier Perrin[2], Fethi A. Rabhi[1], Claude Godart[2]
[1]The University of New South Wales, Australia.
[2]INRIA-LORIA, France

1   INTRODUCTION

Web Service is a new buzzword sweeping through the information systems infrastructure industry. With the advent of the Internet and the Web, the first generation of Web services was born, namely Business-to-Customer (B2C) Web services (e.g., virtual malls, customized news delivery, traffic monitoring, and route planning). More recently, organizations started using the Internet and Web as means to automate relationships between their business processes, i.e., creating Business-to-Business (B2B) Web services. These services allow organizations to form alliances by joining their applications, databases, and systems. The purpose is to share their costs, skills, and resources as well as to offer value-added services. Examples of B2B Web services include procurement, customer relationship management (CRM), finance, billing, traffic information services, accounting, human resources, supply chain, and manufacturing.

The basic technological infrastructure for Web services is structured around XML-based standards and Internet protocols. These standards provide building blocks for service description, discovery, and interaction. Web service technologies have clearly influenced positively the development of integrated systems by providing programmatic access to Web services. They are evolving toward being able to solve critical integration issues, including security, transactions, collaborative processes management, semantic aspects, and seamless integration with existing middleware infrastructures. The infrastructure that is needed to support

Web services is clearly much broader than traditional transaction processing systems.

This chapter introduces some basic concepts related to Web services development in Section 2. Then it provides an overview of existing and emerging standards in Section 3. It describes the role of Web services in integrating Business-to-Business applications in Section 4 and Web service composition in Section 5. The last sections conclude the chapter by providing an overview of current research work and future trends.

2   BASIC CONCEPTS

By definition, a Web service is a self-content, self-describing, loosely coupled, reusable software component that can be published, discovered/located, and invoked via Internet protocols. A Web service is agnostic of operating systems, programming models, and languages. It provides an interface describing how other systems can interact with it using messages. Web services perform functions, which can be anything from simple requests (transformation, storage and/or retrieval of data) to complicated business processes (aggregation, composition, orchestration).

The life cycle of activities related to Web service development, deployment, and enactment is illustrated in Figure 17.1. Briefly stated, these activities are as follows:

- *Wrapping native services*: ensuring that a native/proprietary service (e.g., legacy application) can be invoked by other Web services regardless of its underlying data model, message format, and interaction protocol.

- *Setting outsourcing agreements*: negotiating, establishing, and enforcing contractual obligations between partner services.

- *Assembling composite services*: A service can be elementary or composite. The development of an elementary service is entirely under the responsibility of the provider. The development of a composite service requires the aggregation of other services, which are referred to as component services.

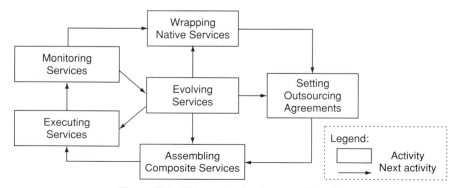

Figure 17.1. Web service development lifecycle

- *Executing services*: This process particularly relates to enacting composite service specifications with regard to execution models satisfying certain practical constraints (e.g., efficiency, availability).

- *Monitoring services*: supervising service executions (e.g., logging service invocations, state changes, and message exchanges) in order to detect contract violations, measure performance, and predict exceptions.

- *Evolving services:* adapting composite services to accommodate organizational changes, take advantage of new technological opportunities, or take into account feedback from monitoring.

In addition, the cycle may refer to other activities such as *service advertisement/discovery*, i.e., generating service descriptions and publishing these descriptions in registries for subsequent discovery. Service descriptions cover several aspects ranging from interfaces to nonfunctional properties and contractual agreements with customers.

Figure 17.2 provides an overview of existing specifications of Web services organized in terms of the issues that they address.

The rest of this chapter is dedicated to presenting in more detail the various specifications that comprose the Web services stack, explaining their relationships with each other, and discussing open research issues and problems.

3   WEB SERVICES INFRASTRUCTURE: AN OVERVIEW

In this section, we first describe the use of SOAP (Simple Object Access Protocol), WSDL (Web Services Description Language), and UDDI (Universal

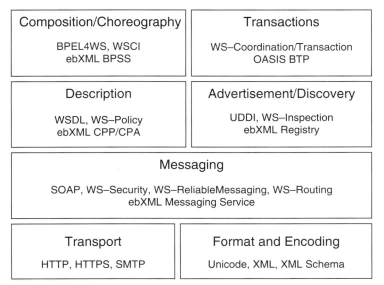

Figure 17.2. *Overview of the Web services stack*

Description, Discovery, and Integration) as building blocks for Web services-enabled applications [1,7]. Then we give a brief overview of other Web service standards.

3.1   Simple Object Access Protocol (SOAP)

SOAP provides an XML-based protocol for structured message exchanges. It relies on existing transport protocols such as HTTP and MQSeries. SOAP features document-based communication among Web services. Document-based communication allows the integration of loosely coupled services. A SOAP message contains two parts: the header and the body. The header includes information such as intended purpose (e.g., service invocation, invocation results), sender's credentials, response type, and so on. The body contains an XML representation of a service invocation request (i.e., name of operation to be invoked, values of input parameters) or response (i.e., results of service invocation). SOAP implementations exist for several programming languages, including Java and C. SOAP implementations provide mappings between SOAP messages and formats understood by service implementations (e.g., Java classes). SOAP implementations typically automatically generate the SOAP header, and provide mappings between the contents of SOAP message bodies and data structures in the host language (e.g., Java objects).

If we take a car rental Web service as an example, the following SOAP request message invokes the operation RentCar using the most stable version (version 1.1):

```
POST /carRenting HTTP/1.1
Host: www.carRenting.com
Content-Type: text/xml; charset="utf-8"
Content-Length: nnnn
SOAPAction: "http://example.com/RentCar"
<SOAP-ENV:Envelope
   xmlns:SOAP-ENV="http://schemas.xmlsopa.org/soap/envelope"
SOAP-ENV:encodingStyle=
                  "http://schemas.xmlsoap.org/soap/encoding">
<SOAP-ENV:body>
        <m:RentCar xmlns:m="http://example.com/RentCar">
           <customer>Rayan Stephan</customer>
           <rentalDate>12/02/2002</rentalDate>
           <returnDate>15/02/2002</returnDate>
        </m:RentCar>
</SOAP-ENV:Body>
</SOAP-ENV:Envelope>
```

This example shows the different parts that make up a SOAP invocation method. Lines 5 and 11–14 specify the method to invoke (RentCar) and its three arguments, which are the customer name, the rental date, and the return date. After a successful invocation, the result is returned in a SOAP response message, such as:

```
HTTP/1.1 200 OK
Content-Type: text/xml; charset="utf-8"
Content-Length: nnnn
<SOAP-ENV:Envelope
    xmlns:SOAP-ENV="http://schemas.xmlsopa.org/soap/envelope"
    SOAP-ENV:encodingStyle=
                    "http://schemas.xmlsoap.org/soap/encoding">
    <SOAP-ENV:Body>
      <m:RentCarResponse xmlns:m="http://example.com/RentCar">
            <rentalFee>356.00</rentalFee>
      </m:RentCarResponse>
    </SOAP-ENV:Body>
</SOAP-ENV:Envelope>
```

3.2   Web Service Description Language (WSDL)

WSDL [29] is an XML-based language for describing the functional properties of Web services. It aims at providing self-describing XML-based service definitions that applications, as well as people, can easily understand. In WSDL, a
service consists of a collection of message exchange end points. An end point
contains an abstract description of a service interface and implementation binding. The abstract description of a service contains (1) definitions of messages
that are consumed and generated by the service (i.e., input and output messages)
and (2) signatures of service operations. Here is an example of an abstract
description:

```
<?xml version="1.0"?>
<definitions name="carRenting" . . . .>
<types>
<schema targetNamespace="http://example.com/carRenting.xsd"
      xmlns="http://www.w3.org/2000/10/XMLSchema">
        <element name="Customer">
          <complexType>
            <all>
              <element name="Name" type="string"/>
              <element name="Gender" type="string"/>
              <element name="CreditCardNo" type="string"/>
            </all>
          </complexType>
        </element>
</schema>
</types>
```

The implementation binding provides a means to map abstract operations to
concrete service implementations. It essentially contains information about the
location of a binding, the communication protocol to use (e.g., SOAP over
HTTP) for exchanging messages with the service, and mappings between the
abstract description of a service and the underlying communication protocol

message types (i.e., how interactions with service occur over SOAP). Here is an example of an implementation binding:

```
<binding name="carRentingSoapBinding"
        type="tns:carRentingPortType">
<soap:binding
        stype="document"
        transport="http://schemas.xmlsoap.org/soap/http"/>
<operation name="RentCar">
<soap:operation soapAction="http://example.com/RentCar"/>
    <input>
        <soap:body use="literal"/>
    </input>
    <output>
        <soap:body use="literal"/>
    </output>
  </operation>
</binding>
```

3.3   Universal Description Discovery and Integration (UDDI)

UDDI is a specification of an XML-based registry for Web services. It defines an interface for advertising and discovering Web services. The UDDI information model, defined through an XML schema, identifies three types of information: white pages, yellow pages, and green pages.

White pages contain general information, such as business name (i.e, service provider's name) and contact information (e.g., provider's phone numbers). Yellow pages contain meta-data that can be used to effectively locate businesses and services based on classification schemes. For instance, UDDI uses the following standard taxonomies to facilitate businesses/services discovery: NAICS (North American Industry Classification System), UNSPSC (Universal Standard Products and Services Code System), and ISO 3166 (the ISO geographical classification system). The green pages contain service access information, including service descriptions and binding templates. A binding template represents a service end point (i.e., a service access interface). It refers to an entity called the tModel. A tModel describes the compliance of a service with a technical specification (e.g., WDSL document, RMI interface, CORBA IDL). For instance, a WSDL document can be registered as a tModel in the UDDI registry and used in the description of a WSDL-complaint service end point to provide access to service operations. The current stable version of UDDI is version 3.

3.4   Other specifications

Other standards in the Web services stack include the following.

3.4.1   WS-Security

WS-Security [14] aims at integrating several existing security-related technologies in a coherent model and providing an XML syntax for this model. This is achieved by defining header elements to be included in SOAP messages. WS-Security does not provide a complete security framework for Web services; however, it does provide mechanisms for ensuring single-message security within SOAP. Three mechanisms are supported in the current specification:

- Propagation of unsigned and signed security tokens in both text and binary formats. Examples of unsigned security tokens include usernames and passwords, while signed tokens include X.509 certificates and Kerberos tickets. Recent extensions provide support for SAML (Security Assertions Markup Language) assertions and XrML (eXtensible rights Markup Language) licenses.

- Message integrity of SOAP messages is provided using the XML Signature specification in conjunction with security tokens.

- Message confidentiality uses the XML Encryption specification in conjunction with security tokens.

3.4.2   WS-Reliability

WS-Reliability [9] and WS-ReliableMessaging [14] are two competing standards that aim at defining SOAP header elements for addressing three issues:

- Guaranteed message delivery through retries

- At most once message delivery through duplicate elimination

- Guaranteed message ordering by attaching sequence numbers to messages within a message group

3.4.3   WS-Coordination and WS-Transaction

Since ACID transactions are not suitable for loosely coupled environments like the Web, OASIS BTP and WS-Transaction/WS-Coordination are proposals for dealing with specific WS aspects of coordination.

WS-Coordination [17] defines a generic framework that can support various coordination protocols. Each protocol is intended to coordinate a different role that a Web service plays in the activity. Some examples of coordination protocols are Completion (a single participant tells the Coordinator either to try to commit the transaction or to force a rollback), 2PC – Two-Phase Commit (a participant such as a resource manager registers for this protocol so that the Coordinator can manage a commit/abort decision across all resource managers), and PhazeZero (the Coordinator notifies a participant just before a 2PC protocol begins).

A Coordination Service propagates and coordinates activities between services. The messages exchanged between participants carry a Coordination Context that contains critical information for linking the various activities within the protocol. A Coordination Service consists of several components: an Activation Service that allows a Coordination Context to be created, a Registration Service that allows a Web service to register its participation in a Coordination Protocol, and a set of Coordination Protocol Services for each supported Coordination Type (e.g., Completion, 2PC).

WS-Transaction [18] is a specification released in August 2002 by Microsoft, IBM, and BEA Systems. It specifies transactional properties of Web Services independently of coordination aspects. It uses two completion patterns:

- atomic transaction (AT)
- business activity (BA)

An *Atomic Transaction* is used to coordinate activities having a short duration and executed within limited trust. It has the classical atomicity property (*"all or nothing"* behavior) from ACID properties.

A *Business Activity* provides flexible transaction properties (relaxing Isolation and Atomicity) and is used to coordinate activities that are long in duration and aimed at applying business logic to handle business exceptions. Actions are applied immediately and are permanent because the long duration nature of the activities prohibits locking of data resources. A Web Service application can include both *Atomic Transactions* and *Business Activities*.

3.5 WS-Policy

WS-Policy [12] provides a framework with an XML-syntax for defining capabilities and requirements of Web services in the form of *policy assertions*. Policy assertions are statements about an XML element or a Web service description that provide indications regarding the text encoding and natural language used in an XML element, the version of a given standard specification used by a Web service, and the mechanisms used for Web service security (e.g., authentication scheme) with reference to the WS-Security specification (see above). A related specification, namely, WS-PolicyAttachement, provides a mechanism for associating policy assertions expressed in WS-Policy to WSDL descriptions and UDDI entries.

4 B2B INTEGRATION FRAMEWORKS

B2B integration frameworks refer to the use of computerized systems for conducting business (e.g., exchanging documents, selling products) among different partners. They provide functions for defining and integrating business processes and for supporting interactions with back-end application systems such as ERPs (Enterprise Resource Planning) [5]. Usually, interactions between partners' external business processes may be carried out based on a specific B2B standard (e.g., EDI, RossettaNet). B2B standards include definitions of the format and semantics of messages (e.g., request for quote), bindings to communication protocols (e.g., HTTP, FTP), business process conversations (e.g., joint business process), and security mechanisms (e.g., encryption, nonrepudiation).

Web services may be coupled with B2B (Business to Business) integration frameworks to capture the semantics of documents and business processes. In this section, we briefly discuss three representative XML-based integration frameworks, namely, eCO, cXML, and RosettaNet [5, 16].

eCO aims at providing a means to access services regardless of the standards and protocols each potential partner adopts. It introduces xCBL (XML Common Business Library) to define information documents. xCBL consists of a set of XML core documents that are used to represent common interactions among partners. It does not target vertical industry domains. Examples of such core documents are purchase orders, invoices, date, time, and currencies. Partners may use and extend these documents (e.g., adding new elements) to develop their own documents. eCO provides some flexibility in the sense that there is no specific set of predefined document schemas. However, this process may complicate integration efforts, since partners need to be aware of newly created document schemas.

cXML (Commerce XML) provides an XML-based schema language for describing business documents. It targets business transactions that involve non-production Maintenance, Repair, and Operating (MRO) goods and services. cXML defines a set of XML DTDs to represent documents. It provides the following elements for describing product catalogs: Supplier, Index, and Contract. The supplier element gives general information about a supplier (e.g., address, ordering methods). The index element describes the supplier's inventory (e.g., product description, part numbers, classification codes). The contract element relates to the negotiation agreements between a buyer and a supplier on product attributes (e.g., price, quantity).

RosettaNet is another B2B integration standard specialized in the areas of Information Technology, Electronic Components, and Semiconductor Manufacturing. RosettaNet is based on two dictionaries: the Business Dictionary and the Technical Dictionary. The Business Dictionary defines vocabulary that can be used to describe business properties (e.g., business name, address, tax identifier). An XML-based schema is used for this purpose. The Technical Dictionary contains properties that can be used to describe characteristics of products (e.g., computer parts).

RosettaNet further recognizes the fact that the business processes governing the interchange of messages must be harmonized and explicitly specified. For this purpose, the RosettaNet standard defines a number of predefined XML-based conversation protocols called PIPs (Partner Interface Processes). A PIP essentially consists of a set of business documents (e.g., purchase order, purchase order acknowledgment) and a set of rules for exchanging messages containing these documents.

In conclusion, a B2B integration framework describes the semantics and structure of service data and operations using XML and domain ontologies. Briefly stated, an ontology defines terms that can be used to describe entities (e.g., service properties, operations) of a specific domain (e.g., healthcare, finance, travel) and relationships among terms. In this approach, an organization creates and publishes the XML documents that describe its offerings, requirements, assumptions, and terms for doing business. Partners can interact with each other after inspecting, understanding, and using each other's definitions. This approach allows the use of services without prior agreement and without the help of external mediators. The establishment of a new relationship with existing partners does not require any additional work for a given partner. This feature is essential to allow the dynamic formation of trading communities. The business process of the trading community is specified by the shared document definitions. The partners in the trading community are interconnected according to the terms of agreed-upon documents, and the business logic implementation on a partner's side is invisible to other trading partners.

5   SERVICE COMPOSITION AND ORCHESTRATION

Web service composition refers to the development of new Web services by interconnecting existing ones according to some business logic, expressed (for example) as a business process model. For example, a composite Web service for travel arrangement could bring together a number of Web services for flight booking, accommodation booking, attractions search, car rental, events booking, etc. in order to provide "one-stop shopping" for its users. Web service composition is a key element of the Web services paradigm, since it provides a means to integrate heterogeneous enterprise applications and to realize business-to-business collaborations.

Orchestration deals with implementation management (what happens behind interfaces, i.e., process execution). Orchestration is therefore a private process, controlled by one party, and defines steps of an executable workflow. Propositions such as BPEL and BPML are clearly at this level. Choreography is more about what happens between interfaces. It can involve static or dynamically negotiated protocols. In this sense, choreography is a public, abstract process, where conversations are composed by equals who define sequences of observable messages [24]. In this section, we describe a representative sample of the ongoing efforts in service composition, orchestration, and choreography standardization.

5.1   Business Process Execution Language for Web Services (BPEL4WS)

The Business Process Execution Language for Web Services (BPEL4WS [Thatte2003]) is a language to model Web service-based business processes. The core concept is the representation of peer-to-peer interactions between a process and its partners using Web services and an XML-based grammar. It is built on top of WSDL (both the processes and partners are modeled as WSDL services).

BPEL4WS – BPEL for short – is a language based on XML that allows control of the process flow (states, coordination, and exceptions handling) of a set of collaborating Web services. For that, it defines interactions that exist within and between organization processes. The language uses either a graph-based or algebraic representation, and offers the ability to manage both *abstract* and *executable* processes. It provides constructs to handle long-running transactions (LRTs), compensation, and exception by using related standards WS-Transaction and WS-Coordination.

BPEL offers an interesting feature that allows independent representation of the interactions between the partners. The interaction protocols are called *abstract* processes, and they are specified in *business protocols*. This concept separates the external behavior of the partners (public and visible message-exchange behavior) from their private internal behavior and implementation. *Executable* processes are represented using the BPEL meta-model to model the actual behavior using the three classical flows: the control flow, the data flow, and the transactional flow. The meta-model it also includes support for the message flow.

As in traditional flow models, the control flow defines the execution flow as a directed acyclic graph. The language is designed to combine the block-oriented notation and the graph-oriented notation. It contains powerful constructors for modeling *structured activities*: aggregation, branching, concurrency, loops, exceptions, compensations, and time constraints. *Links* are used to define control dependencies between two block definitions: a source activity and a target activity. Activities can be grouped within a *scope*, and associated with a scope are three types of handlers: *fault handlers*, *compensation handlers*, and *event handlers*. When an error occurs, the normal processing is terminated and control is transferred to the corresponding fault handler. Then a process is terminated when it completes normally, when a terminate activity is called (abnormal termination), when a fault reaches the process scope, or when a compensation handler is called.

BPEL *basic activities* are handled by three types of messages: <invoke> to invoke an operation on a partner, <receive> to receive an invocation from a partner, and <reply> to send a reply message in partner invocation. One must associate a *partner* with each message, thereby prohibiting message exchange between two internal components for instance. Furthermore, a timeout is not able to be associated with the <invoke> activity, which could block the system if no response were returned.

Data flow management is ensured by using scoped variables. Input and output of activities are maintained in variables, and data are transferred between two (or more) activities thanks to shared data spaces that are persistent across Web services and global to one scope. The <assign> activity is used to copy data from one variable to another.

BPEL also proposes a compensation protocol to handle the transaction flow, particularly long-running transactions. One can define either a fault handler or a compensation handler. Handlers are associated with a scope: a fault handler defines alternate execution paths within the scope, while the compensation handler is used to reverse the work performed by an already completed scope.

On collaboration aspects, BPEL is able to model several types of interactions from simple stateless interactions to stateful, long-running, and asynchronous interactions. *Partner Link Types* are used to model partner relationships, and *correlation sets* represent the conversations, maintaining the state of the interaction. The choreography of the collaborative business processes is defined as an *abstract* process.

For example, given the previous WSDL definitions, we assume for our car rental example that there are three services: the customer service, the rental service, and the credit card service. Here is a simple BPEL process definition, compliant with version 1.1 of June 2003.

```
<!—Process definition —>
<process name="carRentingProcess"
    targetNamespace="http://example.com/bpel/carRenting"
    xmlns="http://schemas.xmlsoap.org/bpel/business-process/"
    xmlns:rns="http://example.com/wsdl/carRenting">
<!—Partners definition. Defines the WS and roles —>
```

```
<!—used by the process. —>
<partners>
  <partner name="customer" partnerLinkType="rns:customer"
    myRole="customerService"/>
  <partner name="rentalOffice" partnerLinkType="rns:rental"
      myRole="rentalRequestor" partnerRole="rentalService"/>
  <partner name="CCChecker" partnerLinkType="rns:credit"
      myRole="creditRequestor" partnerRole="creditService"/>
</partners>

<!—Variables definition. Defines messages sent —>
<!— and received from partners. —>
<variables>
  <variable name="rentalOrder"
messageType="rns:rentalOrderMessage"/>
  <variable name="rentalFee"
messageType="rns:rentalFeeMessage"/>
    <variable name="rentalFault"
messageType="rns:rentalFaultType"/>
</variables>

<!—Data manipulation. In the process, data can be —>
<!—copied and manipulated between variables.—>
<assign>
  <copy>
      <from variable="rentalOrder" part="customerInfo"/>
      <to variable="creditCardRequest" part="customerInfo"/>
  </copy>
</assign>
<!—Sequence including two flows, one for checking —>
<!—inventory, second for checking customer account —>
<sequence>
  <receive partnerLink="customer"
      portType="rns:rentalOrderPT"
      operation="sendRentalOrder" variable="rentalOrder"
      createInstance="yes" />
  <flow>
   <invoke partnerLink="rentalOffice"
     portType="rns:rentalInventoryPT"
     operation="checkINV" inputVariable="rentalRequest"
     outputVariable="rentalResponse" />
   <invoke partnerLink="CCChecker" portType="rns:creditPT"
     operation="checkCRED" inputVariable="creditRequest"
     outputVariable="creditResponse" />
  </flow>
  ...
  <reply partnerLink="customer"
      portType="rns:rentalOrderPT"
```

```
        operation="sendRentalOrder" variable="rentalFee"/>
    </sequence>
</process>
```

5.2   Web Service Choreography Interface (WSCI)

The WSCI specification [2] proposed by Sun, SAP, BEA, and Intalio, is an XML-based language for describing the observable behavior of a Web service during a message exchange in the context of a collaborative business process. This language enables users to describe the sequence of Web service invocations, i.e., the conditions under which an operation can be invoked. The specification is mainly concerned with public message exchanges among Web services, and it supports message correlation, sequencing rules, exception handling, and transactions. Since WSCI defines the flow of messages exchanged by a stateful Web service describing its observable behavior, it does not directly address the issue of supporting executable business processes, as BPEL does. A WSCI document defines only one partner's participation in a message exchange, including the specification of temporal constraints and logical dependencies using constructs to express the flow chart and conditional correlation. Thus, other Web services can unambiguously interact with it according to the intended collaboration. Therefore, a collaboration is described using a set of WSCI documents, one for each partner. There is no private workflow nor global cooperation business process. A WSCI interface is built on top of a WSDL interface that defines stateless operations supplied by a Web service. Therefore, a WSCI interface can be regarded as an augmented WSDL interface that includes operation abstraction, simple sequencing (call, delay, empty, fault, and spawn), message correlation, and properties based on message contents. An action in WSCI maps to a WSDL operation and to a role to perform it. This corresponds to a basic activity in BPEL. A second level aims at defining exceptions, transactions, and compensating transactions, and offers rich sequencing rules: loops, branches, joins, and nested activities (all, choice, foreach, sequence, switch, until, and while). Thus, a stateless WSDL description can be transformed into a stateful message exchange using WSCI. This corresponds to structured activities in BPEL. However, WSCI does not define a transactional protocol but only exposes the transactional capacities of Web services in a collaboration. An extensibility feature of WSCI suggests using RDF to annotate a WSCI interface definition with additional semantics.

5.3   Business Process Management Language (BPML)

BPML [4] from BPMI (Business Process Management Initiative) is a language that provides an abstract model and grammar for describing business processes. BPML allows the definition of both abstract and executable processes, Web services orchestration, and multi-partners collaboration choreography BPML can be used to develop a private implementation of already existing WSCI collaborations. In fact, BPML is more or less at the same level as BPEL and can be used to define a series of activities that a business process performs using a block-structured language. An *activity* is a component performing a specific function, and atomic activities can be composed into complex activities. A BPML specification extends WSCI activity types, adding assign, raise, and synch. A process is a complex activity that can be invoked by other processes. The language includes three process types: nested processes (a process that is defined to execute within another process, such as WfMC nested processes), exception processes to handle exceptional conditions, and compensation processes to support compensation logic. An activity executes within a context, which is similar to a BPEL scope. A context is an environment for execution that allows two activities: (1) definition of a common behavior, e.g., coordination of the execution using signals (such as the raise or synchronize signal) and (2) sharing of properties (data flow exchange between activities). A context is transmitted from a parent to a child, and it can be nested. The language includes a logical process model to express concurrency, loops, or dynamic tasks. The process instantiation is based on the receipt of a message, either in response to a system event and scheduling or invoked from an activity (called or spawned).

5.3.1   ebXML and the Business Process Specification Schema (BPSS)

ebXML (Electronic Business using eXtensible Markup Language) is a global electronic business standard envisioned to define an XML-based framework that will allow businesses to find each other and conduct business using well-defined messages and standard business processes [OASIS and UN/CEFACT]. The ebXML Business Process Specification Schema (BPSS) is part of the ebXML framework B2B suite of specifications aimed at representing models for collaborating e-business public processes. Using XML syntax, BPSS describes public business processes as collaborations between roles, where each role is an abstraction of a trading partner. It also defines relationships and responsibilities. Being abstract, a definition is reusable, since it only defines the exchange of information between two or more partners – business documents and business signals. A business process includes business collaborations, which are a choreographed set of business transaction activities. There are two types of collaborations: binary collaborations between two roles, and multiparty collaborations between three or more roles. Multiparty collaborations are decomposed into binary collaborations.

BPSS does not use WSDL to describe services. Instead, BPSS process models contain service interface descriptions and capabilities for each role. A partner can declare its support for a given role (service interfaces) in a ebXML CPP – Collaboration Protocol Profile, which serves two purposes. Firstly, it supports messaging exchange capabilities, i.e., specific asynchronous request and response operations, each with a defined message content. ebXML uses SOAP with attachments to manage XML document types and MIME attachments. Secondly, it supports generic acknowledgment and exception messages, which allows for reliable and secure messaging service management, e.g., authorization, encryption, certification and delivery. In BPSS, there is no explicit support for describing how data flows between transactions. Instead, BPSS assigns a public control flow (based on UML activity graph semantics) to each binary collaboration. The control flow describes the sequencing of business transactions between the two roles. It can specify sequential, parallel, and conditional execution of business transactions. In addition, BPSS supports a long-running business transaction model based on transaction patterns. A business transaction consists of a request and an optional response. Each request or response may require a receipt acknowledgment. Time constraints can be applied on messages and/or acknowledgments. If a transaction fails, the opposite side is notified so that both sides can decide on the actions that need to be taken. Transactions are not nested, and there is no support for specifying compensating transactions, so a business transaction either succeeds or fails completely. BPSS handles exceptions by defining a number of possible exceptions and prescribing how these are communicated and how they affect the state of the transaction. Then BPSS provides explicit support for specifying quality-of-service semantics for transactions such as authentication, acknowledgments, nonrepudiation, and timeouts.

5.4   WSCL

Web Services Conversation Language (WSCL) is a proposition from Hewlett-Packard related to previous work on e-Speak. WSCL is an XML vocabulary that offers the ability to define the external behavior of the services by specifying the business-level conversations between Web services. One of the main design goals of WSCL is simplicity. As such, WSCL provides a minimal set of concepts necessary for specifying the conversations. A WSCL document specifies three parts: the XML schemas that correspond to the XML documents being exchanged as part of the conversation, the conversation description (the order in which documents are exchanged), and the description of the transactions from one conversation to another. In contrast with BPEL or BPML, WSCL does not specify how the content of the exchanged messages is created. The specification states that typically the conversation description is provided from the perspective of the service provider; however, if can also be used to determine the conversation from the perspective of the user. Although the conversation is defined from the service provider's perspective, WSCL separates the conversational logic from the application logic or the implementation aspects of the service.

6   TRENDS AND OPEN PROBLEMS

Despite the growing interest in Web services, several issues still need to be addressed in order to provide similar benefits to what traditional middleware brings to intraorganizational application integration. Indeed, EAI middleware provides much more than basic features such as service description, discovery, and invocation. In order for Web service technologies to scale to the Internet, several research issues still need to be addressed, including service composition, dependability, privacy, quality of service, mobility, and semantics.

6.1   Process-based integration of services

In spite of the potential opportunities, B2B integration solutions are mainly used by large organizations. One of the main reasons is that the development of integrated services is still, by and large, hand coded, time consuming, and dependent on a considerable low-level programming effort. The integration process is made harder by the fact that the components of integrated service may be heterogeneous, distributed, and autonomous. Developers typically are required to have intimate knowledge of the underlying communication protocols, data formats, and access interfaces. In addition, B2B service integration requires flexibility in order to adapt dynamically adapt to changes that may occur in partners' applications. Businesses must be able to respond rapidly to both operational changes (e.g., increases in a server's load) and market environment changes (e.g., new regulations), which are not easily predictable.

The extension of traditional business process modeling techniques so as to streamline B2B service integration is a natural step in this direction. Indeed, several standardization efforts for process-based integration of Web services are emerging (e.g., BPEL4WS, WSCI, and ebXML BPSS). The momentum gained by the Web services paradigm is reflected by the large number of software development tools that support, or claim to support, the Web services standards. However, the tools and products that efficiently support service composition are still far from mature. The rest of this section provides a quick overview of existing tools and prototypes.

eFlow [6] and CMI (Collaboration Management Infrastructure) [25] are two representative prototype systems for (Web) service composition. Both CMI and eFlow advocate the specification of composite services by using a process model. While CMI argues for the use of state machines to describe the behavior of composite services, eFlow suggests the use of graphs in which the nodes denote invocations to service operations and the edges denote control-flow dependencies. eFlow further introduces the concept of a *search recipe*: a query that is evaluated at run-time (i.e., during the execution of the composite service) in order to retrieve the service that will execute a given service operation. A similar concept is introduced in CMI as well, where it is termed *placeholder*. Search recipes and placeholders provide a mechanism for run-time service selection (see also [9]).

More recently, SELF-SERV [3] has taken the ideas of eFlow and CMI further by refining the concepts of a placeholder/search recipe into that of a *community* (or container). A community is an abstract definition of a service capability that contains a set of policies for managing membership in the community and selects at run-time the service that will execute a given service invocation on behalf of the community. Policies for run-time selection of services are formulated using multiattribute value functions. In addition, SELF-SERV advocates a peer-to-peer model for orchestrating a composite service execution in which the control and data-flow dependencies encoded in a composite service definition are enforced through software components located in the sites of the providers participating in a composition. This peer-to-peer orchestration model, which has its roots in the Mentor distributed workflow engine [20], is an alternative to a centralized model in which the execution is controlled by a central scheduler. From an architectural point of view, Web service composition systems such as eFlow and SELF-SERV provide (1) a tool for designing composite services and translating these designs into an XML-based representation, (2) a tool for assisting the deployment of composite services, and (3) a runtime environment for orchestrating the execution of composite service instances and for handling service selection.

6.2 Dynamic and scalable orchestration of services

The number of services to be integrated may be large and continuously changing. Consequently, if the development of an integrated service requires identifying, understanding, and establishing interactions among component services at service-definition time, that approach is inappropriate. Instead, divide-and-conquer approaches should be adopted, whereby services providing similar capabilities (also called *alternative services*) are grouped together, and these groups take over some of the responsibilities of service integration (e.g., the dynamic discovery of services, based on their availability, characteristics, organizational policies, and resources, that are needed to accomplish the integrated service). In addition, in existing techniques, eventhough the components that contribute to an integrated service can be distributed, they are usually centrally controlled. Given the highly distributed nature of services, and the large number of network nodes that are capable of service execution, novel mechanisms involving scalable and completely decentralized execution of services will become increasingly important.

6.3 Dependable integration of Web services

Traditional transaction management techniques are not appropriate in the context of composite services because the components of such services may be heterogeneous and autonomous. They may not be transactional, and even if they are, their transactional features may not be compatible with each other. In addition, for different reasons (e.g., quality of service), component services may not be willing to comply with constraints such as resource locking until the termination of the composite service execution (as in traditional transaction protocols). Therefore, new transaction techniques are required in the context of Web services. For instance, it is important to extend the description of services by explicitly describing transactional semantics of Web service operations (e.g., specify that an operation can be aborted without effect from a requester's perspective). It is also important to extend service composition models to specify transactional semantics of an operation or a group of operations (e.g., specify how to handle the unavailability of a component service). For instance, at the composite service level, we may specify that, if a service is unavailable, we should try to find an alternative service. The effective handling of transactional aspects at the composite service level depends on exploiting the transactional capabilities of the participating services.

6.4 Privacy in Web services

In applications such as digital governments, there are services that are responsible for collecting data from users and from other services—for instance, those that represent organizations. In real life, privacy policies prevent providers from disclosing data to nonauthorized users or services. There are several issues here: for instance, privacy policy specification for composite services and the privacy-preserving composition of services. If services are going to be used in critical applications, they must provide support for controlling and monitoring violations of privacy policies and service-level agreements. For instance, it is important to look at possible inference techniques (e.g., data mining) and to ensure that privacy is not violated by using these techniques (e.g., aggregation of data from different services and inference of privacy-protected data).

6.5   Web services in mobile environments

The explosive growth of interconnected computing devices (e.g., PDAs, wireless technologies) has created new environments where ubiquitous information access will be a reality. In particular, Web services are poised to become accessible from mobile devices.

Existing service provisioning techniques are inappropriate to cope with the requirements of these new environments. Several obstacles still hinder the seamless provisioning of Web services in mobile environments, including the throughput and connectivity of wireless networks, the limited computing resources of mobile devices, and the frequency of disconnections. Examples of critical issues follow.

- *Context-sensitive service selection.* In addition to criteria such as monetary cost and execution time, service selection should take into account the location of requesters and services and the capabilities of the computing resources on which services are executed (e.g., CPU, bandwidth). This context-aware service selection calls for policies that enable the system to adapt itself to different computing and user requirements.

- *Handling disconnections during service execution.* In a mobile environment, disconnections are frequent. The various causes include discharged batteries, a change of location, or a request from the user to minimize communication costs. To cope with issues related to client or provider disconnection during a service execution, agent-based service composition middleware architecture may be appropriate. In [16], an architecture in which users and services may be represented by delegate agents is proposed. This architecture contains disconnection control policies related to requesters and providers. For example, a delegate agent may be used to collect execution results during disconnection of the user's device and then return these results to the user upon reconnection.

Tuple Spaces are a promising technology for delivering Web services to mobile devices [12]. Indeed, Tuple Spaces provide an effective mechanism for handling two-way asynchronous communications between clients and servers, as opposed to the one-way asynchronous communication mechanism provided by Message-Oriented Middleware (MOM), in which only the server can handle requests asynchronously through its message queue (Section 3). However, more research and development is needed in order to bring Tuple Spaces and other blackboard-based middleware (e.g., JavaSpaces) to the level of maturity and adoption of MOM.

6.6   Optimal QoS-driven service selection

During development of a composite service, the exact set of services to be integrated may not be known at design time. Consequently, approaches are inappropriate in which development of an integrated service requires identifying, understanding, and establishing interactions among component services at design time. Instead, divide-and-conquer approaches should be adopted, whereby services providing similar capabilities (i.e., interoperable services) are grouped together. Services within a group (e.g., "tax declaration services") can then be differentiated statically or at invocation time with respect to organizational and Quality of Service (QoS) parameters such as price, availability, reliability, supported policies, etc. The result of this "grouping" process is that each service operation required by a composite service is potentially provided by multiple interoperable Web services but with different organizational and QoS attributes. The challenge is then to be able to select (especially at run-time), among all the possible alternatives for executing a composite Web service, those that would satisfy certain constraints and maximize certain preferences set by the user for that particular execution. Research in the area of optimal runtime selection of services is under way (see, for example, [31]), but there are still many open issues, such as how to quantitatively compare service offers described in terms of different sets of attributes.

6.7   Semantic Web services

Another effort worth mentioning in the general context of Web technologies is the Semantic Web. The Semantic Web aims at improving the technology that organizes, searches, integrates, and evolves Web-accessible resources (e.g., Web documents, data) by using rich and machine-understandable abstractions for the representation of resources semantics. Efforts in this area include the development of ontology languages such as RDF and OWL [30.]. By leveraging efforts in both Web services and the Semantic Web, the Semantic Web services paradigm promises to take Web technologies a step further by providing foundations to enable automated discovery, access, combination, and management of Web services. Efforts in this area are focusing on providing rich and machine-understandable representation of service properties, capabilities, and behavior, as well as reasoning mechanisms to support automation activities [21]. Examples of such efforts include DAML-S [8], WSMF (Web Services Modeling Framework) [11], and METEOR-S [26]. However, this work is still in its infancy, and many of the objectives of the Semantic Web services paradigm, such as service capability description, dynamic service discovery, and goal-driven composition of Web services still remain to be reached. In particular, service ontologies are needed that would capture both functional (i.e., capability related) and nonfunctional attributes (e.g., price, payment, time, location) [22].

SUMMARY

Web services promise to revolutionize the way in which applications interact over the Web. However, the underlying technology is still in a relatively early stage of development and adoption. While the core standards such as XML, SOAP, and WSDL are relatively stable and are supported in various ways by a number of tools, the standardization efforts in key areas such as security, reliability, policy description, and composition are still under way. The tools supporting these emerging standards are also still evolving. In addition (or perhaps as a consequence), relatively few production-level Web services have been deployed and are being used in practice.

To some extent, these difficulties can be explained by the fact that businesses have already spent considerable resources in the last few years to expose their systems' functionality as interactive Web applications. As a result, they are reluctant to invest more to move this functionality into Web services until the benefits of such a move are clearer. It will probably take another two years before the technology reaches the level of maturity necessary to trigger a widespread adoption [27]. In the meantime, it is important that middleware platform developers integrate the numerous facets of Web services into their products (e.g., facilitating the use of message-oriented middleware for Web service development), while researchers advance the state of the art in challenging issues such as Web service delivery in mobile environments, QoS-driven selection of services, and manipulation of semantic-level service descriptions.

REFERENCES

[1] G. Alonso, F. Casati, H. Kuno and V. Machiraju (2003): Web Services. Springer Verlag.

[2] BEA Systems, Intalio, SAP, Sun Microsystems (2002): Web Service Choreography Interface (WSCI) 1.0, http://www.w3.org/TR/wsci.

[3] B. Benatallah, Q.Z. Sheng, M. Dumas (2003) The Self-Serv Environment for Web Services Composition. *IEEE Internet Computing, 7*(1)*,* 40–48.

[4] BPMI, BPML: Business Process Modeling Language 1.0 (2002), http://bpmi.org/bpml-spec.esp.

[5] C. Bussler (2003): B2B Integration: Concepts and Architecture, Springer.

[6] F. Casati and M.C. Shan (2001) Dynamic and Adaptive Composition of E-Services. *Information Systems, 26*(3), 143–162.

[7] F. Curbera, M. Duftler, R. Khalaf, W. Nagy, N. Mukhi, S. Weerawarana (2002), Unraveling the Web Services Web. *IEEE Internet Computing 6*(2), 86–93.

[8] DAML-S Consortium (2001), DAML Services, http://www.daml.org/services

[9] M. Devarakonda, A. Mukherjee, and B. Kish (1995): Meta-Scripts as a Mechanism for Complex Web Services. In *Proceedings of the 5th Workshop on Hot Topics in Operating Systems (HotOS)*, Orcas Island, WA, USA, May 1995. IEEE Computer Society.

[10] C. Evans, et al. (2003): Web Services Reliability (WS-Reliability) Version 1.0. http://www.sonicsoftware. com/docs/ws_reliability.pdf

[11] D. Fensel, and C. Bussler (2002) The Web services modelling framework WSMF. *Electronic Commerce Research and Application, 1*(2), 113–137.

[12] M. Fontoura, T. Lehman and Y. Xiong (2003): TSpaces Services Suite: Automating the Development and Management of Web Services. In *Proceedings of the Alternate Tracks of the 12th International Conference on the World Wide Web (WWW)*, Budapest, Hungary, May 2003.

[13] M. Hondo, and C. Kaler, (eds) (2002): Web Services Policy Framework (WS-Policy) Microsoft. http://www-106.ibm.com/developerworks/library/ws-polfram

[14] C. Kaler, (ed) (2002): Web Services Security (WS-Security), Version 1.0. http://www-106.ibm.com/developerworks/library/ws-secure

[15] D. Langworthy, (ed) (2003): Web Services Reliable Messaging Protocol (WS-ReliableMessaging). http://xml.coverpages.org/ws-reliablemessaging 20030313. pdf

[16] Z. Maamar, Q.Z. Sheng, B. Benatallah (2004): On composite Web services provisioning in an environment of fixed and mobile computing resources. *Information Technology and Management, 5*(3), in press.

[17] B. Medjahed, B. Benatallah, A. Bouguettaya, et al. (2003) Business-to-Business Interactions: Issues and Enabling Technologies. *The VLDB Journal*, Springer, 2003.

[18] Microsoft, BEA, and IBM (2002a.): Web Services Coordination (WS-Coordination).

[19] Microsoft, BEA, and IBM (2002b.): Web Services Transaction (WS-Transaction).

[20] P. Muth, D. Wodtke, J. Weissenfels, A.K. Dittrich, G. Weikum (1998): From Centralized Workflow Specification to Distributed Workflow Execution. *Journal of Intelligent Information Systems 10*(2), Kluwer Academic Publishers.

[21] S. Narayana and S. McIlraith (2002): Simulation, verification and automated composition of Web services. *Proceedings of the 11th International World Wide Web Conference*, May 2002, Honolulu, USA. ACM Press.

[22] J. O'Sullivan, D. Edmond and A. ter Hofstede (2002): What's in a service? *Distributed and Parallel Databases 12*(2/3), 117–133.

[23] OASIS and UN/CEFACT. Electronic Business XML (ebXML). http://www.ebxml.org

[24] C. Peltz, Web Service Orchestration, HP white paper http://devresource.hp.com/drc/technical_white_papers/WSOrc h/WSOrchestration.pdf

[25] H. Schuster, D. Georgakopoulos, A. Cichocki, and D. Baker (2000): Modeling and Composing Service-Based and Reference Process-Based Multi-enterprise Processes. In *Proceedings of the International Conference on Advanced Information Systems (CAiSE)*, Stockholm, Sweden, pp. 247–263. Springer.

[26] K. Sivashanmugam, K. Verma, A. Sheth and J. Miller (2003): Adding Semantics to Web Services Standards. In *Proceedings of the 12th International Semantic Web Conference (ISWC)*, Sanibel Island, FL, USA, Springer.

[27] B. Sleeper, and B. Robins (2002): The Laws of Evolution: A Pragmatic Analysis of the Emerging Web Services Market. Stencil Group Analysis Memo. http://www.stencilgroup. com/ideas_scope_200204evolution.html

[28] S. Thatte, (ed) (2003): Business Process Execution Language for Web Services version 1.1. http://dev2dev.bea.com/techtrack/BPEL4WS.jsp.

[29] W3 Consortium (2001a.): Web Services Description Language (WSDL) 1.1. Note, W3C. http://www.w3.org/TR/wsdl.

[30] W3 Consortium (2001b.): Semantic Web Activity, http://www.w3.org/2001/sw

[31] L. Zeng, B. Benatallah, M. Dumas, J. Kalagnanam, and Q.Z. Sheng (2003): Quality Driven Web Services Composition. In *Proceedings of the International Conference on the World Wide Web (WWW)*.

Chapter 18

PREDICTING GRID RESOURCE PERFORMANCE ONLINE

Rich Wolski,[1] Graziano Obertelli,[1] Matthew Allen,[1] Daniel Nurmi,[1] and John Brevik[1]

[1]University of California, Santa Barbara

In this chapter, we describe methods for predicting the performance of Computational Grid resources (machines, networks, storage systems, etc.) using computationally inexpensive statistical techniques. The predictions generated in this manner are intended to support adaptive application scheduling in Grid settings, as well as online fault detection. We describe a mixture-of-experts approach to nonparametric, univariate time-series forecasting, and detail the effectiveness of the approach using example data gathered from "production" (i.e., nonexperimental) Computational Grid installations.

1   INTRODUCTION

Performance prediction and evaluation are both critical components of the Computational Grid [20, 8] architectural paradigm. In particular, predictions (especially those made at run time) of available resource performance levels can be used to implement effective application scheduling [13, 38, 42, 12, 43, 9]. Because Grid resources (the computers, networks, and storage systems that make up a Grid) differ widely in the performance they can deliver to any given application, and because performance fluctuates dynamically due to contention by competing applications, schedulers (human or automatic) must be able to predict the deliverable performance that an application will be able to obtain when it eventually runs. Based on these predictions, the scheduler can choose the combination of resources from the available resource pool that is expected to maximize performance for the application.

Making the performance predictions that are necessary to support scheduling typically requires a compositional model of application behavior that can be parameterized dynamically with resource information. For example, consider the problem of selecting the machine from a Grid resource pool that delivers the fastest execution time for a sequential program. To choose among a number of available target platforms, the scheduler must predict the execution speed of the application code on each of the platforms. Grid infrastructures such as Globus [19, 15] provide resource catalogs in which static and therefore precisely known attributes (such as CPU clock speed) are recorded. As such, the simplest approach to selection of the best machine is to query the catalog for all available hosts and then choose the one with the fastest clock rate.

There are several assumptions that underlie this simple example. One assumption is that the clock speeds of the various available CPUs can be used to rank the eventual execution speeds of the program. Clock speed correlates well with execution performance if the machine pool is relatively homogeneous. One of the basic tenets of the Grid paradigm, however, is that a wide variety of resource types is available. If, in this example, a floating-point vector processor is available, and the application vectorizes well, a slower-clocked vector CPU could outperform a faster general-purpose machine, making clock speed an inaccurate predictor of application performance. Conversely, if a scalar integer code is applied, a high-clock-rate vector machine might underperform a slower commodity processor.

A second assumption is that the CPU is the only resource that needs to be considered as a parameter in the application model. If the input and output requirements for the program are substantial, the cost of reading the inputs and generating the outputs must also be considered. Generating estimates of the time required for the application to perform I/O is particularly difficult in Grid settings, since the I/O usually traverses a network. While static CPU attributes (e.g., clock speed) are typically recorded for Grid resources, network attributes and topology are not. Moreover, at the application level, the required network performance estimates are end-to-end. While it is possible to record the performance characteristics of various network components, composing those characteristics into a general end-to-end performance model has proved challenging [36, 16, 53, 17, 6, 30, 37].

However, even if a model is available that effectively composes application performance from resource performance characteristics, the Grid resource pool cannot be assumed to be static. One of the key differentiating characteristics of Computational Grid computing is that the available resource pool can fluctuate dynamically. Resources are *federated* to the Grid by their resource owners, who maintain ultimate local control. As such, resource owners may reclaim their resources or may upgrade or change the type and quantity of resource that is available, etc., making "static" resource characteristics (e.g., the amount of memory supported by a machine) potentially time varying.

Even if resource availability is slowly changing, resource contention can cause the performance, which can be delivered to any single application component, to fluctuate much more rapidly. CPUs shared among several executing processes deliver only a fraction of their total capability to any one process. Network performance response is particularly dynamic. Most Grid systems, even if they use batch queues to provide unshared, dedicated CPU access to each application, rely on shared networks for intermachine communication. The end-to-end network latency and throughput performance response can exhibit large variability in both local-area and wide-area network settings. As such, the resource performance that will be available to the program (the fraction of each CPU's time slices, the network latency and throughput, the available memory) must be *predicted* for the time frame that the program will eventually execute.

Thus, to make a decision about where to run a sequential program given a pool of available machines from which to choose, a scheduler requires

- a performance model that correctly predicts (or ranks) execution performance when parameterized with resource performance characteristics, and

- a method for estimating what the resource performance characteristics of the resources *will be* when the program executes.

In this chapter, we focus on techniques and a system for meeting the latter requirement. In particular, we discuss our experiences in building and deploying the *Network Weather Service* (NWS) [52, 49, 50, 35]—a robust and scalable distributed system that monitors and predicts resource performance online. The predictions made by the NWS are based on real-time statistical analyses of historically observed performance measurement data. Typically deployed as a Grid middleware service, the system has been used extensively [38, 12, 48, 3, 41, 51, 43, 9] to provide resource performance forecasts to Grid schedulers. In this chapter, we describe the architecture of the NWS, the statistical techniques that have proved successful from our collaborations with various Grid scheduling projects, and some of the lessons we have learned from building and deploying a Grid information system capable of managing dynamic data in real time.

2 REQUIREMENTS FOR GRID PERFORMANCE MONITORING AND FORECASTING

As a Grid service, the NWS (as well as any other system that serves dynamically changing performance data) must meet a demanding list of requirements. The system must be able to run continuously so that it can gather a history of available performances from each monitored resource. At the same time, the fluctuations in performance and availability that it is tracking cannot impede its function. Network failures, for example, cannot cause NWS outages, even though the NWS may be using those network links that have failed to gather and serve performance data.

The performance monitoring system must also avoid introducing false correlations between measurements. For example, the typical method for measuring host availability is to use some form of "heartbeat" message to renew a soft-state availability registration [21]. Hosts send a message periodically to a central server to indicate their availability, and missing heartbeats indicate host failure. While this architecture method is robust if the central server is running on a highly available system, it inextricably convolves network failure and host failure. That is, a missing heartbeat or set of heartbeats could be because the host has failed, or because the network linking the host to the central server has failed. For hosts within a cluster, the problem is especially acute. If the network partitions between a cluster and the soft-state registration server, the cluster hosts will appear to have failed when, in fact, they can communicate with each other and with any hosts on the same side of the partition.

Grid performance monitoring systems themselves necessarily have the most restrictive performance requirements of all Grid services. If client applications and services are to use the performance data served by the performance system, in some sense the system must run "faster" than these clients so that the needed data are immediately available. If they are not, clients may waste more time waiting for performance data from the resources they intend to use than they will gain from having the performance data in the first place. That is, the data must be gathered and served in time to be useful. Few other Grid services must operate under such restrictive performance deadlines.

Moreover, the standard technological approaches that have been developed for serving data across a network typically are not optimized to handle dynamically changing data. Most extant systems are designed under the assumption that the rate of queries for the data is substantially higher than the rate at which the data change. For static resource attributes such as processor type, operating system and revision level, static memory capacity, etc. this assumption is reasonable. As an example, queries for operating system type and revision level (which are critical to support for automatic resource discovery) should occur at a higher rate than the administrative OS upgrade frequency in any reasonable setting. However, when historical resource performance is to be used to gauge resource suitability, particularly with respect to load and availability, the opposite data access pattern is typical. Resources update the information base with periodic performance measurements much more frequently than queries are made. Thus query-optimized systems, if not architecturally structural to support more frequent updates than queries, may have trouble coping with the update load introduced by the need to constantly gather performance measurements.

The need to monitor Grid resources constantly without perturbing those resources requires the monitoring system to be ubiquitous yet mostly invisible to users and administrators. Further, a resource monitoring process that has a noticeable impact on running applications will not and should not be tolerated. These issues imply a monitoring system that is powerful enough to provide useful information and yet lightweight enough to not have significant impact on resource performance.

Finally, the Grid performance information system must be able to meet the daunting engineering challenges described in this section at a relatively large scale. While the debate about the feasibility of Internet-wide Grid computing continues, at present Grid systems containing tens of thousands of hosts generating millions of individual performance histories are being deployed. To be effective, Grid performance monitoring systems must be able to operate at least on this scale, in the wide area, while respecting the constraints placed upon resource usage by each resource owner.

3   THE NETWORK WEATHER SERVICE ARCHITECTURE

It is, perhaps, easiest to think of the NWS as a Grid application designed to measure performance and service availability. Resource sensors must be deployed and executed on a large, heterogeneous, and distributed set of resources with widely varying levels of responsiveness and availability. Due to the volatile nature of Grid environments, the NWS is necessarily designed to be portable and scalable, with functional mechanisms for load balancing, redundancy, and failure handling. In this section, we describe the individual components of the NWS as well as the mechanisms that have enabled it to be successfully deployed on Grid architectures around the world and to be compatible with or to work within the most common Grid infrastructures (Condor [46], Globus [19, 15], GrADS [7, 23], etc.).

The NWS is composed of three persistent components and a suite of user interface tools. The set of persistent entities that compose a minimal NWS installation includes one of each of the following: *nameserver*, *memory*, and *sensor*. NWS installations typically include many sensor components, one on each machine that is to be monitored. An installation also includes one or more memory processes, depending on the scale of the installation, and a single nameserver. Each sensor process is responsible for gathering resource information, which is then stored over the network to a memory, the location of which is registered in the nameserver along with other system control information. The relationship between these components is shown in Figure 18.1, and will be more thoroughly explained in the following subsections.

In addition to these persistent components, NWS installations include interface tools that allow users to search, extract, and request forecasts of measurement data. Tools also exist that allow an NWS administrator to control the running state of the entire installation from a single point on the network. These tools are covered in depth at the end of this section.

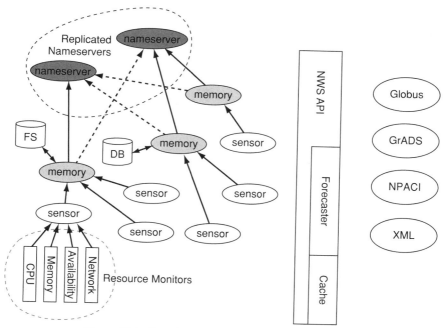

Figure 18.1. Overview of an example NWS installation.

3.1   Nameserver

The nameserver can be considered to be the phone book of the NWS—it keeps a record of every host and activity in the system. As a single source of control and information, NWS users and other NWS entities use the nameserver and stored registrations to perform lookup, search, store, and many other control tasks. Essentially, if an activity, host, or process exists in an NWS installation, information about it can be gleaned from the data stored in the nameserver.

Although there can be multiple nameserver processes, there is only one logical nameserver for each NWS installation. All other NWS components such as memories and sensors are in periodic contact with the nameserver to keep the view of the system current and controllable.

To combat the inevitable downtime of a nameserver or of a machine on which a nameserver is running, a robust failover mechanism has been built into the system. In order to provide robustness, the nameserver is architecturally structured with mirroring capabilities: two or more nameservers, on separate hosts, can be directed to keep their data synchronized. In this case, every update request coming to one nameserver will be forwarded to all others. The nameservers also implement a queue of update requests to tolerate temporary network failures. Nameservers that fail permanently are removed from the mirroring process.

The primary datum kept by the nameserver is called a *registration*. Each registration is a set of flexible key/value attribute pairs, with only a few keys required to construct a valid registration. The required keypairs in every registration are *name*, *objectclass*, *timestamp*, and *expiration*. The former two are used to describe the type of registration and are provided by the registering host, and the latter two are used for management and are added by the name-server upon receipt. The nameserver offers fast search capabilities and updates on the registrations by keeping them ordered in memory and periodically saving a backup to stable storage. Apart from the required keypairs, NWS hosts are free to add new attributes containing whatever control information they require to operate.

Of the required keypairs, *objectclass* is the highest level and the only key-pair that defines the content of the registration itself. Currently, objectclass supports the following values and additional information:

- **nwsHost**. Every host registers itself with the nameserver. *hostType* indicates whether the NWS host is a memory nameserver of the sensor; *ip Address* is the ip address of the nwsHost, as reported by gethostbyname or forced from the command line; *port* is the TCP port on which the host is listening; *started* is the time when the host was executed; *owner* is the login name of the user that started the host; *version* is the NWS version; and *flags* are the options passed to configure upon NWS compilation flags. Other keypairs reflect specific host details (*systemType, releaseName, machineArch, CPUCount*, etc.).

- **nwsSkill**. Every NWS sensor registers a list of its capabilities (called *skills*). It contains the *skillName*, the *option* that can be used when starting an activity, and an informative list of what the options take as arguments (integer, string, . . .).

- **nwsControl**. Currently there are two different controls defined by the *controlName*: *periodic* and *clique*. This objectclass also defines the *host* bound to the control, the *option* that is passed to the control, and the *skillName* that can be started under this control.

- **nwsActivity**. Experiments that are being run in the NWS system are all registered with the nameserver. Objects of this type contain the *control-Name* that started the activity, the *host* running the activity, the *skillName* used for this activity, and the *option* that the skill uses.

- **nwsSeries**. Collections of measurements are called *series*. Objects of this type contain the *host* that ran the experiments, the *activity* generating the series, the measured *resource*, the NWS *memory* that stores the series, the measuring unit for this resource (*label*), and the *option* used for this skill.

The nameserver's responsibility is to store small, independent data items and make them available to users. As a result, it is optimized to make searching and correlating data quick and simple. However, this design is not conducive to storing large sets of data such as measurement series. These data are stored by another process that is designed to deal with the information's specific nature. This component, called the *memory*, is described in the next section.

3.2 Memory

The memory server is responsible for housing measurement data produced by sensors within an NWS installation. The memory receives measurements from sensors and other sources and organizes them into a collection called a *series*. It makes these series available to users through a well-defined interface.

Memories are a very flexible part of the NWS infrastructure and can be used in whatever way is appropriate to the scale of the installation. Users interested in minimizing the network traffic that is used to save measurement data can create a memory on each machine or administrative domain housing sensors. Alternatively, to reduce the cost of retrieving data from a single source, a memory can be place on a nearby central host capable of handling a large number of sensors and measurement series.

The memory registers every series that it is responsible for with the nameserver. In the case of the failure of a replicated nameserver, the memory knows how to contact and utilize backup nameservers. Without the presence of any functional nameserver, it can operate independently–storing measurement data and series registration from newly started sensors. If sensors establish new series with a memory while the nameserver is inaccessible, the memory caches their registrations and forwards them when the nameserver becomes available again.

Upon restart, a memory checks if there are older series in stable storage. If any exist, it creates a limited registration and sends this to the nameserver. This mechanism allows the system to access series that are no longer updated by active sensors but are still addressable by the memory.

By default, memories store measurement data using the file system. Each series is associated with a file named with the fully qualified series name. These files are managed as circular queues, with a size determined by a user parameter.

The first line of the file contains data for managing the circular queue. Each series measurement is stored in a fixed-length, human-readable buffer containing the arrival timestamp, sequence number, expiration timeout, and the timestamp/measurement pair sent by the sensor. As the circular queue becomes full, old values are overwritten.

If data are stored in the file system in this way, the memory keeps a cache of the most frequently accessed series in resident memory to minimize the performance hit of going to the file system. To keep update operations safe, the cache is write-through. Although the cache reduces IO load and increases performance for read operations, the fact that it does not cache write operations results in substantial IO overhead from writes being performed on disk files. Larger installations typically exploit the feature of NWS memories, which, by allowing multiple memory instances within an installation, significantly reduces IO load on any one host running a memory process.

While memories usually store a large enough backlog of data to make accurate resource forecasts, some applications require a longer trace of data. In these cases, memories can use a database instead of a circular-queue filled flat file. In the database, a new table is generated for each series the memory is handling. Each set of measurements is stored in the table with the same information as the flat file design. Data are stored for as long as the database administrator decides to keep the history.

When data are requested from an NWS installation, the memory process is responsible for providing the data. The memory makes no effort to interpret user requests, so users usually talk to the nameserver to discover the name of a series and the memory that houses it. The primary source of data for the memory is the sensor process, which is responsible for running online performance tests. This process is described in the next section.

3.3   Sensor

The NWS sensor component is responsible for gathering resource information from machines, coordinating low-level monitoring activities, and reporting measurements over the network to an NWS memory.

On each machine that houses monitored resources, a single sensor process is deployed. Since single machines house multiple resources, each sensor process has the capability of spawning child processes for measuring each unique resource. Sensors are typically measuring resources available to normal users, so the NWS sensor should be executed using normal user permissions. Running sensors with system privilege is, in fact, discouraged. Starting them can be done manually through automated execution systems (cron, etc.) or at system startup.

To account for unforeseen complications that may cause various resource measurement processes to fail or block, the sensor separates its administrative and measurement components into separate processes. The original parent process is responsible for accepting control messages and starting measurements, while child processes are created to perform the actual measurements. If this approach is not desirable, this feature can be disabled, leaving only one process to handle both measurements and control messages.

If the network between the sensor and memory fails or the memory process becomes temporarily unavailable, the sensor process will begin caching resource measurements until such a time when the memory becomes available. In this way, the sensor is capable of maintaining a consistent view of measured resources without gaps incurred by network or process failures.

The introduction of firewalls often adversely affect distributed systems. NWS sensors can be instructed to use a specified port when conducting network experiments, allowing an administrator to open only two ports in the firewall: one to control the sensor and the other to allow the sensors access to one another while taking network measurements.

A sensor is instructed to start monitoring a resource using a specific skill with some well-specified options. An activity is the process of using a skill at specific interval. An activity generates one or more series measurements, and a single sensor is capable of running any number of activities. The current NWS sensor implementation includes the following predefined skills (note that, due to system limitations, not all skills are available on all architectures):

- **availabilityMonitor**: measures time since the machine last booted.

- **cpuMonitor**: measures the fraction of the CPU available and the current CPU load. Accepts a *nice* level as options.

- **diskMonitor**: measures available disk capacity of a specified disk. Accepts a *path* as option.

- **filesystemMonitor**: monitors performance of a specified file system. Accepts multiple options, including *path*, *fstype* (block/char), *fstmpdir*, *fssize*, and *fsbufmode* (instruct, skill to attempt to avoid file system buffer cache using various methods).

- **startMonitor**: registers the numbers of seconds since the sensor started.

- **tcpMessageMonitor**: monitors bandwidthTcp and latencyTcp to a *target* host. It accepts options to set the *buffer* size of the socket, the *message* size to be used, and the total experiment *size*.

- **tcp ConnectMonitor**: measures the time it takes to establish a TCP connection with a *target* host.

- **memorySpeedMonitor** (experimental): measures attainable memory speed (random or sequential access).

In addition to predefined skills, the sensor has been architecturally structured to make the addition of novel user-defined skills fairly straight forward. A user who wishes to add a new skill needs only to implement a function for measuring a resource of interest, and can rely on existing mechanisms for caching, communication, and control, making the process of adding a new skill as simple and efficient as possible.

Many resources, like CPU, memory, etc. are measured on a single machine. Other resources, in particular network resources, require that two hosts participate in the experiment. Because the NWS uses active network probes, simultaneous tests could interfere with each other. To deal with these different types of measurements, the NWS uses two methods to determine when measurements will be taken.

Periodic skills

Periodic skills need to be run at specific time intervals and are independent (thus running these skills on different hosts at the same time doesn't cause interference in the measurement). Upon starting such skills, the *period* option is used to determine how many seconds pass between experiments. Most predefined skills are periodic skills, since measurement of the CPU, memory, disk, and other independent resources has no effect on other hosts measuring the same resources.

Clique skills

NWS cliques are used to provide a level of mutual exclusion within a group of hosts so that their measurement activities do not interfere with each other. This is a best-effort mutual exclusion mechanism. Upon the start of a clique activity, a token is generated and circulated within the members of the clique. A member can take measurements only if it has the token. Once the member has finished taking all the needed measurements, the token is passed to the next clique member.

Because the network can partition or hosts can fail, the token can get lost. To account for this, the clique protocol implements a mechanism to regenerate the token if knowledge of it is lost. Every clique has a *leader* (by default, the member that starts the token) that keeps track of the time needed to circulate the token. If the leader doesn't receive the token within a reasonable length of time, it regenerates the token and starts a new circulation. Also, if a member of the clique sees a long enough delay between tokens, it becomes the leader and starts a new instance of the token. The clique is timed out after a few multiples of the clique periodicity.

The token system is *best effort* because it considers taking measurements at the right frequency over strict mutual exclusion. The clique protocol ensures that the sensors take their network measurements at roughly the periodicity asked by the activity. Members can starts taking measurements without holding the token if too much time has elapsed. If the token is then received after the sensor's timeout, the token is passed along without taking the measurements. Mechanisms are in place to eliminate multiple tokens circulating at the same time (for example, when a network partition is restored).

3.4   Design considerations

The NWS is expected to provide access to useful data for a large set of heterogeneous and faulty systems. As a result, it is required to be robust, portable, and scalable. Furthermore, sensor processes are run on the machines they are monitoring. If they have high resource requirements, they are likely to degrade application performance and to interfere with their own measurements.

Failure is a complicating factor in the design of NWS processes, since they cannot disregard their responsibilities because a process they report to is unavailable. Passive failure detection is accomplished using heartbeat messages between dependent processes. Heartbeats are used to detect expired registrations and failures in replicated nameservers. Also, the NWS relies heavily on timeouts to aggressively avoid deadlock during communication among NWS processes. Components measure the length of time to send data and receive heartbeats for each host with which they interact. By using forecasting techniques (described in Section 4), the processes use these measurements as a timeseries to compute a perdition and error value. These two pieces of information are combined to form an expected upper bound. These bounds are used to timeout network communication, determine lost clique tokens, and note which processes have not sent a heartbeat message.

The NWS has a number of mechanisms, detailed in the sections describing each component, for handling the failure of the processes on which they depend. First, nameserver replication adds some robustness to the NWS's central point of failure. Additionally, memories and sensors all cache registrations that could not be sent to the nameserver. This means that these processes can be started even when the nameserver has failed, and they can also accommodate temporary nameserver failures. Lastly, sensors cache measurement data so that measurement are not lost when memories fail. These caches can hold a large number of measurements, and can store almost an hour of CPU availability before they start to lose information.

There are a handful of portability issues that have been addressed for the NWS as well. For one, timing out socket communication is not a trivial task. Early versions used alarm signals to interrupt blocking communication system calls. This method is not portable for all OSes and does not interact well with threaded processes. Therefore, the NWS can be configured at compile time to use nonblocking sockets, disabling the use of the alarm signal. Other portability issues come from the use of threads, which are notoriously different across architectures and OSes. Therefore, forking is used in places where threads might be used. To allow users to implement processes that use the NWS within threads, the NWS libraries can be built with an option to add mutexes to synchronize internal calls.

Monitoring the network performance of a set of hosts requires taking $O(n^2)$ measurements, which obviously poses scalability concerns at some level. Observing that, most likely, there are clusters of machines tightly connected (fast local networks) that as a group are connected with wide-area networks, we make the assumption that the statistical properties of the links from machines in one cluster to machines of another cluster are somewhat similar. Hence we do not require all individual measurements from all machines within separate clusters, but can instead elect one (or a few) machines from each cluster and start a *super-clique* among these selected machines. Newer versions of NWS provide a *caching* mechanism that understands this operation and provides a logical view of an all-to-all performance matrix of TCP network measurements. This caching mechanism can be seen in Figure 18.2.

The NWS cache provides another scalability feature. Accessing $O(n^2)$ series requires a user to contact the memory $O(n^2)$ times, thus increasing the time when data are effectively available to unacceptable levels. To address this problem, we have made the assumption that what is really needed is the single prediction

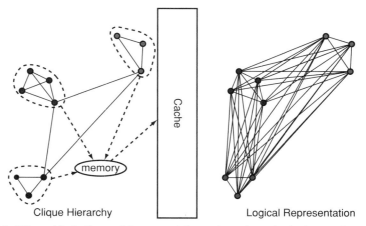

Cache

memory

Clique Hierarchy   Logical Representation

Figure 18.2. Hierarchical clique with connectivity cache reduces both the number of experiments taken and the connectivity graph creation when cliques contain a large number of hosts separated by wide-area networks.

instead of the entire history. The cache works as proxy, collecting the data from the memory and generating the forecasts, then returns the $O(n^2)$ forecasts in one call, avoiding the prohibitive $O(n^2)$ connection cost.

Finally, the components themselves are designed to be able to scale to a large number of hosts. The biggest liability is the nameserver, since it is the most centralized component. The requirements on the nameserver, however, are extremely low, so this liability poses little problem. The worst observed example was a nameserver running on a common desktop Linux machine that served more than 50,000 registrations and hundreds of hosts. In a case where nameservers are frequently accessed, they can be replicated so that different hosts and users can depend on different nameservers. The requirements of memories are not as light as nameservers, so they cannot serve nearly as much information. However, memories are very flexible about where they can be placed, so large systems can easily support a large number of memories.

Sensors have been designed to be lightweight and as nonintrusive as possible on the host being measured. Only under excessive monitoring, due to misconfiguration, may slower or less robust systems be taxed (when the periods of large cliques, file system sensors, and CPU sensors are excessively short). Typically, sensors uses between two and four megabytes of system memory, depending on the number of experiments they run. They spend most of their time waiting for control messages without using the host's processor.

3.5   User interface

There are three main interface applications that are used to interact with an NWS installation: *nws_search, nws_extract*, and *nws_ctrl*. These provide the core command-line interface with the NWS processes.

The nws_search program allows a user to search through the registrations that a nameserver has available. It uses a syntax reminiscent of LDIF, and all the usual operators can be used (&, |, =, >=, <= ...). For convenience, shortcuts have been added that allow users to list standard things like sensors, series, or skills without knowing the registration structure.

The nws_extract program allows the user to retrieve measurement data (series) from an NWS installation. The user specifies the nameserver, the resource they are interested in, and the hosts whose data they want to retrieve. nws_extract will first query the nameserver to find which series name matches the user request, then lookup in the matched object and the contact information of the associated memory, which is then contacted for data retrieval. The series of data is then fed to the forecaster, and the measurements, forecasts, and respective errors are then presented to the user. If the nameserver is unknown, nws_extract can query the first sensor asking to report which nameserver it is using. If the user knows the series names and the memory storing them, using -M and -S they can bypass the nameserver and query the memory directly.

Finally, nws_ctrl allows the user to control processes in an NWS installation. Most importantly, it allows administrators to modify behavior, which is usually specified through command line options at start time. However, there is also a handful of other commands. The following actions are understood by nws_ctrl:

- **test**: performs a simple test of health of a nwsHost. The nwsHost can be *dead* (no connection was made), *unresponsive* (connection was made but there was no response from the sensor), *sick* (the sensor is reachable but it cannot talk to its nameserver), or *healthy* (everything is functioning as expected).

- **register**: instructs the nwsHost to use a different nameserver for registration of objects. This allows the administrator to replace, restart, or move the nameserver process without redeploying the entire NWS installation. If the command is given to a nameserver, it will begin mirroring with the target.

- **memory**: instructs the given sensor to send all new measurements to a different NWS memory.

- **halt**: stops the nwsHost.

- **log**: toggles the verbosity of logging on the specified nwsHost.

- **skill**: asks a sensor to run a particular skill with specified options. Unlike an activity, the results are not taken continuously or sent to the memory but are instead reported directly to the user at his or her terminal.

- **add/remove**: adds or removes a member from a currently running clique. The user needs to specify a member of the clique and the clique name, and the sensor will restart the modified clique with the same options but a different list of members.

- **ping**: runs a single network experiment (tcpMessageMonitor) between the host running the command and the remote sensor, reporting the results directly to the user.

- **start/stop**: asks a sensor to start or stop an activity.

All these processes make use of the well-defined NWS-API to retrieve information and change the behavior of NWS processes. These functions are available to users through the *nws_api* library. It is therefore possible to include the functionality of these programs in a user's application with relative ease. In fact, these programs are invaluable examples of how to interface with the NWS at an application level.

4   THE NWS FORECASTING METHODOLOGY

The forecasting methodology used by the NWS assumes that each resource performance characteristic can be measured quantitatively. Each resource can be described by a stream of performance measurements, and predictions of future measurement values are the quantities that are of interest. Notice that useful qualitative information may be difficult to incorporate under this assumption. For example, it may be possible to know that "less" bandwidth will be available to a desktop machine typically used by a person who frequently downloads images from the Internet than to a machine used by a person who typically works locally. The NWS approach is to gather performance measurements from both machines and then predict future measurement values so that the predictions can be compared quantitatively. For some Grid applications, simply knowing that "less" or "more" resource will be available may be enough to develop an effective schedule. The advantage of using quantifiable resource characterization, however, is that the information is more easily encoded for use by an automatic scheduler. That is, it may be difficult for a scheduling agent to parse and compare the qualities of a resource, but forecast quantities can almost always be compared if the units are compatible.

A second important assumption made by the NWS forecasting method is that performance measurements can be gathered nonintrusively. In particular, any load that the performance monitors introduce does not have a measurable effect on the resource being monitored.

Finally, because the methods are time series based, they assume that the characteristics being measured have an instantaneous value that can be sampled at any given point in time. Not all quantifiable performance characteristics that are useful for scheduling easily conform to this model. For example, it is useful to predict the duration of time that a resource will be available based on previous availability history. Availability, in a time series form, is a series of binary values indicating "available" or "unavailable" at a particular time. Thus, the measurement levels are bimodal. While Markov-based models are adept at predicting modality, time-series analysis tends to be less effective. It is possible to incorporate state-transition models into the NWS forecasting framework, but at present these are not used by the system.

Dynamic Model Differentiation

Rather than relying on a single model, the NWS uses a mixture-of-experts approach to forecasting. A set of forecasting models are configured into the system, each having its own parameterization. Given a performance history of previously observed measurement values, each model is exercised to generate a forecast for every measurement value, based only on the measurement values that come before it. That is, given a performance history of *N* values, a forecast is generated for each. To generate a forecast for measurement *k*, only values up to measurement *k* − 1 will be presented to each forecasting model, for all values $1 \leq k \leq$ *N*. We term this method of replaying a performance history to generate a forecast for each known measurement value *postcasting*.

Postcast errors are generated for each forecasting method by differencing each measurement with the forecast generated for it. By aggregating the postcast errors, each method is assigned an overall accuracy score for the complete history up to the point in time when the forecast is generated. When a single forecast is required, the NWS forecasting system applies the postcasting procedure to all the configured prediction models using the most recent performance history available, and ranks each prediction model in terms of its accuracy. The most accurate model is then chosen to make the requested forecast. Each time a forecast is requested, the NWS recalculates the accuracy ranking using the most recently gathered history. The NWS constantly gathers measurement data from sensors that it controls. Thus, the performance histories that it uses are, typically, up to date at the time a forecast is requested from the system, and the forecaster choice takes into account the "fresh" historical data.

This method of differentiating between competing models based on previously observed accuracy has several advantages. The first is that it is nonparametric. Each individual model may have a specific parameterization, but the complete technique simply takes the constantly updated performance history gathered by the NWS as its only input. A second potential advantage is that it is possible for the system to adapt to changing conditions in cases where the performance response series is nonstationary. For example, if an exponential smoothing predictor with a gain factor of 0.01 is the most accurate predictor at one point in time, and conditions change so that a sliding-window median predictor with a window size of 10 becomes the most accurate (due to a change in the series dynamics) then the system will switch predictors if the change is persistent enough to cause the aggregate error ranking to change. If, however, the forecasters have been exposed to an extensive performance history before the change point, it may take a great deal of time for the better method to garner a lower aggregate error.

To improve the response of the overall technique to changes in the underlying dynamics of each measurement series, the NWS forecasting subsystem also selectively limits the amount of history during postcasting to determine if "old" data is harming accuracy. During the dynamic model-selection phase, a postcast is conducted using all previously available data. In addition, the system conducts postcasts using different windows of previous data (always starting with the most recent data and working backwards in time) and records the "winning" forecaster for each window size. The number of postcast-limiting windows and their sizes are fixed at compile time, but can be changed via configuration parameters when the forecasting subsystem is built. Each window size of previous history is subsequently treated as a separate forecaster, and a final accuracy tournament determines which forecaster will be used.

The pseudocode shown in Figure 18.3 summarizes how NWS forecasts are generated from a given measurement trace. The effect of using this method is that

```
input: T:  measurement trace
       F:  set of forecasting models that take a trace of fixed size and pro-
           duce a forecast of next value
       W:  a set of integer window sizes to limit postcasting

for each window size in W+ (entire history)
       for each forecaster in F
              postcast current forecaster over current window size in T
              (window size slides over all of T)
       record aggregate error for current forecaster
       end for
       record forecaster with lowest aggregate error for this window size
end for

choose forecaster and window size with lowest aggregated error and make
       final forecast using it
```

Figure 18.3. Pseudocode for NWS forecasting methodology.

either the forecaster that has the lowest aggregate error since the beginning of the trace will be chosen as best forecaster, or the forecaster that has the lowest error over an abbreviated history of fixed size will be chosen. If the system has quickly changing dynamics, forecasters that work well over short histories should be more accurate, since they do not include stale data.

5   AN EXAMPLE

To illustrate the types of forecasts that can be generated by the NWS adaptive forecasting technique, we will use the following example. Figure 18.4 depicts an application-level TCP/IP trace from the University of Tennessee (UTK) to the University of California in San Diego (UCSD). The trace times a 64 kilobyte TCP/IP socket transfer and an application-level acknowledgment, and from that timing and data size, it calculates a throughput measure. The socket buffers for this trace are 32 kilobytes, and the buffers used in each communication system call are 16 kilobytes. The entire trace spans the month of June 2000, with one transfer recorded every 30 seconds.

(Note: The actual trace contains a little over 85,000 measurements. As such, the trace data used to generate the graphical figures in this chapter have been decimated. All forecasting and error calculations, however, use the complete trace. We decimate the time series output only for graphical display purposes.)

A companion trace of traceroute data showing the end-to-end gateway traversal indicates that the series is likely not a stationary one. The routes used to connect UTK with UCSD changed from time to time due to routing table misconfigurations and maintenance.

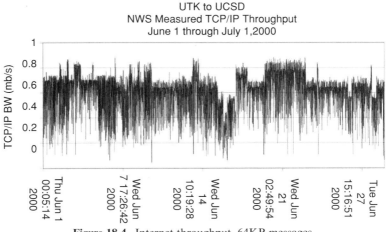

Figure 18.4. Internet throughput, 64KB messages.

In Figure 18.5 we show the NWS forecasts (the light color) superimposed over the measurement series (dark color). After each measurement was gathered, it was passed to the forecasting subsystem, and a forecast (using the method described in Section 4) was generated to produce the forecast trace. From Figure, 18.5 it is clear the the NWS forecasters determine a centralized or smoothed estimate at each step in the series. Figure 18.5 also provides a qualitative depiction of the forecasting error. Each light-colored forecast point is matched vertically with the dark-colored measurement data point it forecasts. The degree to which the dark features are showing (i.e., are not obscured by light-colored features) provides an indication of the overall error.

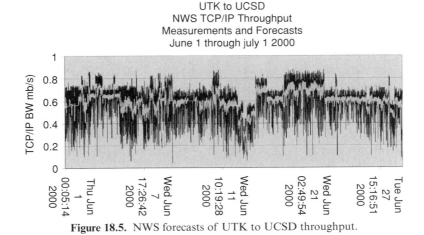

Figure 18.5. NWS forecasts of UTK to UCSD throughput.

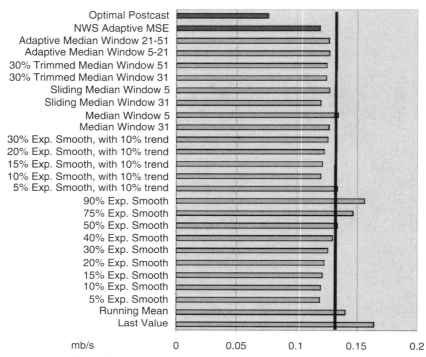

Figure 18.6. NWS forecasts of UTK to UCSD throughput.

More quantitatively, Figure 18.6 details the error performance of the forecasting system. The vertical axis of the graph shows those forecasters that are currently configured into the NSF Middleware Initiative (NMI) [32] release of the NWS and their individual error performance. Error (shown on the horizontal axis) is measured as the square root of the mean square error (MSE). If each NWS forecast is considered to be a conditional expectation of the succeeding measurement, then the forecasting error approximates the conditional sample standard deviation. We do not claim, however, that the conditional expectation or the conditional standard deviation is either an optimal or an unbiased estimates for the true conditional mean and variance—only engineering approximations.

Each of the horizontal bars in Figure 18.6 (except the top two) shows the error performance of a different forecasting model. Notice that one type of model (e.g., exponential smoothing [24]) is used multiple times with different parameterizations (e.g., the gain factor). The entire forecasting suite is similarly populated by different parameterizations of a smaller set of models. The software has been modularized to permit new model types, as well as different modularizations of the included models when it is configured. Currently, the NWS uses 24 model parameterizations (shown in Figure 18.6) in the standard release. The choice of these models is based on our anecdotal experience with effective prediction techniques in the Grid settings, where we or our collaborators have constructed successful schedulers.

The error bar that is second from the top Figure 18.6 shows the error performance of the adaptive NWS technique. That is, this line indicates the true error an

NWS user would have seen from the forecasts generated when the trace was gathered "live." Notice that this performance is equivalent to the minimum error across all configured forecasters. While space constraints prevent us from demonstrating this effect more completely, in all postmortem trace analyses performed by our group since the inception of the project, this phenomenon has been observed. The NWS adaptive forecaster achieves at least equivalent (if not slightly better) error performance as the most accurate of its constituent models. We do not claim that the adaptive forecaster must achieve equivalent accuracy. It is clear that it is possible to construct a series artificially for which the adaptive technique will be less accurate. Our experience, however, is that for empirically observed measurement series taken from Grid systems, this phenomenon occurs in every case.

Also, for space constraints, we have omitted the limited postcast history errors. For this trace, the best overall adaptive performance comes from considering all previous values at any given point in the trace (despite the potential for nonstationarity). That is, the forecasters that adapt based on a shortened window of history are less accurate that the ones that consider all previous measurements.

The error bar marked "Optimal Postcast" at the top of the figure indicates the theoretically maximal forecasting performance (minimum error) that the method could have achieved if the best predictor at each step were known. That is, each time a forecast was generated, if the most accurate prediction made by any predictor in the suite were used, the aggregate error measure shown by the top error bar in Figure 18.6 would have resulted. This measure represents the upper bound on accuracy, since it is the most accurate that the entire suite could have been if perfect foreknowledge of predictor accuracy were possible.

The bottom two error bars are also noteworthy. The bottommost error bar (marked "Last Value") represents the accuracy obtained by simply using the last observed value as a prediction of the next performance measurement at each step. This method corresponds to the typical way in which Grid users make ad hoc estimates without the aid of numerical forecasting techniques. Most users simply "ping" the desired resources or read the most recent performance measurements recorded for those resources by an available monitoring tool, and compare the measurements that they observe to make their scheduling decisions. This method is, by far, the least accurate of those that are available. A second common method is to use a running average as an estimator, based on the assumption that the series is converging to a single mean performance value. The running mean is more accurate than the last value as a predictor, but again, significantly less accurate than other, only slightly more sophisticated techniques.

One possible argument for using the more simple last value or running average techniques is that the computational efficiency of these methods is quite high. The last value requires no computation, and the running average can be calculated as a simple ongoing update. The techniques that we have chosen to incorporate in the NWS implementation, however, come primarily from the signal processing disciplines, making very high-performance versions possible. With careful implementation, each forecast shown in Figure 18.5 required 161 microseconds on an unloaded 750 MHz Pentium III laptop. Thus the additional computational overhead introduced by our implementation of the adaptive methodology introduces negligible performance overhead. More concretely, considering the difference in error performance between the Last Value predictor, the adaptive NWS predictor, and the Optimal Postcast, our implementation halves the error difference between optimal and last value at a cost of 161 microseconds per forecast.

Forecasting Error

For Grid scheduling, the forecasting error can also be used to gauge the value of a particular resource. In Figure 18.7, we show a trace of TCP/IP throughput between adjacent workstations attached to a 100 megabit-per-second Ethernet at the San Diego Super Computer Center (SDSC). The probe size for this trace is 64 kilobytes, with one probe taken every 120 seconds, and the adaptive NWS minimum MSE forecast is superimposed over the measurement trace. The Ethernet segment, however, is also shared by other hosts at SDSC. That is, it is not dedicated to a particular cluster, but rather is a part of the shared, local-area network infrastructure. In Figure 18.8, we show three days' worth of TCP/IP trace data between a pair of cluster nodes at UTK. The nodes are attached via a switched gigabit Ethernet that is dedicated to intracluster communication exclusively. Both figures are plotted using the same scale. Note that the missing values in Figure 18.8 occur when the machine was taken out of service for maintenance.

As expected, the forecast performance of the dedicated gigabit Ethernet link is higher than that for the 100 megabit connection throughout the measurement period. The gigabit link's forecast hovers near 100 megabits per second for most of the trace, while the forecasts for the 100 megabit link are mostly just above 50 megabits. However, the $\sqrt{MSE}$ value (termed the *forecast deviation* in each figure) for the 100 megabit trace is 9.7 megabits per second. For the gigabit trace, it is 64.3 megabits per second. Roughly speaking, as a percentage of the forecast value, the forecast deviation is approximately 20% of the forecast for the 100 MB Ethernet, but 60% for the gigabit link. For programs with malleable granularity that can be controlled by an online scheduler, a more predictable performance response, despite lower absolute performance, may make a resource more valu-

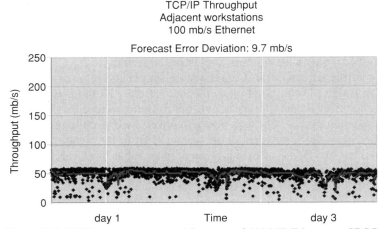

Figure 18.7. NWS measurements and forecasts of 100 MB Ethernet at SDSC.

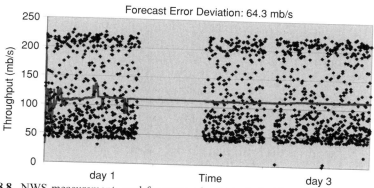

Figure 18.8. NWS measurements and forecasts of switched gigabit Ethernet within a cluster at UTK.

able than a faster, less predictable resource. Data parallel or SPMD (Single Program Multiple Data) programs, for example, have their overall performance defined by the slowest task. In [9] we describe a dynamic scheduling technique for data parallel programs that automatically partitions the workload based on forecast performance levels. For that system, a grossover prediction of delivered performance results is extra work assigned to the potentially slow resource, and as a result, the application executes with less-than-expected performance.

This example also illustrates the role that forecasting can play in detecting faulty resources. For a dedicated gigabit switched network, a forecast value near 100 megabits, with an error deviation of more than 60%, is indicative of a potential problem. When shown these data, the system administrators for the cluster upgraded the system software (several times: hence the dropout in the trace) in an effort to correct a suspected configuration problem. By using the NWS forecasting, it is possible to build an alarm system that would have signaled the potential problem much earlier [29].

6   FORECASTING ERROR AND EMPIRICAL CONFIDENCE INTERVALS

In the previous example, the forecast error deviation permits a ranking of resources by their predictability. For some measurement streams, the forecasting error also can be used to generate a quantifiable bound on the predictability of the measurements in the stream. By treating the MSE as the conditional sample variance, a confidence interval for the forecasted value can be calculated as $(forecast - K * \sqrt{MSE}, forecast + K * \sqrt{MSE})$, where K is a multiplicative factor to be determined. We have used a K value of 3 to bound the predicted execution times of worker tasks in a master–slave distributed implementation of FASTA — a commonly used genetic sequencing application [43]. For the genome sequences we examined, a *K* factor of 3 allowed the scheduler to determine the "dependable" task execution time across a wide range of target resources.

To predict the performance of an individual resource (as opposed to the convolution of data-dependent task execution time with resource performance response, as in the FASTA experiment), smaller multiplicative factors are often effective. For example, we observe that for network throughput, a factor of 2 yields a 90% or better "hit rate" for each succeeding measurement, with the rate being above 95% for most of the measurement streams we have encountered.

Figure 18.9 shows this form of empirical confidence interval as generated by plotting *forecast* +/− (2 * $\sqrt{MSE}$) for the UTK-to-UCSD throughput trace shown previously in Figure 18.4. At each point in time, the prediction interval is formed by making a forecast for the next measurement value, and then adding and subtracting 2 * $\sqrt{MSE}$ for the MSE that has been observed up to that point. The capture rate for this trace is 95.6%. That is, over the entire measurement period, the confidence range predicted by +/− 2 * $\sqrt{MSE}$ captures the next measured value for 95.6% of the total number of measurements. We note that one can also make one-sided predictions using the same idea: For example, if a scheduler (such as the one reported on in [97]) were concerned with the *minimum* available performance, it could determine a K-value to produce lower prediction bounds that have a capture percentage approximately equal to a given value.

The dotted line in Figure 18.9 represents the 5% quantile for the entire trace, with 95% of the measurements falling above this line. If the data were treated as a sample rather than as a time series, this value could be used as an empirical estimate of the minimum throughput level with 95% confidence. By treating the data as a potentially nonstationary series, and recalculating the confidence interval at each time step based on forecasting error, the NWS methodology generates a significantly tighter lower bound than a sample-based quantile method.

As an example of how pervasive this phenomenon is for TCP/IP network throughput, we show the distribution of forecast capture percentages (i.e., the

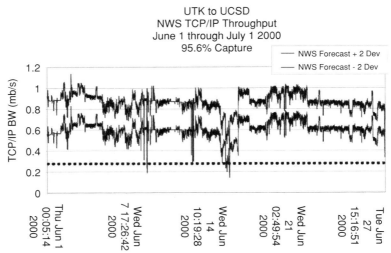

Figure 18.9. Confidence range formed by +-2 deviations.

observed confidence percentage) for a complete Grid system that we monitored during the month of October 2002. The Grid Application Development Software (GrADS) [7, 23] project, as part of its research agenda, maintains a Grid testbed based on stable deployments of the Globus [19, 22] toolkit and the NWS. The purpose of the testbed is to provide support for the development of Grid programming tools and to act as a production Grid environment in which GrADS enabled applications can be tested and evaluated. Globus and the NWS provide the base Grid software infrastructure that GrADS software tools build upon. Approximately 50 users (programmers, graduate students, and project administration personnel) have access to the testbed at any given time, and it is maintained as a permanent resource. Thus, the GrADS testbed constitutes an example of a practical, working Grid.

During the month of October 2002, the GrADS project developed and deployed six GrADS-enabled applications for demonstration at SC02—a prominent high-performance computing conference that takes place annually in November. As such, the October measurement and forecast data for the testbed reflect Grid dynamics in a production computing setting.

The testbed comprises 77 host machines organized into several Linux clusters as well as various independent Unix and Linux machines. Within each cluster, the available networking is either 100 megabit Ethernet or gigabit Ethernet. Clusters at a single site are connected either via local area networking or via the campus network infrastructure (GrADS testbed sites are located at various Universities and two research laboratories). Intersite network connectivity is provided by the Internet, although several of the sites have experimental, high-performance access to an Internet backbone. The GrADS sites are geographically distributed, with machines located at Rice University, UCSD, UTK, the University of Illinois at Urbana-Champaign (UIUC), Indiana University, the Information Science Institute (ISI), and the University of California at Santa Barbara (UCSB).

The NWS provides support for organizing end-to-end network measurements hierarchically. Not all machines must conduct machine-to-machine probes of network connectivity to provide forecasts for the entire resource pool (details on this scaling technique are described in [44] and [52]). For the GrADS testbed, 1234 NWS TCP/IP probe traces are sufficient to provide a complete end-to-end performance forecast report. Finally, the NWS uses a variety of probe sizes ranging from 64 kilobytes per probe to 4 megabytes per probe, depending on the link characteristics at hand. As such, the complete GrADS testbed trace captures a good cross section of available network technologies and probe sizes under Grid computing loads.

Figure 18.10 shows the distribution of capture percentage over the total October trace set when two forecast error deviations are used to form a confidence interval. All network types (intracluster, intrasite, and intersite) are represented. The traces have been sorted from smallest capture percentage to largest. The x-axis depicts trace number and the y-axis shows the capture percentage observed for each trace using $+/- (2 * \sqrt{MSE})$ to form each conditional prediction interval. The smallest capture percentage is approximately 89%. In 1084 of the 1234 traces, however, the predictions capture 95% or more of the future values. We are just beginning to study this phenomenon in detail, but anecdotally the GrADS testbed analysis reflects the common experience reported by NWS users for TCP/IP throughput in different settings.

In Figure 18.11 we show the cumulative distribution of CPU load measurement capture percentage that two deviations generate for the 77 hosts in the

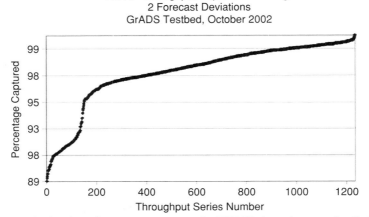

Figure 18.10. Distribution of capture percentages for TCP/IP throughput on the GrADS testbed.

GrADS testbed. The NWS supports a CPU monitor that reports the percentage of CPU cycles that are available to an executing process. The default periodicity (which is what has been used to monitor the GrADS machines) is 10 seconds. Thus, each of the 77 traces contains approximately 250,000 measurements of available CPU fraction at each 10-second time step. The number is approximate, since data may be missing when a machine becomes unavailable as is the case in Figure 18.8. For 75 of the 77 traces, $forecast + / - (2 * \sqrt{MSE})$ also generates a 95% (or higher) confidence interval.

It is clear that the empirical confidence technique warrants more study. Resource characteristics such as TCP/IP round-trip time are not as predictable as throughput or available CPU fraction. We suspect that available nonpaged memory will prove to be similar to CPU measurements in terms of predictability, but

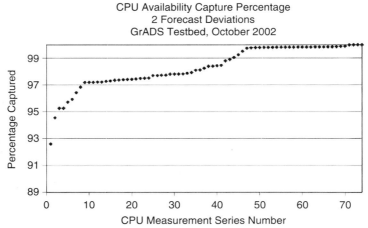

Figure 18.11. Distribution of capture percentages for CPU availability measurements on the GrADS testbed.

the NWS memory sensor has only recently been developed, giving us limited experience with true load characteristics.

7   LESSONS LEARNED FROM DEVELOPMENT AND DEPLOYMENT

Having developed and deployed the NWS in a variety of contexts, we have repeatedly encountered somewhat surprising anecdotes within the user community. While we are hesitant to give these observations the status of "principles," they nevertheless recur with enough frequency to warrant some exposition, if only to provide insight into the successes and failures the system has experienced. Moreover, many of our experiences run counter to the "conventional wisdom" or, in some cases, contradict predicted outcomes made by acknowledged experts. In all cases, however, we present these anecdotes without attribution and acknowledge that any misrepresentation is strictly our responsibility.

7.1   Grid Performance Tools versus Grid Performance Services

Many Grid users install and use individual resource performance monitoring tools to aid in resource discovery. While system administrators clearly understand the need for Grid services such as remote sign-on and file system access, performance monitoring services (particularly for dynamically changing performance data) are often overlooked, since they are used, primarily, to optimize rather than to enable application execution. At the same time, user-level performance tools, particularly for measuring network performance, are plentiful, easy to install, and simple to use. Thus many Grid installations have an administrator-supported infrastructure for secure access, but leave the problem of gauging resource performance to the individual users.

There are two problems with this approach. First, most individual performance monitoring tools are designed for single-user execution. Popular application-level network monitoring tools such as Iperf [26], netperf [28], and nttcp [33] all measure end-to-end network throughput by sending data from a source host to a sink host, and timing the transfer. To ensure that the effects of TCP slow-start [27] do not affect the measurements, these tools (by default) will transfer data continuously for tens of seconds to ensure that steady-state behavior is being observed.

If used occasionally, in isolation (e.g., for performance debugging), the network load introduced by lengthy network probes is negligible. However, if many users each run network probes individually, without coordination, a great deal of unnecessary load may be generated. For example, all hosts at the University of California, Santa Barbara (UCSB) share a common network path (once they exit the campus backbone) to the University of Wisconsin (Wisc) backbone that traverses the Abilene [1] network. While the paths through each campus may differ, all UCSB-to-Wisc transfers share the same route across Abilene and, more importantly, the performance of that route dominates the end-to-end performance. Thus multiple users at UCSB issuing throughput probes to multiple hosts at Wisc will each introduce tens of seconds worth of network load to measure the same artifact: the performance of the cross-country Abilene route. Perhaps more problematically, if enough users issue these probes simultaneously, or if multiple users probe the same host (or issue probes from the same host), the measurements that are generated measure contention between probes.

The NWS solves this problem by using a hierarchy of cliques, as described in Section 3. Cliques at either campus provide intracampus measurements, while a single campus-to-campus probe sequence measures the cross-country throughput. Moreover, the NWS proxy caching layer can automatically generate a virtual fully interconnected network by filling in the "missing" network measurements between hosts at either campus with forecasts taken for the intercampus link. As such, the NWS measures the shared path using a single sequence of measurements but at the same time can present a virtual all-to-all measurement picture to all interested clients by correctly reporting the dominant shared performance for any pair of hosts.

A second problem with the use of tools rather than a service for generating measurements is that user tools are typically designed to require user intervention when resource failure requires the tool to abort. Returning to the network probing example described above, the TCP protocol by default does not include an inactivity timeout. That is, once a TCP handshake has been completed, a network partition will not cause the TCP connection to shut down or abort. The optional KEEP_ALIVE feature of TCP is designed to implement an inactivity abort according to RFC-1122, but the timeout value by default can be no less than 2 hours, which is often too long for Grid applications. The assumption made by most user tools is that the user will manually "time out" the tool and abort it from the command line. Often, due to the need for continuous and historical measurement, these tools are executed repeated within scripts, causing end-point memory and process load.

The NWS TCP throughput probe, however, includes portable timeout mechanisms and an adaptive timeout discovery protocol [4] so that long-running, unattended execution is feasible. However, the engineering effort required to build a portable and reliable timeout mechanism for TCP sockets (without kernel modification) introduces another potential point of confusion. In particular, it may be that the additional mechanisms introduce overhead that affects the quality of the measurements. Indeed, one reason often cited as justification for the use of a particular individual network monitoring tool is that the tool in question is believed, by its user, to be the most accurate among all the available options. In addition, several users, when queried as to why they preferred a particular tool to the NWS as a service, claimed that the tool in question generated more accurate measurements of end-to-end throughput. Questioned further, some speculated that the reason for the loss of accuracy was that the NWS network probe included timeout mechanisms that most applications using TCP sockets do not, and the timeout mechanisms introduced extra overhead.

Figure 18.12 shows a comparison of the throughput measured by three popular user tools – Iperf, netperf, and nttcp – and the NWS throughput measurement service. To generate these data, we ran each different method back-to-back (so that all methods would experience approximately the same ambient network conditions) every 60 seconds over a 72-hour period, resulting in 400 comparable measurements for each technique. We configured all four systems to use the same

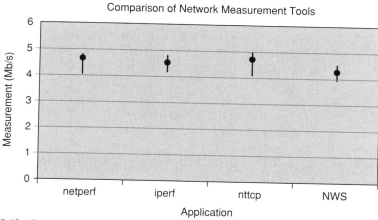

Figure 18.12. Comparison of Internet throughput measurements between a host UCSB and one at the University of Wisconsin.

end-point buffering, which is the one used by default in Iperf, and to transfer the same amount of data. The large circular "dot" for each method marks the median throughput observed, and the bars show the range of values between the first and third quartiles. From these data, it is not possible to conclude that there is any statistical difference between the measurements generated by these methods. The three tools and the NWS service all generate clearly overlapping ranges of values. The NWS probes, however, include all the overhead necessary to implement reliable socket timeouts at the application layer.

As such, we speculate that user-reported perception of tool utility is not based on accuracy but rather on intellectual and manual ease of use. All three of these network measurement tools are well engineered, documented, and simple to understand, install, and use. The NWS is a long-running Grid service designed to support many clients and resources simultaneously. While it does not require special user privileges (each user can in principle install a separate instance of the NWS), it is necessarily more complicated than a simple "ping" tool. As a result, if the local administrator has elected not to install the system, or plans to do so as a low-priority task, we believe users will naturally gravitate towards using tools that they can easily understand, install, and maintain themselves. Subsequent familiarity then breeds a "lore" regarding tool accuracy that, when examined critically, is unverifiable. The cost of this convenience, however, is the wasted resource consumed by redundant measurements. By carefully engineering and structuring the measurement system, a Grid service such as the NWS can yield the same levels of accuracy with greater dependability using significantly fewer resources.

7.2   Network Heterogeneity

Another observation that we have made while developing the NWS and Grid applications that use it [13, 51, 9] is that network performance is truly heterogeneous, and the way in which applications access the network should take this heterogeneity into account to achieve the best possible performance. The use of parallel sockets by applications such as GridFTP [2] and the Internet Backplane Protocol [40] (IBP) illustrates the need to consider such heterogeneity.

For systems such as the TeraGrid [47], where a high-bandwith dedicated network connects nationally distributed computing nodes, the standard congestion avoidance and control mechanisms built into commercially available TCP implementations prevent applications from achieving maximum possible end-to-end throughput. The specific reason is that TCP uses the timing of packet acknowledgments to control the speed with which it will introduce new data into the network, both at start-up and after a packet has been dropped. For networks with high bandwidth-delay products and low drop rates (such as the 40 gigabit/second TeraGrid network), the loss of throughput can be substantial. On these systems, to avoid the need for specially engineered kernel-level TCP stacks, many applications use parallel sockets to circumvent the unnecessary congestion avoidance and control mechanisms.

However, in network settings where the bandwidth-delay product is lower, or where packet loss due to congestion is a possibility, parallel sockets can have the opposite effect. Figure 18.13 compares the performance of the IBP streaming download protocol [40] that uses parallel sockets with a single-socket implementation that uses NWS forecasts for proximity resolution and adaptive timeout discovery [5]. The IBP progress-driven protocol [40] uses parallel sockets and a deadline-driven scheduling algorithm to download segments from a replicated file. Different file segments are fetched in parallel within some prespecified progress window. If the segment at the beginning of the window is late, that segment is fetched in parallel from where it is replicated before new segment transfers are initiated. One simplicity advantage of this approach is that it is completely reactive. That is, it does not require a prediction of future performance levels or failure likelihood, but rather reacts to conditions as they occur.

In contrast, the NWS protocol uses throughput forecasts to rank the replica sites in terms of their download speed. It then maintains a database of forecast response times and of forecast variance so that it can automatically determine

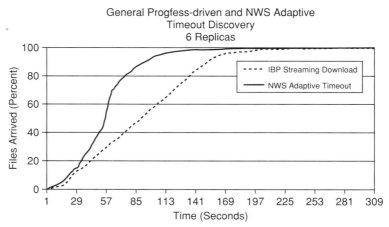

Figure 18.13. Empirical cumulative distribution of file download arrival times for IBP download protocol and adaptive NWS protocol using six replicas.

how long it should wait for each replica to respond. Only one segment of the file is downloaded at a time. The protocol tries the replicas in order of their speed, and switches between them when a timeout occurs [5, 4].

In Figure 18.13, we show the cumulative distribution of file arrival times, where six replicas for each file are distributed across PlanetLab [39], the download point is located at UCSB, and each segment has an artificially induced 5% chance of failing. From Figure 18.13, it is clear that the NWS methodology outperforms the IBP methodology while maintaining the same level of robustness (both systems completely download all files) and using substantially less bandwidth. In this case, the additional network load generated by the IBP protocol through the use of parallel sockets over the Internet slows the individual file transfer times. The adaptive NWS protocol, however, uses the fastest replica when it can and relies on rapid failure discovery and remediation for robustness. Thus parallel sockets, while an excellent choice for dedicated high—bandwidth-delay product networks, yield lower application-level performance over the Internet when compared with a socket scheduling system that uses performance forecasts to control resource usage.

8 MEASURING AND PREDICTING OTHER RESOURCE CHARACTERISTICS

While the empirical and adaptive time series forecasting approach has proved useful in a variety of contexts, there are quantifiable resource characteristics that are not well modeled by a periodic statistical series. Resource availability duration (i.e., resource "lifetime"), for example, is represented as a highly correlated time series with two modes namely, "available" and "unavailable" as depicted in Figure 18.14. Essentially, "available" must be represented as one value (a 1 in the figure) and "unavailable" as another. Further, the prediction of interest is not for the next value but rather for the duration of time that a value will remain constant before it changes.

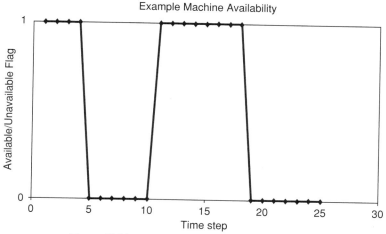

Figure 18.14. Machine availability as a time series.

To make predictions of this type, the NWS requires both the ability to measure the quantity of interest and a different set of forecasting models that are not time series based. In the case of machine availability, we have developed an availability sensor that measures the time between machine restarts, and a process lifetime sensor that can be used to measure processor occupancy in cycle harvesting systems like Condor [46], Entropia [18], and BOINC [10]. These new sensors, which are part of the current system, do not rely on heartbeat messages and soft-state registration to measure availability. Doing so would convolve the observed host availability distribution with the distribution of network partition frequency between the measured site and the storage location where the measurements are captured. That is, sending a heartbeat message to a collector (an NWS *memory* process, in our case) as a measure of host availability records both host failures and failures in the network connecting the host and the collector in a way that cannot be easily separated later. Instead, the sensors send a running accumulation of "up time" so that the effect of missing messages due to network partition can be filtered out of the measurement history.

Predicting machine availability requires forecasting techniques that are substantially more heavyweight than the online time series models. The mode of operation, then, is for the NWS to archive availability measurements and calculate predictions as a background task rather than on-demand, as it does for performance levels.

The type of prediction is also different from what the current system generates. Our initial target is to provide availability predictions to aid process and checkpoint scheduling. Dynamic application schedulers would like to be able to predict when a checkpoint should be taken (so as to minimize checkpoint overhead) and/or to decide if checkpointing is even necessary. For example, a machine with a 99.9% guaranteed availability of 10 minutes can run a 10 minute job to completion 999 times out of 1000 attempts without checkpointing.

This last example also illustrates the nature of the predictions that application schedulers require. Rather than the *mean time to failure*, which is a useful metric in many industrial engineering contexts, the scheduler must estimate how long a resource will be available until the probability of failure exceeds some specified threshold. That is, the scheduler is typically interested in a specific *quantile* from the cumulative failure distribution, rather than the mean. Returning to the example, if the 0.001 quantile of the cumulative machine availability distribution were known, the probability that a machine would be available *at least* as long as the specified duration would be 0.999. An application scheduler, then, requires a prediction in the form of a quantile at a specified level of certainty corresponding to a failure tolerance that either the application or its user is willing to accept.

Moreover, to make a reliable estimate that can be trusted at the given level of certainty, the *confidence bounds* on the estimated quantile must also be determined. Any estimate that is generated from an observed sample of measurements will include random estimation error. If statistical bounds on that error can be calculated, the worst-case bound at the specified level of confidence should represent a conservative *guarantee* of availability.

We have explored both parametric and nonparametric approaches to the problem of generating quantiles and confidence intervals on the estimated quantiles using the NWS. Because of their computational complexity and because they require efficient archival storage, we have not yet incorporated quantile estimation techniques into the NWS forecasting system. Our intention is to do so at some future release, however.

The parametric approach we have taken is to develop automatic software for implementing Maximum Likelihood Estimation (MLE) for various candidate models such as exponential, Pareto, and Weibull. Given a model and a historical trace of availability, the software estimates both the MLE parameters that best describe the data with the model, and the confidence intervals for the fitted model. Figure 18.15 depicts a comparison of model fits for the MLE-determined exponential, Pareto, and Weibull models using availability data gathered from the student instructional machines located at UCSB. At UCSB, the power switch on the machines available to all computer science students is not protected. When using a machine from its console, students routinely "clean off" foreign processes (owned by other students) by power cycling the machine, causing a reboot. Figure 18.5 compares the cumulative distribution of observed availability measurements for the three models.

The dark points depict individual availability durations, and the smoothed lines show the three different models. The Pareto model carries significantly more weight in the tail than the data indicate. It predicts that the 0.8 quantile will occur at approximately 8,000,000 seconds (approximately 92 days). That is, the Pareto model predicts that 20% of the availability durations will be longer than 8,000,000 seconds. From the data, however, only two of the 1765 availability durations lasted that long, making the Pareto overly optimistic. In contrast, the exponential model does not predict that availability durations will last as long as they did. For example, the 0.95 quantile from the data occurs at 2,189,875 seconds (approximately 25 days), meaning that 5% of the measured availability durations were larger than this value. The exponential model predicts the 0.95 quantile to occur

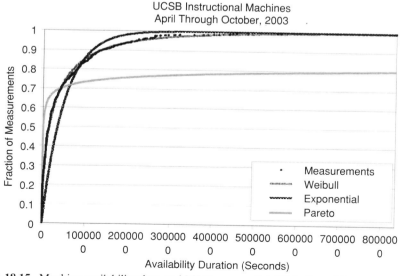

Figure 18.15. Machine availability data and MLE exponential, Weibull, and Pareto models for UCSB instructional machines, April through October 2003.

at 1,495,871 seconds (approximately 17 days), thereby underestimating the possibility of longer durations. The Weibull model, however, fits the data so accurately that its curve is obscured by the data themselves in Figure 18.15. For the 0.95 quantile, this model estimates the duration to be 2,234,657 seconds, missing the measured quantile by 44,782 seconds, or a little over half a day. Maximum Likelihood Estimation is currently the best-known automatic technique for fitting parametric models to observed data for models with a small number of parameters. Thus the Weibull model truly describes the shape of the distribution more accurately than the Pareto or the exponential.

We have also developed software (using goodness-of-fit *p*-values as heuristics) that attempts to determine the best fit automatically. We have examined other availability contexts, including Condor [46], where jobs are terminated when a resource owner reclaims a resource, and an Internet host availability conducted by Long, Muir, and Golding in 1995 [31]. Perhaps surprisingly, we have found that an MLE Weibull model fits the observed availability distributions rather closely. Moreover, previous work with a small number of student and faculty workstations in 2001 [25] also found Weibull models to be effective.

While the Weibull fit was clearly best in our study (see [34] for details), it did not yield the most accurate predictions of future availability durations. The software also generates confidence intervals on the MLE parameters it determines as part of the model-fitting process. From these confidence intervals, it should be possible to calculate the conservative worst-case estimate for the quantile of interest. For quantile prediction, however, it is possible to use nonparametric techniques to estimate a quantile, and confidence bounds for it, without specifying (or indeed knowing) what the underlying distribution is. One such technique uses repeated subsampling of the observed data and *bootstrapping* [14] to estimate the quantile. We have developed a second nonparametric method, which we term the *Binomial Method*, that is based on the binomial distribution. Table 18.1 shows a comparison of the predictive accuracy achieved by using an MLE Weibull and its confidence bounds, bootstrapping, and the Binomial Method to predict future machine availability at UCSB, in the Condor pool, and in the Long, Muir, and Golding study.

Using the first 20 measurements occurring chronologically from each machine trace, we estimated the lower 95% confidence bound on the 0.05 quantile. This number (which is different for each machine) is the minimum duration of time a scheduler could depend upon for each machine with 95% confidence if the methodology used to generate it is effective. For each data set, we identified the individual machine traces with at least 40 measurements so that the number of predictions made would be at least as large as the number of measurements used to "train" the predictor. The number of machines from each data set fitting this criterion is shown in parentheses in the left-hand column.

Table 18.1. Percentage of predictions made correctly using three different quantile estimation methods to estimate the 0.05 quantile with 95% confidence.

Data Set	MLE Weibull	Bootstrapping	Binomial Method
UCSB (16 machines)	56.3%	62.5%	**87.5%**
Condor (87 machines)	95.9%	60.2%	**98.9%**
Long/Muir/Golding (83 machines)	58.0%	53./;.4%	**94.3%**

We then record the number of future measurements that were greater than the estimated 0.05 quantile and report them as a percentage of total number of predictions for each machine (which is greater than or equal to 20 in all cases). Thus, this experiment depicts the empirical accuracy of each estimation method using the first 20 measurements to predict the remaining measurements, where there are at least 20 remaining measurements to predict. Full details from the investigation are described in [11]. From Table 18.1, however, it is clear that the Binomial Method is capable of making accurate, nonparametric estimates of future availability using relatively few measurements.

Thus, using the NWS, we have developed two new functionalities that will eventually be incorporated into the distributed software base. The first is an automatic modeling capability that can generate closed-form probability distributions that "fit" empirically observed availability measurements. We believe this functionality will be crucial to the development of realistic, possibly online simulations of grid, peer-to-peer, and global computing systems. Second using the Binomial Method, the NWS will be able to provide accurate predictions of future availability levels using relatively few measurements.

9   CONCLUSIONS AND FUTURE WORK

There are several ways in which we are currently extending our work beyond the capabilities described in the previous section. We are studying the decay in forecast accuracy (both in terms of the forecast value and the width of the empirical confidence intervals) as a function of time into the future. The current set of NWS forecasting techniques makes predictions for the next time interval. As such, the periodicity with which measurements are gathered defines the time frame for which a forecast is generated. We are attempting to quantify the error associated with multistep forecasting.

We are also investigating methodologies for automatically deriving the multiplicative factor that is needed to generate a given confidence range. The forecasters themselves are nonparametric, but the confidence interval system requires that the multiplicative factor be specified. We believe that the forecasting system must be able to adapt its parameterization automatically to be truly useful in an engineering context.

Finally, the NWS forecasting methodology does not address the problem of translating resource performance response into an estimate of application performance response. Even if resource performance forecasts were perfect, composing resource performance predictions into an application performance prediction can introduce error. To address this problem, we have been investigating ways to generate automatic correlator functions that relate resource performance forecasts to application performance [45]. The goal of this work is to combine a small number of application performance measurements gathered via internal instrumentation with resource performance measurements taken simultaneously from the resources that the application is using. From these simultaneous application-level and resource-level measurements, we derive a correlator for the application that can be used to predict future application performance from resource performance only.

The problem of modeling and predicting resource performance is central to Computational Grid research. Not only is it critical to effective program and system design but also the engineering of dynamic schedulers and fault diagnosis tools requires online access to prediction data as part of the Grid infrastructure. While explanatory models are beginning to emerge, fast statistical techniques applied to real-time performance measurement streams have empirically been shown to be effective. With little added computational complexity, it is possible to make predictions of future performance measurements and to quantify the error associated with these predictions. The resulting prediction accuracy can be substantially better than simply using the last observed value, or averaging — the two most common methods of predicting future performance from historical measurement data. In addition, it is possible to derive empirical confidence intervals, based on forecast error, for some forms of resource performance response. Our experience, described using a small number of representative examples in this chapter, is that these results are general for the resource types we have presented.

One of the unique features of Computational Grid computing is the central role that performance prediction must play with respect to program adaptivity and resource allocation. Despite characteristics that impede rigorous analysis (such as nonstationarity), the work we have described in this chapter reflects the degree to which statistical techniques have proved successful as prediction methods in the Grid settings we have so far encountered.

ACKNOWLEDGMENTS

This work was supported, in large part, by grants from the National Science Foundation, numbered CAREER-0093166, EIA-9975020, ANI-0213911, and ACI-9701333. In addition, the infrastructure development for public release that is discussed has been supported by the NSF National Partnership for Advanced Computational Infrastructure (NPACI) and the NASA Information Power Grid project.

REFERENCES

[1] Abilene. http://www.ucaid.edu/abilene/.

[2] B. Allcock, J. Bester, J. Bresnahan, A. L. Chervenak, I. Foster, C. Kesselman, S. Meder, V. Nefedova, D. Quesnal, and S. Tuecke (2002): Data management and transfer in high performance computational grid environments. *Parallel Computing Journal, 28*(5), 749–771.

[3] B. Allock, I. Foster, V. Nefedova, A. Chervenak, E. Deelman, C. Kesselman, J. Leigh, A. Sim, and A. Shoshani (2001): High-performance remote access to climate simulation data: A challenge problem for data grid technologies. In *Proceedings of IEEE SC'01 Conference on High-performance Computing.* http://www.globus.org/research/papers*/sc01ewa_esg_chervenak_final.pdf.

[4] M. Allen and R. Wolski. Adaptive timeout discovery using the network weather service. In *Proceedings of HPDC-11*, July 2002. http://www.cs.ucsb.edu/~rich/publications/nws-adapt.pdf.

[5] M. Allen and R. Wolski (2003): The livny and plank-beck problems: Studies in data movement on the computational grid. In *Proceedings of SC03*.

[6] H. Balakrishnan, M. Stemm, S. Seshan, and R. H. Katz (1997): Analyzing stability in wide-area network performance. In *Measurement and Modeling of Computer Systems*, pp. 2–12.

[7] F. Berman, A. Chien, K. Cooper, J. Dongarra, I. Foster, L. J. Dennis Gannon, K. Kennedy, C. Kesselman, D. Reed, L. Torczon, and R. Wolski (2001): The GrADS project: Software support for high-level grid application development. *International Journal of High-performance Computing Applications*, 15(4), 327–344.

[8] F. Berman, G. Fox, and T. Hey (2003): *Grid Computing: Making the Global Infrastructure a Reality*. Wiley and Sons.

[9] F. Berman, R. Wolski, S. Figueira, J. Schopf, and G. Shao (1996): Application level scheduling on distributed heterogeneous networks. In *Proceedings of Supercomputing*.

[10] The BOINC project. http://boinc.berkeley.edu.

[11] J. Brevik, D. Nurmi, and R. Wolski (2004): Quantifying machine availability in networked and desktop grid systems. In *Proceedings of CCGrid04*.

[12] H. Casanova, G. Obertelli, F. Berman, and R. Wolski (2000): The AppLeS Parameter Sweep Template: User-Level Middleware for the +Grid. In *Proceedings of IEEE SC'00 Conference on High-performance Computing*.

[13] W. Chrabakh and R. Wolski. GrADSAT: A Parallel SAT Solver for the Grid. In *Proceedings of IEEE SC03*, November 2003.

[14] H. Cramer (1946): *Mathematical Methods of Statistics*. Princeton University Press.

[15] K. Czajkowski, S. Fitzgerald, I. Foster, and C. Kesselman (2001): Grid information services for distributed resource sharing. In *Proceedings 10th IEEE Symp. on High Performance Distributed Computing*.

[16] C. Dovrolis, D. Moore, and P. Ramanathan (2001): What do packet dispersion techniques measure? In *Proceedings of Infocom*.

[17] A. Downey (1999): Using pchar to estimate internet link characteristics. In *Proceedings of ACM SIGCOMM*.

[18] The Entropia Home Page. http://www.entropia.com.

[19] I. Foster and C. Kesselman (1997): Globus: A metacomputing infrastructure toolkit. *International Journal of Supercomputer Applications*.

[20] I. Foster and C. Kesselman (1998): *The Grid: Blueprint for a New Computing Infrastructure*. Morgan Kaufmann Publishers.

[21] I. Foster, C. Kesselman, J. Nick, and S. Tuecke. The physiology of the grid: An open grid services architecture for distributed systems integration. http://www.globus.org/research/papers/ogsa.pdf.

[22] Globus. http://www.globus.org.

[23] GrADS. http://hipersoft.cs.rice.edu/grads.

[24] C. Granger and P. Newbold (1986): *Forecasting Economic Time Series.* Academic Press.

[25] T. Heath, R. Martin, and T. Nguyen (2001): The shape of failure. In *Proceedings of the First Workshop on Evaluating and Architecting System Dependability.*

[26] The iperf tool: http://dast.nlanr.net/Projects/Iperf.

[27] V. Jacobson (1988): Congestion avoidance and control. In *Proceedings of SIGCOMM '88, 18.*

[28] R. Jones. The netperf tool: http://www.netperf.org/netperf/NetperfPage.html.

[29] C. Krintz and R. Wolski (2001): Nwsalarm: A tool for accurately detecting degradation in expected performance of grid resources. In *Proceedings of CCGrid01.*

[30] W. E. Leland, M. S. Taqq, W. Willinger, and D. V. Wilson (1993): On the self-similar nature of Ethernet traffic. In D. P. Sidhu, editor, *ACM SIG-COMM*, pp. 183–193, San Francisco, California.

[31] D. Long, A. Muir, and R. Golding (1995): A longitudinal survey of internet host reliability. In *14th Symposium on Reliable Distributed Systems*, pp. 2–9.

[32] The nsf middleware initiative – http://www.nsf-middleware.org.

[33] New ttcp: http://www.leo.org/~elmar/nttcp.

[34] D. Nurmi, J. Brevik, and R. Wolski (2005): Modeling machine availability in enterprise and wide-area distributed computing environments. *Proceedings of European Conference on Parallel Computing (EUROPAR) August, 2005.*

[35] The network weather service home page – http://nws.cs.ucsb.edu.

[36] V. Paxon and S. Floyd (1997): Why we don't know how to simulate the internet. In *Proceedings of the Winder Communication Conference, also citeseer.nj.nec.com/paxon97why.html.*

[37] V. Paxson and S. Floyd. Wide area traffic: the failure of Poisson modeling. *IEEE/ACM Transactions on Networking, 3*(3), 226–244.

[38] A. Petitet, S. Blackford, J. Dongarra, B. Ellis, G. Fagg, K. Roche, and S. Vadhiyar (2001): Numerical libraries and the grid. In *Proceedings of IEEE SC'01 Conference on High-performance Computing.*

[39] The planetLab home page. http://www.planet-lab.org.

[40] J. S. Plank, S. Atchley, Y. Ding, and M. Beck (2002): Algorithms for high performance, wide-area, distributed file downloads. Technical Report UT-CS-02-485, Department of Computer Science, University of Tennessee. http://www.cs.utk.edu/~plank/plank/papers/CS-02-485.html.

[41] P. Primet, R. Harakaly, and F. Bonnassieux (2002): Experiments of network throughput measurement and forecasting using the network weather service. In *Workshop on Global and Peer-to-Peer Computing on Large Scale Distributed Systems.*

[42] M. Ripeanu, A. Iamnitchi, and I. Foster (2001): Cactus application: Performance predictions in a grid environment. In *Proceedings of European Conference on Parallel Computing (EuroPar) 2001.*

[43] N. Spring and R. Wolski (1998): Application level scheduling: Gene sequence library comparison. In *Proceedings of ACM International Conference on Supercomputing 1998.*

[44] M. Swany and R. Wolski (2002): Building performance topologies for computational grids. In *Proceedings of Los Alamos Computer Science Institute (LACSI) Symposium, 2002*.

[45] M. Swany and R. Wolski (2002): Multivariate resource performance forecasting in the network weather service. In *Proceedings of IEEE SC'02 Conference on High-performance Computing*.

[46] T. Tannenbaum and M. Litzkow (1995): The condor distributed processing system. *Dr. Dobbs Journal*.

[47] The TeraGrid Home Page. http://www.teragrid.org.

[48] S. Vazhkudai, J. Schopf, and I. Foster (2002): Predicting the performance of wide-area data transfers. In *Proceedings of IEEE International Parallel and Distributed Parallel Systems Conference*.

[49] R. Wolski (1998): Dynamically forecasting network performance using the network weather service. *Cluster Computing, 1*, 119–132.

[50] R. Wolski (2003): Experiences with predicting resource performance online in computational grid settings. *ACM SIGMETRICS Performance Evaluation Review, 30*(4), 41–49.

[51] R. Wolski, J. Brevik, C. Krintz, G. Obertelli, N. Spring, and A. Su (2001): Writing programs that run everyware on the computational grid. *IEEE Transactions on Parallel and Distributed Systems, 12*(10), 1066–1080.

[52] R. Wolski, N. Spring, and J. Hayes (1999): The network weather service. A distributed resource performance forecasting service for metacomputing. *Future Generation Computer Systems, 15*(5–6), 757–768.

[53] Y. Zhang, N. Du, V. Paxson, and S. Shenker (2001): The constancy of internet path properties. In *Proceedings of ACM SIGCOMM Internet Measurement Workshop*.

Chapter 19

PERVASIVE COMPUTING: ENABLING TECHNOLOGIES AND CHALLENGES

Mohan Kumar and Sajal K Das
The University of Texas at Arlington

Reducing the complexity of daily life and enhancing human quality of life have been two of the main objectives of computing and communication technologies. Pervasive computing has emerged as a significant research area that will herald the development of user-centric and service-oriented technologies. The Internet is one important step toward making pervasive computing a reality. Through the pervasive Internet, it is possible to access information and networked services anytime, anywhere. The rapid advances made in wireless mobile communications have provided an additional degree of freedom—**mobility**—to users of computing and communication services. The ubiquitous presence of embedded devices, wearable computers, sensor networks, and radio frequency identification (RFID) tags have also made it possible to deploy computing and communication nodes and services, thus enabling pervasive computing environments that aim at providing "what you want, when you want it, how you want it, and where you want it" kinds of services to users and applications. Several important challenges need to be tackled to realize the goals of pervasive computing. In this chapter, we give an overview of various enabling technologies and enumerate some of the challenges of pervasive computing. Several ongoing projects related to this topic are also discussed.

1   INTRODUCTION AND MOTIVATION

Recent advances in computer hardware (including embedded systems), communications technologies, mobile ad hoc and sensor networks, software agents, and middleware technologies have been mainly responsible for the emergence of pervasive computing as an exciting area of research with a wide variety of applications. Pervasive computing encompasses many existing areas in computer science and engineering, such as wireline and wireless communication networks, mobile and distributed computing, embedded computing, agent technologies, middleware, situation-aware computing, and human–computer interfaces. Pervasive computing is about providing "what you want, where you want it, when you want it, and how you want it" services to users, applications, and devices. Pervasive computing paradigms can help meet the challenges encountered in myriad applications in almost all areas of human activity – military, security, transportation, healthcare and telemedicine, crisis management, manufacturing and maintenance, education, entertainment, and others. In pervasive computing environments, hardware and software entities are expected to function autonomously, continually, correctly, and often proactively.

Various enabling technologies such as sensors (e.g., UC Berkeley Motes Sensor Network Platform), Radio Frequency ID (RFID) tags, intelligent appliances, embedded processors, wearable computers, handheld computers, and cell phones will continue to play vital roles in improving human quality of life through the advancement of pervasive computing applications. Tiny intelligent sensors have made it possible to deploy ubiquitous services and thus create smart environments. RFID tags allow subtle integration of objects (e.g., commodities in a superstore or supply-chain management, mechanical objects on an industry floor) into the computing environment. The advances in Internet technologies have allowed us to access information and services in a transparent manner. Additionally, tremendous progress in wireless communications and mobile computing have made "anytime, anywhere" computing and information availability a reality. In the following section, we give an overview of the following technologies: (1) the Internet, (2) mobile and wireless communications, (3) sensor networks, and (4) RFID technology.

The advent of advanced technologies and their associated software tools have resulted in the emergence of several applications. Consider the following three application scenarios to understand where we are headed:

Scenario 1 [15]: A car-accident victim in critical condition needs immediate attention by medical and other personnel who are in geographically distributed locations. Timely and automated actions by ambulance personnel, doctors, and hospital personnel, and their effective collaboration, are essential to save the victim's life. Devices around the victim, such as a street camera, cellular phone, and pocket PC, collaborate to exchange sensory data, recognize the occurrence of an extraordinary event (in this case an accident), and contact an ambulance service. The ambulance, upon arrival, interfaces with the hospital, medical, and other personnel to accomplish the tasks required to save the patient reliably, efficiently, and in a timely manner. In order to accomplish the life-saving mission in this context, real-time collaboration must be established dynamically and autonomously.

Scenario 2: A soldier's personal digital assistant (PDA) contains information about the terrain, strategies, vital data, enemy positions, up-to-date commands from his commander, and shared data with peers. The PDA's connection to the wireless Internet is intermittent and not continuous. It is necessary to provide the PDA with the most relevant data all the time from nearby support stations based on the soldier's current position and the events happening around him. From time to time, the soldier may request new information or advice. The soldier (and his PDA) needs to coordinate with other soldiers (via their PDAs) as well as their command center (a PC or laptop).

Scenario 3: John Smith, a medical surgeon, takes his lunch at the cafeteria. While walking to the cafeteria, he makes notes on his handheld device about a patient he just visited. It is his habit to watch live basketball games and see highlights (and scores) of finished games on his handheld device while at lunch. At the cafeteria, he receives messages and vital information from other doctors, patients, students, and nurses. He also requests the patient records system for the latest patient histories. On some days, he consults remotely with his patients: he listens to sounds and examines images and data provided by remote consultation machines, patients, and nurses. On his walk back to the clinic, he watches his daughter practice soccer at school. All on his PDA!

The aforementioned scenarios use existing basic component technologies—laptops, handhelds devices, street cameras, cell phones, car computers, image and voice recognition systems, and so forth. But the required software and middleware to enable such applications seem difficult to implement. Researchers are still discovering new mechanisms and software/middleware paradigms to glue all these component technologies together. A careful analysis indicates that the above scenarios are based on several challenging technical requirements, including intelligent proactive services; guaranteed quality of service (QoS) and availability of communication channels; adequate authentication and security mechanisms; seamless interaction among heterogeneous entities; the presence of ubiquitous computing devices in the environment; and the like. Thus, despite the advances in hardware and/or communications-related enabling technologies, pervasive computing faces many systems issues and challenges that must be tackled. Exploiting available computing devices, communication technologies, and software services *all the time* and *everywhere* to enhance the quality of human life, ensure security, and utilize resources optimally is a key issue in making pervasive computing possible. To reach this goal, we must address research challenges such as (1) heterogeneity and interoperability, (2) proactiveness and transparency, (3) location-awareness and mobility, and (4) privacy and security. We will discuss these in Section 3 of this chapter.

Several projects in pervasive computing are under way in various universities and research laboratories worldwide. Section 4 discusses a few of these: the Aura project at the Carnegie Mellon University; the Gaia project at the University of Illinois, Urbana Champaign; the Oxygen project at the Massachusetts Institute of Technology; and the PICO and MavHome projects at the University of Texas at Arlington.

2   ENABLING TECHNOLOGIES

Recent years have witnessed significant progress on the technology front to improve human quality of life. The Internet, Due to its pervasiveness, is perhaps the prime contributor to this progress. Mobile and wireless communications have further made it possible to access and exploit Internet-based services anytime anywhere. Additionally, the emergence of sensor networks and RFIDs has enabled us to inject (or distribute) computing capabilities into objects (mechanical, biological, environmental, chemical, etc.) that were traditionally considered to be passive physical objects. The integration of these technologies has led to the ubiquitous presence of computing elements and therefore the all-pervasive Internet and other network-based services.

2.1   The Internet

The Internet has indeed been a great revelation to application designers, service providers, business organizations, and individual users. The tremendous growth of the Internet is due to advances in (1) computer architectures, (2) communication networks, and (3) middleware and application software development. In addition, several technologies such as TCP/IP, Mobile IP, wireless access networks (such as GSM and CDMA) and optical communications, and MEMS (Micro Electro-Mechanical Sensors), as well as software and programming language initiatives such as Java, software agents, and middleware tools, are playing critical roles in the wide applicability of the Internet.

Today, in most homes (in the developed and developing countries), the Internet is considered to be an essential service, just like the television or telephone. For business organizations and industries, the Internet is as important as electricity or telephone service. Many of the applications and services we see today are based on the world wide web (WWW), which is a distributed repository of vast information. With a few exceptions, the Internet is mostly a source of static information that can be accessed on demand.

However, the Internet is not geared for handling dynamically changing information, and it is not a good model for addressing scalability, adaptability, and flexibility issues. Moreover, sustained collaborative interaction and performance (e.g., QoS) for the entire duration of an operation is required to meet the demands of many current applications in telemedicine, defense, transportation, manufacturing, and other areas that employ the Internet. The question is: *can the Internet model meet the demands posed by such applications*? Furthermore, in the current model of the Internet, all processing tasks are carried out at the edge of the network. The principal reasons for this situation are: (1) current solutions are application specific or reactive and thus not scalable, and (2) Internet's best effort end-to-end QoS makes no guarantees about when and whether data will be delivered at all. Therefore, there is a need for transparent but ubiquitous services that can handle dynamic information, act instantly, ensure correct behavior, make immediate decisions, and perhaps prevent undesirable events from happening.

2.2   Mobile and wireless communications

The increased demand for mobility and flexibility in our daily lives has led to the development of wireless LANs (WLANs) and cellular networks. Today WLANs can offer users high bit rates to meet the requirements of bandwidth-consuming services such as video conferences, streaming video, etc. Wireless LANs can be broadly classified into two categories: *ad hoc wireless LANs* and *wireless LANs with infrastructure*. In ad hoc networks, several wireless nodes join together to establish peer-to-peer communication. Each client communicates directly with the other clients within the network. The ad hoc mode is designed such that only clients within transmission range of each other can communicate. If a client in an ad hoc network wishes to communicate outside of the cell, a member of the cell operates as a gateway and performs routing. They typically require no administration. Networked nodes share their resources without a central server.

In wireless LANs with infrastructure, there is a high-speed wired or wireless backbone. Wireless nodes access the wired backbone through access points that allow the wireless nodes to share the available network resources efficiently. Prior to communicating data, the wireless clients and access points must establish a relationship, or an association. In mobile systems, an ongoing connection between a Mobile Host (MH) and a corresponding Access Point (AP) is transferred from one access point to the other through a process called *handoff*. Handoff occurs during cell boundary crossing, weak signal reception, and QoS deterioration in the current cell. Present handoff mechanisms are based only on signal strength and do not take into account the load of the new cell. There is no negotiation of QoS characteristics with the new AP to ensure smooth carryover from the old AP to the new AP. Several methods have been proposed by researchers to ensure seamless handoff in mobile environments.

Since wireless devices need to be small and wireless networks are bandwidth limited, some of the key challenges to the use of wireless networks in pervasive computing environments are data rate enhancements, low power networking, security, radio signal interference, and system interoperability. Improving the current data rates to support future high-speed applications is essential, especially if multimedia services are to be provided. Data rate is a function of various factors such as the data compression algorithm, interference mitigation through error-resilient coding, power control, and the data transfer protocol. With the recent proliferation of outdoor wireless networks and the advent of Free Space Optics (FSO) or wireless optical communications, we are heading in the right direction in terms of data rate requirements. The size and battery power limitations of wireless mobile devices place a limit on the range and throughput that can be supported by a wireless LAN. The complexity and hence the power consumption of wireless devices vary significantly depending on the kind of spread spectrum technology being used to implement the wireless LAN.

A critical factor in pervasive computing is the power consumption associated with wireless communications among resource limited devices. New algorithms have been devised to conserve energy by minimizing wireless communications [20]. Further, the mobility of users increases security concerns in a wireless network. Current wireless networks employ authentication and data encryption techniques on the air interface to provide security for their users.

2.3 Sensor networks

Sensor networks enable us to observe and interact with the physical world in real time and, allow users to monitor the environment, and also to take appropriate actions. Such pervasive instrumentation will be of great value in a range of applications such as security, telemedicine, transportation, crisis management, etc. Thus, sensor networks readily extend to monitoring interactions among hardware and software entities in ubiquitous computing environments. The sensor nodes and their networks are expected to provide sensory services to applications/users continually and autonomously. However, sensor nodes are often low-resource devices with limited CPU power, memory, battery power, and low bandwidth wireless communication channels. Therefore, it is extremely important for sensors to conserve their energy (battery power) in order to prolong their active longevity as well as the lifetime of the entire network. In a sensing application, the observer is interested in monitoring the behavior of a phenomenon under some specified performance requirements (e.g., accuracy or delay). In a typical sensor network, the individual sensors sample or gather local values (measurements), aggregate them in a meaningful way, and then disseminate information as needed to other sensors and eventually to the observer. The measurements taken by the sensors are mostly discrete samples of the physical phenomenon under observation, subject to individual sensor measurement accuracy as well as its location.

Although sensor networks share many of the challenges of traditional wireless networks, including limited energy and bandwidth and error-prone channels, communication in sensor networks may not typically be end-to-end. More specifically, the function of the sensor network may be to report information regarding the observed phenomenon to an observer who is not necessarily aware of the network infrastructure and individual sensors as an end point of communication. Furthermore, energy in sensor networks is more severely limited than in other wireless networks due to the nature of the sensing devices and the difficulty in recharging their batteries. The energy constraint in sensor networks indeed imposes serious challenges in hardware design as well as in communication protocols.

In a pervasive computing framework, tracking of objects (e.g., persons, goods, chemical and biological agents) is extremely important and can be facilitated by using smart devices such as active and passive sensors, motion detectors, RFID tags, digital camera, surveillance equipment, and so on. Such a framework deals not only with the information captured by task-specific sensors, but also with that handled by deployable networks of heterogeneous MEMS (micro-electro-mechanical systems) multisensor nodes (e.g., portable optical or chemical sensors) that communicate via wireless RF and are connected to the Internet backbone. Data coming from these sources need to be aggregated after appropriate transformation and then stored in a specialized server for intelligent decision making. The major design and research challenges in sensor networks include (1) power conservation of mobile sensors, (2) coding and compression of multimedia signals, (3) data fusion to reduce data communication complexity, (4) cooperation among heterogeneous sensor nodes, (5) flexibility on the security level to match the application needs so as to conserve critical resources, (6) scalability, self-organizing, and self-learning of sensor nodes, (7) trust and security decisions based on the utility for the application, keeping mobility and volatility as transparent as possible, and (8) protecting the network from external and internal intrusion.

There are multiple ways for a sensor network to achieve its accuracy and delay requirements, and a well-designed network should meet these requirements while optimizing the energy usage and providing fault tolerance. By studying the communication patterns systematically, the sensor network designer should be able to choose the infrastructure and communication protocols that provide the best combination of performance, robustness, efficiency, and low cost of deployment.

Applications such as sensor fusion, simulation, and remote manipulation, allow users to "see" composite images constructed by fusing information obtained from a number of sensors. Thus, sensors might be viewed as offering network-based services that can be browsed by authorized users. The network may participate in synthesizing the query (for example, by filtering some sensor data or aggregating data). Nodes along the path can take an active role in information dissemination and processing. In this respect, sensor networks are similar to an active network. Application-specific in-network data processing is essential to maximize the performance of sensor networks.

2.4   RFID technology

Radio frequency identification (RFID) is an automatic data capture (ADC) technology that comprises data tokens/tags and mobile scanners/readers equipped with an antenna. The reader detects the presence of an RFID tag within its range. The frequency varies from very low (10–30 KHz) to very high (30–300 GHz). The RFID tags are attached or embedded in objects and programmed with data that identify the object. RFID tags can be read only or a read/write type. The emergence of RFID tags has created an opportunity to enable large numbers of passive objects with no embedded computing resources to be identified and tracked in a networking environment. For example, the nuts and bolts required to assemble a machine part on a manufacturing floor can be tracked with the help of such tags. The use of proxy agents and surrogate services makes it possible to incorporate passive physical objects into any pervasive computing environment. The major challenges include (1) the development of middleware for incorporation of tagged objects into the computing environment, (2) exploiting RFID tags to extract context information, (3) provisioning services, and (4) combining RFID tag information with other sources of information.

2.5   Middleware technologies

Traditionally, agents have been employed to work on behalf of users, devices, and applications [3]. In addition, agents can be effectively used to provide transparent interfaces between disparate entities in the environment, thus enhancing invisibility. Agent interaction and collaboration are critical to the development of an effective middleware for pervasive computing. Software agents in the middleware can be deployed to overcome the limitations of hundreds and thousands of resource-limited devices.

Service discovery is described as the process of discovering software processes/agents, hardware devices, and services. The role of service discovery in pervasive computing is to provide environment awareness to devices and device awareness to the environment. Service provisioning, advertisement, and service discovery are the important components of this module. Although service discovery in mobile environments has been addressed in existing work, service discovery in pervasive computing is still in its infancy. Existing service discovery mechanisms include JINI and Salutation, as well as the International Naming System (INS) [1].

Several new embedded devices and sensors are being developed in the industry and in research laboratories. The architecture of the Berkeley sensor motes and the TinyOS operating system are very good examples of devices and technologies developed for use with embedded networked sensors. The challenge here is to design devices that are tiny (disappear into the environment), consume little or no power (perhaps powered by ambient pressure, light, or temperature), and communicate seamlessly with other devices, humans, and services through a simple all-purpose communication protocol.

Understanding of device and network technologies is important to create a seemingly uniform computing space in heterogeneous environments. The backbone network will probably continue to be the Internet for some time. The challenge is to overcome the Internet's end-to-end architecture and at the same time to allow flexible interactions among network devices, services, and users.

Mobile computing devices have limited resources, are likely to be disconnected, and are required to react (transparently) to frequent changes in the environment. Mobile users desire *anytime anywhere* access to information while on the move. Typically, a wireless interface is required for communication among the mobile devices. The wireless interface can be a wireless LAN, a cellular network, an ad hoc network, a satellite network, or a combination thereof. Techniques developed for routing, multicasting, caching, and data access in mobile environments should also be extended to pervasive environments. A pervasive environment comprises numerous invisible devices, anonymous users, and ubiquitous services. Development of effective middleware tools to mask the heterogeneous wireless networks and mobility effects is a challenge.

Provisioning uniform services regardless of location is a vital component of mobile computing. The challenge here is to provide context-aware services in an adaptive fashion, in a form that is most appropriate to the location as well as to the situation under consideration.

3   CHALLENGES OF PERVASIVE COMPUTING

3.1   Heterogeneity and interoperability

Today's computing world is replete with numerous types of devices, operating systems, and networks. Cooperation and collaboration among various devices and software entities is necessary for pervasive computing. At the same time, the overheads introduced by adaptation software should be minimal and scalable. While it is almost unthinkable to have homogeneous devices and software, it is, however, possible to build software bridges across various entities to ensure interoperability. But then the following question arise: How many such bridges should we create? What about the overheads introduced by the bridges? The Oxygen project [23] envisions the use of uniform hardware and network devices to enable smooth interoperability. The limitations of low resource hardware can be overcome by exploiting the concepts of agents and services. The challenge is to develop effective and flexible middleware tools that mask uneven conditions and to develop portable and lightweight application software.

Network QoS for delivering information and QoS for provisioning services are critical to pervasive computing. For example, in Scenario 1 described earlier, if real-time collaboration is necessary between the ambulance personnel and the doctors in the hospital, multimedia streaming over heterogeneous communication systems must be realized. Such streaming must meet stringent QoS requirements, or else it will be useless. Defining QoS for pervasive computing applications will be a significant challenge to meet. Pervasive computing environments will definitely require service providers to address QoS issues.

3.2   Proactivity and Transparency

The development of computing tools such as the handoff operation in mobile systems have been, in general, *reactive* or *interactive*. On the other hand, the "human in the loop" has its limits, since the number of networked computers will surpass the number of users in the near future. Users of pervasive computing applications may wish to receive "what I want" information and services in a transparent fashion. A thought-provoking paper on active networks [21] envisions a majority of computing devices in the future as being proactive. Proactivity can be provided by the effective use of overlay networks. Active networks can be used to enhance network infrastructure for pervasive computing, ensure network management on a just-in-time basis, and provide privacy and trust [11].

Today, most computing and communication services are also reactive in nature. Most proactive services available today are usually obtrusive and often useless (the online paper clip and pop-up messages are good examples). Ideally, proactive services should be user/application specific and unobtrusive, and must ensure efficient utilization of resources. These requirements can be best described by considering our Scenario 3. Firstly, Dr. Smith's profile must be on his cafeteria's server so that the server can send appropriate information to his device. For example, the server can receive the doctor's schedule a priori from his PDA and determine whether he would be consulting with his patients, his students, or his colleagues. If his schedule is not busy, he may be interested in receiving news or music. Video streaming presented by the proactive server in the cafeteria to the doctor's handheld computer must meet certain QoS requirements in terms of resolution and clarity, brightness, timeliness, etc. In Scenario 1, the cell phone, the PDA and the camera all observe the occurrence of extraordinary events, interact, and make proactive decisions. It will be necessary for users to negotiate QoS to suit their profiles and applications. For example, in Scenario 3, the challenge is how to define proactivity in general and how to tailor proactivity to specific users.

Associated challenges include (1) how to leverage research work in the areas of situation-aware computing, device/user/application profiling, and software agents to enhance proactivity in existing computing devices and (2) how to exploit active network technology to overcome the end-to-end to limitations of the Internet to provide just-in-time services? Profiling can be effectively employed to ensure appropriate proactive services in pervasive systems [12].

3.3   Location Awareness and Mobility

Models of twenty-first century *ubiquitous computing* scenarios [22] depend not only on the development of capability-rich mobile devices (such as web-phones or wearable computers) but also on the development of automated machine-to-machine computing technologies, whereby *devices interact with their peers and the networking infrastructure, often without explicit operator control*. To emphasize the fact that devices must be imbued with an inherent consciousness about their current location and surrounding environment, this computing paradigm is also called *sentient* [12] or *context-aware computing*. "Context-awareness" is one of the key characteristics of applications under this intelligent computing model. If devices can exploit emerging technologies to infer the current activity state of the user (e.g., whether the user is walking or driving, or whether he/she is at office, at home, or in a public environment) and the characteristics of their environment (e.g., the nearest Spanish-speaking ATM), then these devices can intelligently manage both the information content and the means of information distribution.

Location awareness has been perhaps the most widely investigated context, since the current (or future) location of users strongly influences their information needs. Applications in computing and communications utilize such location information in two distinct ways [9]:

Location-Aware Computing. In this category, the information obtained by a mobile device or user varies with location changes. The most common goal on the network side is to automatically retrieve the current or anticipated neighborhood of the mobile user (for appropriate resource provisioning), while on the device side, the typical goal is to discover appropriate local resources. As an example of this category, we can consider the case where mobile users would be automatically provided with local navigation maps (e.g., floor plans in a museum that the user is currently visiting), which are automatically updated as the device changes its current position. For example, in Scenario 1, knowledge of the accident location is critical to providing appropriate responses—to direct the ambulance or to provide network connections via available wireless routers. Similarly, in Scenario 3, appropriate information can be sent to the doctor's device from the closest server if his current location is known or can be predicted.

Location-Independent Computing. In this case, the network endeavors to provide mobile users with a set of consistent applications and services that do not depend on the specific location of the users or on the access technology employed to connect to the backbone information infrastructure. Information about the user's location is required only to ensure the appropriate redirection of global resources to the device's current point of attachment. Such applications are not usually interested in the users' absolute location but only in their point of attachment to the communication infrastructure. An example is cellular telephony, where mobility management protocols are used to provide a mobile user with ubiquitous and location-independent access.

While location-independent computing applications have a fairly mature history, location-aware computing is still at an early stage. Innovative prototypes of location-aware computing environments are still largely experimental and are geared towards specific target environments. The location support systems of different prototypes, as a result, have been mostly autonomous and have always remained at the disposal of the system designers. It is, however, important to realize that the full potential of location-aware computing can be harnessed only if we develop a *globally consistent location management architecture* that caters to the needs of both location-aware and location-independent applications and that allows the retrieval and manipulation of location information obtained by a wide variety of component technologies. This is an important challenge, since location-aware and location-independent applications typically face significantly different *scalability* concerns. In general, location-aware applications do not pose many scalability issues, since they primarily involve local interactions. However, scalability is a critical concern for location-independent network services, which must support access to distributed content by a much larger user set.

In [9], we surveyed the various ways in which context-aware pervasive computing applications are likely to exploit and manage location information, and we used this understanding to debate whether a *universal location management infrastructure* should store location information in a topology-dependent (symbolic) or topology-independent (geometric) format. A detailed analysis of both location-aware and location-independent applications reveals three important points: (1) different systems and prototypes use a wide variety of location resolution technologies, (2) a significant number of location-based applications are primarily interested in resolving the location of a mobile node only relative to the connectivity infrastructure, and (3) obtaining geographical location coordinates requires varying levels of hardware that are absent in many pervasive devices. It seems more preferable for the universal location management infrastructure to manipulate location information in a structured, symbolic form. In cases where geographical coordinates are needed, these may be obtained through the use of access-specific technologies or via appropriate mapping. In the following, we enumerate the objectives of pervasive computing from the viewpoint of the desirable features of a universal location management infrastructure. In particular, we believe that *location prediction, location translation, signaling optimality, and location privacy* are four "must-haves" in a practical pervasive computing infrastructure.

Recall that the basic goal of pervasive computing is to develop technologies that allow smart devices to automatically adapt to changing environments and contexts, making the environment largely imperceptible to the user. The set of candidate applications and their underlying technologies is, however, anything but uniform! Developing a uniform location management infrastructure is thus a challenging task. In the following, we identify five location-related features that a universal architecture must support.

3.3.1 Interoperability across Multiple Technologies and Resolutions

Current prototypes for pervasive applications typically choose a specific location tracking technology that is suitable for their individual needs. Uniform location management architectures must be capable of translating the location coordinates obtained by such systems into a universal format that can be utilized by various application contexts. For example, cellular-based mobile communications will primarily need to resolve the location of a mobile device only up to the point of network attachment. Fleet management and tracking applications may, however, require explicit geometric information. The mobility management infrastructure should thus be capable of efficiently translating such location information between different representations, and also at different granularities (e.g., mobile commerce applications advertising e-coupons may not be interested in the precise hotel room where a given user is located).

3.3.2   Prediction of Future Location

Predicting the user's future location is often the key to developing smart pervasive services. For example, the ATIS active database can be triggered more intelligently by predicting the most likely routes and by warning the client about adverse road conditions along those routes. Prediction of an individual's future position in the indoor office can be very helpful in aggressive teleporting (e.g., supporting follow-me applications). In addition to this explicit service-oriented need for prediction, there is also an implicit need for predictive mobility tracking from the viewpoint of network infrastructure. In several location-independent computing scenarios, the network must meet stringent performance and latency bounds as it ensures uninterrupted access to global information and services, even as the users change their locations. For example, in order to provide quality of service (QoS) guarantees for multimedia traffic (such as video or audio conferencing) in cellular networks, appropriate bandwidth reservations must be made between the hand-held terminal and the serving base station (BS), as well as between the BS and the backbone network. To meet strict bounds on the handoff delay, the network must also proactively reserve resources at the cells where the mobile is *likely* to move. Since many of the tracking technologies do not themselves offer such predictive capabilities, the infrastructure must be capable of constructing such predictive patterns based on the collective or individual movement histories.

3.3.3   Location Fusion and Translation

In certain pervasive computing scenarios, location tracking is achieved through the combination of multiple technologies and access infrastructures. For example, an office application can resolve the location of a user at different levels of granularity using different technologies. As an example, the specific building could be identified through the current wireless LAN cell where the mobile currently resides, whereas an additional ultrasonic system (such as Cricket) [17] may be used to identify the precise orientation and room location of the mobile user. Since the user's complete location reference is obtained only by combining these distinct location management protocols/systems, our global location management framework must efficiently *fuse and merge location information* from two or more distinct network technologies.

The intelligent management of vertical (or intersystem) handoff, on the other hand, often requires the ability to *translate* the mobility and location-related information from one frame of reference to another. For example, when a user switches from a wireless LAN to an overlaid personal communication systems (PCS) network, the system must be able to translate the mobility patterns and location prediction attributes from one system to the other, independent of the representation format utilized by each individual network.

3.3.4   Scalable and Near-Optimal Signaling Traffic

The desire for provably optimal location update and paging strategies in cellular networks is not new. There has indeed been a great deal of work on efficient location management strategies. The world of pervasive devices is soon expected to see a quantum jump in the number of mobile nodes (from millions of cell phones to billions of autonomous pervasive devices) and an even greater variation in their capability (such as power or memory). We must therefore develop efficient and near-optimal signaling mechanisms that minimize any unnecessary signaling load on both the devices and the networking infrastructure.

3.3.5 Security and Privacy of Location Information

Security and privacy management is a key challenge in pervasive networking environments. Notwithstanding the availability of advanced devices and location resolution technologies, users will not embrace a pervasive computing model until a scalable infrastructure is in place to appropriately protect such location information. The problem is not one of simply making such location information either visible or invisible to specific networks; we must allow the user to dynamically configure the scope of location visibility, possibly in multiple representation formats, to individual pervasive services and applications. For example, a user may wish to expose his precise GPS coordinates to emergency response applications (such as 911) but only a much coarser view (say at a granularity of 20 miles) to automobile insurance companies trying to monitor his driving profile. Alternatively, the user may want to specify his network point of attachment (symbolic information) but not his precise in-building location (geometric coordinates) to a pervasive enterprise application.

In a series of works [4, 5, 10, 18], we have developed an *information-theoretic* framework for effective location prediction with optimal signaling cost in wireless mobile networks. In particular, we have shown how the LeZi-update algorithm [4, 5] uses an adaptive learning technique to optimize the signaling associated with location update and paging in a symbolic domain. By treating the movement of a mobile device as a sequence of strings generated according to a stationary distribution, our novel algorithm is able to efficiently store a mobile's entire movement history and also to predict future locations with asymptotically optimal cost. A symbolic representation of location data allows the management infrastructure to deal with an extremely heterogeneous set of networking technologies that possess a wide variety of underlying physical layer and location sensor technologies. Indeed, the ability to accommodate *device heterogeneity* and *technological diversity* is a key to the success of a universal location management scheme. Moreover, we have shown that symbolic information is more amenable to storage and manipulation across heterogeneous databases, and can be exploited to provide necessary functions such as location prediction, location fusion, and location privacy. We have also designed a "hierarchical LeZi-update" algorithm that permits efficient translation of location profiles between heterogeneous systems [13].

4   PERVASIVE COMPUTING PROJECTS

4.1   Aura

Designed for distraction-free pervasive computing, the Aura project [24] focuses on human attention, thus creating an environment that adapts to the user's context and needs. To accomplish this goal, the Aura research spans various individual technologies such as task-driven computing, energy-aware adaptation, intelligent networking, resource opportunism, multifidelity computation, nomadic data access, wearable computers, wireless communication, multimodal user interface adaptability, data and network adaptability, software composition, proxies/agents, collaboration, and smart space. Underlying this diversity, Aura applies two broad concepts, namely, proactivity and self-tuning. Proactivity is a system layer's ability to anticipate requests from a higher layer, whereas self-tuning allows layers to adapt by observing the demands made on them and adjusting their performance and resource usage characteristics accordingly.

The Aura architecture includes already developed but much modified systems such as Odyssey [16] and Coda [14], and other new system components such as Spectra and Prism. Odyssey provides resource monitoring and application-aware adaptation, and Coda supports nomadic, disconnectable, and bandwidth-adaptive file access. Spectra is an adaptive remote execution mechanism that uses contexts to decide how best to execute the remote call. Prism is a new system layer that is responsible for capturing and managing user intentions. Prism, also called the *task layer*, sits above individual applications and services but below the user, providing high-level support for proactivity and self-tuning.

To amplify the capabilities of a resource-limited mobile client and thus to improve user experiences, Aura applies *cyber foraging*. The idea is to dynamically augment the computing resources of a wireless mobile computer by exploiting a wired hardware infrastructure. A surrogate (hardware in the wired infrastructure) assists the mobile computer temporarily. Cyber foraging helps define many challenges such as proactivity for tracking user intent, adaptation for matching the demand and supply of a resource, context awareness to modify its behavior based on the user's state and surrounding, and balancing of proactivity and transparency.

4.2   Oxygen

The goal of the Oxygen project [23] is pervasive human-centered computing based on bringing abundant computations and communications as pervasive and free as air naturally into people's lives. This approach combines integrated user and system technologies that make it easier for people to do more by doing less, wherever they may be.

System technologies include devices, networks and software. Devices technologies provide intelligent space through environmental devices (E21s) that are embedded in homes, offices, and cars to sense and support a local-area computational and communication back-plane. Handheld devices (H21s) are person-centered devices equipped with perceptual transducers, and they can reconfigure themselves through software into many useful appliances in response to speech commands. Flexible, decentralized networks called N21s connect dynamically changing configurations of self-identifying mobile and stationary devices to form collaborative regions. The Oxygen software architecture can adapt to changes, as it relies on control and planning abstractions that provide mechanisms for change.

Oxygen's user technologies directly address human needs. These are perceptual technologies such as the spoken language and visual interaction, and other user technologies including knowledge access, automation, and collaboration that help users perform a wide variety of tasks they want to accomplish in the ways they would to do them like. Speech and vision technologies enable the user to communicate with Oxygen as if they are interacting with another person, thus saving time and effort. Multimodal integration increases the effectiveness of these perceptual technologies. Knowledge access supports improved access to information customized to the needs of people, applications, and software systems. Automation offers natural, easy-to-use, customizable, and adaptive mechanisms for automating and tuning repetitive mundane information functions and control of the physical environment. For example, Oxygen allows users to create scripts that control devices such as doors or heating systems according to their tastes. Collaboration forms spontaneous collaborative regions that accommodate the needs of mobile people and computations and maintains the collaboration context using knowledge access and automation. It provides support for recording and archiving speech and video fragments from meetings, and for linking these fragments to issues, summaries, keywords, and annotations.

4.3   PICO

The Pervasive Information Community Organization (PICO) is a middleware framework that enhances existing Internet-based services [15] with the goal of meeting the demands of time-critical applications such as telemedicine, military, and crisis management. PICO provides automated, continual unobtrusive services and proactive real-time collaborations among devices and software agents in a dynamic heterogeneous environment. PICO deals with the creation of mission-oriented dynamic computing communities that perform tasks on behalf of users and devices autonomously. It comprises two basic building blocks: software entities called *delegents* (intelligent delegates) and hardware devices, called *camileuns* (connected, adaptive, mobile, intelligent, learned, efficient, ubiquitous nodes). The concept of PICO extends the current notion of pervasive computing, that is, that computers are everywhere [22]. Its novelty lies in creating communities of delegents that collaborate proactively to handle dynamic information, provide selective content delivery, and facilitate application interface. In addition, delegents representing low-resource devices have the ability to carry out tasks remotely.

In general, the devices in a pervasive environment provide the services of which they are capable. However, it is necessary to capture the device characteristics in terms of hardware and software and the services they can provide. In the PICO framework, a camileun captures the functional entities of a device. It is an abstract logical representation of a device and provides a link between a device and delegent(s). A camileun is described by the tuple of $C = <C_{id}, F, H>$ where C_{id} is the camileun identifier, F is the set of functionalities, and H is the set of system characteristics.

A delegent provides encapsulation, interface, delegation, adaptation, and manageability for the camileun, user, or application with which it is associated. A delegent *encapsulates* one or more functional units of a camileun. A delegent is goal directed and works by itself or in a community. A delegent responds to sensory inputs, events in the community, and events within itself, and takes appropriate actions based on a set of rules. Delegents work in a community environment where they interact with other delegents and their environments. The modeling of delegents is described here. Delegents not only make camileuns *adaptive* to their surrounding environments but also *condition* them to overcome uneven capabilities of various collaborating camileuns. The set of operational rules, R, defines how a delegent responds to events when it is in a certain state. The operation rules include community engagement, communication, and migration of delegents. Events can be internal or external to the delegents. Each rule consists of a pair of conditional facts and actions.

A community is a collection of one or more delegents working together towards a common goal. Communication and collaboration are essential to the operations of a community, which provides a framework for collaboration and coordination among delegents. A delegent provides a common *interface* to communicate or collaborate with other delegents. Devices are capable of providing services to users and applications. The PICO concept allows the representation of various devices through their respective delegents, who collaborate with each other to provide integrated services.

Communities in PICO are formed either statically or dynamically. Static communities, also called *service provider communities*, are created to provide services in various applications. Dynamic communities are created in response to the occurrence of extraordinary events in the environment. Once a community is formed, its delegents collaborate to carry out the goal of the community.

4.4   MavHome Smart Home

In [7], we defined a smart environment as one that is able to acquire and apply knowledge about its inhabitants and their surroundings in order to adapt to the inhabitants and meet the goals of comfort and efficiency. These capabilities rely upon effective prediction and intelligent decision making with the help of such technologies as robotics, wireless and sensor networking, mobile computing, databases, machine learning and multimedia technologies. With these capabilities, a smart home can adaptively control many aspects of the environment such as climate, water, lighting, maintenance, and multimedia entertainment. Intelligent automation of these activities can reduce the amount of interaction required by the inhabitants, reduce energy consumption and other potential wastages, and provide a mechanism for ensuring the health and safety of the environment occupants [6].

In the MavHome project [8], smart home capabilities are organized into an agent-based software architecture that seamlessly connects needed components while allowing improvements to be made to any of the supporting technologies. The technologies in the MavHome are separated into four cooperating layers. The *physical layer* contains the environment hardware, including devices, transducers, and network equipment. The *communication layer* exchanges information between agents. The *information layer* collects information and generates inferences useful for making decisions. The *decision layer* selects actions for the agent to execute. The MavHome software components are connected using a CORBA interface.

Because controlling an entire house is a very large and complex learning and reasoning problem, the problem is decomposed into reconfigurable subareas or tasks. Thus, the physical layer for one agent may in actuality represent another agent somewhere in the hierarchy, which is capable of executing the task selected by the requesting agent.

Perception of the state of the smart home is a bottom-up process. Sensors monitor the environment (e.g., lawn moisture level) and, if necessary, transmit the information to another agent through the communication layer. The database records the information in the information layer, updates its learned concepts and predictions accordingly, and alerts the decision layer to the presence of new data. During action execution, information flows top down. The decision layer selects an action (e.g., run the sprinklers) and relates the decision to the information layer. After updating the database, the communication layer routes the action to the appropriate effector to execute. If the effector is actually another agent, the agent receives the command through its effector as perceived information and must decide upon the best method of executing the desired action. Specialized interface agents allow interaction with users, robots, and external resources such as the wireless network or the Internet. Agents can communicate with each other using a hierarchical flow. As compared with other projects related to smart homes, MavHome is unique in combining a multitude of technologies from artificial intelligence, machine learning, wireless mobile networking, sensors, databases, robotics, and multimedia computing to create a smart home that acts as an intelligent agent.

5   CONCLUSIONS

In this chapter, we have presented an overview of the enabling technologies for the emergence of pervasive computing and communication infrastructures. While the Internet will perhaps continue to be the backbone of pervasive computing, the tremendous advances in wireless mobile communications allow the creation of ubiquitous networks with very little effort and insignificant cost Moreover, wireless communications offer users the luxury of mobility and provide connectivity on the move. Sensor networks, RFID tags, and embedded devices also help in the deployment of environments that are replete with computing and communicating services. Heterogeneous devices and networks, interoperability among disparate entities, and mobility and security will continue to challenge pervasive computing researchers.

REFERENCES

[1] W. Adjie-Winoto, E. Schwartz, H. Balakrishnan, and J. Lilley, The design and implementation of an intentional naming system, *ACM SIGOPS Operating Systems Review, Proceedings of the Seventeenth ACM Symposium on Operating Systems Principles*, 33(5), 186–201.

[2] G. Banavar, J. Beck, and E. Gluzberg (2000): Challenges: An application model for pervasive computing, in *Proceedings of 6th Annual International Conference on Mobile Computing and Networking (MOBICOM 2000)*, pp. 266–274, Boston, MA, USA.

[3] P. Bellavista, A.Corradi, C. Stefanelli (2000): A mobile agent infrastructure for the mobility support, *Proceedings of the 2000 ACM Symposium on Applied Computing*, pp. 239–245.

[4] A. Bhattacharya and S. K. Das (1999): LeZi-update: An information-theoretic approach to track mobile users in PCS networks, *Proc. 6th Annu. ACM Int. Conf. on Mobile Computing and Networking (MobiCom)*, pp. 1–12.

[5] A. Bhattacharya and S. K. Das (2002): Lezi-update: An information-theoretic framework for personal mobility tracking in PCS networks, *ACM/Kluwer Wireless Networks Journal*, 8(2-3), 121–135.

[6] D. J. Cook and S. K. Das (2003): Health monitoring in an agent-based smart home, International Conf. on Aging, *Disability and Independence (ICADI)*, Washington, Dec.

[7] D. J. Cook and S. K. Das (eds) (2004): *Smart Environments: Architectures, Protocols and Applications*, John Wiley, to appear.

[8] S. K. Das, D. J. Cook, A. Bhattacharya, E. O. Heierman, and T.-Y. Lin (2002): The role of prediction algorithms on the MavHome smart home architectures, *IEEE Wireless Communications* (Special Issue on Smart Homes), 9(6), 77–84, Dec.

[9] S. K. Das, A. Bhattacharya, A. Roy, and A. Misra (2003): managing location in 'universal' location-aware computing, *Handbook of Wireless Internet* (Eds. B. Furht and M. Ilyas), Chapter 17, pp. 407–425, CRC Press.

[10] S.K. Das and C. Rose (2004): Coping with uncertainty in mobile wireless networks, Proceedings of 15th IEEE International Symposium on Personal, *Indoor and Mobile Radio Communications (PIMRC)*, Barcelona, Spain, Sept (Invited Paper).

[11] W.M. Farmer, J.D. Guttman, and V. Swarup (1996): Security for mobile agents, issues and requirements, *Proceedings NISSC'96 National Information Systems Security Conf.*, pp. 591–597, Baltimore, MD, October.

[12] A. Hopper (1999): Sentient computing, The Royal Society Clifford Patterson Lecture, http://www.uk.research.att.com/~hopper/publications.html.

[13] R. Kambalakatta, M. Kumar, and S. K. Das, Profile based caching to enhance data availability in push/pull mobile environments, *International Conference on Mobile and Ubiquitous Computing*, MobiQuitous 2004, Boston, August 22–25, Boston, USA.

[14] J.J. Kistler and M. Satyanarayanan (1992): Disconnected Operation in the Coda File System, *ACM Trans. Comp. Sys.* 5(1), February.

[15] M. Kumar, B. Shirazi, S. K. Das, M. Singhal, B. Sung, and D. Levine (2003): Pervasive Information Communities Organization PICO: A middleware framework for pervasive computing, *IEEE Pervasive Computing*, 72–79.

[16] L.B. Mummert, M.R. Ebling, and M. Satyanarayanan (1995): Exploring weak connectivity for mobile file access, *Proc. 15th ACM Symp. Op. Sys. Principles*, Copper Mountain Resort, CO, December.

[17] N. B. Priyantha, A. Chakraborty, H. Balakrishnan (2000): The Cricket location-support system, *Proceedings of the 6th Annual International Conference on Mobile Computing and Networking*, August, pp. 32–43.

[18] A. Roy, S. K. Das, and A. Misra (2004): Exploiting information theory for adaptive mobility and resource management in future cellular networks,

IEEE Wireless Communications (Special Issue on Mobility and Resource Management), Aug, to appear.

[19] M. Satyanarayanan (2001): Pervasive computing: vision and challenges, *IEEE Personal Computing*.

[20] E. Shih, P. Bahl, and M.J. Sinclair (2002): Wake on wireless: an event driven energy saving strategy for battery operated devices, *Proceedings of the 8th Annual International Conference on Mobile Computing and Networking*, pp. 160–171.

[21] D.L. Tenenhouse (2000): Proactive computing, *Communications of the ACM* 43:5 (May).

[22] M. Weiser (1991): The computer for the 21st century, *Scientific American*, 265(3), 94–104.

[23] http://oxygen.lcs.mit.edu/

[24] http://www-2.cs.cmu.edu/~aura/

[25] http://www.cse.uta.edu/~pico@cse

[26] http://ailab.uta.edu/mavhome/

Chapter 20

INFORMATION DISPLAY

Peter Eades,[1,2] Seokhee Hong,[1,2] Keith Nesbitt,[3] and Masahiro Takatsuka[1,2]
[1]University of Sydney,
[2]National ICT Australia,
[3]Charles Sturt University, Australia

Recent increases in the size of available datasets have created a strong demand for new ways of displaying information. This chapter describes some recent research into information display.

Visualization is the process of generating a picture of a dataset. The data, which may be numerical, ordinal or nominal, is mapped onto visual variables so that they can be visually inspected. The visual variables determine the shapes and appearances of pictorial icons representing the data. These pictures are then placed on a display screen. The main challenge is to convey as much information as possible when these icons are displayed.

In many cases, the data are modeled as a graph, and the visualization process is called *Graph Drawing*. Section 1 of this chapter describes new methods for drawing graphs, aimed at coping with very large data sets.

The underlying display technology for visualization is undergoing rapid changes. In Section 2 we describe some of these new display technologies. These changes take information display beyond the visual; new methods for showing information using the nonvisual senses are described in Section 3.

1 NEW METHODS FOR DRAWING VERY LARGE GRAPHS

Much of the information and data in real-world applications consists of entities and the relationships between the entities, and thus can be modeled mathematically as *graphs*. For example, traditional entity-relationship diagrams and UML diagrams in software engineering can be modeled as graphs. Biological data such as phylogenies can be modeled as trees, PPI (Protein–Protein Interaction) networks can be modeled as graphs, and metabolic (or biochemical) pathways can be modeled as directed graphs. Network data, such as webgraphs, and social network data can be modeled as undirected and directed graphs.

Graph drawing aims to construct good *drawings* (that is, visualizations, or *layouts*) of graphs in two or three dimensions. As the examples given above indicate, Graph drawing systems can be used in many applications such as software visualization, bioinformatics visualization, VLSI design, network data visualization, and social network visualization.

The main challenge in graph drawing is to design efficient algorithms and methods for computing good geometric representations of graphs automatically. There is a great deal of literature in graph drawing, and this research area has been growing for the last decade. Several books are available; see [67, 77, 79, 85]. There is an annual symposium on graph drawing that brings together mathematicians, computer theoreticians, and practitioners.

Further, many fundamental algorithms in graph drawing have been successfully developed and implemented by researchers and software developers. As a result, graph drawing systems and commercial software products are available. These include *GraphViz* from AT&T, *GDToolkit*, *AGD*, *Graphlet*, *TomSawyer Software*, and *ILOG*. For details, see the recent book on graph drawing software [77]. These products are successfully used for software engineering, network data analysis, and visual analysis of bioinformatics data.

The methods and algorithms for graph drawing can be roughly partitioned on the *types* of graphs, *edge representations* and *aesthetic criteria*.

The main types of graphs are trees (rooted trees or free trees), planar graphs, undirected graphs, and directed graphs.

Edges may be represented as straight-line segments, polylines, or orthogonal polylines (of horizontal and vertical line segments). Directed edges normally have arrowheads.

Aesthetic criteria are objective functions for optimization, defining *"good"* visualization of graphs. In general, they measure the readability of a drawing. Sometimes they relate to a specific application domain. For example, when drawing organization charts for a work group, it is important for the boss to be at the top of the page. On the other hand, there are a number of criteria that are independent of the application domain; the most important are the following:

- Minimizing the number of edge crossings

- Minimizing the drawing area (thus maximizing the resolution for a fixed-size screen)

- Maximizing the number of symmetries

- Minimizing the number of bends (in a polyline drawing)

- Minimizing the total edge length

- Uniform edge length

- Good aspect ratio, that is, balancing the width and the height

- Maximizing angular resolution, that is, ensuring that two edges adjacent to a vertex are drawn with enough angular difference

Unfortunately, achieving these aesthetic criteria is very difficult. For example, the problem of constructing a drawing of a general graph with a minimum number of edge crossings is NP-hard. This also holds for most of the other aesthetic criteria.

However, many efficient polynomial time algorithms have been developed for restricted classes of graphs, such as trees and planar graphs.

Also, many practical heuristic approaches have been successfully developed for general graphs. The best known of these heuristic approaches are the *spring algorithms* (or *force directed methods*) for undirected graphs and the *Sugiyama* (or *layered drawing*) *method* for directed graphs. For an overview of each method, see [67]. Both spring methods and Sugiyama methods are popular and widely used in many applications. In the remainder of this section, we describe very recent force-directed methods.

In general, spring algorithms use a physical analogy for graph drawing. For example, the edges of graphs can be replaced by springs to define attractive forces between the two vertices, and repulsive forces can be defined for each pair of vertices to guarantee that they are not drawn too close to each other. Then the system tries to achieve the minimum energy state (or equilibrium state), where the sum of all forces acting on each vertex becomes zero.

Due to the simplicity of the method and the reasonable quality of the drawing, many variations on the spring algorithm have been developed over the last two decades. Early examples include the *spring embedder* by Eades [68], forces using graph theoretic distance by Kamada and Kawai [78], and a *magnetic spring algorithm* by Sugiyama and Misue [86]. These methods differ slightly in terms of the force model and the method to reach equilibrium. For some comparison, see [67].

However, these early methods exhibit relatively high running time, iteratively computing $O(|V|^2)$ forces, where $|V|$ represents the number of vertices in the graph. This limits the size of graphs that such methods can handle in practice: in 1984 Eades reported a limit of about 50 vertices [68], and with 2004 technology these methods can handle a few hundred vertices. For larger graphs, either the quality is poor or the run-time is unacceptable for real-time visualization.

The size of data in practical applications has also grown in the early twenty-first century. For instance, the size of webgraphs is typically measured in the millions. Hence, the scalability of spring algorithms has been a challenging problem.

Recently, many new methods have been successfully developed to solve the problem of drawing very large graphs. Here we briefly describe the main ideas and results. In particular, we review four different approaches:

- Multilevel approach for the force-directed method

- Force-directed method using geometric clustering

- High-dimensional approach

- Spectral method

1.1   Multilevel approach

Walshaw presents a heuristic that uses a multilevel technique combined with a force-directed method [87, 88]. The main idea is to apply a kind of combinatorial clustering (or graph partitioning) method to gradually reduce the size of the graph. If the size becomes small enough, then we can draw the small graph to produce an initial drawing. Then we gradually refine the drawing using a simple interpolation technique and a force-directed method to obtain a drawing of the original graph. More specifically, the multilevel process works as follows.

The first step is to group pairs of vertices to form *clusters*, using a fast heuristic for matching. Then the clusters define a new *coarsened* graph. This step is repeated until the size of the graph falls below some threshold. The second step is to draw the coarsened graph with a random initial drawing. The final step is to successively refine the drawing of the coarsened graph to get a drawing of the original graph, using a simple interpolation technique together with a modified version of the Fruchterman and Reingold force directed method [70].

It is claimed that the running time at each level is approximately $O(|V| + |E|)$ for sparse graphs. However, the total running time may depend on the number of levels of the multilevel process.

The method can compute both two- and three-dimensional drawings, and experimental results have been demonstrated with a number of examples from a few hundred vertices up to 225,000 vertices. The method works very fast, in particular, for 2D drawings of sparse graphs; for example, it takes around 30 seconds for 10,000 vertices. It may takes 10 minutes for the largest graph. For details of experimental results, see [87, 88].

Figure 20.1 shows two examples produced by the method [87]. Figure 20.1a is a drawing of a graph with $|V| = 4970$ and $|E| = 7400$. It takes about 14 seconds. Figure 20.1b shows a drawing of the graph *sierpinski10*, which has $|V| = 88575$ and $|E| = 177147$. It takes about 217 seconds.

Similar ideas were independently used by a number of authors, including Hadany and Harel [74], Harel and Koren [75, 76], and Gajer, Goodrich, and Koburov [71].

Harel and Koren [75, 76] used a *multiscale* technique, with a version of the algorithm of Kamada and Kawai [78]. Their method computes a sequence of improved approximations of the final drawing. Each approximation allows vertices to deviate from their final place by an extent limited by a decreasing constant. As a result, the drawing can be computed using increasingly coarse representations of the graph, where closely drawn vertices are collapsed into a

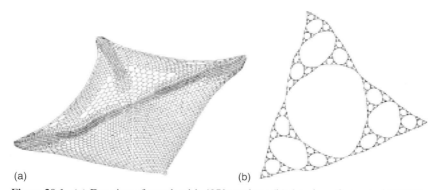

(a)   (b)

Figure 20.1. (a) Drawing of graph with 4970 vertices; (b) drawing of *sierpinski10* [87].

single vertex. Each drawing in the sequence is generated quickly, performing a local beautification step on the previously generated drawing. This method can handle up to a few thousand vertices. For details, see [75, 76].

Gajer, Goodrich, and Koburov also used a similar *multidimensional* technique for drawing large graphs [71]. The algorithm is implemented as a system called *GRIP* [72]. For details, see [71, 72].

1.2 Graph drawing using geometric clustering

Another force-directed approach using *geometric* clustering is presented by Quigley and Eades [83]. The algorithm is an extension of the Barnes–Hut hierarchical space decomposition method [63] to forced directed graph drawing. The main idea is to use a decomposition tree to approximate the force computation between each pair of vertices. Roughly speaking, these pairs approximate forces between vertices based on geometric clustering, defined by the decomposition tree. More specifically, the forces between *close* vertices are computed by the standard direct repulsion between two vertices, whereas the forces between *distant* vertices are computed using a geometric clustering induced by the decomposition tree.

Quigley and Eade's method uses a recursive space decomposition, which induces a geometric clustering of the vertices, and in fact it also induces a graph-theoretic clustering. This graph-theoretic clustering is then used in a force-directed algorithm, and this in turn improves the graph-theoretic clustering. Iterating this process improves both the drawing and the clustering; this process can be useful in applications.

The method was implemented in two and three dimensions using quad-trees and oct-trees [83]. Similar types of decomposition trees can also be used.

The claimed running time to compute the forces (that is, on one level) is approximately $O(|E| + |V| \log |V|)$. Example outputs are illustrated in Figure 20.2 [83].

1.3 A high-dimensional approach

We now describe more recent methods by Harel and Koren [76] for drawing very large graphs using high-dimensional embedding. The main idea of this method is first to draw a graph in very high dimensions (say 50) and then to project the embedding into two or three dimensions.

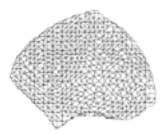 

Figure 20.2. Graph with 2500 vertices on level 6 and the lowest level of the decomposition tree [83].

For the first step, drawing a graph in m dimensions, Harel and Koren choose m *pivot* vertices that are almost uniformly distributed on the graph, using an approximation algorithm of the *k-center* problem. Then the ith coordinate of each vertex is computed based on the graph-theoretic distance from the pivot vertex p_i using breadth-first search. This approach gives a rough but quick initial layout.

For the second step, they use *principal component analysis* (PCA) to choose a good projection of m-dimensional drawing into two or three dimensions. This method transforms a number of correlated variables into a smaller number of uncorrelated variables called *principal components*. The first principal component represents as much variability of the data as possible. Using only the first few principal components, PCA can reduce the dimensions of the data, maintaining the maximum possible variance (see [69]).

More specifically, Harel and Koren compute the first k eigenvectors of the *covariance matrix* (these correspond to the largest eigenvalues) using a simple power-iteration method [89]. Finally, they perform the projection using the direction of the eigenvectors. For details, see [76].

The claimed running time is $O(|V|+|E|)$, and the authors report that the method is rather independent of the structure of the graph (unlike the classical force-directed methods). They present experimental results with graphs of 10^5 vertices drawn in a few seconds, and 10^6 vertices drawn in a minute. Indeed, this method is much faster than the force-directed methods described in the previous sections.

In terms of the quality of the drawings, the method gives reasonable results. However, due to the limitations of linear projections, the 2D drawings have poorer quality compared with those produced by classical force-directed methods. Two sample outputs are illustrated in Figure 20.3 [76]. Figure 20.3 shows the drawing of the *crack* graph with 10,240 vertices and 30,380 edges; this drawing took 0.3 seconds.

For very sparse graphs such as trees, the method does not perform well in terms of the quality of the drawing. Harel and Koren also report that sometimes it is aesthetically better to choose different eigenspaces. The PCA method raises the possibility of creating graph drawing systems that browse views of the graph using different projections onto eigenspaces.

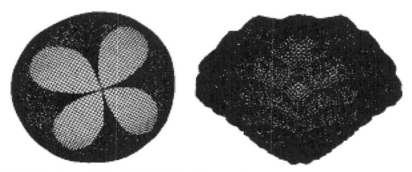

Figure 20.3. Drawings of (a) a 100×100 grid with opposite corners connected, and (b) the *crack* graph [76].

1.4   Spectral method

Spectral methods form part of the toolbox of algebraic graph theory [66] and have been used in many applications such as graph partitioning. The most widely used techniques use eigenvalues and eigenvectors of the *adjacency* matrix or *Laplacian* matrix of the graph.

The spectral graph drawing method was firstly introduced by Hall [73]. Recently, variations have been presented by a number of authors. We briefly review the main idea.

A simple spectral layout method that uses eigenvectors of the Laplacian matrix of a graph is described in [65,90]. Here, the eigenvectors are computed using a simple power iteration method. The layout method has been used for web-graphs and social network data. For details, see [90].

More sophisticated spectral methods for drawing large graphs are presented by Koren et al. [81, 82] and Koren [80].

ACE (Algebraic multigrid Computation of Eigenvectors) constructs a drawing of a graph using eigenvectors of the Laplacian. More specifically, the problem is reduced to minimizing a quadratic energy function, which can be expressed as a generalized eigenvalue problem. They authors present a very fast method for minimizing Hall's energy function [73] using a multiscale approach. For details, see Koren, Carmel, and Harel [81, 82].

It s claimed that ACE can draw graphs with 100,000 vertices in about 2 seconds and graphs of millions of vertices in a minute. However, the authors report that the running time of ACE depends more on the structure of the graph than on the high-dimensional approach. Figure 20.4 shows some results. Figure 20.4a shows the drawing of a folded 100×100 grid with 10,000 vertices and 18,713 edges. Figure 20.4b shows the drawing of a graph with 4,970 vertices and 7,400 edges. Figure 20.4c shows the drawing of the *crack* graph, with 10,240 vertices and 30,380 edges. Figure 20.4d shows the drawing of the *4elt* graph, with 15,606 vertices and 45,878 edges. Figure 20.4e and 20.4f show the drawings of the *dwa512* graph, with 512 vertices and 1,004 edges, drawn using a different choice of eigenvectors.

Koren [80] further extends the spectral approach to graph drawing using *degree-normalized eigenvectors*, which have some aesthetic advantages. He presents an algorithm for computing the degree-normalized eigenvectors quickly. For details, see [80].

1.5   Remarks

We conclude this section with a summary and some remarks on future research directions.

In this section, we briefly discuss current research in graph drawing, concentrating on drawing very large undirected graphs. Several algorithms are available, and we can roughly divide them into two approaches: the fast force-directed methods combined with either a multilevel approach, graph theoretic clustering, or geometric clustering; and spectral approaches that use eigenvectors of matrices associated with the graph. The first approach can handle a few thousand vertices, and the second approach can handle millions of vertices.

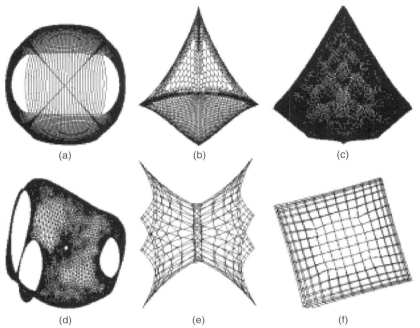

Figure 20.4. Examples of the drawings produced by ACE [81]. See text for details.

It should be noted that these new methods are not currently mature and need extensive evaluation. Some are beginning to be adopted into commercial tools, but at the time of this writing, commercial success has not been achieved. In particular, many authors present experimental results with sparse graphs and with regular structures, thus resulting in good quality drawing quickly. However, few of these methods have been evaluated with real-world data sets with dense graphs and irregular structure. With few exceptions, data such as webgraphs, PPI networks, and social network data have not been thoroughly tested.

Further, there has been no attempt to compare these methods formally. Hence, it would be interesting to conduct an extensive comparison of different approaches for drawing large graphs with real-world data sets.

Furthermore, it may be essential to modify these methods to produce a good-quality drawing of domain-specific data, since many networks and graphs in the real world exhibit special properties. For example, social networks [65] and biochemical pathways [84] exhibit special properties that may be exploited by constraints in force-directed methods. For the properties of special networks, see [64]. This is a challenging topic requiring further research.

Finally, users of real-world applications need good *navigation* methods to accompany the static visualization so that they can interact with the visualizations for further investigation based on their own interests or insights. Thus, future research also should include the design of good navigation methods that support efficient and effective *interaction* methods for the users. This area is also related to the *dynamic* visualizations of graphs, since graphs and networks in the real world are inherently dynamic and thus always changing.

2 NEW VISUALIZATION TOOLS AND TECHNOLOGIES

This section will discuss various visual technologies that are relatively inexpensive but are effective in increasing the accessibility and the amount of information being presented to a user on a screen. This section will also present current issues in utilizing and integrating such technologies to improve the capabilities of visualization.

2.1 High-resolution displays

Due to the marked advances of modern computing technologies, many commodity computer graphics hardware have achieved significant increases in performance and capability, including hardware accelerations of various three-dimensional computer graphics functions [33]. In 2004, many graphics cards commonly support a pixel resolution ranging from $1,024 \times 768$ pixels to $1,600 \times 1,200$ pixels, and further improvements are expected.

In the field of visualization (including both scientific and information visualization), the amount of data being displayed continues to increase, corresponding to the rapid progress of communication and computing technologies. Furthermore, these technological advances now allow scientists and engineers to push the boundaries of data analysis and simulation processes, resulting in the massive amount of data that needs to be visually inspected. In order to display such a large amount of information on a screen, the display system needs a large number of pixels.

Even with the modern commodity computer graphics hardware technologies, it is extremely difficult to provide a high-resolution display capability while maintaining real-time interactivities and three-dimensional complex geometry. In order to achieve super high-resolution displays with inexpensive commodity graphics hardware, Humphreys et al. introduced *WireGL* [35]. WireGL allows *OpenGL* rendering commands to be distributed across a cluster of inexpensive commodity graphics cards. This technology was rolled into a new project named *Chromium* [35]. The novel improvements in Chromium were (1) to provide a mechanism not requiring a user to execute an OpenGL application without modifications, and (2) to introduce a *Stream Processing Unit* (SPU) structure. Once a stream of OpenGL-rendering commands is intercepted by the core module of WireGL, these commands are distributed across a network of graphics hardware by the SPU.

Many distributed rendering or tiled display systems have been developed based on chromium technologies [36–41]. For example, NCSA at the University of Illinois [36], the Visualization Group at the Pennsylvania State University [37], and the *ViSLAB* at the University of Sydney [38] (see Figure 20.5) have developed and packaged chromium-based tiled display systems for scientific visualization. The *VIEWS* development group at LLNL has developed a parallel rendering system using chromium as well as Distributed Multi-headed X (DMX) technologies. With this system, not only the 3D graphics rendered by OpenGL but also other X-windows' widgets can be rendered in a distributed fashion [39].

Figure 20.5. A large tiled display being used in scientific visualization (ViSLAB, The University of Sydney).

Although chromium technology successfully provides distributed-rendering/tiled-display capability, it heavily relies on a fast local network (such as Gigabit Ethernet or Mirinet). Since chromium requires the transmission of many primitive geometry objects over the network, there would be a bottleneck if it were deployed over a cluster of computers on a LAN or a low-bandwidth network. Furthermore, it would be very challenging to provide this distributed rendering service to remotely situated client machines rather than to a tiled display system directly connected to the chromium cluster. In response to this challenge, Bethel et al. have combined chromium technology with a multithreaded scene graph framework [40, 41]. By providing a parallelizable scene graph framework, the rendering process was accelerated by using scene-specific knowledge; this allows the system to reduce the number of geometry objects to be transmitted over the network.

2.2   Augmented displays

One approach to increasing the amount of information conveyed through visualization is to increase the number of visual variables. This approach includes increasing the number of pixels (as described above) and the complexity of pictorial icons used to represent the information. Another approach is to present such pictures within other more information-rich environments. When a piece of information is presented in a context, the contextual information could be used to enhance the original representation and to add extra pieces of information. As a result, the visualization presented in a certain contextual environment could provide more information than the pictures alone can present.

Augmented Reality [42–46] and *Mixed R*eality [47–50] use various information and computing technologies (such as computer graphics, real-time range findings, and human–machine interfaces) to seamlessly integrate the virtual and real-world environments. Research in these fields has been driven by the need to improve the human interface of the computing facilities. The general objective of such research activities is to enhance the human–machine interfaces and user experiences by complementary combinations of the real-world environment and the information/computing technologies.

When visualization of some datasets is required, a user is engaged in inspecting and analyzing the data. The process of data analysis often involves other types of information (such as paper documents, real-world experimental items, and conversational information among colleagues through intense collaboration), all of which exist outside visualized data spaces. Augmented display systems allow visualized information and tangible real-world items to coexist in the same user interaction spaces.

The *Digital Desk* uses a physical desk surface as a projection screen, allowing a user to inspect and interact with the visualized information and the physical object side by side. All user interactions are detected by various sensors, such as stroke sensors and a passive camera, and are communicated back to the visualized information [42]. Feirer et al. developed a knowledge-based augmented reality named KARMA [43]. This system utilized a see-through type *Head Mounted Display* to merge the visualization and real-world spaces.

The above Augmented Reality systems intend to place the visualized information in an environment along with real-world entities. The Mixed Reality system, on the other hand, attempts to place the information, typically images, of the real-world entities in the visualized space. For example, Kanade's *Virtualized Reality* system obtains three-dimensional information about real-world objects through multiple-camera passive range finders, and then places the 3D information in the virtual information space [49].

The Augmented and Mixed Reality systems mentioned above rely on a single visual display such as a desktop surface display or a head-mounted display. The visualization and interaction spaces are usually defined and constrained by this single display device. In order to increase the availability and accessibility of the visualized information and to free a user from spatial constraints, the *Everywhere Display* project at IBM uses the *Multisurface Display Projector* to turn nontethered surfaces into interactive display surfaces [46]. This type of system makes visualized data available and accessible anywhere and anytime, and has great potential to significantly improve how a user interacts with the visualized information.

2.3   Integration of visual technologies

The advances in information and communication technologies have resulted in many research projects that utilize them to create *Computer-Supported Collaborative Work* (CSCW) and *Computer-Mediated Communication* (CMC) in order to support local and remote collaboration. The marked improvements of various advanced visual technologies, as mentioned above, suggest that these new visually enabled technologies must be reevaluated and exploited as core technologies mediating the collaboration processes.

Many visually enabled CSCW or CMC systems [51–59] are designed based on the concept of *WYSIWIS* (What You See Is What I See) [60] and *WYSIWID* (What You See Is What I Do). Many such systems utilize large screen displays, including workbench style displays and "natural" user interfaces [53–57], and some of them are commercially available. However, both the hardware and software of these systems are designed and developed to support *local* intense collaboration. Hence, they fall short in supporting remote intense collaboration. Moreover, many of these systems are still confined to wired input devices that are electro-mechanically or acoustically tracked. Some of the more natural user interfaces (such as *DiamondTouch* [55]) are touch-based interfaces, which require the screen to be touched before any tracking is possible.

The user interaction and communication models of such systems are, however, still based on Norman's gulf model [61]. According to this model, there are two information-processing devices (a computer and a user) connected to each other. The results of computation are passed on to a user via visual and audio output devices. The information from a user is transmitted to the computer through input devices such as a keyboard and mouse.

Norman explained various difficulties of using such systems based on the concept of a "gulf," which prevents a smooth transition between these two information-processing units. This model is useful in explaining the conventional interaction within computing systems. However, in real life, we interact with external objects and pieces of information in a more direct manner. Moreover, when networked interactive systems mediate intense collaboration between multiple parties, a new gulf is introduced between those systems. Therefore, the development of more intuitive user interfaces based on direct manipulation with the help of pervasive user input devices is the major challenge to developing a better visually enabled CSCW system.

Figure 20.6 illustrates a collaborative access table (*CAT*), which uses a passive-range, finder-based natural user input device. A horizontal display, for the computer output, is on the table surface. Cameras capture images of the hands and face of the user, who stands or sits on the left. The system utilizes a stereo range

Figure 20.6. A prototype of a CAT (built by Takatsuka, Eades, and students at the University of Sydney).

finder in order to track the user's hands in a 3D space. By tracking the user's hand and fingertip in the 3D space, the system replaces the mouse clicking function with a simple tapping action on the display surface. In this manner, a user does not have to learn other hand gestures in order to interact with information on the screen.

The uses of various communication-related computing technologies have been studied as the medium of intense local and remote user interactions. A number of computer-based technologies are available to support such systems (such as email, www, on-line chat, and video conferencing). Most of these technologies have been used simply to connect remotely located systems [52]. Hence, disparate users still have to interact with shared information through completely disparate user interaction spaces. The question is whether such technologies are effectively used to provide seamless collaboration. Without careful design and appropriate evaluations, such systems could add an extra "gulf" rather than filling the "gulf" of remoteness.

A clear understanding of the mechanisms of remote intense collaboration and the establishment of a computational framework based on shared visualized information to support the collaboration are the challenges in this field. The successful development of such a visually enabled collaboration system could enhance conventional office management, as well as research management/ collaboration, and could help other research partners better understand each other's activities.

3   BEYOND THE VISUAL: MULTISENSORY DISPLAY

While the majority of work with abstract data displays has focused on the visual sense, there is also increasing interest in displaying abstract data across a wider range of human senses. Many data sets are characterized by their large size and multiattributed nature. By employing multisensory feedback, the goal is to widen the bandwidth between human and computer. With multisensory interfaces, the user can potentially perceive and assimilate multiattributed information more effectively (see Figure 20.7). By mapping different attributes of the data to different senses, such as the visual, auditory, and haptic (touch) sense, it may be possible to better understand large data sets.

This section will consider the display of abstract data using the alternative senses of audition and haptics. This introduction will progress to a consideration of integrating visual, auditory, and haptic displays. The section will then conclude with a discussion of the difficult issues encountered when designing multisensory displays.

3.1   Sound displays

Auditory displays can use sound parameters such as pitch, duration, timbre, and loudness to convey information to the user [1]. All these sound parameters can be controlled in the sound-generation process. The auditory sense is less adept than vision at localizing the position of sounds in space [2]. Nonetheless,

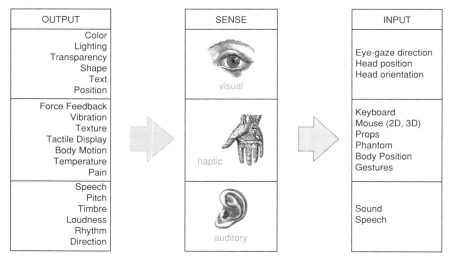

OUTPUT	SENSE	INPUT
Color Lighting Transparency Shape Text Position	visual	Eye-gaze direction Head position Head orientation
Force Feedback Vibration Texture Tactile Display Body Motion Temperature Pain	haptic	Keyboard Mouse (2D, 3D) Props Phantom Body Position Gestures
Speech Pitch Timbre Loudness Rhythm Direction	auditory	Sound Speech

Figure 20.7. Multisensory user interfaces enable a number of different channels of input and output between the user and the computer.

the position of sound is a further parameter that can be used when designing information displays (see Figure 20.8).

A three-dimensional sound display can be achieved in two ways. One approach uses a spatially distributed array of speakers to generate what is called a *sound field simulation* [3]. The alternative approach is called *perceptual synthesis*. In this approach, the synthesized sound can be displayed on simple hardware such as a pair of headphones or loudspeakers. However, perceptual synthesis also requires an appropriate model of the user's head and ear shape, called the *Head-Related Transfer Function*. These functions incorporate the human perceptual

Figure 20.8. A user predicts stock market direction using a combined 3D visual and spatialized auditory display of stock market data [32].
Photo courtesy of CSIRO, Mathematical and Information Science, Canberra.

cues for sound localization into a source signal [3]. The models are complex, user specific, and difficult to generate [4].

The evolving field of study that focuses on displaying abstract data using sound is called *Information Sonification*. The term *information sonification* implies a mapping from the data attributes to the sound parameters [2]. When there is no such mapping, the term *audification* is used. *Audification* describes the direct playing of data as sound [2]. A good example of audification is the playing back of seismic events recorded from an earthquake [5].

In some sample applications of information sonification, sound has been used to assist in debugging software [6], to display scatter plots [7], to help understand parallel program performance [8], and to display computational fluid dynamics data [9].

Sound displays have also been combined with visual displays. For example, auditory signals based on a geiger-counter metaphor were used to display attributes of data collected from a petroleum well [10]. The user of this system could probe attributes of the well data with a sound tool while viewing a visual model of the petroleum well. Sound has also been used to display physiological parameters such as respiratory rate, body temperature, and heart rate, in conjunction with a visual readout of the same data [11].

3.2　Haptic displays

The word *haptic* derives from the Greek and means *to grasp*. The sense of touch differs from vision and hearing in that it relies on action from the user to generate the stimuli. For example, a person must tap against a surface to feel its hardness or move a hand across a surface to feel its texture.

In the real world, the haptic sense is typically used for exploring and handling objects. Exploration tasks involve the extraction of object properties such as shape, mass, and texture and also provide a sense of contact, position, and motion. Handling tasks are dominated by user motor actions such as grasping and object manipulation. For the user, haptic actions require a synergy of sensory exploration and motor manipulation [12].

Direct contact and displacement of the skin with an object provides tactile information, commonly described as touch. However, the human haptic system senses both tactile and kinesthetic information when touching an object [13]. Kinesthetic information provides the sense of position and motion of our limbs and joints. Current tactile displays are inadequate for use in real applications; however, it is possible to integrate force-feedback displays into current virtual environment systems [12]. For example, many platforms use the commercially available Phantom™ force-feedback device [14]. These displays can mimic a range of haptic sensations that the user senses through a combination of tactile and kinesthetic receptors.

The term *information haptization* is used when the sense of touch is used to display abstract data. The term *information tactilization* has also been suggested [15]. The word *haptic* refers to both the *tactile* and *kinesthetic* components of touch. Since most interactions involving the sense of touch rely on a combination of both tactile and kinesthetic feedback, the term *information haptization* is more general.

Although information haptization is a very new domain, some interesting applications have been developed. One of the first uses of force to display information was the *GROPE* project at the University of North Carolina [16]. This display was designed to assist users in molecular docking studies. Haptics has been used to display soil properties such as density, cohesion, and angle of internal friction by allowing the user to move a simulated plough blade through various sandy soils [17]. Force feedback was used to display a small set of properties such as static friction and surface deviations [18]. This approach allowed the user to feel surface textures on simulated surfaces. For example, in this way, different grades of sandpaper can be simulated. In turn, haptics properties such as surface texture, momentum, and compliance have been used to display attributes of stock market data [19] (see Figure 20.9).

In the stock market application, a haptic display is combined with a visual display. The same approach was also used in a control interface developed for a scanning probe microscope [20]. In this application, the user can feel the height and friction of the surface. As well as receiving this haptic information, the user also receives visual data from the surface height and color. In another application, force was used to help seismic interpreters look for patterns in geophysical data [21]. In this system, force feedback helped the user feel subtle features in the seismic data.

3.3   Designing multisensory displays

The term *multisensory* implies that *"more than one sensory modality is used to display the environment"* [1]. If the goal of multisensory display is to *widen the human-to-computer bandwidth*, then it is important that we strive to display different data

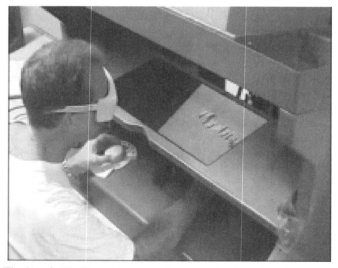

Figure 20.9. The Haptic Workbench incorporates a 3D visual display with the Phantom force-feedback device [14]. This device allows the user to feel attributes such as price momentum on a stock market chart [19].
Photo courtesy of: CSIRO, Mathematical and Information Science, Canberra.

attributes to different senses. This type of display has been characterized as a *complementary display* [22, 23].

Designing *complementary displays* seems a simple enough goal, yet often the senses can interact. For example, using sound in conjunction with haptics can alter the perceived stiffness of a surface [24]. So when a *hard* sound is played on contact, the surface is reported as being harder than when a *soft* sound is played—despite the fact that, in each case, the same haptic model is used to represent the surface contact. Likewise, changing the visual representation of the object can alter the perceived haptic stiffness of a spring. Thick visual representations of a spring feel stiffer than thinner ones, despite the same force being required to compress the spring [12].

Given the problems with multisensory interactions, is it wise to focus only on the visual display of abstract information? After all, some suggest that vision is the dominant sense. While it is true that vision is highly detailed and well suited to comparing objects arranged in space, it is equally true that hearing is effective for monitoring sounds from all directions, even when the source of the sound is not visible. Touch, as has been shown, does equally well as vision at discriminating texture [25]. Morton suggests that haptic texture cues may be more perceptually prominent than visual texture cues when both sources of information are present [25].

Welch and Warren go further: *"The dominance of vision is wrong"* [26]. In fact, different senses are well suited for different kinds of tasks. The problem is that it is not altogether clear what types of abstract data to display to each sense. To address this issue, the designer of a multisensory display must consider the physiological, perceptual, and cognitive capability of each sense.

Understanding the physiology of each sense helps in understanding its performance capabilities and bandwidth. For example, the range of colors that the eye can see or the frequency of sounds that can be heard are limited by the underlying physiology. Perception is dependent on physiology, but multiple levels of neural processing also influence it. For example, the same wavelength of light can appear to be a different color depending on the background color [27]. This difference is a result of the way nerves from the visual receptor cells are organized rather than the actual physiology of the eye's receptors.

The influence of higher neural processes on sensory perception is a general principle and can also be illustrated with hearing and touch [28]. For example, two similar sound frequencies can sound the same and the ability to distinguish them may depend on the musical training of the listener [29]. When displaying a haptic surface with force feedback, the display can give the impression of objects with a soft surface if the display frequency is low [12].

Cognition issues are also important when designing a display to recognize patterns. For example, the haptic sense may not be as useful for remembering complex patterns as the auditory sense. Some users may be more adept at using a particular sense, especially as attention to any single sense can influence performance with that sense [30]. Apart from attention, expectations, context, and knowledge can all influence what we see, hear, and feel [30].

Apart from physiological, perceptual, and cognitive concerns, the designer of multisensory displays must also consider the tasks of the intended user, characteristics of the data themselves, and specifics of the intended display hardware.

Although some attempts have been made to better characterize the design of visual displays [15], auditory displays [31], and even multisensory displays [32], much more theoretical work still needs to occur in these areas.

4.   CONCLUSION

This chapter has described some of the new algorithms and technologies for information display. In most cases, these are untested outside universities and research laboratories. However, it is clear that a number of them will eventually find their way into commercial tools. As more novel concepts in information display are invented and tested, the way that we perceive information will be changed.

REFERENCES

[1] R. Stuart (1996): The Design of Virtual Environments. New York, McGraw-Hill.

[2] G. Kramer (1994): An Introduction to Auditory Display. Auditory Display: Sonification, *Audification and Auditory Interfaces*. Addison-Wesley.

[3] M. J. Evans, A. I. Tew, J. A. S. Angus (1997): Spatial Audio Teleconferencing—Which Way is Better? *International Conference on Auditory Display*, Palo Alto, California.

[4] E. M. Wenzel, M. Arruda, D. S. Kistler, and F. L. Wightman (1993): Localization using nonindividualized head-related transfer functions. *Journal of the Acoustical Society of America*, *94*, 111–123.

[5] C. Hayward (1994): Listening to the Earth Sing. Auditory Display: Sonification, Audification and Auditory Interfaces. G. Kramer, Addison-Wesley, pp. 369–404.

[6] D. H. Jameson (1994): Sonnet: Audio-Enhanced Monitoring and Debugging. Auditory Display: Sonification, Audification and Auditory Interfaces. G. Kramer, Addison-Wesley, pp. 253–266.

[7] T. M. Madhyastha and D. A. Reed (1994): A Framework for Sonification Design. Auditory Display: Sonification, Audification and Auditory Interfaces. G. Kramer, Addison-Wesley, pp. 267–290.

[8] J. A. Jackson and J. M. Francioni (1994): Synchronization of Visual and Aural Parallel Program Performance Data. Auditory Display: Sonification, Audification and Auditory Interfaces. G. Kramer, Addison-Wesley, pp. 291–306.

[9] K. McCabe and A. Rangwalla (1994): Auditory Display of Computational Fluid Dynamics Data. Auditory Display: Sonification, Audification and Auditory Interfaces. G. Kramer, Addison-Wesley, pp. 327–340.

[10] S. Barass and B. Zehner (2000): Responsive Sonification of Well-logs. *International Conference on Auditory Display*, Atlanta, Georgia, USA.

[11] W. T. Fitch and G. Kramer (1994): Sonifying the Body Electric: Superiority of an Auditory over a Visual Display in a Complex, Multivariate System. Auditory Display: Sonification, Audification and Auditory Interfaces. G. Kramer, Addison-Wesley, pp. 307–326.

[12] M. A. Srinivasan and C. Basdogan (1997): Haptics in Virtual Environments: Taxonomy, Research Status, and Challenges. *Computer & Graphics 21*(4) 393–404.

[13] N. I. Durlach and A. S. Mavor, (ed) (1995): Virtual Reality: Scientific and Technological Challenges. Washington, D. C. National Academy Press.

[14] J. K. Salsibury and M. A. Srinivasan (1997): Phantom-Based Haptic Interaction with Virtual Objects. *Computer Graphics and Applications 17*(5), 6–10.

[15] S. K. Card, J. D. Mackinlay, and B. Shneiderman, (ed): (1999): Information Visualization. *Readings in Information Visualization.* San Francisco, California, Morgan Kaufmann.

[16] J. J. Batter and F. P. J. Brooks (1972): GROPE-1. IFIP '71.

[17] D. F. Green and J. K. Salsibury (1998): Soil Simulation with a PHANToM. *The Third PHANToM User's Group Workshop*, Cambridge, Massachusetts, USA, MIT.

[18] D. F. Green (1997): Texture Sensing and Simulation Using the PHANToM: Towards Remote Sensing of Soil Properties. *The Second PHANToM User's Group Workshop*, Cambridge, Massachusetts, USA, MIT.

[19] K. Nesbitt (2002): Experimenting with Haptic Attributes for Display of Abstract Data. *Eurohaptics 2002 International Conference*, Edinburgh, Scotland.

[20] A. Seeger, J. Chen, and R. M. Taylor (1997): Controlling Force Feedback Over a Network. *The Second PHANToM User's Group Workshop*, Cambridge, Massachusetts, USA, MIT.

[21] J. P. McLaughlin and B. J. Orenstein (1997): Haptic Rendering of 3D Seismic Data. *The Second PHANToM User's Group Workshop*, Cambridge, Massachusetts, USA, MIT.

[22] M. R. McGee, P. D. Gray, and S. A. Brewster (2000): Communicating with feeling. *First Workshop on Haptic Human–Computer Interaction.*

[23] L. Y. Pao and D. A. Lawrence (1998): Synergistic Visual/Haptic Computer Interfaces. *Japan/USE/Vietnam Workshop on Research and Education in Systems, Computation and Control Engineering.*

[24] D. E. DiFranco, G. L. Beauregard, and M. A. Srinivasan (1997): The Effects of Auditory Cues on the Haptic Perception of Stiffness in Virtual Environments. ASME Dynamic Systems and Control Division.

[25] A. H. Morton (1982): Visual and Tactile Texture Perception: Intersensory Co-operation. *Perception & Pyschophysics* 31, 339–344.

[26] R. B. Welch and D. H. Warren (1980): Immediate Perceptual Response to Intersensory Discrepancy. *Psychological Bulletin 88*(3), 638–667.

[27] J. Itten (1970): The Elements of Color. New York, USA, Van Nostrand Reinhold.

[28] R. Sekuler and R. Blake (1990): Perception. New York, McGraw-Hill.

[29] G. Kramer, B. Walker, et al. (1997): Sonification Report: Status of the Field and Research Agenda, Prepared for the National Science Foundation by members of the International Community for Auditory Display.

[30] E. B. Goldstein (1989): Sensation and Perception, Brooks/Cole.

[31] S. Barass (1997): Auditory Information Design. Computer Science. Canberra, Australian National University.

[32] K. Nesbitt (2003): Designing Multi-sensory Displays for Abstract Data, School of IT, University of Sydney.

[33] NVIDIA (2003): http://www.nvidia.com.

[34] ATI (2003): http://www.ati.com.

[35] G. Humphreys, M. Eldridge, I. Buck, G. Stoll, M. Everett, and P. Hanrahan, (2001): WireGL: A scalable graphics system for clusters. *Proceedings of SIGGRAPH 2001*, 129–140, August.

[36] G. Humphreys, et al. (2002): Chromium: A Stream-Processing Framework for Interactive Rendering on Clusters, *Proceedings of the 29th Annual Conference on Computer Graphics and interactive techniques*, ACM Press, New York, NY, USA.

[37] NCSA, Display Wall-in-a-Box. (2003): http://www.ncsa.uiuc.edu/TechFocus/Deployment/DBox/overview.html.

[38] PSU, The Pennsylvania State University, High Resolution Tiled Display Wall (2003) http://gears.aset.psu.edu/viz/facilities/displaywall.

[39] ViSLAB, The University of Sydney (2003) http://www.vislab.usyd.edu.au

[40] ASCI VIEWS Visualization project (2003) http://www.llnl.gov/icc/sdd/img/infrastructures.shtml.

[41] E. W. Bethel, et al. (2002): Combining a Multithreaded Scene Graph System with a Tiled Display Environment, *Proceedings of the 2002 IS&T/SPIE Conference on Electronic Imaging and Technology*, The Engineering Reality of Virtual Reality.

[42] E. W. Bethel, et al. (2003): Sort-First Distributed Memory Parallel Visualization and Rendering, *Proceedings of IEEE Symposium on Parallel and Large-Data Visualization and Graphics*, pp. 41–50.

[43] P. Wellnerr (1993): Interacting with Paper on the Digital Desk, *Communications of the ACM*, *36*(7), 87–96.

[44] S. Feiner, B. Macintyre, and D. Seligmann (1993): Knowledge-based Augmented Reality, *Communications of the ACM*, *36*(7): 53–62.

[45] R. Azuma, Y. Baillot, R. Behringer, S. Feiner, S. Julier, and B. MacIntyre (2001): Recent Advances in Augmented Reality. *IEEE Comp. Graph. & App*, *21*(6), 34–47.

[46] A. Fuhrmann, et al. (1998): Collaborative Visualization in Augmented Reality, *IEEE Computer Graphics and Applications*, *18*(4), 54–59.

[47] C. Pinhanez (2001): Using a Steerable Projector and a Camera to Transform Surfaces into Interactive Displays, CHI 2001, March/April, 369–370.

[48] P. Milgram and F. Kishino (1994): A taxonomy of mixed reality virtual displays, *IEICE Transactions on Information and Systems (Special Issue on Networked Reality)*, E77-D(12): 1321–1329.

[49] P. Milgram and H. Colquhoun, Jr. (1999): A Taxonomy of Real and Virtural World Display Integration (Mixed Reality; (eds) Yuichi Ohta and Hideyuki Tamura), Ohmsha Ltd. & Springer-Verlag, pp. 5–30.

[50] T. Kanade, et al. (1999): Virtualized Reality – Digitizing a 3D Time-Varying Event As Is and in Real Time, (Mixed Reality; (eds) Yuichi Ohta and Hideyuki Tamura), Ohmsha Ltd. & Springer-Verlag, pp. 41–57.

[51] M. Hirose, et al. (1999): Building a Virtual World from the Real World (Mixed Reality – Merging Real and Virtual Worlds; (eds) Yuichi Ohta and Hideyuki Tamura), Ohmsha.

[52] R. A. May, II (1999): HI-SPACE: A Next Generation Workspace Environment, Washington State University, Department of Electrical Engineering and Computer Science, May.

[53] H. Ishii and N. Miyake (1991): Towards an Open Shared Workspace – Computer and Video Fusion Approach of Teamworkstation, *Communications of the ACM, 34*(12), 37–50.

[54] S. Coquillart and G. Wesche (1999): The Virtual Palette and the Virtual Remote Control Panel: A Device and an Interaction Paradigm for the Responsive Workbench. In *IEEE Virtual Reality '99 Conference (VR'99)*, Houston.

[55] P. H. Dietz and D. L. Leigh (2001): DiamondTouch: A Multi-User Touch Technology. In *ACM Symposium on User Interface Software and Technology (UIST)*, pp. 219–226.

[56] B. Leibe, T. Stanner, W. Ribarsky, Z. Wartell, D. Krum, B. Singletary, and L. Hodges (2000): The Perspective Workbench: Towards Spontaneous and Natural Interaction in Semi-Immersive Virtual Environments. In *IEEE Virtual Reality 2000 Conference (VR'2000)*, pp. 13–20. New Brunswick, NJ.

[57] I. Rauschert, P. Agrawal, S. Fuhrmann, I. Brewer, H. Wang, R. Sharma, G. Cai, and A. MacEachren (2002): Designing a Human-Centered, Multimodal GIS Interface to Support Emergency Management. In *10th ACM Symposium on Advances in Geographic Information Systems (ACM GIS'02)*, Washington, DC, USA.

[58] A. F. Seay, D. Krum, W. Ribarsky, and L. Hodges (1999): Multimodal Interaction Techniques for the Virtual Workbench. In *Proceeding of CHI'99*.

[59] P. L. Schmalstieg, L. M. Encarnacao, and Z. Szalavar (1999): Using Transparent Props for Interaction with Virtual Table. In *Syposium on Interactive 3D Graphics (I3DG'99)*, Atlanta.

[60] R. Raskar, et al. (1998): The Office of the Future: A Unified Approach to Image-Based Modeling and Spatially Immersive Displays, *SIGGRAPH 98*, Orlando, Florida.

[61] M. Stefik, et al. (1986): WYSIWIS Revised – Early Experiences with Multi-user Interfaces, *CSCW'86*, pp. 276–290.

[62] D. A. Norman (1986): Cognitive Engineering (User Centered System Design; (eds) D. A. Norman and S. W. Draper), Lawrence Erlbaum Associates.

[63] J. Barnes and P. Hut (1986): A Hierarchical $O(n\log n)$ Force-Calculation Algorithm: *Nature 324*(4), 446–449.

[64] S. Bornholdt and H. G. Schuster, (ed) (2003): Handbook of Graphs and Networks: From the Genome to the Internet. Wiley-VCH.

[65] U. Brandes and D. Wagner (2003): Visone -Analysis and Visualization of Social Networks: Graph Drawing Software: pp. 321–340. Springer Verlag.

[66] F. R. K. Chung (1997): Spectral Graph Theory: *CBMS Reg. Conf. Ser. Math.* 92. American Mathematical Society.

[67] G. Di Battista, P. Eades, R. Tamassia, and I. G. Tollis (1999): Graph Drawing: Algorithms for the Visualization of Graphs: Prentice-Hall.

[68] P. Eades (1984): A Heuristic for Graph Drawing. *Congresses Numerantium 42*, 149–160.

[69] B. S. Everitt and G. Dunn, (1991): Applied Multivariate Data Analysis: Arnold.

[70] T. Fruchterman and E. Reingold (1991): Graph Drawing by Force-Directed Placement. *Software-Practice and Experience 21*(11), 1129–1164.

[71] P. Gajer, M. T. Goodrich, and S. G. Kobourov (2000): A Multi-dimensional Approach to Force-Directed Drawings of Large Graphs. *Proceedings of Graph Drawing 2000: Lecture Notes in Computer Science 1984:* pp. 211–221: Springer Verlag.

[72] P. Gajer and S. G. Kobourov (2002): GRIP: Graph Drawing with Intelligent Placement. *Journal of Graph Algorithms and Applications 6*(3), 203–224.

[73] K. M. Hall (1970): An r-dimensional Quadratic Placement Algorithm. *Management Science 17*, 219–229.

[74] R. Hadany and D. Harel (2001): A Multi-Scale Method for Drawing Graphs Nicely. *Discrete Applied Mathematics 113*, 3–21.

[75] D. Harel and Y. Koren (2002): A Fast Multi-Scale Method for Drawing Large Graphs: *Proceedings of Graph Drawing 2000: Lecture Notes in Computer Science 1984:* Springer Verlag: 183-196 (2000) (Journal version: *Journal of Graph Algorithms and Applications 6*(3), 179–202.

[76] D. Harel and Y. Koren (2002): Graph Drawing by High-Dimensional Embedding: *Proceedings of Graph Drawing 2002: Lecture Notes in Computer Science 2528:* Springer Verlag, pp. 207–219.

[77] M. Junger and P. Mutzel, (ed) (2003): Graph Drawing Software: Springer Verlag.

[78] T. Kamada and S. Kawai (1989): An Algorithm for Drawing General Undirected Graphs. *Information Processing Letters 31*, 7–15.

[79] M. Kaufmann and D. Wagner, (ed) (2001): Drawing Graphs: Methods and Models: Lecture Notes in Computer Science Tutorial 2025: Springer Verlag.

[80] Y. Koren (2003): On Spectral Graph Drawing: *Proceedings of COCOON 2003: Lecture Notes in Computer Science 2697*: Springer Verlag, pp. 496–508.

[81] Y. Koren, L. Carmel, and D. Harel (2002): ACE: A Fast Multiscale Eigenvectors Computation for Drawing Huge Graphs: *Proceedings of IEEE Symposium on Information Visualization (InfoVis) 2002:* 137–144

[82] Y. Koren, L. Carmel, and D. Harel (2003): Drawing Huge Graphs by Algebraic Multigrid Optimization. *Multiscale Modeling and Simulation 1*(4), 645–673, SIAM.

[83] A. Quigley and P. Eades (2000): FADE: Graph Drawing, Clustering, and Visual Abstraction: *Proceedings of Graph Drawing 2000: Lecture Notes in Computer Science 1984:* pp. 183–196: Springer Verlag.

[84] F. Schreiber (2002): High Quality Visualization of Biochemical Pathways in BioPath. *Silico Biology 2*(2), 59–73.

[85] K. Sugiyama (2002): Graph Drawing and Applications for Software and Knowledge Engineers: World Scientific.

[86] K. Sugiyama, and K. Misue (1995): Graph Drawing by Magnetic Spring Model. *Journal of Visual Languages and Computing 6*(3): 217–231.

[87] C. Walshaw (2000): A Multilevel Algorithm for Force-Directed Graph Drawing. *Proceedings of Graph Drawing 2000: Lecture Notes in Computer Science 1984:* pp. 171–182: Springer Verlag.

[88] C. Walshaw (2003): A Multilevel Algorithm for Force-Directed Graph Drawing. *Journal of Graph Algorithms and Applications 7*(3), 53–85.

[89] D. S. Watkins (1991): Fundamentals of Matrix Computations: John Wiley.

[90] B. Brandes and S. Cornelsen (2003): Visual Ranking of Link Structures. *Journal of Graph Algorithms and Applications 7*(2), 181–201.

Chapter 21

BIOINFORMATICS
Srinivas Aluru
Iowa State University

1   INTRODUCTION

Ever since the structure of DNA was discovered in the early 1950s, biology has been steadily transforming into a discipline that relates essential life processes to underlying biomolecular data. This discovery has stimulated the growth of molecular biology, the study of how biomolecular sequences influence the functioning of organisms. These developments have brought biology closer to computer science. In many ways, the underlying mechanisms are similar to what we employ in building and programming computers. The characteristics of a life form are coded in its DNA (program), which is processed in each cell (executed) to produce the proteins (outputs) that carry out most of the essential life processes. The field holds immense potential for future discoveries that are unrivaled in significance, such as the possibility of treating diseases and engineering improved crops by altering the genetic composition.

The need to discover biomolecular sequences, to relate those sequences to their structure and function, and to understand evolutionary history through sequence homology (similarity) detection has resulted in a number of interesting problems for computer scientists and led to the development of bioinformatics. Broadly defined, bioinformatics or computational biology is the study of computational methods for furthering biological discovery and applying information technology to solving the problems of biological relevance. The field has experienced an explosive growth in the last two decades, and the accumulated knowledge and importance of the field has reached a stage in which successful advanced graduate programs are being developed to train bioinformaticists. While it is impossible to attempt a comprehensive coverage of this field in a short amount of space, this chapter is intended to provide both a sense of the breadth of the field and a focused study of specific applications, particularly in computational genomics.

2   OVERVIEW OF BIOINFORMATICS

In this section, we present some basic concepts in molecular biology that are
essential for understanding the remainder of the chapter, and we also outline a
number of computational challenges in bioinformatics. The reader should keep in
mind that the discussion is purposefully oversimplified and should refer to a standard textbook [2, 65] for full details.

2.1   Basics of Molecular Biology

In bioinformatics, we are typically concerned with two types of biomolecular
data: DNA (deoxyribonucleic acid) sequences and protein sequences. A DNA
molecule is a sequence made of simpler molecules known as nucleotides. Each
nucleotide consists of a deoxyribose sugar molecule, a phosphate group attached
to the 5′-carbon of the sugar molecule, and a base attached to the 1′-carbon of
the sugar molecule. The different nucleotides are differentiated by the differences
in the bases—Adenine (A), Cytosine (C), Guanine (G) and Thymine (T). For
computational purposes, a DNA sequence can be represented as a string over the
alphabet $\Sigma = \{A, C, G, T\}$, specifying each nucleotide by the first letter of its
name. The sequence is formed by phosphodiester bonds between consecutive
nucleotides: the 5′-carbon of one nucleotide is linked to the 3′-carbon of the previous nucleotide through the phosphate group. Thus, one end of the sequence has
a free 5′ end and the other end has a free 3′ end, giving a directionality to the molecule. It is customary to write a DNA molecule as the sequence of nucleotides
from the 5′ end to the 3′ end.

DNA sequences naturally occur as double-stranded molecules, i.e., two
sequences of nucleotides attached to each other. The two strands are held
together by hydrogen bonds between bases of the corresponding nucleotides. Two
types of base pairings are possible – A with T, involving two hydrogen bonds; and
G with C, involving three hydrogen bonds. For a given nucleotide in one strand,
the corresponding nucleotide in the complementary strand is given by the pairing
$A \leftrightarrow T$ and $C \leftrightarrow G$. The two complementary strands also exhibit opposite directionality. Because of these properties, a double-stranded DNA molecule can be
accurately described as the sequence of one of its strands from its 5′-end to the
3′-end. Note that this would mean two equivalent strings describing the same
DNA molecule. One string (or strand) can be obtained from the other by a *reverse
complementation* operation, which refers to reversing the string and replacing A
with T, T with A, C with G, and G with C. The length of a DNA sequence is
measured in units called *base pairs* (*bp*), where a base pair refers to a pair of corresponding nucleotides on the two strands of a DNA sequence.

DNA is established as the vehicle for passing hereditary genetic information.
The complementarity relation between the two strands of a DNA sequence indicates that one strand is sufficient to recover the entire sequence. This mechanism
makes DNA self-replicating. Several different terms are used to describe DNA
sequences, depending on the role played by particular DNA sequences or the
scale at which these sequences are viewed. The term *genome* refers to the entire
genetic constitution within the nucleus of a cell of a *eukaryotic* organism (organism whose cells have nuclei) or within a cell of a *prokaryotic* organism (organisms

whose cells do not have nuclei). During cell division, the genome is duplicated using the self-replicating mechanism to provide a copy for each resulting cell. The genome is organized into one or more *chromosomes*, where each chromosome is a continuous strand of DNA. A *gene* is a contiguous stretch of DNA along a chromosome that codes for a protein. A *promoter* is a DNA sequence typically located upstream of a gene to aid in its expression. Significant length scales are exhibited in the sizes of genomes. Viruses have the smallest of the genomes, e.g., the virus Bacteriophage λ has an approximate size of 50,000 *bp*. Bacterial genomes are typically 100 times as large or more. Humans, mice, and maize have genomes about 3×10^9 *bp* in size. Plants are known to have some of the largest genomes. For example, the Lily plant has a genome about 100×10^9 *bp* long.

An important function of DNA sequences is to code for protein sequences. Like DNA sequences, proteins are also sequences of simpler molecules, in this case amino acid residues. An amino acid consists of a central carbon atom known as α-carbon, connected to a hydrogen atom, a carboxyl group, an amino group, and a side chain. It is the side chains that distinguish the twenty different amino acids that constitute protein sequences. Amino acid residues are typically denoted by a three-letter abbreviation of their names, such as *Gly* for *Glycine* and *Val* for *Valine*. For computational purposes, we will use a single letter alphabet of size twenty and depict protein sequences as strings over this alphabet.

The mechanism by which a gene codes for a protein is as follows: First, a copy of the gene (or portions of it intended to code for a protein sequence) is made as an RNA (ribonucleic acid) molecule, called messenger RNA, or mRNA for short. Similar to DNA, mRNA is a sequence of nucleotides except that Uracil (U) is used instead of Thymine (T). A *codon* is a consecutive triplet of nucleotides in the mRNA sequence that codes for an amino acid. The many-to-one mapping between the 64 possible codons and the twenty amino acids has been discovered and is common across species (see Table 21.1). Three codons correspond to a STOP signal. The translation typically starts with the codon *AUG*, which codes for the amino acid methanine, and continues until a STOP signal is encountered. The copying of DNA to mRNA is called *transcription*, and the production of protein from mRNA is called *translation*. Together, this process is popularly known as *the central dogma* in molecular biology.

Proteins are responsible for carrying out most of the essential life processes. For example, they act as tissue building blocks (structural proteins) and as catalysts to speed up biochemical reactions (enzymes); they carry out oxygen transport and conduct antibody defense. The three-dimensional structure of proteins is critical to their function. Complex regulatory mechanisms guide the gene-expression process, which together with other factors will ultimately determine the amount of production of the corresponding protein. Multiple forms of the same gene, known as *alleles*, cause differences in *genotype* (genetic difference) between individuals, which will eventually translate into differences in *phenotype* (observable differences, such as color of eyes). Certain variations in a gene sequences may lead to low or nonfunctional proteins and may cause genetic diseases or increase susceptibility to diseases. These differences often arise due to a change in the nucleotide in a single position, also called a *single nucleotide polymorphism (SNP)*. Developing a database of SNPs along the genome is considered vital to pharmaceutical research. Variations within the genome across different

Table 21.1 The genetic code mapping a consecutive triplet of nucleotides (codon) to the corresponding amino acid. Note that multiple codons code for the same amino acid. With the exception of Ser, the first two positions of the codons that code for the same amino acid are identical.

First position	Second Position				Third position
	U	C	A	G	
U	Phe(F)	Ser(S)	Tyr(Y)	Cys(C)	U
	Phe(F)	Ser(S)	Tyr(Y)	Cys(C)	C
	Leu(L)	Ser(S)	Stop	Stop	A
	Leu(L)	Ser(S)	Stop	Trp(W)	G
C	Leu(L)	Pro(P)	His(H)	Arg(R)	U
	Leu(L)	Pro(P)	His(H)	Arg(R)	C
	Leu(L)	Pro(P)	Gln(Q)	Arg(R)	A
	Leu(L)	Pro(P)	Gln(Q)	Arg(R)	G
A	Ile(I)	Thr(T)	Asn(N)	Ser(S)	U
	Ile(I)	Thr(T)	Asn(N)	Ser(S)	C
	Ile(I)	Thr(T)	Lys(K)	Arg(R)	A
	Met(M)	Thr(T)	Lys(K)	Arg(R)	G
G	Val(V)	Ala(A)	Asp(D)	Gly(G)	U
	Val(V)	Ala(A)	Asp(D)	Gly(G)	C
	Val(V)	Ala(A)	Glu(E)	Gly(G)	A
	Val(V)	Ala(A)	Glu(E)	Gly(G)	G

individuals of the same species are very small compared with the length of the genome. For instance, all humans are expected to show over 99.9% identity at the genome level. A typical high-level organism contains several tens of thousands of genes. Genes are conserved across species, and species that are evolutionarily closer exhibit significant gene homologies.

Several experimental procedures have been designed to complement the molecular biological discoveries summarized above. DNA sequences that are several hundred base pairs long can be read using an experimental procedure known as Sanger's method. A number of recombinant DNA techniques have been developed. These include (1) inserting foreign DNA into bacterial genomes for the purpose of cloning, (2) amplifying DNA sequences using the polymerase chain reaction (PCR) method, which corresponds to exponential growth via doubling, (3) artificially converting mRNA sequences to the corresponding DNA sequences, called *complementary DNA* or *cDNA* sequences, and (4) testing for the presence of a particular DNA sequence by using its complementary strand. These and other experimental techniques have been used to deduce DNA and protein sequence data from a plethora of organisms. Such data are deposited in public databases such as GenBank (http://www.ncbi.nlm.nih.gov) and PDB (http://www.pdb.org). Exponential growth in the size of such databases has necessitated computational methods for accessing and analyzing sequence data.

2.2   Computational Challenges

Computational methods and the use of software have become integral parts of a biologist's toolkit. Their use is pervasive, encompassing the discovery, analysis, and interpretation of biological data, aiding in the discovery of biological knowledge, and helping utilize this knowledge in applications in biotechnology and medicine. A systematic study of this interdisciplinary research field has led to a number of important subareas within bioinformatics, some of which are described below.

1. **Alignments and Database Search.** Alignment methods are intended to discover homologies (similarities) of interest between DNA or protein sequences. Alignment algorithms are used to query databases to discover homologous sequences, discover homologous genes within or across species, identify common motifs across multiple protein sequences, and identify overlapping sequences.

2. **Genome Sequencing.** While laboratory sequencing techniques can read DNA sequences several hundred base pairs long, genome sizes of higher organisms are more than a millionfold larger in size. The approach used for genome sequencing is to derive an appropriate number (tens of millions for human and mouse genomes) of random fragments of sequenceable size from the genome. Once these fragments are sequenced, computational methods are designed to assemble the fragments to derive the genome sequence.

3. **Gene Identification and Annotation.** An important first step in understanding the genome of an organism is to identify the locations and structures of its genes and to identify the role of the corresponding protein products (annotation). Computational approaches designed for this problem include ab initio gene prediction methods using hidden Markov models, alignment programs using gene transcriptions such as mRNA and cDNA sequences, and close comparison of related species to identify conserved regions.

4. **Comparative Genomics.** Genome comparisons are useful in identifying conserved genes, promoters, and other sequences; validating and annotating of genome assemblies; and understanding evolutionary histories. Comparative genomics also throws light on genome rearrangements and fast-evolving viruses.

5. **Gene Expression Analysis.** DNA microarrays facilitate profiling of the expression levels of tens of thousands of genes in a single experiment. Such information is used in identifying coregulated genes, inferring gene regulatory networks, identifying genes whose abnormality causes specific diseases, studying developmental genetics, etc.

6. **Phylogenetic Analysis.** The study of the evolution of sequences and species and the deciphering of the evolutionary history connecting known and extinct species is called *phylogenetics*.

7. **Protein Structure Prediction.** The three-dimensional structure of a protein is crucial to its function. The ability of a deformed protein molecule to fold back into its native configuration without external assistance led to the hypothesis that the structure is determined by the sequence itself. Computationally determining the structure of a protein from its sequence is considered a "holy-grail" problem in bioinformatics. A corresponding problem is that of inverse protein folding, the problem of finding a protein sequence that will fold into a desired three-dimensional structure.

8. **Structural Homologies and Docking.** While sequence homologies often translate into structure homologies, the converse need not be true. Furthermore, preservation of important structural motifs is sufficient for functional similarity despite differences in other parts of the structure. While sequence alignment

algorithms are used because of their ease and simplicity, detection of structural homologies and structure-based database searches would be the eventual goal for protein sequences. Similarly, an understanding of protein docking is useful in designing proteins for the effective administration of drugs.

The above list is not meant to be exhaustive but is intended to convey the breadth, importance, and interesting nature of the research problems in bioinformatics and computational biology. Computational techniques have already become an integral part of biological discoveries, and this trend will continue in the future. In the remainder of this chapter, we will focus on specific research problems in an attempt to convey the flavor and excitement of this interdisciplinary research field and the challenging applications it provides for computer science research. We will begin with problems in computational genomics. For a high-level view of the role of algorithmic research in computational genomics, the reader is referred to Karp's recent keynote address [56].

3   BASIC TOOLS OF COMPUTATIONAL GENOMICS

3.1   Alignments

Global Sequence Alignments

Consider the problem of determining whether two DNA sequences are evolutionarily related and detecting the extent of homology (similarity) between them. To model this problem computationally, one must understand the evolutionary mechanisms that could change DNA sequences. Two types of events are of primary interest: mutation, a process that results in substitution of one nucleotide with another; and DNA insertions/deletions, which cause insertion/deletion of a contiguous subsequence. Suppose that DNA sequence A is changed to DNA sequence B through some substitution, insertion, and deletion operations. The homology between sequences A and B can be shown by writing one sequence below the other to clearly indicate matching nucleotides and substitutions. An insertion used in transforming A into B (referred to as an insertion in A) is shown by a sequence of gaps in A corresponding to the inserted subsequence in B. Similarly, a deletion in A is shown by a sequence of gaps in B corresponding to the deleted subsequence in A. For example, Figure 21.1 shows an alignment of DNA sequences $ATGTCGA$ and $AGAATCTA$ obtained by deleting the second base, inserting AA after the third base, and substituting T for the sixth base in $ATGTCGA$.

In order to measure the significance of homology shown by an alignment, a scoring scheme is introduced. The idea is to reward matches and penalize substitutions and insertions/deletions, abbreviated *indels*. A higher score indicates a better alignment. Since the same sequences could be represented using different alignments, the scoring mechanism also provides a way to evaluate how good an alignment is. Thus, the alignment problem can be formulated as a problem of finding the highest scoring alignment between two sequences. The highest score, or optimal score, becomes a measure of the homology between the two sequences.

A	T	G	–	–	T	C	G	A
A	–	G	A	A	T	C	T	A
5	–5	5	–6		5	5	–5	5

Figure 21.1. An alignment between DNA sequences *ATGTCGA* and *AGAATCTA* using a score of 5 for a match, –5 for a substitution, 4 for a gap opening penalty, and 1 for a gap extension penalty.

The above ideas can be formalized as follows: Let Σ be the alphabet, and let '–' denote the gap. A score function $f : \Sigma \times \Sigma \to \Re$ prescribes the score for any column in the alignment that does not contain a gap. Scores of columns involving gaps are determined by an *affine gap penalty function*: for a maximal consecutive sequence of k gaps, a penalty of $h + gk$ is applied. Thus, the first gap in a maximal sequence is charged $h + g$, while the rest of the gaps are charged g each. The term h is called the *gap opening penalty*, and the term g is called *gap extension penalty*. If $h = 0$, the penalty function is called a *constant gap penalty* function. The score of the alignment is the sum of scores over all the columns. The alignment in Figure 21.1 is scored using the simple scoring function, defined as

$$f(c_1, c_2) = \begin{cases} 5, & c_1 = c_2, c_1, c_2 \in \Sigma \\ -5, & c_1 \neq c_2, c_1, c_2 \in \Sigma \end{cases}$$

and an affine gap penalty function that penalizes a maximal sequence of gaps of length k with a penalty of $4 + k$. Then the alignment has a total score of 9.

Let $A = a_1 a_2 \ldots a_m$ and $B = b_1 b_2 \ldots b_n$ be two sequences. An optimal alignment of A and B is computed using a dynamic programming approach. The algorithm uses three tables T_1, T_2, and T_3, each of size $(m + 1) \times (n + 1)$. An entry $[i, j]$ in each table corresponds to the score for optimally aligning $a_1 a_2 \ldots a_i$ with $b_1 b_2 \ldots b_j$, but with the following conditions: In T_1, only alignments in which a_i is aligned with b_j are considered. In T_2, b_j must be aligned with "–", and in T_3, a_i must be aligned with "–." Once the tables are computed, the optimal score for aligning A with B is given by the maximum of $T_1[m, n]$, $T_2[m, n]$, and $T_3[m, n]$.

The top row and leftmost column of each table are initialized to $-\infty$, except in the following cases ($1 \leq i \leq m$; $1 \leq j \leq n$):

$$T_1[0, 0] = 0$$
$$T_2[0, j] = -(h + gj)$$
$$T_3[i, 0] = -(h + gi)$$

A score of $-\infty$ is used to indicate that the alignment is invalid. Consider the task of computing $T_1[i, j]$ for some $i \geq 1$ and $j \geq 1$. The last column of the alignment contains a_i aligned with b_j, which gets a score of $f(a_i, b_j)$. The remaining portion of the alignment must be an optimal alignment between $a_1 a_2 \ldots a_{i-1}$ and $b_1 b_2 \ldots b_{j-1}$. This is given by the maximum of $T_1[i-1, j-1]$, $T_2[i-1, j-1]$, and $T_3[i-1, j-1]$, which can be computed in constant time if these entries are already available. Similar reasoning gives rise to the following recurrence equations:

$$T_1[i,j] = f(a_i, b_j) + \max \begin{cases} T_1[i-1, j-1] \\ T_2[i-1, j-1] \\ T_3[i-1, j-1] \end{cases} \tag{1}$$

$$T_2[i,j] = \max \begin{cases} T_1[i,j-1] - (g+h) \\ T_2[i,j-1] - g \\ T_3[i,j-1] - (g+h) \end{cases} \qquad (2)$$

$$T_3[i,j] = \max \begin{cases} T_1[i-1,j] - (g+h) \\ T_2[i-1,j] - (g+h) \\ T_3[i-1,j] - g \end{cases} \qquad (3)$$

The tables can be filled row by row or column by column. Either way, when a table entry is computed, the entries needed to compute it are already available. As each table entry can be computed in constant time, the algorithm runs in $O(mn)$ time. The tables can be used not only to find the optimal score but also to retrieve one or all optimal alignments. To do this, for each table entry that is being filled, a pointer is maintained that points to the appropriate table entry that resulted in the highest score among all alternatives being considered. If multiple alternatives result in the same highest score, pointers are maintained linking to each of the corresponding table entries. An optimal alignment is recovered from right to left by following the trail of pointers from a highest entry among $T_1[m, n]$, $T_2[m, n]$, and $T_3[m, n]$ to the top left corner of one of the tables. This procedure is often called *traceback*. As each pointer causes a move to the previous row or column or both, an optimal alignment can be retrieved in $O(m + n)$ time. By enumerating all possible paths, all optimal alignments can be enumerated if desired.

Space and Time Reduction Techniques

The time and space requirements of the just-described algorithm for computing sequence alignments are both $O(mn)$. The space requirement can be reduced to $O(m + n)$ using Hirschberg's technique [43, 76] while increasing the run-time by at most a factor of 2. First, note that the entries required for computing row i of the tables T_1, T_2, and T_3 depend only on row $i - 1$ of the tables. By discarding a row as soon as the next row is computed based on it, the space used per table can be reduced to $O(n)$ ($O(min(m, n))$) by choosing B to be smaller of the two input sequences). The total space required for the algorithm is reduced to $O(m + n)$, including the space for storing the input sequences. It is still possible to determine the optimal score because only the last entry of the last row of each of the tables is required to compute it. The only problem with this approach is that the ability to perform traceback and retrieve an optimal alignment is lost. From the biologist's perspective, alignments are crucial.

Hirschberg's strategy uses divide-and-conquer to find both the optimal score and an optimal alignment using only $O(m + n)$ space. Let $A^r = a_m a_{m-1} \dots a_2 a_1$ and $B^r = b_n b_{n-1} \dots b_2, b_1$ denote the reverse of sequences A and B, respectively. Similarly, let T_1^r, T_2^r, and T_3^r denote tables defined similar to T_1, T_2, and T_3 except that entry $[i,j]$ corresponds to an alignment between $a_m a_{m-1} \dots a_i$ and $b_n, b_{n-1} \dots b_j$, i.e., $T^r[i, j]$ denotes the score of an optimal alignment between $a_m a_{m-1} \dots a_i$ and b_n, b_{n-1}, b_j, where a_i is aligned with b_j, etc. Let $k = \lfloor \frac{m}{2} \rfloor$. Compute row k of T_1, T_2, and T_3, and row $k + 1$ of T_1^r, T_2^r, and T_3^r. This is equivalent to filling the top half of the rows of the tables T_1, T_2, and T_3 and the bottom half of the rows of the tables

$T_1{}^r$, $T_2{}^r$, and $T_3{}^r$. Using the space-saving strategy of discarding previously computed rows, the required rows can be computed in $O(mn)$ time and $O(m + n)$ space.

Consider an optimal alignment of A and B. Partition the alignment into two parts by separating the alignment immediately after the column containing a_k. The first part is an alignment between $a_1 a_2 ... a_k$ and $b_1 b_2 ... b_j$ for some j, and the second part is an alignment between $a_{k+1} a_{k+2} ... a_m$ and $b_{j+1} b_{j+2} ... b_n$. Because of affine gap penalties, these need not be optimal alignments, but they would be of the type captured by row k of T_1, T_2, and T_3, and row $k + 1$ of $T_1{}^r$, $T_2{}^r$, and $T_3{}^r$. The value of j and the optimal score can be computed by choosing a value of j that maximizes

$$\max \begin{cases} T_1[k,j] + \max\,(T_1^r[k+1,\,j+1], T_2^r[k+1,j+1], T_3^r[k+1,j+1]) \\ T_2[k,j] + \max\,(T_1^r[k+1,\,j+1], T_2^r[k+1,j+1] + h, T_3^r[k+1,j+1]) \\ T_3[k,j] + \max\,(T_1^r[k+1,\,j+1], T_2^r[k+1,j+1], T_3^r[k+1,j+1] + h) \end{cases}$$

The reason for adding h when combining $T_2[k, j]$ and $T_2{}^r[k+1, j+1]$ or when combining $T_3[k, j]$ and $T_3{}^r[k+1, j+1]$ is to avoid charging a gap opening penalty twice, once at the beginning and once at the end of a maximal sequence of gaps. Let $T[k, j]$ denote the maximum of $T_1[k,j]$, $T_2[k,j]$, and $T_3[k,j]$, and let $T^r[k + 1, j + 1]$ denote the maximum of $T_1{}^r[k + 1, j + 1]$, $T_2{}^r[k + 1, j + 1]$, and $T_3{}^r[k + 1, j + 1]$. The above equation can be simplified to

$$\max \begin{cases} T[k,j] + T^r[k+1,j+1] \\ T_2[k,j] + T_2^r[k+1,j+1] + h \\ T_3[k,j] + T_3^r[k+1,j+1] + h \end{cases}$$

Once the partitioning of an optimal alignment with respect to the middle of sequence A is found, this procedure is applied recursively to each partition. The recursive decomposition is continued until one of the sequences has a single character, which is then solved directly. This leads to the recurrence

$$t(m,n) = O(mn) + t\left(\lfloor \tfrac{m}{2} \rfloor, j\right) + t\left(\lceil \tfrac{m}{2} \rceil, n - j\right)$$

where $t(k, j)$ denotes the run-time for aligning two sequences of lengths k and j, respectively. Solving the recurrence shows that the run-time is $O(mn)$.

Hirshberg's strategy greatly reduces the space required for aligning sequences, making it feasible to perform alignments on very large sequences. Moreover, this strategy confers great practical benefit even for modest-sized sequences because the entire space required may fit in cache memory. While this technique resolves the space problem, the quadratic run-time poses a problem for aligning very large sequences or for carrying out a large number of alignments on short sequences, as is required in many applications. Asymptotically faster sequence alignment algorithms that improve run-time complexity by a log factor have been designed [19, 68]. However, their practical benefits are unclear, and they are rarely used by practitioners.

In most cases, one is interested in an alignment only if a "good" alignment exists, i.e., if the sequences exhibit homology. Consider two sequences of equal length. The ideal score for aligning these sequences occurs when the sequences are identical, yielding a match in every position of the alignment. The quality of an alignment can be measured by its score as a percentage of the ideal score. For simplicity, assume that each match is rewarded by the same score, and assume also a constant gap penalty function, where each gap position is penalized by the same amount. Consider a band in the dynamic programming table around the main diagonal consisting of k diagonals above and below it. Any solution that crosses this k-*band* must have at least $k + 1$ gaps in either sequence and has to miss at least that many matches, limiting the maximum score possible to no more than $(1 - \frac{3k-1}{n})$ fraction of the ideal score. If we are interested in an optimal alignment only if the score is above a certain threshold percentage, the threshold can be used to compute the value of k. For example, if 90% is desired, k can be chosen to be approximately $\frac{n}{30}$. The search space can then be limited to a band of this size without loss of optimal solution if its score is higher than the threshold. The run-time is reduced to $O(kn)$. Such limits can be established for more elaborate scoring schemes and for aligning sequences of different lengths. For a more clever scheme that operates in $O(kn)$ time without a predetermined threshold by using trial and error on k with exponentially doubling values, see [29].

Local Alignments

Given two sequences A and B, the local alignment problem is to find a subsequence of A and a corresponding subsequence of B that exhibit significant homology. Algorithmically, it makes sense to study global alignments first, but the types of alignments used predominantly by biologists are local alignments. Normally, a homologous sequence that is being sought may be a part of a larger DNA sequence, in which case local alignment must be used. In addition, there are several problems that require local alignments. For instance, conserved motifs in protein sequences often indicate structural similarity and functional similarity. When comparing two versions of a conserved gene across species, it is sufficient for the parts of the gene (*exons*) that code for protein to be homologous.

The local alignment problem is computationally modeled as follows: A local alignment between A and B is a global alignment between a subsequence of A and a subsequence of B, scored as presented before. The local alignment problem between sequences A and B is to find an alignment between a subsequence of A and a subsequence of B that results in the highest possible score over all such possible alignments and subsequences [87, 89]. As in the case of global alignments, this problem can be solved using dynamic programming. As before, tables T_1, T_2, and T_3 are created, but with the following difference: An entry $[i, j]$ in each table is used to store the highest score of an alignment between a suffix of $a_1 a_2 \ldots a_i$ and a suffix of $b_1 b_2 \ldots b_j$, with the same restriction on matching a_i and b_j as before. Alignment of empty suffixes is valid in T_1, and is assigned a score of 0. Therefore, Equation (1) is modified in the following way, and Equations (2) and (3) remain the same.

$$T_1[i,j] = f(a_i, b_j) + \max \begin{cases} T_1[i-1, j-1] \\ T_2[i-1, j-1] \\ T_3[i-1, j-1] \\ 0 \end{cases}$$

The maximum score in T_1 is the optimal score. An optimal alignment is retrieved by performing a traceback from a maximum entry in T_1 until a score of 0 is reached. Thus, the local alignment problem can also be solved in $O(mn)$ time.

It is difficult to apply Hirschberg's method to this algorithm to achieve a reduction in space. The following technique was invented by Huang [45] to facilitate space reduction. The algorithm consists of three steps:

1. Compute the optimal local alignment score as before, but only keep track of a largest entry and its position ($[i, j]$) as the tables are filled. Rows are discarded as soon as they are used in computing other rows to save space. This identifies the end of an optimal local alignment.

2. Run a global alignment algorithm on $a_i a_{i-1} \ldots a_1$ and $b_j b_{j-1} \ldots b_1$ to locate a largest entry, which corresponds to the beginning ($[k, l]$) of a subsequence alignment that ends at $[i, j]$. Once again, discard rows as soon as they are no longer needed and remember a largest entry seen so far. This identifies the beginning of an optimal local alignment whose end is discovered in step (1).

3. Run Hirschberg's space-saving global alignment algorithm between subsequences $a_k a_{k+1} \ldots a_i$ and $b_l b_{l+1} \ldots b_j$.

Alignments are one of the most thoroughly studied problem areas in computational biology, dating back to the 1970 introduction of the first global alignment algorithm by Needleman and Wunsch in the context of protein sequence homology [77]. A further study of sequence alignment algorithms can be conducted by referring to the classic text of Sankoff and Kruskal [85]. A good portion of several recent texts in computational biology are devoted to the study of alignment algorithms [22, 37, 71, 81, 87, 96]. Nevertheless, alignments continue to be an active area of research. An important problem area that is not covered here is that of multiple sequence alignments. While pairwise sequence alignments are a fundamental tool used in many computational genomics applications, multiple sequence alignments of a family of related proteins to infer conserved motifs is perhaps the most prevalent direct use of alignments by molecular biologists. Even within pairwise alignments, there are a number of more complex problems, including spliced alignments [66], syntenic alignments [47], and DNA–protein alignments [34, 49, 59, 99]. The sensitivity of an optimal alignment to the particular choice of parameter values used is studied as parametric sequence alignments [27, 38, 78]. To enable fast pairwise alignments for very large sequences, parallel methods have been developed [7, 23, 44, 62, 83].

3.2   Exact Matches

Another standard tool used in computational genomics applications is the identification of exact matching substrings between sequences. Due to evolutionary mechanisms that alter biomolecular sequences and errors introduced by experimental processes, one is rarely interested in exact matches as an end in themselves. Exact matches play a role because they are typically fast—requiring linear time as opposed to the quadratic time of alignment algorithms. As an example, consider the task of finding good local alignments between a query sequence and a database consisting of hundreds of thousands of sequences. It is computationally expensive to do as many pairwise local alignments. If we are interested in a pairwise alignment only if it exhibits significant homology, such an alignment should also contain regions of exact matches. For instance, if an aligning region of 100 *bp* length contains at most four positions of difference, there should be at least an exact match of length 20 in this region. Exact matches can be used as a filter to eliminate large number of pairs that would not yield a good local alignment by performing alignments only on pairs that have an exact matching region larger than a determined threshold. It is in this spirit that many problems related to exact matches find applications in bioinformatics. Below, we provide a brief introduction to three data structures frequently used in computational genomics.

Lookup Tables

A lookup table is a simple data structure that keeps track of the positions of occurrences of substrings of a prespecified length in one or more strings. Lookup tables are used in a number of important bioinformatic tools, including such popular programs as BLAST [4, 5] for database searches and CAP3 [48] for genome assembly.

Let Σ denote the alphabet, and let w denote a prespecified length. The lookup table is an array LT of size $|\Sigma|^w$, corresponding to the $|\Sigma|^w$ possible substrings of length w. Let $f : \Sigma \rightarrow \{0, 1, \dots |\Sigma| - 1\}$ be the one-to-one function such that $f(c) = j - 1$ if c is the jth lexicographically smallest character. For the purpose of the lookup table, any arbitrary ordering of the characters can be taken as lexicographic ordering. Using f, a substring of length w can be treated as a w-digit number in a base $|\Sigma|$ system and converted to its decimal equivalent. We use the notation $F(\alpha)$ to denote the decimal number corresponding to a w-long substring α.

Each entry in the lookup table LT points to a linked list of specific locations within the input set of strings where the substring corresponding to the index for the entry occurs. Let s be a string of length n. It is easy to construct the lookup table for s in $O\left(|\Sigma|^w + n\right)$ time. First, create and initialize each entry to a null list in $O\left(|\Sigma|^w\right)$ time. Then insert substrings one at a time. First compute *index* = $F(s[1..w])$ in $O(w)$ time. Insert the position 1 in the linked list corresponding to $LT[index]$. Using the identity

$$F(s[k+1\dots k+w+1]) = (F(s[k\dots k+w]) - f(s[k])|\Sigma|^{w-1}) \times |\Sigma| + f(s_{k+w+1})$$

$F(s[k+1..k+w+1])$ can be computed from $F(s[k..k+w])$ in $O(1)$ time. Since each starting position $1\dots n - w + 1$ occurs in a linked list, the total size of all linked lists is $O(n)$ (typically $n >> w$). Thus, the size of the lookup table data structure is $O\left(|\Sigma|^w + n\right)$. The lookup table can be easily generalized to a set of strings. Let $S = \{s_1, s_2, \dots, s_k\}$ be a set of k strings of total length N. To create the corresponding lookup table, substrings from each of the strings are inserted in turn. A location in a linked list now consists of a pair giving the string number and the position of the substring within the string. The space and run-time required for constructing the lookup table is $O\left(|\Sigma|^w + N\right)$.

A lookup table is conceptually a very simple data structure to understand and implement. Once the lookup table for a database of strings is available, given a query string of length w, all occurrences of it in the database can be retrieved in

$O(w + k)$ time, where k is the number of occurrences. The main problem with this data structure is its dependence on an arbitrary predefined substring of length w. If the query string is of length $l > w$, the lookup table does not provide an efficient way of retrieving all occurrences of the query string in the database. Nevertheless, lookup tables are widely used in bioinformatics due to their simplicity and ease of use.

Suffix Trees and Suffix Arrays

Suffix trees and suffix arrays are versatile data structures fundamental to string processing applications. Let s' denote a string over the alphabet Σ. Let $\$ \notin \Sigma$ be a unique termination character, and $s = s' \$$ be the string resulting from appending $\$$ to s'. We use the following notation: $|s|$ denotes the size of s, $s[i]$ denotes the ith character of s, and $s[i..j]$ denotes the substring $s[i]s[i + 1] ... s[j]$. Let $suff_i = s[i]s[i + 1] ... s[|s|]$ be the suffix of s starting at i^{th} position.

The suffix tree of s, denoted $ST(s)$ or simply ST, is a compacted tree of all suffixes of string s. Let $|s| = n$. It has the following properties:
1. The tree has n leaves, labeled $1 ... n$, one corresponding to each suffix of s.
2. Each internal node has at least two children.
3. Each edge in the tree is labeled with a substring of s.
4. The concatenation of edge labels from the root to the leaf labeled i is $suff_i$.
5. The labels of the edges connecting a node with its children start with different characters.

The paths from the root to the leaves corresponding to the suffixes $suff_i$ and $suff_j$ coincide up to their longest common prefix, at which point they bifurcate. If a suffix of the string is a prefix of another, longer suffix, the shorter suffix must end in an internal node instead of a leaf, as desired. It is to avoid this possibility that the unique termination character is added to the end of the string. Keeping this in mind, we use the notation $ST(s')$ to denote the suffix tree of the string obtained by appending $\$$ to s'. Throughout this chapter, "$\$$" is taken to be the lexicographically smallest character.

Since each internal node has at least two children, an n-leaf suffix tree has at most $n - 1$ internal nodes. Because of property (5), the maximum number of children per node is bounded by $|\Sigma| + 1$. Except for the edge labels, the size of the tree is $O(n)$. In order to allow a linear space representation of the tree, each edge label is represented by a pair of integers denoting the starting and ending positions, respectively, of the substring describing the edge label. If the edge lable corresponds to a repeat substring, the indices corresponding to any occurrence of the substring may be used. The suffix tree of the string *mississippi* is shown in Figure 21.2. For convenience of understanding, we show the actual edge labels.

Let v be a node in the suffix tree. Let *path-label(v)* denote the concatenation of edge labels along the path from root to node v. Let *string-depth(v)* denote the length of *path-label(v)*. To differentiate this with the usual notion of depth, we use the term *tree-depth* of a node to denote the number of edges on the path from root to the node. Note that the length of the longest common prefix between two suffixes is the string depth of the lowest common ancestor of the leaf nodes corresponding to the suffixes. A repeat substring of string S is *right-maximal* if there are two occurrences of the substring that are succeeded by different characters in

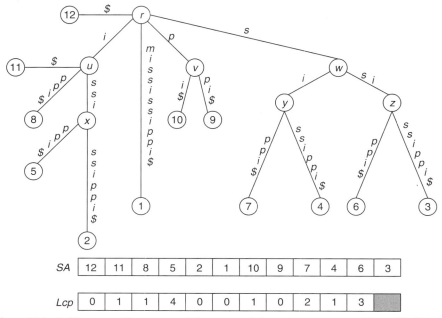

SA | 12 | 11 | 8 | 5 | 2 | 1 | 10 | 9 | 7 | 4 | 6 | 3 |

Lcp | 0 | 1 | 1 | 4 | 0 | 0 | 1 | 0 | 2 | 1 | 3 | |

Figure 21.2. Suffix tree, suffix array, and *Lcp* array of the string *mississippi*. The suffix links in the tree are given by $x \to z \to y \to u \to r, v \to r$, and $w \to r$.

the string. The path label of each internal node in the suffix tree corresponds to a right-maximal repeat substring and vice versa.

Suffix trees can be generalized to multiple strings. The generalized suffix tree of a set of strings $S = \{s_1, s_2,..., s_k\}$, denoted $GST(S)$ or simply GST, is a compacted tree of all suffixes of each string in S. We assume that the unique termination character $ is appended to the end of each string. A leaf label now consists of a pair of integers (i, j), where i denotes the suffix from string s_i and j denotes the starting position of the suffix in s_i. Similarly, an edge label in a GST is a substring of one of the strings. It is represented by a triplet of integers (i, j, l), where i denotes the string number and j and l denote the starting and ending positions of the substring in s_i, respectively. For convenience of understanding, we will continue to show the actual edge labels. Note that two strings may have identical suffixes. This situation is compensated for by allowing leaves in the tree to have multiple labels. If a leaf is multiply labeled, each suffix should come from a different string. If N is the total number of characters of all strings in S, the GST has at most N leaf nodes and takes up $O(N)$ space.

Suffix trees are useful in solving many problems involving exact matching in optimal run-time bounds. Moreover, in many cases, the algorithms are very simple to design and understand. For example, consider the problem of determining if a pattern P occurs in text T over a constant-sized alphabet. Note that if P occurs starting from position i in T, then P is a prefix of $suff_i$ in T. Thus, P occurs in T if and only if P matches an initial part of a path from root to a leaf in $ST(T)$.

Traversing from the root matching characters in P, this can be determined in $O(|P|)$ time, independent of T's length. As another application, consider the problem of finding a longest common substring of a pair of strings. Once the *GST* of the two strings is constructed, the path-label of an internal node with the largest string depth that contains at least one leaf from each string is the answer.

Suffix trees were invented by Weiner [97], who also presented a linear time algorithm to construct them for a constant-sized alphabet. A more space-economical linear-time construction algorithm is given by McCreight [69], and a linear-time online construction algorithm was invented by Ukkonen [94]. A unified view of these three suffix tree construction algorithms can be found in [33]. Farach [25] presented the first linear-time algorithm for strings over integer alphabets. The construction complexity for various types of alphabets is explored in [26].

The space requirement of suffix trees is a cause for concern in many large-scale applications. Manber and Myers [67] introduced suffix arrays as a space-efficient alternative to suffix trees. The suffix array of a string $s = s'\$$, denoted $SA(s)$ or simply SA, is a lexicographically sorted array of all suffixes of s. Each suffix is represented by its starting position in s. $SA[i] = j$ iff $suff_j$ is the ith lexicographically smallest suffix of s. The suffix array is often used in conjunction with an array termed the *Lcp* array, : $Lcp[i]$ contains the length of the longest common prefix between the suffix in $SA[i]$ and $SA[i + 1]$. The suffix and *Lcp* arrays of the string *mississippi* are shown in Figure 21.2. Suffix arrays can also be generalized to multiple strings to contain the sorted order of all suffixes of a set of strings (see Figure 21.3). For linear-time suffix array construction algorithms, see [55, 58]. Techniques for using suffix arrays as a substitute for suffix trees can be found in [1]. Further space reduction can be achieved by the use of compressed suffix trees and suffix arrays and other data structures [28, 36].

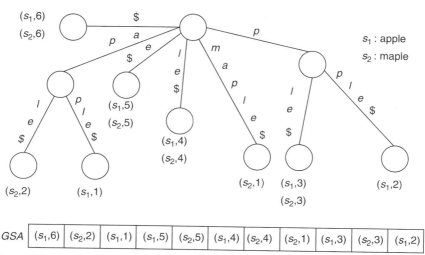

Figure 21.3. Generalized suffix tree and generalized suffix array of strings *apple* and *maple*.

4   APPLICATIONS

4.1   Database Search

Perhaps the most frequently used bioinformatic application is that of searching a database of sequences for homology to a given query sequence. When a new sequence is obtained in the laboratory, the first step in understanding the sequence is often to carry out a database search against as many known sequences as possible. This is important because sequence homology very often translates into functional similarity and immediately provides a way of understanding the newly obtained sequence. To facilitate such searches, large database collections have been developed that include various types of DNA and protein sequences ranging from gene and protein sequences to entire genomes. The most comprehensive such repository in the United States is maintained at the National Center for Biotechnology Information (NCBI; part of National Institutes of Health (NIH)). They have also developed a suite of database search programs commonly known as BLAST, the Basic Local Alignment Search Tool [4, 5]. This collection of programs constitutes the bioinformatic tools most commonly used by molecular biologists. These programs are engineered for speed and employ complex statistics to determine and output the statistical relevance of the generated alignments. The underlying algorithms are not necessarily perfect or optimal. Although we make some BLAST-specific references in some cases, the treatment provided here is more in terms of the issues involved in developing a search program and some computational ways of addressing them.

In principle, a local alignment query can be answered by running a local alignment algorithm on the query sequence and on each of the sequences in the database. The total run-time of such a naive algorithm is proportional to the product of the query sequence length and database size, and is clearly prohibitive and wasteful. Significant savings are realized by first focusing on identifying database sequences that share short exact matching regions with the query, and then processing only such sequences further. We begin with a brief description of the scoring methods employed in practice.

Scoring Schemes

The alignment scoring schemes presented so far relied on simple reward or penalty based on match or mismatch, respectively. In practice, elaborate scoring schemes are constructed to reflect the realities of evolutionary manipulations or functional similarities which the generated alignments are expected to capture. These are developed in the context of aligning protein sequences [3] and are applied to DNA sequence comparison in [90]. Recall that there are twenty different amino acid residues constituting protein sequences. Rather than use a simple match score and mismatch penalty, a symmetric 20×20 matrix is defined to capture the appropriate scores for every possible pair of amino acid residues that may be part of an alignment. The rationale for individualized scores come from preferential substitution of certain types of amino acids. For instance, six of the twenty amino acids are hydrophobic, and substituting one for another is likely to still preserve the protein function. Thus, a high score is awarded for such a substitution, in contrast to when a hydrophilic amino acid is substituted for a hydrophobic one. The most commonly used scoring matrices are the PAM [20] and BLOSUM [42] matrices.

Dayhoff introduced the notion of <u>P</u>ercent <u>A</u>ccepted <u>M</u>utation (PAM) to quantify evolutionary changes within protein sequences. A PAM unit is the amount of evolution that will, on average, change 1% of the amino acids within a protein sequence. A 20×20 transition probability matrix M is defined such that $M[i, j]$ captures the probability of amino acid i changing to amino acid j within 1 PAM evolutionary distance. Longer evolutionary distance probabilities can be determined by computing an appropriate exponent of the matrix—M^{100} gives the matrix for 100 units etc. The score for a PAMk matrix is defined by PAM$k[i, j]$ $= 10 \log \frac{M^k[i,j]}{p_j}$, where p_j is the probability of random occurrence of amino acid j. Smaller evolutionary distances are used for finding short, strong local alignments, while longer evolutionary distances are used for detecting weak, long spanning alignments.

The BLOSUM matrices, short for <u>Blo</u>ck <u>S</u>ubstitution <u>M</u>atrices, are constructed based on local multiple sequence alignments of protein sequences from a related family. BLOSUM matrices are based on the minimum percentage identity of the aligned protein sequences used in deriving them – for instance, the standard BLOSUM62 matrix corresponds to alignments exhibiting at least 62% identity. Thus, larger numbered matrices are used to align closely related sequences and smaller numbered matrices are used for more distantly related ones. Scores in a BLOSUM matrix are log-odds scores measuring the logarithm of the ratio of the likelihood of two amino acids appearing in an alignment on purpose and the likelihood of the two amino acids appearing by chance. A score in a BLOSUM matrix B is defined as

$$B[i,j] = \frac{1}{\lambda} \log \frac{p_{ij}}{f_i f_j}$$

where p_{ij} is the probability of finding amino acids i and j aligned in a homologous alignment, and f_i and f_j denote the probability of occurrence of i and j, respectively, in protein sequences. The scaling factor λ is used for convenience to generate scores that can be conveniently rounded off to integers. The BLOSUM62 matrix is the default matrix used by the BLAST suite of programs, and is shown in Table 21.2.

As for gaps, affine gap penalty functions are used because insertion or deletion of a subsequence is evolutionarily more likely than several consecutive individual base mutations. By using matrices and gap penalty functions derived either directly, based on evolutionary processes, or indirectly, based on knowledge of what types of alignments are biologically satisfactory, it is expected that the alignments generated using computer algorithms reflect biological reality.

Finding exact matches

The first step in query processing is to find database sequences that share an exact matching subsequence with the query sequence. For convenience, the programs designed often look for matches of a fixed length. For instance, BLAST uses a length of 11 for DNA alignments and a length of 3 for protein alignments. When

Table 21.2. The BLOSUM62 matrix.

	A	R	N	D	C	Q	E	G	H	I	L	K	M	F	P	S	T	W	Y	V
A	4	-1	-2	-2	0	-1	-1	0	-2	-1	-1	-1	-1	-2	-1	1	0	-3	-2	0
R	-1	5	0	-2	-3	1	0	-2	0	-3	-2	2	-1	-3	-2	-1	-1	-3	-2	-3
N	-2	0	6	1	-3	0	0	0	1	-3	-3	0	-2	-3	-2	1	0	-4	-2	-3
D	-2	-2	1	6	-3	0	2	-1	-1	-3	-4	-1	-3	-3	-1	0	-1	-4	-3	-3
C	0	-3	-3	-3	9	-3	-4	-3	-3	-1	-1	-3	-1	-2	-3	-1	-1	-2	-2	-1
Q	-1	1	0	0	-3	5	2	-2	0	-3	-2	1	0	-3	-1	0	-1	-2	-1	-2
E	-1	0	0	2	-4	2	5	-2	0	-3	-3	1	-2	-3	-1	0	-1	-3	-2	-2
G	0	-2	0	-1	-3	-2	-2	6	-2	-4	-4	-2	-3	-3	-2	0	-2	-2	-3	-3
H	-2	0	1	-1	-3	0	0	-2	8	-3	-3	-1	-2	-1	-2	-1	-2	-2	2	-3
I	-1	-3	-3	-3	-1	-3	-3	-4	-3	4	2	-3	1	0	-3	-2	-1	-3	-1	3
L	-1	-2	-3	-4	-1	-2	-3	-4	-3	2	4	-2	2	0	-3	-2	-1	-2	-1	1
K	-1	2	0	-1	-3	1	1	-2	-1	-3	-2	5	-1	-3	-1	0	-1	-3	-2	-2
M	-1	-1	-2	-3	-1	0	-2	-3	-2	1	2	-1	5	0	-2	-1	-1	-1	-1	1
F	-2	-3	-3	-3	-2	-3	-3	-3	-1	0	0	-3	0	6	-4	-2	-2	1	3	-1
P	-1	-2	-2	-1	-3	-1	-1	-2	-2	-3	-3	-1	-2	-4	7	-1	-1	-4	-3	-2
S	1	-1	1	0	-1	0	0	0	-1	-2	-2	0	-1	-2	-1	4	1	-3	-2	-2
T	0	-1	0	-1	-1	-1	-1	-2	-2	-1	-1	-1	-1	-2	-1	1	5	-2	-2	0
W	-3	-3	-4	-4	-2	-2	-3	-2	-2	-3	-2	-3	-1	1	-4	-3	-2	11	2	-3
Y	-2	-2	-2	-3	-2	-1	-2	-3	2	-1	-1	-2	-1	3	-3	-2	-2	2	7	-1
V	0	-3	-3	-3	-1	-2	-2	-3	-3	3	1	-2	1	-1	-2	-2	0	-3	-1	4

such an exact length is used (say, w), a lookup table provides a natural and convenient way to find the matches. The lookup table is constructed to index all substrings of length w occurring in database sequences and stored a priori. When a query is issued, all w-length substrings of it are extracted. For each substring, the lookup table entry indexed by it immediately points to the database sequences that contain this substring. Note that in a purely random sequence, the chance of finding a DNA sequence of length 11 is 1 in $4^{11} > 4 \times 10^6$, and the chance of finding an amino acid sequence of length 3 is 1 in $20^3 = 8,000$. In the protein-to-protein version of BLAST, the program does not look for exact matches but rather identifies substrings that may be different than the query substring as long as their nongapped alignment has a score above a specified threshold, as per the amino acid substitution matrix used. In addition, BLAST avoids certain substrings that are known to occur commonly, but the user has the option to request that this filter be turned off.

Generating Alignments

Once a subset of database sequences is identified using exact matches as above, an alignment of each sequence with the query sequence is generated and displayed. This can be done by using full-scale dynamic programming, as explained earlier. In practice, the alignment is obtained by anchoring it at the matching region found and extending it in either direction. As a practical heuristic, the alignment is not continued so as to explore all options, but is stopped once the score falls off a certain amount from the peak score seen.

4.2   Genome Sequencing

Genome sequencing refers to the deciphering of the exact order of nucleotides that make up the genome of an organism. Since the genome contains all the genes of the organism along with promoter and enhancer sequences that play critical roles in the expression and amount of expression of genes, the genome of an organism servers as a blueprint for what constitutes the species itself. Knowledge of the genome sequence serves as a starting point for many exciting research challenges – determining genes and their locations and structures, understanding genes involved in complex traits and genetically inherited diseases, gene regulation studies, genome organization and chromosomal structure and organization studies, finding evolutionary conservation and genome evolution mechanisms, etc. Such fundamental understanding can lead to high-impact applied research in genetically engineering plants to produce desirable traits and in designing drugs targeting genes whose malfunction causes diseases. Over the past one and a half decades, concerted research efforts and significant financial resources directed towards genome sequencing have led to the sequencing of many genomes, starting from the *Haemophilus influenzae* genome sequenced in 1995 [30] to the more recent sequencing of the complex human and mouse genomes [16, 17, 95]. At present, the complete genomes of over 1,000 viruses and over 100 microbes are known. *Arabidopsis thaliana* is the first plant genome to be sequenced, rice genome sequencing is at an advanced stage, and sequencing of the maize genome is currently under way.

The basic underlying technology facilitating genome sequencing is the DNA sequencing methodology developed by Sanger et al. [84]. This method allows laboratory sequencing of a DNA molecule of length about 500 *bp*. However, even bacterial genomes are about 3 to 4 order of magnitudes larger, and the genomes of higher organisms such as human and mouse are about 7 orders of magnitude larger. To sequence a large target DNA molecule, a sufficient number of smaller overlapping fragments of sequenceable size are derived from it and independently sequenced. Once the fragments are sequenced, overlaps are used to computationally assemble the target DNA sequence. This process is called the *shotgun sequencing* approach, and the corresponding computational problem is called *fragment assembly*. In the whole-genome shotgun approach, the target DNA is the entire genome itself. Another alternative is to partition the genome into large DNA sequences of a size on the order of 100, 000 *bp* whose locations along the genome are known from techniques such as physical mapping. Each of these large DNA sequences is then deciphered using the shotgun sequencing approach. While whole-genome shotgun sequencing is quicker, it is computationally more challenging to perform whole-genome assembly than to assemble a few hundred thousand base-pair-long target sequences. However, such whole-genome shotgun assemblies have been carried out for the human and the mouse. For the remainder of this section, we focus on the fragment assembly problem.

FRAGMENT ASSEMBLY

Consider a target DNA sequence to be assembled using the shotgun sequencing approach. We assume that a large number of copies of the same target sequence are available (either as samples or via cloning methods using bacterial artificial chromosomes). Copies of the target sequence are sheared in segments of a defined length and cloned into a plasmid vector for sequencing. Plasmids are circular DNA molecules that contain genes conferring antibiotic resistance and a pair of promoter sequences flanking a site where a DNA sequence can be inserted for replication. The sheared segments are inserted into plasmids and injected into bacteria, a process that allows them to be replicated along with bacteria. The bacteria can be killed using an antibiotic to extract copies of the inserts for sequencing. The inserts are typically a few thousand base pairs long, and about 500 *bp* from each end can be sequenced using Sanger's method. This not only gives two fragments from random locations of the target DNA sequence but also gives the approximate distance between their locations, since the size of the insert can be determined. These distances, known as *forward-reverse constraints* because the two fragments will be on different strands of the genome [48], are crucial in ensuring correct assembly.

Early work on developing the foundations of fragments assembly was carried out by Lander, Myers, Waterman, and others [57, 63, 73, 74]. A number of fragment assembly programs were developed [15, 35, 46, 48, 49, 79, 91]. Based on the experiences gained from these efforts, a new generation of assembly programs have recently been developed for handling whole-genome shotgun sequencing [12, 41, 47, 50, 72, 75]. The discussion provided here is not meant to represent any one particular program but rather is intended to give highlights of the issues involved in fragment assembly and some algorithmic means of handling them.

The primary information available to assemble fragments is the overlap between fragments that span intersecting intervals of the target sequence. DNA sequencing is not error free, but the error rates are quite tolerable, with high-quality sequencing averaging under 1%. Also, the error rates tend to be higher at either end of the sequenced fragment. If the target DNA sequence is not unique—for example, if genomes of several individuals are sampled for diversity—then there are naturally occurring variations that show up in fragments as well. Due to the presence of experimental errors and other differences, potential overlaps between fragments must be investigated using alignment algorithms. It is computationally infeasible to run them on every pair of fragments in a reasonable time frame. On the other hand, the differences are small enough that a good alignment should have exact matching regions. Thus, pairs of fragments that have sufficiently long exact matches are identified, and alignments are carried out only on such pairs. We term these pairs as *promising pairs*. Genomes are known to contain repeats – these range from a large number of copies of short repeating sequences to repeats or tandem repeats of genes that are present in multiple copies to boost the production of the corresponding protein. Repeats mislead assembly software since fragments coming from different parts of the genome may overlap. This is where forward-reverse constraints are useful. In the following, we describe in more detail the computational aspects of shotgun assembly.

Determining the number of fragments

Let $|G|$ denote the length of the target DNA sequence G, and let l denote the average size of a fragment. Let n denote the number of fragments to be derived. The coverage ratio x implied by this sampling is defined as $x = \frac{nl}{|G|}$. Intuitively, the coverage should be sufficient so that overlaps between fragments provide enough information for assembly. It is not possible to guarantee that the fragments will provide complete coverage of *G*. In that case, the fragment assembly program is expected to generate a number of *contigs* (contiguous subsequences) corresponding to the disjoint regions of *G* that can be deciphered from the fragments. Hence, *fragment assembly* is also known as *contig assembly*. Under the assumption that the starting position in *G* corresponding to a fragment is uniformly distributed over the length of *G*, the expected number of contigs and the fraction of *G* covered by the contigs can be estimated [63]. A coverage of 4.6 is enough to cover 99% of *G*, and a coverage of 6.9 is sufficient to cover 99.9% of *G*. As an example, the mouse genome shotgun sequence data consists of 33 million fragments. Assuming an average fragment length of 500 and a 3 billion *bp* genome, the coverage ratio works out to be 5.5. To quickly sequence such a large number of fragments, several high-throughput sequencing machines are typically used.

Finding promising pairs

In a random shotgun sequencing approach using a constant coverage factor (approximately 5–7 in practice), it is easy to see that the number of overlapping pairs of sequences is linear in *n*, provided that repeats do not have an overwhelming presence in the genome. Thus, identifying promising pairs based on exact matches potentially reduces the number of pairwise alignments from $O(n^2)$ to $O(n)$. Most assembly software programs use the lookup table data structure to identify pairs. First, a lookup table is constructed for all the input fragments and their complementary strands using a fixed substring length *w*. Each entry in the lookup table points to a list of fragments that contain a fixed *w*-long substring indexing the entry. Thus, every pair of fragments drawn from this list shares a *w*-long substring. Once a pair is identified, the detected *w*-long match is extended in either direction to uncover a maximal common substring. Some programs further extend the matching region by allowing a small number of errors. One problem with the lookup table is that a pair of fragments having a maximal common substring of $l > w$ bases will have $(l - w + 1)$ common substrings of length *w* within that region. This may cause multiple considerations of the same pair based on the same region, and it is important to find ways of avoiding this possibility. A more elegant strategy using suffix trees will be outlined later.

Aligning promising pairs

Each promising pair is aligned using a pairwise alignment algorithm. Two types of alignments – containments and suffix–prefix overlaps – are of interest, as shown in Figure 21.4. It is typical to reduce alignment time by first anchoring the alignment based on the already found matching region, and extending the alignment at both ends using banded dynamic programming. If one fragment is contained in the other, the shorter fragment need not be used for further overlap computation or in determining which other fragments will be in the same contig. It is, however, used in determining the contig sequence. Based on the alignment score, a measure of overlap strength can be associated with each aligned pair.

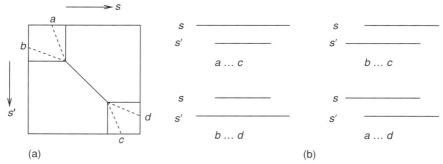

Figure 21.4. The figure shows the pairwise alignment strategy of extending a common substring match at both ends. Also shown are the four types of alignments of interest and their corresponding optimal paths in the dynamic programming table.

Creating contig layouts

This step consists of identifying all the fragments that determine a contig and the layout of these fragments with respect to the contig. One way to do this is to employ a greedy heuristic and consider all good overlaps in decreasing order of overlap strength. The next pair is added to the layout if it does not conflict with the layout determined so far. Forward-reverse constraints can be used to resolve conflicts as well. Another way to address contig layout is to use a graph model, with nodes representing fragments and edges representing good overlaps. Each connected component can then be a contig.

Assembly of contigs

Once the layout of each contig is determined, the exact sequence of the contig is computed by using alignments on the layout. Ideally, one would want a multiple sequence alignment of all the overlapping sequences, but this is time consuming. The pairwise alignments computed earlier can be used to draw the layout, and a simple scheme such as majority voting can be used to determine the base at each location of the contig.

Generating Scaffolds

A scaffold is an ordered collection of one or more contigs. Such an order between contigs can be determined with the help of any available forward-reverse constraints between a pair of fragments, one from each contig. This process allows ordering of some contigs, although there are no overlapping fragments connecting them, and also allows the determination of the approximate distance between the contigs. It is possible to use targeted techniques to fill the gaps later.

The above description is meant to be a generic description of the various phases in genome assembly and the computational challenges in each phase. Clearly, the diverse available genome assembly programs employ different strategies. A modular open-source assembler is currently being developed by the AMOS consortium (http://www.cs.jhu.edu/~genomics/AMOS).

4.3   Expressed Sequence Tag Clustering

Expressed Sequence Tags (ESTs) are DNA sequences experimentally derived from expressed portions of genes. They are obtained as follows: A cell mechanism makes a copy of a gene as an RNA molecule, called the *premessenger RNA*, or pre-mRNA for short. Genes are composed of alternating segments called *exons* and *introns*. The introns are spliced out from the pre-mRNA, and the resulting molecule is called *mRNA*. The mRNA essentially contains the coded recipe for manufacturing the corresponding protein. Molecular biologists collect mRNA samples and, using them as templates, synthetically manufacture DNA molecules. These are known as *complementary DNA molecules*, or *cDNAs* for short. Due to the limitations of the experimental processes involved and due to breakage of sequences in chemical reactions, several cDNAs of various lengths are obtained instead of just full-length cDNAs. Part of the cDNA fragments, of average length about 500–600 *bp*, can be sequenced with Sanger's method. The sequencing can be done from either end. The resulting sequences are called *ESTs* (Expressed Sequence Tags). For a simplified diagrammatic illustration, see Figure 21.5.

It is important to note that the genes sampled by ESTs and the frequency of sampling depend on the expression levels of the various genes. The EST clustering problem is to partition the ESTs according to the (unknown) gene source they come from. This process is useful in several ways, some of which are outlined below:

- *Gene Identification:* Genome sequencing is only a step towards the goal of identifying genes and finding the functions of the corresponding proteins. ESTs provide the necessary clues for gene identification.

- *Gene Expression Studies:* In EST sequencing, genes that are expressed more will result in more ESTs. Thus, the number of ESTs in a cluster indicates the level of expression of the corresponding gene.

- *Differential Gene Expression:* ESTs collected from various organelles of an organism (such as the leaf, root, and shoot of a plant) reveal the expression levels of genes in the respective organelles and provide clues to their possible function.

- *SNP Identification:* The same gene is present in slight variations, known as *alleles*, among different members of the same species. Many of these alleles differ in a single nucleotide, and some of these differences are the cause of genetic diseases. ESTs from multiple members of a species help identify such disease-causing single nucleotide polymorphisms, or SNPs.

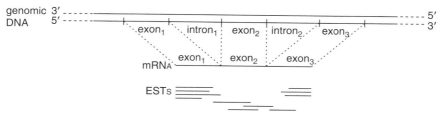

Figure 21.5. A simplified diagrammatic illustration of genomic DNA, mRNA, and ESTs.

• *Design of Microarrays:* Microarrays, also called DNA chips, are a recent discovery allowing gene expression studies of thousands of genes simultaneously. ESTs can be used in designing microarrays to detect the level of expression of the corresponding genes.

EST clustering is an actively pursued problem of current interest [18, 32, 39, 53, 60, 61, 64, 70, 82, 98]. ESTs are fairly inexpensive to collect and represent a major source of DNA sequence information currently available. A repository of ESTs collected from various organisms is maintained at the National Center for Biotechnology Information (http://www.nicb.nlm.nih.gov/dbEST).

If the genome of the organism is available and small, the individuals ESTs can be directly aligned with the genome to determine clustering. However, this situation is rarely the case. As with fragment assembly, the potential overlaps between ESTs from the same gene provide the primary information available for EST clustering. For this reason, fragment assembly software is often used for EST clustering, though there are some subtle differences between the two problems that need to be carefully addressed. One important difference is that ESTs do not sample the gene space uniformly at random, but rather the sampling rate is proportional to the gene expression. It is quite common to have a few very large clusters containing as many as 10% of the input ESTs and to have thousands of single EST clusters. Because of this nonuniform sampling, the number of overlapping pairs can be as high as $\Omega(n^2)$ and are observed to be such in practice. This overlap considerably slows down standard lookup table-based fragment assembly software when applied to EST clustering problems. Furthermore, the space required to store potential overlapping pairs or promising pairs is quadratic, limiting the effectiveness of the software to much smaller data sets.

A suffix tree-based solution can be designed to address these problems [52], and such a solution could be important even for genome assembly when the sampling is purposefully nonuniform [24]. The basic idea is to build a GST of all ESTs and their complementary strands. Common substrings between ESTs can be identified by shared paths in the suffix tree. However, the power of this method lies in directly identifying maximal common substrings and avoiding the generation of pairs based on parts of maximal common substrings. Moreover, the pairs can be generated in nonascending order of the maximal common substring length on an as-needed basis, without having to store any pairs generated so far. This approach will reduce the memory required from quadratic to linear. Below we outline the various steps in EST clustering based on this strategy.

ON-DEMAND PAIR GENERATION

Let the term *promising pair* refer to a pair of strings that have a maximal common substring of length at least equal to a threshold value ψ. The goal of the on-demand pair generation algorithm is to report promising pairs on-the-fly, in the nonincreasing order of maximal common substring length. A pair is generated as many times as the number of maximal substrings common to the pair. The algorithm operates on the following idea: If two strings share a maximal common substring α, then the leaves corresponding to the suffixes of the strings starting with α will be present in the subtree of the node with path-label α. Thus the algorithm can generate the pair at that node.

A substring α of a string is said to be *left-extensible* (alternatively, *right-extensible*) by character c if c is the character to the left (alternatively, right) of α in the string. If the substring is a prefix of the string, then it is said to be left-extensible by λ, the null character. Let *leaf-set*(v) denote the suffixes in the subtree under v. Based on the characters immediately preceding these suffixes, they are partition into five sets, $l_A(v)$, $l_C(v)$, $l_G(v)$, $l_T(v)$ and $l_\lambda(v)$, collectively referred to as *lsets*(v). The algorithm for generation of pairs is given in Figure 21.6. The nodes in GST with string-depth $\geq \psi$ are sorted in nonincreasing order of string depth and are processed in that order. The *lsets* at leaf nodes are computed directly from the leaf labels. The set of pairs generated at node v is denoted by P_v. If v is a leaf, a cartesian product of each of the *lsets* at v corresponding to A, C, G, T, λ with every other *lset* of v corresponding to a different character is computed. In addition, a cartesian product of $l_\lambda(v)$ with itself is computed. The union of these cartesian products is taken to be P_v. If v is an internal node, a cartesian product of each *lset* corresponding to A, C, G, T, λ of each child of v with every other *lset* corresponding to a different character in every other child node is computed. In addition, a cartesian product of the *lset* corresponding to λ of each child node with each of the *lsets* corresponding to λ of every other child node is computed.

Algorithm 1 *Pair Generation*

GeneratePairs
    1. Compute the string-depth of all nodes in the GST.
    2. Sort nodes with string-depth $\geq \psi$ in non-increasing order of string-depth.
    3. For each node v in that order
            IF v is a leaf THEN
                    ProcessLeaf (v)
            ELSE
                    ProcessInternalNode(v)

ProcessLeaf(Leaf: v)
    1. Compute

$$P_v = \cup_{(c_i, c_j)} l_{c_i}(v) \times l_{c_j}(v), \forall (c_i, c_j)\,\text{s.t.}, c_i < c_j \text{ or } c_i = c_j = \lambda$$

ProcessInternalNode(Internal Node: v)
    1. Compute

$$P_v = \cup_{(u_k, u_l)} \cup_{(c_i, c_j)} l_{c_i}(u_k) \times l_{c_j}(u_l), \forall (u_k, u_l), \forall (c_i, c_j)\,\text{s.t.},$$
$$1 \leq k\, l \leq m, c_i \neq c_j \text{ or } c_i = c_j = \lambda$$

    2. Create all *lsets* at v by computing:
        For each $c_i \in \Sigma \cup \{\lambda\}$ do

$$l_{c_i}(v) = \cup_{u_k} l_{c_i}(u_k), 1 \leq k \leq m$$

Figure 21.6. Algorithm for generation of promising pairs.

The union of these cartesian products is taken to be P_v. The *lset* for a particular character at v is obtaining by taking a union of the *lsets* for the same character at the children of v.

A pair generated at a node v is discarded if the string corresponding to the smaller EST *id* number is in complemented form. This avoids duplicates such as generating both (e_i, e_j) and ($ \bar e_i, \bar e_j $) or generating both $(e_i, \bar e_j)$ and $(\bar e_i, e_j)$ for some $1 \leq i, j \leq n$. Thus, without loss of generality, we denote a pair by (s, s'), where $s = e_i$ and s' is either e_j or $\bar e_j$ for some $i < j$. The relative orderings of the characters in $\Sigma \cup \{\lambda\}$ and the child nodes avoid generation of both (s, s') and (s', s) at the same node.

In summary, if v is a leaf,

$$P_v = \{(s, s') \mid s \in l_{c_i}(v), s' \in lc_j(v), c_i, c_j \in \Sigma \cup \{\lambda\}, ((c_i < c_j) \vee (c_i = c_j = \lambda))\}$$

and if v is an internal node,

$$P_v = (s, s') \big| s \in l_{c_i}(u_k), s' \in l_{c_i}(u_l), c_i, c_j \in \Sigma \cup \lambda, u_k < u_l, ((c_i \neq c_j) \vee (c_i = c_j = \lambda))\}$$

CLUSTERING STRATEGY

Consider a partition of the input ESTs into subsets (also called clusters) on which the following two standard operations are supported: *Find*(e_i) returns the cluster containing e_i, and *Union*(A, B) creates a new cluster combining the clusters A and B. These operations can be supported efficiently using a standard Union-Find algorithm [92]. To begin with, each EST is in a separate subset of the partition. At some point during the clustering, let (e_i, e_j) be the next EST pair generated by the on-demand pair generation algorithm. If *Find*$(e_i) = $ *Find*(e_j), the two ESTs are already in the same cluster and they need not be aligned. Otherwise, an alignment test is performed. If the test succeeds, the clusters containing e_i and e_j are merged. Otherwise, they are left as they were. This process is continued until all promising pairs are exhausted. Note that the number of union operations that can be performed is $O(n)$, while the number of pairs can be $\Omega(n^2)$. That means there are $O(n)$ pairs that can lead to the right answer, though one does not know a priori what these pairs would be. The order in which promising pairs are processed does not affect the outcome but does impact the alignment work performed. The least amount of work is performed when each alignment test is a success until the final set of clusters is formed. At this point, no new promising pairs generated will need to be aligned. Thus, based on the intuition that longer exact matches more likely lead to successful alignments, the particular order in which promising pairs are generated should bring enormous savings in execution time.

4.4   Comparative Genomics

Comparative genomics is the comparison and analysis of two or more genomes or of very large genomic fragments to gain insights into molecular biology and evolution. Comparative genomics is valuable because there is significant commonality between genomes of species that may appear very different on the surface. Moreover, coding sequences tend to be conserved in evolution, making comparative genomics a viable tool to discover coding sequences in a genome by merely comparing it with a genome of a related species and identifying the common parts. For instance, approximately 99% of human genes have a counterpart in mice. Based on a study of nearly 13,000 such genes, it has been found that the encoded proteins have a median amino-acid identity of 78.5% [14]. Learning about the subtle genomic differences between humans and mice is a starting point for understanding how these differences contribute to the vast differences between the two species (brain size, for example), and ultimately help us understand how genomes confer the distinctive properties of each species through these subtle differences.

Genome comparisons can be classified into three broad categories, depending on the relationships between the genomes being compared. In each case, a wealth of information can be gained about identifying key functional elements of the genome or subtle differences that have significant implications, some of which are highlighted below:

Individuals from the same species

A single nucleotide difference in a gene can cause a nonfunctional gene (i.e., no protein product) or give rise to a malfunctioning protein that could have serious consequences to health and tissue functioning. Such differences, known as *single nucleotide polymorphisms (SNPs)*, are the cause of genetically inherited diseases such as sickle cell anemia, cystic fibrosis, and breast cancer. They are also known to be responsible for striking hereditarily passed-on differences, including height, brain development and facial structure. Comparative genomics is a valuable tool to reveal SNPs, to help us understand the genetic basis for important diseases, and to serve as the foundation for developing treatments.

Closely related species or conserved regions across species

Closely related species such as different types of microbes can have remarkably different properties, and comparative genomics can help provide the clues that differentiate them. The United States Department of Energy has been supporting research into microbial genomes because of the ability of microbes to survive under extreme conditions of temperature, pressure, darkness, and even radiation. Understanding microbial genomes could enable far-reaching applications such as the cleanup of toxic waste and the development of biosensors. In the category of closely related species, we include species whose genomes are so closely related that a traditional alignment algorithm is capable of elucidating the genomic alignment, even though it may not be computationally advantageous to do so because of the sizes of the sequences. Certain genomic segments across more distantly related species may also have this property, where not only the genes are conserved but also the gene order is also conserved. Comparative genomics study of such regions, known as *syntenic regions*, are carried out between humans and mice [8, 13, 21, 47].

Relatively more distant species

Comparing the genomes of two species is not just a question of applying standard alignment algorithms to sequences much larger in scale. Although most genes may have counterparts across the two genomes, the order is not preserved on a global scale, which is a requirement for classical alignment algorithms to be useful. For instance, it is established that by breaking the human genome into approximately 150 pieces and rearranging the pieces, one can build a good approximation to the mouse genome. Genomic comparisons require taking into account such genomic rearrangements, which include differences in the number of repeats, reversals, translocations, fusions, and fissions of chromosomes [80]. Once such global alignment algorithms are developed and applied, alignments between syntenic blocks can be carried out.

Our discussion of computational methods for comparative genomics will follow the above-mentioned classification. We first describe how alignment algorithms can be extended to solve this problem when it is known that both genes and gene order are preserved. We then describe faster techniques for whole-genome alignments of closely related species.

Alignment-Based Methods

Consider the alignment of two large genomic sequences. If these are from different species, we expect that we are at least dealing with syntenic regions that contain orthologous genes in the same gene order. The order is important for an alignment algorithm to be useful. While the order is not necessary for a gene to play its role, evolution does tend to preserve gene order across these large blocks called syntenic regions. It is only when such an assumption is valid that a direct-alignment algorithm can be designed for genome comparisons.

Even when gene order is preserved, there are differences between a standard alignment and what is required for genomic comparisons. While the genes may be preserved, large intergenic regions may be different. Even when genes are conserved, this may largely apply only to coding regions. Since introns do not participate in the translation of a gene to its corresponding protein product, conservation of exons alone is sufficient to create a highly similar protein product. When aligning two large genomic sequences, it is important to focus on the alignment of regions of similarity and not to penalize for mismatching regions that should not be aligned in the first place. This process can be modeled as the problem of finding an ordered list of subsequences of one sequence that is highly similar to a corresponding ordered list of subsequences from the other sequence. We refer to this problem as the *syntenic alignment* problem.

The syntenic alignment problem can be formalized as follows: Let $A = a_1 a_2$ ... a_m and $B = b_1 b_2 ... b_n$ be two sequences. A subsequence A' of A is said to *precede* another subsequence A'' of A, written $A' \prec A''$, if the last character of A' occurs strictly before the first character of A'' in A. An ordered list of subsequences of A, $(A_1, A_2, ..., A_k)$ is called a *chain* if $A_1 \prec A_2 \prec ... A_k$. The syntenic alignment problem for sequences A and B is to find a chain $(A_1, A_2, ..., A_k)$ of subsequences in A and a chain $(B_1, B_2, ..., B_k)$ of subsequences in B such that the score

$$\left\{\sum_{i=1}^{k} score(A_i, B_i)\right\} - (k-1)^d$$

is maximized (see Figure 21.7).

The function $score(A_i, B_i)$ corresponds to the optimal score for the global alignment of A_i and B_i using scores for matches, penalties for mismatches, and an affine gap penalty function, as described earlier. The parameter d is a large penalty aimed at preventing alignment of short subsequences that occur by chance and not because of any biological significance. Intuitively, we are interested in finding an ordered list of matching subsequence pairs that correspond to conserved exons. One can think of the subsequence between A_i and A_{i+1} and the subsequence between B_i and B_{i+1} as an unmatched subsequence pair. The penalty d can be viewed as corresponding to an unmatched subsequence pair. For a small alphabet size, given a character in an unmatched subsequence, there is a high probability of finding the same character in the corresponding unmatched subsequence. In the absence of the penalty d, using these two characters as another matched subsequence pair would increase the score of the syntenic alignment. The penalty d serves to avoid declaring such irrelevant matching subsequences as part of the syntenic alignment, and its value should be chosen carefully by considering the length of the shortest exons that we expect. Setting d too low increases the chance of substrings, which are too short to be exons, to be considered as matching subsequences. Setting d too high prevents short matching exons from being recognized as matching subsequences.

Based on the problem definition, the syntenic alignment of two sequences $A = a_1 a_2 \ldots a_m$ and $B = b_1 b_2 \ldots b_n$ can be computed by dynamic programming. Basically, we compute the syntenic alignment between every prefix of A and every prefix of B. We compute four tables C, D, I, and H of size $(m+1) \times (n+1)$. Entry $[i,j]$ in each table corresponds to the optimal score of a syntenic alignment between $a_1 a_2 \ldots a_i$ and $b_1 b_2 \ldots b_j$, subject to the following conditions:

- In C, a_i is matched with b_j.

- In D, a_i is matched with a gap.

- In I, a gap is matched with b_j.

- In H, either a_i or b_j is part of an unmatched subsequence.

It follows from these definitions that the tables can be computed using the following recurrence equations:

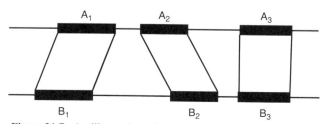

Figure 21.7. An illustration of the Syntenic alignment problem.

$$C[i,j] = f(a_i, b_j) + \max \begin{cases} C[i-1,j-1] \\ D[i-1,j-1] \\ I[i-1,j-1] \\ H[i-1,j-1] \end{cases}$$

$$D[i,j] = \max \begin{cases} C[i-1,j] - (g+h) \\ D[i-1,j] - g \\ I[i-1,j] - (g+h) \\ H[i-1,j] - (g+h) \end{cases}$$

$$I[i,j] = \max \begin{cases} C[i,j-1] - (g+h) \\ D[i,j-1] - (g+h) \\ I[i,j-1] - g \\ H[i,j-1] - (g+h) \end{cases}$$

$$H[i,j] = \max \begin{cases} C[i-1,j] - d \\ I[i-1,j] - d \\ C[i,j-1] - d \\ D[i,j-1] - d \\ H[i-1,j] \\ H[i,j-1] \end{cases}$$

Prior to computation, the top row and left column of each table should be initialized. In table H, the top row is initialized using the penalty d. The top row of I and the leftmost column of D are initialized using the affine gap penalty function. The rest of the initialization entries are set to $-\infty$. After the computation, the maximum value in $C[m, n]$, $D[m, n]$, $I[m, n]$, or $H[m, n]$ gives the optimal score. Using traceback, an optimal syntenic alignment can be reproduced.

Before computing the syntenic alignment, it is important to screen the input sequences for interspersed repeats and low-complexity subsequences using a program such as RepeatMasker [88]. Similar regions consisting of such subsequences are functionally less important than other matches but show strong sequence similarity. In the presence of repeats and low complexity subsequences, the alignment algorithm gives priority to aligning such sequences and may miss aligning the more important subsequences.

The main advantage of the alignment method is that it guarantees finding an optimal solution and is capable of detecting weak similarities. However, its quadratic run-time makes it difficult to apply this method for very large sequences. To alleviate this difficulty, Futamura et al. [31] parallelized the syntenic alignment algorithm. The program produced a syntenic alignment of a gene-rich region on human chromosome 12 (12p13; length 222, 930 bp; GenBank Accession U47924) with the corresponding syntenic region on mouse chromosome 6 (length 227, 538 bp; GenBank Accession AC002397) in about 24 minutes on a 64-processor Myrinet cluster with Pentium 1.26GHZ processors. This region contains 17 genes

[8], and most of the coding regions are identified by the program as 154 matching ordered subsequence pairs spanning 43, 445bp with an average identity of 79%.

Fast Genome Comparison Methods

A number of fast comparison algorithms have been developed for comparing very large-scale DNA sequences from closely related species or syntenic regions from more distantly related species [13, 21, 51, 86]. Generally, these methods perform fast identification of significant local similarities using exact matches. Then alignments are used to extend these similarities or to close gaps in alignments made up of only exact matches. Our presentation here closely follows the work of Delcher et al. [21], who developed the MUMmer program for aligning whole genomes.

MUMmer works on the assumption that long exact matching regions are part of the genomic alignment. This assumption is exploited by identifying unique maximal common substrings between the two sequences called MUMs (Maximum Unique Matches), using them to anchor the alignment, and then further exploring the regions between every pair of consecutive MUMs. The algorithm is composed of the following steps:

1. Fast identification of large MUMs using a suffix tree
2. Computing an ordered sequence of pairs of MUMs to anchor the alignment
3. Aligning regions between consecutive MUMs recursively by using shorter MUMs or dynamic programming-based tools

The first step is the identification of maximal unique matches. To this end, a generalized suffix tree of the two input sequences A and B is constructed in linear time. A maximal common substring that occurs only once in each input sequence corresponds to the path-label of an internal node that has exactly two leaf children, one from each of A and B. However, it is possible that a suffix of such a maximal common substring is also unique and corresponds to a node with similar properties. Recall that the path-label of an internal node in a suffix tree is already right maximal. To ensure that it is left maximal, one only needs to check to make sure that each suffix in the subtree of the node has a different previous character. Thus, a scan of the suffix tree to identify internal nodes with two leaf children and eliminate those that are not left maximal yields the MUMs in linear time. Only MUMs that are larger than a user-specified threshold length are identified to avoid anchoring the alignment on relatively short MUMs that may occur by coincidence.

It may not be possible to use all the MUMs so discovered in anchoring the alignment. A pair of MUMs may cross, allowing the inclusion of only one of them in any viable alignment. To identify a large set of MUMs that does not contain any such pairwise conflicts, the following method is used: the MUMs are first sorted according to their position in genomic sequence A and are labeled 1, 2, ... k in that order, where k is the number of MUMs. The same labeling is applied to the corresponding MUMs on genomic sequence B. A longest increasing subsequence of MUM along B is then sought. This can be solved by a variation of the Longest Increasing Subsequence (LIS) problem [37] that takes into account the lengths of the MUMs so that what is maximized is the total lengths of all the selected MUMs and not the number of MUMs. This can be done in $O(k \log k)$ time.

Once the alignment is anchored using the selected MUMs, one is left with the task of aligning the regions between every consecutive pair of MUMs. The chief advantage of this strategy is the quick decomposition of the original problem into several smaller subproblems. While this should considerably reduce the run-time even if each of the subproblems is addressed using an alignment algorithm such as syntenic alignment, further computational savings can be obtained by recursing on this strategy using shorter MUM threshold length. Also, certain special cases can be readily identified that can be treated separately. Three such special cases are identified here:

- Two MUM pairs separated by a single differing nucleotide – This is classified as a SNP.

- Two MUMs that are consecutive along one genome but are separated in the other – The subsequence separating the two MUMs is treated as an insert.

- Overlapping MUMs – If the intervals spanned by two MUMs along both genomes overlap, this is an indication of a tandem repeat (repeats that occur consecutively with no intervening sequences) separating the two MUMs. The genome that has fewer occurrences of the tandem repeats will restrict the lengths of the MUMs and causes the two flanking matching regions to be identified as two different MUMs.

Once the special cases are identified, the remaining gaps in alignment can be filled by using quadratic time alignment algorithms. If these regions are long enough, a recursive application of MUMs strategy can be applied while eventually closing the remaining gaps using alignment. This method should produce fairly accurate alignments in very short amounts of time. For example, Delcher et al. report alignment of the same human chromosome 12p13 and mouse chromosome 6 syntenic regions described earlier in just 30 seconds [21].

Genomic Rearrangements

The previous algorithms are useful in aligning very closely related genomes where gene order is largely preserved or syntenic regions across genomes within which gene order is preserved. To extend comparative genomics beyond that, computational modeling of genomic rearrangements is needed. Such rearrangements are useful in hypothesizing the relative evolutionary distance between two species and also in identifying syntenic regions that can be aligned using previously described methods. A simple way to model this problem is to consider each genome as consisting of essentially the same set of genes. Each gene is also given an orientation depending on the genomic strand on which it appears. This can be modeled by placing a plus sign in front of each gene that appears on one of the strands and choosing a minus sign for the genes appearing on the complementary strand. Genomic rearrangements are modeled as *inversions*, where inversion of a stretch of the genome is represented by reversing the sequence of genes contained in it and reversing the sign of each gene. The distance between the genomes is then measured as the minimum number of inversions required to convert one genome into the other. These important methods are not described here due to space limitations, largely because the underlying algorithms are different from the exact match and alignment-based methodologies that this chapter is focused on. The interested reader is referred to [9–11, 40, 54, 80, 93].

5 CONCLUSIONS AND FUTURE CHALLENGES

This chapter has aimed at providing a brief introduction to bioinformatics and conveying the flavor of research in computational genomics to readers with little or no familiarity with bioinformatics. The volume of research results that have accumulated so far in bioinformatics and the large number of researchers engaged in research in this area indicate that this field is no longer in its infancy. In fact, it is difficult to provide complete coverage of this area in a medium-sized textbook. The approach taken in this chapter has been to provide a bird's-eye view of computational genomics by looking at a number of challenging research problems in a holistic and integrated manner by focusing on the underlying fundamentals. It is hoped that this approach enabled the coverage of the material in reasonable depth within the scope of a chapter and provided enough understanding to spark the reader's curiosity. The large number of references provided should serve as a starting point for further investigation. For a fairly comprehensive treatment, including recent research directions in bioinformatics and computational biology, the reader is referred to [6].

Many computational challenges remain in bioinformatics, promising decades of interesting work for researchers in this area. Within computational genomics, some of the main challenges can be summarized as (1) sequencing the genomes of many more organisms, (2) understanding the genes and their structure and function within each organism, (3) developing capabilities to compare and analyze a large number of genomes collectively, (4) constructing evolutionary relationships between all known species, known as the *tree-of-life project*, (5) using gene expression studies to understand gene interactions, (6) inferring complex protein interaction pathways and networks, and (7) understanding gene regulatory behaviour as related to its impact on developmental genetics. Computational structure biology is another exciting area that is not covered in this chapter. Computational determination of protein structure from its amino acid sequence is often mentioned as the "holy grail" problem in bioinformatics. Finding sequences that fold into desired structures and understanding the mechanisms of protein–protein docking and protein–drug docking are considered vital to pharmaceutical research. Developing structure databases to enable the search for structural homologies is a difficult problem to address, but may well end up showing that current sequence-based alignment strategies are pursued for computational convenience. Remarkable discoveries await research in computational medicine. One promising area of research is personalized medicine, where an understanding of the complex relationships between the genetic composition of an individual and his or her tendency to develop diseases and response to drugs is expected to lead to the design of targeted treatments with tremendous health care benefits. Progress in solving many such challenges facing modern biology and medicine can only be made by interdisciplinary teams of researchers. Computation will remain an integral part of most potential discoveries and should provide exciting applied problems for computing researchers to work on for decades to come.

REFERENCES

[1] M.I. Abouelhoda, S. Kurtz, and E. Ohlebusch (2004): Replacing suffix trees with enhanced suffix arrays. *Journal of Discrete Algorithms*, *2*.

[2] B. Alberts, A. Hohnson, J. Lewis, M. Raff, K. Roberts, and P. Walter (2002): *Molecular Biology of the Cell*. Garland Science, New York, NY.

[3] S.F. Altschul (1991): Amino acid substitution matrices from an information theory perspective. *Journal of Molecular Biology*, *219*:555–565.

[4] S.F. Altschul, W. Gish, W. Miller, E.W. Myers, and D.J. Lipman (1990): Basic local alignment search tool. *Journal of Molecular Biology*, *215*(3), 403–410.

[5] S.F. Altschul, T.L. Madden, A.A. Schaffer, J. Zhang, Z. Zhang, W. Miller, and D.J. Lipman (1997): Gapped BLAST and PSI-BLAST: A new generation of protein database search programs. *Nucleic Acids Research*, *25*, 3389–3402.

[6] S. Aluru, (ed) (2005): *Handbook of Computational Molecular Biology*. CRC Press, Boca Raton, FL.

[7] S. Aluru, N. Futamura, and K. Mehrotra (2003): Parallel biological sequence comparison using prefix computations. *Journal of Parallel and Distributed Computing*, *63*(3), 264–272.

[8] M.A. Ansari-Lari, J.C. Oeltjen, S. Schwartz, Z. Zhang, D.M. Muzny, J. Lu, J.H. Gorrell, A.C. Chinault, J.W. Belmont, W. Miller, and R.A. Gibbs (1998): Comparative sequence analysis of a gene-rich cluster at human chromosome 12p13 and its syntenic region in mouse chromosome 6. *Genome Research*, *8*, 29–40.

[9] D.A. Bader, B. M.E. Moret, and M. Yan (2001): A linear-time algorithm for computing inversion distance between two signed permutations with an experimental study. *Journal of Computational Biology*, *8*(5), 483–491.

[10] V. Bafna and P.A. Pevzner (1995): Sorting by reversals: genome rearrangements in plant organelles and evolutionary history of X chromosome. *Molecular Biology and Evolution*, *12*, 239–246.

[11] V. Bafna and P.A. Pevzner (1996): Genome rearrangements and sorting by reversals. *SIAM Journal on Computing*, *25*(2), 272–289.

[12] S. Batzoglou, D. Jaffe, K. Stanley, J. Butler, et al. (2002): ARACHNE: A wholegenome shotgun assembler. *Genome Research*, *12*, 177–189.

[13] S. Batzoglou, L. Pachter, J.P. Mesirov, B. Berger, and E.S. Lander (2000): Human and mouse gene structure: comparative analysis and application to exon prediction. *Genome Research*, *10*, 950–958.

[14] M.S. Boguski (2002): Comparative genomics: the mouse that roared. *Nature*, *420*, 515–516.

[15] J.K. Bonfield, K. Smith, and R. Staden. (1995): A new DNA sequence assembly program. *Nucleic Acids Research*, *24*, 4992–2999.

[16] International Human Genome Sequencing Consortium (2001): Initial sequencing and analysis of the human genome. *Nature*, *409*, 860–921.

[17] Mouse Genome Sequencing Consortium (2002): Initial sequencing and comparative analysis of the mouse genome. *Nature*, *420*, 520–562.

[18] E. Coward, S. A. Haas, and M. Vingron. (2002): SpliceNest: visualizing gene structure and alternative splicing based on EST clusters. *Trends in Genetics*, *18*(1), 53–55.

[19] M. Crochemore, G.M. Landau, and Z. Ziv-Ukelson (2002): A subquadratic sequence alignment algorithm for unrestricted cost metrics. In *Proc. Symposium on Discrete Algorithms*, pp. 679–688.

[20] M.O. Dayhoff, R. Schwartz, and B.C. Orcutt (1978): *Atlas of Protein Sequence and Structure*, volume 5. A model of evolutionary change in proteins: matrices for detecting distant relationships, pp. 345–358. National Biomedical Research Foundation.

[21] A.L. Delcher, S. Kasif, R.D. Fleischmann, J. Peterson, O. While, and S.L. Salzberg (1999): Alignment of whole genomes. *Nucleic Acids Research*, 27, 228–233.

[22] R. Durbin, S.R. Eddy, A. Krogh, and G. Mitchison. *Biological Sequence Analysis: Probabilistic Models of Proteins and Nucleic Acids*.

[23] E.W. Edmiston, N.G. Core, J.H. Saltz, and R.M. Smith (1988): Parallel processing of biological sequence comparison algorithms. *International Journal of Parallel Programming*, 17(3), 259–275.

[24] S. Emrich, S. Aluru, Y. Fu, T. Wen, et al. (2004): A strategy for assembling the maize (*zea mays* L.) genome. *Bioinformatics*, 20, 140–147.

[25] M. Farach (1997): Optimal suffix tree construction with large alphabets. In *38th Annual Symposium on Foundations of Computer Science*, pp. 137–143. IEEE.

[26] M. Farach-Colton, P. Ferragina, and S. Muthukrishnan (2000): On the sorting-complexity of suffix tree construction. *Journal of the Association of Computing Machinery*, 47.

[27] D. Fernández-Baca, T. Seppalainen, and G. Slutzki (2002): Bounds for parametric sequence comparison. *Discrete Applied Mathematics*, 118, 181–198.

[28] P. Ferragina and G. Manzini (2000): Opportunistic data structures with applications. In *41th Annual Symposium on Foundations of Computer Science*, pp. 390–398. IEEE.

[29] J. Fickett (1984): Fast optimal alignment. *Nucleic Acids Research*, 12(1), 175–179.

[30] R.D. Fleischmann, M.D. Adams, O. White, R.A. Clayton, et al. (1995): Whole-genome random sequencing and assembly of *haemophilus influenzae* rd. *Science*, 269(5223), 496–512.

[31] N. Futamura, S. Aluru, and X. Huang (2003): Parallel syntenic alignments. *Parallel Processing Letters*, 13, 689–703.

[32] C. Gemund, C. Ramu, B. A. Greulich, and T. J. Gibson (2001): Gene2EST: a BLAST2 server for searching expressed sequence tag (EST) databases with eukaryotic gene-sized queries. *Nucleic Acids Research* 29, 1272–1277.

[33] R. Giegerich and S. Kurtz (1997): From Ukkonen to McCreight and Weiner: A unifying view of linear-time suffix tree construction. 19:331–353.

[34] O. Gotoh (2000): Homology-based gene structure prediction: simplified matching algorithm using a translated codon (tron) and improved accuracy by allowing for long gaps. *Bioinformatics*, 16(3), 190–202.

[35] P. Green (1996): *http://www.mbt.washington.edu/phrap.docs/phrap.html*.

[36] R. Grossi and J.S. Vitter (2000): Compressed suffix arrays and suffix trees with applications to text indexing and string matching. In *Symposium on the Theory of Computing*, pp. 397–406. ACM.

[37] D. Gusfield (1997): *Algorithms on Strings Trees and Sequences*. New York.

[38] D. Gusfield, K. Balasubramaniam, and D. Naor (1994): Parametric optimization of sequence alignment. *Algorithmica, 12,* 312–326.

[39] S. A. Haas, T. Beissbarth, E. Rivals, A. Krause, and M. Vingron (2000): GeneNest: automated generation and visualization of gene indices. *Trends in Genetics, 16*(11), 521–523.

[40] S. Hannenhalli and P.A. Pevzner (1999): Transorming cabbage into turnip: polynomial algorithm for sorting signed permutations by reversals. *Journal of the Association for Computing Machinery, 46*(1), 1–27.

[41] P. Havlak, R. Chen, K.J. Durbin, A. Egan, Y.R. Ren, and X.Z. Song (2004): The Atlas genome assembly system. *Genome Research, 14*(4):721–732.

[42] S. Henikoff and J.G. Henikoff (1992): Amino acid substitution matrices from protein blocks. *Proc. National Academy of Sciences, 89,* 10915–10919.

[43] D.S. Hirschberg (1975): A linear space algorithm for computing maximal common subsequences. *Communications of the ACM, 18*(6), 341–343.

[44] X. Huang (1989): A space-efficient parallel sequence comparison algorithm for a message-passing multiprocessor. *International Journal of Parallel Programming, 18*(3), 223–239.

[45] X. Huang (1990): A space-efficient algorithm for local similarities. *Computer Applications in the Biosciences, 6*(4), 373–381.

[46] X. Huang (1992): A contig assembly program based on sensitive detection of fragment overlaps. *Genomics, 14,* 18–25.

[47] X. Huang and K. Chao (2003): A generalized global alignment algorithm. *Bioinformatics, 19*(2), 228–233.

[48] X. Huang and A. Madan (1999): CAP3: A DNA sequence assembly program. *Genome Research, 9*(9), 868–877.

[49] X. Huang and J. Zhang (1996): Methods for comparing a DNA sequence with a protein sequence. *Computer Applications in Biosciences, 12*(6), 497–506.

[50] D.B. Jaffe, J. Butler, S. Gnerre, and E. Mauceli, et al. (2003): Whole-genome sequence assembly for mammalian genomes: ARACHNE2. *Genome Research, 13,* 91–96.

[51] N. Jareborg, E. Birney, and R. Durbin (1999): Comparative analysis of non-coding regions of 77 orthologous mouse and human gene pairs. *Genome Research, 9,* 815–824.

[52] A. Kalyanaraman, S. Aluru, V. Brendel, and S. Kothari (2003): Space and time efficient parallel algorithms and software for EST clustering. *IEEE Transactions on Parallel and Distributed Systems,* 14.

[53] Z. Kan, E. C. Rouchka, W. R. Gish, and D. J. States (2001): Gene structure prediction and alternative splicing analysis using genomically aligned ESTs. *Genome Research, 11,* 889–900.

[54] H. Kaplan, R. Shamir, and R.E. Tarjan (2000): A faster and simpler algorithm for sorting signed permutations by reversals. *SIAM Journal on Computing, 29*(3), 880–892.

[55] J. Kärkkäinen and P. Sanders (2003): Simpler linear work suffix array construction. In *International Colloquium on Automata, Languages and Programming,* to appear.

[56] R.M. Karp (2003): The role of algorithmic research in computational genomics. In *Proc. IEEE Computational Systems Bioinformatics,* pp. 10–11. IEEE.

[57] J. Kececioglu and E. Myers (1995): Combinatorial algorithms for DNA sequence assembly. *Algorithmica, 13*(1-2), 7–51.

[58] P. Ko and S. Aluru (2003): Space-efficient linear-time construction of suffix arrays. In *14th Annual Symposium, Combinatorial Pattern Matching.*

[59] P. Ko, M. Narayanan, A. Kalyanaraman, and S. Aluru (2004): Space conserving optimal DNA-protein alignment. In *Proc. IEEE Computational Systems Bioinformatics*, pp. 80–88.

[60] A. Krause, S. A. Haas, E. Coward, and M. Vingron (2002): SYSTERS, GeneNest, SpliceNest: Exploring sequence space from genome to protein. *Nucleic Acids Research*, 30.

[61] A. Krause, J. Stoye, and M. Vingron (2000): The SYSTERS protein sequence cluster set. *Nucleic Acids Research, 28*, 270–272.

[62] E. Lander, J.P. Mesirov, and W. Taylor (1988): Protein sequence comparison on a data parallel computer. In *Proc. International Conference on Parallel Processing*, pp. 257–263.

[63] E.S. Lander and M.S. Waterman (1988): Genomic mapping by fingerprinting random clones: a mathematical analysis. *Genomics, 2*, 231–239.

[64] F. Liang, I. Holt, G. Pertea, S. Karamycheva, S. Salzberg, and J. Quackenbush (2000): An optimized protocol for analysis of EST sequences. *Nucleic Acids Research, 28*(18), 3657–3665.

[65] H.F. Lodish, A. Berk, P. Matsudaira, C.A. Kaiser, M. Krieger, M.P. Scott, S.L. Zipursky, and J. Darnell (2003): *Molecular Cell Biology.* W.H. Freeman and Company, New York, NY.

[66] P. A. Pevzner M. S. Gelfand, and A. Mironov (1996): Gene recognition via spliced alignment. *Proc. National Academy of Sciences, 93*, 9061–9066.

[67] U. Manber and G. Myers (1993): Suffix arrays: a new method for on-line search. *SIAM Journal on Computing, 22*, 935–48.

[68] W.J. Masek and M.S. Paterson (1980): A faster algorithm for computing string edit distances. *Journal of Computer and System Sciences, 20*, 18–31.

[69] E. M. McCreight (1976): A space-economical suffix tree construction algorithm. *Journal of the ACM, 23*, 262–72.

[70] B. Modrek and C. Lee (2002): A genomic view of alternative splicing. *Nature Genetics, 30*, 13–19.

[71] D.W. Mount (2001): *Bioinformatics: Sequence and Genome Analysis.* Cold Spring Harbor Laboratory.

[72] J.C. Mullikin and Z. Ning (2003): The phusion assembler. *Genome Research, 13*, 81–90.

[73] E. Myers (1994): *Advances in Sequence Assembly*, chapter in Automated DNA Sequencing and Analysis Techniques (C. Ventner, ed), pp. 231–238. Academic Press Limited.

[74] E.W. Myers (1995): Toward simplifying and accurately formulating fragment assembly. *Journal of Computational Biology, 2*(2), 275–290.

[75] E.W. Myers, G.G. Sutton, A.L. Delcher, I.M. Dew, et al. (2000): A whole genome assembly of *drosophila. Science, 287*(5461), 2196–2204.

[76] E.W. Myers and W. Miller (1988): Optimal alignments in linear space. *Computer Applications in the Biosciences, 4*(1), 11–17.

[77] S.B. Needleman and C.D. Wunsch (1970): A general method applicable to the search for similarities in the amino acid sequence of two proteins. *Journal of Molecular Biology*, *48*, 443–453.

[78] L. Patcher and B. Strumfels (2004): Parametric inference for biological sequence analysis. *Proc. National Academy of Sciences*, to appear.

[79] H. Peltola, H. Soderlund, and E. Ukkonen (1984): SEQAID: a DNA sequence assembly program based on a mathematical model. *Nucleic Acids Research*, *12*, 307–321.

[80] P. Pevzner and G. Tesler (2003): Transforming men into mice: the Nadeau-Taylor chromosomal breakage model revisted. In *Proc. International Conference on Research in Computational Molecular Biology (RECOMB)*, pp. 247–256. ACM.

[81] P.A. Pevzner (2000): *Computational Molecular Biology: An Algorithmic Approach*. MIT Press.

[82] J. Quackenbush, J. Cho, D. Lee, F. Liang, I. Holt, S. Karamycheva, B. Parvizi, G. Pertea, R. Sultana, and J. White (2001): The TIGR gene indices: analysis of gene transcript sequences in highly sampled eukaryotic species. *Nucleic Acids Research*, *29*, 159–164.

[83] S. Rajko and S. Aluru (2004): Space and time optimal parallel sequence alignments. *IEEE Transactions on Parallel and Distributed Systems*, *15*(11).

[84] F. Sanger, S. Nicklen, and A.R. Coulson (1977): DNA sequencing with char-interminating inhibitors. *Proc. National Academy of Sciences*, *74*, 5463–5467.

[85] D. Sankoff and J.B. Kruskal (1983): *Time Warps, String Edits, and Macromolecules: the Theory and Practice of Sequence Comparison*. Reading, MA.

[86] S. Schwartz, Z. Zhang, K. Frazer, A. Smit, C. Riemer, J. Bouck, R. Gibbs, R. Hardison, and W. Miller (2000): PipMaker-a web server for aligning two genomic DNA sequences. *Genome Research*, *10*, 577–586.

[87] J. Setubal and J. Meidanis (1997): *Introduction to Computational Molecular Biology*. PWS Publishing Company, Boston, MA.

[88] A. Smit and P. Green (1999): http://ftp.genome.washington.edu/RM/Repeat Masker.html, 1999.

[89] T.F. Smith and M.S. Waterman (1981): Identification of common molecular subsequences. *Journal of Molecular Biology*, *147*, 195–197.

[90] D.J. States, W. Gish, and S.F. Altschul (1991): Improved sensitivity of nucleic acid database searches using application-specific scoring matrices. *Methods*, *3*, 66–70.

[91] G. Sutton, O. White, M. Adams, and A. Kerlavage (1995): TIGR assembler: A new tool for asembling large shotgun sequencing projects. *Genome Science and Technology*, *1*, 9–19.

[92] R.E. Tarjan (1975): Efficiency of a good but not linear set union algorithm. *Journal of the ACM*, *22*(2), 215–225.

[93] G. Tesler (2002): Efficient algorithms for multichromosomal genome rearrangements. *Journal of Computer and System Sciences*, *65*, 587–609.

[94] E. Ukkonen (1995): On-line construction of suffix-trees. *14*, 249–60.

[95] J.C. Venter, M.D. Adams, E.W. Myers, P.W. Li, et al. (2001): The sequence of the human genome. *Science*, *291*(5507), 1304–1351.

[96] M.S. Waterman (1995): *Introduction to Computational Biology: Maps, Sequences and Genomes*. Chapman and Hall, London.

[97] P. Weiner (1973): Linear pattern matching algorithms. In *14th Symposium on Switching and Automata Theory*, pp. 1–11.

[98] R. Yeh, L. P. Lim, and C. B. Burge (2001): Computational inference of homologous gene structures in the human genome. *Genome Research, 11*, 803–816.

[99] Z. Zhang, W. R. Pearson, and W. Miller (1997): Aligning a DNA sequence with a protein sequence. *Journal of Computational Biology*, pp. 339–49.

Chapter 22

NOISE IN FOREIGN EXCHANGE MARKETS
George G. Szpiro
Jerusalem
Israel

"Noise makes financial markets possible, but also makes them imperfect."

—*Fischer Black*

   This chapter employs a new technique to compare the level of noise in financial markets. The data that are analyzed consist of high-frequency time series of three foreign exchange markets. It is shown that noise in the Dollar–Deutschmark series is least intense, that the Yen–Dollar market has about 10 percent more noise, and that there is about 70 percent more noise in the Deutschmark–Yen time series. On average, the noise level is higher in the late summer and fall than in the winter. The differentials may be related to the amount of news and the timing of its arrival.

1   INTRODUCTION

   Noise, omnipresent in realistic models of nature, is generally considered a nuisance because it keeps researchers from completely explaining natural phenomena and prevents practitioners from making exact predictions. In economics this is more true than in the exact sciences, where conditions can be controlled and experiments can be shielded from outside influences. On the other hand, in economic and in financial markets, noise may be one of the reasons that profits can be made. [2]; [21].

   Usually the variance that remains after the effects of all variables of the model have been taken into account is defined as noise. This remainder is considered to be due to variables that are unknown, or that are disregarded by the model: external shocks, random fluctuations, or the arrival of new information. Market behavior is often described and studied by using autoregressive models with noise,[1]

$$x_t = f(x_{t-1}, x_{t-2}, ..., x_{t-n}) + \varepsilon_t. \tag{1}$$

When confronted with a time-series of observed financial or economic data, the usual procedure is to specify a model, $f(x_{t-1}, x_{t-2}, ..., x_{t-n})$, and then to define noise as the unexplained remainder. Hence, in a fully specified autoregressive time-series, noise is due to factors other than x_{t-j}. While there exist relatively simple methods to estimate and fit linear models to time series, the problem of model specification becomes especially difficult when the data-generating process may be nonlinear.

Recently a new method has been proposed that reverses the process [25] instead of first specifying a model and then defining noise as the remaining variance, the technique permits the measurement of noise even before a linear or nonlinear autoregressive model is specified. All that is required in this case is that the noise's distribution be known. By adapting a method borrowed from theoretical physics—specifically, a well-known algorithm for the determination of the dimension of a chaotic system [14]—the size of the noise can be computed. But we can go one step further. When not only the structure of the model is unknown but, also one has no knowledge about the noise's distribution, the levels of noise in different time series can still be compared, and their relative intensities can be inferred. The only prerequisite in this case is that the noises have the same distributions, and this is the only assumption made in this chapter.

One drawback is that massive amounts of data are needed. Therefore, this chapter applies the methodology to high-frequency time series from foreign exchange markets (containing between several hundred thousand and 1.5 million data points). The intensity of the noise levels in three markets is compared, and then possible differences between months of the year and days of the week are investigated. As will be shown, evidence exists that the noise level is higher in the late summer and fall than in the winter. No significant differences were found for the days of the week.

This chapter provides a first attempt at comparing the amount of noise in financial time series. It does not try to explain the reasons why the level of noise in one series is higher or lower than in another. Further research about the intensity of noise, its timing, and its causes (e.g., arrival of new information, external shocks) is warranted.

The next section explains the difference between two types of noise and discusses the related problem of the tick size in foreign exchange quotes. Section 3 gives a brief description of the method used to measure noise. This method is related to techniques used to search for nonlinear dynamics and "strange attractors" that may underlie financial and economic time-series.[2] Section 4 examines

---

[1]This can be justified by Takens' embedding theorem [27], which states that the lagged values of one variable suffice to characterize the dynamics of a multivariable system.

[2]Some studies that attempted to discover nonlinearities in the foreign exchange rates include Hsieh [16], Meese and Rose [18], Guillaume [15], Evertsz [11], Mizrach [19], Cecen and Erkal [6], and Brooks [5]. On the role of "chartists," who search for simple patterns in one

the database, and Section 5 presents the results. Section 6 concludes with a brief summary of findings and suggestions for further research.

2   MEASUREMENT NOISE VERSUS DYNAMIC NOISE, FINITE TICK SIZES

In experimental science, say, in physics or chemistry, one distinguishes between two types of noise: dynamic noise and measurement noise [20]. The first, dynamic noise δ, derives from outside influences that enter the model,

$$x_t = f(x_{t-1} + \delta_t), \qquad (2)$$

while the latter, measurement noise μ, is due to the finite resolution of the measuring apparatus or to roundoff errors [23],

$$\begin{aligned} x_t &= y_t + \mu_t \\ \text{where } y_t &= f(y_{t-1}). \end{aligned} \qquad (3)$$

Some attempts have been made to distinguish between the two (e.g., [24]). In economics and finance, it is generally believed that the latter noise presents few problems, since the resolution of the measurements is small relative to the numerical values involved. The cost of high-priced goods is generally given to the nearest dollar; for low-priced goods, the dollar is divided into cents. Stock prices are quoted in eighths of dollars; national accounts data involving trillion dollar figures are often given to the nearest million. Exchange-rate data are also quite accurate: the Dollar–Deutschmark exchange rate, for example, is given to four digits after the comma. Hence, with a DM/$ rate of, say, 1.4111, the precision is on the order of 0.007 percent.

Even though price quotes are generally quite precise, they are nevertheless finite. Indeed, the number of possible prices for a good or a commodity must be limited, because if there were an infinite number of pricing possibilities – say, all rational numbers between some upper and lower limits – buyers and sellers would have great difficulty matching their bids. Hence markets can only exist if there is a convention to meet at a finite number of prices. As pointed out above, the cost of a good is usually determined in dollars and cents. If this resolution is too coarse, market participants agree on ticks of, say, tenths or hundreths of a cent. For high-priced goods, on the other hand, dollars and cents may provide too many pricing possibilities for the market, and a convention evolves to trade only at prices rounded to the next five, ten, or hundred units of the currency. The shares of the Swiss newspaper "Neue Zürcher Zeitung," for example, priced at around $40,000, are traded at intervals of 250 Francs (about $180) by market makers in Switzerland.

The size of the tick, seemingly minute when compared to the price of the commodity, does present problems for research, however. In Figure 22.1, we create a

---

dimension, see Allen and Taylor [1]. Engle et al. [10] and Goodhart [13], for example, deal with news in the foreign exchange market. For a survey of the recent literature on exchange rate economics, see Taylor [28].

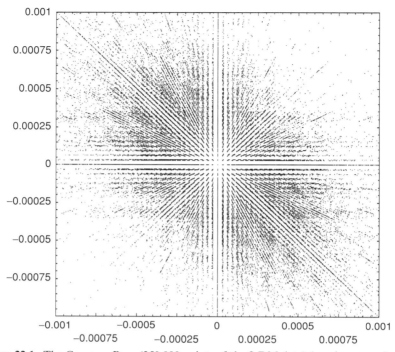

Figure 22.1. The Compass Rose (250,000 points of the $-DM data) (*x*-axis: x_t, *y*-axis: x_{t+1})

large sample of two-dimensional vectors from the $-DM data[3] and plot the x_{t+1}-values against their x_t-values. (In technical parlance, we embed the time series into two-dimensional space.)[4] The pattern that emerges, the so-called "compass rose," was discovered by Crack and Ledoit [7] and further analyzed by Szpiro [26]. As these authors showed, the pattern arises because of the discreteness of the quotes, i.e., the finite resolution of the prices. Finite tick-sizes may lead particular tests to indicate the existence of structure when, in fact, there is none. The problem is compounded by the fact that for such tests – and the method to measure noise uses a variant of such a test – one needs to "embed" the time series in high dimensions. (See Section 3.) As is well known, the lengths of objects generally expand when they are projected upwards into higher dimensions. In fact, the distance between two points grows on average with $\sqrt{d}$, where d is the dimension. Hence, for d=50, the effect of measurement errors increases about sevenfold. In conclusion, it may safely be assumed that noise in financial markets consists of both measurement and dynamic noise.

---

[3]Of the 1,472,241 observations, approximately every sixth vector was used, to give a sample-size of 250,000.

[4]The somewhat visible predominance of points in the North–West and South–East directions is due to the negative correlation between consecutive observations in high-frequency data. [13, 3].

3   CHAOS, DIMENSION, AND MEASUREMENT OF NOISE

The proposed technique [25] borrows from mathematical physics. Specifically, an algorithm is employed that was suggested by Grassberger and Procaccia [14] to measure the dimension of a chaotic system by embedding it in increasingly high dimensions.[5] To illustrate the technique, let us assume a very low-dimensional system and dynamical noise that is uniformly distributed in [−M,+M]. We embed the data into two-dimensional space, take a reference point, and count all neighbors that are contained within a circle of radius r. Let us call this number $C_2(r)$. Now we move to three-dimensional space. When "unfolding" the attractor, we realize that in three-dimensional space the nearest neighbors in the circle are actually downward projections of points that are contained in a cylinder above the circle. The as-yet unknown height M of this cylinder corresponds to the noise level. Let us count the neighbors that are contained in a ball around the reference point and call this number $C_3(r)$. Since the volume of the cylinder is $2M\pi r^2$, and the volume of the ball is $4/3\pi r^3$, the ratio of the number of points in two-dimensional space to those in three-dimensional space gives an indication as to the noise level. In this case, we have

$$C_2(r) = 2M\pi r^2 \quad \text{and}$$

$$C_3(r) = \frac{4}{3}\pi r^3 \tag{4}$$

Computing the ratio, we get

$$\frac{C_3(r)}{C_2(r)} = \eta_{2,3}(r) = \frac{2}{3}\frac{r}{M} \tag{5}$$

We now run a homogenous regression between the ratio $\eta_{2,3}(r)$ and the radius r:

$$\eta_{2,3}(r) = \gamma r. \tag{6}$$

From the last two equations it follows that the level of noise, M, can be computed as

$$M = \frac{2/3}{\gamma}. \tag{7}$$

By adding and subtracting 1.96 standard errors of the γ-estimates, an approximate 95 percent confidence interval can be determined for the estimated noise level. For reasons that will not be discussed here,[6] the regressions are actually run with both r and r^2 as independent variables, and of course the technique must be applied in dimensions much higher than just two or three. As was pointed out above, if the noise distribution is unknown, the numerical results per se have no meaning, but nevertheless do provide an index of the amount of noise present.

---

[5]The algorithm is also used in a test that was devised to search for nonlinearities and chaos in economic time series [4]. There have been numerous attempts to determine whether a chaotic system underlies the data-generating process of financial or economic time series. [22, 12, 16]

[6]See Szpiro [25] for a more detailed description of the method.

Hence, the method can be used to compare relative intensities of noise in different time series, even if the noise's distribution is unknown.

When plotting the results of the computations against the embedding dimension, we will see high levels of noise at first that decrease as dimension increases, and that finally converge to a constant level. The reason for this phenomenon is that in a low-embedding dimension, several "strings" of the system are superimposed on each other, but the system "unfolds" when one moves to higher dimensions [29]. In the present study of the foreign exchange markets, we run the regressions with twenty r-values – for embedding dimensions 1 to 50 – starting with the smallest sphere that contains at least 10^5 data points.

4   DATA

The data for this study consist of the foreign exchange rates in three markets for the time period October 1st, 1992, to September 30th, 1993: the Dollar–German Mark (\$–DM), the German Mark–Yen (DM–Y), and the Yen–Dollar (Y–\$) markets. The data do not consist of actual trades, but of bid and ask quotes, the means of which will serve as proxies for actual trades. The quotes were collected by Olsen & Associates, who made it available to the academic community.[7] The log-differences of the mean between the bid and the ask price were calculated.[8] The series for the \$–DM market consists of 1,472,241 entries (mean 0.00992, variance 835.2, and skewness 531.7). The Y–\$ series has 570,814 entries (–0.02152, 2594.6, –1324.0), and the DM–Y series has 158,979 entries (–0.17354, 3615.1, –23174.0).

An argument could be made to use only data at specified points in time—say, at five-minute intervals—or to employ "business time" to filter the data [8]. The present study uses every observation in the series (i.e., "quote time"), the reason being that a higher frequency of quotes implies more hectic activity or, in other words, a speeding up of time. Furthermore, there seems to be no empirical evidence for intraquote dynamics of any relevance [11].

From the time-series $x_1, x_2, x_3, \ldots$ we derive k-dimensional vectors $\langle x_1, x_2, \ldots, x_k \rangle$, $\langle x_2, x_3, \ldots, x_{k+1} \rangle$, etc., and compute the Euclidean distance between them, for dimensions 1 to 50. A total of $(n-k)(n-k-1)/2$ pairs could be calculated, but we make do with a sample, albeit a large one. For the \$–DM series, the interpair distances of every vector with every 100th other vector were calculated; in the Y–\$, every 15th vector was used; and in the DM–Y, distances were calculated with 4/5ths of the possible vectors. This sampling ensured that an equal amount of pairs (approximately 10^{10}) was used in each market to compute the amount of noise.[9] The pairs were grouped into spheres with radii between 1 and 150. For each embedding dimension, regressions (Eq. 6) were run for twenty consecutive spheres, starting with the smallest one that contained at least 10^5 pairs.

---

[7] Olsen & Associates Ltd., Research Institute for Applied Economics, Zürich.
[8] The results are multiplied by 10^5 in order to receive numerical values that are more manageable.
[9] The method is very computer intensive. The calculation of the 10 billion interpair distances in embedding dimensions 1 to 50, and their grouping into spheres, took more than 200 hours on a Pentium-133 computer for each of the three series.

5 FINDINGS

In Figure 22.2, the results of the noise measurements for the three markets are depicted. Let us recall that since we do not know the distribution of the underlying noise, the numerical values only give an indication as to the relative levels of noise in the three markets, i.e., they represent indexes. As expected, the noise estimates are high in the low embedding dimension, but then gradually decrease as the embedding dimension increases. We see in the figure that in all three examples the estimates eventually converge.[10] From the evidence we conclude that the \$–DM market has a noise index of 12.2 (95 percent confidence interval: ±0.2), the Y–\$ market a level of 13.5 (±0.1), and the DM–Y market a level of 20.7 (±0.1). In other words, with the least noisy \$–DM market as a baseline, we may conclude that the Y–\$ market has about 10 percent more noise, and that there is about 70 percent more noise in the DM–Y time-series.

For comparison purposes, the identical operations are performed with time series whose entries have the same distribution as the original series but whose order is random. The results for the scrambled time series can serve as a benchmark. [4] The only difference in the scrambled series is the removal of any possible structure that existed in the order of the original entries. In Figure 22.3, the estimated noise levels for the scrambled series are presented. Even for low embedding dimensions, these are much higher than in the original series. For the \$–DM market, the level is about 35 (±0.3), and for the other two markets it lies above 45 (±0.5 and ±0.4). Hence, by scrambling the entries, two to three times as much noise was introduced into the series as there was in the original data.

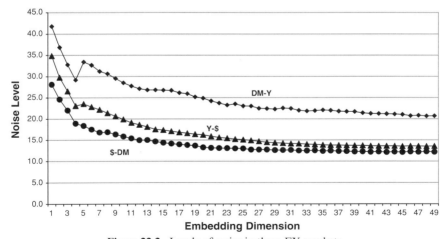

Figure 22.2. Levels of noise in three FX markets

---

[10]Convergence occurs above an embedding dimension of about 35, which would indicate that the time series have dimensions of not more than 17 [29]. However, such dimension estimates may be questioned. [9].

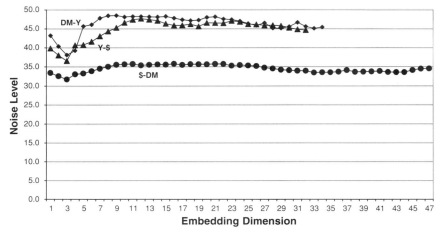

Figure 22.3. Levels of noise in scrambled time series

Let us now turn to more narrow data and compute the noise level within each month of the year, for each of the three markets. Figure 22.4 plots the development of the measured levels of noise against the embedding dimension. Again, the estimates converge,[11] and in Figure 22.5 a summary of the results is presented for embedding dimension 20. On average, the noise level for the months November to January is lower than for the period July to October. A tentative

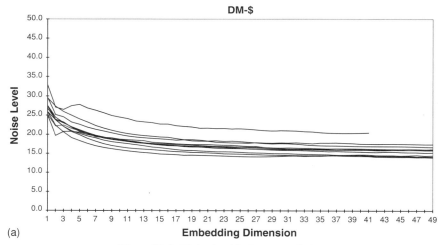

(a)

Figure 22.4. Noise level in intramonth data

---

[11]For some months the calculations were not made for all embedding dimensions up to 50, since there was not a sufficient number of spheres that contain a minimum of 10^5 points. The confidence intervals are again very narrow and won't be given.

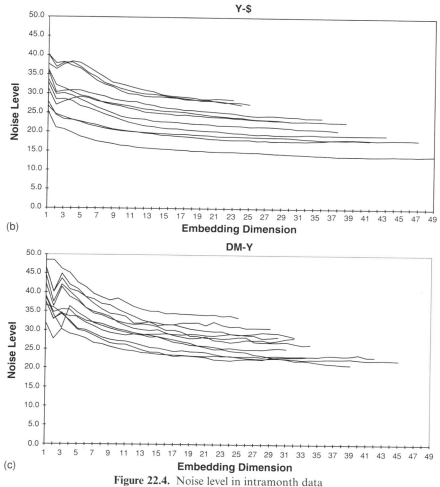

Figure 22.4. Noise level in intramonth data

explanation of this phenomenon could be that more information arrives during the late summer and fall than during the winter.

A comparison between Figures 22.2 and 22.5 shows that the estimates for the single months lie above the results for the whole years (for embedding dimension 20). It may seem surprising that the noise levels, as measured in the monthly data, do not average out to the noise level for the year as a whole. The answer to this puzzle goes to the heart of the nature of noise. The latter is generally defined as the data's variance that is not explained by a certain model. With a better model, unexplained variance decreases, and the data have less noise. In the method used in this chapter, vectors of the time series are compared with previous vectors, and similarities (i.e., closeness in the Euclidean norm) are sought. If one time series is a small subseries of the other, it is more difficult to find similar vectors. On the other hand, the longer the time series, the better known does the underlying structure become. Hence noise decreases. The time series of the data for single months

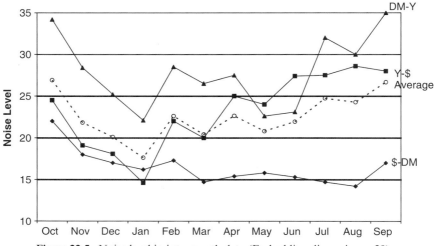

Figure 22.5. Noise level in intramonth data (Embedding dimension = 20)

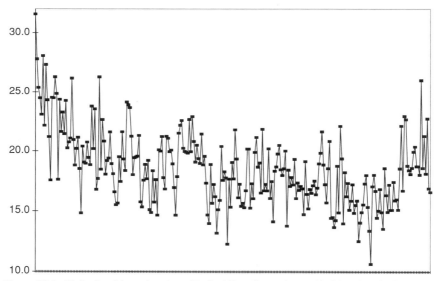

Figure 22.6. Noise level intraday data (Embedding dimension = 20; Mondays indicated by rectangles)

gives less opportunity to "learn" the structure, and a larger part of the data's variance is identified as noise. Incidentally, the reason why an approximately equal number of pairs is used for all markets in the estimations of the noise level for the full year was to counteract this effect.

Finally, we turn to intraday data. The noise level for 258 weekdays for the $–DM data is estimated and depicted in Figure 22.6.[12] Visual inspection does not

---

[12]There were no quotes for two Fridays during the year, 25th of December and 1st of January. For the following analysis, interpolated values were entered for these days.

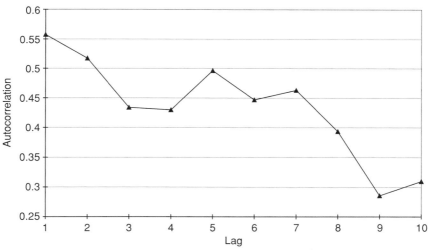

Figure 22.7. Autocorrelation for noise level in intraday data (Embedding dimension = 20)

reveal any significant pattern, and the average noise levels for the days of the week do not differ significantly. However, a common thread may nevertheless run through the days of the week. A plot of the first ten autocorrelations reveals strong "seasonality" for the fifth lag: $\rho = 0.496$ (see Figure 22.7). This suggests that the noise on a certain day of the week is correlated somehow to the same weekday's noise of the previous week. Autocorrelation is especially strong for Tuesdays and Wednesdays ($\rho = 0.519$ and 0.501, respectively). Possible reasons for this phenomenon may be that external shocks (of unknown origin) occur on certain weekdays, or that information arrives at specific times during the week. Further research is warranted.

6   CONCLUSIONS

This chapter employs a new technique to compare the levels of noise present in different time series. Since the method requires very long series, high-frequency data from foreign exchange markets are used. It is shown that of the three markets analyzed, the \$–DM market has the least amount of noise, the Y–\$ market has about 10 percent more noise, and there is about 70 percent more noise in the DM–Y time series. We also see that, on average, there is less noise during the winter than during the late summer and fall. Intraday data show some autocorrelation for the days of the week. The amount of noise may be related to the amount of news that arrives at certain times during the week, during the months, or in various markets.

The analysis presented in this chapter is meant to be an attempt at the comparative study of noise. It does not provide explanations as to why the level of noise in one series is higher or lower than in another. Further research about the intensity of noise and related issues, for example, the arrival and assimilation of new information, is warranted.

REFERENCES

[1] A.L. Helen and P.M. Taylor (1990): Charts, noise and fundamentals in the foreign exchange markets, *Economic J. 100*, 49–59.

[2] F. Black (1986): Noise, *J. Finance 41*, 529–543.

[3] T. Bollerslev and I. Domowitz (1993): Trading patterns and prices in the interbank foreign exchange market, *J. Finance 48*, 1421–1449.

[4] A. Brock, W.A.D. Hsieh, and B. LeBaron (1991): *Nonlinear Dynamics, Chaos, and Instability*, MIT Press, Cambridge.

[5] C. Brooks (1997): Linear and non-linear (non)-forecastability of high-frequency exchange rates, *J. Forecasting 16*, 125–145.

[6] A. Aydin Cecen and C. Erkal (1996): Distinguishing between stochastic and deterministic behavior in foreign exchange rate returns: further evidence, *Economics Letters 51*, 323–329.

[7] T.F. Crack and O. Ledoit (1996): Robust structure without predictability: the compass rose pattern of the stock market, *J. Finance 51*, 751–762.

[8] M. M. Dacarogna, U. A. Müller, R. J. Nagler, R. B. Olsen, and O. V. Pictet (1993): A geographical model for the daily and weekly seasonal volatility in the FX market, *J. International Money and Finance 12*, 413–438.

[9] J.-P. Eckmann and D. Ruelle (1992): Fundamental limitations for estimating dimensions and Lyapounov exponents in dynamical systems, *Physica D 56*, 185–187.

[10] R. F. Engle, T. Ito, and W. L. Lin (1990): Meteor showers or heat waves? Heteroskedastic intra-dayly volatility in the foreign exchange market, *Econometrica 58*, 525–542.

[11] J.G. Carl Evertsz (1996): Self-similarity of high-frequency USD-DEM exchange rates, in *Proceedings of the HFDF Conference* 1996, Olsen & Associates Ltd., Research Institute for Applied Economics, Zürich.

[12] M. Frank and T. Stengos (1989): Measuring the strangeness of gold and silver rates of return, *Review of Economic Studies 56*, 553–567.

[13] C. A. E. Goodhart and L. Figiuoli (1991): Every minute counts in financial markets, *J. International Money and Finance 10*, 24–52.

[14] P. Grassberger and I. Procaccia (1983): Characterization of strange attractors, *Physical Review Letters 50*, 346–349.

[15] M. Dominique Guillaume (1994): A low-dimensional fractal attractor in the foreign exchange markets?, working paper, Olsen & Associates Ltd., Research Institute for Applied Economics, Zürich.

[16] A. David Hsieh (1989): Testing for non-linear dependence in daily foreign exchange rates, *J. Business 62*, 339–368.

[17] _____, (1991): Chaos and nonlinear dynamics: application to financial markets, *J. Finance 46*, 1839–1877.

[18] A.R. Meese and K.A. Rose (1991): An empirical assessment of non-linearities in models of exchange rate determination, *Review of Economic Studies 58*, 603–619.

[19] B. Mizrach (1996): Determining delay times for phase space reconstruction with application to the FF/DM exchange rate, *J. Economic Behavior and Organization 30*, 369–381.

[20] M. Möller, W. Lange, F. Mitschke, N. B. Abraham, and U. Hübner (1989): Errors from digitizing and noise in estimating attractor dimension, *Physics Letters A 138*, 176–182.

[21] F. Palomino (1996): Noise trading in small markets, *J. Finance 51*, 1537–1550.

[22] J. Scheinkman and B. LeBaron (1989): Nonlinear dynamics and stock returns, *J. Business 62*, 311–337.

[23] G.G. Szpiro (1993a): Cycles and circles in roundoff errors, *Physical Review E 47*, 4560–4563.

[24] G.G. Szpiro (1993b): Measuring dynamical noise in dynamical systems, *Physica D 65*, 289–299.

[25] G.G. Szpiro (1997): Noise in unspecified, non-linear time series, *J. Econometrics 78*, 229–255.

[26] G.G. Szpiro (1998): Tick size, the compass rose and market nanostructure, *J. Banking and Finance 22*, 1559–1570.

[27] F. Takens (1981): Detecting strange attractors in turbulence, in D. Rand and L. Young (eds), *Dynamical Systems and Turbulence*, Lecture Notes in Mathematics, Springer Verlag *898*, 366–381.

[28] M.P. Taylor (1995): The economics of exchange rates, *J. Economic Literature 33*, 13–47.

[29] H. Whitney (1944): The self-intersection of a smooth n-manifold in $2n$-space, *Ann. Mathematics 45*, 220–246.

INDEX